FAMOUS FIRST FACTS

INTERNATIONAL EDITION

STEVEN ANZOVIN & JANET PODELL

FAMOUS FIRST FACTS

International Edition

A Record of First Happenings, Discoveries,
and Inventions in World History

The H. W. Wilson Company
New York • Dublin
2000

Library of Congress Cataloging-in-Publication Data

Anzovin, Steven.
    Famous first facts, international edition / by Steven Anzovin and Janet Podell.
        p. cm.
    Includes Indexes.
    ISBN 0-8242-0958-3 (alk.paper)
    1. Encyclopedias and dictionaries. I. Podell, Janet. II. Title.
AG5.A69 2000
031.02--dc21   99-086869

Production Editor: Denise M. Bonilla

Printed in the United States of America

The H. W. Wilson Company
950 University Avenue
Bronx, NY 10452

Visit H.W. Wilson's Web site: www.hwwilson.com

Contents

Preface

Since the first edition of Joseph Nathan Kane's *Famous First Facts* was published by the H. W. Wilson Company in 1933, it has earned a devoted following among readers of reference books on American history. The present volume, *Famous First Facts, International Edition*, was developed in response to suggestions from these readers, who asked for a version that would apply the same format to the world at large.

Famous First Facts, International Edition contains more than 5,000 entries under subject headings ranging alphabetically from Agriculture to Weapons. They represent the entire span of human history, from the earliest known human activity to the social, cultural, and scientific developments of the 20th century. Virtually every nation is represented here, as are international bodies such as the United Nations and NATO. The reader's attention is directed to the section that follows the Preface, entitled How to Use This Book, which describes in detail the classification scheme and the indexing system.

An examination of world events through this kind of focused lens functions something like a newsreel, offering selected scenes that give a quick idea of what happened when. Since history is in many ways a long series of firsts, we have had to make our selections with an eye to considerations of space. In addition to thousands of scientific and technological advances, we have endeavored to include the origins of many ordinary things, such as labor strikes (ancient Egypt), ball games (pre-Columbian Mesoamerica), fast-food restaurants (13th-century China), and e-mail messages (1970s United States).

We would like to extend our gratitude to Michael Schulze, former vice president and director of General Reference for the H. W. Wilson Company, for initiating this project. We would also like to thank senior editor Hilary Claggett and managing editor Gray Young. Jessica Teters, formerly of the Jones Library, Amherst, MA, provided invaluable research assistance, as did Diane Podell Kopperman of the C. W. Post Library, Greenvale, NY. Thanks are also due to the many institutions, agencies, organizations, and librarians who responded so helpfully to our inquiries, and to the sponsors of numerous informative web sites.

No project of this kind is ever truly complete. For future editions, we welcome information on firsts not included in this book. Please direct your correspondence to General Reference, H. W. Wilson, 950 University Ave., Bronx, NY 10452, attention Editor, *Famous First Facts, International Edition*.

Janet Podell and Steven Anzovin
Amherst, Massachusetts
September 1999

How to Use This Book

The entries in this book are classified by general category. The main subject categories are arranged alphabetically. When necessary, the main categories are divided into subcategories. For example, the main category *Language* is divided into subcategories such as *Alphabets and Writing, Authors, Books, Codes, Literary Genres,* and so on. The subcategory *Books,* in turn, contains further subcategories, including *Dictionaries, Encyclopedias,* and *Travel.*

Within this structure of classification, the entries are arranged chronologically. This arrangement has the advantage of enabling the reader to get a sense of how and when a field of endeavor developed.

Each entry begins with a four-digit indexing number, starting with 1001, and an introductory heading in boldface (for example, 1009. Cultured pearls). Please note that the four-digit number is for indexing purposes only and has no connection with the date of the event, which will be found in the text of the entry.

To find a specific entry, the reader may turn to one of the five indexes printed at the back of the volume: the comprehensive Subject Index, which lists alphabetically all major topics mentioned within entries; Years, in which entry headings are arranged chronologically by year; Days, in which entry headings are arranged chronologically by month and day; Names, an alphabetical list of key names from all entries; and Geographical, an alphabetical list of locations by city and nation. Note that geographical locations are identified by their current names; for example, events that took place in Mesopotamia are indexed under Iraq. All five indexes direct readers to the entry's indexing number, making it easy to locate that entry in the main body of the text.

Famous First Facts International

A

AGRICULTURE

1001. Agriculture may have developed in the Solomon Islands or elsewhere in the South Pacific. Excavations at Kilu Cave on Buka Island, the Solomons (part of Papua New Guinea), conducted by archeologists M. Spriggs and S. Wickler, uncovered small flake tools that held traces of starch grains from cultivated taro. The tools have been dated to circa 26,000 BCE.

1002. Farmers' almanac was found at the Sumerian city of Nippur (modern Niffer, Iraq) in 1949. It is an engraved tablet dating from 1700 BCE and contains a father's advice to his son on growing crops.

1003. University to teach rural agriculture was Oxford University in Oxford, England, where a professorship of rural agriculture was established in 1790.

1004. Agricultural research station was built by English agronomist John Bennet Lawes, the founder of the artificial fertilizer industry. In 1843, on his estate at Rothamsted, England, Lawes and the chemist Joseph Henry Gilbert founded Rothamsted Experimental Station, an agricultural research station to study fertilizers and animal nutrition.

AGRICULTURE—AQUACULTURE

1005. Aquaculture was the invention of the Sumerians, who lived in what is now Iraq. Sumerian ponds for breeding fish have been dated to circa 2500 BCE.

1006. Oyster farm of record was started at Lake Lucrin, near Naples, Italy, by the Roman fisherman Sergius Orata circa 110 BCE. Orata built sheltered marine fishponds and provided posts to which the larval oysters could attach and grow.

1007. Seaweed cultivation was developed in Edo (now Tokyo) Bay in Japan circa 1700. Probably the first sea plant grown was laver, a red alga much used in Japanese cuisine.

1008. Fish breeding techniques were developed by a German naturalist named Jacobi in 1733. Wild trout were collected live and placed in artificial ponds. Fish eggs and milt were expressed from the fish at breeding time and mixed in a hatching box; after hatching, the fish fry were moved to larger ponds.

1009. Cultured pearls were the invention of a Japanese businessman, Kokichi Mikimoto. In 1888 he inserted semiglobular mother-of-pearl beads into pearl oysters, hoping that they would form a new pearl around the irritating foreign body, and placed the oysters in a protected inlet. On July 11, 1893, he pulled up a bamboo basket and found in one oyster a semispherical pearl. Mikimoto established a monopoly in the cultured pearl business that destroyed the natural pearl industry. His son-in-law, Tokichi Nishikawa, developed a way to produce the first completely spherical cultured pearls.

AGRICULTURE—CROPS

1010. Cereal crop was wheat. Evidence of its cultivation appears in the human record before 10,000 BCE. It was first grown in Mesopotamia and around the Mediterranean.

1011. Rice is widely thought to have originated in India circa 3000 BCE from strains of the genus *Oryza*. However, a 1996 study by environmental archeologist Syuichi Toyama of Kogakukan University in Japan found that the oldest evidence of rice cultivation comes from sites along the middle Yangtze River in central China, with a median age of 11500 years.

1012. Einkorn domestication occurred in Southwest Asia's Fertile Crescent circa 9000 BCE. According to DNA analysis of 68 lines of cultivated einkorn and 261 wild einkorn lines conducted by Manfred Heun of the Agricultural University of Norway and Francesco Salamini of the Max Planck Institute for Research on Plant Breeding in Cologne, Germany, the exact location may have been the Karacadag Mountains of southeastern Turkey, where wild strains of einkorn are the most closely related to the cultivated varieties. Einkorn (*Triticum monococcum*) is a one-grained form of wheat.

1013. Rye was cultivated in southwest Asia circa 6500 BCE.

AGRICULTURE—CROPS—continued

1014. Beans have been grown around the world since ancient times. Mung and soy beans may have been the first varieties cultivated, probably in China circa 6000 BCE.

1015. Crops cultivated in the New World may have been squashes of the genus *Cucurbita,* a domesticated variety that includes pumpkin and summer squash, according to findings by Bruce Smith of the National Museum of Natural History in Washington, DC, USA. He radiocarbon-dated a cache of seeds found in a cave in Mexico to circa 6000 BCE to 8000 BCE, at least 3,000 years before the beginning of maize cultivation in the Americas.

1016. Barley was cultivated circa 4000 BCE in Egypt, where it was used as animal feed and for brewing beer.

1017. Grape cultivation began at least 6,000 years ago, and probably well before, in the coastal regions surrounding the Black and Caspian seas (in what is now modern Turkey, Iran, Azerbaijan, Kazakhstan, and Russia). The beginnings of winemaking probably date from this period as well, although the first concrete evidence of winemaking dates from 3500 BCE.

1018. Olive cultivation has been traced back to Crete (part of present-day Greece) in the mid-fourth century BCE.

1019. Maize cultivation began around 2700 BCE in the Tehuacán Valley of the central Mexican state of Puebla, some 4,000 to 5,000 years after the beginning of agriculture in the Old World. The date was derived by accelerator mass spectrometry tests announced in 1995. Maize, also called corn, did not emerge as a major food until perhaps 1,000 years after its introduction.

1020. Millet was developed as a crop in China circa 2700 BCE. Millet's resistance to drought made it especially suitable for growing in China's arid western regions.

1021. Orange cultivation began in China no later than 2200 BCE. Oranges are native to China, the Malay islands, and other hot regions of Asia.

1022. Pear orchards may have originated in China circa 2100 BCE. It is certain that the Greeks of the ninth century BCE grew pears.

1023. Cabbage was domesticated from wild cabbage *(Brassica oleracea)* circa 2000 BCE in the eastern Mediterranean and perhaps independently in what is now France. Head cabbage (the *capitata* variety), the most familiar cabbage type in the West today, was not developed as a crop plant until after 1000 CE.

1024. Cacao cultivation began circa 2000 BCE in the highlands of Central America by the precursors of the Toltec and Maya peoples. Cocoa prepared from the roasted cacao beans was used mainly in ceremonial drinks.

1025. Peach cultivation was first accomplished in China, the native habitat of peach trees, near the beginning of the second millennium BCE.

1026. Cotton-producing center in the New World was El Paraíso, a site on the central Peruvian coast. The inhabitants who occupied El Paraíso between 1800 and 1500 BCE manufactured such cotton products as fishing lines, nets, and clothing from wild cotton—cultivation of the plant was not yet practiced—and traded them to neighboring communities.

1027. Apples originated in the forests surrounding Almaty (the city formerly known as Alma-Ata) in Kazakhstan, where ancient cultivars were discovered in 1929 by the Russian botanist Nikolai I. Vavilov. Apple varieties traveled to other regions via the Silk Route and were planted in the Nile delta by order of the Egyptian pharaoh Ramses II in the 13th century BCE.

1028. Oats are one of the most recent grains to be domesticated. The grain was cultivated circa 500 BCE in Asia from wild varieties such as *Avena fatua.*

1029. Banana cultivation is of uncertain origin. The soldiers of Alexander the Great are known to have encountered bananas during their invasion of India in 326 BCE.

1030. Pineapple cultivation originated in the islands of the Caribbean and the northeastern coast of South America, possibly as early as the beginning of the first century CE.

1031. Plum cultivation began at least 2,000 years ago in several places: the Caucasus area between the Black and Caspian seas, the area that is now Syria, and in the Andean highlands of what is now Peru. Wild plums were used in medicinal preparations in Babylonia some 800 years earlier.

1032. Cultivation of potato was begun by Andean farmers circa 200 CE in what are now Peru and Bolivia. The word potato is derived from the Taino word *batata,* meaning sweet potato.

1033. Chinese cabbage was cultivated in China from circa 500 and at about the same time in Korea, where it was used as the basis for kimchi. There are two species of Chinese cabbage, *Brassica pekinensis,* with a cylindrical head and crinkly leaves, and *Brassica chinensis,* or bok choy, with dark, glossy leaves and a thick white stem.

1034. Limes grew in Asia, in and around the islands of Indonesia. They were first seen in Europe at the close of the first millennium CE.

1035. Brussels sprouts commercially grown were cultivated near Brussels, Belgium, perhaps as early as 1200. The first recorded decription of the vegetable *Brassica oleracea,* a relative of broccoli, dates to 1587.

1036. Tomato cultivation began in Mexico in the 12th or 13th century by the Aztecs, from whose word *tomatl* the English word "tomato" is derived. Wild tomatoes are native to the Andean region of South America.

1037. Peanuts were cultivated by the Aztecs and other Mesoamerican peoples. The first Europeans to taste them were members of the first voyage of Christopher Columbus in 1492. The peanut, a legume (*Arachis hypogaea*), was adopted by the Portuguese as a cheap food for slaves and was brought by them to Asia, where it was incorporated into Chinese and Thai cuisine, among others.

1038. Limes in the New World are thought to have originated with Christopher Columbus, who brought the seeds of a number of citrus fruits to the West Indies in 1493.

1039. Pineapples in the Old World were taken to Spain by the crew of Christopher Columbus's second expedition. The explorers came across pineapples on the Caribbean island of Guadeloupe in 1493.

1040. Bananas in the New World were specimens from the Canary Islands imported in 1516 by Friar Tomás de Berlanga (later bishop of Panama), who planted them on the island of Hispaniola (now the countries of Haiti and the Dominican Republic).

1041. Orange cultivation in the New World began when Christopher Columbus introduced Canary Island orange seeds to the island of Hispaniola (now Haiti and the Dominican Republic) on his second voyage, in 1493. Regular cultivation began in 1519 in Panama and in Florida by 1579. Navel (seedless) oranges were developed by Portuguese growers in Brazil.

1042. Tomatoes in the Old World were brought from Mexico to Spain by returning conquistadors early in the 16th century.

1043. Asian spice to be cultivated successfully in the New World was ginger (*Zingiber officinale*), originally native to southeast Asia and used for millennia in Asian cooking and medicine. It was grown by planters in the West Indies, notably Jamaica, soon after the arrival of Europeans. The first shipment of ginger from Santiago in Hispaniola (now the Dominican Republic) arrived Spain in 1547.

1044. Sunflowers were cultivated in the southwestern part of the United States by the indigenous tribes in prehistoric times. They were brought to Europe by the Spanish conquistadors in the 16th century.

1045. Flower cultivated by florists was the tulip. Tulips were imported to Europe in 1554 by the Austrian diplomat Ghislain de Busbecq, who sent a packet of tulip seeds to Vienna from the court of the Ottoman Turkish sultan Suleyman the Magnificent, where he was the ambassador. They were cultivated in Holland at the botanical garden at the University of Leiden by Carolus Clusius (born Charles de L'écluse or Lescluse), an Austrian botanist and former director of the Imperial Herb Gardens in Vienna, who brought tulips with him when he emigrated in 1593. At first they were bred for medicinal purposes, and the Dutch stewed the bulbs like onions. Their beauty then gave rise to the tulip craze. By 1633, the art of breeding and perfecting new varieties of tulips, in specialized combinations of color and size, had become a mass obsession. The market for bulbs, inflated by speculation, crashed in 1637.

1046. Peaches in the New World were brought by the Spanish conquistadors in the 16th century. Peaches were grown in Mexico by the year 1600.

1047. Cultivation of New World crops in Africa was undertaken in 1629 at Portuguese farms near Luanda (in present-day Angola). The crops included maize (corn), sweet potatoes, coconuts, papayas, guavas, and cassava (manioc). Cassava became a staple food in West Africa.

1048. Pears in the New World were brought in the 17th century by English settlers, who planted a pear tree at Eastham, MA, USA, in 1640, and by the French Jesuit missionaries to the native peoples in what is now Quebec, Canada.

1049. Strawberry cultivation began in Europe in the 17th century. Wild strawberries had been eaten since at least the fifth millennium BCE, as attested by seeds found in archeological sites in England, Denmark, and Switzerland. In 1714, a French naval officer, François Frézier, obtained

AGRICULTURE—CROPS—*continued*

five specimens of the Chilean strawberry *(Fragaria chiloensis)* in Chile and brought them back to France. Bred with *F. virginiana,* a strawberry variety imported from Virginia, they produed the first modern strawberry cultivars.

1050. Account of rubber production as it was conducted by the tribal inhabitants of South America was written by Charles-Marie de La Condamine, who came to Peru in 1735 as part of a French scientific team. La Condamine observed local people tapping latex from the rubber tree, *Hevea brasiliensis,* and forwarded rubber samples to France the following year.

1051. Grapefruit appeared in Jamaica, in the West Indies, in the mid-18th century, evidently derived by mutation or cross-breeding from a Malaysian citrus fruit known as the pomelo. Pomelo seeds were imported to the West Indies in 1696.

1052. Grapefruit plantation was established in 1809 in what is now the state of Florida, USA, by Odette Philippe, a French military surgeon. He had taken a liking to grapefruit *(Citrus paradisi)* upon sampling them in the Bahamas, where he had been interned by the British as a prisoner of war.

1053. African violets were first identified in 1892 in the rain forests of German East Africa (now Tanzania and Kenya). A flowering plant of family *Gesneriaceae,* genus *Saintpaulia,* it was probably descended from the Madagascan African primrose. Seeds were brought to Europe and later cultivated as a commercial houseplant.

1054. Avocado cultivation began circa 1900 by American horticulturist George Cullen of Florida, who developed a tree that produced uniform fruit. Mesoamerican peoples had long used the avocado in local cuisine; the word avocado comes from the Nahuatl (Aztec) word *ahuactal,* or "tree testicle."

1055. Macadamia nut orchards for commercial use were planted in Hawaii in 1921. The two species of commercial macadamia nut tree—the smooth-shelled *Macadamia tetraphylla* and the rough-shelled *M. integrifolia*—are native to Queensland, Australia.

1056. Modern rice hybrid that was successful was the rice strain IR-8, bred from a tall Indonesian rice and a dwarf rice from Taiwan. The strain was developed by a multinational team of researchers at the International Rice Research Institute at Los Baños in the Philippines, and was introduced in 1964. IR-8 provided double the yield of most Asian rices and matured earlier as well, enabling some areas to plant two crops in one season.

1057. Black tulip was long sought by breeders but was not achieved until 1979. Dutch horticulturist Geert Hageman obtained the black flower by pollinating a Queen of the Night tulip with pollen from the Winerwald cultivar. It took almost two decades for substantial numbers of black tulips to appear on the market.

1058. Genetically engineered plants were high-yield tobacco plants. The U.S. Department of Agriculture approved them for outdoor testing in 1986.

AGRICULTURE—CROPS—SUGAR

1059. Sugar cane cultivation began on the islands of the South Pacific circa 6000 BCE.

1060. Sugar in Europe produced from sugarcane was imported from Egypt by Venetian traders in 996 CE. Sugarcane probably originated in India, where it was encountered in 325 BCE by Nearchus, an officer in the army of Alexander the Great. Nearchus's account is contained in Arrian's *Indica,* a document of circa 150 CE.

1061. Sugar mill in Europe was invented by Pietro Speciale of Sicily in 1449. His design used three wooden rollers to crush the dried sugarcane sap. The mill was powered by a waterwheel or by a team of oxen.

1062. Sugar cane brought to the New World was unloaded in 1493 from the ships of Christopher Columbus's second voyage at what was to become the city of Santo Domingo, on the island of Hispaniola (now in the Dominican Republic). A sugar mill was built on the island in 1515.

1063. Sugar cane commercial production began in 1636, when a Dutch syndicate introduced the crop *Saccharum officinarum* from Brazil, where it had been grown by the Portuguese, to Barbados, in the West Indies. By 1650 sugar cane was the chief crop in the Caribbean islands.

1064. Sugar from beets (*Beta vulgaris*) was obtained in 1747 by Andreas Sigismund Marggraf, director of the chemical laboratory of the German Academy of Sciences, Berlin, Germany. Previously, all the world's sugar came from sugar cane, which grows only in tropical and subtropical climates. Sugar beets can be grown in cold climates as well.

AGRICULTURE—CROPS—TOBACCO

1065. Cigarettes were rolled in Seville, Spain, circa 1518, when the Spanish began importing cigars from their tobacco plantations in Haiti as a luxury item for the wealthy. (The word "cigar" is probably derived from the Mayan *sik'ar*, meaning tobacco wrapped in maize leaves.) The city's street beggars made their own, thinner versions of cigars, called *cigarrillos*, by pulling pieces of tobacco from discarded cigar butts and rolling them in bits of paper. The name was changed to "cigarettes" after French soldiers began to smoke them during the Napoleonic Wars, in the early 19th century.

1066. Tobacco cultivation by a European was undertaken at the English colony of Jamestown (now in the state of Virginia, USA) in 1612 by John Rolfe, the future husband of Pocahontas, who had arrived from England with 107 other settlers on May 13, 1607. Rolfe was the first settler to come up with a method of curing tobacco, which made it possible to grow tobacco crops for overseas export.

1067. Cigarette factory was founded by Luis Susini in Havana, Cuba, in 1853. This was the first factory to use steam-powered cigarette-rolling machines instead of laborers who hand-rolled the product.

1068. Cigarette-rolling machine was patented in the USA by James A. Bonsack in 1880. It deposited shredded tobacco on a roll of paper, shaped the paper into a long cylinder, and cut the cylinder into individual cigarettes.

AGRICULTURE—EQUIPMENT

1069. Sickle known to archeologists was found in Israel. It was made of antler fitted with flint teeth and dates from circa 5500 BCE.

1070. Hoe was a flaked, sharpened flint set at right angles to a stick and bound to it with gut or cord, in use in Mesopotamia from circa 4000 BCE. Similar hoes were developed in Egypt at about the same period.

1071. Grain drill for planting seed at a set depth was a wooden plow with a seed hopper, invented in Mesopotamia before 2000 BCE. A tube from the hopper released a controlled amount of seed into the furrow as the farmer plowed, thus eliminating the need to sow separately.

1072. Winnowing machine was invented by the Chinese before 40 BCE. The device was a simple hand-cranked fan that blew the chaff away while the seed fell to the ground.

1073. Plow with a moldboard that was curved to turn aside the soil was invented in China sometime in the first century CE. A plow equipped with a moldboard dug deeper furrows than older plows and was better suited to hard, clayey soils. The first European moldboard plows appeared around 1100.

1074. Greenhouses were in use in Rome in the first century CE. The earliest ones were covered with thin sheets of translucent stone. Greenhouses with glass walls are first mentioned by the Roman poet Martial, though not by that name. The word "greenhouse" was coined in the mid-17th century by the English writer John Evelyn, and the first building to be called a greenhouse was erected in 1697 at Chatsworth, England, on the estate of the Duke of Devonshire.

1075. Horse collar was introduced in Europe circa 1000; no more definite place or date is known. A major advance over older forms of harness, the horse collar rested on the horse's shoulders rather than across its chest and allowed the animal to put more force into the pull without being choked. With this invention, horses began gradually to replace oxen as draft animals.

1076. Wheelbarrow was invented in Europe during the late Middle Ages. It is first mentioned circa 1340, as a "wilbarewe."

1077. Wire-screen sifter for grain was invented in England in 1686 by John Newcomb, John Finch, and James Butler. A wooden frame held a large wire screen or sieve that shook and separated grain from chaff.

1078. Horse-drawn seed drill for sowing seed in neat rows in large fields is generally attributed to Jethro Tull of Oxfordshire, England, who invented it in 1701. Tull was trained as a lawyer but preferred farming; he also invented the horse-drawn hoe.

1079. Patent for a moldboard sheathed in iron was issued to Englishman Joseph Foljambe in 1720.

AGRICULTURE—EQUIPMENT—continued

1080. Threshing machine was probably designed in 1732 by British inventor Michael Menzies. A waterwheel turned a shaft on which a set of flails was attached by chains.

1081. Cast iron plow was built by English inventor Robert Ransome, who obtained a patent in 1785.

1082. Mechanical reaper was invented in England by Joseph Boyce, who received a patent in 1799. His reaper was pulled by a team of horses or mules and harvested grains using revolving teeth to press the sheaves against a cutting blade. An American, Henry Ogle, developed a new design in 1826. Ogle's reaper consisted of a straight scythe blade that moved against a series of triangular fingers. The cut grain fell on a collecting board.

1083. Self-sharpening plow was patented by English inventor Robert Ransome in 1803. Ransome later created the first plow made of interchangeable parts that could be repaired in the field.

1084. Haymaker was invented in 1820 by an Englishman, Robert Salmon. His machine used mechanized forks to lift and turn cut grass for drying.

1085. Grain stripper that cut the crop, separated the grain from the stalk, and placed the grain into bins was invented in 1843 by John Ridley and John Bull of South Australia.

1086. Beehive with removable frames was patented by Lorenzo Lorraine Langstroth, a former pastor, in Oxford, OH, USA, on October 5, 1852. Langstroth's hive design revolutionized beekeeping because it was the first that allowed bees to build combs on wooden frames that could be removed, stripped of honey and wax, and then replaced. His key discovery was the "bee space," the minimum air space that bees would not bridge with wax or bee glue. By setting up his frames at this distance, he prevented the bees from building connections between them. This allowed him to remove one frame at a time without damaging the adjacent frames, and enabled him to maximize the amount of honeycomb in the hive.

1087. Self-propelled rotary cultivator was developed in 1855 by the Canadian inventor Robert Romaine of Montreal. A steam engine provided propulsion for the tractor-like vehicle as well as power for the rotary cultivating blades.

1088. Steam-powered plow appeared in the Netherlands in 1862.

1089. Barbed wire was commercially produced beginning on November 1, 1873, in De Kalb, IL, USA, by Joseph Farwell Glidden, who obtained a U.S. patent for his invention on November 24, 1874. In 1875 he co-founded the first company to make the fencing, the Barb Fence Company. Royalties from the patent made him a rich man. The barbs were cut from sheet metal and were inserted between two twisted steel wires. The fencing was sold in rolls and bales. Glidden's cheap fencing made it possible to confine the large herds of cattle that were then being raised on the North American plains.

1090. Mechanical cream separator was invented in 1878 by Carl Gustaf Patrik de Laval, a Swedish scientist, engineer, and inventor with the Klosters-Bruck Steel Works. His design operated by means of centrifugal force. A bowl containing the milk was spun at high speeds, allowing the denser skim milk to rise to the rim of the bowl and flow into a collector. The lighter cream stayed in the center of the bowl. Laval went on to apply his experience to the design of high-speed turbines.

1091. Rotary cultivator was invented in 1912 by an Australian, A.C. Howard. It used revolving blades to stir the top layer of soil around a planted crop, aerating the soil and reducing weeds. Howard introduced a tractor-powered version in 1922.

1092. Coconut processing equipment that extracted the entire meat, milk, and oil from the coconut in one continuous operation was developed by Biotropic, a French company, and marketed beginning in 1990.

AGRICULTURE—FERTILIZATION AND IRRIGATION

1093. Large-scale irrigation project was constructed circa 6000 BCE in Choga Mami (near Mandali in present-day Iraq). Channels cut at right angles to an existing stream directed water to crops. Similar systems were soon developed in China and Egypt.

1094. Water-lifting device was the shaduf, also called the swipe, an upright beam with a long pole pivoted on its top. The pole had a bucket attached to one end and a clay or stone counterweight attached to the other. The shaduf, invented in Assyria (now Iraq) circa 2200 BCE and quickly adopted in Egypt, made the process of irrigation much more efficient than when water was drawn and transferred by hand. It is still used in parts of Africa and Asia.

1095. Synthetic fertilizer was superphosphate, produced in 1817 by James Murray of Ireland. He applied sulfuric acid to bones, which contain calcium phosphate. A process for making superphosphate by applying sulfuric acid to phosphate rock was patented in 1842 by John Bennet Lawes of Rothamsted, England, who then founded the world's first fertilizer factory.

1096. Nitrogen-rich bulk fertilizer was guano, the dried droppings of seabirds, used in South America for centuries and first imported to Europe from the Chincha Islands off the coast of Peru in 1839. Bird guano contains 11 to 16 percent nitrogen, 8 to 12 percent phosphoric acid, and 2 to 3 percent potash. Bats and seals also produce large quantities of guano, but it contains less nitrogen and was not preferred for fertilizer.

AGRICULTURE—PEST CONTROL

1097. Insecticide was pyrethrum (also known as pyrethrin), extracted from powdered chrysanthemum petals by the Chinese circa 100 BCE.

1098. Large-scale use of a pesticide occurred in Europe during the 1840s to aid in eradicating the vine powdery mildew (a common fungus, *Unciluna necator*). Vine powdery mildew had been imported from the New World and was a particular menace to vineyards. Crops were successfully sprayed with lime sulfur and then powdered sulfur.

1099. Organic pesticide was dichlorodiphenyltrichloroethane (DDT), a chlorinated organic chemical first synthesized in 1874 by a German chemist, Othmar Zeidler. Its usefulness as an insecticide was discovered in 1939 by Paul Hermann Müller, a research chemist at the J.R. Geigy Company, Basel, Switzerland, who won the Nobel Prize in Physiology or Medicine in 1948. DDT kills disease-bearing mosquitoes, lice, and fleas, as well as beetles and moths that attack crops. Some species become resistant to it. The chemical was eventually banned in many countries after it was shown to be highly toxic to birds, fish, and mammals.

1100. Biological pest control was initiated on a large scale in the United States in 1886 against the cottony-cushion scale, a tiny insect threatening California's citrus crop. A predatory species of ladybird beetle, *Rodolia cardinalis,* also called the vedalia beetle, was imported from Australia to destroy the pest, and within a year or two had succeeded so well that the technique was adopted around the world.

1101. Systemic pesticide was octamethylpyrophosphoramide, an organophosphate pesticide sold by the trade name Schradan. It was developed during World War II in Germany circa 1944, from research on military poison gas. Schradan was absorbed directly into plant tissue, making the plant itself toxic to pests; however, the pesticide was also poisonous to mammals, including humans.

1102. Modern integrated pest management program in Asia was introduced in Indonesia in 1986 through the Inter-country Program for Integrated Pest Control in Rice in South and Southeast Asia, under the auspices of the United Nations Food and Agriculture Organization. The program aided Indonesian farmers in developing an ecological, low-pesticide approach to controlling pests that attack rice crops.

ANIMALS

1103. Domesticated animal was the dog. Dogs may have been bred by humans as early as 135,000 BCE, according to genetic data derived by American evolutionary biologists at the University of California at Los Angeles, Texas A&M University, and Brigham Young University in Utah, in cooperation with Swedish researchers at the Royal Institute of Technology in Stockholm. Study of a control gene in the chromosomes of 162 wolves from 27 habitats and in 140 domestic dogs of 67 breeds indicated unusual diversity in ancient dogs, an indication of domestic breeding. The earliest known dog breeds are the New Guinea singing dog, the African basenji, the Australian dingo, and the Egyptian greyhound.

1104. Skeleton of a domesticated dog known to archeologists was found at Ain Mallaha, a site in northern Israel that contains remnants of the Natufian culture, circa 9600 BCE. A grave at the site was found to contain two skeletons, one of an elderly woman and the other of a puppy. The woman's hand was resting on the puppy's back.

1105. Ornamental goldfish breeding was started by the Chinese circa 1000 BCE, at the same time that raising carp for food became a common practice (goldfish are a type of carp).

1106. Elephants taken on a sea voyage were probably the 38 elephants who formed a cavalry unit in the army of Hannibal, commander of the Carthaginian armies against Rome in the Second Punic War (218–201 BCE). They were shipped across the Mediterranean from North Africa. Most of them died crossing the Italian Alps in 218. In 801, an elephant that had been

ANIMALS—*continued*

taken by ship from Tunis, in present-day Tunisia, to Italy was given as a present from the caliph Harun al-Rashid to the Frankish king Charlemagne, who had recently been crowned Holy Roman Emperor

1107. Horses in the New World were introduced in 1493 by Christopher Columbus during his second voyage. Twenty horses, all that survived of 34 stallions and mares that left Spain, were landed at the location of the future city of Santo Domingo (now in the Dominican Republic) on the island of Hispaniola.

1108. Horses on the North American mainland were war horses brought by Hernán Cortés in 1519 to the Yucatán to aid in his conquest of Mexico. Horses had lived in the Americas in prehistoric times, but had become extinct at the close of the last ice age.

1109. Animal exterminated by human action in historical times of record was the dodo (*Raphus cucullatus*), a flightless bird formerly native to the island of Mauritius in the Indian Ocean. First described by Portuguese sailors circa 1507, the slow-moving dodos were relentlessly hunted by humans and animals introduced by humans and were extinct by 1681.

1110. Greyhound racing has been practiced since ancient times, notably by the Egyptians and Greeks. The first known greyhound coursing club was founded in 1776 at Swaffham, Norfolk, in England.

1111. Large terrestrial mammal exterminated by human action in historical times was the blaauwbok or bluebuck (*Hippotragus leucophoeus*), a species of southern African antelope hunted to extinction. The last known living specimen was killed in 1799.

1112. Pigeon racing as an organized sport began in Belgium, where it has remained more popular than elsewhere in the world. The first long-distance race of more than 100 miles (160 kilometers) took place in 1818. The world's top event in pigeon racing, the Belgian Concours National, a race from Toulouse to Brussels, was first held in 1881.

1113. Dog show was held at Newcastle upon Tyne, England, on June 28–29, 1859. The organizers were two local sportsmen. Hunting dogs were the only breeds exhibited.

1114. Transatlantic crossing by a bird to be verified by scientists was made by a common tern, *Sterna hirundo*. In August 1917 it was found dead at the mouth of the Niger River in Nigeria, West Africa, wearing a band that had been attached at Eastern Egg Rock, ME, USA, on July 3, 1913.

1115. Coelacanth caught alive was netted in December 1938 in the coastal waters of the Indian Ocean near Cape Town, South Africa, by the fishing trawler *Nerine*. On December 23, Captain Hendrick Goosen invited Marjorie Courtenay-Latimer, a museum curator in East London, South Africa, to check through his catch for unusual specimens. She noticed a fish that she could not identify. It was 5 feet (1.5 meters) long and 126 pounds (57 kilograms), pale mauve blue with iridescent silver markings. On January 3, 1939, J.L.B. Smith, a chemistry teacher at Rhodes University, Grahamstown, positively identified the fish as a coelacanth *(Latimeria chalumnae)*, a lobe-finned fish known from fossils more than 350 million years old. Coelacanths were thought to have become extinct some 65 million years ago. The discovery, termed a "living fossil" by the newspapers, was hailed as the paleontological find of the century. A second coelacanth was caught off the Comoro Islands near Madagascar in 1952.

1116. Large mammal discovered since World War II was *Pseudoryx nghetinhenis,* a new species of bovid (cow) described from recent skulls and hides by British zoologist John Mackinnon, head of the Asian Bureau for Conservation in Hong Kong, in June 1993. The animal, called *saola* by Hmong villagers, was believed to live in the Vu Quang rain forest on the border between Laos and Vietnam, but no live animal was seen or captured by scientists.

ANIMALS—BREEDING AND REPRODUCTION

1117. Hairless dog breeds were developed in the Americas before the third century BCE. Pottery vessels made by the Colima culture of Mexico dating from circa 250 BCE depict dogs with the genetic abnormalities, including missing teeth, warts, and wrinkled skin, characteristic of hairless breeds.

1118. Livestock breeder who applied a scientific program to the development of new breeds was Robert Bakewell of Dishley, Leicestershire, England, considered the founder of modern animal breeding. While the basic principles of breeding have been known since ancient times, Bakewell was the first to use them consistently.

He chose breeding stock only for the most desirable traits; bred the best to the best, on the premise that "like produces like"; inbred animals to reinforce traits; and test-bred animals to determine if they were appropriate for breeding on a larger scale. Bakewell began work with sheep in 1755 and developed a new breed called Leicester. His experiments with beef cattle began in 1760. By 1769, his breed of short-legged, bulky, thickly fleshed cattle were in great demand by other breeders.

1119. Artificial insemination center was founded by Russian biologist Ilya Ivanovich Ivanov in 1901, for the breeding of horses. Semen was collected when a stallion mounted a dummy mare, then was diluted, stored, and inserted into the genital tract of a real mare.

1120. Platypus born in captivity was delivered in 1944 at Healesville Sanctuary, a zoo in Melbourne, Australia. A second platypus birth was not achieved until April 8, 1999, also at Healesville, when twin males were born, the first twin birth in captivity. Platypuses are extremely difficult to raise; as of 1999, none had survived in captivity outside Australia.

1121. Interspecies birth of a cat was announced by Betsy L. Dresser and colleagues at the Cincinnati Zoo in Cincinnati, OH, USA, on February 7, 1989. The kitten, an Indian desert cat (*Felis sylvestris*), an endangered species, was fertilized in vitro (a first for any exotic cat) and was carried to term by an ordinary domestic cat (*Felis catus*).

1122. Big cats born by in vitro fertilization were three tiger cubs delivered in May 1990 by cesarean section on a nine-year-old Siberian tiger at the Henry Doorly Zoo in Omaha, NE, USA. The technique, used for humans and domestic animals, was tailored to tigers by the reproductive physiologists Ann Miller and Leslie Johnston of the New Opportunities in Animal Health Sciences program at the National Zoo in Washington, DC, USA, along with colleagues at the Henry Doorly Zoo. Two of the cubs died from unconnected causes.

1123. Transgenic bull was developed in 1992 by GenPharm International, a small biotechnology company in Mountain View, CA, USA, cofounded by Jonathan MacQuitty. Transgenic animals are genetically engineered to contain human genes. The bull, named Herman, sired the first transgenic calves in 1993. Each calf carried a gene for production in cow milk of human lactoferrin, which is produced naturally in human milk. Important properties of HLF include antibacterial action and iron transport.

1124. Aye-aye born in captivity was a 5-ounce infant delivered on April 6, 1992, at Duke University in Durham, NC, USA, by a pregnant mother brought back from Madagascar in January 1992 by American primatologist Elwyn Simons of the Duke University Primate Center. An aye-aye is a rare prosimian, a near relative of apes and monkeys.

1125. White lion born in the Western Hemisphere was one of three cubs delivered of a white lion mother on March 24, 1994, at the Philadelphia Zoo in Philadelphia, PA, USA. It was also the first white lion born in captivity. At that time, a total of 15 white lions were believed to exist worldwide.

1126. Gorilla born by in vitro fertilization was Timu, a lowland gorilla delivered at the Cincinnati Zoo in Cincinnati, OH, USA, in 1995. It was also the first test-tube birth of an endangered primate. The mother was impregnated with sperm from a gorilla at an Omaha zoo. The process was managed by Betsy L. Dresser and colleagues at the Cincinnati Zoo's Center for Research of Endangered Wildlife.

1127. Cross-breeding of a llama with a camel took place at a government veterinary center in Dubai, United Arab Emirates, in 1997. The baby animal resembled its sire, the camel.

1128. Captive-bred lemurs returned to Madagascar were black and white ruffed lemurs released in November 1997 in the Betampona Reserve, where they joined a small existing population of the rare, endangered animals. The lemurs were bred and raised at the Duke University Primate Center in Durham, NC, USA.

ANIMALS—FOOD AND CLOTHING

1129. Animal domesticated for food was probably the pig, which may also have been the second animal domesticated by humans, after the dog. Pig bones yielding evidence of human consumption between 10,000 and 10,400 years ago were found in a 1994 excavation at Hallan Cemi, an early human settlement in southeastern Turkey.

1130. Cattle herders are thought by some archeologists to have been Africans who lived in Egypt's Western Desert in the eighth millennium BCE. Evidence for this possibility was uncovered at Nabta Playa, near the Sudanese border, where cattle bones were found. It is not yet clear whether these were domesticated cattle or wild cattle taken in hunting.

1131. Domesticated chickens were raised in India some 5,000 years ago. They were bred, chiefly for cockfighting, from wild birds with red feathers that are native to India's jungles.

ANIMALS—FOOD AND CLOTHING—continued

1132. Domesticated pigeons were bred by the ancient Egyptians of the fifth dynasty (about 3000 BCE) for use primarily as food and sacrificial offerings.

1133. Depiction of milking is visible on a frieze unearthed at the Sumerian city of Ur (now Tel-el-Muqayyar, Iraq). It was made circa 2900 BCE.

1134. Beekeeping originated with the Old Kingdom Egyptians circa 2780 BCE. Honey was highly valued, being the main source of sweetening (sugar was unknown in that era).

1135. Domesticated ducks were bred in China from wild mallard ducks some 2,000 years ago.

1136. Beef cattle in North America were introduced in 1550 by the Spanish colonists in Florida (now in the United States).

1137. Sheep-shearing machine was patented by James Highen of Melbourne, Australia, in 1868. The first practical sheep-shearer was used in 1888 at the Dunlop Station. It was patented by Frank Wolseley and John Howard.

ANIMALS—PROTECTION

1138. Law against cruelty to animals appeared in 1641 in the Massachusetts Bay Colony (now the area around Boston, MA, USA), which had been founded 20 years earlier by Puritan immigrants from England. The law stated: "No man shall exercise any Tirranny or Crueltie towards any bruite Creature which are usuallie kept for man's use." However, the idea of compassion towards living creatures was previously expressed in many religions, both eastern and western, and by Greek philosophers such as Pythagoras.

1139. Antivivisection prosecution was launched in Britain in 1874 against a visiting French physiologist who had given a demonstration in which he killed two dogs by injecting them with alcohol. The physiologist was charged with wanton cruelty but was eventually let go. Public outrage over the case led to the passage two years later of the Cruelty to Animals Act.

1140. Law regulating animal experimentation was the Cruelty to Animals Act, enacted in Britain in 1876 after a public furor over experiments on dogs. The law allowed the experiments to continue, but required scientists conducting them to be licensed and to meet a number of conditions intended to avoid the worst suffering.

1141. International animal protection society to campaign on global animal welfare issues was the World Federation for the Protection of Animals, founded in 1953. In 1981 it merged with the International Society for the Protection of Animals, founded in 1959, to form the World Society for the Protection of Animals.

1142. Treaty on the international trade in rare animals was the Convention on International Trade in Endangered Species of Wild Fauna and Flora. It was adopted in 1973 by representatives of 80 nations and later ratified by the governments of most of them. It prohibited commercial trade in 375 endangered species of wild animals and in products derived from them, such as hides, and set up a permitting system for trade in 239 more rare animal species. Rare plants, such as certain species of orchids, were also protected.

1143. Elephant hospital was opened in 1994 within the Thai Elephant Conservation Center near Lampang, Thailand. The founder was Soraida Salwala. The hospital was funded by private donations collected by the organization Friends of the Asian Elephant. Most of the patients were elephants who had been overworked and mistreated in the tourism and illegal logging industries.

ANIMALS—WORK AND TRANSPORTATION

1144. Horse riding was dated to circa 4000 BCE by archeologists David W. Anthony and Dorcas Brown of Hartwick College, Oneonta, NY, USA. They discovered microscopic bit wear—the damage done to a horse's premolar teeth by a bit—on the teeth of horse remains found in burial sites in the steppe grasslands of the Ukraine and Kazakhstan. The bit wear indicated that the horse was ridden with a bridle and a soft bit of bone, leather, or rope in its teeth. The discovery pushed back the beginning of horseback riding some 2,000 years earlier than had previously been thought.

1145. Beasts of burden to be domesticated were the ox and the onager (wild ass), used for agricultural work in Mesopotamia circa 3000 BCE.

1146. Horses for transport were employed by the Sumerians from approximately 3000 BCE. Sumerian wagons were drawn by onagers (*Equus hemionus onager*), a breed of wild ass native to central Asia. The word "onager" derives from the Indo-European root *agro,* meaning "field."

1147. Domesticated camels were tamed in southern Arabia some time before 2500 BCE. However, they did not come into common use as beasts of burden until a camel saddle was developed circa 1400 BCE.

1148. Depiction of a yoke for harnessing draft animals appears in Egyptian tomb paintings dating from 2000 BCE. The yoke was nothing more than a rope tied to the horns of oxen.

1149. Harness was developed in Mesopotamia around 1500 BCE for chariot horses. A leather harness, light, flexible, and responsive, was superior to the yoke for controlling horses during charges. Tandem harnesses that permitted horses and other draft animals to be hitched in single file were developed in both China and Italy by 200 CE. The modern form of harness first appeared in China about the year 500, but was not known in Europe until 1100.

1150. Camel saddle that was practical was developed circa 1400 BCE in northern Arabia. It was mounted over the hump, unlike earlier saddles that were slung over the camel's hindquarters, and was able to carry pack loads on either side and a rider on top. The high saddle also gave an advantage to the mounted warrior, and helped make the camel an effective beast of war for the first time. A later refinement, the Saharan saddle, which was mounted closer to the shoulders, was better adapted for carrying heavy loads and made possible the development of long-range caravans.

1151. Saddle for horses may have been developed in primitive form by the ancient horse-riding peoples of the Ukraine and Kazakhstan, who invented the bridle circa 4000 BCE. The earliest leather saddle of record is known from China circa 200 BCE, during the Han dynasty.

1152. Stirrup was invented by Hindu warriors circa 125 BCE. It consisted of a hanging loop that fitted over the rider's big toe. With their feet braced in stirrups, knights could charge with couched lance and stay in the saddle despite the shock of impact. It was the essential invention leading to the development of heavy cavalry.

1153. Reference to horseshoes was made in Rome during the first century BCE by the poet Catullus, who mentions the casting of a shoe by a mule.

1154. Metal stirrups were produced in China circa 250 CE. Chinese foot stirrups made of cast bronze or iron were in use well before the concept reached Europe via the Byzantine Empire circa 570 CE. The earliest mention of stirrups by a European is in the *Strategikon*, a military

manual written in 580 by the Byzantine general (later emperor) Mauricius Flavius Tiberius. Viking raiders adopted the metal stirrup in the eighth century and brought it to western and northern Europe.

1155. Pigeon post system regularly used for official and military communications was established by the sultan of Baghdad (now in Iraq) in 1150.

1156. Sheepdog trials were held in Wales in 1873. The dogs, primarily border collies, performed versions of their daily tasks—outrun, lift, fetch, drive, pen, and shed—in front of a judge and timekeeper.

1157. Guide dogs trained to assist blind people were the brainchild of a Dr. Gorlitz, director of the Frauendorf Sanatorium near Stettin, Germany (now Szczecin, Poland), where he treated soldiers wounded in World War I. He got the idea from his own German shepherd dog, Excelsior, who, following its herding instinct, helped a partially paralyzed patient to walk. The Austrian War Dog Institute and the German Association for Serving Dogs took up the suggestion and began training dogs for this purpose in 1916.

ANIMALS—ZOOS, AQUARIUMS, AND SANCTUARIES

1158. Zoo may have been the collection of animals owned by Shulgi, ruler of the ancient city of Ur (modern Tel-el-Muqayyar, Iraq) from circa 2097–2094 BCE.

1159. Large zoo was probably the vast animal collection of Wenwang, ruler of the Chinese border state of Chou and considered to be the author of the *I Ching*. Wenwang ruled circa 1150 BCE. During his reign, he founded the Ling-Yu ("Garden of Intelligence"), a 1,500-acre zoo and garden with hundreds of animals.

1160. Zoo in the Western Hemisphere of record was the royal botanical garden and zoo maintained for the ruler Moctezuma II in Tenochtitlán, the capital of the Aztecs (now Mexico City, Mexico). According to descriptions by the Spanish conquistadors led by Hernán Cortés in 1519, the zoo, which required a maintainence staff of 300, displayed jaguars, ocelots, eagles, snakes, and other animals, as well as deformed humans.

1161. Zoo in Europe of the modern type was the Imperial Managerie at Schönbrunn, the summer palace of the Habsburgs, in Vienna, Austria. The zoo was founded in 1752 by the Holy Roman Emperor Franz I for his wife Maria Theresa, and opened to the public in 1765.

ANIMALS—ZOOS, AQUARIUMS, AND SANCTUARIES—*continued*

1162. Public zoo founded as such that is in continuous operation is the London Zoo, founded by the Zoological Society of London in 1826. The original grounds are located in Regent's Park, London, England; a second, larger location was opened at Whipsnade Park, Bedfordshire, England, on May 23, 1931. As of 1998, the zoo housed more than 18,000 individuals of 1,400 species.

1163. Aquarium for public display opened at Regent's Park, London, England, in 1853.

1164. Oceanarium of significant size was Marineland, a privately owned amusement facility and research center near St. Augustine, FL, USA. The attractions included trained dolphins and other marine mammals, who performed in large seawater tanks ringed with seats for the audience, and a series of large aquaria containing sharks, rays, and other fish. It opened to the public on June 23, 1938.

1165. Bear cub sanctuary was established in Turkey in 1998. Created as a joint project of the World Society for the Protection of Animals and the Turkish Ministry of Forests, it was intended as waystation for abused cubs before they were returned to the wild. Turkey, Russia, and other countries in the region have a long tradition of capturing wild bears for training as performers.

ARCHITECTURE

1166. Structures still extant that were not uncovered by archeological excavation are huge stone temples, dating from circa 3250 BCE, located on the Mediterranean islands of Malta and Gozo. The structures are of stone-slab, post-and-lintel construction.

1167. Large stone structure was the Step Pyramid of King Zoser (also called Tosorthros) in Sakkara, the necropolis for the Egyptian city of Memphis. It was built circa 2650 BCE by Imhotep, Zoser's physician and counselor (as well as the first architect and engineer known by name), who recreated in stone the designs of earlier wattle-and-daub structures. The central mastaba—the main rectangular mass covering the tomb—is 200 feet (61 meters) high and is surrounded by six stepped terraces. Underneath are passages and chambers containing thousands of stone vessels and reliefs.

1168. Multi-story building was the ziggurat at the city of Ur (now Tel-el-Muqayyar, Iraq). The stepped baked-brick pyramid, containing internal rooms on several levels, was built circa 2100 BCE at the direction of Ur-Nammu, first king of the third Sumerian dynasty.

1169. Palace was built in Thebes by the 18th-dynasty Egyptian pharaoh Thutmose III, who ruled from 1504 to 1450 BCE and was noted for his extensive construction projects. The palace, designed as a dwelling place with no religious or military function, was enclosed by a wall and contained many small decorated rooms and courtyards.

1170. Portable wooden building of record was the Mishkan ("dwelling place"), the movable desert sanctuary that was constructed by the Israelites after their escape from Egypt, an event dated conjecturally by historians to circa 1250 BCE. According to *Shemot (Names),* the section of the Jewish Bible known in English as the Book of Exodus, the Mishkan had a frame of acacia beams held together with silver sockets. The frame was covered by linen cloths and enclosed within a tent made of goat hair, over which was placed a leather roof. The entire structure was dismantled, transported, and rebuilt whenever the Israelites moved their camp.

1171. Barrel vaults extant, made of mud brick, formed part of the funerary temple of the pharaoh Ramses II, who died in 1213 BCE. The building, called the Ramesseum, was located at Thebes.

1172. Caryatids of Greek design are those of the Treasury of the Cnidians in Delphi, Greece, built circa 550 BCE. *Caryatid* is the generic term for any architectural support, such as a column, that is wholly or partly human in form. Such anthropomorphic supports are known from ancient architecture in Mesopotamia and Egypt, but received their best-known expression in the Erechtheum, an Ionic temple on the Acropolis at Athens, Greece, built by the architect Mnesicles and completed in 405 BCE. The Erechtheum's southern portico is supported by a series of female caryatids. The name is derived from Caryae, a village in Laconia in southern Greece, whose women (according to the Roman writer Vitruvius) had to carry heavy loads as punishment for the town's military alliance with the Persians in 480 BCE.

1173. Buildings with acanthus ornamentation are two structures that are part of the Acropolis in Athens, Greece. On the Parthenon, completed circa 432 BCE, the leaf-shaped ornamentation was used on the pediment plinths. On the Erechtheum, completed circa 405 BCE, acanthus leaves were carved on the frieze. Acanthus ornamentation was first incorporated into the capital of a Corinthian column by Callimachus, a

Greek sculptor of Athens, circa 425 BCE. According to the Roman architect and historian Vitruvius, Callimachus was inspired by acanthus leaves growing around a basket placed upon the tomb of a young girl.

1174. Basilica known from historical records was the Basilica Porcia, built in 184 BCE by Cato the Elder in Rome. The basilica, an architectural form invented by the Romans, was a large, rectangular public building, often with smaller wings at one end, where legal and business affairs were transacted. The interior was divided by colonnades into a central aisle and two side aisles. In most cities, the basilica was constructed near the public square (the agora in Greek cities, the forum in Roman cities). The name is derived from the Greek word *basilike,* meaning "royal." Early Christians adopted the basilica design for their religious buildings.

1175. Basilica still extant is that of Pompeii, Italy. It was built sometime in the second century BCE and served as a combination courthouse and city hall. It was buried in the volcanic eruption that covered Pompeii in 79 CE and unearthed in excavations beginning in the late 19th century.

1176. List of Seven Wonders of the World was compiled by the writer Antipater of Sidon circa 150 BCE, although it may not have originated with him, and was elaborated and modified by later travelers. First on his roster of preeminent manmade structures were the Pyramids of Giza in Egypt, the only one of the Wonders still in existence.

1177. Concrete dome of note was erected over an octagonal room in the Golden House, the palace of the Roman emperor Nero, which was completed in 64 CE. The architects were Severus and Celer. The use of concrete, a fire-resistant material, was prompted by the great fire that had destroyed Rome a few years earlier.

1178. Monumental concrete structure extant was the Pantheon in Rome, Italy, built by order of the emperor Hadrian and completed in 128 CE. (Since 609 it has been formally known as the Church of the Santa Maria Rotonda.) The structure, 143 feet (43 meters) in both diameter and height, is a concrete drum topped by a huge freestanding dome, made of concrete with internal brick arches, that has a central opening 30 feet (9 meters) wide—the largest dome built until the 20th century.

1179. Pagoda evolved from the Buddhist stupa, a hemispherical mound topped by a stack of discs, each of which corresponded to a celestial domain. The first of these monuments was built in India circa 483 BCE. The towering, multistory pagodas most familiar to westerners were developed in China circa 600 CE.

1180. Wooden buildings still extant are in the Horyu Temple complex, a Buddhist temple near Nara, Japan. Founded by Prince Shotoku in 607, the complex includes two large, well-preserved wooden structures, a wooden pagoda and main hall, both built circa 708.

1181. Motte-and-bailey castles were built in the tenth century in the region between the Loire and Rhine rivers that is now divided between France and Germany. In the center was a wooden fortress on a hill (the motte), encircled by a ditch. The land around it (the bailey) was enclosed by a timber palisade.

1182. Stone castles were begun in France during the reign of Geoffroi Grisegonelle, or Geoffrey Greymantle, count of Anjou (960–87). His son, Foulques le Noir, or Fulk Nerra, who ruled from 987 to 1040, was known as *le grand bâtisseur* ("the great builder") because he built a network of fortified stone castles throughout the Angevin territories at intervals of about 20 miles to defend against raids from Brittany in the west and Blois in the east. Langeris, on the Loire River, finished in 992, is thought to have been the first.

1183. Flying buttresses were used in the construction of the Third Abbey Church at the Abbey of Cluny, France. Begun in 1088 under the abbot Hugh of Semur and his architect, Hezelo, the church was an immense structure 615 feet (187 meters) long, with a nave 118 feet (35.9 meters) wide, divided into five aisles to accommodate Cluny's many pilgrims and processions. Above the nave were ribbed barrel vaults 98 feet (29.8 meters) high. The roof supports were not strong enough to hold up the vaults, and after they collapsed in 1125, the builders added a series of external arched buttresses made of stone. The church was dedicated in 1131 and stood until 1798, when it was blown up by anticlericalists during the French Revolution. The earliest building with flying buttresses still extant is Nôtre-Dame de Paris, built between 1163, when the foundation stone was laid, and 1240, when the nave was completed. The narrow stone arched buttresses, ranged along the exterior of the cathedral, were placed at precise points to channel the lateral thrust of the rib vaults away from the walls. The walls of Nôtre-Dame were consequently higher and thin-

ARCHITECTURE—*continued*

ner than in previous stone buildings, and incorporated large areas of material that could not bear weight, such as stained glass. The flying buttresses, with their soaring props and struts, became a characteristic feature of French cathedral design. The original buttresses at Nôtre-Dame were rebuilt several times during the Middle Ages; the current buttresses were restored in the 19th century.

1184. Building in the Gothic style was the Abbey of St.-Denis, located in what is now a suburb of Paris. The traditional resting place of the kings of France, it was founded by King Dagobert I in the seventh century and rebuilt under Abbot Suger in the twelfth century. The reconstruction, completed in 1144, incorporated elements of what is now called Gothic style, including a rose window, large panels of stained glass, ribbed groin vaulting, sculptured ornamentation, and pointed arches. It was the model for the Gothic cathedrals that followed.

1185. Cathedral in the Gothic style was the Cathedral of Nôtre-Dame, begun in 1163 by Maurice de Sully, the bishop of Paris, France, and largely finished by 1235, although construction continued for another century. The cathedral replaced two earlier churches that stood on the site of an ancient pagan temple to Jupiter.

1186. Renaissance architect of importance and the first to apply the principles and building techniques of classical Roman architecture to contemporary Gothic forms was Filippo Brunelleschi of Florence, Italy. Confronted with the problem of adding a dome to the Florence Cathedral, Santa Maria del Fiore, which had remained unfinished for a century because no one had the technical knowledge to complete it, Brunelleschi designed a converging structure of 24 reinforced ribs concealed within inner and outer shells. He also invented a number of machines to aid in the construction work. The finished dome was 367 feet (111.86 meters) high and covered an octagonal space 140 feet (42.7 meters) wide. The cathedral was dedicated on March 25, 1436.

1187. Angled fortifications to protect against bombardment were advocated by the Italian Humanist polymath Leon Battista Alberti. In his book *De re aedificatoria (On the Art of Building)*, promulgated in 1452 and published in 1485, he suggested that serrated walls, especially walls built in a star-shaped design, would withstand artillery bombardment better than flat walls.

1188. Treatise on the theory of architecture was *De re aedificatoria (On the Art of Building)*, published in 1485 by the Italian Renaissance master Leon Battista Alberti. Alberti was the first to present a systematic discussion of architecture as "the art of building" and not merely as an exercise in structural mathematics.

1189. Artillery fortress was Civitavecchia, the papal port near Rome, Italy, on the Tyrrhenian Sea. In 1515, it was equipped with a system of multi-angled bastions that generated overlapping fields of fire.

1190. Royal palace in Europe to integrate public and private functions in one unified structure was the royal palace of Whitehall in London, England. Originally York Palace, the Westminster town house of the archbishops of York from 1245, it was rebuilt in 1530 by King Henry VIII as a replacement for the medieval Palace of Westminster, the first seat of the kings of England. Hans Holbein the Younger assisted in its decoration. It was destroyed by a fire in January 1698.

1191. Prefabricated building is considered to be Nonsuch House. Originally built in the Netherlands, it was taken apart piece by piece and brought to London, England, where it was reconstructed atop London Bridge in 1578. London Bridge, like many urban bridges in medieval and Renaissance Europe, was lined with houses and shops.

1192. Architectural model of Jerusalem was made circa 1590 by the German draftsman and model maker Jacob Sandtner, known for his realistic models of contemporary German cities. His three-dimensional wooden model, now housed in the Bavarian National Museum in Munich, Germany, was an imaginative reconstruction of the ancient walled city as it looked during the Second Jewish Commonwealth, before the destruction of the Second Temple in 70 CE. The model, and many maps of Jerusalem from the same period, were inspired by renewed interest in the Jewish scriptures following the work of Martin Luther.

1193. Sash windows are traditionally held to be the invention of the English architect and designer Inigo Jones. Sliding counterweighted windows were installed at Raynham (or Rainham) Hall in Norfolk, England, in 1630, and Jones is usually considered to be the architect responsible, although there is no documentary evidence of this.

1194. Neoclassic architecture spread widely from France and Britain to the rest of Europe and then the Americas from circa 1750, as a reaction to the decorative excesses of the Rococo style. The early excavations of Herculaneum and Pompeii were of particular influence to the development of Neoclassicism, as they provided numerous unaltered examples of Roman domestic architecture. Probably the first important neoclassic building was the church of Sainte-Geneviève in Paris (now the Panthéon), begun in 1757 by the architect Jacques-Germain Soufflot, who had studied the Greek ruins at Paestum.

1195. Iron-frame building in Europe was the Bibliothèque Sainte-Geneviève in Paris, built between 1843 and 1850 by the French architect Henri Labrouste. It made use of cast-iron supporting columns and arches.

1196. Glass building of importance was the Crystal Palace, constructed in Hyde Park, London, England, in 1851 for the London Great Exhibition. The architect was Joseph Paxton, a gardener and expert in the building of greenhouses and conservatories. Thousands of large sheets of glass, representing one-third of the entire glass output of Great Britain for a year, were fastened onto a frame of prefabricated steel rods to make what was at that time the world's largest building. It was 1,848 feet (563 meters) long and 408 feet (124 meters) wide, and had a central vaulted transept 108 feet (33 meters) high. With a floor area of 23 acres (approximately 92,000 square meters or 9 hectares), it enclosed an area four times that of St. Peter's Basilica in Rome, Italy.

1197. Reinforced concrete structure was a concrete house built in Paris, France, in 1862 by François Coignet. Coignet embedded wrought-iron I-beams into the concrete of roof and floors.

1198. Building of glass bricks of importance was the Glass Pavilion, built in 1914 in Cologne, Germany, by the modernist-socialist architect Bruno Taut.

1199. Geodesic dome was built on the roof of the Carl Zeiss optical works in Jena, Germany, in 1922 to house the world's first planetarium projector. The steel-rod frame of the dome was a highly sub-divided icosahedron, with great circle arcs, composed of 3,480 struts accurate in length to 0.002 inches. The shell was sprayed with successive layers of cement stabilized by steel mesh and backed by a wooden form, a process developed by Franz Dischinger and Ulrich Finsterwalder of the construction firm of Dyckerhoff and Widmann. When completed, it was the world's first thin-shell concrete structure. A geodesic dome is comprised of a complex network of triangles that form a roughly spherical surface. It is the structure with the highest ratio of enclosed area to external surface area.

1200. Use of the term "International Style" was made in 1932 in an exhibition catalog titled *The International Style: Architecture Since 1922,* prepared by the architects Henry-Russell Hitchcock and Philip Cortelyou Johnson for the Museum of Modern Art in New York, NY, USA. In their usage, the International Style referred to the dominant Western building style of the mid-20th century, in which unadorned industrial materials such as glass, steel, and concrete were used to create severely rectilinear buildings.

1201. Geodesic dome with a commercial use was a structure built for the Ford Motor Company in 1953 by the visionary American architect and engineer Richard Buckminster Fuller, who received U.S. patents on the geodesic dome in 1947 and 1954. Not long afterwards, Fiberglas geodesic domes designed by Fuller were put to use in the Arctic to house radar installations on the Distant Early Warning Line.

1202. All-plastic building of large size was the United States Exhibition Building, built in Moscow, Soviet Union (now Russia) in 1959. The building consisted primarily of interlocked fiberglass umbrellas.

ARCHITECTURE—ELEVATORS AND ESCALATORS

1203. Freight elevators were platforms raised by pulley systems or windlasses. They were used to hoist loads for construction projects and were described by the first-century Roman architect and military engineer Vitruvius (Marcus Vitruvius Pollio).

1204. Passenger elevator built for the purpose was a box that allowed King Louis XV of France to ascend from the balcony of his own chambers to the apartment of his mistress, Madame de Chateauroux, at the Palace of Versailles. It was suspended outside the palace, in a private courtyard, by a system of weights that could be manually operated. The elevator was installed in 1743.

1205. Safety elevator was invented in 1852 by Elisha Graves Otis when he was a mechanic at a bedstead factory in Yonkers, NY, USA. It had rails and catches that held the car in place even if the ropes failed. Otis went into the elevator-manufacturing business for himself the

ARCHITECTURE—ELEVATORS AND ESCALATORS—*continued*

following year and installed a freight safety elevator at a New York City address in 1853. In May 1854, at a public demonstration in New York City, he shocked viewers by going aloft in an open elevator whose ropes were then cut in front of their eyes. His first order for a passenger safety elevator came from the E.V. Haughwout and Company store at the corner of Broadway and Broome streets, New York City, in 1857.

1206. Escalator was an endlessly revolving inclined belt to which steps were attached. The design was patented on August 9, 1859, by Nathan Ames of Saugus, MA, USA. The first moving stairway to be put into operation was the Reno Inclined Elevator, designed by Jesse W. Reno, which was installed at Coney Island, New York City, in 1892. The modern form of the escalator was developed by the Otis Elevator Company of New York, NY, USA. The company registered the trade name Escalator in 1900 and installed the first one at the Gimbel Brothers department store in Philadelphia, PA, in 1901.

1207. Electric elevator was installed by the Siemens and Halske Company at the 1880 Mannheim Industrial Exhibition at Mannheim, Germany. It transported passengers to the top of an observation tower.

ARCHITECTURE—HEATING AND COOLING

1208. Central heating system for buildings was used circa 350 BCE by the Lakedaemonians (Spartans) of Greece, who warmed their floors by an arrangement of ceramic pipes filled with air that had been heated by an underground fire. This was the basis for the hypocaust system, used throughout the Roman world in antiquity.

1209. Cooling system for buildings was apparently designed by Leonardo da Vinci for the bedroom of the noblewoman Isabella d'Este, whose home was in Mantua, Italy. Cool air, created by a paddlewheel in an enclosed water-filled chamber, was blown into the room by a bellows. Leonardo da Vinci was a guest in the house in 1500.

1210. Hot-water heating system was sometimes used by the ancient Romans, who nonetheless preferred hot-air heating (the hypocaust system) for most of their buildings. The first hot-water-heated building in more modern times was a castle near Pecq, France, which was outfitted with hot-water pipes in 1777.

1211. Thermostat called by that name was patented in 1830 by chemist Andrew Ure of Glasgow, Scotland. His "heat-responsive element" used a bimetallic bar of dissimilar metals that bent at an angle according to the ambient temperature.

1212. Building with a patented cooling system was Westminster Palace, home of the Houses of Parliament in London, England, where a system that had been patented by the American expatriate inventor Jacob Perkins in 1831 was installed during the building's reconstruction after a destructive fire in 1834. Cool air from the Thames River entered the building through pipes and was pulled in by a draft created by fires maintained in the attics.

1213. Electric radiator was patented in 1892 by two Englishman, Rookes Evelyn Bell Crompton and H.J. Dowsing. It consisted of an enamel-coated metal plate wired to a source of electrcity.

ARCHITECTURE—HOUSES

1214. Houses known to archeologists were found in the village of Zawi Chenui in southeastern Anatolia, on what is now the Turkish-Iranian border. They have been dated to circa 9000 BCE.

1215. Houses made of brick were built in Jericho (now in Palestianian Authority territory) circa 8000 BCE. The bricks, pressed from mud and baked in the sun, were curved along one side and straight on the others, allowing both curved and straight walls. Foundations were made of stone. The simple domed roofs were made of daub and wattle.

1216. Rectangular houses were first built circa 7000 BCE in the city of Jericho (now in the Palestinian-controlled area between Israel and Jordan).

1217. House with an interior courtyard was invented by the Sumerians circa 3000 BCE in what is now Iraq. They developed mud brick houses with bare exterior walls and an open central space, surrounded by dwelling areas with doors and windows opening to the courtyard.

1218. Tract houses were built at Titris Hoyuk, in what is now Turkey, during the third millennium BCE. In the spring of 1997, archeologists Guillermo Algaze of the University of California at San Diego and Timothy Matney of Whitman College, Walla Walla, WA, USA, reported that their team had uncovered a series of houses that shared the same basic design. The houses had mud brick walls built on limestone and fieldstone foundations and were roofed with thatch. The floor plan provided for a central courtyard surrounded by 15 rooms. The courtyard in each house was partitioned into separate areas, one of which contained the family crypt. Evidence of weaving and winemaking was found in some of the houses.

1219. Town house was developed in the Mesopotamian city of Ur (now Tel-el-Muqayyar in Iraq). Starting in 2025 BCE, the inhabitants of Ur began constructing two-story mud brick town houses that featured wooden balconies, paved central courtyards, and staircases made of mud brick. Houses built on this plan can be found throughout the Middle East and the eastern Mediterranean.

1220. House with post-and-lintel construction was the megaron house, which made its appearance in what is now northern Iraq circa 1800 BCE. A megaron house contained a rectangular main room that had four columns, or posts. These posts supported cross beams, or lintels, that carried the roof. Another post-and-lintel arrangement was used for the entrance porch. Post-and-lintel construction was the basic element of classical Greek architecture.

1221. Apartment houses were multiple mudbrick dwellings built for the use of laborers in Rome and its port city, Ostia (in modern Italy), in the first century CE. They were four or five storeys high, with shops and workshops occupying the ground floor. The stairwell was inside.

1222. Home powered by solar cells was "Solar One," built in 1973 by a team of American researchers at the University of Delaware. The home's power system was a photovoltaic-thermal hybrid. Solar cell arrays generated electricity during the day and also acted as flat-plate thermal collectors, with fans blowing the warm air from over the array to phase-change heat-storage bins. Any surplus electricity was fed through a special meter to the local utility. At night, power was purchased from the utility.

1223. Fully computerized house was displayed to the public in Nishi-Azabu, an affluent district in the center of Tokyo, Japan, in December 1989. It was designed by architect Ken Sakamura and cost approximately US$7.1 million to build. It featured computerized windows that automatically controlled the temperature inside the house and a system that retrieved articles from storage.

ARCHITECTURE—SKYSCRAPERS

1224. Structure more than 100 meters tall was the Great Pyramid at Giza (near Cairo, Egypt), which, at 147 meters (481 feet) high, was the tallest man-made structure until 1889, when the Eiffel Tower in Paris was completed at 984 feet (300 meters) high. The Great Pyramid was built by the pharaoh Khufu (also called Cheops), the second king of the Fourth dynasty, circa 2500 BCE.

1225. Building more than 500 feet high was Lincoln Cathedral in Lincoln, England. Completed circa 1307, it was 525 feet (160 meters) high. The cathedral was destroyed by fire in 1548.

1226. Skyscraper was an office building ten stories tall that was built at the corner of La Salle and Adams streets in Chicago, IL, USA, for the Home Insurance Company of New York. The weight of the marble walls was borne by a steel skeleton, the first one ever used in a building. The design also featured a marble balcony supported by four columns of polished granite. The architect was Major William Le Baron Jenney. Construction began on May 1, 1884, and was finished in the fall of 1885. Though this was the first of the modern skyscrapers, it was much shorter than the ancient Pyramid of Cheops in Giza, Egypt, which was as tall as a 40-story building.

1227. Skyscraper more than 1,000 feet high was the Chrysler Building in New York City, NY, USA, completed in 1930. The tip of the 77-story building's spire is 1,046 feet (319 meters) from street level. It was designed by the American architect William Van Alen for the automobile magnate Walter P. Chrysler.

1228. Skyscraper with more than 100 stories was the Empire State Building, completed in 1931 in New York, NY, USA. The steel-framed building measures 1250 feet (381 meters) to the top of its 102 stories. The total height of the building is 1,454 feet (443 meters), including a television mast antenna.

1229. Telecommunications tower higher than 500 meters was the Ostankino Tower in Moscow, the Soviet Union (now Russia), completed in 1967. The unsupported tower stood 537 meters (1,762 feet) high and included an observation deck on the fifth-floor turret that was 360 meters (1,181 feet) high.

1230. Building more than 1,500 feet in height was the World Financial Center in Shanghai, China. On its planned completion in 2001, it was to measure 1,507 feet (460 meters) high.

ART

1231. Artwork extant may have been carved into a lava fragment dated to circa 198,000 BCE. The rock, which contains peculiar markings, was found in northern Israel in 1981 and was examined by American archeologist April Nowell of the University of Pennsylvania, Philadelphia, PA, USA.

1232. Art depiction may be contained in sculptured rock outcrops containing thousands of hole-like indentations at Jinmium in the Kimberley region of Australia, 280 miles southwest of Darwin. Using thermoluminescence tests, an archeological team from the Australian Museum and University of Wollongong dated the rocks at approximately 75,000 years old. The indentations are about 1 inch (3 centimeters) across and are arranged in abstract patterns or groups. One group may depict a four-legged animal, possibly a kangaroo.

1233. African rock art is tens of thousands of engravings and paintings, dating from as early as 4000 BCE, found on rocks in the Sahara. They depict herd animals that were plentiful in the region thousands of years ago, when much of the Sahara was open grassland.

1234. Art presenting a continuous narrative is the Telephos Frieze, part of the Great Altar of Zeus in Pergamon (now Bergama, Turkey), dating from the second century BCE. The frieze is a continuous series of more than 50 carved panels, which were originally painted. It shows a succession of scenes from the life story of a mythological hero named Telephos, who was the legendary founder of the royal dynasty that ruled Pergamon during the Hellenistic period. The Great Altar was the last important structure built at Pergamon before the death of Atalos III, the last Attalid king, and may have been the most spectacular monument of the Hellenistic world. German archeologist Karl Humann headed excavations at Pergamon that began in 1878. Part of the altar was removed from the site and installed at the newly built Pergamon Museum in Berlin, Germany, in 1930.

1235. Renaissance concept of the artist originated in Florence, Italy, in 1435 with the appearance of Leon Battista Alberti's influential book *De pictura,* or *Della pittura (On Painting.* Alberti, himself a painter and a master of many disciplines, elevated the artist from an artisan to a creator whose achievements sprang from the application of a developed intellect, including the mathematical and measurement skills needed to produce paintings with harmonious perspective.

1236. Autobiography of an artist was contained in the second book of *I Comentarii (The Commentaries),* by the Florentine sculptor Lorenzo Ghiberti. After discussing earlier artists of merit, Ghiberti describes his own career and assesses his place in art history. The book was probably completed in 1447.

1237. Book about the High Renaissance was *Le Vite de' più eccellenti architetti, pittori, et scultori italiani (The Lives of the Most Eminent Italian Architects, Painters, and Sculptors),* by Giorgio Vasari, a Florentine writer, painter, and architect. The book was published in 1550. Vasari discussed the history of Italian Renaissance art through biographies of geniuses such as Michelangelo and Raphael. While not always reliable as history, the book is nonetheless a primary source of information about the Renaissance.

1238. Academy of fine arts in Europe was the Accademia del Disegno (Academy of Design), founded in 1563 by the painter and art historian Giorgio Vasari in Florence, Italy. The school's patrons were Grand Duke Cosimo I de' Medici and Michelangelo Buonarroti. Intended to enhance the reputation and social status of artists, the academy was attended by the painters Titian and Tintoretto and the architect Andrea Palladio, among others.

1239. Artist of note to be investigated by the Inquisition was Paolo Caliari of Verona, Italy, better known as Paolo Veronese, who painted biblical and historical scenes peopled with multitudes of characters. In 1573, a Venetian monastery, the Convent of SS. Giovanni e Paolo, commissioned him to paint a version of the Last Supper, showing Jesus and his apostles seated at a table. Veronese's massive canvas, 42 feet (12.8 meters) wide, included some 50 unexpected figures, including German Protestant soldiers, drunkards, animals, and buffoons. The Inquisition charged him with irreverence and demanded his attendance at a tribunal. Questioned about his choice of characters, Veronese said: "I paint pictures as I see fit and as well as my talent permits." Rather than alter the painting in accordance with the tribunal's instructions, he changed the title to *Feast in the House of Levi,* a subject from the Jewish scriptures that was not subject to the same limitations.

1240. Autobiography of a European artist of importance was the *Vita di Benvenuto Cellini (Life of Benvenuto Cellini)*, first printed in Italy in 1728. Cellini was a Mannerist sculptor and goldsmith of high ability—a fact he is ever at pains to remind the reader—but the value of his autobiography is in its extremely frank and lively picture of the late Renaissance courts of Cosimo de' Medici, Francis I of France, and Pope Clement VII.

1241. Surrealist manifesto was *Manifeste du surréalisme,* published in 1924 by the French writer André Breton. In it he laid out the principles of surrealism, including automatism and antirationalism, claiming that this approach to artistic creation perfectly combined dream, impulse, and reality, leading to "an absolute reality, a surreality."

1242. Art holograms were produced circa 1969 by Uri N. Denisyuk, an art professor in the Soviet Union. He created holograms to provide a full record of the appearance of existing three-dimensional artworks.

ART—CRAFTS

1243. Southeast Asian decorative artwork is considered to be the ceremonial axe heads made of highly polished semiprecious stone that have been found throughout Indonesia, the Indochina peninsula, and Malaya. They date from the beginning of the second millennium BCE.

1244. Lacquer was produced in ancient China, perhaps as early as the eleventh century BCE, from the distilled and processed sap of a tree in the cashew family, *Rhus vernicifera.* Its earliest use may have been as a form of ink, since the sap turns black when exposed to air. In later centuries, it was applied decoratively, as a colored and shiny varnish, to all kinds of objects, from kitchen and ceremonial vessels to weapons, carriages, and musical instruments.

1245. Bronze artifacts in sub-Saharan Africa were the *Ukwu* sculptures and ritual objects made circa 900 by the Igbo people of what is now Nigeria. *Ukwu* bronzes mainly depict animals, especially insects and reptiles, with elaborate and minute surface detail. They were cast of high quality alloys of copper, tin, and lead, and carefully finished by chasing. Most were for ceremonial inclusion in the burial chamber of priest-kings and other high officials.

1246. Treatise on crafts by a practicing artisan produced in Europe was *De diversis artibus (Of Many Arts),* also known as *Schedula diversarum artium,* written by an author who called himself Theophilus Presbyter but who was probably a German Benedictine monk and metalworker named Roger of Helmarshausen. The book, which appeared sometime before 1140, described current techniques of craftsmen working in metal, stained glass, ivory carving, manuscript illumination, and wall painting.

1247. Woman silversmith to register her own hallmark was Hester Needham Bateman of London, England, who registered her initials, "H.B.," at the Goldsmiths' Hall in 1761, having taken over her husband's business after his death. Her specialty was elegant tableware.

1248. Fabergé Easter egg was presented on Easter 1884 to the Princess Dagmar, the wife of Tsar Alexander III of Russia. A masterful concoction of flawless, brilliantly colored enamelwork and precious materials, it won the firm of Peter Karl Fabergé a royal warrant to produce an Imperial Egg each year for the tsaritsa. The tradition was continued by Nicholas II, ending only with the Russian Revolution of 1917, after which Fabergé was driven into exile in Switzerland. The eggs are among the rarest and most precious objects in the world and are considered the highest expression of the enameler's, goldsmith's, and toymaker's arts.

ART—EXHIBITIONS

1249. Art exhibition in Europe open to the public was held at the Palais-Royale in Paris by the Académie de Peinture et de Sculpture. The show ran from April 9 to April 23, 1667. From 1671, the exhibition was held biennially in the Louvre.

1250. Exhibition of impressionist paintings was held in Paris, France, in 1874, in the studio of the photographer Nadar (Gaspard-Félix Tournachon). Among the painters who contributed their work to the exhibition were Claude Monet, Pierre-Auguste Renoir, Berthe Morisot, Edgar Degas, and Paul Cézanne. They shared an interest in expressing visual reality through the play of light and color and in reproducing with freshness scenes from ordinary life. The word "impressionism" was originally a derisive term coined by Louis Leroy in the magazine *Le Charivari,* who took it from the title of Monet's 1872 painting *Impression: Soleil levant (Sunrise).*

ART—EXHIBITIONS—continued

1251. International art exhibition was the Venice Biennale, held every two years beginning in 1895. The first exhibition contained 516 art works, shown salon-style. An autonomous agency under Italian law since 1928, the Biennale is partially funded by the Italian government and the city of Venice.

1252. Anti-art movement was Dada, formed circa 1916 by a circle of young artists including Jean Arp, Richard Hülsenbeck, Tristan Tzara, Marcel Janco, Emmy Hennings, and others, who met at Hugo Ball's Cabaret Voltaire, in Zürich, Switzerland. The Dada esthetic prized the expression of absurdity and meaninglessness as an antidote to what members saw as the hypocrisy of traditional art. The movement spread rapidly throughout Germany as well as to Paris and New York. The First International Dada Fair was hosted in Berlin in 1920; it included Marcel Duchamp's famous version of the *Mona Lisa* with beard and goatee.

1253. Modern art festival in South America was São Paulo Modern Art Week, held in São Paulo, Brazil, in February 1922. It included Dadaist and Cubist art, readings, and music, as well as paintings by such female artists as Anita Malfatti and Tarsila do Amaral.

1254. Surrealist exhibition was held in Paris, France, on November 14, 1925. Participants included Paul Klee, Max Ernst, Pablo Picasso, Joan Miró, and other members of the Surrealist group.

1255. Computer art exhibition was held in 1965 at the Technische Hochschule in Stuttgart, Germany.

1256. Havana Bienal was held in 1984 in Havana, Cuba. Considered the most important regular exhibition of contemporary art in and of the Third World, the Bienal by 1994 contained work by more than 200 artists from some 40 countries.

1257. Estonian Biennial was the Saaremaa Bienaal 1995, which took place in Saaremaa, Estonia. The exhibition, entitled "Fabrique d'Histoire," comprised works by 27 artists from 16 countries, with a focus on the Baltic region.

ART—MONUMENTS

1258. Sphinx was the Great Sphinx at Giza, near Cairo, Egypt. Dating from circa 2600 BCE, the recumbent stone colossus, 240 feet (70 meters) long and possessing the body of a lion and the head of a man, was carved from a knoll near the Great Pyramid of Khufu. The paws were carved separately and added later. It is believed to bear the features of the pharaoh Khafre, fourth king of the fourth dynasty. Among Arabs, the Great Sphinx is known as Abu al-Hawl, "Father of Terror." Later sphinxes are found in Mesopotamian and Greek sites.

1259. Obelisks known to archeologists were excavated at Abu Sir, an ancient Egyptian site between Giza and Sakkara, Egypt. They were dedicated to Re, the sun god, and date from the reign of the pharaoh Neuserre, circa 2449–2417 BCE.

1260. Triumphal arch was built in Rome in 196 BCE by Lucius Stertinius. This arch (and two others built during the Roman Republic) was destroyed in antiquity and little is known about it, other than that it contained statuary.

ART—PAINTING AND DRAWING

1261. Paint was applied to the walls of limestone caves in western Europe some 30,000 years ago. The paints used by the makers of the cave artists of France and Spain were produced by crushing minerals to powder. They made dark colors such as black, brown, and violet from manganese, and lighter colors, including yellow, light brown, and red, from hematite and ochre. To make the outlines of animal shapes, they daubed powder on the walls with their fingers or with twigs, moss, fur, or feathers. To achieve broad areas of color, they blew the powder through tubes made of hollowed bones.

1262. Paintings may be wall paintings discovered in a limestone cavern near Avignon in southeast France. The sophisticated images—more than 300 in all—were painted on the rock walls with red, black, and ochre mineral pigments. They depict a diverse menagerie of rhinoceroses, panthers, bears, owls, hyenas, and mammoths, some of which had never been found depicted on cave walls before. The discovery was made in December 1994 at Vallon-Pont-d'Arc by spelunker Jean-Marie Chauvet, a park ranger, with Eliette Brunel-Deschamps and Christian Hillaire. According to radiocarbon tests performed in 1995, the paintings are between 30,300 and 32,400 years old.

1263. Depictions of anatomically correct human have been found on a rock-face at Addaura, Sicily. Painted outlines of animals are accompanied by drawn male figures correctly proportioned and moving gracefully. The figures are up to 15 inches (38 centimeters) high. The paintings have been dated to circa 8000 BCE.

1264. Landscape in art appeared in a Sumerian stele dated to circa 2300 BCE. It depicts the Akkadian conquerer Naramsin in a triumph over Iranian border tribes. Included in the composition are trees and a conical hill.

1265. Attempt to portray continuous movement in a painting was made circa 1900 BCE, when an artist decorating a rock tomb at Beni Hasan, Egypt, created a long, continuous sequence that showed wrestling in action.

1266. Frescoes were created circa 1700 BCE by the Minoan muralists of ancient Crete (part of modern Greece) to adorn palaces and homes. Fresco is a technique of wall painting in which water-based paints are applied to a plastered wall, usually while the plaster is wet. The Minoan frescoes are notable for their lively, naturalistic scenes of ritual bull-leaping, dancing, sports, and dolphins. Early examples of fresco are also known from Ajanta, India (circa 200 BCE), and Dunhuang, China (circa 400 CE).

1267. Landscapes without human figures were painted on the walls of Minoan palaces in Crete and on the nearby island of Thíra (both now part of Greece) circa 1500 BCE. One room in a house at Thíra was completely covered with paintings of flowering hills and flying birds.

1268. Depiction of a flower arrangement showing a bouquet of cut flowers of different kinds appears in a mosaic that decorated the villa of the Roman emperor Hadrian at Tivoli. It dates from the early second century.

1269. Woman miniaturist in Europe was the Spanish nun Ende, whose works date to the late eighth century. She painted an extended cycle of miniature illuminations for a manuscript depicting the Apocalyptic vision of St. John the Divine compiled by the monk Beatus of Liebana circa 786.

1270. Monumental landscape painting extant is "The Riverbank," a silk scroll that was painted in tenth-century China by the Southern Tang scholar and courtier Dong Yuan. More than 7 feet (2 meters) long, the scroll shows a harmonious composition of mountains and water, rendered in brushed ink and light color. It influenced the development of Chinese art for five centuries. It was donated to the Metropolitan Museum of Art in New York, NY, USA, in 1997.

1271. Oil paintings known in Western art are four panels depicting angels and other heavenly beings on the ceiling of the Painted Chamber of the old Palace of Westminster, London, England. The panels were painted in 1264 for King Henry III. They were removed sometime before 1834, when the palace was destroyed by fire, and were subsequently lost. In 1995, two of them were discovered by workers who were cleaning out an old house. The panels were purchased by the British Museum.

1272. Church altarpiece from western Europe showing the Annunciation still extant was painted by Simone Martini in 1333 for the Duomo in Siena, Italy (it is now in the Galleria degli Uffizi in Florence). It shows the angel Gabriel kneeling and holding out an olive branch, symbol of both peace and the city of Siena, to Mary, who is seated and holding a book

1273. Oil painters known by name are traditionally considered to be the Flemish artists Hubert and Jan Van Eyck, the co-founders of the Flemish school of painting in the early 15th century. This opinion is based on the account of them provided by Giorgio Vasari in his 1550 book *Le Vite de' più eccellenti architetti, pittori, et scultori italiani (The Lives of the Most Eminent Italian Architects, Painters, and Sculptors)*. Oil painting went through a two-century period of development before the Van Eycks, but Hubert Van Eyck perfected the technique of layering thin glazes of pigment over a white gesso ground to create the brilliantly luminous colors that distinguish works in oil. Jan was probably the first to use a very clear oil as a vehicle and to thin his paint with turpentine. The first oil painting known with certainty to have been worked on by Hubert and Jan Van Eyck is *The Three Marys at the Tomb*, probably finished circa 1422, and now in the collection of the Museum Boymans–van Beuningen in Rotterdam, the Netherlands.

1274. Painting composed with one-point perspective was *The Trinity*, a fresco painted circa 1425 by Masaccio (Tommaso di Giovanni di Simone Guidi) in the Church of Santa Maria Novella, Florence, Italy. Using mathematical principles developed by the Florentine architect Filippo Brunelleschi, Masaccio succeeded in giving the barrel-vaulted hall depicted in his painting the illusion of depth, height, and volume, with lines converging on a vanishing point fixed at the level of the spectator.

1275. Full-length double portrait is the Flemish artist Jan Van Eyck's painting *The Arnolfini Wedding* of 1434. It commemorates the marriage of Giovanna Cenami and the silk merchant Giovanni Arnolfini, both of Lucca, Italy. A circular mirror on the far wall reflects the couple from behind, and also reveals two wit-

ART—PAINTING AND DRAWING—*continued*

nesses, one of whom is Van Eyck himself. An inscription above the mirror reads *Johannes de eyck fuit hic 1434* ("Jan van Eyck was here 1434"). The work is currently in the collection of the National Gallery, London.

1276. Scientific explanation of perspective in art was set forth by the Italian painter and architect Leon Battista Alberti in his book *De pictura (On Painting),* also known as *Della pittura,* written in 1435. Alberti was a friend of Filippo Brunelleschi, the Florentine architect who is credited with working out the mathematical laws of perspective circa 1410. Alberti's book, much studied by the artists of the early Renaissance, made possible their visually accurate paintings and drawings, which used perspective to create the illusion of three-dimensionality on a flat plane.

1277. Artist to draw freely with pen on paper in Europe was Guasparri di Spinello di Luca Spinelli, known as Parri Spinelli, who lived in Italy from 1387 to 1453. His spontaneous, lively drawings, which included the first regular use of the technique of crosshatching, were unique for the time. Spinelli is also the first European artist to whom a large body of drawings can be confidently attributed. Among his works are studies of draped and undraped male figures, landscapes and cliffs, city scenes, baptisms, standing and seated saints, and many crucifixions.

1278. Woman to paint frescoes known to art historians was Honorata Rodiana, a painter active in Cremona, Italy, in the mid-15th century.

1279. Satirical portrait appears in Michelangelo's *The Last Judgment,* painted in fresco on the altar wall of the Sistine Chapel at the Vatican in Rome, Italy. The work was completed in 1541. Michelangelo depicted a papal official, Biagio da Cesena, as King Minos, the Prince of Hell. The artist also added a satirical self-portrait, painting his own face on the flayed skin of a sinner consigned to damnation.

1280. Caricatures known to have been drawn intentionally as individual works were created by Annibale Carracci of Bologna, Italy, an accomplished painter who lived from 1560 to 1609. The word, which originated with Carracci, is derived from the Italian word *caricare,* "to load."

1281. Women Renaissance artists to attain renown were the Italian painters Sofonisba Anguissola (1535–1625) and Lavinia Fontana (1552–1614). Anguissola, the daughter of a minor noble, worked in the style of the early Italian mannerists and was praised by Michelangelo for her drawing ability. Her self-portraits and paintings of her family earned her commissions from the aristocracy of Milan, Mantua, and Parma. She became a painter at the court of Philip II of Spain and served as art instructor to Queen Isabel. Fontana, from Bologna, studied art with her father, the Mannerist painter Prospero Fontana, and became a renowned portraitist with many clients. Popes Gregory XIII and Clement VIII named her their official painter. Her husband, Gian Paolo Zappi, with whom she had several children, ran their household and served as her business manager.

1282. Dutch painter of note who was a woman was Judith Leyster, who studied under Frans Hals and was a member of the painters' guild in her native city of Haarlem by the time she was 24, in 1633. A brewer's daughter, she painted domestic scenes, portraits, and still-lifes.

1283. Pastellist of renown was Rosalba Carriera, born in 1675, a Venetian painter known for her portraits and miniatures. She began working in pastel circa 1703, using soft sticks of pigment with a gum binder to create a series of small portraits on paper. Achieving wide popularity after moving to Paris in 1620, Carriera created pastel portraits of many royal figures, including King Louis XV and the Holy Roman Emperor Charles VI.

1284. French Impressionist artist who was a woman was Berthe Morisot (1841–1895). A student of Camille Corot, she first exhibited in the Paris Salon of 1864 and showed there regularly for the next decade. In 1868 she befriended the painter Édouard Manet, who later became her brother-in-law; he had a profound effect on her artistic development. Morisot went on to take part in all but one of the Impressionist exhibitions, including the first, held in the Paris studio of the photographer Nadar (Gaspard-Félix Tournachon) in 1874. She is best known for her paintings of women, in domestic or outdoor settings, depicted in jewel-like colors, notably an emerald-like green.

1285. Cave paintings to be discovered were those in the limestone cave at Altamira, near Santander in northern Spain. In 1879, a Spanish nobleman and amateur archeologist, Marcelino de Sautuola, and his twelve-year-old daughter Maria were exploring a large chamber in the cave when Maria looked up and exclaimed *"Toros!"* She was the first to see the colorful Paleolithic paintings of bison on the ceiling. An account of the discovery was published by Sautuola in 1880, but the paintings were not accepted as genuine ancient artifacts until the early 20th century. The paintings may date to circa 20,000 BCE.

1286. Nonrepresentational modern paintings were made in the early 20th century. Art historians do not agree on the question of who was the first painter of nonrepresentational works. Some cite the American artist Arthur Dove, who in 1910 created a series of six paintings on linen, such as *Nature Symbolized, No. 1*, that took their inspiration from landscape but showed no clearly recognizable representational forms. Preference, however, is usually given to the Czech-born painter František Kupka. His 1912 work *Fugue in Red and Blue*, a composition of concentric masses of color and radiating lines, contained no discernible reference to any real object or scene. (Kupka's work, most of which was done in Paris, was not widely known until 1946, when a retrospective of his work was held in Prague.) At approximately the same time, the Russian-born painter Wassily Kandinsky was also experimenting with complete abstraction. An untitled watercolor, which Kandinsky later dated 1910, was thought to be his first nonrepresentational work, but recent scholarship dates the work at 1912 or early 1913. Kandinsky was the most influential early abstract painter and wrote the first theoretical treatise on abstraction, *Concerning the Spiritual in Art* (1912).

1287. Oil pastels were introduced to the world market by a Japanese firm, Sakura Color Products, in 1924. The color sticks, containing pressed pigment in an oil-and-binder base, were called Cray-Pas. They could make a mark on almost any surface and could be worked with solvents and a brush for painterly effects.

1288. Old Master painting sold at auction for more than US$10 million was *Portrait of Duke Cosimo I de' Medici* by Jacopo da Pontormo, dating to circa 1525. Pontormo was an apprentice of Leonardo da Vinci and is considered an early exponent of the Mannerist style. The painting sold at Christie's auction house in New York City on May 31, 1989, for US$32 million.

ART—PRINTMAKING

1289. Woodcut illustration extant was the frontispiece to the *Chin-kang Ching*, a Chinese translation of the Mahayana Buddhist text called the *Diamond Sutra*. The text was printed on six sheets of paper with wood blocks by Wang Chieh in 868. The woodcut illustration shows the Buddha seated amidst a crowd of divine and human figures.

1290. Printed European illustration that has been authentically dated is a 1423 print from a wood engraving entitled "St. Christopher." It was found in the library of the Carthusian monastery in Buxheim, Germany.

1291. Engraving on metal plate as a printmaking technique emerged simultaneously and independently in the Rhine valley of Germany and in northern Italy circa 1450. The first intaglio prints whose dates of execution are known were made in 1446. The Florentine goldsmith Maso Finiguerra (1426-64) was the first master engraver known by name. The first well-known artist to create engravings meant to stand on their own as works of art was another Italian, Antonio Pollaiuolo, whose "Battle of the Nudes" dates to circa 1465.

1292. Drypoint engraving was employed circa 1475 by a German or Flemish artist known as the Master of the Housebook. He is named for a book, dated to that year, that contains drypoint engravings of astronomical scenes, battle scenes, and scenes of daily life. Drypoint is an engraving technique in which a sharp stylus, held like a pencil, is used to incise shallow lines into the surface of a copper plate. The drypoint line leaves a burr that can hold ink for printing.

ART—SCULPTURE

1293. Female figurine of the "Venus" type is the Venus of Lespugue, a figure sculpted from the ivory of a mammoth tusk, found at Lespugue, France, and dating from circa 23,000 BCE. Like all sculptures of this type, it has an exaggerated female anatomy, giving rise to the assumption that it is an artifact of goddess worship or of a fertility cult.

1294. Plaster statues known to archeologists were unearthed at Ain Ghazal on the northern outskirts of Amman, Jordan, the site of the largest early Neolithic settlement in the Near East. In 1984, a team of Jordanian and American researchers noticed plaster objects protruding from the side of a bulldozer cut made some years earlier during highway construction. Two caches of large plaster statues,

ART—SCULPTURE—*continued*

some more than a meter in length, as well as the first known plaster face masks, were removed and shipped to the Smithsonian Institution's Conservation Analytical Laboratory near Washington, DC, USA, where they were restored. The statues have been dated to 6500 BCE.

1295. Metal statue known to archeologists is a copper figure of Pharaoh Pepy I of Egypt, dating from approximately the year 2300 BCE. The statue, 2 feet (0.6 meters) high, was found in the 1890s in the ruins of a temple in Edfu and is now in the collection of the Egyptian Museum in Cairo.

1296. Sculptures in sub-Saharan Africa were terra-cotta objects created by the Nok culture, which flourished in the southern Sudan and northern Nigeria from about 600 BCE to 200 CE. Nok artists made naturalistic sculptures of animals and stylized human figures with tubular heads, trunks, and limbs and perforated eyes of an elliptical or triangular shape. The Nok style influenced the later, more highly developed art of the Ife of western Nigeria. The Nok were also the first known makers of iron in western Africa.

1297. Sculpture of the goddess Aphrodite in the nude was the marble statue *Aphrodite of Cnidus,* made circa 350 BCE by the Athenian sculptor Praxiteles, who thus defied the Greek convention of showing female bodies clothed, except for depictions of prostitutes. Many later representations of Aphrodite, including the *Venus de Milo,* are modeled on this work.

1298. Renaissance sculptor of note who was a woman was Properzia de Rossi, whose marble busts and bas-reliefs decorated churches in her hometown of Bologna, Italy. Her relief *Joseph and Potiphar's Wife* was carved circa 1520.

1299. Public sculpture honoring a car race was *Monument to Levassor, Porte Maillot, Paris,* by the French sculptor Camille Lefebvre, installed in 1907 in Paris. The marble monument commemorates the race from Paris to Bordeaux held in 1895, which was won by Émile Levassor.

1300. Kinetic sculpture that used physical movement was *Mobile: Bicycle Wheel* (1913) by the French artist Marcel Duchamp. It was the first of the artist's "readymades," sculptures incorporating everyday objects. The sculpture consisted simply of a freely rotating bicycle wheel attached to a wooden stool.

1301. Kinetic sculpture in which motion was the main esthetic factor was *Kinetic Sculpture (Standing Wave)* by the Russian sculptor Naum Gabo (born Naum Neemia Pevsner). Completed in Moscow in 1920, the work consisted of a vertical metal rod attached to an electric motor inside the base. The motor caused an oscillation in the rod that produced a wave effect.

1302. Mobiles were invented in Moscow, Russia, in 1920 by the Constructivist artist Aleksandr Mikhailovich Rodchenko. He created kinetic sculptures consisting of flat wooden shapes suspended from the ceiling by wires and animated by air currents.

1303. Welded metal sculpture in which welding was the main assembly process was developed by the Spanish sculptor Julio González. Originally trained as a metalsmith in his father's workshop in Barcelona, Spain, González made contact with Pablo Picasso and other modern artists after moving to Paris in 1900. In 1927 he began a series of forged and welded small figures, and followed in 1931 with a series of female figures made from welded iron rods and bars. In 1934 González made *Maternity,* the first sculpture of welded prefabricated sheet metal, pipes, and other metal parts.

1304. Three-dimensional computer model of an Old Master sculpture was created in 1999 by art historian Jack V. Wasserman of Temple University, Philadelphia, PA, USA, with the help of researchers from the T.J. Watson Center of International Business Machines in Yorktown Heights, NY, USA. The sculpture was the *Florentine Pietà* by Michelangelo Buonarroti, dated to circa 1550. The large marble group depicts the body of Jesus supported by Nicodemus (probably a self-portrait of Michelangelo), the Virgin Mary, and Mary Magdalene. The sculpture, housed at the Museo dell'Opera del Duomo in Florence, Italy, was photographed and laser-scanned in minute detail. The resulting images were assembled into a three-dimensional computer model that could be rotated and examined at close range from any angle.

AVIATION

1305. Treatise on aerodynamics was "On Aerial Navigation," published in 1809 by the English aeronautical pioneer George Cayley. It was the first work to describe practical methods for the design and flight of heavier-than-air craft.

1306. Aeronautical society was the the Société Aerostatique, founded in Paris, France, in 1852.

AVIATION—AIRPLANES

1307. Flying model airplane may be an ancient Egyptian model of a bird in the collection of the Cairo Museum in Egypt. The small model was made of sycamore wood and had a wingspan of 7 inches (18 centimeters). It was unearthed in Sakkara in the late 19th century and is believed to date from circa 300 BCE. According to the Egyptian physician and model bird expert Khalil Messiha, it was carefully designed for flight, with a vertical tail rudder and wings with negative dihedrals for stability. When tested, a reproduction of the wooden bird flew as well as a modern model airplane.

1308. Practical design for a fixed-wing aircraft was proposed (but not built) in 1799 by the English baron, inventor, and aeronautical pioneer George Cayley, who had been fascinated by the challenge of human flight since childhood. His heavier-than-air flying machine featured a fixed wing for lift, tail flaps for stability and control, and a propulsion system (although at that time no engine suitable for aircraft had been invented). Many elements of the design were later incorporated into Cayley's glider designs, one of which flew in 1853.

1309. Radial aviation engine was built in 1903 by the American engineers Charles Matthews Manly and Stephen Marius Balzer for a plane designed by the aviation pioneer Samuel Pierpont Langley. Langley abandoned his airplane project after the Wright brothers became the first to fly a heavier-than-air piloted craft, and the engine was never successfully tested in flight. Radial engines were later used in the majority of prop-driven aircraft.

1310. Pilot's licenses were issued without examination to 16 self-described pilots in December 1909 by the Aero Club de France. The first pilot to pass an examination in order to receive a license was Alfred Leblanc, who received his brevet in 1910.

1311. Woman to receive a pilot's license was Elise Deroche, also known as Baroness de Laroche. She made her first solo flight in 1909, and received her license from the Aero Club de France on March 8, 1910.

1312. Amphibious aircraft was designed and built in 1912 by the German-American engineer Grover Cleveland Loening. The craft, which Loening called an "aeroboat," was an airplane with a boat-shaped keel and pontoon floats in addition to landing gear.

1313. Woman to pilot an airplane over the English Channel was an American, Harriet Quimby. On April 16, 1912, she flew a Blériot monoplane from Dover, England, to Hardelot, France. On July 1, 1912, flying in an aviation exhibition over Dorchester Bay, near Quincy, MA, USA, she fell to her death when her plane suddenly pitched forward and threw her and a passenger from the cockpit.

1314. Aerobats were Petr Nikolaevich Nesterov, a lieutenant in the Imperial Russian Air Service, and Celestin Adolphe Pégoud, a French pilot. On September 1, 1913, Pégoud deliberately flew upside down. Eight days later, Nesterov performed the first complete loop in aviation history.

1315. Airliner was Benoist Airboat No. 43, a biplane flying boat that flew between Tampa and St. Petersburg, FL, USA, on regularly scheduled flights beginning on January 1, 1914. The St. Petersburg–Tampa Airboat Line, the world's first airline with scheduled flights using an airplane, was launched by aircraft builder Thomas Benoist, pilot Antony Jannus, and salesman Percival Fansler. The airline flew every weekday from January to March 1914.

1316. All-metal airplane was the J-1 Blechesel ("Sheet Metal Donkey") a monoplane completed on December 12, 1915, by Hugo Junkers at his aircraft factory in Dessau, Germany.

1317. Long-distance passenger plane was the *Goliath,* designed and built by the firm of Maurice and Henri Farman in Paris, France. It was introduced in 1917 and made regular flights from Paris to London beginning in 1919.

1318. Rocket-propelled airplane was a glider driven by two solid-fuel rockets. The tailless craft was developed by the German rocketry pioneer Alexander Martin Lippisch and first flight-tested on June 11, 1928, in the Rhön Mountains of Germany.

1319. Sport airplane was the Pou du Ciel (Flying Flea), a single-seat aircraft of wooden construction with two wings mounted in tandem. It was invented in 1933–34 by the French aviation pioneer Henri Mignet. A forerunner of the modern microlight aircraft, the Pou was intended to be constructed and flown by anyone of reasonable mechanical skill. Like many modern homebuilt aircraft, it was quite unsafe, and its popularity, initially very high, plummeted as fast as the plane itself when this became widely known. Mignet's 1933 book *Le Sport de l'Air (Aerosport)* was the first to treat aviation as recreation.

AVIATION—AIRPLANES—*continued*

1320. Commercial airliner widely used was the Douglas DC-3 twin-engine monoplane (also known as the C-47 or Skytrain), introduced in 1936 by the Douglas Aircraft Company of California, USA. The durable, stable craft could carry up to 28 passengers or 6,000 pounds (2,725 kilograms) of cargo. Military transport versions of the DC-3 were widely used by the Allies in World War II. Manufacturing ended in 1945, but aging DC-3s are still in use today.

1321. Turbojet aircraft was the German-built He-178, designed by Hans von Ohain with financing from industrialist Ernst Heinkel. It was powered by a centrifugal-flow turbojet, an engine that combined a compressor, combustion chamber, and gas turbine. The inaugural flight of the He-178 took place on August 27, 1939, at Rostock-Marienehe, with Flug Kapitan Erich Warsitz as pilot.

1322. Person to travel more than 500 miles per hour was the World War II German test pilot Hanna Reitsch. In 1941, she made the initial flight test of the prototype rocket-powered Messerschmitt Me 163 Komet fighter-interceptor. Reaching a height of 30,000 feet (9144 meters) within 90 seconds of take-off, the experimental craft achieved a top speed of 500 miles (805 kilometers) per hour.

1323. Ejection seat was a compressed-air piston device installed in the German-built prototype Heinkel He-280 jet fighter. It was first tested with a human being on January 13, 1942, when the test pilot ejected safely at 7,875 feet (2,400 meters) as ice on the wings forced the plane down.

1324. Ejection seat that was propelled by explosives was introduced in the Saab 21 fighter, built in Sweden by the aircraft manufacturer Svenska Aeroplan Aktiebolaget. The first flight test was on July 30, 1943. All modern aerospace ejection seats and escape pods are explosives-propelled.

1325. Ramjet aircraft was the Leduc 0.10, built in France according to the design of French aviation engineer René Leduc. It was successfully launched from another aircraft on April 21, 1949.

1326. Jet airliner was the British Overseas Airline Corporation's De Havilland Comet 1, designed by Geoffrey De Havilland's De Havilland Aircraft Company and first flown in 1952.

1327. Black box flight recorder for recording voice and instrument data was invented in 1958 by David Warren of Melbourne, Australia. The recorder made possible for the first time an accurate determination of events leading up to an aviation accident.

1328. Supersonic jet airliner was a Soviet aircraft, the Tupolev 144 supersonic transport, designed by Alexey Alexeyevich Tupolev. The Tu-144 broke the sound barrier on a test flight in 1969; it achieved Mach 2 in 1970. The plane, which its designers hoped would routinely shorten flight times across the Soviet Union, was beset by technical and financial problems and made only a few commercial flights in the 1970s.

1329. Jumbo jet was the Boeing 747, introduced for flight service by the Boeing Company of Seattle, WA, USA, in 1970. The wide-bodied, two-decked aircraft was taller than a six-story building and could carry up to 490 passengers, more than could easily be handled by the terminal facilities of the time. The first 747s went into transatlantic service for Pan American Airlines beginning on January 21, 1970.

1330. Aircraft powered by human motion that actually flew was the ultra-lightweight *Gossamer Condor,* whose construction materials included Mylar plastic sheeting, cardboard, aluminum tubing, and piano wire. The pilot generated the power by working a set of bicycle pedals. Aeronautical engineer Paul MacCready of Pasadena, CA, USA, led the team that designed and built the plane. On August 23, 1977, bicyclist Bryan Allen pedaled it over a three-mile course to win the US$50,000 Kremer Prize, awarded for milestones in human-powered flight.

1331. Aircraft powered by human motion to cross the English Channel was the *Gossamer Albatross,* designed and built by a team under the direction of Paul MacCready, an aeronautical engineer living in Pasadena, CA, USA. On June 12, 1979, bicyclist Bryan Allen piloted the ultralightweight craft from Folkestone, England, to Cap Gris-Nez, France, in 2 hours 55 minutes.

1332. Solar-powered airplane to cross the English Channel was the *Solar Challenger,* which made the 5.5-hour flight on July 7, 1980. American Stephen R. Ptacek was at the controls of the 210-pound (95-kilogram) plastic and aluminum aircraft as it crossed from Cormeilles-en-Vexin, France, to Manston Air Base, England, at an average speed of 30 miles (48 kilometers) per hour.

1333. Home-built supersonic jet was the work of an American, Jim Bede of Bede Jet. His lightweight, two-seat jet aircraft, built for personal use, had a maximum speed of Mach 1.4 at altitudes up to 45,000 feet (13,716 meters). It was introduced in 1991 at the Experimental Aircraft Association's 39th annual international convention and sport aviation exhibition in Oshkosh, WI, USA.

1334. Ornithopter that actually flew was designed by Jeremy Harris of the Battelle Memorial Institute, Columbus, OH, USA, and James DeLaurier, a professor of aerospace engineering at the University of Toronto, Canada. In late 1991, after 20 years of work, they designed and flew the world's first true ornithopter, an aircraft that flapped its wings and flew like a bird. It weight 8.6 pounds (4 kilograms). The model ornithopter was made of wood, Kevlar, and carbon composites, and was radio-controlled. Each of the wings was 10 feet (3 meters) long and was made of three hinged panels. They were powered by a 1-horsepower piston engine. The first flight lasted 11.5 minutes.

1335. Aircraft powered solely by propfan engines was the Antonov 70, a medium-sized military transport plane built in the Ukraine. It was first flight-tested in 1994. A propfan engine is a hybrid propeller/jet turbine powerplant designed for efficient operation at transsonic speeds (speeds approximating the speed of sound). Its scimitar-shaped props, which have small diameters, rotate at much higher speeds than in conventional prop engines. The An-70's fuel-efficient turbofan engines featured contrarotating propellers, designed by the Stupino Design Bureau, that reduced noise levels and vibration.

AVIATION—AIRPLANES—COMMERCIAL SERVICE

1336. Air transport company was the Aerial Transit Company, incorporated in London, England, on March 24, 1843, by William S. Henson and John Stringfellow. The company proposed to ship freight and passengers on regularly scheduled balloon flights. The concept was too far ahead of its time, and was not commercially successful.

1337. Chartered airplane flight was made by the British pilot Tom Sopwith (Sir Thomas Octave Murdoch Sopwith) on June 28, 1911. Sopwith's biplane was chartered by Wanamaker's, the New York department store, to make a delivery to the deck of the ocean liner *Olym-*

pia, which had sailed for Europe a few hours before. The package dropped by Sopwith's plane contained a pair of eyeglasses for Washington Atlee Burpee, the famous seed dealer, who was a passenger on the ship.

1338. Airline meals regularly available were box lunches served on the Handley Page Transport scheduled route between London and Paris beginning in 1919. The cost was three shillings per meal.

1339. London to Paris scheduled passenger airplane service was inaugurated on August 25, 1919, by Aircraft Travel and Transport of London, England.

1340. Intercontinental passenger service was inaugurated on September 1, 1919, by the French airline Lignes Aériennes Latécoère. Stops were made in Toulouse, France; Barcelona, Spain; and Tangier, Morocco. In 1920, a stop in Casablanca was added.

1341. Airline in continuous operation from its founding to the present day is Koninklijke Luchtvaartmaatschappij NV (KLM, in English Royal Dutch Airlines), founded by Albert Plesman on October 7, 1919, in Amstelveen, The Netherlands. KLM's first scheduled flight took place between Amsterdam and London, England, on May 17, 1920.

1342. Airline ticket and reservation office was opened in Amsterdam, the Netherlands, in 1921 by KLM, the Royal Dutch Airlines.

1343. Commercial pilot who was a woman was the American pilot Ruth Rowland Nichols, employed by the New York–New England Airways carrier beginning in 1932.

1344. Regularly scheduled transoceanic flights were flown by Deutsche Lufthansa AG between Germany and South American cities, notably Buenos Aires, Argentina, beginning in 1934.

1345. Commercial round-the-world airplane flight was a Pan American flight that left La Guardia Field, New York, NY, on June 17, 1947, and returned 309 hours 21 minutes later, having stopped at Newfoundland, London, Istanbul, Karachi, Manila, Bangkok, Calcutta, Shanghai, Tokyo, Guam, Wake, Honolulu, and San Francisco. Actual flying time for the route, which covered a distance of 22,297 miles (35,876 kilometers), totaled 101 hours 32 minutes. The plane carried ten crew members and 21 passengers, each of whom paid US$1,700, and was piloted by Hugh Gordon.

AVIATION—AIRPLANES—COMMERCIAL SERVICE—*continued*

1346. Scheduled commercial jet flight was the British Overseas Airways Corporation scheduled route from London, England, to Johannesburg, South Africa. A De Havilland Comet inaugurated the route on May 2, 1952. Regular jetliner service for passengers was introduced in 1956 by Aeroflot, the airline of the Soviet Union. The first such flight was made by a Tupolev 104 that flew from Moscow to Irkutsk on September 15, 1956. The Tu-104 was the civilian version of the Tu-95, a large turboprop bomber that had first flown the previous year. It was designed by Andrey Nikolayevich Tupolev and Aleksandr A. Arkhangelsky.

1347. Commercial jet airplane pilot who was a woman was Maria Atanassova of the Soviet Union, who was hired by Aeroflot, the Soviet national airline, in 1953 and became a full pilot three years later.

1348. Round-the-world airline service was offered by Qantas Empire Airways, the Australian airline, beginning on January 14, 1958. Two flights on Lockheed Super Constellations were offered: one from Sydney to London flying east, and another from Sydney to London flying west. The eastbound trip took 5.5 days; the westbound trip took 6.5 days.

1349. Transoceanic jetliner service was offered by the British Overseas Airways Corporation with its run from New York, NY, USA, to London, England, inaugurated on October 4, 1958.

1350. Supersonic airliner to enter regular service was the British–French Concorde, which had a maximum cruising speed of Mach 2.04, or 1,354 miles (2,179 kilometers) per hour. Its first regular service flights were on January 21, 1976: a British Airways flight from London to Bahrain, and an Air France flight from Paris to Rio de Janeiro, Brazil.

1351. Supersonic jet service across the Atlantic Ocean was initiated by two Concorde jet aircraft, one from Paris and the other from London, which arrived at Dulles International Airport, Washington, DC, USA, on May 24, 1976, after trips that lasted about three hours each. Regular supersonic flights between France and New York City began on October 19, 1977.

1352. Supersonic airline co-pilot who was a woman was Barbara Harmer, a pilot with British Airways,. On March 25, 1993, she served as first officer on the British–French Concorde supersonic liner from London, England, to New York, NY, USA.

AVIATION—AIRPLANES—FLIGHTS

1353. Flight of a heavier-than-air machine that was mechanically propelled took place on the shores of the Potomac River near Washington, DC, USA, on May 6, 1896. The machine, called an aerodrome by its inventor, Samuel Pierpont Langley, was a 26-pound (12-kilogram) craft 16 feet (4.9 meters) long and was powered by a 1-horsepower steam engine. Repeated launchings from a platform on the riverbank resulted in at least one flight that lasted about a minute and a half.

1354. Airplane flight recognized by most aviation historians took place on December 17, 1903, at Kill Devil Hills, near Kitty Hawk, NC, USA, with Orville Wright at the controls of a motor-powered airplane he had built with his brother Wilbur. The plane, which weighed 745 pounds (338 kilograms) and had a 4-cylinder, 12-horsepower engine, was launched from a monorail after a short run. It remained aloft for 12 seconds and covered 120 feet (37 meters). Three subsequent flights took place that day, of which the longest covered 852 feet (260 meters) in 59 seconds. The average speed was 31 miles (48 kilometers) per hour. However, some historians respect the claim of Gustave Whitehead, who is said to have made four flights, one of which covered a distance of 1.5 miles (2.4 kilometers), in his airplane *No. 21* on August 14, 1901, near Bridgeport, CT, USA.

1355. Complete aerial turn in an airplane was performed by Wilbur Wright on September 20, 1904, at Kitty Hawk, NC, USA.

1356. Launch of a heavier-than-air machine entirely under its own power took place on March 18, 1906, at Montesson, France, when the Romanian aircraft designer Trajan Vuia went aloft in his *Vuia 1*. The plane took off without using a ground-based catapult or launching system and attained an altitude of about a yard (1 meter) for approximately 40 feet (12 meters). The *Vuia 1* was the first monoplane and the first airplane with pneumatic tires.However, some historians of aviation give the credit for the first airplane flight in Europe to a Brazilian pilot, Alberto Santos-Dumont, who flew on September 13, 1906, at Bagatelle Field, Paris, France.

1357. Airplane flight over the ocean was achieved by the French aviation pioneer and inventor Louis Blériot in 1909. On July 25 of that year, Blériot flew the *Blériot XI*, a monoplane design, from Calais, France, to Dover, England, a distance of about 23 miles (37 kilometers). It was also the first flight over the English Channel.

1358. Seaplane flight took place on March 28, 1910, when a seaplane designed by Frenchman Henri Fabre took off from Martigues near Marseilles, France. The first practical seaplanes were designed and piloted the following year by American aviator Glenn Hammond Curtiss.

1359. Flight from Cairo to Calcutta was made by Australian aviator Ross Macpherson Smith in 1918.

1360. Transatlantic airplane flight originated on May 8, 1919, from Rockaway Air Station, Rockaway, NY, USA. A hydroplane, U.S. Navy/Curtiss flying boat NC-4, commanded by Lieutenant Commander Albert Cushing Read, left Rockaway in company with two other planes, both of which failed to finish the trip. Stops were made at Trepassey, Newfoundland, Canada; Horta and Ponta Delgada, in the Azores; and Lisbon, Portugal. The final destination, Plymouth, England, was reached on May 31. The total distance was 4,717 miles (7,590 kilometers); flight time was 53 hours 58 minutes.

1361. Nonstop transatlantic airplane flight originated from Lester's Field, St. John's, Newfoundland, Canada, on June 14, 1919. The pilot, Captain John Williams Alcock, and the navigator, Lieutenant Arthur Whitten Brown, flew a Vickers Vimy that was powered by two 360-horsepower Rolls-Royce engines. They landed at Derrygimla Bog near Clifden, Republic of Ireland, on June 15, a flight of 1,960 miles (3,154 kilometers).

1362. Flight from England to Australia was made by two Australian brothers, Keith Macpherson Smith and Ross Macpherson Smith. They departed from England on November 12, 1919, in a twin-engine Vickers Vimy biplane, accompanied by J.M. Bennett and W.H. Shiers, and landed at Darwin, Northern Territory, on December 10.

1363. London to Delhi scheduled aircraft flight arrived in Delhi, India, on January 8, 1927.

1364. Transatlantic solo airplane flight was made by the American aviator Charles Augustus Lindbergh on May 20, 1927, from New York to Paris. He flew about 3,610 miles (5,808 kilometers) in 33 hours 32 minutes in the *Spirit of St. Louis,* a Ryan monoplane equipped with a single 225-horsepower Wright Whirlwind motor. He left Roosevelt Field, NY, USA, at 7:52 A.M. on May 20 and arrived at 5:24 P.M. New York time the following day at Le Bourget field, Paris.

1365. Transatlantic east-west nonstop airplane flight took place in 1928, when two Germans, Günther von Hünefeld and pilot Captain Hermann Köhl, with Captain James Fitzmaurice of Ireland, left Dublin, Ireland, on April 12 in a single-engine Junkers monoplane. Their destination was New York City, but they crashed in Labrador, Canada, on April 13, and were later rescued.

1366. Flight from the United States to Australia was completed in 1928 by two Australians, Charles Kingsford-Smith and Captain Charles T.P. Ulm, with two American navigators, Harry W. Lyon and James Warner, flying a trimotor Fokker. They had departed from Oakland, CA, USA, on May 31 and made stops at Hawaii and the Fiji Islands before arriving at Brisbane, Australia, on June 8, 1928.

1367. Manned rocket-plane flight took place on September 30, 1929, in Germany, when industrialist and inventor Fritz von Opel, scion of the Opel car manufacturing company, piloted a Hatry glider fitted with 16 solid-fuel rockets for a flight of about 75 seconds, covering a distance of 2 miles (3 kilometers).

1368. Paris to New York nonstop airplane flight was completed in 37 hours and 18 minutes on September 2–3, 1930, when French pilots Dieudonné Coste and Maurice Bellonte flew a Breguet biplane from Le Bourget field in Paris, France, to Valley Stream, Long Island, NY, USA.

1369. Transpacific nonstop airplane flight was made by two Americans, Clyde Pangborn and Hugh Herndon, Jr., who landed at Wenatchee, WA, USA, on October 5, 1931, having flown from Sabishiro, Japan, a distance of 4,458 statute miles (7,173 kilometers), in 41 hours 13 minutes. They flew in a single motored 425-horsepower Bellanca monoplane. This was the last lap of a round-the-world trip.

1370. Transatlantic solo airplane flight by a woman was made by American aviator Amelia Earhart, a native of Atchison, KS, who left Harbor Grace, Newfoundland, Canada, at 5:50 P.M. on May 20, 1932, and arrived at Londonderry, Ireland, at 8:46 A.M. on May 21. She flew 2,026 miles (3,260 kilometers) in 14 hours 56 minutes. Her flight took place exactly two years after that of Charles Augustus Lindbergh, the first pilot to make a solo transatlantic crossing.

1371. Transatlantic westbound solo nonstop flight was achieved by English pilot James A. Mollison, who flew a De Havilland Puss Moth from Portmarnock, Ireland, to Pennefield, New Brunswick, Canada, on August 18, 1932.

AVIATION—AIRPLANES—FLIGHTS—
continued

1372. Round-the-world solo airplane flight was made by American aviator Wiley Hardeman Post in a Lockheed Vega monoplane, the *Winnie Mae.* He took off from Floyd Bennett Field, New York, NY, USA, on Saturday, July 15, 1933, at 5:10 A.M. and landed in Berlin, Germany, at 6:55 A.M. the following day, after a flight of 25 hours 45 minutes. Other stops were at Königsberg, Moscow, Novosibirsk, Irkutsk, Rukhlovo, Khabarovsk, Flat, Fairbanks, and Edmonton. Post returned to Floyd Bennett Field on July 22 at 11:59:30 P.M., making the round-the-world circuit of 15,596 miles (25,094 kilometers) in 7 days 18 hours 49 minutes, of which 115 hours 36 minutes 30 seconds was flying time. His airplane was equipped with a Sperry automatic pilot and a directional radio. Post had previously made a round-the-world flight in the *Winnie Mae,* accompanied by Harold Gatty. Post was thus the first person to fly around the world twice.

1373. Woman to fly solo from England to Australia was the New Zealand aviator Jane Gardner Batten. In May 1934 she flew from England to Australia in 14 days, 23 hours, and 25 minutes; the following year, she also became the first woman to fly the return trip solo.

1374. Transpacific solo airplane flight by a woman was made by the American aviator Amelia Earhart. She left Wheeler Field, Honolulu, Hawaii (then a United States territory), at 10:15 P.M. on January 11, 1935, and arrived at Oakland Airport, Oakland, CA, USA, at 4:31 P.M. the next day, covering 2,408 miles (3,874 kilometers) in 18 hours 16 minutes at an average speed of 133 miles (214 kilometers) per hour.

1375. Round-the-world flight by a commercial airplane was made by the *Pacific Clipper,* of Pan American Airways, which left San Francisco, CA, USA, on December 2, 1941, with a ten-man crew under Captain Robert Ford, and arrived at New York City on January 6, 1942. The plane covered 31,500 miles (50,684 kilometers) in a flying time of 209.5 hours. Because of war conditions, the return trip from New Zealand was over the Coral Sea, Netherlands East Indies, Indian Ocean, Java Sea, Bay of Bengal, Arabian Sea, Persian Gulf, Red Sea, the Nile and Congo rivers, overland to West Africa, thence to Brazil, and finally to New York.

1376. Jet-propelled landing on an aircraft carrier was made on November 6, 1945, by an American pilot, Ensign Jake C. West, in an FR-1 Fireball on the escort aircraft carrier *Wake Island* off San Diego, CA, USA. The Fireball, a U.S. Navy fighter plane, was powered by both a turbojet and a conventional reciprocating engine, and normally used its reciprocating power plant for takeoff and landing, switching over to the jet as either an exclusive or a supplementary propulsive force once it was in the air. As West was landing, the reciprocating engine failed, and he landed using jet power.

1377. Airplane to fly faster than the speed of sound was piloted by an American, Major Charles Elwood "Chuck" Yeager, who flew a Bell X-1, an army rocket airplane, at Edwards Air Force Base, Muroc, CA, USA, on October 14, 1947. The rocket engine was built by Reaction Motors, Rockaway, NJ. The plane attained the speed of 750 miles per hour (1,207 kilometers per hour, Mach 1.06) and an altitude of 70,140 feet (21,377 meters). Alcohol and liquid oxygen were used as fuel, forced into the burners by gaseous nitrogen. The plane was equipped with rockets that could keep it in the air only ten minutes. It had to be dropped from a bomber while at a high altitude. Official announcement of the achievement was withheld until June 10, 1948.

1378. Transatlantic eastward flight by jet airplane was made on July 20, 1948, by 16 Lockheed P-80 Shooting Stars that flew from Mount Clemens, MI, USA, to Odiham, England, under the command of Colonel David Carl Schilling, commander of the U.S. 56th Fighter Group. They traveled a distance of 4,283 miles (6,891 kilometers) in 10 hours 40 minutes. Stops were made at Goose Bay, Labrador; Bluie West Two, Greenland; Keflavik, Iceland; and Stornoway, in the Outer Hebrides, off Scotland.

1379. Round-the-world nonstop flight by an airplane was made in 94 hours 1 minute by a B-50 Superfortress, *Lucky Lady II,* under the command of U.S. Captain James Gallagher. The plane left Carswell Air Force Base, Fort Worth, TX, on February 26, 1949, at 11:21 A.M., carrying a crew of 14. It averaged 249 miles per hour (401 kilometers per hour) on its 23,452-mile (37,734-kilometer) trip. It was refueled four times in the air by B-29 tanker planes and landed on March 2, 1949, at 9:22 A.M.

1380. Transatlantic nonstop jet airplane flight was made on September 22, 1950, by Colonel David Carl Schilling, commanding officer of the U.S. 31st Escort Wing, who flew from Manston, England, to the U.S. Air Force base at Limestone, ME, a distance of 3,300 miles (5,309 kilometers), in a single-engine F-84E Republic Thunderjet. The flight took 10 hours 1 minute. Schilling made three aerial refueling contacts with Air Force tanker planes. Lieutenant Colonel William D. Ritchie, who also took off in an F-84, was forced to bail out over Labrador, Canada.

1381. Transpacific nonstop jet airplane flight was made on July 29, 1952, by a four-jet U.S. RB-45 Tornado bomber from Elmendorf Air Force Base. The plane crossed from Anchorage, AK, USA, to Yokota Air Base, Japan, a distance of 3,460 miles (5567 kilometers), in 9 hours 50 minutes, at an average speed of 350 miles per hour (563 kilometers per hour). The plane was refueled twice in flight by B-29 tanker aircraft. The flight was under the command of Major Louis H. Carrington.

1382. Woman to fly faster than the speed of sound was an American test pilot, Jacqueline Cochran Odlum, who on May 18, 1953, broke Mach 1 (the speed of sound) in a U.S.-built North American F-86 Sabre jet fighter over Edwards Air Force Base, Muroc, CA, USA. In that flight, she attained a speed of 760 miles per hour (1,223 kilometers per hour). She became the first woman to fly at Mach 2 (twice the speed of sound) in 1961.

1383. Round-the-world flights over the North Pole on a regularly scheduled air route began on November 15, 1954, when the Scandinavian Airlines System, using DC-6B planes, inaugurated simultaneous service in both directions between Copenhagen, Denmark, and Los Angeles, CA, USA. The eastbound flight, with 40 passengers, left Los Angeles International Airport at 8:23 P.M. Greenwich Mean Time and arrived at Copenhagen on November 16 at 8:18 P.M. G.M.T., an elapsed time of 23 hours 55 minutes (20 hours 38 minutes' flying time) for the 5,800 miles (9332 kilometers). The westbound flight was made in 24 hours 11 minutes' flying time (27 hours' elapsed time).

1384. Round-the-world nonstop flight by a jet airplane was made by three B-52 U.S. Air Force Stratofortress bombers, which flew 24,325 miles (39,139 kilometers) in 45 hours 19 minutes at an average speed of 525 miles per hour (845 kilometers per hour) under the command of Major General Archie J. Old, Jr., of the 15th Air Force. The takeoff was from

Castle Air Force Base, Merced, CA, on January 16, 1957, and the landing was made at March Air Base, Riverside, CA, on January 18. The planes were refueled in flight by KC aerial tankers. Each eight-engine jet carried a crew of nine. The route was via Newfoundland, French Morocco, Saudi Arabia, the coasts of India and Ceylon, the Philippines, and Guam.

1385. Round-the-world nonstop airplane flight without refueling took place from December 15 to December 23, 1986, when two Americans, Richard Rutan and Jeana Yeager, circled the globe in *Voyager,* a front-and-rear-propeller plane constructed mainly of plastic. The 216-hour, 24,986-mile (40,202-kilometer) circumnavigation began and ended at Edwards Air Force Base, Muroc, CA. Most of the fuel supply was stored in the plane's wings. The plane decreased in weight by roughly 80 percent as the fuel was consumed.

1386. Transatlantic flight by an ultralight airplane was piloted by Eppo Numan, a Dutch artist and restaurateur. He departed from the Netherlands in June 1989 in the *Eppo Windmaster,* a lightweight hang glider with an 80-horsepower motor, and, after many delays, landed in New York, NY, USA, in August 1990. Numan undertook the flight to publicize his concern for the world's environment.

1387. Accurate recreation of the last flight of Amelia Earhart was undertaken by the American pilot Linda Finch in a 1935 Lockheed Electra 10E, the same model of plane flown by Earhart in her failed 1937 attempt to circumnavigate the globe at the equator. Finch departed from Oakland, CA, USA, on March 17, 1997, and returned to Oakland on May 28.

1388. Transatlantic crossing by an robot airplane took place on August 21, 1998, when an Aerosonde robot aircraft, nicknamed "Laima," landed on a field at the Benbecula military range on the island of South Uist in the Outer Hebrides, Scotland, after a 26-hour non-stop flight from Bell Island Airport, St. John's, Newfoundland, Canada. The 29-pound (13-kilogram) aircraft, with a 9-foot (3-meter) wingspan, was powered by a one-cylinder 20cc engine. It guided itself using Global Positioning Satellite data across the 2,000-mile (3,200-kilometer) stretch of the North Atlantic. It was the first unmanned airplane to cross the Atlantic. The Aerosonde flight was conducted by the University of Washington Aeronautics and Astronautics department. The Aerosonde technology was developed by Greg Holland, techni-

AVIATION—AIRPLANES—FLIGHTS—
continued

cal director of the Australian Bureau of Meteorology Research Centre, and manufactured by the American engineering companies The Insitu Group and Environmental Systems and Services.

AVIATION—AIRSHIPS AND BALLOONS

1389. Statement of the principle of hot-air ballooning was made in China circa 200 BCE. A text from that era states: "Take an egg and empty the shell carefully, then ignite a tiny piece of wood in the hole in order to produce a strong air current. The egg will rise in the air by itself and fly away from the spot."

1390. Hot-air balloon was a small test model that was launched inside a room at the Casa de India in Terreiro do Paco, Portugal, on August 8, 1709. It was made by Father Bartholomeu de Gusmão, a Portuguese priest.

1391. Hot-air balloon that was successful was invented by two papermakers, the Montgolfier brothers, Joseph-Michel and Jacques-Étienne, of Annonay, France. In 1782 they discovered that hot smoke captured in a paper or silk bag made the bag rise. On June 4, 1783, the brothers gave the first public exhibition of their discovery in the marketplace of Annonay. Their balloon was made of silk lined with paper. They filled it with hot air from a fire of dampened burning straw and wood. During a ten-minute flight, the unmanned balloon rose to an altitude of about 3,000 feet (914 meters) and traveled more than a mile and a half before settling to the ground.

1392. Hydrogen balloon was made by three French inventors, the physicist and mathematician Jacques-Alexandre-César Charles and the Robert brothers, Nicholas-Louis and Anne-Jean. The balloon was launched over Paris on August 27, 1783.

1393. Animals sent aloft in a balloon were a sheep, a rooster, and a duck, sent aloft by the Montgolfier brothers, Joseph-Michel and Jacques-Étienne, of Annonay, France. On September 19, 1783, in a demonstration for King Louis XVI and a crowd of thousands in the palace courtyard at Versailles, the Montgolfiers sent aloft a 60-foot (18-meter) balloon painted azure blue and decorated with golden fleurs-de-lis. Suspended from it was a basket that carried the three animals. The flight lasted eight minutes. The balloon landed safely about 2 miles

(3 kilometers) away, much to the relief of spectators concerned for the animals' safety. "It was judged that they had not suffered, but they were, to say the least, much astonished," wrote one observer.

1394. Ascent in a hot-air balloon took place in Paris, France, on October 15, 1783, when a 26-year-old physician, Jean-François Pilâtre de Rozier, went aloft in a tethered balloon constructed by the Montgolfier brothers. The first untethered flight was made a few weeks later, on November 21, when Pilâtre de Rozier and an army officer, François Laurent, Marquis d' Arlandes, floated over Paris in a Montgolfier balloon, traveling 5.5 miles (8.8 kilometers) in the course of 25 minutes.

1395. Ascent in a hydrogen balloon was made over France by two of the balloon's inventors, Jacques-Alexandre-César Charles and Nicholas-Louis Robert, on December 1, 1783.

1396. Airship powered by a propeller was developed in 1784 by Jean-Baptiste-Marie Meusnier, a French army general. The balloon was torpedo-shaped, as in later dirigibles, and the propeller was hand-cranked by a crew of three. The airship was capable of a top speed of 3 miles (5 kilometers) per hour.

1397. Flight instrument extant was the barometer carried by American balloonist and physician John Jeffries in his voyage over London, England, in 1784, and again when he and a French companion crossed the English Channel in a balloon on January 7, 1785. Jeffries was the first person from North America to fly.

1398. Woman to ascend in an untethered balloon was Elizabeth Tible, who went aloft on June 4, 1784, over Lyon, France, in a hot-air balloon made by the Montgolfier brothers.

1399. Balloon flight over open water was made by Jean-Pierre François Blanchard, a French aeronaut, and John Jeffries, an American physician, who crossed the English Channel from Dover, England, to the Felmores Forest in France on January 7, 1785.

1400. Balloon used for wartime reconnaissance was launched on June 26, 1794, at Fleurus, Belgium, where French forces under Marshal Jean-Baptiste Jourdan were mounting a counterattack against an assault by Austrian and Dutch soldiers led by Friedrich Josias, prince of Saxe-Coburg. The French soldiers who went aloft were able to report on the movement of enemy troops.

1401. Steam-powered airship was developed by the French inventor Henri Giffard. His craft was a hydrogen-filled bag 144 feet (44 meters) long, powered by a 3-horsepower steam engine he built himself. The engine drove a large propeller at 110 revolutions per minute. In 1852, Giffard launched the airship from the Hippodrome in Paris and attained a speed of 6 miles per hour. Twenty years later, Paul Haenlein, a German engineer, was the first to use an internal-combustion engine to power an airship. The engine used gas from the bag as fuel.

1402. Dirigible capable of powered flight in any direction was *La France,* built by Charles Renard and Arthur Krebs, officers of the French Army's Aérostation Militaire at Chalais-Meudon, France. The hydrogen-filled airship had its first flight on August 9, 1884, circling some 4 to 5 miles (7 to 8 kilometers) over France. *La France* was also the first electrically powered aircraft.

1403. Rigid airship was designed by Hungarian inventor David Schwartz and built in Germany in 1897. It had a hull of aluminum sheet and was powered by a 16-horsepower Daimler engine. The first flight took place on November 13, 1897, when the craft took off from Tempelhof Field in Berlin. It crashed a short time later.

1404. Dirigible that was commercially and militarily successful was designed by Ferdinand, Graf von Zeppelin, a retired German army officer, and manufactured in 1900 by the firm of Luftschiffsbau-Zeppelin. Its aluminum frame, 420 feet (128 meters) long and shaped like a cigar, was covered with fabric. Hydrogen lifting gas was contained in internal fabric cells, which also provided rigidity and support for the frame. A carriage under the hull carried two propellers driven by a 16-horsepower engine.

1405. Zeppelin flight embarked from a floating hangar on Lake Constance, near Friedrichshafen, Germany, on July 2, 1900, with the craft's inventor, Ferdinand, Graf von Zeppelin, at the controls. The German-built dirigible attained a cruising speed of approximately 20 miles (32 kilometers) per hour.

1406. Transatlantic dirigible flight was undertaken by British pilot Major George H. Scott in 1919. On July 2, 1919, he departed from Firth of Forth, Scotland, in a British-made dirigible, the R-34. The craft landed at Mineola, Long Island, NY, USA, on July 6, a flight of 102 hours.

1407. Circumnavigation by air in any sort of aircraft was accomplished by a German airship, the dirigible *Graf Zeppelin,* in 1929. The *Graf Zeppelin* was commanded by Hugo Eckener, a German aeronautical engineer. It carried nine commercial passengers and traveled 19,000 miles in 21 days 7 hours. Eckener also commanded the *Graf Zeppelin* on a polar exploration flight in 1931.

1408. Human ascent into the stratosphere was accomplished by the Swiss-born physician, engineer, and explorer Auguste Piccard and his assistant, Paul Kipfer, with Belgian financing. Seeking a high-altitude platform for the study of cosmic rays, Piccard developed in 1930 a pressurized cabin, the first ever built, to withstand low atmospheric pressures. It was a spherical aluminum gondola equipped with a system for reusing its own air supply. Piccard also developed a high-strength balloon that would rise when only partly inflated at ground level and gradually expand upon ascent as the atmospheric pressure fell. On May 27, 1931, Piccard and Kipfer launched the balloon at Augsburg, Germany, and set a new altitude record of 51,762 feet (15,777 meters). Owing to equipment failures, the flight ended 17 hours later on an Austrian glacier.

1409. Transatlantic commercial airship was the German dirigible LZ-129, named the *Hindenburg,* completed and tested in 1936 by the firm of Luftschiffsbau-Zeppelin in Friedrichshafen, Germany. At 804 feet (245 meters) long, it was the largest airship ever constructed. In May 1936 the Hindenburg began the first scheduled air service across the Atlantic, between Frankfurt am Main, Germany, and Lakehurst, NJ, USA. Seventy passengers traveled on the 60-hour inaugural flight. On May 6, 1937, as it was approaching the docking pylon at Lakehurst, the hydrogen-filled Hindenburg exploded in a fireball that claimed the lives of 35 passengers and crew and one member of the ground crew. It was the first aviation accident with large loss of life.

1410. Transatlantic balloon flight began on August 11, 1978, when Ben Abruzzo, Larry Newman, and Maxie Leroy Anderson, all of Albuquerque, NM, USA, left Presque Isle, ME, in a helium-filled balloon, the *Double Eagle II.* They reached Paris, France, on August 17 after a journey lasting 137 hours 18 minutes.

AVIATION—AIRSHIPS AND BAL-LOONS—*continued*

1411. Transatlantic solo balloon flight was completed on September 18, 1984, by U.S. Air Force Colonel Joe Kittinger. Flying the *Rosie O'Grady's Ballon of Peace,* a 101,000-cubic-foot (2,862-cubic-meter) helium balloon, Kittinger navigated from Caribou, ME, USA, to Montenotte, Italy, a flight of 3,543 miles (5,701 kilometers), in 86 hours.

1412. Transpacific solo balloon flight was completed by the American entrepreneur and balloonist Steve Fossett. On February 18–21, 1995, he piloted a helium balloon 5,430 miles (8737 kilometers) from Seoul, South Korea, to Leader, Saskatchewan, Canada.

1413. Nonstop circumnavigation of the world by balloon was accomplished by Bertrand Piccard, a Swiss psychiatrist, and Brian Jones, an English ballooning instructor, in the *Breitling Orbiter 3,* a hybrid helium and hot-air balloon. The balloon, 180 feet (55 meters) high when fully inflated, was made by Cameron Balloons in Bristol, England. It was launched on March 1, 1999, at Château-D'Oex, Switzerland, in the Swiss Alps. The circumnavigation offically began over Mauritania, in northwestern Africa, at 9 degrees 27 minutes west longitude, where the balloon picked up the jet stream. It then flew eastward across Africa, South Asia, the Pacific Ocean, Central America, and the Atlantic Ocean. The balloon crossed the finish line above Mauritania at 6:00 Greenwich Mean Time (4:54 AM Eastern Standard Time) on March 21, 1999, traveling at a speed of about 130 miles (209 kilometers) per hour, and continued across Africa to Egypt, where it landed in the desert near Luxor, several hundred miles south of the target landing spot near the pyramids of Giza. The trip covered 29,055 miles (46,749 kilometers) in 19 days 21 hours 55 minutes. The mission, which was sponsored by the Swiss watch manufacturer Breitling, was assisted by a 13-member ground crew whose meteorologists used computer modeling and satellite communications to direct the balloon into favorable winds. Bertrand Piccard is the grandson of the pioneer aeronaut Auguste Piccard, the inventor of the pressurized ballon gondola, and the son of the deep-sea explorer Jacques Piccard.

AVIATION—GLIDERS AND KITES

1414. Kites were, according to Chinese legend, invented by the general Han Si circa 150 BCE to frighten the horse nomads attacking China's borders. In reality, kites were in use in Asia perhaps 1000 years earlier. The first European to build a kite may have been the Pythagorean philosopher and scientist Archytas of Tarentum (now Taranto, Italy), circa 370 BCE.

1415. Manned glider flight of record took place in Wiltshire, England, in 1005. According to the account of the twelfth-century English chronicler William of Malmesbury, a Benedictine monk named Eilmer (or Aylmer) strapped wings to his hands and feet and launched himself from a tower of Malmesbury Abbey on a flight of more than a furlong (600 feet, or 183 meters). But, recorded William, "agitated by the violence of the wind and the swirling of air, as well as by awareness of his rashness, he fell, broke his legs, and was lame ever after. He himself used to say that the cause of his failure was forgetting to put a tail on the back part." It is possible that an even earlier manned glider flight was attempted in 875 by Ibn Firnas, a Moor of Córdoba, Spain, but the records are inconclusive.

1416. Manned glider flight that was successful took place in 1853, when the English aeronautical pioneer George Cayley ordered his terrified coachman, whose name was probably John Appleby, to test a large glider of Cayley's design. The coachman sailed some 500 yards (450 meters) across a Yorkshire valley and crash-landed without injury. Appleby, the world's first glider pilot, reportedly shouted back to Cayley, "Please, Sir George, I wish to give notice. I was hired to drive, not fly."

1417. Box kite was invented in 1894 by aeronautical pioneer Lawrence Hargrave. Shaped like a long, open box, it was the first true three-dimensional kite. In a demonstration on November 12, 1894, at Stanwell Park in New South Wales, Australia, Hargrave held on to four box kites and was lifted 16 feet (4.9 meters) off the ground. Hargrave also invented the first compressed-air rotary engine in 1889.

1418. Manned flight by kite that is well-documented was demonstrated by the Australian aeronautical pioneer Lawrence Hargrave, the inventor of the box kite. On November 12, 1894, at Stanwell Park in New South Wales, Australia, he harnessed four box kites to a sling seat, mounted the craft, and flew 16 feet (5 meters) in a strong wind. His kites were later displayed at the Powerhouse Museum in Sydney, Australia.

1419. Glider club was the Darmstadt High School Flying Sport Club, founded in Germany in 1909 by Hans Gutermuth.

1420. Glider pilot who was a woman was Florence Taylor of Australia. On December 5, 1909, she made a short flight at Narrabeen Beach in New South Wales, piloting a craft built by her husband, George Augustus Taylor.

1421. One Sky, One World international kite flying event took place in 1986 at 90 locations in 14 countries, with more than 10,000 kites being flown throughout the day by 40,000 participants. By 1996, the event involved 42 countries and 300,000 kite-flyers. The aim of One Sky, One World was to focus international attention on the need to maintain peace and protect the environment. It was organized by Donald D. Palmer, Jr., a kitemaker of Green Bay, WI, USA.

AVIATION—HELICOPTERS

1422. Helicopter flight took place on November 13, 1907, at Coquainvilliers, France, when Henry Cornu flew a gasoline-powered twin-rotor craft of his own design. The flight lasted only a few seconds, during which the 573-pound (260-kilogram) craft hovered about 6 feet (2 meters) off the ground.

1423. Autogiro was invented by Spanish aeronaut Juan de la Cierva, who made the first successful autogiro flight on June 9, 1923, in Getafe, Spain. He was flying a Deperdussin monoplane with a conventional powered propeller for forward power, as well as a large horizontal freely rotating four-bladed rotor fixed above the cockpit for lift. An autogiro derives upward thrust from unpowered rotors and depends on continuous forward motion for lift, unlike its successor, the helicopter, whose powered rotor allows it to take off and land vertically. Cierva's key discovery was a method of hingeing the rotor blades at the hub so they could respond differentially to the forces involved in rotation, an invention that proved fundamental to helicopter design.

1424. Woman helicopter pilot was the German aviatrix Hanna Reitsch. She flew the German-built FW-61, designed by Heinrich Focke, on July 4, 1937, at Bremen, Germany. It was the first fully-controlled free flight of a helicopter.

1425. Helicopter free flight indoors took place in 1938, when the German aviatrix Hanna Reitsch demonstrated a German-built FW-61 before a large crowd inside the Deutschlandhalle in Berlin.

1426. Helicopter that was successful was the VS-300, constructed in October and November 1939 by Vought-Sikorsky Aircraft, Stratford, CT, USA. A flight of 15 minutes and 3 seconds was made at Stratford on July 18, 1940, by its Russian-American inventor, Igor Ivan Sikorsky. The helicopter had a single main rotor powered by a 70-horsepower Franklin engine and three auxiliary tail rotors for control, one turning in a vertical plane for rudder control and the other two turning in a horizontal plane on outriggers on either side of the tail.

1427. Transatlantic helicopter flight was made by the U.S. Air Force Air Rescue Service in two H-19 (S-55) helicopters that left Westover Air Force Base, Chicopee, MA, USA, on July 15, 1952, and arrived at the Air Force base at Wiesbaden, Germany, on August 4, after 51 hours 55 minutes of elapsed flight time. The leader of the flight was Captain Vincent Howard McGovern, who with copilot Harry Celestine Jeffers piloted the project ship, *Hop-A-Long*. The 3,410-mile (5,487-kilometer) Atlantic crossing was made in 42 hours 25 minutes.

1428. Solo helicopter voyage around the world was completed by Australian pilot Dick Smith in a Bell Model 206L, Long Ranger III. Smith took off on August 5, 1982, from the Bell Helicopter Facility in Fort Worth, TX, and traveled a distance of 35,258 miles before landing in Fort Worth on July 22, 1983. Another circumnavigation was made later that year by two Americans, Ross Perot, Jr., and Jay Coburn, in a helicopter called *The Spirit of Texas*. The flight began on September 1, 1982, in Dallas, TX, USA, and ended in Dallas on September 30. It lasted 29 days 3 hours 8 minutes 13 seconds.

1429. Helicopter powered by human motion was the *Da Vinci 3*, named after Leonardo da Vinci, who first conceived of a rotary-wing flying vehicle in the 15th century. Its first flight, which lasted 6.8 seconds, took place on December 10, 1989, in the gymnasium of the California Polytechnic State University in San Luis Obispo, CA, USA. Maximum height off the ground was 7 inches. Students at the university built the craft out of wood, mylar, and graphite-epoxy. It was powered by the pilot, who pushed bicycle pedals.

AVIATION—PARACHUTES

1430. Parachute was conceived circa 1485 by Leonardo da Vinci in Florence, Italy. A notebook drawing by Leonardo shows a pyramidal parachute with a man hanging below it from a wire rigging, but there is no evidence that he actually constructed it.

1431. Parachutist was Louis-Sébastien Lenormand of France. In 1783, he held two very large umbrellas and jumped from a tree.

1432. Parachutist to jump from a flying craft was André-Jacques Garnerin, a French physicist, army officer, and balloonist. Garnerin designed a white canvas parachute shaped like an umbrella that was approximately 23 feet (7 meters) in diameter, with a basket for the occupant suspended by ropes. On October 22, 1797, he ascended in a hydrogen balloon over Paris to an altitude of 3,200 feet (975 meters), clambered into the basket of the parachute, and cut it loose. He landed safely. It was the first successful descent with a parachute from high altitude.

1433. Emergency parachute jump took place in 1808, at Warsaw, Poland, when a balloon made by the Montgolfier brothers, the French aviation pioneers, burst into flames. The aeronaut was Jordaki Kurapento.

1434. Parachute jump from an airplane was made on March 1, 1912, by U.S. Army captain Albert Berry from a Benoist Pusher plane piloted by Antony Jannus at Jefferson Barracks, St. Louis, MO, USA. Berry jumped from an altitude of 1,500 feet (457 meters) while the plane was traveling at a speed of 50 miles (80 kilometers) per hour.

1435. Parachute jump from an airplane by a woman was made by an American, Georgia Broadwick, 18 years old, on June 21, 1913, over Griffith Field, Los Angeles, CA, from an airplane piloted by Glenn Martin that was flying at an altitude of 1,000 feet (305 meters) and a speed of 30 miles (48 kilometers) per hour. After a drop of 100 feet (31 meters), her parachute opened and she landed in a barley field.

1436. Skydiver was an American aviator, Leslie Irvin. On April 28, 1919, he jumped from an airplane over McCook Field in Dayton, OH, USA, and delayed pulling his chute release to disprove the then-current theory that free-fall would result in unconsciousness.

1437. Pilot to bail out of an airplane flying at supersonic speed was George Franklin Smith of Manhattan Beach, CA, USA, who was propelled into the air when his seat automatically detached itself from an F-100A Super Sabre Jet fighter on February 26, 1955, above Los Angeles International Airport, Los Angeles, CA. He was flying at an altitude of 6,500 feet (1982 meters) at the supersonic speed of 777 miles (1250 kilometers) per hour. His clothes were cut to ribbons, and his socks, helmet, and oxygen mask were stripped off. He felt deceleration of 40 gravities, so that his organs weighed 40 times their normal weight. He landed in the ocean and was rescued by a passing boat off Laguna Beach, CA. He was hospitalized for about six months.

1438. Airplane equipped with its own parachute as standard equipment was the SR-20, a small single-engine plane introduced by the Cirrus Design Corporation, Duluth, MN, USA, in June 1999. The parachute, made by Ballistic Recovery Systems, St. Paul, MN, was packed into a storage area on the roof. In an emergency, it could be deployed by pulling an overhead handle. It was intended to decrease injuries and fatalities to the occupants, rather than to decrease damages to the plane. The SR-20 cost about US$165,000, including US$10,000 for the parachute.

B

BUSINESS

1439. Legal protection for trade secrets was provided in the 18th century BCE by Hammurabi, the king of Babylonia. His code of laws (1792–50 BCE) stipulated that a foster son could never be returned to his original family if his foster father had taught him artisan skills. Handicraft techniques were passed down within families and could not be taught to outsiders.

1440. Pawnshops were known in ancient China circa 1000 BCE and in the classical Mediterranean civilizations from circa 600 BCE.

1441. Bookkeeping manual was *Della mercatura e del mercante perfetto (Of Commerce and the Perfect Merchant)*, written circa 1400 by the Croatian philosopher Benko Kotruljic of Dubrovnik. A French translation appeared in Lyon in 1613.

1442. Treatise on double-entry bookkeeping was the *Summa de Arithmetica, Geometrica, Proportioni et Proportionalita,* published in Italy in 1494 by the mathematician Luca Pacioli. The practice of double-entry bookkeeping had been common in Italy since circa 1400.

1443. Millionaire was Pierre Lorillard, a French-born tobacco merchant who in 1760 opened a successful factory in New York City for the making of pipe tobacco, cigars, chewing tobacco, and snuff. Upon his death in 1843, a French obituary summed up his lavish, nouveau-riche style of life with the term *millionaire,* making him the first person so described.

1444. Boycott was mounted in 1879 in Ireland against Captain Charles Cunningham Boycott, agent for the third Earl of Erne's estates in County Mayo. Boycott was notorious for evicting Irish tenants unable to pay their rent. Under the leadership of Irish nationalist Charles Parnell, the local Irish ostracized him, refusing to work for him, sell him goods, or buy his produce. Boycott was forced to import laborers from Ulster who worked under guard, and within the year he left the country.

1445. Efficiency expert was the American management expert Frederick Winslow Taylor, often called the "father of scientific management." In 1878, Taylor went to work for the Midvale Steel Company in Pennsylvania. In 1881, he attempted to establish, quantitatively, a fair day's work, by making the first scientific time-and-motion studies to determine the optimum efficiency of worker motion and shop environment. The principles he discovered were widely incorporated into the design of modern factories.

1446. Billionaire businessman was John David Rockefeller, who was born to a peddler's family in rural New York State. As a young man in Cleveland, OH, USA, he started an oil refinery and developed it into the Standard Oil Company of Ohio, a giant corporation with a virtual monopoly on the American oil-refining industry. By the time he retired in 1911, Rockefeller was a billionaire.

1447. Privatization campaign was initiated in Chile in 1974 by Augusto Pinochet, the ruler of Chile's military junta. Pinochet had recently overthrown the socialist government of Salvador Allende and, in an effort to shore up the country's flagging economy, returned to private hands most of the industries that Allende had nationalized.

1448. Businessman worth US$100 billion was an American, William Henry "Bill" Gates III, co-founder and chairman of the Microsoft Corporation, a software development company located in Redmond, WA, USA. According to a survey by the international business magazine *Forbes Global,* Gates was worth slightly more than US$100 billion for a brief period in April 1999 (nearly twice what he was worth at the same time in 1998), making him the richest person in the world for the fifth year in a row. Most of Gates's wealth was in Microsoft stock and other securities. *Forbes Global* listed a total of 460 billionaires (in U.S. dollars) worldwide, according to data gathered in April 1999.

BUSINESS—ADVERTISING

1449. Advertisement known appeared in Thebes, Egypt, circa 1000 BCE. It was a notice offering a "whole gold coin" for the capture of a runaway slave called Shem.

1450. Printed advertising poster was produced on the Westminster (now London) press of William Caxton, the English printer, in 1477. It advertised the hot spring cures at Salisbury.

1451. Advertising circular was the *Journal Général d'Affiches,* published beginning on October 12, 1612, in Paris, France.

1452. Prints made for marketing and advertising purposes that have been preserved are five engraved prints by Martinus van den Heuvel, a 17th-century Dutch artist in the employ of the leather industry. The works are dated to circa 1675 and display patterns used in the decoration of gilt leather. The prints were sent to potential customers as a sales promotion.

1453. Advertising agency of record was the William Tayler agency, founded in London, England, in 1786. Tayler placed ads for city businesses in regional newspapers.

1454. International advertising agency was the Australian firm of Gordon and Gotch, founded in Melbourne, Australia, in 1855. Beginning in 1867, the agency opened international offices in England, South Africa, and New Zealand.

1455. Cigarette advertisement showing a woman smoking appeared in the *Southern Tobacco Journal,* Richmond, VA, USA, in 1897. It was considered scandalous.

BUSINESS—HOTELS AND RESTAURANTS

1456. Inns where travelers could find a safe place to lodge overnight were maintained by the Persians (in what is now Iran) along their trade routes, perhaps earlier than the sixth century BCE.

1457. Hostels for pilgrims were operated in Israel for the benefit of Jewish men making the thrice-yearly pilgrimage to the Temple in Jerusalem (the Beit ha-Mikdash). By the year 60 CE, one of these hostels offered medical help to travelers, as well as shelter.

1458. Hospice for Christian pilgrims was founded at Porto, Italy, circa 395 by St. Fabiola, a Roman noblewoman who had converted to Christianity, and St. Pammachius.

1459. Restaurant still extant is the so-called "Chicken Restaurant," which opened in Kaifeng, China, in 1153. Visitors can still eat at this establishment, which has no other name.

1460. Fast-food outlets may have been the short-order restaurants that were observed by the Franciscan friar St. Odoric de Pordenone in Zhengzhou, China, in the early 14th century. Their fare most likely took the form of a spring roll, a leaf of thin dough wrapped around chopped vegetables and quick-fried.

1461. Professional caterers worked in Zhengzhou, China, where they cooked banquets for dinner-party hosts who preferred not to do their own cooking. They were observed soon after 1300 by St. Odoric de Pordenone, a visiting Franciscan friar. Zhengzhou also had numerous restaurants, tea houses, and taverns.

1462. Coffee house known from historical records was the Kivi Han, opened in Constantinople (now Istanbul, Turkey) in 1475.

1463. Restaurant to offer forks for the use of customers was the Tour d'Argent in Paris, France, in the 17th century.

1464. Restaurant known by that term was the Champ d'Oiseau, opened in Paris, France, by A. Boulanger in 1765. The bill of fair was soup and broth. Over the door was a sign advertising these dishes as *restaurants* (restoratives). The word has since passed into a large number of languages.

1465. Family hotel was Low's Grand Hotel, on King Street, Covent Garden, London, England. It opened in January 1774. The proprietor was David Low. Unlike inns, which were mainly eating and drinking establishments with a few extra rooms, the hotel was intended specifically as a temporary residence and catered to families.

1466. Luxury restaurant was La Grande Taverne de Londres, opened by Antoine Beauvilliers in Paris, France, in 1782. It was praised by the gastronome Jean-Anthelme Brillat-Savarin as being the first "to combine the four essentials of an elegant room, smart waiters, a choice cellar, and superior cooking." It catered mainly to the aristocratic class and to well-to-do British travelers, and therefore saw a precipitous decline in business during the French Revolution.

1467. Railway hotels were the Euston and the Victoria, a pair of hotels run by the London & Birmingham Railway Company for its travelers. They opened for business at Euston Station, London, England, in September 1839. The Euston, a fancy establishment, admitted only passengers with first-class tickets. The Victoria was for everyone else.

1468. Major hotel chain was the Statler Company, founded by Ellsworth Milton Statler, a former bellboy and hotel clerk. The first Statler Hotel was opened in 1908 in Buffalo, NY, USA. It featured a private bath in every room, along with many other services for business travelers. Eventually, the chain ran luxury hotels in St. Louis, Cleveland, Detroit, Boston, and New York.

1469. McDonald's restaurant outside the United States was opened on June 1, 1967, in Richmond, British Columbia, Canada. The first McDonald's in Asia was opened in Tokyo, Japan, on July 20, 1971; in Europe, on August, 21, 1971, in Amsterdam, the Netherlands; in Australia, on December 30, 1971, in Sydney; in South America, on February 13, 1979, in Rio de Janeiro, Brazil; and in Africa, on December 18, 1992, in Casablanca, Morocco. By 1998, McDonald's had opened more than 22,000 franchises in 109 countries.

1470. Cyber café was the Electronic Café International, founded by American video artists Sherrie Rabinowitz and Kit Galloway. It opened in Santa Monica, CA, USA, in 1988 and offered computers with modems and other telecommunications gear for the use of patrons, plus a coffeehouse menu and artistic events.

1471. Floating resort hotel was the Four Seasons Barrier Reef Resort, designed by architect Sten Sjostrand. It was built in Singapore in 1988 and moored over the Australian Great Barrier Reef. Later it was renamed the Saigon Floating Hotel and towed to a location off the shore of Singapore. The seven-story structure, which cost approximately US$30 million, had 200 guest rooms, a swimming pool, a tennis court, a nightclub, a sauna, a gymnasium, small shops, several restaurants and bars, a library, fully equipped conference rooms, a post office, sewage treatment plants and holding tanks, facilities for mooring sailboats and yachts, an underwater observatory, and a marine laboratory.

1472. Hotel taller than 1,000 feet was the Baiyoke II Tower in Bangkok, Thailand, completed in 1997. The 89-story hotel reached 1,046 feet (319 meters).

BUSINESS—INDUSTRIAL EQUIPMENT

1473. Oil presses for extracting the oil from olives were in use in Egypt by the year 2500 BCE. The olives were placed inside a cloth bag, which was tied to wooden sticks at both ends. Two people twisted the sticks to squeeze out the oil. The same device was used to extract aromatic oils from a variety of herbs.

1474. Use of compressed air was by the ancient Egyptians, who circa 1500 BCE used foot-operated skin bladders as bellows for smelting and blacksmith work.

1475. Desalination process was described by the Greek philosopher Aristotle circa 350 BCE. The process, used by Greek sailors, involved creating shallow pools for seawater for evaporation, and catching the evaporated water, which was salt-free, by means of a sheet or a sail. A version of this evaporative process is still used in many large desalination plants.

1476. Water-powered sawmill of record was a stone-cutting mill on the Mosella (Moselle) River in Gaul (now France), described by the Gallic-born Latin poet Decimus Magnus Ausonius in his lyric poem about the river written circa 360. It was used to cut marble for the city of Treves. Such mills had probably been in use throughout the Roman Empire for several centuries.

1477. Mechanical wire-drawing equipment was developed in what is now Germany by Rudolf of Nuremberg circa 1350. Previously, wire was made by drawing cut strips of metal by hand through iron dies.

1478. Use of compressed air for materials transport took place in 1474, when vintners in the German city of Nuremberg used pumps to force wine along a pipe from one cask to another.

1479. Steam-powered sawmill was built in 1663 in London, England. Sawyers who feared unemployment rioted at its introduction.

1480. Reaming machine for producing accurate and polished cylinders was invented in 1775 by the English master machinist John Wilkinson.

1481. Hydraulic press was built circa 1796 by the English machinist Joseph Bramah, often considered the father of the machine-tool industry.

1482. Screw-threading metal lathe was invented in 1797 by English master machinist Henry Maudslay, founder of Maudslay & Company in London, England. Maudslay's lathe featured a lead screw that drove the cutting tool carriage at a constant rate geared to the rate of revolution of the spindle, so that threads could be cut with high accuracy.

1483. Mechanized production line was built in 1800 by English machinist Henry Maudslay for the French-born marine engineer Marc Isambard Brunel, who had established the first factory for the manufacture of ship's blocks (pulleys) in Portsmouth, England. Maudslay constructed 43 special-purpose block-manufacturing machines operated in series by only ten men, who could outproduce 100 craftsmen building blocks by hand.

1484. Screws and bolts mass-produced in standard sizes were available in England after 1800, owing to the innovations of machinist Henry Maudslay. In that year, at his workshop in London, he modified his screw-cutting metal lathe to include 28 gear changes that linked the spindle speed with the rate of advance of the tool-cutting carriage. Each gear caused the tool to cut threads to a consistent and accurate pitch, enabling Maudslay and his student Joseph Whitworth to begin the production of threaded metal parts in a variety of standard sizes. In 1841, Whitworth established many of the standard thread pitches that are still in use today.

1485. Shaper was invented circa 1826 by James Nasmyth in Manchester, England. It used a reciprocating cutter or chisel to plane areas of the workpiece to absolute straightness or cut keyways and other precisely shaped holes.

1486. Sewing machine that was practical was invented in 1830 in France by Barthélemy Thimonnier, a tailor from Amplepuis, France. In 1831 he obtained a contract to produce uniforms for the French Army, but his machine was destroyed by a mob of tailors. In 1845 Thimonnier invented a new sewing machine capable of 200 stitches per minute, for which he obtained French and British patents. In 1848 he manufactured the first metal sewing machine.

BUSINESS—INDUSTRIAL EQUIPMENT—
continued

1487. Steam forge hammer was patented in 1842 by the inventor James Nasmyth of Manchester, England. Nasmyth was commissioned by shipbuilder Isambard Kingdom Brunel to forge a huge iron drive shaft for the steamship *Great Britain.* The shaft being too large to forge by manual methods, Nasmyth designed and built a huge hammer powered by steam. His invention, quickly adopted by other manufacturers, enabled the fabrication of larger iron parts than had been possible before.

1488. Vulcanized rubber was successfully produced by American chemist and inventor Charles Goodyear of New York, NY, USA, who obtained a U.S. patent on June 15, 1844, on an "improvement in india-rubber fabrics." He had received a previous U.S. patent on June 17, 1837, for a method of destroying the adhesive properties of rubber by applying bismuth, nitric acid with copper, or other materials.

1489. Desalination plant was built in 1855 by British engineers at the War Office Revictualizing Station at the island of Helgoland (now part of Germany). It employed the distillation process to produce desalted water from seawater for the Royal Navy during the Crimean War.

1490. Synthetic plastic that was widely used in industry was celluloid, invented by the Americans John Wesley Hyatt of Albany, NY, USA, and Isaiah Smith Hyatt of Rockford, IL, USA, who obtained a patent for it on June 15, 1869. This invention won a $10,000 prize offered by Phelan and Collender of New York City for a substitute for ivory in billiard balls. The inventors dissolved pyroxyline and camphor in alcohol, then subjected the mixture to heat and pressure in molds. They began manufacturing it in 1872, organized the Newark Celluloid Manufacturing Company, and obtained a trademark registration on the word "celluloid," a word they coined to mean "cellulose-like."

1491. Electric arc welding with a consumable electrode was developed by the Russian inventor Nikolai Gavrilovich Slavianov in 1890. Coatings on the electrode that added to the strength of the weld were formulated in 1904.

1492. Pneumatic hammer was invented by Charles Brady King of Detroit, MI, USA, in 1890. Brady received a U.S. patent for it on January 30, 1894. The hammer was exhibited at the World's Columbian Exposition in Chicago, IL, USA, in 1893.

1493. Electric arc furnace was invented in 1900 by the French metallurgist Paul-Louis-Toussaint Héroult. Heated by a carbon arc to extremely high temperatures, it was initially used for melting scrap iron, and later in the Hall-Héroult process for the electrolytic refinement of aluminum.

1494. Ammonia factory to produce commercial quantities of the chemical was built at Oppau, Germany, and began production in 1914. It used the Haber-Bosch process, the chief commercial method of producing ammonia, in which nitrogen from the air is directly combined with hydrogen under high pressures and moderate temperatures. Ammonia from this factory was used in the production of artificial fertilizers and, more significantly, as an ingredient in the explosives Germany used in World War I. Had this ammonia not been available, Germany would have been dependent on overseas sources, and probably would not have prosecuted the war.

1495. Electron-beam welding in which a focused high-voltage beam of electrons is used to produce narrow, deep-penetration welds was developed in 1954 by M. Stohr, a researcher at the Saclay Center for Nuclear Research in France.

1496. Computer-aided manufacturing system was developed in 1959 by researchers in the Servomechanics Laboratory at the Massachusetts Institute of Technology, Cambridge, MA, USA. In the first public demonstration, a computer issued instructions in a custom programming language to an automated milling machine, which turned out a batch of aluminum ashtrays.

1497. Steamroller was invented in France by Louis Lemoine. The first demonstration of his new device for flattening ground and roadways was given on May 27, 1959.

1498. Bar code system for marking industrial products was developed in 1970 by Plessey Telecommunications of England.

1499. Nanotechnology company was Zyvex, the world's first company dedicated solely to developing a device called an assembler, a system of unspecified size capable of manufacturing bulk materials or arbitrary structures with atomic precision, getting nearly every atom in the desired place. It was founded by software developer James R. Von Ehr II and began operation in Richardson, TX, USA, in April 1997.

BUSINESS—LABOR

1500. Strike by workers of record took place in Thebes, Egypt, in 1700 BCE. Construction workers building a pyramid organized a work stoppage after their supervisors missed a payday. They had already protested the reduction of value in their wages as a result of economic inflation.

1501. Model factory run on humanitarian principles was New Lanark Mills near Manchester, England, a textile mill that was bought by the Welsh socialist Robert Owen and a group of partners in 1799. Owen improved working conditions in the mill, upgraded the workers' houses, ran a school for the children, operated a store with near-wholesale prices, and restricted the sale of alcohol.

1502. Child labor law was the Health and Moral Apprentices Act, an extension of the Poor Law, proposed by Robert Peel and passed by the British Parliament in 1802. The act was prompted by the unregulated exploitation of child labor in England's mills and factories, where poor children and orphans were often employed for long days and nights without supervision and without concern for their welfare.

1503. Anti-technology riots were mounted in 1811 in Nottingham, England, by bands of unemployed textile craftsmen who called themselves Luddites (after their probably imaginary leader, Ned Ludd). Protesting the mechanization in the textile industry, which had thrown many out of work, the Luddites burned a textile factory owned by Richard Arkwright and smashed a spinning jenny in the house of its inventor, James Hargreaves. Riots continued intermittently for several years, despite severe repression by the government, until rising prosperity undercut the movement.

1504. General union not confined to one trade was the Grand National Consolidated Trades Union, founded in 1833 by Robert Owen, the Welsh manufacturer and utopian reformer. It was intended as a labor union for all workers and found a strong following among London tradesmen. The union was dissolved in 1834 in the face of strong opposition from employers and the British government.

1505. International Communist labor organization was the International Working Men's Association, also known as the First International, founded by union leaders in London, England, on September 28, 1864. Karl Marx was elected to the General Council and immediately assumed control of the organization. The First International was blamed for a wave of strikes that swept through Europe in 1868, leading to fears of a general uprising of labor. In fact, membership in the First International probably never exceeded 20,000, and it could not have organized the widespread labor unrest of the late 1860s and early 1870s. Internal disputes between Communists under Marx and anarchists led by Mikhail Bakunin resulted in the disbanding of the First International at the Philadelphia Conference in 1876.

1506. Factory in which the workers paid for the services of a reader who read aloud to them while they worked was El Fígaro, a cigar factory near Havana, Cuba. The idea came from Saturnino Martínez, publisher of *La Aurora,* a newspaper written for cigar workers. The *lector* read novels and history books as well as news. In May 1866, four months after the arrangement began, the governor of Cuba banned it as subversive. It was continued in the United States by Cuban immigrants to Florida.

1507. Nation to legalize trade unions was Britain, with the passage of the Trade-Union Act of 1871. Previously, some British laws restricting trade unionism had been repealed, but the Trade-Union Act was the first statue to provide explicit legal protection for labor organizations.

1508. Law requiring doctors to report cases of occupational disease was enacted in Britain in 1895. Records of these diseases were maintained by the office of the chief inspector of factories.

BUSINESS—RETAILING

1509. Vending machine was described circa 100 BCE by Hero of Alexandria, the Greek mathematician, engineer, and inventor, who spotted it in an Egyptian temple. It was a coin-operated device that dispensed holy water.

1510. Commercial vending machine was the so-called "honor box" of early 18th-century England. Customers inserted a coin into the mechanical box and received a measure of snuff or tobacco.

1511. Marketing strategy aimed at children was devised in connection with sales of the children's book *A Little Pretty Pocket Book intended for the Instruction and Amusement of Little Master Tommy and Pretty Miss Polly,* published in 1744 in London, England, by John Newbery. Newbery hit upon the idea of offering, for a small additional fee, a toy to go with the book: a red and black ball for boys, and a red and black pincushion for girls. Inaugurating the moralizing approach taken by much subse-

BUSINESS—RETAILING—*continued*

quent marketing to children, Newbery included a letter from a well-known fantasy figure, Jack the Giant Killer, urging children to stick a pin in the red side of their toy whenever they were good, and a pin in the black side whenever they were bad.

1512. Mail-order catalog was produced by Mayer Amschel Rothschild in the Jewish ghetto of Frankfurt am Main, Germany, circa 1765. While still in his teens, Rothschild became an expert dealer in coins. Most of his business was conducted at trade fairs. Since fairs were held intermittently, Rothschild put together a catalog so that he and his customers could do business throughout the year. He later founded the Rothschild banking house.

1513. Shopping mall with numerous shops clustered under a single roof was built in Paris, France, in 1790.

1514. Department store was the invention of Parisian merchant Aristide Boucicaut. Beginning in 1852, he built the Bon Marché, a small piece-goods shop, into a large store with departments for dresses, shoes, and other women's merchandise. Among his retailing innovations were fixed and marked prices, stated policies for merchandise exchanges and refunds, and the practice of setting small retail markups to increase the volume of sales. By 1876 Bon Marché was the largest retail store in the city, with new headquarters featuring skylighted interior courts designed by the engineer Alexandre-Gustave Eiffel and the architect Louis-Auguste Boileau. *Bon marché* means "good buy" in French.

1515. Store lit by electricity was a draper's shop at Newcastle upon Tyne, England. The incandescent Swan lamps were installed in 1882.

1516. Vending machine in modern times was invented by John Glas Sandeman and Percival Everitt of London, England, who obtained a U.S. patent on July 28, 1885, on a machine for automatically delivering prepaid goods, such as postcards, stamped envelopes, and cigarettes. Vending machines selling Tutti-Frutti Gum appeared on the platforms of the New York Elevated Railroad in New York, NY, USA, in 1888.

1517. Used-car dealership opened for business as the Motor Car Company in London, England, in September 1897, with an inventory of 17 automobiles.

1518. Automatic price reductions on merchandise were offered in 1909 at the Automatic Bargain Basement in Filene's, a department store in Boston, MA, USA. After twelve selling days, unsold merchandise was marked down by 25 percent, with additional 25-percent reductions after 18 days and 24 days. Merchandise remaining after a month was donated to charity.

1519. Drugstore chain was C.R. Walgreen & Company, founded in 1909 by Charles R. Walgreen, a registered pharmacist in Chicago, IL, USA. The chain had more than 500 stores by the time of his death in 1939. They featured two drugstore innovations, the lunch counter and the use of open shelves for displaying merchandise.

1520. Laundromat was opened on April 18, 1934, in Fort Worth, TX, USA, by J.F. Cantrell. Four electric washing machines were rented by the hour to those who wished to do their laundry. Hot water and electricity wre supplied, but users were obliged to furnish their own soap. Cantrell called his operation a "washateria."

1521. Rolodex was invented by an American, Arnold Neustadter of Brooklyn, NY, USA, and marketed beginning in 1950. His rotating contact file, with its easily removable alphabetized cards, was an instant success with salespeople.

1522. Retail item priced by a bar code scanner was a package of Wrigley's Juicy Fruit chewing gum. Its bar code was read by a scanner at the checkout counter of the Marsh Supermarket in Troy, OH, USA, on June 26, 1974. The scanner was manufactured by the NCR Corporation.

BUSINESS—TRADE

1523. Long-distance sea trading along regular routes arose independently in numerous places in the world. The earliest evidence for long-distance sea trade was discovered by Stephen Chia of the Universiti Sains Malaysia and Robert Tykot of the University of South Florida in the United States, who tracked similar volcanic glass material from sites in Borneo to Pacific islands 3,500 miles (5,630 kilometers) to the east, indicating the establishment of a regular trading corridor from Southeast Asia to Melanesia and Polynesia. The glass material was dated to circa 4000 BCE.

1524. Sea trade between India and Mesopotamia was established possibly as early as 3000 BCE. Trading vessels traveled between the cities of Harappa and Mohenjo-Daro, in the Indus River valley (in what is now Pakistan), and Babylon (in what is now Iraq), along the coast of the Arabia Sea.

1525. International trade in ice began before circa 2000 BCE, the date of the earliest known ice storage buildings uncovered in Mesopotamia (in modern Iraq). Since it very rarely freezes there, the ice must have been shipped from distant regions.

1526. Caravans across the Sahara were made up of two-wheeled wagons drawn by horses. They were operated by nomadic Berbers, the descendents of cattle-herding pastoralists who lived in the Sahara before 2500 BCE, when the area was still covered with grasses and trees. From about 800 BCE, when the Phoenicians founded the city of Carthage in what is now Tunisia, the Berbers established trade routes that followed oasis lines across the desert. One main route appears to have run from the Fezzan, in present-day Libya, to Gao on the Niger River in modern Mali. A second main route is thought to have run from Morocco to Tichitt, in modern Mauretania. Camels, superior to horses for desert travel, were introduced to North Africa in the first century CE and by the fifth century had entirely replaced horses on caravans.

1527. International maritime law was developed by the inhabitants of the island of Rhodes (part of modern Greece), a center of Mediterranean trade, in approximately 480 BCE. These regulations served as the basis for the *Lex Rhodia,* a set of regulations that governed sea trade in the Byzantine Empire from the seventh century CE onward. Among the important provisions dating from antiquity was the sharing of financial risk among all parties involved in a shipping venture, including the owner of the ship, the owners of the cargo, and the passengers. There were also rules concerning the necessity for written contracts, the necessity for passengers to declare all valuables to the captain, penalties for theft of equipment, penalties for injuries inflicted in fights between sailors, and rewards paid to divers for recovering sunken cargo.

1528. Trade guilds originated in the Greek trading port of Byzantium (now Istanbul, Turkey) in the mid-fifth century BCE. The shipowners of the city organized themselves to set standards for chartering, manning, outfitting, and determining the seaworthiness of ships.

1529. Craft guilds were organized in Rome towards the end of the republican era (first century BCE). Rome recognized a variety of private societies known as *collegia,* which included religious societies and burial associations as well as guilds of tradesmen and craftsmen. Their rights were restricted under the caesars.

1530. Trade between the Mediterranean world and East Africa below the Horn of Africa was under way by the first century CE, as attested by the *Periplus of the Erythrean Sea,* a guidebook compiled in Alexandria, Egypt, circa 100 CE for the use of Greek traders in the Indian Ocean. Readers were advised that such goods as ivory, tortoise shell, rhinoceros horn, and coconut oil were for sale in Azania, a coastal region that correponds to present-day Kenya and Tanzania. The main port was the now-lost city of Rhapta.

1531. Trade between China and southeast Asia was initiated circa 100 CE, during the Han dynasty, in the northern part of what is now Vietnam.

1532. Trade between Rome and China commenced in 166 CE with the arrival in China of a group of Roman merchants.

1533. Trading empire in central Africa was the kingdom of Wagadu, better known as Ghana, from the title of its ruler. It was founded by the Soninke people circa 400 and came to prominence sometime before the year 800. Ghana's wealth came from its control of the trade in salt, gold, and ivory between the Arabs and Berbers in the Sahara region and the black Africans farther southward. It went into eclipse after its conquest by the Muslim Almoravids in the eleventh century. The lands of medieval Ghana are now part of Mauritania and Mali and have no connection with the modern nation of Ghana.

1534. Customs paid by importers were gifts of wine given by French wine merchants to King Aethelred of England circa 1010.

1535. Merchant guild was a fraternal organization of merchants that was formed in the city of Tiel, in what is now Holland, in 1020.

1536. State-run company still in operation, and possibly the oldest company of any kind in continuous existence, is the Bayerische Staatsbrauerei (Bavarian State Brewery), founded in 1040 near Munich, Germany.

1537. International trade fairs still held annually were the fairs of Germany's medieval cities. They include those of Leipzig, begun in 1229; Frankfurt am Main, in 1240 (and perhaps as early as 1050); and Cologne, in 1360.

1538. Company in England chartered by a government to do business and governed by a board of directors was the Company of the Merchants of the Staple. It was formed in 1277, two years after King Edward I of England received from Parliament the right to levy

BUSINESS—TRADE—*continued*

export duties on wool. The Merchant Staplers collected these duties in exchange for a monopoly on the control of England's wool-exporting operations. The "staple"—the town in which all wool exports were required to take place—was eventually fixed as the English outpost at Calais, France.

1539. Shipping tax based on tonnage was levied by King Edward I of England in 1303. The tax for each ship was calculated not by weight but by the number of cargo barrels the ship could hold.

1540. Patent was issued in 1421 in Florence, Italy, to the architect Filippo Brunelleschi, granting him a three-year manufacturing monopoly on his design for a river barge outfitted with a heavy-duty hoist.

1541. General patent law was passed by the city-state of Venice (now in Italy) in 1474.

1542. Multinational corporation that enjoyed long-term success was the East India Company, founded on December 31, 1600, under royal charter from Queen Elizabeth I by 218 knights and merchants of the City of London. The original goal of the company was to loosen the Dutch stranglehold on the Spice Islands trade, but it was more successful in establishing long-term trading agreements on the Indian subcontinent, in Southeast Asia, and in China. By 1834, it had transformed itself from a trading company to the authorized ruler of British possessions in Asia.

1543. Balance of trade and payments for a nation were calculated for England in 1615 by Lionell Cranfield and a Mr. Wolstenholme. The first reference to the figures was included in an essay by Francis Bacon that was written in 1616 and published in 1661. The first use of the term "balance of trade" appeared in *The Circle of Commerce or Balance of Trade* (1621) by Edward Misselden.

1544. Nation to enact a national patent system was England, which in 1623 passed the English Statute of Patents and Monopolies. It granted a "letters patent" to inventors for up to 14 years.

1545. Industrial trade show of importance was held at the Temple d'Industrie in Paris, France, on September 17, 1798, in a building built expressly for the purpose. Organized by the Interior Ministry, which regarded the exhibition as "a first campaign against British industry," it provided a forum for more than 100 exhibitors in all areas of French industry to display their manufactures.

1546. Fruit exporting company of significance was the United Fruit Company, an American firm formed in 1899 from the merger of several smaller companies. The principal founder was Minor C. Keith. United Fruit operated in Caribbean islands, Central America, and Colombia during the early 20th century and built a politically powerful monopoly in the banana and tropical fruit exporting business.

1547. Corporation worth US$1 billion was United States Steel Corporation, founded by the New York financier John Pierpont Morgan in 1901 through the merger of several existing steel companies, including the Carnegie Steel Company and the Federal Steel Company. Ten years earlier, Morgan had created another giant corporation, General Electric, by combining Edison General Electric and the Thomson-Houston Electric Company.

1548. Containerized shipping was invented by an American, Malcolm McLean of Maxton, NC, USA, the owner of McLean Trucking, a large freight-trucking firm. He developed a large shipping container that could be packed with goods at the factory, hauled by truck to a port facility, carried on specially fitted ships to a port terminal, offloaded from the ship, and hitched directly to trucks or loaded on freight cars for cross-continental transport, all without unpacking the container's contents. McLean's first containership, the *Ideal X*, left the port of Newark, NJ, on April 25, 1956.

1549. Free-trade region in modern times was the European Community, established by one of the Treaties of Rome in 1957. The EC, often called the Common Market, established free trade among its members by abolishing tariffs and duties, coordinating their economic policies, and promoting the mobility of labor, capital, and entrepreneurship. Furthermore, all the members (with the exception of Great Britain) pledged to adopt a common currency and a European central bank by 1999. As of 1998, the EC members were France, Belgium, Luxembourg, the Netherlands, Italy, Germany, the United Kingdom, Denmark, Ireland, Greece, Portugal, Spain, Austria, Finland, and Sweden.

1550. Transoceanic cryogenic shipping began in 1959, with the first shipment of liquefied natural gas by cryogenic tanker from Lake Charles, LA, USA, to London, England.

1551. Containership facility was the Elizabeth–Port Authority Marine Terminal, operated by the Port of New York Authority and located on the coast of the state of New Jersey in the United States. It opened for business on August 15, 1962, when Sea-Land Service's S.S.

Elizabethport docked in Newark Bay, Elizabeth, NJ, USA, on the south side of the Elizabeth Channel, south of Port Newark. During its first year, the facility handled 1.4 million metric tons of cargo on 242 vessels and employed 730 people, who earned a total of more than US$4 million.

1552. Free-trade region encompassing North America was created by the North American Free Trade Agreement (NAFTA), adopted between the United States, Canada, and Mexico in 1993. The agreement, which eliminated most trade barriers on products and services, was signed by U.S. president George Herbert Walker Bush, Canadian prime minister Brian Mulroney, and Mexican president Carlos Salinas de Gortari on December 17, 1992, and was effective January 1, 1994.

1553. Commercial ship to sail from China to Taiwan since Taiwan declared its independence from the mainland in 1949 arrived at the southern Taiwanese port of Kao-hsiung on April 19, 1997.

1554. Post for trade between Europe and Africa built since antiquity was the Portuguese fort and warehouse erected in 1448 by order of Prince Henry the Navigator on the island of Arguin, off the Atlantic coast of Morocco. This was the first overseas trading post established by Europeans since the days of the Romans. The Portuguese sold wheat and woolen cloth to the Moorish merchants and Berber tribesmen, who paid for them with black African slaves and gold dust.

C

CITIES AND TOWNS

1555. Walled town was Jericho, on the west bank of the Jordan River, a short distance from the site of the modern city of Jericho. Archeological evidence dates its earliest Neolithic inhabitants to circa 9000 BCE. By 8000 BCE, the town had a massive stone wall and a stone tower protecting as many as 3,000 residents. The biblical Book of Joshua describes the destruction of Jericho's wall by the sound of shofar blasts made by the Israelites as they returned to Canaan, approximately in the 13th century BCE, but no conclusive evidence of it has yet been discovered.

1556. Metropolis was Çatalhüyük, near Konya in south central Turkey. The site is a double mound, partially excavated beginning in 1961 by the British archeologist James Mellaart. The extent and complexity of the site indicates that by 7000 BCE Çatalhüyük may have had as many as 10,000 inhabitants. The settlement contains the earliest murals painted on manmade walls (rather than cave walls), a series of clay-relief leopards discovered by Mellaart in 1961 and dating from circa 6200 BCE.

1557. City in continuous existence is Damascus (Dimashq in Arabic), now the capital of Syria. An urban center existed there circa 3000 BCE at Tall as-Salhiyah, presently a suburb of Damascus. Settlement in the Old City area of Damascus dates from circa 2500 BCE. The first known written reference to Damascus occurs on an Egyptian hieroglyphic tablet from circa 1400 BCE, listing "Dimashqa" among conquered territories.

1558. City planned on a grid was Mohenjo-Daro, built in the Indus Valley about 5,500 years ago in what is now Pakistan. Its streets were laid out along a north–south/east–west grid. The main avenues were about 45 feet (14 meters) wide, wider than those in many modern cities, and the side streets were about 30 feet (9 meters) wide. The ancient city of Titris Hoyuk in southeastern Turkey, which dates to about the same period, also shows evidence of having been built to a master plan specifying street layout and house placement.

1559. City with uniform plot sizes known to archeologists was the ancient Bronze Age city of Titris Hoyuk in southeastern Turkey, near the present-day border with Syria. Building lots dating from circa 2000 BCE were found to come in only two sizes, indicating careful urban planning.

1560. Public park may have been a pleasure ground laid out by the Egyptian pharaoh Ramses III when he built a city in the delta of the Nile River. The park had "wide places for walking" that passed through plantings of flowers and fruit trees. Ramses, who ruled from 1198 to 1166 BCE, is said to have donated more than 500 gardens and groves to the temples of his kingdom.

1561. Utopian town planner was the Greek architect Hippodamus, who lived circa 475–400 BCE. Hippodamus was credited by his Greek contemporaries with inventing the orthogonal or grid plan for cities, applied first during the rebuilding of his hometown of Miletus (now in Turkey) circa 430 BCE. (Similar city plans had

CITIES AND TOWNS—*continued*

been developed in the Indus Valley civilizations, among others, millennia before.) Hippodamus also articulated utopian theories of city planning. His "Hippodamian" towns, limited to 10,000 inhabitants, were designed with straight lines and unambiguous angles that were meant to foster a rational, egalitarian society. No such towns were actually built.

1562. Planned city in South America was Tiahuanaco, located on Lake Titicaca in the Andean highlands of modern Bolivia. Archeologists are not agreed on the founding date for the city, where first construction may have begun as early as 1200 BCE or as late as 200 BCE. The major remaining structures, including the Akapana Pyramid, the gated stone enclosure called the Kalasasaya, and the Palacio were probably built circa 200 CE. An empire centered on Tiahuanaco covered large areas of Bolivia, Argentina, Chile, and Peru.

1563. Major city of the New World was Teotihuacán, located in the northeastern area of the Valley of Mexico. The city was probably founded circa 1 CE and, at the height of its power, circa 600, covered an eight-square mile area (21 square kilometers) and was inhabited by some 150,000 people.

1564. Major settlement built of stone in sub-Saharan Africa was Great Zimbabwe, a complex of granite buildings, including parts dating back to the eighth century, that was built by the Shona people near Lake Kyle. The site occupied some 60 acres (24 hectares) near the present-day city of Masvingo, Zimbabwe. (The name is a Bantu word meaning "stone dwelling.") Among its structures was a fortress and a 30-foot tower surrounded by a wall. The stones were fitted together without the use of mortar. From the eleventh to the 15th century, Great Zimbabwe was an important city in the Karanga empire, Mwanamutapa.

1565. Ghetto took its name from the *ghetto nuovo*, a high-walled cannon foundry on an island within Venice, which was set aside in 1516 as a residential prison area for the Jewish residents of the city. They were allowed to leave during the day, but were locked inside at night, guarded by ten watchmen whose salaries they were required to pay. However, the practice of forcing Jews to live in confined areas had been in effect in various Muslim countries since the 13th century (it was instituted in Morocco in 1280) and had already been adopted in some Christian cities in eastern and central Europe.

1566. City with more than 1 million inhabitants was London, England. The census of 1811 showed London's population to be 1,009,546.

1567. Municipal recreation park was Victoria Park, opened in 1845 in London, England.

1568. Modern city with a downtown commercial area was Chicago, IL, USA, whose old buildings were destroyed in the famous fire of 1871. Burned residential neighborhoods were not replaced because it was too costly to make them fireproof. Instead, between 1885 and 1895 developers turned the area within the Loop (the elevated railway line) into a district of skyscrapers containing space for shops and offices.

1569. City with a woman mayor of record was Argonia, KS, USA. On April 4, 1887, the citizens elected a 27-year-old woman, Susanna Medora Salter, as mayor. She served one year for a salary of US$1.

1570. Kibbutz was Degania, a communal farm established in 1909 in Palestine (now Israel) on the shores of the southern part of the Sea of Galilee. The seven Jewish founders, six men and one woman, intended Degania to be an experiment in radical agricultural collectivism in which all members would share equally in work, housing, food, and profits. Hundreds of kibbutzim were later established in what would become Israel, though not all were modeled after Degania.

1571. City with more than 10 million inhabitants was Tokyo, Japan, which reached that milestone in January 1962. The population of Tokyo had been only 2,777,000 following its devastation by firebombing in 1945.

1572. City with more than 20 million inhabitants was Tokyo, Japan, which in the 1995 United Nations census was home to 27.2 million people. The next nearest city in size of population was Mexico City, Mexico, with 16.9 million inhabitants.

CITIES AND TOWNS—FIREFIGHTING

1573. Firefighting devices were large, water-filled syringes, known to have been used to fight fires in Alexandria, Egypt, circa 100 BCE.

1574. Fireproofing in residential buildings was attempted in ancient Rome after the fire of 64 CE, which destroyed many multistorey apartment dwellings made of mud brick. When they were rebuilt, flat-topped concrete vaults were built into the spaces between the storeys.

1575. Fire extinguisher used water propelled by compressed air. It was invented in Britain by George Manby in 1816.

1576. Steam-powered fire engine was put into service in London, England, in 1829. It could pump a stream of water into a fire from roughly 90 feet (27 meters) away. The engine was not self-propelled and had to be drawn by a team of horses.

1577. Hook and ladder truck that was successful was invented in 1868 by fireman Daniel Hayes of San Francisco, CA, USA. The truck mounted extensible ladders on swivel bases, so that they could be extended toward a burning building from any angle.

1578. Fire truck with an internal-combustion engine that powered both the water pump and the truck itself was introduced circa 1900 by the Waterous Fire Engine Works of St. Paul, MN, USA.

1579. Fire extinguisher for chemical fires was the carbonic acid fire extinguisher, invented in France in 1905 by Alexander Laurent. It produced a foamy solution containing carbonic acid, which effectively smothered oil- and some chemical-based fires, by mixing aluminum sulfate and bicarbonate of soda with a stabilizer.

1580. Snorkel fire truck was introduced by the Chicago Fire Department, Chicago, IL, USA, in 1958. It was equipped with a hydraulic crane, also called a cherry picker, that was mounted on a swivel base. The crane could raise a bucket several stories high for use in rescue or firefighting.

CITIES AND TOWNS—ROADS AND STREETS

1581. Paved streets made of stone were built in the city of Ur (now Tel-el-Muqayyar, Iraq) circa 4000 BCE.

1582. Long-distance road was the Persian Royal Road, which ran east-west across Anatolia for more than 1,500 miles (2,400 km) between the capital city of Susa, Persia (now the village of Shush, Iran), and Smyrna (now Izmir, Turkey), on the Aegean coast, passing through Nineveh and Haran, with a second terminus at Ephesus. Its oldest section dates from the middle of the fourth millennium BCE. The Assyrians extended it further circa 1200 BCE. Beginning in 550 BCE it was reconstructed as a royal road by the Persian kings Cyrus II and Darius I. Although most travelers took three months to cross it, a relay system of couriers was able to deliver messages from one end to the other in nine days. The armies of Alexander the Great marched on the road during their invasion of Persia in the fourth century BCE.

1583. Paved road still extant is a coast-to-coast stone roadway 30 miles (50 km) long, built on the Mediterranean island of Crete by the Minoans circa 2000 BCE, when wheeled carts came into use. The roadway, winding over mountains from Knossos in the north to Gortyna in the south, was built of stone layers paved with sandstone and basalt, and was raised along its center to accelerate drainage. It was about 12 feet (360 cm) wide.

1584. Parking penalty was imposed by the Assyrian king Sennacherib (Sin-akhkhe-eriba), who ruled Nineveh (in modern Iraq) from circa 704 to 681 BCE. Owners of chariots who parked along the royal road were subject to death by impalement.

1585. Paved long-distance road was the Via Appia (the Appian Way), a military and trade road that ran from Rome to the Adriatic coast at Brindisium (modern Brindisi, Italy), a distance of 362 miles (582 km). Construction began under the Roman official Appius Claudius Caecus in 312 BCE. The road, some 20 feet (6 m) wide, was built in two layers: a substratum of large stone blocks joined with mortar, and a top layer made of fitted pieces of lava.

1586. Major intercontinental road was the Silk Road (or Silk Route), a caravan road that stretched 4,000 miles (6,400 km), linking China and Rome. The eastern terminus was the city of Xian. At Dunhuang, the road divided into a northern route that skirted the Takla Makan desert and crossed Turkistan and a southern route through a series of mountain passes into India. Goods, particularly cloth and precious metals, were ferried along the route from one middleman to another. The road also served as a conduit of religious ideas. It was first used circa 100 BCE. The Venetian traveler Marco Polo followed it to China in the 13th century CE.

1587. Major road system in the Americas was begun by the Inca approximately at the beginning of the 13th century. By the 16th century, it comprised about 14,000 miles of roadway in what is now Ecuador, Peru, and Chile, including a coastal highway some 2,250 miles long and a parallel mountain route about 3,400 miles long. The road through the Andes included mammoth retaining walls, bridges suspended on woven cables, staircases and galleries cut into cliffs, stone pavements, and other feats of engineering. The people of each locality were charged with maintaining their section of the highway, as well as maintaining way stations for travelers and stocking them with supplies.

CITIES AND TOWNS—ROADS AND STREETS—*continued*

1588. Mechanical street sweeper was the invention of Edmund Hemming, an Englishman, who in 1699 introduced a street sweeping device similar to the modern carpet sweeper, but on a larger scale.

1589. Road designed for motor vehicles was built in Madagascar by French engineers on the order of the colonial governor, Joseph S. Gallieni, and completed on January 1, 1901. The road connected the port town of Tamatave with the capital city of Antananarivo, and was intended for motor freight traffic.

1590. Traffic lights operated by electricity were installed on August 5, 1914, at Euclid Avenue and East 105th Street, Cleveland, OH, USA, by the American Traffic Signal Company under the direction of Safety Director Alfred A. Benesch. Cross arms were installed 15 feet above the ground and equipped with red and green lights and alternating buzzers. Cleveland inventor Garrett A. Morgan designed an automatic version in 1923.

1591. Roadside telephone for motorist assistance was installed by the Royal Automobile Club of Great Britain in 1919.

1592. Expressway for automobiles was the Avus Autobahn, which opened to traffic on September 10, 1921 in Berlin, Germany. The controlled-access divided highway ran 6.25 miles (10 kilometers) from the Grünewald to the suburb of Wannsee.

1593. Nationwide highway system was the autobahn in Germany. Limited-access expressways had been constructed in Germany beginning in 1921. The Nazis, who came to power in 1933, extended these highways into a network containing some 2,500 miles of roadway that connected all major cities. The massive construction project, intended to boost Germany's capacity for quick military deployment, was rushed to completion in two years.

CLOTHING AND FASHION

1594. Garment to undergo changes of fashion was the *kaunake,* a covering made of the hairy hide of a sheep or goat. It originated in Asia Minor (now Turkey) around the early fourth millennium BCE and was adopted, with local variations, in Mesopotamia and throughout the Mediterranean world, where ideas for styling it were frequently exchanged. It was worn short, long, or belted. The hair on the

outside was combed, shaved in patterns, or cut in strips to produce a decorative effect. By 3200 BCE, a woven woolen version was being worn by people from Central Asia to Western Europe. It ceased to be worn circa 2000 BCE.

1595. Jewelry known to archeologists was found in the tomb, dated to circa 3400 BCE, of the Sumerian queen Pu-abi in the city of Ur (now Tel-el-Muqayyar, Iraq). The sumptuous jewelry, of an extremely high level of craftsmanship, was made of a wide variety of precious materials—gold, silver, carnelian, agate, chalcedony, and lapis lazuli—and formed into beads, rings, bracelets, necklaces, earrings, diadems, amulets, pins, and other items. Fabrication techniques included welding, alloys, filigree, enameling, and stonecutting.

1596. Tattoos of record were found on the body of Ötzi, the so-called Iceman, a 5,300-year-old mummy discovered on September 19, 1991, by Helmut Simon in the Tirolean Ötztal Alps, on the border between Austria and Italy. Fifteen groups of tattoos, including several along the spine, were found on Ötzi's skin. Some of the tattoo sites correspond to acupuncture sites used in Chinese medicine to relieve back pain, leading to speculation that acupuncture or a similar medical discipline was practiced in Europe in Neolithic times.

1597. Cotton clothing was being woven in the Valley of Mexico circa 3000 BCE.

1598. Raincoat that was very nearly waterproof was a garment used by the Celts in Western Europe circa 3000 BCE. It was woven of long-haired wool that shed water.

1599. Corset was invented on the Mediterranean island of Crete during the Minoan Bronze Age, circa 2100 BCE. It was a shaping, waist-cinching garment stiffened with ribs of copper, and was worn by both women and men.

1600. Clothes made of tapestry weaving extant are a glove and robe made in ancient Egypt. They may have belonged to the pharaoh Tutankhamen, in whose tomb they were found. Tutankhamen died in 1352 BCE.

1601. Gloves extant were a pair of white woven linen gloves with wrist drawstrings, found in 1925 during the excavation of the tomb of Egyptian pharaoh Tutankhamen. Tutankhamen died in 1352 BCE.

1602. Parasol was depicted in an Assyrian frieze dating to circa 1350 BCE. A servant or slave is shown holding a long-handled parasol to shade the head of a king.

1603. Sumptuary laws were enacted beginning circa 600 BCE in ancient Lakedaemon (modern Sparta, Greece), whose well-regimented citizens were restricted to what has since become known as a Spartan style of life. Houses were required to be of the simplest possible construction, possession of gold or silver was reserved only to the royal class, and drinking parties were forbidden.

1604. Shawls were worn in India and other parts of Asia at least as early as the third century BCE, when the use of woolen shawls is first mentioned. They were introduced in Europe in 1798, after the return of French troops from Napoléon's campaign in Egypt, and quickly became an essential article of clothing for women.

1605. Brassiere was the *mamillare,* worn by Roman women in the first century CE. The modern bra was invented in 1912 by Madame Cadolle, a Parisian dress designer.

1606. Bikini was probably worn by young women from ancient times. The first known depiction of a scanty two-piece costume dates from circa 300 CE, in the mosaics of the Roman villa of Casale near Piazza Armerina, Sicily.

1607. Pants developed from divided leg coverings worn in the Middle East and Asia in ancient times. In medieval Europe, men in cold climates wore knitted hose until the introduction of breeches, an early form of which was the *braies,* worn in Gaul (now France) in the mid-tenth century.

1608. Pocket was an innovation of the German king and Holy Roman Emperor Henry II (973–1024), who wore one, made of silk brocade, on his white silk tunic.

1609. Medieval sumptuary laws were promulgated by King Philip III of France (reigned 1270–1285). They required nobles and gentlefolk to decrease their private expenditures by restricting the number of fancy garments they could own and the number of courses they could serve at a meal. Fines for breaking these laws were assessed by the royal treasury, with a 16 percent commission going to the informer.

1610. Fashion magazine was published circa 1586 in Frankfurt, Germany.

1611. Law against enhanced bosoms was enacted in the free imperial city of Strasbourg (now in France) in 1370 to stop the custom among fashionable women of using wire corsets and padding their undergarments. The law stated that "no woman should support her bust, whether by arranging her chemise or by lacing her dress" in artificially enhancing ways.

1612. Clothes designer was the 14th-century painter, sculptor, and medalist Il Pisanello (born Antonio Pisano) of Verona, Italy, who made the first scholarly investigation of costume. Pisanello's drawings included many studies of costume and hair design, as well as studies of animals, birds, and plants.

1613. Hoop skirt was the farthingale, introduced circa 1470 in Castile (now in Spain). It was a skirt of heavy material with pliant wooden (or later, whalebone) hoops inserted to give it a full, bell-like shape. The inventor is said to have been Joana, wife of King Henry IV, who wore it to hide an illegitimate pregnancy.

1614. Shirts were sleeveless linen tunics worn in ancient Egypt during the 18th dynasty (1539–1292 BCE). They were made by folding a piece of cloth in half, cutting a neckhole, and stitching the sides partway up.

1615. Ruffed collars were introduced in France circa 1540. Originally the ruff was a modest frill around the neck, created by tightening the top of the shirt with a drawstring. Over the course of some two decades, ruffs became large and elaborate constructions, stiffened with starch, sometimes pleated or crimped, and often with multiple layers of muslin and lace. They were worn by both women and men.

1616. Western European women to wear pants were Spanish courtesans, who experimented with wearing velvet breeches in the late 16th century. The fashion was short-lived.

1617. Clothing patterns in print were included in the *Libro de Geometrica y Traca (Book of Geometry and Tracing),* written by the Portuguese mathematician Joan de Alega (or Alegas) in 1589. The book featured small-scale pictures of patterns meant to be expanded to full size using geometrical techniques.

1618. Beaver skins in the Old World were shipped from Canada to the French port of La Rochelle in 1603.

1619. Waterproof umbrellas of record were oiled silk umbrellas mentioned in a 1637 inventory of goods owned by King Louis XIII of France. There is much evidence of earlier umbrellas and parasols, but most appear to have been used as sunshades, not as protection from rain.

1620. Hoop skirts with panniers that pushed the skirts out to enormous widths—as much as 18 feet (5 meters) across—were introduced in England and France circa 1710. The panniers were originally made of whalebone canes, later of wickerwork.

CLOTHING AND FASHION—*continued*

1621. Dressmaker with a flourishing export business was Rose Bertin, dressmaker to Marie-Antoinette, the queen of France, from 1772. Her elaborately decorated creations, which were displayed by the hundreds in her showrooms, were bought by women of means in Germany, Portugal, Spain, Russia, England, and as far away as the American colonies.

1622. Society model was a rich Parisian lady, Madame de Matignon. Around the year 1775, she entered into an agreement with a businessman, Monsieur Beaulard, who sold hats and headdresses. He supplied her with a new one each morning and next day offered it for sale to women who had seen and admired it.

1623. Parisian couturier was Monsieur Leroy, a former hairdresser who, after the Revolution, switched to dress designing and went into business, in partnership with a prominent dressmaker, Madame Raimbaut. His high-priced shop also sold gloves, scarves, stockings, and other accessories. Among his customers, circa 1800, was Napoléon Bonaparte's wife, the Empress Joséphine, who left him with an unpaid bill of 150,000 francs.

1624. Waterproof raincoat was the mackintosh, invented by the Scottish chemist Charles Mackintosh (or Macintosh) in 1823. He devised a completely water-repellent fabric by cementing two thicknesses of linen or cotton with rubber dissolved in coal-tar naphtha (a substance similar to rubber cement). A vulcanized mackintosh, which was more flexible, less sticky, and lasted longer, was devised by Thomas Hancock in 1843.

1625. Bathing suit for women was a multi-layered costume introduced in France in 1829. It consisted of a linen corset under a long-sleeved tunic, loose bloomers that were enclosed at the ankle, black stockings, and canvas boots.

1626. Paper patterns for clothing printed full size appeared in 1844 in the *Bekleidungskunst für Damen-Allgemeine Muster Zeitung (Women's Fashion Patterns Journal)* of Zürich, Switzerland.

1627. Dry cleaning was done by accident in 1855 when a Parisian dyeworks owner, Jean-Baptiste Jolly, knocked over a table lamp filled with spirit and noticed that the affected parts of the tablecloth appeared to be unusually clean. He thereupon offered to clean his customers' clothes using a chemical process instead of soap and water. He took the garments apart, immersed the pieces in a mixture of turpentine and oil, and restitched them.

1628. Crinolines began to appear around 1850 in France, where they were popularized by the Empress Eugénie, wife of Napoléon III. They were fabric petticoats—originally of horsehair canvas, later of cotton or muslin—shaped by whalebone stays and metal strips. The "cage" crinoline was made entirely of metal. The craze for crinolines lasted for about a quarter of a century.

1629. Woman in Europe to receive official permission to wear pants was the French artist Rosa Bonheur. In 1852, she asked for, and received, permission from the Paris police to wear male clothing while visiting a slaughterhouse to make studies of animals for her paintings. She continued to wear pants afterwards. She was also the first woman to be awarded, in 1865, the Grand Cross of the Légion d'Honneur.

1630. Blue jeans were invented in 1853 by Levi Strauss, a 20-year-old American dry goods salesman of German Jewish extraction. Strauss had arrived three years earlier in San Francisco, CA, USA, where he began making sturdy canvas pants for gold miners. He called them "bibless overalls." In 1853 he opened a pants factory on California Street and switched to indigo-dyed denim fabric. His product was given the name Levis. Another characteristic feature of blue jeans, copper rivets to reinforce stress points, were the idea of Jacob Davis, a Russian Jewish tailor. They were added to Strauss's jeans in 1877.

1631. Bustles for pushing out women's skirts in the rear were popularized by Britain's Queen Victoria in 1869. Bustles started out as gathers of excess cloth, which were eventually replaced by support structures made of wire. The French name was *tournure*.

1632. Gym suit for girls enabling them to take part in vigorous athletic activities consisted of a pair of loose knickers and a jersey. The designer was Margaret Tait, a student at Hampstead Physical Training College in London, England, in October 1892.

1633. Cummerbund originated in India as a long, brightly colored sash wound around the waist. Adopted by the British military during the Raj, it was brought to England and was first seen in London in the summer of 1893.

1634. One-piece bathing suit was worn in public at a California beach in 1909 by Australian-born international swimming star and actress Annette Kellerman, known as the "Diving Venus.". Beachgoers were outraged at her daring attire, but the publicity was good for her films, the first of which was released that year. Esther Williams portrayed Kellerman in the 1952 film *Million Dollar Mermaid.*

1635. Standardized sizes for bras were introduced in the 1920s by dressmaker Ida Kaganovich Rosenthal, a Russian Jewish immigrant to the United States. Rosenthal founded the Maidenform company.

1636. Modern bikini was introduced to the public at a Paris salon on June 26, 1946, a few days after the explosion of an American atomic bomb at Bikini Atoll, by French designer Louis Réard. He called his brief two-piece swimsuit "four triangles of nothing." It was printed with images of newspapers, and modeled by a dancer, Micheline Bernardi.

1637. Trousers with permanent pleats were introduced in 1957 by Arthur Farnworth of the Commonwealth Scientific and Industrial Research Organization, the main research facility of the Australian government. A special fabric treatment held the crease.

1638. Miniskirt was introduced for the spring 1965 season by fashion designer Mary Quant at Bazaar, her boutique on the King's Road in London, England.

1639. Scented suits for men were marketed in Seoul, South Korea, beginning in January 1999. The suits were made of a fabric incorporating tiny capsules that, when touched, released the odor of pine, peppermint, or lavender. The suits sold for up to US$400.

CLOTHING AND FASHION—FASTENERS

1640. Buttons have been found in the ruins of Mohenjo-daro in India, dating to circa 3500 BCE, and were in use by the ancient Greeks and Etruscans from circa 700 BCE. Typically made of wood, bone, or horn, the buttons were fastened by loops, not buttonholes, which were not invented until the 13th century in Europe.

1641. Cut-steel button was introduced by the English inventor and manufacturer Matthew Boulton, one of the inventors of the steam engine, circa 1750. The buttons had a steel base to which were attached small polished steel facets.

1642. Metal snap fastener or press stud was invented by Pierre-Albert Raymond of Grenoble, France, on May 29, 1886. It was first used for fastening gloves.

1643. Zipper that was practical was invented about 1906 by Gideon Sundback of Hoboken, NJ, USA, an American inventor of Swedish ancestry. He obtained a U.S. patent on April 29, 1913, for "separable fasteners." His design consisted of two flexible tapes, each of which carried a row of metal teeth with tiny hooks, and a slider that locked the two rows of hooks together. This fastener was improved upon by later patents obtained on March 20 and October 16, 1917, which were assigned to the Hookless Fastener Company of Meadville, PA, under the name "Talon." The first manufactured garments to incorporate zippers were rubber boots made by the B.F. Goodrich Company, Akron, OH, in 1923. The term "zipper" was coined by the English novelist Gilbert Frankau, who saw the device at a promotional luncheon and exclaimed: "Zip! It's open! Zip! It's closed!" The first fashion designer to use zippers was Elsa Schiaparelli, who added them to garments in her 1930 collection.

1644. Hook and loop fastener was Velcro, invented by the Swiss engineer Georges de Mestral. In 1948, he got the idea after coming home one day from hunting with burdock burrs (*Arctium*) clinging to his clothes. Microscopic examination revealed that the burrs were covered with tiny hooks that caught on any fuzzy surface such as fabric, fur, or hair. Mestral's adaptation, which took him eight years to develop, consisted of two types of nylon fabric, one covered on one side with tiny hooks and the other type with tiny loops. When the hook and loop sides of the fabrics were pressed together, they clung tightly. They could also be easily parted and reattached. Velcro was patented internationally in 1957.

CLOTHING AND FASHION—HATS

1645. Hat-loving society appears to have been the late Minoan civilization of Crete, which flourished between 1580 and 1450 BCE. Illustrations from that era show women in a wide variety of hats of all sizes and shapes, including berets, bonnets, turbans, cornets, and cones, with fanciful ornamentation, including ribbons and feathers. They also wore tiaras, diadems, and crowns.

1646. Elaborate medieval headdresses with absurdly high, cloth-draped horns, curves, and miters came into fashion during the reign (1385–1435) of Isabeau of Bavaria, queen consort to King Charles VI of France. One of these headdresses, the long cone, was named the *hennin* after the first woman to wear it.

CLOTHING AND FASHION—HATS—continued

1647. Top hat was designed and made by John Hetherington, a London haberdasher, in 1797. According to a contemporary news account, he caused a riot the first time he wore his creation on the street and was fined £50 for wearing "a tall structure having a shining luster calculated to frighten timid people." The hat was actually a silk-covered variation of the contemporary beaver-fur riding hat with a wider brim and a lower crown. It caught on as the preferred formal headgear for the British and American male uppe-crust after Prince Albert began wearing a silk-shag version of the top hat in 1850.

1648. Poke bonnet is said to have been invented by an aristocrat named Baroness Oldenburg in 1818. The hood-shaped hat with a wide front brim, tied under her chin and hid most of her face. Poke bonnets were fashionable until the mid-1860s, with a brief return to fashion after they were adopted in England circa 1880 by Catherine Booth for women volunteers of the Salvation Army.

1649. Bowler hat was made by hatmaker Thomas Bowler to the order of the English landowner William Coke, who wanted a hard-crowned hat to protect his head while hunting. Coke tried it on for the first time on December 17, 1849, in the shop of the London hatters, Lock's. He tested the derby's ruggedness by stamping on it twice. The hat passed the test, and Coke bought it for twelve shillings.

CLOTHING AND FASHION—SHOES

1650. High heels were worn circa 2100 BCE by fashionable women at Knossos, on the Mediterranean island of Crete (now part of Greece). They were reinvented in France circa 1600 and eventually became high enough to force the wearers to put their weight on their toes.

1651. Sandals known were made of woven papyrus, leather, and wood and were worn by the nobility of ancient Egypt circa 2000 BCE. The Romans were the first to develop a commercial sandal industry, with shoemakers' guilds manufacturing sandals with designs for the various social classes.

1652. Pairs of fitted shoes with appropriate shapes for the left foot and right foot were made by Roman cobblers in the first century BCE.

1653. Rubber footwear was invented by indigenous peoples of Amazonia circa 1000 CE, centuries before Charles Goodyear's vulcanized rubber shoes of the mid-19th century. The Amazonians dipped their feet and legs in latex, the raw sap of the rubber tree. When it hardened, the latex formed a tough second skin that was waterproof and protected against insects and abrasion.

1654. Standard shoe sizes were probably introduced in England. In 1305, King Edward I adjusted the definition of an inch to mean "three grains of barley, dry and round, placed end to end lengthwise." Shoe sizes were derived from the number of barleycorns needed to measure a particular sole.

1655. Shoelaces used since antiquity were introduced in 1790 in England, to be used in place of the traditional buckles.

1656. Sneakers with rubber soles and plain cloth uppers were sold from the early 1870s by Charles Goodyear of New York, NY, USA, who developed the vulcanized rubber shoe sole, and by many other footwear companies. The first brand of sneakers was Keds, introduced in 1916 by the United States Rubber Company, the successor to Goodyear's shoe company. The first Keds had black soles and high-top brown canvas uppers, mimicking leather shoes. The name was a combination of "kids" and *ped,* the Latin word for "foot."

1657. Running shoes were developed in Germany in 1949 by the designer Adolf Dassler of the Addas Company (now Adidas). The shoes, of lightweight leather with a flexible rubber sole, were marked with the three parallel stripes that distinguish Adidas footwear. Running shoes of the modern variety were introduced in 1962 by New Balance, Boston, MA, USA, a company that specialized in orthopedic shoes. Known as Tracksters, they featured a one-piece rippled sole and a rubber shock-absorber in the heel.

1658. Shoe made from recycled materials was invented in 1990 by Julie Lewis of Portland, OR, USA. She got the idea from a friend who wove rugs from plastic bread bags. Her Deja Shoe was co-designed by Bill Bowerman and was made from recycled polyester and rubber. They were not the first footwear of any kind made from recycled material, however; African and Latin American peoples had long been cutting sandals from the treads of discarded rubber tires.

COMPUTERS

1659. Treatise on computing theory was "On Computable Numbers, with an application to the *Entscheidungsproblem*," published in 1937 by the English mathematician and computing pioneer Alan Matheson Turing. One of the most influential papers in modern mathematics, "On Computable Numbers" proved that a "universal computing machine" (a mathematical construct now called a Turing machine by computer scientists) could solve almost any problem that involved numbers or other symbols.

COMPUTERS—CALCULATORS

1660. Mechanical calculator known to archeologists is the Antikythera Mechanism, dated circa 80 BCE. It was discovered in 1900 in an ancient shipwreck near the island of Antikythera, Greece. The bronze components were so corroded that a working replica was not built until 1981, using parts from a Meccano toy construction set as well as custom-cast bronze gears. The device proved to be an analog computer for modeling the solar and lunar cycles and for predicting eclipses.

1661. Mechnical calculator for astronomical use invented in modern times was the work of German astronomer Wilhelm Schickard, who developed his design in 1624. Little is known of it, however, as his records were lost during the Thirty Years' War.

1662. Adding machine that was practical was the Pascaline, invented in 1642 by the French philosopher, mathematician, and scientist Blaise Pascal. It was inspired by a design described by Hero of Alexandria that computed the distance a carriage traveled. Numbers were entered by turning ten-tooth dial wheels linked to a gear train. Addition and subtraction could be performed on numbers as long as eight digits. The Pascaline was more accurate and faster than manual calculations, but only Pascal knew how to repair the device and it cost more than the human calculators it replaced. The basic principle of the Pascaline is still used in water meters and odometers. The first calculator available for sale, the arithmometer, was invented in 1820 by another Frenchman, Charles Xavier Thomas de Colmar.

1663. Electric tabulating machine was invented by Herman Hollerith of New York, NY, USA. On January 8, 1889, Hollerith received a U.S. patent on a system of recording separate statistical items by means of holes, or combinations of holes, punched in cards, and then counting or tallying such statistical items either separately or in combination by means of electrical counters operated by electromagnets, the circuits being controlled by the perforated cards. The first extensive use of the electric tabulating system was in the compilation of the statistics of population for the eleventh U.S. federal census, in 1890.

1664. Automatic calculator to factor whole numbers into their prime factors was the *machine à congruences* developed in 1919 by the French mathematician and military officer Eugène Olivier Carissan. The brass device consisted of a crank connected to a set of nested, horizontal "congruence rings." Pegs carefully positioned on the rings would give the solution to a problem when the crank was turned; the answer was read by an armature sitting on top of the rings. The device was rediscovered in 1993 at the Observatoire de Bordeaux in Floirac, France, where it had been sitting in a drawer for some 50 years, by Hugh C. Williams of the University of Manitoba in Winnipeg, Canada; Jeffrey Shallit of the University of Waterloo in Ontario, Canada; and François Morain of the École Polytechnique in Palaiseau, France.

1665. Electronic digital calculator was invented by John Vincent Atanasoff, a professor at Iowa State University, Ames, IA, USA. The device was a digital calculator designed to solve linear equations using vacuum tubes for arithmetic units, condensers for memory, and a punch card input/output system. Atanasoff began working on the calculator in September 1939 and performed the first calculations with it in October of that year.

COMPUTERS—HARDWARE

1666. Universal computing machine was the Analytical Engine of British mathematician Charles Babbage, Lucasian Professor of Mathematics at Cambridge University, Cambridge, England, from 1828 to 1839. Seeking a way to reduce the tedium and inaccuracy of calculating logarithms by hand, Babbage tinkered with designs for simpler arithmetic and differential calculators before beginning work in 1834 on the Analytical Engine. This completely mechanical computer, with thousands of meshing ten-tooth gears, was intended to perform any arithmetical operation that could be encoded as instructions on punched cards, a technique Babbage had observed in the card-controlled mechanical looms of Joseph-Marie Jacquard. Babbage developed many of the important features of modern digital computers, including a memory unit for storing numbers; instructions and results that were encoded on an external storage medium;

COMPUTERS—HARDWARE—*continued*

flexible programmability; and sequential control of operations. Most important, the Analytical Engine could make conditional ("if—then") decisions based on the results of its own computations. Babbage lacked the funds to finish his ambitious machine, and it was forgotten until his unpublished notebooks were discovered in 1937.

1667. Computing device with electronic components was constructed in 1930 by Vannevar Bush, a professor at the Massachusetts Institute of Technology, Cambridge, MA, USA. His "differential analyzer" used vacuum tubes in which numerical values could be stored as voltages. Bush, who later served as science advisor to U.S. president Franklin Delano Roosevelt, also designed the "memex device," an electromechanical information appliance. The memex, which was never built, presaged many of the features of the personal computer and the Internet.

1668. Programmable electronic binary computer was invented by construction engineer Konrad Zuse in Berlin, Germany. From 1936 to 1949 Zuse developed a series of four computers. The Z1, built in his parents' Berlin living room, was entirely mechanical, while the Z2, Z3, and Z4 contained electromechanical relays. The Z3 (1941), which could perform a week's worth of calculations in a few hours, was the first fully automated, freely programmable, program-controlled computing machine using binary floating-point arithmetic. All previous calculators had used standard decimal math. German authorities failed to realize the value of his machines until late in World War II. In 1944–45 Zuse calculators were used in the engineering of V-2 rockets, and Zuse himself was briefly assigned to an underground laboratory to develop more advanced computers. Zuse also developed the first algorithmic programming language in 1945–46, called Plankalkul.

1669. General-purpose computer that was fully electronic is usually credited to J. Presper Eckert, Jr., and John W. Mauchly of the Moore School of Electrical Engineering at the University of Pennsylvania, Philadelphia, PA, USA. Their Electronic Numerical Integrator and Computer (ENIAC), was given its first public demonstration on February 14, 1946. The ENIAC was subsequently used by the U.S. Army Ordinance Department at Aberdeen, MD. It was housed in a room 30 by 50 feet (9 by 15 meters), contained approximately 18,000 vacuum tubes, and required 130 kilowatts per hour to operate.

1670. Floppy disk was developed in 1950 by researcher Yoshiro Nakamatsu of the Imperial University in Tokyo, Japan. Nakamatsu licensed the technology to the American computer manufacturer International Business Machines (IBM) Corporation of Armonk, NY, USA, which later developed a commercial version of the technology.

1671. Electronic computer for commercial use was the UNIVAC I (Universal Automatic Computer), introduced by J. Presper Eckert, Jr., and John W. Mauchly in 1951, and manufactured by the Remington Rand Corporation, Philadelphia, PA, USA. It was demonstrated and dedicated at the Bureau of the Census in Philadelphia on June 14, 1951. The key to its success was the use of inexpensive magnetic tape for data input and output. It could retain a maximum of 1,000 separate numbers, accept information contained on magnetic tape at the rate of more than 10,000 characters per second, add, subtract, multiply, divide, sort, collate, and take square and cube roots as needed. More than 50 units were sold in all.

1672. Supercomputer was the Control Data 6600, designed by a team under the American computing engineer Seymour R. Cray at a division of the Control Data Corporation located in Chippewa Falls, WI. The CDC 6600, introduced in August 1963, was far faster than competing mainframe computers of the time. It was purchased by the military to simulate nuclear explosions and break Soviet codes. Scientists also used the 6600 and later Cray-designed supercomputers to model complex phenomena such as hurricanes and the formation of galaxies.

1673. Dot-matrix printer was introduced for computers used during the 1964 Tokyo Olympic Games by Seiko of Tokyo, Japan.

1674. Minicomputer that was commercially successful was the PDP-8, introduced by the American computer manufacturer Digital Equipment Corporation of Maynard, MA, USA, in 1965. The US$18,000 minicomputer was smaller and less expensive than competing mainframe computers, but was almost as powerful. It was purchased primarily by institutions, smaller businesses, and researchers.

1675. Computer modem that was practical was demonstrated by John van Geen at the Stanford Research Institute, Stanford, CA, USA, in 1966. A modem, short for "modulator/demodulator," is a device that converts digital computer information to a signal that can be transmitted to another computer over a telephone line. Van Geen's acoustical coupler modem design was able to receive data signals accurately over telephone lines despite random noise and static, a problem that earlier modem researchers had been unable to solve.

1676. Computer mouse was invented by Douglas C. Engelbart of the Stanford Research Institute, Palo Alto, CA, USA. A mouse is a hand-operated pointing device that enables the computer user to manipulate text or images on a computer screen. Prior to the mouse, the user interacted with the computer screen by typing commands on a keyboard. Engelbart first publicly demonstrated a three-button mouse at the Joint Computer Conference in the Civic Center in San Francisco, CA, USA, in the fall of 1968. The computer system he demonstrated, which incorporated a keyboard, keypad, and window-based graphical user interface, ran a word processor, a hypertext system, and an application for remote collaborative work.

1677. Floppy disk widely used was developed in 1971 by an American, Alan Shugart, for the International Business Machines Corporation of Armonk, NY, USA. The 8-inch (20-centimeter) disk was made of polyester sheet coated with fine magnetic particles and encased in a cardboard sleeve. It was the first form of digital information storage that was cheap, portable, and high density.

1678. Microprocessor was built in late 1970 by the Intel Corporation, Santa Clara, CA, USA, for the Busicom Corporation of Japan. Designed by a team of Intel engineers including Ted Hoff, Stan Mazor, Masatoshi Shima, and Federico Faggin, the Intel 4004 crammed 2300 transistors onto one silicon chip smaller than a thumbtack and ran at a clock speed of 750 kilohertz. It was the first general-purpose computing device that was small enough, cheap enough, and powerful enough to be used as the brain of a wide variety of devices, including computers, calculators, cars, and appliances. Intel announced the 4004 to the public on November 15, 1971.

1679. Personal computer was the Micral, developed in France by Truong Trong Tri for a company called R2E and marketed beginning in May 1973. It was the first fully assembled commercial computer based on a microprocessor, the Intel 8008. The term "microcomputer" was first used in reference to the Micral later that year.

1680. Personal computer kit was the Intel 8008-based Scelbi-8H, marketed in the United States beginning in 1973 by the Scelbi Computer Consulting Company. The kit included 1 kilobyte of programmable random access memory and sold for US$565. The last kit was sold in 1974. The first kit-based personal computer to be commercially successful was the Altair 8800, sold beginning December 19, 1974, when it was featured on the cover of the January 1975 issue of *Popular Electronics* magazine. It was developed by the American electronic engineer Edward Roberts at Micro Instrumentation and Telemetry Systems of Albuquerque, NM, USA. The kit cost US$397. Lauren Solomon, daughter of Les Solomon, publisher of *Popular Electronics,* suggested the name "Altair," which was the destination for the *U.S.S. Enterprise* in that night's episode of the "Star Trek" television series.

1681. Personal computer that was commercially successful was the Apple II, developed by Steven Jobs and Stephen Wozniak of Apple Computer, Cupertino, CA, USA. It featured a 6502 central processing unit, 4 kilobytes of random access memory, an integrated keyboard, a motherboard with slots for expansion, game paddles, and the ability to show color on the screen, a first for personal computers. It sold for US$1,300 beginning in April 1977. The Commodore PET 2001, developed by Commodore Business Machines of Westchester, PA, USA, was shown to the public in January 1977, but it was not marketed to consumers until the summer. It sold for US$595.

1682. Personal computer trade show was the First West Coast Computer Faire, held at the Brooks Civic Auditorium in San Francisco, CA, USA, in April 1977. Approximately 12,750 people attended the event to see the first generation of personal computer technology.

1683. Reduced Instruction Set Computer (RISC) was based on research by computer scientist John Cocke of the Research Division of International Business Machines (IBM), Armonk, NY, USA, in the 1970s. The first RISC computer was IBM's 801 minicomputer, introduced in 1980. Cocke's study of the trade-offs between high performance machine organization and compiler programming language optimization, led him to the realization that a streamlined compiler with fewer instructions could be run on less complex and less expensive microprocessors. The RISC concept was contrary to the established direction of increasingly complex instruction sets and chips as em-

COMPUTERS—HARDWARE—*continued*

bodied in earlier Complex Instruction Set Computer (CISC) microprocessor designs. With fewer kinds of instructions to process, a RISC computer was faster than a CISC computer and tended to be easier to program.

1684. Portable personal computer was the Osborne 1 Personal Business Computer, developed by British entrepreneur Adam Osborne, founder of the Osborne Computer Corporation, and introduced at the West Coast Computer Faire in California in April 1981. The toolbox-shaped computer, which weighed 24 pounds (11 kilograms), featured a Z80A central processing unit, a 5-inch cathode-ray tube display, 64 kilobytes of random access memory, a modem, two floppy disk drives, a keyboard that fit inside the lid of its integrated case, and a selection of business software. The price was US$1,795.

1685. IBM-compatible personal computer was announced by International Business Machines of Armonk, NY, USA, in July 1981 in New York City. The IBM 5150 PC Personal Computer featured a 4.77-megahertz Intel 8088 central processing unit, 64 kilobytes of random access memory, and two floppy disc drives. The operating system was PC-DOS 1.0, a custom version of MS-DOS developed by the Microsoft Corporation of Redmond, WA, USA. The basic computer cost about US$3,000; a version with color graphics cost US$6,000.

1686. Computer with a parallel architecture was the Cray X-MP, designed by Taiwan-born computer engineer Steve S. Chen in 1982 for the American supercomputer manufacturer Cray Research Inc. of Chippewa Falls, WI, USA. Unlike earlier computers, the Cray X-MP used more than one central processor to perform calculations in parallel.

1687. Laser printer for business was the LaserJet laser printer, introduced in the fall of 1984 by the American electronics firm Hewlett-Packard Company of Palo Alto, CA, USA. The printer, which employed a combination of laser scanning and xerographic printing processes, was capable of 300 dots per inch resolution and cost US$3,600. The original research on laser printing was conducted in 1969 by American electronics engineer Gary Starkweather at the Xerox Corporation research facility in Webster, NY, USA.

1688. Year in which the total number of computers in the world exceeded 100,000,000 was 1990. Approximately 93 percent were personal computers.

1689. Underwater personal computer was developed in 1993 by Bruce Macdonald at the Australian Institute of Marine Science. The fully sealed device featured a five-button hand-held keypad that made it possible to type in text with gloved hands.

1690. Electronic memory using a single electron while operating at room temperature was demonstrated by the Hitachi Corporation of Japan in December 1993. The tiny chip required only a single electron to store one bit of information. Previous experiments had required temperatures near absolute zero.

1691. Disk drive to store 1 billion bits of data per square inch was introduced in April 1996 by the American computer company International Business Machines (IBM) of Armonk, NY, USA. The technology was first used in small-format disk drives for portable computers.

1692. Teraflop computer capable of performing a trillion mathematical operations per second was the Janus, built by the Intel Corporation, Santa Clara, CA, USA. The computer, housed in 84 cabinets, contained 9,072 Pentium Pro microprocessors and had hundreds of billions of bytes of memory, enough to generate simulations of complex and massive events in four dimensions with extreme detail. It was installed in July 1997 at Sandia National Laboratories in Albuquerque, NM, USA. The cost was US$55 million.

1693. Disk drive to store 10 billion bits of data per square inch was developed by International Business Machines (IBM) of Armonk, NY, USA, and announced in December 1997. The high-storage disks could store 11.6 billion bits, or 11.6 gigabits, per square inch (or 1.8 billion bits per square centimeter), the equivalent of 725,000 pages of typewritten text.

COMPUTERS—NETWORKS

1694. Computer network was ARPANET, a data communications network developed by American researchers J.C.R. Licklider, Robert Taylor, and other researchers for the U.S. Department of Defense's Advanced Research Projects Agency. The first ARPANET link was put into service on November 21, 1969. It connected a computer in the computer science department at the University of California at Los Angeles, CA, USA, with a laboratory computer at the Stanford Research Institute, Stanford, CA, USA. Over the next decade, ARPANET grew to include many government and university computers.

1695. Electronic mail message was sent in 1971 by American computer engineer Ray Tomlinson of BBN Technologies (now a division of GTE) across the ARPANET, the U.S. Army-built precursor to the Internet. The message was sent by Tomlinson to himself as a test of the ARPANET's messaging capabilities and contained no memorable content.

1696. Electronic mail message to use the @ ("at") sign was the second ARPANET message sent in 1971 by American computer engineer Ray Tomlinson of BBN Technologies. It was an announcement to other ARPANET users of the network's new mail capabilities, and included instructions on how to address mail by appending the @ ("at") sign to the user's log-in name, a technique invented by Tomlinson himself and chosen from the punctuation keys on his Model 33 Teletype.

1697. Computer-to-computer conversation in English was held in October 1972 during the first International Conference on Computer Communications in Washington, DC, USA. One computer at Stanford University in California running the PARRY program (that emulated a psychotic patient) traded canned responses over ARPANET with a computer at BBN Technologies, Boston, running a program called the Doctor (meant to emulate a psychiatrist).

1698. International networking conference was the International Conference on Computer Communications, held in October 1972 in Washington, DC, USA. A demonstration was held of the ARPANET, with network connections among 40 computers. The International Network Working Group was formed to promote an international effort in advanced networking technologies. American computer scientist Vinton Cerf was appointed the group's first chair.

1699. International Internet connections outside North America were established in 1973 at the University College of London, England, and the Royal Radar Establishment in Norway. These hosts were able to communication via ARPANET (the world's first computer network, developed in the United States beginning in 1969) with existing hosts, all of which were then in the United States.

1700. National computer network for military, governmental, and institutional use was commissioned by the U.S. federal government in the early 1970s and put into operation beginning in 1973. Designed by American computer scientists Vinton Cerf and Robert E. Kahn, it was based on ARPANET, the world's first computer network, and employed packet-switching, flow-control, and fault-tolerance techniques developed by ARPANET.

1701. Mailing list was MsgGroup, developed in 1975 for ARPANET, the first internet network, by Steve Walker. The first popular unofficial mailing list was SF-Lovers, a list for fans of science fiction.

1702. Computer network linking two continents was SATNET, the Atlantic Packet Satellite Network, inaugurated in 1976 to connect military and government computers in the United States with those in Europe. It used commercial Intelsat satellites owned by the International Telecommunications Satellite Organization.

1703. Head of state to send an e-mail message was Queen Elizabeth II of England, who was testing a network link between the British Ministry of Defence and the U.S. Department of Defense's ARPANET network. In February 1976, the Queen sent an e-mail of greeting to the DoD's High Order Language Working Group from a computer located at the Royal Signals and Radar Establishment in Malvern, England, using her official net address, ERII. The message was posted when the Queen pressed a red velvet Royal carriage return. Confirmation of reception took an unexpectedly long time, owing to the lengthy address list, and Prince Philip was overheard to remark, "It looks like she broke it."

1704. Personal computer bulletin board was inaugurated in February 1978 by two Americans, Ward Christianson and Randy Suess of Chicago, IL, USA. Called the Computerized Bulletin Board System, it allowed computer users equipped with a modem to log on to the site and exchange information.

1705. MUD (multi-user dominion) was MUD1, invented in 1979 by Richard Bartle and Roy Trubshaw at the University of Essex in Colchester, England. A MUD is a multi-user, interactive simulation, usually a game, that runs over a computer network. The initials also stand for multi-user dimension or dungeon.

COMPUTERS—NETWORKS—*continued*

1706. Total Internet crash took place on October 27, 1980, when the ARPANET (the U.S. Department of Defense's prototype Internet) came to a complete halt because of a status-message virus that was accidentally propagated throughout the network.

1707. Internet domain name system or DNS was introduced in 1984 by researchers at the University of Wisconsin, USA. Previously, packets on the network had to be directed to a numerical address that was hard to remember. Under the DNS, packets were directed to a domain name made up of ordinary words.

1708. Cyberspace description appeared in the 1984 science-fiction novel *Neuromancer* by Canadian writer William Gibson. His concept of a virtual-reality world residing within a global computer network strongly influenced the graphic interfaces designed in the late 1990s for the Internet.

1709. Year in which the number of Internet hosts exceeded 1,000 was 1984.

1710. Guide to E-mail etiquette may have been written by Bernie Greenberg of Symbolics, Incorporated, a developer of artificial intelligence languages and hardware located in Woburn, MA, USA. The tongue-in-cheek guide was posted on April 11, 1984. Among its admonitions: "Idiosyncratic indentations, double-spacing, capitalization, etc., while stamps of individuality, leave one an easy target for parody."

1711. Registered Internet domain was symbolics.com, assigned to Symbolics, Incorporated, a developer of artificial intelligence languages and hardware, located in Woburn, MA, USA, on March 15, 1985. The Domain Name System (DNS) that is now universally used on the Internet was introduced in 1984.

1712. Year in which the number of Internet hosts exceeded 10,000 was 1987.

1713. Computer hacker to be convicted was an American, Donald Burleson, the former director of computer security at a Texas insurance firm, USPA and IRA of Fort Worth, TX, USA. Three days after Burleson was fired in 1985, the company discovered that 168,000 sales records had been erased from its computer system. Burleson used a type of computer virus called a "logic bomb" or "worm" to destroy the computer data. In September 1988, a Fort Worth jury convicted him on third-degree felony charges and sentenced him to seven years' probation and a fine of US$11,800.

1714. Widespread worm attack on the Internet took place on November 2, 1988, when a worm (a form of self-propagating computer virus) was released into the Internet by Robert T. Morris, Jr., a graduate student at Cornell University, Ithaca, NY, USA. The worm replicated much more quickly than expected and within a few hours had shut down some 6,000 of the 60,000 hosts then on the Internet. The cost to repair the damage caused by the worm ranged from US$200 to more than US$53,000 per host site. Morris was later convicted of violating the United States Computer Fraud and Abuse Act.

1715. Internet index was created in 1989 by Peter Deutsch, Alan Emtage, and Bill Heelan of McGill University in Montreal, Canada. Their network software, called Archie, archived File Transfer Protocol (FTP) sites, which at that time accounted for nearly all nodes on the Internet.

1716. Year in which the number of Internet hosts exceeded 100,000 was 1989.

1717. Commercial provider of Internet dial-up access was world.std.com, which began operations in 1990.

1718. Global hypermedia information system was the World Wide Web, invented by English computer scientist Tim Berners-Lee of the Organisation Européene pour la Recherche Nucléaire (CERN), the European Particle Physics Laboratory near Geneva, Switzerland. In his 1980 paper *Enquire-Within-Upon-Everything,* Berners-Lee conceived of a system in which links could be made betwen arbitrary nodes on a network. He wrote a prototype implementation of a web browser and editor with link-creation capability in November 1990, a month after he chose "World Wide Web" as a name for the system over "Information Mesh," "Mine of Information," or "Information Mine."

1719. Year in which the number of Internet hosts exceeded 1,000,000 was 1992.

1720. Web ring was created by Sage Weil, a high-school student from Ashland, OR, USA, in June 1995. Weil wrote software that made it possible to link World Wide Web internet sites anywhere in the world into a ring, or web community.

1721. Copyright law covering the Internet was written by copyright experts from 160 countries who gathered in Geneva, Switzerland, in December 1996 to attend the World Intellectual Property Organization conference. The two treaties, which updated the Berne Convention's protections for music, films, software, and television, were the first to regulate the ability to digitized and distribute intellectual property worldwide via the Internet.

1722. Internet access point in Latin America was completed in mid-1997. The Latin Internet Exchange was located in Santo Domingo, the Dominican Republic, and allowed Internet traffic for the first time to be routed entirely within Latin America, rather than taking the slower and most costly route through network access points in the United States.

1723. Year in which 100 million people connected to the Internet was 1997.

1724. National fiber-optic Internet was CA*net 3, inaugurated in 1998 by Canada. The fiber-optic system offered faster and more reliable connections.

COMPUTERS—SOFTWARE

1725. Computer programmer was English mathematician Augusta Ada Byron King, Countess of Lovelace, the daughter of the poet George Gordon, Lord Byron. In November 1834, she became interested in the computing machines proposed by Cambridge University mathematics professor Charles Babbage. In 1843 she created the first computer program, a method of computing Bernoulli numbers, for use with his Analytical Engine. In an 1843 article she predicted that machines like Babbage's could be used to compose music, make pictures, and assist in scientific research.

1726. Operating system that was commercially successful was the OS/360 system, introduced in 1964 by International Business Machines (IBM) of Armonk, NY, USA. It was the first to be widely adopted among commercial computer users.

1727. Multiuser operating system that was practical was Unix, developed by American computer scientists Ken Thompson, Dennis Ritchie, and Rudd Canaday of Bell Telephone Labs, Holmdel, NJ, USA, between April and June of 1969. A full working implementation of Unix was demonstrated in the summer of 1970 on a Digital Equipment PDP-11/20. The first written documentation for Unix was the *Unix Programmer's Manual,* dated November 3, 1971. Because it allowed any number of users to access a computer at one time, and because it was portable, machine-independent, affordable, and relatively easy to program, Unix became the preferred operating system for large academic and engineering computer installations, and was still growing in popularity in the year 2000. It was also the first collaboratively developed and supported operating system.

1728. Spreadsheet program for manipulating matrices of numbers was the LANPAR program, created in 1970 by Canadian programmers Remy Landau and René Pardo of Lanpar, Limited. The two received a patent for their software, but were unable to protect it against competitors including Lotus Development Corporation, makers of the popular Lotus 1-2-3 spreadsheet, because of irregularities in the patent application.

1729. Personal computer operating system was CP/M (Control Program for Microcomputers), developed by American computer programmer Gary Kildall of Monterey, CA, USA, in 1974. The first version was the CP/M-80 operating system, which simplified the tasks of writing and debugging software for Intel 8080-compatible microprocessors. It was the first operating system suited to computer hobbyists. A version of CP/M was available for the Altair 8800, the first personal computer.

1730. Commercial software for personal computers was a program that enabled the Altair 8800 personal computer to understand software written in the BASIC computer language. It was developed in 1975 by two Americans, William Henry "Bill" Gates III, age 19, and Paul Gardner Allen, age 22, in Seattle, WA, USA. Microsoft, the company they founded to market the software, was the world's first personal computer software company.

1731. Personal computer with a graphical user interface was the Lisa computer, developed by Apple Computer, Inc., of Cupertino, CA, USA, and introduced in January 1983. It featured a 5-megahertz 68000 microprocessor, 1MB RAM, 2MB ROM, an integrated black-and-white monitor, and 720 by 364 bitmapped screen graphics. The operating system, based on innovations developed at Xerox's Palo Alto Research Center in Palo Alto, CA, USA, incorporated icons and windows and was operated with a keyboard and mouse. The software cost Apple Computer US$100 million to develop; the computer itself initially sold for US$10,000. Lisa was an acronym for Local Integrated Software Architecture, and also the name of Apple head Steve Job's daughter.

COMPUTERS—SOFTWARE—*continued*

1732. Encyclopedia on CD-ROM was the *Academic American Encyclopedia,* originally published on paper by Areté in 1979. In 1986, Grolier Publishing of Danbury, CT, USA, released the encyclopedia in a multimedia version called the *Grolier Multimedia Encyclopedia.*

1733. Hypertext computer application was Zoomracks, created by American software designer Paul Heckel and marketed for the Atari ST and IBM PC-compatible personal computers from circa 1986. Zoomracks used a "card-and-rack" metaphor later popularized in Apple Computer's HyperCard program and in many other multimedia programs.

1734. International conference of multimedia publishers was Milia, the International Illustrated Book and New Media Publishing Market, held in Cannes, France, in January 1994. It brought together new media companies in music, books, film, video, software, and images. The conference drew 385 exhibitors from 24 nations. Robert Stein, founder of the Voyager Company, a multimedia publishing firm, gave the keynote address.

1735. Thought control of a computer was achieved in October 1998, when a paralyzed man hospitalized at the U.S. Veterans Affairs Medical Center in Decatur, GA, USA, employed a small electronic brain implant to move the cursor on a computer screen. The implant, a tiny glass capsule coated with neurotropic chemicals extracted from the man's peripheral nerves, was developed by doctors Roy Bakay and Phillip Kennedy of Emory University in Atlanta, GA, USA. When the man thought about moving the cursor, the capsule read the electrical activity in his brain and, via a transmitter in his scalp, sent a command to the computer.

CRIME AND CRIMINAL JUSTICE

1736. Trial by jury developed in England, an outgrowth of the practice of assembling witnesses to give judgment in a case of which they had personal knowledge. Eventually, the jury evolved into a panel that passed judgment after hearing evidence from others. Trial by jury replaced trial by ordeal in England in the 1400s.

1737. Treatise on criminal justice and its reform was *Dei delitti e delle pene (Crimes and Punishments),* by the Milanese economist Cesare Beccaria, published in Italy in 1764. Beccaria, a student of the utilitarian philosophers, denounced the use of torture, humiliation, and secrecy in the punishment of criminals and called for a rational system of progressively ordered penalties.

1738. Prison reformer of note was the English philanthropist John Howard. Upon becoming high sheriff of Bedfordshire in 1773, he toured the local jail, which was appallingly unhealthy, and learned that prisoners were forced to pay their own jailers. Those who could not pay a discharge fee were kept in prison even if they had been acquitted. At his instigation, in 1774 the House of Commons passed prison reform acts that abolished discharge fees and required justices to oversee the health of prisoners. In 1777 Howard wrote the reformist tract *State of the Prisons.*

1739. Probation system for criminals of all ages was legally established as a judicial policy by Boston, MA, USA, in 1878 and by the state of Massachusetts in 1880. This was the first such system in the world.

1740. British jury to consider evidence overseas was the jury in the 1999 war-crimes case of Anthony Sawoniuk, who was accused of participating in the murder of 3,800 Jews in a forest near Domachevo, Belarus, during the Holocaust. The jury visited the town to examine the evidence firsthand.

CRIME AND CRIMINAL JUSTICE— DEATH PENALTY

1741. Drawing and quartering as a punishment for treason was performed on David ap Grufudd, the last native-born prince of Wales, who mounted a rebellion against the English in Wales. In October 1283, before a crowd at Shrewsbury, Salopshire, England, he was briefly hanged on a gallows, cut down while still alive, then disemboweled. His entrails were burned and his body was cut into four parts. Execution by drawing and quartering was used as late as 1803, for seven men who tried to assassinate George III.

1742. Call for abolition of the death penalty was made in 1764 by Cesare Beccaria, an economist and reformer from Milan, Italy, in his book *Dei delitti e delle pene (Crimes and Punishments).* Beccaria's condemnation of excessive punishment was based on utilitarian and humanitarian arguments.

1743. Nation to abolish capital punishment was Austria, in a statute of 1787.

1744. Execution by guillotine of record took place on April 25, 1792, at the Place de Grève in Paris, France, where a convicted highwayman, Joseph Pelletier, was beheaded before a large, boisterous crowd. Invention of the guillotine, originally called the Louisette or Louison, is usually ascribed to the French physician Joseph-Ignace Guillotin, but earlier forms of the guillotine were already in use in Scotland and elsewhere. Guillotin was the first to advocate its use as a humane method of execution that would, in his words, "separate the head from the body in the twinkling of an eye" and that did not distinguish between the upper and lower classes.

1745. Electric chair for executing condemned criminals by electrocution was invented in the United States by Harold P. Brown and Dr. A.E. Kennelly in the 1880s. The first person to die in an electric chair was William Kemmler, alias John Hart, who was put to death on August 6, 1890, at Auburn Prison, Auburn, NY, for the murder of Matilda Ziegler. The execution took eight minutes and required two surges of electricity.

1746. Woman to die in the electric chair was Martha M. Place of Brooklyn, NY, USA, who was electrocuted at Sing Sing Prison, Ossining, NY, USA, on March 20, 1899, for the murder of her stepdaughter Ida.

1747. Gas chamber for executing condemned criminals was the invention of Major D.A. Turner of the U.S. Army Medical Corps. The first person to die in a gas chamber was Gee Jon, a member of a Chinese gang who had been convicted of killing another gang member. He died on February 8, 1924, at a prison in Carson City, NV, USA, where he was exposed to cyanide gas.

1748. English-speaking country to abolish the death penalty was New Zealand, which did so in 1936.

CRIME AND CRIMINAL JUSTICE—DETECTION

1749. Treatise on forensic autopsy of record was *The Washing Away of Unjust Wrongs* (1247), a Chinese manual of post mortem techniques for determining the cause of death by murder, burning, drowning, or other forms of violence.

1750. Forensic postmortem for the determination of the cause of death in a criminal investigation was requested by a magistrate of the Italian city of Bologna in 1302.

1751. Criminal caught by telegraph was the English murderer John Tawell. In 1845, he was seen boarding a train at Slough, England, headed for London. Running along the track was the first public telegraph line, installed by William Cooke and Charles Wheatstone in May 1843. A message was telegraphed from Slough to London, and Tawell was arrested as he disembarked.

1752. Register of fingerprints was instituted by William Herschel, an Indian Civil Service magistrate, at Arrah, India, in June 1859. Herschel required Indians signing official papers to add their palm prints and fingerprints to the document for purposes of identification.

1753. Crime solved using fingerprints of record was committed by Francisca Rojas of Necochea, Argentina, who murdered her children in July 1892 and accused a neighbor of the crime. Bloody fingerprints found at the scene by a police inspector matched those of the mother, not the accused, and she confessed.

1754. Fingerprint bureau in a police organization was the Fingerprint Branch of Scotland Yard, London, England. It was founded in 1901 by Edward Henry, who developed an identification system based on the thumbprint, drawing upon the earlier fingerprinting work of the English eugenicist Francis Galton.

1755. Criminal caught by radio was an American, Harvey Crippen, who in 1910 murdered his wife in London and fled on the liner *Montrose* for Quebec, Canada. He was accompanied by his lover, Ethel le Neve, who was masquerading as his son. The ship's master grew suspicious of them after he saw them holding hands, and radioed Scotland Yard with their description. Chief Inspector Walter Dew hired a fast ship, caught up with the *Montrose* on July 31, 1910, and arrested the pair.

1756. Conviction for murder based on photographic evidence of marks on a bullet was obtained by Arizona lawyer A. J. Eddy in the 1921 murder case of *Arizona v. Hadley*. Eddy was the first to use bullet ballistics in his testimony. The defendant was convicted of first-degree murder based on photographic examination of land-and-groove markings on a bullet from the murder gun.

1757. Retinal print identification system for commercial use was the Eye Printing system marketed by the American company EyeDentify in 1984. It employed an optical device that scanned the back of the eyeball and compared the retinal pattern of blood vessels and markings, as unique as a fingerprint, with images on file in a database.

CRIME AND CRIMINAL JUSTICE—DETECTION—*continued*

1758. Genetic fingerprinting method was developed in 1985 by Alec J. Jeffreys, director of the genetic laboratory at the University of Leicester, England. The method involved analyzing samples of hair, skin, blood, or other bodily residues for DNA sequence unique to an individual. The technique found immediate application in forensic investigation.

1759. Murderer apprehended on DNA evidence alone was Colin Pitchfork, a baker from Leicestershire, England. In 1987, two teenage girls from the area were raped and murdered. Semen recovered from the bodies was analyzed for its unique DNA signature, then compared to DNA from blood samples taken from 5,000 local men. Fearing detection, Pitchfork asked a friend to give blood for him, but the friend later confessed. When Pitchfork was tested, his was the only signature that matched.

1760. Palm identification system was the Palm Recognition System, developed in 1987 for commercial use by Mitsubishi Denki KK (Mitsubishi Electric Corporation) of Japan. An individual placing his or her hand on a sensor plate could be identified from the outline of the hand and the print of the palm, which is as unique as a fingerprint.

1761. Suspect cleared of a crime by DNA evidence was Rodney Buckland, suspected in the 1987 rape and murder of a teenage girl in Leicestershire, England. DNA analysis proved that another man, local baker Colin Pitchfork, was the murderer, and Buckland was set free.

1762. Murderer executed on DNA evidence was American rapist and murderer Timothy Wilson Spencer. DNA collected from his victims matched his and was the main evidence against him. The state of Virginia executed Spencer in April 1994.

1763. Court-ordered wiretap on a computer network was placed by United States officials on a computer at Harvard University, Cambridge, MA, USA, in 1996. It was believed that a student from Argentina, Julio Cesar Ardita, was using the computer to break into U.S. military computers and view files containing engineering information.

1764. Virtual-reality reconstruction of a crime scene was the Interactive Crime Scene Reporting System, developed by two police investigators, Senior Sergeant Adrian Freeman and Sergeant Troy O'Malley, of Queensland, Australia. Using the system, hundreds of photographs of the crime scene taken by a police photographer could be stitched together using the QuickTime VR 3D technology invented by Apple Computer of Cupertino, CA, USA. The result was a "virtual crime scene" that could be viewed on a computer from many angles and with several degrees of magnification. The system was first used to present court evidence in August 1998.

CRIME AND CRIMINAL JUSTICE—GENOCIDE AND WAR CRIMES

1765. Planned genocide on record is described in the biblical Book of Esther, called *Megillat Esther* in Hebrew. The Book of Esther recounts events that are said to have taken place in Shushan, Persia (modern Susa, Iran), during the fifth century BCE. A decree by King Xerxes, known as Akhashverosh in Hebrew, was sent by courier to every province in the Persian empire, ordering the local populations "to destroy, to slay and to exterminate all the Jews, from young to old, children and women, in one day, on the thirteenth of the twelfth month, which is the month of Adar, and to plunder their possessions." A plea for mercy by his queen, Esther, who was herself a Jew, persuaded the king to change his mind, but since a royal decree was irrevocable, he instead granted the Jews permission to defend themselves. Their survival is the basis for the Jewish spring holiday of Purim.

1766. Germ warfare for purposes of genocide may have been attempted by the Spanish conquistador Francisco Pizarro, who is thought to have distributed smallpox-infected blankets to the Inca during his conquest of Peru in the 1530s. In 1763, after a series of Native American uprisings in the Great Lakes area of what is now the United States, Major General Jeffery Amherst, commander of the British Army in North America, suggested to Colonel Henry Bouquet that he distribute to the tribes blankets that had been used by smallpox victims. "Could it not be contrived to send the Small Pox among these disaffected tribes of Indians?" he wrote to Bouquet, who responded on July 13, 1763, "I will try to inoculate [them] with Some Blankets that may fall into their Hands." It is not known whether this strategem was carried out. Another British officer, Captain Ecuyer, the commander of Fort Pitt (now Pittsburgh, PA, USA), claimed to have given two infected blankets to hostile chiefs during the summer of 1763.

1767. Concentration camps known by that name were internment camps set up by the Spanish in Cuba in 1895 to control people opposed to their rule. Camps on a much wider scale were set up by the British during the South African War, also called the Boer War

(1899–1902). Between 1900 and 1902, a network of fifty camps were constructed to confine Afrikaner and Boer women and children and Boer men unfit for service from the republics of Transvaal and Cape Colony. The first two camps were established following a military order of September 22, 1900, to protect the families of Afrikaners who had surrendered voluntarily. Living conditions in the camps were extremely primitive. Of the 136,000 persons interned, 27,927 died, including 22,074 children under 16 years old.

1768. Genocide in the 20th century was the German campaign of extermination against the Herero and Nama tribes in South-West Africa (now Namibia). German attempts at colonization, beginning in the 1880s, were answered in 1904 by a Herero insurrection in which 123 settlers were killed. The German commander, Lothar von Trotha, announced that "every Herero, with or without a rifle, with or without cattle, shall be shot." At the Battle of Waterburg in November 1905, 5,000 Herero were driven into the Kalahari desert to die of thirst. Mass executions and brutal treatment in concentration camps took the lives of thousands more, reducing the Herero population from 70,000 to 16,000 in a few years. The Nama, who joined the rebellion, lost two-fifths of their people.

1769. Genocide squads were the "Special Organizations," squads of criminals and others formed by the Ottoman Turks in 1915 to aid in the extermination of Armenians living within the Ottoman Empire. Mass murders began in January 1915 and accelerated after April 24, 1915, when the Turkish government announced it was "deporting" Armenians to Syria. In fact, the Armenians were being worked to death in concentration camps or murdered outright by the squads, a fact that was well known to foreigners. In many particulars, the Turkish approach to genocide foreshadowed that of the Nazis, who also employed special killing squads and attempted to hide their activities with a variety of euphemisms and cover stories. An estimated 1.4 million Armenians lost their lives in the genocide.

1770. Labor concentration camp whose intended purpose was to kill prisoners through overwork, starvation, harsh treatment, and disease was founded by the Bolshevik regime in 1921 at Arkhangel'sk, Russia. Its name was Holmogor. It was the first of the extensive network of prison camps known collectively as the Gulag, where many millions of Soviet citizens died.

1771. National euthanasia program was Aktion T4, conducted in Nazi Germany by order of Adolf Hitler beginning in October 1939. The decree established "the authority of certain physicians to be designated by name in such manner that persons who, according to human judgment, are incurable can, upon a most careful diagnosis of their condition of sickness, be accorded a mercy death." In the first mass murder, 908 patients were transferred in early 1940 from Schönbrunn, an institution for retarded and chronically ill patients, to a euthanasia center at Eglfing-Haar to be gassed. A total of 70,273 mentally and physically disabled people were murdered in six centers, including the prison Hartheim Schloss, near Linz in Austria, and the notorious Hadamar Psychiatric Clinic. Most victims were secretly put to death by gassing, while others were used for medical experimentation. The next of kin were told that they had died from natural causes. The program was headed by Christian Wirth, an SS officer. Aktion T4 was officially ended on August 23, 1941, after it was denounced on August 3 by the Catholic bishop Clemens von Galen in a sermon in Münster Cathedral, but it was continued unofficially until Germany's defeat in 1945.

1772. Death camp operated for the specific purpose of murdering human beings on an industrial scale was the Chelmno extermination camp in Nazi-occupied Poland, near Lodz. It became operational on December 8, 1941. Polish Jews taken there by the SS were placed in sealed vans and gassed to death by engine exhaust as they were driven to a burial area or crematorium. The first gassing victims also included 5,000 German Gypsies. As many as 360,000 persons were executed in the camp by 1945; only two Jewish inmates were known to have survived the war.

1773. Revolt by prisoners at a Nazi death camp broke out at Treblinka, in eastern Poland. Between 700,000 and 1 million people, virtually all of them Jews, were killed at Treblinka beginning in July 1942, shot to death or murdered in the gas chambers. On July 2, 1943, a group of several hundred Jewish slaves took over the armory and distributed the weapons. They killed a number of Germans and burned several buildings before they were overwhelmed. The camp was shut down a few months later.

CRIME AND CRIMINAL JUSTICE—
GENOCIDE AND WAR CRIMES—*continued*

1774. Nazi death camp to be liberated in World War II was Ohrdruf, near Gotha, Germany, liberated on April 4, 1945, by American soldiers of the XX Corps in the presence of generals Dwight David Eisenhower and George Smith Patton. They found skeletal prisoners, torture equipment, cremation ovens in which corpses were burning, and the stacked-up bodies of hundreds of people who had been shot in the back of the head or starved to death. The victims were Jewish civilians and Polish and Russian prisoners of war.

1775. Definition of rape as a crime against humanity was defined in Article 6(c) of the Charter of the International Military Tribunal at Nuremberg, promulgated on August 8, 1945, at Nuremberg (Nürnberg), Germany, in the aftermath of the Nazi war crimes of World War II. Article 6(c) condemns rape as a "crime against humanity" when committed in a "widespread and systematic manner."

1776. War criminals convicted of crimes against humanity were 19 leaders of Nazi Germany who were tried before the International Military Tribunal in the Nuremberg Trials after World War II. The tribunal, chartered by the Allied nations on August 8, 1946, was charged with seeking justice for three categories of crimes: crimes against peace (that is, beginning a war of aggression); crimes against civilians, including murder, mistreatment, and deportation; and crimes against humanity, involving the persecution and mass murder of a civilian population. The trial began on October 18, 1945, and ended on October 1, 1946. All sessions were held in Germany, the first in Berlin, the rest in Nuremberg (Nürnberg). Three of the 22 defendants were acquitted. Of the 19 who were convicted, four received prison terms, three received life imprisonment, and twelve were sentenced to death and hanged.

1777. Legal definition of genocide was set forth in the Convention on Prevention and Punishment of the Crime of Genocide, a document prepared by the United Nations that went into effect in 1951. Article 2 of the Convention states: "Genocide means any of the following acts commited with intent to destroy, in whole or in part, a national, ethical, racial or religious group as such: (a) Killing members of the group; (b) Causing serious bodily or mental harm to members of the group; (c) Deliberately inflicting on the group conditions of life calculated to bring about its physical destruction in whole or in part; (d) Imposing measures intended to prevent births within the group; (e) Forcibly transferring children of the group to another group."

1778. War criminals indicted for rape were eight Bosnian Serb military and police officers who raped or ordered the rape of Bosnian Muslim women during the Bosnian war. On June 27, 1996, the indictments were announced by the United Nations International Criminal Tribunal for the Former Yugoslavia. It was the first time that sexual assault was treated separately as a war crime by an international tribunal.

1779. Reparations for forced prostitution was paid on November 11, 1996, to Maria Rosa Henson, a Philippine woman who was forced by the Japanese Army during World War II to serve as a prostitute, or "comfort woman." She was imprisoned for nine months in a brothel in the Philippines and forced to provide sex to between 10 and 30 Japanese soldiers each day.

1780. Holocaust reparations from a neutral nation was US$400 paid by Switzerland on November 18, 1997, to Reva Shefer of Latvia. Switzerland agreed to pay reparations after it became known that Swiss banks had laundered stolen gold for the Nazis during World War II and that the banks were holding millions of dollars deposited by Jews murdered in the Holocaust.

1781. Permanent international war crimes court was the International Criminal Court, founded by the United Nations on July 18, 1998. In an assembly in Rome, Italy, 127 nations signed the Final Act and ten signed the ICC statute. The ICC was designed to prosecute such war crimes as genocide, forced pregnancy, and the use of children as combatants.

1782. Genocide conviction by an international court was issued on September 3, 1998, in Rusha, Tanzania, by a United Nations tribunal investigating mass murders in Rwanda. Jean-Paul Akayesu, the former mayor of Taba, a small town in central Rwanda, was judged guilty of genocide for his role in the 1994 killings of more than 2,000 Tutsi villagers, as well as the rape of dozens of Tutsi women. On May 1, 1998, before the same tribunal, former Rwandan prime minister Jean Kambanda became the first person in history to plead guilty to genocide.

1783. Serving leader of a sovereign nation indicted for war crimes by an international tribunal was Slobodan Milosevic, the president of the Federal Republic of Yugoslavia. On May 27, 1999, the International Criminal Tribunal for the former Yugoslavia publicly announced his indictment for "the persecution of the Kosovo Albanian civilian population on political, racial, or religious grounds." A warrant was issued for his arrest. Warrants were also issued for Milan Milutinovic, the president of Serbia; Nikola Sainovic, deputy prime minister of the FRY; Dragoljub Ojdanic, chief of staff of the Yugoslav Army; and Vlajko Stojiljkovic, minister of internal affairs of Serbia. The indictment was submitted on May 22, 1999, by the Prosecutor, Justice Louise Arbour, and approved on May 24 by Judge David Hunt. In the indictment, Arbour noted that it was "the first in the history of this Tribunal to charge a Head of State during an on-going armed conflict with the commission of serious violations of international humanitarian law." Each of the accused was charged with three counts of crimes against humanity and one count of violations of the laws or customs of war. They were also charged with the murder of more than 340 persons identified by name in an annex to the indictment.

CRIME AND CRIMINAL JUSTICE—MURDER

1784. Assassins known by that name were Nizari Isma'ilites, an Iranian Muslim sect whose members considered the murder of their enemies to be a sacred religious duty. The English word "assassins" is derived from the Arab *hashshashin,* the name given to the Nizari Isma'ilites for their supposed habit of smoking hashish to induce visions of paradise before committing terrorist acts. Their first assassination took place in 1092, when they killed the Seljukvizier, Nizam al-Mulik.

1785. Serial killer of record, in acts not associated with war or conquest, may have been Gilles de Laval, the seigneur de Rais, a widely respected knight of France who had served under Joan of Arc. In September 1440 he was arrested on accusations of satanic practices and the torture-murder of some 140 children. He confessed under torture and was hanged at Nantes on October 26, 1440.

1786. Attempted murder by poisoned book may have been committed by the anonymous author of *Chin P'ing Mei (Gold Plum Vase),* written in China during the Ming Dynasty, in 1617 or somewhat earlier. *Chin P'ing Mei* is a naturalistic novel—the first such novel in China, where all prior fiction was based on legend or history—about a wealthy man who enjoys a life of debauchery, graphically described, with his numerous wives and servants. A copy of the book is said to have been sent by the author to one of his political enemies, in the hope that the reader, while turning pages, would moisten his fingers by licking them. The corners of the pages had been painted with poison.

1787. Pirate alleged to have made prisoners walk the plank was Major Stede Bonnet, formerly a magistrate in Barbados, West Indies, who switched to piracy circa 1720 and teamed up with Edward Teach, better known as Blackbeard. He was captured and hanged at Charleston (in what is now South Carolina, USA).

CRIME AND CRIMINAL JUSTICE—POLICE

1788. Organized police force was instituted by Augustus Caesar in Rome. The city had already been divided into wards and precincts, each with its own fire brigade. In the year 6 CE, Augustus added police protection to the brigades' responsibilities. He also ordered the formation of three squads of military police who could be deployed by the prefect of the city.

1789. Chief of police in modern times was Gabriel-Nicholas de la Reynie, who served for three decades as lieutenant-general of police in Paris, France, beginning in 1667, when the post was created. The police force at that time was an extension of the king's authority and included a network of paid informers.

1790. Police station in the modern sense, an operations facility separate from the administrative headquarters, was founded in Paris, France, in 1698. The station was established at the Pont-Neuf, a bridge across the Seine River in central Paris.

1791. Detective bureau was the Police de Sûreté (security police), founded in 1810 in Paris, France, by François-Eugène Vidocq. A former thief himself, Vidocq used his wide knowledge of criminal practices to successfully penetrate the Parisian underworld, using paid agents and informers rather than regular policemen. In 1833, after Vidocq's retirement, the bureau was reorganized and staffed with detective sergeants and inspectors who were members of the Parisian police force.

CRIME AND CRIMINAL JUSTICE—PO-LICE—*continued*

1792. Modern police force was established in parts of London, England, in 1829, when Parliament passed the Metropolitan Police Act. The law provided for a body of salaried, professional, uniformed officers whose responsibilities included preventing crime through frequent patrols, in addition to capturing offenders and serving as watchmen. The officers were called "Bobbies" as a derisive reference to their chief advocate, Robert Peel.

1793. Private detective agency was founded in 1832 in Paris, France, by François-Eugène Vidocq, formerly head of the security police.The agency was called the Bureau des Renseignements au Service des Intérêts Privés, and took on cases that the police were not interested in or that involved sensitive investigations that clients wished to keep private.

1794. Police dog unit to serve as an official part of a police organization was the Canine Police Force, introduced in 1899 in Ghent, Belgium. Trained dogs had already been used informally by police officers and detectives for many years.

1795. United Nations manhunt was conducted in Somalia during the fall of 1993 for Somali clan leader and warlord Muhammad Farah Aydid. Aydid was blamed for the murder of 24 Pakistani UN peacekeeping troops in an ambush on June 5, 1993. The United Nations approved a US$25,000 award for his capture and launched a massive manhunt that involved thousands of UN soldiers and two unsuccessful assaults on clan strongholds. Aydid was never captured; he voluntarily emerged and in October 1993 offered a cease-fire with the release of two UN captives.

1796. Session of the United Nations Commission on Crime Prevention and Criminal Justice was held in Vienna, Austria, in April 1993. Among the issues the commission adressed were national and transnational crime, organized crime, money laundering and other forms of economic crime, drug trafficking, illegal arms sales, terrorism, industrial waste dumping, and corruption.

CRIME AND CRIMINAL JUSTICE—TERRORISM

1797. Woman executed in Russia for political terrorism was Sofia L. Perovskaya, who was co-leader of Narodnaya Volya (People's Will), a revolutionary organization that embraced terrorism as a legitimate means of bringing about political and social change. She was hanged in 1881, along with other members of the group, for killing Tsar Alexander II in a bomb attack.

1798. Airplane hijacking took place on June 16, 1948, en route from Macao, China, to Hong Kong. Chinese bandits led by Wongyu Man enrolled as passengers on a Cathay Pacific Airways flying boat, *Miss Macao,* and attempted to take over the plane in flight, with the aim of kidnapping the passengers for ransom. Shots were fired and the plane crashed, with Wongyu Man the only survivor. In hospital he boasted of the crime to an informer, unaware that his conversations were being tape recorded by the police.

1799. Massacre at the Olympic Games took place on September 5, 1967, during the 20th Summer Olympiad in Munich, Germany. Members of Ailulal Aswad (Black September), the assassination wing of Al Fatah, the military division of the Palestinian Liberation Organization, infiltrated the Olympic Village, killed an Israeli coach and an athlete, and took nine Israeli athletes hostage. The terrorists demanded the release of 236 Palestinians and other terrorists held in Israel. A botched rescue attempt by German police at the Furstenfeldbrück airfield resulted in the deaths of the terrorists and all the hostages, several of whom were killed by stray German bullets. The Black September group (named for the destruction by Jordan of the Palestinian military in September 1970) was founded by Abu Daoud and others and funded by Colonel Muammar al-Qaddafi, the prime minister of Libya. The Olympic operation was masterminded by Ali Hassan Salameh, who was assassinated by the Mossad, the Israeli secret service, in 1979.

1800. International terrorist organization to use skyjacking as its favored terrorist act was the Popular Front for the Liberation of Palestine, founded in 1967 by the militant Marxist-Leninist and Palestinian nationalist Georges Habash. The PFLP's avowed goal was the destruction of the state of Israel. In 1968 the PFLP hijacked 14 Israeli and other commercial airliners.

1801. Terrorist bomb attack on an airplane took place on August 12, 1982, when a bomb went off on a Pan American World Airways airliner traveling from Japan to Honolulu, HI, USA. The blast mortally wounded a Japanese boy, 16-year-old Toru Ozawa, and hurt 15 other passengers. The bomb was a time-delayed device planted by Mohammed Rashid, who had flown from Hong Kong to Japan on the same plane a few hours earlier. Rashid was convicted of the bombing in 1992 by a court in Greece, released by Greece in 1996, and rearrested in 1998 by the United States. The U.S. indictment said that Rashid was a member of a Palestinian terrorist organization, the 15th of May, and that he had planted the bomb together with his wife, Christine Pinter, whose whereabouts were unknown.

1802. Terrorist attack using military poison gas took place in March 1995, when members of the apocalyptic Japanese cult Aum Shinrikyo, at the instigation of its leader, Shoko Asahara, released sarin nerve gas into the Tokyo subway system. Twelve people were killed and 5,500 were injured.

CRIME AND CRIMINAL JUSTICE—THEFT

1803. Highway robber of note who was a woman was Mary Frith, who took the name Moll Cutpurse and, dressed as a man, preyed on victims in and about London, England, beginning circa 1610. Her highway career ended some decades later when she robbed and shot General Fairfax on Hounslow Heath, was pursued and captured, and was forced to pay a large bribe to the Newgate jailers. An autobiography published in 1662, when she was 75, recounted her adventures as a pickpocket, bandit, madam, and fence. "In her time," it was written in the *Newgate Calendar*, "she was superior in the mystery of diving in purses and pockets, and was very well read and skilled too in the affairs of the placket among the great ones."

1804. Theft of the British Crown Jewels was attempted by the Irish adventurer Colonel Thomas Blood during the reign of Charles II. On May 9, 1671, Blood was apprehended at the East Gate of the Tower of London carrying the crown, one scepter, and the orb. Some historians have argued that Blood was in the hire of King Charles II, who planned to raise cash with their secret resale. This speculation is given weight by the fact that Blood received an extremely mild punishment.

1805. Car theft was perpetrated in June 1896 in France. A mechanic hired by the Baron de Zuylen to care for his Peugeot absconded with the vehicle while it was being repaired at the Peugeot shop in Paris. He was later captured and the vehicle was returned.

1806. Modern pyramid scheme was introduced in 1920 by Charles Ponzi, an Italian immigrant to Boston, MA, USA. Enticing investors with promises of "fifty percent profit in forty-five days" for purchasing postal reply coupons, Ponzi in fact sold no coupons and pocketed most of the money, paying back the first investors out of funds he swindled from new ones. He eventually netted US$15 million from 40,000 victims before he was caught and convicted of fraud. Such swindles are now often called Ponzi schemes.

1807. Internet bank robber was Vladimir Levin of St. Petersburg, Russia. Between June and August of 1994, he used valid user IDs and passwords to electronically transfer more than US$10 million from the cash management system of Citibank in New York, NY, USA, to accounts held by Jevgenij Korolkov, Levin's colleague in a multinational hacker ring. The ring was broken in 1995, and Levin was arrested aliong with five accomplices.

1808. Smuggled moon rock was seized by U.S. customs officials on December 7, 1998, in Miami, FL, USA. The rock, brought back by the *Apollo 17* moon mission, had originally been presented to Honduras by American president Richard Milhous Nixon in 1973. The smuggler had failed to declare the rock upon entering the United States.

CULTURAL INSTITUTIONS—LIBRARIES

1809. Library of substantial size was discovered in 1933 at the site of the ancient Mesopotamian city of Mari (now Tall Hariri, Syria). Archeologists uncovered an archive of some 23,600 clay tablets, covered with cuneiform writing, that have been dated to between 2285 and 1755 BCE.

1810. Classification system of all knowledge was constructed in the third century BCE by Callimachus of Cyrene, the Greek poet who headed the royal library at Alexandria, Egypt. His catalog of the library's 500,000 manuscript scrolls, the first of its kind in the world, consisted of 120 scrolls containing bibliographical and critical information on each work. The catalog was arranged by broad categories—including the humanities, the natural sciences, and the social sciences—which were subdivided by subject matter in a way that showed the rela-

CULTURAL INSTITUTIONS—LIBRAR-
IES—*continued*

tionship between areas of knowledge. The catalog, called the *Pinakes (Tiles)* after the ceramic
labels on the bins that held the library's scrolls,
was subtitled *The Tablets of the Outstanding
Works in the Whole of Greek Civilization.*

1811. Library catalog was the *Pinakes (Tiles),*
compiled by the Greek poet Callimachus of Cyrene as an inventory of the contents of the
great library at Alexandria, Egypt. The library
had been founded by Ptolemy I Soter in 306
BCE. When Callimachus became its librarian
some 20 to 25 years later, the collection contained more than half a million volumes in the
form of scrolls, which were grouped together
by subject matter and stored in bins. Each bin
carried a label on a ceramic tile. The *Pinakes,*
named after these tiles, consisted of 120 scrolls,
likewise arranged by subject matter, giving bibliographical information for every book. A typical entry included the title; the name, birthplace, father, teachers, educational background,
and pseudonyms of the author, together with a
brief biography and list of publications; the first
line of the work, a summary of its contents,
and the name of the editor or redactor; and information about the provenance of the scroll.
Callimachus is considered the first bibliogra-
pher.

1812. Libraries in Asia were founded in China
during the Qin (Ch'in) dynasty, circa 221–206
BCE. On imperial order, a copy of every book
was reserved for the emperor's library, and other copies were destroyed.

1813. Modern bibliography of importance was
the *Bibliotheca universalis,* compiled beginning
in 1545 by the Swiss naturalist and encyclopedist Conrad Gesner, known as the "father of
bibliography." Intended as an index by subject
of all known writers, it listed some 1,800 authors alphabetically with the titles of their
works and added Gesner's own annotations and
comments on each entry. It was never completed.

1814. Library with books shelved upright to
display their spines is thought to have been the
private library in Paris, France, of Jacques-
Auguste de Thou, a prominent historian and
politician whose interest in books led to his appointment in 1593 as director of the royal collection, the Bibliothèque du Roi (now the
Bibliothèque Nationale). The practice in most
earlier libraries was to store books flat and fix
them to their shelves with chains.

1815. Public library in Europe was the Bodleian Library at Oxford University, Oxford,
England. It was established November 8, 1602,
with funding from Thomas Bodley, a scholar
and diplomat. The Bodleian Library is entitled
to receive a free copy of every new book published in England.

1816. Treatise on library science was *Advis
pour dresser une bibliothèque (Advice on Establishing a Library),* published in 1627. The
author, Gabriel Naudé, served as librarian to
Cardinal Richelieu and Cardinal Mazarin, the
prime ministers of France, and presided over
the latter's Bibliothèque Mazarine, whose motto
was "Come in, all you who desire to read."
The treatise outlined a classification system that
subsumed all knowledge under the general
headings of theology, medicine, law, history,
philosophy, mathematics, and humanities.

1817. National archive system was the Archives Nationales, created in France in 1789 to
serve as a state-run repository of public records
and documents. The idea of a government's responsibility for maintaining historical records
on behalf of its citizens was an outcome of the
French Revolution.

1818. Library school was opened in the Yonne
district of France by the Abbé Laire at the suggestion of the Ministry of the Interior. Classes
began on April 20, 1799.

1819. Children's library was established in
January 1803 in Salisbury, CT, USA, through
the generosity of Caleb Bingham of Boston,
MA, a native of Salisbury. He donated 150 vol-
umes, the nucleus of the Bingham Library for
Youth.

1820. Carnegie library was inaugurated in
July 1881 in the town of Dunfermline, Scotland. Dunfermline was the birthplace of the
millionaire American industrialist and philanthropist Andrew Carnegie, who paid for the library and more than 2,500 other Carnegie libraries built throughout the English-speaking
world.

1821. International library organization was
the Institut International de Bibliographie,
founded in 1895 in Brussels, Belgium, by librarians Paul Otlet and Henri-Marie Lafontaine.
The organization was later renamed the International Federation for Information and Documentation.

1822. International Congress of Archivists was held in Paris, France, in 1950 under the auspices of the International Council on Archives, which was founded in 1948. The council supports progress in the standardization of archiving and the development of more effective methods of conservation.

1823. Library to possess 100 million items was the Library of Congress, Washington, DC, USA, the chief library of the United States, which acquired its 100 millionth item in 1992. In 1996, its collections included 15 million books, 39 million manuscripts, 13 million photographs, 4 million maps, more than 3.5 million pieces of music, more than half a million motion pictures, and millions of other documents.

CULTURAL INSTITUTIONS—MUSEUMS

1824. Museum known to historians was that of Ennigaldi-Nanna, the daughter of Nabu-na'id (Nabonidus), the last king of Babylonia. Ennigaldi-Nanna was a princess and a priestess of the Old Babylonian god Sin, and ran a temple school circa 530 BCE in the Babylonian city of Ur (now Tel-el-Muqayyar, Iraq). Next to the school was an educational museum containing a collection of labeled antiquities, probably amassed by her father, the first known archeologist. Ur was excavated by British archeologist Leonard Woolley between 1922 and 1934.

1825. University museum was the Ashmolean Museum of Art and Archaeology at Oxford University, Oxford, England. It was founded to house the collection of antiquarian Elias Ashmole, who donated his holdings to the university in 1677. The building, designed by Thomas Wood, was opened to the public in 1683. The Ashmolean was also the first public museum of art, archeology, and natural history in Great Britain.

1826. Museum operated as a public institution was the British Museum in London, England. It was established by act of Parliament in 1753 to house a collection of books, manuscripts, art, and other items donated by the physician and naturalist Hans Sloane. Later, the collections of Edward and Robert Harley, earls of Oxford, and Robert Bruce Cotton were added to the museum's holdings. In 1757, the Royal Library of the Kings of England was transferred to the museum by King George II. The British Museum opened to the public in 1759 at its present location in the Bloomsbury district.

1827. Museum of traditional life was the Nordiska Museet ("Nordic Museum"), located in Stockholm, Sweden. It was designed by Artur Hazilius and opened in 1872. Exhibitions focused on the traditions, crafts, and folklore of Scandinavia.

1828. Open-air museum was the Skansen historical park in Stockholm, Sweden, opened to the public in 1891. Artur Hazilius was the designer.

1829. Children's museum was the Brooklyn Children's Museum, located in Brooklyn, NY, USA. Originally part of the Brooklyn Institute of Arts and Sciences, it was established as an independent institution in 1899, with exhibits designed to instruct children in natural history.

1830. Photographic collection in a museum was installed in 1940 at the Museum of Modern Art in New York, NY, USA, with the assistance of American photographer Ansel Adams.

1831. Interactive museum was the Exploratorium, a hands-on museum of science, art, and human perception located in San Francisco, CA, USA. It was founded in 1969 by physicist Frank Oppenheimer. The permanent collection consisted of more than 800 exhibits, displays, and original artworks, all of which required viewer input and interaction.

1832. Museum of art by women was the National Museum of Women in the Arts, Washington, DC, USA, which opened on April 7, 1987. Its founder and first president was Wilhelmina Cole Holladay.

1833. Multinational art museum was the Solomon R. Guggenheim Museum, based in New York, NY, USA. Under director Thomas Krens, the museum opened satellite institutions in Bilbao, Spain, and Berlin, Germany, in the fall of 1997, and planned for further international expansion after the year 2000.

CULTURAL INSTITUTIONS—ORGANIZATIONS

1834. Club for gentlemen of the kind that became traditional in England was La Court de Bone Compagnie, a group of bon vivants that existed in London, England, in 1413.

1835. Debating society in which members argued the merits of a question and then took a vote to see which side won was the Rota Club, a society that met for some months in 1659 and 1660 at the Turk's Head inn in Westminster (now part of London), England. It was founded by, among others, the writers John Milton, Andrew Marvell, and John Aubrey.

CULTURAL INSTITUTIONS—ORGANIZATIONS—*continued*

1836. Freemason grand lodge was founded on June 24, 1717, in London, England, by the fraternal order of Free and Accepted Masons, the largest worldwide secret society.

1837. Woman to become a Freemason was Maria Deraismes, a feminist and suffragist who joined a French lodge in 1882 and eventually founded one of her own.

1838. Women's organization in Japan was a branch of the Women's Christian Temperance Union, founded in 1886 by the social reformer Kajiko Yajima. The following year, the national legislature enacted the Peace Preservation Law, which prohibited women and children from attending political meetings; it was repealed in 1922.

1839. Service club was the Rotary organization, founded in Chicago, IL, USA, by a lawyer, Paul Percy Harris. The first meeting, which took place on February 23, 1905, was attended by Harris and three friends, a coal dealer, a tailor, and a mining engineer. Subsequent meetings were held in each member's place of business in rotation, so that each could obtain some knowledge of the others' businesses. Community service was also part of the program.

D

DANCE

1840. Dance as communal ritual was practiced at the yearly festivals of Abydos in Egypt, beginning circa 3000 BCE, in which the death and rebirth of the god Osiris was enacted in highly stylized dance, drama, and song. The Abydos festival was also the first known example of a mystery play.

1841. Choreographers known by name were the ancient Greek playwrights Euripides (lived circa 484–406 BCE) and Sophocles (lived circa 496–406 BCE), both of Athens. They are known to have created dances for the Greek choruses of their tragedies. The choreographies were never recorded and are now lost.

1842. Thread-the-needle dance for which there is evidence is depicted in a fresco by Ambrogio Lorenzetti in the town hall of Siena, Italy. It dates from the early 14th century, no later than 1348, and shows nine ladies dancing while another sings and plays the tambourine.

Two of the women hold their arms out to form an arch, through which the others wind in a line, linked hand in hand. This entertainment, once enjoyed all over Europe during communal festivities, is the basis for many children's games.

1843. Dancing master known by name was Domenico da Piacenza, who organized court dances for the princely family of Este in Ferrera, Italy. Piacenza was the author of the first treatise on social dance, *De arte saltandi et choreas ducendi (On the Art of Dancing and Directing Choruses)*, published in 1416.

1844. Morris dancing is known from evidence dating to 1458. Morris dances are ritual folk dances originally performed in rural England by small groups of specially trained men, often wearing white costumes with bells and ribbons. Some examples of Morris-style dancing, such as the horn dance of Abbots Bromley in Staffordshire, England, appear to be very ancient in origin. Morris dancing was performed at the courts of Henry VII, Henry VIII, and Elizabeth I, but declined in popularity after the Puritan revolution of the 1650s. It was revived in 1899 by Cecil Sharp, founder of the English Folk Dance Society, who preserved many dances from extinction. Interest in Morris dancing spread to the United States and Canada after World War II.

1845. Dance notation known to historians were letter-symbols, meant to indicate simple dance steps, in a document dating from circa 1575 discovered in the city archives of Cervera, Spain. Word abbreviations used as dance notations were contained in *Livre des basses danses (Book of Low Dances)*, dated circa 1460, a document in the library of Margaret of Austria.

1846. Minuet was composed in 1653 by Jean Baptiste Lully, an Italian-born French composer in the service of King Louis XIV. Lully is believed to have danced to his own composition, as did the king. The minuet (from the Latin word for "neat"), is a courtly, measured dance that was popular in France and England until circa 1800.

1847. History of dance was *Des ballets anciens et modernes (On Dances Ancient and Modern)*, by Claude-François Menestrier, published in France in 1682.

1848. Can-can dance was performed in Paris, France, in 1842 by Elise Sargent, a dancer at the Jardin Mabille, using her stage name Queen Pomaré (an allusion to Aimata Pomaré, queen of Tahiti, which had just been made a French protectorate).

1849. Polka originated as a folk dance for couples in Bohemia (the modern Czech Republic) circa 1830. It was first seen on stage at the Paris Opéra in 1844 to a composition by Friedrich Burgmuller.

1850. Modern dancer was an American, Isadora Duncan, born Angela Duncan in 1878 in San Francisco, CA, USA. She trained in classical ballet, but rejected it in favor of a personal, freely interpretive style, often based on Greek classical art, that attempted to synthesize music, poetry, and natural imagery into a symbolism of movement. She preferred to dance barefoot, wearing a loose, flowing tunic and scarves. In 1899 she left the United States and traveled to England, Germany, and, in 1905, Russia, where she met her greatest success. Her only important tour of the United States, in 1922, was a complete failure.

1851. Tango as it is danced today probably derived from the Spanish tango and the Argentine *milonga*. Argentine tradition holds that the tango, which was a disreputable dance at first, was popularized circa 1880 at Hansen's Caffee, a café and bar founded in 1877 in Buenos Aires. The first ballroom tango craze swept the Americas and especially Europe in 1915.

1852. Dance notation to precisely indicate movement and rhythm was labanotation, described by its inventor, the Hungarian choreographer Rudolf Laban, in *Choreographie* (1926) and *Kinetographie* (1928).

1853. Mambo was of African and European descent, with its primary roots in English country dance of the 17th century. Later it reached its full development among Haitan-born Cubans. The first recording artist to popularize the mambo as dance music was the Cuban bandleader Dámaso Pérez Prado, the original Mambo King, who introduced it at La Tropicana nightclub in Havana in 1943, and later in a series of international hit recordings released in the early 1950s. Mambo was briefly a dance craze in the United States and Europe in the later 1950s and again in the 1990s.

DANCE—BALLET

1854. Ballet to combine dancing, music, and acting was the *Ballet comique de la reine,* performed on October 15, 1581, at the court of King Henry II and Queen Catherine de Médicis of France for the marriage of the queen's sister, Marguerite de Lorraine. Portraying the conquest of Circe by the King of France, it was the first ballet to carry a single plot through spoken poetry, dancing, music, and acting. The 5.5-hour spectacle cost 3,600,000 gold francs, making it too expensive to perform more than once. It is the first ballet for which there is a complete libretto, published in 1582. The producer was Baltazarini di Belgioioso (also known as Balthasar de Beaujoyeux or Beaujoyeulx), the first great ballet impresario.

1855. Codification of the five basic ballet positions of the feet and arms was made by Pierre Beauchamp, the first choreographer of the Paris Opéra and the director from 1661 of King Louis XIV's Académie de Danse. Many of today's standard ballet terms, including *pas de deux* and *jeté*, were devised by Beauchamp for the system of dance notation he created.

1856. Ballerina to dance professionally was Mlle. Lafontaine, who appeared in 1681 in Jean-Baptiste Lully's *Le Triomphe de l'amour (The Triumph of Love)* at the Paris Opéra. She continued to dance in productions at the Opéra for some ten years, always in costumes with long skirts. Prior to her time, female roles in ballets were performed by young men.

1857. Ballet entirely danced without interruptions for songs or declamatory speeches was *Le Triomphe de l'amour (The Triumph of Love)*, with music by Jean-Baptiste Lully. It was produced at the Paris Opéra in 1681.

1858. Ballerina virtuoso was Marie Camargo, born Marie-Anne de Cupis de Camargo, who starred at the Paris Opéra from 1726 to 1735 and from 1741 to 1751. Renowned for her strength and control, which rivaled that of male dancers, she scandalized balletomanes by raising her skirts above the ankle.

1859. Woman to choreograph her own ballets was the French dancer Marie Sallé, born 1707 in Paris, France. She wrote and performed in her own works, which were noted for their dramatic expressiveness and for their integration of costume, settings, music, and dance styles. Sallé debuted as a performer at the Paris Opéra in 1721 and staged her first important ballet, *Pygmalion* (in which she played the role of Venus) in London and Paris in 1734. In it she danced in loose clothing and with unbound hair, scorning the mask and restrictive costume worn by dancers of the time.

1860. Ballerina to dance on her toes was Maria Taglioni, who went up on point for the first time on March 12, 1832, in *La Sylphide,* at the Paris Opéra. The ballet, which was choreographed by her father, Filippo Taglioni, established the Romantic ballet style of graceful arabesques, jumps, and leaps.

DANCE—BALLET—*continued*

1861. Ballerina to wear a tutu was Maria Taglioni, who wore a light muslin dress with a fitted bodice and a full, airy skirt when she appeared in the premiere of *La Sylphide* at the Paris Opéra on March 12, 1832. The skirt reached to within 12 inches (30 centimeters) of the floor. The dress was designed by Eugène Lami. Most ballet dancers until that time wore cumbersome costumes that inhibited their movements.

1862. Ballets Russes performance was in Paris at the Théâtre du Chatelet on May 19, 1909. The troupe, founded by Russian impresario Serge Diaghilev in 1909, danced *Le Pavillon d'Armide (Armida's Pavilion)* by the Russian choreographer Nikolay Nikolayevich Tcherepnin. Ballerina Anna Pavlova and choreographer Mikhail Mikhaylovich Fokine performed the lead roles. The role of Armida's noble slave was danced by Vaslav Nijinsky. Although it toured throughout Europe, the Ballets Russes never performed in Russia.

1863. Modern ballet choreographer to create unified works coordinating movement, music, theme, setting, and costumes was Mikhail Mikhaylovich Fokine, choreographer of such groundbreaking ballets as *L'Oiseau de feu (The Firebird)* and *Petrouchka* for the Diaghilev Ballets Russes. In 1914, Fokine published a letter in *The Times* of London advocating the creation of dramatic works in which meaning was expressed by the full integration of solo and group movement with the other component arts that make up a ballet. Before Fokine, ballets were considered to be the work of their composers, not their choreographers.

1864. International Ballet Competition was held in Varna, Bulgaria, in July 1964, under the auspices of the Bulgarian Ministry of Culture, and has been held every two years thereafter in cities around the world. Competitions are judged by members of the International Ballet Competitions Rules Committee. Male and female dancers compete in three rounds, displaying their skills in the classical and modern repertoire.

DEATH

1865. Representations of death or of a goddess of death may be the bone and ivory figurines found in the caves of Péchialet and Laugerie Basse in southern France, which date from the Upper Périgordian epoch, circa 20,000 BCE. They are schematized nude figures, nearly faceless, with arms held close to the body.

1866. Autopsy of a well-known individual of record was the postmortem performed on the body of Julius Caesar in 44 BCE by the Roman physician Antistius.

1867. Autopsy by Europeans in the New World was performed in 1533 in Santo Domingo, on the island of Hispañiola (now in the Dominican Republic), to determine whether recently deceased Siamese twins shared a soul or had two separate souls. The attending priest declared that the twins had separate souls. The father was charged for two funerals, but protested and paid for only one.

1868. Scientific effort to relate age and mortality in a large population was undertaken by the astronomer Edmond Halley in 1693. His mortality tables for the city of Breslau, Germany, were the first scientific actuarial tables.

DEATH—BURIAL

1869. Burial known to anthropologists was of remains of a *Homo erectus* dating from circa 400,000 BCE. The burial site, showing definite evidence of interment, was found in a cave near the village of Zhoukoudian, China, just south of Beijing.

1870. Burial ceremony established from evidence at a burial site was performed by Neanderthal peoples in Shanidar Cave, near the village of Shanidar, Iraq. The 60,000-year-old site, excavated in the 1950s, contained the body of a man surrounded by the pollen from what were, at the time of burial, carefully arranged bouquets of cornflowers, hollyhocks, ragwort, daisies, grape hyacinths, yarrow, and St. Barnaby's thistle.

1871. Mummies date from approximately the beginning of the third millennium BCE, when the Egyptians began preserving the bodies of the dead by binding them in cloth wrappings and packing them in charcoal and sand. This method, which relied on the natural effects of aridity to prevent decay, was eventually replaced by more complicated methods involving the surgical removal of organs and the application of preserving agents inside and out.

1872. Coffins came into use early in the third millennium BCE in the Mesopotamian kingdom of Sumer as well as in Egypt, where mummified bodies were placed in a series of coffins within a decorated sarcophagus.

1873. Sarcophagi were used to house the dead by the Egyptians of the first dynasty, circa 3000 BCE. The first stone sarcophagi were used by third-dynasty Egyptians circa 2650 BCE; they were built in the form of mud-brick palaces, complete with false doors and windows. The word "sarcophagus" derives from the Greek words for "flesh-eating stone."

1874. Cemetery of record is a precinct in Giza, Egypt, containing rows of stone structures in which are buried members of the royal household of the pharaoh Khufu (Cheops). The cemetery, close to the Great Pyramid in which Khufu was entombed, was laid out circa 2500 BCE.

1875. Use of canopic jars for holding the embalmed organs of mummified humans took place in Egypt during the Old Kingdom, sometime between the years 2686 and 2160 BCE. They were made variously of faience, stone, clay, or wood. The name is derived from Canopus, the Egyptian city that was a center of worship of the god Osiris.

1876. Necropolis in North America known to archeologists is Monte Albán, an ancient Zapotec city located in Oaxaca state, Mexico. Monte Albán's history dates to circa 700 BCE; among its pyramids, plazas, temples, and ball courts were some 170 sunken tombs for the city's nobles. Many of the tombs were built in the form of small temples. Monte Albán was excavated by Mexican archeologist Alfonso Caso y Andrade from 1931 to 1943.

1877. Mausoleum was the enormous tomb of the Persian satrap King Mausolus of Caria (now in Turkey), one of the Seven Wonders of the Ancient World, completed circa 354 BCE, about two years after his death. The tomb's construction was directed by his sister and widow, Queen Artemisia. It was designed by the Greek architect Pythius and decorated with monumental statues of the king and queen, as well as works by Scopas and other Greek sculptors.

1878. Native American to be buried in Europe of record was Pocahontas, born Matowaka circa 1595 in the Algonkian village of Werowocómoco (in what is now the American state of Virginia). After her conversion to Christianity in 1613, she married the English tobacco planter John Rolfe and went with him to England in June 1616. There she contracted a disease, probably tuberculosis. She died on March 21, 1617, in Gravesend, Kent, where she was buried.

1879. Embalming by injecting the arteries with preservative was originated by William Harvey, the English physiologist, in the early part of the 17th century, when he was making his groundbreaking studies of the human circulatory system. In order to follow the route taken by blood in the body, he injected tinted liquid into his cadavers' arteries. About a century later, English morticians adapted the procedure for use in embalming.

1880. Cast-iron coffin was designed and built by the English master machinist John Wilkinson, known as "the great Staffordshire ironmaster." He died on July 14, 1808, and was buried in the casket in Bradley, Staffordshire.

1881. Treatise on cremation that was influential was *Cremation: The Treatment of the Body After Death,* published in England in 1874 by Henry Thompson, the surgeon to Queen Victoria. It aroused great interest in the practice in Europe and the United States and led to a revival of cremation as a form of burial. Thompson formed the Cremation Society of England, the first organization of secular advocates of cremation, which was instrumental in persuading a British court to rule cremation a legal procedure in 1884. The first crematorium in England was built in 1887.

1882. Crematorium of modern design, in which the deceased is placed in a closed chamber and reduced to ash by high heat, was built in 1875 in Milan, Italy, by its Swiss inventor, Albert Keller. On January 22, 1876, Keller himself became the first person to be cremated at the facility.

1883. Freezing of a corpse for future resuscitation took place in the United States in January 1967. Robert F. Nelson and others interested in cryonics used dry ice to freeze the body of James H. Bedford, a retired psychology professor. The body was placed in storage.

1884. Law forbidding the freezing of humans for future resuscitation was passed in 1990 British Columbia, Canada. The law outlawed the for-profit sale of human cryonics preservation services, forbidding companies to freeze recently deceased individuals in the hope that future technologies could someday bring them back to life.

1885. Space burial took place on April 21, 1997, when small samples of the ashes of 24 people, including two well-known Americans, Timothy Leary and Gene Roddenberry, were carried into space along with Spain's first communications satellite. Leary, a psychologist famous for his espousal of psychedelic drugs,

DEATH—BURIAL—*continued*

died on May 31, 1996. His final request was for "one last far-out trip." Roddenberry, who created the "Star Trek" science-fiction series for American television, died on October 24, 1991. The remains were ejected in lipstick-sized capsules that were expected to orbit the earth for up to ten years before burning up in the atmosphere.

DEATH—SUICIDE

1886. Self-immolation by a Buddhist monk as a political protest occurred on June 11, 1963, when Thich Quang Duc set fire to himself before onlookers and the news media on a street in Saigon, South Vietnam (now Ho Chi Minh City, Vietnam). Quang Duc was protesting the U.S.-backed Diem government's maltreatment of Buddhists. Images of his suicide had a strong effect on world opinion of the American presence in Vietnam. A young Buddhist woman named Nhat Chi Mai had immolated herself as a political protest the month before, but she was not a Buddhist cleric.

1887. Mass cult suicide in modern times took place on November 18, 1978, in Jonestown, Guyana, a utopian agricultural commune founded by a California cult called the Peoples Temple, headed by a minister, Jim Jones. The suicide was touched off by the arrival of a California congressman investigating reports of fraud and abuse. After arranging for the congressman's assassination, Jones ordered his followers to drink poisoned punch. Most of them willingly complied. Those who refused were threatened at gunpoint. The death toll was 913 people, including 276 children.

1888. Death by suicide machine occurred in Detroit, MI, USA, on June 4, 1990, when Janet Adkins of Portland, OR, USA, took her own life using a device that administered a fatal dose of drugs when she pushed a button. The machine was invented by Dr. Jack Kevorkian, a crusader for doctor-assisted suicide. Kevorkian was on hand to assist Adkins, who suffered from Alzheimer's disease. Michigan was selected as the site because at that time the state had no law prohibiting doctor-assisted suicide.

1889. Law specifically permitting assisted suicide was passed in a referendum by voters in Oregon, USA, in 1994. The law included a provision for a mandatory waiting period of 15 days before a physician could write a prescription for a death-inducing medication.

DEATH—VEHICULAR

1890. Ballooning casualties were a 26-year-old French physician and balloonist, Jean-François Pilâtre de Rozier, and a companion, who were killed while attempting to cross the English Channel in a hydrogen-filled balloon in June 1785. The hydrogen exploded and cast the two men 1,500 feet (457 meters) down onto the rocky coast of Boulogne.

1891. Person run over by a train was William Huskisson, a British trade official and promoter of train travel, who was killed on September 15, 1830, at Eccles, Lancashire, England, during a demonstration of the first commercial train service. The demonstration was organized by George and Robert Stephenson and included trains capable of the then-unprecedented speed of 35 miles (56 kilometers) per hour. Huskisson was standing on the main track when he underestimated the speed of an oncoming train and was fatally injured.

1892. Pedestrian killed by an automobile of record was Bridget Driscoll of England. She was attending an early auto show on August 17, 1895, at the Crystal Palace in London, when she apparently panicked and ran into the path of one of the vehicles, driven by Arthur Edsell.

1893. Hang-glider fatality of record occurred on August 10, 1896, at Lichterfelde, near Berlin, Germany, when aviation pioneer Otto Lilienthal died from injuries he sustained after crashing a glider of his design at Stölln, near Rhinow.

1894. Driver fatally injured in an automobile accident of record was an Englishman, Henry Lindfield. On February 12, 1898, en route from London to Brighton with his son as passenger, Lindfield lost control of his Imperial Electric as it descended a hill. The car crashed into a tree, crushing his leg. He died the next day.

1895. Person killed in a motorcycle accident was an Englishman, George Morgan. On February 11, 1899, he was thrown from his motorized tricycle in Exeter, England, and suffered a fatal head injury.

1896. Passenger fatally injured in an automobile accident was James Richer, an Englishman considering the purchase of an automobile. On February 25, 1899, at Grove Hill, Harrow, England, he was being shown the operation of a Daimler eight-seater when the salesman, E. R. Sewell, crashed the vehicle, killing both men.

1897. Airplane accident that was fatal occurred on September 17, 1908, at Fort Myer, Arlington Heights, VA, USA, when a propeller blade struck an overhead wire because a fitting to which the guy wire was attached had worn through. Thomas Etholen Selfridge of the U.S. Army died from a skull fracture and Orville Wright received multiple hip and leg fractures.

1898. Airplane accident involving a woman that was fatal took the life of the American pilot Julia Clark of Denver, CO, USA. She was killed on June 17, 1912, at the Illinois State Fair Grounds, Springfield, IL, when her Curtiss biplane struck the limb of a tree and turned over while she was circling the field at 40 miles per hour on her first flight. Her death was the 151st in heavier-than-air aircraft.

DISASTERS—EPIDEMICS

1899. Epidemic of record took place in Greece during the Peloponnesian War between Athens and Sparta (431–404 BCE). According to the Greek historian Thucydides, a highly contagious disease that had already ravaged parts of northern Africa and Persia struck down a quarter of the Athenian army in 430 BCE, putting an end to its plans for conquest, and devastated southern Greece for four years. The disease has not been identified. Medical historians have suggested smallpox, measles, plague, or typhus.

1900. Smallpox epidemic in Europe of record was the Plague of Antoninus, which decimated Rome, Italy, between 165 and 180, during the reign of the Antonine emperor Marcus Aurelius. It is estimated to have killed one-fourth to one-third of the population. Evidence of earlier smallpox epidemics exists in Egypt (circa 1600 BCE), China, and India.

1901. Outbreak of plague to be documented was the Plague of Justinian, which originated in Egypt in the early part of the sixth century and arrived in 542 in the Eastern Roman capital of Constantinople (modern Istanbul, Turkey), where it killed as many as 10,000 people a day. Over the next 15 years it spread into Western Europe and wiped out many towns. All three forms of plague—bubonic, pneumonic, and septicemic—are spread by fleas that travel in the fur of black rats (*Rattus rattus*). An epidemic of plague may have taken place in Babylon circa 3000 BCE.

1902. Epidemic in Japan was an outbreak of contagious disease, possibly smallpox, that took place in 552. It was probably brought to Japan by visiting Buddhist teachers from Korea. A second epidemic occurred in 585. Between 700 and 1100, Japan suffered 119 deadly epidemics, including smallpox, measles, mumps, dysentery, and influenza.

1903. Outbreak of the Black Death in the Middle Ages began in central Asia or China circa 1340 and struck Europe in 1347, after it was transmitted to a Genoese settlement in the Crimea (in present-day Ukraine) via infected corpses catapulted into the town by an army of Kipchak Turks. The plague spread from the Mediterranean throughout Europe and reached its northern limits in Scandinavia and the Baltic in 1351. The toll of life was estimated by a contemporary chronicler, the French historian Jean Froissart, at approximately one-third of Europe's population, or about 25–30 million people. An estimated 45 million people died in Asia.

1904. Epidemic in the New World of record was the outbreak of smallpox that swept through the Caribbean and Mesoamerica following the first contact with Europeans in 1492. Having no immunity to the disease, Native Americans died in the millions. Smallpox introduced by Europeans, in some cases deliberately, later ravaged the indigenous populations of North and South America.

1905. Epidemic of yellow fever of record took place in South America in the 16th century, although there were undoubtedly many previous epidemics that went unrecorded. Yellow fever is caused by a mosquito-borne virus.

1906. Cholera pandemic began in 1817 in Bengal, India, and spread over much of the world in the next two decades. Cholera is caused by the bacterium *Vibrio cholerae,* which is typically transmitted in contaminated drinking water, especially when there are certain species of zooplankton present. Ingested, it produces severe diarrhea that can be fatal if not treated.

1907. Worldwide pandemic was the influenza pandemic of 1918–19. The infection, popularly known as the "Spanish flu," arose in China and swept through Asia, Australia, Europe, Africa, and the Americas, causing as many as 1 billion people to fall ill and killing an estimated 22 million, more than 1 percent of the world's population at that time.

DISASTERS—EPIDEMICS—*continued*

1908. Epidemic of birth defects caused by a drug was due to the use of Thalidomide, a sedative and antiemetic prescribed in 46 countries between 1959 and 1962. It was soon discovered that women who used the drug in early pregnancy gave birth to babies with phocomelia (seal limbs) and other severe birth defects. Some 12,000 children are believed to have been affected, including about 3,000 in Germany and 500 in Great Britain.

1909. Nationwide poisoning epidemic was suffered by Bangladesh beginning in circa 1975, when a national public health program to dig tube wells was undertaken to provide clean water for villagers who had previously consumed polluted surface water. The program was sponsored by the Bangladeshi government, UNICEF, and other agencies. In the mid-1980s, it was discovered that the majority of the country's 3.5 million to 4 million tube wells contained high levels of arsenic, a serious health hazard affecting some 18 million Bangladeshis, as well as several million Indians in neighboring West Bengal.

1910. Epidemic of mad cow disease took place in Great Britain beginning in 1986. Bovine spongiform encephalopathy (BSE), or mad cow disease, is a fatal infectious disease believed to be transmitted by a prion, or abnormal protein, that causes spongy degeneration of brain tissue. Related to the sheep disease called scrapie, BSE may have arisen in cows because of the common practice of feeding them high-protein supplements made from sheep entrails. Humans can also be infected by a similar disease called Creutzfeldt-Jakob disease, of which one variant is thought to be linked to the ingestion of BSE-infected beef. The first cases appeared in England in 1993.

1911. World AIDS Day was held on December 1, 1988, after the World Summit of Ministries of Health on Programs for Aids Prevention called for social tolerance of those with AIDS and a greater exchange of information on the disease.

DISASTERS—NATURAL

1912. Famine of record was chronicled in the "Stele of Famine," an engraving found in an Egyptian tomb and dated to circa 2700 BCE. "There is a lack of crops and all kinds of food," reads the stele. "Torn open are the chests of provisions, but instead of contents there is air." The crop failure lasted seven years and caused an unknown number of deaths.

1913. Tidal wave of record was the massive wave that followed the explosive eruption of Thíra (Santorini), a volcanic island in the Aegean Sea, circa 1500 BCE (or perhaps as early as 1600 BCE). This was one of the largest volcanic explosions in historical times. The tidal wave damaged several Minoan cities on nearby Crete, and may have led to the legends of the fall of Atlantis.

1914. Volcanic eruption accurately described was the eruption of Mount Vesuvius that destroyed the Roman towns of Pompeii and Herculaneum on August 24, 79 CE. The historian Pliny the Younger witnessed the event from about 20 miles away and wrote a detailed account of the eruption and the earthquakes, ash cloud, and tidal wave that accompanied it.

1915. Flood to cause massive loss of life of record hit England and the Netherlands in 1099. A combination of high tides and storm surges flooded coastal England and the Lowlands, killing as many as 100,000. A sea flood that took place in 1228 in Friesland (now in the Netherlands) also drowned an estimated 100,000 people.

1916. Earthquake to cause massive loss of life of record was the great earthquake that occurred in Shaanxi Province, China, on January 24, 1556. An estimated 830,000 people were killed, making it the most deadly quake of all time. Most of the victims died when massive landslides carried away their homes, which had been carved into loose clay cliffs.

1917. Avalanche to kill more than 1,000 people of record occurred at Plurs, Switzerland, on September 4, 1618. It completed buried the town and killed everyone in it except for four villagers who were away at the time.

1918. Landslide to kill more than 1,000 people of record buried more than 2,240 villagers in Chiavenna, Italy, on September 16, 1618.

1919. Tidal wave to cause massive loss of life of record struck Awa, Japan, in 1703. Created by an earthquake far out to sea, the huge wave killed more than 100,000 people.

1920. Tidal wave to kill more than 10,000 people of reliable historical record was a tidal wave that hit Japan in 1707. Contemporary Japanese reports put the death toll at 30,000.

1921. Storm to kill more than 100,000 people of record was the storm of October 7, 1737, that hit the province of Bengal in India. Contemporary records put the death toll at 300,000.

1922. Famine to kill more than 1 million people of reliable historical record was the famine of 1769–70 that occurred in Bengal, India, following the failure of the monsoon. There were no crops that year, and at least 3 million, and perhaps as many as 10 million, died of starvation. Severe famines in southern Asia in 917–18 and in China in 1333–38 may have been as deadly, but there are no reliable casualty figures.

1923. Flood to cause more than 1 million deaths engulfed Honan province in China in the fall of 1887, when the Yellow River washed away its 70-foot (21-meter) levees. Eleven major cities and some 300 villages were washed away, and 50,000 square miles of farmland remained underwater for weeks. The death toll has been estimated at between 900,000 (those directly killed by the flood) and 6 million (including deaths from famine and disease). This was the deadliest flood of historical record.

1924. Volcanic eruption of the 20th century in which there was large loss of life was the eruption on May 7, 1902, of La Soufrière on the island of St. Vincent in the Caribbean. A rain of ash and pyroclastic flows caused 1,565 deaths. The next day, Mount Pelée on nearby Martinique exploded, killing as many as 40,000 people.

1925. Avalanche of the 20th century to kill 10,000 people occurred in the Italian Alps on December 13, 1916. Many villages were buried, causing an estimated 10,000 casualties.

1926. Landslide to kill more than 100,000 people hit Kansu, China, on December 16, 1920. More than 180,000 were killed when loess cliffs of western China, home to hundreds of thousands of cave-dwelling peasants, were dislodged by an earthquake and fell into the valleys below. This is the deadliest landslide of record.

1927. Tornado to cause more than 500 deaths of record was the tornado of March 18, 1925, which cut a kilometer-wide path for some 200 miles (320 kilometers) through Missouri, Illinois, and Indiana, USA. The tornado traveled at speeds of up to 73 miles (117 kilometers) per hour and followed a slight topographic ridge on which a series of mining towns were built. Because it lacked a distinct funnel, the tornado was difficult to see from a distance, and few people in the path had any advance warning. Many children were killed when their schools were destroyed. The death toll has been variously given as 689 or 695; 2,027 people were injured.

1928. Storm to kill 1 million people was the huge cyclone of November 13, 1970, that pounded East Pakistan (now Bangladesh). Storm surges covered vast stretches of the coastal plain, killing millions of livestock and destroying more than 1 million acres of rice paddies. Hardest hit were the offshore islands, many of which were completely stripped of human life. No accurate official death toll has ever been established, but reasonable estimates place the count at up to 1 million. Relief from the Pakistani government, located in Karachi 2,000 miles (3,200 kilometers) to the west, was slow in coming. This inaction led directly to political rebellion and the formation in 1971 of the independent state of Bangladesh.

1929. Town buried by a volcano in modern times was a fishing village on the Icelandic island of Heimaey. An eruption in 1973 buried nearly the entire village in lava, ash, and hot mud. The villagers were evacuated in time and all survived but one man caught by the lava while searching for liquor in his cellar.

DISASTERS—SINKINGS AND WRECKS

1930. Marine disaster costing more than 10,000 lives was the sinking of the Spanish Armada in 1588, the fleet assembled by Spain's King Philip II to support his planned invasion of England. Initially, the Armada was composed of some 130 ships crewed with 8,000 seamen and carrying 19,000 soldiers. On the night of August 7, while the Armada warships were anchored in the English Channel, the English launched fire ships into their midst, breaking the Spanish formation. A battle the next morning resulted in heavy Spanish casualties. The remaining ships were forced by the prevailing winds to sail the long way home around the tip of Scotland. Storms wrecked many, and only 60 vessels returned to Spain. The total loss of life was approximately 14,000.

1931. Train wreck took place on November 8, 1833, near Heightstown, PA, USA. A broken axle derailed a Camden & Amboy train carrying 24 passengers, killing two—the first passenger fatalities in a train accident—and injuring the rest.

1932. Passenger liner sunk by a submarine was the luxury passenger liner R.M.S. *Lusitania,* owned by the Cunard Line and in 1907 built by the firm of John Brown and Company, Clydebank, Scotland. The *Lusitania,* commanded by Captain William Thomas Turner, departed from New York, NY, USA, on May 1, 1915. That same day, Germany published a warning that any ship "flying the flag of Great

DISASTERS—SINKINGS AND WRECKS—
continued

Britain" was subject to attack in waters near the British Isles and Ireland. On the afternoon of May 7, 1915, the *Lusitania* was steaming unescorted, without taking any precautions against German submarine attack, near the headland of Kinsale, Cork, Ireland. It was spotted by Lieutenant Commander Walter Schweiger of the U-boat *U-20,* who ordered a single torpedo to be fired at a range of 2300 feet (700 meters). It struck amidships on the starboard side of the liner and exploded. A second explosion, probably of the ship's boilers, did even more damage. The *Lusitania* sank in 20 minutes, with the loss 1,198 people, including 128 American citizens.

1933. Rail accident in which more than 500 people were killed took place on December 12, 1917, when an overloaded troop train derailed in Modane, France. The official death toll was 573, but as many as 1,000 soldiers may have died.

1934. Train disaster caused by the use of narcotics of record occurred on June 22, 1918, when an empty troop train smashed into a wooden circus train stalled on the tracks outside Ivanhoe, IN, USA, killing 68 circus performers and personnel and many animals. Alonzo Sargent, the engineer of the troop train, had taken "liver pills" containing opium, and had slept through several warning lights and signals.

1935. Crash of a passenger airliner occurred on December 14, 1920, when a British airplane hit a house just north of London and burst into flame. The aircraft, which had just taken off, was operated by Handley Page Continental Air Services and carried six passengers and two crew members. Four of the passengers survived.

1936. Airliner collision took place over Poix, France, on April 7, 1922, when a Farman Goliath owned by Grands Express Airlines hit a DH-18 operated by Daimler Airways.

1937. Refugee ship disaster of record occurred on February 24, 1943, when the overcrowded Romanian ship *Struma,* carrying 769 Romanian Jews fleeing the Nazis, sank in a storm off Istanbul, Turkey. Everyone on board was drowned. The ship had previously been denied entry to Palestine (now Israel) by British authorities.

1938. Accidental sinking of ships carrying prisoners of war of record took place on September 12, 1944, in the South China Sea, when three American submarines, the *Growler,* the *Sealion,* and the *Pampanito,* torpedoed two Japanese troop ships, the *Kachidoki Maru* and the *Rakuyo Maru.* Unknown to the American vessels, and in defiance of the Geneva Convention, the unmarked Japanese transports were conveying 2,218 Australian and British prisoners of war to an internment camp on Formosa (now Taiwan). A total of 1,274 Allied POWs lost their lives. Of the 944 survivors, 114 were rescued by the submarines; the rest were picked up by other Japanese ships.

1939. Marine disaster costing the lives of more than 10,000 noncombatants was the sinking of the *Cap Arcona,* a German luxury liner, and a second ship, the *Thielbeck,* in the harbor of Lübeck, Germany, on May 3, 1945. British bombers destroyed both ships, which were carrying survivors of the Nazi death camps. An estimated 14,000 people, mostly Jews, lost their lives.

1940. Refugee ship fire to cause large loss of life occurred in China on December 3, 1948, when the Chinese ship *Kiangya,* carrying refugees from the civil war between Nationalist and Communist forces, hit a sea mine off Shanghai. The ship burned before sinking, killing some 3,000 people.

1941. Ferry to sink with large loss of life was the South Korean passenger ferry *Chang-Tyong-Ho.* On January 9, 1953, it sank off Pusan, with the loss of 349 passengers and crew.

1942. Nuclear submarine lost at sea was the U.S.S. *Thresher* (SSN-593). On April 10, 1963, the American-built sub went down during a test dive about 220 miles off the coast of Boston, MA, USA. On board were 129 men under the command of Lieutenant Commander John W. Harvey; all hands were lost. A subsequent investigation by the U.S. Navy identified the likely cause of the disaster as a faulty silver-brazed weld in an engine-room seawater system. At pressure, the weld failed, leaking seawater into the electrical system and causing a reactor shutdown that left the submarine without propulsion and unable to blow its ballast tanks.

1943. Warship to sink with nuclear weapons aboard was the U.S.S. *Scorpion* (SSN-589), an American-built, nuclear-powered, fast attack submarine. On May 22, 1968, the *Scorpion,* with 98 crewmen under the command of Commander Francis A. Slattery, sank about 400 miles (644 kilometers) southwest of the Azores in more than 10,000 feet (3050 meters) of water. The sub's armament included two nuclear-tipped torpedoes. The cause of the disaster has never been determined, although it is known that the U.S. Navy had put the *Scorpion* on an experimental low-maintenance program.

1944. Aviation disaster in which more than 500 people were killed was the runway collision of two fully loaded Boeing 747 jumbo jets, one owned by Pan American Airlines and the other by Royal Dutch Airlines (KLM). The accident occurred on March 27, 1977, at Los Rodeos Airport on Santa Cruz Tenerife in Spain's Canary Islands. The planes, which had recently been refueled, were located at opposite ends of the airport's single runway and could not see one another because of a heavy fog. As the Pan Am pilot taxied slowly into takeoff position, the KLM pilot, apparently not hearing orders from the tower to hold his position, accelerated for take-off, plowed into the Pan Am aircraft at high speed, and exploded. The death toll was 576, including everyone aboard the KLM jet and all but 45 of the 396 people aboard the Pan Am jet.

1945. Traffic accident in which more than 2,000 people were killed took place in the Salang Tunnel in Afghanistan on November 3, 1982. A fuel tanker hit a Soviet Army truck and exploded within the narrow confines of the 1.7 mile (2.7 kilometer) tunnel, killing as many as 3,000 people.

DISASTERS—VARIOUS

1946. Sports arena disaster was the collapse of a stand during a gladiatorial event at the Circus Maximus during the reign of the emperor Antoninus Pius (138–161). Roman records claimed that 1,162 people were killed.

1947. Disastrous flood caused by war occurred in 1642 at Kaifeng, China, when anti-Ming rebels under Li Tzu-cheng destroyed the seawall there. More than 300,000 people lost their lives in the ensuing flood.

1948. Explosion to cause great loss of life in peacetime occurred in Brescia, Italy, in 1769. More than 3,000 people were killed when stores of black powder in the state arsenal exploded, possibly after a lightning strike.

1949. Smog disaster of record took place in London, England, in 1873. A probable atmospheric inversion trapped a dense fog mixed with smoke from burning coal, creating a lethal smog that killed an estimated 1,150 people, mostly young children and the elderly.

1950. Severe famine caused by government ideology was the disastrous Soviet famine of 1932–34, the result of Josef Stalin's policy of forced farm collectivization and crop export, exacerbated by the murder of tens of thousands of *kulaks* (rural landowners). While millions of peasants starved to death across Russia, Ukraine, and Belarus, the Soviet Union was exporting millions of tons of grain to prove to the world that the Communist system of agriculture was a success. No confirmed death toll has ever been released, but historians of the post-Soviet era cite figures as high as 20 million.

1951. Firestorm in history was caused by the firebombing of Hamburg, Germany, by the Allies between July 24 and August 3, 1943. Flames at the center of the fire reached 1,400 degrees F (800 degrees C) and loomed 15,000 feet (4,570 meters) above the city. All oxygen in the city was consumed as the fire's tornado-like winds exceeded 150 miles (240 kilometers) an hour. Some 30,482 people died in the inferno, including 5,586 children.

1952. Circus fire with large loss of life took place in Hartford, CT, USA, on July 6, 1944. One hundred-sixty-eight people were killed and 487 were injured when a fire consumed the main tent at the Ringling Brothers Circus.

1953. Nuclear power plant disaster was the partial fuel core melt-down that took place on December 12, 1952, at the Chalk River experimental NRX reactor facility near Ottawa, Canada. The core problems were caused by the failure of four neutron-absorbing control rods to descend into the core and moderate the reaction. Pressure build-up inside the containment area caused a four-ton gas-holder dome to be thrown four feet through the air, jamming it into the superstructure. Radiation was released into the atmosphere, and millions of gallons of radioactive waste water were pumped out of the bottom level of the plant and into shallow trenches near the Ottawa River. The reactor core was buried as radioactive waste. Among the clean-up engineers was future American president Jimmy Carter.

1954. Major nuclear power plant accident occurred on the northwest coast of England in 1957, when a fire at a gas-cooled plutonium separation plant used to produce the fuel for nuclear weapons released more than 20,000 curies of radioactive iodine into the atmosphere. Cabinet papers released in 1988 revealed that British prime minister Harold Macmillan kept the accident a secret so as not to endanger an agreement with the United States to share classified nuclear information.

DISASTERS—VARIOUS—*continued*

1955. Nuclear waste disaster to cause large loss of life was the explosion in the Mayak Chemical Combine, a Soviet nuclear weapons facility located near Lake Kystym in the province of Chelyabinsk (now part of Russia). On September 29, 1957, an explosion with the force of 75 tons of TNT blew the 2.5-meter-thick lid off an underground tank farm containing high-level nuclear waste. Approximately 20 million Ci of radiation was released into the atmosphere, some of which formed into a radioactive cloud 5 miles (8 kilometers) wide that came down on an area containing some 270,000 inhabitants. No records were kept on the exact number of deaths resulting from radiation exposure, but it is believed to be in the thousands. The area, considered to be the most polluted on earth, is under permanent quarantine.

1956. Soccer (association football) disaster with large loss of life took place in Lima, Peru, on May 24, 1964. Rioting that followed an unpopular ruling in a game between Peruvian and Argentinian teams took the lives of more than 300 spectators and injured more than 500.

1957. Pesticide disaster in Europe was the poisoning of the Rhine River originating near Bingen, West Germany (now Germany), on June 18, 1969, when a large quantity of the organochlorine pesticide endosulfan was released into the water. Tens of thousands of fish were killed. The government of the Netherlands, located downstream from the spill, held the government of West Germany responsible, although no immediate culprit was ever discovered.

1958. Chemical disaster to cause large loss of life occurred at Bhopal, India, in December 1984, when 45 tons of the toxic gas methyl isocyanate escaped from an insecticide plant owned by an Indian subsidiary of the American chemical company Union Carbide Corporation. As many as 2,500 people living near the plant were killed, and about 50,000 other people suffered temporary injuries. A later investigation showed the plant was unsafe and understaffed.

1959. Pipeline fire to cause large loss of life was the result of an unsuspected leak in a liquid petroleum pipeline near Uta, in the Ural Mountains of the Soviet Union (now Russia). On June 3, 1989, the fuel exploded and destroyed two passenger trains running alongside on the Trans-Siberian railroad. Some 500 people were killed and 723 were injured.

1960. Human stampede to cause massive loss of life of record occurred on July 2, 1990, when Muslims on pilgrimage to Mecca, Saudi Arabia, panicked inside an overheated pedestrian tunnel. More than 1,450 people were trampled to death.

E

EDUCATION

1961. State-run gymnasium was built in Athens (in modern Greece) in 590 BCE. The students were young freeborn men, ages 16 to 18, who were trained in physical development, including gymnastics, running in armor, wrestling, and boxing. They also learned skills necessary for military and civic activities, including singing and dancing (for participation in public festivals), riding horses, and driving chariots. Upon graduation, the student, if he passed an examination, became a citizen-cadet in the Athenian army.

1962. Medieval educational center to transmit the Greek scientific heritage was the Academy of Gondeshapur (or Jundi Shahpur) in southwest Persia (modern Iran). Founded by excommunicated Nestorian Christians in the mid-fifth century CE, Gondeshapur attracted an international body of scholars and became a great center of cultural exchange, especially under the Sasanian king Khosrow I Anushirvan (531–579). It included a language school, where Greek medical and scientific manuscripts were translated; a famous hospital that combined ideas from Persian, Indian, and Greek medicine; and an academy for students of ethics, philosophy, astronomy, law, finance, and Zoroastrian religion.

1963. Hornbooks for teaching reading to young children appeared in Europe at the end of the 15th century. A woodcut illustration from a book published in Basel, Switzerland, in 1508 shows the figure of Wisdom holding up a rectangular wooden plate on which are shown the letters of the alphabet. Later versions also displayed the Lord's Prayer. The texts were covered with a thin sheet of transparent horn for protection.

1964. Grade levels in schools were introduced by the religious and educational reformer Philipp Melanchthon during the early years of the Protestant Reformation in Germany, beginning in the 1520s. At Eisleben, where he founded secondary schools on which many others were modeled, the curriculum was taught in three stages, the student being required to master the material at each stage before being allowed to move on.

1965. Call for universal literacy in modern times was made by the Christian reformer Martin Luther in *Dass man Kinder zur Schulen halten solle (Discourse on the Duty of Sending Children to School)*, published in 1530, and in numerous letters to mayors of German cities and princes of German states. An important tenet of Luther's evangelical doctrine held that people of every class and of both sexes should be able to read and understand the Bible without the need for interpretation by clerics.

1966. Public schools in the modern era were established in 1543, when Maurice, Duke of Saxony, opened three schools on his lands. They were funded by the sale of properties belonging to monasteries that had been shut when the churches became Lutheran. The educational plan was provided by Philipp Melanchthon in his 1528 book *Unterricht der Visitatoren (Instructions for Visitors)*, which was adopted by newly established schools in numerous German cities. Literacy for the children of laborers and farmers was stressed by Martin Luther as a spur to piety, since it enabled ordinary people to read the Bible.

1967. Practical theory of pedagogy was proposed by Jan Ámos Komenský (in Latin, Johann Amos Comenius), a Protestant minister who led educational and social reforms in Poland, England, Sweden, and the Netherlands after he was exiled from Moravia (now the Czech Republic) during the religious persecutions of the 17th century. In his *Didactica Magna (The Great Didactic)*, written in 1638, he outlined a comprehensive plan of education involving four progressive levels from infancy to young adulthood, with the curriculum and teaching methods fitted to the needs and abilities of each age group.

1968. Illustrated school textbook was the *Orbis Sensualium Pictus (The Visible World in Pictures)*, published in 1658 by the Moravian (Czech) educational visionary Jan Ámos Komenský, better known by his Latinized name, Johann Amos Comenius, who was then in exile in Amsterdam, the Netherlands. The book was intended for use in teaching Latin, and provided drawings to convey the meanings of Latin phrases.

1969. Normal school for training teachers was the Institute of the Brothers of the Christian Schools, founded at Reims, France, in 1685 by St. Jean-Baptiste de la Salle, who opened two others in Paris soon thereafter. These schools trained the members of the teaching order he had founded in 1684. The first known organized class for training teachers was started in Lyon, France, in 1672.

1970. Primer for teaching reading in English was *The Protestant Tutor*, published in London, England, circa 1685. Primers were originally collections of religious texts, including the Lord's Prayer and the Ten Commandments, compiled for the use of ordinary people. With the addition of the alphabet, word lists, and the catechism, the primer became useful for beginning readers in Protestant schoolrooms.

1971. Educational reformer to stress individual development was Johann Heinrich Pestalozzi, who put into practice the ideas expressed in Jean-Jacques Rousseau's philosophical novel *Émile, ou Traité de l'éducation*. At his school and teacher-training institute at Yverdon, Switzerland (1805–25), he experimented with learning methods that involve the senses and that stimulate children to observe, think, and respond (rather than simply to memorize and recite). This required the development of a new skills on the part of teachers, including the preparation and delivery of lessons and the ability to guide a class discussion.

1972. National teacher-training program was instituted in Prussia (now part of Germany) in 1809 by Carl August Zeller, who sent 17 men to Yverdon, Switzerland, to study under the educational modernizer Johann Heinrich Pestalozzi. By 1840, Prussia's schools were staffed by teachers trained in 38 state-run institutions and in university courses. Standards for secondary-school teachers were raised with the introduction of a mandatory practice year in 1826 and mandatory examinations in 1831.

EDUCATION—*continued*

1973. Kindergarten had its opening in 1837 in Blankenburg, Prussia (now in Germany). It was originally called the Child Nurture and Activity Institute, but it was later renamed the Kindergarten by its founder and director, the German philosopher of education Friedrich Fröbel.

1974. Correspondence course was carried out by the educator Isaac Pitman of Bath, England, who had developed an improved system of shorthand. In January 1840 he advertised for students, offering prepaid lessons through the mail at a cost of one shilling each. Shortly afterwards, he began offering the lessons for nothing more than the cost of postage. He was soon overwhelmed with students and had to recruit volunteers to help correct their work.

1975. Correspondence school was a language school established in 1856 by Charles Toussaint and Gustav Langenscheidt of Berlin, Germany. Reading, writing, grammar, and pronunciation lessons in French, English, and other languages were sent out to enrollees by mail.

1976. National school system to require manual training as part of the curriculum was that of Finland, where it was called *sloyd,* from a Swedish word meaning "handiwork." Sloyd education included metalworking, woodworking, gardening, and handcrafts such as basket weaving. Promoted by the educator Uno Cygnäus, it was made a required part of the curriculum of rural Finnish schools in 1866 and of urban schools in 1872.

1977. Montessori school was the Casa dei Bambini (Children's House), a preschool for children between ages three and six that was opened in 1907 by Maria Montessori, an Italian physician and educator, in a slum neighborhood of Rome. Montessori developed an alternative educational system that respected the individuality of children and sought to develop their creativity with special sets of learning devices. About 60 pupils attended the first year. Montessori was Italy's first woman doctor.

1978. High school for space scientists was the European Space School, founded at Brunel University in West London in 1989. It was designed to train future space scientists, engineers, and entrepreneurs, offering a program covering planetary science, physics, astronomy, life sciences, rocketry, remote sensing, and related subjects.

1979. Satellite-delivered digital video system for education was developed in 1992 by Mexico's Monterrey Institute of Technology and Higher Studies. The approximately 4,000 ITESM faculty members were able to make two-way contact with 48,000 students at 26 campuses across Mexico via teleconferencing links. Classes were broadcast from the main Monterrey campus or from a truck stationed at any satellite campus.

1980. Computerized robot to grade essays on a standardized test was the E-rater, invented in 1996 by Jill Burstein and other scientists at the Educational Testing Service, Princeton, NJ, USA. It was used for the first time in February 1999 to help score responses to the Graduate Management Admission Test (GMAT), given to American business-school applicants. The robot was programmed to look for such things as errors in spelling and grammar, inaccurate sentence structure, and illogical or disorganized arguments. Each test was graded by a human reader as well as the electronic reader. If their results differed by more than one point on a grading scale of 0 to 6, a second human reader was asked to arbitrate. The introduction of electronic scoring was intended to save labor costs and time and to reduce the subjectivity of human grading.

EDUCATION—COLLEGES AND UNIVERSITIES

1981. Permanent institution of higher education in the liberal arts was founded in Athens, Greece, circa 393 BCE by Isocrates, an orator, pamphleteer, and teacher of rhetoric and political philosophy. In his academy, a conservative institution dedicated to producing the future leaders of the Hellenic world, he trained the general Timotheus, the Cypriot ruler Nicocles, and the historians Ephorus and Theopompus, among other notables. Isocrates was seen by rival philosopher Plato as the quintessential Sophist, willing to espouse any cause merely for the pleasure of argument.

1982. University in China was the imperial university founded at the court of the Han emperor Wudi in 124 BCE, when 50 students came to study the Confucian classic texts with a faculty of five scholars. Within 75 years, the enrollment had reached 3,000. The chief purpose of the university was to educate men for the national civil service.

1983. University in the Western world was founded on February 27, 425, by the Roman emperor Theodosius II in the city of Constantinople (now Istanbul, Turkey). The faculty consisted of 31 teachers. One lectured in philosophy, two in law, and 28 in Greek and Latin grammar, rhetoric, and literature. Though it was under Christian auspices, the institution had a major role in preserving the classics of pagan Greece and Rome.

1984. University still in existence is the Islamic University of Qarawiyin in Fez, Morocco. It was founded in 859. The chief center of Islamic learning after the Christian conquest of Spain, it declined in the 18th and 19th centuries, but was revived after Moroccan independence.

1985. Scholarly societies were the *universitates* that were organized in Bologna (in present-day Italy) in the eleventh century. These were groups of foreign students—meaning anyone from outside Bologna—who had come to hear lectures at the city's *studium generale,* or forum of scholars. They banded together mainly for protection, since as outsiders they had no rights as citizens. The four original groups were Roman, Tuscan, Lombard, and Ultramontane ("beyond the Alps"), which covered everyone else. Each was governed by a rector in consultation with a council. They were accorded formal legal status in 1158 by Emperor Frederick I Barbarossa.

1986. University in Europe was the University of Bologna, Italy. Numerous European cities in the tenth century hosted a *studium generale,* a place of higher education where students—mostly grown men already employed by the government or the Church—gathered to hear lectures by scholars. The foreign students at Bologna, where the scholarly specialty was civil and canon law, began to organize themselves into guilds, called *universitates,* towards the end of the eleventh century. They were given official recognition by Emperor Frederick I Barbarossa in 1158, and instruction was extended to medicine and philosophy in 1200. Some historians of education give precedence to the medical school that was founded at Salerno, Italy, in the ninth century, though it was never known as a university. The first university in Central Europe was Prague University, founded on April 7, 1348, by Charles IV, King of Bohemia, in what is now the Czech Republic.

1987. University in Africa was founded circa 1320 at Timbuktu (now in Mali) by the Mali emperor Mansa Musa. Teaching was conducted in Arabic. The Muslim traveller Leo Africanus visited the city in 1514 and wrote, "Here are a great many doctors, judges, priests, and other learned men, bountifully maintained at the king's cost. And hither are brought diverse books out of Barbary, which are sold for more money than any other merchandise." In subsequent centuries, Timbuktu was sacked and abandoned, and little remains of the university or libraries.

1988. University professor who was a woman is likely to have been Dorotea Bocchi, who succeeded her father as professor of medicine at the University of Bologna, Italy, circa 1390. Some years earlier, lectures were delivered at the university by the scholar Novella D'Andrea, who was concealed from the male students behind a curtain.

1989. University in the New World was the Autonomous University of Santo Domingo, now in the Dominican Republic. It was founded in 1538, when Santo Domingo was still the main seat of Spanish colonial administration in the New World. Two years later, the University of Michoacán was founded in Mexico.

1990. Woman to earn the degree of Doctor of Philosophy was a noblewoman, Elena Lucrezia Piscopia Cornaro, of Venice, Italy, who received the doctorate from the University of Padua in 1678, though she was not allowed to attend lectures and studied privately.

1991. Modern university was the University of Halle, Germany, founded by the Elector Frederick III of Brandenburg (later King Frederick I of Prussia) in 1694. Although it was specifically Lutheran at its founding, its faculty, from an early date, embraced rational scientific investigation and claimed the right of free inquiry. Halle was also the first university where lectures were given in the vernacular language rather than in the traditional Latin. It merged with the University of Wittenberg to form the Martin Luther University of Halle-Wittenberg in 1817.

1992. Scholar of African descent to earn a doctorate from a European university was Anton Wilhelm von Amo, born in Guinea and raised in Germany. He received his degree from the University of Wittenberg in 1734 with a dissertation on the psychology and physiology of sensations.

EDUCATION—COLLEGES AND UNIVER-
SITIES—*continued*

1993. Technical college was the École Centrale des Travaux Publics (Central School of Public Works), founded by the National Convention in Paris in 1794. In 1795 the name was changed to the École Polytechnique. As conceived by Lazare Carnot and Gaspard Monge, it was intended to provide technical and mathematics training for scientists; under Napoléon, it was transformed into a military school for artillery and other technical officers.

1994. College to enroll women and men on equal terms was Oberlin Collegiate Institute, Oberlin, OH, USA, which opened on December 3, 1833, with 44 students, 29 men and 15 women. Equal status was granted to women on September 6, 1837, when 30 men matriculated along with four women: Elizabeth Smith Prall of New York City, Caroline Mary Rudd of Huntington, CT, Mary Hosford of Oberlin, OH, and Mary Fletcher Kellogg of Jamestown, NY. On August 25, 1841, the first three of these women graduated with the B.A. degree, having pursued a classical course equivalent to that at Yale University. On March 21, 1850, the name of the school was changed to Oberlin College. It was the first school in the United States to advocate the abolition of slavery and to accept African-American men and women on equal terms with white students.

1995. College for women was Mount Holyoke College, South Hadley, MA, USA, chartered on February 11, 1836, and opened on November 8, 1837, as the Mount Holyoke Female Seminary, with 80 students who paid $64 a year for tuition and board. They were required to do co-operative household tasks. The first principal was Mary Lyon, who served until 1849. The first commencement, at which four women were graduated, was held on August 23, 1838. Another women's college chartered in 1836 was Wesleyan College, Macon, GA, USA, originally known as the Georgia Female College, which graduated its first class of eleven women on July 16, 1840. An earlier claim is made for the Elizabeth Female Academy, Washington, MS, USA, which existed from 1818 to 1843.

1996. European university to admit women as students was the University of Zürich, Switzerland, which began accepting women applicants in 1865.

1997. Foreigner to be appointed professor in a German university was Willoughby D. Miller, an American, who was appointed professor of operative dentistry in 1884 at the University of Berlin, where he had previously done graduate work in chemistry and physics.

1998. Woman appointed to the faculty of a French university was the physicist Marie Curie, born Maria Sklodowska in Warsaw, Poland. On May 13, 1906, she was appointed to the Sorbonne to fill the professorship that had formerly been held by her husband Pierre, who had been killed in a traffic accident.

1999. Modern university in the Caribbean was the University of the West Indies, founded in Jamaica in 1949. Branch campuses were later opened in Trinidad, Barbados, and Guyana.

2000. Long-distance university without classrooms was the Open University, headquartered in Milton Keynes, England. Originally called the University of the Air, it was founded by Labor Party leader Harold Wilson, the former and future prime minister, to make higher education available to everyone in the country, regardless of age, social background, or educational experience. The institution opened in 1971 with 24,000 students who enrolled in courses that were broadcast on television by the British Broadcasting Corporation. By 1999 it was the largest university in Britain, with 125,000 undergraduate students and 40,000 graduate students, and offered most of its programs on videotape and on the Internet.

2001. On-line course of study was offered in 1981 by the Western Behavioral Sciences Institute's School of Management and Strategic Studies in San Diego, CA, USA.

2002. Nation to put all its universities on the Internet was Canada, which began its NetNorth university-networking effort in 1984. The program was completed a year later, on the centennial anniversary of the day that the last spike was driven on the cross-Canada railroad.

2003. Internet university to receive accreditation was Jones International University, headquartered in Englewood, CO, USA, which offered courses on the Internet. On March 5, 1999, it received accreditation from the North Central Association of Colleges and Schools, an American accreditation agency, as the first "cyber university," and was authorized to award the degree of Master of Business Administration (MBA). The courses were taught by professors at American colleges and were open to students anywhere in the world. The president of Jones International University was Pamela S. Pease.

EDUCATION—DISABILITIES

2004. Method for teaching the deaf to speak, read, and write was developed circa 1560 by the Spanish Benedictine monk Pedro Ponce de León. Although the exact details of his approach have been lost, it is believed that he used a combination of techniques, including letter-tracing and molding the lips of his students with his hands. His greatest success was with Gaspard Burgos, a prospective monk who was both deaf and mute, whom he taught to make confession. Burgos later wrote several books.

2005. Deaf person educated in lip-reading and speaking appears to have been Luís de Velasco, a nobleman of Castile, Spain, who had been born without the sense of hearing. Sometime around the year 1620, he became the student of Juan Pablo Bonet, a priest who served as his older brother's secretary. Bonet taught him to understand lip movements and to communicate orally himself.

2006. School for deaf education was founded in 1760 in Paris by a French cleric, Charles-Michel de l'Épée. He taught his pupils a system of sign language, derived from simple signs used by the deaf community of Paris, that included a method of finger-spelling French words. From l'Epée's system developed French Sign Language, the first modern sign language for the deaf and the basis for American Sign Language.

2007. School for blind children was the Institution Nationale des Jeunes Aveugles (National Institution of Blind Youth), established in Paris, France, by Valentin Haüy. The school opened in 1784 with twelve students. Haüy, a professor of calligraphy, was moved to start the school when he saw blind men compelled to earn their livings as objects of ridicule in freak shows.

2008. Reading system for blind people was created by Valentin Haüy of Paris, France, founder of the first school for blind children. In 1793, Haüy, a calligrapher by trade, created an alphabet of raised letters that his students could comprehend through their fingertips. One of his students was Louis Braille, who later became the inventor of a reading system that replaced raised letters with combinations of raised dots.

2009. Education for children with mental retardation was undertaken by the French physician Jean-Marc-Gaspard Itard, an ear specialist who worked at a school for deaf children. From 1801 through 1805 he supervised the education of a feral child, an eleven-year-old boy who had spent years living alone in a forest and who was unable to talk. Itard's account of his work was published in 1807 as *Rapports sur le sauvage de l'Aveyron (The Wild Boy of Aveyron)*.

ELECTRONICS

2010. Electron tube diode was invented in 1904 by English electrical engineer John Ambrose Fleming, a professor at University College in London. Known variously as the vacuum diode, kenotron, thermionic tube, Fleming valve, and thermionic valve, the electron tube diode was a sealed glass tube containing a heated metal cathode and an unheated anode. It was able to regulate the direction of current passing through it depending on the polarity of an external voltage applied to the anode. The work was based on observations made on the movement of voltage across a diode by the American inventor Thomas Alva Edison in 1883. Fleming was the first to use the diode in an important application for radiotelephony, as an electronic rectifier for converting alternating-current radio signals into direct-current signals detectable by a telephone receiver.

2011. Radar was developed as early as 1904 by the German engineer Christian Hulsmeyer, who obtained European patents for "an obstacle detector and ship navigation device" based on the reflection of radio waves from distant metallic objects. There being no pressing need at that time to detect distant enemies—the airplane had yet to be used in war—the German military showed no interest in Hülsmeyer's process. During the 1930s the British independently developed their own radar technology and used it effectively to detect approaching German bombers in World War II.

2012. Electronic amplifier tube was invented in 1907 by the American electronics engineer Lee De Forest. His triode, or audion, added a zigzag wire called a control grid between the two electrodes of the tube diode invented by English electrical engineer John Ambrose Fleming in 1904. De Forest applied a small negative voltage to the control grid and was able to control and amplify the larger voltage flowing through the tube. The audion tube became the key component of all electronic technology that required amplification, including radio, radiote-

ELECTRONICS—*continued*

lephony, radar, television, and early computer systems, until the invention of the transistor in 1947. In 1912 De Forest first demonstrated the principle of cascaded amplification when he linked several audion tubes in sequence, amplifying a tiny signal to enormous power.

2013. Military radar experiment took place at the Naval Research Laboratory (NRL) in Washington, DC, USA, in 1922. A ship floating down the Potomac River was detected as it passed between a radar transmitter on one shore and a radar detector on the other.

2014. Photoelectric cell or tube was publicly demonstrated on October 21, 1925, by the Westinghouse Electric and Manufacturing Company at the Electrical Show at Grand Central Palace in New York, NY, USA. The photoelectric cell, which is sensitive to light, was used to count objects as they interrupted a light beam in passing, to open doors as a person or car approached, and to perform similar functions.

2015. Printed circuit was the invention of Paul Eisler, an Austrian expatriate living in England, who handbuilt the first such unit in his London bedroom in 1936. Eisler was unable to arouse much interest in England for his invention, but electronics firms in the United States were quick to adopt the process and first used printed circuits in proximity fuses for antiaircraft shells.

2016. Transistor was invented at the Bell Telephone Laboratories, Murray Hill, NJ, USA, by three Americans, John Bardeen, Walter Houser Brattain, and William Shockley. The first demonstration took place on June 30, 1948. The essential element of the device was a tiny wafer of germanium, a semiconductor. Transistors perform the same functions as vacuum tubes, but occupy a fraction of the space and operate on greatly reduced amounts of power. The three inventors shared the Nobel Prize in Physics in 1956.

2017. Laser was the invention of two Americans, Charles Hard Townes of New York, NY, USA, and Arthur Leonard Schawlow of Madison, NJ, USA. In 1951, Townes, a physicist with Columbia University, New York City, first conceived of the maser, a practical device for amplifying the stimulated emission of microwaves, basing his idea on the earlier work of English physicist Paul Dirac and others. Townes and his brother-in-law Schawlow developed the first "optical maser," or laser, in September 1957. They filed for a U.S. patent on July 30, 1958, which was granted on March 22, 1960. Gordon Gould, a graduate student at Columbia, independently conceived of the laser in October 1957, but did not apply for a patent until April 1959. The word "maser" is an acronym for "microwave amplification by stimulated emission of radiation." The word "laser" is an acronym for "light amplification by stimulated emission of radiation."

2018. Integrated circuit was invented independently by two Americans, Jack Kilby of Texas Instruments, Dallas, TX, USA, and Robert Noyce of Fairchild Semiconductor, Mountain View, CA, USA. On September 12, 1958, Kilby tested a working integrated circuit. Between March and June of 1959, Noyce improved on Kilby's cruder device by designing the first reliable, mass-produceable integrated circuit. Noyce was awarded the U.S. patent after a ten-year lawsuit between the two men.

2019. Epitaxy fabrication was invented in 1960 by American researchers J.J. Kleimack, H.H. Loar, I.M. Ross, and H.C. Theuerer at the Bell Telephone Laboratories in Holmdel, NJ, USA. Epitaxy was a new method of depositing a crystalline substance, such as silicon, in a thin layer upon the surface of a crystal of the same substance. It was the key technology in developing inexpensive manufacturing processes for semiconductors. Another Bell Labs researcher, A.Y. Cho, perfected molecular beam epitaxy, an ultra-high vacuum technique that could produce single-crystal growth one atomic layer at a time, enabling the construction of extremely precise components.

2020. Working laser was demonstrated in public on July 7, 1960, by Theodore Harold Maiman, a researcher at the Hughes Aircraft Company in Malibu, CA, USA. Maiman designed a ruby cylinder with polished ends. It was partially silvered on the outside with a small hole at one end for the beam to exit. When illuminated by a powerful xenon lamp, the ruby emitted a coherent beam of red light.

2021. Liquid crystal display was developed in 1968 by a research group under George Heilmeier at RCA's David Sarnoff Research Center in Princeton, NJ, USA. Liquid crystals are organic substances that reflect light when voltage is applied. In the typical LCD display, a layer of liquid crystal material is sandwiched between two layers of glass; voltage is applied by a pattern of transparent electrodes bonded to the inner surfaces of the glass, causing the LCD crystals in the electrified region to sharply change their index of reflectivity, creating an image that can be seen only in the presence of reflected light. The first commercial use of LCDs was in a wristwatch marketed by Bulova in 1970.

2022. Twisted nematic liquid crystal display (LCD) was developed in 1970 at Hoffmann–La Roche, Inc., in Switzerland, and first used in watch and calculator displays in 1971. The twisted nematic LCD had better contrast and was visible across a wider viewing angle than earlier LCDs.

2023. Ultraviolet solid-state laser was developed by Sony KK of Tokyo, Japan, and announced in late 1993. The laser generated a 1-watt continuous-wave beam at a wavelength of 266 nanometers.

2024. Saser for the amplification of sound by the stimulated emission of radiation was invented in 1994 by Jean-Yves Prieur and colleagues at the University of Paris–South in Orsay and the Pierre and Marie Curie University. The device, an inch-long rod of ordinary glass, chilled almost to absolute zero to eliminate vibrations from heat, was found to amplify sound the way that lasers amplify light.

2025. Three-dimensional display screen was demonstrated by researchers at Sanyo Electric of Osaka, Japan, in 1996. The display was less than an inch thin but produced the illusion of looking into a box some 8 inches (20 centimeters) deep, even when seen from a wide range of angles. Viewers were not required to wear special 3D glasses.

ELECTRONICS—CONSUMER

2026. All-transistor portable television was a small set with an 8-inch (20-centimeter) screen introduced in 1960 by the Sony Corporation, a consumer electronics firm founded in Tokyo, Japan, in 1946 by Masaru Ibuka and Akio Morita.

2027. Home video tape recorder was introduced on June 7, 1965, by the consumer electronics manufacturer Sony KK of Tokyo, Japan. The unit, which could record only in black and white, sold for US$995.

2028. Videocassette recorder for home use was the Betamax, which was sold by the consumer electronics manufacturer Sony KK of Tokyo, Japan beginning in 1969, with international distribution beginning in 1972. It was built into a console that also contained a Sony color television set. The tape was contained in a plastic cassette to make it easy to handle.

Sony had marketed the first open-reel video tape recorder for home use, the TCV-2010, beginning in 1966. The device required a separate camera set up on a tripod, as well as a separate microphone to record sound.

2029. Videodisc was the Capacitance Electronic Disc (CED), developed in 1969 by RCA, New York, NY, USA. It was based on sound recording technology and employed a disc, engraved with grooves of recorded analog video and audio signals, that was read by a capacitance-sensitive stylus riding in the grooves. The device was commercially unsuccessful.

2030. Electronic pocket calculator was a battery-powered model introduced on August 20, 1971, by Texas Instruments, Dallas, TX, USA. It weighed about 2.5 pounds (1.1 kilograms) and cost US$149. It could add, subtract, multiply, and divide, displaying the results in an LED (light-emitting diode) window.

2031. VHS videocassette recorder was introduced in Japan and the United States by the Japan Victor Company (JVC) on September 19, 1976. JVC also announced the availability of a compatible video camera at the same time. VHS stands for Video Home System; it is a half-inch helical-scan format similar to the technically superior Betamax system introduced by Sony KK in 1969. Unlike Sony, JVC energetically licensed its system, and VHS eventually supplanted Betamax in the marketplace.

2032. Compact disc players were manufactured by the Japanese firm Sony using technology pioneered in 1979 by the Dutch firm Philips. To make CD recordings, sounds were digitally rendered on magnetic tape as electronic signals in binary form. These signals were encoded as microscopic pits in the reflective surface of a 5-inch (12.7-centimeter) disc made from plastic and aluminum. The sound was played back by focusing a laser beam on the spinning disc. When the beam encountered the pits, it was reflected back at an angle to a detector that converted it into an analog signal for output to a hi-fi stereo system.

2033. Flat-screen pocket television was patented in 1979 in Japan by Matsushita Denki Sangyo KK (Matsushita Electric Industrial Company), founded by Konosuke Matsushita in 1918. The hand-held device featured a tiny liquid-crystal display screen.

ELECTRONICS—CONSUMER—*continued*

2034. Videodisc system that was commercially successful was introduced in 1979 by the Philips Company, the Netherlands. The Philips LaserVision media was an optical disc, approximately the size of a long-playing vinyl record, in which digital video and audio signals were encoded by a laser in the form of microscopic pits. In the LaserVision playback unit, a low-power laser beam reflecting off the pits translated the video and audio data into signals that could be played on a television set.

2035. Personal stereo cassette player was the Walkman, designed by Masaru Ibuka and Akio Morita, founders of the consumer electronics manufacturer Sony KK of Tokyo, Japan. It was launched in Japan on July 1, 1979, at a price of US$169, and was introduced internationally beginning in December 1979.

2036. Camcorder for the consumer market was the Betamovie, introduced in Tokyo, Japan, in October 1982 by Sony KK. It combined a video camera and a Betamax videocassette recorder in one battery-powered unit, allowing up to 3 hours and 35 minutes of recording time.

2037. Pocket television was the Watchman, introduced by Sony KK of Japan in 1984. It was a black-and-white set with a screen measuring 2 inches (5 centimeters) in diameter.

2038. Pocket videocassette recorder and television was the Video Walkman, introduced in Japan by Sony KK in 1988. The 2.5-pound (1-kilogram) device incorporated a small liquid crystal display (LCD) color television screen and a compact 8-millimeter videocassette recorder in a battery-powered package that could fit comfortably in a large pocket.

2039. Handheld video game was the Game Boy, introduced in Japan in 1989 by Nintendo Company, Ltd.

ELECTRONICS—SOUND RECORDING

2040. Sound recording device to be designed was the "paléophone," a type of phonograph conceived by a French poet and inventor, Émile-Hortensius-Charles Cros, in 1877. On April 30, 1877, Cros deposited papers detailing his invention with the French Academy of Sciences, but a practical working version was never constructed. The first practical sound recording device was the phonograph, demonstrated on December 7, 1877, by two Americans, Thomas Alva Edison and John Kreusi.

2041. Phonograph was designed by American inventor Thomas Alva Edison of Menlo Park, NJ, USA, who secured a U.S. patent on February 19, 1878, on a "phonograph or speaking machine." His original idea had been to invent a telegraph repeater, and he had given construction directions to one of his mechanics, John Kreusi, on August 12, 1877. The first cylinder, operated by a hand crank, was wrapped in tin foil, with which two needles fastened to diaphragms made contact. The first verse recorded on the new instrument was "Mary Had a Little Lamb." A clock spring motor and waxlike record were invented some ten years later.

2042. Dictation device was the treadle-powered Graphophone, patented in the United States in 1885 by Chichester Bell and Charles Tainter. Similar to the Edison phonograph, it recorded sound on wax-coated cylinders with vertical cut grooves. On May 13, 1887, Bell and Tainter founded the American Graphophone Company, with financing from court and congressional reporters James Clephane, Andrew Devine, and John H. White, to sell their device as a dictation machine.

2043. Phonograph record of the modern disk type was invented by Emile Berliner of Washington, DC, USA, and first publicly demonstrated before the Franklin Institute in Philadelphia, PA, USA, on May 16, 1888. Berliner's "Gramophone" record was a flat disk in which the grooves were cut in a lateral spiral, making it much easier to duplicate for the mass market than Edison's recording cylinder.

2044. Jukebox was a coin-operated phonograph player installed in the Palais Royale, San Francisco, CA, USA, on November 23, 1889, by Louis Glas. The first widely successful jukebox manufacturer was the Rudolph Wurlitzer Company of North Tonawanda, NY, USA. The company's most popular model was the Wurlitzer Model 1015, designed in 1946 by Paul Fuller. Among its novel features were curved plastic tubes containing a fluid with a low boiling point. Small heaters kept the fluid bubbling. Wurlitzer sold 56,246 of the Model 1015 at US$750 each.

2045. Magnetic wire recording device was the Telegraphone, patented in 1898 by the Danish electrical engineer Valdemar Poulsen. It recorded speech and other sounds by the alternating magnetization of a length of piano wire. The telegraphone could record up to 30 minutes of audio; the wire moved at a speed of 84 inches (213 centimeters) per second. It was first displayed publicly at the 1900 Paris Exhibition.

2046. Mass-produced double-sided recording discs were manufactured by the Odeon Company of Germany in 1904. These were based on the "Red Seal" 10-inch discs developed by the Victor Company in 1901.

2047. Recording tape was patented by Fritz Pfleumer of Germany in 1928, and developed as a commercial product in 1934 by Interessengemeinschaft Farbenindustrie Aktiengesellschaft (I.G. Farben). The idea of using a strip of fabric impregnated with iron filings as a recording medium was first proposed by an Englishman, Oberlin Smith, in 1888.

2048. Tape recorder was the Blattnerphon, developed in 1929 by German film producer Louis Blattner. Blattner used it to add synchronized sound to the films he made at Ellstree Studios in England. The recording medium was steel tape; audio output was enhanced with electronic amplification.

2049. Tape recorder to use plastic tape was the Magnetophon, a machine introduced in 1935 by the Allgemeine Elektricitäts Gesellschaft of Berlin, Germany. The tape, which recorded at a speed of 30 inches per second (approximately 750 millimeters per second), was lighter and easier to handle than the steel recording tape or wire used in earlier devices.

2050. Tape recording of a live concert took place on November 19, 1936, in England, using German-built BASF/AEG tape recording equipment. The performer was the British conductor Sir Thomas Beecham, artistic director at Covent Garden.

2051. Recording of piano on tape was made of a 1940 recital at the Vatican, Rome, Italy, by the Polish virtuoso Mieczyslaw Horszowski.

2052. Long-playing (LP) phonograph records that were successfully manufactured were made by Columbia Records, Bridgeport, CT, USA, a division of the Columbia Broadcasting System, and introduced to the public on June 21, 1948, at the Waldorf-Astoria Hotel, New York, NY. CBS engineer Peter Goldmark was the inventor of the nonbreakable Vinylite plastic disks, which played at a speed of 33.3 revolutions per minute. One side of a 12-inch LP played for 23 minutes, compared to 4 minutes for one side of a standard 78-rpm record; 78s were quickly supplanted by the new technology.

2053. Tape cassette was developed by the Dutch electronics firm Philips NV in 1961. It was first shown to the public in Berlin, Germany, in 1963.

2054. Recording on audio CD to sell 1 million copies worldwide was *Brothers in Arms*, released on May 17, 1985, by the British rock group Dire Straits, led by Mark Knopfler. The disc passed the international million-sales mark in 1986.

2055. Digital Audio Tape (DAT) was developed in the early 1980s by several Japanese consumer electronics manufacturers, including Sony KK, the Japan Victor Corporation, and JVC's parent company, Matsushita Denki Sangyo KK (Matsushita Electric Industrial Company, Ltd.). In February 1987, the Japanese electronics firm Aiwa was the first to bring a DAT product to the market. DAT offered purer sound reproduction than analog tape, but the cassettes were more expensive and incompatible with older systems.

ENERGY—ALTERNATIVE

2056. Windmills are first mentioned in Arabic writings of the ninth century, which refer to horizontal windmills constructed in 644 by a Persian millwright named Abu Lu'lu'a on the Iran-Afghanistan border. These early windmills, like the watermills they were based on, were horizontal in orientation. The sails radiated from a vertical drive shaft and were driven by wind blowing through the mill building. The millstones were mounted above the sails and were directly attached by an axle to the drive shaft.

2057. Tidal-powered mill was built in England in 1100.

2058. Fuel cell was described by English chemist Humphry Davy in 1802. A fuel cell is a device that uses electrochemical reactions to generate electricity; Davy's design contained a carbon anode and aqueous nitric acid as the cathodic reactant.

2059. Waterwheel turbine was invented in 1827 by French engineer Benoît Fourneyron. Pursuing an idea for a more efficient waterwheel suggested by his engineering teacher, Claude Burdin, Fourneyron designed a small, 6-horsepower turbine with blades or vanes set at angles in a rotor. Water flowing through the turbine was directed outward from the hub toward the rim at greater pressure than could be achieved by an ordinary waterwheel. In 1837 Fourneyron demonstrated a small but high-powered water turbine of 60 horsepower capacity that was capable of 2,300 revolutions per minute.

ENERGY—ALTERNATIVE—*continued*

2060. Fuel cell that was practical was invented in 1839 by English chemist William R. Grove. His fuel cell design produced electric current from hydrogen and oxygen reacting on two platinum electrode strips immersed in acidified water.

2061. Methane plant was built to provide fuel for a leper colony near Bombay, India, in 1857.

2062. Solar cell was developed in 1883 by Charles Fritts, an American inventor. Fritts constructed the first true solar cells using junctions formed by coating the semiconductor selenium with a thin layer of gold. When direct sunlight hit the cell, electrons were driven across the potential difference between the two layers, generating a weak current. Fritts's devices transformed less than 1 percent of the absorbed sunlight into electricity.

2063. Geothermal power station to produce electricity went into operation in Larderello, Italy, in 1904. It generated power from steam heated by geothermal activity below the plant. The hot springs in the region had been used by the Etruscans for baths at least as early as circa 700 BCE.

2064. Heat pump that was practical was invented in 1927 by the British chemist T.G.N. Haldane, who used it to heat his home in Scotland and his laboratory in London.

2065. Silicon solar cell in which silicon replaced inefficient selenium in the semiconductor layer was invented by an American, Russell Ohl, in 1941. While Ohl's cells were not much more efficient at converting light to electricity, further refinement over the next decades led to cells with 15 percent efficiencies or better.

2066. Solar furnace of commercial size was constructed in 1946 in Meudon, France. It employed a large concave mirror to focus sunlight on a heating chamber. The furnace was capable of reaching temperatures in excess of 5,000 degrees Fahrenheit.

2067. Solar cells that were practical were announced in May 1954 at the Bell Telephone Laboratories in Holmdel, NJ, USA, by three American researchers, Gerald L. Pearson, Daryl Chapin, and Calvin Fuller. Their silicon solar cell converted 6 percent of the sunlight falling directly on it into electricity, which was six times the conversion efficiency of earlier designs.

2068. Solar thermal power plant was an experimental installation completed in 1960 at the desert capital of Ashkhabad (now Ashgabat, Turkmenistan). More than 1200 mirrors arranged in concentric circles concentrated sunlight on a central steam boiler that ran a standard generator.

2069. Tidal electric generator plant of commercial significance was the Rance River Power Station, located in the estuary of the Rance River in the Gulf of St.-Malo, Brittany, France. Construction was begun in 1961 and completed in 1967. It consisted of a dam equipped with reversible turbines that turned whether the tide was going in or out. The plant's 24 power units were each capable of generating 10,000 kilowatts of electricity.

2070. Power plant using solar cells was dedicated in the United States on June 7, 1980, by Governor Scott Matheson at Natural Bridges National Monument, UT, USA. The US$3 million photovoltaic system had 266,029 solar cells mounted in twelve long rows. They produced a 100-kilowatt output that supplied current for six staff residences, maintenance facilities, a water sanitation system, and a visitors' center. The plant was a joint venture of the U.S. National Park System, the U.S. Department of Energy, and the Massachusetts Institute of Technology's Lincoln Laboratory. It was 38 miles (61 kilometers) from the nearest power line.

2071. Amorphous silicon solar cell was introduced in 1987 by the Sanyo Corporation of Japan. Rather than requiring a substrate of expensive and difficult-to-manufacture crystalline silicon, the cells were based on a less expensive amorphous (noncrystalline) silicon, manufactured depositing silicon-hydrogen vapor as a thin film.

2072. Commercial-scale thermal solar energy installations were nine operating 30,000-kilowatt solar electric generating units owned by Luz International Ltd. of California, USA. Constructed from 1984 to 1990, the plants used solar heat-collection elements, sun sensors, and computer controls developed by company founder Arnold J. Goldman to produce steam for conventional electrical generation. The first plant had an installed cost of US$5,979 per kilowatt of capacity, compared with US$3,011 per kilowatt for the ninth. The falling price of natural gas and oil sent Luz International into bankruptcy as it was building its tenth plant.

2073. Portable fuel cell that was practical was announced in 1992 by Sanyo Electric, Hyogo Prefecture, Japan. Sanyo's design, based on the reaction of phosphoric acid with hydrogen absorption metal, generated 250 watts of electricity from a 57-liter cell weighing about 60 pounds.

2074. Commercial electric plant using poultry litter as fuel was designed by Lifschutz Davidson and located in Suffolk, England. It began operation in 1993.

2075. Wave-powered electricity generator for commercial use was anchored to the seabed and began operation in August 1995 near the mouth of the River Clyde, Scotland. Called the Osprey, for Ocean Swell Powered Renewable Energy, the 8,000-ton steel structure was designed to generate 2 megawatts of electricity from the rising and falling action of waves and another 1.5 megawatts from a wind turbine fixed to the top of the structure. The Osprey was first used commercially to power desalination plants.

2076. Solar service stations for electric vehicles were two stations in Germany and two in the Netherlands. They were owned by Anglo/Dutch comglomerate Royal Dutch Shell and opened on March 4, 1999. The stations were designed to allow the recharging of electric vehicles by solar power generated on-site, with supplemental power available from the local grid.

ENERGY—ELECTRICITY

2077. Description of static electricity was recorded circa 600 BCE by Thales of Miletus (in present-day Turkey), the Greek (or possibly Phoenician) philosopher, scientist, and geometer, who lived circa 636–546 BCE. He produced static electricity by rubbing amber ("elektron" in Greek) against his clothing, noting that it first attracted and then repelled light objects.

2078. Electric generator was invented by the German physicist and engineer Otto von Guericke in 1663. His generator created static electricity by rubbing a rotating ball of sulphur. In 1672, Guericke observed that the spinning ball began to glow as an electric charge was built up, a process called electroluminescence; he was therefore the first person to create and observe artificial light from an electrical device.

2079. Conduction of electricity along a wire was achieved in 1729 by the English inventor Stephen Gray (or Grey). He created a static charge by rubbing his hands on a corked glass tube and transmitted the charge about 490 feet (150 meters) through a hemp thread wrapped in silk to an ivory ball. Gray was the first to show the difference between a conductive material (hemp) and a nonconductive material (silk).

2080. Storage device for electricity was the Leyden (or Leiden) jar, invented by the German inventor Ewald Georg von Kleist in 1745 but named by the Dutch physicist Pieter van Musschenbroek of the University of Leiden, who discovered it independently in 1746. The Leyden jar is a device for storing static electricity. The basic design developed by Kleist and Musschenbroek was similar: a glass jar partly filled with water, with a cork pierced by a wire or nail that was long enough to reach the water. Static electricity generated by a friction device was found to travel along the wire and accumulate in the jar. The stored charge could be released by touching the wire, producing a shock. The Leyden jar was a forerunner of the modern capacitor.

2081. Battery was the voltaic cell or pile, invented in 1800 by Italian physicist Alessandro Giuseppe Antonio Anastasio Volta, professor of physics at the Royal School of Como, Lombardy (now Italy), for whom the volt is named. It consisted of alternating zinc and silver disks separated by pads soaked in an electrolyte, either sodium hydroxide or brine. The first practical dry-cell battery able to produce a large and useful current was the lead-acid cell invented in 1859 by Gaston Planté of France. It was the ancestor of the modern automobile battery.

2082. Electromagnet was invented in 1820 by the French physicist and astronomer Dominique-François-Jean Arago. He wrapped copper wire in a spiral and showed that passing an electric current through it attracted iron filings. When the current was removed, the fillings dropped off.

2083. Electromagnet that could support more than its own weight was invented in 1823 by the English physicist William Sturgeon, lecturer in science at the Royal Military College, Addiscombe, Surrey. After coating a 7-ounce iron bar to insulate it, he wrapped the bar with copper wire attached to the terminals of a voltaic cell (an early form of battery). Current running through the bar generated a magnetic field strong enough to lift 9 pounds of iron.

ENERGY—ELECTRICITY—*continued*

2084. Hydroelectric generator was built by Aristide Bergès of France. On September 28, 1869, he channeled water from a fall in the Alps to turn a dynamo, which supplied direct current electricity to machines in his workshop.

2085. Electric generator that was commercially successful was the Gramme dynamo (short for dynamoelectric generator), invented circa 1869 by the Belgian-born Zénobe-Théophile Gramme, a French engineer and inventor. It was demonstrated before the French Academy of Sciences on July 17, 1871. A later model of Gramme's dynamo could be reversed from a generator to a direct-current electric motor.

2086. Electric company was the Edison Electric Light Company, 65 Fifth Avenue, New York, NY, USA, incorporated on October 15, 1878. Three thousand shares with a par value of US$100 each were issued for the express purpose of financing Thomas Alva Edison's work on the incandescent lamp. The Edison Electric Illuminating Company was incorporated on December 17, 1880, with a capitalization of US$1 million for the purpose of furnishing electric light in New York City. The first president of the company was Norvin Green.

2087. Transmission of electricity through high-voltage cable was developed by the French inventor Marcel Deprez. On February 6, 1883, in a crowded public demonstration in Paris, he transmitted power from a dynamo to an electric motor via a transmission line that looped from Paris to Le Bourget and back to Paris.

2088. Power transmission installation using alternating current was made in 1890 at Telluride, CO, USA, by the Westinghouse Electric and Manufacturing Company. The generator was a 100-horsepower, 88.33-cycle, single-phase, 3,000-volt unit driven by water power. A 3-mile (5-kilometer) transmission line was erected and a single-phase synchronous motor was installed at the end of the line. The motor lacked a starting torque, and a necessary adjunct was a starting motor to bring the unloaded synchronized motor to its normal speed.

2089. Underground hydroelectric plant was completed in 1898 in huge tunnels behind Snoqualmie Falls near Seattle, WA, USA.

2090. Alkaline dry cell battery was developed by the American inventor Thomas Alva Edison in 1914 at his laboratory in West Orange, NJ, USA. It used an alkaline electrolyte of basic nickel-iron and nickel-cadmium, not an acid electrolyte, as in lead storage-cell batteries. Edison did not commercialize the alkaline cell, and it did not become widely used until the 1970s.

ENERGY—ELECTRICITY—ILLUMINATION

2091. Arc lamp was invented by English experimentalist Humphry Davy. In 1807, he produced the first controlled electric arc between two charcoal rods set 4 inches (10 centimeters) apart. The rods were connected to a battery of 2,000 cells.

2092. Incandescent lamp was patented in Great Britain by Frederick de Moleyns in 1841. It used carbon powder heated between two platinum wires to produce a brief light. The first light bulb with a filament was the work of the British inventor Joseph Swan, whose bulb design of 1860 (improved in 1880) employed carbonized cotton filaments in a vacuum inside a glass bulb. On October 21, 1879, Thomas Alva Edison of Menlo Park, NJ, USA produced a very similar design. Ultimately, Swan's and Edison's patents were merged.

2093. Electric rail and street lamps were developed in 1876 by the Russian electrical engineer Pavel Nikolayevich Yablochkov, who was commissioned by the Russian government to develop a method of illuminating the Moscow–Kursk rail line for safe travel by the tsar, who feared nighttime attacks by anarchists. His "Yablochkov candle" was an arc lamp with consumable carbon electrodes that operated on alternating current. It was also used for street lighting in Russia and Europe before the advent of the mercury-vapor lamp around the turn of the century.

2094. Private home fully illuminated with electric lights was the house in Porchester Gardens, England, belonging to English electrical pioneer Rookes Evelyn Bell Crompton. He equipped it with electric lights in 1879.

2095. Building illuminated by neon lamps was the Grand Palais in Paris, France, which in 1910 was outfitted with neon tube lamps developed by the French engineer and chemist Georges Claude.

2096. Electric discharge lamp that found wide application was the neon tube, invented in 1910 by the French physicist Georges Claude. In 1909, Claude had found that passing a high-voltage electrical current through a tube filled with the inert gas neon produced a deep red light, and he shortly developed a commercial version of the tube appropriate for illumination and signage.

2097. Fluorescent lamp successfully developed was made by American electrical engineer and inventor Arthur Compton at the General Electric Company, Schenectady, NY, USA, in 1934. His fluorescent bulb sent electric current through an argon-filled glass tube that was coated on the inside with phosphor. Mercury vapor inside the tube emitted ultraviolet waves that were changed by the phosphor into visible light. General Electric displayed the lamps at the 1939 New York World's Fair.

2098. Electronic light bulb was developed by InterSource Technologies of Sunnyvale, CA, USA. Called the E-Lamp, the bulb contained a small radio transmitter that excited gas plasma within the bulb, which in turn excited phosphors coating the bulb's inner surface. With no filament to break, the E-Lamp was capable of lasting as long as 20,000 hours and used 75 percent less electricity than equally bright incandescent light bulbs. It was commercially available beginning in 1993.

ENERGY—FOSSIL FUELS

2099. Oil seeps were known to the Sumerians, who collected oil from the surface deposits at Tuttul (now Hit, Iraq) from circa 3000 BCE. Crude oil was used by the Greeks, the Persians, the Chinese, and peoples of the Americas for various purposes. Oil distillation was developed by the Arabs, probably around 800. An oil well was drilled unintentionally in 1818 at the mouth of Troublesome Creek, near Monticello, KY, USA, by American salt miners.

2100. Natural gas wells were drilled in China circa 1003. Gas from shallow wells was vented through bamboo pipes and used to fuel kiln and forge fires.

2101. Illumination by gas was developed in 1792 by the Scottish engineer William Murdock. Murdock was working for the engineering firm of Matthew Boulton and James Watt in Birmingham, England, when he began experimenting with coal gas as an illuminant. (Coal gas is a mixture of hydrogen, methane, and carbon monoxide produced by heating bituminous coal.) In 1792 he lighted his cottage and offices in Redruth, Cornwall, with coal gas, using gas burners he invented of simple pipes with perforated ends. These were the first gas jet lighting fixtures.

2102. Large building illuminated by gas was James Watt's foundry in Birmingham, England, outfitted in 1803 with coal gas lighting by the Scottish engineer William Murdock, the inventor of gas illumination. A small plant on-site provided the gas.

2103. Public power utility was the London Gas Light and Coke Company, chartered in London in 1812. Using large coke-processing plants around the city, it produced coal gas for illumination and distributed it through underground pipes to customers.

2104. Kerosene distilled from bituminous shale and cannel coal for illuminating purposes was obtained by an American, Dr. Abraham Gesner, who secured a U.S. patent on March 27, 1855, covering his process. The product was manufactured by the North American Kerosene Gaslight Company at Newton Creek, NY, USA. Gesner received U.S. patents on June 27, 1854, on a process for obtaining kerosene by heat distillation. The name "kerosene" is derived from *keros,* the Greek word for wax, referring to the use of paraffin in the distillation process.

2105. Oil well that was commercially productive was made on August 27, 1859, at Titusville, PA, USA, by Edwin Laurentine Drake and E.B. Bowditch, who opened a 70-foot shaft in an area that was known to contain oil-bearing shale. Drake and Bowditch worked for the Seneca Oil Company and were prospecting for a supply. The Titusville well produced some 400 gallons per day.

2106. Multistep crude oil refining was a distilling process developed in 1873 by the Russian chemist A.A. Tavrisov in Baku, Russia.

2107. Synthetic gasoline plant was built in Germany in 1927. It employed the Fischer-Tropsch process, in which carbon monoxide and hydrogen generated from a mixture of coke and steam were catalyzed to produce hydrocarbons. Alternatively, a slurry of heavy oil and coal was catalyzed in a hydrogen atmosphere. The resulting hydrocarbon mixture was separated into various products, including gasoline, by fractional distillation.

2108. International oil pipeline was completed in July 1934. It ran from the oilfields of Kirkuk in northern Iraq to the port of Tripoli in Syria.

ENERGY—FOSSIL FUELS—*continued*

2109. Fluid catalytic cracking process was developed by the French chemist Eugène Houdry in 1937 and commercialized by the American petrochemical firm Sun Oil Company (from 1971 the Sun Company, Inc., or Sunoco) from 1937 to 1942. Catalytic cracking, in which heavy gas oils were converted into lighter high-octane fuels such as gasoline, employs catalysts such as clay to speed the conversion process.

2110. Commercial petrochemical plant for fluid catalytic cracking was Powdered Catalyst, Louisiana (PCLA) No. 1, which went on line in Baton Rouge, LA, USA in 1942. It was built by Catalytic Research Associates, a consortium formed in 1938 by Standard Oil of New Jersey, Standard Oil of Indiana, M.W. Kellogg, and the German chemical firm I.G. Farben. Fluid catalytic cracking is now the primary petroleum refining process.

2111. Oil-from-coal plant was built in 1954 in the company town of Sasolburg, northern Free State province, South Africa, by the South African Coal, Oil, and Gas Corporation Ltd. (now Sasol, Ltd.). The first petrochemical plant to process significant quantities of oil from coal, it was located near the vast coal reserves near the Vaal River. The Sasol plant also produced gasoline and other petrochemical products.

2112. Horizontal oil drilling was achieved by the French petrochemical firm Société Nationale Elf Aquitaine and the French Oil Institute (IFP) in 1980. A horizontal pipeline was used to tap the vast natural gas deposits at Lacq, France.

2113. Underwater natural gas production station was Skuld, completed in September 1988 by the French petrochemical firm Société Nationale Elf Aquitaine. The automated plant was situated 360 feet (167 meters) deep in the North Sea off Norway.

2114. Subsea gas pipeline in Asia was a 440-mile (708-kilometer), 28-inch (72-centimeter) pipeline leading from the Yacheng 13-1 gas development in the South China Sea to Hong Kong, China. The line was the world's second longest seabed gas pipeline, after Zeepipe in the North Sea. It was built and operated by ARCO China Inc., with partners China National Offshore Oil and Kufpec (China). The pipeline began operation in 1995.

ENERGY—NUCLEAR

2115. Nuclear reactor in Europe was the F-1 (for "Physics-1"), designed by a team of Soviet physicists under Igor Vasilyevich Kurchatov. It went critical (began producing power) on December 25, 1946, at the Kurchatov Institute in Moscow. The F-1, which was copied from an American design, was graphite moderated and initially operated at a power level of 10 watts. It was also the first Soviet nuclear reactor.

2116. Civilian nuclear power plant was constructed by Soviet engineers at Obninsk, about 55 miles (88 kilometers) from Moscow. The 5-megawatt plant went on-line on June 27, 1954.

2117. Nuclear power plant of substantial generating capacity to produce electricity for a civilian power grid was Calder Hall, brought on-line in 1956 in England. Construction was supervised by the principal designer, Christopher Hinton. Calder Hall was a gas-cooled reactor design, fueled with graphite-moderated slugs of natural uranium metal encased in aluminum and cooled with carbon dioxide gas.

2118. Nuclear reactor in Asia was Apsara, a large-scale nuclear reactor brought on-line at Trombay, India, on August 4, 1956, by the Atomic Energy Establishment, Trombay (AEET), now the Bhabha Atomic Research Centre. The AEET was formally inaugurated by Pandit Jawaharlal Nehru on January 20, 1957. The founder of the AEET was Indian physicist and mathematician Homi Jehangir Bhabha, the prime architect of the Indian civilian nuclear-energy program. India's first nuclear plant for commercial power production was the 420-megawatt Tarapur Atomic Power Station in Maharashtra, commissioned in 1969.

2119. Breeder reactor was the United Kingdom Atomic Energy Authority Technology Prototype Fast Reactor, an experimental plant built at Dounreay, Scotland, in 1959. It was closed in March 1994.

2120. Tokamak that was operational was developed by Soviet nuclear physicist Lev Andreyevich Arzimovich (or Artsimovitch) at the Kurchatov Institute in Moscow, and first operated in 1963. Arzimovich's design for a toroidal magnetic confinement chamber in which superheated plasma could be brought to fusion temperatures was the basis for the majority of later controlled-fusion experiments. The tokamak, an abbreviation of the Russian phrase *toroidal kamera magnetik,* was first proposed by Soviet physicists Andrey D. Sakharov and Igor Y. Tamm in 1950.

2121. Fast breeder reactor of commercial size was the Superphénix, built in the foothills of the Jura mountains of France. A breeder reactor is a nuclear fission power plant that produces as much as or more plutonium fuel than it consumes. The Superphénix contained five to ten times as much plutonium as an ordinary nuclear reactor, as well as 5,000 metric tons of highly explosive liquid sodium used as a coolant. Fifty-one percent of the project was funded by France, the other 49 percent by Italy and a German-led European consortium. The Superphénix entered service in 1984. Plagued by technical difficulties, the plant generated electricity for only ten months between 1984 and 1994, then had a brief period of productivity from September 1995 until December 1996. In August 1997, French prime minister Lionel Jospin ordered the plant to be closed.

2122. Temperature of 100 million degrees Kelvin was achieved in October 1988 by the Joint European Torus, a multinational western European venture located at Culham, England. This temperature, ten times hotter than the interior of the sun, was considered the minimum necessary to develop a sustained controlled fusion reaction.

2123. Fusion reactor to generate 10 megawatts of power was the Tokamak Fusion Test Reactor at the Plasma Physics Laboratory of Princeton University, Princeton, NJ, USA. This power level, considered an important milestone by fusion power developers, was achieved in 1994. The TFTR was fueled with a mix of deuterium and tritium and sustained the 10-megawatt power level for one second.

2124. Stellarator of large scale was the Large Helical Device, built at Japan's National Institute of Fusion Science. A prototype magnetic-containment fusion reactor, the stellarator provided an alternative to the tokamak (donut-shaped) reactor design. The Large Helical Device was first injected with high-energy plasma on March 31, 1998.

ENGINEERING

2125. Hydraulic engineer known by name was Eupalinus of Megara, Greece, famous for the water tunnel he built on the Aegean island of Samos circa 550 BCE. Samos Tunnel was described by the Greek historian Herodotus as one of the three greatest engineering feats in the Greek world. Intended to carry fresh water from distant springs to the island's capital city, the aqueduct, which was 6 feet (2 meters) square, tunneled through Mount Castro for 3,300 feet (1,000 meters). The tunnel was drilled with hammer and chisel by teams of slaves working from both ends. A jog in the tunnel was needed to join the two sections, which missed connecting by 16 feet (4 meters). Water flowed through clay pipes laid in a trench in the floor.

2126. Surveyors of record were Roman professionals called *gromatici*, who were active from the third century BCE. Their main instrument was the groma, a sighting device that had two wooden arms, set at right angles to each other, from which plummets were suspended.

2127. Engineering school was the École des Ponts et Chaussées, founded in Paris, France, in 1747. The first director was civil engineer Jean-Rodolphe Perronet, renowned for his graceful stone bridges.

2128. Nuclear engineer was the Hungarian-born American physicist Eugene Paul Wigner, one of the founders of quantum mechanics. Trained as an engineer at the Berlin Institute of Technology in Germany, Wigner emigrated to the United States in 1930. He worked at the Metallurgical Laboratory at the University of Chicago in 1942, helping Enrico Fermi to engineer the first atomic pile, and in 1943 designed the first pile for the Hanford Engineer Works in Washington state. In 1946 he was director of research and development at the Clinton Laboratories (later the Oak Ridge National Laboratory) in Tennessee.

ENGINEERING—AQUEDUCTS AND CANALS

2129. Aqueduct was constructed in 691 BCE at the orders of Sennacherib (Sin-akhkhe-eriba), king of Assyria. It was a sloping limestone masonry channel designed to transport fresh water 34 miles (54 kilometers) from a distant river, the Great Zab, to the gardens of Nineveh. An arched bridge 30 feet (9 meters) high supported the channel over a valley 900 feet (274 meters) wide. Aqueducts of simpler design and shorter length were probably built in ancient Persia, India, Egypt, and elsewhere in the region as early as circa 1000 BCE, but none are known in detail.

2130. Suez canal was constructed by the emperor Darius I of Persia circa 500 BCE to increase commerce with Egypt by forming a waterway between the Red Sea and the Mediterranean. The canal, which took several years to build, ran from the Nile River delta to the port of Suez on the Persian Gulf. It remained in use for nearly twelve centuries. The route of the modern Suez Canal, completed in 1869, follows it closely. There may have been yet an earlier canal at Suez circa 2000 BCE.

ENGINEERING—AQUEDUCTS AND CANALS—*continued*

2131. Canal in China of importance was the Grand Canal, a system of waterways that stretched across northern China for 1,085 miles (1,747 kilometers). It was used chiefly for transporting grain to highly populated areas. Its oldest part, the Shan-yang Canal, was built in ancient times, in the third or fourth century BCE. A large-scale expansion project, undertaken some seven centuries later using conscripted laborers from the army, brought the total to 600 miles by the year 610. Further expansion and renovation has continued intermittently to the present day.

2132. Roman aqueduct was the Aqua Appia, built in 312 BCE under the direction of the censor Appius Claudius Caecus to serve the city of Rome. It was 10 miles (16 kilometers) long and mainly ran underground or as a stone-lined ditch from its source, springs on the Lucullan estate, to a central distribution point in the city. A short stretch of less than a foot was raised above ground. Eventually, the Roman aqueduct system included eleven aqueducts totaling 298 miles (479 kilometers) in length. They brought water to the city from sources as far away as 56 miles (90 kilometers).

2133. Raised aqueduct of great length was the Aqua Marcia, commissioned by the Roman Senate in 144 BCE and completed by Marcius Rex, the praetor, in 140 BCE. It was built completely of stone and ran 57 miles (91 kilometers) from springs in the region of the upper Anio to the city of Rome. About 7 miles (11 kilometers) of the acqueduct were high above ground, raised on arched columns; the rest ran through tunnels and channels cut into the virgin rock.

2134. Lock for river navigation was in use in China by 70 CE. It was simply a dam in which a section could be removed. The rush of water through the opening carried the boat over the shallows below the lock.

2135. Pound lock on a canal was built in 1373 at Vreeswijk, the Netherlands, where the Utrecht canal meets the Lek River. This early pound lock was a basin enclosed by inner and outer gates, which could be alternatively raised or lowered to adjust the water level to that of the river or the canal.

2136. Canal connecting the Atlantic to the Mediterranean was the Canal du Midi, also known as the Canal du Languedoc, completed in France in 1692. It linked the Bay of Biscay at Toulouse with the Mediterranean coast, a course of 150 miles (241 kilometers) over mountainous terrain requiring the construction of 100 locks, three major aqueducts, and the first important canal tunnel. The chief engineer was Pierre Riquet.

ENGINEERING—BRIDGES

2137. Stone bridge was the Pons Aemilius, built across the Tiber Riber in Rome, Italy, in 179 BCE.

2138. Suspension bridge was mentioned in the account of Fa-hsien, a Chinese monk of the fourth century. Fa noted the existence of a rope bridge over the Indus River in India which was already very ancient when he crossed it in 399. Similar bridges were invented independently in the Americas, notably in the Andes region of South America, and were probably in use by about the same time.

2139. Suspension bridge with iron chains was a bridge over the Indus River in India that used iron chains instead of rope for its main cables. This was crossed in 630 by Xuanzang, the renowned Chinese traveler and scholar of Buddhism, and later described in the chronicle of his travels, *Ta-T'ang Hsi-yü-chi (Records of the Western Regions of the Great T'ang Dynasty)*.

2140. Open caisson was first employed to build the Pont Royal bridge in Paris, France, completed in 1685. The engineer, Jules Hardouin Mansart, had the piling foundations excavated within an open caisson, a watertight box, higher than the water level, that was lowered to the riverbed.

2141. Bridge incorporating iron structural members was the work of a French engineer named Garbin, who in 1755 oversaw the construction of a three-arch bridge over the Rhône River at Lyon. One of the arches was built of iron girders and connecting angles. The entire bridge was intended to be built in iron, but the cost was too high.

2142. Bridge constructed entirely of cast iron was the Coalbrookedale Bridge over the River Severn in Coalbrookedale, Shropshire, England. It was designed by Thomas Pritchard and erected by John Wilkinson and Abraham Darby III. The bridge's five arch ribs were cast in two 70-foot (21-meter) halves to make a single semicircular arch spanning 143 feet (44 meters). No nuts, bolts, or screws were used in its construction; it was assembled entirely with cast dovetailed joints, pegs, and keys. It opened for traffic on January 1, 1781.

2143. Closed or pneumatic caisson for underwater excavation was first used in 1850 to construct the foundation of a bridge at Rochester, England. Unlike the open caisson, the pneumatic caisson was closed at the top; air was pumped in to raise the pressure inside and keep out the water. Conditions tended to be drier inside, and it could be used in deeper water, but workers who spent much time in the higher pressure of a pneumatic caisson risked getting the bends.

2144. Steel bridge was the Eads Bridge over the Mississippi River at St. Louis, MO, USA, the work of the American engineer James Buchanan Eads. The steel, rolled at Andrew Carnegie's mills, had a strength of 60,000 pounds (27,000 kg) per square inch. The bridge's three arch spans, all longer than 500 feet (152 meters), were set into place using timber cantilevers, also making it the first steel cantilevered bridge. It was opened on July 4, 1874.

2145. Reinforced concrete bridge was the Vienne River Bridge at Châtellerault, France, completed in 1899 by French engineer and architect François Hennebique. The three-arched bridge's center arch spanned more than 160 feet (49 meters). However, the bridge was not connected to the abutments by hinges that would allow it to expand and contract with changes in temperature, and the arches cracked in three places.

2146. Bridge with piers sunk in the open sea was the Golden Gate suspension span, San Francisco, CA, USA. Construction was officially started on January 5, 1933. Joseph Baermann Strauss was appointed chief engineer. The length of the main structure of the bridge was 8,940 feet (2,725 meters), with towers 746 feet (227 meters) above water and a minimum clearance of 220 feet (67 meters). The Golden Gate Bridge was the first built across the outer mouth of a major ocean harbor.

2147. Rail bridge higher than 500 feet was the bridge at Vresk, Iran, completed in 1938. It stood 500 feet (152 meters) above the lowest point of the gorge it spanned.

2148. Suspension bridge spanning more than 5,000 feet was the Great Belt bridge in Denmark. Completed in 1997, it spanned 5,328 feet (1,624 meters).

ENGINEERING—CONCRETE

2149. Concrete may have been invented by the ancient Greeks on the island of Thíra, where a mixture of stone aggregate and lime mortar was used as a building material. The first people to develop the use of concrete in architecture were the Romans, who mixed their mortar with volcanic earth from Mount Vesuvius. One of the earliest large-scale applications known was located at Puteoli (modern Pozzuoli, Italy), whose concrete harbor was built in 199 BCE.

2150. Cement to bind stone was used in various formulas from early antiquity, but it was the Romans of circa 150 BCE who devised a cement recipe strong and water-resistant enough for truly permanent construction. The classic Roman *pozzolana* cement consisted mainly of slaked limestone mixed with clayey volcanic ash mined near what is now the Italian city of Pozzuoli. Many of the Roman construction projects built with pozzolana still stand after two millennia.

2151. Hydraulic mortar was formulated by English civil engineer John Smeaton, considered the founder of his profession in Britain. While experimenting with underwater mortar mixtures in 1756 for the third rebuilding of the Eddystone Lighthouse, he discovered the best recipe was powdered limestone admixed with clay.

2152. Portland cement was patented in 1824 by mason Joseph Aspdin in Leeds, England. He named his mixture of burned limestone and clay after the limestone called portland stone, which it resembled. A superior formulation of portland cement was developed by another Englishman, Isaac Charles Johnson, circa 1850.

2153. Patents for reinforced concrete were issued to Joseph Monier, a French gardener. Monier inserted steel wire mesh into wet concrete flowerpots and tubs and found that the mesh matrix gave superior tensile strength to the concrete. He obtained a French patent for this innovation in 1867 and also was granted later patents for the use of reinforced concrete in bridge and building construction.

2154. Reinforced concrete building system was patented in France in 1892 by engineer and architect François Hennebique. Inspired by the mesh-reinforced concrete flower tubs of Joseph Monier, Hennebique developed a structural system in which concrete slabs and structural beams were reinforced with embedded iron stirrups and bars. Hennebique's system was used to construct an apartment building in Paris and a number of innovative bridges.

ENGINEERING—CONCRETE—*continued*

2155. Moon concrete incorporating actual lunar material gathered by the United States Apollo space program was developed in 1986 by American engineer T.D. Lin for the National Aeronautics and Space Administration. The moon concrete was expected to find use in future construction projects on the lunar surface.

ENGINEERING—DAMS

2156. Dam known to archeologists is an earthen dam faced with stones, built circa 3200 BCE in Jordan.

2157. Masonry dam of record was constructed on the Nile River at Kosheish, Egypt, circa 2900 BCE. It was 49 feet (15 meters) high and was used to control the water supply for the city of Memphis.

2158. Dam still extant in continuous use is a rock-filled dam on the Orontes River in Syria. It is thought to date from 1300 BCE.

2159. Arch dam was the Dâra Dam, built by the Byzantine Romans on the present-day border between Syria and Turkey circa 550 CE, during the reign of the emperor Justinian. The dam was curved so that its convex (arched) side faced the water; pressure from the water served to tighten the structure and press it securely against the banks.

2160. Dam higher than 1,000 feet was the Rogun Dam at Vakhsh, Tajikistan. Planned for completion in 2000, it stood 1,099 feet (335 meters) high.

ENGINEERING—ENGINES AND MOTORS

2161. Turbine was a toy called the aeolipile, built circa 75 CE by the Greek inventor Hero of Alexandria and described in his book *Pneumatica*. His device, a primitive but workable form of the reaction turbine, was a hollow ball with nozzles fastened at opposite ends and pointing in opposite directions. The ball was mounted on a pivot that turned on two hollow tubes extending from a steaming cauldron. As the steam flowed through the tubes and escaped from the nozzles, it caused the ball to spin.

2162. Piston engine was invented in 1673 by Christiaan Huygens, the Dutch scientist. His design had one piston and was powered by gunpowder. When a small charge in the cylinder was detonated, it pushed the piston, which turned a crank. It is considered by some to be the first crude internal combustion engine.

2163. Steam engine was patented in 1698 by English military engineer Thomas Savery. Savery, a master miner, was seeking a way to pump water out of flooded coal mines that was less costly than the horse-powered pumps then in use. In his patent, he described his machine as a "new Invention for Raiseing of Water and occasioning Motion to all Sorts of Mill Work by the Impellent Force of Fire." It consisted of a steam boiler and a separate pumping vessel with an intake valve at the bottom. When pressurized steam was introduced into the vessel, a vacuum was created that drew water up from below and expelled it from an outlet at the top of the vessel. A water sprinkler condensed the steam and added to the pumping effect. Savery's engine could not work under high pressure and thus lacked the power and efficiency of later pumps. A design for a steam engine much like Savery's was described in *De' spiritali* (1606) by the Italian natural philosopher Giambattista della Porta.

2164. Commercially successful steam engine was the atmospheric-pressure piston engine of Thomas Newcomen, which superseded the less-efficient engine of Thomas Savery. Newcomen's main improvement was a piston that separated the condensing steam from the water. The piston was connected to one end of a rocking beam, which was attached at the other end to the pumping rod at the mine shaft. The first recorded Newcomen engine was built in 1712 near Dudley Castle, Staffordshire, England.

2165. Watt steam engine was built by James Watt in 1765. Watt added a separate steam condenser to the design of Thomas Newcomen; this improved efficiency by eliminating the need to heat and cool the cylinder with each stroke. Watt also invented a way for his steam engine to rotate a shaft, an idea that led directly to the motor vehicle.

2166. Steam engine still in working order is the Smethwick Engine, built in 1779 by the Birmingham Canal Company, England, from a design by James Watt. Until 1891, it pumped water on the canal at Smethwick, England. The engine is now in the collection of the Birmingham Museum of Science and Industry.

2167. Gas turbine patent was granted in England in 1791 to the inventor John Barber. Rotary power from Barber's engine was supplied by a turbine rotor driven by two jets of hot gas. Compressors forced pressurized air into a fuel-fired combustion chamber that was supposed to generate enough power to drive the compressors and the rotor with a moderate load. However, no working engine was ever built.

2168. Internal-combustion engine of the modern type was invented by Captain Samuel Morey of Orford, NH, USA, who received a U.S. patent on April 1, 1826, "on a gas or vapor engine." His engine had two cylinders, 180-degree cranks, poppet valves, a carburetor, an electric spark, and a water cooling device. He employed the vapor of spirits of turpentine and common air. A small tin dish contained the spirits, and the only heat he used was from a common table lamp. A rotary movement was obtained by means of a crank and flywheel, as in a steam engine.

2169. Direct-current electric motor was invented by Thomas Davenport of Brandon, VT, USA, in July 1834. Davenport, a prosperous blacksmith, had traveled to the Penfield Iron Works in Crown Point, NY, USA, to purchase some iron. He saw one of the first electromagnets there, and was so fascinated that he bought it on the spot. After several months of experiments, he built the first practical electric motor. It consisted of a rotating disk with two electromagnets as the spokes, supported by a spindle rising from a base on which were fixed two other electromagnets. When Davenport rapidly switched the direction of the current back and forth, the disk spun at speeds up to 30 revolutions per second. Davenport obtained a patent on the device in 1835.

2170. Internal-combustion engine that was commercially successful was patented in 1860 by the Belgian-born engineer Jean-Joseph-Étienne Lenoir. Experimenting in his Paris workshop, Lenoir independently developed the first workable internal-combustion engine. It was a two-stroke-cycle, converted steam engine fueled by a mixture of coal gas and air and using an ignition system of his own design. By 1865 more than 1,400 were in use in France and Britain to power pumps, printing presses, and other low-power machines, as well as the first automobile and motorboat. The Lenoir engine was eventually supplanted by superior four-cycle designs.

2171. Four-stroke internal-combustion engine in which every gasoline explosion drove four strokes of the piston was developed in 1876 by German inventor Nikolaus August Otto. His single-piston design, which used coal gas fuel, was first displayed publicly at the 1878 Paris Exposition. Otto did not invent the four-stroke cycle—that was patented in 1862 by the French engineer Alphonse-Eugène Beau de Rochas—but he was the first to build a practical engine based upon it.

2172. Two-stroke internal-combustion engine was developed by the English inventor Dugald Clerk in 1879 for the manufacturing firm of Sterne & Company. His efficient design, which generated two strokes of the cylinder for every explosion, was fueled by coal gas. It received an English patent in 1881. Descendants of Clerk's engine were widely used in lightweight gasoline-powered machines, such as lawn mowers and mopeds.

2173. Alternating-current electric motor was developed in the 1880s by the Serbian-American inventor and electric-power pioneer Nikola Tesla, who developed the technology behind alternating-current (AC) electric power transmission. Tesla was an employee of the Continental Edison Company in Paris, France, when it occurred to him that a rotating magnetic field could be made to do work. In 1883, while on assignment in Strassburg, Germany, he constructed a prototype induction motor. This is generally considered the ancestor of the modern electric motor.

2174. Spark plug were invented in France in 1885 by the Belgian-born engineer Jean-Joseph-Étienne Lenoir, developer of the first practical internal combustion engine. His sparking device was very similar to those still in use today.

2175. V-block engine was the invention of the German engineers Gottlieb Wilhelm Daimler and Wilhelm Maybach, who built the first engine of this type in 1889. Its two cylinders were arranged in a "V" at an angle of 17 degrees; at top speed, the engine generated 600 rpm and produced 1.5 horsepower.

2176. Diesel engine was patented by French-born German engineer Rudolf Christian Karl Diesel in 1892 and first described in 1893 in his treatise *Theorie und Konstruktion eines rationellen Wäremotors (Theory and Construction of a Rational Heat Motor)*. Unlike earlier internal combustion designs, Diesel's highly efficient four-stroke engine did not use an ignition system; combustion was achieved by compressing air during one part of the cycle until it was sufficiently hot to spontaneously ignite the fuel. The first commercially viable prototype was a 25-horsepower model developed in 1897 by Diesel with the assistance of Maschinenfabrik Augsburg and the Krupp family conglomerate.

2177. Carburetor was invented by the German engineer Wilhelm Maybach in 1893. The model for all modern carburetors, it prepared the fuel-air mixture for injection in the combustion cylinder. The first carbureted gasoline engine was the Phoenix, developed by Maybach and his partner, Gottlieb Wilhelm Daimler.

ENGINEERING—ENGINES AND MOTORS—*continued*

2178. Radiator was developed in 1897 by Wilhelm Maybach in Germany. His design consisted of a honeycomb of cooling ducts through which hot air from the engine was drawn by a fan.

2179. Diesel engine built for commercial service was a two-cylinder 60-horsepower unit built in September 1898 in the plant of the St. Louis Iron and Marine Works, St. Louis, MO, USA. The engine, which drove a direct-current generator, was erected and operated in the Second Street plant of the Anheuser Busch brewery. Adolphus Busch bought Rudolf Diesel's American patent rights in 1897 for a sum of approximately US$250,000.

2180. Starter motor for an automobile was introduced in 1931 by French inventor Maurice Gondard.

2181. Afterburner for a jet aircraft engine was developed in 1945 by the aviation division of Rolls-Royce Limited (now Rolls-Royce Motor Holdings Limited), of Derby, Derbyshire, England. The afterburner is a second combustion chamber near the rear of the engine. Extra fuel is injected into the chamber and burned when additional thrust is needed.

2182. Rotary internal-combustion engine was the Wankel engine, developed by the German engineer Felix Wankel in 1954–56 at the NSU Motorenwerk AG in Neckarsulm, Germany. Wankel, a specialist in sealing technologies, replaced the reciprocating pistons and cylinders of other engine designs with a rotor shaped like a curved equilateral triangle. A single turn of the rotor, which is sealed into the engine, creates three chambers of dynamically changing size. A complete cycle of intake, compression, expansion, and exhaust takes place in each chamber with every turn. An output shaft connected to the rotor provides power.

ENGINEERING—MACHINES

2183. Simple machine still in use is the dalu, an animal-powered irrigation device consisting of a goatskin bag drawn by rope over a pulley. It is known to have been used by the Sumerians circa 3500 BCE in lower Iraq. The dalu is still in use in rural areas of Libya.

2184. Homeostatic machine that adjusted itself to changing external conditions was the south-pointing carriage, invented in China circa 300 CE (but ascribed in an official Chinese history to the Duke of Zhou, who is supposed to have developed the device circa 1030 BCE). The first machine to incorporate a differential gear, the south-pointing carriage was a wheeled vehicle topped by a jade statue. The statue's raised arm pointed south no matter which way the wheels of the carriage were turned. Power from the wheels was applied to continually adjust the position of the jade figure.

2185. Water mill of record was the water-driven quern, in use in Greece and Asia Minor before 100 BCE, and first mentioned in a Greek poem written circa 85 BCE. A quern is a mill in which grain is ground between a fixed concave stone and a turning convex stone that fits into it.

2186. Device to transmit power through gearing was the undershot, horizontal-shaft water mill, described circa 27 by the Roman architect and military engineer Vitruvius (Marcus Vitruvius Pollio). The mill's waterwheel was connected by a right-angle gear to a vertical shaft to which was fixed a grinding wheel.

2187. Hydraulic press was invented by the French scientist, mathematician, and philosopher Blaise Pascal circa 1647. It was a device consisting of a piston and cylinder filled with a fluid liquid. Pressing on the piston produced a compressive force upon a stationary anvil. Modern versions of the hydraulic press are widely used in industry. It was reinvented in the late 18th century by the English engineer Joseph Bramah. Pascal was also the inventor of the syringe.

2188. Micrometer that was accurate enough for precise measurement and adjustments was built by master machinist Henry Maudslay at his shop in London, England, circa 1800. Using his screw-cutting metal lathe, which was capable of cutting threads of extremely fine pitch, he fashioned a micrometer that was ten times more accurate than existing models.

2189. Programmable logic controller was invented by the Austrian-born American engineer Odo J. Struger in 1958–60 at the Allen-Bradley company in Milwaukee, WI, USA. A programmable logic controller, or PLC, is a simple electronic device that allows precise numerical control of machinery. It is widely used to control everything from washing machines to roller coasters to automated manufacturing equipment.

ENGINEERING—TUNNELS

2190. Canal tunnel was the tunnel constructed by engineer Pierre Riquet for the Canal du Midi in France, completed in 1681. Most of the tunnel's length of 515 feet (157 meters) was blasted with black powder charges inserted into holes drilled into the rock; this marked the first known use of explosives for a major tunneling project.

2191. Underwater tunnel was drilled under the Thames River in London, England, under the direction of French-born marine engineer Marc Isambard Brunel. Tunneling through the soft, wet ground under a body of water had been considered impossible until Brunel's invention of the drilling shield, a rectangular screw-tipped iron casing that was forced through yielding earth by means of hydraulic jacks. Miners removed earth through doors in the face of the shield, or could step through and work in front of it. The tunnel was begun in 1825 and completed in 1842.

2192. Mountain tunnel of note was the Mount Cenis (or Fréjus) Tunnel linking France and Switzerland. The tunnel ran for 7 miles (12 kilometers) under Mount Cenis in the Alps and was completed in December 1870. It was built by the French engineer Germain Sommeiller, who invented a compressed-air rock drilling machine for the project, and was one of the first to make use of Alfred Nobel's new invention, dynamite.

2193. Automobile tunnel was the Holland Tunnel between New York, NY, and Jersey City, NJ, USA, beneath the Hudson River. Construction began on October 12, 1920. The tunnel, which was named for the chief engineer, Clifford Milburn Holland, consisted of two tubes 9,250 feet (2,819 meters) long, of which 5,480 feet (1,670 meters) passed under the river, and was designed to accommodate 1,900 motor vehicles an hour. The ventilation system changed the air 42 times an hour; it was the first ventilation system designed to accommodate the exhaust of motor vehicles. The tunnel was opened on November 12, 1927. In the first hour, 20,000 people walked through the tunnel from shore to shore. Vehicular traffic was allowed through on November 13, 1927.

2194. Undersea tunnel was the Kanmon rail tunnel linking the islands of Honshu and Kyushu in Japan. The tunnel, which runs 2.25 miles (3.5 kilometers), nearly all underwater, was begun in 1936 and completed in 1944.

2195. Road tunnel longer than 10 miles that was not an underwater tunnel was the tunnel at St. Gotthard, Switzerland, completed in 1980. It was 10.14 miles (16.32 kilometers) long.

2196. Rail tunnel longer than 50 kilometers was the tunnel at Seikan, Japan, completed in 1988. It was 53.90 kilometers (33.49 miles) long. This was also the first undersea tunnel longer than 50 kilometers.

2197. Tunneling machine that could turn 90 degrees was developed by the Taisei Corporation, Ishikawajima-Harima Heavy Industries, and Tokyo Electric Power, all of Japan. The tunnel borer possessed two shields, a smaller spherical subshield in front of a larger conical shield. The spherical subshield could pivot as much as 90 degrees and begin tunneling in a new direction. The machine was first tested in 1993 in a tunnel connecting a stormwater detention pond and a pump station in Kawasaki, Japan.

2198. Underwater link between Great Britain and Europe was the Channel Tunnel, also known as the "Chunnel". It ran from Folkestone, England, under the English Channel to Calais, France. Construction began in December 1987 by Eurotunnel, an Anglo-French consortium. Primarily a rail link, it contained two railroad tunnels and a network of smaller service tunnels. Of the Chunnel's 31 mile (50 kilometer) length, 24 miles (38 kilometers) were under water. In May 1994, the Chunnel was opened to traffic in an inaugural ceremony attended by Queen Elizabeth II of England and President François Mitterrand of France.

ENTERTAINMENT—BEAUTY CONTESTS

2199. Beauty contest with an official panel of judges was the Concours de Beauté, held on September 19, 1888, at Spa, Belgium. Twenty-one finalists were chosen from 350 contestants. The winner was Bertha Soucaret of the French island of Guadeloupe in the Lesser Antilles.

2200. Swimsuit beauty contest was held at Maroubra Beach in Sydney, Australia, on February 18, 1920, sponsored by the Sunday Times of Sydney. The contest was won by Edith Pickup, a 14-year-old who, the paper raved, exhibited "the true charm of fresh girlishness."

2201. Miss World contest was held at the Lyceum Ballroom in London, England, on April 19, 1951. The competition, held in conjunction with the Festival of Britain, was devised by the publicity agent Eric Motley of Mecca, Ltd. Kiki Haakonson of Sweden was the first winner. This was also the first beauty contest in which the contestants appeared in bikinis.

ENTERTAINMENT—CIRCUSES

2202. Circus monkey was General Jackoo, billed as "The Military Monkey," a simian outfitted in a British army uniform. He debuted in 1768 at Astley's Amphitheatre in London, England.

2203. Modern circus was Astley's Amphitheatre, founded in 1769 on the outskirts of London, England, by Philip Astley, a former horsebreaker with a dragoon regiment. Astley was an expert rider and performed his own tricks, such as waving a sword while riding with one foot on the saddle and one on the horse's head. His wife also performed equestrian stunts. In 1770, other acts were added, including acrobats, ropedancers, aerialists, clowns, strongmen, and a freak show. Astley opened 18 similar one-ring amphitheaters throughout Europe.

2204. Circus in Europe was founded in Vienna, Austria, in 1780 by Juan Porte, a Spanish-born performer and impresario.

2205. Circus known by that name was the Royal Circus, founded in 1782 in London, England, by trick rider Charles Hughes.

2206. Circus clown was Joey, a comic persona created by the London actor Joseph Grimaldi. Joey, the prototype of later circus clowns, mixed innocence and slyness in one character and got most of his laughs doing pratfalls and other slapstick routines. He first appeared in the pantomime production *Harlequin and Mother Goose* at London's Covent Garden Theatre in 1806.

2207. Circus elephants were Baba and Kiouny, who were displayed in 1816 at Antoine Franconi's Cirque Olympique de Franconi in Paris, France. The pachyderms performed such tricks as catching objects with their trunks, opening bottles, and turning the handle of a hurdy-gurdy.

2208. Circus trailer belonged to Antoine Franconi, the circus impresario, who founded the Cirque Olympique de Franconi in Paris, France, in 1805. Sometime in the first half of the 1830s, Franconi ordered a traveling van that housed a kitchen, a bedroom, and a dining room.

2209. Flying trapeze act was performed on November 12, 1859, by aerialist Jules Léotard at the Cirque Napoléon in Paris. Léotard, who invented the trapeze for his act, worked without a net. He used a pile of mattresses instead. His act was the subject of the popular song "That Daring Young Man on the Flying Trapeze." Léotard's best-known innovation was his costume, a close-fitting, stretchy suit of knitted jersey that reached to the wrists and ankles.

2210. Human cannonball in a circus act was a woman who called herself Zazel. She appeared for two years at West's Amphitheatre, London, England, starting on April 2, 1877.

2211. Three-ring circus was founded in the United States in 1882 by P.T. Barnum to showcase his recent purchase of the elephant Jumbo. It enabled three acts to perform simultaneously, with additional activities taking place on smaller platforms between the rings and along a track surrounding the rings.

2212. Roller coaster was invented by an American, Lemarcus Adna Thompson, a former Sunday school teacher, and put in operation in June 1884 by the L.A. Thompson Scenic Railway Company at Coney Island, NY, USA (now part of New York City). It traveled along a wooden and steel track 450 feet (138 meters) long at a speed of 6 miles (10 kilometers) per hour. The cars started from a peak and ran downgrade, the momentum carrying the cars up an incline. The passengers got out, the attendants pushed the train over a switch to a higher point on a second track, and the passengers returned. The highest drop was only 30 feet (9 meters). Thompson obtained a U.S. patent on January 20, 1885, on a roller-coasting structure and another patent on December 22, 1885, on a gravity switchback railway. The first high-speed roller coaster was The Cyclone, which opened at Coney Island on June 26, 1927. Its one-and-a-half minute ride hit speeds of up to 60 miles (97 kilometers) per hour.

2213. Ferris wheel was invented in 1892 by George Washington Gale Ferris, an American railroad and bridge engineer. It was erected on the Midway at the World's Columbian Exposition in Chicago, IL, USA, in 1893. It consisted of 36 cars, each capable of holding 60 passengers. The highest point of the wheel was 264 feet (80 meters). The total weight of the wheels and cars was 1,905 metric tons, of the levers and machinery 2,000 metric tons, and of the passengers per trip 136 metric tons.

2214. Human cannonball family act were the Zacchinis, a family of Italian circus performers who started the cannonball act in 1922, using a cannon they built in Malta. The cannonballers included five of the nine children of Ildebrando Zacchini, an Italian gymnast who founded the Circus Olympia in the early 1900s. The stunt involved a large cannon barrel fitted with a hidden launch pad that was pushed forward by a blast of compressed air, shooting the performer across the tent and into a net at a speed of 90 miles per hour. A small quantity of black gunpowder was ignited at the same time to produce an impressive roar. Members of the family performed the act at circuses throughout Europe and the United States. The last to fly was Ildebrando's grandson Hugo, who retired in 1991.

ENTERTAINMENT—MAGIC

2215. Ventriloquist known by name as a professional performer was Louis Brabant, valet to King François I of France (reigned 1515–47). Ventriloquism or voice-throwing is a skill with an ancient and widespread past, and has been practiced since antiquity in most areas of the world.

2216. Magician whose act included mind-reading tricks using visual and verbal cues provided by accomplices in the audience was Philip Breslaw, who performed at the Haymarket Theatre in London, England, in 1781.

2217. Magician to use electricity in his act was Jean-Eugène Robert-Houdin of Blois, France. Beginning in 1845, he performed in Paris theaters, baffling audiences with brilliant sleight-of-hand. His mind-reading tricks were created with the help of electric signaling devices. He also used specially designed boxes with hidden supports and other conjuring equipment.

2218. Books that explained magic tricks were *Confidences d'un prestidigitateur (Disclosures of a Conjurer)*, published in 1859, and *Les Secrets de la prestidigitation et de la magie (Secrets of Conjuring and Magic)*, published in 1868. Their author was the master French sleight-of-hand artist Jean-Eugène Robert-Houdin.

ENTERTAINMENT—SPECTACLES

2219. Mock naval battle of record was staged in Rome by Julius Caesar in 46 BCE. Caesar ordered an artificial lake to be constructed in Rome's Campus Martius for the purpose. The opponents played out a sea battle between the navies of Egypt and Tyre. The mock naval battle, or *naumachia*, became a favorite entertainment of the Romans, who allowed the combatants—convicted criminals or prisoners of war—plenty of realism, including death.

2220. Sports spectacular was a three-day event held by the Emperor Titus to celebrate the opening of the 50,000-seat Colosseum in Rome in 80 CE. Gladiators in combat were featured on the first day, together with a staged "hunt" that ended the lives of 5,000 wild animals, including elephants, hippos, lions, and tigers. The games on the second day included chariot races, horse races, boxing matches, and circus performances. On the third day, the floor of the arena was flooded to make a "sea" on which a mock naval battle was fought by 3,000 men. The contests and spectacles continued for a total of 100 days.

2221. Tournament between armed knights was held in France in 1066 and was called the *haslitude*, or "spear game." Some texts name Baron Geoffroi de Preully as the originator. In its earliest form, the tournament was a war game that ended in a *mêlée*, or free-for-all.

2222. Peep shows were miniature scenes painted inside a box by the Italian Renaissance master Leon Battista Alberti in 1437. Viewers peeked through a hole in the front of the box at a glass panel comprising the rear of the box. Alberti painted scenes in perspective on the glass and lit it from behind in various ways to suggest sunlight or moonlight.

2223. World's Fair was the London Great Exhibition, which opened May 1, 1851, in Hyde Park. Originally proposed by art critic Sir Henry Cole as a means to promote British industry, trade, and progress to the world, the fair also had the backing of Prince Albert, the husband of Queen Victoria. It was housed in the Crystal Palace, a huge glass and iron pavilion designed by Joseph Paxton. The Great Exhibition lasted 141 days, featured 14,000 exhibitors, and attracted more than 6 million visitors from all over the world. The term "world's fair" was first applied to the Great Exhibition by English poet and novelist William Makepeace Thackeray.

ENTERTAINMENT— SPECTACLES— *continued*

2224. International ice show star was the German ballerina and skater Charlotte Oelschlägel, who went under the stage name Charlotte. Already popular in Germany, she came to the United States in 1915 to perform in *Flirting in St. Moritz,* the first modern ice show held in North America, at the Hippodrome in New York City.

2225. Performance of a *Son et lumière* **show** took place in 1952 at the Château de Chambord near Blois, France, by Paul Robert-Houdin, the château's curator. *Son et lumière* ("Sound and Light") was a multimedia production in which a prerecorded soundtrack of music and narration was combined with a display of spotlights and other visual effects, including smoke and fireworks, to present the history of a famous site.

2226. Edition of the *Guinness Book of World Records* was published in 1955 by Guiness PLC of London, England (formerly of Dublin, Ireland), a brewery better known for its Irish stout. It was originally a collection of trivia intended to help beer drinkers settle pub arguments.

2227. Performance of a *Son et lumière* **show in Britain** was presented in 1957 at Greenwich Palace in London, England.

2228. Performance of a *Son et lumière* **show in Africa** was staged at the Pyramids of Giza near Cairo, Egypt, in 1961.

2229. Performance of a *Son et lumière* **show in the United States** was produced in Philadelphia, PA, USA, in 1962, at Independence Hall, the site of the adoption of the Declaration of Independence in 1776 and the meetingplace of the Constitutional Convention in 1787.

2230. Performance of a *Son et lumière* **show in Asia** took place in 1965 at Shah Jahan's 17th-century compound, the Red Fort, in Delhi, India.

2231. Humor museum was Un Nouveau Muse . . . Pour Rire (A New Museum for Laughs), which opened on April 1, 1993, in Montreal, Canada. The museum offered exhibitions on the history of comedy, including the birth of political satire in ancient Greece, the physical comedy of the silent screen era, and the commedia dell'arte of 16th-century Venice.

2232. World's fair with a marine theme was Expo 98, held in Lisbon, Portugal, in 1998. The theme of the expo, "The Oceans: A Heritage for the Future," was expressed in six thematic pavilions. Most of the 146 nations pavilions also had watery themes.

ENTERTAINMENT—TRAVEL

2233. European luxury casino and seaside resort was the Sea Bathing and Circle of Foreigners Company, better known as the casino at Monte-Carlo in Monaco. A charter to build a gambling resort on the French Riviera was granted by Prince Charles III of Monaco in 1856, and the resort opened for business in 1861. An opera house, sporting club, and other amenities were later added, making Monte-Carlo the world's premiere playground for the wealthy and famous. The casino operating company was taken over by the government in 1967.

2234. Package tour of Europe was arranged in 1856 by the English travel packager and missionary Thomas Cook, who with his son John Mason Cook later founded the first worldwide travel agency, Thomas Cook and Son. The firm was so successful that grand tours are often called Cook's Tours.

2235. Economy package tour was a "Whitsuntide Working Men's Excursion" arranged by the travel packager and missionary Thomas Cook. The six-day excursion to Paris, France, departed from London, England, on May 17, 1861. It was the first such tour in which fare, accommodations, and meals could all be paid for in advance. The cost was about 46 shillings per person.

ENVIRONMENT

2236. Incinerators were constructed circa 2500 BCE in the city of Mohenjo-Daro, located in the Indus Valley in present-day Pakistan. Evidence of mass burning of solid waste was unearthed by British archeologist Robert Eric Mortimer Wheeler, former director-general of archeology for the government of India, during excavations in the mid-1970s.

2237. Treatise on human ecology was *De aëre, aquis, et locis (Air, Waters, and Places)*, attributed to the Greek physician Hippocrates (circa 460 BCE to 377 BCE). The book investigated the effects on health of diet and environment.

2238. Waste-disposal law known to historians was promulgated in ancient Athens in 320 BCE. The law forbade residents from simply throwing waste out into the street, instead requiring them to bury it or dispose of it outside the city in open pits.

2239. Description of global warming was the work of two scientists. In 1827, the French mathematician and physicist Jean-Baptiste-Joseph Fourier speculated on an atmospheric process in which the earth's temperature could be raised by reflection of the sun's heat from an upper layer of the atmosphere, analogous to how the air inside a greenhouse is heated by the sun's energy. In 1908, the Swedish chemist Svante August Arrhenius argued that carbon dioxide added to the atmosphere by burning fossil fuels was creating a greenhouse effect, thereby warming the globe.

2240. Environmental lawsuit was mounted in the copper-smelting town of Swansea, Wales, in 1832. Claiming that slag and fumes were destroying the land near the copperworks, a group of farmers pursued an indictment for public nuisance against John Henry Vivian, co-owner of the area's giant Hafod smelting firm. A trial was held the following year that ended in victory for the copperworks owners.

2241. National public health legislation was the Public Health Act of 1848, passed by the British Parliament to prevent the spread of cholera. A National Board of Health was established, with local boards responsible for the regulation of water supply, sewerage, and polluting businesses.

2242. Species import ban was the Destructive Insects Act of 1877, passed by the British Parliament to prevent the import of the Colorado beetle, a pest native to North America. Introduced to potatoes in the 1850s by Colorado miners, the beetle quickly spread eastward to the Atlantic coast and was poised to hitch a ride overseas. The bill gave British officials the power to restrict or prohibit the landing of any crop that might contain the beetle.

2243. Environmental restoration plan for an industrial site was prepared in 1943 by the landscape architect G. A. Jellicoe for a quarry, the Hope Valley Cement Works, in England's Peak District. The plan called for a recreational use of the land, with boating, fishing, and camping facilities, once the quarry was played out.

2244. Country to depend mainly on water from desalination was Kuwait, which has few natural sources of fresh water. With wealth gained from selling its oil reserves, Kuwait built its first large land-based desalination plant in 1948 to supply desalted Persian Gulf water to Kuwait City. The plant's original capacity, 1.2 million gallons a day, was upgraded to 5 million gallons per day in 1958. Additional plants have since been built to serve the country's rapidly growing worker population and to supply water for Kuwait's two major industrial parks. By the year 2000, countries in the Middle East accounted for about three-quarters of the world's desalination capacity.

2245. City in North America to use seawater as its sole water supply was Key West, FL, USA. In 1967, it began drawing water from a large desalination plant capable of producing more than 2 million gallons of fresh water from salt water every day.

2246. International environmental conference was the United Nations Conference on the Human Environment, organized by the UN General Assembly and held in Stockholm, Sweden, in June 1972. Attended by delegations from 114 governments, it produced several landmark documents, including a Declaration on the Human Environment, an Action Plan for the Human Environment, and a Resolution on Institutional and Financial Arrangements. The United Nations Environment Programme was created later that year to coordinate environmental activities within the United Nations system

2247. Latin American country with an environmental ministry was Venezuela. In 1977, that country formed a Ministry of Environment and Renewable National Resources to deal with environmental problems stemming from the country's oil and mineral boom.

2248. International environmental law that was comprehensive and enforceable was the 1982 United Nations Convention on the Law of the Sea. It was also the first legal instrument that provided for a system of settling disputes arising from the international use of seas and oceans.

2249. Jungle canopy walkway for tourists was opened in Malaysia's Kinabalu National Park in Borneo in 1989. Designed by biologist Illar Muul, the 300-foot (90-meter) walkway allowed visitors to see plants and animals that live only in the rain forest's uppermost branches, with minimal environmental impact on the treetop environment.

ENVIRONMENT—*continued*

2250. Goldman Environmental Prizes were awarded in 1990 by the American philanthropists Richard and Rhoda Goldman to a grassroots environmentalist from each continent. The winners were Robert Brown, Australia; Lois Gibbs, United States; Janet Gibson, Belize; Harrison Ngau Laing, Malaysia; János Vargha, Hungary; and Michael Werikhe, Kenya. The annual prize was worth US$125,000 in 1999.

2251. Earth Summit was the United Nations Conference on Environment and Development, also called the Earth Summit, held in 1992 in Rio de Janeiro, Brazil, to address urgent problems of environmental protection and socioeconomic development. The largest intergovernmental conference in history, it was attended by more than 100 heads of state. The assembled leaders signed the Convention on Climate Change and the Convention on Biological Diversity, endorsed the Rio Declaration and the Forest Principles, and adopted Agenda 21, a 300-page plan for achieving sustainable development in the 21st century.

2252. Green Cross organization was founded by the former Soviet leader Mikhail Gorbachev in 1993 to "help create a sustainable future by cultivating harmonious relationships between humans and the environment." Green Cross organizations are active in 21 countries. These include: Argentina, Bolivia, Burkina Faso, Czech Republic, Estonia, France, Germany, Hungary, Italy, Ivory Coast, Japan, South Korea, Netherlands, Poland, Russia, Swaziland, Sweden, Switzerland, United Kingdom, United States, and Venezuela. The organizations in Germany and the United States have adopted the name "Global Green."

2253. Ultraviolet (UV) radiation increase over a populated area owing to the shrinking of the earth's ozone layer over the Antarctic was announced by American and Argentine researchers in 1993. According to John E. Frederick of the University of Chicago and colleagues, who monitored UV levels at a research station in Ushuaia, Argentina, on the southern tip of South America, biologically harmful UV frequencies increased significantly during the Southern Hemisphere summers of 1990 and 1992.

2254. Comprehensive study of worldwide biodiversity was the Global Biodiversity Assessment, issued by the United Nations Environment Programme in November 1995. The study, the first comprehensive, peer-reviewed report of its kind, found that human activities posed an increasing threat to the biological diversity of plants and animals in most ecosystems.

2255. Human action to affect the earth's planetary motion was the transfer between 1950 and 1998 of 2,400 cubic miles of water from the world's oceans to 10,000 man-made reservoirs. The discovery was announced in 1996 by Benjamin Fong Chao, a geophysicist at the NASA Goddard Space Flight Center in Greenbelt, Maryland, USA. Most of the water was transferred from equatorial regions to mid-latitude regions, concentrating the mass of water nearer the earth's axis. This shift in mass made the earth spin slightly faster.

2256. List of the world's most endangered historical sites was released in 1996 by the World Monuments Watch of the World Monuments Fund, a nonprofit organization based in New York, NY, USA. The Fund's first annual compilation of the world's 100 most endangered historical sites was assembled by eight architectural preservationists who chose from 253 nominations in 70 countries. The list was selected every two years from cultural sites including historic structures, groups of buildings, historic districts, archeological sites, public art, and cultural landscapes.

2257. Deep underground nuclear waste storage site was the Waste Isolation Pilot Plant, located in salt beds 2,150 feet (655 meters) under the desert near Carlsbad, NM, USA. The site, created to store hundreds of thousands of barrels of radioactive wastes from nuclear weapons production, was licensed for plutonium storage by the U.S. government on May 13, 1998.

ENVIRONMENT—PARKS AND RESERVES

2258. National park was land set aside in 1879 in what is now Royal National Park, Australia.

2259. National parks service was the Dominion Parks Branch, established by the Canadian government in 1911. It was the predecessor to the current Canadian parks service, Parks Canada.

2260. National park in Africa was Virunga National Park in the Democratic Republic of the Congo (formerly Zaire). Originally encompassing an area of 3,012 square miles (7,800 square kilometers), the park was founded in 1925 as Albert National Park. It is home to one of the few remaining populations of mountain gorillas.

2261. Freshwater national park was established in 1980 by Malawi in the southern region of Lake Malawi, the southernmost of the major lakes of East Africa's Great Rift Valley. The park was created to protect the lake's 500 to 1,000 species of brilliantly colored freshwater tropical fish from poachers.

2262. Wilderness park in a mall was the American Wilderness Experience, which opened in 1997 at the Ontario Mills shopping mall in San Bernardino County, CA, USA. Simulated biomes recreated five separate natural environments.

ENVIRONMENT—POLLUTION

2263. Urban air pollution afflicted London, England, as early as 1273, when coal smoke provoked complaints from well-to-do residents. In 1306, King Edward I made it a capital offense to burn coal in the city.

2264. Treatise on air pollution was *Fumifugium, or the Inconvenience of the Aer and Smoke of London Dissipated* by the diarist John Evelyn, written in London, England, in 1661. Evelyn, a favored councillor of Charles II, proposed various remedies for London's persistent smog problem, none of which were implemented until the 19th century.

2265. Air pollution abatement device was a damper designed to reduce the production of smoke from chimneys, invented in France in 1715.

2266. Water pollution law was passed in 1856 in London, England, to control waste dumped into the Thames River.

2267. Catalytic converter for automobile engines to reduce exhaust emissions was invented in 1907 by a Frenchman, Michel Frenkel. Frenkel's converter was originally intended to reduce the smell of exhaust fumes. In 1974, the American automobile manufacturer General Motors of Detroit, MI, USA, was the first company to equip cars with a modern catalytic converter to absorb air pollutants.

2268. Oil spills on the ocean took place beginning in January 1942, when German U-boats began sinking Allied military oil tankers off the eastern seaboard of North America. Between January and June of that year, an estimated 590,000 tons of oil was released into the Atlantic Ocean, an amount greater than the combined tonnage of all the commercial oil spills worldwide from 1945 to 1978.

2269. Oil spill from a commercial tanker of significance occurred on March 18, 1967, when the tanker *Torrey Canyon,* under Italian-born captain Pastrengo Rugiati, broke up on shoals off the coast of Cornwall, England. The ship spilled some 119,000 tons (830,000 barrels) of Kuwaiti crude oil into the ocean, creating a slick that at full extent was 35 miles long and almost 20 miles wide. The tanker, which still contained thousands of tons of oil, was destroyed later that month by three days of massive bombing raids.

2270. Nation heavily polluted by nuclear waste was Kazakhstan. According to a 1992 study by Kazakhstani researchers, more than half of Kazakhstan's arable land was occupied by nuclear-test and research sites, raising the typical background level of radiation to 25 to 500 times the permissible level. In the most affected areas, many residents exhibited high white blood cell counts, a symptom of low-level radiation poisoning, and average life expectancy dropped by two years from 1948 to 1992.

2271. International regulation of greenhouse gas emissions was the Kyoto Protocol, agreed to by representatives of 159 nations, as well as environmental groups, industry associations, and other nongovernmental organizations, on December 10, 1997, in Kyoto, Japan, during the United Nations Conference on Climate Change. Signers of the protocol were legally obligated to reduce emissions of waste industrial gases, mainly carbon dioxide, that were believed to cause global warming through the greenhouse effect. The major industrialized nations were asked to make the largest cuts in emissions: the European Union agreed to cut its emissions of six greenhouse gases 8 percent below their 1990 levels; Japan was to reduce its emissions 6 percent below 1990 levels; and the United States was to cut its emissions 7 percent below 1990 levels. The treaty required approval by each signatory's government before full implementation.

EXPLORATION

2272. Westerner to visit India may have been a Greek sea captain, Scylax of Caryanda, who was commissioned by King Darius I of Persia to make a voyage of exploration down the Indus River, circa 515 BCE. The trip took two and a half years.

2273. Detailed account of a long sea voyage was *Ta peri okerinou (On the Ocean)*, by the Greek explorer and geographer Pytheas. In 324 BCE Pytheas headed westward from Massilia (now Marseilles, France) along the Mediterranean coast, passed through the Straits of Gibraltar, followed the Atlantic coast to what is now Brittany, crossed the English Channel, spent time in Cornwall, circumnavigated Britain, crossed the North Sea, visited Scandinavia, and possibly got as far as the Baltic Sea before returning home, having traveled some 8,000 miles. His account, which contained observations of daily life in Cornish villages, no longer exists, but is quoted and paraphrased in the work of others.

2274. Native Americans to cross the Atlantic may have been a group of men who were shipwrecked in 62 CE in northern Europe, probably in France. They were most likely fishermen from the American or Canadian coast who had been blown out to sea in a storm. The tribal chieftain in whose lands they were found sent them on to Quintus Metellus Celer, governor of Cisalpine Gaul (the northern part of present-day Italy), with the message that they must have come from India. A similar incident took place in 1508, according to the Venetian historian Pietro Bembo.

2275. Discovery of Greenland by Europeans took place in 982, when the Viking known as Erik the Red (born Erik Thorvaldson) sailed west from Iceland after he was banished for killing a man. He was searching for western land visible from the mountaintops of Iceland. Erik rounded the southern tip of Greenland and settled near the present location of Julianehb. He spent three years exploring the coast, then returned to Iceland, where he spread the word about a vast unclaimed land he called "Greenland" in a successful effort to make the land more attractive to settlers.

2276. European traveler to reach the Chinese frontier may have been a Spanish Jew, Benjamin of Tudela. Over a 13-year period, probably beginning in 1159, he traveled to Provence, Genoa, Rome, southern Italy, Corfu, Constantinople, the Aegean islands, Damascus, Baghdad, Jerusalem and other cities in the Holy Land, and Egypt. His account of his travels, *Massaot* (published in English in 1907 as *The Itinerary of Benjamin of Tudela*), includes descriptions of places in Asia, including the western parts of China, though historians do not know whether he visited them personally.

2277. Major Chinese voyage of exploration and diplomacy left China in 1405 under the command of Zheng He, a Muslim-born officer in the service of Emperor Yongle. His fleet comprised 300 ships, many of them of immense size, including the Treasure Ship, a nine-masted junk more than 400 feet long. Some 27,000 men went with him. The mission of the expedition was to collect tribute, make diplomatic contacts, and extend China's prestige and commercial influence. In the course of two years, the fleet visited ports in what are now the countries of Vietnam, Thailand, Malaysia, India, and Sri Lanka. Zheng He later made seven other voyages, which took him through the Persian Gulf and the Red Sea and down the east coast of Africa almost as far as Mozambique.

2278. International and multicultural academy for explorers was founded at Sagres, Portugal, in 1420 by Prince Henry the Navigator (Henrique o Navegador). The academy brought together Christian, Jewish, and Muslim experts in oceanography, astronomy, mathematics, cartography, and nautical instrumentation. Hundreds of mariners were trained there. Its facilities included a mapmaking studio, an observatory, an archive of reports by travelers, and (at nearby Lagos) a shipbuilding factory. Between 1420 and 1460, dozens of expeditions based at Sagres made exploratory voyages down the coast of West Africa.

2279. Explorers to pass Cape Bojador since antiquity were the Portuguese captains Gil Eanes and Alfonso Gonçalvo Baldaia, whose carracks rounded the cape in 1434 in an expedition sponsored by Prince Henry the Navigator. The cape, located on the Atlantic coast of Africa in what is now the nation of Western Sahara, was considered by European sailors of that era to be the point of no return.

2280. European expedition to round the southern tip of Africa was led by the Portuguese mariner Bartolomeu Dias, a squire of the royal household of King João of Portugal. Dias departed from Lisbon in August 1487 with two caravels and a supply ship and headed along the North African coast toward the Gulf of Guinea, then down the western coast. On Janaury 6, 1488, his ships were blown out to sea by a storm. Hoping to regain the coast,

Dias sailed east but saw only empty ocean until, turning north, he sighted land on February 3. It took him some time to realize that the expedition had been blown all the way around the southern tip of Africa without sighting it.

2281. Expedition of Christopher Columbus was organized with the intention of finding a westward route to Asia. Columbus himself, whose original last name was probably Colón, was a cartographer and navigator from Genoa, Italy, who had secured the sponsorship of Queen Isabella and King Ferdinand of Spain. His first expedition left Palos, Spain, on August 3, 1492, carrying 120 men, and headed southwestward to the Canary Islands off the African coast, where one of his three ships underwent repairs. Departing again on September 6, the fleet crossed the Atlantic Ocean and on October 12 made landfall in the archipelago now called the West Indies, probably on the island of Guanahani (now San Salvador). Searching for evidence that he had reached Cathay (China) or Cipangu (Japan), Columbus landed on October 24 at Cuba and on December 6 at Ayti (present-day Hispaniola, divided between Haiti and the Dominican Republic), where he built a fort, La Navidad. The two ships still afloat— the third had run aground—headed homeward on January 16 and were separated in a storm. Columbus, in the *Niña,* arrived in Lisbon March 13 and in Palos on March 15. This was the first of four voyages under the command of Columbus.

2282. Letter containing a description of America was written by the explorer Christopher Columbus. On March 14, 1493, having docked in Lisbon, Portugal, at the end of his first voyage to the New World, he dispatched two letters of identical content, one to Raphael Sanchez and the other to Luis de Santangel, describing his encounters and discoveries.

2283. New World inhabitants forcibly taken to the Old World were seven bewildered Taino islanders, Arawakan Indians from Hispaniola brought by Christopher Columbus to Spain aboard the *Niña* and the *Pinta.* Upon their arrival on March 15, 1493, the Taino were taken to the Royal Palace in Barcelona, where they were displayed to King Ferdinand and Queen Isabella.

2284. European traveler to set foot on the North American continent after the Vikings whose name is known was John Cabot (also spelled Caboto, Cabotto, Caboote, Gabote, Calbot, or Talbot), a mariner who was probably born in Genoa, Italy. In 1496, King Henry VII of England granted Cabot a charter to sail west to Asia and set up a spice-trade monopoly.

Cabot's ship, a 70-foot caravel called the *Mathew,* embarked from Bristol, England, on May 20, 1497, and arrived on the coast of what is now Newfoundland on June 24. After planting the English and Venetian flags, Cabot and his men spent a few hours exploring the landing site, then returned to their ship. It is possible that Basque whalers or other European fishermen touched on the continent after Leif Eriksson and before Cabot, but there is no reliable evidence of their explorations.

2285. Direct sea voyage from Western Europe to Asia was accomplished by a fleet under the command of the Portuguese mariner Vasco da Gama. His fleet of four vessels set sail from Lisbon, Portugal, on July 8, 1497, and, after rounding the Cape of Good Hope, arrived on May 20, 1498, in the city of Calicut (now Kozhikode, Kerala state), the most important trade port on India's Malabar coast.

2286. European explorer to land on the South American continent was Christopher Columbus. During his third voyage, in which he sought a route south of Cuba to Cathay (China), his ships entered the Gulf of Paria and saw the South American mainland on August 1, 1498. On August 5, 1498, Columbus planted the Spanish flag on the Paria Peninsula, in what is now Venezuela.

2287. Explorer saved by an eclipse was Christopher Columbus. In 1503, during his fourth voyage to the New World, he and his men were stranded for months on the island of Santo Domingo (now Hispaniola, divided between Haiti and the Dominican Republic) after their caravels were disabled by shipworm. On February 29, 1504, to forestall an attack by the local residents, Columbus invited their chiefs to attend a nighttime meeting on the beach at Santa Gloria Bay, where he promised that any attack would be avenged by God. As proof, he asked them to look at the moon, which began to disappear. The result was a promise of assistance from the chiefs. Columbus had in his possession an almanac, written by the Spanish Jewish astronomer Abraham Zacuto, that contained astronomical tables from which he was able to calculate the time of the eclipse.

2288. Eyewitness account by a European traveler of life in the African interior was that of Alvise Ca' da Mosto (or Cadamosto), the author of *Il Libro della prima navigazzione per ocean alle terre de'negri della bassa etiopia* (The Book of the First Ocean Voyage to the Land of the Blacks of Lower Ethoiopia). Ca' da Mosto, a trader and mariner from Venice, was commissioned by Portugal's Prince

EXPLORATION—*continued*

Henry the Navigator to explore the west coast of Africa in 1455. He entered the Gambia River and continued inland for 60 miles. Among the observations he made there was the silent trade between Berbers, who carried rock salt in caravans from the Sahara Desert, and African villagers, who paid for the salt with gold. Ca' da Mosto was also the first European to land at the Cape Verde islands, in 1456. His book appeared in 1507.

2289. European explorers to see the Pacific Ocean were Spanish soldiers led by the conquistador Vasco Núñez de Balboa. Embarking from Acla, Panama, on September 11, 1513, in search of a rumored southern sea and an empire of gold, Balboa, 106 Spaniards, and many Native American bearers hacked their way across the narrowest part of the isthmus, east of the present-day Panama Canal. Balboa sighted the Pacific for the first time as the expedition reached the peaks of the Panamanian cordillera on September 25 or 27. Arriving at the shore of the Gulf of San Miguel, probably on September 30, Balboa reportedly marched into the surf and shouted, "By the grace of God, I claim all that sea and the countries bordering on it for the King and Castile!"

2290. Journey across North America of record was completed in 1536 by four members of the disastrous 1528 Spanish expedition to Florida: a Moorish slave named Estevánico; his owner, a Spanish nobleman named Andrés Dorantes de Carranca; a captain named Alonso del Castillo Maldonado; and Alvar Núñez Cabeza de Vaca. Shipwrecked on the coast of the Florida panhandle, the four were enslaved by local Native Americans, but escaped after four years and made their way from village to village through what is now the southern United States and northern Mexico. In March 1536, after crossing the entire width of North America, they met a company of Spanish raiders on the Rio Sinaloa. Cabeza de Vaca recounted the journey in *Naufragios (Shipwrecks)*, published in 1542.

2291. European travelers in Japan were several Portuguese traders, passengers on a Chinese ship that foundered off the island of Tanega, near southern Kyushu, in 1543. They brought with them the first guns ever seen in Japan, which were eagerly copied, as well as samples of sugarcane.

2292. Voyage around Cape Horn was led by Jakob Le Maire, commanding the Dutch ship *Eendracht,* and navigator Willem Corneliszoon Schouten. Both were employed by the Compagne Australe, a trading firm owned by Le Maire's father. A competing Dutch company, the powerful Verenigde Oostindische Compagnie, owned all Dutch rights to passage through the Straits of Magellan to the East Indies; the Le Maire/Schouten expedition set out in search of a more southerly route. Departing from the Netherlands on June 14, 1615, the ship rounded the stormy southernmost tip of South America on January 29, 1616. Schouten named the headland "Cape Horn" after Hoorn, his Dutch hometown. When the *Eendracht* arrived in Java, then a Dutch colony, it was confiscated by the local VOC representative, who did not believe that it had not gone through the Straits of Magellan.

2293. European explorer to see New Zealand was the Dutch navigator Abel Janszoon Tasman, who sighted the South Island on December 13, 1642. He sailed his ships, the *Heemskerk* and *Zeehaen,* into but not through the strait between North Island and South Island, and departed New Zealand from North Cape on January 4, 1643. The Maoris he encountered did not let him land. Tasman did not recognize New Zealand as a complex of islands; he believed it was part of Terra Australis, a legendary southern continent.

2294. European explorer to land on Easter Island (Rapa Nui) was the Dutch navigator Jakob Roggeveen, who landed on the remote island on Easter Sunday, 1722. At that time, Easter Island was home to about 4,000 people of Polynesian heritage, whose ancestors had arrived from the Marquesas circa 400. The island is now governed by Chile.

2295. Scientific exploration of the Amazon River in South America was accomplished by the French mathematician and naturalist Charles-Marie de La Condamine. In 1743, after spending eight years in Peru with a geographic expedition charged with determining the length of an arc of meridian at the equator, La Condamine embarked on a journey down the Amazon that took him from what is now Ecuador across the continent to Brazil. The trip, by raft, lasted four months.

2296. European explorer to cross North America north of Mexico was Alexander Mackenzie, the Scottish-born Canadian fur trader and explorer. Mackenzie left Fort Chipewyan on Lake Athabasca (in what is now the province of Alberta), in 1793. Following the Peace, Parsnip, Fraser, Blackwater, and Bella Coola rivers, he crossed the Rocky Mountains and reached what is now Dean Channel on the Pacific coast of British Columbia on July 22, 1793.

2297. European explorer to visit Timbuktu and return with an account of his observations was the French traveler René Caillie. He disguised himself as an Arab merchant and entered Timbuktu (now in Mali) in April 1828, expecting to find the golden city of learning and culture described in *The History and Description of Africa,* a famous 16th-century travel book by al-Hasan ibn Muhammad al-Wezzan al-Fasi (known in the West as Leo Africanus). Instead, Caillie wrote, "the city is nothing but a mass of ill-looking houses built of earth. Timbuktu and its environs present the most monotonous and barren scene I ever beheld."

2298. European explorers to sight Mount Kilimanjaro were the German missionaries and explorers Johannes Rebmann and Ludwig Krapf, who sighted the snowcapped volcano in May 1848. Kilimanjaro is the highest mountain in Africa and is located in northeastern Tanzania.

2299. European explorer to cross the Australian continent was John King, a member of the Burke and Wills expedition that set out north from Melbourne, Australia, in 1860. Four members of the group—Robert Burke, William Wills, King, and Charles Gray—reached the tidal marshes at the edge of the Gulf of Carpentaria, on the northern coast of the continent. On the return trip, madness and hunger claimed the lives of Burke, Wills, and Gray. King survived with the help of aborigines, who traded food for birds he shot with his rifle. He was rescued by a relief party in 1861.

2300. European explorer to find the source of the White Nile was John Hanning Speke, the Scottish explorer, who in 1858 was the first European to see Lake Victoria, the largest lake in Africa, and to correctly identify it as the Nile's source. Speke found the outlet from which the Nile flowed, Ripon Falls, on July 28, 1862. Lake Victoria is mainly in Tanzania and Uganda.

2301. European explorer to cross Africa from coast to coast was the English explorer Verney Lovett Cameron, a naval officer. With the sponsorship of the Royal Geographical Society, he led an expedition in 1873 from Zanzibar to locate and aid the missionary David Livingstone, lost somewhere in East Africa. Soon after his arrival, Cameron learned that Livingston had died. He then pushed on to Lake Tanganyika, followed the lake's outlet to the Congo-Zambezi watershed, and, after an arduous journey, arrived at the Atlantic coast of Africa near Benguela, Angola, on November 7, 1875.

2302. Person to complete the "Explorer's Grand Slam" was British explorer David Hempleman-Adams, who over a period of 15 years visited the North and South magnetic and geographic poles on foot and scaled the highest mountains on all seven continents. The last of his destinations was the geographic North Pole, which he reached on April 28, 1998.

EXPLORATION—CIRCUMNAVIGATIONS

2303. Circumnavigation of Africa was sponsored by Necho II, an Egyptian pharaoh of the 26th dynasty, circa 580 BCE. According to the Greek historian Herodotus, the expedition was successful, for Necho's captains returned to report that they had seen the sun move to the north as they rounded the southern tip of Africa. A later, unsuccessful attempt was led by Eudoxus of Cyzicus, a Greek navigator of the second century BCE. With the sponsorship of the king of Egypt, Ptolemy III Euergetes (reigned 246–222 BCE), he embarked with three ships from Gades (now Cádiz, Spain) and sailed down the west coast of Africa. The expedition was lost somewhere near the Gulf of Guinea.

2304. Circumnavigation of Britain was probably accomplished by the Greek explorer and astronomer Pytheas of Massalia (now Marseilles, France) circa 324 BCE. According to the Greek historian Polybius, Pytheas was the first to give an accurate estimate of the circumference of Britain—4,000 miles (6,400 kilometers)—and visited a place he called Thule, possibly present-day Iceland or Norway.

2305. Circumnavigation of the world was accomplished by an expedition that was sponsored by Spain and led by the Portuguese-born captain-general Ferdinand Magellan. Seeking a westward sea route past the continent of South America to the Spice Islands (modern Indonesia), Magellan embarked with five ships and a crew of 280 men from the port of Sanlúcar, Spain, on September 20, 1519. In November 1520 the fleet made the perilous passage

EXPLORATION— CIRCUMNAVIGA-
TIONS—*continued*

through the Strait of Magellan, the first ships to do so, and headed west into the southern Pacific, not reaching land again until March 1521. On April 27, 1521, Magellan was killed in a battle on the island of Mactan (now part of the Philippines). After many hardships, one of the ships, the *Vittoria,* under the command of the Basque seaman Juan Sebastian del Cano (also spelled d'Elcano or El Cano), arrived in Seville, Spain, on September 8, 1522. The 18 Europeans aboard—about half of the 35 men from the original crew who survived the trip—were the first humans to circumnavigate the world.

2306. Sea captain to circumnavigate the world was the English mariner, pirate, and explorer Francis Drake. At the end of 1577, at the request of Queen Elizabeth I, he sailed west from Plymouth, England, with five small ships (soon reduced to three) and 164 men. Passing through the Strait of Magellan, Drake scourged the Spanish-occupied west coast of South America, sailed as far north as Vancouver, Canada, anchored at present-day San Francisco, CA, USA, concluded a treaty with the sultan of the Spice Islands, rounded Africa, and returned to Plymouth harbor on September 26, 1580, with his ship, *The Golden Hind,* laden with gold, jewels, and spices.

2307. Woman to circumnavigate the world was Baré, whose full name is unknown. Disguised as a man, she sailed as a botanist's assistant on the French ship *Étoile* in an expedition to Tierra del Fuego in 1767, then to Tahiti (where her ruse was discovered), and finally back to France.

2308. Circumnavigation of the world from west to east was accomplished in 1772–75 by an expedition under the commanded of the English explorer and navigator James Cook. Seeking to confirm reports of an unexplored southern continent, Cook's ship, the *Resolution* and a consort ship, the *Adventure,* left Plymouth, England, on July 13, 1772. The two vessels rounded Africa, crossed the Antarctic Circle to 70 degrees south latitude in January 1773, headed east to New Zealand, and explored the South Pacific. They returned to England in July 1775.

2309. Circumnavigation of Australia was completed by the English navigator Matthew Flinders in 1803. Commanding the *Investigator,* Flinders sailed north from Port Jackson (now Sydney) on July 22, 1802. After charting the east coast of Australia and the Gulf of Carpen-

taria on the north, he charted the western and southern coasts, passing Van Diemen's Land (Tasmania), which he had circumnavigated in 1795. The *Investigator* returned to Port Jackson on June 9, 1803.

2310. Circumnavigation of Antarctica was successfully completed in 1819–21 by a Russian expedition under Fabian Gottlieb von Bellingshausen (in Russian, Fadey Fadeyevich Bellingsauzen), an Estonian-born Russian naval officer and scientist. Commanding the sloops *Vostok* and *Mirny,* von Bellingshausen led a close-in circumnavigation of the ice-bound continent and may have been the first to spot Antarctica itself, on January 28, 1820, although that honor was also claimed by the English explorer Edward Bransfield and the American captain Nathaniel Palmer. In January 1821 Bellingshausen discovered and named two islands, Peter I and Alexander I, the first land definitely sighted within the Antarctic Circle. These were believed to be part of the mainland until 1940, when an American expedition discovered ice channels separating them from Antarctica proper.

2311. Polar circumnavigation of the earth was completed on April 11, 1982, when Ranulph Fiennes and Charles Burton of the British Transglobe Expedition returned to the North Pole after a circumnavigation through the South Pole.

EXPLORATION—POLAR

2312. Sighting of Antarctica has been claimed by Europeans from Russia, England, and America, but may in fact have taken place circa 650 CE by a Maori navigator. According to Maori legend, a war canoe under the command of the mariner Ui-te-Rangiora sailed south from New Zealand and encountered the Antarctic icepack.

2313. Expedition to sail around the northernmost point of Asia was led by Semyon Ivanov Dezhnev, a Russian trader and explorer. In 1648 Dezhnev and a group of Russian adventurers sailed in small boats several hundred miles through the Arctic Ocean along the northern coast of Siberia, rounded Siberia's forbidding northeastern tip, threaded down through the Bering Strait (the narrow channel between Siberia and North America), and finally entered the Pacific Ocean. This route, icebound for most of the year, was not traveled again until 1878. On this voyage, Dezhnev may also have been the first European to see Alaska.

2314. European explorer in North America to reach the Arctic by land was Samuel Hearne, an English Canadian in the employ of the Hudson's Bay Company. In 1770–72, he was sent on an expedition north from Fort Prince of Wales to search for a possible overland route to Asia. In July 1770 Hearne arrived at the mouth of the Coppermine River, which empties into the Arctic Ocean. Hearne was accompanied on the 5,000 mile round trip through the Northwest Territories only by an Indian guide and the guide's eight wives.

2315. Navigation of the Northeast Passage was accomplished by an expedition under Nils Adolf Erik Nordenskjöld, a Swedish geologist, geographer, mineralogist, and explorer. An experienced Arctic sailor, Nordenskjöld made several voyages to Spitsbergen Island, Greenland, the Kara Sea, and the mouth of the Yenisei River in Siberia before captaining the *Vega* in 1878 in a voyage around the Arctic coast of Europe and Siberia to the Bering Strait and the Pacific Ocean.

2316. International Polar Year was organized in 1882 by the eleven member nations of the first International Polar Commission, which met in 1879 in Hamburg, Germany. Several research stations for oceanographic, meteorological, and geophysical work were set up in the Arctic. One station for Antarctic research was established by Germany on Britain's South Georgia, an island in the South Atlantic. A second International Polar Year took place in 1932–33.

2317. Explorers to winter in Antarctica were the members of the Belgian exploration vessel *Belgica*, under the command of Adrien Victor Joseph, Baron de Gerlache de Gomery. It was the first purely scientific expedition to the southern continent. In 1898, the ship became locked in pack ice. The crew, the first humans to survive a winter in Antarctica, spent the next 13 months learning how to deal with the intense cold. Gerlache's mate on the *Belgica* was Roald Amundsen, who later led the first expedition to reach the South Pole.

2318. Expedition to sail through the Northwest Passage took place in 1903–05, when the 47-ton sloop *Gjöa*, with a crew of six commanded by the Norwegian polar explorer Roald Engelbregt Gravning Amundsen, sailed east to west along the northern Canadian coast, ending at Herschel Island in the Yukon.

2319. Explorer to reach the South Pole was Roald Engelbregt Gravning Amundsen of Norway. Amundsen's expedition departed from Norway in June 1910, and sailed to the Bay of Whales, Antarctica, where they organized a base camp. On October 19, 1911, Amundsen set out with four colleagues, along with 52 sled dogs. They arrived at the South Pole on December 14, 1911.

2320. Dogsled crossing of the Northwest Passage was accomplished by Knud Johan Victor Rasmussen, an explorer and ethnologist of Danish and Eskimo descent. Rasmussen set out to observe and collect information on every known Eskimo group in an effort to establish the ethnological unity of Eskimo culture. He departed by dogsled on September 7, 1921, from Upernavik, Greenland, crossed northern Canada and the Arctic pack ice, and reached Point Barrow, AK, USA, on May 23, 1924. His book *Across Arctic America* (1927) detailed his journey.

2321. Flight over the North Pole was long credited to an American, U.S. Navy lieutenant Richard Byrd, who claimed to have overflown the pole on May 9, 1926. Evidence found in Byrd's diary and published in 1996 indicated that Byrd probably turned back 150 miles short of his goal and lied about it. The first undisputed overflight of the North Pole was achieved by Italian explorer Umberto Nobile, Norwegian explorer Roald Amundsen, and American coalmining heir Lincoln Ellsworth on May 12, 1926.

2322. Vessel to cross the Northwest Passage west to east was the Royal Canadian Mounted Police patrol ship *St. Roch*. In 1942, it became only the second vessel ever to navigate the Northwest Passage across the top of Canada and the first to do so from west to east.

2323. Women to winter in Antarctica were Edith "Jackie" Ronne and Jennie Darlington, who spent the year 1947 at East Base on Stonington Island with their husbands, explorer Finn Ronne and pilot Harry Darlington, as part of a private 23-person expedition.

2324. Airplane flight to land at the North Pole was made by a ski-wheeled U.S. Air Force C-47, which landed on May 3, 1952. It took off from Fletcher's Ice Island, about 115 miles (185 kilometers) from the pole, carrying ten American military officials and scientists. It was piloted by Lieutenant Colonel William Pershing Benedict of San Rafael, CA, USA, and copilot Lieutenant Colonel Joseph Otis Fletcher of Shawnee, OK, USA.

EXPLORATION—POLAR—*continued*

2325. Discovery of the North Pole is thought by many to have been made on April 6, 1909, by a dogsled expedition led by American explorer Robert Edwin Peary, who was accompanied by his African-American assistant, Matthew Alexander Henson, and four Eskimos. Henson is believed to have actually set foot on the pole first, although Peary is shown in photographs holding a flag at the site. This claim was disputed by Frederick A. Cook, who maintained that he had reached the pole by dogsled on April 21, 1908. Both claims were ruled incorrect in 1997 by American historian Robert M. Bryce, who said that neither explorer succeeded in reaching 90 latitude N. The first person known for certain to have set foot on the pole was another American, Lieutenant Colonel Joseph Otis Fletcher of Shawnee, OK, USA, who arrived by plane on May 3, 1952.

2326. Woman to fly over the North Pole was the American explorer, geographer, military advisor, and heiress Louise Arner Boyd. Boyd began her career as a polar explorer in 1924 at the age of 37 and financed a number of her own expeditions, including one to search for the Norwegian Arctic explorer Roald Amundsen, who disappeared during a rescue mission in 1928. In 1955, when she was 68 years old, she chartered an airplane and flew over the North Pole.

2327. Airplane flight to land at the South Pole carried an American expedition that landed on October 31, 1956, at 8:30 A.M. Greenwich time. U.S. Navy rear admiral George John Dufek and six officers landed in the *Que Sera Sera,* a twin-engine Douglas R4D Skytrain transport plane. The flight was part of Operation Deepfreeze, commanded by Admiral Richard Evelyn Byrd and undertaken in connection with the International Geophysical Year 1957–58. Dufek, commander of the Naval Support Force, was in charge of logistic support for the scientific body of the expedition. He became the first American to set foot on the South Pole.

2328. Explorer to set foot on both the North and South Poles was an American, Dr. Albert Paddock Crary. On May 3, 1952, he visited the North Pole by aircraft. On February 12, 1961, he reached the South Pole by tracked vehicle as part of a scientific expedition.

2329. Surface ship to reach the North Pole was the Soviet nuclear-powered icebreaker *Arktika,* formerly the *Leonid Brezhnev,* built in 1974 at the Baltic Shipbuilding and Engineering Works, Leningrad, USSR (now St. Petersburg, Russia). Under the command of Captain O. G. Pashnin, the ship reached the geographic North Pole on August 17, 1975.

2330. Expedition to cross Antarctica by dogsled and foot was the Trans-Antarctica Expedition, led by an American, Will Steger, and a Frenchman, Jean-Louis Étienne. The 3,741-mile (6,019-kilometer) journey, which began on August 1, 1989, traversed the continent from the Antarctic Peninsula, crossed the South Pole, and ended at a Soviet base on the eastern coast in 1990. Financing was provided primarily by adventure product manufacturers including DuPont and W.L. Gore & Associates.

2331. Traverse of Antarctica on foot took place in 1989–90, when Reinhold Messner and Arved Fuchs trekked 1,800 miles (2,896 kilometers) without vehicles or sled dogs across the southern continent. The two men departed on November 13, 1989, walking and skiing from the coast to the South Pole. From there they proceeded to McMurdo Bay on the Ross Sea, where they arrived on February 12, 1990.

F

FAMILY—BIRTH

2332. Depiction of a pregnant woman known is the "Venus of Laussel," a figure carved in relief on the wall of a limestone cave in Laussel, France. Her left hand rests on her belly and her right hand holds a curved horn. The image was carved during the Gravettian period, circa 25,000 to 20,000 BCE.

2333. Depiction of a woman in labor may be the figure engraved on the walls of Le Gabillou cave in the Dordogne region of southern France, dated to approximately 13,000 BCE. It shows a reclining woman with a pregnant belly and raised legs. Another cave in France, La Magdelaine, contains a relief from about 10,000 BCE of two pregnant women in postures suggestive of labor.

2334. Pregnancy test was developed circa 1500 BCE by the ancient Egyptians, who understood that a substance in the urine of a pregnant woman causes seeds to germinate. A similar test was used to determine the sex of the baby. The pregnant woman would urinate over two piles of seeds, one of barley, the other of wheat; the barley grew faster if the baby was a girl, the wheat if the baby was a boy.

2335. Cesarean operation of record, though its authenticity is questioned, was said to have been performed circa 1500 in Sigershauffen, Switzerland, by a pig gelder, Jacob Nufer, to prevent his wife and baby from dying in childbirth. Surgical childbirth, performed on a dying woman in the hope of saving the baby, was done in ancient Rome and is mentioned in the Talmud. The name *caesar*, from which the words *czar (tsar)* and *kaiser* are derived, comes from the Latin word *caedere*, "to cut," and is thought to have been adopted by the ancient Roman family of the Julii after one of its members was born surgically.

2336. Manual for midwives was *The Garden of Roses for Pregnant Women and for Midwives*, written by Eucharius Roslin at the request of Catherine, Duchess of Brunswick, and published in Worms, Germany, in 1513. An English edition, *The Byrthe of Mankynde*, was published in 1555.

2337. Incubator for premature babies was a warming box invented in 1588 by the Italian natural philosopher Giambattista della Porta.

2338. Woman to write a book on childbirth was Louise Boursier (1563–1636), teacher, author, and midwife to the French court for 27 years. She delivered the future Louis XIII and six children of King Henry IV. In 1609, she wrote a book on midwifery and childbirth practices that was expanded in 1759 by her descendant, Angélique le Boursier du Courdray, who was also a midwife.

2339. Cesarean birth fully documented was performed by the German physician Jeremiah Trautmann in 1610. The mother died 25 days later, probably from peritonitis.

2340. Obstetrical forceps for use in childbirth were the invention of Peter Chamberlen, a surgeon of French Huguenot ancestry who practiced in England and who assisted Queen Anne, wife of King James I, and Queen Henrietta Maria, wife of King Charles I, when they gave birth. In approximately the year 1630, Chamberlen devised an instrument with two straight metal blades that could be inserted into a laboring mother's vagina, allowing the physician to pull the baby out by the head, if necessary.

2341. Physician to teach obstetrics and midwifery on a scientific basis was William Smellie of Lanark, Scotland. In 1739, after many years' experience as an obstetrician, Smellie began lecturing in London. He encouraged his students to be present as observers when he assisted at births and made leather-covered dummies on which they could practice. He was also the first scientist to make exact measurements of the human pelvis.

2342. Artificial insemination of a human being of record took place in France in 1785. French physician M. Thouret of the University of Paris used a tin syringe to transfer his own semen to his wife, who he believed was sterile. She successfully conceived and bore a healthy child.

2343. Ether as an anesthetic in childbirth was introduced by Walter Channing, dean of the medical school and professor of midwifery and medical jurisprudence at Harvard University. The first patient upon whom he used it successfully was Fanny Longfellow, whose delivery he attended in 1847 at the Boston Lying-In Hospital, Boston, MA, USA.

2344. Queen to deliver a child under anesthesia was Queen Victoria of England. In 1853, at her request, she delivered her seventh child, Prince Leopold, under chloroform.

2345. Quintuplets known to survive infancy were the Dionne quints—Emilie, Yvonne, Cecile, Marie, and Annette—of Callander, Ontario, Canada. The five identical girls developed from three successive twinnings of a single embryo; the sixth sibling died in the third month of pregnancy. They were born on May 28, 1934, to Elzire Dionne, who already had six children, and her husband Oliva. Allen R. Dafoe was the attending physician. The infants weighed an average of 2 pounds 11 ounces each.

2346. Birth to be televised for the public took place in the United States on December 2, 1952, and was televised by KOA, Denver, CO, USA, over 49 stations of the National Broadcasting Company. The birth was that of Gordon Campbell Kerr, who weighed 5 pounds 7 ounces. He was delivered by cesarean section in the hospital delivery room of the Colorado General Hospital of the University of Colorado Medical School in Denver. The parents were

FAMILY—BIRTH—*continued*

Lillian Kerr and John R. Kerr of Denver. The telecast was part of the "March of Medicine" program, presented in conjunction with the annual clinical meeting of the American Medical Association.

2347. Nonuplets of record were born on June 13, 1971, to 29-year-old Geraldine Brodrick in Sydney, Australia. Brodrick had taken experimental pituitary hormone treatment to address what was believed to be a serious hormone imbalance (in fact, her medical problems were the result of an undiscovered tumor). All nine of the infants died soon after birth.

2348. Test-tube baby was born to Lesley Brown of Bristol, England, who gave birth to Louise Brown in Oldham General Hospital, London, England, on July 25, 1978. Louise was conceived in vitro on November 10, 1977, with the aid of gynecologist Patrick Steptoe and physiologist Robert Edwards, who fertilized an egg from Lesley Brown with sperm from her husband and implanted the fertilized egg in her womb.

2349. Test-tube twins conceived through in-vitro fertilization, Stephen and Amanda Mays, were delivered by Radmila Mays on June 5, 1981, at the Queen Victoria Medical Centre, Melbourne, Australia.

2350. Test-tube triplets conceived through in-vitro fertilization, two girls and a boy, were born on June 8, 1983, at Flinders Medical Centre, Adelaide, Australia.

2351. Frozen embyro to come successfully to birth was a baby known to the public as "Zoe," delivered on April 11, 1984, at the Queen Victoria Hospital, Melbourne, Australia. The embryo was conceived in vitro under the supervision of researchers Linda Mohr and Alan Frounson, frozen in liquid nitrogen for two months, then thawed and placed in her mother's womb for normal development.

2352. International program to promote safe birth was the Safe Motherhood Initiative, launched in 1987 at the International Conference for Safe Motherhood in Nairobi, Kenya. Backed by the World Health Organization, the United Nations Population Fund, UNICEF, the World Bank, the Population Council and the International Planned Parenthood Federation, the Safe Motherhood Initiative was intended to raise awareness of the fight against maternal mortality.

2353. Septuplets to survive birth were four boys and three girls, born to Bobbi and Kenny McCaughey in December 1997 at the Iowa Methodist Medical Center in Des Moines, IA, USA. The cesarean-section deliveries were performed within a six-minute period by doctors Paula Mahone and Karen Drake.

2354. Childbirth streamed live on the Internet occurred on June 16, 1998, at the Arnold Palmer Hospital for Women and Children in Orlando, FL, USA. The mother, Elizabeth Oliver, gave birth to a boy named Sean at 10:40 A.M. Eastern Daylight Time after labor was induced at 6 A.M.. The attending doctor was Steve Carlin. A live video feed of the birth was digitized and streamed to AHN.com, a World Wide Web site sponsored by America's Health Network, a healthcare information television cable network based in Orlando. Some 1.4 million people worldwide linked to the web site and viewed the birth as it occurred.

2355. Octuplets known to have survived birth were born at St. Luke's Episcopal Hospital in Houston, TX, USA, to Nkem Chukwu, age 27, and Iyke Louis Udobi, her husband, both of whom were American citizens born in Nigeria. The children were conceived with the use of fertility drugs. One daughter, Chukwuebuka Nkemjika, was born twelve weeks prematurely on December 8, 1998. The others were born by cesarean section on December 20 and ranged in weight from 10.3 ounces to 1 pound 16 ounces. Five were girls: Chidinma Anulika, Chinecherem Nwabugwu, Chimaijem Otito, Chijindu Chidera, and Chinagorom Chidiebere. Two were boys: Chukwubuikem Maduabuchi and Chijoke Chinendum. The tiniest baby, Chijindu Chidera, died of heart and lung failure a few days later.

FAMILY—BIRTH CONTROL

2356. Contraceptives to avoid pregnancy were used by women in ancient Egypt circa 1500 BCE. They made wads of plant fibers and covered them with a jelly that inhibited conception. One such jelly was made of crocodile dung and sour milk; another was made of honey, dates, and powdered acacia spikes. The active ingredient, found in both milk and acacia, was lactic acid.

2357. Comprehensive treatise on contraception and birth was *On Midwifery and the Diseases of Women,* written circa 150 CE by the Greek gynecologist, obstetrician, and pediatrician Soranus of Ephesus (modern Selçuk, Turkey). It contained detailed descriptions of many birth control practices, as well as accounts of podalic (feet-first) and breech (posterior-first) births. In the West, it was considered the standard work on women's and infants' health until the dawn of scientific medicine in the 16th century.

2358. Condoms were described by the Italian physician Gabriele Fallopio (also known by the Latinized version of his name, Fallopius), in 1564. They were made from the washed intestines of pigs and other domesticated animals and were intended to prevent the spread of sexually transmitted diseases, not as a method of birth control.

2359. Recommendation that condoms be used for birth control was contained in the French publication *L'Escole des Filles,* which appeared in Paris in 1655. The anonymous author suggested the use of a linen sheath to prevent conception.

2360. Manual on birth control written for the use of ordinary people was *Every Woman's Handbook,* by the radical journalist Richard Carlile, published in London, England, in 1826.

2361. Vaginal cap method of contraception, the forerunner of the modern diaphragm, was invented in 1838 by the German physician Friedrich Wilde. It was found to be only moderately effective, and did not become widely popular until the introduction of effective spermicides in the post-World War II period.

2362. Abortion by vacuum aspiration was described circa 1865 by gynecologist James Young Simpson of Edinburgh, Scotland. The method was called "dry cupping," and involved applying suction to the uterus to draw out the unborn baby. The modern procedure of vacuum aspiration, widely used in the latter part of the 20th century in countries that allowed abortion, was a refinement of dry cupping.

2363. Family planning clinic offering contraceptive information to women was opened in 1882 in Amsterdam, the Netherlands, by Aletta Jacobs. Jacobs was the first woman admitted to a Dutch university, from which she graduated in 1879; the first woman to practice medicine in Holland; and the first Dutch woman to claim the right to vote, in 1883. Her clinic prescribed the use of the Dutch cap, a rubber barrier that fits over the cervix.

2364. Vasectomy as a means of contraception was introduced by Dr. Harry Sharp of Indianapolis, IN, USA, in 1899. Vasectomies were performed earlier by Felix Gruyon, a French surgeon, to speed the healing of prostate operations. A British surgeon, Sir Astley Cooper, laid the groundwork for human vasectomies in 1823 through an experiment in which he severed the vas deferens of a dog. The dog retained the urge to mate but sired no pups.

2365. Pamphlet on birth control from a feminist perspective was "Family Limitation," written in 1914 by the American family planning advocate Margaret Sanger.

2366. Modern nation to make abortions freely available was the Soviet Union, which offered women free abortions on demand beginning in 1920. Following World War II, in which more than 20 million Soviets were killed, abortions were prohibited by Josef Stalin. They were eventually legalized again, after which abortion became the Soviet Union's most common method of birth control.

2367. Intrauterine device (IUD) that was practical was the contraceptive coil invented by the German researcher Ernst Grafenberg in 1928. It was a small spiral of silver thread designed to be inserted into the uterus, where, as a foreign body, it attracted large numbers of the woman's white blood cells. The white blood cells also destroyed fertilized eggs before implantation.

2368. Rhythm method of birth control was proposed in 1929 by physician Hermann Knaus of Berlin, Germany, and independently a few months later by the Japanese doctor Kyusaku Ogino. Both noted that ovulation occurs at a predictable time in the menstrual cycle of most women, and that understanding the pattern or rhythm of a woman's cycle allows her to avoid intercourse at the times when she is likely to become pregnant. In 1964, physicians John and Evelyn Billings of Australia were the first to propose that observation of the cyclical changes in cervical mucus could aid women in predicting their most and least fertile days.

2369. State-supported family planning clinics were opened in the cities of Mysore and Bangalore, in the Indian state of Mysore, in 1930.

2370. Birth-control pill was developed over a five-year period by Gregory Pincus, a biochemist at the Worcester Foundation for Experimental Biology, Shrewsbury, MA, USA, and John Rock, a gynecologist at Harvard Medical School, Cambridge, MA, USA. It used synthetic progesterone and estrogen to repress ovula-

FAMILY—BIRTH CONTROL—*continued*

tion in women. Clinical tests were performed in 1954. The project was initially commissioned and funded by birth-control pioneer Margaret Sanger and heiress Katherine Dexter McCormick. The contraceptive was intended to be "without danger, sure, simple, practical, suitable for all women, and ethically acceptable for the couple." The first brand to be authorized for sale by prescription was Enovid-10, made by the G.D. Searle Company, Chicago, IL, USA, which received approval by the U.S. Food and Drug Administration on May 9, 1960.

2371. Copper IUD was designed in 1970 by Chilean physician Jaime Zipper. Copper added to a plastic IUD resulted in less uterine bleeding.

2372. Country to limit births as national policy was the People's Republic of China, which instituted a one-child-per-couple population-control policy in 1979. Severe penalities were imposed on the family if more children were born. Circa 1988, rural familes were allowed to have a second child if the first was a girl. This was in reaction to increased rates of infanticide of girl babies, especially in rural areas.

2373. Abortion pill developed through medical research was RU 486 (mifepristone), an artificial steroid discovered by French researcher Étienne-Émile Baulieu. When taken during the early stages of pregnancy, RU 486 blocks the action of the hormone progesterone, halting pregnancy, triggering menstruation, and flushing the embryo out of the uterus. It was available for sale in France on September 23, 1988.

2374. Condom designed to be worn by women was a soft plastic pouch that was introduced in the United States under the brand name Reality in 1993. The manufacturer was the Female Health Company, Chicago, IL, USA.

2375. Thermoformed plastic condom was invented by Robert Miller and colleagues at the Canadian pharmaceutical and medical supply firm of Ortho-McNeil Inc. The condom was made of formed polyesterurethane that the company claimed was stronger and more virus-resistant than rubber. Ortho received a patent for the product on October 17, 1995.

FAMILY—CHILDREN

2376. Dolls were made in prehistory; many scholars believe that the doll was the first toy. The earliest known dolls were found in ancient Egyptian burial sites dating from circa 3000 BCE; they were made from painted wood with hair of stringed beads.

2377. Written record of wet-nursing was contained in a Sumerian lullaby, found on a cuneiform tablet dated to the period of the Third Dynasty of the city of Ur (modern Tel-el-Muqayyar in Iraq), circa 2100–2004 BCE. A wet-nurse is a nursing woman who breast-feeds another woman's child for pay or services.

2378. Contract terms for wet-nursing are first specified in the Code of Hammurabi, the Babylonian law document dated to circa 1792–50 BCE.

2379. Baby bottles known were pottery containers found on the island of Cyprus and dated to circa 900 BCE. Instead of a nipple, the baby suckled a piece of cloth.

2380. Depiction of a potty appears on a Greek wine jug from Athens in the late fifth century BCE. It shows a large bowl set on a thick base. A little child sits in the bowl, with its legs dangling out of two holes in front. The jug is now in the British Museum.

2381. Depiction of a child riding a "kiddie car" was a woodcut illustration that accompanied the "Versehung des Leibs," a treatise, in verse form, on how to take care of children. It was written by a German monk in the 15th century.

2382. Orphan export program was instituted by King James I in 1619 to provide colonists and cheap labor for the English settlements in America while reducing the number of state-supported orphans in England's cities. Orphans and street children were seized and herded aboard transports by gangs who were paid per child delivered. In 1627 alone, some 1,500 children were transported to the Virginia colony.

2383. Baby carriage was owned by the family of William Cavendish, the third Duke of Devonshire, of Chatsworth, England, and was made there in 1733 by William Ken. Commercial manufacture of baby carriages began in London in 1850.

2384. Talking doll was patented in 1823 by Johann Nepomuk Maelzel, the German maker of musical instruments and mechanical toys. When the doll was squeezed, air was forced through shaped chambers inside the body that made sounds approximating the words "mama" and "papa."

2385. Perambulator of the modern type, with four wheels, a deep cradle-like body, and a retractable hood, was invented in 1848 by a New Yorker, Charles Burton. Regular manufacture began in London, England, in 1850.

2386. Playground of the modern type with apparatus designed for play was opened in 1859 in Queen's Park and Philips Park, Manchester, England. The playground featured horizontal bars and swings.

2387. Mass-produced infant formula available on the market was introduced in Germany in 1867 by Baron Justus von Liebig. Called Liebig's Soluble Food for Babies, it was advertised as containing the same ingredients as mother's milk. Liebig began marketing the product internationally in 1868.

2388. Stuffed toy bear was the teddy bear, named after U.S. president Theodore Roosevelt. Two different toymakers—Morris Michtom of Brooklyn, NY, USA, and Margaret Stieff of Germany—were inspired to make cuddly bear dolls after they saw a cartoon that first appeared in the *Washington Evening Star* on November 18, 1902. It showed Roosevelt, a prodigious hunter, deciding not to shoot some bear cubs and their mother.

2389. Boy scout troop officially registered was the first Glasgow Scout Troop, founded on January 26, 1908, in Glasgow, Scotland, by Captain Robert Young. Members were drawn from four local schools: Hillhead High, Glasgow High, Glasgow Academy, and Kelvinside Academy.

2390. Raggedy Ann doll was a handmade rag doll that John Gruelle gave to his young daughter Marcella in 1915 when she was dying of tuberculosis. Gruelle, who was a political cartoonist for the *Indianapolis Star* in Indianapolis, IN, USA, made up stories about the doll. He later published a collection of these stories, which made the doll so popular that it was manufactured commercially beginning in 1918.

2391. Mass-produced cereal food for infants was Pablum, developed in 1928 by the Canadian pediatrician Alan Brown of the Hospital for Sick Children in Toronto. Pablum contained vitamin-enriched, finely milled grain that was precooked to make it easy to prepare and digest.

2392. Disposable diapers were Boaters, invented in 1950 by Marion Donovan, a mother from New York, NY, USA. They consisted of an absorbent pad attached to a waterproof backing and were fastened on the baby with snaps. The first mass-market disposable diapers were Pampers, introduced in Peoria, IL, by Procter and Gamble of Cincinnati, OH, in 1961. They cost ten cents each. After consumers complained about the price, the company withdrew them from the market and reintroduced them in Sac-ramento, CA, USA, in 1966 for six cents each. The first disposable diapers with adhesive tabs to replace safety pins were Kimbies, made by Kimberly-Clark, Dallas, TX, in the early 1970s. Procter and Gamble's Luvs, introduced in 1976, were the first to come with an elastic fit.

2393. Child whose parents had both flown in space was Yelena Andrianovna Nikolayeva, born on June 8, 1964, in what was then the Soviet Union and is now Russia. She was the daughter of Soviet cosmonauts Valentina Vladimirovna Nikolayeva Tereshkova, who in 1961 had become the first woman to fly in space, and Andrian Nikolayev, who had piloted the *Vostok 3* spacecraft in August 1962.

2394. Collapsible baby stroller that was successful on the international market was the Aprica, introduced by the Kassai Company of Japan in 1970. Marketing in North America began in 1980.

FAMILY—MARRIAGE

2395. Marriage and divorce laws extant were part of the Babylonian law code promulgated by Hammurabi (1792–50 BCE) in what is now Iraq. Married couples were required to execute a prenuptial marriage contract setting forth their responsibilities for debts, maintenance, and labor. The husband had the power to divorce his wife, but was obliged to return her dowry. If the couple had children, the mother retained custody of them and was entitled to child support from their father, but she was not free to remarry until the children were grown. A woman who was accused of being a "bad wife" could be exiled or enslaved by her husband. She could bring suit against him for cruelty in the hope of winning a legal separation and the return of her dowry, but her decision would be influenced by the knowledge that if she lost her suit, she would be executed by drowning.

2396. Diamond engagement ring of record was presented in 1477 to Mary, daughter of Charles the Bold, Duke of Burgundy, at her home in Ghent (now in Belgium), by Archduke Maximilian, son of Holy Roman Emperor Frederick III. The golden ring was set with diamonds in the shape of the letter *M*.

2397. Personal ad placed by an individual in search of marriage is thought to have been the notice that appeared on July 19, 1695, in the *Collection for the Improvement of Husbandry and Trade,* an English periodical. It said: "A Gentleman about 30 Years of Age, that says he has a Very Good Estate, would willingly Match Himself to some young Gentlewoman that has a fortune of £3,000 or thereabouts, and he will make Settlement to Content."

FAMILY—MARRIAGE—*continued*

2398. Bridal suite in a hotel was opened in 1844 by the Irving House, New York, NY, USA.

2399. Alimony payments were mandated under the Matrimonial Causes Act, passed by the British Parliament in 1857. It specified that husbands had a responsibility to provide for their former wives after the marriage was ended in divorce or annulment.

2400. Marital property reform law allowing wives to retain control of their own assets was enacted in Sweden in 1920. The law gave wives and husbands separate control of their own property and provided for a fair division of jointly owned property if the marriage ended.

FINANCE—BANKING

2401. Banking regulations are contained in the Code of Hammurabi, the collection of Babylonian laws from the second millennium (1792–50) BCE. One law pertains to embezzlement: "If any one be on a journey and entrust silver, gold, precious stones, or any movable property to another, and wish to recover it from him; if the latter do not bring all of the property to the appointed place, but appropriate it to his own use, then shall this man, who did not bring the property to hand it over, be convicted, and he shall pay fivefold for all that had been entrusted to him." Another covers banking contracts: "If any one give another silver, gold, or anything else to keep, he shall show everything to some witness, draw up a contract, and then hand it over for safe keeping. If he turn it over for safe keeping without witness or contract, and if he to whom it was given deny it, then he has no legitimate claim. If any one deliver silver, gold, or anything else to another for safe keeping, before a witness, but he deny it, he shall be brought before a judge, and all that he has denied he shall pay in full."

2402. Banker of record was Pythius, who operated a merchant banking business for Greek traders circa 600 BCE in what is now western Turkey.

2403. Municipal bank was a pawnshop opened in 1198 in Freising, Bavaria (now in Germany). The first public pawnshop in Europe, it was organized to provide state-regulated competition to the pawnshops operated as private enterprises. It accepted pledges and made loans at reasonable interest.

2404. Joint-stock bank capitalized by a group of stockholders was the Bank of San Giorgio in Genoa, Italy, a flourishing center of the import-export trade in the Mediterranean in the late 13th century.

2405. Bank exchange where financial and commercial transactions could be carried out were columned arcades, or loggias, built in Italian cities, of which the Loggia dei Mercanti, opened in Bologna in 1382, may be the first.

2406. Central bank was the Bank of England, chartered by act of Parliament in 1694 as a joint-stock company. Located in London, it was originally founded to assist in paying the national debt incurred from wars in Ireland, France, and the Low Countries during the reign of William III. Subsequently it served as the chief banker and lender and controller of the money supply for the British government, as well as the lender of last resort for commercial banks.

2407. Savings bank was opened in Brunswick, Germany, in 1765. It was the first to serve private individuals, rather than businesses or municipalities.

2408. Bank clearinghouse to limit net payments among banks by offsetting their mutual transactions in London, England, in 1773 and in the United States in 1853. Earlier forms of the clearinghouse that were limited to trade were in use by Asian and European financiers circa 1300.

2409. Presidential bank in India was the Bank of Bengal, founded in 1806 by the British to supplement and westernize India's traditional, caste-based financial system. It was the first of several presidential banks.

2410. Global banking crisis began during the Panic of 1857, which started in the United States. A collapse in the value of railroad securities, coupled with the binding of bank assets in nonliquid railroad investments, forced some 1,415 American banks to suspend specie payments. Many banks went under. This created a money-market panic for investors in Great Britain and Europe. Germany was hit especially hard; many newly created German industrial banks failed.

2411. Postal giro system was established by Austria in 1883. The postal giro (from Latin *gyrus,* "turn around") is a service in which banks authorize direct transfer of funds among account holders via the mail. The practice did not spread to other countries until 1906, when Switzerland and Japan established similar postal giro systems.

2412. Credit union in the Western Hemisphere was founded in 1900 by legislative reporter Alphonse Desjardins in Lévis, Quebec, Canada.

2413. World bank was the International Bank for Reconstruction and Development, affiliated with the United Nations. It entered into force on December 27, 1945, when it was subscribed to by 21 countries, whose subscription amounted to US$7,173 million. The first loan was made on May 9, 1947, to France—a 30-year loan of US$250 million at 3.25 percent and of US$150 million at 3 percent.

2414. Bank to issue a credit card was the Franklin National Bank, Franklin Square, NY, USA, which did so on April 15, 1952. Customers charged their purchases to the bank, which made the payments and then billed the cardholder. The service was later extended to the bank's branches.

2415. Bank credit card to gain national acceptance was BankAmericard (later called Visa), issued by the Bank of America, San Francisco, CA, USA, in 1959. There was no membership fee or service charge. Full-scale services were offered to cardholders and merchants.

2416. Bank to install an automatic teller was the Chemical Bank, New York, NY, USA, which placed its first automatic teller machine (ATM) in operation at Rockville Center, Long Island, NY, on January 1969. A coded card inserted in an opening dispensed an envelope containing a set sum of cash.

2417. Third World country to default on its foreign debt was Mexico, whose treasury secretary, Jesus Silva Herzog, announced on August 20, 1982, that the country could not repay a US$60 billion foreign debt. The Mexican default led to similar defaults by some two dozen other countries.

2418. Virtual financial services company was First Virtual Holdings Inc., which opened for business exclusively on the Internet in 1994. It offered secure internet commerce services based on e-mail transactions. The company's physical headquarters were in San Diego, CA, USA.

FINANCE—INSURANCE

2419. Actuarial table was invented by the ancient Romans circa 220 CE. Mortality tables that calculated the risk of death for people at various ages were constructed for the Roman burial societies, which financed funeral expenses and paid pensions to the families of the deceased.

2420. Fire insurance company was the Hamburger General-Feur-Cassa (or Feuerkasse), established in December 1676 by the Ratsherren (city council) of Hamburg (now in Germany). Subscribers, mainly brewers and other business owners, held regular policies and paid fixed premiums. In case of fire, the policyholders received no more than 0.25 percent of the value of the lost property per annum.

2421. Marine insurance underwriters were active in London, England, in the late 17th century. The prominent insurance house Lloyd's of London got its start in 1688 at Edward Lloyd's London coffeehouse, located near the docks, a convenient meeting place for underwriters, bankers, merchants, shipowners, and captains.

2422. Life insurance company of record was founded in 1706 by the Bishop of Oxford and the financier Thomas Allen in London, England. The company, called the Amicable Society for a Perpetual Assurance Office, collected annual premiums from policyholders and paid the nominees of deceased members from a common fund.

2423. State-sponsored social security system was instituted beginning in 1883 by the German Reichstag under the leadership of Chancellor Otto von Bismarck, who hoped that a comprehensive program of social services would weaken the popularity of the German Social Democratic Party. The program began with a sickness insurance law that provided industrial workers with guaranteed medical care and cash benefits during illness. An 1884 law established compulsory worker accident insurance for selected industries. Pension funds for trade, industrial, and agricultural workers were founded in 1889; the funds were administered by the Imperial Insurance Office.

2424. Old age pension plan was passed in Germany in 1889 and enacted beginning on January 1, 1891. The Old Age Insurance Act required workers to pay premiums to a pension fund if they were over the age of 16 and earned more than 2,000 marks (approximately US$500) per year. Employers contributed an equal amount. Workers could collect their pensions beginning at age 70.

FINANCE—MARKETS

2425. Stock market was probably that of France, which began circa 1200, although centralized commodities trading may have developed even earlier in China and India. Trading in commercial bills of exchange at regional fairs was first regulated during the reign (1268–1314) of Philip IV (Philip the Fair).

FINANCE—MARKETS—*continued*

2426. Stock exchange was founded by the Van de Buerse (or Bursen) family of financiers in Bruges, Belgium. Circa 1450, bankers began to gather in front of their house, under the family's sign of three purses ("bursen"), to engage in securities trading. The word "bourse," French for stock market, derives from their name.

2427. Stock market brought down by speculation mania was the British stock market in 1720, during the South Sea Bubble, which ruined many British investors and greatly embarrassed the government. The main culprit was the South Sea Company, incorporated in 1711 to sell slaves and goods to Spain's American colonies. With Parliament's approval, in 1720 the company assumed the British national debt, planning to raise funds mainly by the rapid growth of its stock price and not by its trade business, which was much less successful than was generally known. Shareholders were promised huge returns on their investments, which led to heated speculation in South Sea stock and the quick rise and precipitous collapse of the British stock market. An inquiry revealed that several members of Parliament had speculated in the market and had received bribes from the company.

2428. Stock exchange known by that name was the London Stock Exchange, founded in 1773 by stockbrokers who had been exchanging securities on an informal basis. In 1801 a stock-exchange building was constructed in Chapel Court, Bartholomew Lane, London. Official rules for the exchange were established in 1802.

2429. Currency board in Africa was the West African Currency Board, established in the British West African colonies in 1912. It governed the issue of currency, mainly silver coins and bank notes, in the colonies of Nigeria, the Gold Coast (now Ghana), Gambia, Togoland, and the British Cameroons.

2430. Stock exchange member who was a woman was Irish-born Oonagh Keogh, who on July 9, 1925, was admitted to the floor of the Dublin Stock Exchange over the protests of several members of the Exchange Committee. Keogh's father was a trader, and she initially acted as the recorder of his transactions, later taking over his business when he became ill.

2431. West African money market was created in 1954, when the British colony of Gold Coast (now Ghana) issued a tranche of 90-day treasury bills.

2432. Japanese company to sell stock on United States stock exchanges was Sony KK, a consumer electronics firm founded in Tokyo, Japan, in 1946 by Ibuka Masaru and Morita Akio. Sony offered stock to American investors beginning in 1963 and was listed on the New York Stock Exchange beginning in 1970.

2433. Women to trade on the floor of the London Stock Exchange were allowed beginning in 1973.

2434. Day on which the Dow Jones industrial average broke 10,000 points was March 16, 1999. The Dow is an index of the stock performance of 30 prominent corporations, and its fluctuations are viewed as signs of market strength and decline at the New York Stock Exchange in New York, NY, USA. At 9:50 A.M., shortly after trading began, the Dow broke the 10,000 mark, reaching a high point of 10,001.78. It then pulled back, and by the close of trading, it was down to 9,930.47, a loss of 28.30 points for the day.

2435. Day on which the Dow Jones industrial average broke 11,000 points was May 3, 1999, 24 days after it crossed the 10,000-point mark. It rose 2.09 percent to reach 11,014.69.

FINANCE—MONEY

2436. IOU promissory note known to archeologists is a rock tablet about the size of a human palm. The text, scratched on the rock in the Akkadian cuneiform language, was written in Mesopotamia about the year 3,000 BCE. It contains a promise by two brothers, Pirhum and Samas-Musezib, to pay a certain merchant a quantity of fine barley or 2.5 shekels. The tablet is now in the collection of Smith College in Northampton, MA, USA.

2437. Government coinage is traditionally held to have been instituted circa 560 BCE by Croesus, the last king of Lydia, the fertile and wealthy region of western Anatolia (now Turkey). According to the Greek historian Herodotus, the Lydians were "the first to strike and use coins of gold and silver" with a fixed value. Croesus' coins were made first of electrum, an alloy of gold and silver, and then of pure gold on one side and pure silver on the other. They were stamped with the facing heads of a lion and a bull.

2438. Bill of exchange is mentioned in the *Discourse on Banking*, written circa 390 BCE in Athens, Greece, by Isocrates, an orator, pamphleteer, and teacher of rhetoric and political philosophy. He describes the practice of placing a sum in the hands of a banker and receiving a letter that could be used to secure funds from other bankers in distant cities.

2439. Penny called by that name was a silver coin minted circa 790 in Mercia (one of the kingdoms of Anglo-Saxon England) under the rule of King Offa. Probably first struck in Canterbury, the coins displayed the design influence of old Roman coinage as well as the deniers of the Carolingian Franks. They bore the king's name and title and the name of the minter.

2440. Paper money was issued in China in 994, during the Song dynasty, when metal for coinage was in short supply. To answer the need for an exchange medium, Chang-ho, the emperor's coinage official, ordered the imperial treasury to pay merchants in paper certificates that could later be exchanged for hard currency, with a three-year time limit. The certificates were known as *chia-tzu,* "credit money." Exchange notes that could be freely circulated without a time limit were introduced in 1189.

2441. Numismatics treatise was the *Chuan Chih (A Treatise on Coinage),* written in 1149 by the Chinese economist and collector Hung Tsun.

2442. Florin or *fiorini d'oro* was minted in Florence, Italy, in 1252. The gold coin, widely used and imitated in Europe, the Middle East, and northern Africa until the 17th century, was marked with a lily and a figure of John the Baptist. It weighed about 3.5 grams.

2443. Mill-driven coin press was invented by Leonardo da Vinci in Italy circa 1500. His water-driven press was able to produce more uniform coins more quickly; these were known as "milled money." Similar designs were adopted throughout Europe over the next two centuries.

2444. Shilling was issued in England by Henry VII in 1504. This coin, originally called a testoon, was worth one-twentieth of a pound sterling, or twelve pence, and bore a profile of Henry VII engraved by Alexander Bruchsal. It was renamed the shilling during the reign of Edward VI. No longer used in the United Kingdom, the shilling (now valued at 100 cents) is the basic monetary unit in the former British East African colonies of Kenya, Somalia, Tanzania, and Uganda.

2445. Thaler was struck in 1519 from silver mined at Joachimsthal in Bohemia (now Jáchymov, Czech Republic) under the authority of the Count of Schlick. The coin was known as the Joachimsthaler, or thaler, which became in various languages the daler, dalar, daalder, tallero, and, in English, the dollar.

2446. Mint fully mechanized was the mint in Paris, France, where milled coins were produced in 1645. The milled coins were more uniform and more attractive, and were harder to counterfeit.

2447. Bank notes were issued in 1658 by the Riksbank of Stockholm, Sweden.

2448. Check of record was issued in 1659. It was an order to pay a Mr. Delboe £400, issued to the London goldsmiths Morris and Clayton.

2449. Guinea was first minted in 1663 in England. The coins, made of gold mined in what is now the Republic of Guinea in West Africa, were initially worth £1.

2450. Copper coins in England were issued by the government in 1672. Earlier issues of copper coins were from private minters, not the state. The milled coinage was stamped with the image of Britannia.

2451. Dollar coin so denominated was the silver dollar issued by the British Sierra Leone Company in 1791, three years before the United States issued its first silver dollar. It was worth ten *macutas* (the local unit of value) and bore the image of a crouching lion.

2452. Coins minted with steam-powered machinery were copper two-penny and one-penny pieces minted in 1797 by Matthew Boulton, the steam engine pioneer, at his works in Birmingham, England. The British government provided Boulton with an initial contract for 50 tons of coins; eventually some 4,200 tons of copper coins were produced. Boulton went on to supply steam-powered minting machines to Russia, Spain, Denmark, Mexico, India, and the British Royal Mint.

2453. Copper-nickel coins were minted by Belgium in 1860. A cupronickel alloy with 25 percent nickel offered several advantages over pure copper, silver, or nickel, including less oxidation, higher durability, and lower cost to mint. Cupronickel coins replaced silver coinage in Britain in 1947. The alloy was used in the American nickel in 1866 and was later adopted as the outer layer in the dime and quarter.

2454. Cash register was invented in 1879 by James J. Ritty, a businessman from Dayton, OH, USA. While he was traveling to Europe by steamship, Ritty observed the workings of a recording device that marked the revolutions of the ship's propeller and gave the officers an accurate daily record of the speed of the boat. When he returned to the United States, he invented a machine for registering receipts of

FINANCE—MONEY—*continued*

cash and totaling them. It was not accurate, but the following year, 1880, he produced a machine that gave some evidence of being practical. In 1884 the National Cash Register Company took over the business.

2455. Traveler's checks were devised in 1891 by Marcellus Fleming Berry, who was then general agent of the American Express Company. In the first year, 248 checks amounting to US$9,120 were sold.

2456. Coins minted in Canada were struck on January 2, 1908, at the opening of the Canadian branch of the British Royal Mint in Ottawa, Canada. Governor-General Earl Grey struck the first coin, a gold sovereign. The first bronze penny was struck by the Countess of Grey. Silver coins were struck beginning on February 19. Previously, coins for Canada were minted in Britain.

2457. Billion-pound loan was the Third War Loan, issued by Great Britain in 1917 to pay for World War I expenses. The funds were raised within six weeks.

2458. Nation in Oceania to have its own modern coinage was Fiji, beginning in 1934. The coins were minted at the Royal Mint, London, England, in British denominations.

2459. Smart card was patented in France by Roland Moreno in 1975. The smartcard is a type of credit or debit card with an embedded microchip that stores information on commercial transactions or other data, such as personal identity information. The data can be read and modified with simple electronic equipment. The first widespread implementation of smart card technology was put in place by France Télécom in the mid-1980s, when the company converted all its coin-operated pay phones to work with smart cards.

2460. Plastic money were banknotes made of a tough, flexible polymer, issued by the Reserve Bank of Australia on January 27, 1988, to mark the bicentennial of the arrival of the first British convicts. The AU$10 note featured the likeness of Andrew Barton ("Banjo") Paterson, author of the song "Waltzing Matilda."

2461. Electronic cash cards were introduced in Swindon, England, in July 1995 by a British financial services company, Mondex International. The cards, contained embedded microchips that could be programmed with a cash value up to $1,000. Cash value could be replenished at automated teller machines or through special telephone equipment. Cash value could also be transferred from one card to another.

2462. Digitally drawn currency note was issued by the central bank of Switzerland in 1996. The 50-franc bill, which was designed using a computer, incorporated more than 20 anticounterfeiting features and included a raised triangle at one end to help blind people (and vending machines) identify the bill.

2463. Cashless community in which electronic cash cards replaced bills and coins was Guelph, Ontario, Canada, which began the community-wide experiment in September 1997. Equipment for making financial transactions with the cards was installed throughout the town, making it possible for residents to use them in place of cash for store purchases, parking meters, pizza deliveries, taxicabs, municipal buses, vending machines, and pay phones. The cards, which carry cash value programmed into a microchip, were supplied by Mondex Canada, a subsidiary of Mondex International, which had introduced the cards in England two years earlier.

2464. Unified currency in Europe was the euro, officially adopted by the member nations of the European Union on January 1, 1999. On that date, the exchange rate of each national currency was locked to that of the euro. International trading in the new unified currency began on January 4. The first coins were minted in France on May 11, 1998. Each coin design bore on one side a symbol of the European Union, and on the other the national symbols of the country in which it was minted. Both coins and notes were slated to enter circulation on January 1, 2002.

FINANCE—TAXES

2465. Sales tax of record was introduced in ancient Rome by Augustus Caesar to maintain the *aerarium militare,* a military treasury he instituted in 6 CE. Called the *centesima rerum venalium,* it was a 1 percent general sales tax on all goods purchased at auction.

2466. Income tax was the *catasto,* instituted in 1427 by the Commune of Florence (now in Italy) for all the domains under Florentine rule. Each household was required to file a declaration stating real estate holdings, debts, credits, and a list of its members. The supplied information was used by the clerks of the Commune to calculate a taxable amount that was to be paid yearly. The *catasto* record books, which have been preserved, represent the most comprehensive picture of the economic state of any community before modern times.

2467. Graduated income tax was introduced in 1799 in Britain by Prime Minister William Pitt to help pay for the Napoleonic Wars. Incomes were taxed at a sliding scale that topped out at a rate of two shillings to the pound (10 percent) on incomes of £200 per annum and above. Incomes below £60 were exempt. The tax was abolished after the defeat of Napoléon in 1815.

2468. National gasoline tax was levied by the United States government beginning in 1932.

FOOD AND DRINK

2469. Vegetarian of record was Ötzi, the so-called Iceman, a 5,300-year-old mummy found on September 19, 1991, by Helmut Simon in the Tirolean Ötztal Alps, on the border between Austria and Italy. Analysis of Ötzi's hair and stomach contents, performed by Stephen Macko of the University of Virginia in the United States, indicated that he had not eaten meat or dairy products in months, suggesting that he lived primarily on a vegetable diet, although it is not certain that he did this out of choice.

2470. Doctrine of the Five Flavors in Chinese cuisine is traditionally ascribed to the sage I Yin circa 2000 BCE. The Five Flavors are sweet, sour, bitter, hot, and salt.

2471. Vegetarian principles were set forth in the Hindu work *Atharva Veda,* one of the early Indian texts in Sanskrit, dating from circa 1000 BCE. The eating of meat was held to be an offense against one's ancestors.

2472. Food purity law was an Indian statute passed in 300 BCE that imposed a fine for selling impure oil and adulterated grains.

2473. Food purity law still observed is the "Reinheitsgebot," ordered by Duke Wilhelm IV of Bavaria (now in Germany) in the year 1516. The law stated that the only ingredients permitted for brewing beer were water, malted barley, malted wheat, hops, and water. The action of yeast in brewing beer was unknown at the time. This law still applies to modern German beers.

FOOD AND DRINK—ALCOHOL

2474. Beer from malted barley was brewed in Mesopotamia before 4000 BCE.

2475. Wine was produced by the Sumerians in what is now western Iran nearly 5,500 years ago, according to evidence discovered by Virginia R. Badler of the University of Toronto, Canada. Her research at Godin Tepe, a military outpost inhabited from 3500 BCE to 3100 BCE, revealed a reddish residue of grapes inside pottery vessels possibly used for issuing alcoholic rations to troops.

2476. Legal regulation of the trade in alcoholic beverages is first mentioned in the Code of Hammurabi, the Babylonian law document dated to circa 1792–50 BCE. The code fixed a fair price for beer and forbade tavernkeepers (who apparently were mainly women) to allow or promote disorderly conduct or treasonable assembly, under pain of death. Tavernkeepers were ordered to bring the offenders to the palace for trial.

2477. Advanced beer-brewing methods began with the ancient Egyptians, who were making beer at least as early as 1500 BCE. According to electron microscopy examination of bread remains and the linings of beer vessels from tombs and settlements, Egyptian beer-making was a two-step process. Cereal grains were first malted and roasted to provide color, sweetness, and flavor, then mixed in water with cold sprouted grains. Second, the batch was decanted and fermented to produce beer.

2478. Distilled liquor was made by the Chinese from rice beer some time before the beginning of the ninth century BCE.

2479. Whisky was Scotch whisky. The practice of distilling a potent spirit from malted barley is first mentioned in a document dated to 1494, and attributes its invention to a Scottish monk, John Cor.

2480. Wine cooler was described by Blasius Villafranca in his *Methodus Refrigerandi,* published in Rome, Italy, circa 1550. According to Villafranca, Italian monks kept their wine bottles in a container filled with water to which saltpeter (potassium nitrate) had been added, causing an endothermic chemical reaction that chilled the water. This produced such an intensely cold drink that it "made the teeth chatter."

2481. Bottled beer was introduced in 1586 (or possibly in 1602) by Alexander Nowell, the Puritan dean of St. Paul's Cathedral in London, England, who was also the author of the standard Anglican catechism. Nowell made the discovery that ale will keep longer if stored in glass bottles sealed with corks.

2482. Rum was refined from molasses by Spanish sugar plantation owners circa 1600 (perhaps as late as 1650) in Barbados. The dark-brown spirit was originally called "rumbullion," which was soon shortened to rum.

FOOD AND DRINK—ALCOHOL—continued

2483. Champagne was invented circa 1675 by Dom Pierre Pérignon, a Benedictine monk of the Champagne region in France. He is traditionally credited with discovering the process of fermenting slightly sweetened wine a second time in the bottle to create a sparkling, effervescent drink. Dom Pérignon used tightly driven corks to stopper the bottles and force the carbon dioxide back into the wine, becoming the first vintner to cork his bottles.

2484. Grog or watered rum was concocted, according to legend, in 1740 by the British admiral Edward Vernon, known as "Old Grog" for his coat of Grogham, a water-resistant fabric of gummed silk and wool. A pint of grog was issued twice daily to British sailors until July 1970.

2485. Cocktail is said to have been served in 1776 by Betsy Flanagan, a barmaid in Halls Corners, Elmsford, NY, USA, who decorated the bar with tail feathers. An inebriate called for a glass of "those cocktails," so she prepared a mixed drink, and inserted one of the feathers.

2486. Beer-pump handle for pumping brew from kegs was patented on May 9, 1785, by the English machinist Joseph Bramah.

2487. Brewery in the Western Hemisphere in continuous operation was the Molson Brewery in what is now Alberta, Canada. It was founded in 1786 by John Molson.

2488. Whisky distillery officially sanctioned by the Crown was founded in 1823 by the Scottish distiller John Smith at Glenlivet, Scotland. The modern distillery there still produces the best-selling single-malt Scotch whisky.

2489. Modern lager beer was a clear, golden-hued brew, known today as "pilsner," produced in 1842 in the town of Pilsen in Bohemia (now in the Czech Republic). Pilsen was granted brewing rights by King Wenceslas in 1295.

2490. Martini was mentioned in O.H. Byron's *Modern Bartender's Guide,* published in New York, NY, USA, in 1884. A martini is a cocktail made of gin or vodka and vermouth, with a dash of bitters. The origin of the name is in dispute. Byron called the drink a "Martinez" and described it as a Manhattan (a whisky cocktail sweetened with vermouth) but made with gin rather than whisky. It was first called a "Martini" in the American mixologist Henry Johnson's 1888 book *How to Mix Drinks in the Present Style.* The martini did not become "dry" until after World War I, when it became the fashion to use unsweetened French vermouth instead of the sweet Italian variety.

FOOD AND DRINK—COFFEE AND TEA

2491. Tea was brewed in China 4,700 years ago, according to Chinese tradition. The emperor Shen Nung is said to have first infused the beverage in 2737 BCE when leaves from the plant *Camellia sinensis* fell into water he was boiling.

2492. Reference to tea that is authenticated is in the *Erh Ya,* a Chinese dictionary compiled circa 350 BCE.

2493. Treatise on tea and its uses was *The Classic of Tea* by Lu Yu, published in China in 780. It was the first book to describe fully the preparation and uses of tea.

2494. Coffee used as a stimulant probably began circa 800, possibly by members of the Galla people in Ethiopia, who ate coffee berries wrapped in animal fat, but the exact circumstances are obscure. According to one story, a goatherd named Kaldi noticed that his flock was unusually frisky. Sampling the berries of the bush on which they were feeding, he experienced a rush of energy and exhilaration so pleasurable that he felt obliged to share his experience with everyone he knew.

2495. Coffee drinking probably began in Yemen circa 1000, when wild coffee bushes (*Coffea arabica*) were imported from Kaffa, Ethiopia (from which coffee gets its name). The Arabs invented the process of boiling the coffee beans to make a drink, which they called *qahwa* (Arabic for "that which prevents sleep").

2496. European author to write about tea was the Venetian geographer Gian Battista Ramusio, in his *Delle navigationi e viaggi (Of Voyages and Travels),* published in 1559.

2497. Coffee sweet and light was offered circa 1683 at the Viennese coffeehouse of the Polish-born entrepreneur Franz Georg Kolshitsky. Sugar and cream or milk were added to make the bitter brew more appealing. He is also credited with first serving coffee with the grounds strained out, now known as "Viennese style."

2498. Iced tea was introduced in 1904 by an Englishman named Richard Blechynden at the Louisiana Purchase Exposition in St. Louis, MO, USA. Instant powdered tea for making iced tea was put on the consumer market in 1945, having been developed for military use.

2499. Instant coffee mass-produced for the consumer market was introduced in 1906 by George Constant Washington, an English chemist living in Guatemala. Washington's brand was called Red E Coffee. Water-soluble instant coffee was first developed in the laboratory by a Japanese-American chemist, Satori Kato of Chicago, IL, USA, in 1901.

2500. Freeze-dried instant coffee was invented in 1937 by the Nestlé and Anglo-Swiss Condensed Milk Company (now Nestlé SA) of Vevey, Switzerland. Nescafé, as the product was called, was marketed beginning in 1938.

FOOD AND DRINK—COOKBOOKS

2501. Cookbook known to historians is *Hedypatheia (Pleasant Living),* completed circa 350 BCE by a Greek, Archestratus. It is mentioned in the most famous cookbook of classical Greece, the *Deipnosophistai (The Learned Banquet),* written in the second century BCE by Athenaeus.

2502. Cookbook in English was probably *The Form of Cury,* author unknown, compiled in England circa 1150. Its 196 recipes were derived primarily from French sources. The word "cury" in the title does not refer to the spicy Indian dish but is an obsolete term for cooked food.

2503. Printed cookbook was *De Honeste Voluptate ac Caletudine (Concerning Honest Pleasure and Well-being)* by Bartolema Scappi, also called Bartolomeo Sacchi, a librarian in the Vatican at Rome, Italy. Printed in 1485 (some sources give 1475), it contained mainly recipes for desserts.

2504. Cookbook known to have been written by a woman was *The Queen-like Closet; or Rich Cabinet,* written by Hannah Wooley and published in England in 1670.

2505. Recipes to be tested in an organized way before they were published were printed in *Beeton's Book of Household Management,* by Isabella Beeton, published in London, England, in 1861.

2506. Cookbook with standardized measurements was the *Boston Cooking School Cook Book,* edited by Fannie Merritt Farmer, and published in Boston, MA, USA, in 1896. Cookbooks traditionally used directions no more specific than "a handful" or "a cupful."

FOOD AND DRINK—DAIRY

2507. Butter is mentioned (as *ghee,* or clarified butter, a staple of Indian cuisine) in the Indian sacred texts called the *Rig Veda (Wisdom of the Verses),* many of which date to circa 1200 BCE. Butter from cow, goat, sheep, camel, horse, or yak milk was first developed in prehistory by herding peoples, probably independently in several regions.

2508. Cheese mentioned by name in an historical account was brie, the creamy French cheese with a crusty rind. Chronicles of the court of Charlemagne, king of the Franks from 768 and Holy Roman Emperor from 800 to 814, mention brie as a favorite cheese at the emperor's table. Reportedly, Charlemagne had a standing order for a supply to be sent from the Abbey of St. Germain-des-Prés near Paris to his fortress at Aix-la-Chapelle; he enjoyed it after dining while listening to readings from St. Augustine's *City of God,* his favorite book.

2509. Powdered milk was invented by the horse peoples of the Central Asian steppe. It is first recorded as being used circa 1200 by the cavalry of Genghis Khan. The riders spread horse milk out in the sun to dry, then ground it into a powder. To reconstitute the powder, it was mixed with water in a flagon and hung from the saddle, where by the end of the day it had fermented into the popular Mongol drink, koumiss.

2510. Cheese factory went into service in Bern, Switzerland, in 1815.

2511. Condensed milk was commercially produced in 1851 by Gail Borden of Brooklyn, NY, USA (now part of New York City), who received a U.S. patent on August 19, 1856, on an "improvement in concentration of milk," although the patent office doubted the value of the invention. The first condensery was established at Wolcottville, CT, USA, in 1856. It was not successful, and another attempt was made at Burrville, CT, in May 1857, but that was also a failure. A third attempt was made with an enlarged factory at Wassaic, NY, in June 1861. This venture was successful and later developed into the Borden Company, with factories throughout the United States.

2512. Centrifugal cream separator was made by Wilhelm C.L. Lefeldt and Carl G.O. Lentsch of Schöningen, Germany. An American patent was granted to them on September 25, 1877, for an "improvement in centrifugal machines for creaming milk." Their device consisted of an electric rotator that forced the heavy milk to the base of the pan. In 1879, two Americans,

FOOD AND DRINK—DAIRY—continued

David M. Weston and Edward Burnett, of Boston, MA, USA, introduced a more efficient design that was first used on the Deerfoot Farm, Southborough, MA, USA. It made 1,600 revolutions a minute and had a 26-inch (66-centimeter) bowl. The machine had to be stopped to draw off the cream and skim milk after separation.

2513. Centrifugal cream separator with a continuous flow was invented by Carl Gustaf Patrik de Laval of Stockholm, Sweden, who received an American patent for it on October 4, 1881.

2514. Pasteurized milk was produced in Paris, France, in 1885 by Louis Pasteur, the French scientist who invented the process. Seeking to reduce the level of bacterial organisms in fresh milk, which can cause such diseases as brucellosis and tuberculosis in humans, Pasteur adapted the "pasteurization" method he had developed for the beer and wine industries to prevent excess fermentation. He quickly heated the milk to a temperature sufficient to destroy pathogens but not high enough to damage the milk itself. Most pasteurized milk today is heated to at least 161 degrees F (72 degrees C) for 15 seconds or more.

2515. Ice cream cone is an American invention, said to have originated at the Louisiana Purchase Exposition in St. Louis, MO, USA, in 1904. Charles E. Menches, a young ice cream salesman, gave an ice cream sandwich, as well as flowers, to the young lady he was escorting. Lacking a vase for the flowers, she took one of the layers of the sandwich and rolled it in the form of a cone to act as a vase. The remaining layer was similarly rolled to hold the ice cream, resulting in the invention of the ice cream cone. Similar claims have been made by other concessionaires.

2516. Containers of yogurt with fruit mixed in were marketed in Paris, France, by Isaac Carasso in 1926 under the brand Dannone, after his son Daniel. Carasso had begun his yogurt-making business in Barcelona, Spain, in 1919. The Dannone brand was renamed Dannon when Carasso brought his business to the United States in 1941.

FOOD AND DRINK—PACKAGING

2517. Cannery was the House of Appert, opened in 1810 at Massey, near Paris, France, by a Parisian, Nicolas Appert. Appert developed the process of vacuum canning after entering a national competition to find new ways to preserve food for the French army and navy.

He successfully packed a variety of foods, including soups, stews, preserves, and produce, in sealed glass jars that were sterilized by boiling. His findings were published in 1810 in *L'Art de conserver, pendant plusieurs années, toutes les substances animales et végétales* (The Art of Preserving All Kinds of Animal and Vegetable Substances for Several Years).

2518. Metal cans were patented in 1810 by the English inventor Peter Durand (or Duran). His patent covered a number of containers for preserving foods through heat, including tin-coated iron cans, other metal cans, pottery, and glass. Until 1865, tin cans were made of metal so thick that they had to be opened with a hammer and chisel.

2519. Steam sterilization of cans began in 1874, with the invention of the autoclave by an American, A.K. Shriver. It was a large pressure-sealed container in which empty cans could be sterilized with steam before being filled with food and sealed.

2520. Self-heating cans were developed in 1941 by the H.J. Heinz Company of Pittsburgh, PA, USA. They were solely for military use, being considered too expensive and dangerous for regular consumers.

2521. Milk carton was invented in 1951 by Swedish industrialist Ruben Rausing. Also called the tetrahedral carton or Tetra-Pak, it was composed of several bonded layers of waxed paper, aluminum, and plastic.

2522. Food irradiation for preservation was first patented in the United States in 1905. The technique was developed to a practical level in 1943 by Bernard E. Proctor and other researchers at the Massachusetts Institute of Technology in Cambridge, MA, USA. Radioactive cobalt or another source of ionizing radiation was used to briefly irradiate meat, killing microorganisms and retarding spoilage. The process was found to be quick, effective, and energy-efficient. In 1958, the Soviet Union became the first country to allow the irradiation of commercial food products.

2523. Pull-top aluminum can for packaging carbonated and alcoholic beverages was introduced by Alcoa (the Aluminum Company of America) in 1962. The first product to be sold in a tab-top can was Schlitz beer.

FOOD AND DRINK—PREPARED FOODS

2524. Bread was flatbread formed from moistened stone-ground grain. The dough was baked on heated flat stones or under a bed of ashes. Early evidence of bread baking dates from Neolithic times, circa 10,000 BCE, and has been found in many areas of Africa, the Middle East, and Asia.

2525. Olive oil factory known to archeologists was discovered in 1998 on what is now submerged land off Israel's northern coast by marine archeologists Ehud Galili and Jacob Sharvit of the Israel Antiquities Authority. Four large holes dug into the seafloor were found to be filled with thousands of olive pits; also unearthed at the site were grinding tools, woven reed baskets, stone basins, and other olive-oil production equipment. Carbon dating put the site at circa 4500 BCE.

2526. Commercial bakeries developed in ancient Rome from circa 200 BCE. A bakery uncovered in the ruins of Pompeii (buried in 79 CE by a volcanic eruption) still contained the remains of baked loaves.

2527. Salted herring as a commercial product was introduced by William Beukelszoon of Biervliet (now in the Netherlands) in circa 1260. He cured the herring in the traditional method, by gutting and salting, and sold it by the barrel.

2528. Pasta is thought to have originated in China. According to legend, the idea was brought from China to Italy by the Venetian traveler Marco Polo in 1295. Another possible route was through India, Persia, or the Arab countries, all places where noodles were eaten in the early 13th century.

2529. Barbecue originated circa 1610 in a method of salting and smoking meat practiced by the Carib Indians on the island of Haiti (now the island of Hispaniola, divided between Haiti and the Dominican Republic). The meat was spread over a greenwood frame, called *barbacoa* in Spanish.

2530. Sandwich was not invented, but was made popular, by British politician John Montagu, the fourth earl of Sandwich and the first lord of the Admiralty during the American Revolution. A habitual gambler, Montagu spent a full 24 hours at cards one day in 1762, eating only beef between slices of toast so he did not have to leave the table for a meal.

2531. Carbonated water was invented by English chemist Joseph Priestley, who 1772 demonstrated a small carbonating device before the College of Physicians in London, England.

2532. Soft drink business was started by Jacob Schweppe, a jeweler in Geneva, Switzerland, in partnership with Jacques and Nicholas Paul. Schweppe developed a carbonating device based on the work of Joseph Priestley and Antoine Lavoisier, and used it to produce artificial mineral waters. He began selling his soda water in 1794. Later he moved the business to London. The drink was bottled in round containers that could not stay upright so that the corks would stay wet, tight, and gas-proof.

2533. Canned fish was sardines, introduced by Joseph Colin of Nantes, France, circa 1819. Canned salmon was the invention of John Moir of Aberdeen, Scotland, who began selling the product circa 1825. Anchovies in a tin were first marketed in Norway in 1841.

2534. Self-rising flour ready-mixed with leavening and salt was developed by an Englishman, Henry Jones, who marketed it beginning in 1845.

2535. Frozen meat for commercial sale was introduced in 1857 by James Harrison of Geelong, Australia, using equipment based on the gas vapor-compression refrigeration systems independently invented by the Americans Jacob Perkins and Alexander C. Twinning. The first meat-packing plant capable of packaging refrigerated and frozen meat was opened in Sydney in 1861, and Australian frozen meat was first shipped to England in 1879.

2536. Food product to be pasteurized was wine, in 1863, when mass spoilage was threatening to ruin the French winemaking industry. The emperor Napoléon III commissioned the eminent chemist and microbiologist Louis Pasteur, then director of the École Normale Supérieure in Paris and an expert in fermentation, to solve the problem. He recommended heating the wine to 135 degrees F (57 degrees C) to kill the bacteria responsible for the spoilage.

2537. Margarine was produced commercially in 1869 by the French chemist Hippolyte Mège-Mouriès. He developed a butter-like combination of animal fats (mainly lard) churned with milk solids and salt. It had the advantage of a higher melting point than butter and kept better at room temperature.

2538. Margarine factory was opened in 1871 in Oss, the Netherlands, by the butter merchants Jan and Anton Jurgens. They purchased margarine manufacturing rights from Hippolyte Mège-Mouriès, the French chemist who invented the first practical margarine-making process.

FOOD AND DRINK—PREPARED FOODS—*continued*

2539. Artificial flavoring was the phenolic compound synthetic vanillin, a vanilla substitute synthesized in 1874 by two German chemists, Wilhelm Haarman and Ferdinand Tiemann.

2540. Chop suey is of obscure origin. It may have been the invention of Lihung Chang, a chef for the Chinese ambassador to the United States, who devised the glutinous dish of bamboo shoots, water chestnuts, bean sprouts, onions, mushrooms, and meat or fish over rice, in either 1888 or 1896. The name probably derives from *jaahp-seui,* meaning odds and ends.

2541. Condensed soup for the consumer market was invented in 1897 by the American chemist John T. Dorrance of the Joseph Campbell Preserve Company, a cannery in Camden, NJ, USA. His double-strength condensed soups had the advantage of being cheaper to distribute and sell because water, the weightiest part of the formula, was added by the consumer. The low-priced canned soups first appeared on the market in 1898, already sporting the company's characteristic red and white labels. In 1914, Dorrance became president of the company, which changed its name to the Campbell's Soup Company in 1924.

2542. Frozen food for the mass market was developed by Clarence Birdseye, an American biologist from Brooklyn, NY, USA. In 1916, Birdseye began to experiment with methods of retaining the flavor and nutrition of cabbage and fish over long periods by quick-freezing them in brine. In 1924, in Gloucester, MA, USA, he perfected the belt-freezer, a device that subjected food to quick-freezing by pressing it between refrigerated plates. He received a patent for his invention on August 12, 1930. Frozen foods with the Birdseye trademark were first marketed in Springfield, MA, in 1930. Birdseye sold his trademark in 1929 to the Postum Company, later the General Foods Corporation, for US$22 million.

2543. Vitamin to be commercially synthesized and manufactured was vitamin D, which was manufactured by Mead, Johnson and Company, Evansville, IN, USA, beginning in 1927 and was marketed in the spring of 1928. It was made by exposing a solution of ergosterol to ultraviolet light.

FOOD AND DRINK—SNACKS AND SWEETS

2544. Cake of record was a small, well-wrapped sesame-honey cake found in the grave of Pepionkh, who lived in ancient Egypt circa 2200 BCE.

2545. Candy was produced in Egypt circa 1000 BCE. It was a confection of fruit, nuts, spices, and honey.

2546. Frozen desserts were enjoyed by the ancient Romans, who mixed fruit juice with snow brought down from the mountains by runners. A recipe for a milk-based frozen dessert was introduced to Italy in 1295 by Marco Polo, who described the Chinese method of preparing sherbet, or fruit ice with a milk base. The first ice cream parlor was opened in Paris in 1670 by a Sicilian, Francisco Procopio; he mainly sold fruit ices. The most popular modern flavors of ice cream—vanilla, chocolate, and strawberry—were probably invented by a cafe-owner named Tortoni in Paris circa 1790. The first modern ice cream factory was built in 1851 by Jacob Fussell, a milk dealer in Baltimore, MD, USA.

2547. Hot cocoa was long enjoyed by the indigenous peoples of Mexico and Central America, although in a form more bitter than the hot cocoa consumed today. The Aztecs favored an unsweetened beverage called *xocoatl* (Nahuatl for "bitter water") made from cocoa beans fermented in the pod. These were roasted and then ground to a paste with vanilla and other flavors. The paste was formed into dried cakes that were broken into hot water and whipped to produce a foaming hot cocoa drink. Xocoatl was first sampled by the Spanish conquistadors in 1519.

2548. Recipe for a wedding cake was contained in an English cookbook published in 1769. It called for a white-glazed cake with two layers of icing, the inner one containing ground almonds. The white wedding cake with multiple decorated tiers is mainly a British invention and was popularized during the Victorian era.

2549. Beet sugar factory opened in Silesia (now part of Germany) in 1801, using an extraction process developed by the German organic chemist Franz Karl Achard.

2550. Chocolate for eating produced by a commercial process was introduced in 1819 by François-Louis Cailler of Vevey, Switzerland. He developed a machine to prepare unsweetened chocolate in blocks for cooking.

2551. Chocolate cocoa and candy were produced in 1828 by the Dutch chocolatier Konraad Johannes van Houten. He patented a process for removing the cocoa butter from ground and roasted beans to obtain powdered chocolate. The cocoa powder was easily measured and dissolved quickly in warm water or milk, unlike the chocolate chunks previously used for chocolate beverages. Heating the butter with ground chocolate and sugar, van Houten produced a mixture that solidified into a candy when cooled.

2552. Chewing gum was "State of Maine Pure Spruce Gum," manufactured in Bangor, ME, USA, in 1848 by John Curtis and his brother on a Franklin stove. In 1850 they moved to Portland, ME, where they made paraffin gums under the brand names Licorice Lulu, Four-in-Hand, Sugar Cream, Biggest and Best, and White Mountain, and spruce gums under the names Yankee Spruce, American Flag, Trunk Spruce, and 200 Lump Spruce.

2553. Milk chocolate prepared with the addition of dried milk was invented in 1876 by Daniel Peter of Vevey, Switzerland.

2554. Sugar cubes were patented in England in 1878 by Henry Tate, owner of the Silvertown Sugar Refinery of London and later the founder of the Tate Gallery (paid for with the proceeds from his sugar business).

2555. Bubble gum was invented by an American, Frank Henry Fleer, founder of the Frank H. Fleer Corporation of Philadelphia, PA, USA. In 1906 he developing a chewing gum called Blibber-Blubber. The recipe was perfected in 1928 by company employee Walter Diemer, who called his product Dubble Bubble for its ability to make large bubbles. Successful market testing began in Philadelphia on December 26, 1928.

FOOD AND DRINK—SPICES AND SAVORIES

2556. Onions as a savory foodstuff were known to many ancient peoples. The earliest known depictions of onion-eating are frescoes of laborers eating raw onions in an Egyptian tomb dated to circa 3200 BCE.

2557. Mustard used as a spice was probably brown or Oriental mustard (*Brassica juncea*), known since prehistory from the Himalayan region in what are now India, Tibet, and Nepal. Indian texts from circa 3000 BCE mention concoctions of ground dried mustard seed.

2558. Pickles were produced by 2000 BCE in the Fertile Crescent (now Iraq), when farmers stored unwashed cucumbers and other cucurbits in brine. The bacteria that adhered to the unwashed fruit set off the pickling process. Modern picklers use sanitary yeast pickling cultures developed by the American agricultural chemist John Etchells.

2559. Dijon mustard was introduced circa 1200 in the town of Dijon, France. It derived its unique flavor from the addition of verjuice, the extract of unripe grapes, to a paste of ground brown mustard seed and vinegar.

2560. Mayonnaise is of uncertain origin. The creamy sauce, an emulsion of egg, oil, vinegar, and lemon juice, may have been introduced circa 1757 to France by the Duc de Richelieu, who had recently won a battle at Mahón (thus, mayonnaise) on the island of Minorca (now part of Spain). Or the word mayonnaise may derive from the French *moyeunaise,* meaning "of the yolk."

2561. Worcestershire sauce was concocted by English druggists John Wheeley Lea and William Perrins in 1835. The formula for the spicy sauce was given to them by Lord Sandys, British governor of Bengal. The ingredients were anchovies, shallots, chilies, cloves, tamarinds, garlic, sugar, molasses, vinegar, and salt.

2562. Bouillon cubes containing meat extracts were developed in 1899 in Frey Bentos, Paraguay, under the brand name Oxo.

2563. Monosodium glutamate (MSG) was discovered in Japan in 1908 by Kikunae Ikeda, who found that savory soup made from seaweed contained high levels of the substance, a white, crystalline sodium salt of glutamic acid. MSG, now produced commercially by the fermentation of ammonium salts in molasses or a starch, is widely used as a flavor enhancer in Chinese and Japanese cuisine and in many packaged food products.

2564. Vegemite was invented by Australian Fred Walker in 1908, and marketed by Fred Walker & Company. Walker was seeking a food that would stay edible during long excursions into the dry, hot outback. The dark, savory paste was made of a mixture of yeast, onions, celery, water, and salt.

G

GAMES

2565. Board game was unearthed by the British archeologist Leonard Woolley during his excavation of Ur (modern Tel-el-Muqayyar in Iraq) in 1926. The boards and pieces belong to a pachisi-like game dating from circa 3000 BCE.

GAMES—*continued*

2566. Go may date from as early as circa 2300 BCE, according to legend, and probably originated in China, where it is called *wiqi*. The first confirmed historical mention of an early form of the game, called *yi*, is in the Chinese Zuo Zhuan chronology for the year 546 BCE. Go was first played in Japan in 735 CE at the Imperial court and later became the unofficial national game. Go is a game of strategy in which two players try to capture territory on a board by placing black or white stones so as to surround and capture the stones of their opponent.

2567. Backgammon developed from an ancient Roman game, *ludus duodecim scriptorum* ("the game of twelve lines"). It was probably influenced also by the Indian game of pachisi and by Egyptian games. A similar game appears to have been played in Babylon circa 2000 BCE.

2568. Checkers evolved from games played in ancient Egypt circa 1600 BCE. Checkers adopted the 64-square chessboard in Europe circa 1150 CE, and the modern rules were essentially in place by circa 1500.

2569. Counting game is thought to have been *mancala* (also spelled *mankala*), which is played throughout Africa under a variety of names. It is a counting game involving the distribution of seeds or stones into a series of cups. Although there are specially made mancala boards, of which the earliest known are Egyptian stone boards dating from circa 1400 BCE, the game can be played with depressions dug into the earth.

2570. Military game known was *alquerque,* a checkers-like game found in 1925 during the excavation of the tomb of the Egyptian pharaoh Tutankhamen. The game, which dates from circa 1355 BCE, was played by two people on a board incised with five diagonal lines. Each player maneuvered an "army" of twelve pieces along vacant intersections. As in checkers, pieces could be captured by jumping over them.

2571. Dominoes were played sometime around the twelfth century in China, where they were derived from dice games. A similar game, the parent of the game now familiar in the West, was apparently invented separately in 18th-century Italy.

2572. Checkers book was written by Antonio Torquemada and published in Valencia, Spain, in 1547.

2573. Jigsaw puzzle was invented circa 1760 independently in France and England; the English inventor was John Spilsbury (or Spillbury). In both countries, they were made from maps glued to a wooden board and then cut up along the national boundaries, and were intended to aid in teaching geography. The oldest extant jigsaw puzzle, "Europe divided into its kingdoms," was made by Spilsbury in 1766.

2574. Crossword puzzle was prepared by an American, Arthur Wynne, and was published in the Sunday supplement of the *New York World* of December 21, 1913.

2575. Mah-jongg originated in China, where variations of it were played in the different provinces during the 19th century. It is played with a set of tiles bearing Chinese symbols and scenes. The game was adapted for English-speaking players by Joseph P. Babcock, an American businessman who had lived in Shanghai. He imported the first of his copyrighted sets to the USA in 1920.

2576. Computer game was SPACEWAR, invented by Steve Russell, a graduate student at the Masschusetts Institute of Technology, Cambridge, MA, USA, and first demonstrated publicly in 1962 at the university's Spring Open House. The game was based on the science-fiction stories of E.E. "Doc" Smith. Players used joysticks to control a computer graphics display showing two spaceships shooting at each other. The processing was done by a Digital Equipment Corporation PDP-1 minicomputer.

2577. Video game that was commercially successful was the arcade game Pong, an electronic version of ping-pong created by 29-year-old American computer engineer Nolan K. Bushnell. Pong was introduced in 1972 by Bushnell's company, Atari Corporation. Bushnell placed the first unit in Andy Capp's Tavern in Sunnyvale, CA, USA, where it was an instant hit. Pong became a national craze in the United States, making Bushnell a multimillionaire and inaugurating the video game industry. An early, noncommercial version of Pong was invented in 1958 by William Higinbotham, head of instrumentation design at the Brookhaven National Laboratory, Upton, NY. It was not patented.

2578. Video game designer of renown was Shigeru Miyamoto, who joined the Japanese firm of Nintendo in 1977 as the company's first staff artist. Miyamoto was the creator of the Donkey Kong (1981), Super Mario Brothers (1985), and Zelda series of arcade and video games, which by the year 2000 had generated more than US$10 billion dollars in sales and royalties. Miyamoto's games were notable for their playability, visual ingenuity, appealing characters, and relative lack of violence.

2579. Trivia board game of international popularity was Trivial Pursuit, invented on December 15, 1979, by two Canadians, photo editor Chris Haney and sportswriter Scott Abbott. It was a simple race-type board game in which players were required to answer trivia questions about a wide range of general topics. The rights were later purchased by U.S. game company Selchow and Righter, which markets the game in 33 countries.

GAMES—CARD GAMES

2580. Card games probably originated in China no later than 969. In that year, according to Chinese accounts, the emperor Mu Tsung expressed his frustration with scholars and government officials who played cards, even though, in the emperor's opinion, it was a pastime that invited bad luck. The earliest Chinese card games were played with paper money made by block printing.

2581. Card games in Europe were introduced in the 12th or 13th century, in association with gambling. They were already widespread in France by 1254, and by 1397 had become so popular that working people were forbidden by official decree to waste time on them on work days.

2582. Tarot cards for telling fortunes appeared in 14th-century Italy and France, probably from an Asian or Middle Eastern source.

2583. Printed playing cards were probably the first pictures printed in quantity in Europe. References to wood blocks being used for the printing of cards can be found in German documents dating from 1402.

2584. Playing cards using the four modern suits of diamonds, hearts, spades, and clubs appear to have been introduced in the Provence region of France circa 1440. The four suits are thought by some historians to have originated in India.

2585. Poker-type card game was *primera,* a three-card game played in Spain from circa 1500, and perhaps as early as 1200. It was a betting game, and hands included pairs, three of a kind, and three of a suit, called a flux. By circa 1700 primera had evolved into a game variously known as *poque* in France and *pochen* in Germany; both words mean "bluff."

2586. Euchre family of card games appears to have developed from *triomphe,* a Spanish game that is known to have been played early in the 16th century.

2587. Cribbage was developed from an earlier game, Noddy, by the English poet and dramatist Sir John Suckling (1609–1642), a man who was known at court as "the greatest gamester both for bowling and cards."

2588. Bridge card game developed from the partnership game whist (originally called whisk, from "whisking up the tricks"), popular in England in the 17th and 18th centuries. Whist was succeeded in 1896 by bridge whist, in 1904 by auction bridge, and in 1925 by contract bridge.

2589. Compendium of rules for a game was published by the English lawyer Edmond Hoyle, whose first book was *A Short Treatise on the Game of Whist* (1742). It was extremely popular in the card-obsessed society of 18th-century London and was commonly used to settle disputes on the rules of the game. The book went through 13 editions in his lifetime and many more after his death. Modern editions of rule books "by Hoyle" include his standardized rules for other popular games, including piquet, brag, quadrille, chess, and backgammon. The expression "according to Hoyle" still means to conform strictly to the rules.

2590. Pinochle is derived from bezique, which has been credited to Gustav Flaker, a schoolteacher from Sweden who is said to have invented the game in the early 1800s for a contest.

2591. Playing deck with double-headed face cards of record was a pack printed in Germany in late 1813 to commemorate the key Allied victory over Napoléon at the Battle of Leipzig. Depicted as the kings were the monarchs of the four participating Allies (Austria, Prussia, Russia, and Sweden). The jacks were the Allied commanding generals (Prince Karl Philipp Schwarzenberg, General Gebhard Leberecht Blücher, General Leonty Leontyevich Bennigsen, and the Swedish crown prince Jean Bernadotte). The queens were the Roman goddesses Ceres, Diana, Flora, and Pomona. A joker depicting Napoléon was not included in the deck.

2592. Book on poker was a rule book written in London circa 1875 by Robert C. Schenck, U.S. minister to Great Britain.

GAMES—CARD GAMES—*continued*

2593. Rummy card games are widely thought to have developed from *conquian* (also called *cooncan*), a Mexican game dating to the mid- to late 19th century. Another theory is that they derive from an American poker variant called whiskey poker. Rummy's remote ancestor, however, appears to have been the Chinese tile game known to English-speakers as mah-jongg, which also requires players to form related sets.

2594. Rule book of bridge was compiled by John Collison of London, England, who had learned the game while in Constantinople (now Istanbul, Turkey) in 1885. In February 1886 he published a short pamphlet titled *Biritch, or Russian Whist.*

2595. International bridge match was held at Almack's club in London, England, on September 15, 1930. In the 200-hand match, an American team headed by Ely Culbertson defeated a British team captained by Walter Buller.

2596. Canasta was played in the late 1940s in Uruguay, from which it was imported to the USA. Canasta is one of many forms of rummy.

GAMES—CHESS

2597. Chess-like game was the Indian game *chaturanga,* which was invented sometime after 600 CE. Like chess, chaturanga was played on a 64-square board. Two armies, each with pieces representing soldiers, horses, chariots, and elephants, maneuvered to capture enemy pieces. The modern game of chess developed in its present form in Europe circa 1450, after the moves of the pieces were standardized.

2598. International chess tournament was organized in London in 1851 by Howard Staunton, the top British player and editor of the first chess magazine in English. The tournament was won by Adolf Anderssen of Germany.

2599. World chess champion was the Austrian grandmaster Wilhelm Steinitz. He became the first player to earn the official title of "World Chess Champion" when he defeated Johannes Zukertort in London in 1886.

2600. World chess champion who was a woman was Vera Francevna Stevenson-Menchik of the Soviet Union. She defended the title seven times from 1927 to 1944.

2601. World chess champion defeated by a computer under championship conditions was Russian-born Gary Kasparov, the world's ranking grandmaster. On February 10, 1996, in Philadelphia, PA, USA, he lost the first game of a six-game match against Deep Blue, a chess-playing computer developed by a team of International Business Machines (IBM) researchers based in Yorktown Heights, NY, USA. On May 11, 1997, Deep Blue won a six-game rematch with Kasparov, after he resigned the sixth and final game after just 19 moves.

2602. Black chess player to become a grandmaster was Maurice Ashley of Brooklyn, NY, USA, a Jamaican-born immigrant who had been playing and studying chess since his teens. He earned the rank of grandmaster on March 15, 1999, in a tournament sponsored by the Manhattan Chess Club. The title of grandmaster is awarded by the International Chess Federation.

GAMES—GAMBLING

2603. Dice were fortunetelling devices made of bone. The practice of playing dice games appears to have originated in Egypt, where marked cubes have been found in tombs dating from the beginning of the second millennium BCE. Some ancient Egyptian dice were altered for cheating.

2604. Reference to dice games in literature occurs in the epic Hindu poem, the *Mahabharata,* whose earliest material is dated to circa 1302 BCE.

2605. Public lottery with cash prizes is thought to have been La Lotto de Firenze, which took place in 1530 in Florence, Italy.

2606. Book on gambling techniques was *Liber de ludo aleae (Book of Games and Chance),* written circa 1563 by the Italian physician, mathematician, and astrologer Gerolamo (Girolamo or Geronimo) Cardano. It is the first mathematical study of games of chance, such as cards or dice, and presents an early outline of probability theory.

2607. National lottery was instituted in England during the reign of Queen Elizabeth I. A royal proclamation issued in 1567 offered 400,000 lottery tickets at ten shillings each, with a top prize of £5,000 in cash and goods, as well as many smaller prizes. Drawings began on January 11, 1569. Proceeds from the lottery were used to fund public works.

2608. Casino game is likely to have been the card game called faro, which probably originated in Italy and was popularized in the 17th century by King Louis XIV in France. Its name derives from the picture of an Egyptian pharaoh displayed on one of the cards.

2609. Craps game was introduced in New Orleans, LA, USA, about 1813 by Bernard Xavier Philippe de Marigny de Mandeville, who had seen the dice game of hazards played in France. As a common nickname for a Creole man was Johnny Crapaud, the game became known as Crapaud's game, which later was abbreviated to "craps." Mandeville lost a fortune at the game. He was obliged to cut a street through his property and to sell lots on both sides to obtain funds to pay his debts. Maps show this street as Craps Street, later changed to Burgundy Street.

2610. Modern lottery run by a national government was Lotto, the national lottery of Italy, where weekly drawings began in 1863.

2611. Craps bookie was John H. Winn of New York, NY, USA. In 1907, Winn developed the informal dice game called private craps, in which players make bets with one another on the outcome of a roll of the dice, into a casino game called open craps, in which a bookmaker takes bets in exchange for a fee.

GARDENS

2612. Reference to a windbreak for protecting a garden occurs in a legend that was current in Sumeria (now Iraq) in the third millennium BCE. A man named Shukallituda consults the goddess Inanna after his carefully tended garden is destroyed by wind-driven blasts of sand. The goddess advises him to plant trees that will serve as a windbreak and provide shade as well.

2613. Representation of a plant growing in a pot appears on the stone altar of the temple of Hagar Qim in Malta, which was built circa 2000 BCE. It shows a long-stemmed plant with leaves extending on both sides.

2614. Botanical garden of record was the temple garden at Karnak, Egypt, built circa 1500 BCE. It also provided fruit, vegetables, and medicinal herbs for the temple priests.

2615. Tree of which there is historical record appears to be a pipal tree that stands at Anuradhapura, Sri Lanka, where it was planted circa 245 BCE. According to tradition, this tree was transplanted from Bodh Gaya, India, where it was a shoot of the famous Bo tree under which Siddhartha Gautama meditated continuously until he attained enlightenment and became a Buddha.

2616. Topiary gardening appeared in Rome in the first century. According to the historian and scientist Pliny the Elder, the art of shaping shrubs and hedges, known in Latin as *romora tonsilis,* was the invention of one Caius Martius, who trimmed cypress trees.

2617. Garden plan extant for a European garden is a drawing of the garden maintained by the monastery of St. Gall, in present-day Switzerland, circa 820. The drawing shows a compound based on the *villa rustica,* the Roman agricultural estate. It contained an 18-bed vegetable garden, a physic garden for medicinal flowers and herbs, and an orchard containing 14 kinds of fruit trees that were planted among the graves in the monastery's cemetery.

2618. Gardening book was *Hortulus (The Little Garden),* a poem by Walahfrid Strabo, a monk who lived at the monasteries of St. Gall and Reichenau in present-day Switzerland during the first half of the ninth century.

2619. Turkish horticultural treatise was *Revnaki Rostan (Beauty of the Gardener),* which appeared in 1070. It included a recommendation for keeping insect pests to a minimum in an ornamental garden by planting mustard.

2620. Lawn-care manual was *Opus ruralium commodorum (The Advantages of Country Living),* a book on husbandry by the Italian Petrus de Crescentius (or Crescenzi) that appeared in 1306. The author recommended laying turf cut from a meadow on ground prepared by weeding and scalding, then pounding it with mallets and with one's feet.

2621. Bonsai was developed in China perhaps as early as circa 1 CE and reached its full development in Japan after circa 1100. A bonsai plant was first depicted in the *Kasuga-gongengenki,* a scroll painted in 1309 by the Japanese artist Takashina Takakane. The first show of bonsai in the West was at a Paris exposition in 1878. Bonsai means "tray-planted " in Japanese, and refers to the art of growing and shaping dwarf shrubs and trees in planters.

2622. Orangery with glass walls, for sheltering citrus trees during Northern European winters, was built in 1619 by the French Huguenot engineer Salomon de Caus for Frederick V, Elector Palatine of the Rhine, in Heidelberg, Germany. The walls were framed in wood, with space for glass windows. The entire building, 280 feet long and heated by four furnaces, was assembled over the Elector's grove of 400 or-

GARDENS—*continued*

ange trees every September and remained in place until April, when it was taken down. Previous orangeries, dating from the mid-16th century, were heated rooms or sheds without access to sunlight.

2623. Traps for human trespassers in gardens were described by the Scottish landscape gardener John Claudius Loudon, author of *An Encyclopaedia of Gardening,* first published in 1822. He described a "barbarous contrivance," something like a large rat trap, that was set in market gardens. It was designed to crush the leg of the thief who was caught in it. There was also a "humane" version that merely broke the leg.

2624. Hydroponic garden was planted in 1860 by two German agronomists, Ferdinand Sachs and Gustav Knopp. They grew various plants in a box without soil; the plant roots were suspended in a flowing solution of water and essential minerals.

2625. Organic gardening originated with the English agricultural scientist Albert Howard in the 1930s. In place of synthetic and possibly dangerous insecticides and fertilizers, he advocated a program of soil enrichment and nontoxic pest-control techniques.

2626. Botanical garden display under a geodesic dome was a tropical rainforest display that opened in 1960 at the Missouri Botanical Garden in St. Louis, MO, USA. The geodesic dome, designed by Richard Buckminster Fuller, housed streams, waterfalls, and some 1,200 species of plants in a natural setting. It was called the Climatron.

GOVERNMENT AND POLITICS

2627. Political sex scandal of record took place circa 1400 BCE in the ancient Mittanite city of Nuzi (now Yorghan Tepe, Iraq), according to Akkadian-language cuneiform tablets unearthed in 1927–28 by archeologist Edward Chiera of the Harvard Semitic Museum, Cambridge, MA, USA. Kushshihar, the mayor of Nuzi, was accused of immoral behavior with a young woman, Humerelli, and of making improper use of public property in the course of their affair. He was apparently put on trial, but the tablet containing the verdict has not been found.

2628. Civil service examinations to select Chinese civil servants by merit were introduced during the Han dynasty in 124 BCE, when an imperial university and a system of schools were founded to teach Confucian political and social ideals to students hoping for a career in government. Under the previous dynasty, the Ch'in, candidates for civil service jobs were placed by recommendation, rather than examination. A system of centralized public written examinations open to all was in place during the Tang dynasty (618–906 CE). Exams lasted several days. In order to avoid the possibility of favoritism in grading, all the completed tests were copied by a scribe to conceal the identity of the candidates from the examiners.

2629. Government bulletins regularly issued were the *tipao,* reports concerning matters of government that were sent from correspondents in Beijing to provincial officials stationed in Korea, Mongolia, and other farflung parts of the Han empire (202 BCE through 221 CE). They were revived during the T'ang dynasty, beginning in 618, and were eventually sent out by an official news agency. The *tipao* were written out by hand until the 17th century, when they were typeset using wooden type.

2630. Politician to offer a chicken in every pot was Henry IV (Henri de Navarre), king of France from 1589 to 1610 and the first of its Bourbon rulers. He is reputed to have said: "I want my people to have a fowl simmering in their pot every Sunday."

2631. Government complaint box of record, from which complaints would be passed directly to the national ruler, was the *meyasubako,* periodically posted at the residence of the eighth Tokugawa shogun, Yoshimune, a reformer who ruled Japan from 1716 to 1745. By this means Yoshimune hoped to hear the unfiltered complaints of the people, especially on matters of bribery and corruption.

2632. Ombudsman was Lars August Mannerheim, appointed by the old Swedish Riksdag in 1809 to handle public complaints against the government. Mannerheim took office on March 1, 1810, with the official title of *Justitieombudsman,* and served until 1823. The word *ombudsman* means "agent" in Swedish.

2633. Public opinion poll for political purposes was taken in the United States during the presidential election of 1824. The results appeared on July 24, 1824, in the *Harrisburg Pennsylvanian.* The four candidates were Andrew Jackson of Tennessee, John Quincy Adams of Massachusetts, William Harris Crawford of Georgia, and Henry Clay of Kentucky. The poll put Jackson in first place, and indeed Jackson won the popular vote with 153,544 votes to Adams's 108,740, but since none of the candidates received a majority of the electoral vote, the election was decided in the House of Representatives, and Adams was the winner.

2634. National government to have a World Wide Web presence was the government of the United States. In 1993, the federal government established World Wide Web sites for the White House (http://www.whitehouse.gov) and e-mail addresses for the president (president@whitehouse.gov) and the vice president (vice-president@whitehouse.gov).

GOVERNMENT AND POLITICS—ELECTIONS

2635. Free election in North America took place on May 18, 1631, when John Winthrop was elected governor of the English colony of Massachusetts. Some scholars maintain that the Virginia Assembly was selected by means of votes in 1619.

2636. Woman to vote in an election of record was shopowner Lily Maxwell of Manchester, England. A ratepayer, she was accidently listed in the voting register for the by-election of November 26, 1867. She arrived at the polls with a protective escort of suffragists and cast her vote for the Liberal candidate, Jacob Bright.

2637. Free, democratic elections in Central America that were considered entirely honest were those held in Costa Rica in 1890, in which José Joaquín Rodríguez was elected president.

2638. Voting machines were invented by an American, Jacob H. Myers, and first authorized for use in the United States. New York State was the first to approve such machines on March 15, 1892, under an act "to secure independence of voters at town meetings, secrecy of the ballot and provide for the use of Myers' automatic ballot cabinet." The machines were first employed on April 12, 1892, at Lockport, NY, USA.

2639. National voting rights for women were granted by New Zealand on September 19, 1893, when the House of Representatives passed the Electoral Act. The legislators had been presented with a petition containing the names of 31,872 women, gathered under the auspices of the Women's Christian Temperance Union. Women first went to the polls in the national elections of November 28, 1893.

2640. Free election in which Muslim fundamentalists obtained a majority took place in Algeria in June 1990, when the fundamentalist Islamic Salvation Front took a majority of the municipal and provincial councils. It was Algeria's first multiparty election since winning independence from France in 1962.

2641. Incumbent African president defeated in a democratic election was Mathieu Kérékou, president of Benin from 1972 to 1991. A committed Marxist-Leninist, Kérékou participated in the 1967 military coup that overthrew President Hubert Maga. On October 26, 1972, a second coup ended with Major (later General) Kérékou assuming the roles of president, prime minister, and minister of national defense. Widespread dissatisfaction with Benin's socialist government led in March 1991 to multiparty presidential elections in which Kérékou was defeated by Nicéphore Soglo.

2642. Free multiparty elections in the Arabian peninsula were held in 1993 in the Republic of Yemen, the nation formed by the 1990 merger of the Yemen Arab Republic, or North Yemen, and the People's Democratic Republic of Yemen, or South Yemen. These were also the first elections in Arabia in which women were allowed to vote.

2643. Nonracial democratic elections in South Africa were held on May 2, 1994. The African National Congress swept the election with a 62 percent margin over its opponents, the National Party and the Inkatha Freedom Party, winning 252 seats in the 400-seat National Assembly and control of seven of nine regional legislatures. Some seven out of ten South Africans voted. The leader of the ANC, Nelson Rolihlahla Mandela, became South Africa's first president elected on a nonracial basis.

GOVERNMENT AND POLITICS—LAWS AND RIGHTS

2644. Law code has been ascribed to Ur-Nammu, first king of the third Sumerian dynasty, whose capital was the city of Ur (now Tel-el-Muqayyar in Iraq). The original list of laws, now lost, was probably carved on a stela circa 2100 BCE; it is known only from copies made by Old Babylonian scribes more than 1200 years later. It lists the compensation to be paid for various bodily injuries, and prescribes penalties for adultery, witchcraft, runaway slaves, and rape.

2645. Constitution in the New World was the first constitution of colonial Connecticut, known as the "fundamental orders," drawn up by Roger Ludlow and adopted on January 14, 1639, in Hartford, CT, USA, by representatives of the towns of Wethersfield, Windsor, and Hartford. Ludlow was influenced by a sermon delivered May 31, 1638, by the Reverend Thomas Hooker at Hartford's Center Church. The constitution established a general assembly and governor's office and guaranteed political freedom for adult men.

GOVERNMENT AND POLITICS—LAWS AND RIGHTS—*continued*

2646. Law guaranteeing freedom of speech was promulgated by Sweden in 1766. Under the law, censorship of books and periodicals was abolished, and all Swedish citizens were allowed access to official documents kept by state or municipal agencies.

2647. Written national constitution outside of the United States was that of Poland, approved by the Sejm (Diet) on May 3, 1791, and signed that day by King Stanislaw II August Poniatowski. It contained a liberal bill of rights and set up a constitutional monarchy. Russia, which opposed the new constitution, immediately invaded Poland and crushed the rebellion that followed. Four years later Poland was partitioned by Russia, Prussia, and Austria.

2648. Constitutional guarantee of free speech was the First Amendment to the Constitution of the United States, proposed by Congress in September 1789 and ratified by the states on December 15, 1791. The text of the First Amendment reads: "Congress shall make no law respecting an establishment of religion, or prohibiting the free exercise thereof; or abridging the freedom of speech, or of the press; or the right of the people peaceably to assemble, and to petition the Government for a redress of grievances." It was authored by James Madison. Although many other nations have based their constitutions on that of the United States, few have chosen to include such a sweeping guarantee of freedom of speech.

2649. Uniform national law code was the Code Napoléon (the Napoleonic Code), commissioned in 1800 by Napoléon Bonaparte, then First Consul of France, and drafted by a council under Jean-Jacques Régis de Cambacérès. The stated intent of the new code was to create an internally consistent body of laws which owed nothing to custom and everything to common sense, rationality, and logic. The Code Napoléon, declared the Code Civil of France in 1804, dealt with personal rights, property rights, and laws of succession and contract; criminal statues were added in 1811. Still the basis of law in France, it is also in use in countries such as Haiti, Bolivia, and the province of Quebec in Canada, where French culture was influential.

GOVERNMENT AND POLITICS—LEGISLATURES

2650. Parliament was the Althing of Iceland, founded in 930 CE, approximately 80 years after Vikings settled the island. The Althing served as national general assembly, legislative body, and law court, and was open to all adult male heads of household. It convened at Thingvellir at the height of midsummer. The Althing survived in truncated form after Iceland's acceptance of Norwegian sovereignty in 1262 and Danish control in 1380, but was abolished in 1800. In 1874 it was restored to legislative status. The Althing voted to reestablish Iceland as a free republic in 1944, severing all ties with Denmark. Some historians claim that the Tynwald Court, the legislative assembly of the Isle of Man (now part of England), may be as old as circa 890 and thus predate the Althing.

2651. Parliament on the European continent was the Riksdag, established in Sweden in 1435.

2652. European legislator of African descent was Mathieu Louisi, elected on August 22, 1848, to represent Guadeloupe in the French National Assembly. He served one term.

2653. Women elected as members of a Parliament were 19 women legislators who campaigned in Finland's national elections of March 15–17, 1907, the first following the introduction of universal and equal suffrage. The MPs took their seats in the Riksdagen on May 23. Most of them belonged to the Social Democrat Party.

2654. Woman to become a member of the British Parliament was Lady Astor, born Nancy Witcher Langhorne in Danville, VA, USA, the daughter of a Confederate officer in the Civil War. She succeeded her second husband, Waldorf Astor, in the House of Commons when he moved to the House of Lords in 1919 after becoming Viscount Astor of Hever on the death of his father. She was elected on the Tory ticket to represent the Plymouth constituency, took her oath of office on December 1, 1919, and served until 1945. But although Lady Astor was the first woman to serve in Parliament, she was not the first to be elected. Constance Markiewicz of Ireland successfully ran for office in 1918, the year in which women were granted the right to do so, but she refused to take her seat as a gesture of grievance against England.

2655. Woman to become a member of the Australian Parliament was the political and social reformer Edith Dircksey Cowan. In 1921, at the age of 60, she ran as an endorsed Nationalist and was elected to the Lower House in the first Western Australian election in which women were allowed to run for office, defeating the previous attorney general. She was only the second woman to be elected a parliamentary official in the history of the British Empire.

2656. Aboriginal Australian elected to the Australian Parliament was Neville Bonner, a member of the Jagera clan. He was elected to the Senate in 1972 on the Liberal Party ticket and served until 1983.

2657. Live broadcast from the British Parliament took place on June 9, 1975, when proceedings in the British House of Commons were broadcast by the British Broadcasting Corporation.

2658. Direct election of the European Parliament took place in the nine member states from June 7 to June 10, 1979, when national representatives to the EP were chosen by direct universal suffrage for the first time. The 410 representatives elected met in the Palais de l'Europe in Strasbourg, France, in July. Previously, representatives had been selected by the national parliaments of the member nations.

2659. Woman to become president of the Parliamentary Assembly of the Council of Europe was Leni Fischer, a member of Germany's parliament, who was elected on January 20, 1996. The Council of Europe was founded on May 5, 1949, to advance European unity.

GOVERNMENT AND POLITICS—MOVEMENTS

2660. Black nationalist movement was organized by the African-American Quaker, antislavery advocate, and merchant Paul Cuffe (1759–1817), captain of the brig *Traveler*. A native of Cuttyhunk Island, Massachusetts, Cuffe sailed to Sierra Leone in 1810 and began efforts to form a sugar-trading cooperative between the United States, England, and small West African nations. He encouraged free blacks to emigrate to Sierra Leone and in 1815 financed a small colony of 38 former slaves with his own funds.

2661. Theorists of socialism were active in France and England in the late 18th and early 19th centuries. The possibility of an industrialized state run on scientific principles by experts, with the goal of improving the condition of even the poorest members, was explored by Claude-Henri de Rouvroy, comte de Saint-Simon, in his *Nouveau Christianisme (New Christianity)* (1825) and other works. His contemporary, Francois-Marie-Charles Fourier, proposed the creation of cooperative agricultural settlements, called phalanges, whose members would share the responsibilities and the benefits of their collective efforts. The Welsh reformer Robert Owen built a model workers' community near Manchester, England, and in 1825 financed an experimental cooperative village in New Harmony, IN, USA. Some historians trace the origins of socialist ideas to Plato's *Republic* in the fourth century BCE.

2662. Anarchist was the French political radical and social philosopher Pierre-Joseph Proudhon. In his radical economic tract *Qu'est ce que la propriété? (What Is Property?)*, written in 1840, Proudhon coined the word "anarchism" to describe a society unfettered by any sovereign authority, which he believed was the inevitable goal of an advanced nation, and declared himself to be an anarchist. He added, "As man seeks justice in equality, so society seeks order in anarchy. Anarchy—the absence of a sovereign—such is the form of government to which we are every day approximating."

2663. Labor party called by that name was the Queensland Labour Party, established in 1890 at the instigation of the Queensland Provincial Council of the Australian Labour Federation. Australia's first MPs from the Queensland Labour Party, elected in 1892, were T. J. Ryan and G. J. Hall. In 1904, Australia became the first nation to have a Labour government, which was led by Prime Minister John Christian Watson. The first Labour government in Britain was not elected until 1945, during the political turmoil following the end of World War II. Under Prime Minister Clement Attlee, the party established the National Health Service, a system of universal welfare, stronger state control of industry, and a full labor program.

2664. European politician to adopt a platform of anti-Semitism was Karl Lüger, demagogic leader of the Austrian Christian Social Party and mayor of Vienna from 1897 to 1910. A liberal and modernizer in other areas, Lüger found it politically expedient to espouse a demogogic program of anti-ethnicism and anti-Semitism.

2665. World Zionist Congress was held in August 1897 in Basel, Switzerland. The first international meeting dedicated to the establishment of a modern Jewish national state, it was organized by the Austrian journalist Theodor Herzl, the father of political Zionism. The con-

GOVERNMENT AND POLITICS—MOVE-MENTS—*continued*

gress was attended by 204 delegates from Russia and central and eastern Europe, as well as a smaller number from western Europe and the United States. The delegates adopted a resolution calling for "a publicly recognized home for the Jewish people in Palestine."

2666. Modern political party for Africans was the African National Congress, founded by Pixley Seme in the Cape Province (now part of South Africa) on January 8, 1912. Originally called the South African Native National Congress, its goal was to preserve and extend voting rights for persons of color. It was known as the African National Congress from 1923.

2667. Meeting of the Palestine Liberation Organization was held in May 1964 in Jordanian-occupied Jerusalem (now part of Israel), when 422 Palestinian Arab leaders under the chairmanship of Ahmad Shuqeiri set up an organizational structure for a national council, executive committee, national fund, and armed force, and adopted a charter calling for the destruction of Israel and the establishment of an Arab state in its place.

2668. Green Party seats in a national government were won in the Bundestag (lower house) elections of March 6, 1983, by 27 members of *Die Grünen* (The Greens, or Green Party) of West Germany (now Germany). *Die Grünen* was founded in Germany in 1979 as a radical environmentalist, pacifist, and antinuclear protest movement by Herbert Gruhl, Petra Kelly, Gert Bastian, and others. In the 1983 election, the party won a 5.6 percent share of the vote, the first evidence that environmentalism might have a real base of political support in Europe.

2669. International Conservative Congress was held in Washington, DC, USA, in September 1997. It was attended by some 90 notable political conservatives from four continents, who discussed the international aspects of conservatism. The event was sponsored by the American conservative magazine *National Review*, as well as several American conservative institutions and foundations.

GOVERNMENT AND POLITICS—MOVE-MENTS—COMMUNISM

2670. Communist may have been the French revolutionary François-Noël Babeuf (also known as Gracchus Babeuf). Babeuf was a minor figure in the French Revolution who is remembered mainly for advocating, through his newspaper *Le Tribun du peuple (The Tribune of the People),* a ruthless final revolution in which all private property would be abolished, ushering in an era of universal equality under a dictatorship of the people. His ideas, coupled with the militant tactics he adopted in insurrections against the French revolutionary government, bore a remarkable resemblance to those of the Russian Marxist Vladimir Ilyich Lenin. Babeuf went to the guillotine on May 27, 1797.

2671. Communist secret society was the League of the Just, formed by Joseph Moll and mostly German-born followers of Karl Marx and Friedrich Engels. The first meeting was in June 1847 in London, England. When Marx and Engels agreed to join the League later that year, it was reconstituted as the Communist League, the first true Communist political party.

2672. Communist political platform was contained in the *Manifest der Kommunistischen Partei (The Communist Manifesto),* drafted in Paris, France, in 1848 by Karl Marx and Friedrich Engels. It was written at the request of the Communist League, the first Communist political party, which promptly adopted it as its politcial platform. After offering a version of world history as a centuries-long process of economic class struggle, the authors espoused a revolution of the proletariat in which all private property would be abolished. The *Manifesto* ends with the famous call: "The proletarians have nothing to lose but their chains. They have a world to win. Workingmen of all countries, unite!"

2673. Communist revolution that was successful was the Russian Revolution of 1917, also known as the Bolshevik Revolution and the October Revolution. Events throughout that year, including abortive coups in February and July, contributed to the collapse of constitutional liberalism in Russia and the seizure of power by the Bolsheviks under the militant Marxist Vladimir Ilyich Lenin. The revolution is typically dated from November 6–7 (October 24–25, Old Style calendar). On that night the Bolsheviks assumed control of Petrograd (later Leningrad, now St. Petersburg). The nearly bloodless revolution was immediately ratified by the Second All-Russian Congress of Soviets of Workers' and Soldiers' Deputies, and a national communist government was declared.

GOVERNMENT AND POLITICS—STATES AND EMPIRES

2674. Regional superpower was ancient Egypt, which dominated northeastern Africa and much of southeastern Asia for half a millennium during the period of the Old Kingdom, circa 2700–2200 BCE.

2675. Empire was the Akkadian Empire, established by Sargon of Akkad, who conquered Sumer in ancient Mesopotamia (present-day Iraq) in 2334 BCE. The empire he established extended west into Anatolia (in Turkey) and east into present-day Iran. It collapsed circa 2180 BCE, possibly due to a harsh drought.

2676. African state outside Egypt of record was Cush (or Kush), a kingdom in the southern part of Nubia along the valley of the Nile, reaching from the Second Cataract into what is now Sudan. It is mentioned in Egyptian documents circa 1990 BCE and flourished particularly during the interruption of Egypt's military excursions during the Second Intermediate Period (1785–1540 BCE). Royal tombs at Kerma, the capital, contained wooden furniture inlaid with ivory, copper weapons, jewelry, and ceramic goods, as well as evidence that the Cushites practiced mass live burials during the funerals of their kings.

2677. Large political state in Asia was organized circa 1760 BCE in China by the Shang dynasty, traditionally considered to be the second Chinese dynasty (after the semi-mythical Hsia dynasty). Centered in north-central China, the Shang empire extended north to what is now Shantung province and west to the present Honan province. Shang kings were the first to call themselves Sons of Heaven. The dynasty ended circa 1100 BCE.

2678. Confederation of Greek city-states to embark on a joint military adventure was assembled to fight the Trojan War, which took place circa 1185 BCE. Although the legend repeated in Homer's *Iliad* gives the cause as the abduction of Helen, wife of King Menelaus of Sparta, by Paris, son of King Priam of Troy, the more likely reason for the attack on Troy was the desire of the early Greeks to eliminate the city as a controller of trade between the Mediterranean and the Black Sea area. Troy stood at the entrance to the Dardanelles, at the present-day site of Hissarlik, Turkey.

2679. Empire to span multiple continents was the Persian Empire, which at its height covered some 2 million square miles of land in Africa, Europe, and Asia. It was formed in the sixth century BCE when Cyrus the Great conquered Media, a kingdom in the northwestern part of what is now Iran, and combined it with his own kingdom of Parsa (in southwestern Iran). Under the rule of Darius I, who ruled from 522 to 486 BCE, the empire was extended by further military conquests until it covered more than 2,500 miles between the present-day countries of Libya and Pakistan, reaching as far north as the Caucasus mountains and as far south as the Arabian Sea. Darius was the first to use the title "king of kings." The Persian empire continued until the year 330 BCE, when it was overthrown by Greek armies under Alexander the Great.

2680. Republic was the Roman Republic, founded circa 509 BCE after the despot Lucius Tarquinius Superbus, last of Rome's seven kings, was deposed, legendarily by Lucius Junius Brutus but possibly by Etruscan forces under Lars Porsenna, king of Clusium. To replace the monarchy, the Romans founded a government led by two annually elected magistrates and military leaders, the consuls, who performed executive duties while the Roman Senate, which had already been established under the kings, formulated the law for ratification by citizen voters in popular assemblies. The Romans called their new political system the *res publica* (public thing). Lucius Junius Brutus is usually held to have been the first consul elected.

2681. Democracy of notable influence was founded in ancient Athens, at first, circa 570 BCE, under Solon, who established a constitution giving voting power to a popular assembly of freeborn male citizens, and in its ultimate form in 508 BCE under the archon and reformer Cleisthenes. Cleisthenes reorganized Athenian society so that all the villages, or demes, of Attica could supply proportional representation to a new Council of Five Hundred, a kind of senate.

2682. Empire in sub-Saharan Africa was Ghana, first of the major trading empires of western Africa, which dominated the upper Senegal-Niger region between circa 800 and 1240. The ancient kingdom, not to be confused with the modern African republic of Ghana, occupied lands now part of Mali and Mauritania. According to tradition, Ghana was founded circa 400 by a king called the *ghana* (the title given to all later Ghanaian rulers). At the height of its power, Ghana derived its great wealth from import-export taxes on the traffic in alluvial gold from southern Africa to the Muslim caravan routes to the north, and by acting as the middleman for the trade in salt that moved south to pay for the gold.

GOVERNMENT AND POLITICS—STATES AND EMPIRES—*continued*

2683. Slavic state was Moravia, in the area of eastern Europe now occupied by the Czech Republic and Slovakia. Slavs moved into the area in the sixth century and gradually displaced the previous inhabitants, mainly Avar tribal peoples, beginning in circa 650. The Slavs took the name Moravians from the Morava River. A kingdom known as Moravia, nominally in fief to the Holy Roman Emperor, was established circa 818 under Prince Mojmír I, who reigned until 846. In 863, Moravia became the first Slavic state to fully adopt Christianity.

2684. Islamic state was Medina, the Arabian village (then called Yathrib; now in Saudi Arabia) to which Muhammad fled in 622 after he was rejected by his hometown of Mecca, and where he became established as a leader and prophet. From Medina he led his followers on raids against neighboring Arab tribes, conquering them and incorporating them into his federation.

2685. Muslim dynasty was the Umayyad dynasty, founded by the caliph Mu'awiyah I in 661 in Damascus, Syria. The Umayyad caliphs established an Islamic empire extending into Europe, Africa, Central Asia, and India. In 750, the Umayyad family was replaced by the Abbasids, but the Umayyad line continued in Spain until 1031.

2686. Andean empire was that of the Chimú people, who ruled the coastal areas of Peru between circa 1200 and 1465. The Chimú established a highly stratified society that was notable for its large-scale irrigation systems and elaborate network of roads. The Chimu capital, Chan Chan, founded by the legendary Chimú leader Tacayhamo, was located near present-day Trujillo, Peru. In 1465–70, the Chimu were conquered by the Inca.

2687. Thai capital was Sukhothai, in what is now Thailand's Chao Phraya River basin, or Central Plain. Located about 8 miles from the present-day Thai town of the same name, it was founded circa 1220 as the center of a newly independent Thai state.

2688. Black African state to be well documented was the Solomonid kingdom of Ethiopia, founded in 1270 by Yikunno Amlak, a man from the Amhara region, and extended by his grandson, the warrior king Amda Siyon (1314–44). The family claimed the throne as descendants of the Queen of Sheba and Solomon, king of Israel. The kingdom was a Christian state with a population of farmers, a class of nobles with quasi-feudal powers, and an itinerant royal court. Church documents and court chronicles provide most of the historical evidence.

2689. Global empire was that of the Portuguese, who employed their superior navigational skills to establish colonies in North Africa (1448), West Africa (circa 1490), India (1505), Brazil (1530), and China (1557).

2690. Empire to unite the Indian subcontinent was the Mogul (also spelled Mughal) Empire, founded by Babur, born Zahir ud-din-Muhammad, a Muslim descendent of the Mongol conquerors Genghis Khan and Tamerlane. A commander of genius as well as an able statesman and poet, Babur achieved his first whirlwind victories in India in April 1525 with the help of artillery purchased from the Ottoman Turks. By 1529 Babur had secured dominion over a vast area of northern and central India from Qandahar to the borders of Bengal. The Mogul dynasty that he established ruled India until the region was made a British colony in 1857. In English, the word "mogul" has come to mean any powerful ruler.

2691. African state to be ruled as a colony of a European state was Angola, formerly a Portuguese colony carved from the kingdoms of the Ndongo and the Kongo in the 17th century. Trade with Portugal, mainly in slaves, began in 1483; the first move to colonize the area began in 1575, when the Portuguese government granted Paulo Dias de Novais the right to conquer the interior. Expansion of the slave trade led to uprisings in the mid-17th century that were put down by the Portuguese, but the conquest of Angola was not completed until 1920. It remained under Portugal's control until November 1975.

2692. Independent nation in the New World was the United States, which declared its independence from Great Britain on July 4, 1776.

2693. Constitutional republic was the United States of America. The U.S. Constitution was signed at the end of the Constitutional Convention, which met at Philadelphia, PA, from May 25 to September 17, 1787, and was ratified on June 21, 1788. It was declared to be in effect on March 4, 1789.

2694. Independent nation in Latin America was Haiti, which declared its independence from France on January 1, 1804, after a rebellion led by former African-American slaves Jean-Jacques Dessalines and Henri Christophe routed Napoléon's forces on November 9, 1803. In 1825, in return for an indemnity of close to 100 million francs, France became the first nation to officially recognize Haitian independence. Haiti was also the first independent French-speaking republic, and the first African-American republic, in the New World.

2695. Republic in Africa was Liberia, created in 1822 by the American Colonization Society as a home for freed African slaves from the United States. Independence was declared in 1847 by Joseph Jenkins Roberts, Liberia's first black governor, and Liberia became a republic the following year.

2696. Muslim country to adopt a secular government was Turkey, after its establishment as a republic in 1923. During the next few years, under the leadership of its first president, Mustafa Kemal Atatürk, Turkey abolished the caliphate, closed the country's religious schools and courts, outlawed a number of Islamic organizations, provided for the legal emancipation of women, and switched from Arabic script to the Latin script used by Western languages. In 1926, the Islamic law, the *Shari'a,* was entirely replaced by secular law codes derived from those of Switzerland, Italy, and Germany.

2697. Non-Western nation to become fully industrialized was Japan, which undertook to convert from a feudal agricultural economy to full industrialization in the late 19th century and had completed the process of becoming an industrialized nation, comparable to those in the West, by circa 1930.

2698. British civilian medal conferred on a country was the George Cross awarded on April 15, 1942, to Malta, a member of the British Commonwealth, by King George VI. The medal honored Malta's stoic resistance to German aerial attacks during World War II.

2699. Sub-Saharan African colony to gain its independence was Ghana, comprising the former British colony known as the Gold Coast and the UN Trust Territory of Togoland, which became an independent nation on March 6, 1957, under prime minister Kwame Nkrumah. In 1960, Ghana was declared a republic, with Nkrumah as its first president.

2700. Fundamentalist Islamic republic was founded in Iran in 1979 by Muslim religious leader Ayatollah Ruhollah Khomeini (born Ruhollah Musawi in 1930 in Khomein, Iran). Khomeini, a strict Shi'ite fundamentalist, had been exiled from Iran since 1964, but his charismatic influence over Iranian politics grew throughout the 1970s. On February 1, 1979, he returned to Teheran in triumph two weeks after the collapse of the regime of Mohammad Reza Pahlavi, the last shah of Iran, and assumed control of Iran's Islamic revolution. A referendum in December 1979 established Iran as an Islamic state under Islamic law, with Khomeini as its leader for life.

2701. Tribal state in Canada with self-government was formed from mainly wilderness land in British Columbia, which became the national territory of the Nisga'a Native Americans under a pact reached on July 16, 1998, with the Canadian federal government. The treaty gave the Nisga'a, a tribe of some 5,800 members, the deed to approximately 1,930 square kilometers of land, as well as a cash settlement and a form of self-government.

GOVERNMENT AND POLITICS—SYMBOLS

2702. Representations of flags and flag-like objects called vexilloids appear on Egyptian pottery from circa 3500 BCE.

2703. Crowns known to historians were the crowns of the kings of Upper and Lower Egypt. The crown of Upper Egypt was a white cone with a serpent in front. The crown of Lower Egypt was a red cap with a tall straight crown in back and a spiral crown in front. These were combined into one double crown when Upper and Lower Egypt were united, an event traditionally ascribed to the pharaoh Menes of the First Dynasty circa 3100 BCE.

2704. Flag still extant is a metal flag found in Iran that dates from the third millennium BCE. It was attached to a metal pole and capped by a finial in the shape of an eagle.

2705. Great Seal showing a monarch seated on a throne together with royal insignia was introduced in Europe by Emperor Henry II of Germany, who ruled from 1002 to 1024. The first European monarch to use a two-sided seal was Edward the Confessor of England, who ruled from 1042 to 1066.

2706. European heraldry originated in the twelfth century, when the widespread use of chain-mail body armor and helmets made it necessary for knights to display some form of identification. The first man to bear a shield with a heraldic device appears to have been Geoffrey, Count of Anjou, who is reported to have received from his father-in-law, King Henry I of England, a shield on which lions were painted, sometime around the year 1130. A French enamel from the same era shows Geoffrey carrying just such a shield.

GOVERNMENT AND POLITICS—SYMBOLS—*continued*

2707. Heraldic device worn by an English king was the shield showing three golden lions that was worn by King Richard I, known as Coeur-de-Lion, or Lion-Hearted, who came to the throne in 1189.

2708. Flag of a people was the flag of Denmark, the Dannebrog, which is older in origin than any other nation's. The design, a white cross on a red field, has been used in Denmark since the 14th century. An old Danish tradition maintains that on June 15, 1219, in answer to a prayer, the Dannebrog appeared in the sky over the battlefield where the Danes were losing to their enemies, the Estonians, and came down to earth, where the Danes gained the victory.

2709. National flag was the flag adopted on June 14, 1777, by the Second Continental Congress of the United States of America, during its war of independence against Britain.

GROOMING AND COSMETICS

2710. Cosmetics were current among fashionable women and men in ancient Egypt, perhaps the first truly fashion-conscious society, during the fourth millennium BCE. The Egyptians applied lip color, cheek rouge, skin cream, and body paint. Kohl, a black ointment made from antimony, was used to make the eyes look bigger and the eyelashes thicker, and was also formed into sticks for use as eyebrow pencils. A green eye shadow was made from ground malachite, to which beetle shells were added for a glitter effect. Prescriptions for blending combinations of ingredients to alleviate particular problems appear on clay tablets from 3000 BCE.

2711. Nail polish was devised in China, probably during the third millennium BCE. Different colors were assigned to people of different social strata.

2712. Manicure set was found in a 4,000-year-old tomb at Tel-el-Muqayyar, Iraq, the site of the ancient Mesopotamian city of Ur. It contained gold nail-care instruments. Another set of personal care items from the same era was found in the ruins of Tepe Gawra (near modern Mosul, Iraq). It consisted of four items—a pointed toothpick, a makeup applicator, an ear scoop, and a wand—with holes bored in their handles, held together by a ring.

2713. Tampons were made in ancient Egypt and Mesopotamia of softened papyrus pith and water reeds.

2714. Tallow soap is said by the Roman historian Pliny the Elder to have been made in 600 BCE by the Phoenicians, who did so by boiling goat tallow and wood ashes in water.

2715. Book on cosmetics was the *Medicamina faciei (Cosmetics),* written circa 2 BCE by Ovid, the Roman poet (born Publius Ovidius Naso in what is now Sulmona, Italy). The book, of which only 100 lines of verse remain, appears to have been a witty exposition on the art of feminine allure. It includes detailed recipes for women's cosmetics, such as a face pack of barley-bean flour, eggs, and mashed narcissus bulbs.

2716. Public bathing on a wide scale was practiced by the ancient Romans, as evidenced by the many examples of *thermae*—public bathhouses—that still survive in areas once within the Roman Empire. Best known are the large imperial *thermae* in Rome, such as the Baths of Agrippa (27 CE), the Baths of Titus, built in 81 CE, and the huge Baths of Caracalla, completed circa 217 and designed to serve 1,600 bathers at once. Most *thermae* contained several rooms, in which the bather progressed from hot to cold baths. Bathing was considered so important that bathhouses were constructed in every important Roman or Roman-influenced settlement, including such out-of-the-way places as Herod's Palace atop Masada in the arid Judean wilderness.

2717. Cold cream was invented by the influential physician Galen of Pergamon (now Bergama, Turkey), who circa 180 CE mixed water, beeswax, and olive oil into a face cream that was effective in cooling and softening the skin.

2718. Handkerchief was the *muscinium,* introduced by the Romans circa 300 CE. It was used mainly to wipe the nose.

2719. Luxury spa was a mineral spring at Spa, near the Belgian town of Liège, which became a fashionable destination for upper-class Europeans in the 16th century.

2720. European ruler to bathe regularly of record was Queen Elizabeth I of England, who reigned from 1558 to 1603. She was considered eccentric for her habit of bathing as often as once a month—a practice few of her subjects emulated. Regular bathing was not considered healthful by most Europeans until the 19th century.

2721. Facial tissues of rice paper were used by the Japanese for centuries. An English traveler visiting Japan in 1637 wrote that "the Japanese blow their noses with a certain soft and tough kind of paper which they carry around with them in small pieces, which, having used, they fling away as a filthy thing."

2722. Wrapped soap for sale was Old Brown London Soap, offered by London chemist John Atkinson in 1892.

2723. Bathroom scale for home use was introduced by a German company, Jas Ravenol, in 1910. The scale was called the Jarasco scale.

2724. Makeup specifically for movie actors was a semiliquid tan greasepaint, available in a range of tones, developed for the American movie industry in 1910 by Max Factor.

2725. Cosmetics entrepreneur of note was Helena Rubinstein, a Polish-born cosmetician who began selling a homemade beauty aid, Creme Valaze, at her beauty salon in Melbourne, Australia, in 1902. By 1917, she had opened salons in London, Paris, and cities in the United States. Eventually her company operated research laboratories where dermatologists and chemists invented hundreds of new items, of which the most famous was waterproof mascara. Rubinstein was the first cosmetics entrepreneur to develop a line of medicated skin-care products and the first to station saleswomen in department stores to give demonstrations for customers.

2726. Talking bathroom scale was introduced by the Malaysian inventor H.S. Ong in 1984.

GROOMING AND COSMETICS—HAIR

2727. Combs for styling hair and holding it in place have been found in Egyptian tombs from the fourth millennium BCE.

2728. Wigs were worn by the Egyptians. By 3000 BCE, they were shaving their heads and putting on wigs made of human hair and plant fibers. Wigs served to establish social status, with the most elaborate headpieces reserved for royalty.

2729. Shampoo was diluted citrus juice, used by the Egyptians from about 2500 BCE.

2730. Curling iron for styling hair was an iron bar that was heated in fire and used to make curls on the heads and beards of upper-class Assyrians circa 1500 BCE. Assyrian officers did not go to war without having their hair groomed.

2731. Hair styling was practiced circa 1500 BCE by the Assyrians, who applied it to both heads and beards. Using techniques of cutting, layering, oiling, tinting, curling, dyeing, and perfuming, they created elaborate hairdos that were regulated by sex, occupation, and social rank.

2732. Hair lightening was practiced by dark-haired Greek men and women of the fourth century BCE, who bleached and powdered their hair in an attempt to look blond.

2733. Male hairdresser to style women's hair appears to have been one Monsieur Champagne, whose services were in demand by affluent Frenchwomen in the mid-17th century. Shortly thereafter, the first hairdressing academy to train both women and men was opened in Paris.

2734. Permanent wave hairstyle was introduced by the German hairdresser Karl Ludwig Nessler on October 8, 1906, at his Oxford Street salon in London, England. His method for styling hair with permanent curls and bobs required women to sit for up to six hours with heavy brass rollers in their hair. The style did not catch on internationally until 1915, when it was adopted by the American ballroom dancer Irene Castle.

2735. Commercial hair dye was developed in 1909 by Eugène Schueller, a French chemist, using the ingredient paraphenylenediamine. The company he founded to market the product, the French Harmless Hair Dye Company, became a giant in the cosmetics industry after its name was changed to L'Oréal.

2736. Blow dryer for hair was developed simultaneously and independently in 1920 by two American companies, the Racine Universal Motor Company and Hamilton Beach, both of Racine, WI, USA. The companies were working on developing electric blenders, and both were aware that women were already using home vacuum cleaners to dry their hair. Combining these two technologies, plus a heating coil, yielded the earliest blow driers. The first widely successful model was introduced in the Sears-Roebuck fall-winter 1951 catalog. It featured a nozzle attached to a pink plastic bonnet that fit over the head.

GROOMING AND COSMETICS—MIRRORS

2737. Hand mirrors made of metal sheets, bent slightly convex and polished smooth, were current in Sumeria and Egypt during the Bronze Age, circa 3500 BCE. They were set into handles made of gold, wood, ivory, and other materials.

GROOMING AND COSMETICS—MIRRORS—*continued*

2738. School for mirror artisans to train them in techniques of polishing metal with sand was opened in Greece in 328 BCE.

2739. Full-length mirrors of highly polished metal were made in Rome during the first century. Silver was the preferred material, because of its fidelity in reflecting true colors.

2740. Glass mirrors were made by skilled Venetian glass artisans circa 1300.

2741. Glass mirrors free of distortion were made possible by a technique of rolling out smooth planes of glass that was patented by Bernard Perrot, a French glass artisan, in 1687.

2742. Freestanding full-length mirror was the cheval glass, invented in France in the late 18th century. The mirror was mounted in a frame supported by four feet. It was adjustable both for height, through a pulley and counterweight system, and for angle.

2743. Silvered hand mirror made by chemically depositing a thin film of silver on glass was invented in 1835 by Baron Justus von Liebig, a pioneering German chemist and professor at the University of Giessen.

GROOMING AND COSMETICS—PERFUME

2744. Perfume bottles date from circa 1000 BCE in Egypt, where there was already a 2,000-year-old tradition of making perfumes from flowers, spices, oils, and honey.

2745. Guild of perfume makers was founded in the twelfth century in France, where they were called *parfumeurs*.

2746. Perfume containing alcohol was "Hungary Water," made in 1370 for Queen Elizabeth of Hungary. It was made of scented floral oils blended in an alcohol solution.

2747. Eau de cologne was created in Cologne, Germany, in 1709 by Jean-Baptiste Farina, an Italian-born barber. The formula included bergamot oil, lemon spirits, and orange bitters in an alcohol base.

2748. Designer perfume was Chanel No. 5, developed by perfumier Ernst Beaux in Biarritz, Switzerland, and introduced on May 5, 1921, by the Paris coutourier Gabrielle "Coco" Chanel. The number 5 was chosen by Chanel because the product was to be sold beginning on the fifth day of the fifth month. (Other accounts have it that it was the fifth fragance she tested.) The perfume, in its revolutionary cubic glass bottle, was so successful that it formed the financial basis of Chanel's fashion business.

GROOMING AND COSMETICS—SHAVING

2749. Shaving instruments were implements found in nature, including flints, shells, and shark's teeth. Their earliest use appears to have been in Asia and Africa some 20,000 years ago.

2750. Razors were used in Egypt in the fourth millennium BCE, crafted from copper and gold.

2751. Clean-shaven society was that of the ancient Romans. Roman legend as reported by the historian Livy had it that the metal razor was introduced circa 550 BCE by Lucius Tarquinius Priscus, the fifth king of Rome, and that it became the custom for Roman men to shave beginning circa 500 BCE.

2752. Professional barbers were those of ancient Rome, who were organized into guilds in 303 BCE.

2753. Safety razor was a blade equipped with a metal guard along one edge. It was invented in 1762 by Jean-Jacques Perret, a French barber.

2754. Safety razor to be commercially manufactured was the Star Safety Razor, made by Kampfe Brothers, New York, NY, USA, in 1880. It consisted of a short portion of a hand-forged blade of a barber's straight razor inserted in a frame with full safety features.

2755. Electric shaver was invented by an American, Colonel Jacob Schick, who recognized that soldiers in the field needed a razor that did not require soap or hot water. He patented a tiny electric motor in 1923 and received U.S. patents on his "shaving implement" on November 6, 1928. The first razors manufactured by the Schick company of Stamford, CT, were delivered on March 18, 1931.

2756. Disposable razor was the Bic Disposable, developed by the Bic Company of France, and marketed worldwide beginning in 1975. It contained a single blade and a cheap plastic handle, and was designed to be thrown away after a few shaves.

GROOMING AND COSMETICS—TEETH

2757. Toothbrush was a twig with one end frayed to make a brush, a device used by people all over the world. The oldest ones extant are Egyptian, from the beginning of the third millennium BCE.

2758. Toothpaste was used by the Egyptians circa 2000 BCE. They ground pumice stones and mixed the powder with wine vinegar.

2759. Toothbrushes with bristles were a Chinese invention, dating from 1498, and were made with hog bristles. The handles were made of bone or bamboo.

2760. Toothpaste tube was the invention of a dentist, Dr. Washington Wentworth Sheffield of New London, CT, USA, who was seeking a method of packaging toothpaste that was more hygienic than the porcelain jars then in use. In 1892, he introduced a flexible, collapsible metal tube.

2761. Toothbrush with synthetic bristles was Dr. West's Miracle Tuft Toothbrush, made by the E.I. du Pont de Nemours and Company of Wilmington, DE, USA, and first introduced to the retail trade in September 1938. The bristles were made of nylon, but were stiff enough to hurt the gums. Du Pont introduced a soft-bristle brush in the 1950s.

2762. Electric toothbrush was the Broxodent, made by the Squibb Company, an American firm. It went on sale in 1961. A cordless electric toothbrush made by General Electric came on the market the following year.

H

HEADS OF STATE—EMPERORS AND EMPRESSES

2763. Emperor known by name was Sargon of Akkad, the Semitic conqueror of Sumer in ancient Mesopotamia (present-day Iraq). What little is known about Sargon comes from copies made by Babylonian scribes of long-lost Akkadian court documents. According to tradition, the baby Sargon (the name means "True King") was found floating in a basket in the river by a gardener. From humble beginnings, he rose to become cupbearer to the ruler of the Sumerian city of Kish. After usurping the throne of Kish, he defeated the Sumerian king Lugalzaggisi of Uruk (the biblical city of Erech). In 2334 BCE, he founded a dynasty that lasted 146 years. It was centered in the capital city of Agade, which has never been located. Sargon pursued conquests as far west as Anatolia (in Turkey) and as far east as Iran, and established a wide network of trading agreements. The Akkadian Empire's collapse, circa 2180 BCE, may have been due to a harsh drought that brought a flood of refugees into the area.

2764. Chinese ruler to invoke the Mandate of Heaven to justify his right to rule was Wu Wang, the founder of the Chou dynasty, who came to power in 1111 BCE by overthrowing the last Shang emperor, Chou Hsin. Because Chou Hsin was notorious for debauchery and cruelty, Wu Wang declared that his mandate to rule had been withdrawn by Heaven, which required a virtuous king whose rule would produce a harmonious society.

2765. Emperor of Japan was Jimmu Tenno, held to be a direct descendant of the Japanese sun goddess, Amaterasu. According to semi-historical accounts in early Japanese myth-chronicles, he conquered areas of Honshu along the Inland Sea and circa 660 BCE established a capital at Yamato.

2766. Emperor of India was Candragupta (or Chandragupta), a member of the Maurya tribe who was raised as a cowherd and lived as a slave until his owner, a Brahmin politicians, had him tutored in military tactics. He gathered a mercenary army and by the year 325 BCE was emperor of Magadha (modern Bihar). He became the ruler of the Punjab circa 322 BCE after the death of Alexander the Great and the subsequent withdrawal of the Greeks. In 321 BCE he founded the Maurya dynasty. During his reign, his army of 600,000 men conquered the whole of India, repelling an invasion by Alexander's successor, Seleucus I Nicator, circa 305 BCE. He became a Jain and fasted to death, following Jain custom, circa 297 BCE after India was stricken by a famine.

2767. Buddhist national leader was the Indian emperor Asóka, third ruler of the Maurya dynasty, who ascended to the throne circa 273 BCE. By 261 BCE, his kingdom included most of southern and central India as well as Afghanistan and Baluchistan. The bloody conquests of his early career apparently sickened Asóka, and in 261 he renounced violence and converted to Buddhism, which he made the state religion. Asóka then instituted a reign of unusual liberalism and tolerance. His "rock edicts," inscribed pillars of rock erected throughout the kingdom, admonished people to plant trees, dig wells, be kind to children, and establish hospitals. Missionaries from Asóka's realm, including his own son, are believed to have brought Buddhism to Sri Lanka and Thailand. A Hindu revolt circa 180 BCE destroyed the Maurya empire and virtually ended Buddhism in India.

HEADS OF STATE—EMPERORS AND EMPRESSES—*continued*

2768. Emperor of China was Qin Shi Huangdi (also transliterated Ch'in Shih Huang Ti), founder in 221 BCE of the Qin (Ch'in) empire, from which the modern state of China takes its name. Shi Huangdi, born Zheng, was the ruler of the small state of Qin. In a masterful series of conquests, he subdued six rival states and granted himself an imperial title that means "First August Emperor of Qin." He died in 210 BCE and was buried in a tomb that took 36 years to construct. A modern excavation of his tomb unearthed 7,000 terracotta soldiers, perhaps representing an army to command in the afterlife.

2769. Emperor of Rome was Gaius Octavius (also known as Octavian), grandnephew of Julius Caesar. In his will, Caesar adopted Octavian and made him his heir, which gave the younger man sufficient influence with the legions to take control of Rome and eventually the entire Greco-Roman world in the power struggle that followed Caesar's assassination. Octavian was given the honorary name Augustus Caesar by the Roman Senate on his accession in 27 BCE. He ruled as emperor until 14 CE.

2770. Empress of Japan was Suiko Tenno, daughter of one emperor and widow of another, who was placed on the throne by her uncle, Soga Umako, in 592 during a power struggle among Japan's feudal clans that was exacerbated by a war between the followers of Japan's indigenous Shinto religion and supporters of the newly imported religion of Buddhism. Suiko succeeded in encouraging the spread of Buddhism while she placated Shintoists by making offerings to the traditional gods. The country was governed by Suiko's nephew, the crown prince and regent Shotoku.

2771. Empress of China to rule in her own right was Wu Ze-tian, also called Wu Zhou. Originally one of numerous imperial concubines, she succeeded, through assassination and intrigue, in becoming empress in 655, ruling in place of her invalid husband, Gao Zong, for 23 years. In 690 she proclaimed herself emperor after deposing both of her sons. Her reign lasted 15 years.

2772. Woman to rule the Byzantine Empire was Irene, who ruled the Byzantine Empire from 797 to 802 CE. After the death of her husband Leo IV in 780, she assumed the regency and was co-emperor with her ten-year-old son, Constantine VI. As he matured, Constantine challenged her control and had her banished from court from 790 to 792. In 797 she took her revenge by having him arrested and blinded. Her period as sole ruler—with the title of emperor, not empress—ended when she was deposed in 802 and exiled to Lesbos.

2773. Holy Roman Emperor was Charlemagne (also known as Carolus Magnus, Charles the Great, and Charles I), who as king of the Franks from 768 to 814 united the greater part of western Europe in one empire. On December 25, 800, at St. Peter's Basilica in Rome, Italy, he was crowned Holy Roman Emperor by Pope Leo III, who in a surprise move placed a crown on his head and pronounced him "Augustus and emperor" of all Christian lands, including those of Byzantium. The coronation came as a shock to Charlemagne, who had expected Leo to consecrate his son as King of the Franks and the Lombards.

2774. Khmer emperor was Jayavarman II (posthumously known as Paramesvara), who founded the Khmer, or Cambodian, Empire in 802. Jayavarman II ascended to the throne with Javanese backing in 800 but declared Khmer independence in 802. He established his capital near Angkor Wat circa 840, near the end of his rule.

2775. Emperor of Mali was Sundiata (or Mari Diata), a member of the Mandingo tribe who, according to oral tradition, was one of twelve brothers in the royal family of the kingdom of Kangaba, on the Upper Niger River. He came to power in 1235 after defeating the usurper who had assassinated his brothers. Over the next two decades he continued to annex neighboring kingdoms and built a vastly rich empire that lasted until the 16th century and controlled most of the West African trade in gold.

2776. Emperor of Songhai was Sonni Ali, who became ruler of the small Songhai kingdom on the upper Niger River (in present-day Mali) circa 1464 and expanded it into an empire, beginning with his conquest of the Tuareg occupiers of Timbuktu in 1468. Songhai became a center of commerce and remained so until its conquest by the Moroccans in the late 16th century. At its peak, it reached from the Atlantic coast in Senegal eastward into what is now Niger.

2777. Tsar to travel outside Russia was Peter the Great. To further his plan of modernizing the country and building its military power, he organized the Grand Embassy, a group of 250 members of the Russian elite, who were sent to western Europe in 1697 on a fact-finding tour. The tsar accompanied them, sometimes using the alias Sergeant Pyotr Mikhaylov. In addition to visiting educational and political institutions, hiring specialists in a variety of fields to assist Russian projects, studying shipbuilding, and trying his hand at working as a shipyard carpenter (first at Saardam, Holland, in the shipyard of the Dutch East India Company, and then at Deptford, England, for the Royal Navy), he conducted diplomatic negotiations with England, Holland, and Austria.

2778. Emperor of the Ashanti was Osei Tutu, who brought into federation, circa 1698, a number of Ashanti kingdoms in the area that is now Ghana. He was the first to sit on the Golden Stool, symbol of the king's temporal and spiritual power. The empire continued to expand after his death and became wealthy in the 18th century as a supplier of slaves to European purchasers.

2779. Emperor of France was Napoléon Bonaparte, who had earlier declared himself consul for life. He was proclaimed emperor of France on May 28, 1804, and received the crown from Pope Pius VII in a lavish ceremony on December 2, 1804, at Nôtre-Dame de Paris. At the climactic moment, Napoléon famously seized the crown from the pope and set it on his own head.

2780. European-born emperor of a North American country was Ferdinand Maximilian Joseph, an Austrian archduke who with French backing became emperor of Mexico in 1864. Maximilian originally had the support of Mexican conservatives as well as French troops in Mexico, but in 1867, when pressure from the United States led French emperor Napoléon III to withdraw his army, Maximilian unwisely decided to stay and defend the city of Querétaro against Republican forces under former Mexican president Benito Pablo Juárez. On May 14, 1867, Maximilian was betrayed and captured. He was executed on June 19.

HEADS OF STATE—PRESIDENTS

2781. President of a nation was the first president of the United States of America, George Washington, who was inaugurated in the Federal Building on Wall Street in New York City and served from April 30, 1789, to March 4, 1797. He was not, however, the first person to be known as the president of the United States. After the adoption of the Articles of Confederation in 1781, the presidents of the sessions of the Continental Congress signed themselves "President of the United States in Congress Assembled." The first to do so was Thomas McKean of Delaware.

2782. Constitutional president of Mexico was Guadalupe Victoria (born Manuel Félix Fernandez in Tamazuela, Mexico), a military leader in the Mexican independence movement, who served as the elected president of Mexico from 1824 to 1829.

2783. President of the Argentine republic was Bernardino Rivadavia, elected president of the United Provinces in 1826. Although an enlightened and able leader who founded museums and universities, he was unable to pacify the provinces, which were often at war, or to garner the support of the provincial caudillos (leaders). He was forced to resign in 1827. His birthday is now a national holiday.

2784. President of Ecuador was Juan José Flores, elected on May 13, 1830, after Ecuador seceded from Gran Colombia and became a separate, independent republic.

2785. President of Colombia was Francisco de Paula Santander, a confederate and later opponent of Simón Bolívar, who fought to liberate Colombia (then called New Granada) from Spanish rule. Santander was called to serve as the new nation's first president on April 1, 1833. His administration ended in 1837.

2786. Constitutional president of Honduras was Francisco Ferrera, a pro-clergy conservative who assumed power on January 1, 1841. Honduras had declared its sovereignty and independence on November 5, 1838.

2787. President of Liberia was Joseph Jenkins Roberts, an American-born son of free African-Americans from Virginia. Liberia was created in 1822 by the American Colonization Society as a home for freed African slaves from the United States. Roberts, Liberia's first black governor, declared independence for the country in 1847 and was elected its first president. He stepped down in 1856 to become president of Liberia College, but served again as president from 1872 to 1876.

2788. President of a Central American country born in the United States was the adventurer and filibuster William Walker. In 1856, Walker was invited by a revolutionary faction to seize power in Nicaragua, which he did with the help of Cornelius K. Garrison and Charles Morgan, officials of Cornelius Vanderbilt's Accessory Transit Company. Walker was president of Nicaragua from July 12, 1856, to May 1, 1857, when he surrendered to the U.S. Navy and fled the country.

HEADS OF STATE—PRESIDENTS—*continued*

2789. Civilian president of Mexico was Benito Pablo Juárez, a liberal-democratic reformer who served from 1861 to 1872. A Zapotec Indian of Oaxaca province, Juárez served as minister of justice, head of the Supreme Court, and as effective vice president during the turbulent period during and after the reign of the conservative caudillo Santa Anna. Juárez led the successful resistance to the invasion in 1864 of French forces supporting Ferdinand Maximilian Joseph as emperor of Mexico.

2790. President of Brazil was Marshal Deodoro da Fonseca, first of a succession of Brazil's "coffee presidents," so-called because they depended heavily on the support of the wealthy coffee growers. Fonseca was a leader of the effort to establish a Brazilian republic after the abdication of King Pedro II on November 15, 1889, and in 1891 was elected president under Brazil's new constitution, closely modeled after that of the United States. He resigned in November 1891.

2791. President of Cuba was Tomás Estrada Palma, elected in 1902 during the interim period between the two American occupations of the island, in 1899–1901 and 1906–09.

2792. Constitutional president of Panama was Manuel Amador Guerrero, who took office following the declaration, with U.S. support, of Panamanian independence from Colombia in 1903.

2793. Democratic president of Uruguay was José Batlle y Ordóñez, the democratic reformer, journalist, and leader of the Colorado Party. His election as president in 1903 led to a civil war with an opposition group called the Blanco Party. In 1905, free elections were held, and Batlle y Ordóñez was again elected to the presidency. He stepped down in 1907, but was reelected in 1911 and served until 1915.

2794. President of the Republic of Portugal was Manoel José de Arriaga, elected by the new Constituent Assembly on August 24, 1911. His short administration was marred by the increasing factionalism of Portuguese politics, which ultimately led to a series of coups, assassinations, and a civil war between royalists and democrats.

2795. President of China was Sun Yixian (in Wade-Giles, Sun Yat-Sen), the founder of the Kuomintang, the Chinese nationalist movement. In December 1911, during the revolution that overthrew the Manchu Dynasty, he was voted the first provisional president of the Republic of China by revolutionary delegates meeting at Nanking. Sun resigned on February 12, 1912, in favor of Yuan Shikai, who had the backing of the government ministers.

2796. President of Czechoslovakia (the modern Czech Republic) was the philosopher, political theorist, and national hero Tomás Masaryk, the leading figure of Czech nationalism. He was elected on November 14, 1918, and reelected in 1920, 1927, and 1934. He resigned in 1935.

2797. President of independent Poland was Józef Klemens Piłsudski, the Polish statesman, revolutionary, and military leader, who was elected on November 14, 1918, and served until May 29, 1923. Pilsudski was the leading figure in setting Polish foreign policy between the wars.

2798. Prime minister of independent Latvia was Karlis Ulmanis, leader of the Latvian Farmers' Union, who formed a government after independence was declared on November 18, 1918. He served as prime minister from 1918 to 1921, again in 1925–26 and 1931–32, and once more from 1934 to 1940 (the last four years as president also). He disappeared in 1940 after his arrest by the Soviets, who annexed Latvia on August 3 of that year. The first president of Latvia in the post-Soviet era of independence was Guntis Ulmanis, also a leader of the Latvian Farmers' Union, elected on July 7, 1993.

2799. President of independent Finland was Kaarlo Juho Stahlberg, principal writer of the Finnish constitution. A professor of administrative law at the University of Helsinki, he was a leading member of the National Progressive Party and was elected president of newly independent Finland in 1919. He served a single term, until 1925.

2800. President of independent Estonia in its period of freedom between the world wars was August Rei, who served as president of the constituent assembly that was elected in April 1919. On June 15, 1920, Rei oversaw the adoption of a new constitution. The first president of Estonia following the breakup of the Soviet Empire was Lennart Meri, who took office after the elections of September 1992.

2801. President of Turkey was Mustafa Kemal Atatürk, the Turkish national hero and founder of the modern Republic of Turkey. He was elected president by the provisional Grand National Assembly in Ankara on April 23, 1920, while still a rebel against the Ottoman government of Sultan Mehmed VI in Istanbul. The sultanate was abolished in 1922, and the Turkish republic was proclaimed on October 29, 1923. Mustafa Kemal Atatürk served as its leader until his death on November 10, 1938.

2802. President of the federal republic of Austria was the political philosopher and activist Michael Arthur Josef Jakob Hainisch. An advocate of Anschluss (the incorporation of Austria into Germany), he was elected Austria's first federal president in December 1920 as a compromise candidate with no strong political base. He was reelected in 1924 and served until 1928. Hainisch was one of the vocal supporters of Austria's unification with Nazi Germany in 1938.

2803. Constitutional president of Spain was the Spanish statesman Nicetor Alcalá Zamora, formerly the prime minister, elected by the National Assembly on December 11, 1931. He was deposed in February 1936 and went into exile.

2804. President of the Republic of Ireland (Éire) was the Gaelic scholar Douglas Hyde, the first professor of modern Irish at University College, Dublin, and the leading 20th-century conservator of the Irish tongue. On June 25, 1938, he was inaugurated as the first president of the Irish Republic, having been nominated unanimously by all parties. He served a seven-year term.

2805. President of Syria was the nationalist Shukri al-Kuwatli, leader in the 1930s of the anti-French National Bloc movement (later the National Party). When Syria was granted independence in 1943, he was able to garner enough support to win the presidency. He was ousted in the army coup of 1949, but after a period of exile returned to Syria and was reelected in 1955.

2806. President of the modern Republic of Iceland was Sveinn Björnsson, a member of the Althing, Iceland's minister to Denmark during the 1920s and 1930s, and the regent for the Danish king during World War II. When Iceland declared its independence from Denmark in 1944, Björnsson was elected the republic's first president. He was reelected in 1945 and 1949.

2807. President of the Philippines was Manuel Roxas y Acuña, leader of the liberal wing of the Nacionalista Party (later the Liberal Party), who assumed the presidency on July 4, 1946, the date that the Republic of the Philippines declared its independence. Roxas had served in the pro-Japanese government of José Laurel during World War II, but his postwar political career was assured by his friendship with the American general Douglas MacArthur. Roxas served until his death in 1948.

2808. President of South Korea was Syngman Rhee, a longtime advocate for Korean independence. Rhee had spent World War II in Washington, DC, and had the political support of United States. When the Republic of Korea (South Korea) was established on August 15, 1948, Rhee became its first president, and won reelection in 1952, 1956, and 1960. Rhee's increasingly dictatorial rule, plus the likelihood that he fixed the election of 1960, sparked widespread rioting and forced him out of office on April 27, 1960.

2809. President of Israel was Belarus-born Chaim Azriel Weizmann, head of the World Zionist Organization from 1917 to 1946. He was president of the state of Israel from February 1949 to November 1952.

2810. President of Indonesia was Sukarno, president of the United States of Indonesia when it achieved independence from the Netherlands on December 27, 1949. He had declared Indonesia's independence, and his presidency, on August 17, 1945, before the union with the Netherlands was officially dissolved. Sukarno's controversial regime was marked by bizarre political excess as he attempted to impose a Marxist-inspired program under the name "Guided Democracy." Following a bloody coup and near-civil war, of which Sukarno himself was the likely instigator, he was replaced by the military commander Suharto in March 1968 and was placed under lifelong arrest.

2811. Constitutional president of the Republic of Egypt was the anti-Western nationalist, socialist, and modernizer Gamal Abdel Nasser, who came to power following a coup on July 23, 1952, in which he and a group of young officers, including his successor Anwar Sadat, ousted King Farouk. After a brief puppet regime run by Nasser behind the scenes, he became prime minister in 1954. In January 1956 the charismatic Nasser was the only candidate on the presidential ballot under a new constitution that established Egypt as a socialist Islamic state. He died in office in 1970.

HEADS OF STATE—PRESIDENTS—continued

2812. President of independent Tunisia was the moderate nationalist Habib ibn Ali Bourguiba, who shepherded Tunisia through the process of winning independence from France in 1956. Bourguiba's Neo-Destour Party (later the Democratic Constitutional Assembly), won independent Tunisia's first elections in 1957, and he was installed as president. Bourguiba was made president for life by the Tunisian National Assembly in 1975 and served until 1987.

2813. President of Guinea was Ahmed Sékou Touré. A forceful speaker on nationalist issues, Touré was elected several times to the French-controlled National Assembly, but was denied his seat until 1956. Guinea declared its independence on October 2, 1958, the first Francophone nation in Africa to do so, and Touré was elected president. He served until 1984.

2814. President of the European Parliament was the French minister of foreign affairs Robert Schuman, in 1958 unanimously elected the first president of the European Economic Community Joint Assembly (EEC, ECSC, Euratom), now the European Parliament. He served until 1960. On May 9, 1950, Schuman gave a speech in which he articulated the first practical proposal for European economic unity, whereby the coal and steel industries of France and the Federal Republic of Germany would be administered by a joint institution that would also be open to all European countries. May 9 is now known as Schuman Day, the date on which the European Union celebrates its birthday.

2815. President of Senegal was the statesman and poet Léopold Sédar Senghor. In the 1930s, Senghor went to France, where he earned a reputation as a poet and literary theorist, notably as one of the founders of the Negritude movement. Senghor was captured by the Nazis during World War II and interned for two years in a concentration camp. A founder of the Senegalese Progressive Union (later called the Socialist Party), Senghor was unanimously elected president of the new Republic of Senegal in 1960. He retired from office on December 31, 1980.

2816. President of the Ivory Coast (Côte d'Ivoire) was Félix Houphoüet-Boigny, a founder of the African Democratic Rally, which worked to promote civil rights for black Africans in French-held territories. Houphoüet-Boigny served two terms as a Cabinet minister under the French before becoming president of Côte d'Ivoire in 1960, in which office he remained through six terms until his death in 1993.

2817. President of the United Republic of Cameroon was Ahmadou Ahidjo, who served from 1960 to 1982 and is remembered for achieving independence and for guiding the consolidation of the southern half of the British Cameroons with the larger French colony of Cameroon in 1961. He was reelected for five consecutive terms before resigning on November 6, 1982.

2818. President of the Democratic Republic of the Congo was Joseph Kasavubu, head of the Alliance des Ba-Kongo (Abako Party), who was elected in June 1960 and served until 1965, when he was deposed in a coup by his former political ally, Colonel Joseph Mobutu (Mobutu Sese Seko). Kasavubu had formed a political alliance with the first prime minister, Patrice Hemery Lumumba, but wrested control of the government from him in September 1960.

2819. President of independent Madagascar was Philibert Tsiranana, leader of the Social Democratic Party (Parti Social Démocrate). He was elected to lead the provisional government of the newly independent nation (then known as the Malagasy Republic) after it proclaimed its independence from France on October 14, 1958. Full independence was attained on June 26, 1960. Tsiranana served until 1972. The Malagasy Republic changed its name to the Democratic Republic of Madagascar on December 21, 1975.

2820. President of independent Niger was Hamani Diori, the leader of the Progressive Party of Niger, who served in that office from August 1960, to April 15, 1974, when a disastrous famine led to his ouster by Lieutenant Colonel Seyni Kountche, the army chief of staff.

2821. President of the Republic of Chad was N'Garta François Tombalbaye, a trade unionist with strong support in the southern region of the country. When Chad achieved complete independence from France on August 11, 1960, Tombalbaye became the first president of the republic.

2822. President of the Central African Republic was the educator David Dacko, who became president in 1959 and on August 13, 1960, oversaw the achievement of independence for the Central African Republic, formerly a protectorate of France. Dacko was replaced in 1965 by the commander of the army, Jean-Bedel Bokassa. On Sept. 21, 1979, Dacko pledged to restore the republic after ousting the brutal Bokassa, but was in turn overthrown in a coup of September 1981.

2823. President of the Republic of Mali was the radical socialist Modibo Keita, leader of the Sudanese Union-African Democratic Assembly. On September 22, 1960, the organization founded the independent Republic of Mali, with Keita as president. Keita's eight years of alignment with the Communist bloc led to deep disaffection in the army, and on November 19, 1968, a coup led by Lieutenant Moussa Traoré overthrew the Keita regime.

2824. President of independent Gabon was Léon M'ba. Gabon, formerly the French Congo, achieved independence from France on August 17, 1960, and M'ba, who had served as prime minister, was elected president in 1961. He alienated the Gabonian Army by declaring a one-party regime just before the 1964 elections and was ousted during the coup that quickly followed. French troops were required to restore him to office, where he remained until his death in 1967.

2825. President of independent Mauritania was Moktar Ould Daddah, the first person from his country to gain a university education. Daddah devoted his political career to the achievement of national unity. As president of the Executive Council, he was the choice for prime minister in 1959. When Mauritania attained independence from the French Community in 1961, Daddah was elected to the presidency, where he served until his one-party government was overthrown in 1978 in an army coup led by his successor, Lieutenant Colonel Mustafa Ould Salek.

2826. President of Togo was Sylvanus Olympio, leader of the Committee of Togolese Unity. He was elected president of the French colony's first territorial assembly in 1946. Togo achieved independence from France in 1960, and Olympio was elected president in 1961. On January 13, 1963, he was assassinated during a military coup sparked by disaffection with his authoritarian rule and his increasing alienation from leaders in the northern part of the country. He was the first black African leader to be killed in a military coup in the postwar period.

2827. President of Tanzania was Julius Kambarage Nyerere. In 1961, Nyerere was the chief negotiator for Tanganyikan independence and in 1962 served as the first prime minister of independent Tanganyika, formerly a British colony. He was elected president of Tanganyika later that year, and in 1964 became the first president of the United Republic of Tanzania (the union of Tanganyika and Zanzibar).

2828. President of Rwanda was Grégoire Kayibanda, leader of the Parti du Mouvement de l'Emancipation du Peuple Hutu (Party for Hutu Emancipation). When Rwanda declared its independence in July 1962, Kayibanda, having already established an all-Hutu provisional government, became president of the country. His ascension to power triggered a mass exodus of Tutsi, who were fearful of Hutu discrimination. In 1973, Kayibanda was overthrown by disaffected Hutu officers under Juvénal Habyarimana.

2829. President and prime minister of the Yemen Arab Republic (North Yemen) was Abd Allah as-Sallal, an officer in the Yemeni Army. On September 27, 1962, he led a coup that overthrew Saif al-Islam Muhammad al-Badr, imam of Yemen and as-Sallal's former patron. In November 1967, as-Sallal was ousted in his turn by a coup while he was out of the country.

2830. Democratically elected president of the Dominican Republic was Juan Bosch, a historian and essayist. In 1939 Bosch founded the country's first political party, the Dominican Revolutionary Party. In 1963, after the assassination of longtime dictator Rafael Trujillo, he won a landslide victory in an open election. He was ousted seven months later by the army. Elections resumed in 1965, but Bosch, who was never again elected, said that they were tainted by vote fraud.

2831. President of Nigeria was the U.S.-educated politician, scholar, poet and journalist Nnamdi Azikiwe, known popularly as "Zik of Africa." A founder of the National Council of Nigeria and the Cameroons, he became president in 1963 and served until 1966.

2832. President of Zambia was the nationalist educator and statesman Kenneth David Kaunda, leader from 1960 of the United National Independence Party. UNIP dominated elections held in 1964, and, following Zambia's declaration of independence, on October 24, 1964, Kaunda became executive president. He served until November 2, 1991.

HEADS OF STATE—PRESIDENTS—*continued*

2833. President of Botswana was Seretse Khama. The hereditary chieftain of the Ngwato (or Mangwato) people of the British protectorate of Bechuanaland (now Botswana), Seretse married a white Englishwoman, and in the ensuing scandal was forced by the colonial authorities to renounce the chieftainship. He entered politics as the head of the Democratic Party and became prime minister in 1965. Following the achievement in 1966 of Botswanan independence, which Seretse helped to negotiate, he served as president from 1966 until his death in 1980.

2834. President of Gambia was Dawda Kairaba Jawara, leader of the People's Progressive Party. A veterinarian turned politican, he was prime minister from 1962 to 1970 and served as president from April 24, 1970, when Gambia became a republic. Jawara won six successive free elections before being ousted in a coup in 1994.

2835. President of Equatorial Guinea was Francisco Macías Nguema. He was elected in 1971, following Equatorial Guinea's declaration of independence on October 12, 1968. Macías's authoritarian regime was overthrown in 1979 by Lieutenant Colonel Teodoro Obiang Nguema Mbasogo.

2836. Woman to become president of a nation was Isabel Martínez De Perón (born María Estela Martínez Cartas) of Argentina. She was the running mate of her husband, Juan Perón, on his election to the presidency in 1973, and succeeded him on July 1, 1974, the day of his death. During her tenure, Argentina was brought to the brink of anarchy. She was put under house arrest in a military coup on March 24, 1976.

2837. President of Benin was Major Mathieu Kérékou. Benin (formerly Dahomey) proclaimed independence in 1960. Kérékou, at that time a radical socialist, assumed control of the government in 1972 and renamed the country the People's Republic of Benin in 1975. He was elected president by the National Assembly in 1980. In 1990, the country's name was changed again to the Republic of Benin in the wake of the collapse of the Soviet Union's eastern European empire.

2838. President of the People's Republic of Angola was writer and physician António Agostinho Neto. A militant nationalist and Marxist, he was fully radicalized in 1960 when Portuguese colonial troops arrested him for political activism while he was treating a group of patients. When the patients protested, many were killed. Agostinho was detained in Portugal but escaped and rejoined the Movimento Popular de Libertação de Angola, the Cuban-backed Angolan liberation movement that he had helped found in the mid-1950s. He was elected its president in 1962. When Angola achieved its independence from Portugal in 1975, the MPLA gained control of the central region, and Neto was declared president of the country.

2839. President of the Seychelles was James R. Mancham, elected to head a coalition government in 1975. The Seychelles, a British crown colony from 1903, became a fully independent member of the Commonwealth of Nations in 1976. In 1977, Mancham was deposed in a coup led by his socialist prime minister, France-Albert René.

2840. President of independent Cape Verde was Aristides Pereira. Cape Verde declared its independence from Portugal on July 5, 1975. Pereira was defeated for relection in 1991.

2841. President of the European Parliament who was directly elected was Simone Veil of France. She served as president at the EP's headquarters in Strasbourg, France, from July 1979 until 1982.

2842. Woman to become president of a nation in a democratic election was Vigdís Finnbogadóttir, elected president of Iceland on June 30, 1980. She was the first elected female head of state (as distinct from prime minister), and the first female president who did not succeed her husband.

2843. President of Djibouti was Hassan Gouled Aptidon. He was elected to the presidency in 1981 and again in 1987.

2844. Woman to become president of Malta was Agatha Barbara, a longtime member of Parliament and three-time cabinet minister, who was elected president on February 16, 1982.

2845. President of Burkina Faso (formerly the French colony of Upper Volta) was Captain Thomas Sankara, a reformer who lead a coup against the government of Jean-Baptiste Ouedraogo on August 4, 1983. In 1984, Sankara renamed the country Burkina Faso, which means "Land of Incorruptible People".

2846. President of Communist Poland who was chosen in a free representative election was Lech Wałesa, the plainspoken leader of Solidarnosc (Solidarity), Communist Poland's first independent labor union. Wałesa was a national hero for his stubborn resistance in the 1970s and 80s to the Soviet-backed Communist regime. The first free presidential elections were held in 1990, after Solidarity had won a majority of seats in the Sejm (the Polish parliament) in 1988. Wałesa won in a landslide victory and served until 1995.

2847. President of independent Kazakhstan in the post-Soviet era was the communist moderate Nursultan Abishevich Nazarbayev, formerly a member of the Supreme Soviet and the Politburo, who took office in 1990. Kazakhstan became fully independent from the Soviet Union in 1991.

2848. Woman to become president of Nicaragua was Violeta Barrios de Chamorro, the publisher of the newspaper *La Prensa* and leader of the Unión Nacional Opositora (National Opposition Union). She was elected on February 25, 1990. The election constituted a popular referendum on the legitimacy of the Sandinista revolutionary Communist regime that had taken power in 1979. Chamorro's husband, Pedro Joaquín Chamorro Cardenal, was assassinated in 1978 for writing editorials that attacked the right-wing Somoza government, which the Sandinistas overthrew.

2849. President of independent Lithuania was pianist and musicologist Vytautas Landsbergis, a founding member of Sajudis, Lithuania's independence movement. The chairman of the Lithuanian parliament, he became president of independent Lithuania on March 11, 1990, the day he declared his country's independence from the Soviet Union. Lithuania was illegitimately annexed by the Soviets under Josef Stalin in 1940. The first president of Lithuania following the final withdrawal of Soviet troops on August 31, 1994, was Algirdas Brazauskas, chairman of the Lithuanian Democratic Labour Party.

2850. President of Namibia was Samuel Nujoma, the leader of the South West Africa People's Organization, who was sworn in as the country's first president by United Nations secretary-general Javier Pérez de Cuellar on March 21, 1990. From 1916, Namibia was under the colonial rule of South Africa, which agreed to grant Namibia independence according to a UN-sponsored regional peace treaty. On November 14, 1989, voters in Namibia elected 72 delegates to a constituent assembly that later drafted a constitution for the newly independent nation.

2851. Woman to become president of the Republic of Ireland (Éire) was Mary Robinson, an international lawyer with feminist and socialist views, who was elected in November 1990 and retained her post for many years. In May 1993, she visited Queen Elizabeth II at Buckingham Palace in London, England, thus becoming the first head of state of the Republic of Ireland to pay a courtesy call on a British monarch.

2852. President of Uzbekistan was Islam Karimov, chief of the Communist Party of Uzbekistan during the last years of Soviet rule. Uzbekistan declared its independence from the Soviet Union in 1991.

2853. President of independent Georgia was Zviad Gamsakhurdiya, elected in 1990 in the first free elections ever held in that country. Georgia declared its independence on April 9, 1991. Gamsakhurdiya attempted to impose authoritarian rule over the country and was deposed in January 1992.

2854. Democratically elected leader of Russia was Boris Nikolayevich Yeltsin, sworn in as president in June 1991 after the first direct, popular elections in Russia's history.

2855. President of independent Slovenia was Milan Kucan, formerly a leader of the Yugoslav Communist Party. He was elected in 1990 in Slovenia's first free multiparty elections. Slovenia seceded from Yugoslavia on June 25, 1991. After a ten-day battle, occupying Yugoslav forces (mainly Serbs) were driven out on October 25, 1991.

2856. President of Azerbaijan was Ayaz Mutalibov, leader of the Communist Party of Azerbaijan, who became president when Azerbaijan declared its independence in August 1991.

2857. President of Moldova was Mircea Snegur. The independent Republic of Moldova, formerly the Moldavian Soviet Socialist Republic, declared its sovereignty in 1990 and became fully independent on August 27, 1991.

2858. President of Kyrgyzstan was the democratic reformer Askar Akayev. Kyrgyzstan (formerly the Kirgiz Soviet Socialist Republic, or Kirgiziya) proclaimed its independence from the former Soviet Union on August 31, 1991.

HEADS OF STATE—PRESIDENTS—continued

2859. President of Tajikistan was the authoritarian pro-Communist leader Rahman Nabiyev, who took office when Tajikistan declared its independence on September 9, 1991. In August 1992, Nabiyev was forced from office as violent opposition demonstrations spread to several major cities.

2860. Leader of independent Turkmenistan was Saparmurad Niyazov, a leader of the Communist Party of Turkmenistan. He became president when the Republic of Turkmenistan declared its independence from the former Soviet Union on October 27, 1991. In 1994, Niyazov's presidency was extended until 2002 by a near-unanimous vote, a reflection of his tight control of the political system.

2861. President of independent Ukraine was Leonid Kravchuk, an economic reformer elected to the presidency in December 1991. Ukraine, formerly the Ukrainian Soviet Socialist Republic, declared its sovereignty on July 16, 1990, and its full independence on August 24, 1991. One of Kravchuk's first acts was to appoint Ukraine's first prime minister, Leonid Kuchma.

2862. President of the Czech Republic was the playwright and human-rights activist Václav Havel. Havel was the most prominent and articulate leader of the movement for Czech independence from the Czechoslovak federation. A principal architect of the "Velvet Revolution," in which the Soviet-supported Communist government agreed to share power with noncommunist parties, Havel served as interim president of Czechoslovakia from December 1989 to July 1992. When the Czech Republic was formed on January 1, 1993, Havel was elected to the presidency by the Chamber of Deputies.

2863. President of independent Slovakia was Michal Kováč, elected in February 1993. Previously he had served as finance minister and parliamentary leader in the Czechoslovak Communist government. Slovakia and the Czech Republic declared independence separately on January 1, 1993.

2864. President of Eritrea was Isaias Afwerki, the secretary-general of the Eritrean People's Liberation Front. The EPLF was a mainly Christian secessionist party seeking independence from Ethiopia, which had assumed control of Eritrea in 1962. With the collapse of Ethiopia's Marxist government in the early 1990s, the EPLF formed a provisional government. Eritrea's new National Assembly elected Afwerki as president on May 21, 1993, and full independence was declared on May 24.

2865. Black African president of South Africa was Nelson Rolihlahla Mandela, founder of the African National Congress, the chief black African opposition group to the former apartheid regime in South Africa. Mandela was a political prisoner from 1964 to 1990, during which time he won tremendous international prestige. Released by then-president F.W. de Klerk on February 11, 1990, Mandela reassumed the leadership of the ANC and worked with de Klerk to dismantle the apartheid system. On May 2, 1994, Mandela was elected president in South Africa's first non-racial elections. He was sworn into office on May 10, 1994.

2866. President of the Republic of Belarus was Alyaksandr Lukashenka, elected on July 10, 1994. Formerly the Belorussian S.S.R., Belarus became an independent republic in 1990, after the collapse of the Soviet Union, and adopted its first constitution in March 1994. In November 1996, the pro-Russian Lukashenka forced through a controversial referendum that altered the constitution to give him wider powers and an extended term.

2867. President of the Palestinian Authority was Yasir Arafat (born Muhammad Abd ar-Ràuf al-Qudwah al-Husayn), the chairman of the Palestine Liberation Organization. He was elected on January 20, 1996, garnering over 88 percent of the vote in the Gaza and West Bank elections, in which about 1 million Palestinians participated.

2868. Woman to become president of Switzerland was Ruth Dreifuss, formerly interior minister, who was elected by the Swiss Parliament in the fall of 1998 for the standard one-year presidential term. She was also the first Jewish person to hold that office.

2869. Eastern European country to elect a woman as president was Latvia. On June 17, 1999, in Riga, Latvian legislators elected Vaira Vike-Freiberga to the presidency. She was only the second democratically elected president since Latvia's declaration of independence from the former Soviet Union in 1991.

HEADS OF STATE—PRIME MINISTERS

2870. Prime minister is traditionally held to be Robert Walpole, the favored minister of George I and George II of Great Britain, who served in Parliament from 1721 to 1742. Historically, however, the unofficial term "prime minister" had been used to slur unpopular ministers beginning with the reign of Queen Anne. Formally, Walpole was first lord of the treasury; he rejected the title of "prime minister" as a term of abuse. The PM was finally officially acknowleged by Parliament in 1937. Nonetheless, the brass plate on the entrance to 10 Downing Street in London still reads "First Lord of the Treasury."

2871. Prime minister of Denmark's first parliamentary government was Adam Wilhelm, Count Moltke. The former minister of finance and the exchequer under King Christian VIII, Moltke formed a representative government in 1848 when Christian's successor Frederick VII renounced the monarchy. The constitution of June 5, 1849, was introduced with his guidance.

2872. Prime minister of Sardinia-Piedmont under the constitution of March 5, 1848, was the liberal Piedmontese writer and politician Count Cesare Balbo, a notable figure in the Italian Risorgimento.

2873. Prime minister of Hungary was the Magyar patriot and national hero Count Lajos Batthya'ny, a leader in the movement for Hungarian independence from the Austrian Habsburg monarchy. A parliamentary government was approved by Emperor Ferdinand and took office on April 7, 1848, with Batthya'ny as premier, but political tensions between the Austrian monarchy and Hungarian nationalists persisted, and a civil war erupted. Batthya'ny was wounded and captured by Austrian forces on January 3, 1849, convicted of sedition, and executed by firing squad on October 6.

2874. Prime minister of New Zealand was English-born Henry Sewell, a solicitor and colonial official. A member of the newly created House of Representatives, he was made premier on May 7, 1856, but resigned just six days later for lack of political support. Subsequently, he held a variety of other ministerial posts.

2875. Prime minister of independent Romania was the Moldavian statesman, reformer, and historian Mihail Kogalniceanu. He served as prime minister under Prince Alexandru Ion Cuza from October 1863 to February 1865, engaged primarily in carrying out land reforms, including the expropriation of monastic properties.

2876. Prime minister of the Dominion of Canada was John Alexander Macdonald, a reformer and one of the chief movers in bringing about the Dominion through the union of New Brunswick, Nova Scotia, and Quebec (including what is now Ontario). Macdonald served two terms, 1867–73 and 1878–91.

2877. Prime minister of Japan was Prince Ito Hirobumi, who served as premier in 1885–88, 1892–96, 1898, and 1900–01. Ito was one of the drafters of the Meiji Constitution (1889) that brought a modern system of government to Japan, and was also the principal figure in the establishment of the Diet, the Japanese parliament, in 1890.

2878. Prime minister of Australia after its establishment as a commonwealth was Edmund Barton, a leader of the Australian federal movement. He became prime minister in 1900 and served until 1903.

2879. Prime minister of the Union of South Africa was the Boer statesman and military leader Louis Botha. Botha, chairman of Het Volk (People's Party), served as prime minister of the Transvaal in 1907 before being chosen in 1910 by a national convention as prime minister of the new Union of South Africa, a post he held until his death in 1919.

2880. Prime minister of Yugoslavia was Stojan Protic, the Serbian statesman, newspaper editor, and Radical Party leader. He was named the first prime minister of the Kingdom of Serbs, Croats, and Slovenes (later Yugoslavia) in 1918, serving until 1919, and again from February to May of 1920. It was Protic who drafted the reply to Austria-Hungary's war ultimatum that followed the assassination of Archduke Franz Ferdinand in Sarajevo on the eve of World War I.

2881. Prime minister of Northern Ireland was James Craig, the first Viscount Craigavon, a leader of the Unionist Party, who served as first prime minister from June 22, 1921, to November 24, 1940.

2882. Premier of Thailand was Luang Phibunsongkhram, born Plaek Khittasangkha. A Thai revolutionary who helped abolish the absolute monarchy, Phibunsongkhram was the minister of defense before becoming premier in December 1938. Phibunsongkhram was an admirer of Italian and Japanese fascism and allied his country with Japan during World War II. After the war, he adopted a strong anti-Communist policy. He was ousted in a coup in 1957 and fled to Japan, where he died in 1964.

HEADS OF STATE—PRIME MINISTERS—*continued*

2883. Prime minister of Sri Lanka was Don Stephen Senanayake, founder of Sri Lanka's cooperative-society movement and an advocate of agricultural and technological modernization. Sri Lanka (formerly Ceylon) became independent of Great Britain in 1947. Senanayake served as prime minister from 1947 to 1952.

2884. Prime minister of India was Jawaharlal Nehru, a leader of the Indian independence movement, who became prime minister after the partition of India and Pakistan on August 15, 1947. A steadfast supporter of parliamentary government, Nehru established India's nonaligned stance in international affairs. He served in office until his death on May 27, 1964, at New Delhi.

2885. Prime minister of Pakistan was Liaquat Ali Khan, a lawyer who served as the longtime assistant to Muhammad Ali Jinnah, the leader of the Indian Muslim independence movement. He was general secretary of the Muslim League from 1936 to 1947, when he became the prime minister of the newly formed country of Pakistan. He was assassinated in 1951 by Muslim extremists who were disappointed by his failure to pursue a military confrontation with India.

2886. Premier of North Korea was Kim Il-sung, born Kim Song Ju in 1912 near Pyongyang. Kim was a Soviet-trained military commander who had led Korean Communist rebels against the Japanese occupation forces during World War II. After the war, with Soviet backing he established a provisional government in the Communist-held north, and in 1948 declared himself premier of the newly formed Democratic People's Republic of Korea. Kim's iron rule, which lasted until his death in July 1994, was maintained through a cult of personality modeled after those of the Communist tyrants Josef Stalin and Mao Zedong.

2887. Prime minister of independent Myanmar was U Thakin Nu, the Burmese independence leader and politician. On January 4, 1948, when Burma (now Myanmar), formerly a British colony, became an independent republic, U Nu was named prime minister. He served from 1948 to 1956, from 1957 to 1958, and from 1960 to 1962.

2888. Prime minister of Israel was David Ben-Gurion, born David Gruen in Plonsk, Poland, in 1886. The leading Zionist of his day, and the statesman most responsible for the formation of the modern Jewish state, he delivered the speech declaring Israel's independence on May 14, 1948, in Tel Aviv. He served as prime minister from 1948 to 1953 and again from 1955 to 1963.

2889. Prime minister of Sudan was Isma'il al-Azhari, Sudanese statesman and leader of the National Unionist Party. The NUP won the elections of 1953, and Azhari became the first Sudanese prime minister in January 1954. He saw the government through independence, achieved on January 1, 1956, but lost his post to a military government in 1958. In 1965 he returned to power as president of the Supreme Council of the Sudan, but was again deposed by a military coup on May 25, 1969.

2890. Prime minister of Ghana was Kwame Nkrumah, founder of the Convention People's Party. He was born in the Gold Coast (a former British colony, now Ghana). On February 8, 1951, in the Gold Coast's first general election, Nkrumah was elected to Parliament directly from the prison cell where he was serving a term for political dissidence. When independent Ghana was formed from the Gold Coast and the British Togoland trust territory in March 1957, Nkrumah was made prime minister. His government was ousted by a military coup in 1966.

2891. Prime minister of Malaysia was Prince Abdul Rahman Putra Alhaj. He served as premier and foreign minister of newly independent Malaya (formerly a British colony) from August 1957 to 1970. The name of the country was changed to Malaysia in 1963.

2892. Prime minister of Nigeria was Sir Abubakar Tafawa Balewa, a leader of the Nigerian Northern Peoples Congress. Balewa, a nationalist and reformer, became his country's first premier in 1958. The following year, after Nigeria's pre-independence elections, he became prime minister in a coalition government and thus was the first leader of independent Nigeria. He was killed in an army coup in 1966.

2893. Prime minister of Singapore was Lee Kuan Yew, who dominated Singaporean politics for three decades and was the figure most responsible for his country's remarkable prosperity. A British-educated lawyer, he helped negotiate the terms of Singapore's independence status within the Commonwealth of Nations, and was sworn in as prime minister on June 5, 1959. In August 1965, Singapore became a fully sovereign state. Lee continued as prime minister until his resignation in November 1990.

2894. Prime minister of the Democratic Republic of the Congo was Patrice Hemery Lumumba, an African nationalist widely admired in the 1960s. He formed the first government of the newly independent Democratic Republic of the Congo (formerly a Belgian colony) on June 23, 1960, and served as the first prime minister until September 1960. On January 17, 1961, he was assassinated by his political enemies.

2895. Prime minister who was a woman was Sirimavo Ratwatte Dias Bandaranaike, leader of the Sri Lanka Freedom Party of Ceylon (now Sri Lanka). She succeeded her husband, Solomon West Ridgeway Dias Bandaranaike, who was prime minister from 1956 until his assassination by a Buddhist monk in 1959. She served as prime minister from July 1960 to 1965, from 1970 to 1977, and again after her daughter, Chandrika Kumaratunga, was elected president of Sri Lanka in November 1994.

2896. Prime minister of Sierra Leone was Milton Augustus Striery Margai, founder of the Sierra Leone People's Party. With British backing and support from conservative chiefs, he was made chief minister in 1953. After independence was granted by Great Britain in 1961, he headed a coalition government until his death on April 28, 1964.

2897. Prime minister of Algeria was Ahmed Ben Bella, the Algerian freedom fighter and cofounder of the National Liberation Front. With the support of Colonel Houari Boumedienne, chief of the Army of National Liberation, Ben Bella became prime minister in 1962, in the chaotic days following the end of the French-Algerian War and the establishment of the Algerian Republic. On June 19, 1965, a coup led by Boumedienne toppled the government, and Ben Bella was imprisoned.

2898. Prime minister of independent Jamaica was Alexander Bustamante, leader of the Jamaican Labour Party. He became prime minister in the elections of April 1962, and oversaw the process by which Jamaica became independent with full dominion status within the British Commonwealth on August 6, 1962. He announced his retirement before the general elections of February 21, 1967, the first held by Jamaica since independence.

2899. Prime minister of independent Uganda was Apollo Milton Obote, leader of the Uganda People's Congress. He served as prime minister of the new nation from 1962, when it achieved independence, to 1970. Obote was elected to the presidency in 1966. In 1971, he was driven out in a coup led by the army officer Idi Amin, who had earlier aided Obote in actions against Bugandan tribal separatists. While Amin devastated the country, Obote built up an army in neighboring Tanzania. When Tanzanian forces deposed Amin in 1979, he returned and was elected to a second presidential term in May 1980.

2900. Prime minister of the Republic of Trinidad and Tobago was Eric Eustace Williams, a native of Trinidad. Founder of the People's National Movement in 1955, the principal nationalist party in the islands, he achieved the premiership in 1962 after the PNM handily won the national elections of December 1961 and the former British colony won its independence. He served until 1981.

2901. Prime minister of Kenya was Jomo Kenyatta, born Kamau Ngengi. One of the most successful African nationalists, he negotiated Kenya's independence from Great Britain in 1962 and formed a provisional government that took power officially on December 12, 1963. In 1964, under a revision to the constitution, Kenyatta was made president, a post he held until his death in 1978.

2902. Premier of Belize was George Price, leader of the People's United Party. Price, formerly first minister, became premier in 1964. Belize, formerly called British Honduras, became independent on September 21, 1981.

2903. Prime minister of independent Lesotho was Chief Leabua Jonathan, leader of the Basutoland National Party. Lesotho had become a constitutional monarchy in 1964. The Basutoland National Party won the first general elections, held in 1965, and Jonathan became prime minister under King Moshoeshoe II. He served in that post until 1985.

2904. Prime minister and president of Guyana was Linden Forbes Sampson Burnham. The British installed him as prime minister of British Guiana in 1964, and when the country, renamed Guyana, won its independence in May 1966, Burnham became its first premier. In 1980, after elections widely regarded as fraudulent, he became Guyana's first president, a post he held until his death in 1985.

HEADS OF STATE—PRIME MINIS-TERS—*continued*

2905. Prime minister of Malawi was Hastings Kamuzu Banda, who accepted the premiership when Malawi achieved independence from Great Britain in 1964. Banda assumed the post of president when Malawi became a republic on July 6, 1966. Banda proclaimed himself president for life in 1971 but left office in 1994 after losing that year's presidential elections.

2906. Prime minister of Libya was Colonel Muammar al-Qaddafi, who in September 1969 led the coup that overthrew the government of King Idris I. Qaddafi proceeded to oust most foreigners, to nationalize the oil industry, and to establish an Islamic socialist regime according to theories laid out in his *Green Book,* an Arabist imitation of Mao Zedong's *Red Book.* An eccentric and impulsive ruler, Qaddafi earned widespread enmity for supporting international terrorism.

2907. Prime minister of Bangladesh was Mujibur Rahman (also known as Sheikh Mujib), founder of the Awami League and leader of the East Bengal independence movement. He was proclaimed prime minister in January 1972, after East Pakistan became the independent nation of Bangladesh on December 16, 1971. Rahman was assassinated in a coup d'état in January 1975.

2908. Prime minister of independent Suriname was Henck Alphonsus Eugène Arron, financier and leader of the National Party Alliance, who headed Suriname's first constitutional parliament following elections held in 1973. Suriname, formerly Dutch Guiana, won full independence from the Netherlands in 1975. Arron was deposed in a coup in 1980.

2909. Prime minister of Dominica in the Lesser Antilles was Patrick Roland John, who served briefly as first prime minister of the newly independent island republic from November 3, 1978, to May 1979, when he was ousted in a political scandal over a rumored plan to invade Barbados.

2910. Prime minister of the Islamic Republic of Iran was Mehdi Bazargan, an opposition leader during the reign of Mohammad Reza Pahlavi, the last shah of Iran. After the overthrow of the shah by Ayatollah Ruhollah Khomeini in 1979, Bazargan was named prime minister on February 5, 1979. He resigned on November 6, following the capture of the U.S. embassy in Teheran by Iranian extremists.

2911. Woman to serve as prime minister of Great Britain was Margaret Hilda Thatcher, born Margaret Roberts. She assumed the leadership of the Conservative Party in 1975, becoming the first woman to lead a major British political party, and formed her first government after the elections of May 1979.

2912. Prime minister of St. Vincent and the Grenadines in the Lesser Antilles was the centrist Milton Cato, head of the St. Vincent Labour Party, which in December 1979 won the first elections following the achievement of independence on October 27, 1979.

2913. Prime minister of Zimbabwe (formerly Rhodesia) following its reconstitution was the Marxist nationalist Robert Gabriel Mugabe, who served from 1980 to 1987. Mugabe, cofounder of the Patriotic Front of Zimbabwe (later the Zimbabwe African National Union Popular Front), had been a guerrilla leader in the Rhodesian civil war before his party won a landslide victory in the elections of 1980. On December 31, 1987, Mugabe also became Zimbabwe's first executive president.

2914. Leader of a modern Muslim nation who was a woman was the politician Benazir Bhutto, head of the Pakistan People's Party, who served as prime minister of Pakistan from December 1, 1988, to August 1990 and from October 1993 to November 1996. Her first term was cut short when her government was dismissed by the president of Pakistan, Ghulam Ishaq Khan, after corruption charges were leveled against her. Khan's successor, President Farooq Leghari, dismissed her second government, also on charges of corruption and mismanagement.

2915. Premier of France who was a woman was Edith Cresson, a socialist and political ally of French president François Mitterrand. She served as prime minister from May 15, 1991, to April 2, 1992.

2916. Woman to become prime minister of Poland was Hanna Suchocka, a professor of constitutional law and member of Poland's parliament, the Sejm. In 1992, after the fall of Poland's Communist regime, she became prime minister after winning the support of three parties, the Christian National Union, the Liberal Democratic Congress, and her own Democratic Union. Her coalition lasted until October 1993.

2917. Canadian prime minister who was a woman was Kim Campbell (Avril Phaedra Campbell), who took office as prime minister on June 25, 1993, and served until November. A native of British Columbia, she was selected at a convention of the Progressive Conservative Party to replace outgoing PM Brian Mulroney.

2918. Premier of Nunavat was Paul Okalik, selected in April 1999 to head the newly created territory of Nunavat, a semi-autonomous region of northern Canada inhabited mainly by Inuit (Eskimos).

HEADS OF STATE—ROYALTY

2919. Pharaoh of ancient Egypt was Menes (also known as Mena or Min), the first king of the first Egyptian dynasty, who ruled circa 3100 BCE (some sources give a later date of 2925 BCE). Ancient historians, including Herodotus, credited him with uniting Lower and Upper Egypt into one kingdom by conquest and founding the capital city of Memphis. According to Manetho, an Egyptian chronicler of the third century BCE, Menes reigned 62 years and was killed by a hippopotamus. He has been identified by some modern historians as a composite figure, a combination of the early Egyptian kings Narmer and Aha, whose tombs were found near Abydos in the late 19th century.

2920. King of Korea was Tangun, in legend the son of the god Hwanung and a human woman whom Hwanung had created from a bear. According to Korean chronicles, Tangun ruled circa 2333 BCE and is credited with inaugurating a Korean national religion that anticipated elements of Buddhism and Taoism. His birthday is celebrated as a national holiday.

2921. Pharaoh who was a woman was Hatshepsut, a queen of the 18th dynasty. She ruled for a year following the death circa 1504 BCE of her husband and half-brother, Thutmose II. In 1503 BCE, she was succeeded by his son, Thutmose III.

2922. Reference to King David outside the Bible was discovered in 1993 at the ancient mound of Tel Dan in northern Israel by Avraham Biran of Hebrew Union College–Jewish Institute of Religion and Joseph Naveh of the Hebrew University. They unearthed a chunk of basaltic rock bearing the phrases "House of David" and "King of Israel." The writing has been dated to circa 850 BCE, approximately a century after David's death, which took place circa 962 BCE.

2923. King of united Armenia was Tigranes II the Great, the most powerful king of ancient Armenia, who ruled from circa 95 to 55 BCE. During his reign, he extended Armenian control east into what is now Azerbaijan and southwest as far as present-day Syria. Almost all of this territory was lost to the Romans after Tigranes surrendered to the Roman general Pompey, who invaded Armenia in 66 BCE.

2924. King of Italy was the German chieftain Odoacer, who overthrew the general Orestes, last Roman ruler of the western Roman Empire, and was declared King of Italy by his troops on August 23, 476.

2925. King of France was Clovis I, Merovingian founder of the Kingdom of the Franks, who was crowned in 481. By 508 he had extended his rule to encompass most of what is now northwestern and central France, had established his capital in Paris, and had chosen Roman Catholicism as the state religion.

2926. King of Tibet was Gnam-ri srong-brtsan, formerly the lord of Yar-lung and one of several princelings who controlled parts of what is now Tibet. Towards the end of the sixth century, he extended his power over neighboring princedoms and Chinese tribes and began a program of military conquest.

2927. Muslim caliph was Abu Bakr, originally from Mecca in Arabia (now Saudia Arabia), who was the close advisor and deputy of Muhammad, the founder of Islam. He was also the father of Muhammad's favorite wife and the man who accompanied Muhammad when he escaped from Mecca to Medina in 622. When Muhammad died on June 8, 632, Abu Bakr was named *khalifat rasul Allah* ("successor of the prophet of God") by the Muslims of Medina (although Shi'ite Muslims say that Muhammad had designated his son-in-law, Ali ibn Abi Talib, as his successor). The term *caliph* as a title indicating the civil and religious head of the Muslim state came into use sometime later, probably after the accession of Abu Bakr's successor, Umar ibn al-Khattab. In the two years of his reign, Abu Bakr suppressed rival religious claimants, conquered the tribes of central Arabia, and extended Islamic conquests into Syria and Palestine.

HEADS OF STATE—ROYALTY—continued

2928. King to call himself "King of the English" was Offa, king of the Anglo-Saxon kingdom of Mercia from 757 to 796. Offa declared himself "rex anglorum," or king of the English, and was the first English king to be treated as an equal by the kings of Europe. Some historians prefer to cite Aethelstan, ruler of the West Saxon kingdoms of Wessex and Mercia. On September 4, 925, he was crowned *Rex Totii Britanniae* ("king of all Britain").

2929. King of Germany was Louis the German, crowned king of Bavaria in 825. A Frankish-born king of the Carolingian dynasty (he was the son of Louis I, the first Holy Roman Emperor), he spoke German and cultivated German culture.

2930. Biography of a European king was *Vita Karoli Magni (Life of Charles the Great),* a biography of Charlemagne written circa 830 by Einhard, a favorite of the court. Written in Latin and modeled after the style of Suetonius, the ancient Roman author of the *Lives of the Caesars,* Einhard's book presented in brief form the events and achievements of the reign of Charlemagne and offered intimate glimpses of the king's personal habits and tastes.

2931. King of Scotland north of the Forth and Clyde rivers was Kenneth I MacAlpin, who united Dalriada and the Pictish kingdom after succeeding his father circa 834. Additional lands were added to the Scottish kingdom into the 13th century.

2932. King of Norway was Harald I Fairhair, hereditary ruler of southeastern Norway. According to the Icelandic saga *Heimskringla,* written by Snorri Sturluson circa 1225, Harald declared himself king of united Norway circa 890 after his decisive victory over the princes of the western districts at the Battle of Hafrsfjörd.

2933. King of Vietnam was Ngo Quyen, a renowned military commander, who liberated the country from Chinese forces in 939 and whose tactics were studied and admired by later Vietnamese leaders, including Ho Chi Minh. Ngo Quyen established a dynasty that lasted until 954.

2934. Woman to rule a part of Russia was Princess Olga (or Helga), who served as regent of the Principality of Kiev (the present-day Ukraine) from 945 to 964 after the assassination of her husband. She converted to Christianity during her regency—the first of the pagan Kievan royal family to do so—and was eventually canonized by the Orthodox Church as its first Russian saint.

2935. Ruler of Luxembourg was Siegfried, Count of Ardennes. In 963 he traded his holdings for Lucilinburhuc ("Little Fortress"), a castle built in Roman times on the Alzette River, at the location of what is now Luxembourg city. This castle gave its name to the tiny domain of Luxembourg, which was gradually accreted by Siegfried's heirs over the next century. The first count of Luxembourg was Conrad, a descendant of Siegfried, who assumed that title in 1060.

2936. Sultan was the Muslim conqueror Mahmud of Ghazna (now Ghazni, Afghanistan), whose full name was Yamin al-Daula Abùl-Qasim Mahmud ibn Sebüktigina. Between 998 and 1030, he carved out a kingdom encompassing modern Afghanistan, Iran, and northwestern India. Mahmud was the first to use "sultan" as a title of political as well as spiritual authority.

2937. King of all Sweden was Olof Skötkonung, ruler of Västergötland, who proclaimed himself king of the entire country circa 1000. At about the same time, he was baptized by missionaries from Norway, making Olof the first Christian Swedish ruler.

2938. King of Hungary was István I (Stephen I, also called St. Stephen), who succeeded his father as duke of Hungary in 997. He was crowned king on December 25, 1000, by Pope Sylvester II. (The crown is now a Hungarian national treasure.) Born a pagan, he was reared as a Christian, was canonized in 1083, and is Hungary's patron saint.

2939. King of Poland was Bolesław I, prince of Great Poland from 992, who was crowned by Emperor Otto III in 1000 and had himself crowned again by the archbishop of Gniezno on December 25, 1024, to consolidate his sovereignty over lands he had conquered in the meantime. He established Poland as an independent kingdom and created an independent Polish Catholic Church.

2940. King of Myanmar was Anawrahta (or Aniruddha), who reigned circa 1044–77 from his capital Pagan on the Irrawaddy River. Anawrahta is credited with uniting the northern and southern regions of Myanmar (formerly called Burma) into a single kingdom and with introducing the Theravada form of Buddhism.

2941. King of Portugal was Afonso I, also known as Afonso Henriques, who used the title of king circa 1139 but whose independent sovereignty was not formally accepted by Christian Spain until 1179.

2942. Woman to rule Georgia was Queen Tamara, who was proclaimed king in 1184 after the death of her father, King Giorgi, with whom she had served as co-ruler since 1178. During the 24 years of her reign, she extended the Georgian empire throughout the region of the Caucasus, from Azerbaijan to Circassia, and presided over a flowering of culture that was ended, soon after her death, by the Mongol invasions.

2943. Inca was Manco Capac, founder circa 1200 of the Inca dynasty at Cuzco, Peru. Little is known about Manco Capac, but legend holds that he and his followers emerged from a series of caves near the village of Paqari-tampu, south of Cuzco.

2944. Woman to rule France was Blanche of Castile (originally Blanca de Castilla), who became regent of France in 1226, after the death of her husband, King Louis VIII. She served until 1234, when her son, Louis IX (the future St. Louis), came of age. She acted as regent again during the years 1248 through 1252, while Louis was in the Holy Land at the head of a Crusader army, and raised the money to ransom him after he was captured by the Muslim leader Baybars I.

2945. Woman to rule Luxembourg was Countess Ermesinde, who governed Luxembourg from 1226, when her husband died, to 1237, when her son took the throne as Henry V.

2946. Muslim leader who was a woman was Raziya, or Raziyyat-ud Din, daughter of Iltutmish, the sultan of Delhi (now in India). Despite the Muslim prohibition against woman rulers, Iltutmish named her to succeed him, which she did after his death in 1236, becoming queen of Delhi In 1240 she was deposed and imprisoned, and later that year was killed in battle while trying to regain the throne.

2947. Prince of Wales was Llywelyn ap Gruffudd, ruler of Gwynedd, one of the early kingdoms from which present-day Wales was constituted. Llywelyn styled himself "Prince of Wales" circa 1258, after he had consolidated his rule of Gwynedd over the claims of his brothers. In 1267 the title was acknowledged by King Henry III of England in the Treaty of Montgomery, which assured Llywelyn the fealty of the other Welsh lords.

2948. Sultan of the Ottoman Empire was Osman I (in Arabic, Uthman), also called Osman Gazi, born in 1258 in a small Turkmen state in the Anatolia region of what is now the modern state of Turkey. At the head of an army of Ghazis (Muslim frontier warriors), Osman established a long-lived dynasty and carved an empire out of areas under Byzantine control. His descendants extended the Ottoman conquests to include all of modern Turkey and most of Iraq, Iran, and the Middle East, as well as parts of northeast Africa and eastern Europe. The Ottoman Empire lasted until its dissolution after World War I.

2949. King of the Lao people was Fa Ngum (or Fa Ngoun), who conquered an area encompassing present-day Laos as well as parts of Thailand and Vietnam. Fa Ngum formed a unified Laotian state called Lan Xang ("a million elephants"), with its capital at Luang Prabang on the upper Mekong River, and reigned over it from circa 1316 to 1373, when he was deposed.

2950. Aztec priest-king was Acamapichtli, not a native Aztec himself but a prince of the neighboring Culhuacán state, who was asked by the Aztecs to rule over them circa 1376 after the founding of their capital city, Tenochtitlán, in the Valley of Mexico.

2951. Woman to rule the Scandinavian countries was Margrete of Denmark (also known as Margaret), the daughter of Denmark's King Valdemar IV and the wife of Norway's King Haakon VI. In 1376, when her father died, she became regent of Denmark for her young son Olaf, and in 1380, when her husband died, she became regent of Norway. Olaf died seven years later, and Margrete was elected sovereign by both countries. She was also proclaimed ruler by the Swedish nobles who had risen to depose their king, whom Margrete took prisoner. In 1396 the Union of Kalmar united all three Scandinavian countries (as well as Finland, which was then part of Sweden) under Margrete's absolute sovereignty.

2952. Woman to rule Poland was the nine-year-old Hungarian-born Queen Jadwiga (or Hedvig), who was crowned king of Poland in 1384 after the death of her father, Louis the Great of Hungary and Poland. Three years later, she married Jogaila, Grand Duke of Lithuania, thus assuring the conversion to Christianity of the Lithuanians and founding the Jagiellonian dynasty that united Poland and Lithuania for nearly 200 years.

2953. Tsar of all Russia was Ivan IV, known as "the Terrible," who reigned from 1547 to 1584. The coronation took place in Uspensky Cathedral in the Kremlin, Moscow. (The term *tsar*, sometimes transliterated as *czar*, was derived from the ancient Roman title *caesar*.) A ruler of unusual cruelty and ruthlessness, Ivan

HEADS OF STATE—ROYALTY—*continued*
crushed the remaining independent principalities of Russia, created the first Russian police force, and began the system of serfdom. According to legend, he gouged out the eyes of the architects who built St. Basil's Cathedral in the Kremlin so that nothing like it could never be built again.

2954. King and Queen of Spain were Ferdinand II of Aragon and Isabella I of Castile, who became Catholic rulers of a united Spain on January 2, 1492, after Ferdinand's conquest of Granada, the last Muslim kingdom on the Iberian peninsula. Isabella reigned until her death in 1504, Ferdinand until his death on January 23, 1516.

2955. Wife of Henry VIII of England was Catherine of Aragon, the daughter of the Spanish rulers Ferdinand II of Aragon and Isabella I of Castile. The marriage took place on June 11, 1509. While it initially appeared to be happy, Catherine did not give birth to a living male heir. In 1527 Henry asked for an annulment from Pope Clement VII, who, fearing the anger of Catherine's nephew Charles V, the Holy Roman Emperor, did not grant it. Henry then had the Archbishop of Canterbury, Thomas Cranmer, annul the marriage. Papal jurisdiction was ended in England by act of Parliament and the king became head of an independent Church of England. In pursuit of a male heir, Henry married five more times. Catherine spent her last years in isolation.

2956. Woman to rule England in her own right was Mary I, born Mary Tudor, also known as Bloody Mary, the daughter of King Henry VIII and Catherine of Aragon. Her reign lasted from July 20, 1553, to her death on November 17, 1558. The last Catholic sovereign of England, she was noted mainly for her persecution of Protestants. Lady Jane Grey, who was put on the throne for nine days immediately after the death of Edward VI, is sometimes cited as the first English queen, but she never consolidated power in her own right, and was executed by Mary in 1554.

2957. Coronation of a monarch conducted in English was that of King James I, which took place in Westminster Abbey, London, England, in 1603. Previously, the service had been conducted in Latin as set out in the *Liber Regalis,* the book of the service for the coronation of Edward II in 1307.

2958. King of England and Scotland was King James VI of Scotland, who became King James I of England. He assumed the throne of Scotland in 1567. When Queen Elizabeth I died childless, James succeeded to her throne as well. The first Stuart king of England, he ruled from 1603 to his death in 1625, and was the first monarch to call himself "King of Great Britain."

2959. King of Bhutan was Sheptoon La-Pha, a Tibetan Buddhist priest who became *dharma raja,* or master of spiritual affairs, and assumed control of what is now Bhutan circa 1650. The current kings of Bhutan are descended from Ugyen Wangchuk, who in 1907 was elected *druk gyalpo,* or hereditary king.

2960. Sultan of Oman was Oman Ahmad ibn Sa'id, previously the governor of Suhar. He was elected imam and sultan in 1749. The dynasty he established, the Al Bu Sa'id dynasty, produced all of Oman's subsequent sultans, as well as the rulers of Zanzibar up to 1964.

2961. Emir of Kuwait was Sabah bin Jabir bin Adhbi, elected in what is now Kuwait City circa 1758 by chieftains of the Utub confederation, a group of Arabian families that had arrived in the region circa 1700. The Al-Sabah family still rules present-day Kuwait.

2962. King of Hawaii was Kamehameha I, born Paiea on the island of Hawaii circa 1758. Kamehameha carefully consolidated his power with a mixture of negotiation and conquest over a period of 28 years, assuming control of all the islands of Hawaii in 1810. He ruled until his death in 1819.

2963. King of Belgium was Leopold I, in full Léopold-Georges-Chrétien-Frédéric. Leopold was elected King of the Belgians in 1831 and reigned until 1865, during which time Belgium was formally emancipated from the Netherlands. A committed neutralist, Leopold was famous for pursuing diplomacy through matchmaking. Among the marriages he arranged was that between his niece Victoria, queen of England, and his nephew Prince Albert of Saxe-Coburg-Gotha.

2964. Constitutional monarch of modern Greece was Otto, an Austrian-born Catholic royal chosen as king of Greece by a congress of the European powers held in London in 1832. His unpopular reign began on February 6, 1833. A revolt in 1843 forced him to grant a constitution that guaranteed that later kings would be Orthodox Christians. Otto's penchant for picking the losing side in regional conflicts led to his ouster on October 23, 1862.

2965. British monarch to live in Buckingham Palace was Queen Victoria. The royal family took up residence in the palace on July 13, 1837. Originally built for the dukes of Buckingham in the 17th century, the palace was purchased in 1761 by King George III as a London home for his new wife, Charlotte Sophia of Mecklenburg-Strelitz. Today the palace is the official London residence of the British sovereign in the City of Westminster.

2966. King of Luxembourg was William III (Willem Alexander Paul Frederik Lodewijk), king of the Netherlands and a member of the house of Nassau, the hereditary rulers of the Grand Duchy of Luxembourg. The tiny nation was granted full sovereignty and independence by the Great Powers on May 11, 1867. William III, who had become king of Luxembourg in 1849, retained the crown until his death on November 23, 1890.

2967. Kaiser of a united German Reich was Wilhelm I, born Wilhelm Freidrich Ludwig, the Hohenzollern king of Prussia. He was proclaimed Kaiser of the newly unified German Empire on January 18, 1871, at German military headquarters in Versailles (captured during the Franco-Prussian War). Wilhelm I's reign was marked mainly by his collaboration with chancellor Otto von Bismarck in strengthening Germany's dominance in central Europe. He ruled until his death on March 9, 1888, in Berlin.

2968. King of Romania was Carol I, a German prince, born Karl Eitel Friedrich, Prinz von Hohenzollern-Sigmaringen. He was the cousin of the French emperor Napoléon III. Carol was elected Prince of Romania by plebiscite in April 1866 and reigned as king from May 1881 to his death in October 1914.

2969. King of modern Bulgaria was Ferdinand, born Ferdinand Karl Leopold Maria in Austria in 1861. Elected prince of Bulgaria on July 7, 1887, he declared himself king on October 5, 1908, upon proclaiming the full independence of Bulgaria from the Ottoman Empire. In World War I, Bulgaria made the mistake of allying itself with Germany, and Ferdinand was forced to abdicate on October 4, 1918.

2970. King of independent Montenegro was Nicholas I, who proclaimed himself king on August 28, 1910, when Montenegro declared independence from the Ottoman Empire. Nicholas is noted for firing the first shot of the First Balkan War on October 8, 1912, when Montenegro declared war on Turkey.

2971. King of independent Egypt was Fùad I, born Ahmed Fuad Pasha. The sultan of Egypt from 1917, Fùad assumed the kingship after Britain unilaterally declared Egyptian independence in 1922. In 1923, he promulgated Egypt's first constitution, which he abrogated in 1930 and then restored under pressure from nationalist elements in 1935. Fùad I served as king until his death in 1936.

2972. Constitutional monarch of Thailand was King Prajadhipok (or Phrapakklao). During his reign (1925–35) in Thailand (then called Siam), he allowed a democratic revolution to abolish the absolute monarchy and adopt a constitution. Prajadhipok abdicated on March 2, 1935, to be replace by an authoritarian military government.

2973. King of Albania was Ahmed Bey Zogu (Ahmed Zog), who was proclaimed King Zog I on September 1, 1928, after serving as president for nearly three years. In 1925, he began an association with Mussolini's Italy that ended in 1939 with his exile and Albania's loss of independence.

2974. King of Saudi Arabia was Abd al-Aziz ibn Abd ar-Rahman ibn Faysal ibn Turki Abd Allah ibn Muhammad al Sa'ud, known as Ibn Sa'ud, the descendant of a family that had held power over large areas of Arabia for 150 years. He was crowned in 1932, when he created the kingdom of Saudi Arabia from lands he had conquered during a protracted period of warfare. He opened Saudi Arabia to U.S. oil companies the year after his coronation.

2975. King of independent Iraq was Faysal (or Faisal) I, the son of Husayn ibn Ali, who from 1916 to 1924 was ruler of the Hejaz and Grand Sharif of Mecca. British kingmakers seeking a leader for Iraq, then under British mandate, chose Faysal as a potential ruler because he had impeccable pan-Arab credentials and no stake in local Iraqi politics. He was crowned in August 1921 and presided over Iraq's full achievement of independence on October 3, 1932, less than a year before his death on September 8, 1933.

2976. British monarchs to visit the United States were King George VI and his consort, Queen Elizabeth, who crossed from Canada to the United States at Niagara Falls on June 7, 1939, as part of a tour following the king's coronation on May 12. They visited New York City and Washington, DC, before recrossing the border on June 12.

HEADS OF STATE—ROYALTY—*continued*

2977. King of Jordan was Abdullah ibn Husayn, from 1921 emir of Transjordan under the British mandate. On May 25, 1946, two months after the end of the mandate, he declared himself king of the state of Jordan, known formally from 1949 as the Hashemite Kingdom of Jordan. Abdullah ibn Husayn was assassinated in 1951 and was succeeded by his grandson, Hussein ibn Talal, in 1953.

2978. King of independent Libya was Idris I, born Sidi Muhammad Idris al-Mahdi as-Sanusi. The head of the Sanusiyah, an Islamic mystical brotherhood based in his birthplace of Cyrenaica, Idris was on the brink of consolidating power as ruler of Libya when the Italian invasion of 1922 forced him to choose exile in Egypt. He returned in Libya in 1947, and was chosen as the constitutional monarch of Libya when the country declared its independence in December 1951. In September 1969, a coup led by Colonel Muammar al-Qaddafi overthrew the government while Idris was out of the country, and he returned to exile in Egypt.

2979. Televised coronation was that of Queen Elizabeth II of England, which took place on June 2, 1953, at Westminster Abbey in London.

2980. King of independent Morocco was Sidi Muhammad ben Yusuf, sultan from 1927, who oversaw negotiations with France that led to Moroccan independence in 1956 and adopted the title King Muhammad V the following year. He abdicated the throne in 1960 in favor of his son, Hassan II. Morocco's first parliamentary elections were held in 1977.

2981. King of independent Swaziland was King Sobhuza II of the Dlamini clan, Ngwenyama ("Lion") of the Swazi nation from December 22, 1921, when Swaziland was a British High Commission territory. He oversaw adoption of a new constitution and independence from Great Britain in 1967, then repealed the constitution and restored the full powers of the monarchy in 1973. Sobhuza held the polity together primarily by kinship ties: he had at least 70 wives and perhaps 500 children. He died in 1982.

2982. Sheikh of independent Bahrain was Sheikh Isa ibn Sulman al Khalifah, who declared Bahrain's independence in August 1971. Previously, Bahrain had been a British protectorate. Al Khalifah was the latest in a line of sheikhs who had ruled the country since 1783.

2983. Sultan of independent Brunei was Pengiran Muda Hassanal Bolkiah, who succeeded his father, Omar Ali Saifuddin, in 1967. Brunei, one of the wealthiest nations in the world on a per capita basis, achieved its independence from Britain on January 1, 1984.

HEADS OF STATE—VARIOUS

2984. Doge of Venice was Orso, elected in 727 in a brief interlude of Venetian independence during the period of Byzantine control of the Venetian lagoon, which ended circa 751.

2985. Imam of Oman was Julanda ibn Mas'ud, an Ibadi preacher who headed the Kharijite Islamic sect in Oman. He was chosen in 751 by religious leaders and the chiefs of the major tribes, inaugurating a period of religious leadership that ended in 1154, but was revived in 1428.

2986. Shogun to assume military control of Japan was Yoritomo Minamoto, a noble who in 1192 established the shogunate (*bakufu* in Japanese), or national military government, centered at the city of Kamakura. During the 700-year period of the shogunate, the shogun was often the true power in the country, ruling on behalf of the Japanese emperor. The word *shogun* is an abbreviation of *sei-i tai shogun,* which means "barbarian-conquering generalissimo," a title originally bestowed on the Japanese warlords who pacified the Ainu peoples of the island of Hokkaido in the eighth century.

2987. Governor-general of Brazil was Tomé de Sousa, appointed by John III, King of Portugal, in 1549. Sousa, who had had a distinguished military career in Portugal's African and Indian colonies, founded the first Brazilian capital, Bahia (Salvador), and established a basic administration for the huge territory. He served until 1553.

2988. Governor-general of the Dutch Republic was the Archduke Matthias of Habsburg, declared the formal head of government in 1577 by the States-General, which met in Brussels. He served until 1581. Real power in the republic, which included Belgium and some areas of what is now Germany and was known formally as the United Provinces of the Netherlands, was exercised by Prince William of Orange.

2989. Leader of united Afghanistan was Ahmad Shah Durrani, born Ahmad Khan Abdali, a hereditary chief of the Afghan Abdali tribe. Chief bodyguard of the Persian conqueror Nader Shah, Durrani was elected leader by the Afghan chiefs after Nader Shah's death, and was crowned in 1747 at Qandahar. He established an empire that extended far into present-day India.

2990. Leader of independent Paraguay was José Gaspar Rodríguez Francia ("El Supremo"), the isolationist autocrat who became dictator of Paraguay in 1814 and was ruler for life from 1816 to 1840. He closed the country to outsiders, banned foreign travel and trade, and personally managed nearly every aspect of Paraguay's society and economy.

2991. Leader of independent Chile was Bernardo O'Higgins, the Chilean patriot and military leader. Chilean revolutionary forces supported by Argentina and led by O'Higgins defeated Spanish colonial forces at the Battle of Chacabuco on February 12, 1817, after which O'Higgins was proclaimed supreme director. He declared Chilean independence on February 12, 1818. Growing political opposition forced him to resign in 1823.

2992. Leader of free Ecuador was Antonio José de Sucre, who is considered the liberator of his country. Sucre was the chief general of Simón Bolívar in the struggle for South American independence from Spain. Offered the presidency of Bolivia, he served two years and then returned to Ecuador in 1828, where he was assassinated on June 4, 1830.

2993. Leader of united, independent Argentina was Juan Manuel de Rosas. De Rosas was head of the provincial militia of Buenos Aires in the 1820s. During a period of political unrest, he arranged to be elected governor by the Buenos Aires legislature on December 5, 1829. From 1835 to 1852 he united the provinces of what is now modern Argentina under an authoritarian rule modeled after Napoléon's. He was overthrown by a coalition of Argentinians, Brazilians, and Uruguayans at the Battle of Caseros on February 3, 1852.

2994. Leader of the independent Dominican Republic was the caudillo Pedro Santana, who defeated the followers of the patriot Juan Pablo Duarte and emerged as the leader of the Dominican Republic after it declared independence from Haiti in February 1844.

2995. Leader of independent Guatemala was the conservative nationalist Rafael Carrera, who established himself as dictator in 1838, following the collapse of the United Provinces of Central America, a brief-lived federation that Guatemala had joined in 1823. Carrera declared Guatemalan independence in March 1847. He became president for life in 1854, and he occupied the leadership until 1865.

2996. Chancellor of Germany was Otto von Bismarck, born Otto Eduard Leopold, Prinz von Bismarck, the Prussian statesman who played the leading role in unifying the German states into an empire and positioning that empire as the most powerful force in Europe. He served as the first chancellor of Germany—a post created especially for him—from January 1871 until his ouster by Kaiser Wilhelm II in 1890.

2997. General secretary of the Communist Party of the former Soviet Union was Josef Stalin, born Iosif Vissarionovich Dzhugashvili in Georgia in 1879. In 1922, Stalin won the post of general secretary of the party's Central Committee, which he retained until his death on March 5, 1953. After the death of Vladimir Ilyich Lenin in 1924, Stalin used his position to expand his power until by the mid-1930s he was the supreme leader of the Soviet Union—and, in the assessment of many historians, the most powerful tyrant in history.

2998. Fascist dictator was Benito Amilcare Andrea Mussolini, founder and leader of the Italian Fascist Party, the world's first fascist political body. The term *fascism* was taken from the fasces, an axe bundled with wooden rods by a red band, which was the symbol of state power in ancient Rome. In 1919 Mussolini called his new party a "Fasci di Combattimento" (Band of Fighters), and offered himself as a dictator who could make Italy a great power again. The central fascist idea of a unified, militant state under a supreme leader was quickly taken up in Germany, Japan, and many other countries. Prime minister of Italy from 1922, Mussolini in 1925 declared himself dictator of a future Italian empire. Initially admired in Europe, he formed a disastrous alliance with German Nazi leader Adolf Hitler in 1936. On July 24, 1943, with the Allies set to invade the Italian mainland, he was deposed and imprisoned by his own party. The Germans reinstated him in a puppet regime in northern Italy, where on April 28, 1945, near Dongo, he was shot and killed by Italian Communists. His body was hung upside down in the Piazza Loreto in Milan.

HEADS OF STATE—VARIOUS—*continued*

2999. Leader of independent Cyprus was Makarios III, born Mikhail Khristodolou Mouskos, archbishop and Cypriot primate of the Greek Orthodox Church. Makarios, a supporter of union with Greece, was a principal negotiator in the talks that led to Cyprus's full independence from Great Britain, achieved on August 16, 1960. He was president of Cyprus from December 13, 1959, until his death in 1977.

3000. Ruler of independent Mozambique was Samora Machel, military commander and party leader of the Frente de Libertação de Moçambique (Mozambique Liberation Front), or Frelimo. Machel led Frelimo in its successful guerilla war against Portuguese rule. Mozambique achieved independence in June 1975 and a government was formed under Machel, who moved the country toward Soviet-style collectivization.

3001. Chief executive of Hong Kong under restored Chinese sovereignty was the shipping magnate Tung Chee-hwa, who won a landslide victory in the election of December 1996. He was the first Chinese leader of Hong Kong since 1842, when the city became a British crown colony.

HISTORY

3002. Narrative secular history book of importance was *The History of the Greco-Persian Wars,* written before 425 BCE by Herodotus of Halicarnassus (now Bodrum, Turkey), often called "the father of history." Divided into nine books (but not by Herodotus himself), it tells the story of the wars between Greece and Persia between 499 and 479 BCE. Although Herodotus borrowed material from early authors—notably Hecataeus of Miletus, a Greek ethnographer and geographer of the early fifth century BCE—his book was the first secular historical narrative that was an organic whole, and the first to include primary material, such as the texts of dialog and speeches by important historical figures. *The History of the Greco-Persian Wars* set the standard for all subsequent history writing.

3003. Chinese historical archive still extant is the compilation of diverse documentary records known as the *Shu Ching (Classic of History),* of which the oldest chapters, containing the sayings of the ancient legendary emperors, appear to date from no later than the fourth century BCE.

3004. Chinese historian of importance was Sima Qian (in Wade-Giles, Ssu-ma Ch'ien), successor to his father as royal astronomer at the Han imperial court, where his duties included the maintenance of state chronicles. In 105 BCE he began writing the *Shih chi (Historical Records),* the first comprehensive history of China. It included a set of tables showing the comparative chronology of the various states and kingdoms, a chronological outline and a detailed account of important events in each state, biographical articles, chapters on government and politics, and the author's critical observations.

3005. Chinese woman historian was Ban Zhao, who completed a celebrated history of the Han dynasty, the *Han shu (Han Documents, or History of the Former Han Dynasty),* that was begun by her father, Ban Biao, and continued by her brother, Ban Ku. The work, which contains more than 800,000 words, was an exhaustive account of the Han empire from its origins in 206 BCE to the rebellion of Wang Mang in 9 CE. All of China's later dynastic histories took it as a model. Ban Zhao, who was widowed in her youth, was also a poet and essayist; her book *Nu jie (Lessons for Women)* appeared in 106.

3006. History of Japan was the *Kojiki (Chronicle of Ancient Things),* a compilation of historical and mythological accounts gathered from oral tradition and written down in the year 712 by order of the Empress Gemmei. It included a twelve-century history of the imperial court from its origins in the seventh century BCE to the end of Empress Suiko's reign in the seventh century CE. The *Kojiki* was followed eight years later by an official chronicle, the *Nihon shoki,* also called the *Nihon gi (Chronicles of Japan),* that covered much of the same ground and was modeled on Chinese imperial histories. It was commissioned by Gemmei's daughter, the Empress Gensho. Because the Japanese language did not yet have a written form of expression, the *Kojiki* was written in Japanese using Chinese characters, the *Nihon shoki* in Chinese.

3007. Arabic history of the world was *Tàrikh ar-Rusul wa al-Muluk (History of Prophets and Kings),* completed in Baghdad, Iraq, circa 915 by the Qur'anic scholar Abu Jafar Muhammad ibn Jarir at-Tabari. The *History* commences with Creation and the stories of biblical rulers before relating the life of Muhammad and the subsequent deeds of the Umayyad and Abbasid caliphs. It ends in the year 915.

3008. History of Iceland in Icelandic was the Íslanedabokk (The Book of the Icelanders), written by a priest, Ari Thorgilsson, circa 1125, and covering events from the first settlement of Iceland in the ninth century.

3009. History of West Africa was the *Tarikh al-Fettach,* written in Arabic by Mahmout Kati, a scholar from Timbuktu (in present-day Mali). The work, begun in 1519, included histories and legends of West African tribes and kingdoms, among them Songhai and Ghana.

3010. Account of the Andean world from an insider's perspective was the *Nueva corónica y buen gobierno,* written in Peru circa 1613 by the Andean historian Felipe Guamán Poma de Ayala (born Waman Puma), a descendent of Incan lords in the Huánuco region. The nearly 1200-page manuscript described the history of the Inca empire from its earliest origins to the conquest and colonization of the Andes by Spain. The last section is a discussion of good and bad aspects of the Spanish viceroyal government.

3011. Written history in Zulu was the 1922 work *Abantu abamnyama lapha bavela ngakhona (The Black People and Whence They Came),* by Magema Fuze, published in South Africa.

HOLIDAYS AND CELEBRATIONS

3012. New Year's festival was celebrated in the civilizations of Mesopotamia (now Iraq) from circa 2000 BCE. Civilizations chose various dates, usually at or near the fall or spring equinox.

3013. Zoroastrian holidays were seven holidays instituted by Zarathushtra, the founder of the religion, in the sixth century BCE (or perhaps many centuries earlier, as some historians believe). Six of these days, the *gahambars,* honor one of the Amesha Spentas, or "holy immortals," beings of creative power who are considered independent aspects of the Creator God, Ahura Mazda. The seventh Amesha Spenta, who is associated with fire, is celebrated in the holiday No Ruz ("new day"), which anticipates the eventual triumph of good over evil. These festivals continue to be observed by Zoroastrian communities in Iran and India.

3014. Dragon Boat races in China originated in 278 BCE, when the poet and courtier Qu Yuan drowned himself in the Mi-Lo River after the kingdom from which he had been exiled was conquered by a neighboring state. The festival, held on the fifth day of the fifth month in the Chinese lunar calendar, commemorates the race of the fishermen who rushed to retrieve his body. Qu Yuan was the first Chinese poet known by name.

3015. Chanukah (also transliterated in English as Hanukkah), the Jewish Festival of Lights, was celebrated by Yochanan ben Mattityahu, head of the Temple in Jerusalem (the Beit ha-Mikdash), circa 164 BCE. Chanukah commemorates the reconsecration of the Temple after it was used for idol worship by the Hellenized Syrians under Antiochus IV Epiphanes. (The word *chanukah* means "dedication" in Hebrew.) It also marks the victory of the rebellion for religious freedom, the first of record, led by Jewish guerrilla fighters under Yehudah ben Mattityahu, known as ha-Maccabi (the Hammer).

3016. New Year to begin on January 1 was decreed by the Roman republican calendar beginning in 153 BCE. The Julian calendar, instituted in 46 BCE, was the first calendar widely adopted to set the New Year at that date.

3017. Epiphany (Adoration of the Magi) was celebrated on January 6 by the Egyptian Gnostics in the late second century CE, according to Clement of Alexandria. This was believed to be the date when Jesus showed himself to be the Son of God at his baptism in the Jordan, as well as the date of the first manifestation of his divinity before the Magi (the Adoration of the Magi) and of his first miracle at Cana. (The word "epiphany" is from the Greek *epiphaneia,* or "manifestation.") The date also marks a pagan Egyptian festival celebrating the overflow of the Nile. In the Eastern Church, Epiphany was established as the last of the twelve days of Christmas, and was second in importance only to Easter. The Western Church institutionalized observance of the holiday by circa 380.

3018. St. Valentine's Day derived from the merger of the ancient Roman festival of Lupercalia, a fertility holiday celebrated on February 15, and the feast day of St. Valentine, who was martyred on February 14, 269. During Lupercalia, couples were matched by having young men draw the names of young women from a box. This is the probable origin of the tradition of sending valentines.

HOLIDAYS AND CELEBRATIONS—continued

3019. Santa Claus originated in the historical figure of St. Nicholas, an early Christian bishop who lived in Myra (now Demre, Turkey) circa 260–323, and whose relics were long kept in the basilica there. Numerous miracles are attributed to Nicholas, but he is most often remembered for distributing gifts to children on Christmas eve.

3020. Up-Helly-Aa fire festival in the Shetland Islands originated in the legendary funeral accorded the Viking chieftain Haki, who died circa 320. Mortally wounded, he lay down in his ship, surrounded by the bodies of his warriors slain in battle. The remnant of his followers set the ship ablaze and allowed it to go out to sea. The event is commemorated each January at Lerwick, a town on the Shetland island of Mainland and the northernmost town in Britain, where a replica of a Viking longship is burned after a ceremonial procession.

3021. Easter was observed by the early Christians on the same day as the first seder of Pesach (Passover), celebrated by Jews on the night of the 14th of Nisan. In the Western Church, Easter was fixed on the first Sunday after the first full moon following the vernal equinox by the first ecumenical Council of Nicaea, convened in 325 at what is now Iznik, Turkey. Today, the Eastern Church calculates the date of Easter using the same formula, but according to the Julian calendar. The English term "Easter" was first used by the Venerable Bede, writing circa 725 in Northumbria, England. He claimed that Easter derived from Eostre, the Anglo-Saxon goddess of spring.

3022. Sunday sabbath was celebrated in 325, when the First Council of Nicaea, convened by the Roman Emperor Constantine at what is now Iznik, Turkey, ordained the change. Previously, the sabbath had been celebrated on Saturday, the seventh day, in accordance with Jewish religious practice. The First Council of Nicaea also fixed the date of Easter.

3023. Christmas was celebrated in the western Roman Empire by circa 336, according to a Roman almanac of the time. The date of December 25 as the day of the birth of Jesus was probably settled upon to coincide with a Roman solar holiday, the *natalis solis invicti,* held on the winter solstice. The eastern churches were slower to accept that date, and the Armenian Church never has, preferring to celebrate the birth of Jesus on January 6. The custom of giving gifts on Christmas probably derived from another Roman holiday, the Saturnalia.

3024. Mention of the Feast of the Nativity of record was contained in a Roman almanac called the Philocalian Calendar, or the Chronographer of 354, which claims that a festival in honor of the birth of Jesus was observed on December 25 by the church in Rome in the year 336. As far as is known, the date of December 25 is not based in historical fact, but reflects the belief among the early Christian chronologers that Jesus was conceived on March 25 (the spring equinox, also considered to be the day of the creation of the world), and was born nine months later on December 25.

3025. Halloween evolved from All Saints' Day, celebrated on November 1. References to All-Saints' Day date from the reign of Pope Gregory III, 731–741, and in 837 Pope Gregory IV ordered its observance throughout western Christendom. In Britain, All Saints' Day was known as All Hallows, with the evening before known as Halloween. This holiday coincided with the ancient Celtic holiday of Samhain, an agricultural festival in which villagers dressed as spirits of the dead, and over time the two merged.

3026. Feast of Orthodoxy originated in 843, when the Byzantine empress Theodora restored the worship of icons, repeatedly barred by religious authorities beginning in 730. The feast, held on the first Sunday of Lent, is observed by members of the Eastern Orthodox Church, as well as Eastern Catholics who follow the Byzantine Rite.

3027. Eisteddfod was held in 1176 at Cardigan Castle in Wales. It was a tournament of bards, the traditional Celtic poet-musicians who chanted their poetry aloud. The annual assembly ceased in the 17th century, but competitions in poetry continued to be held privately. An annual arts festival called the Eisteddfod has been held each summer in Wales since the 19th century.

3028. Printed New Year's greeting appeared at the end of a twelve-page pamphlet printed by Johannes Gutenberg at Mainz (in modern Germany) in December 1454. It read: *Eyn gut selig nuwe Jar (a good, blessed new year).* The pamphlet was entitled *Eyn Manung der Cristenheit widder die Durken (A Warning to Christendom against the Turks).*

3029. Christmas trees evolved from the ancient European pagan practice of tree worship. In medieval Germany, worshippers erected a "paradise tree" hung with apples on December 24th, the feast day of Adam and Eve. In later centuries, the tree was decorated with such Christian symbols as wafers, candles, and stars. The first written reference to a Christmas tree notes their use in Strasbourg (now in France) in 1605.

3030. Guy Fawkes Day was celebrated informally after the execution of the British soldier and terrorist conspirator Guy Fawkes, a member of the Gunpowder Plot of 1605. Fawkes, a Catholic, was enlisted to blow up the Parliament building, with King James I and the chief ministers inside, as a reprisal for anti-Catholic repression in England. Although Fawkes managed to plant a large cache of gunpowder under the Parliament building, the plot was never carried out. He was arrested on November 4, 1605, and executed in front of Parliament on January 31, 1606. Guy Fawkes Day is held on November 5 (the day Parliament was to be destroyed) and is celebrated with fireworks, masquerades, and the burning of Guy Fawkes effigies.

3031. Australia Day began with a flag-raising ceremony to mark the first anniversary of the First Fleet's arrival at Sydney Cove on January 26, 1788. Observed on January 29, Australia Day now includes activities that celebrate Australia's diverse cultural heritage, as well as naturalization and citizenship ceremonies.

3032. Bastille Day commemorates the events of July 14, 1789, when an angry mob of Parisians stormed the Bastille, an ancient fort used as a prison by the Bourbons, and captured it from the authorities. This was the defining event of the French Revolution. July 14 was formally made a national holiday in 1880.

3033. Columbus Day was celebrated in the United States on October 12, 1792, to mark the tricentennial of the day in when Christopher Columbus made his first landfall in the New World, probably on the West Indian island of Guanahani (now San Salvador). Annual celebrations began in 1893 during the World's Columbian Exposition in Chicago, IL, USA. The holiday is also celebrated in Spain and most Latin American countries.

3034. Canada Day (Dominion Day) was celebrated on July 1, 1868, the anniversary of the formation of the Dominion of Canada under the British North America Act of 1867. Originally called Dominion Day, the name was changed in 1982 following the patriation of the Canadian constitution. Canada Day is celebrated with patriotic activities and fireworks.

3035. Bank holidays officially determined by national legislation were set in England, Wales, and Ireland by the Bank Holidays Act of 1871 (with a supplemental act of 1875). The official bank holidays were Easter Monday, Whitmonday (the first Monday of August), the first weekday after Christmas and Boxing Day. Banks were already required to close on Christmas and Good Friday by common law.

3036. Arbor Day was celebrated in the United States on April 10, 1872, in the state of Nebraska. Governor Julius Sterling Morton suggested the holiday and helped celebrate it by having more than 1 million trees planted throughout the state. Arbor Day did not become a legal holiday in Nebraska until April 22, 1885, Morton's birthday. Arbor Day is celebrated in nearly all U.S. states and in a number of other countries, including South Korea, where it is a national holiday observed on April 5.

3037. Labor Day was inaugurated in the United States in 1882 by the Knights of Labor, one of the first labor unions. The first holiday to honor working people, it is observed on the first Monday in September in the USA, Puerto Rico, and Canada.

3038. International socialist workers' holiday was May Day, designated by the Second International Socialist Congress, meeting in Paris, France. It was first celebrated on May 1, 1889. With the growth of socialism, May Day became a day of demonstration and protest for left-wing parties in Europe and North America, and was the primary state holiday in Communist countries.

3039. Pan American Day was occasioned by the founding of the Pan-American Union at the First International Conference of American States, held in Washington, DC, USA, in 1889–90. The anniversary of the founding, on April 14, is celebrated by the member countries of the General Secretariat of the Organization of American States.

3040. United Nations Day was celebrated on October 24, 1947, by resolution of the UN General Assembly. It commemorates the date that the UN Charter was put into effect.

HOLIDAYS AND CELEBRATIONS—*continued*

3041. Kwanzaa was invented by the African-American educator Ron Karenga as a seven-day celebration of African culture. The first Kwanzaa was held on December 26, 1966, in Long Beach, CA, USA. The holiday has since seen gradual adoption worldwide among people of African-American descent. Kwanzaa is a Swahili word meaning "first fruit."

3042. Caribana Festival was held in the summer of 1967, during the Canadian centennial festivities in Toronto. Celebrating the spirit of the West Indies, especially Trinidad and Tobago, Caribana is the largest Caribbean carnival festival in North America. It is held yearly during the last two weeks of July and the first weekend in August.

3043. International Earth Day took place on April 20, 1990. It was organized by American environmental activist Denis Hayes, who had organized the original Earth Day in the United States in 1970. An estimated 200 million people in 140 countries participated.

3044. Helsinki Human Rights Day took place on August 1, 1992. The Helsinki Final Act of the Conference on Security and Cooperation in Europe was adopted in 1975 by 33 European nations, the United States, and Canada, all of which agreed to respect a common set of human rights and fundamental freedoms.

3045. International Festival of the Sea was held in Bristol, England beginning in May 1996. The first maritime festival ever held in Britain, it featured a reconstruction of John Cabot's ship *The Matthew,* which in 1997 reenacted Cabot's 1497 voyage to the North American mainland.

3046. National Internet holiday was "la Fête de l'Internet," held in France on March 20 and 21, 1998. Internet-related events were staged around the country, including interactive chats with politicans, web-only artworks, "web-vans" cruising the streets offering Internet education and access, and a speech by French president Jacques Chirac available exclusively from a governmental web site.

3047. Country to officially celebrate the year 2000 was the island of Kiribati in the Pacific Ocean. In 1995, President Teburoro Tito adjusted the International Date Line, which had bisected the main island, so that it ran directly to the west of the Line Islands, a Kiribati possession. Other nearby nations, such as Tonga and the easternmost parts of New Zealand, are at least an hour east of the line. Therefore, Kiribati was the first country to reach 12:01 AM on January 1, 2000.

HOME

3048. Housekeeping magazine was *The Englishwoman's Domestic Magazine,* a monthly magazine published in London by Samuel Beeton with the assistance of his wife, Isabella Beeton, beginning in 1852. The price was twopence a copy. The contents covered sewing, cooking, and other practical matters.

3049. Household management book was *Beeton's Book of Household Management,* by Isabella Beeton, published in London, England, in 1861. It was a collection of articles written for her husband's monthly magazine, *The Englishwoman's Domestic Magazine.* Mrs. Beeton, the eldest of 21 children and herself the mother of four, offered practical suggestions on every aspect of running a middle-class English home, including cleaning, cooking, planning menus, keeping household accounts, hiring and supervising servants, choosing a wardrobe, and making good conversation.

HOME—APPLIANCES

3050. Heating stoves were introduced in China circa 600 BCE.

3051. Iron for smoothing clothes was used by the ancient Greeks circa 300 BCE to create pleats in their garments. It was nothing more than a heavy heated iron bar that was laid down on the fold to press it.

3052. Mechanical ventilating fan was invented in China circa 180 CE. It was a rotary ceiling fan meant to draw cool air upward into the room. Power was provided by servants turning a crank. A water-powered ventilating fan was invented by Leonardo da Vinci in 1500, and a similar device was used in England in 1533 to provide ventilation for a mine.

3053. Cast-iron stoves appeared in Alsace (in modern-day France) in 1490, along with stoves constructed of brick and tile.

3054. Washing machine of record was constructed by John Hoskins of England. According to an account published in 1677 by the scientist Robert Hook, the soapy laundry was put in a coarse-weave bag and squeezed under a cylinder turned by a handwheel. A more efficient system was invented in 1758 by English inventor William Bailey, in which the wet wash was agitated in water before it was squeezed dry. The first electric washing machine for consumer use was the Thor, invented by an American, Alva J. Fisher, in 1907, and manufactured by the Hurley Machine Company.

3055. Pressure cooker was the "steam digester," invented in 1679 by Denis Papin, the French engineer who first conceived of the steam engine. The steam digester was a vessel with a tight, self-sealing lid, able to contain steam at high pressure. When pressurized, the boiling point of water inside the vessel was raised well above normal, enabling quick cooking of tough foods. A meal cooked by this method was served in London on April 12, 1682, to the members of the Royal Society. Papin also invented the first pressure safety valve, to prevent the vessel from bursting.

3056. Masonry stove with an efficient design was the work of a Swedish architect, Baron Carl Johan Cronstedt, who developed his stove in 1767. Masonry stoves were used to heat houses in Europe at least from 1557, when the first patent for such a stove was granted.

3057. Cooking stove that was practical was the invention of Benjamin Thompson, Count von Rumford, an American-born physicist and government administrator who lived in England and Bavaria (now part of Germany) after serving as a British spy and military officer during the American Revolutionary War. Rumford's scientific exploration of the physics of heat energy influenced his 1790 design for a firebrick cooking stove that made efficient use of heat.

3058. Clothes dryer was invented in France circa 1799. Clothes were put into a perforated drum (similar in concept to the drums inside modern electric and gas clothes dryers), and was turned by a handle over a flame. Skill was required to avoid incinerating the clothing.

3059. Coffee percolator for leaching boiling water through coffee grounds was invented circa 1800 by Jean-Baptiste de Belloy, the archbishop of Paris, France.

3060. Gas stove that was practical was installed in 1826 in the kitchen of James Sharp, head of a gasworks in Northampton, England. It was intended for roasting meat and had a circle of burners at the bottom and a set of hooks on top. Sharp, who had designed the stove himself, eventually started a factory to manufacture his invention and installed one in 1834 at the Bath Hotel in Leamington, England.

3061. Electric cooktop was invented by an American, George B. Simpson of Washington, DC, USA, who received a patent on September 20, 1859, on an "electrical heating apparatus" that he called an electroheater. The machine generated heat by passing currents of electricity over coils of platina or other metallic wire.

3062. Carpet sweeper that was practical was invented in 1876 by Melville Reuben Bissell, owner of a china shop in Grand Rapids, MI, USA. Bissell was allergic to the packing straw on which his shop relied, and looked for a way to keep it picked up. Although the idea for carpet-sweeping had been introduced earlier, none of the early sweepers worked well. Bissell devised the "broom-action" principle, by which the application of variable pressure on the handle made the sweeper responsive to different grades of floor coverings. He obtained a patent on September 19, 1876, and organized the Bissell Carpet Sweeper Company.

3063. Dishwasher was invented in 1886 by an American, Josephine Cochrane, of Shelbyville, IL, USA. Her initial design was a large copper tub outfitted with removable wire dish racks. Hot soapy water was pumped over the dishes by turning a crank. The Cochrane dishwasher was patented in the United States in December 1886 and won an award at the 1893 World's Columbian Exposition in Chicago.

3064. Electric oven went into use in 1889 at the Hotel Bernina in Samaden, Switzerland. The oven used German silver resistance-coil as heating elements. Power was supplied by the hotel's own hydroelectric generator. The commercial manufacture of electric ovens was started two years later by the Carpenter Electric Heating Manufacturing Company, St. Paul, MN, USA.

3065. Electric toaster was invented by the Crompton Company of Chelmsford, England, and put on the market in 1893.

3066. Refrigerators manufactured for home use went on the market in Chicago, IL, USA, in 1913.

HOME—APPLIANCES—*continued*

3067. Pop-up toaster was developed by mechanic Charles Strite of Stillwater, MN, USA. On May 29, 1919, he applied for a U.S. patent on a device that could toast and eject bread when positioned over a fire. The first pop-up electric toaster was introduced in 1926 by the McGraw Electric Company, Minneapolis, MN. A model that was equipped with an automatic toast ejector was marketed the same year by another Minneapolis firm, Waters Genter Co.

3068. Air conditioner for home use was designed in 1927 by Willis Haviland Carrier of Buffalo, NY, USA. Carrier, an engineer, received a patent in 1906 for air-conditioning machinery.

3069. Electric blanket was introduced by the Thermega Company, London, England, in 1927. However, the Thermega blanket lacked a thermostat, and thus could not be adjusted to individual preferences. The Simons Company of Petersburg, VA, USA, marketed the first thermostatically controlled electric blanket in 1946.

3070. Motorized clothes dryer was an invention of J. Ross Moore of Devil's Lake, ND, USA. To spare his mother from having to go outside to hang up the laundry in bone-chilling winter weather, he built an oil-heated drum that he set up in a shed next to the house. Beginning in 1930, he worked on a series of crude drying machines. He eventually sold the idea to the Hamilton Manufacturing Company, Two Rivers, WI, USA, which began selling dryers in 1938.

3071. Espresso machine was introduced by Gaggia, the Italian appliance manufacturer, in 1946.

3072. Food processor was the Kenwood Chef, the brainchild of English inventor Kenneth Wood. His combination mixer, juicer, slicer, food mill, and pasta-maker was marketed in Great Britain beignning in 1947.

3073. Microwave oven for commercial food preparation was introduced by the Raytheon Company, Lexington, MA, USA, in 1947. It was based on research into microwave-generating magnetron tubes by Raytheon scientist Percy Spencer. Spencer was standing near a magnetron when he noticed that a candy bar in his pants pocket had melted, although he had felt no heat. The first microwave oven for home use was the Tappan Oven, which was sold in the United States beginning in 1952 by the Tappan Corporation, Tappan, NY, USA, for US$1,295.

HOME—FURNISHINGS

3074. Lamps in the form of simple torches made of resinous sticks may have originated as far back as 70,000 BCE. Handmade sandstone lamps that probably held wads of moss saturated with animal fat were found at Pekarna, Moravia (now in the Czech Republic), and dated to approximately 30,000 BCE. Lamps from the fourth millennium BCE that were made from hollowed-out conch shells were found at the Mesopotamian city of Ur (Tel-el-Muqayyar, Iraq). The Phoenicians and Greeks eventually replaced shell lamps with pottery lamps in the form of shells. Flat saucers with floating wicks were used, in various forms, in ancient Egypt, China, Southeast Asia, Japan, India, Israel, and Polynesia.

3075. Floor coverings were made of plaited rushes and were used in Mesopotamia from circa 4000 BCE.

3076. Metal lamps were found at the archeological dig at Ur (Tel-el-Muqayyar, Iraq) and date from the fourth millennium BCE. They were made of gold, silver, and copper.

3077. Table is of ancient origin. The earliest preserved wooden examples are from circa 1500 BCE in Egypt.

3078. Tapestry known to archeologists was woven in linen by the ancient Egyptians. The tomb of Thutmose IV, an 18th-dynasty pharaoh who reigned from 1400 to 1390 BCE, was found to contain three tapestry fragments, the oldest known. Two depict cartouches of Egyptian pharaohs, and the third is marked with hieroglyphs.

3079. Oriental carpet design is known from a stone carving from the Assyrian palace of Khorsabad (in modern Iraq). Dating from circa 700 BCE, the carving shows a small rug with a central pattern of quatrefoils framed by a border of lotus flowers.

3080. Carpeting extant is a wool knotted-pile carpet in a Scythian royal grave at Pazyryk in the Altai Mountains of Kazakhstan. It was discovered during excavations beginning in 1929. The red-and-ochre carpet, which dates to circa 400 BCE or earlier, shows a checkboard design surrounded by borders of riders, elk, and griffins.

3081. Lanterns enabling lights to be carried outdoors without being doused by the elements were made during the Roman era. The earliest type was made of clay and had an open front that shed light from a pottery lamp inside. These were superseded by metal lanterns with horn windows. Examples of these, dating from the first century CE, were found at Pompeii and Herculaneum, in southern Italy.

3082. Papal throne was the wooden seat thought to have been occupied by St. Peter when he assumed the title of Bishop of Rome sometime before 64 CE, the date of Peter's martyrdom. According to Roman Catholic tradition, the chair itself has been preserved in the Vatican vaults. A holiday called "St. Peter's Chair at Rome" is celebrated by the Roman Church on January 18, the supposed date of Peter's ascension to the throne.

3083. Silk tapestry known to scholars is fragments of Chinese *k'o-ssu* (cut silk) tapestry found in desert oases around Turfan in the Sinkiang Uighur Autonomous Region of China, once an important stop along the Silk Route. The fragments, which depict repeating patterns of flowers, vines, birds, and animals, are thought to date to the T'ang period (618–907CE).

3084. European tapestry still extant is the Cloth of St. Gereon, originally created for the Church of St. Gereon in Cologne, Germany. It is a seven-color wool tapestry depicting medallions with fighting bulls and gryphons. Most scholars date the work to circa 1000, based on its decorative ornaments, which resemble those in illuminated books of the time. Fragments of the tapestry are stored at museums in Germany, France, and England.

3085. Silk carpet extant is a Timurid carpet made in Persia (now Iran) and dating from circa 1400. It was displayed publicly at the International Carpet Fair in Philadelphia, PA, USA, from October to November 1996.

3086. Lamp with a chimney to draw the flame upward and produce a better light was invented by the Italian artist and polymath Leonardo da Vinci circa 1500. It was made of metal.

3087. Wallpaper of record was put up on the walls of the Master's Lodgings at Christ's College in Cambridge University, Cambridge, England, soon after the building was built in 1509. It bore a black-and-white pinecone design, meant to imitate a cloth wall hanging, and had been impressed with a woodblock on the backs of various documents, which were turned to face the wall. In all likelihood, the wallpaper was the work of Hugo Goes, a York printer.

3088. Modern oil lamp was the Argand burner, named after its inventor, the Swiss physician Aimé Argand. He introduced a sleeve-like wick that was fitted between inner and outer metal tubes. It created a circular flame, which was fed by air moving up the inner tube. A glass chimney increased the draft. The result was a clean-burning lamp with bright illumination. Argand patented his invention in England in 1784.

3089. Folding metal-framed furniture was invented by the German-born American furniture designer George Hunzinger, who set up a store in 1855 in Brooklyn, NY, USA. Hunzinger obtained his first patent in 1860 for an extension table permanently incorporating eight leaves. His 1866 design for a folding-reclining armchair was immensely successful. In 1897 he patented a convertible lounge chair that became a day bed. Other Hunzinger innovations included folding metal chairs, the ancestors of the modern director's chair.

3090. Modern product designer was the English industrial designer Christopher Dresser (1834–1904), who specialized in household goods, including metalwork, glass, ceramics, carpets, furniture, and wallpaper. His designs for metal kitchenware and tableware—including spoon warmers, teapots, candlesticks, tureens, and tankards—were influenced by Japanese and Chinese art, and their streamlined melding of form and function make them a precursor of modernist design movements of the 20th century. Dresser was the first industrial designer to recognize the benefits of mass-producing household goods by machine, since it would make well-designed utensils available to people of modest means. He was also the first to stamp his full name on his products, rather than a maker's mark. His book *The Art of Decorative Design* was published in 1862.

3091. Tubular steel chair was invented by the Hungarian-born designer and architect Marcel Breuer in 1925, while he was form master in the woodshop at the Bauhaus, the school of design, architecture, and applied arts founded by Walter Gropius in Weimar, Germany. The chair had a simple bent tubular frame of polished steel, with a cane seat and back. It is probably the most copied chair design in history.

3092. Foam-rubber padded seating was installed in the Shakespeare Memorial Theater, Stratford-upon-Avon, England, in 1932. The cushions were made of a molded latex-air mixture developed in 1929 by Dunlop Latex Development Laboratories of Fort Dunlop, Birmingham.

HOME—FURNISHINGS—*continued*

3093. Vinyl shower curtains were introduced by the B. F. Goodrich Rubber Company of Akron, OH, USA, in 1938. They were made of lightweight Japanese silk coated with Koroseal, a material developed from polyvinyl chloride by a Goodrich staff scientist, Dr. Waldo Semen. Unlike rubberized curtains and oiled silk, Koroseal was resistant to the effects of steam, soap, and hot water. Within a few years the company was producing shower curtains made from vinyl alone.

3094. Waterbed was invented in 1965 by Charles Hall, a student at the University of California at Berkeley, CA, USA, and first shown that year at the Cannery Gallery in San Francisco. He later founded a company to bring his invention to the market.

3095. Inflatable chair was developed by Italian designers in Milan, Italy, in 1966. North American consumers got their first look at the chairs, which were made of clear polyvinyl film, on March 12, 1967, during a program called "At Home 2001," hosted by American news anchor Walter Cronkite and broadcast by the Columbia Broadcasting System.

HOME—HOUSEWARES

3096. Candles were in use in both Egypt and Crete by the beginning of the third millennium BCE. Candlesticks from that era have been found in both locations.

3097. Pots had their origin in large hollow rocks. Soapstone, a soft stone (steatite) that is easily carved and is a good conductor of heat, was used for making cooking pots in Egypt in the 17th century BCE.

3098. Wok was in use in China for stir-frying and rice cooking from circa 1000 BCE. The thin-walled, bowl-shaped pan, which requires less fuel to reach a high temperature than other pan types, was well-adapted to setting directly in a wood fire and on Chinese-style stoves.

3099. Thimbles were bronze examples found in the ruins of Pompeii and Herculaneum in Italy, which were destroyed by volcanic eruption in 79 CE. Their design is identical to that of modern thimbles.

3100. Fork evolved from the simple skewer, and was known to the ancient Romans, who used a serving fork with two tines. The first written mention of a fork dates from circa 1090, when a historian of the Ducas family of Byzantium (present-day Turkey) described a small golden fork used by the daughter of Constantine X Ducas, Eastern Roman emperor from 1059 to 1067.

3101. Enameled cookware was made in Delft, the Netherlands, in 1609. Enameling—the process of glazing metal, usually tin, cast iron, or molded steel—was known to the ancients, who employed it mainly for jewelry and other decorative work. Durable coatings for kitchen use were not developed until the modern era. Enameled iron pots were made in Germany in 1788, and saucepans were marketed in England beginning in 1799.

3102. Matches for creating a flame were made in Paris, France, in 1805 by Jean Chancel. They were thin splints of wood tipped with a mixture of potassium chlorate, sugar, and gum. The heads ignited when they were dipped into sulfuric acid.

3103. Friction matches were the invention of an Englishman, John Walker, who owned a pharmacy in the town of Stockton-on-Tees. In 1826, while experimenting with ways to improve the combustion in hunting guns, Walker happened to scrape against the floor a stick with which he had mixed potash and antimony. It ignited. In April 1827 he began selling "sulphuretted peroxide strikables," long sticks tipped with potassium chloride, antimony sulfide, gum arabic, and starch, which he called "Friction Lights." They were intended to be scraped along the inner side of a folded piece of sandpaper.

3104. Rubber bands were produced by Messrs. Perry and Company of London, England, in 1845, after Stephen Perry received a patent for them.

3105. Safety pin was invented by Walter Hunt of New York, NY, USA, who obtained a patent on April 10, 1849. Within the space of three hours, he conceived the idea, made a model, and sold his patent rights for US$100. The pins were manufactured in New York City.

3106. Safety matches were patented in 1855 by Johan Edvard Lundström of Jönköping, Sweden, using a preparation of red phosphorus. Previous varieties of friction matches sometimes ignited spontaneously because the combustible materials were combined in the match head. Lundström's safety matches divided the combustible materials between the match head and the striking surface. They were first produced in 1855 by the Jönköpings Tandsticksfabrik.

3107. Synthetic plastic was Parkesine, invented circa 1855 by Alexander Parkes of Birmingham, England. A compound of chloroform, camphor, and castor oil, Parkesine was a thermoplastic easily molded and formed into household articles. It was first manufactured in 1866 by a company Parkes formed for that purpose in London. Parkesine was chemically similar to celluloid, patented by two Americans in 1869.

3108. Can opener designed for the purpose was invented in 1858. It combined a sharp hook for piercing the can with a blade for enlarging the hole. The inventor was Ezra J. Warner of Waterbury, CT, USA. A patent for a can opener with a cutting wheel was issued in 1870 to another American inventor, William W. Lyman. Electric can openers appeared on the market in the United States in December 1931.

3109. Matchbooks containing cardboard matches were made by the Diamond Match Company at its Barberton, OH, USA, factory in 1896 under a patent granted on September 27, 1892, to Joshua Pusey, an attorney from Lima, PA. Although the patented design had the striking surface on the inside cover, the manufacturer moved it to the outside to prevent fires.

3110. Paper clip is usually attributed to Johann Waller (or Vaaler), a Norwegian inventor, who in 1900 developed an inexpensive clip made of wire and first patented it in Germany.

3111. Household detergent was Persil, introduced in 1907 by Henkel & Cie. of Dusseldorf, Germany.

3112. Cellophane is credited to the Swiss chemist J.E. Brandenberger, who created it in 1911. While working for a French textile company, he was given the job of finding a fabric that would repel dirt for use in tablecloths. He came up with the idea of combining cotton with a preparation of cellulose, a fibrous plant substance, which he processed with carbon disulfide into thin flat sheets. He received European and United States patents on his product in 1913. Cellophane was widely used in packaging until the 1960s, when it was largely replaced by plastic.

3113. Aerosol can was invented in 1926 by Erik Rotheim of Norway. He packaged a liquid in a pressurized container with a valve that released the contents when a lever was pressed.

3114. Cellophane transparent tape was invented by Richard Gurley Drew of St. Paul, MN, USA, who obtained a patent on May 27, 1930, on "adhesive tape." The patent was assigned to the Minnesota Mining and Manufacturing Company of St. Paul, better known as 3M. The tape was introduced to the market on September 8, 1930. The tape was developed from an earlier invention of Drew's, pressure-sensitive masking tape for use by car body shops.

3115. Aerosol product was an insecticide spray developed in 1941 by two U.S. government research chemists, Lyle D. Goodhue and W.N. Sullivan. The "bug bomb," as it was called, was used by the U.S. Navy and Marines during World War II to reduce military fatalities from malaria.

3116. Plastic container for kitchen use was a clear polyethylene water tumbler invented in 1945 by Earl S. Tupper, a Massachusetts, USA, chemist. This was the first household product made entirely of plastic. In 1948 Tupper began marketing Tupperware, a line of resealable, leak-proof polyethylene containers.

3117. Nonstick cookware was developed by the French engineer and inventor Marc Grégoire. In 1954 he patented a process by which polytetrafluoroethylene (PTFE, also called Teflon), a very slippery, heat-resistant, and non-reactive plastic, could be bonded to aluminum. In 1956 he founded the T-Fal Company, which marketed the first nonstick frying pan.

3118. Plastic bags were developed in Sweden by Akerlund & Rausing, at the suggestion of a salesman named William Hamilton. The first bags were introduced for commercial use in August 1960 as bags for the Strom shoe store chain, which had had trouble with its shoes tearing through paper bags.

HUNTING AND FISHING

3119. Big-game hunting is usually considered to have begun in Europe around 40,000 BCE, but it may have begun much earlier. In 1997, archeologists unearthed heavy wooden spears about six feet (1.8 meters) long from an openpit mine in Schoeningen, Germany. The spears, which have been dated to circa 400,000 BCE, were most likely used to kill large prey such as mastodon and elk.

3120. Arrowheads were used in western Europe as early as 40,000 BCE. Small, pre-formed flint projectile points have been found in Mousterian sites of that period. Bows and arrows were first pictured in rock paintings in southern Spain and the Sahara dated to 8000 BCE.

HUNTING AND FISHING—*continued*

3121. Net hunters known to anthropologists are the Gravettian people, who populated much of Europe some 29,000 to 22,000 years ago. In 1997, an American-Czech team of researchers presented evidence that people who lived in the Gravettian settlements at what are now Pavlov and Dolni Vestonice in the southern Czech Republic wove capture nets for hunting game.

3122. Whaling was practiced by Inuit and Aleut peoples of the North Pacific as early as 3000 BCE, according to archeological evidence of bone harpoons, float bladders, and other primitive whaling gear. They hunted small whale species that could be easily beached and stripped of blubber and meat.

3123. Treatise on hunting was *Kynegetikos (Hunting Man)*, probably written circa 375 BCE by the Greek historian Xenophon. It described the techniques of hunting on horseback and claimed that the hunt was the proper training for war.

3124. Factory ship for whaling was built by the Basque whaling captain François Sopite Zaburu in 1596. Zaburu constructed a brick furnace (called a tryworks) on the deck of his whaling ship. At sea, the tryworks was used to melt whale blubber into whale oil, which was stored in barrels. Previously, whales were killed and towed to factories on shore, where their blubber was stripped and boiled down. Basque whalers voyaged widely in pursuit of whales, and may have been the first Europeans after Leif Eriksson to land on the North American coast.

3125. Whaling town was Smeerenburg ("Blubbertown"), built beginning in 1619 on Spitsbergen, an island north of Norway above the Arctic Circle. It was founded by Dutch whaling syndicates on a site earlier used by the English Muscovy Company. The town provided a trading and outfitting base for whalers hunting the Greenland right whale and other polar whale species. A lengthy period of extreme cold beginning in the mid-1650s temporarily shut down the arctic whaling trade; Smeerenburg was abandoned around 1665.

3126. Global treaty to regulate fishing on the high seas was adopted in New York, NY, USA, by the United Nations Conference on Straddling Fish Stocks and Highly Migratory Fish Stocks on August 4, 1995. The treaty made it legally binding for nations to conserve and sustainably manage high-seas fisheries and reach peaceful agreements in fishing disputes. It was signed by 25 nations.

I

INTERNATIONAL RELATIONS

3127. Statement of the principle of medical neutrality in wartime was made by the Muslim leader Saladin, sultan of Egypt, Syria, Yemen, and Palestine, whose full name in Arabic is Salah ad-Din Yusuf ibn Ayyub. In October 1187, after his armies defeated the Crusaders and captured Jerusalem (in present-day Israel), Saladin ordered the doctors on both sides to help the wounded, regardless of whether they were Christian or Muslim.

3128. Reference to the Iron Curtain was contained in *Through Bolshevik Russia* (1920), a travel book by Mrs. Philip Snowden, who wrote: "We were behind the 'iron curtain' at last." Probably the phrase was in informal use before that. Nazi officials were fond of using it: Josef Goebbels did so in remarks of February 25, 1945, as did Count Schwerin von Krosgk, foreign minister in the Dönitz government that was briefly in power after the death of Adolf Hitler. In a radio statement of May 7, 1945, he warned that "the iron curtain in the east moves closer and closer." On March 5, 1946, Winston Churchill used the same phrase in a speech at Westminster College in Fulton, MO, USA, and the coinage is often attributed to him.

3129. International oil embargo was imposed by the United States on Japan, in response to the Japanese occupation beginning July 26, 1941, of military bases in southern Indochina (now Vietnam). It was this action, more than any other, which led the Japanese Navy, desperate to secure new supplies of petroleum, to plan the attack on Pearl Harbor on December 7 of that year.

3130. Oil embargo in peacetime was the temporary embargo on crude oil shipments to the United States and the Netherlands in December 1973 by the Arab members of the Organization of Petroleum Exporting Countries, meeting in Teheran following the October 1973 Yom Kippur War between the Arab states and Israel. OPEC members, including Iraq, Kuwait, Saudi Arabia, the United Arab Emirates, and Libya, hoped to use the embargo to pressure Western nations to withdraw their support for the Jewish state.

3131. Visit by an American president to a country on the U.S. list of terrorist states took place on October 27, 1994, when President William Jefferson Clinton visited Damascus, Syria, to meet with that country's president, Hafez al-Assad.

3132. Visit made by South Korean tourists to North Korea after the division of Korea into two hostile states in 1948 was made by 780 travelers who took went on a five-day guided tour of North Korea's scenic Diamond Mountains in November 1998. The group's cruise ship, which also carried 200 international journalists, departed from and returned to the South Korean port of Donghae.

3133. British prime minister to address the Parliament of the Irish Republic was Tony Blair. On November 26, 1998, he spoke in Dublin before 226 Irish legislators in a joint session of the Seanad (Senate) and the Dáil (lower house) regarding the prospects for peace between England and Ireland.

INTERNATIONAL RELATIONS—ALLIANCES

3134. Political association of Arab states was the Arab League, founded in Cairo, Egypt, on March 22, 1945. The founding members were Egypt, Iraq, Lebanon, Saudi Arabia, Syria, Transjordan (now Jordan), and Yemen. Later members included Algeria, Kuwait, Libya, Morocco, Somalia, the Sudan, Tunisia, the United Arab Emirates, and the Palestine Liberation Organization.

3135. Call for a united democratic Europe was issued by Winston Churchill, then recently the prime minister of England. In a speech of September 19, 1946, at Zürich, Switzerland, Churchill proposed the creation of a "United States of Europe" with an elective government, unified economy, and integrated military structure. On May 8–10, 1948, the Hague Congress called for a united democratic Europe and the creation of the Council of Europe, which first met on May 5, 1949, in London, England, and was later based in Strasbourg, France.

3136. Regional cooperative in Oceania was the South Pacific Commission, formed in 1947 and now including Australia, France, the United Kingdom, New Zealand, and the United States—nations with dependencies in the South Pacific—and 21 island states and territories. The SPC was intended to promote health, social, and economic development in the region.

3137. Peacetime alliance of European and North American nations was the North Atlantic Treaty Organization, formed in response to the military threat posed by the Soviet Union. It was established on August 24, 1949, following the signing of the North Atlantic Treaty in Washington, DC, USA, on April 4, 1949, by Belgium, Canada, Denmark, France, Iceland, Italy, Luxembourg, the Netherlands, Norway, Portugal, the United Kingdom, and the USA. Greece and Turkey joined NATO in 1952, West Germany (now Germany) in 1955, and Spain in 1982. The main headquarters of NATO's military command, the Supreme Headquarters Allied Powers in Europe, is located in Brussels, Belgium. In December 1950, the American general Dwight David Eisenhower was appointed NATO's first Supreme Allied Commander, Europe. In Article 5 of the North Atlantic Treaty, the members "agree that an armed attack against one or more of them in Europe or North America shall be considered an attack against them all; and consequently they agree that, if such an armed attack occurs, each of them, in exercise of the right of individual or collective self-defense recognized by Article 51 of the Charter of the United Nations, will assist the Party or Parties so attacked by taking forthwith, individually and in concert with the other Parties, such action as it deems necessary, including the use of armed force, to restore and maintain the security of the North Atlantic area."

3138. Plan for European economic and monetary union or EMU was devised at the Hague Summit in December 1969 by France and Germany. Within a year, France decided to back out of the plan, and after several months of negotiation, it was shelved until 1992, when EMU became a legal requirement of the Treaty on European Union.

3139. National nuclear-free zone was established in New Zealand in 1984.

3140. Regional nuclear-free zone was the South Pacific Nuclear Free Zone Treaty (Treaty of Rarotonga), signed in 1986 at Rarotonga, the Cook Islands, by New Zealand and other nations of the South Pacific.

3141. Continental nuclear-free zone was the African Nuclear Weapons Free Zone, established on April 11, 1996, following the signing of the Treaty of Pelindaba by 49 of the 53 members of the Organization of African Unity.

3142. Non-NATO ally of the United States in the Western Hemisphere was Argentina, who gained that distinction in October 1997. The title gave Argentina preferential access to surplus American military equipment. Other non-NATO allies of the United States were Israel, Egypt, Jordan, Japan, South Korea, and Australia.

INTERNATIONAL RELATIONS—ALLIANCES—continued

3143. Former Warsaw Pact nations to join NATO were Poland, Hungary, and the Czech Republic, which formally joined on March 12, 1999. The North Atlantic Treaty Organization (NATO) is a military alliance of Western nations, formed in 1949 to protect western Europe from attack by the Soviet Union. Poland, Hungary, and Czechoslovakia were among eight nations that had joined the Warsaw Pact, an alliance controlled by the Soviet Union, in 1955, when they were under Communist regimes. Those regimes were overthrown in 1989. Two years later, the Warsaw Pact was dissolved and the Soviet Union was disbanded. The invitation to all three countries to join NATO was made in 1997, when the organization had changed its mission to one of containing regional conflicts and combatting terrorism. The ceremony in which they accepted membership, marking their progress in establishing democratic rule, took place at Independence, MO, USA, at the Harry S. Truman Presidential Library, 52 years to the day after President Truman sent a message to Congress calling for American support of countries struggling against communism. The foreign ministers who signed the agreement were Jan Kavan of the Czech Republic, Janos Martonyi of Hungary, and Bronislav Geremek of Poland.

INTERNATIONAL RELATIONS—DIPLOMACY

3144. Diplomatic contact between Africa and China took place in 629, when a mission from the Shunai kingdom, located in what is now Somalia, arrived in Changan (present-day Xian, China), headquarters of the Tang dynasty.

3145. British ambassador to the United States was George Hammond. He was appointed on July 5, 1791.

3146. Woman accredited as a minister to a foreign power was Rosike Schwimmer of Hungary, a socialist, pacifist, and feminist, who on November 25, 1918, was appointed minister to Switzerland by the brief-lived, leftist Hungarian Republic. She resigned in 1919 and was forced to flee the country in 1920 after the conservative counterrevolution led by Miklós Horthy assumed control of the government.

3147. International civil service was established along with the formation of the League of Nations, which took place at the Paris Peace Conference in 1919. League of Nations operations required a secretariat of several hundred, including administrative, clerical, and custodial personnel, as well as many experts in various aspects of international diplomacy and law. Personnel were drawn from Great Britain, France, Switzerland, and about 40 other nations.

3148. Woman accredited as an ambassador was Aleksandra Mikhaylovna Kollontay (born Aleksandra Domontovich), a Russian Marxist feminist who headed the Soviet diplomatic missions to Norway, Mexico, and Sweden between 1923 and 1945. In 1944 she negotiated the armistice between the Soviet Union and Finland.

3149. Telephone hot line between nations was instituted on June 20, 1963, by the United States and the Soviet Union. It was intended to provide an emergency communications link between the leaders of the two superpowers. The hot line was never actually used.

3150. Ambassador to Arctic aboriginal peoples was the Inuit activist Mary May Simon, who on October 31, 1994, was appointed Canada's first ambassador for circumpolar affairs. The first Inuit (Eskimo) to hold an ambassadorial position, her task was to raise awareness of, and promote solutions to, the social, economic, and ecological challenges facing the Arctic peoples of the world's circumpolar nations—Canada, the United States, Russia, Finland, Sweden, Norway, Iceland, and Denmark.

INTERNATIONAL RELATIONS—LAWS AND RIGHTS

3151. Comprehensive text on international law was De Jure Belli ac Pacis (On the Law of War and Peace), written in Paris in 1625 by the Dutch jurist Hugo Grotius (born Huigh de Groot). Drawing on biblical, classical, and contemporary sources, it set forth the basis of modern international law. Grotius insisted on the existence of a "natural law" for nations that allowed for just wars but also provided for the rights of individuals.

3152. International copyright agreement was the International Convention for the Protection of Literary and Artistic Works, usually referred to as the Berne Convention, adopted in 1886 by an international conference in Berne, Switzerland. Each of the signatories agreed to protect works first published in other signatory countries, as well as honor the rights of unpublished artists.

3153. International court was the Permanent Court of Arbitration, founded at The Hague, the Netherlands, in 1899. According to its charter, the Permanent Court was to provide "the settlement of disputes between States by judges of their own choice and on the basis of respect for law." It was composed of a panel of jurists appointed by the member governments. Arbitrators were selected by the litigants. The Court arbitrated 20 cases between 1902 and 1932. After the formation of the League of Nations, many nations turned to its Permanent Court of International Justice, established in 1921. It operated until 1945, rendering 32 judgments and 27 advisory opinions. In 1945 the Permanent Court of International Justice was superseded by the International Court of Justice, which is under the auspices of the United Nations.

3154. International Congress of Comparative Law met in Paris, France, in 1900. Attendants proposed an international law code to be enacted by national legislatures. A general code of international law has never been implemented.

3155. Nonviolent act of civil disobedience of international significance of international significance was the *satyagraha* (Hindi for "truth force"), led by the Indian-born lawyer Mohandas K. Gandhi on March 22, 1907, in Johannesburg, South Africa. Gandhi and his followers were protesting South African racial laws that forced Indians to carry residence permits at all times.

3156. International treaty prohibiting racial discrimination was the Convention on the Elimination of All Forms of Racial Discrimination, signed by member nations of the United Nations on December 21, 1965, and entered into force on January 4, 1969. The convention signatories resolved "to adopt all necessary measures for speedily eliminating racial discrimination in all its forms and manifestations, and to prevent and combat racist doctrines and practices in order to promote understanding between races and to build an international community free from all forms of racial segregation and racial discrimination."

3157. International laws to protect privacy of personal information went into effect on October 25, 1998, enacted by six of the 15 members of the European Union, with the rest expected to follow suit. The law, a directive of the EU that had to be supplemented by individual statutes in each member nation, prohibited commerce in personal data, such as credit-card transaction records, telephone records, and magazine subscription lists. The law also prohibited any company doing business in the EU from transmitting personal data to any nation without such privacy protection, including the United States.

INTERNATIONAL RELATIONS—SUMMITS AND CONFERENCES

3158. Hemispheric diplomatic conference was the Congress of Panama, held in 1826 at the invitation of Simón Bolívar, president of Gran Colombia and Peru (now Bolivia and parts of several other South American nations). Bolívar had imagined a general conference leading eventually to the unification of all the territories of Latin America, but only Colombia, Peru, Mexico, and some areas of Central America sent representatives. A treaty of alliance was signed that proposed the future establishment of a biannual continental congress and a common army and navy. Civil war in 1827 put an end to Bolívar's hopes.

3159. Modern congress of nations in the Americas was the First International Conference of American States, held in Washington, DC, USA, in 1889–90. After 1910 it was known as the Pan-American Union. In 1948, the Ninth International Conference of American States, held in Bogotá, Colombia, established the Organization of American States as the successor to the Pan-American Union.

3160. Arms limitation conference was the Conference on the Limitation of Armaments, which assembled at Memorial Continental Hall in Washington, DC, USA, from November 12, 1921, to February 6, 1922. Nine nations took part in the conference: the United States, Great Britain, France, Italy, Japan, China, Holland, Belgium, and Portugal.

3161. International disarmament conferences of major scope were the Disarmament Conferences held at Geneva, Switzerland, between 1932 and 1937. Sponsored by the League of Nations, the first conference, held in February 1932, was intended to provide a framework by which the 60 attending nations could reduce armaments while guaranteeing security. Disagreements over appropriate levels and proportions of armaments and profound distrust between France and Germany forced the session into deadlock.

3162. General conference of the United Nations Educational, Scientific and Cultural Organization took place in 1947. UNESCO General Conferences meet every two years in Paris, France.

3163. Meeting of the nonaligned movement took place on April 18–24, 1955, at the Bandung Conference, held in Bandung, Java, Indonesia. The conference was organized by Indonesia, Myanmar (Burma), Ceylon (Sri Lanka), India, and Pakistan. Delegates were sent from

INTERNATIONAL RELATIONS—SUMMITS AND CONFERENCES—continued

29 Asian and African states that had been former colonies of European powers. The conference condemned colonialism "in all its forms" and advocated forming a "third force" to offset the Cold War rivalry of the United States, Soviet Union, and China. Among the leaders of the nonaligned movement were Jawaharlal Nehru of India, Gamal Abdel Nasser of Egypt, and Josip Broz Tito of Yugoslavia.

3164. African–African American Summit was held in April 1991 in West Africa by African and American government officials, diplomats, businesspeople, and religious leaders from the United States and Africa.

3165. Heads of state to meet in an on-line chat session were Prime Minister Mahathir Mohamad of Malaysia, Yasir Arafat of the Palestinian Authority, and President Fidel Ramos of the Philippines. They met for ten minutes in an on-line interactive chat session on January 17, 1996.

3166. International meetings of ministers in Antarctica took place on January 25, 1999, when ministers and senior officials from 24 nations, all of which were signatories of the 1959 Antarctica Treaty, gathered at the Scott Base on the Ross Ice Shelf. The international meeting was arranged by New Zealand to discuss proposed safeguards for the Antarctic environment.

INTERNATIONAL RELATIONS—TREATIES

3167. Treaty in which the entire world was partitioned was the Treaty of Tordesillas, signed by ambassadors from Spain and Portugal on June 7, 1494, at Tordesillas, Spain. It split the globe into two parts, with the line of demarcation running 370 leagues west of the Cape Verde Islands, about 48 degrees of longitude west of Greenwich. Spain was granted all territory on the eastern side of the line, Portugal all territory on the western side, and both countries were prevented from claiming land already under Christian rule. The dividing line on the other side of the globe was left unspecified. The treaty was an extension of bulls issued on May 4, 1493, by Pope Alexander VI. It was not recognized by later European colonial powers.

3168. Peace treaty among European powers to arbitrate world trade was the Treaty of Breda, signed at Breda, the Netherlands, on July 3, 1667, by the Dutch Republic (the Netherlands), its allies, France and Denmark, and its opponent, England. The treaty put an end to the second Anglo-Dutch War, a contest over commercial rivalries in Asia and the Americas. The French gave up three West Indian islands to the English in exchange for Acadia (Nova Scotia) and the retention of French Guiana. The English gave up possession of Surinam to the Dutch, acquired some of their African trading posts, and retained control over New York and New Jersey, the former Dutch colony of New Netherland. The Dutch kept their position in the East Indies and won additional shipping rights within European waters.

3169. Treaty between a South American country and a North American country was the Treaty of Peace, Amity, Navigation and Commerce, signed on May 31, 1825, between the United States and Colombia. Its main provision was to guarantee the United States access to Colombian ports, and vice versa.

3170. International agreements on the humane treatment of soldiers and civilians in wartime were signed at the first Convention for the Amelioration of the Wounded in Time of War, held in Geneva, Switzerland, in August 1864. The Geneva conventions, as they are commonly known, were initiated by Jean-Henri Dunant, the founder of the Red Cross. The agreement reached at the first convention provided that hospitals for the wounded or medical personnel could not be considered military targets; that all wounded combatants had to be treated impartially; and that the Red Cross symbol would identify protected personnel and equipment. By 1867, the first Geneva convention had been ratified by the European great powers. Later conventions, held in 1906 and 1929, extended the protections.

3171. Antiwar treaty of international importance was the Kellogg-Briand Pact, also called the Pact of Paris, signed on August 27, 1928, in Paris, France, and eventually accepted by most nations of the world. The multilateral treaty required the signatories to "renounce the resort to war as an instrument of national policy." It was drafted by the French foreign minister, Aristide Briand, and the U.S. secretary of state, Frank B. Kellogg. Fundamental flaws in the pact—it allowed for wars of "self-defense" and made no provision for peace enforcement—rendered it worthless as a deterrent to conflict.

3172. Signatories of the Warsaw Pact were Albania, Bulgaria, Czechoslovakia (now Slovakia and the Czech Republic), Hungary, East Germany (now Germany), Poland, Romania, and the Soviet Union (now the Commonwealth of Independent States). The pact was primarily a military alliance imposed on the smaller states by the Soviet Union as a reaction to the remilitarization of West Germany and its acceptance into the North Atlantic Treaty Organization in 1954. The text was drafted by Vyacheslav Mikhailovich Molotov, the Soviet foreign minister. It was signed at the Warsaw Conference in Warsaw, Poland, on May 14, 1955.

3173. Country to attempt to withdraw from the Warsaw Pact was Hungary. On October 31, 1956, at the height of the October Hungarian uprising against communist rule, Prime Minister Imre Nagy told Soviet deputy premier Anastas Ivanovich Mikoyan that Hungary was planning to withdraw from the military alliance. The following day, Soviet tanks entered Hungary and troops began to crush the rebellion. A new puppet communist regime was installed that pledged Hungary's continued participation in the pact. Nagy was lured out of sanctuary in the Yugoslav embassy and executed.

3174. Nuclear weapons test moratorium was observed, unofficially, from November 1958 to September 1961, by the three nuclear powers, the United States, the United Kingdom, and the Soviet Union.

3175. Treaty to govern the use of a continent was the Antarctic Treaty, signed in Washington, DC, USA, on December 1, 1959 by representatives of the governments of Argentina, Australia, Belgium, Chile, France, Japan, New Zealand, Norway, South Africa, the Soviet Union, the United Kingdom, and the United States. The treaty, which was enacted on June 23, 1961, prohibited signatories from claiming sovereignty over any part of the continent and reserved the entire landmass for free, nonpolitical, and nonmilitary scientific investigation.

3176. Nuclear arms–control treaty was the Nuclear Test Ban Treaty, formally the Treaty Banning Nuclear Weapons Tests in the Atmosphere, in Outer Space and Under Water. It was signed in Moscow on August 5, 1963, by the United States, the Soviet Union, and the United Kingdom. The treaty banned tests of nuclear weapons above ground, in the ocean, and in outer space, but did allow testing underground. It made no allowance for verification of compliance. More than 100 nations ratified the treaty. Two nations that did not were France and the People's Republic of China, both of which continued to conduct aboveground tests.

3177. Country to withdraw from the North Atlantic Treaty Organization (NATO) was France, during the presidency of Charles de Gaulle. Fearing that under NATO France was losing its ability to pursue an independent foreign policy, de Gaulle announced in a speech on September 9, 1965, that he would "end the subordination that is described as integration." In February–March 1966, France ended its military ties with NATO. These were restored in December 1995.

3178. Treaty on the use of space was the Treaty on Principles Governing the Activities of States in the Exploration and Use of Outer Space, Including the Moon and Other Celestial Bodies, endorsed by the United Nations General Assembly on December 19, 1966. The treaty was signed by the United States, the Soviet Union, the United Kingdom, and other countries beginning on January 27, 1967. Signatories were prohibited from placing weapons of mass destruction into space, and agreed not to claim sovereignty over other celestial bodies.

3179. Nonproliferation treaty for weapons of mass destruction was the Treaty on the Nonproliferation of Nuclear Weapons, agreed to on July 1, 1968, by representatives of the United Kingdom, the United States, the Soviet Union, and 59 other nations. It went into force on March 5, 1970. France and China ratified the treaty in 1992. The signatories agreed not to sell or give nuclear weapons to nonnuclear states or to assist them in developing such weapons. It was renewed on May 11, 1995, by 178 nations.

3180. Strategic Arms Limitation Treaty (also called SALT I) between the United States and the Soviet Union was signed in Moscow by President Richard M. Nixon and General Secretary Leonid Brezhnev on May 26, 1972, culminating negotations that began in November 1969. SALT I and its successors were designed to slow the arms race in strategic nuclear weapons.

3181. Treaty banning the use of the weather as a weapon of war was signed on May 18, 1977, by the United States, the Soviet Union, and 29 other nations. The signatories agreed not to attack each other by initiating artificial storms, earthquakes, or tsunamis.

3182. Peace treaty between an Arab nation and Israel was the Camp David Accords between Israel and Egypt, signed on September 18, 1978, by Israeli prime minister Menachem Begin and Egyptian president Anwar Sadat at Camp David, near Washington, DC, USA. Among its provisions was the withdrawal of Is-

INTERNATIONAL RELATIONS—TREATIES—*continued*

rael from the Sinai Peninsula, which it had captured from Egypt in 1967 during the Six-Day War. A peace treaty between Israel and the Palestinians was signed on September 13, 1993, by Yasir Arafat, chairman of the Palestinian Liberation Organization, and Israeli prime minister Yitzhak Rabin at the White House in Washington, DC, USA. Both parties officially recognized each other for the first time, and Israel granted the Palestinians limited but increasing political autonomy in exchange for a modification of the PLO charter, which did not acknowledge the right of the Jewish state to exist.

3183. Open Skies treaty was signed on March 24, 1992 by representatives of 24 nations attending the Conference on Security and Cooperation in Europe, held in Helsinki, Finland. The treaty provided for mutual aerial inspections of military and other facilities and dealt with such issues as territorial openness, use of observation aircraft, sensors on board these aircraft, and the quotas of annual inspection flights for each country. Reciprocal aerial inspections were first proposed by U.S. president Dwight David Eisenhower in 1955.

3184. Treaty between the North Atlantic Treaty Organization (NATO) and Russia was signed by NATO officials and Russian president Boris Nikolayevich Yeltsin on May 27, 1997. The cooperative pact gave Russia a consultative role in NATO decisions. In return, Russia did not put obstacles in the way of several former Soviet-bloc countries who were applying to join NATO.

3185. Land mine treaty was signed in Ottawa, Canada, on December 3, 1997, by representatives of more than 120 nations. Nations that ratified the treaty pledged to destroy all stockpiles of anti-personnel land mines within four years and to clear all mines from their territory within 10 years. The United States, China, and Russia did not sign the treaty, citing the need to protect the security of their personnel and installations overseas.

INTERNATIONAL RELATIONS—UNITED NATIONS

3186. General association of nations was the League of Nations, founded after World War I at the Paris Peace Conference in 1919 at the instigation of U.S. president Woodrow Wilson (although the United States never officially joined). It was headquartered in Geneva, Switzerland. The League's main purpose was to maintain stable international relations and to prevent another world conflict. In theory, the Covenant of the League of Nations provided for collective security, international arbitration, and a permanent court of justice for its members. In practice, the League lacked any power to discipline member states and failed completely in its mission. It was disbanded in 1946.

3187. Meeting to establish the United Nations took place at the Dumbarton Oaks mansion in Washington, DC, USA, from August 21 to October 7, 1944. Representatives of China, Great Britain, the Soviet Union, and the United States met to discuss the establishment of an international organization for maintaining peace and security. On October 9, the participants made public their "Proposals for the Establishment of a General International Organization," which formed the basis for the United Nations Charter signed in 1945 at the San Francisco Conference.

3188. United Nations conference was the United Nations Conference on International Organization, often called the San Francisco Conference, which took place in San Francisco, CA, USA, beginning on April 25, 1945. Fifty nations attended. UNCIO finalized the structure and mission of the organization and produced the final text of the Charter of the United Nations.

3189. Member nations of the United Nations were the following, who signed the United Nations Charter on June 26, 1945, at the San Francisco Conference in San Francisco, CA, USA: Argentina, Australia, Belgium, Bolivia, Brazil, Belorussian SSR (now Belarus), Canada, Chile, China, Colombia, Costa Rica, Cuba, Czechoslovakia (now Slovakia and the Czech Republic), Denmark, Dominican Republic, Ecuador, Egypt, El Salvador, Ethiopia, France, Greece, Guatemala, Haiti, Honduras, India, Iran, Iraq, Lebanon, Liberia, Luxembourg, Mexico, the Netherlands, New Zealand, Nicaragua, Norway, Panama, Paraguay, Peru, the Philippines, Poland, Soviet Union (now Russia), Saudi Arabia, South Africa, Syria, Turkey, Ukrainian SSR (now Ukraine), United Kingdom, United States, Uruguay, Venezuela, and Yugoslavia.

3190. Chairman of the United Nations Atomic Energy Commission was H. V. Evatt, an Australian minister of foreign affairs, appointed in 1946. He presided over the first meeting of the agency, at which American financier Bernard Baruch presented a U.S. proposal for giving international responsibility for regulating the development of nuclear energy to the United Nations. Evatt rejected modifications offered by Andrei Gromyko of the Soviet Union and seconded by the American physicist J. Robert Oppenheimer, and the plan was abandoned.

3191. Secretary general of the United Nations was Trygve Halvdan Lie, a Norwegian statesman and diplomat who had been foreign minister of the Norwegian government in exile during World War II. On February 1, 1946, Lie was elected to a five-year term as secretary general, the highest office in the United Nations. During his tenure, he came into repeated conflict with the Soviet Union, which threatened to veto his reelection for a second term. The General Assembly appointed Lie for an additional three years in 1950 over the protests of the Soviets. Thereafter, Soviet bloc nations refused to recognize him as secretary general. He resigned on November 10, 1952.

3192. Meeting of the United Nations General Assembly took place in Flushing Meadow, NY, USA, on October 23, 1946. The United Nations Charter, which had been adopted in June, entered into force the following day. The General Assembly is comprised of representatives of all members of the United Nations. It is convened yearly or by special session.

3193. International maritime organization was the Inter-Governmental Maritime Consultative Organization, founded in 1948 by the United Nations Maritime Conference. The goal of the agency was to develop and facilitate the adoption of regulations and procedures for international shipping. On May 22, 1982, the name was changed to the International Maritime Organization.

3194. United Nations embargo was an embargo on arms and strategic materials shipments to China and North Korea, adopted by the United Nations General Assembly in 1951 in support of the UN military action in Korea (the Korean War).

3195. President of the United Nations General Assembly who was a woman was an Indian diplomat, Vijaya Lakshmi Pandit, born Swarup Kumari Nehru in 1900. She served in the United Nations from 1953 to 1954. She was the sister of Jawaharlal Nehru, the leader of the Indian nationalist movement. In 1937, as minister for local self-government and public health, she became the first Indian woman to hold a cabinet portfolio.

3196. Secretary general of the United Nations from an Asian nation was the teacher, diplomat, and champion of nonalignment U Thant, born in Burma (Myanmar) on January 22, 1909. On November 3, 1961, following the death of United Nations secretary general Dag Hammarskjöld, Thant was named acting secretary. He was elected in his own right on November 30, 1962, and retired in 1971.

3197. Representative of a nongovernmental organization to address a plenary session of the United Nations General Assembly was Yasir Arafat, chairman of the Palestine Liberation Organization. Arafat spoke before the General Assembly on November 22, 1974, when the General Assembly passed resolution 3237 (XXIX), giving observer status to the PLO. This enabled the organization to maintain an office in New York but did not give it the same privileges as UN member states.

3198. World Heritage List sites were officially announced in 1978 under the International Convention for the Protection of the World Cultural and Natural Heritage, adopted by the United Nations Educational, Scientific and Cultural Organization in 1972. They included: L'Anse aux Meadows National Historic Park and Nahanni National Park in Canada; Galapagos National Park and the Old City of Quito in Ecuador; the Rock-hewn Churches of Lalibela and Simien National Park in Ethiopia; Aachen Cathedral in Germany; the Historic Center of Cracow and the Wieliczka Salt Mines in Poland; the Island of Gorée in Senegal; and Mesa Verde National Park and Yellowstone National Park in the United States. The World Heritage Committee, consisting of representatives from 21 nations, administers the Convention. The Committee named twelve sites in 1978, 45 in 1979, 28 in 1980, 26 in 1981, 24 in 1982, 29 in 1983, 23 in 1984, 30 in 1985, 31 in 1986, 41 in 1987, 27 in 1988, seven in 1989, 17 in 1990, 22 in 1991, 20 in 1992, 33 in 1993, 29 in 1994, 29 in 1995, 37 in 1996, and 46 in 1997.

3199. Ranking of countries by human development was published in *The Human Development Report 1990* by the United Nations Development Programme. The report assessed the impact of development on the lives of people in 130 countries; the three main factors considered were life expectancy, educational access, and standard of living.

INTERNATIONAL RELATIONS—UNITED NATIONS—*continued*

3200. International Year of the World's Indigenous People was 1993. The event was declared by the United Nations to draw attention to such issues as the right of indigenous peoples to possess or repossess ancestral lands or receive compensation for them, the right to establish autonomous governments, and the right to international arbitration of conflicts between indigenous peoples and national governments.

3201. Condemnation of anti-Semitism by the United Nations took place on March 9, 1994, when the United Nations Human Rights Commission cited the practice of anti-Semitism as a violation of human rights. It was the first time in the history of the UN that such a proclamation was made.

3202. Director-general of the World Trade Organization was the Italian diplomat Renato Ruggiero, who began his tenure on May 1, 1995. The WTO, which is administered by the United Nations, is the successor to the General Agreement on Tariffs and Trade (GATT) and began with 104 national members. The agency's headquarters are in Geneva, Switzerland.

3203. Secretary-general of the United Nations from a black African nation was the professional civil servant Kofi Atta Annan, born in Kumasi, the Gold Coast (now Ghana). Annan was descended from the hereditary paramount chiefs of the Fanti people. In 1997 he succeeded Boutros Boutros-Ghali to become the seventh secretary-general of the United Nations.

3204. Deputy secretary-general of the United Nations was Louise Frechette, Canada's former deputy minister of national defense, named to that post in January 1998 to aid Secretary General Kofi Atta Annan in the redesign of the United Nations administrative structure.

L

LAND TRANSPORTATION

3205. Wind-driven vehicle was designed by the Italian physician and engineer Guido da Vigevano in 1335 for his patron, King Philip VI of France, who was seeking innovative military gear for a possible crusade to the Holy Land. A book by Guido depicts a self-propelled, windmill-powered battle wagon. The wagon was never built, as far as is known.

3206. Organization to promote human-powered transportation was the International Human Powered Vehicle Association, which held its first land speed championships in 1975. The IHPVA is an association of national associations and organizations, dedicated to promoting improvement, innovation, and creativity in the use of human power, especially in the design and development of human-powered vehicles. In 1999, the IHPVA had member associations in Australia, Belgium, Finland, France, Germany, Great Britain, the Netherlands, North America, and Switzerland.

3207. Transcontinental trip by a solar-powered vehicle was completed by Hans Tholstrup and Larry Perkins in the *Solar Trek,* a custom car powered by a 1 kilowatt photovoltaic array mounted on the hood, roof, and trunk. In 1983, the *Solar Trek* drove from Perth to Sydney, Australia, covering 2,500 miles (about 4,000 kilometers) in less than 20 days.

LAND TRANSPORTATION—ANIMAL-POWERED

3208. Coach with side doors and a spring carriage is thought to have been produced in Kocs, Hungary, circa 1450.

3209. Bus service was offered in Paris, France, in 1662, at the encouragement of the philosopher and mathematician Blaise Pascal. The horse-drawn omnibuses, called *carrosses à cinq solz,* seated eight. According to Pascal's proposal, they were to "circulate along a predetermined route in Paris at regular intervals regardless of the number of passengers." The service began operation on March 16, 1662, and was initially popular, but when a fare was introduced, ridership declined. The Latin word *omnibus* means "for everyone."

3210. Carriage propelled by dogs was invented circa 1885 by a Frenchman, Monsieur Huret. His three-wheeled carriage was propelled by dogs running in treadmills incorporated into the rear wheels.

LAND TRANSPORTATION—MOTOR VEHICLES

3211. Motor vehicle has had several inventors. The first independently maneuverable, self-propelled vehicle was a three-wheeled tractor invented by French military engineer Nicolas-Joseph Cugnot in 1769. Its power plant was a two-piston steam engine, designed by Cugnot, that was the first to use high-pressure steam without the need for condensation. Intended as an artillery hauler, Cugnot's tractor anticipated the self-propelled guns of 20th-century warfare.

3212. Motor vehicle accident took place in Paris, France, in 1769, when the three-wheeled steam tractor invented by military engineer Nicolas-Joseph Cugnot collided with and knocked down the wall of a building.

3213. Motorized bus service opened in 1831, when the *Infant,* a ten-seat steam-powered wheeled carriage designed by Walter Hancock, began carrying passengers between Stratford-upon-Avon and London, England. Hancock conceived of his enterprise not as a transportation business—passengers were not required to pay a fare—but as as means of dissipating social prejudices.

3214. Electric vehicle was constructed in 1837 by Scottish inventor Robert Davidson, who operated a carriage powered by voltaic cells between Edinburgh and Glasgow at a speed of 4 miles (6 kilometers) per hour.

3215. Motorcycle was built circa 1868 by American inventor Sylvester Hayward Roper of Roxbury, MA, USA. Roper's steam-powered, two-wheeled velocipede was road-tested about 17 years before the gas-powered Reitwagen of the German engineers Gottlieb Wilhelm Daimler and Wilhelm Maybach. It was not commercially successful.

3216. Motorcycle with an internal-combustion engine was invented by the German engineers Gottlieb Wilhelm Daimler and Wilhelm Maybach. In the mid-1880s, working out of Daimler's home in Bad Cannstatt, Germany, they designed a lightweight, carbureted gasoline engine suitable for a one-person vehicle. In 1885, Daimler fitted the air-cooled, single-cylinder design to a homebuilt bicycle made of oak and called it the Reitwagen ("Riding Wagon"). It was capable of speeds up to 7 miles per hour (12 kilometers per hour). A motorized tricycle had been invented in 1884 by Edward Butler in England, but it was not gasoline powered.

3217. Motorcycle to be mass-produced was the Hildebrand & Wolfmüller of 1894, with a 2.5 horsepower, water-cooled, four-stroke parallel twin engine developed by the German engineers Heinrich and Wilhelm Hildebrand, Alois Wolfmüller, and Hans Geisenhof. Several hundred were sold.

3218. Bus with an internal-combustion engine was a twelve-seater, 5-horsepower vehicle built by Benz that plied a route from Siegen to Deutz in Germany beginning on March 18, 1895. It was operated by the Netphener Omnibus company, which charged 70 pfennig to ride the entire route. The first driver was Hermann Golze. The service proved uneconomical and was terminated in December of that year.

3219. Motorcycle designed to be a motor vehicle and not just a bicycle with a motor was the Indian motorcycle, manufactured in Springfield, MA, USA, by the Hendee Manufacturing Company, founded by American inventor George M. Hendee. Three motorcycles were built in 1901. The following year, production was increased to 143. The engines were made by the Aurora Machine Company, Aurora, IL, USA, and were mounted to the motorcycle frames in Springfield. The machines were first publicly demonstrated on June 1, 1901, in a hill-climbing exhibition.

3220. Motor home was built for the German physician and motoring enthusiast E.E. Lehwess in 1902. Called the *Passe-Partout,* the 25-horsepower vehicle was designed by the firm of Panhard and Levassor of Paris, France, and featured a compact kitchen and sleeping area. Lehwess planned to drive his motor home around the world but abandoned it when the engine broke down near Gorky, Russia.

3221. National speed limit was set in England in 1903. The limit was 20 miles (32 kilometers) per hour.

3222. Motorized trailer to be commercially produced was a mahogany-paneled model manufactured by Eccles Motor Transport Ltd., Birmingham, England, in 1919. It slept two people and was equipped with rudimentary kitchen facilities.

3223. Snowmobile was invented in 1922 by Joseph-Armand Bombardier of Valcourt, Quebec, Canada. The vehicle was an ordinary sleigh outfitted with a Model T automobile engine driving a snow propeller. Bombardier founded the first snowmobile manufacturing company in 1937.

3224. Woman to motorcycle from the United States to Tierra del Fuego was an American, Catharine Rambeau, a 54-year-old grandmother from Michigan. The trip of 14,312 miles (23,028 kilometers) began in Lantana, FL, USA, on December 11, 1988, and ended on December 19, 1989, in Ushuaia, Argentina.

LAND TRANSPORTATION—MOTOR VEHICLES—AUTOMOBILES

3225. Automobile intended primarily as personal transportation was invented by the Belgian-born French engineer Jean-Joseph-Étienne Lenoir, one of the inventors of the internal-combustion engine. Lenoir converted his two-cycle engine from coal gas to liquid fuel and, in 1862, attached it to a carriage. In September 1863, this first automobile made a 6-mile (9.7-kilometer) trip on public roads in under three hours.

3226. Head of state to order an automobile was Tsar Alexander II of Russia, who in 1864 ordered a vehicle from the Belgian-born French engineer Jean-Joseph-Étienne Lenoir, the inventor of the first automobile. It is not known whether Alexander ever actually rode in his car.

3227. Seat belt was patented by American inventor E.J. Claghorn in 1885, for a belt designed to restrain passengers in vehicles moving at speed.

3228. License plate for an automobile was issued in 1889 to Leon Serpollet of Paris, France.

3229. Production automobile with a gas-powered internal-combustion engine was the *Stahlradwagen,* introduced by the German engineer Gottlieb Wilhelm Daimler in 1889. This was the first four-wheeled, gasoline-fueled car that was practical to own and operate. It was powered by the first V-engine, a two-cylinder design capable of producing a speed of about 11 miles (18 kilometers) per hour.

3230. Electric car was the Electrobat, manufactured in 1891 by the firm of Morris and Salom of Philadelphia, PA, USA. The first electric car using modern technology was the Electric Vehicle One, or EV1, marketed by General Motors, Detroit, MI, USA, beginning on December 4, 1996. The first models were leased to customers in Los Angeles, CA, USA, at a price tag of US$34,000. The two-seater coupe was powered by a 137-horsepower, three-phase induction motor that ran on stored energy in a lead-acid battery pack. The EV1 could travel 70 to 90 miles between chargings, which took three to twelve hours.

3231. Drivers' licenses were issued in France beginning in 1893. License cards were also a French innovation. By order of the Ministère des Travaux Publics, all French drivers were required to obtain one beginning on March 10, 1899.

3232. Automobile club was the Automobile Club de France, founded in Paris in 1895.

3233. Gas station was opened in Bordeaux, France, in December 1895. The proprietor, A. Barol, offered gasoline, oil changes, repair services, and parking.

3234. Car with an electric starter instead of a crank was the British-made Arnold, sold beginning in 1896.

3235. Bumpers were installed as an experiment on a Czech-built automobile, the Präsident, in 1897, but fell off after a short trip. Rubber bumpers were first patented by English automotive manufacturer F.R. Simms in 1905, and were factory equipment on the Simms-Welbeck model of that year.

3236. Taxicabs outfitted with meters for calculating the charge to customers were operated by Friedrich Greiner in Stuttgart, Germany, beginning in May 1897. An earlier motorized cab service was started in Stuttgart by a driver named Dütz in 1896, but his two Benz-Kraftdroschkes lacked taximeters.

3237. Sedan with a fully enclosed body was the 1898 Renault, built at Boulogne-Billancourt, France, by Renault Frères, the firm founded by Louis Renault and his brothers Marcel and Fernand. The top-heavy, short-wheelbase vehicle was said to resemble "a top hat on wheels."

3238. Rent-a-car business was started in 1918 in Chicago, IL, USA, where the owner of a used-car lot set aside twelve cars to be rented to customers. The business became the Hertz Drive-Ur-Self System in 1923, after it was purchased by John D. Hertz, who built it into a nationwide chain.

3239. Subcompact car designed to be fuel-efficient was the Volkswagen Beetle, dubbed the "people's car" by its early supporter, Adolf Hitler. The manufacturer, Volkswagen AG, located in Wolfsburg, Germany, was originally operated by the Nazi-run Deutsche Arbeitsfront (German Labour Front). Austrian automotive engineers Ferdinand Porsche and his son Ferry designed the car in 1934 after Hitler urged him to create a car that most Germans could afford. It was notable for its small size, light weight, rounded, unglamorous look, and rear-mounted, air-cooled engine.

3240. Front-wheel-drive car in regular production was the Citroën Model 7, introduced on March 24, 1934, by the French automotive firm of Citroën (now a unit of Peugeot SA) and first shown to the public at the 1934 Paris Motor Show. The Citroën Model 7's front-wheel-drive system was designed by André Lefebvre.

3241. Diesel passenger car was the 1936 Mercedes-Benz manufactured by the automaker Daimler-Benz AG of Stuttgart, Germany.

3242. Plastic car was manufactured by the Ford Motor Company, Dearborn, MI, USA, in August 1941. Fourteen plastic panels were mounted on a tubular welded frame. Windows and windshield were of acrylic sheets, which resulted in an approximately 30 percent decrease in weight. On January 13, 1942, a U.S. patent was obtained by Henry Ford on the automoile body construction, an auto body chassis frame made from steel tubes or pipes designed for use with automobiles made from plastics.

3243. Production automobile with a fiberglass body was the 1957 Lotus Elite, designed by Colin Chapman, founder of Lotus Cars, Ltd., of England. It featured a glass-fiber reinforced monocoque chassis, the first in a production car. (In monocoque construction, the vehicle body is integral with the chassis.) The streamlined design achieved a drag coefficient of 0.29, the lowest of any car of its time. Production of the car was discontinued in 1962.

3244. Japanese auto manufacturer to export cars to the U.S. market was Nissan Jidosha KK, or Nissan Motor Company, Ltd., headquartered in Tokyo, Japan. The company exported its Datsun 310 model to the United States beginning in 1958. First-year sales were 83 vehicles.

3245. Hatchback automobile was the Renault 4, introduced by the state-controlled automotive manufacturer Régie Nationale des Usines Renault of Boulogne-Billancourt, France, in September 1961.

3246. Car with hidden headlights was the Lotus Elan, introduced in 1962 by Lotus Cars, Ltd., of England. The Elan featured headlights that folded away into the body to present a completely streamlined profile to the wind.

3247. Production automobiles with seat belts were introduced by Volvo Aktiebolaget of Göteborg, Sweden, in 1963. The belts were the three-point type.

3248. Car with a rotary engine was the Cosmo Sport 110S L10A coupe, introduced in 1967 by the Toyo Kogyo Company of Japan (known as the Mazda Motor Corporation from 1984). It was powered by a twin-rotor engine designed by Felix Wankel. Only 343 units were built of the original model.

3249. Car with a computer chip was the 1968 Volkswagen 1600, built by Volkswagen AG of Wolfsburg, Germany. A microprocessor controlled the electronic fuel-injection system.

3250. Headlight washer/wiper was introduced by the Swedish carmaker Saab-Scania Aktiebolag in its Sonett lll model, which debuted at the 1970 New York Auto Show. The Swedish Automobile Association awarded its Gold Medal to Saab for this safety innovation.

3251. Turbocharged engine for a mass-produced automobile was introduced by the Swedish carmaker Saab-Scania Aktiebolag in 1976, and went into production in 1978. The Saab 99 Turbo model was the first to integrate a variable-boost turbocharger into a family car, providing extra power and low-end torque. The 2.0-liter turbo engine was rated at 135 horsepower.

3252. Japanese-owned automobile factory in the United States was built by Honda Giken Kogyo KK (Honda Motor Company, Ltd.), founded by Honda Soichiro in 1948. Under its U.S. subsidiary, the American Honda Motor Company, Honda opened a plant in 1982 in Marysville, OH, USA, to assemble its popular Honda Accord model. Honda's corporate headquarters are in Tokyo, Japan.

3253. Joint venture between Japanese and American automobile manufacturers was inked in 1983 by General Motors of Detroit, MI, USA, and Toyota Jidosha KK (Toyota Motor Company, Ltd.) of Toyota City, Japan. The two companies agreed to assemble jointly designed cars in a factory in California. The venture was approved on December 22, 1983, by the U.S. Federal Trade Commission.

3254. Anti-skid system for consumer production cars was the Electronic Traction Control system introduced by Volvo Aktiebolaget of Göteborg, Sweden, for its 1985 line. Rather than using an anti-lock braking system to equalize wheel rotation during a skid, the Volvo design monitored the difference in rotation between drive and non-drive wheels and throttled back on the flow of gas to the engine until all four wheels were turning at the same speed.

3255. Production automobile fueled by methanol was the Chevrolet Lumina Variable Fuel Vehicle, manufactured by the American automobile manufacturer General Motors of Detroit, MI, USA. The first vehicles were delivered in June 1992.

LAND TRANSPORTATION—MOTOR VEHICLES—AUTOMOBILES—*continued*

3256. Mass-produced aluminum automobile was the Audi A2, introduced in Europe in 1995 by Audi AG, owned by Volkswagen AG of Wolfsburg, Germany. The car had an aluminum space-frame and engine components designed and manufactured with the help of the Aluminum Company of America (Alcoa). Aluminum was attractive to automakers because it was strong, lightweight, and corrosion-resistant.

3257. Real-time car navigation system was put into operation by Japan in 1995–96. Known as the Vehicle Information and Communication System, it consisted of a transmitting and receiving device installed in the car which provided the driver with exact information on the car's location. Each device broadcast a unique signal that was tracked by a satellite-based positioning system. The car's position was relayed to the receiver and displayed to the driver on a small computer screen. Japan spent US$610 million in 1995–96 on developing this and other approaches to real-time navigation for motor vehicles. A second navigation system used car cell phone lines to transmit information, but was not as popular.

3258. Electric car to be mass-produced using modern technology was the Electric Vehicle One, or EV1, marketed by the American carmaker General Motors of Detroit, MI, USA, beginning on December 4, 1996. The first models were leased to customers in Los Angeles, CA, at a price tag of US$34,000. The two-seater coupe was powered by a 137-horsepower, three-phase induction motor that ran on stored energy in a lead-acid battery pack. The EV1 could travel 70 to 90 miles between chargings, which took 3 to 12 hours.

3259. Self-guided car was the Argo, developed by researchers at the University of Parma in Italy and sponsored by the Italian National Research Council. The first trials of the computer-controlled vehicle, which could steer itself to its destination on an ordinary road while avoiding obstacles, were held in June 1998.

3260. Family car with its own video entertainment system available as a factory-installed option was the 1999 Oldsmobile Silhouette minivan, offered by the American auto manufacturer General Motors, headquartered in Detroit, MI, USA. The van could be equipped with a 5-inch (13-centimeter) LCD screen and a video tape player.

3261. Production car with a night-vision system was the Cadillac 2000 DeVille, introduced in fall 1999 by the American auto manufacturer General Motors, headquartered in Detroit, MI, USA. Behind the front grille was an infrared sensor that could detect people or animals ahead of the car. A heads-up display (HUD) projected against the inner windshield alerted the driver to a potential accident situation.

3262. Fuel cell car that was practical was developed by the international automobile manufacturer DaimlerChrysler and publicly introduced on March 17, 1999, in Washington, DC, USA. Called the NECAR 4, it used advanced fuels cells built by Ballard Power Systems of Vancouver, Canada, to turn liquid hydrogen into electricity and water. Methanol or suitable reformulated gasoline could also be used in the fuel cell. The five-seater design, based on the Mercedes A-Class car, had a range of 280 miles between refuelings. It was expected to be introduced as a commercial product in 2004.

LAND TRANSPORTATION—RAILROADS

3263. Wheeled carts on rails were in use in Europe from at least the 14th century. The first known wheeled vehicles to run on rails were mine carts on wooden rails used in Germany circa 1430.

3264. Steam locomotive was built by the Cornish engineer inventor Robert Trevithick. After developing a high-pressure steam engine superior to others of the period, he constructed a series of steam-powered street carriages, and in 1803 designed a larger and more powerful carriage that ran along rails. It was built at the Penydaren Ironworks in South Wales, owned by Samuel Homfray. On February 21, 1804, the locomotive proved its hauling power by pulling ten tons of iron and 70 men along 10 miles (6 kilometers) of track.

3265. Steam locomotive in regular use was the *Blucher,* put into service in 1814 on the coal-hauling railway at Killingworth, England. It was invented by George Stephenson as an improvement on John Blekinsop's "steam boiler on wheels," a precursor to the locomotive. The *Blucher* was capable of pulling 30 tons of coal at 4 miles (6 kilometers) per hour.

3266. Steam locomotive passenger service was inaugurated on September 27, 1825, when English inventor George Stephenson's locomotive *Active* (later renamed the *Locomotion*) pulled 28 cars and 450 passengers along the Stockton and Darlington Railway, owned by entrepreneur Edward Pease. The train was preceded by a horseman carrying a flag with the inscription "Periculum privatum utilitas publica" (The private danger is the public good). After the flagman left the 8-mile (12.9-kilometer) track, Stephenson allowed the engine to reach the unheard-of speed of 15 miles (24 kilometers) per hour.

3267. International rail line was built by Belgium and France in 1830–31 from Liège, Belgium, to Cologne, France (now in Germany). The Belgian national rail system, one of the first in Europe, was designed by English railroad pioneer George Stephenson.

3268. Train station was the Crown Street Station in Liverpool, England, which served the Liverpool and Manchester Railway. The station, built in 1830, was a single train shed, open at both ends. The Mount Clare train station in Baltimore, MD, USA, was built the same year. The small, brick, polygonal structure has been preserved as a historical site.

3269. All-steam railway service was offered by the Liverpool–Manchester Railway in England beginning on September 15, 1830.

3270. Iron railroad track of the modern "inverted T" type was invented by English engineer Charles Vignoles, circa 1835.

3271. Concourse in a train station was designed in 1847 by architect Leyonce Reynaud for the Gare du Nord in Paris, France. The concourse was elevated above the platforms and allowed passengers to move from one to another without having to cross the tracks.

3272. International railroad in North America was the Atlantic and St. Lawrence Railroad, construction of which began on July 4, 1846. The first trains ran from Portland, ME, USA, to Montreal, Canada, on July 18, 1853, covering 292 miles (470 kilometers) in less than twelve hours. On August 5, 1853, the line was leased to the Grand Trunk Railway of Canada for 999 years.

3273. Railway speed limit was imposed in Britain on July 5, 1865, as part of the Locomotives and Highways Act. The limit was 2 miles per hour.

3274. Dining-car service was offered to sleeping-car passengers by the Great Western Railway of Canada in 1867.

3275. Electric locomotive that was practical was developed by Werner von Siemens and Johann George Malske. A circular electrified track was set up for it at the Berlin Fair in Germany in 1879.

3276. Funicular railway was a small tram powered by twin 45 horsepower steam engines, constructed in 1879–80 to bring passengers up the steep heights of Vomero in Naples, Italy.

3277. Orient Express service began on October 5, 1883, when the first train departed Paris, France, for Contantinople in the Ottoman Empire (now Istanbul, Turkey). Europe's first transcontinental rail express and the first luxury rail service from Europe to Asia, it was operated by La Compagnie Internationale des Wagons-Lits et des Grands Express Européens, a firm owned by the Belgian entrepreneur Georges Nagelmackers. The original route extended some 1,700 miles (2,740 kilometers) and included stops at Munich, Vienna, Budapest, and Bucharest. Passengers took a ferry over the Black Sea from Bulgaria to Constantinople until 1889, when the rail link was completed. The Orient Express was discontinued in 1977.

3278. Railway in China stretched between Tanghshan and Tianjin, and was opened in November 1888.

3279. Country to electrify its main-line tracks was Italy, where a process of electrification began in 1902. By the end of the century, 50 percent of Italy's rail system was electric.

3280. Diesel locomotive was introduced in 1912 by the Swiss firm of Sulzer AG in Winterthur, Switzerland. The 85-metric-ton engine was capable of generating 1,200 horsepower. However, the locomotive was unreliable and was never put into regular service.

3281. Diesel locomotive in regular service was operated in Tunisia beginning in 1921. The engine was actually a diesel-electric hybrid built in Sweden.

3282. Bullet train line was opened on October 1, 1964, in Japan, along a specially built 320-mile (515-kilometer) stretch of track between Tokyo and Osaka. Trains running along the *shinkansen,* Japanese for "New Trunk Line," were capable of attaining a top speed of 130 miles (209 kilometers) per hour. It was the first rail line to use prestressed concrete ties and very long lengths of welded steel track.

3283. Mag-Lev train was the German Transrapid 07 (TR07), running on a 20-mile (31.5-kilometer) experimental track near Bremen, Germany. The train, managed by the Magnetbahn Versuchs- und Planungsgesellschaft mbH and built in 1988 at the Thyssen Transrapid System GmbH plant in Kassel, Germany, levitated above its single-rail track on a "magnetic cushion" that eliminated

LAND TRANSPORTATION—RAILROADS—*continued*

friction and enabled it to travel at a maximum speed of 342 miles (550 kilometers) per hour. It was capable of carrying 60 first-class passengers. Regular service between Berlin and Hamburg was planned for 2005.

3284. Country whose rail system was completely electrified was Switzerland. In the year 2000, less than 0.4 percent of Swiss rail operations were powered by other energy sources.

LAND TRANSPORTATION—SUBWAYS

3285. Subway was built in London, England, at the instigation of city solicitor Charles Pearson, who first proposed the idea in 1843. Construction of 3.75 miles (6 kilometers) of underground railway between Farringdon Street and Bishop's Road, Paddington, was authorized by Parliament in 1853. The Metropolitan Railway was opened on January 10, 1863, employing steam locomotives running through arched brick tunnels that had been dug under the London streets. The London underground carried 9,500,000 passengers in its first year, despite the noxious fumes of the coke- and coal-burning trains.

3286. Pneumatic subway was invented by Alfred Ely Beach and was known as the Beach Pneumatic Underground Railway of New York, NY, USA. The company was incorporated for freight traffic on June 1, 1868, and for passenger traffic on May 3, 1869, with a capital stock of US$5 million. The system was opened to the public on February 26, 1870; it was the first subway system in the Western Hemisphere. The tunnel was 312 feet long and ran from the west curb line of Broadway at Warren Street down the middle of Broadway to a point south of Murray Street. It consisted of a circular tube nine feet in diameter. The straightaways were built of brick masonry, and the curves were built of iron plate. The cars, which were well upholstered, carried 22 persons each. They were propelled by a rotary blower that drove a blast of air through the tunnel against the rear of the car, carrying it along "like a sailboat before the wind."

3287. Electric subway was the tube line in London, England, that ran from King William Street in the City of London under the Thames River to Stockwell, a distance of 3 miles (5 kilometers). The line was opened by the Prince of Wales on November 4, 1890. Earlier underground trains burned coal.

3288. Subway on the European continent was built in Budapest, Hungary, where a 2.5-mile (4-kilometer) electric subway was opened in 1896. The cars were built on the trolley model, running singly instead of in train.

LAND TRANSPORTATION—WHEELS AND TIRES

3289. Wheel may have been in use on the steppes of Russia and Kazakhstan as early as 3500 BCE, according to archeological work done in 1995 by archeologists David W. Anthony and Dorcas Brown of Hartwick College, Oneonta, NY, USA. They excavated graves left by a Bronze Age proto-Aryan culture that settled the steppes from the Urals to the Tien Shan Mountains in western China. Within the graves were traces of spoked wheels mixed with the skulls and bones of sacrificed horses. These are the first spoked wheels known and appear to have come from the first chariots. Similar wheels did not appear in Mesopotamia until circa 2000 BCE.

3290. Depiction of a wheel is on a Sumerian clay tablet that contains a pictograph of a sledge with solid wheels. The tablet was found in excavations of the city of Erech (also called Uruk) in Iraq and dates from circa 3200 BCE.

3291. Roller bearings for wooden wagon wheels were introduced in Europe circa 100 BCE, probably first in Germany or France. The bearings themselves were carved wooden hardwood rollers in a grooved wooden casing, with animal fat used as a lubricant

3292. Pneumatic tires consisting of an air-filled lining and a protective cover were patented in England in 1845 by the Scottish engineer Robert William Thomson. His leather tires were called "Aerial Wheels" and were successfully installed on a horse-drawn brougham.

3293. Rubber tires made of solid rubber were installed on horse-drawn hansom cabs in London, England, in 1881.

3294. Pneumatic automobile tire were made in 1895 by Michelin & Cie., a French rubber-manufacturing company run by the brothers André and Édouard Michelin. Previously, all cars had solid tires. Interest was generated in their invention after the Michelins entered a car equipped with air-filled tires in the 1895 Paris–Bordeaux road race.

3295. Steel-belted radial-ply automobile tire was the Michelin X, introduced in 1948 by the Compagnie Générale des Établissements Michelin of Clermont-Ferrand, France.

LANGUAGE

3296. Grammarian known by name was the Indian scholar Panini, whose book *Astadhyayi*, written circa the fifth century BCE, explicated according to systematic rules the old form of Sanskrit used in the Hindu religious texts known as the *Vedas*.

3297. Comparative linguist was William Jones, a British jurist of Welsh descent who mastered 28 languages. As judge of the high court in Calcutta, India, from 1783 to 1794, he studied Hindu law in the original Sanskrit. In 1786, in a lecture delivered at the Bengal Asiatic Society, which he had founded, he developed the theory that Greek, Latin, and Sanskrit share a basic vocabulary and are derived from a common ancestor. This hypothesis was confirmed by later scholars, who named the parent language Proto-Indo-European.

3298. Comprehensive study of Proto-Indo-European was *Vergleichende Grammatik des Sanskrit, Zend, Griechischen, Lateinischen, Litthauischen, Altslawischen, Gotischen und Deutschen (Comparative Grammar of Sanskrit, Zend, Greek, Latin, Lithuanian, Old Slavic, Gothic, and German)*, written by German linguist Franz Bopp between 1833 and 1852. It detailed the structure of what scholars consider the ancestor (now extinct) of Sanskrit, Greek, Latin, the Romance languages, the Germanic languages, and the Celtic languages.

3299. Artificial language to attract a significant number of speakers was Vollapük, introduced in 1880 by its inventor, the German clergyman Johann Martin Schleyer. Its students numbered in the hundreds of thousands, but many of them eventually switched to Esperanto, the first artificial language to have a lasting influence. Esperanto, meaning "one who hopes," was developed over the course of 15 years by Ludwik Lejzer Zamenhof, an oculist in Warsaw, Poland, who hoped that an international language would lead to tolerance and understanding among the nations. Introduced in 1887, it combined elements of Latin, Greek, the Romance languages, and the Germanic languages. Grammar and spelling were simplified and verb irregularities were eliminated.

3300. Universal system for phonetic transcription was the International Phonetic Alphabet, developed from concepts proposed by the Danish linguist Otto Jespersen and further developed circa 1895 by Paul Passy and others. The IPA was intended to help students quickly pronounce unfamiliar languages by providing a single, uniform method of transliteration.

3301. Artificial language based entirely on English was Basic English, a simplified form of English with a minimal vocabulary. It was developed in 1932 by the British scholar C.K. Ogden.

3302. Ancient language revived for modern use was Hebrew (Ivrit), the national language of the state of Israel. Hebrew, the original language of the Jews, was supplanted by Aramaic in daily speech after the Babylonian exile circa 586 BCE. It was, however, carefully preserved through the centuries as the holy language of the Torah and other Jewish religious texts. In the early 20th century Biblical Hebrew was expanded into a modern language through the efforts of the Lithuanian-born Zionist and linguist Eliezer Ben-Yehudah (born Eliezer Yitzhak Perelman in 1858), called "the father of modern Hebrew." Ben-Yehudah moved to Palestine in 1881, where he edited a number of Hebrew periodicals and founded the Hebrew Language Council, later called the Academy of Hebrew Language. His life's work was contained in *The Complete Dictionary of Ancient and Modern Hebrew*, published in 17 volumes between 1910 and 1959. Hebrew was adopted as the official language of Israel in 1948.

3303. Voice reader for reading printed matter aloud was invented by an American, Raymond Kurzweil. It was first demonstrated publicly on January 13, 1976, and was tested by the National Federation for the Blind. The machine, manufactured by Kurzweil Computer Products, Cambridge, MA, USA, converted ordinary printed materials, including books, magazines, and typewritten correspondence, directly into spoken English at 150 words per minute. It used a camera to scan the pages into a computer that analyzed the letters and pronounced them.

3304. Global language was English. Spread first throughout the British Empire and later by the dissemination of American culture, commerce, and mass media in the decades after World War II, by 1990 English was widely acknowledged as the first truly worldwide language, spoken by a significant number of people in every country. In 1997 English was the official language of 54 countries, French was the official language of 33 countries, and Arabic was the official language of 24 countries.

LANGUAGE—*continued*

3305. Language spoken by more than 1 billion people was Guanhua, or Mandarin Chinese, the standard dialect in China. According to estimates by Sindey S. Culbert of the University of Washington, Seattle, WA, USA, in 1997 there were 1.034 billion Guanhua speakers. English speakers numbered only 500 million.

3306. Language to have its entire literature available on computer was Yiddish. Beginning in January 1999, the National Yiddish Book Center in Amherst, MA, USA, digitized 35,000 books in Yiddish by running the pages through an automatic scanning machine, making it possible to reproduce any of the books electronically in 30 seconds. Most of the world's Yiddish-speaking Jews were killed by the Nazis and their collaborators during the Holocaust (1938–45). The center was founded by Aaron Lansky in 1980.

LANGUAGE—ALPHABETS AND WRITING

3307. Picture writing known to archeologists is the ideographic writing developed in Sumer circa 3400 BCE. It employed pictures as signifiers and was used primarily for accounting. At the height of its development Sumerian picture-writing included as many as 1,200 separate ideograms, often marked on clay envelopes that enclosed small clay shapes representing animals or other property. Pictographic inscriptions from the same period (and possibly a century or two earlier, according to some scholars) have been found on clay pots at an ancient royal cemetery in Abydos, Egypt.

3308. Inscription identifying a historical personage by name is on a small slate ceremonial slab of ancient Egyptian origin dating to circa 3100 BCE. Known as the palette of King Narmer, it was unearthed by J.E. Quibell in 1898 at Hierakonpolis (modern Kawm al-Ahmar, Egypt). An individual named "Men" is twice named on it; this was probably Menes, the pharaoh credited with unifying Egypt. He is pictured smashing in the head of an enemy with a club.

3309. Written language that used symbols was developed from earliest forms of picture-writing in several areas of the Middle East at the end of the fourth millennium BCE. Written Sumerian, a linear cuneiform system developed circa 3100 BCE in the city-state of Sumer (now in present-day Iraq), was probably the earliest. The symbols were composed of wedge-shaped marks inscribed in clay tablets by the end of a reed or stylus.

3310. Calligraphy was the cursive hieratic script that had developed from Egyptian hieroglyphic writing by circa 2500 BCE). The earliest examples, from the Egyptian fifth dynasty (circa 2494–2345 BCE), were written with brush and ink on papyrus. Hieratic was at first written vertically; the writing direction switched from right to left circa 2000 BCE. Hieratic script was employed mainly for priestly writings.

3311. Script written in regular horizontal lines was Linear A, a Minoan syllabic script from ancient Crete (part of present-day Greece) dating to about 1850 BCE. It was written from left to right. While the approximate phonetic meanings for the Linear A symbols are known (from its transliteration in samples of Linear B, the earliest known Greek writing), the actual language in which Linear A is written is unknown.

3312. Pictographic script in Asia was jiaguwen, a pictographic script inscribed on oracle bones from the Chinese Shang dynasty (circa 1760–1100 BCE). Used exclusively for divination, the characters were inked onto turtle shell or ox bone and then inscribed over the ink with a needle. When thrown into the fire, the shell or bones cracked into pieces, which then could be retrieved and read for omens.

3313. Alphabet emerged between 1700 BCE and 1500 BCE in the eastern Mediterrean area, in present-day Lebanon, Syria, and Israel, among people speaking one of the Semitic languages, identified by most scholars as North Semitic. Its letters represented consonants only. The earliest specimen known appears on a cuneiform tablet discovered in 1949 by a French archeological team under Claude-Frédéric-Armandat Schaeffer at the site of the ancient city of Ugarit (now Ras Sharma, Syria). The tablet has been dated to circa 1450 BCE and is inscribed in the 30-letter Ugaritic alphabet apparently invented in the city and used nowhere else.

3314. Alphabetic inscription in a writing system ancestral to modern Western alphabets was discovered in 1923 on the sarcophagus of Ahiram, king of the ancient Phoenician seaport of Byblos (biblical Gebal, present-day Jubayl, Lebanon) circa 1000 BCE. The inscription, in the earliest known Phoenician alphabetic script, was an epitaph for Ahiram, and reads: "Made by Ittoba'l, the son of Ahiram, king of Byblos, for Ahiram, his father, as his eternal (dwelling-) place. If there be a king among kings and a governor among governors and an army commander up in Byblos who shall uncover this sarcophagus, let his judicial staff be broken, let his royal throne be upset! May peace flee from Byblos, and he himself be wiped out!"

3315. Writing in a Western alphabet is the Marsiliana Tablet, from Etruria (the modern region of Tuscany, Italy), now in the Museo Archeologico in Florence, Italy. The inscription on the tablet, which dates from the eighth century BCE, is in the Etruscan language, written in the characters of the Greek alphabet as it was originally constituted, with 22 letters drawn from the Semitic alphabet plus four others.

3316. Alphabet to include vowels as individual letters was early Greek. By the middle of the fourth century BCE, all the local variations of the Greek alphabet in use in the Greek city states had standardized the single 24-character alphabet of classical Greek, which included separate characters for the sounds of *a, e, i, o,* and *u.* The alphabets used in all modern European languages are descended in some fashion from the Greek alphabet.

3317. Punctuation was used in Greece circa 350 BCE, when literary texts written on papyrus began to use the *paragraphos,* a line placed under the first words of a new topic. This evolved into the modern practice of dividing a text into paragraphs.

3318. Punctuation system was developed by the Greek scholar Aristophanes of Byzantium, called "the father of punctuation." He is credited with inventing the first extensive punctuation system circa 200 BCE when he was head of the great library at Alexandria, Egypt. His innovations included diacritical marks, accents, and an early form of the period.

3319. Shorthand was invented by a Roman former slave named Marcus Tullius Tiro in 63 BCE. He used his system of rapid writing to record speeches made in the Senate, including those of the orators Cicero and Seneca. His system was taught in Roman schools throughout the empire and was used for many centuries after his death.

3320. Writing system invented in the New World is known from La Mojarra Stela 1, an inscribed basalt monument discovered in 1986 in Veracruz, Mexico, and dating to circa 159 CE, during the little-known period between the disappearance of the Olmec culture and the rise of the Mayan culture. The main text on the front face, decoded by anthropologists Terrence Kaufman of the University of Pittsburgh, Pittsburgh, PA, USA, and John Justeson of the State University of New York, Albany, NY, USA, contains political, astronomical, and calendrical references that enable it to be dated with precision. It was written in the hieroglyphic system known as epi-Olmec, of which there are only four known legible texts. At approximately the same time, the Mayan civilization of Mexico and Central America developed its own hieroglyphic system. With some 800 pictorial characters, Mayan writing contains a mixture of logograms, or glyphs denoting one entire word, and phonetic signs for syllables. Some glyphs are both logograms and phonetic signs, and also stand for more than one word or concept. Nearly all examples of Mayan writing were destroyed by the Catholic priests following the conquest of the Yucatán by Spanish conquistadors circa 1540, but a few codices (bound books) and inscriptions survived. By 1960, the main features of Mayan writing had been discovered by the Soviet linguists Yury Valentinovich Knorozov and Tatiana Prouskouriakoff and the German scholar Heinrich Berlin.

3321. Writing in runes is known from Danish inscriptions dated to the third century CE. Runic scripts were used by many Germanic tribes.

3322. Autograph handwritten by a known individual in Europe that can be authenticated is that of Rodrigo Díaz de Vivar, known as El Cid, the Castilian war leader and Spanish national hero. The signature is dated to 1096.

3323. Book about shorthand in English was *Characterie: an Arte of Shorte, Swifte, and Secrete Writing by Character* (1588) by Timothy Bright.

3324. Typewritten letter was sent by John P. Sheldon, editor of the *Michigan Gazette* in Detroit, MI, USA, to U.S. secretary of state Martin Van Buren in Washington, DC, USA, on May 25, 1829. It had been typed on the "typographer," an early typewriter invented by William Austin Burt of Mount Vernon, MI.

3325. Writing by brain wave was accomplished as part of an ongoing program of research with disabled patients conducted by psychologists at the University of Tübingen, Germany. Totally paralyzed individuals suffering from amyotrophic lateral sclerosis were connected to brain-wave readers. Trained via biofeedback to use their slow cortical potential brain waves to move a cursor on a computer screen, the patients were able to pick out letters on a graphic keyboard and spell messages. A description of the program was given in an article in the March 1999 issue of the British science journal *Nature.*

LANGUAGE—AUTHORS

3326. Author known by name was Enheduanna, an Akkadian princess born circa 2300 BCE. Her father was Sargon, conqueror of Sumer and the first emperor known by name, who appointed her as priestess at the temple of the moon god in Ur (present-day Tel-el-Muqayyar, Iraq). Two clay tablets signed with her name have survived. Both contain poems in honor of Inanna, the goddess of war and fertility.

3327. Literary critic was the Greek philosopher Plato (428–348 BCE), who in his work *Politeia (The Republic),* written circa 375 BCE, banished poets from his ideal polity on moral grounds, claiming that literature is a misleading simulation of reality that renders its readers morally unfit for an authentic understanding of the world.

3328. Critical edition of the works of Homer was prepared by Zenodotus of Ephesus, the Greek grammarian who, circa 284 BCE, became the first superintendent of the royal library at Alexandria, Egypt, the greatest repository of manuscripts in the ancient world. Using the library's collection of Homeric manuscripts, which he was able to compare, Zenodotus edited both the *Iliad* and the *Odyssey.* He divided each epic into 24 books and changed lines that he thought were out of place, inaccurate, or inauthentic. His emendations were considered to be too subjective, and some of them were restored by a later editor, the third Alexandrian librarian, Aristarchus of Samothrace.

3329. Bards belonged to one of the three elite classes among the ancient Celts in continental Europe and on the British islands. Their role was to compose and chant verses about historical and mythical events. The other two classes, which appear to have overlapped somewhat, were the Druids, who served as the religious, legal, and lore-keeping authorities, and the seers, who specialized in divination and prophecy. The earliest mention of bards comes in the writings of Timagenes of Alexandria in the mid-first century BCE, possibly from source material taken from Posidonios of Apamea, his contemporary.

3330. Biography written by a woman may have been *The Life of St. Radegund,* written in 610 by a Frankish nun, Baudonivia. The author lived at the convent founded by Radegund at Poitiers, in present-day France, in 552, and compiled the source material for the book from people who knew her. Radegund was a Thuringian princess who was married to her captor, the Merovingian king Chlotar, before becoming a nun.

3331. Woman to write professionally was Christine de Pisan, who took up writing as a way of supporting her three children after the death of her husband, a courtier, in 1389. In addition to many poems, she wrote a biography of King Charles V; books examining the effects of France's wars; a treatise of moral instruction for women; and an autobiography. Altogether, her works fill some 15 volumes. Many were commissioned by patrons among the nobility. With her poem *Épistre du dieu d'amours (Letter from the God of Loves)* of 1399, followed in 1405 by *Le Livre de la cité des dames (The Book of the City of Ladies),* she initiated the literary defense of women against their condemnation by medieval male authors and their general maltreatment.

3332. Literary salon where aristocratic writers, both male and female, discussed matters of cultural importance was begun in 1623 by Catherine d'Angennes, Marquise de Rambouillet, at the Hôtel de Rambouillet, her palatial home in Paris, France. A semi-invalid, Madame de Rambouillet directed the salon for 25 years from her bed in an elegant drawing room.

3333. Woman intellectual in the New World was Sister Juana Inés de la Cruz (born Juana Ramírez de Asbaje), a 17th-century nun of New Spain (now Mexico). A child prodigy, she learned to read at the age of 3, mastered Latin at 9, and at 17 astounded scholars with her learning. As a nun at the Convent of the Sisters of San Jerónimo, in Mexico City, she served as archivist, secretary, and treasurer, and had time left to continue studying and to write poems and plays. Eventually she was charged with intellectual vanity and was forced to give up her library of 4,000 books and her collection of scientific and musical instruments. Three volumes of her writings were published in Spain between 1689 and 1700.

3334. Copyright law securing to authors the benefits of their work, and limiting those benefits to a certain period of time, was enacted in England in 1710 and was known as the *Statute of Anne.* The length of time was set at 21 years, subsequently extended to 28.

3335. Society for the protection of dramatists' rights was La Société des Auteurs Dramatíques, founded in 1777 by the French dramatist Pierre-Augustin Caron, known as Beaumarchais, the author of *The Barber of Seville* (1775) and *The Marriage of Figaro* (1784). Beaumarchais was involved in numerous legal and artistic disputes and saw the need for such a society to protect his own work.

3336. Literary agent to establish a regular practice was A.P. Watt of Aberdeen, Scotland, and London, England. In 1875 he started an agency to represent authors in negotiations with publishers. Among his clients were the British authors George Macdonald and Walter Besant.

3337. President of the Soviet Writers' Union was the Russian short-story writer and novelist Maksim Gorky, born Aleksey Maksimovich Peshkov. He was elected to that post in 1934, where he helped develop the tenets of Socialist Realism in literature that all union members were required to follow.

3338. Black African member of the Académie Française was the poet Léopold Sédar Senghor, the first president of independent Senegal. Senghor was author of several poetry collections, including *Chants d'ombre (Songs of Shadow)*, published in 1945, *Hosties noires (Black Offerings)*, which appeared in 1948, *Ethiopiques* (1956), and *Oeuvre poétique (Poetical Work)*, published in 1990. He also assembled the first collection of writings by proponents of the Negritude literary movement of the 1930s and 1940s. Senghor was inducted into the Académie in 1984.

LANGUAGE—BOOKS

3339. Book extant was made in first-century CE Rome. It was a book about the Macedonian wars, written in Latin. All previous texts were inscribed on clay, stone or metal surfaces, or written on scrolls.

3340. Printed book was the *Mugu chonggwang tae dharani-gyong (Dharani Sutra)*, a Korean woodblock-printed scroll dating to circa 704.

3341. Multivolume printed book series was a 130-volume collection of Chinese classics printed for Fong Tao, a Chinese minister, beginning in 932.

3342. Book written in the Americas known to historians is the Dresden Codex, or Codex Dresdensis. This Mayan book, which has been dated to circa 1100, contains astronomical tables of astonishing accuracy. It is believed to be a copy of earlier texts dating from the fifth to ninth century, and is one of only four Mayan codices known to have survived the Spanish conquest of the Yucatán in 1540. The Sächsische Landesbibliothek, the state library of Saxony, located in Dresden (now in Germany) acquired the codex in the early 19th century and first published it in 1848. The codex is made of fig-bark paper folded like an accordion and bound with the skin of a jaguar.

3343. Picture books were made in the early 14th century by German monks. They consisted of parchment and paper pages on which were depicted scenes from the Bible, with identifying captions. Often there were several illustrations juxtaposed on a page. These books, which were produced for several centuries, later acquired the name *Bibliae Pauperum (Bibles of the Poor)*, on the assumption that they were displayed in churches for the edification of illiterate worshipers. Another possibility is that they were used by priests who were themselves not well educated or who were too poor to buy the texts.

3344. Book printed in Europe known to bibliographers was a copy of a German religious poem called the "World Judgment." All that remains of it are two pieces cut from a single page. Analysis of the paper and typeface has led scholars to conclude that the book was 74 pages long and that it was printed between 1444 and 1447 at Strassburg, Germany (now Strasbourg, France), where Johannes Gutenberg is known to have operated an experimental printing press.

3345. Bookplate to identify the owner of a book dates from Germany circa 1450, contemporaneous with the invention of the printing press. The label itself is undated.

3346. Reference to a reading group appeared in a French work from the 15th century, *Les Évangiles des quenouilles (The Gospels of the Distaffs)*. It describes a group of women who assemble in a house on a series of winter evenings to spin yarn and hold a lively discussion while they take turns reading aloud from favorite books.

3347. Text printed in Europe bearing a date was a papal indulgence printed in 1454 at Mainz (now in Germany). Authorized by Pope Nicholas V, it offered remittance of punishment for sin in exchange for donations to the Christian military campaign against the expansionist Ottoman Turks, who had captured Constantinople the previous year. Of the four issues that were printed, three appear to have been printed by Johannes Gutenberg or his former partner,

LANGUAGE—BOOKS—*continued*

Johann Fust, and the fourth by Peter Schöffer. Another text from the year 1454, printed by Gutenberg in December, was a pamphlet entitled *Eyn Manung der Cristenheit widder die Durken (A Warning to Christendom against the Turks).*

3348. Best-seller was the Bible, which has been continuously in print since Johannes Gutenberg's first typeset edition, made circa 1455. An estimated 3.5 billion copies of the Bible in various languages have been sold since then. The entire Bible has been translated into about 350 languages. Parts of the Bible have been translated into more than 2,000.

3349. Book printed in Europe that survives in its complete form was the Gutenberg Bible, also called the 42-line Bible and the Mazarin Bible (because the first copy known to bibliographers was part of the library of Cardinal Mazarin of France). Some 40 copies are still extant. The three-volume Latin work, printed in 42-line columns, was set by six compositors in a majestic Gothic type. It was designed by Johannes Gutenberg and printed on his press at Mainz (in present-day Germany), probably with the assistance of Johann Fust and Peter Schöffer. Though it bears no date, it cannot have been printed later than 1456, the date of a handwritten notation in one of the surviving copies.

3350. Book printed in color was the Mainz Psalter, designed by the printer Johannes Gutenberg in Mainz (in modern Germany). After Gutenberg's business was taken over by his financial backer, the prominent goldsmith Johann Fust, the printing of the Psalter was completed by Fust and Peter Schöffer, Gutenberg's foreman. The Psalter was printed in black and red ink with two-color initials. It was finished on August 14, 1457.

3351. Colophon in a printed book was added to the last page of the Mainz Psalter of 1457 by its printers, Johann Fust and Peter Schöffer. The inscription ran as follows: "The present copy of the Psalms, adorned with beauty of capital letters and sufficiently picked out with rubrics, has thus been fashioned by an ingenious method of printing and stamping without any driving of the pen, and to the worship of God has been diligently completed by Johannes Fust, citizen of Mainz, and Peter Schöffer of Gernsheym, in the year of the Lord 1457 on the Vigil of the Assumption." The printing was completed in Mainz, Germany, on August 14, 1457.

3352. Illustrated books printed in Europe were made by Albrecht Pfister of Bamberg, Germany. The earliest of his books to incorporate woodcut illustrations were the *Ackermann von Böhmen* (1460), by Johannes van Saaz, and the first dated book printed in German, Ulrich Boner's *Der Edelstein* (1461), a collection of fables. In many of Pfister's surviving books, the woodcut pictures have been colored in by hand.

3353. Printed book with a separate title page was the *Bul zu dutsch (Papal Bull in German),* issued by Pope Pius II and printed in 1463 in Mainz by Peter Schöffer. The first to display information about the location and date of printing and the name of the printer, in addition to the title and author, was the *Calendarium* of Regiomontanus, an astronomical and astrological calendar printed at Venice in 1476 by Erhard Ratdolt and his associates. (Regiomontanus was the pen name of the German astronomer and mathematician Johann Müller.) This was also one of the first printed books decorated with borders and fancy initial letters.

3354. Book printed in the English language was the *Recuyell of the Historyes of Troye,* a translation by William Caxton of *Recueil des histoires de Troye,* a French work by Raoul Le Fèvre. Caxton, an English wool merchant and trade official who had learned the art of printing in Germany, published the book in 1475 in the Flemish city of Bruges (now in Belgium). It contains what is probably the first engraving to appear in a printed book.

3355. Book printed in England that bears a date was *The Dictes or Sayengis of the Philosophers,* printed in 1477 by William Caxton on the printing press he had set up the year before. It was located in the Almonry, near Westminster Abbey, in the city of Westminster (now part of London). Caxton went on to publish first editions of works by Geoffrey Chaucer, John Gower, and Thomas Malory.

3356. Printed book decorated with type ornaments was the *Arte di ben morire* of Capranica, printed in Verona, Italy, in 1478 by G. and A. Alvise. Type ornaments are also known as fleurons.

3357. Illustrated book in English was an encyclopedia, *The Myrrour of the worlde,* which contained woodcut illustrations. It was published in 1481 by William Caxton at Westminster (now part of London), England.

3358. Printed editions of Greek classics were published by Aldus Manutius (born Aldo Manuzio, or Mannucci), Italy's first important printer. In 1490 Manutius founded the Aldine Press in Venice, Italy, where he also formed a scholarly academy, the "Neacademia" or Aldine Academy, to produce small-format, inexpensive editions of the Greek classics. Marcus Musurus of Crete was the academy's leading scholar. In March 1495 Manutius printed his first dated book, the *Erotemata* by Constantine Lascaris. Over the next two decades the Aldine Press issued 27 first editions of Greek authors, including works by Aesop, Aristotle, Aristophanes, Euripides, Herodotus, Homer, Plato, and Sophocles.

3359. Book printed in the Western Hemisphere was the *Breve y mas compendiosa doctrina christiana en lengua mexicana y castellana (Brief Compendium of the Christian Doctrine in the Language of Mexico and Castile)* by Juan de Zumárraga, the first bishop and archbishop of Mexico. It was printed in Mexico City in 1539.

3360. Book auction of record was held in the Netherlands in 1599.

3361. Book illustrated with photographs was *The Pencil of Nature,* published in six parts between 1844 and 1846 by the English scientist, inventor, and photographic pioneer William Henry Fox Talbot. It contained 24 calotypes (a photographic process, invented by Talbot, that used paper negatives), of scenes in and around his studio in Reading, some of which may have been taken by Benjamin Bracknell Turner.

3362. Book manuscript written on a typewriter was the manuscript of *The Adventures of Tom Sawyer,* by the American author Mark Twain (pseudonym of Samuel Langhorne Clemens). It was typed on a Remington typewriter in Hartford, CT, USA, in 1875. Twain's *Life on the Mississippi* was also typewritten that same year. Twain did not publicize his use of the typewriter, as he did not want to write testimonials or explain the operation of the machine to the curious.

3363. Commercial book club was founded in Germany in 1919. It reprinted editions of the classics for its members. Like later book clubs, it used the "negative option" system, in which monthly shipments of books were automatically sent to subscribers unless subscribers returned a refusal card by mail.

3364. Nazi book burning took place on the evening of May 10, 1933, at the square of Unter den Linden across from the University of Berlin in Germany. In the presence of Nazi officials, thousands of torch-carrying university students set fire to a mountain of 20,000 books, including works by Thomas Mann, Ernest Hemingway, Albert Einstein, Sigmund Freud, Helen Keller, Margaret Sanger, Marcel Proust, H.G. Wells, Karl Marx, and Émile Zola. Addressing the crowd, Nazi propaganda minister Josef Goebbels announced that the flames "not only illuminate the final end of an old era, they also light up the new."

3365. Book set into type completely by electronic composition was *The Long Short Cut,* a 192-page suspense novel by Andrew Garve, which was published by Harper and Row, New York, NY, USA, in April 1968. The book was produced by Haddon Craftsmen of Scranton, PA, who used an RCA Videocomp and computer system.

3366. Book to sell at auction for more than US$10 million was *The Gospel of Henry the Lion,* an English illuminated manuscript dating from circa 1173. It sold for US$10,841,000 at Sotheby's auction house in London, England, on December 6, 1983.

LANGUAGE—BOOKS—DICTIONARIES

3367. Vocabulary list known to archeologists is a list of Akkadian words from the seventh century BCE, found in Mesopotamia.

3368. Dictionary for tourists was printed in 1480 by the pioneering English printer William Caxton at his print shop in Westminster (now part of London, England). It was a 36-page bilingual dictionary in English and French, defining terms most used by travelers.

3369. Rhyming dictionary was *Manipulus Vocabulorum. A Dictionarie of English and Latine wordes, set forthe in suche order, as none heretofore hath ben,* published in 1570. The compiler was Peter Levens.

3370. Dictionary of the English language published as a separate volume was *A Table Alphabeticall, conteyning and teaching the true writing and understanding of hard usuall English wordes, borrowed from the Hebrew, Greeke, Latine, or French &c.* Published in London, England, in 1604, it was the work of two schoolmasters, Robert Cawdrey and his son Thomas. They plagiarized extensively from an earlier work, *The English Scholemaister, teach-*

LANGUAGE—BOOKS—DICTIONARIES—
continued

ing all his schollars of what age soever the most easie short & perfect order of distinct readings & true writinge our Englishe tonge, by Edmund Coote, which had appeared in 1596.

3371. Dictionary called by that name was *The English Dictionary: or, an Interpreter of hard English Words,* published in England in 1623 by Henry Cockeram.

3372. Thesaurus in English had its roots in the *Essay towards a Real Character and a Philosophical Language* by Bishop John Wilkins, published in England in 1668. It contained tables of words related by concept. The first widely successful thesaurus was *Thesaurus of English Words and Phrases* by Peter Mark (or Marc) Roget, produced in 1852. It was the first truly comprehensive classification by concept of synonyms, antonyms, and verbal equivalents.

3373. Encyclopedic dictionary was the *Lexicon Technicum,* published in 1704, which was also the first important encyclopedic work in English. It was edited by John Harris, an English theologian and scientist, who described it as "an universal English dictionary of arts and sciences: explaining not only the terms of art, but the arts themselves." Entries were arranged alphabetically, illustrated with clear engraved plates, and had bibliographies appended to the longer articles. Harris was also the first encyclopedia compiler to enlist the aid of experts, including the naturalist John Ray and Sir Isaac Newton.

3374. Dictionary of English slang was *A Classical Dictionary of the Vulgar Tongue,* by Captain Francis Grose, published in England in 1785.

3375. Edition of the *Oxford English Dictionary* was *A New English Dictionary on Historical Principles,* published in 10 volumes from February 1, 1884, to April 19, 1928, by the Clarendon Press of Oxford, England. The chief editor was James Murray. The title was changed to *Oxford English Dictionary* for the revised, twelve-volume 1933 edition. The *OED* is considered the definitive dictionary of English.

LANGUAGE—BOOKS—ENCYCLOPE-
DIAS

3376. Philosophical encyclopedia was a work by Speusippus, an Athenian scholar of the fourth century BCE, in which he set forth the teachings of his teacher, the philosopher Plato, who was also his uncle.

3377. Encyclopedia for young adults appeared circa 183 BCE under the title *Praecepta ad filium (Advice to His Son).* The author was Marcus Portius Cato, better known as Cato the Censor or Cato the Elder. The encyclopedia was a collection of letters in which Cato attempted to summarize various kinds of knowledge that a young man would find helpful in building a successful life.

3378. Encyclopedia of importance was Pliny the Elder's encyclopedia of the physical world, *Historia naturalis (Natural History),* completed in Rome circa 77 CE and widely influential up to the end of the medieval period. The work, divided into 37 "books," indiscriminately mixes accurate contemporary knowledge about the sciences, agriculture, medicine, and the arts with numerous myths, fallacies, and fantasies, many of which were accepted without question by later scholars and persist to the present day. The errors in *Natural History* were first detailed by an Italian, Niccolò Leoniceno, in 1492.

3379. Encyclopedia compiled in Asia known by name was the *Huang-lan (Emperor's Mirror),* compiled in China by imperial order circa 220. The actual text is no longer extant.

3380. Jewish scientific encyclopedia was the *Yesodei ha-tevunah u-migdal ha-emunah (The Foundations of Understanding and the Tower of Faith),* a compilation of articles in Hebrew on the arts and sciences, made in 1110 by Avraham bar Hiyya, an astronomer, mathematician, and philosopher active in the Islamic civil service in Barcelona, Spain.

3381. Encyclopedia compiled by a woman was the *Hortus deliciarum (Garden of Delights),* compiled circa 1160 by Herrad of Landsberg, the abbess of Hohenburg, in Alsace, Germany, for the purpose of educating the nuns in her convent. The encyclopedia contained biblical stories and historical accounts, illustrated with 636 illuminated miniatures.

3382. Encylopedia of ancient Mexico was the *Historia general de las cosas de Nueva España (General History of the Things of New Spain),* by the Spanish Franciscan missionary Bernardino de Sahagún. It was published in Spain in 1569. Sahagún, who was a missionary in Mexico from 1529, assembled a wide range of ethnographic information on Aztec life, mainly derived from interviews with Aztec notables, into an authoritative compendium. It was printed in Nahuatl-language pictographs as well as in Spanish.

3383. Encyclopedia for children was the *Pera Librorum Juvenilium (Collection of Juvenile Books)* produced by the German professor Johann Christoph Wagenseil in 1695. The next such work did not appear until 1853; it was the *Petite Encyclopédie du jeune âge (Small Children's Encyclopaedia)*, published by Librarie Larousse in Paris, France.

3384. General encyclopedia in the English language was the *Encyclopaedia Britannica; or, A Dictionary of Arts and Sciences,* which combined short entries on a wide variety of subjects with longer essays on important topics. The project was the brainchild of Andrew Bell and Colin Macfarquhar, both printers in Edinburgh, Scotland, who paid £200 to William Smellie, a printer, antiquary, and natural historian, to compile the work. It was published in three volumes between 1768 and 1771.

3385. Modern encyclopedia for children was *The Children's Encyclopaedia,* published in Britain in 1910. The American edition, published two years later, was called *The Book of Knowledge.* The editor was Arthur Mee, an English journalist and writer.

3386. Visual encyclopedia for children was *I See All,* written and edited by the English journalist and reference-book author Arthur Mee. It contained thousands of small illustrations with brief captions. *I See All* was issued in several volumes between 1928 and 1930.

3387. International encyclopedia in Japanese was the *Buritanika Kokusai Daihyakka-jiten (Britannica International Encyclopedia),* published in 28 volumes between 1972 and 1975.

3388. Encyclopedia distributed via data network was the *Academic American Encyclopedia,* from 1986 known as the *Grolier Multimedia Encyclopedia,* originally developed by the publishing firm of Arete and later sold to Grolier Publishing of Danbury, CT, USA. The content of the *Academic American Encyclopedia* was licensed internationally to commercial data networks beginning in 1983.

3389. Year more encyclopedias were distributed on CD-ROM than in print was 1995.

LANGUAGE—BOOKS—TRAVEL

3390. Travel writer may have been Wen-Amon, an Egyptian priest of Thebes, Egypt, whose account of a difficult voyage, *The Story of Wen-Amon,* was written in Thebes circa 1070 BCE. The author was sent by his superiors to buy cedar logs from Lebanon to make a ceremonial barge. En route, at the coastal settlement of Dor (in present-day Israel), his money was stolen by a member of the seafaring Tsekser tribe. He retaliated by robbing another group of Tsekser. At the Phoenician city of Byblos (now Jubayl, Lebanon), he was put under house arrest for eight months—not because of his piracy, since his rank as a priest conferred immunity from arrest, but because he had to write home for more money. On the way home with his purchase, his ship ran away from a Tsekser war fleet in a storm, was blown off course, and landed him on Cyprus, where he narrowly escaped execution.

3391. Russian travel writer was Daniel of Kiev, called in Russian Daniel Kievsky or Daniil Polomnik (the Pilgrim). In the early twelfth century, most likely the year 1106, he left the Russian monastery where he served as abbot and traveled from Constantinople via Cyprus to the Holy Land, staying in Jerusalem (in present-day Israel) for more than a year and visiting the Dead Sea, Hebron, and Damascus. He described his journey in *Puteshestvie igumena Daniila.*

3392. Vocabulary list for travelers to a foreign country was an untitled 26-page list of words in both English and French, printed by William Caxton in Westminster (now part of London), England, in 1480.

3393. Travel book illustrated with original photographs was *Égypte, Nubie, Palestine et Syrie (Egypt, Nubia, Palestine, and Syria)* by the French journalist and photographer Maxime Du Camp. The book chronicled the trip he took in 1849–51 to the Middle East with the novelist Gustave Flaubert. Du Camp took 200 calotypes (a photographic process that used paper negatives) while traveling and included 125 in the book. It was published in 1852 in Lille, France, by Louis-Désiré Blanquart-Evrard.

3394. Travel guidebooks that were internationally popular were the Baedeker guidebooks, issued by the publishing firm of Karl Baedeker of Coblenz, Germany, beginning in 1854. The first volume was a guide to Germany and the Low Countries. Its information was carefully checked by Baedeker, who paid incognito visits to the places discussed. Baedeker was also the first to develop a starred rating system for hotels and restaurants. The Baedeker guides were eventually published in German, French, and English and covered most areas of the world. Widely considered to provide impartial and trustworthy assessments of places of interest to travelers, the guides featured fine printing, accurate maps, distinctive red bindings, and articles written by distinguished scholars and critics. The first English-language Baedeker appeared in 1861.

LANGUAGE—CODES

3395. Specimen of cryptology known is a hieroglyphic message from about 1900 BCE carved into the rock wall of a tomb at Menet Khufu, Egypt, belonging to Khnumhotep II, a courtier of the pharaoh Amenemhet II. The message describes monuments built by Khnumhotep. In various places, the scribe substituted rare hieroglyphic symbols for ones in common use, probably in order to impress viewers and command their attention.

3396. Transposition cipher was produced by a device called the skytale, used by the army of the Greek city-state of Sparta. The message was written on a long strip of parchment or leather that had been wound onto a wooden staff. The unwound strip was illegible to anyone except a person possessing a staff of exactly the same girth on which the strip could be correctly rewrapped. This was the earliest form of encrypted correspondence. The Greek historian Thucydides mentions an episode in 475 BCE when Sparta used the skytale to recall its eminent general, Pausanius, who was about to commit treason by joining the invading Persians.

3397. Treatise on cryptography was a chapter of a longer work on military technology called *On the Defense of Fortified Places*. It was written circa 360 BCE by Aeneas of Stymphalis, also known as Aeneas Tacticus (the Tactician), who lived in Arcadia (now part of modern Greece). Among the methods he suggested for maintaining communications security was to conceal a message within a book by making pinpricks near the appropriate letters.

3398. Treatise on cryptanalysis appears to have been the *Kitab al-mu'amma (Book of Secret Language)*, written by the Arab philologist al-Khalil ibn Ahmad, author of the first Arabic dictionary, in Basra (in modern Iraq) circa 750. The book is now lost. He and subsequent Muslim scholars are considered the founders of the science of cryptanalysis.

3399. Nomenclator combining elements of codes (word substitutions) and ciphers (alphabet substitutions) for purposes of communications secrecy was a collection of substitution lists, known as keys, dating from circa 1379. It was used by Gabrieli di Lavinde, secretary to Clement VII, who was the first of the antipopes to reign at Avignon, France, during the Great Schism in the Roman Catholic Church.

3400. Cipher wheel was invented circa 1466 by the Italian scholar and artist Leon Battista Alberti, famed as the first Renaissance man. The device consisted of two attached copper circles, a large fixed wheel displaying the alphabet plus the numerals 1 through 4, and a small movable wheel displaying a randomly rearranged version of the alphabet. The cipher could be shifted frequently during the encoding of a message, making its decipherment very difficult. The four numerals could be used to place enciphered codes into the message. This was the first use of a polyalphabetic coding system. Alberti was also the author of the first known frequency table, which enabled cryptanalysts to decipher messages based on the frequency or rarity of various letters.

3401. Secret service to specialize in codebreaking was the Council of Ten, the state security committee that oversaw the government of Venice (in modern Italy) from 1310 through 1797. In 1506 it hired as its cipher secretary the cryptanalyst Giovanni Soro, author of a book on solving ciphers in Italian, French, Spanish, and Latin, who was known throughout Europe for his ability to read encrypted messages. He provided Venice's ambassadors with a general cipher that allowed them to communicate privately with one another, as well as with individual ciphers that only his office could interpret. The Council of Ten offered rewards for advances in cryptography and operated a school for codebreakers.

3402. Printed cryptology book was the *Polygraphia,* by the German abbot Johannes Trithemius, published posthumously in July 1518. It included the first square table, an alphabetical diagram that allows an encrypter to change ciphers with each letter. Trithemius was famous during his lifetime for his bibliographies, biographies, histories, and particularly for his fascination with occult lore, which earned him the reputation of a magician. The third volume of his manuscript *Steganographia (Hidden Writing)* purported to be a work of occult astrology, featuring tables containing the names of demons and spirits opposite lists of numbers. It was banned by the Roman Catholic Church and is still used as a conjuring text by people interested in magic. However, the names and numbers were eventually proven to be elements of a cryptogram, and the book turned out to be a collection of messages written in code.

3403. Cryptogram written in the New World by a European was a letter written in Mexico on June 25, 1532, by the Spanish conquistador Hernán Cortés. A set of symbols was substituted for the alphabet, and proper names appear in code.

LANGUAGE—ENGLISH

3404. Prose work in English was the law code of King Aethelberht I of Kent, England, written circa 600 CE. The king had been converted to Christianity by St. Augustine of Canterbury in the year 597.

3405. Poet in English whose name is known was Caedmon. According to the Venerable Bede's *Ecclesiastical History,* written circa 725, Caedmon was an illiterate shepherd in Northumbria (now Yorkshire, England) sometime in the second half of the seventh century, no earlier than 658. He received, in a dream, a visit from a figure who instructed him to sing of "the beginning of things" and gave him the ability to speak verses in the Anglo-Saxon language, also known as Old English. St. Hilda, founder of the nearby monastery of Streaneshalch (now called Whitby), invited him to become a lay brother and gave him the lifelong task of making poems from sacred texts that were read to him by the monks. The only remnant of his work that remains is a nine-line fragment of his original dream poem, the *Hymn* to the Creation.

3406. Epic poem in English was *Beowulf,* composed in Old English circa 700–750. The earliest European vernacular epic, it relates the story of the Swedish warrior hero Beowulf, leader of the Geats, and his battles with the monster Grendel, Grendel's mother, and, as an aging king, with a fire-breathing dragon. The text is known only from a single manuscript, now called the *Beowulf Manuscript,* which dates from circa 1000 and is preserved in the British Library. The epic did not appear in print until 1815.

3407. Novellas in English were written by Geoffrey Chaucer, who incorporated them into *The Canterbury Tales,* completed circa 1395. The book contains 24 tales, framed by a lively narrative in which a group of pilgrims, on their way to the shrine of Thomas à Becket in Canterbury, agree to engage in a storytelling contest.

3408. King of England after the Norman Conquest who could read and write English was Henry V, who reigned from 1413 to 1422. The kings of England after the Conquest in 1066 were of Norman stock and they spoke, wrote, and read French. Henry, born in 1387 and educated chiefly by his uncle, Henry Beaufort, bishop of Winchester, was also literate in English. He insisted on the use of English in his official documents, and when he invaded France in 1415 to enforce his territorial claims, he made a point of dictating a letter in English.

3409. English-only rule was probably the resolution adapted in 1422 by the brewers of London, England, who declared their intention to follow the example set by King Henry V by using the English language, rather than Latin or French, in their transactions.

3410. Autobiography in English was *The Book of Margery Kempe,* dictated over the course of four years by the illiterate Mrs. Kempe in a lively colloquial style. She was the wife of a well-to-do merchant in Lynn, England, the mother of 14 children, and a religious mystic, although some of her contemporaries attributed her visions to emotional disturbance. The book, completed circa 1436, describes the visions and the pilgrimages she made to shrines in Spain, Germany, Rome, and Jerusalem.

3411. Proposal to purify the English language from foreign elements was made in the mid-15th century by Reginald Pecock, bishop of Chichester, who objected to the extensive intrusion of Latin words into English. He urged the replacement of Latinate words such as "impenetrable" and "inconceivable" with newly coined Anglicisms such as "ungothroughsome" and "nottobethoughtable." Pecock was also a theologian whose preference for reason over scriptural authority resulted in his imprisonment for heresy.

3412. Publisher in English was William Caxton, who set up England's first printing press in England in 1476. His shop was located near Westminster Abbey, in a town that is now part of London. He was both printer, editor, translator, and publisher. In addition to works in English by the poets Geoffrey Chaucer, John Gower, John Lydgate, and Thomas Malory, he printed French works that he had rendered into English himself. Of the various dialects of English spoken on the island, Caxton chose the version spoken in London to reproduce in print, giving it the prestige that eventually led to its standardization.

LANGUAGE—ENGLISH—*continued*

3413. Secular play in English was *Fulgens and Lucrece,* written circa 1490 by the English dramatist Henry Medwall. Medwall was chaplain to Cardinal John Morton, Archbishop of Canterbury, and his dramatic works are believed to have been written to entertain the cardinal's entourage. *Fulgens and Lucrece* concerns two suitors and their pursuit of a woman who must choose between them.

3414. Glossary of English words explained in English was a list of words found in an English translation of the Bible. It was called "A table expoundinge certeyne wordes," and was compiled for William Tyndale's English translation of the Pentateuch, printed in 1530. Its purpose was to allow any person literate in the English language to understand the meaning of the Scriptures.

3415. Comedy written in English was *Ralph Roister Doister,* a five-act play in doggerel and song penned circa 1553 by the English translator, educator, and clergyman Nicholas Udall. Based on the works of the Roman playwrights Terence and Plautus (especially Plautus' comedy *Miles Gloriosus*), it employed stock comic types to portray the rowdy life of 16th-century London. The play was probably first performed by Queen Mary's Chapel Royal at Windsor Castle or by the pupils of Westminster School in London, where Udall was schoolmaster.

3416. Blank verse in English was contained in *Certain Bokes of Virgiles Aenaeis,* a translation of Books II and IV of Vergil's *Aeneid* by the English poet Henry Howard, Earl of Surrey. It was published in 1557, ten years after Surrey was executed on a trumped-up charge of treason against Prince Edward, the son of King Henry VIII. Surrey's innovative use of unrhymed iambic pentameter (blank verse) was inspired by the works of Italian poets, including Petrarch. Surrey was also the first to develop the sonnet form later used by William Shakespeare.

3417. Dramatic tragedy in English was *The Tragedie of Gorboduc,* written by the English playwrights Thomas Norton and Thomas Sackville. It was first acted in 1561. Inspired by the bloody revenge dramas of the Latin playwright Seneca, it is the earliest known English tragedy, as well as the first English drama in blank verse (unrhymed iambic pentameter, the form used by Seneca).

3418. Children's book in English that was not a school text was a book of verses entitled *A Booke in Englyssh Metre, of the great Marchant Man called Dives Pragmaticus, very preaty for Children to reade.* It was printed by Alexander Lacy and was published in London, England, in 1563.

3419. Autobiography in English by a man was *A book of songs and sonnetts with longe discoorses sett with them, of the chylds lyfe, together with a young mans lyfe,* written by Thomas Whythorne circa 1576. Whythorne, a composer, recounted his school days and adult career as a music master.

3420. Satire in English was *The Steele Glass,* written in 1576 by the English adventurer, playwright, poet, and prose writer George Gascoigne. It was written in blank verse, the first time that verse style had been used for an original nondramatic work in English.

3421. Play by William Shakespeare was the chronicle play *Henry VI, Part I,* the first of three parts. It was first performed in 1589 and was published in the First Folio of 1623. The play, concerning the early career of England's Henry VI, was based primarily on material from Raphael Holinshed's *Chronicles of England, Scotland and Ireland.* Some scholars have proposed that *Henry VI, Part I* was actually written after parts II and III, but the relative lack of polish in *Henry VI, Part I* suggests that it is the earlier work.

3422. Domestic tragedy in English was the late Elizabethan drama *Arden of Feversham,* written circa 1591 by an unknown author. A precursor of the melodrama, it tells the tale of the murder of a husband by his wife and her lover, and their eventual punishment.

3423. Diary in English known to historians was kept by Lady Margaret Hoby, an English Puritan of the landed gentry. She began the diary in 1599, setting down her daily activities but rarely recording her personal feelings.

3424. Poet laureate of England was the playwright and lyric poet Ben Jonson, who in 1616 was granted an annual pension by King James I as recompense for his literary services to the crown. A second such pension, to Sir William Davenant, was granted in 1639. The position became a regular court appointment in 1668, when John Dryden, the preeminent poet, translator, and literary critic of his generation, received the title; he is thus considered the first official poet laureate. His stipend, like those of all poets who held the title from 1630 to 1790, included a "butt of canary wine" each year.

3425. Publication in English printed in the American colonies extant was a document printed on August 11, 1645, in the Massachusetts Bay Colony port of Boston (now Boston, MA, USA), in which the colonial leaders justified to their constituents the conflict with the Narragansett Indians. It was entitled *A declaration of former passages and proceedings betwixt the English and the Narrowgansets, with their confederates, Wherein the grounds and justice of the ensuing warre are opened and cleared. Published, by order of the Commissioners for the united Colonies.*

3426. Woman to write professionally in English was the 17th-century adventuress, dramatist, novelist, and poet Aphra Behn, born in 1640. Employed as a spy in the Netherlands by King Charles II, she landed in debtors' prison in England and began writing to pay her way out. Her influential novel *Oroonoko, or the History of the Royal Slave,* published in 1688, was the first important English romance by a woman. It recounts the tale of an enslaved African prince whom Aphra knew in the English colony of Suriname, where she was raised. Between 1670 and 1689 she wrote 15 successful comedic plays, notably *The Forc'd Marriage* (1671) and *The Rover* (produced in two parts in 1677 and 1681), and also penned a large number of poems.

3427. Book in the English language written by a woman known by name was *The Midwives Book or the Whole Art of Midwifery,* by Jane Sharp. It was published in England in 1671.

3428. Novel in English that was successful both commercially and as a literary work was *Robinson Crusoe* by Daniel Defoe, published in 1719. The tale of an Englishman shipwrecked on a remote island, it was also the first realistic novel and the first adventure novel in the English language.

3429. Children's fiction book in English was *The History of Little Goody Two-Shoes; Otherwise called, Mrs. Margery Two-Shoes.* It was published in London, England, by John Newbery, sometime between the year 1744, when Newbery began specializing in children's books, and 1766, when the third edition of the book appeared. The author is unknown.

3430. Printed collection of nursery rhymes was *Tommy Thumb's Pretty Song Book,* published in two volumes in London in 1744. It contained the earliest known versions of such nursery rhymes as "London Bridge is falling down," "Hickory, dickory dock," and "Sing a song of sixpence."

3431. Book of Mother Goose nursery rhymes was *Mother Goose's Melody: or Sonnets for the Cradle,* published in London, England, in 1781 by the firm of John Newbery. It contained 51 rhymes, including "Ding Dong Bell," "Hush-a-bye baby on the tree top," and "Jack and Jill." The editor may have been the playwright Oliver Goldsmith. The book was sold as "the most celebrated Songs and Lullabies of old British nurses." The name Mother Goose was probably borrowed from Charles Perrault, the French writer of fairy tales, whose collection *Contes de ma mère l'oye (Tales of My Mother Goose)* appeared in 1697.

3432. Melodrama in English was *A Tale of Mystery,* translated for the London stage in 1802 by Thomas Holcroft. It was an adaption of the popular French melodrama *Coelina, ou l'enfant du mystere (Coelina, or The Child of Mystery),* written in 1800 by the French dramatist Guilbert de Pixérécourt, considered the most important popularizer of the genre.

3433. Censored edition of Shakespeare was the *Family Shakespeare,* edited in 1807 by Harriet Bowdler, sister of the English doctor and social reformer Thomas Bowdler, who published an expanded 1818 version titled *Family Shakspeare.* The Bowdlers' concern was to prepare an edition that no parent would hesitate to read to a child. Their practice was to delete or paraphrase any part of Shakespeare's work that, in their view, might damage the morals of the young. The 1818 *Family Shakspeare* was in fact a popular and financially successful edition. By 1838, the word "bowdlerize" had entered the language as a term meaning "expurgate for moral purposes."

LANGUAGE—LITERARY GENRES

3434. Literature for children was found on Sumerian clay tablets from the period of the Third Dynasty of the city of Ur (modern Tel-el-Muqayyar in Iraq), circa 2100–2004 BCE. Excavated at sites believed to be schools, these texts fall into five categories: lullabies; proverbs and fables; stories of schoolboys' lives; writing exercises; and dialogs or debates.

3435. Epic is the ancient *Epic of Gilgamesh.* It relates the futile search for immortality of a heroic Sumerian king, Gilgamesh, who was probably based on a historical king of the same name who ruled the city of Uruk (Erech) circa 2200 BCE. The fullest extant version, though not the earliest, is on twelve fragmentary Akkadian-language tablets discovered by British archeologist Austen Henry Layard in 1845–51 during

LANGUAGE—LITERARY GENRES—continued

his excavation of the 2,600-year-old library of
the Assyrian king Ashurbanipal (Asur-bani-apli)
at Nineveh, in present-day Iraq. The original
date of the epic is circa 2000 BCE. Gilgamesh
is also the first important literary hero.

3436. Literature known to archeologists was
that of Sumeria. A cuneiform tablet dated to
circa 2000 BCE, unearthed in the Sumerian city
of Nippur (modern Niffer, Iraq), contained a
list of some 21 documents, including early versions of the parts of the Gilgamesh epic, several hymns to Enlil, Inanna, and other Sumerian
gods, and lamentations over the destruction of
the cities of Sumer and Nippur itself. This was
the first literary catalog.

3437. Didactic verses are found in the later
Upanishads, written circa 500 BCE. The *Upanishads* are compilations of teachings, in Sanskrit, by the sages of early Hinduism.

3438. Fables with morals are attributed to the
Greek author Aesop in the mid-sixth century
BCE. Although Aesop is said variously to have
served King Croesus of Lydia and King Lycurgus of Babylon, his existence has not been con-
clusively documented. A volume of fables bearing his name, collected by Demetrius Phalareus,
first appeared in the fourth century BCE.

**3439. Epic poem in a vernacular European
language** known to historians was *Beowulf,*
written in the Old English (Anglo-Saxon) language circa 700 CE. It tells the story of
Beowulf, a warrior hero who defeats a series of
monsters in combat until, in his old age, he is
mortally wounded by a dragon. A single version of the poem remains, dating from about
the year 1000.

3440. Novel was *Genji monogatari (The Tale
of Genji),* completed by Murasaki Shikibu (a
pseudonym) in Kyoto, Japan, circa 1010 CE.
Murasaki was a lady in the court of the empress Joto Mon'in. Her long and complex novel, the first important work of Japanese literature and usually considered the finest, relates
the love life of the royal prince Genji while ex-
quisitely describing the refined society of
Heian-period Japan. Murasaki probably took
her pseudonym from a character in her book, a
young girl of surpassing beauty. The first English version was translated by Arthur Waley
and published in 1935.

3441. Sagas evolved in Iceland in the mid-
twelfth century, when oral storytelling was
largely replaced on farmsteads by the practice
of reading aloud, called *sagnaskemmtun (saga
entertainment).* Subjects for sagas included
kingly biographies, Germanic myths, and the
adventures of Iceland's early settlers, especially
their blood feuds. They were written in Old
Icelandic, a language closely related to Old
Norse.

3442. Minstrel tale known to historians was
König Rother (King Rother), a medieval German romance dating from circa 1160 that was
popular among wandering minstrels of central
Europe. The tale, which relates the quest of
Rother to marry a princess and rescue his loyal
retainers from the emperor of Constantinople, is
notable for its combination of Byzantine and
Germanic story elements.

3443. Legal drama was contained in *Njála
(Njal's Saga),* generally considered the greatest
of the 13th-century Icelandic sagas. Several
powerful scenes are set in the court of the
Althing, the early Icelandic parliament, in
which the argument of fine points of law deter-
mines the fates of the main characters.

3444. Picaresque novel in which a hero, often
of a rascally and footloose character, has a series of adventures, including brawls, romances,
and intrigues, was *La Vida de Lazarillo de
Tormes y sus Fortunas y Adversidades,* published in Burgos, Spain, in 1554. The work has
most often been attributed to Diego Hurtado de
Mendoza. The rambling plot concerns the
young rascal Lazaro, who serves under a succession of hypocritical masters. The Spanish
term for such a novel, *novela picaresca,* is derived from *pícaro,* "rogue."

3445. Modern epic poems were written in the
mid-16th century. *La Araucana,* a verse epic
about the revolt of the Araucanian Indians
against the Spanish in Chile, was composed by
Alonso de Ercilla y Zúñiga, a young courtier
who had served in Chile as a captain in the
Spanish army and whose sympathies had been
won over by the Araucanians. His poem, in 39
cantos, was published in installments, beginning
in 1569 and ending in 1590, and inspired several others. *Os Lusíadas (The Lusiads),* an epic
history of Vasco da Gama's discovery of the
sea route to India, was written in Lisbon in
1572 by Luís Vaz de Camoẽs, Portugal's national poet.

3446. Stream of consciousness as a literary technique was used by the English comic novelist Laurence Sterne in *The Life and Opinions of Tristram Shandy, Gentleman,* written between 1760 and 1767. Told mainly in the first person, the book is an eccentric parody of novelistic and autobiographical forms that was strongly influenced by John Locke's theory of the association of ideas.

3447. Gothic novel was *The Castle of Otranto,* published in 1764 by the English writer Horace Walpole. A seminal work of the proto-Romantic imagination, it contains most of what were to become the conventions of the Gothic genre: a dark ruined castle, an innocent heroine in peril, a sinister villain, and mysterious, supernatural events.

3448. Science-fiction novel was *Frankenstein; or the Modern Prometheus,* published in 1818 by English writer Mary Wollstonecraft Shelley. It relates the Gothic tale of Victor Frankenstein, a scientist who creates a living monster from parts of corpses and is ultimately destroyed by his creation.

3449. Short story in the modern era is subject to debate, but many critics give credit to three stories in Washington Irving's 1819–20 collection *The Sketch Book of Geoffrey Crayon, Gent.* These are "The Legend of Sleepy Hollow," "Rip Van Winkle," and "The Spectre Bridegroom."

3450. Novel to be serialized was *The Pickwick Papers,* the first novel by the English writer Charles Dickens. Beginning in the spring of 1836, it was published in installments, over the course of 20 months, by the publishing house of Chapman and Hall, London.

3451. Modern detective story is usually considered to be the American writer Edgar Allan Poe's short story "The Murders in the Rue Morgue." It was first published in April 1841 in *Graham's Lady's and Gentleman's Magazine,* a literary magazine edited by Poe himself. Poe's atmospheric tale of a series of gruesome murders was the first of several to feature his French amateur detective, C. Auguste Dupin.

3452. Modernist poetry is usually considered to be the work of French poet Charles Baudelaire. The 100 poems in *Les Fleurs du mal (The Flowers of Evil),* published in 1857, vividly depict a debased urban demimonde in which the poet obsessively seeks for new experiences to ease the bleakness of his world.

3453. Police procedural or *roman policier* was invented by the French author Émile Gaboriau, the author of 21 novels and collections of writings. Gaboriau's most famous works were his policiers, including *Le Crime d'Orcival (The Crime of Orcival),* written in 1867, and *Monsieur Lecoq* of 1868. The latter, which concerned the problem of identifying an unknown prisoner, introduced the detective Lecoq, who exhibited some of the deductive powers of Arthur Conan Doyle's later creation, Sherlock Holmes.

3454. Detective novel was *The Moonstone,* by William Wilkie Collins, published in 1868. In it, a sober English detective investigates a series of mysterious deaths linked to a cursed family jewel.

3455. Surrealist text was "Les Champs magnétiques" ("Magnetic Fields"), a short piece by the French writers André Breton and Philippe Soupault. It was published in 1920 in the Parisian literary review *Littérature,* which Breton cofounded. The first example of the Surrealist technique of automatic writing, DdLes Champs magnétiques was, according to Breton, created by a method of "pure psychic automatism . . . the dictation of thought, free from any control by the reason and of any aesthetic or moral preoccupation."

3456. Booker Prize was awarded in 1969 to *Something to Answer For,* a novel by P.H. Newby. The full name of the award is the Booker McConnell Prize; it was set up in 1968 by Booker PLC, a group of companies specialising in food distribution, and is administered by the National Book League. It is awarded to the best full-length novel written in English by a citizen of the United Kingdom, the Commonwealth, Ireland, Pakistan, or South Africa. Publishers are invited to submit entries with scheduled publication dates between January and November of the award year.

LANGUAGE—LITERARY GENRES—REGIONAL

3457. Latin American novel was the 1816 work *El periquillo sarniento (The Itching Parrot),* a scathing, picaresque satire of the conservative Mexican middle-class. It was written by the dramatist, pamphleteer, and political activist José Joaquín Fernández de Lizardi, a leader of Mexico's national liberation movement. He published his radical political views under the pseudonym "el pensador mexicano" ("the Mexican thinker").

3458. Brazilian novel was *A moreninha (The Little Brunette),* by Joaquim Manuel de Macedo, published in 1844.

LANGUAGE—LITERARY GENRES—RE-
GIONAL—*continued*

**3459. Caribbean Spanish-language poet who
was a woman** was the Puerto Rican poet Lola
Rodríguez de Tío. Her works first appeared in
1876 in the collection *Mís Cantares (My
Songs).* "Cuba y Puerto Rico Son" ("Cuba and
Puerto Rico Are"), first published in the 1893
collection *Mi Libro de Cuba (My Book of
Cuba),* was her best-known poem.

**3460. Novel in an African vernacular lan-
guage** was *Moeti oa bochabela (The Traveler
to the East),* written in Sesotho by the writer
Thomas Mokopu Mofolo, a native of Basutoland (now Lesotho), and published in 1907. An
allegorical novel about an African man's spiritual journey, it was influenced by John Bun-
yan's English classic, *Pilgrim's Progress.*
Mofolo's best-known work was the 1925 book
Chaka, a biographical novel about the 19th-
century Zulu king Shaka. It was banned for 15
years by Christian missionaries who disap-
proved of its frank portrayal of pagan African
customs.

3461. Caribbean novel in English of importance was *Jane: A Story of Jamaica* by E.G. de
Lisser, published in 1913 by Lisser's own publishing company, Pioneer Press, in Jamaica.

3462. Anti-apartheid novel was *In a Province*
(1934), by the South African writer Laurens
van der Post.

LANGUAGE—MYTHS AND LEGENDS

3463. Flood story occurs in the mythology of
Mesopotamia, dating from the fourth millennium BCE. A Sumerian legend known as Eridu
Genesis tells of a worldwide flood brought by
the gods for the purpose of killing all human
beings. A humble and good man named
Ziusudra, of Shuruppak in modern-day Iraq,
was forewarned by the god Enki and built a
ship, in which he saved himself, his family, and
"the seed of all living things"; he reestablished
life on earth and eventually received the gift of
immortality. In the Akkadian version, which is
part of the Gilgamesh epic, the survivor's name
is Utnapishtim.

3464. Written versions of the Greek myths
were set down by the Greek poet Hesiod in his
Theogony, circa 700 BCE. The collection included the now-famous myths of Chaos and Gaea,
the rebellion of Cronos against Uranus, the sub-
duing of the Titans, the rise to power of Zeus,
and the spread of evil through Pandora's box,
as well as many other stories of the Greek gods
and goddesses.

3465. Lost-slipper motif in a folktale appears
to have originated in a story about Rhodopis, a
celebrated Thracian prostitute (and the first
prostitute who is known by name) who lived in
Egypt in the sixth century BCE. According to
the story, an eagle flew away with one of her
slippers and took it to the city of Naukratis,
where he dropped it in front of the pharaoh
Ahmose II. The fascinated pharaoh searched his
kingdom to find its owner, but though he succeeded in fitting the slipper to the foot of
Rhodopis, she did not return his interest.

3466. Sighting of a mermaid was reported in
320 BCE by the Greek historian Megasthenes,
who had been sent by the Macedonian ruler of
Babylon, Seleucus Nicator, on a diplomatic
mission to the Indian emperor Candragupta
Maurya. On his return, he described having
seen near Sri Lanka a creature that was half
woman, half fish.

3467. Bestiary in European literature was the
Physiologus, usually considered to have been
written in Alexandria, Egypt, or Yehudah (Judah; present-day Israel) sometime before 300
BCE. The author wrote in Greek and may have
been either of two fourth-century bishops, St.
Basil the Great or Epiphanius of Constantia.
The book collects 48 fables or tales, each of
which links one animal, plant, mythical beast
(such as the unicorn), or stone with a biblical
text. It was widely disseminated and translated,
with a Latin edition appearing as early as circa
350.

3468. Major source of international folktales
was probably the *Pañca-tantra (Five Chapters),*
also spelled *Panchatantra* and known to English readers as *The Fables of Bidpai.* The
book, written in Sanskrit, was composed in India sometime between 100 BCE and 500 CE. It
took the form of a lesson in politics and world-
ly success, delivered by a learned man to three
princes through animal fables in verse and
prose. Beginning in the sixth century, it was
translated into a series of languages, including
Persian, Syriac, Arabic, Hebrew, Greek, Latin,
numerous Slavic and Romance tongues, Turkish, and Indonesian, giving rise to many local
versions of its stories.

**3469. Reference to the King Arthur legend
in literature** occurs in a poem, *Y Gododdin,* by
the Welsh poet Aneirin. In describing a battle
that took place circa 600 in northern England
between a Saxon army and a group of Celtic
warriors, the author compares the Welsh hero
Gwawrddur to Arthur.

3470. Reference to the King Arthur legend in a historical work is contained in the *Historia Brittonum (The History of Britain),* written circa 800, probably by a Welshman named Nennius. It describes twelve battles fought by Arthur against Saxon invaders, of which the twelfth was called The Battle of Mount Badon. Two earlier writers, Gildas in the sixth century and the Venerable Bede in the eighth century, refer to the leader of the Britons at the Battle of Mount Badon as Ambrosius Aurelianus.

3471. Legend of Prester John appeared in 1145, when Bishop Hugh of Gebal, Syria (now Jubayl, Lebanon) wrote a report to the papal court then at Viterbo, Italy, describing an Arabian priest-king who had defeated Persia's Muslims on the battlefield and had nearly succeeded in capturing Jerusalem for the Christians. This report was described the same year in the *Chronicon* of the German bishop Otto of Friesling. By the 1300s, the legend of Prester John had become associated with the region that is now Ethiopia. His name and kingdom appeared on a map drawn in 1459 by Fra Mauro, a Venetian monk.

3472. Version of the Holy Grail legend appeared in *Perceval, ou Le Conte du Graal (Perceval, or the Romance of the Grail),* one of five Arthurian romances penned by the French poet Chrétien de Troyes between 1165 and 1180. Troyes's works stressed the fantastical aspects of the Arthur legend.

3473. Keeper of the Holy Grail was Joseph of Arimathea, a Samarian of the first century CE who is mentioned in the New Testament. Numerous medieval Christian legends, notably those related in Robert de Borron's verse romance *Joseph d'Arimathie* (circa 1200) and Thomas Malory's *Morte D'Arthur* (circa 1450), cite Joseph as being entrusted with the Grail, the cup said to have been used by Jesus at the Last Supper.

3474. Appearance in literature of legendary Germanic heroes occurred in the *Elder Edda,* or *Poetic Edda,* a collection of lays in the Old Norse language, compiled in Iceland circa 1270 from earlier material in oral tradition. Siegfried, the protagonist of Richard Wagner's 19th-century opera cycle *Der Ring des Nibelungen,* appears in the *Elder Edda* as Sigurd. (He appears also in the *Nibelungenlied,* a poem written in Germany circa 1200, but the version in the *Elder Edda* is thought to be older.)

3475. Reference to the Robin Hood legend in English literature occurs in *The Vision of Piers Plowman,* a long dream-poem composed by William Langland of Shropshire, England, circa 1377. Two lines spoken by a character named Sloth go as follows (translated into modern English): "I do not know my paternoster perfectly as the priest sings it, But I know rhymes of Robin Hood and Randolph, Earl of Chester." The earliest poem in which Robin Hood figures as a character himself is a ballad known as *Robin Hood and the Monk,* which dates from about the year 1450.

3476. Witchcraft encyclopedia was the *Malleus Maleficarum (Hammer of the Witches),* published in 1486 by two Dominican friars, Jakob Sprenger, dean of the University of Cologne, Germany, and Heinrich Kramer, professor of theology at the University of Salzburg, Austria. The book purported to be a guide to satanic practices, such as night-riding and pacts with the Devil, and was also intended as a practical textbook for Christian authorities charged with identifying witches and exterminating them. It went through many editions and was considered authoritative by Catholics and Protestants well into the 18th century.

3477. Witch image of an old crone with a long nose and a tall black hat originated with a woman who was born in 1488 in Knaresborough, Yorkshire, England. Known in adulthood as Mother Shipton, she was a noted psychic and seeress.

3478. Reference to Utopia occurs in the title of a book by the humanist Christian philosopher Thomas More, Lord Chancellor of England, that was published in December 1516. Its full title is *Libellus vere aureaus, nec minus salutaris, quam festivus, de optimo reipublicae statu deque nova insula Utopia (On the Highest State of a Republic and on the New Island Utopia),* though it is now known simply as *Utopia.* The book contrasted the cruel social and political conditions of Europe with the possibilities of an ideal life on an imaginary island off the New World. The inhabitants of the island, all devout Christians guided by reason, practice a form of communism in which everything is shared except for spouses. The word *utopia* is Greek for "nowhere."

LANGUAGE—MYTHS AND LEGENDS—
continued

3479. Faust legend was contained in the *Faustbuch* (1587), author unknown, which contained tales supposedly narrated by the real Faust, a necromancer who died circa 1540 in what is now Germany. The legend of Faust as a rationalist who sells his soul to the devil in return for knowledge was given its now-familiar form in *The Tragicall History of Dr. Faustus* (1607) by the English playwright and poet Christopher Marlowe.

3480. Collection of folktales from oral tradition compiled by folklorists was *Kinder- und Hausmärchen (Children's and House Tales)*, published in Germany between 1812 and 1815. The compilers were two brothers, Jacob and Wilhelm Grimm. Most of the stories, some 200 in all, were told to the Grimms by ordinary people living in the countryside; before their publication, they were rewritten and annotated. The work is better known in English as *Grimm's Fairy Tales.*

3481. World Dracula Congress took place in Romania in May–June 1995. Attendees discussed literary and historical aspects of the myth of the vampire, whose widespread impact on popular culture began with the 1897 gothic novel *Dracula* by Bram Stoker.

LANGUAGE—NAMES

3482. Personal name to survive in written records was inscribed on clay tablets in Sumer circa the 34th century BCE. The name was En-lil-ti.

3483. Family names were first adopted in China in 2852 BCE, by imperial decree.

3484. Person to adopt a symbol as a name was the pop musician and performer Prince Rogers Nelson, born in Minneapolis, MN, USA, who used the stage name Prince. In 1992 he adopted as his name a glyph combining the medical symbols for male and female.

LANGUAGE—TEXTS

3485. Etruscan writing is an inscription known as the Marsiliana Tablet, dating from the eighth century BCE. The language of the Etruscans, who lived in what is now Tuscany, in northern Italy, is not closely related to any other known language; hence its extant texts, including some 11,000 inscriptions but no literature, remain largely incomprehensible.

3486. Persian writing known is an inscription carved in the sixth century BCE on a rock face at Behistun, Persia (now Bisitun, Iran), in Old Persian. The cuneiform script was invented by order of Darius I, who needed a written language in order to record the events surrounding his accession to the throne of Persia in 529 BCE. The text was also inscribed in Babylonian and Elamite.

3487. Tamil writing consists of inscriptions dating from the third century BCE. The first literary works were written in the first century CE. Known collectively as *cankam,* or "literary academy," they include more than 2,000 poems, including poems about love and war. Tamil, a branch of the Dravidian family of languages, is the official language of Tamil Nadu state in southern India.

3488. Sinhalese writing known appears on rock inscriptions from circa 200 BCE. The earliest extended prose works, dating from the tenth century, were paraphrases of Buddhist writings in the Pali language. Sinhalese is spoken in Sri Lanka.

3489. Pali text appeared in the first century BCE in Sri Lanka, where the sayings of the Buddha were committed to writing. Pali is a literary language that originated in India in the fifth century BCE and that was used in the composition of the sacred texts of Theravada Buddhism.

3490. Scandinavian writing known, and the earliest examples of writing extant in any Germanic language, are runic inscriptions from the Scandinavian countries and southeastern Europe, of which the oldest are dated to 200 CE. They include statements of ownership or manufacture, memorial declarations, and incantations, carved into wooden and metal objects. The first Scandinavian poet whose name is known was the ninth-century skaldic poet Bragi the Old, whose language, Old Norse, was current in both Norway and Iceland. Norwegian, Danish, and Swedish began to emerge from the parent language in the eleventh century. Manuscripts in Danish, which gave rise to Norwegian, are extant from the 13th century, and Swedish prose is considered to begin with a New Testament translation from 1526.

3491. Coptic writing was employed in letters written in the early fourth century by St. Anthony of Egypt, the first Christian monk. Coptic developed from ancient Egyptian and was used as a literary language by Christian theologians from the fourth to the eighth century.

3492. African written language known was the Ethiopian language Ge'ez, a literary language related to classical Arabic. The first use of it was made in the fourth century, to translate Christian works from the Greek. No longer in use for compositions, Ge'ez remains the liturgical language of the Ethiopian Orthodox Church.

3493. Irish Gaelic writing appears on tomb inscriptions in Ogham script, made with knife strokes on stone, in the fourth century. The earliest extant poem in Irish Gaelic may be the *Amra Choluim Chille (Eulogy of St. Columba),* written in 597 by Dallán Forgaill, Ireland's chief bard. The first collection of Irish Gaelic writing was *Leabhar na Huidhre (The Book of the Dun Cow),* an anthology of legends, historical tales, sagas, poems, and religious material that was compiled at Clonmacnoise monastery circa 1100. Some of the texts were already three or four centuries old.

3494. Armenian writing was a translation of the Bible, made circa 410. It is known as the Mesropian Bible after St. Mesrop Mashtots, the priest who had invented an alphabet for the Armenian language about ten years earlier, and who later wrote a number of prayers, hymns, and theological commentaries.

3495. Georgian writing dates from the fifth century, after the development of a script based on the Greek alphabet, which was used for inscriptions and a translation of the Gospels. The first work written in Georgian, circa 480, was a biography of St. Shushanik. The earliest epic poem was *Vepkhis-tqaosani (The Knight in the Panther's Skin),* by Shota Rustaveli, composed in the twelfth century. Georgian, the official language of the Republic of Georgia, belongs to the Kartvelian (South Caucasian) language family.

3496. Text in the Avestan language is the *Gathas,* a group of 17 hymns composed by Zarathushtra, the founder of the religion. They form the oldest part of the *Avesta,* a collection of prayers, hymns, liturgies, and other scriptures that were transmitted orally for hundreds of years until about the fifth century CE, when an alphabet was invented in Sasanian Persia (modern Iran) for the purpose of recording them. No other literature exists in the Avestan language. The entire *Avesta* ran to 21 volumes, nearly all of which were entirely destroyed in the mayhem that attended the successive conquests of Persia by the Arabs, Turks, and Mongols. The oldest extant manuscript dates from 1323.

3497. Kannada writing appears in sixth-century inscriptions. The first literary work extant was the *Kavirajamarga (Royal Road of Poets),* a treatise on poetic rhetoric that dates from circa 850. The first work of fiction was the *Lilavati,* by Nemicandra, a royal love story written in 1370. Kannada, also known as Kanarese, belongs to the Dravidian family of languages and is the official spoken language of Karnataka state in southern India.

3498. Welsh writing known is *Y Gododdin,* a poem about the fate of the warriors whom Mynyddawg Mwynfawr of Caereidyn (near modern Edinburgh, Scotland) sent on a mission to capture a Saxon fortress. The author was Aneirin, one of the five great bards of the sixth-century Cymry, or Welsh, identified by the historian Nennius. Another of their number was Taliesin, the author of mythological works in the Celtic tradition. The first Welsh grammar was *Cambrobrytannicae Cymraecaeve linguae institutiones et rudimenta,* a work in Latin that set forth the principles of the Welsh language and of Welsh bardic poetry. It was written by Siôn David Rhys, a physician at Cardiff, Wales, and was published in 1592.

3499. Mon and Khmer writing developed from Indian alphabets. Several hundred early inscriptions in Old Khmer and Old Mon have been found on monuments from early-seventh-century Cambodia, Thailand, and Vietnam. These were the basis for the Thai and Burmese writing systems.

3500. Telugu writing is extant from the year 633. The first literary work in Telugu, written in the tenth or eleventh century by Nannaya and Tikkana, is a religious text based on the *Mahabharata,* the ancient Hindu epic poem. Telugu, a Dravidian language, was the court language of the Vijayanagar empire (14th through 16th centuries) and is the official language of India's Andhra Pradesh state.

3501. Turkish writing appeared in the Orhon (or Orkhon) inscriptions, carved on two monuments near the Orhon River in northern Mongolia. They are epic narratives of early Turkish history, encompassing the origins of the Turks as the nomadic Mongolian tribe of T'u-chïeh and its victory over the Chinese emperor Hsüan Tsung under the leadership of two brothers, Kül and Bilge. The monuments were made in 732 and 735, after the brothers' deaths. The first poet of note to write in Turkish was Yunus Emre (1238–1320), a Bektashiyah Sufi mystic who is considered the founder of Turkish literature in the Islamic era.

LANGUAGE—TEXTS—*continued*

3502. Italian writing may be an eighth-century riddle from Verona, although scholars disagree on whether the language is truly Italian or is a Latin vernacular. The first lengthy documents in recognizable Italian are tenth-century court records from Montecassino, in which the testimony of the witnesses is given in Italian. The first Italian literary work of importance is considered to be the Tuscan *Ritmo Laurenziano (Laurentian Rhythm)* of circa 1190.

3503. Javanese writing began in the eighth or ninth century with translations and poetic renderings of Sanskrit works, including the *Mahabharata* and the *Ramayana.*

3504. Malayalam writing dates from the late ninth century. Its literature began in the 13th century. Malayalam, one of the Dravidian languages, is the official language of India's Kerala state.

3505. Bulgarian writing emerged in 893 at Preslav (now Veliki Preslav), where clerics trained by Sts. Cyril and Methodius, the inventors of the Cyrillic alphabet, translated Christian religious texts for use in missionary work among the Slavs. Old Bulgarian was the first of the Slavic languages to receive a written form.

3506. Spanish writing known consists of short glosses on two Latin texts from Rioja and Castile, both dating from the tenth century. The first major work in Spanish was the epic poem *Cantar de mío Cid (Song of My Cid),* written circa 1140 by an unknown author in Castilian, which is the basis for modern Spanish. The earliest extant copy, the *Poema del Cid,* is from circa 1307.

3507. Dutch writing was used in parts of the *Wachtendonck Psalm Fragments,* preserved from the early tenth century. The first poet to write in Dutch is considered to have been Heinrich von Veldeke (Henric van Veldeke), born in Lorraine (in the modern Netherlands), who is known as the founder of both German court epic poetry and Dutch poetry. His *St. Servatius* was written circa 1180 in the Limburg dialect of Old Dutch; his *Eneit,* a retelling of the Aeneas legend, was written circa 1185 in Franconian, a form of Middle High German. The earliest Dutch plays, known as the *Abele spelen* ("seemly plays"), date from the 14th century and had secular themes.

3508. Bengali writing appeared in the *caryapadas,* or "lines on proper practice." These were didactic verses in Old Bengali, probably composed in the tenth century. Bengali is the language of Bangladesh and the state of West Bengal, India.

3509. Korean writing appeared in the tenth century in the Silla kingdom, in a genre of poetry known as *hyangga,* written in the Korean language but expressed in Chinese characters. A Korean script, Hangul, was invented in 1443.

3510. Malay writing known consists of seventh-century inscriptions from the Indonesian island of Sumatra, written in a southern Indian script. The first substantial works, shaped by the conventions of Sanskrit poetry, were written during the rule of Airlangga, emperor of eastern Java from 1019 to circa 1049.

3511. Russian writing developed after the invention in the ninth century by Sts. Cyril and Methodius of a Slavic script, which was eventually transmitted, by way of Bulgaria, to the Russian princely capital at Kiev (in modern Ukraine). The earliest Russian manuscripts were translations from Greek religious works. The oldest known is the *Ostromirovo evangeliye (The Ostromir Gospel),* which carries a date of 1057.

3512. Gujarati texts were written in the twelfth-century Indian kingdom of Gujarat by Hemacandra, a scholar and teacher of the Jain religion, whose first book, the *Arhanniti (Jaina Politics),* appeared in 1125. His works, some of which were written in Sanskrit, include books of philosophy, science, epic poetry, and grammar. Gujarati is the official language of the Gujarat state.

3513. Polish writing known appears on a papal bull received in 1136 by the Archbishop of Gniezno, which contained a list of names in an early form of Polish. Manuscripts in Polish are extant from the 14th century.

3514. Hindi writing of importance was *Prthviraj Rasau,* an epic poem about the last Hindu king of Delhi, written in the twelfth century. The author was Chand Bardai. Hindi is the official language of the Republic of India.

3515. Oriya writing of substantial size was the *Madala-pañji (Drum Chronicle)* from the twelfth century, concerning events at the temple of Jagannatha in Puri, India, one of the important centers of Hindu pilgrimage. Oriya is the official language of the state of Orissa.

3516. Portuguese writing known was the text of an agreement made in 1192, dividing property among the heirs of a prosperous Portuguese family. In the 16th century, standard Portuguese developed in the Lisbon area from Gallego-Portuguese, the linguistic unit comprising Galician and old Portuguese. Brasileiro, or the Brazilian Portuguese dialect, began diverging from the mother tongue soon after Portuguese colonization began in 1530.

3517. Hungarian writing was employed in the *Halotti beszéd (Funeral Oration)*, a translation from the Latin, which appeared in a volume of church documents, the *Pray Codex*, late in the twelfth century. The oration is the first example of literature in any of the Uralic languages, a family of some 21 related languages spoken in northeastern Europe and northern Asia. The first extant poem is Hungarian is *Magyar Mária-siralom (Old Hungarian Lament of the Virgin Mary)*, written towards the beginning of the 14th century. The first play in Hungarian was *A három körösztény leányról (On Three Christian Virgins)*, a translation, made circa 1520, of a Latin play by the tenth-century German nun and poet Hrosvitha.

3518. Assamese writing appeared in the *Prahlada-caritra*, about the legendary king Prahlada, written in the 13th century by Mena Sarasvati. Assamese is the official language of the Indian state of Assam.

3519. Czech writing was individual words found in eleventh-century texts written in Old Church Slavonic. The first substantial use of Czech came in the composition of hymns written in Bohemia in the late 13th century. The earliest secular work in the Czech language was a 14th-century poem about Alexander the Great, *Alexandreis*, a version of a Latin poem by Gautier de Châtillon.

3520. Marathi writing of importance was the *Jñaneshvari*, a verse commentary in Old Marathi on the Hindu religious poem *Bhagavadgita*, written circa 1290. The author was the mystic Jñanadeva. Marathi is the official language of the state of Maharashtra, India.

3521. Amharic writing consists of hymns and chronicles commemorating the warrior king Amda Tseyon ("Pillar of Zion"), who defeated a number of Muslim kingdoms in the early 14th century and who is considered by some to be the founder of Ethiopia. The first novel in Amharic, published in 1908, was *Libb Wallad Tarik (Imaginative Story)*, by Afawarq Gabra Iyasus (Afeworq Gabre-Eyesus). Amharic and Oromo are the two modern languages of Ethiopia.

3522. Kashmiri writing dates from the 14th century, when it was used by the poet Lalla to write love poems to the god Shiva. Also from the 14th century, or possibly from the 15th, are 94 stanzas in Kashmiri that occur in a work of Indian philosophy, the Sanskrit book *Mahanaya-prakasha (Illumination of the Highest Attainment)*. Kashmiri is spoken in Jammu and Kashmir state, northern India.

3523. Maithili writing of importance was the 14th-century *Varna-ratnakara*, by Jyotishvara. Maithili, one of several languages spoken in the Bihar state of India, was for centuries a language used by scholars.

3524. Vietnamese writing began to appear in the 15th century, after the development of a script based on Chinese characters that was used by the poets Nguyen Trai, Emperor Le Thanh Tong, and Nguyen Binh Khiem. A romanized script was adopted in the 17th century.

3525. Estonian writing known dates from the 1520s, when it was used in the text of the Kullamaa prayers. The first prose work in Estonian, from 1535, was a version of the Lutheran Church's catechism, translated from German. Estonian is one of the family of Uralic languages from northeastern Europe and northern Asia.

3526. Rumanian writing was used in the 15th and 16th centuries for translating Slavonic religious texts. The two main branches of Rumanian are Daco-Rumanian (spoken in Rumania and Moldova), of which the earliest written example dates from 1521, and Aromanian (spoken in parts of Greece, Albania, Bulgaria, and Yugoslavia), which is first recorded in 1731.

3527. Scottish Gaelic collection of writings was the *Book of the Dean of Lismore*, compiled by two brothers, Duncan MacGregor and James MacGregor, and completed in 1526, though containing material some 200 years older. The collection included heroic ballads and bardic poems by Scottish and Irish poets. The first printed book in Scottish Gaelic was *Foirm na Nurrnuidheadh*, a translation by Bishop John Carswell of liturgical materials by the Protestant reformer John Knox. It was published in 1567.

3528. Punjabi writing was the *Janam-sakhi (Life Story)*, a collection of anecdotes about the life of Guru Nanak, the founder of the Sikh religion. It was compiled by his follower Bala some years after Nanak's death in 1539. A special alphabet, Gurmukhi, was invented by Nanak's successor, Guru Angad, to be used for writing Sikh scriptures in Punjabi. The language is spoken in northwestern India and Pakistan.

3529. Finnish writing was used in a primer that was published circa 1543 by Mikael Agricola, Finland's first Lutheran bishop. Literature in the Finnish language, one of the Uralic languages, is considered to date from Agricola's translation of the New Testament in 1548.

LANGUAGE—TEXTS—*continued*

3530. Lithuanian writing was a catechism published in 1547 in Königsberg, East Prussia (now Kaliningrad, Russia). The author was Martynas Mazvydas. A second catechism was published in 1595 by Mikalojus Dauksa, whose prayerbook in Lithuanian was issued in 1599. Lithuanian grammars by Danielius Kleinas appeared in 1653 and 1654.

3531. Nahuatl grammar was published in Mexico in 1547 by Andres de Olmo. Nahuatl, the classical version of the Nahua Uto-Aztecan language family, was the spoken tongue of the Aztec civilization.

3532. Urdu writing was used for the poetry composed in the 16th century in the kingdoms of Golconda and Bijapur in India. Urdu developed as a literary language from Hindustani under the strong influence of Persian, and is now the official language of Pakistan.

3533. Tagalog writing appeared in Christian texts printed by the Spanish after their conquest of the Philippines in the 16th century. Probably the first significant work of modern fiction in Tagalog was *Florante at Laura,* an epic romance written by Francisco Balagtas in the early 19th century.

3534. Latvian writing of importance was a catechistic work, the *Catechismus Catholicorum,* which appeared in 1585. A dictionary of Latvian by Georgius Mancelius was published in 1638, and a Latvian grammar, by Johann Georg Rehehausen, in 1644.

3535. Swahili writing was written in Arabic script and dates from 1652. The first known epic poem in Swahili was the *Hamziya,* a court poem in the Kingozi dialect, commissioned by Bwana Mkuw II, king of the island of Pate, near present-day Kenya. It was composed by Sayyid Aidarusi in 1749. The first novel was *Uhuru wa Watumwa (Freedom for the Slaves),* a work of historical fiction by James Mbotela, published in 1934.

3536. Grammar and primer in an indigenous North American language were aids to the teaching of the Algonkian language spoken by the Native Americans of the Massachusetts area, prepared by the Puritan minister John Eliot, pastor of the church at Roxbury in the Massachusetts Bay Colony (now part of Boston, MA, USA), and printed at Cambridge by Marmaduke Johnson. The grammar, a 66-page work that was published in 1666, was entitled *The Indian Grammar Begun; or, an Essay to Bring the Indian Language into Rules, for the Help of Such as Desire to Learn the Same, for the Furtherance of Gospel Among Them.* The primer, published in 1669, was *The Indian Primer; or, The Way of Training Up of Our Indian Youth in the Good Knowledge of God, in the Knowledge of the Scriptures and in an Ability to Read.* This may have been a republication of an earlier edition printed in Cambridge by Samuel Green in 1653, of which no copies have survived. The Algonkian language was represented by English characters.

3537. Pashto writing appeared in the lyric poems written by Khushhal Khan Khatak, chief of the Pashtun Khatak tribe in the 17th century and its leader in wars against the Mughal rulers of India. Pashto is one of two official languages of modern Afghanistan.

3538. Slovak writing emerged after the scholar Anton Bernolák published his grammar of Slovak in 1790. The first piece of noteworthy literature was *Slávy dcera (The Daughter of Sláva),* by Jan Kollár, a sonnet cycle that celebrated Slavic culture and unity.

3539. Hausa writing dates from the reign (1804–17) of Usman dan Fodio (Uthman ibn Fudi), Muslim founder of the Fulani empire in what is now Nigeria. The earliest works, which were written using Arabic characters, addressed various religious, legal, and political disputes.

3540. Native North American language to be given its own written form was the Cherokee language. The inventor of its written form was Sikwayi (also called Sequoyah), a Cherokee silversmith born circa 1776 in the East Tennessee settlement of Tuskegee. His father was Nathaniel Gist, a French trader. Sikwayi, though illiterate, was fascinated by books, and understood the immense advantage that a system of writing gave to European settlers. Over many years, he developed a syllabary in which 85 characters derived from English, Hebrew, and Greek were assigned to serve as symbols for Cherokee sounds, allowing the Cherokee to write in their own language for the first time. Although his writing was at first considered witchcraft, the syllabary was adopted by the Tribal Council in 1821 and was used to produce the first Native North American newspaper in 1828. Specimens of Sikwayi's writings are preserved in the Sequoyah Birthplace Museum near Vonore, TN, USA.

3541. Xhosa writing appeared in South Africa in the mid-19th century, when the Lovedale Missionary Institution, based in Glasgow, Scotland, set up a printing press at Alice. The first collection of poetry, published in 1927, was *Imihobe nemibongo (Songs of Joy and Lullabies)*, by Samuel Edward Krune Mqhayi, who was also the author of early volumes of history, biography, and fiction.

3542. Yoruba writing emerged after 1875, when the Church Missionary Society, operating in Lagos, Nigeria, developed a standardized script. It was first used in a translation of the Christian Bible, completed in 1900. The first book of poetry in Yoruba, J. Sobowole Sowande's *Iwe Ekini Sobo (Sobo's First Book)*, was published five years later. The first novel was *Ogboju Ode Ninu Igbo Irunmale (The Forest of a Thousand Demons)*, by the Yoruba chief Daniel Olorunfemi Fagunwa, published in 1938.

3543. Zulu writing dates from the early years of the 20th century. The first novel, *Insila ka Shaka (The Bodyservant of King Shaka)*, was published in South Africa in 1930. Its author, John Langalibalele Dube, was the first president general (from 1912) of the South African Native National Congress, forerunner of the African National Congress, and a prominent educator and journalist.

3544. Somali writing began to be published in Somalia in the 1950s and 60s. Cali Xuseen Xirsi was the first author to produce written, rather than oral, poetry. In 1974 Faarax M.I. Cawl produced the first novel of note, *Aqoondarro waa u nacab jacayl (Ignorance Is the Enemy of Love)*.

LANGUAGE—TEXTS—ARABIC

3545. Arabic book was the Qur'an, the holy book of Islam. The edition that is read today is based on the compilation of Zayd ibn Thabit, one of Muhammad's secretaries, who was commissioned by the caliph Uthman ibn Affan (also known as Uthmar or Othmar) to create an authoritative text. It was issued circa 651. Since recitation of the Qur'an in Arabic is a religious requirement, the language was introduced to many new areas with the spread of Islam and was adopted as the official language in many parts of North Africa and the Middle East.

3546. Dictionary of Arabic was the *Kitab al-ayn (Book Beginning With the Letter Ayn)*, compiled by the Arab philologist al-Khalil ibn Ahmad in Basra (in modern Iraq) circa 750.

3547. Arab poet to write in a colloquial style was Abu al-Atahiyah, born Abu Ishaq Isma'il ibn al-Qasim ibn Suwayd ibn Kaysan in al-Kufah, a village in what is now Iraq. His pseudonym means "father of craziness." His lack of education enabled him to avoid poetic convention and to adopt a freer mode of expression. The poems of his later years were collected in the *Zuhdiyat* some 250 years after his death in 826.

LANGUAGE—TEXTS—CHINESE

3548. Chinese writing originated during the Shang dynasty, China's first historically documented era, which lasted from approximately 1760 BCE to 1100 BCE. Tortoise shells and ox bones from that period carry inscriptions of family names and similar records, as well as questions posed to the gods.

3549. Chinese prose work is likely to have been the *I Ching (Book of Changes)*, a collection of 64 hexagrams that were intended as an aid to divination, together with suggested interpretations and commentaries. The hexagrams are combinations of solid lines (representing *yang*, the male cosmic principle) and dotted lines (representing *yin*, the female cosmic principle), whose interactions are thought to represent all possibilities. The oldest part of the *I Ching* is attributed to Wen-wang, ruler of the ancient state of Chou, who is said to have written it between 1144 and 1141 BCE, during his imprisonment by the last ruler of the Shang dynasty.

3550. Book of poetry in a Chinese language was the *Shi Jing (Book of Poetry)*, a collection of 305 poems drawn from oral tradition. It formed an important part of the program of education propounded by Kongfuzi (Confucius) in the fifth century BCE. Scholars believe that the poems were written down over a long period from the twelfth century to the seventh century BCE, when they were first compiled, and that they continued to undergo changes until the era of Kongfuzi. They fall into four main types: folk ballads, festivity chants, historical poems, and temple hymns.

3551. Poet in a Chinese language known by name was Qu Yuan, a courtier from a noble family of the southern state of Ch'u. He was the author of some 25 works, of which the most famous is *Li Sao (The Lament)*. This was an autobiographical poem describing his downfall at the hands of his political enemies, which cost him his position at court, and recounting his wanderings through legendary and magical realms. Qu Yuan died in 278 BCE.

LANGUAGE—TEXTS—CHINESE—*continued*

3552. Woman poet in a Chinese language of note was Ts'ai Yen (Wen-chi), who lived at the turn of the first century CE. She was the author of the 108-line poem *Pei-fen Shih (The Lamentation)*, the first to be written in the five-word *shih* style. The poem vividly describes her experiences as a captive of the invading Tartars, who kept her as a hostage for twelve years, during which she bore two children as the wife of a Tartar chieftain, until she was ransomed by a family friend.

LANGUAGE—TEXTS—FRENCH

3553. French writing was used in 842 in the Oaths of Strasbourg, an agreement confirming the alliance of Louis the German and Charles the Bald against Lothair. The three of them were brothers, the sons of King Louis I and the grandsons of Charlemagne, whose Holy Roman Empire was in dispute among them. The Oaths were made public in two versions, one German and the other French. According to some scholars, the second version was actually in a form of Latin. If so, the first writing in Old French is a translation, made in 882, of a Latin text on the life of St. Eulalia by the poet Aurelius Clemens Prudentius.

3554. Woman poet to write in French was Marie de France, a French-born author who probably lived in England. Her collection of love stories in verse, *Lais*, appeared circa 1170, and her collection of fables, *Ysopet*, in 1180. Her poetry was the model for the "Breton lay," a romantic tale with magical and mythological aspects, which became popular in both French and English literature.

3555. Prose works in the French language were two tales dating from about 1200, *Joseph d'Arimathie* and *Merlin*. Both had originally been composed in verse by the poet Robert de Borron, and both concerned aspects of the Holy Grail and Arthur legends.

3556. Novel in the French language is considered to be *Petit Jehan de Saintré*, a romance of the Anjou court, written by Antoine de la Sale and published in 1456.

LANGUAGE—TEXTS—GERMAN

3557. German writing was a translation of parts of the New Testament into Gothic, made circa 375 by Ulfilas (or Wulfila), bishop of the Goths and Visigoths, whom he converted to the Arian form of Christianity (in which Jesus is not considered identical with, or equal to, God). He invented the Gothic alphabet for the purpose. Old High German, the ancestor of modern German, emerged about four hundred years later, when it was used both for the translation of Christian texts and for the recording of pagan hymns and stories.

3558. Woman poet to write in German was Hrosvitha, a Benedictine nun from a highborn Saxon family. Beginning circa 960, she began writing plays on Christian themes, in Latin, that were intended to be read by the nuns with whom she lived in the convent at Gandersheim, Germany. She also wrote histories, biographies of saints, and Christian legends in verse.

3559. German prose work of importance was *Der Ackermann aus Böhmen (Death and the Plowman)*, written circa 1400 by Johannes von Tepl in Prague, now in the Czech Republic. The book is in the form of an argument between a plowman—who stands for every man—and Death, with God as the judge of their rhetorical success.

LANGUAGE—TEXTS—GREEK

3560. Greek writing known to archeologists developed on the island of Crete, where a local script called Linear A, used for writing the local Minoan language, was adapted for use with Greek. Inscriptions in this script, called Linear B, appear on pottery vases made in Crete circa 1500 BCE and on clay tablets from both Crete and mainland Greece. The script was syllabic, rather than alphabetic. The decipherment of this script in 1952 by two British scholars, Michael Ventris and John Chadwick, is considered one of the great feats of linguistics. The first known inscription written in alphabetic Greek was discovered on a wine jug from Athens dating to circa 740 BCE. It reads: "Whoever of all dancers performs most nimbly will win this vase as a prize."

3561. Greek prose work aside from law codes dating from the seventh century BCE was the cosmographical work *Heptamychos* by Pherecydes of Soros, one of the Seven Wise Men of Greece, who lived in the mid-sixth century BCE. He is said to have been the teacher of the great mathematician and philosopher Pythagoras and to have originated, in the West, the idea of metempsychosis, or transmigration of souls.

LANGUAGE—TEXTS—HEBREW

3562. Hebrew writing known consists of inscriptions from the twelfth century BCE. The earliest substantial text is the Gezer Calendar, a description of the agricultural year that was written in Gezer, Israel, in the late tenth century BCE, the era of King Solomon.

3563. Dictionary in the Hebrew language was the *Makhberet*, a lexicon of the Torah and other biblical books compiled by the poet and philologist Menakhem ben Saruq in Córdoba, Moorish Spain, circa 950.

3564. Printed book in Hebrew is thought by scholars to have been a commentary on the Torah by the 13th-century Spanish scholar Rabbi Moshe ben Nakhman (known as the Ramban, or Nachmanides), printed by Manasseh Obadiah and Benjamin of Rome between 1469 and 1472, probably at Rome, Italy. The first to carry a date of publication was the *Perush ha-Torah*, the commentary on the Torah by the twelfth-century French scholar Rabbi Shlomo Yitzhaqi (known as Rashi), printed at Reggio di Calabria by Abraham ben Garton ben Yitzhak, and completed on February 17, 1475. It was followed shortly thereafter by a code of Jewish law, the *Arba Turim* of Jacob ben Asher, whose four volumes were completed at Piovi di Sacco on July 3, 1475, by Meshullam Cusi and his sons.

LANGUAGE—TEXTS—JAPANESE

3565. Japanese writing known, dating from circa 440 CE, is an inscription written on a sword. Until the ninth or tenth century, the Japanese made use Chinese script, modified and adapted in a variety of ways. They then developed two syllabic systems, *hiragana* and *katakana*, in which the Chinese characters were simplified and given phonetic values. *Hiragana*, particularly, was the favored script of educated women at court. Both systems, augmented by Chinese characters where needed, are used in modern Japanese.

3566. Collection of poetry in Japanese was the *Manyoshu (Collection of Ten Thousand Leaves)*, an anthology of some 4,500 poems in the short *tanka* and long *choka* forms. It was compiled sometime after the year 759.

LANGUAGE—TEXTS—LATIN

3567. Latin writing known is a four-word inscription in Greek characters on a cloak pin called the Praeneste Fibula, which has been identified as a Roman object from the seventh century BCE. The inscription reads *manios:med:fhefhaked:numasioi*, which means "Manius made me for Numerius." Latin evolved from Etruscan.

3568. Epic translated into Latin was the *Odyssia* (circa 235 BCE), a translation into traditional Roman Saturnian verse of Homer's *Odyssey*. The author was Lucius Livius Andronicus, a freed Greek slave who is often called the "father of Roman literature." It was probably written as a school text to introduce Roman students to Greek literature. Andronicus himself is the first known teacher of Latin.

3569. Epic composed in Latin was the *Annales*, which recounts the history of Rome from the time of its legendary founding by Aeneas. For many years it was honored as Rome's national epic. Its author was Quintus Ennius, who also wrote numerous tragic plays modeled on those of the Greeks, as well as epigrams that are the first elegiac couplets ever written. Ennius, born in southern Italy, was made a Roman citizen in 184 BCE and is considered the founder of Latin literature.

LANGUAGE—TEXTS—SANSKRIT

3570. Sanskrit text and the oldest of the sacred Hindu writings of India is the *Rig Veda (Wisdom of the Verses)*, a collection of 1,028 hymns recited by priests during fire sacrifice. It is divided into ten books, each composed by a different sage. Books two through seven date approximately from 1200 BCE. The others were composed over the course of several centuries. These hymns are considered to have been divinely revealed. Later forms of Vedic literature include *Brahmanas*, explanations of rites and sacrifices, and metaphysical or philosophical texts known as *Aranyakas* and *Upanishads*.

3571. Sanskrit grammar was the *Astadhyayi*, by Panini, a scholar of the fifth century BCE. This book, probably the first extant grammar of any language, was a comprehensive study of Vedic Sanskrit, an Indian language that had developed over the course of some 1,400 years and that had been used in the composition of the *Vedas*, the earliest Hindu sacred texts.

LANGUAGE—TEXTS—YIDDISH

3572. Printed text in Yiddish was *Almekhtiger Got (Almighty God)*, a translation of the Passover hymn *Addir Hu*, which was printed at the end of a Passover Haggadah that was published in Prague (in the modern Czech Republic) in 1526.

LANGUAGE—TEXTS—YIDDISH—*continued*

3573. Yiddish writing consists of glosses added in the mid-eleventh century in the margins and between the lines of Hebrew bibles and commentaries. The first complete sentence extant was a rhymed blessing written in a *makhzor,* or prayer book for holy days, from the German city of Worms, dated 1272–73. Manuscripts in Yiddish, including glossaries of the language, appeared in the late 14th century.

3574. Yiddish play to be performed was *Serkele,* written in 1826 by Shloyme Etinger (also spelled Solomon Ettinger) and first performed by students at the rabbinical academy in Zhitomir, the Ukraine. The text of the play was not published until 1861.

3575. Yiddish literary annual was *Die Yiddishe Folkbibliothek (The Yiddish Folk Anthology),* published in Kiev, the Ukraine, in 1888–89. The editor was Sholem Aleichem (born Sholem Yakov Rabinowitz), often called "the Jewish Mark Twain" for his sharply observant tales, rich in vernacular humor, of life in the Jewish villages of Eastern Europe. *Die Yiddishe Folkbibliothek* published the works of, among others, the classic Yiddish authors Sholem Abramovitz and Yoyel Linetski. Sholem Aleichem also wrote the first children's fiction in Yiddish, the story cycle *Motl Peyse dem Khazns (Adventures of Mottel, the Cantor's Son).* The first Motl story appeared in 1907.

LANGUAGE—WRITING IMPLEMENTS

3576. Seals for fastening and recording originated in the fifth millennium BCE in the preliterate culture of Mesopotamia, where they were used to identify containers, such as jars and sacks. The seal, bearing a particular mark or symbol, was pressed into a piece of clay that had been molded over the jar stopper or around the rope by which the sack was tied.

3577. Stylus for inscribing marks on wet clay tablets was made from sharpened reeds in Sumer circa 3500 BCE. The Sumerians had a patron goddess of writing and accounting, Nissaba, who was originally the goddess of grass plants, including reeds.

3578. Ink was invented by the Egyptians sometime in the 28th century BCE. It consisted of carbon soot mixed with gelatin from boiled animal hides. This preparation was formed into sticks, which were liquified in water as needed.

3579. Brush and ink for writing were employed by the Chinese at least as early as circa 1000 BCE, and are still the preferred tools for writing Chinese characters.

3580. Reed pen was invented circa 300 BCE, by the Egyptians, who used papyrus and other reeds, sharpened at one end, to write with ink on papyrus paper.

3581. Metal pen was known in Roman times. A bronze pen-point was found during the 19th-century excavation of Pompeii, Italy, the Roman town that was buried in a volcanic eruption in 79 CE.

3582. Quill pen cut from the tail or wing feather of a large bird, typically a goose, may be as old as the reed pen, but the first mention of one in literature is in the *Etymologiae (Etymologies)* of St. Isidore of Seville, an encyclopedia and glossary dating from circa 600.

3583. Depiction of a lead pencil was a woodcut of a carved wooden lead-holder holding a piece of sharpened graphite, shown in a 1565 book by the Swiss naturalist and encyclopedist Conrad Gesner. Gesner was also the first to identify graphite (compressed carbon) as a separate mineral.

3584. Pencil factory was opened by the entrepreneur Friedrich Städtler in Nuremberg (Nürnberg), Germany, in 1660.

3585. Typewriter patent was issued on January 7, 1714, by Queen Anne of England to inventor Henry Mill for a device capable of reproducing handwriting in a form similar to printing. The machine was never built and few details of its construction are known.

3586. Rubber eraser possibly originated in Portugal circa 1725, but the first verifiable mention of a rubber eraser dates from 1752, when a member of the Académie Française suggested that caoutchouc gum (a natural rubber produced by the South American rubber tree, *Hevea brasiliensis*) was useful for erasing black marks on paper. The term *rubber,* coined in 1770 by the English chemist Joseph Priestley, derives from this use.

3587. Patent on colored ink was issued in England in 1772.

3588. Steel pen point capable of being manufactured by machine was invented in 1828 by John Mitchell of Birmingham, England. His design, though durable, lacked flexiblity and was hard to write with. It was improved in 1830 by another Englishman, James Perry, who added a central and two side slits that gave additional pliability to the nib.

3589. Pencil with an attached eraser was patented by Hyman L. Lipman of Philadelphia, PA, USA, who received a U.S. patent on March 30, 1858. The pencil had a groove into which was "secured a piece of prepared rubber, glued in at one end."

3590. Typewriter that was practical was invented in 1867 by Christopher Latham Sholes of Milwaukee, WI, USA. The machine was patented in the United States on June 23, 1868, and was known commercially as The Type-Writer, a word coined by Sholes. This machine had a movable carriage, a lever for turning paper from line to line, and a converging type bar. The keyboard, similar to that of a piano, had two rows of black walnut keys with letters painted in white. The machine had all the letters in capitals, figures from 2 to 9, a comma, and a period. It was manufactured by E. Remington and Sons of Ilion, NY, USA, under contract dated March 1, 1873. The first machine was completed on September 12, 1873. A few years later, the firm sold its typewriter business to Wyckoff, Seamans and Benedict, who afterward organized the Remington Typewriter Company.

3591. Typewriter to be marketed was that of the Danish inventor Malling Hansen. In October 1870, a Copenhagen firm introduced the "Skrivekugle," a commercial typewriter based on his design.

3592. Fountain pen that was practical was invented by Lewis Edson Waterman and was manufactured in 1884 by the L.E. Waterman Company in New York, NY, USA. The first year, about 200 fountain pens were manufactured. They were originally manufactured by hand. Waterman also invented the machinery to produce fountain pens in commercial quantities.

3593. Ballpoint pen was patented on October 30, 1888, by John J. Loud of Weymouth, MA, USA. The patent was on a pen having a spheroidal marking point capable of revolving in all directions.

3594. Stenography machine to be commercially viable was the Stenotype, invented in 1906 by an American court reporter, Ward Stone Ireland. The machine had 22 silent keys that were pressed in various combinations to create letter groups and abbreviations.

3595. Mechanical pencil was the Ever-Sharp Pencil, invented in 1915 by Hayakawa Tokuji of Japan. In 1912 Hayakawa founded a metalworks company to make snap buckles, later called the Sharp Corporation after the pencil, his most successful early product. After World War II Sharp became better known as an electronics manufacturer.

3596. Ballpoint pen widely used was the Biro, developed in 1938 and patented on June 10, 1943, by Lazlo Biro, a Hungarian expatriate living in Buenos Aires, Argentina. The Biro boasted a smooth writing action owing to its accurately ground ball, which rotated smoothly in a brass seat, and was preferred by air crews because it was not affected by changes in atmospheric pressure and could write at any angle. However, the ink used in the early Biros was too heavy, causing the pen to skip. Biro sold the United States patent rights during World War II to the Eversharp Company.

3597. Correction fluid for typists was invented by an American, Betsy Nesmith, in 1951. As a typist working with a new IBM typewriter, she sought a means of obscuring smudges and errors, and developed a white tempera paint that covered black typewriter ink and dried quickly on paper. Later she founded the Liquid Paper Company to market her product.

3598. Felt-tip pen was the Pentel, marketed in 1960 by the Stationery Company of Tokyo, Japan.

3599. Computerized pen was patented in 1998 by a British company, British Telecommunications Plc in Surrey, England. The instrument, called a "Smartquill," used a spatial sensor and built-in handwriting recognition software to read its owner's writing. The writing could be recorded as an electronic text file for transmission to a desktop computer, printer, modem, or advanced mobile telephone.

M

MAPS AND CHARTS

3600. Maps of record were made by the Babylonians on clay tablets. The earliest known was found at Nuzi, Iraq, and dates to circa 2300 BCE, probably during the reign of Sargon. It shows towns and topographical features, and indicates three of the four cardinal directions, north, east, and west.

MAPS AND CHARTS—*continued*

3601. City map was that of the Sumerian city of Nippur (modern Niffer, Iraq). American archeologists from the University of Pennsylvania excavated the city from 1889 to 1900 and found a clay tablet, dating from circa 1500 BCE, that showed the walls, moat, parks, and gates of the city and identified the important temples.

3602. Road map was drawn circa 1150 BCE in Egypt. It shows the gold mines worked by Egypt between the Nile and the Red Sea. Roads, houses, and religious sanctuaries are indicated by name; the mines and other features are shown in color.

3603. World map is traditionally considered to be the work of the Greek philosopher and astronomer Anaximander of Miletus (now in Turkey), who circa 550 BCE engraved a circular map of the known world on a stone tablet. The map is only known from references in later Greek works.

3604. Periplus for mariners, describing coastal waters and landmarks, was written in Massilia (now Marseille, France) circa 525 BCE. It showed routes and harbors along the Atlantic coast. The earliest periplus still extant dates from circa 350 BCE and describes the coast of the Mediterranean, parts of the Atlantic coast in modern Spain and Morocco, and a large part of the Black Sea coast. It is attributed, erroneously, to the Greek explorer Scylax of Caryanda, who lived 150 years before.

3605. World map still extant was created by the Babylonians in Iraq circa 500 BCE. The clay tablet contains a circular map depicting Babylonia and two adjacent kingdoms surrounded by an ocean and several unknown islands. At the center of the map is the city of Babylon.

3606. Time-series graphic dates from circa 1000 and appears in a European astronomy text. It plots the inclinations of the sun, moon, and known planets over a 30-month period. It is the first known graphic to show values changing over time.

3607. Sea chart of southern Asian and Indian waters was a sailing chart, the earliest known Chinese map of the seas, that portrays the seventh voyage (1431–33) of the admiral and diplomat Zheng He (or Cheng Ho). The chart shows his voyage beginning in the Chinese city of Nanking and reaching ports along the Arabian and east African coasts. In addition to sea routes, the chart contains detailed sailing instructions and is remarkably accurate at depicting the coasts of China and nearby regions of Asia.

3608. Map of any part of the Americas may be the Vinland Map, a chart tentatively dated to circa 1440. It contains a representation of Greenland and a jagged island labeled as "Island of Vinland, discovered by Bjarni and Leif in company." The labeled island corresponds to the area of Newfoundland, Canada, where Vikings under Leif Eriksson settled circa 1000. The map's authenticity has been a matter of sharp debate among experts. Scientists have used various methods to determine the actual age of its parchment and ink, with contradictory results. Proton-beam analyses performed in 1995–96 by Thomas Cahill of the University of California, Davis, appeared to confirm that the Vinland Map is not a hoax but is the same age as the *Tartar Relation,* a set of 15th-century documents with which it was discovered sometime in the first part of the 20th century. The map first came to the attention of scholars after it was purchased in 1957 by American arts patron Paul Mellon from a rare book dealer in Geneva, Switzerland. Mellon gave the map to Yale University Press, which in 1965 published *The Vinland Map and the Tartar Relation,* the first book to contain a depiction of the map. The book was co-authored by R.A. Skelton, superintendent of the British Museum Map Room, George R. Painter, the British Museum's assistant keeper of printed books, and Thomas Marston, curator of Medieval and Renaissance Literature at Yale University.

3609. Modern treatise on geography was written circa 1440 by the Italian architect and mathematician Leon Battista Alberti. It included his explanation of methods for surveying and mapping the city of Rome.

3610. Printed map in Europe was the so-called "T-O" map of St. Isidore of Avila, Spain, pictured in his multivolume encyclopedia *Etymologiae (Etymologies),* written circa 600. A woodcut of the map was included in the first printed edition of the work, which appeared in Augsburg (now in Germany) in 1472. The T-O map is in the form of a circle enclosing a T. The inside of the circle is divided by the T into thirds representing the continents of Asia, Europe, and Africa. The circle is the Encircling Ocean (the Atlantic, Indian, and Pacific Oceans) and the T is the Mediterranean Sea.

3611. Ephemeris was *Ephemerides,* published by the German astronomer Regiomontanus (Johann Müller) in Nuremberg in 1474. It contained tables of the daily positions of the celestial bodies and was intended for use by navigators and astronomers.

3612. Terrestrial globe extant was constructed by the German mapmaker Martin Behaim, who had received a commission for it from the city council of his hometown of Nuremberg. The globe was built over the course of a year and was finished in 1492. It was a hollow shell about 20 inches (50 centimeters) in diameter. Maps in six colors, drawn by painter Georg Glockenthon, were pasted around the exterior. Behaim's globe showed a number of mythical islands and an enlarged Asia separated from western Europe only by a narrow body of water, much as Columbus expected to find. It was known in Germany as Behaim's *Erdapfel* ("earth apple"). Globes are thought to have been constructed in antiquity by the Greeks, but no examples survive.

3613. Map showing the Spanish discoveries in the New World was a world map, dated to 1500, drawn by Juan de la Cosa, a Spanish navigator and geographer. Cosa sailed with Christopher Columbus on his second voyage in 1493 and on a later voyage to the northeastern coast of South America in 1499. His world map showed the Caribbean Sea and the route of John Cabot's voyage to Canada.

3614. Map to use the name "America" for the New World was in the *Cosmographiae Introductio,* a world map by the geographer Martin Waldseemüller (also called Ilacomilus or Hylacomylus) of Württemberg (now Germany) In April 1507, at St. Dié in the Vosges Mountains of Alsace, Waldseemüller printed one thousand copies of the map using twelve woodcut blocks. The book contained an account by the Italian explorer Amerigo (Americus) Vespucci of his discoveries in South America. Waldseemüller labeled the New World "America" in his honor.

3615. Map to name North and South America was published by Gerardus Mercator in Germany in 1537. The map was shaped like two hearts, one pointing up showing the Western Hemisphere, and one pointing down showing the Eastern Hemisphere.

3616. Maps showing Australia were prepared with the help of Portuguese mariners well before the Dutch explorers who visited in the late 17th century. The *Boke of Idrography* (1542) by Frenchman Jean Rotz, a leading member of the Dieppe school of cartographers, showed a large land mass called "Java-la-Grande" in the area of the Pacific where Australia would be. The maps show coastal place names in Portuguese and attach Portuguese flags to the land, indicating that the information had been conveyed from Portuguese explorers who had charted the northern coast of Australia.

3617. Mercator projection was invented by Gerardus Mercator, born Gerhard Kremer in 1512 in Rupelmonde, Flanders (now Belgium). With two associates, the mathematician Gemma Frisius and the master engraver Gaspar a Myrica, Mercator published a series of popular globes and maps and developed a new projection geometry for flat maps in which the lines of longitude and latitude were always at right angles to each other—a great convenience for navigators plotting a course. The first world map incorporating the Mercator projection was published in Germany in 1569.

3618. Atlas of the modern type was the 1570 collection *Theatrum orbis terrarum (Epitome of the Theater of the World)* of Abraham Ortelius, a cartographer, engraver, and book dealer in Antwerp, Belgium. It contained 70 maps engraved in a uniform style. Ortelius borrowed the concept from Gerardus Mercator, who first used the term *atlas* to mean a book of maps or charts. On the cover of his map folios, Mercator printed a picture of Atlas, the Greek Titan who bore the world on his shoulders.

3619. Map of the Alps to show accurate placement and topography of individual mountains was prepared in 1578 by Johannes Stumpf, a geographer and doctor living in Berne, Switzerland. It was the first map to show the names of such peaks as the Eiger, the Jungfrau, and the Schreckhorn.

3620. Meteorological map of the world to be published was prepared in 1686 by Edmond Halley, the English astronomer. It displayed the direction and distribution of prevailing winds over the oceans.

3621. Mapping survey of a country was conducted in France by Cesar-François Cassini in 1744.

3622. Map of the moon was was published in 1647 in the *Selenographia,* by Johannes Hevelius (born Jan Heweliusz) of Gdansk, Poland. Earlier moon drawings had been made by many astronomers, starting with Galileo in 1609, but Hevelius's map was the first to depict the entire visible surface of the moon in detail. The first map containing many of the names we use today for lunar features, such as Mare Tranquilitatis (Sea of Tranquility), was made by the Italian Jesuit astronomer Giovanni Battista Riccioli and published in his *Almagestum novum* (1651).

MAPS AND CHARTS—*continued*

3623. Weather maps were made by the German explorer and naturalist Friedrich Wilhelm Karl Heinrich Alexander von Humboldt during his 1799 exploration of the Orinoco River basin in Venezuela. At regular intervals each day, Humboldt measured the air temperature, used his thermometer to estimate the altitude (the higher the land, the lower the temperature at which water boils), and took compass readings of his position. The isothermic charts he drew of his results were the first weather maps.

3624. Epidemic map was prepared by the English physician John Snow, who used a street map of central London to plot neighborhood deaths from cholera for September 1854. He used a dot to indicate each address where a death occurred. The greatest number of dots were clustered around the location of a water pump on Broad Street, indicating the source of the epidemic. Snow removed the pump's handle, preventing the further spread of the disease.

3625. International map of the world was proposed in 1891 by the International Geographic Union. The map was to be based on common world specifications with a scale of 1:1,000,000, and was to be prepared by cooperative effort of the union members. A similar resolution was adopted by the United Nations Economic and Social Council in 1953. A map meeting these specifications was not published until 1992, when the Digital Chart of the World was completed as a cooperative project by cartographic organizations in Australia, Canada, Great Britain, and the United States.

3626. Highly detailed map of Antarctica was prepared from 8,000 images gathered in the fall of 1997 by Radarsat, a Canadian earth-observing satellite employing synthetic aperture radar. The data revealed ice flows and rough terrain where earlier maps were featureless, and provided more clues to the exact shape of the Antarctic continent, which is buried under a thick layer of ice.

3627. Three-dimensional map of Mars was released publicly on May 27, 1999, by the U.S. National Aeronautics and Space Administration. The map, assembled from laser-ranging data collected by the Mars Global Surveyor orbiter, revealed an egg-shaped planet with a crater-pocked southern hemisphere and a relatively smooth northern hemisphere.

MAPS AND CHARTS—STAR CHARTS

3628. Portable star map known to astronomers is the Tunhuang manuscript, made in China circa 940.

3629. Printed astronomical charts were drawn by Su Sung in China circa 1064. He received his commission as a result of the Council of Kaifeng, a convention of four scholars (astronomer, meteorologist, chronicler, and astrologer) who met in that city in 1054 to discuss the appearance of a temporary "guest star" in the constellation known to them as Thiem-Kuan. This was the supernova that produced the Crab Nebula in the constellation known in the West as Taurus.

3630. Book of printed star charts was an Italian book, *De Le Stelle Fisse (Of the Fixed Stars)* by Alessandro Piccolomini, published in 1540. The stars were identified by letters.

3631. Star atlas to include coordinates was published in 1588 by Giovanni Paolo Gallucci.

MATERIALS—GLASS AND CERAMICS

3632. Pottery is the slab-built, cord-pattern ware of the Jomon culture of Japan, which dates to circa 10,000 BCE and first appeared on Kyushu, the southernmost of the four main Japanese islands.

3633. Potter's wheel is unknown, but a likely place of origin is China during the Neolithic age. Wheel-made pots have been found in archeological sites from the Ta-wen-k'ou culture, which appeared during the fifth millennium BCE. The people of Sumeria (modern Iraq) and Anatolia (modern Turkey) used the potter's wheel in the fourth millennium.

3634. Pottery kiln of the standard type, in which the vessels are separated from the fire, was developed in Mesopotamia circa 4000 BCE. The vessels were placed in a chamber with a perforated floor and the fire was built in a hearth directly below it.

3635. Synthetic material of any kind appears to be Egyptian faience, so-called because it was later produced in large quantities in Egypt, although it was originally created in Mesopotamia circa 4000 BCE. It was developed as a substitute for the vivid blue stone called lapis lazuli. It was made by dusting copper ore over a talc stone and firing them until they fused into a hard blue substance.

3636. Potter's wheel was invented circa 3250 BCE by the Sumerians, who lived in what is now southern Iraq. The earliest design was a simple tournette that was turned by hand. It may have been the earliest machine to use a wheel. The familiar kickwheel-powered potter's wheel was not invented until circa 400 BCE, possibly by the ancient Greeks.

3637. Glass objects known are beads found in Mesopotamia, at the Akkadian cities of Ur, Eridu, Eshnunna, and other sites. The oldest ones are dated to circa 2400 BCE.

3638. Glassmaking formula is contained in a tablet from Akkadia inscribed in the 17th century BCE. It was intended as a reference for other glassmakers, and was couched in obscure phrases as a way of keeping the formula a secret from the uninitiated. The formula was used to make the glass found in the ruins of the palace at Tell Atchana, Babylonia (now in Iraq), the residence of Hammurabi's son.

3639. Glass bottle known to archeologists dates from Egypt circa 1450 BCE and bears the cartouche of Thutmose III, a pharaoh of the 18th dynasty.

3640. Molded glass was developed in Alexandria, Egypt, circa 300 BCE.

3641. Blown glass artifacts were created by the Phoenicians in what is now Lebanon circa 10 BCE. The early glassblowers used a blowing iron, a tube about 5 feet (1.5 meters) long, to blow air into a ball of molten glass. As it expanded, the blob was rolled back and forth on a flat surface to give it shape, manipulated with another iron rod to make a handle or spout, or hot-fused with other glass shapes. This process is essentially the same as glass artisans use today.

3642. Window glass was produced by the ancient Romans. The first known example of window glass was a cast-glass bathhouse window found in the ruins of the town of Pompeii, buried in a volcanic eruption of August 24, 79 CE.

3643. Porcelain was developed in China beginning in the T'ang dynasty (circa 618–907 CE). True hard-paste (completely nonporous) porcelain was developed during the Yüan dynasty, circa 1279, from powdered *petuntse,* a feldspathic rock, mixed with kaolin clay.

3644. Stained glass on a large scale was used to create large windows in the choir and ambulatory of the Abbey of St.-Denis, near Paris, France, which was rebuilt between 1137 and 1144, according to the account of the Abbot Suger, who supervised the work. The large windows contained a series of medallions painted with religious scenes; the facade also contained a stained-glass rose window, probably the first in a church. Little of the original stained glass remains.

3645. Porcelain made for the Chinese imperial council was known as *shu fu,* after the Chinese characters for "central palace." The dishes were white, with a bluish glaze, and were made at Ching-te-chen during the Yüan dynasty, circa 1300.

3646. Glass factory in the Americas was established in 1592 in the town of Córdoba del Tucumán, Argentina. Most glass products from the factory, which included glassware and thick window panes, were made from broken glass originally fashioned in Europe.

3647. Cut glass was made by the ancient Romans, but in a fairly primitive form. Cut glass was developed to a high level of artistry circa 1600 by Caspar Lehmann, gem engraver to Emperor Rudolf II, in Prague, Bohemia (now capital of the Czech Republic). Lehmann worked heavy glass with cutting, grinding, and polishing wheels, scribers, chisels, and other tools, producing highly individual works that marked the beginning of the Baroque style known as "Bohemian glass." He received a patent for his cut-glass process in 1609.

3648. Porcelain manufactured in Europe was produced circa 1707 at the Meissen factory near Dresden in Saxony (now in Germany) by alchemist Johann Friedrich Böttger and physicist Ehrenfried Walter von Tschirnhaus (or von Schirnahaus). Deposits of kaolin (white china clay), the main ingredient in porcelain, had recently been discovered in Saxony. Böttger and von Tschirnhaus combined kaolin with a powder made from local feldspathic rocks to produce a true hard-paste (completely nonporous) porcelain formula similar to that long known in China. Meissen porcelain is also known as Dresden porcelain.

3649. Bone china was developed circa 1800 by Josiah Spode and Josiah Spode II at their pottery factory at Stoke-upon-Trent, Staffordshire, England. By adding bone ash to hard-paste porcelain, the Spodes produced china that was more resistant to chipping than standard porcelain.

3650. Glass fiber was invented in France in 1836 by Ignace Dubus-Bonnel, who received a patent for the "weaving of glass, pure or mixed with silk, wool, or linen, and made pliable by steam." He displayed the world's first woven glass fabrics at the 1839 Paris Exhibition. The draperies shrouding the hearse that carried Napoléon Bonaparte's ashes for reburial in Paris in 1840 were made of Dubus-Bonnel's glass fabric containing embedded metallic particles.

MATERIALS—GLASS AND CERAMICS—
continued

3651. Tempered glass manufacturing process was patented by the French glassmaker François Royer de la Bastie on June 13, 1874.

3652. Float glass was manufactured in 1959 by the Pilkington Brothers glass works in Doncaster, England. The float glass process, invented by Alastair Pilkington, was the first in which completely flat plate glass could be inexpensively produced without the need for grinding and polishing.

3653. Thermoplastic ceramics were developed in 1990 by Japanese materials scientist Fumihiro Wakai at the University of Osaka, with support from the Japanese chemical firm of Mitsubishi Kasei Kogyo KK. Heating the ceramic causes it to elongate.

MATERIALS—METALS

3654. Copper tools such as hammers and knives were fashioned circa 8000 BCE in part of Europe and Mesopotamia.

3655. Gold artifacts date from circa 4500 BCE and were found in Mesopotamian sites in what is now Iraq. Gold can be collected from the sand and gravel of streams and riverbeds in a nearly pure metallic state and is easily worked.

3656. Smelted artifacts were discovered at the site of Tepe Yahya, located northeast of Dowlatabad in southeastern Iran. The artifacts date from circa 3800 BCE and were probably produced by the accidental smelting of copper with tin, forming a new mixture—bronze—with better properties than copper alone.

3657. Bronze artifact known to archeologists is a bronze rod dating from circa 3700 BCE. It was found in the pyramid at Maydum (now Medum) in Egypt.

3658. Advanced bronze artifacts were unearthed by American and Thai archeologists in 1974 at the village of Ban Chiang Dao in northwest Thailand. They found graves containing a bronze spearhead, a bronze anklet, and bronze bracelets dated circa 3600 BCE, as much as 500 years before articles of similar quality were made in Mesopotamia.

3659. Iron artifacts are beads made from meteoric iron. They were found at Jirzah, Egypt, and date from before circa 3500 BCE.

3660. Welding of dissimilar metals dates from circa 3500 BCE. The two metals were fused by repeated hot hammering, folding, and rehammering. The process was employed in parts of Europe and Asia in making weapons and jewelry.

3661. Smelted iron artifact known to archeologists is a dagger blade set in a bronze hilt, known from fragments found at Tell al-Asmar (modern Eshnunna, Iraq) and dating from circa 2700 BCE.

3662. Wrought iron was probably invented by the Hittites of Anatolia (now Turkey) circa 1400 BCE. They smelted iron oxide with charcoal at high temperatures, producing an iron sponge with a small carbon content. The hot iron and slag was removed from the furnace and worked with a hammer to expel the slag and create a ductile mass of iron. Similar methods for forging wrought iron developed independently in Africa and southeast Asia.

3663. Metallurgy textbook was *De re metallica (On Metals)* by Georgius Agricola (born Georg Bauer), a scholar and scientist of Saxony (now in Germany). Published posthumously in 1556, it established the science of metallurgy and remained the standard text on the subject until the 19th century.

3664. Coke-smelted iron was produced in 1709 by ironmaster Abraham Darby in Coalbrookdale, England. Coke, a form of coal, burned hotter and more efficiently than charcoal, and yielded iron that could be cast into shapes with thin walls, such as steam-engine boilers.

3665. Isolation of platinum was made by Antonio de Ulloa, the Spanish metallurgist, in 1748. Deposits were first noted in the 16th century by Spanish miners in the alluvial deposits of the Río Pinto, Colombia. The name platinum comes from the Spanish *platina del Pinto,* silver of the Pinto.

3666. Nickel obtained in a pure sample was prepared by the Swedish chemist and mineralogist Axel Fredrik Cronstedt in 1751. He isolated the hard, silvery metal, now widely used as an alloy and in coinage, from an ore that German miners called Kupfernickel ("Old Nick's copper").

3667. Discovery of chromium was made in 1797 by the French chemist Nicolas-Louis Vauquelin in lead ore from Siberia. In 1798 he prepared a pure sample of the metal from the brilliantly colored mineral crocoite, naming the new metal chromium (from the Greek word *chromos,* or hue).

3668. Extraction of beryllium in its oxide form was made from a sample of beryl in 1798 by the French chemist Nicolas-Louis Vauquelin, professor of chemistry at the Paris Faculty of Medicine. The metal was formerly known as glucinium for its sweet taste (however, it is highly toxic in solution). Beryllium was first isolated in its pure state in 1828 by Friedrich Wöhler of Germany and Antoine Bussy of France.

3669. Aluminum was unknown in pure form to the ancients, but they did suspect the existence of a metal in common compounds found in clay. A small amount of the pure metal was first prepared in 1825 by the Danish physicist Hans Christian Oersted by reducing anhydrous aluminum chloride with potassium amalgam. In his report to the Royal Danish Academy, Oersted noted that his sample formed "a lump of metal which in color and luster somewhat resembles tin."

3670. Corrugated iron was invented in 1829 by Henry Robinson Palmer, an engineer with the London Dock Company. The sheets were manufactured by the firm of Richard Walker—Carpenter and Builder and were used to build dockside storage sheds in London, England. Corrugated iron could be adapted for walls, partitions, and doors, and was the first sheeting material useful for roofing.

3671. Aluminum in commercial quantities was produced by the French industrial chemist Henri Sainte-Claire Deville in 1854, at his plant near Paris. In 1855, bars of the metal were first displayed to the public at the Paris Exposition Universelle.

3672. Mass production of steel was made possible by the British industrialist and inventor Henry Bessemer, who announced it before the British Association for the Advancement of Science in Cheltenham, Gloucestershire, England, in 1856. The Bessemer process, in which air was blown into molten iron, was capable of producing large quantities of mild steel that could be used to fabricate plate, rod, and other metal parts that previously had been made of brittle cast iron, or that had been impossible to make from iron at all.

3673. Monel was developed in 1905 in New Jersey, USA, and is now a trademark of the International Nickel Company of Canada. Monel, an alloy of nickel and copper in a ration of 66 percent to 31.5 percent (with trace amounts of other metals), is noted for its resistance to seawater corrosion.

3674. Stainless steel was discovered accidentally in 1914 by British metallurgist Harry Brearley. Brearley had been experimenting with various steel alloys for Sheffield cutlery manufacturers and was in the habit of discarding samples in a scrap heap outside his shop. Some months later, he noticed that one sample, an alloy of 0.4 percent carbon and 13 percent chromium, was still uncorroded. This was the first of a line of chromium-based stainless steels, the most common of which is the 18/8 grade, steel containing 18 percent chromium, 8 percent nickel, and 0.2 percent carbon.

3675. Factory to obtain uranium from gold was built in 1952 at Krugersdorp, South Africa, a mining and industrial center where gold was first discovered in 1887. The plant closed in the mid-1980s, when the major gold ore deposits in the region had been worked out and the world market for uranium declined.

MATERIALS—MINERALS

3676. Mineralogy textbook was *De natura fossilium (On Natural Fossils)* published in 1546 by Georgius Agricola (born Georg Bauer), a German scholar and scientist considered "the father of mineralogy." It contained the first classification system for "fossils" (the 16th-century term for minerals) based on the resemblance of various mineral crystals to the Platonic solids. Agricola was the first to recognize the existence of mineral compounds.

3677. Mineral separation by flotation was the froth flotation process, developed in 1903 by Charles Potter and Guillaume Delprat of New South Wales, Australia. Potter and Delprat created a suspension of minerals in water, added a surfactant (soap), and agitated the suspension. The more wettable minerals were concentrated in the froth on the surface of the water, allowing them to be skimmed off. The less wettable minerals settled to the bottom of the tank.

3678. Star of Africa was the diamond known as Cullinan I, cut from the original Cullinan Diamond discovered in the Premier Diamond Mine in Transvaal, South Africa, on January 25, 1905. It was named for Thomas M. Cullinan, chairman of the Premier Diamond Company. When extracted, the raw diamond weighed 3,106 carats and was the largest diamond ever found. The government of the Transvaal presented the uncut stone as a gift to King Edward VII of England in 1907. The pear-shaped Cullinan I, called the "First Star of Africa" or "Greatest Star of Africa," was, at 530.2 carats, the first and largest of the 9 major and 96 minor stones, all flawless, cut from the

MATERIALS—MINERALS—*continued*

original stone by the firm of I.J. Asscher and Company of Amsterdam, the Netherlands. It is set in the royal scepter of the British monarchy. The "Second Star of Africa," the Cullinan II, is set in the British imperial crown.

MATERIALS—MINING

3679. Hard-rock mining operation was begun in the turquoise mines of the Sinai peninsula (now part of Egypt) before 3400 BCE. The blue semi-precious gemstone is found in ancient Egyptian artifacts, including the bracelets of Queen Zer, which constitute some of the world's oldest examples of jewelry.

3680. Coal mine known by name is the Fushun mine of northeastern China, dug circa 1000 BCE. Coal from that mine is believed to have been used to feed the fires of local copper smelters. Coal was in use in Wales before circa 2000 BCE, but it may not have been mined.

3681. Gold rush in the New World began in 1692, when treasure seekers from São Paulo struck gold in the area called Minas Gerais (its Portuguese name means "general mines"). A consignment of Brazilian gold weighing one and a half tons reached Lisbon in 1699.

3682. Safety fuse was invented in 1831 by an Englishman, William Bickford. His fuse was a cotton cord containing a core of black powder and wrapped with cloth. The exact burning time for a set length of the fuse was known, so detonation times could be calculated precisely.

3683. Blasting cap was invented by the Swedish chemist Alfred Nobel in 1865. It made possible the first safe and controlled use of nitroglycerin for mining and other industrial purposes.

3684. Dynamite mining demonstration took place on July 14, 1867, at Merstham Quarry in Redhill, Surrey, England, when Alfred Nobel, the inventor of dynamite, detonated a quantity of the stable nitroglycerin-based explosive to test its applicability to mining. Modern formulations of dynamite are still widely used in mining operations.

3685. Detonating cord was patented in France in 1908. Called *cordeau détonant,* it consisted of a rolled lead tube with a core of TNT. It detonated at a the rapid velocity of 16,000 feet (4,900 meters) per second. A later American version, with the trade name Primacord, was wrapped in flexible layers of cloth and is widely used in mining and blasting.

3686. Mining claim on the ocean floor was filed in December 1997 on 1,974 square miles (5,110 square kilometers) of the Bismarck Sea belonging to Papua New Guinea by Nautilus Minerals Corp., a Papua New Guinea company run by Australians. The volcanically active site, approximately a mile (1.6 kilometers) deep, was believed to contain rich deposits of iron, zinc, copper, silver, and gold.

MATERIALS—PAPER

3687. Paper was made from papyrus, a water plant native to Egypt that grows some 15 feet (4.6 meters) high. The ancient Egyptians pulled the woody fibers from this plant and pressed them together to make flat sheets. Scrolls were made by pasting sheets together. Papyrus fibers were also used to make ropes, cloth, and sails. The earliest papyrus known, a blank sheet, was found in a tomb from approximately 2800 BCE.

3688. Parchment was in wide use in the ancient world from at least circa 2500 BCE, about the time of the invention of papyrus paper. Parchment is a writing material made from the treated skins of animals, most often sheep. A parchment that could be used on both sides, manufactured using special cleaning, stretching, straightening, and whitening techniques, was first developed circa 200 BCE in the Greek city of Pergamon (modern Bergama, Turkey), from which the word "parchment" is derived. The use of two-sided parchment led directly to the invention of the codex, or bound book, which replaced the scroll and the wax or clay tablet.

3689. Rag paper was the invention of Ts'ai Lun, an official of the imperial court in China during the Han dynasty. In the year 105 CE, he produced a sheet of paper by soaking and pressing a mixture of fibrous materials, including mulberry bark, fish nets, rags, and hemp waste. He reported his new process to the emperor Ho Ti and was rewarded with a noble title. The earliest known specimens of paper, nine letters dating from circa 130 CE and written in Sogdian script, were found in 1907 by Sir Aurel Stein in a watchtower of the Great Wall in Chinese Turkestan.

3690. Paper mill in the Muslim world was established in 751 in Samarkand (now in Uzbekistan).

3691. Paper mill in Europe is thought to have been the mill at Fabriano (in modern Italy), built circa 1270, which was noted for its introduction of animal glue as the medium for sizing the sheets.

3692. Watermark was first used at the paper mill at Fabriano, Italy, circa 1270. It was made by twisting fine wire into a distinctive shape and laying it on the paper-molding screen, producing an image on the sheet that was only faintly visible. Watermarks were eventually by mills used to identify the size or quality of a batch of paper and as the manufacturer's insignia.

3693. Carbon paper was the invention of Ralph Wedgwood of London, England, who received a patent for it on October 7, 1806. He applied ink to thin sheets of paper and dried them between blotters.

3694. Wood pulp paper was invented in 1840 in Germany by Friedrich Gottlob Keller, who developed a papermaking process in which ground wood waste replaced pulped rags. Wood pulp paper was cheaper than rag paper, but it was far more acidic and turned yellow and brittle with age.

3695. Corrugated paper was invented by Albert L. Jones of New York, NY, USA, who received a U.S. patent on December 19, 1871, on an "improvement in paper for packing." His patent covered corrugated sheets only and made no mention of backing or facing sheets. Later a facing sheet was applied to one side, and then to both sides, making single-face and double-face corrugated cardboard. Jones assigned his patent to the Thompson and Norris Company of Brooklyn (now part of New York City), NY, USA, which was the first manufacturer of corrugated paper. Corrugated paper boxes came into use about 1890.

MATERIALS—TEXTILES

3696. Evidence of weaving known to archeologists is four small pieces of clay, dated to 25,000 BCE, that carry impressions of woven cloth. These were unearthed in 1995 at a site called Pavlov in the Czech Republic by Jim Adovasio of Mercyhurst College in Erie, PA, USA, and colleagues. The clay impressions are 10,000 years older than any other known woven artifacts.

3697. Cord known to archeologists is three fragments of twisted plant fibers found near the Sea of Galilee in Israel. The cord's discoverers, Daniel Nadel of the Stekelis Museum of Prehistory in Haifa, Israel, and colleagues, date them to 17,300 BCE.

3698. Cloth fragment known to archeologists was discovered in 1988 in Cayonu in southeastern Turkey by a team of archeologists from the University of Chicago and Istanbul University, Turkey. The calcium-encrusted, semi-fossilized fragment, probably made of linen, measures 3 inches by 1.5 inches (7.6 by 3.8 centimeters). It may have served as a grip for the handle of a bone tool. Radiocarbon dating of artifacts found nearby indicated that the cloth dates from circa 7000 BCE.

3699. Cloth made of animal fiber dates from the middle of the seventh millennium BCE. Remnants of wool clothing were found, attached to human bones, at the mound of Çatalhüyük, in present-day Turkey. Wool cloth has also been found at Stone Age lake-dwelling sites in Switzerland.

3700. Depiction of tapestry weaving is a painting dated to circa 3000 BCE in the necropolis of Beni Hasan, Egypt. It depicts a high-warp loom of the kind used to produce fine tapestries.

3701. Silk was first produced from the silkworm, the moth caterpillar *Bombyx,* in China, possibly as early as 2500 BCE. More than a millennium passed before the Chinese began exporting cloth made of silk, and an understanding of sericulture did not appear in any other place until India adopted it circa 140 BCE. Sericulture in Europe was started in Constantinople (now Istanbul, Turkey) by the Byzantine emperor Justinian I circa 550 CE, when, at his request, two Nestorian Christian monks spirited a number of silkworms out of China.

3702. Printed cloth may have originated in Africa. A fresco illustration from the rock tombs at Beni Hasan, Egypt, dating from circa 1900 BCE, shows Bedouins from northern Africa wearing garments that go over one shoulder and fall to below the knee. They appear to have been printed with brightly colored patterns, including combinations of dots, stripes, zigzags, and blocks. Early printed fabrics dating from circa 400 BCE have been found in India. Fabric printing was also developed in pre-Columbian Mexico and Peru.

3703. Brocading technique is soumak, a herringbone-like brocade method most often applied to flat-woven rugs, saddle pads and bags, and the like. The earliest known example was found in charred fragments excavated at Gordion, near Ankara, Turkey, dating from circa 600 BCE.

3704. Knotting as a technique of making carpets is known from royal graves at Pazyryk, in the Altai Mountains of Siberia (now in Kazakhstan), that date to circa 400 BCE. The knots were used to make appliqué patterns on felt bags and clothing and to create a woollen carpet with a checkboard design surrounded by borders of elk and mounted huntsmen.

MATERIALS—TEXTILES—*continued*

3705. Cashmere garments of soft goat's wool were woven in Kashmir (now a province of India) beginning in the 16th century and perhaps in the 15th, when Kashmir's prince, Zayn-ul-Abidin, is said to have invited Turkistani weavers to teach his subjects.

3706. Lace was developed in the late 15th century in Italy and Flanders (the area that is now Belgium and the Netherlands). In 1457, Duchess Giovanna Dandolo established a lacemaking center on the island of Burano, near Venice.

3707. Lace pattern books for perusal by ladies of the court were published by a Venetian clothier, Matio Pagano, and Pierre de Quinty of Cologne (now in France). Both books appeared in 1527.

3708. Lace factory was set up in 1595 by a Venetian noblewoman, Duchess Morosina Morosini, under the direction of Catina Gardin. It employed 130 craftswomen.

3709. Tartan plaids as emblems of Scottish clans are first mentioned circa 1500, but it is unlikely that tartans were widely adopted before 1600. Highland dress, with its characteristic tartan kilt and sash, is first depicted in the painting *Highland Chieftain* (1660) by English artist John Michael Wright.

3710. Cotton thread was produced commercially by James and Patrick Clark in 1806 in Paisley, Scotland, as a substitute for silk thread, which was unavailable in Britain because of the Napoleonic blockade.

3711. Woven elastic webbing containing rubber thread was developed circa 1830 by the firm of Rattier et Guibal in Paris, France, with the assistance of the rubber manufacturer Thomas Hancock. The webbing found its first wide use in the manufacture of corsets.

MATERIALS—TEXTILES—MACHINERY

3712. Vertical two-bar tapestry loom was invented in ancient Egypt before circa 1600 BCE. The earliest known depiction of a vertical two-bar loom of the kind still preferred for weaving tapestries was found in sites dating from the 18th dynasty (1567–1320 BCE).

3713. Spinning wheel of a primitive type was in use in India by circa 1300 BCE, and was refined in China with the addition of a treadle by circa 200 CE. It did not appear in Europe for another millennium, with the first authenticated evidence of a spinning wheel dating from 1268 in Paris, France. The familiar form of spinning wheel still in use today, with a bobbin, vertical distaff, and foot treadle, was introduced in Saxony circa 1500.

3714. Knitting machine was a frame machine that knit wool. The first item of clothing it produced was coarse woolen stockings. It was invented in 1589 by William Lee, a clergyman at Calverton in Nottinghamshire, England. Lee requested a patent from Queen Elizabeth I, but was turned down because she feared that his invention would hurt the livelihood of England's hand-knitters. Lee emigrated to Rouen, France, where, with the help of King Henry IV, he set up a knitting industry.

3715. Machine to spin yarn on more than one spindle was the spinning jenny, invented circa 1764 by James Hargreaves, a poor, uneducated spinner from Lancashire, England. Observing a spinning wheel that was accidently overturned by his daughter, Jenny, he conceived of a machine in which a single person could simultaneously spin multiple strands of thread on many upright spindles. Hargreaves's first spinning jenny was cranked by hand and had eight spindles; subsequent versions had as many as 120 spindles. Hargreaves received an English patent for his invention on July 12, 1770. The jenny was responsible for automating an important segment of the British textile industry. Some historians credit an earlier inventor, Thomas Higgs, with developing a similar machine circa 1760.

3716. Power loom was developed in 1784 by the English clergyman and inventor Edmund Cartwright and patented in 1785.

3717. Automated loom was the Jacquard loom, also called the Jacquard attachment, patented in 1804 by the French weaver Joseph-Marie Jacquard, who developed the earlier work of Jacques de Vaucanson. Actually a device that could be attached to any appropriately modified loom, it used hooks to control the individual warp yarns. The hooks in turn were precisely controlled by a revolving chain of punched cards, with the pattern of holes determining the pattern of the weave. It was the first device to automatically produce intricate woven patterns such as brocade and damask, and forms the basis for all modern mechanical looms. The punched-card system developed by Jacquard was also one of the fundamental innovations leading to the development of the digital computer.

3718. Silkscreen printing for fabrics was developed by French printers in Lyon in the late 19th century. Samuel Simon of Manchester, England, patented a silkscreen press for textiles in 1907.

MATERIALS—TEXTILES—SYNTHETIC

3719. Synthetic dye was mauve, a dye produced from coal tar in 1856 by William Henry Perkin, a English chemistry student. Seeking a synthetic substitue for the malaria medicine quinine, Perkin created a dark tarry substance that, when applied to silk, imparted a purplish hue. It was the first aniline dye.

3720. Synthetic indigo was developed in 1880 by German chemist Adolf von Baeyer, chemistry professor at the University of Munich. The method consisted of a synthesis of indoxyl by fusion of sodium phenylglycinate in a mixture of caustic soda and sodamide. Synthetic indigo dye has largely replaced natural indigo, which is obtained by fermenting leaves of the tropical plant *Indigofera.*

3721. Synthetic fiber was an extrusion of nitrocellulose (cellulose nitrate) made by the physicist Joseph Swan at Newcastle upon Tyne, England, in 1883. Swan, the inventor of an incandescent electric bulb, needed a strong fiber for use as a filament. He made threads of artificial silk by injecting nitrocellulose through a tiny hole into a coagulating fluid. His wife used the thread to crochet mats and doilies.

3722. Synthetic fiber produced in a factory was rayon, a fiber derived from cellulose. It was patented in 1884 by Count Louis-Marie-Hilaire Bernigaud de Chardonnet, who began producing it commercially in 1892 at Besançon, France.

3723. Synthetic fiber suitable for making cloth was viscose rayon, whose components were patented by C.S. Cross in 1892 and C.H. Stearn in 1898. Previous forms of rayon were useful for making fringes and tassels, but could not be dyed or woven into fabric. By July 1905, viscose rayon was being commercially produced at a factory near Coventry, England.

3724. Synthetic fiber produced entirely from chemicals was nylon, invented by Dr. Wallace Hume Carothers, a chemist at E.I. du Pont de Nemours and Company, Wilmington, DE, USA, who obtained a U.S. patent for it on February 16, 1937. The patent covered synthetic linear condensation polymers capable of being drawn into strong, pliable fibers, as well as the process for making them.

3725. Synthetic fabric that was waterproof and breathable was Gore-Tex, a fabric developed by Wilbert L. Gore and his son Robert Gore in 1969. Derived from polytetrafluoroethylene (PTFE, also called Teflon), which Wilbert Gore had helped develop at E.I. du Pont de Nemours and Company, Wilmington, DE, USA, Gore-Tex was a laminated fabric that allowed water vapor to pass through while completely blocking water droplets. Gore-Tex was used in sports clothing, shoes, electronics, and medical applications.

MATHEMATICS

3726. Sexagesimal number system was invented by the ancient Babylonians sometime in the third millenium BCE. Based on the number 60, and developed for calendrical use, it survives today in the 360 degrees of a circle and in the division of time into hours, minutes, and seconds.

3727. Magic square is believed to have been invented in China in the 22nd century BCE. A magic square is a grid in which each space is filled by a number and in which every row of numbers—vertical, horizontal, and diagonal—adds up to the same sum. According to legend, the Emperor Yü, founder of the first Chinese dynasty circa 2200 BCE, saw one laid out on the back of a tortoise that emerged from the Yellow River.

3728. Treatise on mathematics was the Rhind papyrus, an ancient Egyptian scroll containing an extensive set of mathematical tables and problems. It was copied by the scribe Ahmes circa 1650 BCE. The scroll was named for the Scottish antiquarian and collector Alexander Henry Rhind, who purchased it in Egypt in 1858.

3729. Woman mathematician of record was Theano, the wife of Pythagoras. She taught on the faculty of the commune he founded in 539 BCE at Crotone in southern Italy, and is credited with having identified the "golden section," an ideal proportion in which a line is divided into two unequal parts, of which the first is to the second as the second is to the whole.

MATHEMATICS—*continued*

3730. Irrational number known to mathematicians was the square root of 2, usually rounded to 1.414. The Greek mathematician and philosopher Pythagoras was the first to demonstrate circa 530 BCE that the square root of 2 cannot be expressed as a simple fraction or as a decimal with a finite number of decimal places.

3731. Treatise on geometry was the *Elements,* written by the Greek mathematician Hippocrates of Chios circa 460 BCE. His work is lost, but is believed to have been incorporated into Euclid's more comprehensive *Elements,* written circa 300 BCE. The Greek philosopher Simplicius, writing in the late Roman period, refers to the efforts of Hippocrates efforts to square the circle.

3732. Mathematical definition of a circle is the 15th preliminary definition contained in the *Elements* of Euclid, written in Alexandria, Egypt, circa 300 BCE

3733. Method of finding prime numbers was the Sieve of Eratosthenes, invented circa 240 BCE by the Greek mathematician and astronomer Eratosthenes of Cyrene (present-day Shahhat, Libya). It finds prime numbers—positive integers larger than 1 that can only be divided by themselves and 1—by taking some arbitrary number and striking out the multiples of all primes less than or equal to the square root of that number. This process of elimination works well for relatively small values but, until the advent of computers, was impractical for large ones.

3734. Calculation of pi (π) is credited to the Greek mathematician, scientist, and engineer Archimedes, who lived from 287 to 212 BCE in Syracuse, Sicily. In one of Archimedes' nine extant manuscripts, *Measurement of the Circle,* he shows how he obtained a value for π of approximately 3.14 by averaging the lengths of polygons with 96 sides drawn just inside and outside the circumference of a circle and dividing that by the circle's diameter. The number received its name from the Greek letter π, the first letter of the Greek word *perimetros,* or perimeter. Archimedes' method is also the first known example of a standard procedure for calculating an integral.

3735. Treatise on trigonometry was the *Almagest,* completed circa 140 CE by Ptolemy (in Latin, Claudius Ptolemaeus), the Alexandrian astronomer and mathematician. Primarily a work of astronomy, it also contained the first tables of the chords of a circle, calculated accurately to five places, and a section on the solution of triangles that implied the law of sines.

3736. Woman mathematician to win renown was Hypatia, born circa 370 CE in Alexandria, Egypt. Although all her works are lost, we know from the letters of her friend Synesius of Cyrene, later bishop of Ptolemais, and from the Suda lexicon, a booklist of circa 900, that she wrote commentaries on the *Arithmetica* of Diophantus of Alexandria, on the *Conics* of Apollonius of Perga, and on the astronomical canon of Ptolemy. She was also the head of Alexandria's Neoplatonic school of philosophy. She was murdered by a Christian mob in 412.

3737. Mathematician to use algebra known to historians was the pioneering Hindu mathematician Aryabhata I of Kusumapura, India. His mathematical compendium, the *Aryabhatiya,* written entirely in verse and completed in 499, contained 33 rules in arithmetic, algebra, and plane trigonometry and gave an accurate value for π to four places.

3738. Use of zero as a place holder in positional base notation was adopted from Hindu mathematics by the Arabic mathematician Muhammad ibn Musa al-Khwarizmi, who lived circa 780–850 in Baghdad (now in Iraq). Khwarizmi's work on Hindu numeration, *Algoritmi de numero Indorum (Al-Khwarizmi on the Hindu Numbers),* in which he explained the modern use of zero, is known only in a Latin translation. In this work, Khwarizmi introduced Hindu numerals into Western mathematics. Earlier uses of zero can be found in ancient Egyptian and Mayan documents, but it was used only as a marker for an empty position within a number.

3739. Use of the terms "billion" and "trillion" was made by the French mathematician Nicholas Chuquet in 1485. Chuquet used *billion* to mean "one million million." Today the American meaning, "one thousand million," is more common.

3740. Common algebraic symbols such as the plus and minus signs and the square-root sign were invented in Germany circa 1450. They came into more general use after they were adopted circa 1486 by the German mathematician Johannes Widman of the University of Leipzig.

3741. Equal sign was used by the English physician and mathematician Robert Recorde in his book *The Whetstone of Witte* (1557). Recorde proposed the "=" sign to replace the hodgepodge of abbreviations and symbols formerly used by mathematicians to denote an equation.

3742. Treatise advocating the use of the decimal system was the pamphlet *La Thiende (The Tenth)*, published in 1585 by the Dutch engineer, inventor, and mathematician Simon Stevin. In it, Stevin described the use of decimal fractions for common calculations and proposed their general adoption "for all accounts that are encountered in the affairs of men," such as in surveying, astronomy, and general measurement.

3743. Systematic algebraic notation was used in *In artem analyticem isagoge (Introduction to the Analytical Arts)*, written in 1591 by the French mathematician François Viète. He inaugurated the modern practice of using letters for algebraic expressions as well as variables. Viète's notation employed capital vowels for unknown variables (A, E, I, etc.) and capital consonants for parameters (unspecified constants).

3744. Logarithm tables were published in 1614 by the Scottish mathematician John Napier in his *Mirifici Logarithmorum Canonis Descriptio (Description of the Marvelous Canon of Logarithms)*. Napier discovered that he could perform multiplication and division of real numbers by adding and subtracting corresponding numbers derived by raising a base very close to 1 to the power of the real number, then finding the real number that corresponded to the result.

3745. Exponent symbols as numerical superscripts for powers of x were invented by the French mathematician and philosopher René Descartes and first used in his work *La Géométrie*, which appeared in the Netherlands in 1637 as a postscript to his *Discours de la méthode (Discourse on Method)*. This was also the first work to follow the modern practice of denoting variables by lowercase letters at the end of the alphabet (x, y, z) and known unspecified quantities by lowercase letters at the beginning of the alphabet (a, b, c).

3746. Slide rule for arithmetical calculation by the use of sliding, logarithmically graduated scales, was invented by the Englishman Robert Bissaker in 1654. In his design, the slide worked between parts of a fixed stock.

3747. Treatise on binary mathematics was written in March 1679 by the German mathematician and philosopher Gottfried Wilhelm von Leibniz, who invented the binary (base-2) numeration used in modern computing.

3748. Treatise on calculus was *Nova Methodus pro Maximis et Minimis (New Method for the Greatest and the Least)*, an exposition of the basic methods of both integral and differential calculus, published in 1684 by the German mathematician and philosopher Gottfried Wilhelm von Leibniz. Unknown to Leibniz, integral calculus had been invented independently in 1666 by the English scientist Isaac Newton, who called it the "method of fluxions." Newton did not publish his discovery until 1687, in Book I of the *Philosophiae Naturalis Principia Mathematica (Mathematical Principles of Natural Philosophy)*. Newton accused Leibniz of plagiarism, a charge Leibniz hotly denied. In 1713, the Royal Society of London settled the matter of priority in Newton's favor, based on an investigative report that was secretly written by Newton himself. Nonetheless, it is Leibniz's methods and notation that are used today by mathematicians.

3749. Woman mathematician of renown since antiquity was Maria Gaetana Agnesi, born in 1718 in Milan (then a crown land of the Hapsburgs, now in Italy). In 1748, she published *Instituzioni analitiche ad uso della gioventù italiana (Analytical Institutions for the Use of Italian Youth)*, a massive text on algebra, analytic geometry, and calculus that was widely reprinted and translated. It contains the first descriptions of the cubic (the Agnesi curve) and sine curve (the Witch of Agnesi) that bear her name. In 1750 Pope Benedict XIV appointed her professor at the University of Bologna.

3750. Modern slide rule was invented in 1859 by a French artillery officer, Amédée Mannheim. The Mannheim rule was adaptable for general calculations (most previous slide rules were intended for specific applications, such as carpentry) and had scales on one face only. Results were indicated by the position of a cursor. It was used worldwide after 1880, when it was exported from France to other countries.

3751. Woman to earn a doctorate in mathematics was Sofya Vasilyevna Kovalevskaya (née Krukovskaya), also known as Sonya Kovalevsky, who left Russia for Germany as a young woman to study physics and mathematics. Though no German university allowed women to enroll, the University of Göttingen conferred the doctoral degree on Kovalevskaya in 1874 on the strength of her thesis on partial differential equations, undertaken for her private teacher, Karl Weierstrass. She later became a professor at the University of Stockholm.

MATHEMATICS—*continued*

3752. Topology book was written by the American mathematician Oswald Veblen. His book *Analysis Situs* (1922) was the first to provide systematic coverage of the basic ideas of topology, the branch of mathematics describing the properties that an object retains under deformation. Veblen, a founder of the Institute for Advanced Study, Princeton, NJ, USA, became a professor of the school of mathematics there in 1932.

3753. Fields Medal for exceptional achievement by mathematicians under 40 years of age was established by the will of John Charles Fields, a Canadian-born research mathematician at the University of Toronto, and was adopted in 1932 by the International Congress of Mathematicians in Zürich, Switzerland. The Fields Medal is considered to be the "Nobel Prize" of mathematics. The first Fields Medals were awarded in 1936 to the Finnish mathematician Lars Valerian Ahlfors of Harvard University, Cambridge, MA, USA, and to Jesse Douglas of the Massachusetts Institute of Technology, Cambridge, MA, USA.

3754. Significant mathematical problem solved by computer was the four-color map problem, formulated in 1852 by the English mathematician Francis Guthrie. Guthrie claimed that a maximum of four colors were required to color any map so that no contiguous areas had the same color, but did not provide a complete proof. That eluded mathematicians until 1976, when it was provided by Wolfgang Haken and Kenneth Appel of the University of Illinois, USA. They used a computer to check all the possible coloring combinations of a set of 1,936 fundamental maps, and, by a process of simplifying each map, found that there was no map that required more than four colors. Testing each of the fundamental maps required as many as 500,000 logical operations; the complete proof took more than 1,000 hours of computer time.

3755. Factoring of a 100-digit number was accomplished on October 11, 1988, when Mark Manasse of the Systems Research Center of the Digital Equipment Corporation in Palo Alto, CA, USA, and Arjen Lenstra of the University of Chicago, Chicago, IL, USA, announced that they had succeeded in fully factoring a huge number, 11 to the 104th power plus 1. They used the "quadratic sieve" factoring method invented by Carl Pomerance of the University of Georgia at Athens, GA, USA. The work was calculated by a network of hundreds of computers in the United States, Europe, and Australia.

3756. Mathematical proof of Fermat's last theorem was announced in June 1993 by British mathematician Andrew Wiles of Princeton University, Princeton, NJ, USA, at the Isaac Newton Institute in Cambridge, England. Fermat's last theorem, proposed in 1637 by Pierre Fermat, is an extension of the Pythagorean theorem. It states that no number raised to any power higher than two can be the sum of two other numbers raised to like powers. Mathematicians seeking to prove the deceptively simple theorem, the most famous unsolved problem in mathematics, had been frustrated for centuries. Wiles's 200-page proof was so specialized that only a few dozen mathematicians in the world could understand it. It was published in the May 1994 issue of *Annals of Mathematics*.

3757. Encyclopedia of integer sequences was published in 1995 by Neil J.A. Sloane of AT&T Bell Laboratories in Murray Hill, NJ, USA, and Simon Plouffe of the University of Quebec in Montreal, Canada. Each entry in the encyclopedia gave the first dozen or more numbers from a particular sequence, the sequence's name, a mathematical formula showing how to obtain successive terms, and citations indicating where the sequence had appeared in the mathematical or scientific literature.

MEDICINE—ANESTHESIA

3758. Anesthetic was an elixir of opium, which was employed by the Egyptians by 1500 BCE to dull the senses of patients undergoing trepanning, an operation to relieve brain pressure by drilling a hole in the skull. Herbal anesthetics were known to a variety of ancient civilizations, including the Egyptians, who used an extract of nepenthes; the Inca, who chewed coca leaves; and the Babylonians, Hebrews, and Greeks, who used a preparation made from mandrakes.

3759. Medieval doctor to advocate the use of anesthesia was Theodoric Borgononi of Lucca, Italy, a 13th-century physician and Dominican friar. Before operating, he applied sponges soaked in preparations of opium or mandragora, both of which are narcotics, to the mouths and noses of his patients.

3760. Discovery of the anesthetic properties of nitrous oxide (laughing gas) was made by the English chemist Sir Humphry Davy in 1799. Nitrous oxide, a gas, had been discovered 25 years earlier by Joseph Priestley. Davy, who was in the habit of experimenting on himself, inhaled some to see whether it would make him ill. He experienced euphoria combined with insensitivity to pain, followed by hysterical laughter and tears, and finally unconsciousness.

3761. Modern use of anesthesia in surgery took place in Kii Province, Japan, in 1805. The physician was Hanaoka Seishu, who performed a breast-cancer operation on his wife. Hanaoka's anesthetic, called "Tsusen san," was prepared from datura (mandragora), aconite (wolfsbane), and other traditional Chinese medications. It is likely that this was the first successful major operation under general anesthesia. The first surgery under general anesthesia in the West took place in Jefferson, GA, USA, on March 30, 1842, when Crawford Williamson Long removed two small cysts from the neck of James M. Venable while the patient inhaled sulfuric ether from a towel. Both doctor and patient had previously experimented with ether as an intoxicant. Long was eventually persuaded to stop using anesthesia by local residents who suspected him of using witchcraft or poison and who threatened to lynch him if he continued.

3762. Modern use of anesthesia in dentistry is credited to the dentists Horace Wells of Hartford, CT, USA, and William Thomas Green Morton of Boston, MA, USA. Wells was present at a stage show featuring nitrous oxide (laughing gas), recognized its anesthetic potential, and on December 11, 1844, himself underwent a painless wisdom tooth extraction after inhaling the gas. However, he was unable to provide exact dosages in his public demonstrations, which were failures. The use of ether was pioneered by Morton, who painlessly extracted a bicuspid from Eben Frost on September 30, 1846.

3763. Hospital to use anesthesia in surgery was Massachusetts General Hospital in Boston, MA, USA, where ether was used in an operation that took place on October 16, 1846. The patient, Gilbert Abbot, was rendered unconscious by the anesthetist, William Thomas Green Morton, who had developed the use of ether in his local dentistry practice. A tumor was then removed painlessly from Abbot's neck by John Collins Warren, professor of surgery at Harvard Medical School, who afterwards declared, "Gentlemen, this is no humbug." The operation took 25 minutes.

3764. Local anesthetic was cocaine, used in 1884 by Carl Koller, an Austrian ophthalmologic surgeon, to block pain during eye, nose, and throat operations.

MEDICINE—BOOKS AND TREATISES

3765. Extensive treatise on dental problems was the Ebers Papyrus, an Egyptian document dated to circa 1700 BCE but incorporating material perhaps 2000 years older. It described various tooth diseases and offered formulas for soothing poultices containing olive oil, dates, onions, and beans. These were to be applied "against the throbbing of the blisters in the teeth."

3766. Medical texts known are two scrolls from Egypt, the Edwin Smith Papyrus and the Georg Moritz Ebers Papyrus. Both date from the middle of the second millennium but are thought to contain material from about 3000 BCE, and both are named for scholars who acquired them in the 19th century. The Edwin Smith Papyrus explains the diagnosis and treatment of numerous ailments. The Ebers Papyrus is a compilation of household remedies for a variety of troubles.

3767. Text of Chinese medicine was the *Huang Ti Nei ching* (*The Yellow Emperor's Classic of Internal Medicine*), written in China about the year 300 BCE and usually called the *Nei ching*. It was also the first treatise on acupuncture. Chinese medicine is based on the restoration of balance to the *ch'i* (life force) and other physico-spiritual properties.

3768. Yoga textbook was the four-volume *Yoga Sutras*, whose first three volumes were written in India in the second century BCE. The author was Patañjali, although that name is likely to have been a pseudonym; it is also given as Gonardiya and Gonikaputra. The book presents eight aspects of yoga: restraint from negative actions, observance of positive actions, practice of postures, regulation of breathing, abstraction of the senses, concentration, meditation, and trance.

3769. Medical text written by a woman is attributed to Metrodora, a Greek, probably of the first century CE. The book concerns diseases of the uterus, stomach, and kidneys.

MEDICINE—BOOKS AND TREATISES—
continued

3770. Texts of Ayurvedic medicine were the *Caraka-samhita,* a medical text from the first century CE, and the *Susruta-samhita,* a surgical text from the seventh century, although the material in both is older by many centuries (Susruta, a surgeon, performed plastic surgery, lithotomies, and cataract operations circa 49 BCE). Ayurveda, meaning "science of life" in Sanskrit, is a system of medicine that attributes disease to an imbalance in the *doshas,* three physical forces corresponding more or less to bile, phlegm, and wind. Its principles had their origin in the *Atharvaveda,* a collection of magical lore dating back to circa 1500 BCE, which was brought to India from Iran by the invading Aryans along with the three other Vedas that became the sacred texts of Hinduism.

3771. Treatise on medicine written in medieval Europe was probably *The Book of Remedies,* the earliest medical work written in Italy. It was composed in Hebrew by an Italian Jewish physician, Shabbatai Donnolo, and published in 975.

3772. Japanese medical book extant was the *Ishinho,* compiled by a Chinese immigrant, Tambano Yasuyori, in 30 volumes that were completed in 982.

3773. Illustrated surgical treatise was included in the eleventh-century Spanish medical and surgical encyclopedia *At-Tasrif liman ajaz'an at-Tàalif (The Method),* whose Latin translation, *De chirurgia (On Surgery),* became the leading textbook on surgery in the West. The last chapter of this work showed illustrations of hundreds of surgical instruments, including many invented by the author, Abul Kasim, or Abu al-Qasim Khalaf ibn Abbas az-Zahrawi (also called Albucasis), court physician to the caliph in Córdoba. The first surgical treatise to include depictions of actual operations was the *Manual of Military Surgery* by Hans von Gersdorff, published in 1517, which contained woodcut illustrations.

3774. Treatise on human anatomy based on dissection was *Anathomia Mundini,* by Mondino de' Luzzi. Heavily reliant on the ancient and inaccurate teachings of Galen, the book was published in 1316 and printed for the first time in 1478. The author, who taught at the University of Bologna, Italy, introduced the systematic study of anatomy into medical training.

3775. Textbook of dentistry was *Artzney buchlein wider allerlei Krankeyten und Gebrechen der Tzeen (Little Medicinal Book for All Kinds of Diseases and Infirmities of the Teeth),* published in Germany in 1530. The author is unknown. It was written in German for the surgeons and barbers who handled the mouth problems that physicians refused to treat. The subjects included drilling, filling, and extraction. The first comprehensive treatise was *Le chirurgien dentiste, ou, traité des dents (The Surgeon Dentist, or Treatise on the Teeth,* 1728), by the eminent French oral surgeon Pierre Fauchard, which covered anatomy, morphology, pathology, transplantation, and much else.

3776. Treatise on human anatomy with accurate illustrations was *De humani corporis fabrica (On the Human[s Bodily Works),* published in Basel, Switzerland, in 1543. It was the work of the Belgian-born physician and medical pioneer Andreas Vesalius and Jan Stephan van Calcar, a young Belgian artist who had studied with the painter Titian in Venice. To produce the striking illustrations, Vesalius dissected a series of executed criminals supplied by the city authorities while Calcar stood by and drew what Vesalius laid bare.

3777. Comprehensive treatise on pathology and physiology was *Medicina,* published in 1554 by Jean François Fernel, professor of medicine at the University of Paris in France. It was the earliest systematic treatise on physiology and pathology (terms coined by Fernel), providing a methodical study of disorders arranged by organ.

3778. Treatise on dental anatomy was *Libellus de dentibus (Pamphlet on the Teeth),* published in 1563 by the Italian anatomist Bartolomeo Eustachio.

3779. Works on comparative embryology were *De formato foetu (Of the Formation of the Fetus),* published in 1600, and *De Formatione ovi et pulli (Of the Formation of Eggs and Chicks),* published in 1621. They were written by the anatomist and surgeon Hieronymus Fabricius ab Aquapendente (born Geronimo or Girolamo Fabrizio in Acquapendente, Italy), professor of surgery and anatomy at the University of Padua from 1562 to 1613. *De formato foetu* compared the development of the fetus in dogs, cats, horses, and humans, and contained the first detailed description of the placenta. *De Formatione ovi et pulli* contained the first detailed description of the fetal development of birds. Fabricius was also the first to show that the pupil of the eye changes its size, the first to fully describe the action of the vocal chords, and the first to investigate the semilunar valves of veins.

3780. Treatise on basal metabolism was *De statica medicina (On Medical Measurement),* published in 1614. The author was the Italian physician Santorio Santorio (also known by the Latin name Sanctorius), a pioneer in the use of scientific measurement in medical research.

3781. Treatise on sign language was *Of The Art of Signs,* written in Italy in 1616 by G. Bonifacio.

3782. Dentistry textbook in English was *The Operator for the Teeth,* by Charles Allen, published in England in 1685.

3783. Treatise on occupational medicine was *De Morbis Artificum Diatriba (Diseases of Workers),* published in 1700. The author was the Italian physician Bernardino Ramazzini, the founder of the specialty of occupational medicine. The book describes illnesses brought on by workplace exposure to hazardous materials, including such toxic metals as mercury. More than 50 occupations were covered.

3784. Treatise on autopsies was *De Sedibus et Causis Morborum per Anatomen Indagatis (The Seats and Causes of Diseases as Investigated by Anatomy),* published in 1761 by the Italian physician Giovanni Morgagni. Morgagni presented detailed anatomical findings in the postmortems of some 700 of his patients.

3785. Scientific treatise on histology was *Traité des membranes (Treatise on Membranes),* written in 1800 by the French physician Marie-François-Xavier Bichat. In it he described 21 kinds of tissues that form the organs of the body.

3786. Scientific treatise on public health was *Report . . . on an Enquiry into the Sanitary Condition of the Labouring Population of Great Britain,* written in London in 1842 by physician and social reformer Edwin Chadwick. It was the first to irrefutably link infectious disease and child mortality with polluted water supplies and lack of sanitation.

MEDICINE—BOOKS AND TREATISES— PHARMACOPOEIA

3787. Pharmacopoeia of medicinal herbs dates from about 2100 BCE and was found at Nippur (now Niffer, Iraq). It consists of a small clay tablet inscribed with the cuneiform writing of ancient Sumer. Scholars believe that it represents one physician's records of medications he prescribed to patients, including salves made of oil, wine, and crushed herbs. The earliest Chinese herbal appears to date from approximately the same era, although it is attributed by tradition to Shen Nung, the legendary emperor of the 28th century BCE, who is also said to have founded Chinese agriculture. A catalog of medicinal plants bearing his name described 365 species of herbs.

3788. Pharmacopoeia widely used was *De materia medica,* a five-volume work by the Greek pharmacologist Pedanius Dioscorides, published in 77 CE. Dioscorides did his research on medicinal plants during his travels as a surgeon in the army of the Emperor Nero of Rome. He described about 1,000 medicines derived from vegetable, animal, and chemical sources and gave botanical descriptions of 600 plants, peppermint and cannabis among them. *De materia medica* was translated into many languages and became a standard reference work that was relied on for some 1,500 years.

3789. Pharmacopoeia adopted officially by a government was the *Dispensatorium (Dispensary)* of Valerius Cordus, published in 1546 and made legally binding for physicians practicing in Nuremberg (now in Germany).

3790. National pharmacopoeia in English that all preparers of drugs and medications were required to follow was published in England in 1618 under the title *London Pharmacopoeia.*

3791. International pharmacopoeia was the *Pharmacopoea Internationalis,* published by the World Health Organization of the United Nations in 1951.

MEDICINE—DENTISTRY

3792. Dental bridges were sets of two or three teeth connected by gold wire that were made by the Egyptians circa 3000 BCE, probably to fill gaps in the teeth of corpses being prepared for the afterlife. The first bridges known to have been intended for use by living people were made by Phoenician goldsmiths in Sidon (in modern Lebanon) circa 500 BCE. They created prosthetic appliances made of natural teeth and ivory false teeth bound together with gold wire. They also used wire to stabilize teeth loosened by gum disease.

3793. Description of tooth decay was contained in a Sumerian text of circa 3000 BCE. It blamed the gnawing action of tiny "tooth worms" for dental decay and toothache.

3794. Acupuncture for dental problems was used as a pain-reducing treatment for dental caries by Chinese practitioners beginning circa 2700 BCE.

MEDICINE—DENTISTRY—*continued*

3795. Dentist known by name was Hesi-Re, a contemporary of the Egyptian pharoah Zoser (circa 2650 BCE), who was called "chief of the toothers and the physicians." Neferites, who lived in Egypt circa 2600 BCE, constructed the first known set of false teeth. The work of anonymous Egyptian dentists, preserved in mummified bodies, includes ivory dentures, gold crowns, drained abscesses, and tooth fillings.

3796. Jaw drilling was done by the Egyptians circa 1600 BCE to allow pus to escape from abscessed teeth.

3797. Dentures in Europe were constructed in the ninth century BCE by the Etruscans in what is now central Italy. Real teeth extracted from corpses, or false teeth sculpted from pieces of bone and ivory, were fixed into gold settings that fit inside the mouth.

3798. Iron tooth of record was found in the jaw of a 1,900-year-old skeleton of a man unearthed in the ancient cemetery at Chantambre, France, by archeologist Louis Girard of the University of Bordeaux. The carefully fitted tooth was evidence that Roman-era dentistry was more technologically advanced than had been thought.

3799. Dental implant operations in which artificial teeth made of nonorganic materials were implanted into the jawbone were done by the Mayas of South America. The earliest example known is a piece of a mandible from circa 600, found in Honduras, that contained three pieces of shell, carved to look like teeth and inserted into empty incisor sockets.

3800. Use of silver amalgam to fill dental cavities was introduced by the Chinese in the seventh century. It is mentioned in a pharmacopoeia by Su Kung that appeared in 659.

3801. Oral surgeon of importance was Abul Kasim (known in the West by his Latinized name, Albucasis), physician at the court of the Spanish caliph in Córdoba. He was the author, circa 1000, of the encyclopedia work *At-Tasrif liman ajaz'an at-Tàalif (The Method)*, which recorded his own advances in the use of cauterization, ligation, and extraction in oral surgery. He invented a number of instruments for scaling teeth to prevent periodontitis. The first person to be known by the title of dental surgeon was Pierre Fauchard, author of *Le chirurgien dentiste (The Surgeon Dentist)*, published in France in 1728.

3802. Japanese dentists were Tambano Furiyori and his son Tambano Kaneyasu, members of a family of medical practitioners who were descended from the prominent physician and Chinese emigrant Tambano Yasuyori. Kaneyasu was the first person to be named (circa 1250) as the dentist of the imperial court, a position that continued to be filled by his descendents. The family's accumulated knowledge was eventually published in 1531 under the title *Chikayasu's Dental Secrets.*

3803. Dentures retained by adhesion and atmospheric pressure, rather than by springs, were invented by Japanese dentists circa 1500. They were made of fruitwood and carved to match a model of the patient's mouth that had been made from a beeswax impression. Embedded in the wooden base were replacement teeth made of bone, marble, or metal. The earliest example of an upper denture is preserved at the Buddhist temple at Wakayama, whose founder, the nun Nakaoka Tei, is reputed to have crafted them for herself.

3804. King to practice dentistry was King James IV of Scotland, who learned how to extract and cauterize teeth from a barber who had treated him in 1503. He acquired a set of dental instruments and practiced on his own household and courtiers.

3805. Women admitted to a guild of dentists were allowed to join the Barber-Surgeons' Company of England in 1544, soon after it was chartered by King Henry VIII.

3806. Dentists with professional credentials were trained in Paris, France, beginning in 1699, when King Louis XIV authorized the College of Surgeons to require dentistry students to pass a two-year course in mouth surgery and tooth restoration. Graduates were allowed to advertise themselves as "tooth experts."

3807. Dental drill for cavities was a hand-operated metal utensil with which the practitioner, using a twisting motion, dug the decayed matter out of the tooth. Pierre Fauchard, a dental surgeon in Paris, France, described the tool in his classic and influential work *Le chirurgien dentiste (The Surgeon Dentist),* which was published in 1728.

3808. Porcelain dentures were invented by two Parisians, an apothecary, Alexis Duchâteau, and a dentist, Nicolas Dubois de Chémant. The latter received a French patent in 1789 for his improved porcelain dentures, which were known as "incorruptibles" because, unlike organic materials such as ivory, porcelain resisted stains, odors, and disintegration. He also made porcelain noses. Individual porcelain teeth were created by in 1830 by another Parisian dentist, Giuseppangelo Fonzi.

3809. Dentist's chair made for the purpose was constructed circa 1790 by Josiah Flagg, a dentist in Boston, MA, USA, who practiced restorative dentistry, orthodontics, endodontics, and oral surgery, and prepared his own prosthetics and pharmaceuticals. It was a wooden chair in the Windsor style, to which he attached an adjustable wooden headrest and a tray to hold instruments. A reclining model, equipped with a lamp and mirror, was invented by James Snell in 1832. James Beall Morrison made a tilting chair in 1868, and the Buffalo Dental Manufacturing Company made a version in 1875 whose back could be lowered.

3810. Powered dental drill was invented in 1790 by John Greenwood of New York, NY, USA. It was adapted from the spinning wheel and made some 500 rotations per minute. Power was obtained by means of a foot treadle. Greenwood was George Washington's dentist.

3811. Identification of fluoride as a tooth-decay preventive was made in 1802 by dentists in Naples, Italy, who noticed that many of their patients from the surrounding countryside had teeth that were both free of cavities and discolored by yellow spots. Some detective work revealed that these patients came from places where the soil and water contained high levels of fluoride.

3812. Dentistry journal was the *American Journal of Dental Science,* founded by Chapin A. Harris, a dentist in Baltimore, MD, USA. The first issue was published on June 1, 1839, and mailed to subscribers in 23 states and five foreign countries. In 1841 the journal was taken over by the American Society of Dental Surgeons, which had been organized by Harris and Horace H. Hayden the previous year; it was the world's first nationwide dental society.

3813. Silver amalgam tooth filling in modern times was developed in France circa 1845 by Thomas W. Evans, an American dentist who later became the dentist to Emperor Louis Napoléon. His formula mixed silver with tin and trace amounts of copper.

3814. Woman dentist with a degree from a dental school was Lucy Beaman Hobbs, who received her D.D.S. degree on February 21, 1866, from the Ohio College of Dental Surgery in Cincinnati, OH, USA. The school had denied her admission when she first applied. She studied privately with one of its graduates and

opened her own practice before she was allowed to enroll. Marie Grubert, who graduated from the same school not long afterward, became the first woman to serve as an officer of a dental society when she was elected vice president of the Mississippi Valley Association of Dental Surgeons in 1872.

3815. Dental spittoon with running water was the Whitcomb Fountain Spittoon, made by the S.S. White Company of Philadelphia, PA, USA, in 1867. The basin was flushed by jets of water from a pipe around its circumference. Patients could collect water for rinsing from a faucet shaped like a swan. The device also featured cupholders and a tray for holding instruments.

3816. Dental drill powered by electricity was manufactured by the S.S. White Company of Philadelphia, PA, USA. Its inventor, George F. Green of Kalamazoo, MI, USA, obtained a patent on January 26, 1875, on "electro-magnetic dental tools" used for sawing, filing, dressing, and polishing teeth. The motor was inside the handpiece, which made it too heavy for comfortable use. The company also manufactured a drill operated by a foot treadle, invented by James Beall Morrison.

3817. Recognition of the true cause of tooth decay was made by the American-born physician, dentist, and medical researcher Willoughby D. Miller, professor of operative dentistry at the University of Berlin, Germany. A trained chemist who studied with the pioneering bacteriologist Robert Koch, he recognized that acids formed by the fermentation of carbohydrates in the mouth destroyed the tooth enamel, allowing microbes to enter and attack the dentine. This discovery raised the possibility that the teeth could be preserved through preventive hygiene, including the use of toothpastes and mouthwashes. Miller explained his theory in *Microorganisms of the Human Mouth,* published in 1890.

3818. Dental X-rays were made by C. Edmund Kells of New Orleans, LA, USA, a dentist and inventor. He built the first X-ray machine in the United States in 1896, shortly after the discovery of radiography by the German scientist Wilhelm Conrad Röntgen. His was also the first dental office in the nation to use electricity supplied from a power station, rather than by batteries, and to make use of compressed air during treatment. His inventions included a dental and surgical suction pump, elevator brakes, a fire extinguisher, and many other patented devices.

MEDICINE—DENTISTRY—*continued*

3819. International dentistry assocation was the Fédération Dentaire Internationale (International Dental Federation), founded in Paris, France, in 1900 at the third International Dental Conference. The IDF published the first issue of the *International Dental Journal,* the first global dentistry journal, in 1950.

3820. Free dental clinic for poor children was probably a program set up in Rochester, NY, USA, in 1901 by the Rochester Dental Society. It eventually received funding from George Eastman, the founder of the Eastman Kodak Company, and became the Eastman Dental Dispensary. Another free children's clinic was founded in 1902 in Strassburg, Germany (now Strasbourg, France) by Dr. Ernst Jessen.

3821. Dental hygienist was trained in 1905 by Alfred Civilion Fones, a dentist in Bridgeport, CT, USA, to teach his patients techniques for home oral prophylaxis. In 1913, he started the Fones Clinic for Dental Hygienists, many of whose graduates were hired by school districts to instruct children in proper toothbrushing habits. Connecticut began licensing dental hygienists in 1917.

3822. Tooth decay vaccine was announced in April 1998 by a team of British researchers uinder Julian Ma and Tom Lehner of the Guys Hospital Dental School in London, England. The vaccine, derived from genetically modified tobacco plants, was painted directly on teeth. It contained antibodies that destroyed *Streptococcus mutans,* the bacteria that causes most tooth decay.

MEDICINE—DISEASES

3823. Physical handicap in an adult of record was found through detailed study of a partial cranium of a young female adult, dated to circa 400,000 BCE, that was discovered in Morocco in 1971. Analysis by Jean-Jacques Hublin of the Museum of Man in Paris, France, found that the skull possessed a fetal abnormality—an abnormally rounded, relatively smooth bone at the back of the head—that indicated severe musculoskeletal dysfunction in the rest of the body.

3824. Person with dwarfism of record was unearthed in 1963 at Romito Cave near the modern city of Cosenza, Italy. The 11,150-year-old skeleton belonged to a male of about 17 years of age who exhibited a rare type of dwarfism called acromesomelic dysplasia. The remains were discovered and analyzed by David W. Frayer and colleagues of the University of Kansas, USA. A second skeleton found at the site may have been the dwarf's mother.

3825. Cases of schistosomiasis known to medical researchers were those of Egyptians who lived circa 1000 BCE. Their mummified kidneys showed evidence of damage caused by *Schistosoma,* a parasitic blood fluke that lives in aquatic snails and causes debilitating illness in humans.

3826. Description of epilepsy was found on a Babylonian medical text written in cuneiform on a baked brick tablet circa 650 BCE. It attributed epileptic seizures to demonic possession.

3827. Description of disease as a matter of science rather than religion or magic was made by the Greek physician Hippocrates (circa 460 BCE to 377 BCE). In discussing epilepsy, he wrote: "It is not any more sacred than other diseases, but has a natural cause, and its supposed divine origin is due to man's inexperience. Every disease has its own nature, and arises from external causes."

3828. Occupational disease of record was a case of lead poisoning described by the Greek physician Hippocrates (fourth century BCE), or by someone writing under his name, in the treatise *Epidemics,* part of the medical anthology known as the Hippocratic Collection. The patient earned his living as a metal extractor.

3829. Description of clinical depression and bipolar disorder was given by the second-century Greek physician Aretaeus of Cappadocia (in modern Turkey) in his four-volume treatise *On the Causes and Indications of Acute and Chronic Diseases.* Of patients with depression, he wrote that they "become peevish, dispirited, sleepless, and start up from a disturbed sleep. Unreasonable fears also seize them. . . . They complain of life and desire to die." This work and another by Aretaeus, *On the Treatment of Acute and Chronic Diseases,* remained unknown until 1554, when their manuscripts were discovered. Aretaeus also gave closely observed descriptions of spinal paralysis, cerebral paralysis, asthma, pneumonia, diptheria, tetanus, pleurisy, and diabetes, which he named.

3830. Description of lead poisoning was included in the *Epitomes iatrikes biblio hepta (Medical Compendium in Seven Books),* written by the Greek physician and encyclopedist Paul of Aegina circa 680 CE. A compendium of all the medical knowledge known in the West, it mentions the specific symptoms of lead poisoning, such as "lead palsy" in the hands, blindness, and convulsions. Lead in the ancient world was found mainly in water pipes, where it leached into drinking water, and in the shops of craftsmen who manufactured lead objects.

3831. Treatise on smallpox was *De variolis et morbillis (Treatise on the Small Pox and Measles),* written circa 900 by the Persian doctor Abu Bakr Muhammad ibn Zakariyà ar-Razi (known in Latin as Rhazes), the leading Muslim physician of the era.

3832. Contagious disease to be brought under control in Europe was leprosy, a disfiguring disease caused by the bacillus *Mycobacterium leprae.* Beginning in the 14th century, people suffering from leprosy were confined in leper houses, known as lazarettos, run by the monasteries of St. Lazarus. This was a reaction to more brutal measures, such as the order by King Philip the Fair in 1313 to burn alive all lepers in France. An estimated 19,000 of these hospices were founded throughout western Europe. The isolation of lepers succeeded in eradicating the disease in France by 1656, when the country's lazarettos were closed. In other places, the lazarettos were converted into places of confinement for plague victims, mentally ill people, and syphilitics.

3833. Cases of syphilis are in dispute. Archeological evidence shows that the disease was suffered by Native Americans many centuries before European contact, leading to the widespread belief that the disease was transmitted to the rest of the world following the voyages of Christopher Columbus in 1492. The first cases in Europe were reported in 1494 in Naples (now part of Italy) while the kingdom was under attack by the armies of Charles VIII of France. The disease appears to have been spread by soldiers of the defending Spanish army who had sailed with Columbus. However, some medical investigators beleive that syphilis existed earlier in the Old World, perhaps in a less virulent strain that was consiered a form of leprosy.

3834. Description of syphilis was written in 1519 by the German nobleman and Protestant activist Ulrich von Hutten, who described the symptoms he had suffered as a young man, including inflamed boils as big as acorns. The first medical description was contained in *Syphillis sive morbus Gallicus (Syphilis or the French Disease),* a rhymed treatise dated 1530 by the Veronese physician Girolamo Fracastoro. Fracastoro named the disease and provided the earliest theory of its contagion and treatment.

3835. Germ theory of disease was contained in the 1546 work *De contagione et contagiosi morbis (On Contagion and Contagious Diseases)* by the Veronese physician Girolamo Fracastoro. Fracastoro offered a remarkably accurate model of the origin and transmission of infectious diseases that anticipated the germ theory developed by Robert Koch and Louis Pasteur in the 19th century.

3836. Vitamin-deficiency disease to be cured was scurvy, caused by the lack of adequate vitamin C (ascorbic acid) in the diet. Mariners on long sea voyages were among the first to suffer from the disease. In 1753, scurvy's cause was identified by the Scottish naval surgeon James Lind, who found that giving sailors a daily drink of orange, lemon, or lime juice (all good sources of vitamin C) could completely cure and prevent the disease. Vitamin C itself was not isolated and identified until 1928. The researcher who accomplished it, the Hungarian chemist Albert von Szent-Györgyi, won the 1937 Nobel Prize in Medicine or Physiology. Two other vitamin-deficiency diseases, rickets and beriberi, which are caused by a lack of Vitamin D and Vitamin B, respectively, were first described in tenth-century China.

3837. Occupational carcinogen to be identified was soot. The prevalence of cancer of the scrotum in men who had been chimney sweeps during childhood was noted in 1775 by Sir Percivall Pott, a surgeon in London, England.

3838. Outbreak of botulism on record took place in Wildbad, Germany, in 1793, when paralysis struck 13 people, six of whom died. The illness was traced to a smoked sausage that all 13 had shared. In 1896, the Belgian scientist Émile van Ermengem identified the cause of these paralytic outbreaks as the soil microorganism *Clostridium botulinum,* which produces a deadly nerve toxin in food that has been smoked, cured, or canned at insufficient temperatures.

3839. Treatise on color blindness was *Extraordinary Facts Relating to the Vision of Colours,* published in 1794 by English chemist John Dalton, the formulator of the first scientific atomic theory. Dalton himself was color-blind, and attributed the condition (wrongly) to discoloration of the aqueous humor, the liquid medium of the eyeball.

3840. Disease known to be caused by a specific microbe was anthrax, caused by *Bacillus antracus,* a bacterium. In work published at Breslau, Germany (now Wroclaw, Poland), in 1876, the German microbiologist Robert Koch demonstrated that anthrax developed in mice only when injected with that bacterium, proving

MEDICINE—DISEASES—*continued*

for the first time that diseases weren't caused by mysterious substances but by specific micro-organisms. His investigations also elucidated for the first time the complete life cycle of a bacterium. For this and other work, Koch was awarded the 1905 Nobel Prize in Physiology or Medicine.

3841. Disease proven to be transmitted by insects was the tropical disease elephantiasis, a disorder of the lymph glands that results in disfiguring scarring and swelling. In 1879, Patrick Manson, a Scottish physician practicing in southern China, recognized that the disease is caused by a parasite, the nematode worm *Filaria bancrofti,* and demonstrated that the parasite is spread through the bites of mosquitoes.

3842. Recognition of the vector of malaria was made by Ronald Ross, surgeon-major with the British Army's Indian Medical Service at a hospital in Begumpett, India. His research, from 1892 to 1898, located the malarial parasite in the intestinal tract of the *Anopheles* mosquito and confirmed that malaria is transmitted by its bite. He was awarded the Nobel Prize in Physiology or Medicine in 1902. The parasite itself had been discovered and identified in 1880 by the French pathologist Charles-Louis-Alphonse Laveran, then working as an army surgeon in Algeria. Laveran received the Nobel Prize in Physiology or Medicine in 1907. Related work was done independently in Italy by Giovanni Grassi.

3843. Description of anaphylaxis was offered by the French physiologist, bacteriologist, and pathologist Charles Robert Richet in 1902. He coined the term to describe the severe, sometimes fatal reaction to a second injection of or other exposure to an antigen such as bee venom. For his work on the immune system, he won the 1913 Nobel Prize in Physiology or Medicine.

3844. Case of Alzheimer's disease of record was described by Alois Alzheimer, the physician who identified it. The patient was Auguste D., a German woman who died in 1906. Her files, lost for decades, were rediscovered in the 1990s at the University of Frankfurt, and in 1997 slides of her brain tissue were tracked down to a collection at the University of Munich.

3845. Induced cancer was deliberately produced in 1915 by two Japanese chemists, Katsusaburo Yamagiwa and Koichi Ichikawa, when they coated the ears of rabbits with coal tar. The tar caused skin cancers to form.

3846. Radiation-induced cataracts were discovered by the American opthalmologist David G. Cogan in 1946 while examining survivors of the Hiroshima and Nagasaki atomic bombs dropped on Japan at the end of World War II. Cogan wrote the first major treatise on neuro-ophthalmology, *Neurology of the Visual System* (1966).

3847. HIV infections may have occurred as early as 1950, according to analysis of a blood sample of a Bantu man from Léopoldville, Belgian Congo (now Kinshasa, Democratic Republic of Congo). An analysis performed in 1986 showed that the man had been infected with human immunovirus 1 (HIV-1) in 1959. In 1998, projections derived from DNA sequences of the virus by Toufo Zhu of the Aaron Diamond AIDS Research Center, New York, NY, USA, indicated that HIV-1 may have begun evolving in humans as much as a decade earlier.

3848. Human cancer-causing virus to be discovered was the Epstein-Barr virus, a herpes virus that also causes acute infectious mononucleosis. It was isolated in 1964 by the British scientists M.A. Epstein, Y.M. Barr, and B.G. Achong from cells grown from tissues involved with Burkitt's lymphoma, a lymphatic cancer prevalent among Ugandan children that was described by Denis Parsons Burkitt in 1958.

3849. Identification of the AIDS virus was announced by two scientific teams in March 1983. The human immune deficiency virus (HIV), the retrovirus that causes AIDS, was isolated and reported by Dr. Robert Gallo of the National Cancer Institute in Bethesda, MD, USA, and by Dr. Luc Montagnier at the Institute Pasteur in Paris, France. AIDS is an abbreviation for *acquired immunodeficiency syndrome.*

3850. Diagnostic test for AIDS was developed in 1985 by Luc Montagnier and colleagues of the Pasteur Institute, Paris, France. It was a sandwich-type immunoenzymatic detection method.

3851. World Conference on Breast Cancer was held July 13–17, 1997, in Kingston, Ontario, Canada. Some 600 scientists, health professionals, activists, environmentalists, breast cancer survivors, and women with breast cancer attended. The conference was sponsored by the New York City-based Women's Environment and Development Organization and the Kingston Breast Cancer Conference Committee.

MEDICINE—EDUCATION

3852. Medical school in Europe to operate on an organized basis was founded at Salerno, in what is now Italy, in the ninth century. It educated students from three continents—Europe, Africa, and Asia—and occasionally allowed women to study.

3853. Licensing requirement for physicians was imposed circa 1250 in Salerno, Italy, when the faculty of the medical school there was given the authority to administer a licensing examination to all physician candidates in the southern Italian kingdom of Naples.

3854. Dentistry instruction as a formal discipline began in 1580 at the University of Paris, in France.

3855. Licensing requirement for dentists was enacted in 1685 by the electorate of Brandenburg-Prussia (an area now divided between Germany and Poland). Various kinds of practitioners, including tooth extractors, hernia operators, oculists, and lithotomists (who removed bladder stones), were required appear before the Collegium Medicum in Berlin to have their skills and knowledge evaluated.

3856. Clinical teacher was the Dutch physician Hermann Boerhaave (1668–1738). A professor at the University of Leiden, he founded the modern system of teaching medical students at the patients' bedside.

3857. Veterinary school was founded in France in 1761.

3858. Nursing school was the Deaconess Institute, founded in 1836 by Theodor Fliedner to train Protestant women in nursing techniques as a way of giving charitable service to the poor. The school was located at Kaiserswerth, near Düsseldorf, Germany. Within the space of 30 years, it trained some 1,600 women. One of them was an Englishwoman, Florence Nightingale, who went on to establish nursing as a profession.

3859. Dental college was the Baltimore College of Dental Surgery in Baltimore, MD, USA, founded by two dentists, Horace H. Hayden and Chapin A. Harris, who served as its first president. The faculty also included two physicians. The college opened on November 3, 1840, with five students, two of whom completed the two-year course of study and graduated with the degree of D.D.S. It eventually became the School of Dentistry at the University of Maryland, Baltimore.

3860. Medical school for women was the Boston Female Medical School, Boston, MA, USA, which was organized through the initiative of Samuel Gregory. It opened on November 1, 1848, with twelve pupils and two teachers. On May 24, 1856, the school was incorporated as the New England Female Medical College, with power to confer degrees. In 1874 it was absorbed by the Boston University School of Medicine, founded the previous year as a school of homeopathy, which thus became the first coeducational medical school in the world.

3861. School for professional nurses was the Nightingale Training School for Nurses, founded by Florence Nightingale at St. Thomas's Hospital, London, England. The first class, consisting of 15 students, enrolled in June 1860. Nightingale founded the school with £50,000 donated by the public in honor of her lifesaving work during the Crimean War, when, as superintendent of the British Army's female nurses, she harassed the military authorities into cleaning up the filthy conditions in its hospitals.

3862. Postgraduate center for psychiatric education was the Salpêtrière Hospital in Paris, France. Under the direction of Jean-Martin Charcot, the leading neurologist of his time, the Salpêtrière began in 1882 to train such outstanding neurologists and psychiatrists as Sigmund Freud, who attended in 1885. It was Charcot's lectures on the organic basis of hypnosis that sparked Freud's interest in the psychology of neurosis.

3863. Geriatrics department in a medical school was established in 1982 at the Mount Sinai Medical Center in New York, NY, USA, by American physician Robert Butler.

3864. Veterinary chiropractic school was founded by Sharon Willoughby in Hillsdale, IL, USA, in 1990. The school taught veterinarians how to apply techniques of chiropractic joint adjustment to animals.

3865. Virtual autopsies could be performed on an Internet web site created in October 1998 by medical staff and students at Leicester University in England. The site presented data from seven actual autopsies. Visitors to the site could investigate each patient's medical history and examine detailed images prepared by a real pathologist to produce their own postmortems.

MEDICINE—EQUIPMENT

3866. Sterilization by steam was practiced by the Chinese before the year 980, when Lu Zanning described it in his *Discourse on the Investigation of Things*. He advocated the application of steam to the bedding and other belongings of people who had died from contagious fevers.

3867. Wheelchair of record was designed by Flemish nobleman Jehan Lhermite for the ailing Philip II of Spain, who died in 1598.

3868. Modern wheelchair designed for hospital use was the Merlin Chair, built in Belgium circa 1770 by Joseph Merlin, a Belgian maker of musical instruments. It was a three-wheeled invalid chair, with a double tire on the two front wheels. The outer tires were turned by the hands to propel the chair, as in modern designs. The Merlin chair was probably inspired by the wooden chair built in 1760 by the French cabinetmaker Jean-François Oeben for the ailing Duc de Bourgogne. Merlin was also the inventor of the roller skate.

3869. Stethoscope was invented in 1816 by the French physician René-Théophile-Hyacinthe Laënnec, who called it a "plectoriloc." It was a wooden cylinder, 9 inches (23 centimeters) in length, that amplified the sounds made by the heart and lungs. For ease in carrying, stethoscopes were made in three parts that were screwed together. They were made binaural in 1852, when an American, George P. Cammann, added the two earpieces.

3870. Endoscope allowing physicians to see deeper into bodily orifices was the speculum, invented by Pierre Segalas of France in 1827. It was a wand with a mirror attached to one end. A candle illuminated the mirror.

3871. Hypodermic syringe was invented sometime around 1835 by Charles Gabriel Pravaz, a French doctor who specialized in orthopedics. The cylinder was made of silver. The contents were pushed through the needle by the turning of a screw. Pravaz's syringe was used to inject ferric chloride into aneurysms to encourage clots to form.

3872. Modern stethoscope was invented in 1839 by the Czech physician Josef Skǒda. He improved on previous single-tubed designs by adding a second tube that enabled the practitioner to listen through the stethoscope with both ears.

3873. Ophthalmoscope was invented in 1851 by the physiologist and physicist Hermann von Helmholtz, who was then a professor of physiology at the University of Königsberg, Germany. The device, a spyglass fixed to an inclined mirror, allowed physicians to send light to the back of a patient's eye and to receive a magnified view of the retina and other inner structures of the eye.

3874. Clinical thermometer in current use was invented in 1866 by the physician and medical historian Sir Thomas Clifford Allbutt of Leeds, England. His short mercury thermometer, which registered temperature in a few minutes, replaced previous thermometers that were 12 inches long and took 20 minutes to work.

3875. Life-support system to provide the physical requirements of human survival in environments where they are lacking was devised by the French physician and engineer Paul Bert, a pioneer in aerospace medicine, who designed portable oxygen supply systems for balloonists and mountaineers. The first test of his ideas was made in 1875, when two balloonists on a high-altitude flight inhaled humidified oxygen from tubes made from cow intestines. One died and the other survived.

3876. Surgical adhesive bandage was Hansaplast, invented by the German pharmacist Paul Beiersdorf in 1882. His plaster-coated bandage was waterproof and provided good protection, but it did not let the wound breathe.

3877. Centrifuge for medical use was the hematocrit, invented by Swedish physician Sven Hedin in 1889. Basing his work on a proposal by another Swedish doctor, Magnus Gustav Blix, Hedin constructed a rotating device with a large flywheel attached to a smaller wheel that could hold tubes of blood. Turning the flywheel made the small wheel spin at a high rate. Centrifugal force acting on the blood samples forced the heavier blood cells to separate out from the blood plasma and accumulate at the bottom of the tubes, where they could be measured and counted.

3878. Small bandage with built-in adhesive was the Band-Aid, the invention of Earle Dickson, of the Johnson and Johnson Company, New Brunswick, NJ, USA. In 1921, while preparing a dressing for his accident-prone wife, Dickson came up with the idea of a small, ready-to-apply bandage made of a wad of sterile gauze backed by a strip of surgical adhesive. Dickson's key innovation was the use of a removable nonstick material to protect the sticky side of the adhesive tape. Another Johnson and Johnson employee, W. Johnson Kenyon, suggested the name "Band-Aid."

3879. Pyroelectric ear thermometer was invented by Jacob Fraden, a physician in San Diego, CA, USA, and introduced in 1990. It read a patient's temperature by measuring infrared heat from the eardrum.

MEDICINE—HOSPITALS

3880. Hospitals in Asia of record were the Brahmanic hospitals established in Sri Lanka circa 431 BCE.

3881. Military hospitals were built by the Romans circa 100 BCE.

3882. Christian hospitals were founded after the abolition of pagan healing temples in 331 CE by the Roman emperor Constantine after his conversion. The first of note was founded in Cappadocia (now part of Turkey) by St. Basil of Caesarea in 370.

3883. Public hospital in Europe was founded in Rome, Italy, circa 396 by the Christian convert St. Fabiola, a wealthy woman who financed the project by selling her property— some accounts say she converted her home into a hospital—and who nursed the sick herself. Her teacher, St. Jerome, wrote of her: "Often did she carry on her own shoulders persons infected with jaundice and filth. Often too did she wash away the matter discharged from wounds which others, even though men, could not bear to look at." Some also credit Fabiola with being the first known woman surgeon.

3884. Medieval hospital in Europe was the Hôtel Dieu of Lyon, France, founded in 542 by Childebert I, King of the Franks. Similar hospitals were founded in French cities throughout the Middle Ages and were an outgrowth of the infirmaries run by monasteries. Typically, they were unventilated halls in which sick people lay crowded together in dirty beds or on piles of straw, and the emphasis was less on treatment than on effecting salvation.

3885. Islamic hospital was built during the reign of the Umayyad caliph al-Walid I (705–715), probably in Damascus, Syria. Another was built in the environs of Baghdad (in present-day Iraq) by the city's founder, Abu Ja'far al-Mansur, the second Abbasid caliph, sometime after 762.

3886. Hospital to keep charts for patients was opened in Baghdad (in modern Iraq) in the tenth century, together with an associated medical school with an international body of faculty and students. The staff of 24 physicians included bonesetters, surgeons, and oculists. The medications, therapy, and diet given to each patient were recorded on charts.

3887. Teaching hospital was the Pantokrator, founded in 1136 by John II, the Emperor of Byzantium, at his capital, Constantinople (now Istanbul, Turkey). In addition to the hospital, which accommodated 50 patients, the Pantokrator included a pharmacy, a home for 24 elderly men, a residence for lepers, and a monastery, whose abbot and monks served as administrators of the facilities. The staff included five pharmacists, five laundresses, two cooks, two bakers, a latrine-cleaner, and four pallbearers.

3888. Isolation hospital for plague victims was built at the Italian city of Ragusa (now Dubrovnik, Croatia) in 1377, under orders from the city's health board.

3889. Military hospital in Europe since antiquity was built by the Spanish at Mechelen in Brabant (now Malines, Belgium) during Spain's campaign to control the Netherlands (1572–1659). In addition to treating wounds received on the battlefield, the physicians and surgeons treated infectious diseases, particularly syphilis, and stress disorders.

3890. Free dispensary for the poor was opened in 1635 in Paris, France. The first director was the physician and journalist Théophraste Renaudot, physician to King Louis XIII. Renaudot also founded the first medical advisory clinic, in 1630.

3891. Hospital for unwanted newborns was the Foundling Hospital of London, England, established in 1741. Newborn babies whose mothers could not raise them were left there to be given a home and taught a trade.

3892. Clinical rounds in hospitals for the purpose of teaching medical students were initiated by the Scottish physician John Rutherford, professor at the Edinburgh Medical School. Beginning in 1750, he daily brought groups of students to a special ward in the city's infirmary that had been set aside for that purpose.

MEDICINE—HOSPITALS—*continued*

3893. Protestant hospital was founded in 1836 by the German Lutheran pastor and reformer Theodor Fliedner at Kaiserswerth, near Düsseldorf, Germany. At the same time, he established a nursing order for Protestant women, the order of deaconesses, and founded a motherhouse and training school for them, the Deaconess Institute.

3894. Women's hospital founded by women was the Woman's Hospital of New York, NY, USA. On February 10, 1855, a constitution was adopted by 30 women who formed the Woman's Hospital Association. The Woman's Hospital was opened with 40 beds on May 4, 1855, with Dr. James Marion Sims as resident surgeon. A permanent building was opened on December 5, 1906.

3895. Women's hospital staffed by women physicians was the New York Infirmary for Women and Children, incorporated in New York, NY, USA, on December 13, 1853, "to provide for poor women the medical advice of competent physicians of their own sex." Its first location was a one-room infirmary in Tompkins Square. On May 12, 1857, a hospital was opened. The founder and chief physician was Dr. Marie Elizabeth Zakrzewska.

3896. Teaching and research hospice for the dying was St. Christopher's Hospice, founded in London, England, in 1967 by a group of doctors and nurses headed by physician Dame Cicely Saunders. The staff was a community team of health care professionals and lay volunteers, organized by Saunders on Christian principles.

3897. Solar-powered hospital was a remote medical clinic in Waramuri, Guyana. In 1983, a photovoltaic system designed and installed by NASA's Lewis Research Center and the Solarex Corporation was installed in the tiny clinic. The 1.8 kilowatt system fed electricity to a vaccine refrigerator, indoor lighting, doctor's examination light, and a radio. Similar systems were installed later that year in medical clinics in Pedro Vincente Maldonado, Ecuador; Kibwezi, Kenya; Ikutha, Kenya; and Chikwakwa, Zimbabwe.

3898. National railway hospital was India's Lifeline Express, conceived by India's first prime minister, Jawaharlal Nehru, and implemented in 1991 by the IMPACT India Foundation, with the support of the Indian government and three United Nations agencies, the United Nations Development Programme, UNICEF, and the World Health Organization. Lifeline Express consisted of three medically equipped railcars that brought doctors into the country's remote districts.

MEDICINE—IMAGING

3899. Prehistoric painting to show the heart of a mammal is an image of an elephant or mammoth, painted in red lines on the wall of El Pindal Cave in Asturias, Spain, some 30,000 years ago. The heart is not anatomically correct, but is drawn in the same symmetrical shape as the hearts on Valentine's Day cards.

3900. Anatomically correct image of the human heart known to archeologists is a ceramic container made about 3,000 years ago by one of the Olmec peoples in what is now south-central Mexico. The container, 7 inches (18 centimeters) tall, appears at first glance to be a male figure divided down the middle, with three cylindrical shapes protruding from its shoulders. It can also be viewed as a representation of a human heart, complete with a pulmonary artery, an aorta, and a superior vena cava—the heart's three major blood vessels—and an interventricular sulcus, the crease that separates the right and left ventricles. The image was identified by a cardiologist and amateur art historian, Dr. Gordon Bendersky of Elkins Park, PA, USA, who said that its existence supports the theory that the Olmec was the first Mesoamerican civilization to practice human sacrifice through removal of the victim's heart.

3901. Image of human tissue made from life was a daguerreotype made by Englishman Alfred Donne in 1845. It showed tissue samples as seen through a microscope.

3902. X-ray photograph of human anatomy was made by Wilhelm Conrad Röntgen (or Roentgen), the discoverer of X rays, on December 22, 1895, in Würzburg, Germany, and sent to physicist Franz Exner in Vienna, Austria. The radiograph shows the bones of a woman's hand, and is traditionally assumed to be of Röntgen's wife. However, Röntgen did not label it himself.

3903. Electrocardiogram of the electrical activity of the human heart was produced in 1903 by the Javanese-born Dutch physiologist Willem Einthoven, a professor at the University of Leiden. That year, he invented the string galvanometer, or Einthoven galvanometer, a device for recording the fluctuations of electrical potential of the heart muscles as a graph on paper. Einthoven was the first to recognize that certain markings in the electrocardiogram were characteristic of various kinds of heart disease.

3904. Arteriogram was an X-ray image of human arteries taken by two Portuguese doctors, the neurologist António Caetano de Abreu Freire Egas Moniz and Renaldo Dos Santos, in 1927.

3905. Electroencephalogram or printed recording of the electrical activity of the brain was produced by the German psychiatrist Hans Berger in 1929 using his invention, the electroencephalograph. He was the first to observe and name the alpha and beta types of brain waves.

3906. CAT scan was performed in 1972 to diagnose the brain tumor of a patient at the Atkinson Morley's Hospital in Wimbledon, England. Computerized axial tomography (CAT) was developed by the British electrical engineer Godfrey Hounsfield of Electrical and Musical Industries (EMI) Ltd. and by the South African-born American physicist Allan McCormack. They shared the 1979 Nobel Prize in Physiology or Medicine. The mathematical principles on which their work was based were discovered by the Austrian mathematician J. Radon in 1917.

3907. Magnetic resonance image of a human body was made of the chest cavity of Dr. Lawrence Minkoff on July 3, 1977, by American researcher Dr. Raymond Damadian, founder of the FONAR Corporation in Melville, NY, USA. Working independently, Damadian and Paul C. Lauterbur of the University of Illinois at Urbana-Champaign, IL, USA, developed the application of magnetic resonance imaging (MRI) technology to noninvasive medical diagnosis. MRI scanners produce detailed images of soft tissues, including blood vessels, blood flow, cartilage, bone marrow, muscles, ligaments, the spinal cord, and fluids in the brain and spine, that do not show up well or at all on X rays. The first functional MRI scanner was called the Indomitable and was designed by Damadian.

3908. Comprehensive digital atlas of the human body was the Visible Human Project, led by Americans Victor Spitzer and David Whitlock of the University of Colorado Health Sciences Center in Denver, CO, USA. The body of an executed murderer, 39-year-old Joseph Paul Jernigan, was sliced into ultrathin cross-sections. Detailed, 3D-navigable views of these cross-sections were made by photography, magnetic resonance imaging, and computer tomography. In 1997, these views were made available to medical schools, hospitals, and researchers on CD-ROMs and specialized computer networks. (A woman's body was incorporated into the atlas at a later date.) The program was financed by the National Library of Medicine, a unit of the National Institutes of Health.

MEDICINE—IMMUNIZATION

3909. Inoculation against smallpox appears to have been carried out by a Taoist monk in China in the tenth century BCE. He placed into the nostril of the patient a cloth pad that had been impregnated with attenuated smallpox germs.

3910. Vaccine that was successful was the smallpox vaccine, developed by the physician Edward Jenner in 1796. As a country physician in Berkeley, Gloucestershire, England, Jenner had noticed that milkmaids who contracted cowpox, a mild pox-like disease of cattle, were immune to the related but much more serious disease of smallpox. (The Latin name for cowpox is *vaccinia,* from which the word "vaccination" is derived.) In May 1796, Jenner used pus from the cowpox lesions on the finger of a dairymaid, Sarah Nelmes, to inoculate an eight-year-old boy, James Phipps. Phipps quickly developed a mild case of cowpox. Two weeks later Jenner inoculated Phipps with material from a smallpox lesion, with no effect—the cowpox inoculation had provided immunity to smallpox. Jenner's initial 1797 report on his findings was rejected by the Royal Society. In 1798 he privately published *An Inquiry into the Causes and Effects of the Variolae Vaccinae, a Disease Known by the Name of Cow Pox,* which gave a full description of his vaccination process.

3911. Rabies vaccine was devised between 1880 and 1885 by the French chemist and microbiologist Louis Pasteur, who isolated the virus that causes rabies in the saliva and spinal cords of infected animals and progressively weakened it until it was effective as a vaccine. His first test on a human being took place on July 6, 1885. The patient was Joseph Meister, a nine-year-old boy from an Alsatian village who had been bitten by a rabid dog on the way to school. Pasteur injected him with the vaccine over the course of twelve days, and he survived (he later became the doorman at the Pasteur Institute in Paris). Shortly afterwards, Berger Gupille, a 14-year-old shepherd, was saved by the vaccine after he fought off a rabid dog who was attacking children. By the following March, Pasteur had treated 350 people infected by rabies, of whom only one had died.

MEDICINE—IMMUNIZATION—*continued*

3912. Poliomyelitis vaccine was produced by American researcher Dr. Maurice Brodie of New York, NY, USA, in February 1933. It was obtained from the spinal cords of rare Indian monkeys that had been infected with poliomyelitis. The spinal cords were excised and made into an emulsion that was treated with formalin to kill the virus. The first polio vaccine widely used was developed in 1952 by another American researcher, Jonas Edward Salk, director of the Virus Research Laboratory at the University of Pittsburgh's School of Medicine.

3913. Vaccine to be chemically synthesized was SPf66, an antimalarial vaccine developed by Manual Patarroyo of Colombia, who donated the rights for its use to the World Health Organization in 1995. All previous vaccines were made biologically, by attenuating or killing the bacteria that produce disease.

3914. AIDS vaccine tested internationally was Aidsvax, developed by American pharmaceutical firm Vaxgen, Inc. On June 3, 1998, the company received approval from the U.S. Food and Drug Administration to conduct clinical trials involving 5,000 uninfected volunteers in some 40 clinics in the U.S. and Canada and 2,500 volunteers in 16 clinics in Thailand.

MEDICINE—MEDICINES

3915. Use of bicarbonate of soda as an antacid was introduced by the Sumerians in the mid-fourth millennium BCE.

3916. Medicine kit may have been carried by Ötzi, the so-called Iceman, a 5,300-year-old mummy found on September 19, 1991, by Helmut Simon in the Tirolean Ötztal Alps, on the border between Austria and Italy. Among the effects Ötzi was carrying were two balls of birch fungus (*Piptoporus betulinus*) pierced with thongs. Ingesting birch fungus can bring on bouts of diarrhea; the fungus also contains an oil that is toxic to some parasites. Reseachers believe that Ötzi ate doses of the fungus to control an infestation of intestinal whipworm parasites, which were found in his colon.

3917. Asthma medication that was effective was ephedrine, an alkaloid drug derived from the horsetail plant, especially the species *Ephedra sinica*. It was known as an decongestant and asthma treatment in Chinese medicine from circa 3000 BCE. In 200 CE, a Chinese doctor named Zhang Zhongjing was the first to advocate its use in print in his compendium of all the medical knowledge then known in China. Synthetic ephedrine was developed by Western doctors and used as a bronchodilator and nasal decongestant beginning in the 1920s. Most modern over-the-counter remedies for hay fever still contain ephedrine.

3918. Narcotic drugs were known to early humans in the form of poppy juice and other substances. The first narcotic of record was opium elixir, used by several ancient peoples, including the Egyptians. An Egyptian medical text of circa 1500 BCE warned against excessive use of the drug as an anesthetic during trepanning (an operation in which the skull was opened to relieve pressure on the brain) because of the uncontrollable delusions it produced. The earliest evidence of human use of the poppy comes from 5,000-year-old burial sites in Granada, Spain.

3919. Cough lozenges were hard candies made with honey, which has throat-soothing properties. The Egyptians used them from about the beginning of the first millennium BCE.

3920. Anticoagulant to maintain the flow of blood, even in air, was hirudin, contained in the saliva of certain species of leeches, notably *Hirudo medicinalis* in Europe, *Hirudo troctina* in Africa and the Middle East, and *Gnathobdella ferox* in Asia. Application of leeches for bloodletting was practiced in ancient India; the first Western citation is contained in the works of the Greek physician Nicander of Colophon (in modern Turkey) circa 130 BCE. Use of leeches reached its height in Europe between 1825 and 1840.

3921. Public pharmacy was opened in Baghdad (now capital of Iraq) circa 770.

3922. Epsom salt (magnesium sulfate) was named in 1695 by the English physician and naturalist Nathaniel Grew, who dug up a quantity of the compound at Epsom Springs, a natural hot spring whose water was prized by the British for its medicinal qualities.

3923. Isolation of morphine was accomplished in 1805 by German chemist Friedrich Wilhelm Adam Ferdinand Serturner, who first called it "principium somniferum," but in a published report referred to it as "morphium." Morphine is the active ingredient in opium, a narcotic derived from the juice of the opium poppy.

3924. Codeine was derived from opium in France in 1832 by the chemist Pierre-Jean Robiquet. Codeine is used medicinally as a painkiller, antispasmodic, and sedative.

3925. Barbiturate was derived from barbituric acid, synthesized in 1864 by the German chemist Adolf von Baeyer. The first barbiturate to be sold commercially in a medicinal preparation was the sedative Veronal, marketed in the United States in 1903. Barbiturates are organic compounds that depress the nervous system.

3926. Petroleum jelly or petrolatum, a semisolid gel derived from petroleum and used as a lubricant and skin emollient, was developed in 1870 by Robert Augustus Chesebrough, a chemist from Brooklyn, NY (now part of New York City), USA, after a trip to the Pennsylvania oil fields, where he was shown a gummy waste product that was thought to heal wounds. He coined the word "Vaseline" for his gel and registered it in the United States on May 14, 1878, as a trademark. On May 10, 1880, he organized the Chesebrough Manufacturing Company, New York City, which he headed until 1909.

3927. Heroin was developed from the addictive painkiller morphine, an extract of the dried milky juice of unripe opium poppy seedpods, by Farbenfabriken vormals Friedrich Bayer and Company, Barmen, Germany (now Bayer AG, Leverkusen), in 1898. Also called diacetylmorphine, it was made by treating morphine with acetic anhydride. Heroin was initially believed to be a stronger and supposedly nonaddictive form of morphine—the trade name *heroin* was meant to convey the impression of heroic effectiveness as a pain reliever—but the drug proved to be even more addictive than morphine and therefore unsafe for analgesic use.

3928. Aspirin is usually considered to have been formulated in a marketable compound in 1899 by the German chemist Felix Hoffman of Farbenfabriken vormals Friedrich Bayer and Company, Barmen, Germany (now Bayer AG, Leverkusen). However, the real discoverer of aspirin was another chemist, Arthur Eichengreen. Eichengreen's contribution was deliberately obscured by Bayer during the Nazi period because he was a Jew.

3929. Chemotherapeutic drug that effectively treated an infectious illness was atoxyl, a synthetic arsenic derivative discovered in 1905 by a British scientist, Harold Thomas. Although it was highly toxic, it was useful in combatting African trypanosomiasis (also called African sleeping sickness), a lethal inflammation of the nervous system transmitted by the tsetse fly and caused by the parasitic protozoans *Trypanosoma gambiense* and *Trypanosoma rhodesiense.*

3930. Treatment for syphilis was mercury, administered orally. It was somewhat effective in killing the syphilis bacterium but was more often fatal to the patient. The first successful antisyphilis drug was arsphenamine (trade name Salvarsan), an arsenic compound developed in 1909 by the German bacteriologist Paul Ehrlich. A week-long course of penicillin was found to be the most effective treatment in studies conducted in 1943 by the American physician John Friend Mahoney.

3931. Synthetic drug to treat bacterial infections was arsphenamine, an arsenic-based chemical compound marketed under the name Salvarsan. It attacks *Treponema pallidum,* the sexually transmitted microorganism that causes syphilis. Salvarsan was developed in 1909–10 by the German bacteriologist Paul Ehrlich, head of the Royal Institute for Experimental Therapy at Frankfurt am Main, who had already shared the 1908 Nobel Prize in Physiology or Medicine for his work in immunology.

3932. Chemical anticoagulant was sodium citrate, whose action in preventing blood clotting was discovered in Belgium shortly before World War I. The first transfusion of human blood kept liquid with sodium citrate took place on March 27, 1914, at l'Hôpital St.-Jean in Brussels.

3933. Isolation of insulin was achieved in 1921 by two Canadian biochemists, Frederick Grant Banting and Charles H. Best, at the University of Toronto. Lack of insulin, or the inability of cells to receive it, causes the disease diabetes mellitus, in which the blood sugar rises to dangerous levels. Banting and Best tested insulin preparations on diabetic dogs before trying it successfully, on January 11, 1922, on a 14-year-old boy, Leonard Thompson.

3934. Sulfa drug was Prontosil, the trade name for sulfamidochrysoidine. In living tissue, the Prontosil molecule forms para-aminobenzenesulfonamide (sulfanilamide). Its effectiveness was demonstrated in 1928 by the chemist and pathologist Gerhard Domagk, director of the I.G. Farbenindustrie (Bayer) Laboratory for Experimental Pathology and Bacteriology, Wuppertal-Elberfeld, Germany. Investigating the antibacterial action of azo dyes, he found that the red dye Protonsil prevented the death of mice infected with streptococci and controlled staphylococcic infections in rabbits. The discovery was announced in 1932 and earned Domagk the 1939 Nobel Prize in Physiology or Medicine, but the Nazi regime in Germany prevented him from accepting it. In 1936

MEDICINE—MEDICINES—*continued*

the English physician Leonard Colebrook and his colleagues made the first clinical use of Prontosil, employing it to treat septicemia (blood poisoning) and puerperal, or childbed, fever.

3935. Amphetamine to be sold commercially in a medicinal preparation was Benzedrine (amphetamine sulfate). Its manufacturer, the American pharmaceutical company Smith, Kline, and French, introduced it in 1932 in its Benzedrex inhaler, which was marketed to people with clogged sinuses. Amphetamine, a stimulant that does not occur in nature, was invented in 1887.

3936. Patient to be given penicillin was an American, Anne Sheafe Miller. In February 1942, Miller was admitted to New Haven Hospital in New Haven, CT, USA, with a life-threatening streptococcal infection. After 27 days of conventional treatments, she was given a penicillin preparation manufactured by Merck Laboratories of New Jersey, USA, and she quickly recovered.

3937. Tranquilizer commercially available was reserpine, an alkaloid isolated in 1952 by the British biochemist Robert Robinson and the Swiss pharmacologist Emil Schittler from extracts of the plant genus *Rauwolfia*. Powdered *Rauwolfia serpentina* root had long been known in India and elsewhere as a calmative. Commercial quantities of reserpine were first manufactured in 1953 by Ciba AG in Basel, Switzerland.

3938. Medicine produced using recombinant DNA was human insulin, produced in 1978 by the City of Hope Medical Center, Duarte, CA, USA, in a joint venture with the American biotechnology firm Genentech. The insulin was created using bacteria that had been implanted with human DNA. The U.S. Food and Drug Administration approved use of the bioengineered insulin in 1982.

3939. Human antibodies produced artificially were announced by American researchers Henry Kaplan and Lennart Olson on July 29, 1980, at the Stanford University Medical School, Stanford, CA, USA. Kaplan and Olson, seeking a method of manufacturing pure human antibodies to help diagnose and treat disease, created a line of antibody-producing hybrid cells by fusing bone-marrow cancer cells with human spleen cells.

3940. Drug to prevent cancer was tamoxifen citrate, a selective estrogen receptor modulator, developed by Zeneca Pharmaceutical (now Astrazeneca) under the trade name Nolvadex. In April 1998, the National Cancer Institute (NCI) released findings from the National Adjuvant Breast and Bowel Project's Breast Cancer Prevention Trial that showed tamoxifen cut the risk of breast cancer nearly in half among more than 13,000 women at high risk for the disease. On October 29, 1998, the U.S. Food and Drug Administration approved tamoxifen for the reduction of breast cancer risk in healthy women considered to be at high risk.

MEDICINE—PRACTITIONERS AND RESEARCHERS

3941. Physician known by name appears to have been Imhotep, the Egyptian genius who built the Step Pyramid for King Zoser circa 2650 BCE and who is thus also known as history's first architect and engineer. His medical services were rendered in his capacity as royal magician and astrologer. A century after his death, Imhotep was elevated to the Egyptian pantheon as god of medicine, afterwards becoming identified with the Greek god of medicine, Asclepius.

3942. Malpractice regulation for physicians is included in the Code of Hammurabi, the collection of Babylonian laws from the second millennium (1792–50) BCE. Penalties were prescribed for any physician who killed a patient while opening an abscess. For the death of a patient who was a slave, the doctor had to make good the loss to the owner by furnishing a living slave. For the death of a patient who was free, the doctor paid by having both of his hands cut off.

3943. Description of the circulatory system that was reasonably accurate is contained in the Ebers Papyrus, one of the earliest medical texts. It was compiled in Egypt circa 1500 BCE but contains material that is much older. The author of the papyrus demonstrates familiarity with the system of blood vessels and the functioning of the heart.

3944. Researcher to conduct human dissections for scientific purposes was the Pythagorean philosopher Alcmaeon, who lived during the sixth century BCE in Croton (the modern Crotone, Italy). He was also rumored to have practiced vivisection, the dissection of living animals.

3945. Gynecologist who was a woman was the Athenian physician Agnodice, who is traditionally considered to have practiced circa 350 BCE. As did many later woman physicians, she dressed as a man when seeing patients. She is credited with achieving a role, that of physician, forbidden to her by law. Modern historians believe that Agnodice may not have been a historical figure. The only source for her tale is Hyginus, a Latin author of the first century CE.

3946. Anatomist to dissect human cadavers was Herophilus, the founder of the science of anatomy in the West, who lived in the scholarly community at Alexandria, Egypt, in the fourth century BCE. He described the ventricles of the brain, recognized the difference between sensory nerves and motor nerves, and studied the reproductive organs, pancreas, spleen, liver, and duodenum, which was given its name by him. None of his nine books survived the burning of the Alexandria library in 272 CE.

3947. Western physician to take a pulse was the Greek physician Herophilus, one of the founders of the science of anatomy, who was part of the community of scholars in Alexandria, Egypt, in the fourth and third centuries BCE (he died circa 280 BCE). He timed the pulse using a water clock.

3948. Jewish physician known was Rufus of Samaria (present-day Israel and the Palestinian Authority), who lived circa 100 CE. He was the author of commentaries on Hippocrates, written in Greek.

3949. Endocrinologists lived in China in the second century CE. By adding minerals and other substances to human urine, they extracted steroid and pituitary hormones that were reduced to crystalline form for consumption by patients.

3950. Physicians in Japan were Koreans who arrived in response to an invitation from the emperor of Japan. The first, Kimbu, came in 414 CE, the second, Tokurai, in 459.

3951. Muslim physician of note was Abu Bakr Muhammad ibn Zakariyà ar-Razi, known in the West as Rhazes, who served as chief physician at hospitals in Rayy, Persia (his birthplace, now in Iran, circa 865), and Baghdad. His book *Kitab al-hawi (Comprehensive Book)* covered the medical knowledge of Greece, Syria, Persia, and India. In addition to being an innovator in medicine and dentistry, he was an important philosopher and an alchemist.

3952. King to practice curing of the "king's evil" by touching the swollen lymph glands on the neck of a person afflicted with scrofula, a form of tuberculosis, was Edward the Confessor, king of England from circa 1042 to 1066. The custom is said to have been started by a young woman who was told in a dream to ask the king to wash her neck with water, with the result that the skin opened, pus flowed out, and healthy skin grew over the wound. Although later monarchs of England doubted that the touching was effective, the practice continued until 1712, and in France until 1830, with many thousands of people receiving the touch. King William III of England told each person he touched, "May God give you better health and more sense."

3953. Description of pulmonary blood circulation was given circa 1250 by Ibn an-Nafis, the Syrian-born director of the Nasiri Hospital in Cairo, Egypt. He deduced logically that, contrary to the teachings of Galen, blood passes through the lungs on its way from the right to the left ventricle of the heart. No progress came of this recognition, however, nor of its rediscovery circa 1553 by the Spanish physician Miguel Serveto (Michael Servetus), until it was established experimentally by the English physician William Harvey, who described it, together with many other aspects of the heart and circulatory system, in his *Exercitatio Anatomica de Motu Cordis et Sanguinis in Animalibus (An Anatomical Exercise Concerning the Motion of the Heart and Blood in Animals)* in 1628.

3954. Woman physician to receive university training was Costanza Calenda. In 1422 she obtained a degree from the University of Naples, Italy.

3955. Forensic pathologist of record was the Florentine physician Antonio Benivieni (circa 1443–1502). Records of 15 autopsies he performed have been preserved. In a case of carcinoma of the stomach, he wrote: "My kinsman, Antonio Bruno . . . wasted away through lack of nourishment till little more than skin and bone remained. The body was cut open for reasons of public welfare. It was found that the opening of his stomach had closed up and it had hardened down to the lowest part with the result that nothing could pass through to the organs beyond, and death inevitably followed."

3956. Toxicologist was the iconoclastic German-Swiss physician Paracelsus (original name Philippus Aureolus Theophrastus Bombast von Hohenheim), who lived in the first half of the 16th century. His experiments with poisons confirmed that their effectiveness was caused by biochemical action.

MEDICINE—PRACTITIONERS AND RE-
SEARCHERS—*continued*

**3957. Anatomist since antiquity to dissect
human bodies** was Mondino dei Liucci (also
called Raimondino dei Liuzzi and Mundinus,
his Latin name), teacher of anatomy and surgery at the University of Bologna, Italy, in the
early 14th century, who dissected cadavers during his lectures. His book *Anathomia Mundini*
appeared in 1316.

3958. Anatomist to break with Galen was the
Flemish doctor Andreas Vesalius (the Latinized
version of his birth name, Andreí van Wesel;
his birthplace, Brabant, is in modern Belgium).
Beginning in 1537, Vesalius, who had received
his medical degree from the University of Padua, Italy, served as lecturer in surgery at the
universities of Padua, Basel, Pisa, and Bologna.
The conventional practice of lecturers at the
time was to discourse on the teachings of the
ancient Greek physician Galen while students
watched a cadaver being dissected by the lecturer's assistants. The lecturer himself did not
examine the cadaver or presume to contradict
Galen. Vesalius broke with tradition by doing
his own dissections and studying anatomy directly from the human body.

**3959. Military surgeon to treat gunshot
wounds without cautery** was Ambroise Paré,
a surgeon in the royal army of France. The
standard treatment for gunshot wounds called
for the surgeon to cauterize them with boiling
oil. In 1537, while treating wounded men on
the battlefield, Paré ran out of oil and, with
grave misgivings, had to make do with a mixture of turpentine, egg yolks, and oil of roses.
He discovered that the men whose wounds had
been scalded suffered far more pain, inflammation, swelling, and fever than the others. His
superior method of treatment was described in
his 1545 book *La Méthod de traicter les playes
faites par les arquebuses et aultres bastons à
feu (The Method of Treating Wounds Made by
Harquebuses and Other Guns),* which was itself an innovation, since it was written in
French rather than Latin. Paré also abandoned
the practice of cauterizing blood vessels with a
hot iron during amputations, replacing it with a
method of tying arteries with a ligature.

**3960. Skeleton prepared by a medical re-
searcher** still extant was prepared in 1546 by
the Flemish physician Andreas Vesalius (born
André Van Wesel in Brabant, modern Belgium), whose thoroughgoing dissections of cadavers resulted in the publication in 1543 of *De
humani corporis fabrica (On the Human's Bodily Works),* the first accurately illustrated anatomy text. The skeleton remains in the possession
of the University of Basel, Switzerland, where
Vesalius taught for a time.

3961. Modern epidemiologist was the 16th-
century French physician Guillaume de Baillou
(or Baillon), also known by the Latin name
Ballonius, who became dean of the medical
faculty at the University of Paris in 1580. He
was the author of a comprehensive survey of
epidemics that took place between 1570 and
1579.

**3962. Physician to use precise measuring in-
struments** in medical research and treatment
was Santorio Santorio (in Latin, Sanctorius),
professor of medical theory at the University of
Padua, Italy, from 1611 to 1624. Santorio was
an adherent of the iatrophysical theory, which
held that the body is essentially a machine.
Adapting inventions made by his friend and
colleague Galileo Galilei, he began using a
pulse clock in 1602 and a clinical thermometer
in 1612. He conducted a 30-year experiment,
using a scale, to study the effects of perspira-
tion and excretion on his own body weight, and
produced the first scientific examination of basal metabolism, *De statica medicina (On Medical Measurement),* in 1614.

3963. Pharmacists to practice as professionals
belonged to the Society of Apothecaries, founded in London, England, in 1617. Nonmembers
were barred from preparing and selling medicines.

3964. Religious order of nurses was the
Daughters of Charity of St. Vincent de Paul,
who founded the group in Paris, France, in
1633, together with St. Louise de Marillac, its
first superior. The members were young Roman
Catholic women who were trained to help the
poor, particularly with nursing care. They did
not take religious vows and were the first congregation of Catholic women to undertake charitable activities outside the cloister.

**3965. Physician to specialize in occupational
medicine** was the Italian physician Bernardino
Ramazzini, professor at the universities of Modena (1682–1700) and Padua (1700–1714). He
was the first to recognize the influence on
health of occupational hazards and to insist that
doctors should familiarize themselves with their
patients' ways of earning a living.

3966. Chiropodist to use the title was David Low, an Englishman who made his living as a corn-cutter, removing corns from people's feet for a guinea each. (He had earlier been a hotelier and had founded the first hotel in London.) The word "chiropodist" appeared in *Chiropodologia,* Low's textbook on foot care, which was published in 1785.

3967. Physician to understand the necessity for hygiene was Joseph Clark, a doctor in Dublin, Ireland, in the 1790s. Clark succeeded in reducing the death rate from puerperal fever in the city's maternity wards by requiring the staff to pay more attention to cleanliness. In 1829, Robert Collins, Clark's son-in-law, introduced the use of chlorine solutions to disinfect hospital maternity rooms.

3968. Professional organization of pharmacists was the Pharmaceutical Society of Great Britain, founded in London, England, in 1841.

3969. Woman physician in modern times to earn a degree from a medical school was Dr. Elizabeth Blackwell, a native of Bristol, England, who came to the United States in her youth. Most of the medical schools to which she applied refused to admit her because she was female. On January 23, 1849, she received her M.D. degree from the Geneva Medical College (later known as Hobart College), Geneva, NY, USA, receiving the highest grades in her class. She did graduate work at St. Bartholomew's Hospital, London. In 1853 she opened a private dispensary in New York City, the New York Infimary for Indigent Women and Children, with an all-female staff. She later founded two institutions of medical education for women, the Infirmary Medical School in New York and the London School of Medicine for Women, where she became professor of gynecology.

3970. Woman physician in England was Elizabeth Garrett Anderson, who earned her license to practice medicine from the Society of Apothecaries in 1865, although she had had to study privately because no British medical school accepted women. In 1870 she received her medical degree from the University of Paris. She was the founder of the New Hospital for Women and its associated women's medical school.

3971. Japanese woman to become a physician was Ginko Ogino, who graduated from Kojuin, a school of Western medicine, in 1882 and qualified to practice medicine in 1885.

3972. Hindu woman to earn a medical degree was Anandibai Joshee of India, who became a physician in 1886.

3973. Woman physician in Australia was Constance Stone. Barred from entering the medical school at Melbourne University, she studied overseas, earned a degree in 1890, and became a registered doctor.

3974. Woman to be awarded the British Order of Merit was the British nurse Florence Nightingale. In 1907, at the age of 87, Nightingale was awarded the Order of Merit by King Edward VII in recognition of her service in the Crimean War and in developing British medicine.

3975. Nation with a substantial number of women physicians was Russia, where there were some 1,500 women doctors practicing in 1914, a tenth of the total number. Women were allowed to attend Russian medical schools beginning in 1872.

3976. Flying bush doctor was St. Vincent Walsh, a physician based in Queensland, Australia, who beginning in May 1928 used a de Havilland airplane to reach patients in remote areas of the outback. The air medical service was arranged by John Flynn of the Queensland Presbyterian Mission.

3977. White witch doctor of note was South African former model Chris Reid. A student of black African traditional medicine, Reid, known professionally as Ntombhe Mhlophe, was officially recognized in 1994 as the first white practitioner of his craft.

MEDICINE—PROSTHETIC DEVICES

3978. False eyes were developed by ancient Egyptian physicians circa 2000 BCE, and were made of fired clay.

3979. Written record of a prosthesis was contained in the *Rig Veda,* the ancient sacred poem of India, which dates to circa 1500 BCE. It describes how the warrior queen Vishpla lost her leg in battle and was fitted with an iron leg, after which she returned to battle.

3980. Iron hand was fashioned by artisans in 218 BCE for the Roman general Marcus Sergius, who had lost his right arm in the Second Punic War against Carthage (in present-day Tunisia). The iron hand was designed to hold his shield, enabling him to return to the campaign.

3981. Mechanical prosthetic arm was designed in 1508 by Götz von Berlichingen, a German mercenary knight. Having lost his right arm at the Battle of Landshut in 1508, Götz ordered an iron hand that could grip and release by means of catches and springs. The hand was suspended from his arm with leather straps.

MEDICINE—PROSTHETIC DEVICES—
continued

3982. Glass eyes were invented circa 1625 by the German surgeon Joannis Scultetus, who developed them as a consequence of his treatment of head injuries in the Thirty Years' War (1618–148).

3983. Artificial eardrum was a piece of pig bladder, meant to approximate the action of the tympanic membrane. The bladder was stretched across a small horn made from elk's hoof and inserted into the ear. It was invented by German physician Marcus Banzer in 1640.

3984. Below-knee leg prosthesis was introduced in 1696 by Dutch surgeon Pieter Andriannszoon Verduyn (or Verduuin). The non-locking device made it easier to walk than did simple wooden legs or prostheses that locked for walking.

3985. Artificial hip was developed in 1972 by English orthopedic surgeon John Charnley. It was made mainly of high-density polyethylene and featured a functional, low-friction hip socket.

MEDICINE—PSYCHIATRY AND PSYCHOLOGY

3986. Drug treatment for mental illness was the administration of opium and olive oil to individuals "possessed by demons," as recommended in the Code of Hammurabi, the Babylonian law document dated to circa 1792–50 BCE.

3987. Asylums for the mentally ill are thought to have been founded in the Islamic lands of the Middle East in the eighth century.

3988. Insane asylum in Europe was Bethlem in London, England, founded as the priory of St. Mary of Bethlehem in 1247. Bedlam, as it was later known, accepted its first mentally ill inmates in 1403.

3989. Use of the term "psychology" in a work written in English appeared in "Observations on Man, His Frame, His Duty, and His Expectations," published in 1749 by the English philosopher and physician David Hartley. In that book, he attempted to construct an associative model for such complex mental processes as reasoning, imagining, and remembering.

3990. Hypnosis has been practiced by shamans and other healers since prehistory. In 1774, the Swabian physician Franz Anton Mesmer was the first to introduce hypnotic practices to modern medicine. Mesmer developed a theory of disease based on "animal magnetism," in which illness was caused by blockages to the flow of an invisible fluid in the body (somewhat analogous to the flow of current in a magnetic field). Mesmer's cures often required him to put the patient into a state of trance, a practice that his followers called *mesmerism*. James Braid, a Scottish surgeon, in 1841 coined the term "hypnosis."

3991. Humane treatment of the mentally ill was pioneered in 1788 by Vincenzo Chiarugi, head of a hospital for the insane at Florence, Italy. He was closely followed by Philippe Pinel, who was responsible for unchaining the patients at the Bicêtre asylum for men in Paris, France, where he was appointed chief physician in 1792, and the female inmates of Salpêtrière, where he became the director in 1794. Pinel was perhaps the first physician in modern times to view people with insanity as suffering from an illness rather than as criminals, beasts, or cases of demonic possession.

3992. Refuge for mentally ill patients where they were guaranteed humane treatment in a home-like environment was the York Retreat, founded in 1796 by William Tuke, a tea merchant in York, England, and operated for many years by his family. The Tukes were members of the Society of Friends, better known as Quakers.

3993. Phrenologist was the German-born Viennese physiologist Franz Josef Gall (1758–1828). Gall was the first to correctly ascribe brain functions to localized areas of the cerebrum. He extended this insight with the mistaken notion that the mental faculties and personality of an individual could be determined by what he called cranioscopy, the examination of the bumps and depressions in the skull. This technique is now called phrenology, a word coined by Gall's followers. In 1802, his lectures on the subject were condemned as sacrilegious by the Austrian government, and in 1805 Gall left Vienna for Paris.

3994. Work of experimental psychology was *Beiträge zur Theorie der Sinneswahrnehmung (Contributions to the Theory of Sense Perception),* written between 1858 and 1862 by the founder of experimental psychology, Wilhelm Wundt. Wundt was then a lecturer in physiology at the University of Heidelberg, Germany.

3995. Course in scientific psychology was offered in 1862 by Wilhelm Wundt. Wundt, known as the founder of experimental psychology, was then a lecturer in physiology at the University of Heidelberg, Germany. He introduced experimental methods borrowed from the natural sciences and advocated the use of introspection as the means to gain insight into psychological processes. Wundt's lectures were published in 1863 as *Vorlesungen über die Menschen und Thierseele (Lectures on the Mind of Humans and Animals)*.

3996. Psychologist to relate known physiological facts to psychological phenomena was the Scottish philosopher Alexander Bain, often considered the father of psychology. In works such as *Mind and Body: The Theories of Their Relation* (1873), he developed theories of voluntary and spontaneous behavior and compound and constructive mental association. He was the first to observe that behavior resulting in pleasurable consequences tends to be repeated and behavior resulting in painful consequences tends not to be.

3997. Psychology journal was *Mind*, edited beginning in 1876 by the Scottish philosopher and pioneering psychologist Alexander Bain.

3998. Experimental psychology laboratory of importance was founded at the University of Leipzig, Germany, in 1879 by Wilhelm Wundt, regarded as the founder of experimental psychology. Wundt, who held the chair of philosophy at the university, conducted the first systematic investigations of the immediate experiences of consciousness.

3999. Psychoanalyst was the Viennese physician Josef Breuer, credited by Sigmund Freud with being the founder of psychoanalysis. Breuer, a specialist in hysteria, was the first to find that memories of traumatic events could be released under hypnosis, thereby causing relief of the hysterical symptoms caused by the repressed memory. In 1895, Breuer and Freud co-authored *Studien über Hysterie (Studies on Hysteria)*, the first study of this process.

4000. Treatise on psychoanalysis in which the term was used was *Die Traumdeutung (The Interpretation of Dreams)*, published in Vienna, Austria, in 1899 by Sigmund Freud, considered by most to be the founder of psychoanalysis (a term he coined in 1896). In this work he offered his interpretation of the function of dreams and the sexual symbolism of dream imagery and events, calling dreams "the royal road to a knowledge of the unconscious." *Die Traumdeutung* also introduced such characteristic Freudian concepts as the libido, displacement, the Oedipus complex, and the Electra complex.

4001. Standardized intelligence test was invented in 1905 by Alfred Binet, director of the psychological laboratory at the Sorbonne in Paris, France, with his colleague Théodore Simon. The French Ministry of Public Instruction requested Binet to devise a test for selecting children who, it was thought, lacked the intelligence to be educated in the public schools. Binet and Simon produced a series of scaled tasks that were considered to typify the intellectual development of children of different ages, and assigned a "mental age" to children taking the tests according to the level of the tasks they could successfully complete. A child whose mental age was well below his or her chronological age was considered to be a poor candidate for standard school education.

4002. Behaviorist was the American psychologist John Broadus Watson, professor of psychology at Johns Hopkins University, Baltimore, MD, USA, and founder of behaviorism. Watson held that human behavior was psychology's only subject matter, that the goal of the psychologist was nothing more than the prediction and control of behavior, and that that goal could best be pursued in a laboratory setting by investigation of conditioned responses in subjects. His first major work was *Behavior: An Introduction to Comparative Psychology* (1914).

4003. Woman psychoanalyst was a physician, Karen Danielsen Horney, who was trained in psychoanalysis circa 1915 by Karl Abraham, a close associate of its originator, Sigmund Freud. During Horney's more than 30 years in practice in Germany and the United States she found reason to reject various tenets of Freud's theories, especially those dealing with the psychology of women, and to propose that people's neuroses are caused by anxiety arising from social, cultural, and familial circumstances.

4004. Shock therapy for treating mental illness was insulin-shock therapy, developed by Manfred Sakel at the University Neuropsychiatric Clinic in Vienna, Austria, as part of his research into the treatment of morphine addicts, and introduced in 1934. The method, which involved the inducement of convulsions by lowering the patient's blood sugar level, was eventually replaced by electroshock therapy.

4005. Electroshock therapy to treat mental illness was introduced in Rome, Italy, in 1937, when physicians Ugo Cerletti and Lucio Bini attached electrodes to the temples of a schizophrenic patient and applied an alternating electric current of 80 volts for 0.2 seconds. The pa-

MEDICINE—PSYCHIATRY AND PSYCHOLOGY—*continued*

tient stiffened, relaxed, began to sing loudly, and lapsed into silence, but, overhearing the doctors discussing their plans for a second attempt, he interrupted, saying: "Not another one! It's deadly!" However, the sessions were continued, and after several more, the patient's hallucinations and convulsions are said to have abated.

4006. Hotel with a staff psychologist was the Nob Hill Lambourne in San Francisco, CA, USA, a hotel catering mainly to business travelers, which began offering a therapy service in February 1998. By calling the front desk, the hotel's guests could make appointments with a local psychologist, Dr. Charmian Anderson, for phone therapy sessions, which were billed at the rate of US$2 a minute. The hotel received 20 percent of the fee.

MEDICINE—PUBLIC HEALTH

4007. Municipal board of health was established in Milan, Italy, shortly after the arrival in 1348 of the epidemic of plague known as the Black Death. Similar boards were established throughout Italy. They kept records of deaths and had legal authority to take measures to combat contagion, including isolating the sick and preventing travelers from entering the town.

4008. European city with a municipal health officer employed in a secular capacity was Lübeck, Germany, which hired a physician for the job in the 14th century.

4009. Quarantine was imposed by the doge of Venice in 1403 against the Black Death, a measure that was largely successful. Ships wishing to enter the city were forced to wait a period of 30 days to determine if their crew or goods were infected. In 1423 an island near the city was designated a quarantine station, or lazaretto. In 1485 the wait was set at 40 days (*quarantina*, in Italian), the period of time Moses spent on Mount Sinai and Jesus spent in isolation in the wilderness.

4010. Ambulance designed specifically to move hurt people safely was created in 1792 by Baron Dominique-Jean Larrey, Napoléon's military surgeon. His *ambulance volante* (flying ambulance) was a covered cart, mounted on a carriage with springs and pulled by a fast horse. Its purpose was to move wounded soldiers from the battlefield to field hospitals set up in the rear.

4011. Water purification plant was a sand filtration plant, built in 1829, used to purify water from the Thames River for consumption by Londoners.

4012. International medical relief organization was the Red Cross, officially formed at the Geneva Convention of 1864 and still headquartered in Geneva, Switzerland. It was based on the ideas of the Swiss humanitarian Jean-Henri Dunant, who had advocated the formation of national voluntary societies for humanitarian aid during wartime. The Red Cross also performs such peacetime duties as first aid training and disaster relief. Red Crescent societies were first formed in Muslim countries after 1906.

4013. Antitoxin laboratory operated by a public health department was established in September 1894 by the Department of Health of New York City, USA. The director was American physician William Hallock Park. This was the first such laboratory in the world to provide for the free distribution of antitoxin to the poor.

4014. City with a chlorinated water supply was Pola, Italy, which began a chlorination program in 1896. Chlorine was added to kill cholera germs, which are spread by infected water.

4015. Motorized ambulances were put into service in 1900, when they were adopted for military use by the French Ninth Army Corps and for civilian use by the city of Alençon, France.

4016. Mosquito-eradication project to control disease was undertaken by U.S. Army engineers in Havana, Cuba, in the aftermath of the Spanish-American War, when yellow fever ravaged the American troops. After an army commission headed by Walter Reed confirmed by experiment that yellow fever is carried by mosquitoes, work crews under the direction of chief sanitary officer William Crawford Gorgas began operations in February 1901 and succeeded in wiping out the disease in Havana in three months' time by destroying the mosquitoes' habitat, chiefly through swamp drainage. Gorgas was later in charge of mosquito-eradication efforts in Panama, where an epidemic of yellow fever had halted progress on the Panama Canal. Work was resumed after the death rate from the disease was cut to 6 per thousand from a high of 176.

4017. International organization for promoting health was the World Health Organization, founded on April 7, 1948, following proposals made by delegates from Brazil and China at the conference in San Francisco, CA, USA, that formed the United Nations in May 1945. The first WHO assembly took place between June 24 and July 24, 1948. Dr. Andrija Stampar of Yugoslavia was appointed as president and Dr. Brock Chisholm of Canada was appointed as director-general. Headquarters were located in Geneva, Switzerland. Initially, WHO focused on eliminating major diseases such as malaria, yaws, tuberculosis, leprosy, and smallpox. Since 1978, the organization has concentrated on improving primary health care by educating people in hygiene and providing essential drugs, sanitation, and nutrition.

4018. International standards for food quality were published by the Codex Alimentarius Commission, a joint commission of the United Nations Food and Agriculture Organization and World Health Organization. Established in 1963, the commission has compiled comprehensive definitions of foods and food additives, set requirements for food composition, quality, and labeling, and recommended restrictions on residual pesticides in foods. Some 120 nations subscribe to its provisions.

4019. Country to make seat belts compulsory in all automobiles was Czechoslovakia (now the Czech Republic and the Republic of Slovakia), which enforced a seat belt law from January 1969.

MEDICINE—PUBLIC HEALTH—DRUGS AND TOBACCO

4020. Intoxicating drug is alcohol, which was produced in the form of beer and wine by the earliest civilizations.

4021. Marijuana smoking became popular in India circa 2000 BCE. *Cannabis sativa,* the marijuana plant, was probably introduced from China, where it had been brewed for tea for 1,000 years or more. Indians of all classes dried the leaves and buds and smoked them in pipes or threw them on the fire. Marijuana was brought to the New World by the Spanish in 1545.

4022. Europeans to smoke tobacco were Rodrigo de Jerez and Luis de Torres, two members of the crew of Columbus' first voyage. In November 1492, about three weeks after Columbus landed in the New World, Jerez and Torres were sent on a three-day expedition across Cuba. On their return, they reported how the natives wrapped dried leaves in "a musket formed of paper," and after lighting one end "drank smoke" through the other. Both men tried it for themselves, and Rodrigo de Jerez later became so addicted to smoking—the first European to develop a nicotine addiction—that he was imprisoned for his "devilish habit" by the Inquisition.

4023. Anti-smoking crusader was King James I of England. Tobacco, imported from the English colony at Jamestown, VA, USA, beginning in 1613, made nicotine addicts of many of his subjects. He was critical of tobacco smokers and wrote a pamphlet entitled *Counterblaste to Tobacco.*

4024. Connection between tobacco and cancer was made by John Hill, a London physician, in 1761. Among his patients were many who indulged in snuff, a powdered form of tobacco that was inhaled through the nose. Hill noticed a tendency among heavy snuff-users to develop nasal polyps, which can become cancerous.

4025. International drug trade could be said to have begun in 1779 with the importation of Indian-grown opium into China by the British East Indian Company, which used the revenues gained to purchase Chinese tea for export to England. China quickly banned the opium trade, making it a capital offense to smoke the drug, but the effort was unsuccessful and in fact merely increased corruption among trade officials.

4026. National effort to prevent drug addiction was made by China in the 19th century, when the East India Company was engaged in a three-way trade that involved importing opium into China from India and using the proceeds to buy Chinese tea for export to England. The opium trade had been banned in China since 1799, but corrupt officials allowed it to continue. The situation worsened in 1839, when other nations also began selling opium and the Canton government ordered all foreign-owned opium destroyed. England's refusal to comply was one of the factors that led to the outbreak of the first Opium War (1839–42).

4027. Self-help program for substance abusers was Alcoholics Anonymous, the first of the twelve-step rehabilitation programs for people with addictions. It was founded in New York, NY, USA, on June 10, 1935, by a stockbroker, William Griffith Wilson, and a surgeon, Robert Holbrook Smith, who recognized the need for mutual support in their struggles to remain sober. The twelve-step model, emphasizing anonymity, group discussion, and reliance on a "higher power," has been adopted for use with other kinds of addiction.

MEDICINE—PUBLIC HEALTH—DRUGS AND TOBACCO—continued

4028. Synthetic hallucinogen was LSD, or D-lysergic acid diethylamide, also known as LSD-25. The mind-altering effects of LSD were discovered by Swiss chemist Albert Hofmann in 1943 when he accidentally ingested a small amount. The drug increased his pulse rate and blood pressure, caused visual and auditory hallucinations, and induced acute feelings of euphoria and terror. Hofmann had synthesized the drug during his study of ergotamine and ergonovine, alkaloids derived from ergot, a fungal disease of rye and other cereals caused by the ascomycete fungus *Claviceps purpurea*. Ergot was long known to have unusual and sometimes dangerous psychotropic effects when eaten.

4029. Methadone maintenance program for heroin addicts was a unit established in 1965 at the Manhattan General Hospital in New York, NY, USA, with funding from the city[s commissioner of hospitals. It was operated by Dr. Vincent Dole of the Rockefeller University and a psychiatrist, Dr. Marie Nyswander. The two had done research demonstrating that high doses of methadone, a synthetic narcotic, controls the drug cravings of heroin and morphine addicts and enables them to function normally.

4030. Nicotine chewing gum was Nicoret, developed in 1986 by the Swedish pharmaceutical firm Pharmacia Les Theraputics AB to aid smokers trying to kick the cigarette habit.

MEDICINE—PUBLIC HEALTH—SANITATION

4031. Latrines have been found in sites on Scotland's Orkney Islands dating from circa 2800 BCE. They were simple stone seats carved with drain channels.

4032. Sewage system was constructed circa 2500 BCE in the city of Mohenjo-Daro, located in the Indus Valley in present-day Pakistan. Every house in the city had drains for kitchens, bathrooms, and indoor toilets, which were connected to a system of brick-lined pipes installed under the main streets. Access was afforded through covered manholes.

4033. Sewer still in use is the Cloaca Maxima ("Great Sewer"), a large underground channel built for the city of Rome. Construction began circa 500 BCE when a stream draining into the Tiber River was lined with stone; the channel was completely enclosed with a barrel vault in the third century BCE. Some lengths of it (now lined in concrete instead of stone) are integrated into the storm drainage system of the modern city.

4034. City to require a privy in each house as a public sanitation measure was Frankfurt am Main, Germany, in 1481. Houses on public streets were ordered to move their pigsties from the front to the rear and to keep them clean.

4035. Flush toilet in primitive form may have been developed in Minoan Crete (part of modern Greece) circa 2000 BCE. However, the flush toilet's invention is usually credited to the English courtier, wit, and poet John Harrington, circa 1594. One of the first was installed at the palace of his godmother, Queen Elizabeth I, at Richmond, Surrey. Harrington penned in 1596 a salacious mock epic titled *The Metamorphosis of Ajax* (a pun on the slang term "jakes"), for which Elizabeth banished him from court.

4036. Galvanized metal trash can was invented in 1883 by Eugène Poubelle, the Paris prefect of police, whose name was adopted as the French word for trash can.

MEDICINE—SURGERY

4037. Brain surgery was trepanation, an operation in which the physician opens a hole in the skull. Modern surgeons perform the operation to relieve excessive fluid pressure in the cranial cavity. Ancient physicians may have opened the skull to provide a way for disease to "escape" from the body. According to archeological evidence announced in 1999, the earliest known trepanation was performed as early as circa 7300 BCE on a 50-year-old man living in what is now Ukraine. The skull was found in 1953 by Russian archeologist A.D. Stolyar, and was radiocarbon dated in 1995 by Malcolm C. Lillie of the University of Hull in Britain. Marks on the skull indicated that the patient healed well and lived many years after the operation.

4038. Hemostatic technique to stop surgical bleeding was cautery. The Georg Moritz Ebers Papyrus, one of the earliest Egyptian medical texts (dating from circa 1600 BCE), advises the practitioner to deal with bleeding during an abscess operation by using a knife heated in fire.

4039. Surgery to repair a cleft lip was accomplished in China during the Ch'in dynasty, in the late third century BCE.

4040. Surgery to repair perforated or obstructed intestines was performed by the Hindu surgeon Susruta in India in 49 BCE. To suture the wound, he used the severed heads of giant ants, whose jaws still exercised enough gripping pressure to hold the parts together. Susruta used steel instruments, and his equipment included 20 sharp instruments and 101 blunt.

4041. Surgical procedure in North America of record has been dated to circa 300 CE, according to a Paleo-Indian skull showing evidence of cranial surgery to relieve a non-trauma-induced soft tissue lesion (sinus pericranii). The remains were unearthed in Alameda County, CA, USA. The skull is the earliest and only conclusive evidence of invasive surgery from prehistoric North America.

4042. Plastic surgery was described in the *Susrutu Sambita,* a medical text compiled in India no later than the fifth century. The book describes cases of disfigurement caused by the loss of a nose and explained a method of grafting skin from the forehead and cheek to repair some of the damage.

4043. Tonsillectomy was first described in the *Epitomes iatrikes biblio hepta (Medical Compendium in Seven Books),* written by the Greek physician and encyclopedist Paul of Aegina circa 680.

4044. Barber surgeons began to practice in 1163, when Pope Alexander III issued a decree forbidding Christian clergy from shedding blood. This rule prevented monks from assisting one another with bloodletting, the deliberate opening of a vein, which was then considered an important aspect of maintaining health. The job was taken over by barbers.

4045. Treatise on military surgery was the *Buch der Wund-Artzney (Book of Wound Surgery),* published in Strasbourg (now in France) in 1497. The author was Hieronymus Brunschwig.

4046. Appendectomy to remove an inflamed appendix took place in 1736. The surgeon was Claudius Aymand of Britain.

4047. Gynecological surgery that was successful took place in Danville, KY, USA, in 1809. The patient, Jane Todd Crawford, had a huge ovarian tumor that threatened her life. The local doctor, Ephraim McDowell, performed the operation on a kitchen table, while the patient sang hymns to distract herself from pain. The removed cyst weighed 15 pounds (7 kilo-

grams). Although the surgery did not take place under antiseptic conditions, Mrs. Crawford did not contract an infection, and lived another 31 years. Fear of infection discouraged further operations of this kind for several decades.

4048. Use of antisepsis was developed between 1845 and 1848 by Ignaz Philipp Semmelweis, assistant at the obstetric clinic in Vienna, Austria. Semmelweis noted that women who came to the clinic to give birth died of puerperal (childbed) fever at far higher rates than those who gave birth at home. He further observed that many women died after being examined by medical students who had recently performed autopsies on other victims of the fever. Reasoning that the students were passing infection to his patients, he ordered them to wash their hands in an antiseptic solution of chlorinated lime. Mortality rates in the ward dropped from 18.27 to 1.27 percent. Despite this success, Semmelweis's theories were not accepted by the European medical establishment in his lifetime, and he died of an infection he received during an operation.

4049. Antiseptic surgery was pioneered by the English surgeon Joseph Lister at the Royal Infirmary in Glasgow, Scotland. Seeking a way to reduce the high rate of death from the infection of wounds during surgery, he began to pour carbolic acid (known to be effective in cleaning sewers and combating typhoid contagion) on bandages, ligatures, instruments, and the wounds themselves, with spectacular success. His first trial of antisepsis took place in Glasgow on August 12, 1865. The patient, eleven-year-old James Greenlees, had been run over by a cart. Lister set his badly broken leg and dressed it with a bandage saturated with carbolic acid and linseed oil. It healed without infection.

4050. Treatise on antiseptic surgery was "On the Antiseptic Principle in the Practice of Surgery," by the English surgeon Joseph Lister, who introduced antiseptic techniques at the Royal Infirmary, Glasgow, Scotland, in the 1860s. The book was published in 1867.

4051. Surgeon to use gloves to prevent infection was Dr. Nicholas Senn, a surgeon at the Milwaukee Hospital, Milwaukee, WI, USA. After experimenting with the antiseptic carbolic spray advocated by Joseph Lister, and finding it inadequate, Senn began looking for other ways to curb the spread of germs in the operating room, including the use of boiled cotton gloves. He also required the audience to keep its distance—operating rooms of that era were often crowded with onlookers—and ordered the

MEDICINE—SURGERY—*continued*

patient's skin to be disinfected near the place of incision. These ideas, which led to a steep decline in mortality among surgery patients, were discussed in his influential book *Principles of Surgery,* published in 1890.

4052. Heart operation in which a wound in the heart was successfully stitched closed with sutures was performed on September 9, 1896, at the Frankfurt City Hospital in Frankfurt, Germany. The surgeon, Dr. Louis Rehn, used three silk sutures to close a knife wound in the heart of a patient who had been stabbed in a bar fight. Until that time, heart wounds were almost invariably fatal.

4053. Laparoscopic surgery employing a tube outfitted with lenses and surgical instruments inserted into the body through a small incision was performed in 1901 on the abdomen of a dog by Georg Kelling, a surgeon from Dresden, Germany.

4054. Vascular sutures were developed by the French-born American surgeon Alexis Carrel in 1902. He received the 1912 Nobel Prize in Physiology or Medicine for his technique, in which delicate blood vessels were sewn together with specialized needles and catgut—a necessary precursor to organ transplantation and open heart surgery.

4055. Laparoscopic surgery on a human being was performed in 1910 by Hans Christian Jacobaeus, a professor of medicine at the Caroline Institute in Stockholm, Sweden, who was investigating the causes of the accumulation of fluid in the peritoneal cavity.

4056. Prefrontal lobotomy was performed in 1936 by Portuguese neurologist António Caetano de Abreu Freire Egas Moniz with an associate, Almeida Lima. Egas Moniz bored two holes into the skull of his patient (a paranoid psychotic) and destroyed the surface of the frontal lobe of the cerebrum, whence, he reasoned, the patient's obsessive thought patterns emanated. Egas Moniz recognized the drastic side effects of the operation and advocated its use only as a last resort. As a pioneer in the new field of psychosurgery, he shared in the 1949 Nobel Prize in Physiology or Medicine.

4057. Operation to cure congenital heart disease took place on November 29, 1944, at the Johns Hopkins Hospital in Baltimore, MD, USA. The surgeon was Alfred Blalock. This form of surgery, subclavian-pulmonary artery anastomosis,, corrects a fatal congenital heart defect in babies, called Fallot's tetralogy or blue baby syndrome, that prevents sufficient oxygen from entering the blood. Babies with this condition have a bluish cast to their skin. The operation was planned by Blalock and pediatric specialist Helen Brooke Taussig, known as the founder of pediatric cardiology.

4058. Corneal graft or refractive lamellar keratoplasty was developed in 1949 by ophthalmic surgeon José Barraquer of Bogotá, Colombia. The procedure uses tissue from another part of the eye to rectify the curvature of the cornea, improving vision for patients with severe myopia or hypermetropia.

4059. Pacemaker successfully implanted in a patient was put into the chest of Arne Larsson on October 9, 1958, at the Karolinska Institute, Stockholm, Sweden, by Dr. Ake Senning. Larsson received his first pacemaker on October 8, but it stopped working a few hours later, and he was given a second one in another operation the following day. The pacemaker's designer was Dr. Rune Elmqvist.

4060. Radiation surgery was performed in Sweden on July 3, 1971. Using a gamma-ray beam composed of 179 beams of cobalt radiation, surgeons destroyed a brain tumor in a patient who remained conscious throughout the operation.

4061. Radial keratotomy to correct myopia by surgical flattening of the cornea was invented in Japan in 1955, but was not practiced in its modern form until 1973, when Svyatoslov Fyodorov, director of the Moscow Research Institute of Eye Microsurgery, set up a large clinic to perform the procedure on thousands of patients every year.

4062. Robotic brain surgeon was developed by engineers and doctors at the Federal Institute of Technology and the University Hospital in Lausanne, Switzerland. The robot, called Minerva, had a computer-controlled manipulator arm that could be outfitted with various surgical tools. Tips of the tools could be positioned by the arm to within small fractions of a millimeter. In September 1992, the robot was used to drain cysts in the brains of two cancer patients.

4063. Heart surgery broadcast on the Internet took place on August 18, 1998, when Dr. Robert Lazzara of the Providence Seattle Medical Center, Seattle, WA, USA, performed bypass surgery on Gloria Snoddy, age 57, and Charles Sheridan, age 52. Video images of the procedures were digitized and uploaded to the World Wide Web.

4064. Open-heart surgery streamed live on the World Wide Web was a coronary bypass operation performed on August 19, 1998, at a hospital in Houston, TX, USA. The patient's first name was given as Rena. The surgeon was Dr. Denton A. Cooley. The operation took 3 hours 40 minutes. It was viewed by more than 150,000 people on AHN.com, a web site operated by a cable TV channel, America's Health Network, based in Orlando, FL, USA. This was the first live surgery of any kind to be streamed on the Internet. Other live transmissions pioneered on the same web site include the birth of a child, on June 16, 1998; a hair transplant, on September 30, 1998; a knee operation, on November 11, 1998; surgery on a herniated disk, on December 3, 1998; brain surgery, on January 7, 1999; repair of an aneurysm, on February 18, 1999; and a knee replacement operation, on February 23, 1999.

4065. Magnetic surgery system was developed in the United States and first employed in late 1998 to perform a brain tumor biopsy in an area of the brain that is very difficult to reach directly. Superconducting magnets guided the surgical instrument to the tumor along a complex path that avoided areas of the brain that surgeons wanted to leave untouched. Magnet-resonance images were used as a map to the tumor. The procedure was performed on a 31-year-old man at the Barnes-Jewish Hospital in St. Louis, MO, USA, on December 17, 1998. The surgical team was led by neurosurgeon Ralph Dacey of the Washington University School of Medicine in St. Louis.

MEDICINE—SURGERY—TRANSPLANTS

4066. Artificial heart in an animal was implanted in a dog in 1937 by a Russian physician.

4067. Organ transplant from one human to another that was successful was performed by Dr. Richard Harold Lawler of the Little Company of Mary Hospital, Chicago, IL, USA, on June 17, 1950, in a 45-minute operation witnessed by 40 visiting surgeons and doctors. A healthy kidney was removed by Dr. James Ward West from the body of a woman who had died. Dr. Lawler transplanted the kidney into the renal pedicle of a patient from whom a polycystic left kidney had been removed.

4068. Heart-lung machine was developed by John H. Gibbon, Jr., of Philadelphia, PA, USA. The machine was a pump that kept blood oxygenated and circulating. It was first used successfully on May 6, 1953, when Gibbon closed a hole between the two upper chambers of a patient's heart (an atrial septal defect).

4069. Liver transplant was performed in the United States as an experimental procedure on March 1, 1963, by a team led by surgeon Thomas Earl Starzl at the University of Colorado Health Sciences Center, Denver, CO, USA. Starzl went on to perform scores of hepatic transplants, including the first baboon-to-human liver transplant. He was the author of *Experience in Hepatic Transplantation* (1969), the first full published account of liver grafting.

4070. Transplant of an animal organ into a human being took place at the University of Mississippi Medical Center in Jackson, MS, USA, on January 23, 1964, when a team of twelve doctors headed by Dr. James D. Hardy transplanted the heart of a chimpanzee into the body of a 64-year-old patient. The patient, whose name was not made public, died 90 minutes later.

4071. Heart transplant was performed at Groote Schuur Hospital in Cape Town, South Africa, by senior cardiothoracic surgeon Christiaan Neethling Barnard. On December 3, 1967, Barnard and a team of 20 surgeons replaced the heart of grocer Louis Washkansky with a heart taken from a woman who had become an accident victim. Washkansky, who was administered a potent course of immunosuppressant drugs to aid his body's acceptance of the new organ, died 18 days later of double pneumonia.

4072. Transplant of an artificial heart into a human being took place at St. Luke's Episcopal Hospital in Houston, TX, on April 4, 1969. American surgeon Dr. Denton A. Cooley implanted the world's first entirely artificial heart into Haskell Karp, age 47, from Skokie, IL. The prosthetic heart was made of Dacron and plastic. Karp lived with the heart for three days, when it was replaced by a transplanted human heart. He died on April 8.

4073. Transplant of artificial skin took place at Massachusetts General Hospital, Boston, MA, USA, on April 23, 1981. Doctors reported that an artificial skin composed of cowhide, shark cartilage, and plastic was applied with successful results to ten burn patients, three of whom would have died without the treatment. The artificial skin was developed by Ioannis V. Yannas and a team of researchers at the Massachusetts Institute of Technology, Cambridge, MA.

MEDICINE— SURGERY— TRANS-PLANTS—*continued*

4074. Transplant of an artificial heart that was intended to be permanent was performed in the United States on December 2, 1982, when a team of doctors at the University of Utah Medical Center, Salt Lake City, UT, USA, headed by Dr. William C. DeVries, implanted a mechanical heart into Barney B. Clark, 61, a retired dentist from Des Moines, IA. The device, called the Jarvik-7, was designed by Dr. Robert K. Jarvik. Clark survived for nearly four months before dying of vascular collapse on March 23, 1983.

4075. Transplant of a baboon heart into a human being was performed by Dr. Leonard L. Bailey at the Loma Linda University Medical Center, Loma Linda, CA, USA, on October 16, 1984. The patient was a 15-day-old baby girl known to the public as "Baby Fae." Her body rejected the transplant and she died on November 15.

4076. Transplant of a baboon liver into a human being took place at the University of Pittsburgh Medical Center, Pittsburgh, PA, in July 1992. A team of surgeons led by Thomas Earl Starzl transplanted the liver of a baboon into a 35-year-old patient infected with human immune deficiency virus (HIV) whose liver had been destroyed by hepatitis B. A human liver could not be used because it too would have been destroyed by the hepatitis. The patient died two months later, apparently of unrelated causes.

4077. Hand transplant that was successful took place on September 23, 1998, at the Edouard Herriot Hospital in Lyon, France. In a 13.5-hour operation, Australian businessman Clint Hallam, who had lost his wrist and hand in a logging accident in 1989, received a replacement forearm and hand donated from a brain-dead patient whose identity was not disclosed. The six-doctor medical team was led by microsurgeons Jean-Michel Dubernard of Lyon and Earl Owen of Sydney, Australia.

MEDICINE—TREATMENTS

4078. Hyperthermia for treating tumors originated with the Egyptians of the third millennium BCE. A papyrus from that era records the use of heated plates to raise the temperature of tumors.

4079. Recommendation to treat physical disorders with exercise and massage appears in the *Huang Ti Nei ching (The Yellow Emperor's Classic of Internal Medicine),* a Chinese treatise dating from 2700 BCE. The book advises "breathing exercises, massage of skin and flesh, and exercises of hands and feet" to alleviate paralysis, chills, and fever.

4080. Case of mouth-to-mouth resuscitation on record may be the episode recounted in the book of II Kings of the Jewish scriptures (the Bible), in which the prophet Elisha, who lived in Israel in the ninth century BCE, is said to have revived the child of a woman who had given him shelter. According to the text, the child was out in the fields with the reapers when he complained of head pain—a possible case of heatstroke. He died, and his mother went to the prophet for help. After praying to God, Elisha "lay upon the boy, placing his mouth upon his mouth, his eyes upon his eyes, and his palms upon his palms. He stretched himself out over him, and warmed the flesh of the boy. . . . The lad sneezed seven times, and the lad opened his eyes."

4081. Health resorts were the temples of healing established in ancient Greece beginning circa 800 BCE. Located in pleasant surroundings, usually near mineral springs, they were called *asklepeia,* after Asklepios (in Latin, Aesculapius), the physician of legend who was said to have been slain by Zeus because his cures were robbing the Underworld of its population. Patients would bathe, make sacrificial offerings, and take naps in the temple. While they napped, priests in the guise of Asklepios would come to them, accompanied by flute music, to attempt visionary healings. In later centuries, more reliance was placed on special diets, exercise, and drinking, as well as bathing in, the mineral waters.

4082. Electrotherapy was invented by the Greeks in the fifth century BCE, using a sea creature, the electric ray *(Torpedo nobiliana).* Electric rays, also known as torpedo fish, have organs on the sides of their heads that emit up to 220 volts of electricity. The Greeks, although they had no understanding of electricity, applied electric rays to the bodies of people suffering from a variety of illnesses, including heart trouble and headache, in the hope that the electric shocks would stimulate them to heal.

4083. Plaster of Paris for medical use to stabilize broken bones in casts was used circa 900 CE by the Persian doctor Abu Bakr Muhammad ibn Zakariyà ar-Razi (known in Latin as Rhazes), the leading Muslim physician of the era.

4084. Popular health diet was devised at the medieval medical school at Salerno (in modern Italy) circa 1100. It was based on the idea that the world is constituted of four elements—earth, air, fire, and water—that manifest themselves in the human body as temperamental "humors." People with an excess of a particular humor were advised to preserve their health by choosing foods that would balance, rather than aggravate, their natures. Foods were classified as moist, dry, warming, or cold. The diet was popularized throughout Europe by crusaders who had been treated at Salerno.

4085. Clinical trial to test the efficacy of a particular medical treatment using a control group was conducted in 1747 by the Scottish physician James Lind, who was then a naval surgeon with Britain's Royal Navy. Seamen on extended voyages had long suffered from a wasting disease called scurvy, and more British sailors died of scurvy than of wounds received in battle. Although scurvy was known to be the consequence of a lack of fresh fruits and vegetables in the sailors' diet, it was not clear which foods would prevent it, or in what amounts. Lind's trial involved six pairs of sick sailors, each pair receiving a different treatment for 14 days. The pair who recovered quickest ate a daily ration of a lemon and two oranges. Lind's results, published in 1753 in his *Treatise of the Scurvy*, were not heeded by the Royal Navy until 1795, when it decreed that all British sailors should routinely be given drinks of citrus juice. The active ingredient, Vitamin C, was not identified until 1928.

4086. Cardiac stimulant was digitalis, a preparation made from the common or purple foxglove plant (*Digitalis purpurea*). Long known as a herbal remedy for dropsy (general edema), its effects in strengthening the heartbeat were first clinically tested by the English physician and botanist William Withering and publicized in his 1785 treatise *An Account of the Foxglove, and Some of Its Medical Uses: With Practical Remarks on Dropsy, and Other Diseases.*

4087. Modern massage technique was Swedish massage, developed by Per Henrik Ling, a Stockholm physician, in the early 19th century. Ling derived his principles of massage treatment from ancient Chinese, Egyptian, Greek, and Roman techniques and from his interest in the fledgling sport of gymnastics.

4088. Apparatus used to treat respiratory failure was the iron lung, invented by two Americans, Philip Drinker and Louis Agassiz Shaw, who made the original model in April 1927. It consisted of a cheap galvanized iron box with a bed made from "garage creepers" and two household vacuum cleaners with hand-operated valves as the source of alternate positive and negative pressure. The Consolidated Gas Company of New York donated US$7,000 to Harvard University, Cambridge, MA, USA, to produce a second model, which was first used on October 12, 1928, at the Children's Hospital, Boston, MA, USA, to help a little girl suffering from respiratory failure caused by poliomyelitis. The machine was manufactured by Warren E. Collins.

4089. Cardiac catheterization was performed in 1929 by the German surgeon Werner Theodor Otto Forssmann. He passed a thin, flexible rubber tube, 0.125 inch (3.2 millimeters) in diameter and 2.5 feet (76 centimeters) in length, up a vein in his own anesthetized arm and into the right atrium of his heart. Cardiac catherization enables physicians to measure blood flow, examine narrowed arteries and veins, and administer drugs directly to the heart muscle. Forssmann later injected an iodine-based contrast medium into his heart and took the first cardiac X-ray photographs. He shared the 1956 Nobel Prize in physiology or medicine with two Americans, Andre F. Cournand and Dickinson W. Richards, who perfected his technique.

4090. Kidney dialysis was performed on a human being in 1943 at the Municipal Hospital, Kampen, the Netherlands, by Willem Johan Kolff, employing an artificial kidney of his own design. A cellophane membrane enclosing blood flowing from the patient was washed through a dialyzing saline solution, removing waste products and fluids and balancing the blood plasma electrolytes.

4091. Monoclonal antibodies were produced in 1975 by the immunologists Georges Köhler of Germany and César Milstein of Argentina. They found that a strain of cultured myeloma cells could be hybridized with normal, antibody-producing B cells from the spleen of an immunized mouse, resulting in cells able to produce a single type of antibody (termed a monoclonal antibody) and also to multiply indefinitely like a cancer cell. This led to the industrial production of a variety of monoclonal antibodies for pharmacological use.

MEDICINE—TREATMENTS—*continued*

4092. Transdermal patch for the delivery of medication through the skin was Scopoderm TTS, introduced in 1981 by Ciba Geigy of Switzerland and Alza Corporation of the United States. Scopoderm TTS was a small patch, worn on the arm, that containing an anti-motion-sickness drug; the drug was absorbed directly through the skin in small, continual doses.

4093. Ultrasonic disintegrator used in medicine was the endoscopic ultrasonic disintegration system for destroying kidney stones, invented in 1982 by medical researchers Christian Chaussy, Egbert Schmied, and Walter Brendel, all of Munich, Germany. It used focused and tuned ultrasound transmitted to the kidney area via a small surgically inserted metal rod.

4094. Gene therapy was conducted in the United States on September 14, 1990, by W. French Anderson, chief of the Molecular Hematology Branch of the National Heart, Lung, and Blood Institute in Bethesda, MD, USA, and Drs. Kenneth Culver and Michael Blaese. The gene procedure was intended to correct a genetic immunodeficiency disease, adenosine deaminase deficiency, inherited by a four-year-old girl. Samples of her white blood cells were cultured and exposed to an engineered retrovirus that carried a healthy version of the gene that produces adenosine deaminase. The virus transferred the gene to her cells, which were then reinjected into her.

4095. Health-care facility with a labyrinth was designed by Victoria Stone and was constructed at the California Pacific Medical Center, San Francisco, CA, USA, in 1997. It measured 36 feet (11 meters) in diameter and had a path of about one-third of a mile (half a kilometer). Some people claimed that walking the labyrinth had a calming effect.

MEDICINE—TREATMENTS—BLOOD

4096. Blood transfusion was developed by the Incas of Peru circa 1300, centuries before effective transfusion techniques were practiced in Europe. Key to the Incas' success was the fact that all the indigenous peoples of the Andean region have the same blood type, O RH-positive.

4097. Blood transfusions in Europe were attempted without success by an Italian physician, Giovanni Colle, in 1628. Many of his patients died from receiving blood from donors of different and incompatible blood groups.

4098. Blood transfusion in Europe in which the patient survived was performed in 1667 by Jean-Baptiste Denis, medical consultant to King Louis XIV of France. The patient was a boy and the donor a lamb. The boy probably survived because most of the lamb's blood clotted before it entered his bloodstream.

4099. Blood types to be discovered were A, B, and O, described in 1901 by the Austrian physician and immunologist Karl Landsteiner, a research assistant at the Vienna Pathological Institute. Landsteiner was the first to show that differences between blood types were due to distinctive antigens carried by the red blood cells, and that matching the antigen type between blood donor and blood recipient ensured a successful transfusion. Landsteiner also developed the standard alphabetic nomenclature for blood groups. In 1902 he described the AB blood type, and in 1927 the rare blood types M and N.

4100. Blood bank was founded by Soviet physician Sergey Yudin in 1931 at Moscow's Sklifosovsky Institute, an emergency hospital.

4101. Prenatal blood transfusion was performed at the National Women's Hospital in Auckland, New Zealand. On September 20, 1963, physician George Green administered blood to an unborn child during labor.

4102. Artificial blood was Fluosol DA, developed by Ryochi Naito of Japan in 1979. Saito himself was the first person to receive a transfusion of the substance. Its first use in an emergency operation came in April 1979, when a man with a rare blood type received a Fluosol DA transfusion at a hospital in Fukushima, Japan. Fluosol DA was a petroleum-derived fluid that could carry hemoglobin and mixed readily with natural blood.

MEDICINE—VISION AIDS

4103. Eyeglasses are generally credited to the Italian lens grinder Armato (or Salvino) degli Armati, whose gravestone claims that achievement for him, in 1287. Other authorities attribute the invention to an Italian monk, Nicolas Bullet, in 1285, and to a Florentine, the Dominican monk Alessandro di Spina, circa 1299. Chinese oculists were making spectacles at about the same time, so it is not clear which country has priority.

4104. Depiction of eyeglasses is in a 1352 portrait of Hugh of Provence by Tommaso da Modena, a northern Italian painter.

4105. Contact lenses were imagined by the Italian artist and scientist Leonardo da Vinci, who sketched his designs for them in 1508. The corneal contact lens was conceived of by the French philosopher René Descartes in 1632.

4106. Reading glasses with concave lenses clearly designed for the correction of myopia were depicted in the portrait of Pope Leo X painted in 1517 by the Italian artist Raphael.

4107. Eyeglass frames were invented by an optician in London, England, in 1727. Spectacle cases were first known in Europe circa 1710.

4108. Bifocal eyeglasses were invented by Benjamin Franklin of Philadelphia, PA, USA, who was annoyed at having to carry two pairs of glasses. He took a frame and equipped it with lenses that consisted of two parts with different focusing powers. On May 23, 1785, from Passy, France, he wrote to George Whatley, "I have only to move my eyes up and down as I want to see distinctly far or near." Inasmuch as ordinary spectacles in the colonies cost as much as US$100 each, his invention did not receive a ready popular response.

4109. Contact lenses for correcting defective vision were developed by the German biophysicist Adolf Eugen Fick in 1887–88, when he was a professor at the University of Würzburg. His lenses, intended to correct irregular astigmatism that could not be improved by eyeglasses, were fitted by making a cast of the patient's eye and pouring glass into the mold. They covered all the surface of the eye between the lids and were highly uncomfortable. Edouard Kalt, an optician in Paris, France, experimented with similar lenses at about the same time. The first glass contact lenses were produced in Wiesbaden, Germany, in 1887 by F.E. Müller, a glassblower.

4110. Plastic contact lenses were made of polymethylmethacrylate by Theodore Obrig and introduced in 1936 by the Interessengemeinschaft Farbenindustrie Aktiengesellschaft (I.G. Farben) of Germany. Like their glass predecessors, they covered the entire surface of the eye.

4111. Artificial lens for surgical insertion into the eye was developed in 1952 by English ophthalmologist Harold Ridley. It was made of polymethylmethacrylate and was used in place of the natural lens of the eye in cases where diseased lenses had to be removed.

4112. Soft contact lens was invented by the Czech macromolecular chemist Otto Wichterle. In 1961, he developed a new polymer, HEMA, that could absorb water and therefore stay moist on the eyeball. Using homemade equipment incorporating an Erector set and a phonograph, he spun-cast a small amount of HEMA into a flexible clear lens. Bausch & Lomb purchased the rights to Wichterle's patent in 1966 and began marketing commercial soft-contact lens products in 1971. Wichterle was persecuted for his involvement in anti-Communist protests during the Prague Spring of 1968, but in 1990, after the fall of the communist regime, he was appointed head of the Czechoslovak Academy of Science. In 1993, after the formation of the Czech Republic, he was made honorary head of the Czech Academy.

MILITARY

4113. Alcoholic beverages in military rations may have been used by Sumerian troops as early as 3500 BCE, according to evidence discovered by Virginia R. Badler of the University of Toronto, Canada. At Godin Tepe in western Iran, a military outpost inhabited from 3500 BCE to 3100 BCE, containers bearing chemical traces of beer and wine were found in a storeroom along with small clay balls that were used as missiles. Soldiers were probably issued alcoholic rations and ammunition at the site.

4114. Border wall constructed by the inhabitants of a region to stop outsiders from invading their country was the Medean Wall, built in the fourth millennium BCE between the rivers Tigris and Euphrates in what is now Iraq.

4115. Medal for military valor known to historians was the "Gold of Honor", an award bestowed in Egypt for valor. Archeological evidence found at Qan-el-Kebri, Egypt, indicates that the "Gold of Honor" was awarded by the pharaohs of the 18th dynasty, beginning circa 1440 BCE. It is the first known award of any kind.

4116. Treatise on siegecraft was *On the Defense of Fortifications,* also called *How to Survive Under Siege,* a work by Aeneas Tacticus (Aeneas the Tactician) of Stymphalis, Arcadia (in modern Greece), written circa 360 BCE. The work included information on tunneling, signalling, ciphering, defending against battering rams, deploying mercenary troops, and planning an evacuation.

4117. Illustrated manual of military technology was *Bellisfortis,* written and illustrated in 1402 by Conrad Kyeser of Eichstätt, Germany, and covering a thousand years of European weaponry.

MILITARY—*continued*

4118. Military academy in Europe was the Schola Militaris, founded in 1616 in Siegen, Germany, by Count John of Nassau-Siegen to train Dutch army officers. The first director was Johan Jakob von Wallhausen.

4119. Military-industrial complex in the modern sense developed in revolutionary France during the 1790s, when scientists and engineers were paid to give their attention to the advancement of military technology.

4120. National code of the laws of war was *The Lieber Code, Instructions for the Government of Armies of the United States in the Field by Order of the Secretary of War, General Orders No. 100,* drafted by the German-born American political philosopher and jurist Francis Lieber in Washington, DC, USA, on April 24, 1863. Intended for the use of the United States armed forces during the American Civil War, the Lieber Code formed the basis for all important international formulations of the rules of war, including the Hague Conventions.

MILITARY—ARMED FORCES

4121. Medical officers in the armed forces were appointed by Julius Caesar in 48 BCE to treat the legionnaires of Rome. Each legion was assigned a complement of 17 doctors, who were paid as noncommissioned officers.

4122. Slave army that was widely successful was that of the Mamluks (or Mameluks), slave soldiers under the early Muslim caliphs. The first Mamluk army was assembled in Baghdad (now in Iraq) under the Abbasid caliph al-Mu'tasim circa 835, and the practice was soon adopted throughout the Muslim world. Mamluks served under Saladin and were instrumental in expelling the Crusaders from the Levant (present-day Lebanon). In 1260, under the slave general Baybars, they defeated invading Mongol cavalry under Hulegu at Ain Jalut, in what is now the Palestinian-controlled West Bank. It was the first important reverse suffered by a Mongol army. Mamluks established a dynasty in Egypt and Syria that ruled from 1250 to 1517 and was politically influential into the late 18th century.

4123. Armored soldiers in sub-Saharan Africa were those of Kanajeji Sarki, king of the Hausa state of Kano (now in Nigeria), who by 1410 was ruler of much of West Africa. His cavalry wore metal helmets and chain mail fabricated by artisans of the Mamluk dynasty in Egypt, and their chargers were protected by tightly quilted armor.

4124. National standing army in Europe was that of Sweden, founded in 1527 during the reign (1523–60) of Gustav I Vasa.

4125. Modern army to use military drill was the army of the Netherlands, which pioneered the use of continuous volleys of gunfire laid down by rotating ranks of musketeers, for which constant practice was essential. The idea was adapted begining in 1594 by the Dutch leaders Maurice and William Louis of Nassau from Roman tactics as described by the second-century writer Aelianus.

4126. Army drill book was *The Exercise of Arms,* published in Amsterdam, the Netherlands, in 1607. Using sequences of illustrations by the Dutch artist Jacob de Gheyn, who based them on drawings by John, Count of Nassau-Siegen, the book laid out proper drill for the use of pikes, muskets, and arquebuses.

4127. Military air force was the Compagnie d'Aérostiers, a company of balloonists founded in 1794 by Louis Bernard Guyton de Morveau for the government of France during the Revolution. The Compagnie conducted aerial reconnaissance that aided French armies in several battles in the mid-1790s.

4128. African army with standardized training and tactics was the military force created by Shaka Zulu in what is now coastal South Africa circa 1816, when he became commander of the Zulu, then a small group with perhaps 1,500 members. He organized the army into officered regiments, instituted a conditioning program of long-distance runs that enabled his soldiers to travel 50 miles in a day, and stopped the use of spears in favor of sharp knives that were effective in hand-to-hand combat. A team of boys accompanied each regiment to carry equipment. In battle, Shaka typically combined a frontal attack by one regiment with a pincer movement by two others, keeping a fourth in reserve. These innovations, together with Shaka's use of capital punishment to discipline the Zulus, allowed him to carry on wars of extermination against neighboring clans and to expand the Zulu territory into an empire.

4129. Army with a trained nursing staff to treat its wounded was the British Army, during the Crimean War. With more than half of the army's wounded soldiers dying for lack of food, water, and medical care in dirty, rat-infested hospitals, the British secretary of state in 1854 asked the health reformer Florence Nightingale to organize a nursing unit. She and a group of 38 nurses succeeded in bringing down to 2.2 percent the death rate at the hospital in Üsküdar (Scutari, Turkey).

4130. Modern air force was a tiny unit established under the Office of the Chief Signal Officer of the United States Army on July 1, 1907. The Aeronautical Division was commanded by Captain Charles de Forest Chandler and consisted of one noncommissioned officer, one enlisted man, and, eventually, one aircraft, the Wright military flyer of 1909.

4131. Independent air force was the Royal Air Force, established in Great Britain on April 1, 1918. It was coequal with the British army and navy as a separate armed service with its own ministry and secretary of state.

4132. NATO joint military exercises in a former Warsaw Pact nation took place in September 1994, when approximately 1,000 soldiers from 13 countries on opposite sides of the Cold War held war games in Poland. The exercises were conducted under the Partnership for Peace, a plan by which applicant countries from eastern Europe could become limited NATO partners. The Partnership for Peace became official NATO policy in January 1994, when it was announced at a summit in Brussels, Belgium, by NATO secretary-general Manfred Woerner.

4133. Joint peacetime military exercises between Brazil and Argentina took place from October to December 1996. The two rival countries signed an agreement of military cooperation earlier that year that also formalized cooperation on space technology and energy.

MILITARY—INTELLIGENCE

4134. Intelligence-gathering operation of record is described in the Torah (also called the Jewish scriptures). In chapter 13 of the book *Bamidbar (In the Desert)*, known in English as the Book of Numbers, God says to Moses: "Send men to scout the land of Canaan, which I am giving to the Israelite people." Twelve spies were chosen for the reconnaissance mission, one from each of the tribes of Israel. After 40 days, they came back with a discouraging report. The traditional date for this event is the Jewish year 2449. Historians generally date the Exodus to circa 1250 BCE.

4135. Cryptanalyst of record is Daniel, the Jewish prophet, whose narrative is given in the biblical book that bears his name. A citizen of the state of Judah (now modern Israel and the Palestinian Authority), Daniel was among the Jews taken captive by the Babylonians during their invasion under Nabu-kudurri-usur (Nebuchadrezzar) in 597 BCE. He succeeded in deciphering the meaning of the cryptic Aramaic message, *mene mene tekel upharsin*, that appeared on the palace wall at the banquet held by Bel-shar-usur (Belshazzar), the crown prince, correctly deducing that it referred to the imminent conquest of Babylonia (modern Iraq) by the Persians.

4136. Spy ring whose existence is supported by historical record was employed by the Persian leader Cyrus the Great, who ruled from 559 to 530 BCE. In 539, in preparation for his siege of Babylon, Cyrus recruited a group of dissident Babylonian priests to enter the city and help him subvert the rule of the last Babylonian king, Belshazzar, a follower of the old Babylonian god Sin. In return, the priests, all followers of Marduk, were to receive various privileges from Cyrus. The gambit appears to have succeeded, because the city surrendered without a fight.

4137. Woman cryptanalyst known was Gorgo, the wife of Leonidas, king of the Greek city-state of Sparta in 480 BCE. According to the Greek historian Herodotus, the Spartans received a set of blank wooden tablets from a Greek man living in Persia. Under its wax coating was a message—undetected until Gorgo ordered the wax scraped off—alerting the Spartans to the impending invasion by the Persians under Xerxes. Leonidas was killed in the famous three-day doomed defense of the pass of Thermopylae, but the Persians were turned back the following year at Plataea and Salamis.

4138. Treatise on espionage is contained in *Ping-fa (The Art of War)*, written circa 400 BCE by the Chinese military philosopher Sun Tzu. It describes the various kinds of spies and discusses the creation of intelligence and counterintelligence organizations. Sun Tzu paid particular attention to the techniques and benefits of psychological warfare.

4139. Military intelligence agency was organized in Prussia (now part of Germany) under Frederick the Great (ruled 1740–86). This was the first national intelligence office run for military rather than for strictly political ends.

4140. Modern war won through superior military intelligence concerning the target nation was the Franco-Prussian War. In the period of tension that preceded its outbreak in July 1870, a massive espionage effort was organized by Wilhelm Stieber, chief of Prussian military intelligence. Some 30,000 of his agents entered France, gathering information about roads, railways, bridges, and supply centers, and assessing the economic situation of each village and town. The invasion succeeded in a matter of months.

MILITARY—INTELLIGENCE—*continued*

4141. Sound recordings used to transmit coded messages in wartime were messages sent in 1915 from Radio WSL in Sayville, NY, USA, which was operated by Telefunken AG, a subsidiary of the German firm Allgemeine Elektricitäts Gesellschaft. WSL regularly exchanged traffic with its sister station, Radio POZ in Nauen, Germany. German agents used Telegraphone wire recorders to speed up recorded messages about Allied shipping plans so that the words would become an unintelligible buzz. The messages then were transmitted to Nauen, where Telegraphone recorders were used to slow the messages back down so they could be understood. The station's espionage activities were accidentally discovered by an amateur radio experimenter in New Jersey named Charles Adgar. Investigating what hobbyists were calling "the Nauen buzz," Adgar slowed down the buzz on a home-built recording machine and clearly heard the messages. One transmission turned out to contain the command to sink the passenger liner *Lusitania,* torpedoed by a German U-boat on May 7, 1915, with the loss of more than 1,200 lives. On July 6, 1915, the U.S. Navy seized the radio station for violation of the U.S. Neutrality Act.

4142. Electromechanical cryptographic decoder was the Colossus I, an early computer built by Alan Matheson Turing, Maxwell H.A. Newman, and T.H. Flowers at the Government Code and Cipher School (GC and CS) center at Bletchley Park, near London, England. Upon their completion in December 1943, several Colossus computers were used to decipher German military messages encrypted on the Enigma machine, the most advanced mechanical cryptographic device of the time. The Colossus contained 1,500 vacuum tubes and miles of wiring connected by electromechanical relays, all managed by a small army of WRENs (members of the Women's Royal Naval Service). The Colossus is sometimes cited as the first electronic computer, but it contained some mechanical systems, and it was not a general-purpose calculator.

4143. Overthrow of a democratic foreign government arranged by the U.S. Central Intelligence Agency was the Guatemalan coup of June 1954, which ousted leftist Jacobo Arbenz Guzmán, the democratically elected president of Guatemala. Arbenz Guzmán enjoyed the support of Guatemalan Communists and was attempting to raise export taxes and expropriate lands claimed by the United Fruit Company, a U.S. agribusiness and the largest landowner in Guatemala. Fearing that Arbenz Guzmán was preparing to establish the first communist regime in the Americas, Presidents Harry S. Truman and Dwight David Eisenhower approved secret plans to destabilize his government by "psychological warfare and political action" and "subversion" and replace him with a more compliant leader. The CIA organized an insurgent guerrilla army of exiles under Colonel Carlos Castillo Armas and embarked on a disinformation campaign to dishearten the Guatemalan military. Arbenz Guzmán fled the country on June 27, 1954. Armas assumed control and dismantled Arbenz Guzmán's reform program. From this action sprang the CIA's long history of counterrevolutionary activities in Latin America, which continued into the 1990s. In 1997, the CIA declassified some 1,400 pages of secret archives detailing the Guatemalan destabilization program and the agency's role in the 1954 coup.

4144. Reconnaissance satellite system were the Corona satellites, launched by the United States beginning in early 1959. In twelve years of highly classified operation, 145 Corona satellites were placed in low polar orbits by rockets launched from California. Each contained high-resolution cameras designed to photograph Soviet territory and eject film canisters to the earth.

4145. Signal intelligence satellite was the *SolRad* satellite, launched by the United States into orbit atop a Navy Transit-2A navigation satellite in 1960. Ostensibly designed to monitor solar radiation, *SolRad* in fact contained a secret signal intelligence payload developed by the U.S. Naval Research Laboratory to discover the nature and location of Soviet air defense radars.

MILITARY—UNIFORMS

4146. Military unit to wear a complete uniform was the Yeoman of the Guard, an organization of 50 soldiers formed in 1485 to serve as the bodyguard for King Henry VII of England. They wore a distinctive set of clothes, including a brimmed hat, a tunic with a ruffed collar, and breeches that reached to the knee. The unit is still in existence and the Tudor uniform is still worn.

4147. Military regulation concerning uniforms was an order given by King Henry VIII of England to the earl of Shrewsbury in 1534. The king instructed the earl to raise an army, and further instructed him to outfit the soldiers in uniforms of blue, except for a red stocking on the right leg.

4148. Military uniform designed by an artist was the striped blue, red, and yellow uniform worn by the Swiss Guards, the security force at the Vatican in Rome, Italy. It was designed by Michelangelo in the mid-16th century and is still worn today, with few changes.

4149. Naval uniform was worn by the seamen who defended England against invasion by the Spanish Armada in 1588. All of them wore blue jackets.

4150. Uniforms in military khaki were adopted by units of the British Army under the Raj, and later became standard issue to many armies worldwide, including the United States Army. In 1846, Lieutenant Harry Lumsden, commanding a unit of Sepoy irregulars called the Queen's Own Corps of Guides, adopted uniforms of "mud-color" (which is the meaning of *khaki* in Parsi) to help his men blend in with the dusty terrain of the North-West Frontier. Regular units of the British Army first began wearing khaki in 1857, and adopted it service-wide in 1902.

MILITARY—WAR

4151. Depiction of organized warfare was found in cave paintings at many sites in northern Australia by Paul Tacon, an anthropologist at the Australian Museum in Sydney, and Christopher Chippendale, an archeologist at the University of Cambridge in England. The sites dated from three periods: 10,000 to 6,000 years ago; 6,000 to 3,000 years ago; and 3,000 years ago to the present. Recent sites contained more depictions of battle than older sites.

4152. Battle for which a precise date is known took place in Mesopotamia (in present day Iraq) between Lydians and Medes. A total solar eclipse occurred just as the battle reached its height, and the terrified combatants laid down their arms. Astronomers have calculated that this eclipse took place on the afternoon of May 28, 585 BCE.

4153. Germ warfare has been employed since at least circa 550 BCE, when the Assyrians hit upon the idea of poisoning enemy wells with rye infected with the toxic fungus ergot. The first use of germ warfare to result in significant loss of life occurred during the siege of the Genoese settlement at Kaffa (now Feodosiya, Ukraine) in 1347, when Kipchak Turks hurled bodies of corpses infected with bubonic plague over the walls. The Black Death subsequently spread throughout Europe and resulted in 25–30 million deaths.

4154. Woman to wear armor while leading men in battle was Queen Tomyris, chief of the Massegetai, a nomadic tribe living on the eastern shore of the Caspian Sea (in present-day Iran and Turkmenistan). In 529 BCE, according to the Greek historian Herodotus, the queen's son committed suicide when he was captured by the invading Persians, and Tomyris avenged him by killing the Persian leader Cyrus the Great in combat.

4155. Treatise on war was the *Ping-fa (The Art of War)*, written circa 450 BCE by the Chinese strategist and general Sun Tzu (born Sun Wu). It contains detailed instructions on strategy and tactics, with particular emphasis on maintaining flexibility of action, as well as advice on military intelligence and the political ramifications of warmaking.

4156. Scalping was practiced by the Scythians of what is now southern Russia, according to the Greek historian Herodotus, writing circa 425 BCE.

4157. Troop transport capable of moving a large body of soldiers was the *Siracusa*, built in 280 BCE for King Gerone II of Syracuse, Sicily. It was a four-masted ship with 20 banks of oars, big enough to carry 4,000 troops and eight siege catapults.

4158. Woman to lead a rebellion against the Roman Empire was Boudicca (or Boadicea), queen of the Iceni, a Celtic tribe living in what is now Norfolk, England, during the Roman occupation of Britain. After the death of her husband in 60 CE, the Romans forcibly annexed the tribe's territory, subjected Boudicca to a public flogging, and raped her two daughters. Boudicca took revenge by leading the Iceni and their allies in a rebellion in which, according to the Roman historian Cornelius Tacitus, they killed 70,000 local townsfolk and Roman soldiers, including most of the IX Legion. The Iceni were defeated a year later. Boudicca either died of wounds or took poison.

4159. Military victory of Islam was the Battle of Badr, which took place in Arabia (modern Saudi Arabia) in 624. Two years earlier, Muhammad, the founder of Islam, had been invited by the ruling clans of Yathrib (now called Medina) to immigrate to their city to escape the hostility of the merchants of Mecca, his hometown. From Medina, he led a number of raids on Meccan caravans. On March 16, 624, his forces, though outnumbered, attacked a Meccan caravan returning from Syria. The bat-

MILITARY—WAR—*continued*

tle that followed was won by the Muslims, who regarded their victory as a sign of approval from God. A year later, the Meccans launched a revenge attack on Medina, resulting in a draw.

4160. Crusade was inspired by a speech given by Pope Urban II on November 18, 1095, at Clermont, France. Responding to an appeal from Alexius Comnenus, the Byzantine emperor, for help against the Seljuk Turks, Urban called for a military campaign to restore Christian sovereignty over Jerusalem. Four armies under French leaders arrived in Constantinople (modern Istanbul, Turkey) in 1096 and mounted successful attacks on the cities of Nicaea and Antioch before besieging Jerusalem. The city fell on July 15, 1099, and its Muslim and Jewish inhabitants were massacred. Crusader kingdoms were set up in four regions of the conquered territories.

4161. Jewish martyrs massacred by the Crusaders were the communities of the Rhineland and lands to the east—areas that are now part of Germany, France, the Czech Republic, Slovakia, and Hungary—through which the Christian army passed in the spring of 1096 on its way to the First Crusade. They included the communities of Speyer, Worms, Neuss, Mainz, Bachrach, Mehr, Xanten, Cologne, Troyes, Metz, Regensburg, Prague, and Pressburg (Bratislava). In addition to the thousands of Jews who were killed, many more committed suicide to avoid forced baptism.

4162. Fortress in the New World was Paramonga, built by the Chimú people circa 1200 in what is now Peru. It consisted of a series of three walls, with bastions at the corners, enclosing a central hill.

4163. Invasion of Japan was attempted in 1274 and again in 1281 by the Mongols under Kublai Khan. Both attempts ended in defeat. On the night of August 14, 1281, a typhoon struck the Mongols' vast fleet—3,500 ships carrying 100,000 men—as it approached Japan. The fleet was destroyed, while the defending navy was spared. This apparent miracle gave rise to the idea of the *kamikaze,* or "divine wind," a word later applied to the Japanese suicide pilots of World War II.

4164. Cannon used in warfare were employed in 1331 during the siege of Cividale del Friuli, the seat of the Lombard dukes in Italy, by a Germanic army. The invaders were repelled by primitive bombards fired from the town walls.

4165. Commander to coordinate mobile armored artillery, infantry, and cavalry as one tactical unit was the 15th-century Bohemian general and national hero Jan Zizka, victorious commander of the Hussites in the Hussite Wars against the Catholic forces of the German emperor Sigismund. Under Zizka's leadership, the well-disciplined peasant armies of the Hussites destroyed Sigismund's army in a battle near Prague (now in the Czech Republic) in 1420. Zizka's most striking innovation was the use of mobile artillery mounted in armored, horse-drawn wagons—an ancestor of the armored tank invented nearly 500 years later.

4166. Major land battles decided by firepower took place in the mid-15th century. In 1453, the Ottoman Turks under Sultan Mehmed II used enormous bombards to break through the walls of Constantinople (thereafter called Istanbul), whose fall marked the end of the Byzantine Empire. The year 1453 also saw the close of the Hundred Years' War, in whose last stages the French successfully used siege artillery to push the English out of their fortresses in Guyenne and Gascony.

4167. War to receive news coverage was the invasion of the kingdom of Naples (in present-day Italy) by the French under King Charles VIII in 1494. The campaign, from preparation to defeat, was described in printed news pamphlets that reproduced letters sent home by participants. The first war covered by a professional journalist was the skirmishing in the Netherlands between British forces and those of revolutionary France, which was written up by England's John Bell in 1793–94 in his *The Oracle or Bell's New World,* largely as a promotional gimmick.

4168. Major land battle decided by volley fire was the Battle of Breitenfeld on September 17, 1631, when Catholics and Protestants fought near Leipzig, Germany. The Protestants, led and trained by King Gustavus Adolphus of Sweden, defeated the forces of the Holy Roman Emperor by using tactics developed by the Dutch army. His well-drilled musketeers were deployed in long lines with rotating ranks, one rank firing while the previous rank was reloading. They were thus able to pour almost continuous volleys of gunfire into the deep square formations taken by their opponents.

4169. Brazilian general of African descent was Henrique Dias, who fought for the Portuguese in the 1630s in their defense against the invading Dutch. In 1633 he was named commander-in-chief of a company of black soldiers and defeated the Dutch in battles at Arecise, Pernambuco, and Cinco Pontus.

4170. World war that involved all four hemispheres was the Sugar War between the Netherlands and Portugal, which took place beginning in 1645, after Portuguese-speaking sugar planters rose up in rebellion against Dutch Calvinist rule in Brazil. Armed conflicts took place in Angola, the island of Timor, and India. When the war ended, the Dutch had won most land battles and naval engagements and had gained control of the Spice Islands, but the Portuguese maintained control of Brazil, Angola, and Goa.

4171. Guerrilla war is as old as organized warfare, and is well-documented from ancient Persian, Greek, Roman, and Mongol accounts of battle. The first war in which the term "guerrilla" was applied to irregular combatants was the Peninsular War (1808–14), in which Spanish partisans fought against the French occupying army under Napoléon. As many as 30,000 guerrillas pursued classic partisan tactics: blocking or destroying roads and bridges, ambushing columns of enemy soldiers from hidden positions, and intercepting military messengers.

4172. Military clash between China and a western power was the first Opium War (1839–42), brought on by China in an attempt to end the illegal and disruptive opium trade, which was operated by British traders. Hostilities broke out in 1839 when Chinese imperial commissioner Lin Tse-hsü seized all British-owned opium warehouses in Canton. In 1842, a British fleet conquered Shanghai, laid siege to Nanking, and sailed up the Yangtze River, forcing China's capitulation. The Treaty of Nanking, signed August 29, 1842, ended the conflict, but ceded Chinese ports, trade privileges, and special legal rights to Britain.

4173. Civil war to cause 20 million deaths was the Taiping Rebellion, a civil war in China that took place between 1850 and 1864. The conflict, between the Ch'ing dynastic authorities and the fanatical peasant followers of a religio-communistic movement begun by Hung Hsiu-ch'üan, the self-proclaimed emperor of a new Taiping T'ien-kuo (Heavenly Kingdom of Great Peace), caused the deaths of 20 million Chinese and the fatal weakening of the Chinese state. The rebellion was finally put down with the aid of American and British forces.

4174. Telegraph used in warfare was employed by the British in the Crimean War (1853–56), a conflict between Russia and the British, French, and Ottoman Turks on the Crimean Peninsula (now the autonomous Republic of Crimea in the southern Ukraine). The telegraph system used was developed by William O'Shaughnessy, an assistant surgeon with the East India Company. O'Shaughnessy was also instrumental in installing the first telegraph network in India.

4175. War to receive extensive newspaper coverage was the Crimean War (1853–56), fought in what is now Ukraine between Russia and an alliance composed of Ottoman Turkey, France, England, and Sardinia-Piedmont. Reports telegraphed from the combat zone by William Howard Russell appeared in *The Times* of London.

4176. Battle decided by the use of breech-loading infantry rifles was the Battle of Königgrätz, also called the Battle of Sadowa (now Hradec Králové, Czech Republic), which took place on July 3, 1866, during the Seven Weeks' War between Prussia and Austria. Firing from prone positions, Prussian forces armed with bolt-action, breech-loading needle guns inflicted 40,000 casualties on Austrian troops, who stood erect to fire muzzle-loaders. Previously, breechloaders had been used in the American Civil War, but without decisive effect.

4177. Defeat of a European colonial power by African military forces was inflicted on Italian colonial units by the Ethiopian army under King Menilek II (also spelled Menelik) at the Battle of Adowa in 1896. The battle was fought in north-central Ethiopia, which Italy claimed as a protectorate under the Treaty of Ucciali, signed with Menilek in 1889. On March 1, 14,500 poorly organized Italians engaged an Ethiopian army of 100,000 and were crushed; the remaining colonial units were forced to retreat and many were killed along the way. An estimated 70 percent of the Italians were killed, wounded, or captured.

4178. Casualty of World War I can plausibly be claimed to be the Archduke Franz Ferdinand, heir apparent to the Austro-Hungarian Empire. He and his wife, the duchess of Hohenburg, were assassinated on June 28, 1914, in Sarajevo (now the capital of Bosnia-Herzegovina), by a disaffected Bosnian Serb, Gavrilo Princip. The assassination prompted a declaration of war by Austria-Hungary against Serbia on July 28, and World War I ensued as a network of alliances drew in all the major powers.

MILITARY—WAR—*continued*

4179. Germ warfare in modern times was employed by Germany against the Allies during World War I. In the United States and Romania, horses and cattle destined for France were inoculated by German spies with glanders, a lesion-producing disease that can be transmitted to humans. By 1916 Germany was stockpiling other pathogens, including *B. anthracis* and *B. mallei.*

4180. Battle with more than 1 million casualties was the First Battle of the Somme in World War I, a huge Allied assault against entrenched German troops that took place from July 1 to November 13, 1916, along a 21-mile (34-kilometer) front north of the Somme River in France. British infantry sustained massive losses of 60,000 men on the first day of the attack, mainly from German machine gun emplacements. After more than four months of bloody fighting, no conclusive gains were made by either side. In all, casualties totaled approximately 1,265,000—650,000 German, 420,000 British, and 195,000 French.

4181. Massed tank attack was at the Battle of Cambrai, France, during World War I. On November 20, 1917, the British Third Army, supported by 474 tanks (of which only about 330 saw combat), attacked three German divisions posted along the Hindenburg line. The tanks quickly overran the enemy with little loss to British forces, but the British commander, General Sir Julian Byng, failed to consolidate his gains with adequate cavalry and infantry support, and the tanks themselves were too slow for effective pursuit. Within two weeks the Germans had recaptured most of their lost territory.

4182. Supreme War Council of the World War I Allies was held on December 1, 1917. Representatives from the United States, France, Great Britain and Italy held their first meeting at Versailles, France, to discuss the broad coordination of strategy and the establishment of a unified military command.

4183. Germ warfare against civilians in modern times was waged by Japan's secret "731 Unit" against China before and during World War II. Beginning in 1932, Japan began a program of infecting civilian Chinese prisoners in Manchuria with anthrax, meningitis, shigella, and other diseases. In 1938, Japanese aircraft began dropping diseased fleas, feathers, and cotton wadding onto Beijing, the central city of Nanjing (Nanking), and several smaller communities. At its height, the Japanese biological warfare program employed 3,000 people and occupied several extensive research and production plants. In all, some 10,000 Chinese may have been killed by biological agents.

4184. Attack of World War II was the faked assault on August 31, 1939, by the Germans on their own radio station at Gleiwitz, on the border with Poland. The subterfuge was masterminded by Gestapo chief Reinhard Heydrich, head of the Reich Security Central Office, and was intended to provide a pretext for Adolf Hitler's long-planned invasion of Poland on the following day. Prisoners from a nearby concentration camp were dressed in Polish uniforms, then murdered and arranged in attacking positions outside the radio station. The Germans then made a broadcast in Polish from the station.

4185. Shot of World War II was fired at dawn on September 1, 1939, by the German battleship *Schleswig Holstein* at the Polish Westerplatte Garrison in Gdansk (Danzig), Poland.

4186. Declaration of war in World War II was that of Great Britain, which declared war on Germany on September 3, 1939. Australia, New Zealand, and France declared war on the Nazi state the same day. Germany had begun the war on September 1 with its surprise attack on Poland, but did not formally declare war.

4187. Battle with more than 2 million deaths was the Battle of Stalingrad (now Volgograd, Russia) in World War II, which took place from August 19, 1942, to February 2, 1943. Confident of an easy victory, the German Sixth Army under Friedrich Paulus entered the bombed-out city in early September but was stymied by Red Army defenders who, entrenched in the ruins, inflicted huge losses on the Germans while suffering even greater losses themselves. A counteroffensive by the Soviets on November 19 trapped and decimated the Sixth Army and elements of the Fourth. Paulus surrendered on January 31, 1943, disobeying Hitler's direct order to commit suicide rather than submit. According to later Soviet estimates, the total Axis battle deaths, including German, Romanian, Hungarian, and Italian troops, were 800,000. Soviet battle deaths, not including civilians, were in excess of 1,100,000. Of the 91,000 Axis troops who surrendered, fewer than 6,000 were repatriated; the rest were killed immediately or soon died in

Soviet internment and labor camps. There are no reliable statistics for civilian deaths, although of the 500,000 residents of Stalingrad before the battle, only 1,500 remained in the city at the end.

4188. Allied soldier killed in combat on D-Day may have been Lieutenant Daniel Brotheridge of the British Sixth Airbourne. He was killed shortly after midnight on June 6, 1944, while taking a bridge in Benouville, France.

4189. Meeting of American and Soviet troops in World War II took place on April 25, 1945, when elements of the U.S. 273rd Infantry Regiment contacted Soviet troops in the village of Leckwitz on the Elbe river in eastern Germany. A monument commemorating that event was placed at the nearby city of Torgau.

4190. American flag to fly over the defeated Nazi empire was made in May 1945 by an Austrian tailor under the direction of Private Rollie Noble and other American soldiers stationed in Linz, Austria, according to an account by the American general George Smith Patton. The flag was stitched together from a red Nazi banner, white material from an old Austrian flag, and blue-dyed fabric for the field of stars.

4191. Use of the term "cold war" was made publicly in a speech on October 24, 1948, by the American financier and presidential adviser Bernard Baruch before a committee of the U.S. Senate.

4192. United Nations military action was during the Korean War. On June 25, 1950, with the aid and approval of the Soviet Union, the Democratic People's Republic of Korea (North Korea) mounted a surprise invasion of the Republic of Korea (South Korea). In emergency session, the United Nations Security Council adopted a resolution calling for aid in stemming the North Korean advance. On June 27, U.S. forces entered the conflict on the side of South Korea by direct order of President Harry S Truman, who called it a "United Nations police action." Eventually, the Korean War also involved troops from Australia, Canada, Great Britain, Turkey, and ten other UN member nations.

4193. Destruction of a nuclear reactor as an act of war took place on June 7, 1981, when Israeli warplanes used air-to-ground missiles to destroy the Osirak civilian nuclear reactor in Iraq. The raid was ordered because Israelis feared that Iraqi leader Saddam Hussein was secretly using the reactor for the production of weapons-grade nuclear materials.

4194. War lasting more than three centuries was a conflict between the Isles of Scilly (now part of Britain) and the Netherlands, begun in 1651 over trade and territorial rights. Although the actual fighting ended some years later, the war was not officially declared at an end until a peace proclamation was carried to Scilly by the Dutch diplomat Jonkheer Huydecoper on April 17, 1986.

4195. Deployment of the NATO rapid reaction force in a member country took place in late 1990 when the air arm of the Allied Command Europe Mobile Force was deployed to Turkey after that country asked for help in deterring the threat posed by Iraq and to demonstrate NATO's solidarity with Turkey in the Persian Gulf crisis. The ACE force in Turkey included squadrons of aircraft from Germany, Italy, and Belgium.

4196. Deliberate use of environmental warfare occurred during the 1991 Persian Gulf War between Iraq and a United Nations-sanctioned alliance of Western and Arab forces, including those of Saudi Arabia. In hopes of wreaking havoc on Kuwait and polluting the desalination plants on the Gulf coast of Saudi Arabia, Iraqi president Saddam Hussein ordered the release of an estimated 1.45 million tons of Kuwaiti oil into the Persian Gulf from the Sea Island storage facilities on January 25, 1991. Near the end of the war, the Kuwaiti oil fields were set on fire by Iraqi forces, spewing tons of petrochemical smoke and particulates into the atmosphere. While devastating for the local environment, the action failed as an act of war, having no significant impact on the Allied war effort or on the economy of Saudi Arabia.

4197. United Nations–sanctioned force sent uninvited to a sovereign country were the combat troops, primarily from the United States, Canada, and France, sent to Somalia in 1991 by unanimous vote of the Security Council to establish order so that humanitarian aid deliveries could be distributed by international agencies. On March 26, 1993, the Security Council transferred command from the U.S.‡led Unified Task Force to the UN Operation in Somalia (UNOSOM II), a UN-led operation. UNOSOM II was also the first UN military operation authorized to use force under the provisions of Chapter VII of the United Nations Charter.

MILITARY—WAR—*continued*

4198. Ethnic violence in the former Soviet Empire erupted in October 1992 in the semiautonomous North Ossetian republic (in the North Caucasus) between Ossetian nationalists seeking independence and civilians from the Ingush ethnic minority. Several hundred people were killed before some 3,000 Russian troops were sent to quell the violence.

4199. Peacekeeper to die in Somalia was an American, Private First Class Domingo Arroyo, a 21-year-old Marine from Elizabeth, NJ, USA. In January 1993, during Operation Restore Hope, a mainly American peacekeeping mission, he was shot by an unknown gunman while on night patrol at the airport near the Somali capital of Mogadishu.

4200. Offensive operation by NATO was an air attack on four Bosnian-Serb warplanes carried out over Bosnia on February 28, 1994, by American F-16 fighters. The Bosnian-Serb aircraft, which were brought down after being warned to leave a no-fly zone patrolled by NATO forces, had just bombed a Bosnian munitions factory at Novi Travnik.

MILITARY—WAR—AIR

4201. Kites used in warfare were deployed by the Chinese army circa the first century BCE against the horse-riding nomads who were attacking China's borders. To divert their attention and lower their morale, the Chinese sent up arrays of kites, to which were attached lightweight musical instruments that made howling, keening, and rattling noises in the wind. The kites also served to channel the nomads' attack to locations favorable to the Chinese.

4202. Aerial bombardment of a city took place on August 22, 1849, during an unsuccessful revolt against Habsburg rule by the city of Venice. The Austrian besiegers, facing an enemy protected by a natural moat, tried to inflict long-distance damage on the city by lofting unmanned balloons equipped with time-delayed explosive charges. Austria ceded Venice to Italy in 1866 after its defeat by Prussia.

4203. Military aircraft was the Wright military flyer of 1909, built by American aviation pioneers Wilbur and Orville Wright for the U.S. Army Signal Corps as an observation and signaling craft. It was a biplane design powered by a 32-horsepower engine and twin pusher props. The flyer could not get into the air on its own and required a primitive catapult launching system driven by a weight dropped from a tower. The first public demonstration

was given on July 27, 1909, at Fort Myer, VA, USA, before a crowd of 10,000, including the American president, William Howard Taft. Orville Wright was the pilot, with U.S. Army lieutenant Frank Purdy Lahm as passenger; flight time was 1 hour 12 minutes 37.8 seconds.

4204. Airplane bombing experiment was made over Lake Keuka, Hammondsport, NY, USA, on June 30, 1910, by Glenn Hammond Curtiss under the auspices of the *New York World* newspaper. Curtiss released lead missiles attached to colored streamers from a height of 50 feet (15 meters) toward a target 500 feet by 90 feet (152 meters by 27 meters). He scored ten hits and four misses. The tests were witnessed by Admiral William Wirt Kimball.

4205. Use of airplanes in war took place in Libya on October 23, 1911, during the Italo-Turkish War, when an Italian pilot flew a Blériot XI from Tripoli to survey the Turkish lines at El Azizia.

4206. Bombing raid from an aircraft was mounted on November 1, 1911, during the Italo-Turkish War of 1911–12. An Italian pilot, Giulio Gavotti, flying over Tripolitania (northern Libya) in an Etrich-Taube monoplane, dropped a grenade-type bomb by hand on a column of Turkish soldiers.

4207. Aviator wounded in combat by ground fire was Captain Montu of the Italian Army Aviation Corps. On March 31, 1912, during the Italo-Turkish War of 1911–12, Montu was hit by rifle fire as he and the pilot, Lieutenant Rossi, conducted a bombing raid on the fortress of Tobruk, in Libya.

4208. Pilot captured during war was Lieutenant Moizo of the Italian Army Aviation Corps. On September 11, 1912, his aircraft, a Nieuport, came down behind the Turkish lines at El Azizia, Libya.

4209. Aerial bombardment of a city by airplane took place on August 30, 1914, when German aircraft dropped bombs on Paris, France, two weeks after the start of World War I. Damage to the city was minimal.

4210. Airplane pilots killed in combat were two German officers, Wilhelm Sclienting and Fritz von Zangen. Both were killed in France on October 5, 1914, in the fiery crash of their unarmed Aviatik, after it was riddled with bullets from a French Air Corps Voisin biplane that was equipped with a forward machine gun. The biplane was piloted by Joseph Franz. Troops on both sides watched the episode from the ground trenches.

4211. Bombing raids were mounted against the Zeppelin works at Friedrichshafen, Germany, by the British Royal Naval Air Service on October 8 and November 21, 1914. Storage of highly flammable hydrogen gas at the site added greatly to the destructive power of the bombs; most of the facility was destroyed. The attacks were launched from bases in Belgium, making them the first bombing raids to cross a national border.

4212. Fighter plane in regular production was the Vickers F.B.5 Gunbus, a pusher-type biplane developed between 1913 and 1915 by Vickers, Ltd., in Britain. Armed with a machine gun fired by a gunner/observer in a tiny forward compartment, it was put into service over France in early 1915.

4213. Heavy night bomber was the Handley Page 0/400, a four-engine biplane designed and built for the British Royal Navy Air Service by the firm of Frederick Handley Page. The bomber saw service in World War I from December 1915 onward. It carried a crew of four and a maximum bomb load of 1,800 pounds (815 kilograms).

4214. Theorist of air warfare was the Italian general Giulio Douhet, commander of the Aeronautical Battalion, Italy's first air force, from 1912 to 1915. He was the author of the first work of air strategy, *Il dominio dell' aria (Command of the Air)*, which appeared in 1921 and was widely influential. Douhet proposed the concept of air superiority and outlined how future wars could be won by unrestricted air attack on the enemy's urban and industrial centers, thus causing a general breakdown in society and loss of morale.

4215. Airplane bombing experiment to sink a battleship took place on July 21, 1921, near Hampton Roads, VA, USA, in an Army bombing demonstration conducted by the U.S. Army general William "Billy" Mitchell. The target was the *Ostfriesland,* a former German battleship. Martin bombers dropped seven 2,000-pound (908-kilogram) bombs on the battleship and nearby, causing it to turn on its port side and sink stern first within 21 minutes. This was the first of several demonstrations by Mitchell with the goal of persuading military leaders to strengthen the air power of the U.S. armed forces.

4216. Troop movement by airplane was the transport in April 1923 of 280 fully armed British Sikh troops from Kingarban to Kirkuk, Iraq, a trip of 75 miles (121 kilometers). A fleet of twelve-seater Vickers Vernons was used. The troops were deployed to put down a Kurdish rebellion.

4217. Woman to serve as a combat pilot was Sabiha Gokchen, a member of the Turkish Flying Corps. In 1937 she bombed Kurdish rebels in eastern Turkey. For her service, she was awarded the Flying Medal set with brilliants by her adoptive father, Mustafa Kemal Atatürk, the Turkish national hero and founder of the modern Republic of Turkey.

4218. Bomb to land on German soil in World War II was inadvertently dropped on the island of Helgoland on December 3, 1939, by a British Wellington bomber of 115 Squadron returning from an attack on German shipping in the North Sea.

4219. Electronic warfare in the air got its start in World War II, and especially in the air war over Germany. A German radar guidance system for aircraft (the Knickebein system), which provided navigation for night bombers based on signals from ground transmitters, was deployed beginning in February 1940. In response, the antiradar system Asperin, which jammed Germany's Knickebein, was developed by the Allies in September 1940. The use of electronic guidance, detection, jamming, and antijamming systems developed rapidly over the course of the war.

4220. Glider assault was the aerial attack during World War II by a German glider-borne force against Eben-Emael, a massive Belgian fortification anchoring the Albert Canal defensive line. At dawn on May 10, 1940, nine DFS 230B-1 assault gliders carrying 78 paratroopers of the XXII.Landungs-Division (German 22nd Air Landing Division) touched down on the roof, quickly overpowering the 850 Belgian defenders and forcing the surrender of the fort a few hours later.

4221. Paratrooper assault on a fortified area was the capture on May 10, 1940, of the bridges near the town of Moerdijk, the Netherlands, by airborne troops of the German XI.Fliegerkorps.

4222. Air battle that was strategically important was the Battle of Britain, the air attack by Nazi Germany on Great Britain that lasted from July 10 to October 31, 1940. Had the Luftwaffe not been beaten back by the Royal Air Force, it is likely that Germany would have invaded England or at least would have been able to dictate surrender or neutrality terms, and thus consolidate its hold on Europe. Several factors account for Britain's victory in the battle: Britain was defending its home territory; Britain used radar to detect incoming German bombers;

MILITARY—WAR—AIR—_continued_
British fighters used superior high-octane aviation fuels; and German Reichsmarschall Hermann Göring, head of the Luftwaffe, was unable to adopt a long-term and effective strategy of attack.

4223. Aircraft units staffed entirely by women were formed in the Soviet Union in 1941–42 in response to the German invasion of June 1941. The all-woman units consists of three regiments: a fighter regiment flying Yak-1s; a bomber unit flying Pe-2 light bombers and Po-2 night bombers; and the Night Witches regiment, a nighttime reconnaissance and light bomber unit.

4224. Major airborne assault was Operation Mercury, the invasion of Crete by German forces during World War II. On May 20, 1941, 15,000 airborne and parachute troops of IX.Fliegerkorps under Generaloberst Kurt Student were landed on the island by 700 transport aircraft and 80 DFS 230B-1 assault gliders. The defending British troops, mainly New Zealanders and Australians supported by Cretan civilians, were defeated, but not before the elite German Seventh Parachute Division had suffered losses greater than the total number of Germans killed in the war to that date.

4225. Woman to be awarded the Iron Cross was the German test pilot Hanna Reitsch. As Nazi leader Adolf Hitler's favorite pilot, she received both the Iron Cross second class, awarded to her in 1941 for developing a way to cut the cables dangled by British barrage balloons, and the Iron Cross first class, which she received in 1942 after barely surviving the crash of a prototype rocket-powered Messerschmitt Me 163 Komet.

4226. Women pilots to down enemy aircraft in combat were members of the Soviet Air Force's 586th Fighter Aviation Regiment, the world's first all-woman air combat and reconnaissance unit. On September 24, 1942, Olga Yamshchikova shot down a German Junkers Ju 88 bomber over Stalingrad in the Soviet Union (now Volgograd, Russia). On or about the same date, Valeria Khomyakov, piloting a Yak-1 fighter, shot down a Ju 88 over Saratov in what is now western Russia. Over the course of the war, the 586th shot down 38 enemy aircraft.

4227. Chaff to jam radar was used by the Allies beginning in July 1943. Code-named "Window," the technique involved dumping foil strips out of an aircraft to create a false radar signature that would fool enemy detection systems.

4228. Blimp lost in combat was the _K-74_, a U.S. Navy blimp. It was shot down by a German submarine, the _U-134_, on July 18, 1943, while on convoy duty in the Atlantic.

4229. Jet fighter was the English-built Gloster Meteor. It entered service on July 27, 1944, a few weeks before Germany introduced its own jet fighter, the Me-262. It was powered by a centrifugal-flow turbojet based on the designs of Frank Whittle. The Meteor was used to intercept V-1 "buzz bombs," but it was less effective against enemy fighters or bombers.

4230. Jet bomber was the twin-engined Arado Ar 234B-2 "Blitz," built for the German Luftwaffe in 1944 and fielded in early 1945, when it flew mainly reconnaissance missions. It was capable of a top speed of 460 miles (740 kilometers) per hour. Only 274 were built.

4231. Rocket-propelled warplane was the Messerschmitt Me 163 Komet fighter, employed by Nazi Germany in the last months of World War II. The tailless airframe was based on designs by Alexander Martin Lippisch; the liquid hydrogen-peroxide rocket engine was developed by Helmuth Walter. Although the Me 163 could outperform most other aircraft of its day, it was inadequately armed and tended to explode on landing.

4232. Atomic bomb explosion over enemy territory took place on August 6, 1945, over Hiroshima, Japan. Most of the city was destroyed and approximately 80,000 people were killed, with as many as 100,000 more losing their lives as a result of radiation poisoning and other secondary factors. The bomb, one of only two functional nuclear devices in existence at that time, was dropped from the _Enola Gay,_ a U.S. Army Air Force B-29 long-range heavy bomber. The pilot was Colonel Paul Warfield Tibbets, Jr., of Miami, FL, USA, and the bombardier was Major Thomas W. Ferebee of Mocksville, NC, USA.

4233. Supersonic bomber was the U.S.-built B-58 "Hustler," developed by Convair and first flight tested on November 11, 1956. The slim-bodied, delta-winged craft, which carried nuclear weapons and fuel in a large pod under the fuselage, was capable of a maximum airspeed of Mach 2.1.

4234. Stealth aircraft was the U.S. Air Force's SR-71 _Blackbird,_ a strategic reconnaissance craft. It was designed by Clarence Leonard "Kelly" Johnson at Lockheed Advanced Development Company as a replacement for the aging U-2 spyplane, which Johnson had also designed. The SR-71, which entered service circa 1965, was a twin-engine jet aircraft with a sleek titanium fuselage shaped to produce the smallest possible radar signature. It was the fastest, highest-flying aircraft of its time (excepting the X-15 series of rocket craft), capable of operating at altitudes in excess of 85,000 feet (26,000 meters), well above the operational range of nearly all ground-to-air defense systems.

4235. Destruction of an attacking missile by a defensive missile in combat occurred on January 18, 1991, when a SCUD missile launched from Iraq during the Gulf War was blown out of the sky over northern Saudi Arabia by an American-made Patriot antimissile missile.

4236. Multinational coordinated air strikes by NATO were carried out on November 21 and 23, 1994, when fighter-bomber aircraft from the United States, Great Britain, the Netherlands, and France attacked Serbian missile batteries. NATO aircraft also bombed an airfield in Serb-held Croatia, a launching area for Serbian attacks against Muslim safe areas.

4237. Woman fighter pilot to fire a missile in combat was Lieutenant Kendra Williams of the U.S. Navy air wing based on the U.S.S. *Enterprise* aircraft carrier. On the night of December 16–17, 1998, she launched a laser-guided missile from her FA/18 Hornet jet fighter at an anti-aircraft emplacement in Iraq.

MILITARY—WAR—SEA

4238. Naval battle of record was fought in 664 BCE between the Greek city-state of Corinth, on the Greek mainland, and the Ionian Sea island of Corcyra (modern Corfu), a breakaway Corinthian colony.

4239. Admiral who was a woman was Queen Artemisia I of Halicarnassus in Asia Minor (the modern Bodrum, Turkey), who commanded five ships in the fleet of the Persian king Xerxes when he invaded Greece in 480–479 BCE. As described by the Greek historian Herodotus, she warned Xerxes, in vain, against attempting a direct naval confrontation with the Greeks, and persuaded him to cancel the entire campaign after his defeat in the battle of Salamis. During the battle, her own ship rammed and sank another belonging to one of her allies, King Damasithymos of Calyndia, with whom she had an ongoing quarrel.

4240. Warship known from archeological evidence is the Marsala Ship, a wreck discovered in 1969 in the harbor of Marsala in western Sicily, Italy. Honor Frost and the international team of marine archeologists who excavated the site concluded that the original ship was approximately 110 feet (33.5 meters) long and 16 feet (5 meters) wide. The presence of ballast stones and the lack of cargo in the wreck indicated that it was a war galley, probably used for scouting or for ramming smaller craft. It is believed to have been one of the swift "Liburnian" ships with 17 sweeps per side used by the ancient city-state of Carthage in the Battle of the Aegates Islands (241 BCE), the last battle of the First Punic War between Carthage and the Roman Republic. Also found in the wreck were remains of marijuana (*Cannabis sativa*) stems, which may have been chewed by the oarsmen.

4241. Rams for striking and sinking enemy vessels were used in the prows of Greek galleys circa 300 BCE, according to many depictions of ram-equipped warships in Greek art. Later they were adopted by the Romans and other Mediterranean seafarers. The first ram known to archeologists that can be definitively dated is the Athlit Ram, constructed circa 175 BCE. It was discovered by the Israeli marine archeologist Yehoshua Ramon in 1980 in shallow water off the coast of Athlit, Israel. The ram was made of a heavy wooden armature of approximately 7 feet (2.3 meters) in length, over which was fitted a thick bronze shell that had been custom-cast to fit the wood. The bronze was decorated with symbols identified with two Hellenistic Egyptian kings, Ptolemy V Epiphanes and Ptolemy VI Philometor. The latter reigned between 204 and 164 BCE.

4242. Muslim navy was founded by Abd Allah ibn Sa'd ibn Abi Sarh, the governor of southern Egypt, and Mu'awiyah ibn Abi Sufyan, the governor of Damascus (in modern Syria), to assist the Muslim attack on the Byzantine Empire. The navy captured the Mediterranean islands of Cyprus in 649 and Rhodes in 654. It scored its first defeat of a Byzantine fleet in 652 off Alexandria, Egypt, and inflicted a worse defeat on the Byzantines in 655 off Anatolia's Lycian coast (part of modern Turkey) in the Battle of Dhat as-Sawari, also called the Battle of Lycia. Mu'awiyah went on to become caliph and the founder of the Umayyad dynasty of Muslim rulers.

4243. Naval battle in which Greek fire was used was the Battle of Cyzicus, which took place off the Byzantine capital of Constantinople (modern Istanbul, Turkey) in 673. A large Muslim fleet was destroyed by Greek fire, an ancient forerunner of napalm, that was hurled by catapult from Byzantine ships. Greek fire an incendiary compound and a forerunner of napalm.

MILITARY—WAR—SEA—*continued*

4244. Viking raid known to historians was an attack in 793 by Danish raiders on the church and monastery of Lindisfarne, a small island in the west North Sea off the English Northumberland coast. The Viking period is traditionally dated from this event.

4245. Naval battle fought with cannon broadsides was an engagement fought on August 10, 1512, off the coast of Brest, France, between an English fleet under Sir Edward Howard and a defending French fleet commanded by a Welshman, Sir Piers Morgan. The ships traded broadside for broadside until the French flagship exploded next to one of the English ships, resulting in the deaths of 1,600 men.

4246. Major naval battle decided by firepower was the Battle of Lepanto, fought by the Ottoman Turks and several Christian states of western Europe over possession of the island of Cyprus. The battle took place on October 7, 1571, in the Gulf of Patras, near Lepanto (Návpaktos), Greece, and involved about 170,000 men. It matched the allied fleets of Spain, Venice, and the papacy, commanded by the Spanish general Don Juan de Austria, against the Muslim fleet, commanded by Ali Pasha, Muhammad Saulak (the governor of Alexandria), and Uluj Ali (the dey of Algiers). The opponents were fairly evenly matched in terms of ships, but the European allies had more than 1,800 artillery pieces, the Turks 750. In four hours of fighting, the Turks lost some 200 galleys and 30,000 men. Within six months they rebuilt their fleet, and Venice surrendered Cyprus to the Turks two years later.

4247. Ironclad ships were the *kobukson,* or "Turtle boats," designed and paid for by the Korean admiral Yi Sun-Shin in 1591–92 in anticipation of an invasion by Japan. Like the later ironclads of the American Civil War, the Turtle boats were clad and decked in iron sheet and were armed with cannon. They also were equipped with spikes to repel boarders, an iron ram, slits for archers, and the ability to lay down a screen of oily smoke,which issued from a hollow statue of a turtle's head that was fixed to the bow. During battle, the sails were lowered, and the craft became a galley, rowed by 14 to 20 men. The rudder was worked by a ten-man team. The Turtle boats destroyed both the invading Japanese fleet of 1592 and a second one in 1597.

4248. Naval battles in which ironclad vessels participated took place in 1592, during the invasion of Korea by the Japanese warlord Toyotomi Hideyoshi. The Japanese arrived with 300,000 troops in a fleet numbering more than 200 ships under Ukida Hideiye. They were met by the Korean admiral Yi Sun-Shin with the a small fleet of ironclad warships, called *kobukson,* or "Turtle boats," which could be both sailed and rowed. In a series of encounters between May and September, the Turtle boats destroyed the Japanese fleet without losing any of their own. In 1597, a second Japanese invasion fleet was decimated by Turtle boats, with the loss of some 300 Japanese ships and 50,000 sailors and soldiers. It was the largest naval engagement until the 20th century.

4249. Smokescreen in a battle created deliberately was introduced by the Korean navy in 1592, during its defense against a sea invasion by the Japanese. The invasion was repelled by Admiral Yi Sun-Shin's *kobukson,* or "Turtle boats." These armored vessels, the first ironclad ships, were each equipped with a wooden box, carved in the shape of a turtle's head, that projected from the bow. Sulfur and saltpeter were kept burning in the box, producing billows of smoke that issued from the statue's mouth.

4250. Major naval battle fought by the Dutch navy was the Battle of Gibraltar Bay, fought on April 25, 1607, off the coast of Spain near Algeciras. Some 25 ships under Jacob van Heemskerk, seeking to stop Spanish attacks on Dutch East Indies trading vessels, met and destroyed a similar fleet under Don Juan Alvarez d'Avila.

4251. Submarine built for use in war was the *American Turtle,* built in 1776 by American inventor David Bushnell of Saybrook, CT, USA. The vessel, which was large enough to accommodate one operator, had a 24-inch (61-centimeter) two-bladed wooden screw propeller, operated by hand, that enabled it to travel forward or in reverse at 3 knots. A crank operated the rudder aft. Water was admitted for descent and forced out with a hand pump for surfacing. Another screw, on the bottom, moved the submarine vertically. On September 7, 1776, during the American Revolutionary War, Ezra Lee used the craft to attach a torpedo time bomb to the hull of the British flagship, the 64-gun H.M.S. *Eagle,* in New York Harbor. An explosion resulted, but no serious damage occurred, as the bomb had drifted away from the ship.

4252. British ship to bear the initials H.M.S. for "His/Her Majesty's Ship" was the H.M.S. *Phoenix* in 1789.

4253. Ironclad warship in modern times was the French single-decker *La Gloire,* designed by Stanislas-Charles-Henri-Laurent Dupuy de Lôme and commissioned in Toulon, France, in 1860. It had an iron-braced wooden frame clad with iron plate 4.7 inches (12 centimeters) thick. The ship's deck was iron and was outfitted with 36 muzzle-loading rifled guns.

4254. Iron-hulled warship was the H.M.S. *Warrior,* designed by Isaac Watts, completed in 1861 at the Thames Iron Works, Blackwall, England, and commissioned on August 1, 1861, under Captain A.A. Cochrane. It was the brainchild of First Sea Lord Sir John Pakington and Admiral Sir Baldwin Wake Walker, who sought a new iron battleship to counter the French ironclads that entered service beginning in 1858. The *Warrior* was the largest warship of its time, 418 feet (128 meters) long and 58.4 feet (17.8 meters) wide, dwarfing its French counterparts and every wooden man-of-war ever built. Its primary armament was 26 breechloading 68-pounders, augmented by four 40-pounders and eight massive guns throwing 110-pound shot. Although possessing powerful steam engines capable of propelling the ship at 14.1 knots, the *Warrior* was also rigged with three masts. Originally assigned to the Channel Fleet, the *Warrior* saw active duty until 1900, after which it was used as a storage hulk and floating oil jetty. In 1978 a restoration effort was initiated and in 1987 it was put on permanent display at the Naval Base, Portsmouth, England.

4255. Naval battle between ironclad vessels was the action at Hampton Roads, VA, USA, on March 9, 1862, between the U.S.S. *Monitor,* the revolutionary turreted vessel designed and built by American inventor John Ericsson and commanded by Lieutenant John Lorimer Worden, and the large Confederate ironclad ship *Virginia* (formerly the *Merrimac*), commanded by Commodore Franklin Buchanan. The three-hour battle ended inconclusively, after both ships sustained damage and Worden was blinded by flying iron splinters. The *Virginia* was the first to retire, and the battle was interpreted by both sides as a victory for the *Monitor.*

4256. Periscope was invented by Thomas Doughty, acting chief engineer of the United States Navy, in 1864. During Nathaniel Prentiss Banks's Red River expedition, Doughty was on the turreted gunship *Osage.* Annoyed by bushwhackers and snipers who could not be seen yet did deadly work, Doughty rigged up a sheet-iron tube extending from a few feet above the deck to the engine room below, with an internal arrangement of mirrors that allowed him to see the shore. When attacked, he would signal the gunners to fire.

4257. Modern conflict in which an Asian power defeated a European power was the Russo-Japanese War, a conflict between Russia and Japan over control of Manchuria and Korea. Fighting began on February 8, 1904, at Port Arthur in Manchuria (now Lu-shun, China). A series of humiliating defeats for Russia culminated in May 1905 with the complete destruction of the Russian Baltic fleet by the Japanese Navy, commanded by Admiral Togo Heihachiro, at the Battle of Tsushima, south of the Sea of Japan. A peace treaty mediated by U.S. president Theodore Roosevelt was signed at Portsmouth, NH, USA, on September 5, 1905.

4258. Battleship powered by steam turbines was the H.M.S. *Dreadnought,* launched by Britain in 1906. The ship was 526 feet (160 meters) long, displaced 18,000 tons, and carried a crew of about 800. The four propeller shafts were powered by steam turbines and produced a maximum speed of 21 knots, a major increase in performance over earlier warships of its size. It was also the first "all-big-gun" battleship with no smaller secondary cannon. The main battery consisted of ten 12-inch (300-millimeter) guns in five armored turrets. Two dozen 3-inch (78 millimeter) rapid-firing guns were retained for use against light attack craft. Despite its impressive size and performance, it was obsolete by World War I and was sold for scrap in 1920.

4259. Use of aircraft carriers in war took place during the Mexican Revolution, when United States forces occupied the Mexican port of Veracruz in April 1914. Five seaplanes were carried aboard two American warships, the battleship U.S.S. *Mississippi* and the cruiser U.S.S. *Birmingham,* and were used to fly reconnaissance missions over Mexican positions held by troops under General Victoriano Huerta. The planes did not launch from deck but were lowered over the side to the water.

4260. Submarine blockade was mounted against the British Isles by German U-boats beginning on February 2, 1915. The blockade was not especially effective until Germany began to wage unrestricted submarine warfare in early 1917, a decision that brought the United States into the war and ultimately led to Germany's defeat.

MILITARY—WAR—SEA—*continued*

4261. Aircraft carrier adapted from a conventional warship to see service in war was the British warship H.M.S *Furious,* built in 1917 by Harland & Wolff Ltd., Belfast, Ireland. The turbine-powered vessel, 743.3 feet (226.6 meters) long and 95.8 feet (29.2 meters) wide, was outfitted with a single 18-inch (457-millimeter) gun that was soon removed to make room for an extension of its forward flight deck. It could carry a full complement of 36 aircraft. On July 18, 1918, the *Furious* saw action in the first important carrier raid, the successful British attack on the German Zeppelin airbase in Tondern, Schleswig-Holstein (now part of Germany).

4262. Landing of a plane on a ship under way was achieved by British pilot E.H. Dunning. On August 2, 1917, he landed his Sopwith Pup on the warship H.M.S *Furious,* the first ship regularly used as an aircraft carrier.

4263. Aircraft carrier with a through-deck runway was the H.M.S. *Argus,* a British passenger liner that was converted in 1918 by the Royal Navy for carrier use. Unlike earlier carriers, which were fitted with short flight decks in the forward part of the ship, the *Argus* possessed a flight deck extending from bow to stern. This "through-deck" design enabled it to launch heavier, larger aircraft, and was adopted by all later carriers.

4264. Aircraft carrier attack was launched from the waters of the Baltic Sea on July 18, 1918, when British naval vessels, including the H.M.S. *Furious,* the first aircraft carrier in regular use, mounted a successful attack on the German Zeppelin airbase in Tondern, Schleswig-Holstein (now part of Germany).

4265. Aircraft carrier built as such from the first design phase was a Japanese carrier, the *Hosyo,* with 7,470 tons displacement. Commissioned in December 1922, it carried 21 aircraft.

4266. Naval shot of World War II was fired at 4:47 AM on September 1, 1939, when the German battleship *Schleswig Holstein* unleashed a barrage on the Polish Westerplatte Garrison, a complex of barracks and workshops on the port canal of Gdansk, Poland. Under constant fire, the Westerplatte nonetheless held out for a week before surrendering.

4267. Civilian ship sunk in World War II was the Donaldson Atlantic Line passenger liner *Athenia* of 13,581 tons, sunk west of Scotland on September 3, 1939, by the German submarine U-30. The U-boat's captain, Leutnant Julius Lemp, mistook the ship for an armed merchant cruiser. The ship was carrying evacuees from Britain to the USA. Some 1,300 survivors were rescued by British destroyers; 118 passengers were drowned.

4268. U-boat captured in World War II was the U-39, brought to the surface on September 14, 1939, in the mid-Atlantic by depth charges released from the British destroyers *Firedrake, Faulkner,* and *Foxhound.* The U-39 had just fired two torpedoes at the British aircraft carrier *Ark Royal.*

4269. Warship sunk by air attack in wartime was the German light cruiser *Königsberg,* sunk at Bergen, Norway, on April 9, 1940, by aircraft from the British carrier H.M.S. *Ark Royal.*

4270. Aircraft carrier to be sunk by surface ships was the H.M.S. *Glorious,* commanded by Captain D'Oyly-Hughes. It was sunk on June 8, 1940, en route from Narvik, Norway, to Scapa Flow in the Orkneys, by bombardment from German warships *Scharnhorst, Gneisenau,* and *Hipper.* A total of 1,207 British personnel were lost.

4271. Japanese naval casualty in World War II was the merchant ship *Awajisan Maru.* On December 8, 1941, it was sunk by Royal Australian Air Force planes off Koto Bharu, Malaya (now Malaysia).

4272. Sea battle fought solely by air power was the Battle of the Coral Sea (a large area of the Pacific Ocean between Australia and New Caledonia), which took place on May 4–8, 1942, between U.S. Navy Task Force 17, under command of Rear Admiral Frank J. Fletcher, and Vice Admiral Takeo Takagi's Japanese Carrier Striking Force, which was converging on Port Moresby, New Guinea. American and Japanese planes took off from carriers 180 miles away from each other; no surface ships ever sighted ships of the opposing force. The Japanese lost 39 ships, including the carrier *Shoho,* and many aircraft. The United States lost the aircraft carrier *Lexington* and suffered severe damage to the carrier *Yorktown.* The battle was a strategic victory for the United States.

4273. Nuclear-powered submarine was the U.S.S. *Nautilus,* built by the Electric Boat Company, a division of the General Dynamics Corporation, Groton, CT, USA, under the supervision of U.S. Navy captain Hyman George Rickover. The submarine, launched on January 21, 1954, on the Thames River at Groton, was commissioned on September 21, 1954, tested under nuclear power on January 17, 1955, and completed on April 22, 1955. Its crew consisted of eleven officers and 85 enlisted men. The first commander was Eugene Parks Wilkinson. The steam turbines were powered by a liquid-cooled nuclear reactor. The *Nautilus* was 323 feet (99 meters) long overall. Its displacement was 3,747 tons (3,399 metric tons) submerged.

4274. Nuclear-powered warship was the U.S.-built cruiser U.S.S. *Long Beach,* launched on July 14, 1959. It was powered by two Westinghouse C1W nuclear power plants that could drive the 16,602-ton vessel at up to 30 knots. Armament consisted of guided missiles and antisubmarine weapons.

4275. Submarine equipped with ballistic missiles was the nuclear-powered U.S.S. *George Washington,* commissioned on December 30, 1959, at Groton, CT, USA, on the Thames River. The cost of construction was approximately US$110 million. The first commander was James Butler Osborn. It went on patrol duty on November 15, 1960, from Charleston, SC, USA, and returned on January 21, 1961, having traveled 67 days underwater. The *George Washington* was equipped with 16 vertical Polaris missile tubes that were fired below the surface. The Polaris missiles could be equipped with nuclear warheads.

4276. Nuclear-powered aircraft carrier was the American carrier U.S.S. *Enterprise,* completed on December 20, 1961. It was 1,101 feet (336 meters) long and 252 feet (77 meters) wide, with an 85,350-ton (77,412-metric-ton) full-load displacement. The carrier, built by the Newport News Shipbuilding and Dry Dock Company, Newport News, VA, USA, had a complement of 440 officers and 4,160 enlisted men. It was equipped with eight pressurized water-cooled nuclear reactors and was capable of steaming for five years without refueling. Its flight deck was large enough to accommodate four football fields, and each of its four propellers was the height of a two-story building.

MONEY

4277. Hyperinflation took place in China circa 1166. Paper money was issued in abundance several times between 1020 and 1160 to cover cash shortages, fueling inflation. In 1160, the emperor Gao Zong, first emperor of the Southern Sung dynasty, instituted a reform of the currency by replacing the old, worthless notes with a new issue. By 1166 this new issue had a nominal value of 43,600,000 ounces of silver, but as cash was almost as worthless as the old. China experienced several more periods of hyperinflation before abandoning paper currency altogether circa 1455.

MOVIES

4278. Motion picture was taken by the French photographer Louis Le Prince, an early researcher in motion pictures. In 1885 (or possibly 1887), Le Prince reportedly captured moving outlines on a wall at the Institute for the Deaf, New York, NY, USA, but no evidence of this movie exists. A 2.125-inch (55 millimeter) wide roll of film, taken by Le Prince in early October 1888, is the first surviving motion picture of record. It shows the garden of the house of his father-in-law, Joseph Whitley, in Roundhay, Great Britain.

4279. Movie studio was a frame cabin covered with black roofing paper, built on Thomas Alva Edison's property in West Orange, NJ, USA, in 1892. The structure was built so that it could be pivoted to enable the stage to secure the maximum sunlight. It was called a "revolving photographic building" and was completed on February 1, 1893, at a cost of US$638. Its nickname was "Black Maria."

4280. Movie to be copyrighted consisted of 47 successive frames showing a man named Fred Ott sneezing extravagantly. Ott was a mechanic who worked at the laboratories of Thomas Alva Edison. The images were filmed on February 2, 1893, at the Edison studio, West Orange, NJ, USA, by William Kennedy Laurie Dickson. The copyright was recorded as follows: "Edison Kinetoscopic Record of a Sneeze, January 7, 1894. Entered in the name of W.K.L. Dickson, under No. 2,887, January 9, 1894." The movie is more popularly known as *Fred Ott's Sneeze.*

4281. Motion picture of importance is usually agreed to be *La Sortie des ouvriers de l'usine Lumière (Workers Leaving the Lumière Factory),* shot in 1895 by the French film pioneers Louis and Auguste Lumière. It was first shown in Paris that year.

MOVIES—*continued*

4282. Movie recorded on film to be shown on a screen was exhibited by the American inventor Woodville Latham, who demonstrated his Pantoptikon at 35 Frankfort Street, New York, NY, USA, on April 21, 1895. A continuous roll of film, with hole perforations on the sides for spokes of the sprocket, was reeled in front of an electric light contained in a projector of the magic lantern type. On May 5, 1895, Latham filmed a staged bout of four minutes' duration between Young Griffo and Battling Charles Barnett on the roof of Madison Square Garden, New York City. The film was exhibited on May 20 at 153 Broadway, New York City, after which it was shown in a tent on Surf Avenue on Coney Island for the rest of the summer.

4283. Movies shown commercially were several one-minute films screened on December 28, 1895, in the basement of the Grand-Café in Paris, France. The movies were made by the French film pioneers Louis and Auguste Lumière and showed scenes from daily Parisian life, including a crowded street, the arrival of a train, and a company of marching soldiers.

4284. Film director who was a woman was the French film pioneer Alice Guy Blache, who directed her first film in 1896 in Paris. Blache directed, produced, and/or supervised nearly 300 films in her career, many with her own production company, the Solax Company, which she founded in 1912. She directed the first sound film by a woman in 1906. In 1953 she was recognized by France as the world's first woman filmmaker and made a knight of the French Legion of Honor.

4285. Narrative film to tell a story was *Fée aux Choux,* conceived and directed by the French film pioneer Alice Guy Blaché, a secretary for the Léon Gaumont film equipment company. It was shown in 1896 at the International Exhibition in Paris. The one-minute film, produced to help sell the newly invented motion picture projector, was based on an old French fable about a fairy who makes children in a cabbage patch. *L'Affaire Dreyfus (The Dreyfus Affair),* produced in 1899 by Georges Méliès, is often erroneously cited as the first narrative film. *La Fée aux Choux* was also the first film directed by a woman.

4286. Films synchronized with speech were several short films, including one featuring Sarah Bernhardt as Hamlet, produced by the Gaumont Company of France and screened at the Paris Exposition on June 8, 1900. Speech was provided by carefully synchronizing an amplified record player to play along with the film.

4287. Film composer to create a score especially for a motion picture was Romolo Bachioni (or Bacchini). In 1906 he wrote original music for the Italian films *Malio dell'Oro* and *Pierrot Innamorato.*

4288. Feature-length motion picture was *The Story of the Kelly Gang,* produced by the theatrical company of J. and N. Tait in Melbourne, Victoria, Australia. It recounted the life story of the bushranger Ned Kelly. The 65-minute film, which cost 450 Australian pounds to make, opened at the Melbourne Athenaeum Hall on December 26, 1906.

4289. Double feature was shown at the Glacarium in Melbourne, Australia, on May 15, 1911. The films were *The Last Chord* and the Italian production *The Fall of Troy.*

4290. Cinematographer of lasting influence was George William "Billy" Bitzer, who photographed movies for the Hollywood director D.W. Griffith from 1913 to 1924. Bitzer is credited with developing most of the techniques of modern film photography, including long shots, close-ups, fade-outs, iris shots, and soft-focus shots. He was also the first to shoot a movie entirely by artificial light and to achieve mood effects using candlelight and firelight. As a young man, during the Spanish-American War, he became the first cameraman to film a war.

4291. Dramatic films shot in Africa were made in 1913 by the German big-game hunter turned filmmaker Hans Hermann Schomburgk. On an expedition to the German West African colony of Togoland (an area now divided between the Republics of Togo and Ghana), he made several short features, the best known of which was *The White Goddess of the Wangora,* starring Meg Gehrts.

4292. Tracking shot in which the movie camera was mounted on a mobile platform was invented by the Russian cinematographer Nikolay Kozlovsky for the 1913 film *The Twilight of a Woman's Soul,* directed by Yevgeny Bauer. The shot appears in the opening reel.

4293. Film archive was the Dansk Statens Arkiv for Historiske Film og Stemmer, founded at the Royal Library in Copenhagen, Denmark, on April 9, 1913, at the instigation of the journalist Anker Kirkeby and the film producer Ole Olsen of Nordisk Films.

4294. Color feature film was *The World, the Flesh, and the Devil,* a British production directed by F. Martin Thornton. It opened at the Holborn Empire in London, England, on April 9, 1914. The color system used was called Kinemacolor, an additive process developed by Charles Urban circa 1906. It involved a single black-and-white film strip onto which each frame had been exposed twice, once for blue-green tints, and once for red-orange tints. The film was projected at double speed (32 frames per second) through a glass filter, half blue-green and half red-orange, that rotated in synchrony with the film. All the frames shot for blue-green were projected through the blue-green part of the filter, and likewise for red-orange. When the film was viewed on the screen, the eye combined the hues into an approximation of lifelike color.

4295. Movie studio to produce 100 feature films was the Paramount Pictures Corporation, founded in Hollywood, CA, USA, in 1914 by W.W. Hodkinson and now owned by Viacom Inc. In 1921, Paramount made 101 films, the most ever made by any movie studio.

4296. Commercial talking motion picture was *Der Brandstifter (The Arsonist),* a German film released in 1922. The first Hollywood movie with sound and image fully integrated was *Lights of New York,* a gangster movie made in 1928 by the Warner Brothers studio.

4297. Film studio in China of importance was the Mingxing studio, which began releasing films in 1922. The early productions were mainly Chinese versions of Hollywood genres such as musicals and adventure serials.

4298. Freeze frame was used as the final image of *La Roue (The Wheel),* a 1922 film by French director Abel Gance. *La Roue* was the story of a group of railway workers and, more generally, about the depersonalization and routinization of life brought on by 20th-century technology. The frozen frame showed the death of the oldest worker, Sisif.

4299. Movie shown on an airplane was screened in April 1925 on a British Imperial Airways flight. The film was the 1925 silent special effects epic *The Lost World,* from the book by Arthur Conan Doyle about dinosaurs in the modern world.

4300. Movie accompanied by prerecorded sound to be released as a feature film was presented on August 5, 1926, at an invitation performance at the Warner Theatre, New York, NY, USA. On August 6, a gala premiere was held at which seats sold for US$10. The show used the Vitaphone system, meaning that the film did not carry a sound recording but was synchronized with disc phonograph records of the musical score. The main feature was *Don Juan,* directed by Alan Crosland, which starred John Barrymore, Mary Astor, Warner Oland, Estelle Taylor, and Myrna Loy. The musical score was played by the New York Philharmonic Orchestra. It was preceded by a number of short features showing performances by Mischa Elman, Efrem Zimbalist, a marimba band, and other musicians.

4301. Movie with both sound and color was Warner Brothers' Vitaphone Technicolor film *On with the Show,* exhibited on May 28, 1929, at the Winter Garden, New York, NY, USA. The cast included Betty Compson, Joe E. Brown, and Ethel Waters. It was directed by Alan Crosland and was based on a story by Humphrey Pearson.

4302. National film archive was the Reichsfilmsarchiv, founded in Nazi Germany in February 1935.

4303. Woman cinematographer to receive sole credit for the camerawork in a feature film was Galina Pushkova, for the 1946 Soviet film *Songs of Abay.*

4304. Film made by a studio outside the United States to win an Academy Award was *Hamlet,* directed by Laurence Kerr Olivier, who also starred in the title role. At the 1949 Academy of Motion Picture Arts and Sciences awards ceremonies held in Los Angeles, CA, USA, *Hamlet* won five Oscars, including one for Olivier as best actor.

4305. Slow motion action sequence was employed in *Shichinin no samurai (The Seven Samurai),* an epic 1954 film by the Japanese director Akira Kurosawa. In an early scene, the samurai leader Kambei (played by Takashi Shimura) rescues a little boy and kills his kidnapper, who collapses in slow motion.

4306. Movie premiered simultaneously in major cities throughout the world was *On the Beach,* an adaptation of the novel by the English-born Australian novelist Nevil Shute, which had its premiere in the United States on December 17, 1959, at New York City's Astor Theatre and in 17 other cities around the world.

MOVIES—*continued*

The 134-minute film was produced by Stanley Kramer and written by John Paxton. It starred Gregory Peck, Ava Gardner, Fred Astaire, and Anthony Perkins. It told the story of the extinction of the human race after a nuclear war.

4307. Film directed by an African to be distributed outside Africa was *Borom Saret,* a short fiction film directed by the Senegalese writer and filmmaker Ousmane Sembène. It was released in 1963. His 1966 feature *La Noire de . . . (Black Girl),* about the enslavement of an African servant girl, was the first produced by an African filmmaker.

4308. Holographic movie was produced in 1969 by American physicists A.D. Jacobson and colleagues. It was a 70-millimeter, 30-second holographic film of tropical fish swimming in an aquarium.

4309. IMAX film was screened at the EXPO '70 world's fair in Osaka, Japan. IMAX is a giant-screen film technology developed between 1967 and 1970 by the IMAX Corporation, founded by three Canadians, Graeme Ferguson, Roman Kroitor, and Robert Kerr. The IMAX film format is ten times larger than standard 35-millimeter film and is projected with special equipment onto a large, curved screen that seems to envelop the audience.

4310. Multiplex hologram in which a short sequence of motion picture film was superimposed onto a single hologram, creating a still image that appeared to move in time as well as three-dimensional space, was developed in 1972 by American physicist Lloyd Cross. His multiplex hologram, also called an integral hologram, produced 360-degree animated holographic scenes viewable in ordinary white light. Sequential frames of standard motion-picture footage of a moving subject were recorded on special holographic film. When viewed, the composite images appeared to the human eye as a three-dimensional moving image. Cross's best-known multiplex hologram was "Kiss II," created in 1974 with Pam Brazier. It combined 540 motion picture frames of Brazier winking and blowing a kiss into a single holographic image that "played" as it was viewed from different angles.

4311. Holographic film system was developed in 1976 by Soviet filmmaker Victor Komar in Moscow. It incorporated a modified movie camera, a special projector with a mercury-cadmium lamp for illuminating the holographic film, and a holographic screen. Four people could view the film at one time. The first movie created with Komar's system was a 47-second monochrome short of a young woman holding a bouquet of flowers in front of her face. Viewers could move their heads and see the woman's face behind the flowers, as if the projected image were actually three-dimensional. Komar produced the first full-color holographic film in 1984.

4312. Feature film released on CD-ROM was the 1966 British film *A Hard Day's Night,* directed by Richard Lester and starring the Beatles. In 1993, the film was converted to Apple Computer, Inc.'s QuickTime digital movie format by The Voyager Company, a multimedia publisher in New York, NY, USA, and distributed commercially on CD-ROMs formatted for Apple Macintosh computers. As viewed on a computer screen, the movie could be displayed at a maximum of 320 pixels by 240 pixels.

4313. Feature film broadcast on the Internet was *Wax: Or the Discovery of Television Among the Bees,* a cult science-fiction film by American director David Blair. Blair uploaded the film in digital video format on May 22, 1993, for viewing worldwide.

4314. Film to earn US$1 billion worldwide was *Titanic,* an epic romance about the doomed luxury liner. The 1997 film was written, produced, and directed by American filmmaker James Cameron and distributed by two American studios, Paramount Pictures and Twentieth Century Fox. As of March 2, 1998, the film had earned US$575.7 million in the international box office and US$427 million in North American theaters, for a total of US$1,002,706,625. It was the highest grossing film of all time as well as the highest grossing film in more than 50 countries.

4315. Feature film to premiere simultaneously in a theater and on the Internet was *Dead Broke,* a low-budget drama written and directed by the American filmmaker Edward Vilga and starring Paul Sorvino, Tony Roberts and John Glover. On May 5, 1999, it was available for viewing anywhere in the world via the World Wide Web site of iFilm Network, an on-line community of independent filmmakers and film fans, while simultaneously the film was downloaded by satellite feed to a digital projection system at the Tribeca Film Center, a physical theater in New York, NY, USA.

4316. Movie to make more than US$100 million in 5 days was *Star Wars: Episode 1—The Phantom Menace,* which opened in North America on Wednesday, May 19, 1999. By midnight Sunday, May 23, it had grossed an estimated US$105.7 million at the box office. That total eclipsed the US$98.8 million, five-day box-office record set by the Steve Spielberg film *Jurassic Park: The Lost World* when that film opened in North America in May 1977. *Star Wars: Episode 1—The Phantom Menace* also broke the world record for the US$200 million mark, earning that sum on June 1, after just 13 days in theaters. A prequel to the first *Star Wars* trilogy of space fantasy films released between 1977 and 1983, the film was written and directed by the American filmmaker George Lucas.

4317. Digital projection of a major motion picture took place on June 18, 1999, when four theaters in the United States—two in New Jersey and two in California—screened the popular science fantasy film *Star Wars: Episode 1—The Phantom Menace* using experimental filmless digital projection systems from competing manufacturers CineComm and Texas Instruments. In both systems, a computerized projector delivered images to the screen directly from a motion graphics file stored on a high-capacity hard disk or downloaded from a satellite transmission.

4318. Major motion picture to be produced and exhibited entirely with digital technology was Walt Disney Pictures' animated feature *Tarzan,* based on the Edgar Rice Burroughs story. Produced and mastered entirely digitally using animation, composition, and editing software, it began a run using filmless digital projection systems at three U.S. theaters—one in Orlando, FL, one in Burbank, CA and one in Irvine, CA—on July 23, 1999.

MOVIES—ACTORS

4319. Movie star was the American actor Max Aronson, known variously as Bronco Billy, Max Anderson, and Gilbert M. Anderson. His first film appearance was in 1903 in *The Great Train Robbery,* in which he played the roles of the bandit, the brakeman, and the passenger who was shot. His first starring role was in *The Messenger Boy's Mistake,* for which he was paid 50 cents an hour. The first woman to become a movie star was the American actress Florence Lawrence, who started performing in films in 1907, first for the Edison company and then for the Vitagraph Company. In 1909 she went to the Biograph Company and was featured as "The Biograph Girl." Later she became known as "The IMP Girl," working for the Independent Moving Picture Company.

4320. Movie character with worldwide appeal was the Little Tramp, created by the English-born filmmaker and actor Charles Spencer Chaplin for his second film, *Kid Auto Races at Venice* (1914), and fully embodied in *The Tramp* (1915) and many later films. With his distinctive costume (fraying frock coat, baggy trousers, derby hat, and cane), jaunty walk, and air of endearing pathos, the Tramp was the first important character created exclusively for the cinema.

4321. Voice double was Hungarian tenor and cantor Joseph Diskay, who supplied the singing voice for Swedish actor Warner Oland in the pioneering Hollywood talkie *The Jazz Singer* (1927). Oland, who played a cantor, was unable to muster an adequate vocal performance for the *Kol Nidre* (the prayer that opens the evening service of the Jewish holiday of Yom Kippur), so Diskay was asked to sing into a microphone off-camera while Oland moved his lips in synchronization.

4322. Performer in a foreign language film to win the Academy Award for Best Actress was Sophia Loren (born Sofia Scicolone), the internationally popular Italian actress. She received the 1961 Academy Award at ceremonies in Los Angeles, CA, USA, for Vittorio de Sica's film *La ciociara* (released in English as *Two Women*), in which she played the mother of a teenage girl during World War II.

4323. Performer in a foreign language film to win the Academy Award for Best Actor was Roberto Benigni, the Italian comic actor and director, for his performance in the 1998 film *Life Is Beautiful,* a tragicomedy about the Holocaust. He received the award during the Academy Award ceremonies in Los Angeles, CA, USA, on March 21, 1999.

MOVIES—ANIMATIONS

4324. Animated picture machine was the Zoetrope, the "Wheel of Life," patented on April 23, 1867, by the American inventor William E. Lincoln of Providence, RI, USA, who assigned it to Milton Bradley and Company, Springfield, MA, USA. It consisted of a horizontal wheel with a series of animated drawings showing successive steps at right angles to the circumference. The drawings were viewed through a slit and, when the wheel revolved, appeared to show animation.

MOVIES—ANIMATIONS—*continued*

4325. Flip book was patented by Henry Van Hoevenbergh of Elizabeth, NJ, USA, who obtained a U.S. patent on May 16, 1882, on an "optical toy." The flip book was a series of successive drawings bound together in book form that, when riffled front-to-back, appeared to show animation. Flip books are now a standard tool for teaching animation, and are also treated as animated art in their own right.

4326. Animated cartoon was the American artist and filmmaker James Stuart Blackton's *Humorous Phases of Funny Faces,* containing about 8,000 drawings showing a man rolling his eyes and blowing smoke at a girl, a dog jumping over a hoop, and similar scenes. The final scene was a chalk-type drawing that the artist started as a sketch of one object, but that ended as a sketch of another. The film was released by Vitagraph in 1906.

4327. Animated character to appear in a series of cartoons was Fantôche, a hapless stick-figure man created by the pioneering French animator Emile Cohl, who worked for a time at the Gaumont Studio in Paris. Fantôche first appeared in the humorous 1909 short *Le Cauchemar du Fantôche (Fantôche's Nightmare).* In all, Cohl made about 250 animated films, most of which are lost.

4328. Animation made by the cel process using clear sheets of celluloid or acetate was *The Artist's Dream,* also known as *The Dachshund,* released on June 12, 1913, by Pathé Frères. It was produced by John Randolph Bray of New York, NY, USA, who received a U.S. patent for the technique on August 11, 1914. The cartoon showed Bray drawing a dachshund that ate sausages until he exploded. The drawings were made on transparent celluloid, with the colors painted on the reverse side, and were photographed with a regular color camera. The Brewster color process was used.

4329. Animation in color was *The Debut of Thomas Kat,* the story of a kitten taught by his mother to catch mice who confidently and tragically tackled a rat. The cartoon was produced by the Bray Pictures Corporation, New York, NY, USA, and was released in 1916 by Paramount.

4330. Feature-length animated film was *El Apóstol (The Apostle),* a political satire on the career of Argentine president Hipolito Irigoyen, released in 1917 by the pioneering Latin American filmmaker Federico Valle. The one-hour film required 50,000 finished drawings; the lead animator was Diogenes Tabora. No prints of the film are known to exist. Walt Disney's *Snow White and the Seven Dwarfs* (1937) is often erroneously cited as the first feature-length animation. It was, however, the first feature-length film made using the technique of cel animation.

4331. Animation with sound was "Steamboat Willie," an animated film produced in Hollywood, CA, USA, by Walt Disney. The world's first sound cartoon, it had a sound track that ran the entire length of the film and was accurately matched with the visuals. It was first shown on September 19, 1928, at the Colony Theatre, New York, NY, USA. This was also the first film to depict the antics of Mickey Mouse.

4332. Feature-length animated film directed by a woman was *Die Geschichte des Prinzen Achmed (The Story of Prince Achmed),* completed in Berlin, Germany, in 1926 by animator Lotte Reiniger, with technical assistance from her husband, the film producer Carl Koch. The 65-minute-long film was adapted from a story in *The Arabian Nights* and used a rare technique in which the characters were black paper cutouts animated against a translucent colored background. *Die Geschichte des Prinzen Achmed* was also the first film created with a multiplane animation stand, a device that enables several levels of animated material to be filmed at the same time.

4333. Feature-length animated film made by the cel process was Walt Disney's *Snow White and the Seven Dwarfs,* based on the fairy tale. It was first exhibited on December 21, 1937, at the Cathay Circle Theatre, Los Angeles, CA, USA. The running time was 75 minutes.

4334. Computer-generated short film was *Catalog,* a seven-minute collection of abstract computer-generated animations created in 1961 by American computer researcher and film special effects artist John Whitney, Sr., founder of Motion Graphics Incorporated. Whitney used a mechanical analog computer with slit-screen capabilities of his own invention to generate the swirling full-color images, which were set to the jazz music of Ornette Coleman.

4335. Digital computer animation was created in 1963 by Edward Zajac of Bell Laboratories, Holmdel, NJ, USA. It consisted of a simulated trip around the globe based on satellite still photographs.

4336. Animated film to win an award at the Cannes International Film Festival was the 1973 animated feature *Fantastic Planet,*, a futuristic story of a rebellion by oppressed humanoids against a race of gigantic androids. It was co-produced in France and Czechoslovakia (now the Czech Republic) and co-written and designed by René Laloux and Roland Topor. The film won a Special Jury Prize.

4337. Feature film incorporating digital computer graphics was the American-made 1976 science fiction thriller *Futureworld,* written and directed by Michael Crichton. Digital computer graphics were used to create an animated image of the head of American actor Peter Fonda. The animation was shown on a computer monitor in the film.

4338. Feature film that was entirely computer-animated was *Toy Story,* 81 minutes long, released on November 21, 1995, by Walt Disney Pictures, Burbank, CA, USA. It was produced at Pixar Corporation and directed by former Disney animator John Lasseter. The plot involves the adventures of two dolls, a cowboy and a space hero, who are rivals for the attention of a young boy. *Toy Story* was one of the year's top-grossing films, earning close to US$300 million worldwide in its first twelve months of release.

MOVIES—FESTIVALS

4339. Film festival was held in Monaco in 1898.

4340. Annual film festival was started in Venice, Italy, on August 6–21, 1932, as a tourist attraction in connection with an international art fair held at the same time. It was presided over by Count Volpi de Misurata, the finance minister under Benito Mussolini. Participating nations were Italy, France, Germany, Great Britain, the former Soviet Union, and the United States. In later years the festival became a propaganda event in support of fascist ideology.

4341. Grand Prix of the Cannes International Film Festival was awarded to the best films from the participating nations at the first Cannes event in 1946. They were: *The Red Earth,* directed by Lau Lauritzen (Denmark); *The Lost Weekend,* directed by Billy Wilder (United States); *Symphonie Pastorale,* directed by Jean Delannoy (France); *Brief Encounter,* directed by David Lean (Great Britain); *Neecha Nagar,* directed by Chetan Anand (India); *Open City,* directed by Roberto Rossellini (Italy); *Maria Candelaria,* directed by Emilio Fernandez (Mexico); *The Prize,* directed by Alf

Sjöberg (Sweden); *The Last Chance,* directed by Leopold Lindtberg (Switzerland); *Men Without Wings,* directed by M. Cap (Czechoslovakia); and *The Great Turning Point,* directed by Friedrich Ermler (former Soviet Union).

4342. Film to win the Palme d'Or at the Cannes International Film Festival was the 1955 American film *Marty,* written by Paddy Chayefsky and starring Ernest Borgnine. The Palme d'Or (Golden Palm) is currently the top prize in the festival, held yearly at Cannes, a resort city of the French Riviera.

4343. Film festival in the Western Hemisphere held annually and continuously was the San Francisco International Film Festival, inaugurated in 1957 in San Francisco, CA, USA. The festival, now under the auspices of the San Francisco Film Society, is noted for its eclectic mix of programs.

4344. African film festival was the Fespaco African film festival, first held in 1969 in the French protectorate of Upper Volta (now Burkina Faso). The Fespaco festival takes place every two years and features entries in French, English, Arabic, and many African languages. The festival's prize for best film is the Stallion of Yennenga.

4345. Acapulco Black Film Festival was held from June 24 to 29, 1997, in Acapulco, Mexico. The festival was designed to present and honor international, classic, and independent black cinema.

MOVIES—GENRES

4346. Movie comedy was *Fred Ott's Sneeze,* which also contained the first movie closeup. All 47 frames show a closeup of Ott, a mechanic with a gift for comedy, sneezing his head off for the camera. The action was recorded on February 2, 1893, at the Edison studio, West Orange, NJ, USA. William Kennedy Laurie Dickson was the project supervisor.

4347. Slapstick movie comedy was *L'arroseur Arrosé (The Sprinkler Sprinkled),* a short film made by Auguste and Louis Lumière in France in 1895. It featured some mischief inflicted by a child on a man trying to water his lawn.

4348. Science fiction film was *Le voyage dans la Lune (A Trip to the Moon),* a 14-minute film made in 1902 by the French director Georges Méliès, in which a team of pompous astronomers makes a lunar excursion in a rocket. The special effects, including the landing of the rocket in the eye of the Man in the Moon, were the first in the history of film.

MOVIES—GENRES—*continued*

4349. Movie western was *The Great Train Robbery,* made in 1903 in the woods outside Paterson, NJ, by Edwin S. Porter. The movie, though only twelve minutes long, was a piece of nonstop action, ending with the shooting of the four robbers by a posse of vigilantes recruited at a barn dance. It was the first movie to use elliptical technique (the deliberate skipping of nonessential material to keep the story moving at a fast pace).

4350. Newsreel was *Day by Day,* produced beginning in 1906 by the English filmmaker Will G. Barker. The newsreel, showing daily events of London street life, was shown at the Empire Theater in Leicester Square.

4351. Underground film was *Un Chien andalou (An Andalusian Dog),* produced in Paris, France, in 1928 by filmmaker Luis Buñuel and Surrealist painter Salvador Dali. The film, financed by Buñuel's mother, had no coherent narrative, but instead presented a series of striking, often disturbing short scenes drawn from the personal obsessions of the two filmmakers. It was the first such film to be seen widely.

4352. Movie musical in which singing and dancing were completely integrated into the story line was *Broadway Melody,* a Hollywood movie released by MGM in 1929. It starred Bessie Love and Charles King.

MOVIES—MOVIE THEATERS

4353. Movie exhibition in a theater to a paying audience was held on April 23, 1896, in Koster and Bial's Music Hall, 34th Street, New York, NY, USA. Thomas Alva Edison's Vitascope depicted a series of short scenes, including a ballet scene, a burlesque boxing match, surf breaking on the shore, and a comic allegory entitled *The Monroe Doctrine.* The images were about half life size and were shown in conjunction with other acts. The audience called for Edison, but he did not appear and refused to take a bow.

4354. Movie theater was opened in Piccadilly, London, England, in May 1896, but it burned down not long after. The first movie theater to run shows on a regular basis was Vitascope Hall, in New Orleans, LA, USA, where the first show took place on June 26, 1896. Tickets cost ten cents each. The theater, which had been converted for the purpose by William T. Rock, seated 400 viewers and showed short movies, usually comic pieces or scenic landscapes.

4355. Movie theater in Asia was probably the Denki-kan Electric Theatre in Tokyo, Japan, which began showing movies in 1903.

4356. Movie palace with seating for thousands of spectators was the Gaumont-Palace in Paris, France, a converted stage theater with room for 5,000 patrons. It opened in 1910.

4357. Newsreel theater was the Embassy, on Broadway and 46th Street, New York, NY, USA, which opened on November 2, 1929.

4358. Multiplex theater was the Regal Twins in Manchester, England. In 1930, it began to offer audiences two different films in two separate theaters.

4359. Drive-in movie theater was opened on June 6, 1933, in Camden, NJ, USA, by Richard Milton Hollingshead, Jr., and Willis Warren Smith of Riverton, NJ. Two shows were presented nightly. Nine rows of inclined planes accommodated 500 cars. The sound equipment was supplied by the RCA-Victor Company, Camden, NJ.

MUSIC

4360. Musical notation was included in instructions on a Sumerian clay tablet on tuning the nine-string Babylonian lyre to a heptatonic scale. The tablet was unearthed in the ancient city of Ur (now Tel-el-Muqayyar, Iraq) and has been dated to circa 1800 BCE. It was deciphered in 1966 by French archeologist Jacques Duchesne-Guillemin.

4361. Organist appears to have been Thäis, who lived in the third century BCE in Alexandria, Egypt. Her husband, Ctesibius (or Ktesebios), invented the hydraulic organ, the world's first mechanical musical instrument, which she learned to play.

4362. Musical notation using letters of the alphabet from A to G is credited to St. Odo (also spelled Oddo), the abbot of Cluny, France, from 927 to 942.

4363. Troubadour of note was William IX, Count of Poitiers, Duke of Aquitaine and Gascony (also called Guilhem VII of Poitiers), who died in 1127. William, an adventurer who led a failed Crusade in 1101 and was twice excommunicated for licentiousness, wrote eleven stanzaic poems in the Provençal language that were intended to be sung. Troubadour songs, which most often took the form of love poems to idealized noblewomen, were among the first secular songs created in Europe.

4364. Orchestra is considered to be the group of instruments, including violins and other stringed instruments both bowed and plucked, keyboards, and wind instruments, that was assembled in 1607 by Claudio Monteverdi for the premiere performance of his opera *La favola d'Orfeo (The Fable of Orpheus)*, presented that year at the Carnival in Mantua, Italy,

4365. Band known by that name was an ensemble of 24 violinists at the court of King Charles II of England in the second half of the 17th century (1660–85). The group was called the "king's band." The military band, consisting of wind, brass, and percussion players who accompany soldiers on parade, was a German innovation of the 15th century.

4366. Composer to write more than 100 hours of music was the English early Baroque composer Henry Purcell (1659–95), according to a survey in *Classical Music* magazine. Purcell was composer in ordinary to King Charles II, and wrote works for every state occasion. His known compositions include more than 150 songs and short vocal works, 8 harpsichord suites, 13 Fantasias, 2 In Nomines, 5 Pavans, 22 sonatas, 3 overtures, 1 violin sonata, 1 opera, 5 semi-operas, and incidental music to 43 plays.

4367. Encyclopedia of music was the *Musikalisches Lexikon (Musical Lexicon)* of 1732, published by the German composer and music scholar Johann Gottfried Walther.

4368. Orchestra of the modern type with separate sections for brass, wind, strings, and percussion, was organized in 1743 at the court of Karl Theodor, the elector palatine of Mannheim (now in Germany). The Mannheim orchestra was renowned for its ability to deliver such virtuosic effects as abrupt dynamic changes, lengthy crescendos, and quickly ascending melodic figures.

4369. Orchestra still in existence is the Gewandhaus Orchestra (originally known as the Grosses Concert) of Leipzig, Germany. It gave its first performances in 1743.

4370. Composer able to make a living entirely by writing music of his own choice was Ludwig von Beethoven, the German-born composer. Beethoven's financial future—and his complete creative freedom—was secured in 1809, when the archduke Rudolf, Prince Lobkowitz, and Prince Kinsky, all of Vienna, Austria (where Beethoven had taken up residence in 1792), offered him an annuity of 4,000 florins if he promised not to leave the city. The stipend enabled Beethoven to concentrate on writing such works as his *Ninth Symphony* and the *Missa Solemnis*.

4371. Conductor to use a baton was the German early Romantic composer, violinist, and conductor Louis Spohr (born Ludwig Spohr) of Brunswick (now in Germany). During a career spanning more than 50 years (1802–57), Spohr toured Italy with the violin virtuoso Niccolò Paganini, and conducted the opera in Frankfurt am Main, toured England six times, and served as court conductor at Kassel.

4372. Musical encyclopedia in English of importance was the *Dictionary of Music and Musicians* by the English musicologist and critic George Grove. The first edition was published between 1879 and 1789. In 1980, a thoroughgoing revision was published as *The New Grove Dictionary of Music and Musicians*.

4373. Music by indigenous American peoples to be recorded was two disk recordings of "Indian Songs," both titled "Three Melodies from the Ghost Dance." They were listed in the first catalog, dated November 1, 1894, of the United States Gramophone Company, Washington, DC, USA. No examples of these recordings are known to have survived.

4374. One-armed pianist of international stature was the Viennese performer Paul Wittgenstein (brother of the philosopher Ludwig Wittgenstein), who lost his right arm in World War I. The composer Maurice Ravel wrote his last major work, the Piano Concerto in D, for the left hand (1931), for Wittgenstein. Richard Strauss, Sergey Sergeyevich Prokofiev, and Benjamin Britten also wrote left-handed works for him.

4375. Pope to become a recording star was Pope John Paul II. In 1992, a recording of his voice reciting the rosary sold more than 1 million copies in Spain as a two-CD set. Another CD, *Abba Pater*, which contained the voice of the Pope chanting prayers and other material in five languages over music by Italian composers, was released on March 23, 1999, by the Sony Classical label and was a best-seller among Catholics worldwide.

MUSIC—JAZZ

4376. Composer of jazz music was William Christopher "W.C." Handy, also known as the "father of the blues," whose "Memphis Blues" was composed in 1911 and published on September 27, 1912. An African-American born in Florence, AL, USA, he was the first to combine the blues with ragtime, creating the earliest jazz compositions.

4377. Jazz record sold to the public was recorded in the United States by the Original Dixieland Jass Band, a group of five white musicians led by cornetist Nick La Rocca, the son of an Italian cobbler. The session was recorded on a Victor 78 disk by the Victor Company in New York, NY, USA, in February 1917. It featured two tunes, "Dixieland Jass Band One-Step" and "Livery Stable Blues," in which La Rocca made his horn sound like a horse whinnying.

4378. European jazz musician to win international recognition was Jean-Baptiste "Django" Reinhardt, the Belgian-born Gypsy (Rom) jazz guitarist. Reinhardt, who lost two fingers in a caravan fire in 1928, devised alternate fingerings that aided his development as a masterful improvisor. In all, he made some 800 recordings beginning circa 1930, and toured internationally through the 1930s and after World War II.

4379. Jazz festival was held in Newport, RI, USA, in 1954. The promoter was jazz aficionado George Wein. In 1971 the festival was moved to New York City.

MUSIC—MUSICAL COMPOSITIONS

4380. Hymns still sung in their unchanged form may be the Hindu hymns composed in Sanskrit and collected in the Vedas, of which the earliest, the *Rig Veda,* dates to approximately 1500 BCE. Transmitted by oral tradition until they were committed to writing in the tenth century CE, they have been preserved very much intact and are chanted by Brahmin priests on sacred occasions. Another early hymn of approximately the same period is a Hurrian-language composition found on a tablet, dating to circa 1400 BCE, from the site of the ancient city of Ugarit (now Ras Shamra, a mound on the Mediterranean coast of northern Syria). The tablet included lyrics and musical notation consisting of interval names and number signs. An inscription identified the text as a song to the moon goddess Nikkal.

4381. Gregorian chant as presently known was created by the merger of Gallican chant (as developed in the Frankish kingdom) and the *Cantus romanus,* a liturgy developed circa 600 to accompany the text of the Roman Catholic mass and the canonical hours during the time of Pope Gregory I (Gregory the Great or St. Gregory). Monks of the St. Gall abbey in Switzerland are often credited with combining the two chant forms circa 778, although it is more likely that a gradual period of assimilation occurred.

4382. Hymn for which an exact date is known is the "Heyr Himna Smiour (Hear, the Maker of Heaven")" by the Icelandic bard Kolbein Tumason, who composed it in 1208 CE.

4383. Canon known is *Sumer is icumen in,* an anonymous Middle English lyric dating from circa 1260. The song is written for six voices, of which two provide a repeating bass pattern and the other four participate in a cyclical repetition of the main melody. The canon is also sung to an alternate set of words, *Perspice christicola,* a Latin poem for Easter. The word "canon" comes from the Latin *canones,* meaning "rules," and refers to a musical composition in which multiple voices imitate the lead voice, often with variations; rounds and catches are forms of canon.

4384. Polyphonic mass by a known composer was *La messe de Nôtre Dame (The Mass of Our Lady),* written by Guillaume de Machaut in the 14th century (he died in 1377). Machaut was canon of the cathedral of Reims, France. In addition to the mass, he set many of his own poems to music. Polyphony is the combination of two or more lines of melody.

4385. Psalms in metrical form were the work of the French poet Clément Marot, valet de chambre to King Francis I. In 1539, he published a collection of 30 psalms that he had translated into French and recast in metrical versions. Another edition, *Trente Pseaulmes de Dâvíd (Thirty Psalms of David),* appeared in 1542. Marot's rendering of the psalms was denounced as heretical, and he went into temporary exile in Geneva, Switzerland. The Protestant leader John Calvin, who was seeking alternatives to the Roman Catholic liturgy, had some of the psalms set to music for congregational singing in the church at Geneva in 1562.

4386. Concerti were published in a 1587 collection of church music and madrigals titled *Concerti,* by the Venetian composers Andrea and Giovanni Gabrieli. These Baroque-era vocal-instrumental pieces, for up to 16 parts, did not include a solo for instrument, as did all concertos from the mid-18th century onward.

4387. Orchestration employed in a musical composition, in which the score specifies the use of particular instruments, was pioneered early in the 17th century by the Italian composer Claudio Monteverdi (1547–1643).

4388. Performance of the oratorio *Messiah* by the German-born English composer George Frideric Handel took place in Dublin, Ireland, on April 13, 1742.

4389. Nocturne was invented by the Irish composer and piano virtuoso John Field, who published a series of 20 nocturnes for piano in 1814. Field's short, reflective pieces, characterized by a leisurely melody over a chromatic accompaniment, strongly influenced the Polish composer and pianist Frédéric Chopin, who later published his own collection of 19 nocturnes.

4390. Impressionist musical composition was *Printemps (Spring)*, an orchestral composition by the Paris composer Claude Debussy that received its premiere in 1887. The faculty of the Paris Conservatoire, where Debussy had been a student, attacked its "vague Impressionism." The term had been current in the visual arts since the 1870s.

4391. Symphony incorporating continuous choral and orchestral elements was the *Symphony No. 8 in E Flat Major*, completed in 1907 by the Austrian composer Gustav Mahler. It was written to be performed by eight soloists, a double choir, and full orchestra, and is known popularly as the "Symphony of a Thousand."

4392. Recording of a complete symphony was made in 1914 by the Berlin Philharmonic, conducted by Arthur Kikisch. The orchestra's complete recording of Beethoven's *Fifth Symphony* occupied eight single-sided 78 rpm discs.

4393. Musical composition to incorporate a phonograph recording in a live performance was *Pini di Roma (Pines of Rome)* by the Italian composer Ottorino Respighi, first performed in 1924. The score called for a gramophone recording of a nightingale at the end of the nocturne movement.

4394. Live electronic music was *Imaginary Landscape no. 1*, produced by the American composer John Milton Cage in 1939 at the radio studio of the Cornish school in Seattle, WA, USA. It consisted of two players operating variable-speed turntables, a muted piano, and cymbals.

4395. Musique concrète was *Étude aux chemins de fer (Railroad Etude)*, composed in 1948 by Pierre Schaeffer, a composer, radio engineer, and broadcaster in Paris, France. The piece was the first to involve the manipulation of prerecorded ("concrete") sounds. It was first broadcast over French radio on October 5, 1948.

MUSIC—MUSICAL INSTRUMENTS

4396. Musical instrument known to archeologists may be a flute unearthed in 1997 in a cave near Idrija, Slovenia, that had once been occupied by Neanderthals. The flute was made of the hollowed femur of a bear, with four drilled holes along one side. It has been dated to at least circa 43,000 and possibly as early as 82,000 BCE. Some archeologists believe the bone was actually chewed and punctured by animals, probably wolves, although it may still have been used as a flute by early humans.

4397. Whistles known to anthropologists were found at Upper Paleolithic sites of the Aurignacian period, circa 25,000–22,000 BCE, at Istállósko, Hungary. They were made from perforated finger and toe bones.

4398. Harps were musical bows, having the same shape as hunting bows, but equipped with strings that could be plucked to produce sound. Harps were played circa 3000 BCE in Egypt and Sumer. A tomb at Ur (modern Tel-el-Muqayyar, Iraq) was found to contain three harps, each with 12 to 15 strings.

4399. Lyres known to archeologists were box lyres of Sumerian origin dating to circa 3000 BCE. The instruments measured about 3.5 feet (1.1 meters) in length, with one arm longer than the other. Contemporary Sumerian reliefs show large lyres played with two hands by seated musicians, similar to the method of playing the modern harp.

4400. Lutes were played in Egypt and Mesopotamia, where a long-necked lute appears in Babylonian artwork from the middle of the third millennium BCE. Lutes with bodies made of wood rather than skin originated in Arab cultures in the Middle East, where they were known as *al-oud* ("the wood"), the source of the English word "lute."

4401. Trumpet known was found in 1922 by British archeologists excavating the ancient Egyptian tomb of King Tutankhamen. It was made of silver in the form of a short straight tube, 18 inches (46 centimeters) long, that lacked a separate mouthpiece. Tutankhamen's tomb has been dated to circa 1350 BCE.

MUSIC—MUSICAL INSTRUMENTS—*continued*

4402. Harmonicas and other wind organs, including the accordion and concertina, are descended from the southern Chinese sheng, a kind of mouth organ consisting of a lacquered gourd fitted with a mouthpiece and a dozen or more vertical pipes. Metal reeds in the gourd sounded when air was blown through; notes in a pentatonic scale were made by fingering holes in the pipes. Dating from before 1100 BCE, it appeared in Europe by circa 1700 CE.

4403. Banjos originated in Africa, possibly in ancient times. The word is thought to be derived from *mbanza,* the name for a similar instrument in the Kimbundu language of northern Angola.

4404. Two-tone bells were the zhong bronze bells found in Chinese tombs dating mainly from the late Chou dynasty of circa 600–255 BCE. The truncated, clapperless bells each had two tones, either a third or a minor third apart, played by striking them on their sides precisely at two different places. Although zhong bells were first unearthed circa 1900, their secret was not discovered by Chinese musicologists until 1977.

4405. Organ was the hydraulus, or water organ, invented by Ktesebios (or Ctesibius) of Alexandria circa 250 BCE. The water organ was a small instrument, a mechanical adaptation of the panpipes. Wind was supplied to the pipes via a wind reservoir pressurized by a lever-operated piston pump. The lower part of the wind reservoir, which had no bottom, was immersed in water. Air escaping into the water from around the bottom edge of the reservoir served to maintain an equal pressure of air inside, thus providing a steady flow of air. A primitive keyboard directed the air to the desired pipe. A hydraulus was unearthed in 1931 at Aquincum, near Budapest, Hungary.

4406. Bowed instrument known was the rabab, also called the rababah or Arab fiddle, the ancestor of the European rebec. A lute-sized instrument with a membrane stretched over the body, no fingerboard, and two or three strings, it was typically stroked with a bow. It dates from before the tenth century CE and was played in the Middle East, Africa, Central Asia, and northern India.

4407. Stringed instrument played by a keyboard was the eschiquier, mentioned in the account books for the year 1360 of King John II the Good of France. The eschiquier was a stringed keyboard instrument like "an organ that sounds by means of strings," according to the description, but no examples are extant, and it is not known whether it was an early form of clavichord, harpsichord, or piano.

4408. Violin was a modification of an earlier stringed instrument, the viol. Violins were first made in Italy during the second half of the 16th century by Gaspare da Saló in Brescia and by Andrea Amati in Cremona. Amati's earliest known violin was made in 1564.

4409. Oboe was invented by French instrument-maker and musician Jean Hotteterre in 1657. He modified the treble shawm, the oboe's immediate predecessor, by narrowing the bore, reducing the size of the finger holes, and cutting a more narrow reed that was inserted directly into the top section of the instrument. The oboe was immediately popular with 18th-century composers for its voice-like expressivity and rich dark tonal color.

4410. Stradivarius violin was crafted in its now-familiar modern shape by Antonio Stradivari (also called Stradivarius) in 1665, while he was a student in the workshop of the Amati family in Cremona, Italy.

4411. Clarinet was invented circa 1690 by flute-maker and musician Johann Christoph Denner in Nuremberg (now in Germany). Experimenting with improvements to the single-reed chalumeau, Denner added an additional two keys to the chalumeau's seven fingerholes, opening up a higher register of notes, the clarino, from which the clarinet gets its name.

4412. Pianoforte was invented by Bartolomeo di Francesco Cristofori, a harpsichord maker in the employ of the Medici family in Florence, and introduced in 1709. By modifying the hammer action in a related keyboard instrument, the clavichord, he made it possible for the first time to obtain variations in the sound, depending on the degree of pressure applied to the keys. Cristofori called his instrument a *gravecembalo col piano e forte* ("harpsichord with soft and loud") for its ability to play at a range of volumes depending on how hard the keys are pressed, an ability that the harpsichord does not possess. It was the first keyboard instrument with all the elements of the modern piano.

4413. Electrified musical instrument was the Clavecin Electrique, an electric harpsichord created in 1761 by the French abbot and inventor J.B. Delaborde of Paris, France.

4414. Metronome was invented by Dietrich Nikolaus Winkel of Holland circa 1812. Like modern versions, Winkel's metronome consisted of a clockwork-driven pendulum that could be set to mark any musical tempo with a click for every beat. The design was improved in 1815 by the German inventor Johann Nepomuk Maelzel.

4415. Modern bow for playing musical instruments was invented by François Tourte in Paris, France, circa 1800. He was the first to use pernambuco, or brazilwood, for the stick of his violin bows and to shape the stick in a concave curve to keep the strands of horsehair in tension. A frog, or screw, could be turned to tighten the tension on the horsehair.

4416. Accordion was invented in 1821 by a German, Friedrich Buschmann, who adapted the basic principle of the floor-standing, bellows-driven reed organ to portable use. Buschmann's original design had right-hand buttons for treble chords, instead of a keyboard as in modern models, and lacked the now-standard left-hand buttons for bass chords.

4417. Concertina was patented in 1829 by Charles Wheatstone in London, England. He capped a hexagonal bellows with end pieces fitted with buttons for selecting pitches from its brass or steel reeds. Pairs of reeds were matched so that the same note would sound both on the press and on the draw of the bellows.

4418. Tuba was patented in 1835 by instrument-maker Johann Gottfried Moritz of Berlin, Germany, and bandmaster Wilhelm Wieprecht. Moritz's design was a bass tuba. The modern tuba is closer in design to the bass tuba invented in 1845 by the Belgian-born Parisian instrument-maker Antoine-Joseph Sax (also known as Adolphe Sax), who also invented the saxophone.

4419. Saxophone was patented in 1846 by the Belgian-born Parisian instrument-maker Antoine-Joseph Sax (also known as Adolphe Sax), who had been seeking ways to improve the tone of the bass clarinet. The saxophone was first adopted by French military bands.

4420. Modern transverse flute was invented in 1847 by the German flute-maker Theobald Böhm of Munich. His design replaced the traditional conical bore with a cylindrical bore and introduced the current system of levered key and ring mechanisms. Transverse flutes, held sideways, were known in Greece and Etruria as early as the second century BCE.

4421. Steinway piano was developed in 1859 by the German-born piano maker Henry Engelhard Steinweg and manufactured in Steinweg's factory in New York, NY, USA. Steinweg began calling himself Steinway beginning in 1865, and his company became Steinway & Sons.

4422. Music synthesizer powered by electricity was the Telharmonium, also known as the Dynamophone, invented by Thaddeus Cahill and first demonstrated publicly in 1906 at Telharmonic Hall in New York, NY, USA. The huge, 200-ton instrument, consisting of 140 dynamos and tone mixers powered by electrically driven gears, was controlled by an organ-style keyboard and foot pedals. When the player pressed the keys, current produced by the dynamos was converted into musical tones. The machinery itself was so noisy it had to be placed in the basement of the building. The sound was transmitted by telephone lines to subscribing restaurants, hotels, and homes, marking the first use of electronic equipment to distribute music.

4423. Musical instrument to create sound with electromagnetic fields was the theremin, also called the thereminvox or etherphone, invented in 1918 by Leon Sergeyevich Theremin (also known as Lev Termen) of the former Soviet Union. The theremin created an electromagnetic field from two radio tubes oscillating at audible frequencies. A variety of pitches and harmonics could be produced as the performer's hands moved in the space around the theremin's metal antennas, creating an undulating sound experienced by listeners as either soothing or threatening.

4424. Electric guitar to be widely marketed was the Rickenbacker Electro Spanish guitar of 1935, designed by Adolph Rickenbacker (also spelled Rickenbacher), George Beauchamp, and Doc Kauffman of the Electro Company, Los Angeles, CA, USA. It was made of cast Bakelite, a synthetic resin, and featured a one-piece body, molded fittings, and a bolt-on neck. A patent was filed by Beauchamp in 1936 and granted in 1939. Credit for the first electric guitar of any kind is claimed by several inventors. Between 1920 and 1924, acoustical engineer Lloyd Loar experimented with microphone

MUSIC—MUSICAL INSTRUMENTS—*continued*

pickups for acoustic guitars, and in the early 1930s he designed for the Vivi-Tone company an acoustic-electric Spanish-neck guitar made out of solid wood. Les Paul electrified acoustic guitars in 1929 using a phonograph needle. George Beauchamp patented the electrified Fry Pan Hawaiian guitar, which was made of solid aluminum, in 1931, the same year that Dobro introduced its own electric solid-body Hawaiian guitar.

4425. Museum of brass instruments was the Trumpet Museum, founded near Pottstown, PA, USA, in 1980 by Franz Streitwieser, inventor of the Clarin horn. The collection contained some 750 brass instruments as well as other antique horns from around the world.

4426. International pipe organ festival was celebrated in Toulouse, France, in October 1996. Some 10,000 people attended the festival's 21 concerts.

4427. Grand piano without strings was the Disklavier Gran Touch Digital Grand Piano, a US$15,495 instrument introduced in 1997 by Yamaha of Japan. Pressing the keys caused hammers to move, as in an ordinary piano, but instead of striking piano strings, the hammers passed over optical sensors that caused the instrument to generate digitally sampled piano sounds.

4428. Two-lid piano was invented by the pianist, conductor, and inventor Daniell Revenaugh of Berkeley, CA, USA. Along with the traditional upper lid, Revenaugh's piano boasted a lid that could be lowered from the piano's undercarriage. The lower lid was intended to capture and project potentially lost sound from the underside of the instrument. The instrument saw wide recital use in 1997.

MUSIC—OPERA

4429. Comic opera is considered to have been *Le jeu de Robin et Marion (The Play of Robin and Marion),* by Adam de la Halle, also known as Adam le Bossu (the Hunchback). The play, the story of a shepherdess courted by a knight, was enhanced at strategic points by the addition of popular songs. It was performed before the French court resident at Naples, Italy, in 1283. Another play by the same author, *Le jeu de la feuillée (The Play of the Greensward),* is the first French comedy. Adam de la Halle came from Arras, France, and belonged to the group of poets known as the Trouvères.

4430. Opera known by that name was *Dafne,* a version of the Greek myth of Daphne and Apollo, with music by the Florentine ducal choirmaster Jacopo Peri and text by the poet Ottavio Rinuccini. It was first performed in 1597 in Florence, Italy, in the home of Giovanni Bardi, Count of Vernio, who had commissioned it. The play, which was called in Italian *un opera in musica* ("a work in music"), was the outgrowth of research into Greek dramatic forms that was undertaken by the Camerata, a group of scholars and musicians founded by Bardi in 1580. Peri's music, most of which no longer survives, was probably performed by an ensemble consisting of harpsichord, cello, lute, and viola da gamba. The text was published in 1600.

4431. Opera whose music is still extant is *Euridice,* by Jacopo Peri and Ottavio Rinuccini, a setting of the Greek myth of Orpheus and Eurydice. It was written in honor of the wedding of Marie de Médicis of Italy to King Henry IV of France and was given its first performance on October 6, 1600, at the Pitti Palace in Florence.

4432. Castrato of note was Antonio Bernacchi, who began singing in operas in his hometown of Bologna, Italy, in 1607. He specialized in making elaborate ornamental improvisations on the melody. The castrati were male singers whose testicles had been surgically removed before adolescence to prevent the deepening of their voices. The voice that resulted was usually supple, powerful, and capable of a wide range of octaves. Such singers often played female roles.

4433. Opera house was the Teatro di San Cassiano, opened in 1637 in Venice, Italy, by the Tron family. It was the first venue in which operas were performed for the general public, rather than for a select and wealthy audience. The most prominent composer to write operas for San Cassiano was Claudio Monteverdi, whose *L'incoronazione di Poppea (The Coronation of Poppea)* was presented there in 1642.

4434. Opera in English was *The Siege of Rhodes Made a Representation by the Art of Prospective in Scenes, And the Story sung in Recitative Musick,* produced in 1656 by the English poet and theatrical impresario William Davenant (also spelled D'Avenant). Davenant's staging introduced two innovations to the English theater: painted stage sets—the work was conceived as a visual spectacle more than a musical one—and a female performer.

4435. Opera in French was *Pastorale d'Issy,* written in 1659 by the poet Pierre Perrin and the composer Robert Cambert. The first French opera performed in full was Cambert and Perrin's *Pomone,* which opened the Académie Royale de Musique in Paris on March 3, 1671.

4436. Opera diva to gain an international reputation was Francesca Cuzzoni, a soprano from Parma, Italy. After a brief career in Venice and Bologna, she went to London, where she appeared in George Frideric Handel's *Ottone* in 1723. Her popularity was rivaled by that of another Italian soprano, Faustina Bordini, who came to London in 1726.

4437. Operetta of note was *Orphée aux Enfers (Orpheus in the Underworld),* with music by Jacques Offenbach and a libretto by Hector Crémieux and Ludovic Halévy. It was premiered on October 21, 1858, at the Bouffes-Parisiens theater in Paris, where it became a smashing success. Offenbach was the manager of the theater, which he had taken over with the intention of producing a new form of musical entertainment. According to a contemporary newspaper account, the theater was "consecrated to openhearted laughter, to fantasy, to light and smart melody, to bold refrains."

4438. Rock opera was *S.F. Sorrow,* released by the Pretty Things, a British rock band, in 1968. The plot, concerning the downfall of one Sebastian F. Sorrow, was based on a short story by the group's singer, Phil May. The group played the opera in its entirety for the first time at a concert in London, England, in September 1998, in connection with the album's reissue on CD after three decades out of print.

MUSIC—POPULAR

4439. Collection of folk ballads was *Reliques of Ancient English Poetry,* edited by Bishop Thomas Percy and published in England in 1765. Percy was at a friend's house when he rescued a tattered manuscript from the fire; it turned out to be a 15th-century manuscript of English and Scottish ballads. To these he added other ballads, songs, and romances discovered in attics and libraries.

4440. Communist song of international popularity was "L'Internationale," the anthem of every international Communist conference and the national anthem of the former Soviet Union until 1944. It was based on an 1871 poem that was written in Paris by the French teamster Eugène Pottier and set to music by another French laborer, Pierre Degeyter. The first line reads *"Debout, les damnés de la terre"* ("Arise, the wretched of the earth").

4441. Cabaret was the Chat Noir, which opened in Paris, France, in 1881.

4442. Wartime song popular with both sides of the conflict was the World War II hit "Lili Marlene." Composed in 1938 by German songwriter Norbert Schultz, it was based on the 1923 poem "Song of the Sentry" by Hans Leip. The first recording was made by Swedish singer Lale Andersen. In 1941, German troops began playing the song on their radio stations, and it was picked up by the British Eighth Army in North Africa. "Lili Marlene's" English lyrics were written by Tommy O'Connor.

4443. Rock and roll song was probably "Rocket 88," recorded in 1951 by American performer Jackie Brenston for Chess Records, Chicago, IL, USA.

4444. Rock concert is usually considered to be the Moondog Coronation Ball, held on the night of March 21, 1952, at the Cleveland Arena in Cleveland, OH, USA. It was organized by disc jockey Alan Freed and attracted a mainly African-American audience, each of whom paid US$1.50 to get in. Several acts were scheduled to appear, but only Paul "Hucklebuck" Williams was able to perform before the show was shut down by the Cleveland fire marshal.

4445. Worldwide rock-and-roll hit was "Rock Around the Clock," recorded on April 12, 1954, by the American group Bill Haley and the Comets. The song sold an estimated 25 million copies worldwide.

4446. Beatles recording to become a hit was "Love Me Do," released in England in October 1962 on the EMI label. The song quickly went to Number 1 in the music charts in Liverpool, the Beatles' hometown. They had made an earlier record for the Polydor label in Germany.

4447. Reversed sounds in a popular recording were used in the song "Rain," also titled "niaR," the B side of a 45 released on June 10, 1966, by the British pop group The Beatles. The technique was accidentally invented by Beatles member John Lennon.

4448. Rock music festival was the Monterey International Pop Festival, held on June 15–18, 1967, at the Monterey, CA, USA, fairgrounds. Promoter Alan Pariser and booking agent Ben Shapiro assembled the largest roster of British and American rock and soul acts up to that time, including the Who, the Grateful Dead, Otis Redding, Jefferson Airplane, Big Brother and the Holding Company with Janis Joplin, and the Jimi Hendrix Experience. More than 50,000 fans attended the nonprofit event, which inaugurated a decade of ever-larger rock festivals.

MUSIC—POPULAR—*continued*

4449. African song that was an international pop hit was "Soul Makossa," a synthesis of Afropop with American and French influences, recorded by the Cameroonian instrumentalist Emmanuel Dibango N'Djocké, also known as Manu Dibango, in 1972.

4450. Music video was produced by Bruce Gowers to accompany a performance of "Bohemian Rhapsody" by the British glam-rock group Queen. Freddie Mercury (born Frederick Bulsara) was the lead singer and performer. The seven-minute video was first shown on the British television program "Top of the Pops" on December 20, 1975.

4451. Aboriginal Australian performer to achieve international success was singer Archie Roach, frontman for the rock group Yothu Yindi. Roach's hit album *Charcoal Lane* (1990) mixed indigenous sounds, storytelling, and social protest with elements of rock, blues, country, reggae, and dance pop. Roach toured North America in 1992.

4452. Rock concert on Mount Everest was held on May 19, 1998, at Kalapathar, Nepal, 18,208 feet above sea level. The concert was sponsored by the Namaste Cultural Studio Company and featured Nepali and Japanese entertainers.

N

NEWS AND MEDIA

4453. Eyewitness report to become a best-seller was a letter Christopher Columbus wrote to the monarchs of Spain in March 1493, describing his voyage across the Atlantic, from which he had just returned. By April 1, the letter had been printed and distributed throughout Barcelona. By April 29, this letter, or another written at about the same time, was circulating in a Latin translation in Rome, where it was so popular that it went through three editions. Before the year was out, printed copies had been published in Paris, Antwerp, Basel, and Florence.

4454. Advice column appeared in the first issue (dated June 27, 1693) of the first magazine for women, *The Ladies' Mercury,* published by London bookseller John Dunton. The entire magazine, filling both sides of a single sheet, was devoted to the advice column, which offered expert replies to questions submitted by readers on matters of love, marriage, and sex.

4455. Gossip columnist and the first person to write a signed newspaper column of any kind was John Hill, who wrote about celebrity scandals and other society news for two London papers, the *London Advertiser* and the *Literary Gazette,* from 1751 to 1753, using the name "The Inspector." Hill is better known as a botanist and the author of the 26-volume work *The Vegetable System.*

4456. War correspondent was the English newspaper publisher John Bell, owner of *The Oracle or Bell's New World.* To attract readers, Bell spent 1793–94 in the Netherlands, from which he sent back eyewitness reports of the fighting between the British and the French. His accounts were the more interesting because he traveled with the enemy army, rather than his own, but he made his observations from a safe distance.

4457. Investigative reporter was James Gordon Bennett of New York, NY, USA, the Scottish-born founder and editor of the daily *New York Herald.* In April 1836 he wrote a series of articles about the murder of Ellen Jewett, a prostitute. He paid repeated visits to the crime scene, where the police allowed him to view the victim's body and to check through her belongings, and interviewed people who knew her. He concluded that the man accused of the murder was innocent (he was, in fact, acquitted) and that the real killer was a woman who lived in the same house. The *Herald* enjoyed a steep rise in circulation as a result of his articles.

4458. War correspondent to file dispatches by telegraph from a combat zone was William Howard Russell, who covered the Crimean War, in what is now part of Ukraine, from 1853 to 1856 as a reporter for *The Times* of London. He was the first reporter to deliver eyewitness accounts of events he witnessed on the battlefield.

4459. Poster kiosks were pillars especially erected for posting handbills and announcements, installed in 1854 in Berlin, Germany.

4460. War photographers to produce a substantial body of work were British photographers Roger Fenton and Marcus Sparling, who were sent by the British government to cover the siege of Sevastopol (October 17, 1854–September 11, 1855) during the Crimean War. Their purpose was to influence public opinion, which had been negatively affected by articles in *The Times* of London that described in detail the horrors of battle and the suffering of soldiers. Fenton and Sparling used a horse-drawn van converted to a darkroom. Of the 360 photographs that survive, none shows actual combat.

4461. Staff cartoonist on a newspaper was Francis Carruthers Gould, who was hired in 1888 by the *Pall Mall Gazette* of London, England, to draw editorial and political cartoons.

4462. War photographer who was a woman was the pioneering American photojournalist Margaret Bourke-White, born Margaret White in New York City in 1906. In 1941, as a photographer for *Life* magazine, she became the first woman photographer officially attached to the U.S. armed forces. She covered the Allied Italian campaign, the siege of Moscow, and the final defeat of Nazi Germany.

4463. Televised trial was the trial of Adolf Eichmann, the Gestapo official who built the Nazi system of organized mass murder and torture that killed millions of Jews and other targeted populations between 1938 and 1945. Eichmann, who had escaped from Nazi Germany to Argentina, was captured there by Israeli agents in May 1960. His trial, which took place in the District Court in Jerusalem from April 11 to August 14, 1961, was televised in Israel and was recorded on tape. He was convicted of all 15 counts brought against him and sentenced to death. The judgment was confirmed on appeal and Eichmann was hanged on May 31, 1962.

4464. All-news radio station that was successful was probably XETRA, which broadcast from Tijuana, Mexico, for an audience living in Los Angeles, CA. Its owner, Gordon McLendon, changed it from a rock-and-roll format to an all-news format on May 6, 1961. The station's staff of twelve newscasters wrote their stories from information provided by wire services, recycling them on the air every seven and a half minutes.

4465. All-news television network was Cable News Network, headquartered in Atlanta, GA, USA. It was founded in June 1980 by Robert Edward Turner III, better known as Ted Turner, head of the Turner Broadcasting System. CNN used satellite feeds to provide live coverage of global events, supplied by a network of news bureaus in cities worldwide. The network broadcast 24 hours a day.

NEWS AND MEDIA—COMICS

4466. Comic strip published as a booklet was *The Adventures of Dr. Festus* by the artist and writer Rodolphe Töpffer of Geneva, Switzerland. It was published in 1829. Töpffer created a series of absurdly comical stories told by means of lithographed drawings, which were bound into small albums.

4467. Comic strip in a magazine was "Those Cheap Excursions!," which appeared on June 7, 1890, in *Comic Cuts,* a weekly English humor periodical edited by Houghton Townley.

4468. Comic strip with an ongoing character was "The Yellow Kid," by the artist Richard Outcault. Its main character was a mischievous New York slum child with a bald head and, for clothing, a bright yellow nightshirt on which different bits of text appeared. A comic strip starring the Kid began appearing in the Sunday supplement to the *New York Journal* on October 24, 1897. "The Yellow Kid" was also the first comic strip to be printed in a newspaper.

4469. Comic books featuring color cartoons previously published in newspapers were published in 1904 by Cupples and Leon, New York, NY, USA. The books were 10 inches high and 15 inches long, contained 40 pages, and retailed for 75 cents. The titles of some of the books were *Alphonse and Gaston and Their Friend Leon* and *Happy Hooligan* by Frederick Burr Opper, *The Naughty Adventures of Vicious Mr. Jack* by James Swinnerton, and *The Katzenjammer Kids* by Rudolph Dirks

4470. Comic strip in a daily newspaper was "A. Piker Clerk," a strip about horseracing, which began appearing in the sports pages of the *Chicago American* in 1904, printed in black and white. The artist and author was Claire Briggs.

4471. Comic strip with an adventure hero was "Tarzan," based on the character created by the American novelist Edgar Rice Burroughs. The strip, designed by Canadian-born artist Harold Foster, aimed for pictorial realism, rather than cartoonish caricatures. It first appeared in several papers on September 27, 1931. The strip was drawn on Sundays by Foster and on weekdays by Rex Mason.

4472. Comic book superhero was Superman, the brainchild of writer Jerry Siegel and artist Joseph Shuster, both of whom were American high school students in Cleveland, OH, USA. The first issue was published by Detective Comics (DC) in June 1938.

NEWS AND MEDIA—MAGAZINES AND PERIODICALS

4473. Magazine was probably the *Erbauliche Monaths-Unterredungen (Edifying Monthly Discussions),* which appeared in Hamburg, Germany, between 1663 and 1668. The publisher was the poet and theologian Johann Rist.

4474. Periodical continuously published to the present day was *Philosophical Transactions of the Royal Society,* published in London, England. The first number appeared on March 6, 1665.

4475. Magazine for popular entertainment was Jean Donneau de Vizé's *Le Mercure Galant,* founded in Paris, France, in 1672. It featured celebrity news (that is, accounts of goings-on at court), poems, short anecdotes, and other light-hearted material.

4476. Illustrated magazine was *Memoirs for the Curious; or an account of what occurs that's rare, secret, extraordinary, prodigious and miraculous through the world, whether in Nature, Art, Learning,* a monthly that might best be described as the *National Geographic* of its day. The first number appeared in London, England, in 1701.

4477. Women's magazine edited by a woman was *The Female Tatler* of London, England. The editor was Mary de la Rivière Manley, who used the pseudonym "Mrs. Crackenthorpe." The magazine, which made its first appearance in July 1709, specialized in scandalous revelations about people's private lives.

4478. Magazine known by that name was Edward Cave's *The Gentleman's Magazine,* which began publication in London, England, in 1731. The original meaning of the word *magazine* is "warehouse" or "collection of supplies." *The Gentleman's Magazine* was a collection of previously published articles.

4479. Children's magazine was a tiny volume entitled *The Lilliputian Magazine; or the Young Gentleman and Lady's Golden Library,* which was published monthly in London, England, from June 1751 through July 1752. Each issue presented humorous fare for children, including riddles, jokes, and tales. The editor was John Newbery, the children's book publisher.

4480. Magazine in a Native American language was the *Siwinowe Kesibwi* ("The Shawnee Sun"), a monthly, first printed on February 24, 1835, on the press of Jotham Meeker, an American missionary at the Shawnee Baptist Mission in Kansas. Johnston Lykins was editor.

4481. Picture magazine was the *Illustrated London News.* It began weekly publication in London in 1842. Each issue contained 32 woodcut engravings, including some based on daguerrotypes; these were afterwards superseded by photographs. The magazine was the brainchild of Herbert Ingram, a Nottingham news agent.

4482. Magazine to put a hologram on its cover was *National Geographic,* published from Washington, DC, USA. The March 1984 issue incorporated a small white-light transmission hologram on the front cover. Nearly 11 million copies were printed and distributed worldwide, making it the first hologram to be mass distributed. The cover of the December 1988 issue was entirely a hologram. The front showed a double laser image of glass models of the earth, one whole and one exploding, as a statement of the world's environmental fragility. The spine featured holographic text, and the back cover was a holographic advertisement. The front cover image was made using a pulsed laser with an exposure of seven-billionths of a second. American Bank Note Holographics of Elmsford, NY, USA, embossed the holograms onto a plastic roll and transferred them to a 30-inch wide roll of special aluminum foil. The foil was laminated roll-to-roll to the magazine's regular cover stock and covered with a gold-tinted scratch-resistant coating at Manville Forest Products in Monroe, LA, USA.

4483. Online, peer-reviewed journal was *The Online Journal of Current Clinical Trials,* a joint venture of the American Association for the Advancement of Science in Washington, DC, USA, and the nonprofit Online Computer Library Center in Dublin, OH. It debuted in April 1992 and was available only in an electronic format. The first editor was Edward J. Huth. Subscribers could be notified by fax whenever an article of interest to them appeared on-line.

NEWS AND MEDIA—NEWSPAPERS

4484. News posters to keep the public informed about current events were published in Rome in 59 BCE. They were parchment sheets called *acta diurna populi Romani* ("daily transaction of the Roman people") and *acta senatus* ("transactions of the Senate"). They carried information about government affairs, including battles, executions, and decrees, as well as announcements of deaths, births, and marriages. The text was handwritten in multiple copies and posted on buildings in Rome and other cities, where they were recopied by scribes. When Julius Caesar became consul in 59 BCE, his first action was to require the *acta* to be published on a daily basis.

4485. Handwritten newsbooks and newsletters were used in western Europe in the 15th century to circulate accounts of such events as battles, disasters, royal weddings, and royal deaths. The earliest known printed versions include a write-up of a tournament that was printed in Italy circa 1470 and reports printed in Italy and Germany in the 1470s concerning the military struggle between the kingdoms of Europe and the Ottoman Empire.

4486. News sheet printed in the New World extant is an account of an earthquake and a storm that wracked Guatemala. It was printed in 1541 in Mexico City, Mexico, where a printing press had been set up two years earlier.

4487. Newspapers published regularly were the handwritten gazettes that circulated in the mercantile Italian city of Venice in the 16th century. Each consisted of a single sheet folded to make four pages, on which were written a selection of brief news items. A specimen exists from 1547. During the 1550s the gazettes were distributed once a week, usually on Saturday.

4488. Printed newspapers published regularly were the weekly German newspapers *Relation: Aller Fürnemmen und Gedenkwürdigen Historien,* edited in Strasbourg (now in France) by the printer Johann Carolus, or the *Aviso Relation oder Zeitung,* printed by Lucas Schulte and edited by Heinrich Julius, Duke of Brunswick-Wolfenbüttel. The earliest surviving issues of both newspapers are dated January 1609. They had title pages and consisted of short entries arranged by place of origin.

4489. Japanese newspapers were the *kawaraban,* broadsheets printed from tile or wooden blocks, which became popular during the Tokugawa shogunate circa 1615. These printed papers were preceded by *yomiuri,* a transaction in which a consumer paid to hear the news read aloud.

4490. Newspaper in the English language was printed in Amsterdam, Holland, under the title *Corrant out of Italy, Germany, Etc.* The first issue was published on December 2, 1620. The publisher was Pieter van den Keere. The opening sentence was: "The new tydings out of Italie are not yet com." The front page contained four articles about military events that had taken place the previous November in Hungary, Moravia, and Bohemia.

4491. Newspaper published in England was published during the summer of 1621 by Thomas Archer, a London stationer, who was punished with imprisonment because he had failed to obtain a publishing license and to submit his news reports to official censors. The earliest extant copy of a newspaper printed in England is dated September 24, 1621, and entitled *Corante, or weekely news from Italy, Germany, Hungary, Poland, Bohemia, France and the Low Countreys.* The publisher was one N.B., either Nathaniel Butter or Nicholas Bourne.

4492. Newspaper in England that was successful was the *Weekley Newes,* which was published in London by Nathaniel Butter, Nicholas Bourne, and Thomas Archer from August 2, 1622, through 1625. The price was 1 groat. Since publication of domestic news brought with it the risk of prosecution, the paper printed foreign news only. From September 1622 it was edited by Thomas Gainsford, who introduced a new format by grouping together news items on the same subject.

4493. Official newspaper of a government was *La Gazette* (later *La Gazette de France*), France's first newspaper, published weekly in Paris beginning on May 30, 1631, by the physician Théophraste Renaudot. *La Gazette* printed only news personally approved by Renaudot's patron, Cardinal Richelieu.

4494. Newspaper in continuous publication to the present day is the Swedish official gazette, the *Post-och inrikes tidningar,* published beginning in 1645 by the Royal Swedish Academy of Letters.

4495. Commercial newspaper in continuous publication is a Dutch paper, the *Haarlems Dagblad/Oprechte Haarlemsche Courant.* It was first issued under the title *Weeckelycke Courante van Europa* on January 8, 1656, in Haarlem, Netherlands, where it is still published.

4496. Newspaper published in the British colonies in America was *Publick Occurrences Both Forreign and Domestick.* It was founded by Benjamin Harris, an English newspaper publisher who had gone the colonies to escape prosecution for printing embarrassing political information. The first issue of his American newspaper was published in Boston, MA, on September 25, 1690, with a front-page story that began: "The Christianized Indians in some parts of Plimouth, have newly appointed a day of Thanksgiving to God for his Mercy in supplying their extream and pinching Necessities

NEWS AND MEDIA—NEWSPAPERS—*continued*

under their late want of Corn & for His giving them now a prospect of a very Comfortable Harvest. Their Example might be worth mentioning." However, an item on the third page contained an embarrassing rumor about the king of France, and the newspaper was immediately suppressed by the governor of Massachusetts.

4497. Evening newspaper was Ichabod Dawks's one-page London news sheet, *Dawks's News-Letter.* The paper was published between four and five o'clock in the afternoon every Tuesday, Thursday, and Saturday, and was circulated to subscribers at the rate of ten shillings a quarter. The first issue was published on June 23, 1696.

4498. Daily newspaper in continuous publication is the *Wiener Zeitung,* published in Austria. It was first issued in 1703.

4499. Sunday newspaper in English was *The Observer,* founded in 1791 in England and noted for its broad international coverage.

4500. Asian newspaper in English was the *Canton Register,* published beginning on November 8, 1827, in Guangzhou, China.

4501. Egyptian newspaper was *Al-Waqai al-Misriyah,* founded in 1828.

4502. Weekly Australian newspaper was the *Sydney Herald,* first issued in 1831 by John Fairfax and associates. The paper became a daily in 1840 and changed its name to the *Sydney Morning Herald in 1842.*

4503. Afro-Brazilian newspaper published by and for Brazilians of African descent was *O Homem de Cor,* which ran for five issues in 1833.

4504. Army newspaper for soldiers in the field was put out for United States troops during the Mexican War. The title was *The American Flag.* The first issue appeared on June 6, 1846, at Matamoros, Mexico.

4505. African national newspapers were *Ikhwezi (The Morning Star), Isigidimi samaXhosa (The Xhosa Messenger), Imvo zaba Nshundu (Opinions of the Black People),* and *Izwi labantu (Voice of the People),* which appeared in what is now South Africa beginning in the mid-19th century.

4506. Daily newspaper in Japan was the *Yokohama Mainichi,* founded in 1870.

4507. Socialist women's newspaper was *Die Gleichheit (Equality),* edited by Clara Zetkin (born Clara Eissner), a friend of the Marxist activists Vladimir Ilyich Lenin and Rosa Luxemburg. The first number appeared in Stuttgart, Germany, in 1892.

4508. Shipboard newspaper was the *Transatlantic Times,* printed by radio pioneer Guglielmo Marconi on November 15, 1899, aboard the American passenger liner S.S. *St. Paul.* He set up a radio receiver to pick up news broadcast from his transmitter station on the Isle of Wight, then printed a four-page newspaper and sold it to passengers for one dollar, with the proceeds going to charity.

4509. Daily shipboard newspaper was the *Cunard Daily Bulletin,* printed beginning October 1902 from news received by radio aboard the Cunard liners S.S. *Campania* and S.S. *Lucania.*

4510. Newspaper illustrated exclusively with photographs was the *Daily Mirror,* published in London, England, by the press baron Alfred Harmsworth (Lord Northcliffe) beginning in 1903.

4511. Tabloid newspaper that was successful was the *Daily Mirror,* published in London, England, by the press baron Alfred Harmsworth (Lord Northcliffe) beginning in 1903. The price was one halfpenny. It had a smaller format than regular newspapers and relied heavily on photographs.

4512. Zulu newspaper was *Ilanga lase Natal (The Natal Sun),* which began publication in 1904 in Durban, South Africa. The publisher, John Langalibalele Dube, was an American-educated minister and novelist.

NEWS AND MEDIA—SERVICES

4513. News agency paid to collect information about events was a private group of correspondents who delivered news to the merchants and traders of Venice (in modern Italy) during the early 16th century. Reports concerning anything that might affect shipping—especially the movements of the Ottoman Turkish fleet—influenced prices in Venetian markets. A professional news service was started by Christoph Scheurl, a German lawyer and traveler, in 1536, and another was opened at about the same time by Jeremias Crasser of Augsburg.

4514. Modern news service was Agence Havas, founded in 1835 in Paris, France, by Charles-Louis Havas, a translator and distributor of articles from foreign papers. Agence Havas is now the Agence France-Presse (AFP), the major French wire news service.

4515. Wire news service was established by Agence Havas of Paris, France, when it sent its first news item by telegraph in 1845. Within a decade, all the news agencies of Europe began to set up wire services to speed transmission of stories to their newspaper clients.

4516. Newspaper cooperative was founded in New York, NY, USA, in 1846, when six newspapers agreed to co-sponsor the reporters who were sent to cover the Mexican War. The organization was called the New York Associated Press.

4517. Communist wire service was the Soviet news agency Tass, short for Telegrafnoe Agentsvo Sovetskovo Soyuzam ("Telegraph Agency of the Soviet Union"). Tass was formed in 1925 to distribute the Soviet versions of domestic and world news. It was disbanded in 1991 during the collapse of the Soviet Union.

NOBEL PRIZES

4518. Woman to win a Nobel Prize was the Polish-French physicist Marie Curie. She shared the 1903 Nobel Prize in Physics with Henri Becquerel and her husband, Pierre Curie, "in recognition of the extraordinary services they have rendered by their joint researches on the radiation phenomena." In 1911 she became the first woman to win the Nobel Prize in Chemistry, the first woman to be the sole winner of a Nobel Prize, and the first person to win the Nobel Prize twice.

4519. Nobel Prize winner to win the award twice was the Polish-born French physicist Marie Curie. She shared the 1903 Nobel Prize in Physics for the discovery of radioactivity with Pierre Curie, her husband, and physicist Henri Becquerel. In 1911, Curie was awarded the chemistry prize "in recognition of her services to the advancement of chemistry by the discovery of the elements radium and polonium, by the isolation of radium and the study of the nature and compounds of this remarkable element." It was the first time that a woman was the sole winner of a Nobel Prize and the first time that the Nobel Prize in Chemistry was awarded to a woman.

4520. Industrial scientist to win a Nobel Prize was Irving Langmuir, an American chemist employed by the General Electric Company, Schenectady, NY, USA, from 1909 to 1950. Langmuir's research into molecular films and their underlying physical chemistry earned him the 1932 Nobel Prize in Chemistry.

4521. Nobel Prize winner to win twice in the same field was physicist John Bardeen of Champaign, IL, USA. He and two co-winners, Dr. William Shockley and Dr. William Houser Bralton, received the Nobel Prize in physics at Stockholm, Sweden, on December 10, 1956, for their work on semiconductors and the discrepancy of the transistor effect. Bardeen also shared the 1972 prize with Leon N. Cooper and John Robert Schrieffer for their explanation of superconductivity leading to more efficient transmission of electrical power.

4522. Nobel laureate who was the sole winner of awards in two different categories was American biochemist and peace activist Linus Carl Pauling of the California Institute of Technology, Pasadena, CA, USA. He was presented with the award for chemistry on December 10, 1954, at Stockholm, Sweden, and the Peace Prize on December 10, 1963, at Oslo, Norway. The awards were worth $35,000 and $50,000, respectively.

NOBEL PRIZES—CHEMISTRY

4523. Nobel Prize in Chemistry was awarded in 1901 to Dutch chemist Jacobus Henricus van't Hoff "in recognition of the extraordinary services he has rendered by the discovery of the laws of chemical dynamics and osmotic pressure in solutions."

4524. Nobel Prize in Chemistry winner from North America was Theodore William Richards of Harvard University, Cambridge, MA, USA, who won the prize in 1914 "in recognition of his accurate determination of the atomic weight of a large number of chemical elements." The prize of 146,900 Swedish kroner was presented on November 12, 1915, in Stockholm.

4525. Nobel Prize in Chemistry winner from Latin America was the Argentinian biochemist Luis F. Leloir of the Institute for Biochemical Research in Buenos Aires. He was awarded the 1970 Chemistry prize "for his discovery of sugar nucleotides and their role in the biosynthesis of carbohydrates."

4526. Nobel Prize in Chemistry winner from Oceania was John Warcup Cornforth, born in Sydney, Australia, who was awarded the 1975 prize "for his work on the stereochemistry of enzyme-catalyzed reactions." He shared the prize with the Bosnia-born Swiss chemist Vladimir Prelog.

NOBEL PRIZES—CHEMISTRY—*continued*

4527. Nobel Prize in Chemistry winner from Asia was Kenichi Fukui of Kyoto University, Japan. He shared the 1981 Chemistry prize with American chemist Roald Hoffman "for their theories, developed independently, concerning the course of chemical reactions," specifically, the role of orbital bonds in organic chemistry.

NOBEL PRIZES—ECONOMICS

4528. Nobel Prize in Economics was awarded in 1969 to Ragnar Anton Kittil Frisch, a professor of economics at the University of Oslo, Norway, and Jan Tinbergen, professor of economics at the Netherlands School of Economics (now part of Erasmus University), Rotterdam, and the University of Leiden. The prize was in recognition of their work in econometrics, the application of mathematical models and statistical techniques to economic data.

4529. Nobel Prize in Economics winner from North America was the American economist Paul Anthony Samuelson, a presidential economic adviser during the presidential administrations of John F. Kennedy and Lyndon B. Johnson. Samuelson won the 1970 award for improving the analytical methods used in economic theory. He was the author of the classic textbook *Economics,* published in 1948.

NOBEL PRIZES—LITERATURE

4530. Nobel Prize for Literature was awarded in 1901 to French poet René-François-Armand Sully Prudhomme, "in special recognition of his poetic composition, which gives evidence of lofty idealism, artistic perfection, and a rare combination of the qualities of both heart and intellect."

4531. Woman to win the Nobel Prize for Literature was the Swedish novelist Selma Ottiliana Lovisa Lagerlöf, who was awarded the literature prize in 1909. Her historical novels, such as *Herr Arnes Penningar* (1904) and the Löwensköld trilogy (1925–28), *Löwensköldska ringen (The Ring of the Löwenskölds), Charlotte Löwensköld,* and *Anna Svärd,* were noted for their grounding in Norse legend and family saga. She was also the first woman to become a member of the Swedish Academy, in 1914.

4532. Nobel Prize for Literature winner from Asia was Indian poet Rabindranath Tagore, winner of the 1913 prize "because of his profoundly sensitive, fresh and beautiful verse, by which, with comsummate skill, he has made his poetic thought, expressed in his own English words, a part of the literature of the West."

4533. Nobel Prize for Literature winner from North America was the American writer Sinclair Lewis, author of *Main Street, Babbitt, Arrowsmith, Elmer Gantry,* and other satirical novels of American life. He was awarded the prize in 1930 "for his great and living art in painting life, with a talent for creating types with wit and humor."

4534. Nobel Prize for Literature winner from Latin America was Chilean poet Gabriela Mistral (born Lucila Godoy y Alcayaga), winner of the 1945 Literature prize "for her lyric poetry which, inspired by powerful emotions, has made her name a symbol of the idealistic aspirations of the entire Latin American world."

4535. Nobel Prize for Literature winner from the Middle East was Shmuel Yosef Agnon, born Shmuel Yosef Halevi Czaczkes, who shared the prize with the German-Swedish poet Nelly Sachs in 1966. He was a Ukrainian-born citizen of Israel. The leading figure in modern Hebrew fiction, he was the author of such novels as *Hakhnasat kalah (The Bridal Canopy),* published in 1919, and *Tmol shilshom (The Day Before Yesterday),* published in 1945. His work primarily dealt with the conflict between the traditional Jewish life of the European shtetls (Jewish villages) and the moral confusions of the modern world.

4536. Nobel Prize for Literature winner from Oceania was the Australian novelist Patrick Victor Martindale White. He was awarded the 1973 prize "for an epic and psychological narrative art which has introduced a new continent into literature."

4537. Nobel Prize for Literature winner from Africa was the Nigerian playwright and novelist Akinwande Oluwole "Wole" Soyinka, who won the prize in 1986. It was the first international honor in literature ever won by a black African writer. Soyinka's first play was *The Swamp Dwellers,* produced in London in 1958, when he was a student at the University of Leeds, in England. His later plays were critical of African authoritarianism. Soyinka spent two years during the 1960s in a Nigerian prison for his opposition to the war in Biafra, and in 1994 he went into self-exile as a protest against the Nigerian leadership. In March 1997 he was charged by the Nigerian government with treason.

NOBEL PRIZES—PEACE

4538. Nobel Prize for Peace was awarded in 1901. It was divided equally between Jean-Henri Dunant, the Swiss founder of the International Committee of the Red Cross and the originator of the Geneva Convention (Convention de Genève), and Frédéric Passy, founder and president of the first French peace society, the Société française pour l'arbitrage entre nations.

4539. Woman to win the Nobel Prize for Peace was the Austrian political activist Bertha Félicie Sophie, Freifrau von Suttner, born Bertha Félicie Sophie Gräfin in Prague (now in the Czech Republic) in 1843. A friend of Alfred Nobel, she influenced him to found the Nobel Peace Prize, and was in 1905 the first woman to receive it for her work in the international peace movement and as the author of *Die Waffen nieder (Lay Down Your Arms)*, a popular pacifist work published in 1889 under the pen name Bertha Oulot.

4540. Nobel Prize for Peace winner from North America was American president Theodore Roosevelt. The prize was awarded in 1906 for his service in the cause of peace in concluding the treaty between Russia and Japan at the end of the Russo-Japanese War.

4541. Nobel Prize for Peace winner from Latin America was Carlos Saavedra Lamas, the Argentinian minister of foreign affiars, awarded the 1936 prize for his service in mediating an armistice and peace agreement ending the Chaco War between Paraguay and Bolivia.

4542. Professional soldier to be awarded a Nobel Prize for Peace was the American general and statesman George Catlett Marshall, U.S Army chief of staff during World War II and sponsor of the postwar European Recovery Program, popularly known as the Marshall Plan. He received the prize on December 10, 1953, at Oslo University, Oslo, Norway.

4543. Nobel Prize for Peace winner from Africa was Albert John Mvumbi Lutuli, a Zulu chief, educator, and president of South Africa's African National Congress from 1952 to 1967. He was awarded the 1960 prize for his peaceful opposition to apartheid.

4544. Nobel Prize for Peace awarded to the United Nations Armed Forces was accepted by United Nations secretary-general Javier Pérez de Cuellar in Oslo, Norway, on December 10, 1988. By that date, more than 500,000 UN peacekeepers from 58 countries had been involved in 15 peacekeeping operations since 1948. United Nations peacekeeping forces, which are nonviolent except in self-defense, are intended to reduce strife in crises and allow time for the development of negotiated solutions.

NOBEL PRIZES—PHYSICS

4545. Nobel Prize in Physics was awarded in 1901 to the physicist Wilhelm Conrad Röntgen of Munich University, Munich, Germany, discoverer of x-rays (also called Röntgen rays), "in recognition of the extraordinary services he has rendered by the discovery of the remarkable rays subsequently named after him."

4546. Nobel Prize in Physics winner from North America was Albert Abraham Michelson of the University of Chicago, Chicago, IL, USA, awarded the prize in 1907 "for his optical instruments of precision, and the spectroscopic and metrologic investigations which he carried out by means of them." Michelson was one of two scientists who made the first precise and accurate measurement of the speed of light.

4547. Nobel Prize in Physics winner from Oceania was Australian-born scientist William Lawrence Bragg, who with his father William Henry Bragg shared the 1915 prize "for their services in the analysis of crystal structure by means of X-rays."

4548. Nobel Prize in Physics winner from Asia was Japanese physicist Hideki Yukawa of Kyoto Imperial University and Columbia University, New York, NY, USA, awarded the 1949 Physics prize "for his prediction of the existence of mesons on the basis of theoretical work on nuclear forces."

NOBEL PRIZES—PHYSIOLOGY OR MEDICINE

4549. Nobel Prize in Physiology or Medicine was awarded in 1901 to German physiologist Emil Adolf von Behring of Marburg University, Marburg, Germany, "for his work on serum therapy, especially its application against diphtheria, by which he has opened a new road in the domain of medical science and thereby placed in the hands of the physician a victorious weapon against illness and deaths."

NOBEL PRIZES—PHYSIOLOGY OR MEDICINE—*continued*

4550. Nobel Prize in Physiology or Medicine winner from North America was Alexis Carrel of the Rockefeller Institute for Medical Research, New York, NY, USA, awarded the prize in 1912 "for his work on vascular ligature and on the grafting of blood vessels and organs."

4551. Nobel Prize in Physiology or Medicine winner from Oceania was Howard Walter Florey, born in Adelaide, Australia, who shared the 1945 prize with Alexander Fleming and Ernst Boris Chain "for the discovery of penicillin and its curative effect in various infectious diseases."

4552. Nobel Prize in Physiology or Medicine winner from Latin America was Bernardo Alberto Houssay of Argentina's Instituto de Biología y Medicina Experimental in Buenos Aires. He shared the 1947 prize with two Americans, Gerty and Carl Cori, "for his discovery of the part played by the hormone of the anterior pituitary lobe in the metabolism of sugar."

4553. Woman to win the Nobel Prize in Physiology or Medicine was the Czech-born American researcher Gerty Theresa Cori (born Gertrude Radnitz) of Washington University, St. Louis, MO, USA, who shared half the 1947 prize with her husband Carl Ferdinand Cori "for their discovery of the course of the catalytic conversion of glycogen."

4554. Nobel Prize in Physiology or Medicine winner from Africa was Max Theiler, a physician born in South Africa. He was awarded the 1951 prize "for his discoveries concerning yellow fever and how to combat it."

4555. Nobel Prize in Physiology or Medicine winner from Asia was the Japanese-born researcher Susumu Tonegawa, of the Massachusetts Institute of Technology (MIT), Cambridge, MA, USA. He won the 1987 prize "for his discovery of the genetic principle for generation of antibody diversity."

P

PHILOSOPHY

4556. Western philosopher is traditionally considered to have been the Greek (or possibly Phoenician) philosopher, scientist, and geometer Thales of Miletus (in present-day Turkey), who lived circa 636–546 BCE. Thales' reputation as a thinker rests entirely on accounts set down after his death; no works of his own survive. Aristotle, who lived two centuries later, described him as a materialist and monist, the first to reject a mythological explanation for the existence of the universe and to claim that everything is derived from a single physical substance.

4557. Philosopher to advocate teaching and social activism as a way of life was the Chinese philosopher Kongfuzi (in Wade-Giles, K'ung Fu-tzu), known in the West as Confucius (died 479 BCE). He believed in character-building through universal education, teaching as a vocation, and the ethical necessity of having scholars dedicate themselves to the improvement of society in accordance with Confucian ideals.

4558. Cynic was Antisthenes of Athens, Greece, a disciple of Socrates, who lived circa 445–365 BCE. As the founder of Cynicism, he preached a philosophy of simple living unfettered by the conventions, hypocrisies, and injustices of society.

4559. Skeptic was Pyrrho of Elis (modern Ilia, Greece), who lived circa 365–275 BCE. He was the founder of the more influential of the two ancient branches of Skepticism (the other was academic or dogmatic Skepticism). Pyrrho held that because the arguments for or against any supposedly known fact are equally valid the only reasonable position is the withholding of belief in any knowledge. Once reconciled to not knowing anything, an individual would attain serenity of mind. None of Pyrrho's works survive, and his thought is known primarily from writings of Sextus Empiricus dated to circa 200 CE.

4560. Epicurean was Epicurus of Samos, who lived circa 341–270 BCE. Epicurus advocated living a simple, retiring life of serene moderation and reasonableness. In 306 BCE he established a school in Athens, Greece, which admitted women and even slaves.

4561. Stoic was Zeno of Citium, the founder of the Stoic philosophy, who was born in Cyprus and lived circa 333–262 BCE. According to Zeno, happiness lies in living with courage and dignity in conformance to the divine plan by which nature is governed. The name of his philosophy derives from the Stoa Poikile ("painted colonnade"), the landmark in the city of Athens, Greece, where he gave his lectures beginning circa 310 BCE.

4562. Yin-Yang philosophical school flourished in Ch'i (now Shantung, China) in the third century BCE. Its leading philosopher was Zou Yan (Tsou Yen; died circa 260 BCE), who combined the concept of the mutual complementarity of Yin and Yang with the theory of the Five Agents (metal, wood, water, fire, and earth). The idea of Yin-Yang is ancient and its origin is unknown. It presents the natural world as a duality of principles—earth, femaleness, and passivity, on the one hand, and heaven, maleness, and activity, on the other.

4563. Attempt to reconcile Judaism and philosophy was made in 175 BCE by Aristobulus of Paneas, a Jewish philosopher in Alexandria, Egypt, whose book *An Explanation of the Mosaic Scripture* sought to prove that the principles of Greek philosophy were from divine revelation in the Torah. The first such attempt to have a lasting effect was made by Moshe ben Maimon (known as the Rambam, or Maimonides) in *The Guide of the Perplexed,* published in 1195 in Arabic under the title *Dalalat al-hàirin* and translated into Hebrew as *Moreh nevukhim.* The Spanish-born Maimonides, physician to the vizier at Cairo, Egypt, held intellect and rationalism, rather than mysticism, to be the true ways of knowing God.

4564. Commentary on the *I Ching* extant was written by the Chinese philosopher Wang Bi circa 248 CE. His metaphysical commentary on the Confucian mystical classic, often used as a book of divination, was penned when he was in his early 20s.

4565. Islamic philosopher was Ya'qub ibn Ishaq as-Sabah al-Kindi, who lived in the ninth century (he died circa 870) in the area that is now Iraq. The first Muslim thinker to make use of Greek rationalism and science, he was the author of more than 270 works in Arabic on a wide variety of subjects, including natural philosophy, mathematics, logic, medicine, and astrology, with particular attention to questions of knowledge, both scientific (acquired through observation and logic) and revealed (as in the Qur'an), and of the nature of creation and the soul.

4566. Islamic philosopher with a following in the West was Muhammad ibn Muhammad ibn Tarkhan ibn Uzalagh al-Farabi, known in the West as Alpharabius or Avennasar, the first Neoplatonist philosopher in the Muslim world. Of Turkish birth, he spent his adult life in Damascus, Syria, where he died circa 950. He applied Aristotelian and Platonic ideas to the consideration of the perfect Islamic state, which he envisioned as governed by a philosopher-king.

4567. Humanist was the Italian poet Francesco Petrarca (Petrarch), who lived mainly in Italy from 1304 to 1374. Considered by many to be the "father of the Renaissance," he was the first to offer a synthesis of classical culture and Christian philosophy. In such works as *Secretum meum,* completed in 1343, he argued that secular achievements did not necessarily preclude an authentic relationship with God—in fact, he insisted that God had given humans their vast intellectual and creative potential to be used to the fullest.

4568. Modern encyclopedia of philosophy was the *Encyklopädie der philosophischen Wissenschaften im Grundrisse (Encyclopedia of Philosophical Knowledge in Outline),* published in 1817 by the German philosopher Georg Wilhelm Friedrich Hegel. As well as reviewing the history of philosophic inquiry in the West, it also contained the most comprehensive review of Hegel's own philosophic system.

4569. Existentialist work is usually considered to be *Enten-Eller: et-livs fragment (Either/Or: A Fragment of Life),* written in 1843 by the Danish religious philosopher Sören Aabye Kierkegaard. It presented a philosophy based on the need to make fully thought-out choices for every life decision, the core tenet of existentialism.

4570. Philosophy café or *café philo* was the Café des Phares in Paris, France, where in 1992 philosopher Marc Sautet organized a regular philosophy discussion group. The concept caught on and by 1997 there were more than 20 such cafés in and around Paris, as well as many in Belgium, England, Greece, Switzerland, Japan, and the United States.

PHOTOGRAPHY

4571. Photo interview was of an 1886 conversation between the French scientist Eugène Chevreul and Nadar (born Gaspard-Félix Tournachon), a French journalist, caricaturist, and portrait photographer. Nadar took photographs of Chevreul throughout the interview and later published 21 of them. Captions underneath each picture contained Nadar's questions and Chevreul's answers.

4572. Photography booth was invented by a Hungarian entrepreneur, Anatol Marco Josepho, and patented in Germany on January 13, 1924. It consisted of a small booth with a seat for one or two subjects, a box camera with a wide-angle lens, and a compact darkroom. An attendant operated the camera and developed the photographs.

PHOTOGRAPHY—*continued*

4573. Paparazzo was the American photographer Weegee, born Usher (Arthur) Fellig in Zloczew, Austria (now Poland) in 1899. In 1923, having emigrated to the United States, Fellig joined Acme Newspictures (which later became United Press International Photos), and in 1935, he began a career as a freelance press photographer working out of police headquarters in lower Manhattan. Fellig's photos had a raw immediacy that derived in part from his aggressive pursuit of sensational subjects—dead gangsters, crime victims, and the like—and from his habit of arriving at the scene before the police did (thanks to his constant monitoring of police radio).

4574. Photographic pictorial biography was *Lincoln: His Life in Photographs,* a biography of American president Abraham Lincoln published in 1941 by the Hungarian-born journalist Stefan Lorant.

PHOTOGRAPHY—CAMERAS AND FILM

4575. Camera obscura was known to Chinese astronomers circa 400 BCE. They observed solar eclipses by allowing sunlight to be projected through a pinhole into a darkened room, where an inverted image of the event could be seen on the opposite wall. The camera obscura was also described by Aristotle less than 100 years later.

4576. Magic lantern is often attributed to the German Jesuit priest Athanasius Kircher, who was supposed to have invented this precursor to the film projector circa 1654, but in fact types of magic lanterns had long been known in China, and variants of the device were essential to the traditional shadow puppetry of Java, Bali, and Thailand.

4577. Photographic process that was practical was the daguerreotype, invented in 1839 by Louis-Jacques-Mandé Daguerre. By exposing a silvered metal plate in a camera, developing the image with mercury vapor, then fixing it with salt, Daguerre developed the first method of permanently reproducing photographs. The process was made public on January 9, 1839, at a meeting of the French Academy of Sciences.

4578. Portrait camera was invented by the Viennese photographer Friedrich Voigtländer, with a fast double combination lens, the first designed specifically for portrait photography, by mathematician Josef Max Petzval. The conical-shaped brass camera, shaped rather like a small cannon, took circular daguerreotypes about 3.5 inches (9 centimeters) in diameter. It was introduced to the market on January 1, 1841.

4579. Color photography process was invented circa 1850 by an American, Levi Hill, a former Baptist minister of Westkill, NY, USA. The complicated developing process Hill used to produce what were called "Hillotypes" was described in his 1856 book *A Treatise on Heliochromy.* Long dismissed as a fraud who secretly hand-colored his photographs, Hill was vindicated in 1986 when Joseph Boudreau, the chairman of the photography department at Paier College of Art in Hamden, CT, USA, recreated Hill's process and produced his own Hillotypes.

4580. Flash powder was developed in 1887 by two German photographer-chemists, Adolf Mietke and Johannes Gaedicke. Their volatile mixture was composed of magnesium, potassium chlorate, and antimony sulfate, and created an extremely bright flash when ignited.

4581. Camera to use film rolls was Kodak No. 1, a fixed-focus box camera, announced in June 1888 by American inventor George Eastman of Rochester, NY, USA. It weighed 22 ounces and had a lens fast enough to make instantaneous exposures. It used a roll of film of 100 exposures and took a round picture 2.5 inches in diameter. It did not require a table or tripod for support. The camera was covered by a U.S. patent dated September 4, 1888, and the name Kodak was registered on the same date.

4582. Anastigmatic lens that was commercially successful was the Protar f.7.5 lens, manufactured in 1889 by the Carl Zeiss Works, Jena, Germany, from a design by German physicist Paul Rudolph. An anastigmatic lens provides a clear image edge-to-edge; earlier lens types often only provided a sharp focus for light coming through the center of the lens.

4583. Color photographic process that was practical was invented in 1893 by the Irish scientist John Joly at Trinity College, Dublin. Previously, color photographs were taken through three filters of red, blue, and green. Joy invented a single filter that was ruled with thin lines of the three colors at about 200 lines per inch. A transparency created by photographing through this filter could be viewed through an identical filter to see a vivid, accurate color image.

4584. Thirty-five-millimeter camera that was commercially successful was the Leica 1, invented by German mechanical engineer Oskar Barnack in 1913 and introduced in 1924 by the Ernst Leitz optical firm of Wetzlar, Germany. Its small size, light weight, and precision craftsmanship made it especially appealing to professional photographers. Barnack is also credited with standardizing the size and aspect ratio of the 35-millimeter film format.

4585. Stroboscopic lamp for high-speed photography was invented in 1927 by Harold Eugene "Doc" Edgerton, an American-born graduate student at the Massachusetts Institute of Technology in Cambridge, MA, USA. Edgerton's stroboscope, or strobe, emitted a bright light for a tiny fraction of a second. Previous researchers had conceived of a fast-flashing light, but Edgerton was the first to synchronize a strobe light to the shutter of a camera and develop the techniques of high-speed photography. His stop-action photographs of the splash of a single milk droplet, a bullet in mid-flight, and other previously invisible events revealed a world of unknown natural phenomena. The holder of 47 patents, Edgerton also invented specialized sonar, underwater cameras, and high-intensity lamps.

4586. Single lens reflex (SLR) 35 millimeter camera was the Kine Exakta, designed in June 1932 by Karl Nuchterlein at the Ihagee Kamerawerk, Steenbergeen and Company, Dresden, Germany. It was exhibited at the Leipzig Spring Fair in March 1936 and was in production from April 1936. The Russian-built "Cnopm" camera, sometimes cited as the first SLR, did not go into production until the end of 1937. The Kine Exacta was the first camera to resemble the modern SLR and boasted such innovations as a small but bright viewfinder, a fast multi-speed shutter, built-in synchronization with an accessory flash attachment, and a bayonet mount for interchangeable lenses.

4587. Instant camera was the Polaroid camera, invented by an American, Edwin Herbert Land, and demonstrated on February 21, 1947, at a meeting of the Optical Society of America at the Hotel Pennsylvania, New York, NY, USA. The camera contained a specially prepared photographic paper with "pods" of developer and hypo sandwiched with the film. The turning of a knob squeezed open one of the pods, which developed the negative and made the print. The picture was produced in about one minute.

4588. Digital still camera was the Mavica, developed by Sony KK of Tokyo, Japan, and announced on August 24, 1981. It stored photographs not on film but on an internal magnetic disk as digital files that could be displayed on a TV screen. A consumer version of the Mavica was introduced in 1988.

PHOTOGRAPHY—PHOTOGRAPHS

4589. Photograph was made in 1826 by Joseph-Nicéphore Niepce, a French physicist who had invented photoengraving ten years earlier. It shows the view from an upper window of his house. The image was formed on a pewter plate inside a camera obscura over the course of an eight-hour exposure. The photograph is preserved at the University of Texas, USA.

4590. Printed photograph extant was made by the French photography pioneer Joseph-Nicéphore Niepce in February 1827. Some months earlier, in a three-hour exposure, he had copied an engraved portrait of Cardinal d'Amboise onto a pewter plate. After having the plate etched and inked, he pulled two paper prints, both of which are still in existence.

4591. Photography studio in Europe open to the public began operation on March 23, 1841, on the roof of the Royal Polytechnic Institute in London, England. Crowds gathered to have their portraits taken by owner Richard Beard and chemist John Frederick Goddard in the circular studio, lit by blue-glazed windows that gave an eerie look to the pictures.

4592. Photographs of a historic event were taken by German photographers Hermann Biow and Carl Ferdinand Stelzner of the ruins of Hamburg, Germany, after a fire destroyed much of the city on May 5–8, 1842.

4593. Art photographs deliberately conceived to convey abstract esthetic ideas were a series of daguerreotypes titled "The Lord's Prayer", produced by the English photographer J.E. Mayall in 1845. In 1851, another series of large daguerreotypes "to illustrate poetry and sentiment" were displayed by Mayall in the Crystal Palace for the London Great Exhibition. They were not a popular or critical success.

4594. Underwater photograph of record was taken in 1856 by William Thompson, who lowered a waterproofed camera to a depth of 20 feet (6 meters) in Weymouth Bay, England. The photograph was exposed for ten minutes. It was first displayed in public at a meeting of the London Art Society.

PHOTOGRAPHY—PHOTOGRAPHS—continued

4595. Aerial photographs were views of Paris from a balloon taken in 1858 by Nadar (born Gaspard-Félix Tournachon), a French journalist, caricaturist, and portrait photographer. Nadar had already patented the idea of aerial photography for mapmaking in 1855. A well-known satirical lithograph by Honoré Daumier depicts Nadar with a camera flying over Paris in his large balloon, *Le Geant.* It was titled *Nadar Élevant la Photographie à la Hauteur de l'Art (Nadar Raising Photography to the Height of Art).*

4596. Underground photographs were taken circa 1862 by the French photographer Nadar (Gaspard-Félix Tournachon) in the catacombs and sewers of Paris, France. Nadar used an electric arc light powered by a Bunsen battery for illumination.

4597. Photographs showing action were taken by the English photographer Eadweard Muybridge in 1877 on a stock farm owned by Leland Stanford at Palo Alto, CA, USA. Stanford, the governor of California, hired Muybridge to determine whether or not a fast-trotting horse ever has all four hooves in the air simultaneously. Muybridge set up a series of twelve cameras with wire-tripped shutters. This enabled him to take a series of photographs at regular intervals, in rapid succession, of a racehorse in action. The results showed that a running horse is indeed completely airborne in the course of its gallop.

4598. Infrared photograph taken in the dark with a short exposure was made in the Eastman Kodak Research Laboratories in Rochester, NY, USA, on October 7, 1931. A photograph was taken with a one-second exposure, in apparently total darkness, of a group of 50 visitors to the laboratories. The room was flooded with invisible infrared rays, and a new photographic emulsion sensitive to infrared was used.

POPULATION

4599. Human societies destroyed by overpopulation were most likely those founded on several Polynesian islands, notably Mangareva (now part of the Gambier Islands, in the Tuamotu Archipelago of French Polynesia), which was settled circa 1000 CE. According to archeologists, Mangareva initially thrived and established a vital trade with nearby Pitcairn and Henderson islands. As the population increased, resources, especially wood for boats, grew scarce. Civil war broke out and the starving people turned to cannibalism. Communication

and commerce among the islands ended circa 1450. A small population on Mangareva survived, but, without trade from the larger island, the isolated inhabitants of Pitcairn (a few hundred) and Henderson (about 50) died out circa 1600.

4600. Year the world population exceeded 500 million was 1500.

4601. National birth registry was started by Sweden, which made the registration of births mandatory in 1686.

4602. Treatise on human population growth was *Various Prospects of Mankind, Nature, and Providence,* written by the Scottish cleric Robert Wallace in 1761. Wallace, anticipating the theories of Thomas Malthus, maintained that the increase in human beings would mean that "the earth would at last be overstocked, and become unable to support its numerous inhabitants." To solve the problem, he predicted that women would be cloistered, men would be castrated, and people would be executed when they reached a certain age.

4603. Treatise on human population growth that had a wide influence was the pamphlet *An Essay on the Principle of Population as It Affects the Future Improvement of Society, with Remarks on the Speculations of Mr. Godwin, M. Condorcet, and Other Writers,* written in England in 1798 (and later revised and expanded) by the Anglican minister Thomas Malthus. In it he proposed that population growth, which he claimed must increase geometrically, would sooner or later outstrip the amount of food available, leading inexorably to poverty and the breakdown of society.

4604. Year the world population exceeded 1 billion was 1804.

4605. Year the world population exceeded 2 billion was 1927.

4606. Year the world population exceeded 3 billion was 1960.

4607. Year the world population exceeded 4 billion was 1974.

4608. Country with more than 1 billion people was China. In 1987, China's population was 1,104,193,000.

4609. Year the world population exceeded 5 billion was 1987.

4610. Country to have more suburbanites than city and rural dwellers combined was the United States, which achieved that distinction in 1990.

4611. Year the world population exceeded 6 billion was 1999.

POPULATION—HUMAN ORIGINS

4612. Animal believed to be the ancestor of apes, monkeys, and humans is *Catopithecus,* a lemurlike animal that lived in northern Africa approximately 36 million years ago. Skull, jaw, and teeth fossils of *Catopithecus* were discovered in 1995 in Egypt's Fayum Desert by Elwyn Simons and a team from Duke University, Durham, NC, USA. A claim has also been made for *Eosimias,* a tiny animal whose fossilized jaw, found in China, was dated to about 40 million years ago. The status of *Eosimias* as an anthropoid is in dispute.

4613. Hominid species known to be an ancestor of modern humans was *Australopithecus afarensis,* discovered in the late 1970s by the American paleoanthropologists Donald Johanson and Timothy White at sites in Laetoli, Tanzania, and Hadar, Ethiopia. Fossil and DNA analysis of the most complete skeleton, a small female nicknamed "Lucy," suggest that all modern humans are related to her. In 1994, gerontologist Robert C. Walter of the Institute of Human Origins in Berkeley, CA, USA, conducted a single-crystal laser-fusion analysis of the ratio of two forms of argon in grains of local volcanic ash taken from the Hadar site. He obtained an age of 3.18 million years for the Lucy fossil. Related *A. afarensis* fossils at the site were dated to 3.4 million years ago. Fossils of another species, *Australopithecus anamensis,* are suspected of being even older. They were discovered in 1995 by a team under British paleoanthropologist Meave Leakey near Lake Turkana in northern Kenya.

4614. Tools were used by Australopithecines millions of years before the emergence of modern humans. The earliest known stone tools made by humans or their direct ancestors were found in the desiccated fossil fields of Gona, Ethiopia, by a team led by Ethiopian paleoanthropologist Sileshi Semaw. Their discoveries were announced in 1995. The tools were dated to 2.6 million years BCE.

4615. Meat-eating hominids may have lived in Africa as long as 2.5 million years ago, according to evidence published in the journal *Nature* on January 15, 1999. Analysis of carbon-13 in australopithecine tooth remains, performed by Matt Sponheimer of Rutgers University in New Brunswick, NJ, USA, and Julia A. Lee-Thorp

of the University of Cape Town in South Africa, indicated that hominids of that era were probably eating small herbivores, who concentrate that isotope in their bodies from grasses and sedges.

4616. Fossils of *Homo erectus* were the fossils of a human-like skull and femur discovered in 1891 at Trinil, Java (now part of Indonesia), by the Dutch anatomist Eugene Dubois. The femur was ape-like in some details but was straighter than the femurs of apes, indicating an upright posture. Dubois classified his find as *Pithecanthropus erectus,* Latin for "ape man erect." In 1940 the remains were recognized as the first *Homo erectus*/7 *H. erectus* was the immediate ancestor of modern humans and lived in the middle Pleistocene Epoch, about 1 million to 500,000 years ago.

4617. Human use of fire took place at least 1 million years ago and perhaps as many as 1.5 million years ago, according to fossil remains found in a cave in Swartkrans, South Africa. South African anthropologists C.K. Brain of the Transvaal Museum in Pretoria and Andrew Sillen of the University of Cape Town discovered 270 burned fragments of animal fossils, mostly antelope bones, at the site. Hominids had apparently made campfires there repeatedly, judging by the distribution of bones. The previously accepted date for human use of fire had been 500,000 BCE.

4618. Evidence of cannibalism was found in 1995 in Atapuerca in northern Spain by a Spanish team directed by Eudald Carbonell of the University Rovira i Virgili in Tarragona. The team found hominid remains, dating to circa 780,000 BCE, that showed clear evidence of having been butchered for meat.

4619. Human footprints known to anthropologists were found in 1995 in sand dunes at West Coast National Park, near Cape Town, South Africa, and announced in August 1997 by geologist David Roberts and paleoanthropologist Lee Berger of the University of Witwatersrand in Johannesburg. The three footprints are believed to have been left in wet sand by a woman 5 feet 3 inches (1.6 meters) tall. They were dated by a variety of techniques to circa 115,000 BCE.

4620. Skeleton of a black African known to anthropologists is believed to be Asselar Man, a skeleton found in 1927 by M.V. Besnard and Théodore Monod near Asselar, French Sudan (now the Republic of Mali). The remains date from circa 5000 BCE.

POPULATION—MIGRATION AND SETTLEMENT

4621. Hominids in Asia probably belonged to one of two early human species, *Homo habilis* or *Homo ergaster*. Fossils of hominid teeth—an upper incisor and a fragment of lower jaw with a premolar and adjacent molar—were found between 1984 and 1988 during the excavation of Longgupo Cave, near Wushan in the eastern Szechwan province of China. The dig was conducted by scientists from the Institute of Vertebrate Paleontology and Paleoanthropology in Beijing and the Chongqing Museum of Natural History. The hominid remains were dated by Chinese anthropologists to between 1.78 and 1.96 million years BCE.

4622. Hominid remains in Europe were discovered in 1991 in the republic of Georgia by Leo Gabunia of the Georgian Academy of Sciences and a team of German and Georgian scientists. They located the mandible of an early hominid, probably a *Homo erectus* dating to as early as 1.6 million years ago, in the foundation of a medieval house in the deserted town of Dmanisi. Accompanying the jawbone were stone tools, the skulls of two saber-toothed tigers, and the rib of an ancient elephant.

4623. Site of human habitation in Europe is the cave of Le Vallonet, on the coast of France near Roquebrune-Cap-Martin. When the French archeologist Henri de Lumley excavated the inner chamber of the cave in 1959 and 1962, he found Paleolithic pebble, flint, and bone tools. They have been dated to as early as 1.3 million years BCE.

4624. Humans in Siberia may have arrived circa 300,000 years ago, much earlier than previously was thought. Excavations begun in 1982 by Russian archeologists Yuri A. Mochanov and Svetlana Fedoseeva uncovered tool-making activities at the Diring Yuriak site on the Lena River, 87 miles (140 kilometers) from the city of Yakutsk, Russia. The tools were dated using the thermoluminescent technique and evaluated by the American geoarcheologist Michael R. Waters of Texas A&M University.

4625. Humans in Australia may have arrived earlier than 135,000 years ago, according to research by Richard L.K. Fullagar and colleagues at the Australian Museum in Sydney. At that period, an ice age had lowered the sea level, making it easier for people from southeast Asia to reach Australia. Fullagar found stone sharpened artifacts at a northwestern Australian site known as the Jinmium rock shelter, and used thermoluminescent techniques to date them to circa 116,000 to 176,000 years ago.

4626. Humans in the Americas crossed the Bering Strait from Siberia about 30 millennia ago. The earliest evidence of human occupation in the New World, derived from analysis of the mitochondrial DNA of Central American indigenous peoples, has been dated at circa 29,000 BCE.

4627. Human remains in the Americas may be two thigh bones of a woman that were unearthed in 1959 on Santa Rosa Island off Santa Barbara, CA, USA. Dating performed in the late 1990s suggested that the bones were approximately 13,000 years old, about 1,400 years older than the next oldest human remains known from the New World, and supporting theories that the woman or her ancestors may have arrived in North America by maritime colonization from Polynesia or Southeast Asia rather than overland across the Bering Strait. Previously, the oldest remains known to archeologists belonged to the so-called "Midland Woman," found near Midland, TX, USA, in 1953. In 1992, Curtis R. McKinney of Southern Methodist University in Dallas, TX, used a radioactive uranium-decay process to date her remains to 9,600 BCE, plus or minus 800 years. Midland Woman may be the only known representative of the Clovis people.

4628. Human habitation in the Americas known to archeologists was found in the mid-1970s at Monte Verde in Chile by geologist Mario Pino of the Southern University of Chile in Valdivia. The site has been dated to 10,500 BCE. However, many paleoanthropologists consider that the first New World culture that has been definitively dated is the Clovis culture of circa 9,000 BCE, named for Clovis, NM, USA, where sharp, fluted projectile points of chalcedony or obsidian and other artifacts were first unearthed in the early 1930s.

4629. Site of organized human activity in North America that has been documented was discovered by archeologist Michael Kunz atop a mesa in northern Alaska in 1978. Radiocarbon evidence obtained by Kunz and his associate Richard Lanier indicated that the site was a prehistoric hunting outpost used by a previously unknown culture dating from 7700 to 9700 BCE. Artifacts at the site included stone spear heads and hunting tools.

4630. Permanent settlement known to archeologists is the village of Zawi Chenui in southeastern Anatolia on the Turkish-Iranian border. It was inhabited before 9000 BCE.

4631. Cities on the Indian subcontinent were Harappa and Mohenjo-Daro, begun circa 3500 BCE in the valley of the Indus River in what is now Pakistan. They were rediscovered by accident in the 1850s, when British railroad builders working on the East India Railway dug up two mounds of earth and brick to use as roadbed fill. The mounds were recognized in the 1920s as the remains of ancient cities.

4632. Human construction in the New World known to archeologists is the Watson Brake complex, an oval grouping of eleven earthen mounds located in the floodplain of the Ouachita River near Monroe in northern Louisiana, USA. According to Reca Bamburg Jones and archeologist Joe W. Saunders of Northeast Louisiana University, who published an examination of the site in September 1997, the mounds date to circa 3400 BCE, some 1,900 years earlier than the next-oldest site, the 3,500-year-old mounds at Poverty Point in northeast Louisiana.

4633. Cities in the Americas known to archeologists were Andean desert sites at Pampa de las Llamas-Moxeke and Taukachi-Konkan, both in the Casma Valley in Peru. Dated at circa 1500 BCE, well before the earliest known great pre-Columbian civilizations, the two urban sites housed several thousand inhabitants.

4634. Meso-American culture of importance was the Olmec culture, which dominated what is now the southern Veracruz and adjacent Tabasco regions of the Mexican Gulf Coast from circa 1150 BCE to circa 400 BCE. Best known for their monumental stone carvings of stylized heads, some 10 feet (3 meters) tall, the Olmecs also constructed pyramids and ceremonial centers marked by great mounds, carved stelae, and altars with many depictions of a jaguar god. *Olmec* is the Nahuatl word for "inhabitant of rubber country," referring to the rubber trees that grow in the region.

4635. Voyage of colonization known to historians was a Carthaginian expedition that took place circa 500 BCE under the leadership of Hanno, who wrote an account of it. A group of men and women left Carthage (in present-day Tunisia) in 60 ships, headed westward, passed through the Strait of Gibraltar, and set down six colonies along the coast of what is now Morocco, of which the first was Thymiaterion (now called Kenitra). The expedition is thought to have reached as far south as Sierra Leone and possibly to Cameroon.

4636. Anglo-Saxons to arrive in England after the Celts appealed for help against attacks by the Picts and Scots were the Jutes, who arrived from the area that is now northern Germany and southern Denmark circa 449 (the date given by the Venerable Bede, England's first historian). Their leaders were two brothers, Hengest and Horsa (both of which mean "horse"). They were followed by the Saxons, the Angles, the Frisians, and other Germanic tribes from the same region.

4637. Settlers in Madagascar were Austronesians thought to have arrived from Indonesia circa 700. The island's population has a combined Asian and African ancestry and its language, Malagasy, is a member of the Malayo-Polynesian family, modified by aspects of the Bantu languages spoken in parts of Africa.

4638. Muslim settlement in East Africa took place during the second half of the eighth century CE, when Shi'ite Muslims from southern Arabia settled along the coastline in what is now Somalia and Kenya. Muslim trading businesses were soon established on offshore islands such as Kilwa and Pemba (both in modern Tanzania), importing cotton, silk, glassware, and pottery, and exporting ivory, leopard skins, tortoise shells, ambergris, mangrove poles, and African slaves. The Arab historian Abu al-Hasan Ali al-Mas'udi, who visited in 916, mentioned an island, possibly Pemba, that was inhabited and ruled by Muslims.

4639. Humans in New Zealand were the Maoris, a Polynesian people from the eastern Pacific. According to archeological evidence, they reached New Zealand circa 800. Maori traditions place the colonization date at closer to 1400.

4640. Settlement in Iceland was made in the ninth century by Irish monks, who used it as a place of hermitage. The first permanent settlement was founded in 874 by a Norwegian couple, Ingólfur Arnarson and his wife, who built a homestead where the city of Reykjavik now stands.

4641. European traveler to sight North America was probably Bjarni Herjölffson, a trader from Iceland, according to the *Groenlendinga saga (Tale of the Greenlanders)* in the *Flateyjarbók (Songbook),* a collection of Icelandic sagas and tales dated to the 13th century. Bjarni was on his way to Greenland about the year 986 when his ship was blown off course by a storm. He and his men found

POPULATION—MIGRATION AND SETTLEMENT—*continued*

themselves near an unknown tree-covered land, which they did not stop to investigate. His account of this adventure inspired Leif Eriksson to undertake a voyage of exploration some years later.

4642. Settlers in Greenland left Iceland in 986 in a fleet of 25 ships under the leadership of Erik the Red (Erik Thorvaldson), who had discovered Greenland (now part of Denmark) four years earlier. About half the ships were lost en route. The 350 settlers who arrived on Greenland's southwestern coast established a Norse settlement that survived until the late 15th century. A church built at Brattahlid (Tunigdliarfik) circa 1000 by Erik's wife was the first Christian church in the New World.

4643. European settlement in North America was Vinland, founded by the Icelandic Viking explorer Leif Eriksson circa 1000 somewhere on the northeastern coast of North America, most likely on the coast of Newfoundland. It was, according to the account given in the Icelandic *Eiríks saga (Saga of Erik)* and the *Groenlendinga saga (Tale of the Greenlanders),* a land with hardwood forests, ample pastureland, and wild grapes. Leif and his crew wintered there and returned to Greenland in the spring with a cargo of timber. A group of colonists led by Leif's brother Thorvald and sister Freydis and by the Icelander Thorfinn Karlsefni returned to the area in 1004 and again circa 1007 and settled at L'Anse aux Meadows, Newfoundland, Canada, where they left house sites and other remains discovered in 1963 by Helge Ingstad. The settlement was abandoned by 1015.

4644. Child born of European parents in North America was Snorri Thorfinnson, the son of Thorfinn Karlsefni and Gudrid, widow of Leif Eriksson's brother Thorstein Eriksson. They were among 130 settlers from Greenland who arrived at L'Anse aux Meadows, Newfoundland, Canada, circa 1007 to colonize a region they called Vinland, which had been explored by Leif some years before.

4645. Peoples of the Canary Islands were the Guanches and the Canarios, aboriginal peoples who settled the islands in Neolithic times. Their culture, which had developed crafts, writing (which has never been deciphered), and a monotheistic religion, was completely destroyed and the people decimated after Spanish invaders under the Norman-French adventurer Jean de Béthencourt claimed the islands for Spain in 1404.

4646. Jews in the New World were Marranos, Spanish Jews who had converted to Christianity in order to escape torture and death under the Inquisition. Marranos took part in Columbus's voyage of discovery in 1492 and in later Spanish and Portuguese explorations. The first Jewish settlement in the New World was Jodensavanna, founded circa 1640 in Suriname (formerly Dutch Guiana) by Sephardic Jews from Holland. Prayer services were held in the synagogue for some 230 years, even after the rest of the village had been reclaimed by the jungle. The first permanent Jewish settler in North America was Jacob Barsimson of Holland, who landed at the Dutch colony of New Amsterdam (the future New York City) on August 22, 1654.

4647. Town founded by a European in the New World was La Isabela, a settlement established on the West Indian island of Hispaniola by Christopher Columbus on January 2, 1494, during his second voyage. The town, in the modern Dominican Republic, is now a ruin.

4648. Permanent European settlement in the New World was Santo Domingo, now the capital of the Dominican Republic, on the island of Hispaniola. It was founded on August 4, 1496, by Bartolomeo Columbus, the brother of Christopher. Originally called Nueva Isabela, after Queen Isabela, it was renamed after being destroyed by a hurricane and rebuilt in 1502. As the capital of the Spanish colony of Santo Domingo, it was the first seat of European colonial administration in the New World.

4649. Colonial palace in the New World was the Alcázar de Colón, also called the Virreinal Palace, in Santo Domingo, Dominican Republic. It was started in 1510 by Christopher Columbus for his son, Diego, and became the center from which the Spanish conquests in the New World were governed. The 22-room building is a mixture of the Mudejar-Gothic and western Mediterrean Renaissance styles.

4650. European settlements in South America were founded in 1510. One, Nombre de Dios, was founded by the explorer Diego de Nicuesa on the Caribbean coast of present-day Panama, near the mouth of the Chagres River. The other, San Sebastien de Urabá, was founded by Alonso de Ojeda on the Gulf of Urabá, in present-day Colombia. These were the first Spanish settlements on the mainland of the Americas. Neither lasted long. The colony at Urabá was transferred to Darién, a region of the Isthmus of Panama, by Vasco Nuñez de Balboa. Renamed Santa María de la Antigua del Darién, it became the first permanent European settlement in South America.

4651. European to join a Native American people was the Spanish conquistador Gonzalo Guerrero, who was accepted into the Maya culture of the Yucatán in Mexico as a warrior circa 1510. According to an account by Diego de Landa, an early bishop of Yucatán, Guerrero taught the Maya how to build fortifications in the European style that were better able to withstand gunpowder weapons, enabling them to resist Spanish efforts at conquest. He was killed by Spanish forces in Honduras in 1536.

4652. European settlement on the west coast of the New World was Panamá, founded by the Spanish colonial administrator Pedro Arias Dávila in 1519 on the Bay of Panama (in fact, on the southern side of the isthmus). It was the center of Spanish shipping and military activities in the area until it was destroyed in 1671 by the English privateer Sir Henry Morgan. A new Panama City was built nearby.

4653. Conquistador to conquer a part of the New World for the Spanish crown was Hernán Cortés, formerly an administrator in the Spanish colony of Cuba, who left the island on February 18, 1519, with a fleet of eleven ships and an army of 508 soldiers and 16 horses. They landed a few weeks later at Tabasco, in present-day Mexico, and took the Aztec capital city of Tenochtitlán with the help of indigenous allies. On August 13, 1521, after a series of battles, the Aztec empire collapsed and Cortés became the ruler of its entire territory.

4654. European industry in the Americas was probably glassmaking. Glass was being made by Spanish craftsmen in Puebla, Mexico, circa 1535.

4655. Spanish settlement in North America was a fort founded by the conquistador Pedro Menéndez de Avilés circa 1565 near what is today St. Augustine, FL, USA. The fort predated the colonization of Jamestown, VA, in 1607 and the Pilgrims' landing at Plymouth, MA, in 1620. A remnant of the structure was unearthed in 1993 by anthropologist Kathleen Deagan and colleagues of the Florida Museum of Natural History.

4656. European city in southern Africa was the Portuguese-built São Paulo de Luanda (now Luanda, Angola), founded in 1576 by Paulo Dias de Novais, the grandson of Bartolomeu Dias. The first African city south of the equator, it became a major port for the Portuguese slave traffic to Brazil.

4657. English-speaking colony in the New World was the island of Newfoundland (now a province of Canada), which was claimed for England by Sir Humphrey Gilbert in 1583. It was used as a summer base for cod fishermen from Ireland and western England. The French made a similar claim, for the same purpose.

4658. Mexican–American trail was El Camino Real de Tierra Adentro ("Royal Road of Interior Land"), a 1,500-mile (2,414-kilometer) trail that ran from Mexico City to Santa Fe (in what is now New Mexico, USA). It was established by Juan de Oñate in 1598, with the original terminus at San Juan Pueblo.

4659. Permanent English settlement in America was established at Jamestown, VA, USA, on May 13, 1607, with the arrival of 105 male colonists who had been sent out by the London Company from Blackwell, England, on December 19, 1606. Among them was the explorer Captain John Smith, who was one of seven men who formed the first English colonial council in North America. The first women allowed at Jamestown came in 1621. The following year, 347 of its 1,240 inhabitants were killed in an attack by Native Americans, and many others died of starvation over the winter.

4660. English settlement in India was Pettapoli, founded in 1611 on the coast of the Bay of Bengal. In the same year, England's East India Company founded its first South Indian trading station on the same coast, at Machilipatnam. In 1639 the station was transferred to Madras, where it became the first of the company's Indian locations to be fortified.

4661. Colony financed by a lottery was Jamestown, the first permanent English settlement in America, founded in what is now Virginia, USA, in 1607. Its sponsor, the Virginia Company of London, raised funds for the struggling colony by running lotteries in English towns, after receiving the crown's permission in 1612.

4662. Continuous settlements of Asians in North America were the shrimping villages established circa 1760 in the bayou country of Louisiana, USA, by Filipino immigrants. Most of these had been sailors on Spanish galleons working the routes between Manila, the Philippines, and Spanish settlements in Mexico.

4663. Convicts deported to Australia arrived from England aboard six British transport vessels under the command of Arthur Phillip, Australia's first governor. The youngest convict was nine years old, the oldest 82. Most had been convicted of stealing and petty crimes.

POPULATION—MIGRATION AND SETTLEMENT—*continued*

The complement of convicts was divided as follows: the *Scarborough,* with 208 men; the *Alexander,* with 195 men; the *Lady Penrhyn,* with 101 women; the *Charlotte,* with 88 men and 22 women; the *Friendship,* with 76 men and 21 women; and the *Prince of Wales,* with one man and 49 women. The passage took 252 days, during which 40 of the convicts and five of their children died of disease. The ships arrived on January 20, 1788, at Australia's Botany Bay, but Phillip, finding the area unsuitable for a penal colony, continued 10 miles north to Sydney Cove (Port Jackson), where the convicts were landed between January 27 and February 6.

4664. European child born in Australia was Thomas Whittle, Jr., the son of Thomas Whittle, a Royal Marine, and his wife. The boy was born aboard ship as the First Fleet entered Sydney Cove (Port Jackson) on January 26, 1788.

4665. African Pygmies to visit Europe were six Mbuti—two women and four men—transported from the Ituri Forest (in what is now the Democratic Republic of the Congo) to England in 1905 by Colonel James Jonathan Harrison. The pygmies were displayed at the London Hippodrome in June of that year, then toured the country, with visits to Buckingham Palace and the House of Commons. They returned to the Congo in 1907.

4666. Jewish city founded in Israel in modern times was Tel Aviv. It was founded in Palestine in 1909 by residents of the Jewish quarter of the ancient Mediterranean port city of Jaffa and was formally incorporated in 1950, after the Israeli War of Independence. In Hebrew, Tel Aviv means "hill of Spring." The name was taken from the title of a novel by Theodor Herzl, the founder of modern Zionism.

4667. Australian real estate owned by aborigines in modern times was the slum of Redfern in Sydney, sold in 1973. In 1998 it was home to about 500 aborigines, the only such enclave in Australia's largest city.

POSTAL SERVICE

4668. Complaint by a postal deliverer was recorded in Egypt circa 2300 BCE. In part, it read: "The messenger, before going to wild foreign countries, leaves all his property to his children for fear of the Asiatics and wild beasts. And what sort of life is he living in Egypt? Soon after his coming back he has to go again and when he is leaving he is troubled with many sorrows again."

4669. Centralized postal system with relay stations for organizing and forwarding mail was put into effect in Persia by King Cyrus the Great during the sixth century BCE. Couriers were sent in stages along the empire's main military roads, including its chief highway, the 1,500-mile (2,400-kilometer) Persian Royal Road.

4670. Postal service to carry private mail began circa 1550 in what is now Germany, when the noble house of Thurn und Taxis, holder of the government postal monopoly for the Holy Roman Empire, was authorized by Emperor Charles V to carry letters sent by individuals. The Thurn und Taxis service, which had begun by carrying royal mail for the Holy Roman emperor Maximilian I from 1489, continued to operate until 1867.

4671. Prepaid envelopes were developed during the reign of King Louis XIV of France. In 1653 a private post was established. According to tradition, a M. de Valfyer came up with the idea of selling *formes de billet,* or blank form letters, together with envelopes to which postage was already attached.

4672. Postal system to carry prepaid mail was the Penny Post system, the creation of the English postal reformer Sir Rowland Hill, a former schoolmaster. In 1837 he published a pamphlet entitled *Post Office Reform; its Importance and Practicability,* in which he argued persuasively in favor of instituting a postal system based on prepayment by the sender, in which a fixed fee of one penny would be charged to send a half-ounce letter anywhere within Great Britain. The system then in use required the person receiving the letter to pay the cost, which was calculated according to the weight of the letter as well as the distance it had traveled. Hill's plan was accepted by the government and went into effect in May 1840.

4673. Christmas cards were sent out in 1843 by the London museum director Henry Cole. His three-panel cards bore the now-standard inscription, "A Merry Christmas and a Happy New Year."

4674. Prepaid postcards were issued on October 1, 1869, in Austria. They were invented by Emmanuel Hermann of the Neustadt Military Academy

4675. International postal congress met on September 15, 1874, in Bern, Switzerland. Representatives of 22 states attended, including Germany, Great Britain, France, Italy, the United States, and Egypt. The conference produced the Treaty Concerning the Establishment of a

General Postal Union, the first agreement governing the international post, on October 9, and established a General Postal Union (later the Universal Postal Union) on July 1, 1875. The Universal Postal Union is now an agency of the United Nations.

4676. Postage meter was the invention of Karl Uchermann of Norway, and was manufactured in Oslo. The first meters were adopted by the Norwegian postal service in 1903.

4677. Junk mail was sent out in 1905 by druggist Lunsford Richardson of Selma, NC, USA, the inventor of Vicks VapoRub mentholated ointment. After the U.S. Post Office overturned its rule requiring mail to be addressed to a specific individual, Richardson mailed out hundreds of advertisements bearing only the designation "Boxholder."

4678. International dogsled mail left Lewiston, ME, USA, on December 20, 1928, with Alden William Pulsifer, postmaster of Minot, ME, in charge, and arrived on January 14, 1929, at Montreal, Canada. The mail traveled in a regular eight-foot mushing sled weighing 200 pounds (91 kilograms), pulled by six blackhead Eskimo dogs. They averaged 9 miles (14.5 kilometers) an hour and covered from 40 to 60 miles (64 to 97 kilometers) a day. The mail pouch contained 385 letters in government-stamped canceled envelopes. The trip was not an official one. The sled returned to Lewiston on February 2, 1929, having passed through 118 cities and covered 600 miles (965 kilometers), of which 90 percent was bare of snow.

POSTAL SERVICE—AIRMAIL

4679. Letter sent by airmail was sent on January 7, 1785, by Benjamin Franklin, the American scientist and statesman, while he was stationed in Europe as a treaty negotiator for the Continental Congress. The letter crossed the English Channel from Dover, England, to the Felmores Forest, France, in a hot-air balloon flown by the French balloonist Jean-Pierre François Blanchard and an American physician, John Jeffries. This was the first aerial sea voyage.

4680. Airmail flight by airplane took place in India on February 18, 1911, when Henri Becquet flew some 6,000 pieces of mail from Allahabad to Naini Junction, a distance of 5 miles (8 kilometers), in a Humber-Sommer biplane.

4681. Regular airmail service began in German South West Africa on May 18, 1914, with a route between Swakopmund and Windhoek.

4682. International military airmail route was briefly operated by the Italian Army between Brindisi, Italy, and Valona, Albania, from May to June 1917.

4683. Regular civil airmail service was operated by Austria beginning in March 1918 under the supervision of former military pilot A.R. von Marwil. The route included stops in Vienna; Lvov, Proskurov, and Kraków, Poland; and Odessa (now in Ukraine).

4684. International airmail service was inaugurated on March 3, 1919, between Seattle, WA, USA, and Victoria, BC, Canada, a distance of 74 miles, by American pilot and entrepreneur Edward Hubbard of the Hubbard Air Service, who piloted a Boeing Type C open cockpit biplane with pontoons. Airplane designer William Edward Boeing was a passenger on the flight. Regular service under contract began on October 14, 1920, and continued under successive contracts until June 30, 1937.

4685. Transpacific airmail flight and the first air crossing from California to the Philippines was made by the *China Clipper* of Pan American Airways, commanded by an American, Captain Edwin Charles Musick. The plane left San Francisco, CA, USA, on November 22, 1935, at 3:46 A.M. and made stops at Honolulu, Midway, Wake, and Guam, landing at Manila, Philippine Islands, on November 28 at 11:31 P.M., having covered 8,210 miles (13,210 kilometers) in 59 hours 48 minutes. It carried 58 sacks of mail containing 110,865 letters. The return trip started on December 1, 1935, from Manila and was completed on December 6 at 10:37 A.M. at San Francisco. The eastbound flight was made in 63 hours 24 minutes. The total flying time was 123 hours 12 minutes.

4686. Letter to circumnavigate the world by commercial airmail was dispatched from New York, NY, USA, on April 19, 1937. It was routed via San Francisco, Hong Kong, Penang, Amsterdam, and Brazil and was returned to New York on May 25, 1937.

4687. Transatlantic airmail service was inaugurated by Pan American Airways on May 20, 1939, when the *Yankee Clipper,* a 4-engine, 38-metric ton flying boat, took off from Manhasset Bay, Port Washington, NY, USA, at 9:07 P.M. It made one stop at Horta, in the Azores, and arrived at Lisbon, Portugal, on May 21 at 8:42 P.M. The elapsed time was 26.5 hours, the flying time 20 hours 16 minutes. It was commanded by Captain Arthur Earl La Porte and carried a crew of 14, 3 airline employees, and 1,680 pounds (762 kilograms) of mail.

POSTAL SERVICE—AIRMAIL—*continued*

4688. Airmail service by jet aircraft was begun by Avro Canada in 1950. The first flight was between Toronto and New York City on April 18.

POSTAL SERVICE—STAMPS

4689. Postage stamps designed to be affixed to letters as a sign of prepayment were printed by the British government in 1834 and were put into use on May 6, 1840, in London, England, when the world's first prepaid postal system, the Penny Post, went into operation. Sixty-four million of the one-penny "Penny Black" stamps were printed using equipment designed by American inventor Jacob Perkins. Blue stamps costing two pennies were also printed. Both designs showed Queen Victoria's profile. The stamps were the invention of Sir Rowland Hill, the postal reformer who had convinced Britain to adopt the new system. The stamps were printed in sheets and had to be cut apart with knives or scissors.

4690. Stamp collector known was a young woman who placed a notice in the *Times* of London in 1841 soliciting canceled postage stamps so that she could decorate her dressing room with them.

4691. Postage stamps with serrated edges that allowed them to be easily separated by hand were issued in Britain in 1854. The serrations were made by machine.

4692. Stamp dealer of record was Jean-Baptiste Constant Moëns, a bookseller of Brussels, Belgium. He began his philately business circa 1855.

4693. Stamp catalogs or lists for stamp collectors were issued in 1861 by two French philatelists, Oscar Berger-Levrault and Alfred Potiquet. By 1862, catalogs were also available from Frederick Booty, J.E. Gray, and Mount Brown in England and from the Belgian dealer Jean-Baptiste Constant Moëns, the first professional stamp dealer.

4694. Stamp albums for keeping stamp collections were introduced in Paris, France, in 1862 by Justin Lallier.

4695. Stamp magazine was the *British Monthly Intelligence,* which started and folded in 1862.

4696. Handbook for stamp collectors was *De la Falsification des Timbres-Poste,* published in 1863 by the Belgian stamp dealer Jean-Baptiste Constant Moëns. It contained suggestions on how to recognize forged stamps, and how to judge the value of authentic ones.

4697. Commemorative postage stamp was issued in 1888 by New South Wales, then a British colony, to celebrate the centenary of its founding. New South Wales became a province of the Commonwealth of Australia in 1901.

4698. Airmail stamps were issued on an experimental basis in 1917 by Italy and on a regular basis in 1918 by the United States.

4699. Stamp depicting basketball was issued in the Philippines in 1934.

PRINTING TECHNOLOGY

4700. Printed object was the Phaistos disk, discovered on July 3, 1908, by British archeologists excavating the ancient Minoan palace at Phaistos, Crete (part of modern Greece). It is a baked clay disk about 6.5 inches (16.6 centimeters) in diameter. The disk contains a spiral of 241 signs, never deciphered, that were created by impressing individual characters into the soft clay with a set of stamps. The Phaistos disk has been dated to circa 1700 BCE, some 2,500 years earlier than printing began in China.

4701. Rub printing process was t'a pen, invented circa 200 CE in China. T'a pen was a simple block printing process in which reproductions of important Confucian texts were created by laying sheets of rice paper onto stones carved with the texts, rubbing the back of the paper with a dark substance such as charcoal, and peeling it away to create a print. The process was also employed by Buddhist pilgrims used to copy religious texts inscribed in relief on marble pillars: they would make an impression of the carving by applying ink and pressing sheets of damp paper against the stone. A similar process was used to make copies of religious seals on which were carved images and prayers.

4702. Printer known by name was Wang Chieh, who used inked wood blocks to print the *Chin-kang Ching (Diamond Sutra),* a Chinese version of a popular Mahayana Buddhist text. The text was printed on six sheets of paper pasted together. A seventh sheet displayed the earliest printed illustrated frontispiece, which is also the earliest dated woodcut. The entire roll was 16 sheets long and about 1 foot wide. It contains the first imprint, in the form of a statement at the end, declaring that it was "printed on May 11, 868, by Wang Chieh, for free general distribution, in order in deep reverence to perpetuate the memory of his parents."

4703. Movable type was invented in China between 1041 and 1048 by Bi Zheng, described by the chronicler Shen Kua as "a man of the common people." He carved the characters of the Chinese language into individual blocks of clay, which he then hardened by baking. To print from these characters, he set them into an iron form, coated them with a mixture of paper ash, wax, and pine resin, and impressed them on sheets of paper. The type was kept in wooden cases in Bi Zheng's shop, where he oversaw a team of assistants.

4704. Printing press was designed and constructed by Johannes Gutenberg (full name, Johann Gensfleich zur Laden zum Gutenberg), a German metalworker and gem cutter then living in Strassburg (now Strasbourg, France). The first reference to it was made in a lawsuit brought against Gutenberg by the heirs of one of his financial backers in 1439. It was modeled on earlier papermaking presses, as well as on presses for making cheese, wine, and oil. The type was laid flat on a wooden platen and the paper was pressed down on it with a heavy screw that was turned by a handle.

4705. Typeface made in Europe in a non-Roman alphabet was the Greek font made circa 1465 by Conrad Sweynheym and Arnold Pannartz, two German printers who operated their press at the monastery of Subiaco, near Rome, Italy. They used it in their edition of the works of the third-century Christian writer Lactantius (Lucius Caecilius Firmianus), completed on October 29, 1465. The first book entirely printed in Greek was the *Bactrachomyomachia (Battle of the Frogs and Mice),* printed at Brescia circa 1474, probably by Thomas Ferrandus. The first printed Greek book that carries a date was a grammar by Constantinus Lascaris, the *Epitomé,* printed by Dionysius Paravisinus in Milan in 1476.

4706. Music printed from movable type was printed in 1476 by Ulrich Hahn, in Rome, Italy. He printed examples of plainsong (chant with a single melody) using red ink for the staff lines and black ink for the notes. This required two impressions on the paper. The first polyphonic music to be printed from movable type was *Harmonice Musices Odhecaton A,* a book of chansons printed in Venice in 1501 by Ottaviano del Petrucci. His method required multiple impressions painstakingly registered. In 1525 Pierre Haultin became the first to succeed in printing both notes and staff on paper in a single impression.

4707. Italics for typesetting were invented before 1500, as printers sought more compact typefaces that could be used in small-format books. The first significant use of italics in a book was as the body type for the Aldine Virgil, a pocket-sized edition printed in 1501 by the Aldine Press of Venice, Italy, under the master printer Aldus Manutius. The letters were designed and cut by Francesco Griffo, who modeled them after the handwriting of scribes in the papal chanceries. The slanted italics were reserved for lowercase only; uppercase letters were printed in roman.

4708. Licenses for printing presses were imposed in 1502 by Spain, which required approval by the court or the Church for the granting of a license.

4709. Printing press in the New World was co-founded in 1539 in Mexico City, Mexico, by Juan de Zumárraga, Mexico's first Roman Catholic bishop.

4710. Woman printer of note was Charlotte Guillard of Paris, France, who worked in the printing businesses of the two husbands she outlived and who afterwards ran her own shop. She died in 1556.

4711. Machine for printing wallpaper was invented in 1785 by a Frenchman, Christophe-Philippe Oberkampf.

4712. Lithograph was created in 1796 by the German playwright Aloys Senefelder in Prague (now the capital of the Czech Republic). Lithography is a printing technique based on the principle that grease and water do not mix. Experimenting with various printing methods as a way to inexpensively reproduce musical scores, Senefelder wrote in reverse on a flat slab of limestone with a greasy chalk, wetted the stone, then rolled ink onto the writing. He discovered that only the greasy marks held ink, and that the ink could be transferred to a sheet of paper pressed against the stone.

4713. Steam-powered printing press was developed by the German engineer Friedrich Koenig between 1803 and 1814. Koenig envisioned a completely mechanized printing system in which the movements of the platen and bed and the inking process were all geared to a steam engine.

PRINTING TECHNOLOGY—*continued*

4714. Flatbed press was invented in 1811 by Friedrich Koenig in England. It consisted of a flat printing bed onto which was fixed an inked printing plate. Above the bed was a rotating cylinder that was wrapped with sheets of paper. As the bed moved forward in a straight line, the cylinder was brought into contact with the plate and rolled along it, resulting in an inked impression on the paper.

4715. Steam-driven rotary press was installed in 1814 at the *Times* of London. The first stop-cylinder press driven by a steam engine, it employed two inked cylinders, each of which printed one sheet as the press bed moved back and forth. As many as 1,100 sheets per hour could be printed. The press was designed by the German engineers Friedrich Koenig and Andreas Bauer.

4716. Photoengraving was the creation of Joseph-Nicéphore Niepce of Chalon-sur-Saône, France, a lithographer. Since Niepce could not draw well, he sought ways of copying designs through the action of sunlight. In 1822 he succeeded in transferring an engraved image onto a plate coated with bitumen of Judea, a form of asphalt that hardens in the presence of light. The dark areas that remained were washed away with turpentine.

4717. Screen printing was invented in 1852 by the English scientist, inventor, and photographic pioneer William Henry Fox Talbot. Talbot was seeking a method of preparing photographic images for printed reproduction, and was experimenting with exposing images onto a steel etching plate coated with a photosensitive medium. Talbot's key insight was to break up the image into a mesh of small dots. He stretched a screen, a piece of thin black tulle cloth, between the subject and the covered steel plate, then uncovered the plate to expose it to the subject. The exposed image on the plate retained the mesh of the cloth. The plate, when etched, retained an evenly pitted texture that varied in depth according to the gray values of the image. The pitted areas held ink effectively and accurately reproduced the image when printed. Talbot's process was the forerunner of rotogravure.

4718. Roll-fed rotary press was the high-speed newspaper press invented by an American, William Bullock, in 1865. It was a fully mechanized, steam-driven printing system, which incorporated a cylindrical platen with stereotyped typeform. The paper was supplied from a large roll and was cut automatically after printing. Bullock's press was capable of printing 12,000 newspapers per hour.

4719. Letterpress halftone reproduction of a photograph was the work of the Canadians William Augustus Leggo and George Edouard Desbarats, two of the inventors of the halftone printing process. The reproduction, of a photo depicting Prince Arthur, a son of Queen Victoria, appeared in the first issue of the *Canadian Illustrated News* on October 30, 1869.

4720. Newspaper folding device was invented by the Americans William Bullock and Richard Hoe in 1870. They folded the output from Bullock's rotary newspaper press and could handle up to 12,000 papers an hour.

4721. Halftone printing plate for reproducing photographs in books, magazines, and newspapers was the work of Frederic Eugene Ives, a photographer at Cornell University, Ithaca, NY, USA, who received the first U.S. patent for the halftone printing screen and process on February 8, 1881. Earlier printers had conceived the idea of reproducing photographs by dividing them up into lines that could be transferred to a printer's plate. Ives was the first to devise a consistent method of producing halftones that could be applied to large printing operations. In 1878, he converted a photographic negative into a dot-screen gelatin relief from which he made a printing plate with good fidelity to the original image. The first halftone using the Ives process was printed in the June 1881 issue of the *Philadelphia Photographer*.

4722. Linotype machine was invented by German-born American inventor Ottmar Mergenthaler of Baltimore, MD, USA, who obtained a patent on August 26, 1884, on a "matrix making machine." The first Linotype machine to be used commercially was a blower machine installed on July 1, 1886, by the Mergenthaler Linotype Company in the printing plant of the *New York Tribune* and used to cast type for the July 3 issue. The machine had a keyboard assembling mechanism, a mechanism for casting a full line of type in a single bar, and a matrix lifting and distributing device. When the matrix was released from a vertical tube that resembled a pipe of an organ, it was carried by air blast along an inclined chute to its place in the assembling line of matrices.

4723. Machine capable of casting individual letters of type was the Monotype typesetter, invented by Tolbert Lanston of Washington, DC, USA. Lanston received five patents for it on June 7, 1887. The machine cast new type, letter by letter, from matrices that were used over and over.

4724. Xerography was invented by Chester Floyd Carlson, an American research physicist from New York, NY, USA. Xerography is the process of making dry paper duplicates based on principles of photoconductivity and electrostatics. Carlson saw the need for a high-volume copying process that was more economical and easier to handle than photostats and carbon copies. On October 22, 1938, in Astoria, NY, USA, Carlson made the first electrophotographic image on wax paper pressed against an electrostatically charged, sulfur-coated zinc plate dusted with fine dark powder. The image consisted of the message "10-22-38 Astoria." Carlson obtained a U.S. patent for the process, which he called xerography, on October 6, 1942.

4725. Copy machine that was commercially successfully was the Model 914, introduced in 1950 by the Haloid Company of Rochester, NY, USA. It used the xerographic duplicating process. An earlier Haloid copier, the Model A, was too slow and complicated to be successful. In 1961, Haloid changed its name to the Xerox Corporation.

4726. Color xerographic copier was marketed by Canon of Japan in 1973. An American firm, the Xerox Corporation, also introduced a plain-paper color copier in 1973.

R

RELIGION

4727. Portrait of a shaman is thought to be a figure painted on the wall of the Trois Frères cave at Lascaux, France, which dates to approximately 15,000 BCE. The figure is a creature with a shape that is generally human, but with a tail, a furry skin, large owlish eyes, and antlers on its head. It appears to be dancing. Historians believe that it is associated with a ritual performance to bring good fortune on a hunting expedition or to bring healing to a sick person.

4728. Religion known to archeologists is that of the Aborigines of northwestern Australia's Arnhem Land. Rock paintings of a mythical being called the Rainbow Serpent, dated to 6000 BCE, are believed to be icons of a religion inspired by sightings of a rare fish washed ashore when the sea level rose at the end of the last ice age.

4729. Mother goddess known was the Sumerian deity Ninhursag, who, in addition to being the goddess of stony ground (her name means "lady of the mountain"), had charge of the birth and death of living creatures, plant, animal, and human. She had several alternate names and identities, including Nintur ("lady birth giver"), Ninlil ("lady of the storm"), Ninmakh "exalted lady"), Dingirmakh ("exalted deity"), and Aruru ("dropper," referring to childbirth). The Sumerian culture, located in what is now Iraq, dates from the mid-fourth millennium BCE.

4730. Religion to offer divine judgment and salvation was the Egyptian worship of Osiris, the first deity who was said to function as a savior. Its foundation was an ancient legend in which the good king Osiris is murdered and dismembered by his brother, resurrected by his wife, Isis, and installed as the god of the dead after fathering Horus, his son. A funeral ritual based on this legend was performed for pharaohs by 2400 BCE and for commoners by 1400 BCE. During the embalment process, the story was recited, culminating in the incantation "As you do not die, Osiris, so this man does not die." It was expected that dead people, once revived in the afterlife, would be judged by Osiris according to the quality of their deeds and character, undergoing a final death if they failed the test, but receiving salvation and passing into immortality if they were proven to be *maa kheru* ("true of voice").

4731. Religious text extant is inscribed on the inner walls of the mortuary pyramid at Saqqarah, Egypt, belonging to the fifth-dynasty king Unas, who died circa 2325 BCE Known as the first of the Pyramid Texts, it contains magic spells, incantations, hymns, and prayers for the protection of the king in the afterlife.

4732. Legend of a resurrected deity whose cycle of life and death is identified with the yearly cycle of nature and fertility was that of Osiris, the Egyptian god of the dead. His murder at the hands of his brother Set and resurrection through the magical aid of his wife Isis was identified with the change of the seasons and the annual flooding of the Nile, the source of Egypt's agricultural irrigation. The first known depiction of Osiris was made circa 2300 BCE. The Sumerians in Mesopotamia (modern Iraq) had a similar myth, that of Tammuz (Dumuzi, in Akkadian), whose cult involved the annual reenactment of his marriage to the goddess Inanna and his descent to the underworld.

RELIGION—*continued*

4733. Verses in honor of a deity extant are two poems written on clay tablets in the 23rd century BCE and signed by Enheduanna, princess of Akkad and priestess in the temple at Ur (modern Tel-el-Muqayyar, Iraq). Both poems celebrate the goddess Inanna.

4734. Evidence of Chinese religion comes from the oracle bones used during the Shang dynasty (circa 1760–1100 BCE) to pose questions to the spirit world. The question was written out on the leg bone of an ox or the shell of a tortoise, which was then heated. The pattern of cracks that resulted was thought to communicate the answer.

4735. Prayer of thanksgiving for crops is mentioned on an inscribed Sumerian tablet from 1700 BCE that was found at Nippur (modern Niffer, Iraq). The text, considered the first farmers' almanac, presents a father's advice on agriculture. It includes instructions to pray to the deity Ninkilim "on the day the seed breaks through the ground."

4736. Monotheistic religious reformer was the 18th-dynasty Egyptian pharaoh Akhenaton (also spelled Akhnaton or Ikhnaton, also known as Amenhotep IV), who reigned from 1353 to 1336 BCE. He promoted a monotheistic cult of the sun god Aton (Akhenaton means "one useful to Aton") and obliterated mention of the older Egyptian gods, especially Amon, from public inscriptions. However, the Aton cult lasted only a few years after his reign, ending with the death of his son-in-law, Tutankhamen.

4737. Atheistic religious movements arose in India in the sixth century BCE. Jainism, founded by Vardhamana Mahavira, envisioned the salvation of the individual soul as the consequence of an ascetic life leading to detachment from material things. Although Jainism does not recognize a Supreme Being or Creator, the rites performed by lay people in Jain temples include veneration of Mahavira, other Jain saints, and Hindu deities. Buddhism, founded by Siddhartha Gautama, taught that all concepts of God and the individual soul are illusory and that recognition of the suffering inherent in all existence should give rise to a way of life based on compassion, truthfulness, mindfulness, and strong mental and physical self-discipline. The widely popular variant form known as Mahayana Buddhism ("the greater method") interpreted Buddhist teachings in a way that allowed for the worship of the Buddha and of aspiring buddhas, known as *bodhisattvas,* as deities.

4738. Druid known by name was the Celtic chieftain Divitiacus, whose tribe, the Aedui, occupied an area in Gaul that is now part of the Burgundy region of France. In 60 BCE he addressed the senators of Rome, asking for their help in repelling incursions by Germanic tribes. The unanticipated result was the invasion and takeover of Gaul by a Roman army under Julius Caesar. The word "druid" is derived from Celtic words meaning "oak knowledge" and refers to a class of men and women in Celtic tribal society who served as naturalists, oral historians, judges, teachers, diviners, doctors, and religious authorities. The first account of their activities occurs in historical books by the Syrian Greek philosopher Posidonios of Apamea, a friend of the Roman statesman Marcus Tullius Cicero, who met Divitiacus during his visit to Rome.

4739. Account of Germanic religion of importance was provided by the Roman historian Cornelius Tacitus in his ethnographic book *Germania,* also called *De origine et situ Germanorum.* Written circa 98 CE, the book drew on eyewitness reports to describe the rituals, customs, and political organization of several Germanic tribes on Rome's Rhine frontier. The first direct evidence comes from alliterative poems in the Old Norse language, particularly the *Elder Edda,* also known as the *Poetic Edda,* which was composed in Iceland circa 1270, though it contained 300-year-old material from the Scandinavian mainland. It includes a history of the Norse gods, the "Völuspá" ("Prophecy of the Seeress"), and poems about the sayings and doings of Odin, Loki, Thor, and the rest of the Norse pantheon.

4740. Druze imam was Hamzah ibn Ali, who in 1017 founded the Druze (or Druse) religion in Cairo, Egypt. The Druze religion is based on the tenet that the Egyptian Fatimid caliph al-Hakim was a messianic figure, the final incarnation of God, who will redeem his followers on Judgment Day. The sect takes its name from Muhammad ibn Isma'il ad-Darazi, the first missionary of the group, who in 1021 publicly proclaimed Druze doctrine in the main mosque of Cairo, causing a riot in which he was probably killed.

4741. Baha'i leader was Mirza Hoseyn Ali Nuri, known as Baha' Allah ("Glory of God"). In 1853 he was exiled from Iran for spreading the teachings of Mirza Ali Mohammad of Shiraz, a prophet known as the Bab ("gateway"), who was executed for heresy by Iran's Muslim Shiite leadership. In 1867, while he was in Constantinople (now Istanbul, Turkey), Baha'

Allah declared himself the messenger of God long awaited by the Bab's followers, who thus became the founding members of the Baha'i religion. Baha'i is a universalist faith that emphasizes the unity of all religions and the equality of humankind.

4742. Treatise on animism was *Primitive Culture* (1871) by the British anthropologist Edward Burnett Tylor, the first man to hold the chair of anthropology at Oxford University. Tylor, who coined the term "animism," provided the first systematic descriptions and analyses of the religions of tribal peoples.

4743. Celebration of the Mysteries at Eleusis in modern times was performed in 1981 by the American feminist theologian Carol P. Christ and a small group of followers. The Mysteries were originally celebrated at Eleusis, near Athens, Greece, by the ancient Greeks and Romans in honor of Demeter, the Grain Goddess, and her daughter, Persephone. The last known celebration was in 400 CE.

RELIGION—BUDDHISM

4744. Buddhist missionaries were the 60 original *bhikkus,* or monks, who joined the monastic order formed by Siddhartha Gautama circa 528 BCE. He instructed them to travel in all directions as nomadic teachers, saying: "Wander forth, *bhikkhus,* for the good of the many, for the happiness of the many, out of compassion for the world."

4745. Buddhist monks were the five disciples to whom the newly enlightened Buddha addressed his first sermon, the *Dhammacakkappavattana-sutta (Discourse Setting in Motion the Wheel of Doctrine),* in Varanasi (Benares), India, circa 528 BCE. After hearing this lesson, they received his permission to become *bhikkus,* or "sharers" (i.e., monks), and after hearing the Buddha's second sermon, the *Anattalakkhana-sutta,* on the doctrine of "no-self," they attained the status of *arhats,* or "perfected ones." They were shortly joined by a young convert, Yasa, and four of his friends, and then by another 50 of their acquaintances, who together formed the beginning of the *sangha,* the Buddhist monastic community.

4746. Statement of Buddhist doctrine is said to have been made by Siddhartha Gautama, the Buddha, at a deer park in Sarnath, near Benares (now Varanasi), India, circa 528 BCE. Having succeeded through meditation in reaching the state of *nirvana,* or enlightenment, the Buddha (according to traditional accounts) made the decision to remain in the world to teach others, and sought out the five companions with whom he had formerly shared an ascetic life. Finding them at the deer park, he gave his first lesson, called the *Dhammacakkappavattana-sutta (Discourse Setting in Motion the Wheel of Doctrine).* In this sermon, he proclaimed the Four Noble Truths, involving the individual's escape from suffering in this world through the rejection of the illusory self, the renunciation of all material cravings and attachments, and the following of the Eightfold Path—right understanding, right thought, right speech, right action, right occupation, right effort, right mindfulness, and right concentration.

4747. Buddhist monastery was Jetavana, built in a garden outside the walls of Shravasti, India (then the capital of the kingdom of Kosala) in the late sixth century BCE. It was constructed by a banker, Anathapindika, and presented by him to the Buddha (Siddhartha Gautama), whose headquarters it became.

4748. Buddhist nun was Mahapajapati Gotami, the aunt of Siddhartha Gautama, the Buddha. She and a number of her friends became *bhikkunis* (sharers, or nuns) circa 495 BCE, after the Buddha paid a visit to his original family, the chieftains of the Sakya people, in the northeast Indian town of Kapilavastu.

4749. Buddhist Council is traditionally said to have met at Rajagriha (now Rajgir, India) circa 483 BCE, soon after the death of Siddhartha Gautama, the Buddha. At this meeting, 500 *arhats,* or "perfected ones," are said to have compiled and recited texts containing instruction on Buddhist precepts and rules for monastic life. Historians doubt that this council actually took place. If they are correct, the first council was the one held about a century later at Vaishali, which was intended to resolve a dispute over the permissibility of leniencies in monastic life.

4750. Buddhist monastic rule was the *vinaya,* or "discipline," a set of rules attributed to the Buddha, Siddhartha Gautama, who is said to have drawn them up before his death circa 483 BCE. Since he named no successor, the rules were intended to serve as permanent guidelines for the Buddhist monastic community, the *sangha.* They outline a democratic system in which decisions are made by the assembled monks in council. The chief *vinaya* text is the *Patimokkha (Requirements),* which is recited communally every fortnight in monasteries of the Theravada school.

RELIGION—BUDDHISM—*continued*

4751. Buddhist monument was the stupa built circa 483 BCE at the cremation site of Gautama Buddha in Kusinara (the modern Kasia, India). The stupa was a hemispherical mound surrounded by a gated, circular balustrade, and topped by a stack of discs, each of which corresponded to a celestial domain.

4752. Schism in Buddhism arose early in the fourth century BCE with the establishment of the Mahasanghika school (meaning "great community"). Its adherents emphasized the transcendent nature and infinite purity of the Buddha, attributing his earthly life as Siddhartha Gautama to an illusion. They also adopted more lenient monastic rules and introduced revised interpretations of many points of Buddhist teaching. Their viewpoint eventually developed into Mahayana Buddhism, the syncretic movement that took hold in China, Korea, Tibet, Mongolia, Japan, and Vietnam, in which the Buddha became the head of a pantheon of deities. Theravada Buddhism, the "doctrine of the elders," was generally followed in Sri Lanka, Thailand, Cambodia, and Laos.

4753. Buddhist inscriptions were the "rock edicts" of India, made by order of Asóka, third emperor of the Maurya dynasty, to explain to his people the moral tenets of Buddhism, which he embraced circa 261 BCE. These explanations and instructions, centering on compassion, honesty, and nonviolence, were inscribed on the rock walls of caves, on cliffs, and on stone pillars, in a variety of Prakrit languages (Middle Indo-Aryan) derived from Sanskrit. Since Buddhist oral teachings were not written down until the first century CE, the rock edicts constitute the first historical evidence for Buddhist ideas.

4754. Establishment of Buddhism as a state religion was made by Asóka, the third Maurya emperor of India, soon after his own conversion circa 261 BCE. He died between 238 and 232 BCE. The last Maurya emperor was murdered some 50 years later, and Buddhism was disestablished and became a persecuted sect.

4755. Country outside India to accept Buddhism was Sri Lanka, which received a team of missionaries circa 251 BCE. These were a prince and princess of India, Mahendra and Sanghamittha, who had been sent by the Indian emperor Asóka, himself a convert from Hinduism who had made Buddhism the state religion of India. Through persuasion and example, the emissaries succeeded in convincing the king of Sri Lanka, Devanampiya Tissa, to accept Buddhism, along with his family and eventually his subjects. Since Buddhism became extinct in India in the ninth century, Sri Lanka has been the country with the oldest continuous Buddhist tradition.

4756. Biography of the Buddha was the *Mahavastu (Great Story),* an anonymous Sanskrit work from the second century BCE, with later additions. It contains descriptions of many miraculous and legendary events associated with the life of Siddhartha Gautama, the founder of Buddhism.

4757. Images of the Buddha were introduced in Buddhist art in the first century CE in two different locations, Gandhara (an area now part of northwestern Pakistan and eastern Afghanistan) and Mathura (in what is now the state of Uttar Pradesh, India). The statues made in Gandhara were influenced by Greco-Roman depictions of gods and emperors. Those made in Mathura were influenced by the local tradition of Hindu statuary. Before this time, Buddhist art did not depict the Buddha himself, but relied on symbols, such as the Bodhi tree, the footprint, the swastika, the wheel, the vase of flowers, and the stupa.

4758. Buddhist site of importance in China is the cave-temples at Yungang in northern Shanxi province, carved circa 460 CE in the sandstone cliffs at Yungang at the order of the emperor Wencheng of the Northern Wei dynasty (circa 386–535). Each of the five caves, commemorating the first five Northern Wei emperors, contained a colossal Buddha or bodhisattva, thus linking the power of the emperors with devotion to Buddha. Nine other religious caves at the site are of later, nonimperial origin. Buddhist missionaries entered China in the first century CE; the first Chinese woman to become a Buddhist nun was Zhong Lingyi, in 317.

4759. Zen Buddhism is said by tradition to have originated in the fifth century BCE with Mahakashyapa, an Indian disciple of the Buddha who achieved enlightenment in an instant when the Buddha held up a flower. In 520, the Indian monk Bodhidharma brought the concept of spontaneous enlightenment to Kuang, China (modern Canton), where it attracted adherents who developed it into a school of Buddhism called Ch'an, a word derived from the Sanskrit *dhyana,* meditation. The Chinese character for *Ch'an* is pronounced "zen" in Japan.

4760. Introduction of Buddhism to Tibet was made by its second king, the military leader Srong-brtsan-sgam-po, who began his rule in 629. Among his wives were two Buddhist women, one from Nepal, the other from China. In order to have Buddhist texts translated into the Tibetan language, he arranged for a scholar to devise a script, based on an Indian model.

4761. Buddhist monastery in Tibet was built at Bsam-yas (Samye) during the reign of Khri-srong-lde-btsan (Khrisong Detsen). It was completed in 749 under the supervision of Padmasambhava (Guru Rinpoche), the famed Indian teacher of Tantric Buddhism. Seven Tibetans were in the first group to be ordained as monks there.

4762. Buddhist priest to be married was the Japanese priest Shinran, founder in 1224 of the Jodo Shinshu, or True Pure Land sect, a devotional branch of Buddhism that teaches the possibility of rebirth in a paradise called the Pure Land through the recitation of the name of Amitabha, "the Buddha of Infinite Light." Though Buddhist priests were required to be celibate, Shinran married a woman named Eshinni after he was exiled for promoting his religious reforms.

4763. Dalai Lama was Dge-'dun-grub-pa (Gendutrup), abbot from 1391 of Tashilhunpo monastery in central Tibet, a monastery of the Gelukpa school. He was considered the first Gelukpa *tulku*—an enlightened being who manifests an aspect of the Buddha—and was known by the title Gwelya Rinpoche. Subsequent *tulkus* were held to be his reincarnation. The third Gwelya Rinpoche was given the title Dalai Lama in 1578 by the Mongol leader Altan Khan, with whom he had formed an alliance, and it was retrospectively given to his former incarnations. (The Mongolian word *dalai* means "ocean," the word *lama* means "the higher one.") Between 1642, when the fifth Dalai Lama took office, and 1959, when the Chinese invaded Tibet, the Dalai Lama was also the temporal ruler of Tibet.

4764. Popularizer of Zen Buddhism in the West was Daisetsu Teitaro Suzuki, a disciple of the Japanese Zen master Soen who lived in the United States from 1897 to 1909 and intermittently thereafter. His lectures and writings, including *Outline of Mahayana Buddhism*, published in 1907, attracted a wide audience and helped prepare the way for the contemporary American interest in Zen.

RELIGION—BUDDHISM—SCRIPTURES

4765. Buddhist religious texts originated as oral teachings that were compiled in India over the course of five centuries, beginning with the life of Siddhartha Gautama, the Buddha, who died in 483 BCE. They were committed to writing in Sri Lanka in the first century BCE, using the literary language Pali. The texts are divided into three sections and hence are called the *Tipitaka (The Three Baskets)*. The earliest part, the *Vinaya Pitaka (Basket of Disciplines)*, outlines the rules for monastic life; the second, *Sutta Pitaka (Basket of Discourses)*, relates discourses, teachings, and sermons of the Buddha; the third is the *Abhidhamma Pitaka (Basket of Special Doctrine)*. A Sanskrit version, the *Tripitaka*, was written down later.

4766. Buddhist manuscripts extant are the Kharosthi scrolls, 29 fragments of manuscripts written on birch bark in the Indian Gandhari dialect of Prakrit and in the Kharosthi script, in the holdings of the British Library in London, England. The exact location of their discovery is unknown, but was probably Afghanistan. The scrolls are believed to date to circa 100 CE. The texts include Gandhari versions of such verse compilations as the *Rhinoceros' Horn Sutra* and the *Songs of Lake Anavatapta.*

4767. Important text of Mahayana Buddhism was the *Saddharmapundarika-sutra (Lotus Sutra)*, written in Sanskrit in southern India in the first century CE. It portrays the Buddha as a divinity who takes various forms, offers a multiplicity of teachings, and practices magical actions, all for the purpose of bringing other beings to enlightenment. In China and Japan, the translated *Lotus Sutra* became the object of veneration by several Buddhist sects.

4768. Printed edition of the Buddhist canon was prepared by printers in Chengdu, Szechwan province, China, in 985, on the commission of the emperor Taizong. The edition of the *Tripitaka*, the Buddhist scriptures, took twelve years to complete and required 130,000 wood blocks.

4769. English translations of early Buddhist texts were translated from the Pali language by the English scholar Thomas William Rhys Davids, founder of the Pali Text Society, who became interested in Buddhism when he was stationed in the British civil service in Ceylon (now Sri Lanka). His book *Buddhist Suttas from the Pali* was published in 1881.

RELIGION—CHRISTIANITY

4770. Christians were individual Jews living in Jerusalem in 33 CE who were persuaded that the preacher and reformer known as Yeshua, or Yehoshua, had returned from the dead to manifest himself as the *Moshiach,* or "anointed one" (in Jewish theology, a descendant of King David who will save Israel from its enemies). The Hebrew name Yeshua was later changed to its Greek form, Iesous, from which was derived the name Jesus. The title *Moshiach* ("messiah" in English) was translated into Greek as Christos, from which was derived the title "Christ." The designation "Christians" to identify those who agreed with this view of Yeshua—a minority of the Jewish population— was first used in the Galatian city of Antioch, Asia Minor (now Turkey), circa 35–40 CE.

4771. Christian martyr was St. Stephen, a Hellenized Jew and follower of Jesus who was stoned by Jews outside the city of Jerusalem circa 36 CE for declaring that worship in the Beit ha-Mikdash (the Temple) was an act of idolatry.

4772. Center of Christian missionary activity was Antioch, a city in the Roman province of Galatia (now in Turkey), where Saul of Tarsus, a tentmaker and rabbi who had adopted the Greek name Paul, attempted circa 40 CE to convince both Jews and pagan Greeks that the recently executed Jesus of Nazareth was in fact the messiah whose coming was expected at any moment by the Jews. Paul, later known as St. Paul, had already done some missionary work in Syria and his homeland of Cilicia. His converts among the Gentiles increased after he abolished the requirement to live by Jewish law, including the practice of circumcision.

4773. Gnostic with something approaching a documented history was Simon Magus, a first-century Jewish adept of magic from Samaria. According to the account given in the New Testament, he became a convert to Christianity, evidently for the purpose of obtaining a magical ability to transmit the Holy Spirit. One of numerous Christian and Hellenistic followers of the religio-philosophical movement known as Gnosticism, he popularized the idea that evil came into the world through the breaking of the monotheistic unity of God. Later adherents developed the notion of a duality of good and evil and of the redemptive power of esoteric knowledge conveyed through divine revelation.

4774. Gospel was the Gospel of Mark, written, according to scholars, sometime between the execution of St. Peter in 64 and the fall of Jerusalem to the Romans in 70. Although it was the earliest gospel to be composed, and is thus considered the best source of information on the life of Jesus, it is placed second in the New Testament canon, after that of Matthew. The author, who wrote in Greek, was identified by the second-century bishop Papias as Peter's secretary. The word "gospel" is derived from the Anglo-Saxon words for "good story."

4775. Christian church order was the *Didache (Teaching),* also known as the *Teaching of the Twelve Apostles,* the earliest surviving work of Christian patristic literature. Written in Greek, the *Didache* is thought to have been compiled in Syria in the second century CE from materials already in use among Christians in various localities, including rules on prayer, the Eucharist, baptism of converts, and appointment of bishops. It also took up moral questions and described signs by which to detect the imminence of the Second Coming.

4776. Christian institution of higher learning was the School of Alexandria, founded circa 150 by Pantaenus, Clement, and Origen in Alexandria, Egypt. It was best known for teaching an allegorical method of interpreting Greek literature and myths in the light of orthodox Christian doctrine.

4777. Heretical Christian sectarian movement was Montanism, also known as the Cataphrygian Heresy. It was founded in the mid-second century by Montanus, a Phrygian convert who was recognized throughout Asia Minor (modern Turkey) as having prophetic and charismatic powers, which were also claimed by some of his followers. Montanus preached that he had initiated a new age, the Age of the Holy Spirit, superseding the Age of the Son (Christianity), and required a strict standard of morality in preparation for the end of the world.

4778. Christian creed was the Apostles' Creed, a set of affirmations concerning the life, death, and divinity of Jesus and fundamental aspects of Christian doctrine. It is thought to have originated in the questions which a second- or third-century bishop would put to a prospective convert before baptism (although some scholars believe that it developed from a second-century Greek hymn). By the year 1200, it was accepted by the western branch of the Roman Catholic Church, though not by its eastern branch, as a formal statement of faith. In composition, it predates the Nicene Creed, accepted at the Council of Nicaea in 325.

4779. Christian church built for the purpose may be a basilica discovered in June 1998 in Aqaba, Jordan, by a team of Jordanian and American archeologists led by Thomas Parker of North Carolina State University, NC, USA. Unlike older churches, it was not built originally for another purpose, such as housing. The building has been tentatively dated to circa 280.

4780. Christian monk is considered to have been St. Anthony of Egypt (also spelled Antony and Antonios). From circa 286 CE to 305, he lived alone on the mountain Pispir (now called Dayr al-Maymun) in the Egyptian desert, becoming the first Christian hermit and the first of the Desert Fathers. The demonic temptations that, according to legend, he withstood there later became the subject of much Christian art. Other Christians who came to the desert to follow his example were later organized by him into loose communities, earning him the title of founder of Christian monasticism.

4781. Establishment of Christianity as the state religion was made in Armenia in 303, when King Tiridates III, having been converted by St. Gregory the Illuminator, made adherence to Christianity the law of the land.

4782. Celibacy rule for Christian priests was promulgated by the Council of Elvira, held at Elvira, Spain, circa 306 CE. Spanish priests and bishops, including those already married, were required to give up sexual relations. The rule requiring all priests in the Roman Catholic Church to remain unmarried and celibate was established at the first and second Lateran Councils, held at Rome in 1123 and 1139.

4783. Legal recognition of Christians in the Roman Empire was issued in Rome by the ailing emperor Gaius Galerius Valerius Maximianus, a brutal persecutor of Christians. On his deathbed, and fearing that his illness was the revenge of the Christian god, Galerius proclaimed an edict of toleration on April 30, 311.

4784. Christian monastery was founded by St. Pachomius at Tabennisi, on the east bank of the Nile River in Upper Egypt. Pachomius, an Egyptian, was a former soldier in the Roman army, where he was converted to Christianity. In about the year 314 he decided to become one of the many Christian hermits who were living in the Egyptian desert, some in solitude, others in informal collectives. Over the next few years he brought together a group of hermits at Tabennisi to live as an organized community, sharing meals, work, and prayer.

4785. Historian of the Christian church was Eusebius of Caesarea, who lived circa 260–340. His *Ecclesiastical History,* begun during the Roman persecutions and revised several times between 312 and 324, is the principal source of information on the early Christian church and its relation to the Roman Empire.

4786. Rule book for Christian monastic life was the *Rule* of St. Pachomius, a book written circa 315 that set forth the daily routine of his monastery at Tabennisi, Egypt, and established a structure of authority for running it. The first of its kind in Christianity, it was used by Pachomius as the foundation for eleven monasteries and nunneries that attracted some 7,000 people.

4787. Ecumenical Christian creed was the Nicene Creed (also called the Niceno-Constantinopolitan Creed). It was formulated in 325 at the First Council of Nicaea (now Iznik, Turkey), convened by the Roman Emperor Constantine the Great, and modified at a second council held in Constantinople (now Istanbul, Turkey) in 381. The only creed accepted as authoritative by the Roman Catholic, Eastern Orthodox, Anglican, and major Protestant churches, the Nicene Creed held that God the Father and God the Son are consubstantial and coeternal and that Arianism, the doctrine in which Jesus is a being created by and subservient to God, was heretical.

4788. Formal attempt to define the nature of Jesus was undertaken in 325 at Nicaea (now Iznik, Turkey) by a council of delegates from the various Christian churches, summoned and presided over by Constantine the Great, the emperor of Rome, though he was not yet a baptized convert. The council adopted a creed, known as the Nicene Creed, that defined Jesus as "of one substance" with God, condemning as heresy the view held by Arius of Alexandria that Jesus was a created being, not fully divine. This was the first of the Church's ecumenical councils.

4789. Stylite was the Syrian pillar hermit St. Simeon, called Simeon Stylites or Simeon the Elder, who lived near Aleppo, Syria, in the fifth century. Simeon was so revered as a miracle-working monk that the people constantly importuned him for cures and wonders. To escape them, in 420 he erected a pillar 6 feet (2 meters) high, topped with a small platform that became his dwelling place. Later he built a column 50 feet (15 meters) high; the platform atop this pillar had a railing for safety and could be

RELIGION—CHRISTIANITY—*continued*

reached by a long ladder. Disciples and converts were sometimes allowed to come up, bringing food and gifts, but Simeon himself reportedly never came down and died on the platform in 459.

4790. Convent in Europe was the women's monastery at St. John's, founded by Bishop (later St.) Caesarius at Arles (now in France) in 512. It was headed by his sister, St. Caesaria, the first abbess. The first illuminated books copied and illustrated by women may have been created here, according to Caesarius' instructions: "Between psalms and fasts, vigils and reading, let the virgins of Christ copy holy books beautifully."

4791. Archbishop of Canterbury was St. Augustine of Canterbury, also called Austin, who was probably born in Rome circa 550. The founder of the Christian Church in southern England, as well as of Christ Church, Canterbury, England, he was consecrated bishop of the English by St. Virgilius at Arles, France, in 597.

4792. Christian missionaries in China belonged to a Nestorian delegation that arrived in 635, headed by the Persian bishop A-lo-pen. At Ch'ang-an (modern Xian) they were granted an audience with Emperor T'ai Tsung, who gave them funds to built a monastery. The community lasted until the early tenth century. A stone monument, set up in 781 and discovered by Jesuit missionaries in 1625, records the beginnings of the mission.

4793. Christian writer in Arabic was the Syrian bishop, theologian, and linguist Theodurus Abu Qurrah (also known as Theodore abu Kurra), who lived from 750 to 825. Theodurus Abu Qurrah was a Melchite monk at the monastery of St. Sabas near Jerusalem, where circa 780 he began writing on philosophic Christian theology for an Arabic-speaking audience.

4794. Christian scholastic to attempt a scientific construction of theology, adducing logical reasons for things that had hitherto been matters of faith, was St. Anselm of Canterbury, abbot of the monastery of Bec, France, and later archbishop of Canterbury, England. His *Monologium* (1077) identified God as absolute perfection that can be understood by human reason. In his *Proslogium (Address),* he offered the first ontological argument for the existence of God, asserting that the ability of the human mind to conceive of God implies the existence of God. The scholastics were also called the Schoolmen.

4795. Crusading order of knights were the Knights of Malta, originally known as the Hospitallers of St. John of Jerusalem. The Knights were founded in a Benedictine hospital in Jerusalem and dedicated to the care of Christian pilgrims to the Holy Land. The order was formally recognized by Pope Paschal II on February 15, 1113, five years before the founding of the Knights Templars. The Knights also pledged to make war on Islam and through the 14th and 15th centuries preyed on Muslim shipping from their home bases in Rhodes and, from 1530, in Malta. Since 1961 they have been known as the Sovereign Military Hospitaller Order of St. John of Jerusalem, of Rhodes and of Malta.

4796. Christian radical reformer was Arnold of Brescia (Arnaldo da Brescia), former prior of the monastery in Brescia, Italy, who called for an end to the exercise by the Church of temporal power, and for a reversal of widespread corruption among the clergy. He was condemned as a schismatic in 1139 and as a heretic in 1141, and was executed for participating in the rebellion against papal rule that produced a short-lived republic in Rome.

4797. Book of Christian mysticism by a woman to be read widely was *Scivias (Know the Ways of the Lord).* It was written between 1141 and 1152 by the visionary, composer, and naturalist St. Hildegard of Bingen, the abbess of Rupertsberg, near Bingen (now in Germany). Her mystical book of knowledge contains 26 apocalyptic visions with vivid color illuminations painted under her direct guidance. Several images depict her receiving a mystical insight from heaven as a colorful flash of light piercing her head or eyes, leading some medical historians to associate her visions with migraines.

4798. Missionary society supported by lay people, rather than by a religious establishment, was the Company for Propagating the Gospel in New England and Parts Adjacent in North America, founded in England in 1649 to support the work of John Eliot. Eliot was a Puritan minister who emigrated in 1631 to the Massachusetts Bay Colony (now Boston, MA, USA), where he became pastor of the Roxbury church and began a campaign to convert the Massachusetts Indians to Christianity.

4799. Sunday school was established in 1780 in Gloucester, England, by social worker and journalist Robert Raikes. Raikes opened his religious school on Sunday because many poor children worked in factories the other six days of the week. Local women were hired to teach reading and the Anglican church catechism.

4800. Christian college in Africa was Fourah Bay College, founded in 1827 for the education of Anglican clergy in Sierra Leone, then a British colony. It is now part of the University of Sierra Leone.

4801. Mormon church was organized on April 6, 1830, at Fayette, NY, USA, by Joseph Smith. The church's doctrines were based on the *Book of Mormon,* a narrative about the journey of an ancient Israelite family from Jerusalem to America, where some of them, builders of a disappeared civilization, receive teachings from the risen Jesus and others become the ancestors of the American Indians. The text was said to have been translated by Smith, with divine aid, from a set of golden plates on which it had been recorded in an Egyptian language.

4802. Ecumenical conference was the World Student Christian Federation, organized in 1895 by the American Methodist missionary John Raleigh Mott, the student secretary of the International Committee of the Young Men's Christian Association. The conference was attended primarily by young Protestant missionaries.

4803. International ecumenical missionary organization was the International Missionary Council, established at the Edinburgh Conference of 1910 with the aim of promoting the Christian faith worldwide and applying its teachings to social problems. The International Missionary Council was absorbed in 1961 by the World Council of Churches.

4804. Unification Church teachings were preached by Sun Myung Moon in 1946, when he was a member of the Presbyterian Church in what is now North Korea, and described in his book *Divine Principle,* published in 1952. Moon founded the Holy Spirit Association for the Unification of World Christianity (the Unification Church) in Seoul, South Korea, in 1954. His theology revolves around the need to restore God's kingdom on earth through a perfected, sinless family.

4805. Meeting of the heads of the Anglican and Catholic churches took place on March 23, 1966, when Arthur Michael Ramsey, the Archbishop of Canterbury, head of the Church of England (Anglican Church) met with Pope Paul VI in Rome, Italy. The Anglican and Roman Catholic churches parted ways in 1534.

RELIGION—CHRISTIANITY—ORTHODOX

4806. Patriarchates of the Orthodox Church were the two patriarchates established by the Council of Chalcedon (now Kadeköy, Turkey) in 451. One was Jerusalem, whose Christian community, which vanished after the city's devastation by the Romans in 130, had recently been reconstituted. The other was Constantinople (formerly Byzantium; now Istanbul, Turkey), whose bishop had been recognized since 381 as the equal of the bishop of Rome (the pope) as a consequence of the transfer of the imperial capital from Rome to Byzantium 50 years earlier.

4807. Ban on the use of icons in Christian worship was proclaimed in 730 by the Byzantine emperor Leo III, called Leo the Isaurian, who considered the veneration of religious images to be idolatrous. He enforced the ban over the objections of the Patriarch of Constantinople, Germanus I, and of many followers of Eastern church. The Iconoclastic Controversy continued for more than a century, with icon veneration restored in 787, banned again in 815, and restored for good in 843. Objections to religious images in Christian worship were voiced as early as the fourth century by Eusebius, Asterias, Epiphanius, and other prelates.

4808. Orthodox monastery was the Great Laura, established in 963 by St. Athanasius the Athonite (also called Athanasius of Trebizond) on Mount Athos, in northeastern Greece. With help from the Byzantine emperors Nicephorus II Phocas and his successor, John I Tzimisces, Athanasius succeeded in organizing the solitary hermits who already occupied the mountain into a monastic community under the rule of an abbot. So many Greek and Russian Orthodox monasteries were eventually built on Mount Athos that it was declared a theocratic republic in 1927.

4809. Orthodox saint from Russia was St. Olga (or Helga). During her reign as regent of the principality of Kiev (now part of Ukraine) from 945 to 964, she became a Christian convert and worked to make other converts. The country became entirely Christian during the reign of her grandson Vladimir.

4810. Patriarch of Moscow was St. Job, previously Metropolitan of Moscow, who was elevated by Patriarch Jeremiah of Constantinople (now Istanbul) in 1589. The Patriarch of Moscow is the leader of Russian Orthodoxy. His most notable act was the choice of Boris Godunov as tsar after the death of Tsar Fyodor in 1598. St. Job was canonized in 1989.

RELIGION— CHRISTIANITY— ORTHO-DOX—*continued*

4811. Patriarch of Moscow who was not Russian by birth was Metropolitan Alexis of Leningrad (now St. Petersburg), born Aleksey Mikhailovich Ridiger in 1929 in Tallinn, Estonia. He was elevated to Patriarch Alexis II of Moscow and All Russia, the leader of Russian Orthodoxy, on June 7, 1990. The election was the first (and last) under the Soviet system in which the patriarch was chosen without government pressure.

4812. Pope to visit a mainly Christian Orthodox country was Pope John Paul II (Karol Wojtyla). In May 1999, he made a three-day visit to Romania, whose citizens belong primarily to the Romanian Orthodox church. Pope John Paul and Romania's Orthodox Patriarch Teoctist attended a common prayer service on May 7, then made a joint appeal for Christian unity before a crowd of several thousand well-wishers.

RELIGION—CHRISTIANITY—PROTESTANT

4813. Protestant hymnbook was a collection of 89 hymns in the Czech language. It was published in Prague, Bohemia (the present-day Czech Republic), on January 13, 1501, for the group Unitas Fratrum, pacifist followers of the Protestant leader Jan Hus. The book was also the first Christian hymnbook to be printed in a commonly spoken language, rather than in Latin.

4814. Date in the Protestant Reformation is considered to be October 13, 1517, when Martin Luther, an Augustinian prior, parish preacher, and professor at the University of Wittenberg, Germany, nailed to the door of the Wittenberg church (or, according to some scholars, sent to the bishops) a document known as the *Ninety-five Theses,* in which he condemned, on theological grounds, the practice of selling papal indulgences. The name "protestant" was applied to Luther's reform movement in 1529. There had already been various calls for reform within the Church for some 400 years.

4815. Major statement of Protestant theological doctrine was *Loci communes rerum theologicarum,* published in Germany in 1521. Its author, Philipp Melanchthon, was professor of Greek at the University of Wittenberg, where he was a friend and colleague of Martin Luther, professor of biblical exegesis. *Loci*

communes was the first systematic explanation of Luther's evangelical interpretations of sin, law, and grace and their differences from the interpretations current in the Roman Catholic Church.

4816. Protestant liturgies of different kinds were created in 1523. In Germany, Martin Luther issued an altered version of the Latin Mass, the *Formula missae et communionis,* which was followed in 1526 by the *Deutsche Messe,* a service in which Latin prose was replaced by metrical paraphrases in German. In Switzerland, Huldrych Zwingli rejected the entire rite and substituted a program of readings from the New Testament.

4817. Protestant reformer to abolish the Mass was Huldrych Zwingli, priest at the Grossmünster in Zürich, Switzerland. Beginning in 1523, he instituted a series of changes in worship, including the removal of images from the church and the elimination of organ music, both of which he said were without biblical foundation. The Mass was replaced by a Communion service accompanied by readings from the New Testament.

4818. Adult baptisms in modern times were conducted in January 1525 in Zürich, Switzerland, by Konrad Grebel, founder of the radical Anabaptist movement called the Swiss Brethren, in defiance of the rulings of the Zürich city council, which required infant baptism.

4819. Anabaptist church was founded at Zollikon, near Zürich, Switzerland, on January 21, 1525, when Konrad Grebel, Felix Manx, and a number of like-minded people broke away from Huldrych Zwingli's reform movement over the issue of obedience to a government decree requiring them to perform infant baptism, wihch they believed to be invalid. The Anabaptists refused to recognize state authority in spiritual matters and were persecuted as a result. The movement includes the Mennonites, the Amish, and the Hutterites.

4820. Lutheran churches were founded in Germany after Martin Luther began his dissident evangelical movement within the Roman Catholic Church. These early churches adopted as their basic statement of faith the Augsburg Confession, a document written chiefly by Luther's colleague Philipp Melanchthon and presented on June 25, 1530, to the Holy Roman Emperor Charles V as an explanation of Lutheran theology.

4821. Anglican Communion church was the Church of England, which asserted its independence from the Roman Catholic Church in 1534, when Parliament, under pressure from King Henry VIII, replaced papal authority over the church with the authority of the monarch. The arrangement became permanent in 1558 with the accession of Henry's Protestant daughter, Queen Elizabeth I.

4822. Calvinist (Reformed) church was the community of French Protestant refugees that assembled in the 1530s in Geneva, Switzerland, and that was headed from 1536 by one of their number, John Calvin (born Jean Cauvin). His theology was distinguished by its assertion that the atonement for sin effected by the death of Jesus was efficacious only for a minority of believers, the "elect," who were predestined for salvation.

4823. Hymnbook containing hymns in English was *Goostly Psalmes and Spiritualle Songes*, a collection of 24 hymns compiled by Miles Coverdale and published in London, England, in 1539. Nine of the hymns were in Latin and 15 in English, most of them translations of German songs. The book was banned by the Church as soon as it was published.

4824. Protestant heretic to be martyred for his beliefs was the Spanish physician Miguel Serveto (Michael Servetus), the author of books refuting the concept of the Trinity, arguing against infant baptism, and urging a complete reconstitution of organized Christianity. He was burned in effigy by the Roman Catholic Inquisition in France after he escaped during his trial, but was rearrested in Geneva, Switzerland, in 1553 at the instigation of the Protestant leader John Calvin, who successfully sought his conviction and execution.

4825. Presbyterian church was founded by the French followers of John Calvin, known as Huguenots, in 1559, when the Reformed Church of France adopted an organizational structure in which leadership was provided by ministers and lay elders who made decisions collectively. Presbyterian churches are Reformed (Calvinist) churches governed by courts and councils, rather than by a hierarchy of persons.

4826. Puritans were clergymen within the Church of England who sought to purge the church of residual Catholicism after the accession of Queen Elizabeth I. They also balked at having to obey her orders in matters of liturgy, vestments, and, ultimately, of the entire structure of church government, which they wished to change from episcopal hierarchy to presbyterian collegiality. From 1565 they were known as Puritans, or Precisians. Some broke away to establish independent congregations; among these Separatists were the refugees who eventually settled in Plymouth, MA (in the future USA), and became known as the Pilgrims. Other Puritans attempted reform from within and were rebuffed. Eventually they became allied with the parliamentary attack on the monarchy that resulted in civil war and the execution of King Charles I.

4827. Unitarian church was the Minor Reformed Church of Poland, founded in 1565 after the Polish Reformed Church was rent by a schism over the legitimacy of the Trinity. Poland had become a refuge for persecuted Italian and Spanish humanists who questioned the Trinity, the divinity of Jesus, and the doctrine of atonement. The first Unitarian church to be known by that name was founded in Transylvania (now Romania) in 1568, when Bishop Ferenc Dávid changed the Great Church at Kolozsvár from Calvinist to Unitarian worship. He ultimately turned against the idea that Jesus, as a human being, should be worshipped at all, and was condemned to life in prison for "Judaizing activities."

4828. Protestant service in the New World was conducted in 1579 by the English mariner Francis Drake aboard his ship the *Golden Hind*, anchored in what is now San Francisco Bay, San Francisco, CA, USA.

4829. Baptist church was founded in 1609 in Amsterdam, the Netherlands, by a group of English Separatists led by John Smyth. Smyth contended that Scripture supported the practice of baptism only for adult believers. Accordingly, he baptized himself and 36 others, including Thomas Helwys, who organized the first English congregation when he returned to London in 1611. Helwys's group held to the Arminian doctrine that the death of Jesus produced atonement for everyone and not only for the predestined elect, and thus became known as General Baptists. A more strictly Calvinist group, the Particular Baptists, was founded in England in 1638.

4830. Quaker meetings were held in the Midland and northern counties of England beginning in 1649, when members of the Seekers, a Puritan Separatist group, gathered to hear the preaching of George Fox, a Leicestershire workingman. Fox had experienced revelations concerning the presence of God as the "inward Light" within each individual, which needed no

RELIGION—CHRISTIANITY—PROTESTANT—*continued*

mediation from ministers or organized churches. The congregations formed from these assemblies called themselves the Society of Friends. The term "Quakers" was originally applied to them in ridicule.

4831. Anglican saint was King Charles I, who was beheaded by order of Parliament on January 30, 1649. The Church of England claimed that Charles was a martyr for the faith because he was executed for resisting the religious reforms demanded by the Puritan political faction, which controlled Parliament. St. Charles's Day was celebrated beginning in 1661. Mention of it was removed from the English Prayer Book in 1859.

4832. Moravian Church community was formed in Herrnhut, a village built in 1722 on the estate of Count Nicholas Ludwig von Zinzendorf in Saxony (now part of Germany) as a refuge for the Bohemian Brethren, who had been meeting in secret since the group's suppression in 1620. They were descendants of the fellowship group Unitas Fratrum, founded in 1457 in Bohemia (now part of the Czech Republic) by followers of the reformer Jan Hus. Eventually the group was constituted as the Moravian Church, with a particular vocation as missionaries.

4833. Methodist religious group was a society of Anglican students at the University of Oxford, England, who earned the name by their methodical practice of Bible study, worship, and good works. Their leader, John Wesley, began traveling through Britain and Ireland in 1738, preaching a variant of Church of England doctrine that emphasized the saving power of the Holy Spirit. The Methodists gradually took on a separate identity from the Church of England and became completely independent in 1795.

4834. Anglican priest who was not of European descent was Philip Quaque (or Kweku), an African born in Cape Coast (part of modern Ghana) in 1741. Taken to England as a young teenager, he was educated by the Church of England's Society for the Propagation of the Gospel in Foreign Parts, received ordination as a priest in 1765, and married Catherine Blunt, an Englishwoman. In February 1766 he returned to Cape Coast, where he was employed as " Missionary, Catechist and Schoolmaster." He taught religious school in his native land, with mixed success, for 51 years.

4835. Bible society was the British and Foreign Bible Society, co-founded in 1804 in London, England, by Thomas Charles, a Welsh Methodist. The Society undertook to prepare low-cost vernacular Bible translations and distribute them internationally.

4836. Protestant religious order was the order of deaconesses, or female diaconate, founded by the Lutheran pastor Theodor Fliedner at Kaiserswerth, near Düsseldorf, Germany, in 1836. The women of the order were trained in nursing techniques. Fliedner subsequently opened one hundred deaconess homes in Protestant countries.

4837. Universal Week of Prayer was inaugurated by the World Evangelical Alliance of London, England, for the first week of January 1846. The week was intended as a time of repentance and reflection, similar to the ten-day period between Rosh Hashonah and Yom Kippur for the Jews, from whom the idea was borrowed.

4838. Adventists were the followers of William Miller, a farmer and soldier from Pittsfield, MA, USA, who proclaimed in 1831 that the Second Coming would occur in 1843. The Millerite movement, which combined conservative Protestant doctrines with millenarian hopes, continued to flourish after the expected date came and went. Members of the group established a formal church, the Advent Christian Church, in 1861. The Seventh-Day Adventist Church was founded two years later.

4839. Salvation Army activities were undertaken by William Booth, an English revivalist preacher who had left the Methodist New Connection to do his own preaching and social outreach work, starting in the poverty-stricken Whitechapel section of London in 1864. In 1878 he changed the name of the group from the Christian Mission to the Salvation Army, an all-volunteer religious organization that he ran on a military model with himself as general, in partnership with his wife, Catherine.

4840. Jehovah's Witnesses were members of a study group, the International Bible Students Association, that was started in 1872 by Charles Taze Russell, a haberdasher in Pittsburgh, PA, USA. Eventually, Russell taught that the Second Coming had occurred invisibly in 1874 and that Armageddon, followed by the establishment of the Theocracy, God's eternal kingdom on earth, was imminent. The current name was adopted in 1931.

4841. World Methodist Council met as the Ecumenical Methodist Conference in London, England, in 1881. The organization, known under its present name from 1951, fosters cooperation among Methodist groups worldwide and develops guidance on Methodist doctrine, education, and other concerns. Organizational offices are located in Switzerland and the United States.

4842. Pentecostal churches were an outgrowth of the Holiness Movement, a 19th-century Methodist-influenced revival effort in American Protestant churches. Beginning on January 1, 1901, students of Charles Parham at the Bethel Bible College in Topeka, KS, USA, were "baptized in the Spirit" and began speaking in tongues in the manner described in the New Testament book of Acts. Their subsequent evangelization campaign received a major boost in 1906 from William J. Seymour, whose Apostolic Faith Gospel Mission in Los Angeles, CA, attracted sympathizers of all races and classes. Separate communities began to form when the energetically charismatic style of Pentecostal worship was rejected by the established churches.

4843. Anglican woman priest was Florence Tim-Oi Lee, a deaconess of Macao. During World War II, she received an emergency ordination on January 25, 1944, from Bishop R.O. Hall of the Diocese of Hong Kong, who sought to remedy the fact that there were no ordained priests in Macao capable of giving communion. After the war, Tim-Oi Lee was forced to resign her ministry by the Chinese House of Bishops. She worked as a laborer under the Chinese Communist government until she managed to escape to Canada in 1981.

4844. Director of the World Evangelical Fellowship who was not from the West was Agustin Vencer, Jr., the general secretary of the Philippine Council of Evangelical Churches. was elected at the organization's general assembly in Manila, the Philippines, on June 25, 1992.

4845. Global evangelical rally was the Praying Through the Window campaign, sponsored by the evangelistic initiative AD 2000, headquartered in Colorado Springs, CO, USA. The event was held in October 1993 and rallied an estimated 21 million Christians to offer on-site and home-based intercessory prayer for people within the so-called 10/40 Window, a rectangular area on the globe extending from 10 degrees to 40 degrees north of the equator and dominated by Buddhist, Islamic, and Hindu countries. A second Praying Through the Window event was held in 1995.

4846. Anglican women priests to be officially ordained were 32 candidates who became priests on March 12, 1994, at Bristol Cathedral in England. Women's ordination was approved at the General Synod of the Anglican Church in 1975. Following the controversial move, several hundred members of the clergy threatened to convert to Roman Catholicism.

RELIGION—CHRISTIANITY—ROMAN CATHOLIC

4847. Pope is considered to have been St. Peter, born Shimon (in Greek, Simon), probably in the Galilee region of Israel (then Roman-occupied Palestine). A fisherman, he became the leader of the disciples of Jesus and was given the name Cephas ("rock," or *petra* in Latin, from which the name Peter is derived). He also became the first martyred pope when he was crucified upside-down by Roman authorities circa 64 CE. The term "pope," meaning "father," was originally applied to all bishops, but came to apply only to the bishop of Rome. The first exercise of papal jurisdiction by the bishop of Rome was made by St. Victor, pope from 189 to 199, who excommunicated the bishops of Asia Minor for continuing to celebrate Easter according to the Jewish calendar.

4848. Antipope was St. Hippolytus, a conservative church leader who was consecrated by a dissident group in 217 or 218 CE and reigned during the pontificates of saints Calixtus (218–222), Urban I (222–230), and Pontian (230–235). Hippolytus was exiled in 235 to the mines of Sardinia by the Roman emperor Maximinus, where he was reconciled with Pontian (who had also been exiled). Both agreed on a single successor, St. Anterus.

4849. Catholic index of forbidden books was contained in a decree issued in the year 405 by Pope Innocent I. Pope Gelasius I issued a more comprehensive decree containing lists of banned and recommended books in 496. The first *Index Librorum Prohibitorum,* the official index of works forbidden by Church authorities as dangerous to the faith, was issued in 1559 by the Sacred Congregation of the Roman Inquisition at the Vatican, Rome, Italy. The Index was last revised in 1948 and ceased publication in 1966.

4850. Abbey in Western Europe was Montecassino, in present-day Cassino, Italy. It was founded in 529 by St. Benedict of Nursia, author of the rules that govern the daily operations of many Roman Catholic monasteries and convents. His abbey plan, on which most others are modeled, was based on a central cloister

RELIGION—CHRISTIANITY—ROMAN
CATHOLIC—*continued*
that gave access to the church, dormitory, refectory, library, and chapter house. It also made provision for an infirmary, kitchen, brewery, workshops, garden, and numerous other facilities.

4851. Pope to be assassinated was John VIII, elected pope on December 14, 872 CE, as the successor to Adrian II. He was murdered on December 16, 882, in Rome, apparently by members of a political conspiracy.

4852. Pope tried for heresy after his death was the Roman-born Pope Formosus, who was elected on October 6, 891, and died in 896 in the midst of a political struggle over control of the city. Shortly after his death, his body was disinterred by his enemies and, at a bizarre trial popularly known as the "Cadaver Synod," his successor Pope Stephen VII convicted the corpse of heresy. Formosus's fingers of consecration were cut off and the body was thrown into the Tiber River.

4853. Catholic saint canonized by a pope was St. Ulrich, bishop of Augsburg, Germany, from 924 to his death in 973. The siege of Augsburg by the invading Magyars in 955 failed because of Ulrich's fortification of the city. His canonization by Pope John XV in 993, at Rome, is the first such action on record. Previously, saints were recognized by popular acclaim, and their veneration was regulated by the local bishop. By church law enacted in the early 13th century, all canonizations came under the authority of the pope.

4854. French-born pope was Sylvester II (Gerbert of Aurillac), who was born near Aurillac, in Auvergne, France, circa 945. He was elected on April 9, 999, and died in 1003. A politically astute leader, he was also a renowned mathematician, scholar, and teacher, and was an especially gifted musician who built several organs.

4855. Flagellation sects in which Christians did public penance for sin by scourging themselves and one another with whips were founded in the mid-eleventh century by St. Peter Damian (Pier Damiani), the Italian ascetic and reformer.

4856. Pope born in England was Adrian (or Hadrian) IV, born Nicholas Brakespear (or Breakspear) circa 1100 at Abbot's Langley, near St. Albans, Hertfordshire, England. He was elected pope on December 4, 1154.

4857. Christian mendicant orders were the Franciscans, founded in Italy by St. Francis of Assisi in 1210, and the Dominicans, founded in France by St. Dominic de Guzmán in 1216. Members of these orders, known as friars, followed the way of life modeled by St. Francis, owning no property, living in poverty, and working for their livelihoods, resorting to begging if necessary. The Dominicans specialized in preaching and education.

4858. Rule for Christian monastic life written by a woman was the work of St. Clare of Assisi, who created it for the Poor Clares, the order of Franciscan nuns founded by her in 1212. Her convent near Assisi, Italy, was initially required to follow an adaptation of the rules of St. Benedict. In 1253, just before Clare's death, permission was granted by Pope Innocent IV for the adoption of her rule, which stressed penitential prayer, poverty, and penance.

4859. Official Christian inquisition was instituted by Pope Gregory IX in 1231 for the purpose of eradicating heretics, particularly the Cathari and Waldensians in Italy and France. The campaign was also directed at practitioners of witchcraft and alchemy. Interrogators were granted the right to use torture against accused people in 1252.

4860. Inquisition directed against Jews was initiated in 1247 in Vienne, France, by two Franciscan friars who were attempting to prove the ancient lie that Jews sacrificed Christian children in order to use their blood in making matzah for Passover. The inquisition was terminated by order of Pope Innocent IV, who had declared blood libels false. The Jews of Vienne were expelled by this order in 1253.

4861. Oberammergau passion play performance was produced in 1364 by the residents of Oberammergau, Germany, who had promised the previous year to mount a theatrical presentation of the death of Jesus once each decade if their village escaped the epidemic of the Black Death that was raging through Europe. The pageant, still produced and performed by local residents every ten years, is one of the few examples of the medieval passion play to continue into the present day, although it has been revised several times to remove anti-Semitic elements.

4862. Antipope during the Great Schism was Clement VII, born Robert of Geneva in 1342 in Switzerland. A cousin of the French king, he was the leader of a group of French-born cardinals who ruled invalid the election on April 8, 1378, of Italian-born Pope Urban VI. On September 20, 1378, at Fondi in the Papal States, the rebellious cardinals elevated him to the papacy. While Urban VI stayed at the Vatican, Clement VII ruled from the papal residence in Avignon, France. The rivalry between the two popes, called the Great Schism, sowed spiritual and political confusion throughout Europe for 40 years.

4863. Auto-da-fé took place in 1481 at Seville, Spain. The auto-da-fé (the phrase means "act of faith") was a public ritual in which people accused of apostasy or heresy by the Inquisition, having been tortured before their convictions, were tied to stakes and burned alive. Most of the victims were converted Jews and Muslims who were suspected of practicing their religions secretly, a capital crime. Protestants and members of the mystical sect called the Illuminati were also burned. The executions were carried out by the civil government to prevent the Church from having to shed blood. The last auto-da-fé took place in Mexico in 1850.

4864. Catholic priest ordained in the New World was the Spanish-born Bartolomé de Las Casas, a soldier, planter, and lay teacher of catechism. He was ordained a priest in either 1512 or 1513 in the colony of Santo Domingo, Hispaniola (in the present-day Dominican Republic), and became a missionary to the Indians and an outspoken defender of their rights. In 1522 he joined the Dominicans. From 1544 to 1547 he was bishop of Chiapas, Mexico. After his return to Spain he wrote the first book about slavery in the New World, the *Brevísima relación de la destrucción de las Indias (A Brief Report on the Destruction of the Indies)* (1552).

4865. Cathedral in the New World was the cathedral of Santo Domingo (now in the Dominican Republic), built between 1514 and 1542 to house the New World's first Roman Catholic archdiocese. The cathedral contains three arched cloisters. During the colonial period, the main cloister was used as the ecclesiastical cemetery.

4866. Easter Mass in Central America was celebrated on April 24, 1519, in Tenochtitlán, the capital of the Aztecs (now Mexico City, Mexico). Among those attending were Moctezuma II, priest-king of the Aztecs, and the Spanish conquistador Hernán Cortés.

4867. Seminary in the New World was the Colégio de la Santa Cruz de Santiago Tlatelolco in Mexico City, Mexico, founded in 1536 by Spanish Franciscan Juan de Zumárraga, Mexico's first Roman Catholic bishop.

4868. Catholic monastic order founded after the beginning of the Protestant Reformation was the Society of Jesus (the Jesuits), an order devoted to missionary and educational work. It was founded in 1539 by St. Ignatius of Loyola, formerly a Spanish knight, and received approval from Pope Paul III in 1540. The order, with a highly centralized authority, combined a special vow of obedience to the Pope with a flexible rule that allowed its members to undertake foreign missions.

4869. Catholic martyrs who were Japanese were 26 converts who were put to death at Nagasaki on February 5, 1596, by order of the shogun, Hideyoshi Toyotomi. Hideyoshi banned Christianity earlier that year for fear that Portuguese and Spanish missionaries were preparing the ground for a Western invasion of Japan. As many as 4,000 Catholics were executed by 1651, many of them after prolonged torture.

4870. Scientist executed by the Catholic Church was the Italian philosopher and scientist Giordano Bruno, born Filippo Bruno in 1548 in Nola, Campania, Italy. Bruno was a steadfast advocate of the Copernican theory, which had been declared heretical by the Roman Catholic Church. He was seized by the Inquisition in Venice. After spending seven years in prison, during which he refused to recant his beliefs, he was burned at the stake on February 17, 1600, in Rome. On hearing his death sentence, he reportedly said, "Perhaps your fear in passing judgment on me is greater than mine in receiving it."

4871. European buried in the Imperial City in Beijing, China, was Matteo Ricci, a Jesuit priest and missionary who was the first Westerner to establish missions in China and who wrote the first important Western works on that country since Marco Polo. When Ricci died in Beijing on May 11, 1610, at the age of 57, he was granted the right to be buried in the Imperial City by special order of Emperor Wanli — the first of the very few Europeans ever given that honor.

4872. Catholic saint from the New World was Rosa de Lima, a Peruvian. She was canonized in a ceremony in the Vatican on August 30, 1617.

4873. Christian missionaries in Tibet were the Jesuits Johannes Grueber and Albert d'Orville. On October 8, 1661, while en route from Beijing, China, to Rome, Italy, they became the first Europeans to enter the capital city of Lhasa, Tibet.

RELIGION—CHRISTIANITY—ROMAN
CATHOLIC—*continued*

**4874. Catholic bishop of African descent in
the New World** was Francisco Xavier de Luna
Victoria, who was appointed bishop of Panama
in 1715.

4875. Vatican Council of the Roman Catholic
Church was convened in Rome, Italy, by Pope
Pius IX on December 8, 1869. After heated debate, and with the urging of Pope Pius, the
council instituted the *Pastor Aeternus,* the dog-
ma of papal infallibility. The council's work
was cut short when Piedmontese troops occupied the Vatican in 1870, but it was never formally dissolved. A second Vatican Council was
held in 1962–65.

**4876. Doctor of the Church who was a wom-
an** was the Spanish nun and mystic Teresa of
Ávila, born Teresa de Cepeda y Ahumada in
1515 in Ávila, Spain. She was canonized in
1622 and elevated to the status of doctor of the
church in 1970 by Pope Paul VI.

4877. Pope born in Poland was John Paul II,
born Karol Wojtyla on May 18, 1920, in
Wadowice, Poland. Made archbishop of Kraków in 1964 and cardinal of the Church in
1967, he was elected pope on October 16, 1978
and invested on October 22. John Paul II was
the first non-Italian pope since the Dutch-born
Adrian VI, who was elected in 1522 and served
a single year.

4878. Pope to visit a Communist country was
John Paul II, born Karol Wojtyla in Wadowice,
Poland, and elected pope in 1978. In June
1979, John Paul II paid a highly publicized visit to his homeland, then under the political
leadership of Edward Gierek, general secretary
of the Polish Communist party. The pope spoke
on 32 occasions to crowds of as many as one
million people.

**4879. Catechism of the Catholic Church
since the Renaissance** was promulgated by the
Vatican in 1992, under Pope John Paul II. The
first new catechism since 1566, it presented the
Church's teachings on such modern subjects as
abortion, euthanasia, birth control, drunken
driving, drug abuse, environmental damage, and
genocide.

**4880. Catholic member of the British royal
family since the 17th century** was Katherine,
Duchess of Kent, who converted from Angli-
canism to Catholicism and took full communion on January 14, 1994. She was the first
member of the British royal family to adopt
Catholicism since the year 1688.

**4881. Gypsy (Rom) to be beatified by the
Catholic Church** was Ceferino Jiménez Malla,
also known as El Pele, an illiterate horse-trader
who lived near the city of Barbastro in Aragon,
Spain. In August 1936, during the Spanish Civil War, he was shot by a Republican firing
squad for coming to the aid of a priest who
was being assaulted. Jiménez Malla's beatification by Pope John Paul II took place at the
Vatican in Rome, Italy, on May 4, 1997, attended by 3,000 Rom. Beatification, in Roman
Catholicism, is the second step in the process
leading to possible canonization as a saint.

RELIGION—CHRISTIANITY—SCRIP-
TURES

4882. Christian Bible was the Jewish Bible
translated into Greek. This translation, the Septuagint, or "seventy"—so called because it was
reputed to have been made by a committee of
70 Jewish scholars—was originally produced
for the use of the Greek-speaking Jewish community in Alexandria, Egypt. It took the trans-
lators a century to complete the task, starting
with the Torah (the five books of Moses) in the
mid-third century BCE. The Septuagint was
adopted by Christian groups in the first and
second centuries CE and was used as the basis
for later translations into Old Latin, Coptic,
Ethiopic, Armenian, Georgian, Slavonic, and
Arabic.

4883. English translation of a biblical text
still extant was a rendering into Old English of
the Ten Commandments, together with some of
the accompanying laws of personal conduct and
social organization from the Book of Exodus.
They appeared in the law code of Alfred the
Great, king of Wessex (now part of England)
from 871 to 899. Alfred, a man of learning,
made his own translations of theological and
historical works from Latin and is thought to
have translated 50 of the Psalms.

4884. English translation of the Bible appeared in 1382 under the sponsorship of the
English religious reformer John Wycliffe. Wycliffe, like the Protestant reformers and transla-
tors who came after him, intended to subvert
the Church's control over access to scripture by
making the text available in the vernacular. The
chief translator appears to have been Nicholas
of Hereford.

4885. Printed edition of the Bible was the
Gutenberg Bible, printed in Latin in Mainz (in
modern Germany) on the press invented by Johannes Gutenberg. It bears no date, but one
copy carries a handwritten notation of August
15, 1456, the day on which its owner, Heinrich

Cremer, finished binding it. The printing was done either by Gutenberg himself or, as some scholars believe, by his former partner, Johann Fust, and an associate, Peter Schöffer. It is also known as the 42-line Bible and the Mazarin Bible. Some 40 copies are known to exist.

4886. Polyglot Bible in which the text contained parallel translations in several languages was the *Complutensian,* printed in 1514–17 at the University of Alcalá de Henares, Madrid, Spain, and published in 1522. Its patron was Cardinal Francisco Jiménez de Cisneros, the archbishop of Toledo. On the Old Testament pages, versions of the Masoretic text (Hebrew), the Targum of Onkelos (Aramaic), the Vulgate (Latin), and the Septuagint (Greek), all appeared in parallel columns. The New Testament pages included the Greek original and the Vulgate.

4887. New Testament printed in English was a translation by the English humanist scholar William Tyndale, then in exile in Cologne, Germany, who printed it in July 1525 with the financial support of London merchants. He had earlier tried to translate the Bible into English in England, but had been prevented by Church authorities. The Cologne printing was suppressed by Church officials in Germany, but a second printing, made at Worms, was widely disseminated, and was brought to England in 1526. Tyndale was arrested in the Dutch (now Belgian) city of Antwerp while working on an English translation of the Pentateuch, and was strangled and burned at the stake in on October 6, 1536. Fifty thousand copies of Tyndale's New Testament were already in circulation.

4888. Translation of the complete Christian Bible into a modern European language was made by Martin Luther, the religious reformer whose activities led to the Protestant Reformation. In 1534 he published his German version of the Christian Bible. His New Testament in German had appeared in 1522.

4889. Printed edition of the complete Christian Bible in English was printed in 1535 in Zürich, Switzerland. The translation was made by the English cleric Miles Coverdale, an Augustinian friar living in the Flemish city of Antwerp (now in Belgium). It went through three printings abroad before its first printing in England, which was made by James Nycholson in Southwark (now part of London) in 1537.

4890. Catholic edition of the Bible in a vernacular language was the Douai-Reims Bible, a rendering of the Latin Vulgate into English. Although ordinary individuals were barred by the Church from reading the Bible to prevent unauthorized interpretations, the publication of several Protestant translations motivated William Cardinal Allen to assemble a group of exiled Roman Catholic scholars at a seminary in Douai, a town in the Spanish Netherlands (now in France), to produce a version that would reflect Catholic teachings. The chief translator was Gregory Martin. The New Testament was published in 1582, the Old Testament in 1609–10.

4891. Edition of the King James Version of the Bible was published in England in 1611. The translation, whose stately cadences and poetic vitality had a lasting effect on writers in English, was completed over the course of seven years by 47 scholars working at Westminster, Oxford, and Cambridge. The project was under the sponsorship of King James I.

4892. Bible translated into an indigenous American language was *The New Testament of Our Lord and Saviour Jesus Christ,* completed in 1661 by John Eliot, sometimes called the "Apostle to the North American Indians." Bearing a dedication in English to England's King Charles II, it contained 130 printed leaves without pagination and two title pages, one in English and the other in the Algonkian language. The text was in double columns with marginal references. The first complete Bible in any Native North American language was *The Holy Bible, Containing the Old Testament and the New, Translated into the Indian Language,* prepared by Eliot in 1663. Both Bibles were printed in Massachusetts by Samuel Green and Marmaduke Johnson. These were the first Bibles printed in North America.

4893. New Testament printed in Asia may have been a New Testament reportedly printed in Japanese by resident Jesuits at Miyako, Japan, in 1613. No copy or independent account of this publication exists. The first printed New Testament known with certainty to have existed was published in 1715 in the Tamil language of Malaysia by the Lutheran missionary Bartholomäus Ziegenbalg.

4894. Illuminated Bible manuscript from the modern era was the St. John's Bible, commissioned by St. John's Abbey, a Benedictine monastery near Collegeville, MN, USA. The scribe was Donald Jackson, the Queen of England's calligrapher. The Bible was written on 1,150 sheets of calfskin vellum with a goose

**RELIGION— CHRISTIANITY— SCRIP-
TURES—**continued

quill, using inks made of ground minerals. Each page was designed by computer. By request of the abbey, the illustrations stressed Christianity's connections to Judaism and Islam and featured women far more than was typical of medieval illuminated Bibles. The first two pages to be completed were shown to the public in New York, NY, in March 1999. All seven volumes were expected to be finished in 2004 and to be made available on CD-ROM.

RELIGION—CONFUCIANISM

4895. Confucian text was the *Lun yü (Conversations)*, known in English as the *Analects*, a collection of the sayings and teachings of the Chinese sage Kongfuzi (Confucius), compiled by the second generation of his followers, circa 450 BCE. In the main, these were ethical teachings about the individual's social, religious, and political responsibilities in building a harmonious society. In 1190, the *Lun yü* and three other Confucian texts were published, with a commentary, by the philosopher Chu Hsi, who helped to bring about a revival of interest in Confucianism.

4896. Explicator of orthodox Confucianism was the Chinese philosopher Mengzi (in Wade-Giles, Meng-tzu), known in the West by the Latinized form of his name, Mencius, who studied as a youth (circa 350 BCE) with the grandson of Kongfuzi (Confucius). In his system, four feelings inherent in human nature—commiseration, shame, courtesy, and the sense of right and wrong—are developed by education into the four virtues of humaneness, righteousness, decorum, and wisdom. He identified the common people as the most important part of the nation and required rulers to take full responsibility for ensuring their material welfare and their educational and spiritual development.

4897. Establishment of Confucianism as the state religion was decreed by the Chinese emperor Wudi, an emperor of the Han dynasty, who ruled from 140 to 87 BCE. He was an autocratic ruler, rather than the benevolent ruler required by Confucius (Kongfuzi), but appreciated the Confucian emphasis on the performance of religious rituals and sacrifices by the emperor, in his role as Son of Heaven, as a way of maintaining the proper balance between nature and society. The Confucian classic literature was taught in the many schools that were opened during Wudi's reign to educate future government officials.

4898. Deification of K'ung Fu-tzu (Confucius) began in 58 CE, when the government schools of China were required by imperial order to offer sacrifices to the author of the texts that formed their curriculum. The Confucian system was not itself a religion, but a comprehensive philosophy of social order in which religious rituals, including sacrifices to deities and ancestors, had an important place.

4899. Neo-Confucian philosopher was the Chinese writer Chou Tun-i (1017–1073), creator of a metaphysical system that synthesized humanistic Confucian principles with Taoist concepts drawn from the *I Ching (Book of Changes)*. His major works were the *T'ai-chi-t'u shuo (Explanation of the Diagram of the Great Ultimate)* and the *T'ung-shu (Explanatory Text)*.

RELIGION—HINDUISM

4900. Evidence of Hinduism in its earliest form comes from clay figures and seals used by the people of the Indus valley civilizations circa 2500 BCE. One seal appears to show a horned male deity sitting in a yoga position among animals, much as the deity Shiva is shown in later Hindu depictions. There are also figurines of females, similar to later depictions of Hindu goddesses. Other significant motifs include ritual bathing and phallic veneration.

4901. Caste system in Hinduism evolved from the four socioreligious classes of Indian society mentioned in the *Rig Veda,* the earliest of the Hindu religious writings, dated to the middle of the second millennium BCE. The four groups, called *varnas,* are the Brahmans, the class of priests and teachers; the Kshatriyas, the warrior and princely class; the Vaishyas, comprising traders and cultivators; and the Shudras, who do menial work.

4902. Hindu religious text is the *Rig Veda (Wisdom of the Verses),* a collection of hymns that is the earliest part of the Vedas, the sacred revealed literature of Hinduism. It was written in Sanskrit, probably as early as circa 1500 BCE.

4903. Statement of the Hindu doctrine of karmic reincarnation appears in the *Brihadaranyaka Upanishad.* The word *Upanishad,* which means "session," in the sense of a learning session, refers to 108 collections in Sanskrit of teachings by various Hindu sages, made approximately between 1000 and 500 BCE. The *Brihadaranyaka Upanishad,* one of the earliest, is attributed to the sage Yajñavalkya. It contains the first discussion of *samsara,* the cycle of birth and rebirth that every soul must undergo; of *moksha,* liberation from this cycle; and of *karma,* the determination of the conditions of rebirth according to the acts a person committed in his or her previous life.

4904. Statement of the Hindu doctrine of *Brahman* appears in the *Chandogya Upanishad,* one of the earliest of the *Upanishads,* 108 volumes of Indian religious teachings collected between the tenth and fifth centuries BCE. The *Chandogya Upanishad* explicates the idea of *Brahman,* the ultimate, immortal, unchanging reality that constitutes the ground of all existence, and of *Atman,* the individual self. The relationship between them is expressed in the Sanskrit phrase *tat tvam asi,* or "That Thou Art," meaning that the Absolute and the Self are in fact identical.

4905. Hindu heresies arose in India in the sixth century BCE. One was Jainism, founded by Vardhamana Mahavira; the other, Buddhism, founded by Siddhartha Gautama. Both rejected the authority of the Hindu scriptures called the Vedas and the sacrificial rituals associated with them, together with the idea of a creator deity and the hierarchical caste system.

4906. Authoritative Hindu law code was contained in the *Manava-dharma-shastra,* popularly known as the *Manu-smrti (Laws of Manu)* in acknowledgment of its attribution to Manu, India's legendary first man. In 2,694 stanzas, the book discussed the arrangement of Indian society and the activities incumbent on Hindus at different levels and conditions within it. One section, probably codified in the first century BCE, was devoted to the laws of kingship and similar matters.

4907. Statement of the Hindu doctrine of *dharma* appears in the series of religious law books known as the *dharma sutras* and *dharma shastras,* of which the most important was the *Manava-dharma-shastra,* better known as the *Manu-smrti (Laws of Manu),* dated to about the first century BCE. *Dharma* is the concept of social order, requiring each person to carry out specific ethical, religious, and practical responsibilities, and to observe specific customs and restrictions, based on his or her hereditary placement within the hierarchical structure of Hindu society.

4908. Hindu temple known to archeologists was a one-room shrine built at Sanchi, in Madhya Pradesh state, during India's Gupta Empire, between 320 and 540. Depictions in art of the Hindu deities date from the same period.

4909. Hindu poet-saints of the *bhakti* **devotional movement** lived in southern India beginning in the sixth century, wandering from temple to temple and singing ecstatic hymns they composed in the Tamil language. They belonged to two groups: the Nayanars, devotees of the deity Shiva, and the Alvars, devotees of Vishnu. The first known by name was a sixth-century Nayanar woman, Karaikkal Ammaiyar. The "way of *bhakti*" involving a close emotional connection between worshipper and deity, had already been developing for several centuries.

4910. Hindu monastic order was Dasnami, founded by the eighth- or ninth-century theologian Shankara, the leading exponent of the Advaita Vedanta school of Hindu philosophy. The order's four monasteries, apparently modeled on those of the Buddhists, were Sringeri, Dvaraka, Badarinatha, and Puri. Its members were Saivites, for whom the deity Shiva is the principal representation of God.

4911. Juggernaut was the immense wooden chariot used by Hindus during Rathayatra, the annual chariot festival. During this holiday, which takes place in June or July, statues are removed from their sanctuaries and taken in procession through the streets in wheeled vehicles 44 feet high, pulled by hundreds of men. The word "juggernaut" is a corruption of the name Jagannatha ("Lord of the World"), one of the forms of the Hindu deity Krishna (himself an incarnation of Vishnu), who is worshipped during Rathayatra at the twelfth-century temple of Puri, in India's Orissa state, and at Shrirampur, in West Bengal state.

4912. Hindu text translated into English was the *Bhagavad Gita (Song of God),* a poem of 700 verses, cast in the form of a dialogue between Arjuna, a warrior prince, and Krishna, a charioteer who represents the divine, and exploring the immanence and transcendence of God and the dilemma of ethical human conduct. It dates from the first or second century CE and was incorporated into the Indian epic called the *Mahabharata.* It was translated into English by Charles Wilkins in 1785.

4913. Modern Hindu reform movement was the Brahmo Samaj ("society of Brahma"), founded by the religious, social, and educational reformer Ram Mohun (or Rammohan) Roy in Calcutta, India, in 1828. The Bengali-born Roy, a Brahmin and a sometime employee of the British East India Company, was a linguist who had read the Jewish, Christian, and Muslim scriptures in the original languages. The Brahmo Samaj advocated a monotheistic, West-

RELIGION—HINDUISM—continued

ern-influenced version of Hinduism, purged of polytheism, the caste system, and traditional customs such as child marriage and the practice of burning widows to death on their husbands' cremation pyres.

4914. Prophet to declare that all religions are true was Ramakrishna Paramahansa (born Gadhadhar Chatterji), from 1859 a priest at the temple of Kali, the Hindu goddess of creation and destruction, at Daksineshvar, near Calcutta, India. Ramakrishna was a visionary mystic who perceived God in all things and who was said to have achieved complete union with *Brahman*, the eternal and unchanging reality of God. After studying Islam and Christianity, he came to the conclusion that all religions are one, that all are ultimately derived from the teachings of the Vedanta school of Hinduism, and that a person should seek God by following the religion he or she inherited.

4915. Modern Hindu reform movement that rejected Western influence was the Arya Samaj ("Aryan society"), founded in 1875 by Dayananda Sarasvati, a Gujarati Brahmin and member of the ascetic Sarasvati sect. The intention of the Arya Samaj was to reassert the original authority of the Vedas, India's earliest scriptures, in the belief that they represented pure monotheism that had been corrupted by polytheism and idol worship over the course of 3,000 years. Other religions, such as Christianity and Islam, were held to be offshoots of monotheistic Hinduism.

4916. Westerners to promote Hindu ideas were the leaders of the Theosophical Society, organized in New York in 1875 by Helena Blavatsky, a Russian with an interest in esoteric religions and occult ideas of all kinds. Blavatsky and her colleague Annie Besant, an Englishwoman, claiming to act under the guidance of spiritual mentors in the Himalaya, founded chapters of the society in India, Europe, and the United States. Besant's books introduced Hinduism to many readers in the West. The enthusiasm of the Theosophists, and their conviction that Hinduism was superior to Christianity, were factors in the awakening of nationalist sentiments in India.

4917. Hindu missionary in the West and the first person to present Hinduism as a universal faith was Vivekananda (born Narendranath Datta), a Bengali disciple of the famous mystic Ramakrishna. In 1893, Vivekananda traveled to the United States to speak at the World Parliament of Religions, part of the World's Colum-

bian Exposition, in Chicago, IL. During a four-year lecture tour of the USA and England, he promoted Ramakrishna's view that all religions are true and that all spring from Hinduism, specifically from the philosophy called Vedanta. In many cities, his followers founded Vedanta educational centers. On his return to India, Vivekananda founded the Ramakrishna Mission, an organization that combined religious education with social service and advocacy of social and political reform.

RELIGION—ISLAM

4918. Muslim ritual to be established was the *salat*, the prayer ritual, consisting of statements of faith, recitations from the Qur'an, and a sequence of postures, including standing, bowing, sitting, and prostration (kneeling while touching the forehead and palms to the floor). It originated with Muhammad, the founder of Islam, during his residency at the Arabian city of Mecca (in modern Saudi Arabia) between 620 and 622. It is now required five times daily and is one of the five "Pillars of Islam." The others are *shahada* (profession of faith), *zakat* (giving alms), *saum* (fasting), and *hajj* (undertaking a pilgrimage to Mecca).

4919. *Jihad* was the successful "holy war" led in 624 by Muhammad, the founder of Islam, against the inhabitants of the city of Mecca. The Qur'an states that it is the religious duty of every Muslim to spread Islam by waging war against the enemies of the faith, whether by the heart, the tongue, the hand, or the sword.

4920. Convert to Islam may have been Abu Bakr (573–634), the father-in-law of Muhammad. His conversion occurred before 622, the year he accompanied Muhammad on his journey from Mecca to Yathrib (now Medina, Saudi Arabia). After Muhammad's death, Abu Bakr was chosen as his successor. His claim as first convert is doubted by some Islamic historians.

4921. Mosque was the Prophet's Mosque, built in 622–634 by Muhammad, the founder of Islam, in the courtyard of his clay brick house in Medina (now in Saudi Arabia). The mosque, intended as a place of worship for Muhammad's followers, was open at the sides, with a simple roof supported by pillars made from the trunks of palm trees. A pulpit, the minbar, was built on the wall facing Mecca, from which Muhammad proclaimed Islamic law. The original buildings were razed in 706 by the caliph al-Walid I and a permanent mosque was erected on the site.

4922. Muslim expulsion of Jews took place in Arabia (now Saudia Arabia) during the lifetime of Muhammad, the founder of Islam, after his relocation from Mecca to Medina (then called Yathrib) in 622. The inhabitants of Medina, most of whom were tribal Arabs, included several clans of Jews, who had founded the city. Although Muhammad regarded himself as a prophet in the Jewish tradition, his claims were ridiculed by the Jews of Medina, who refused to convert. In 624, soon after the Battle of Badr, which established Muhammad and his followers as a military power, the Muslims besieged the Jewish clan of Qaynuqa' and forced them to leave the city. They expelled the an-Nadir clan in 625. After the surrender of a third clan, the Qurayzah, in 627, they massacred its men and enslaved its women and children.

4923. Tolerated minorities under Islam were several small Christian and Jewish communities living in Arabia near the Gulf of Aqaba (in an area that is now part of Jordan). In 630, their region was conquered by the Muslims under Muhammad. Although the Muslims required all pagans in their conquered territories to convert to Islam or be killed, they made an exception for the Christians and Jews, recognizing them as "people of the book" who had sacred scriptures and who accepted divine revelation through prophets, even though they did not accept Muhammad as a prophet. They were assigned the status of *ahl adh-dhimma*, minorities with a protected but second-class status in Islamic society. Later, when the Muslims invaded Iran and India, they assigned the same status to the Zoroastrians and Hindus. *Dhimmis* throughout the early Islamic world were required to pay a poll tax, the *jizyah*.

4924. Expansion of Islam outside Arabia was undertaken by the caliphs who succeeded Muhammad, the founder of Islam, after his death in 632. Under Abu Bakr, Muslim forces conquered the Sasanian city of al-Hirah (now An Najaf, Iraq) in 633. Under Umar ibn al-Khattab, they pressed northward into Byzantine and Sasanian lands, capturing Damascus in 636 and Jerusalem in 637. An invasion force sent by Umar in 639 took control of Egypt and moved westward into northern Africa. Under Uthman ibn Affan, the Sasanian Empire was overthrown and Persia became Muslim. This expansion continued until, by 714, the Muslim empire reached from Spain in the west to India in the east.

4925. Civil war in Islam developed after Egyptian soldiers assassinated the third caliph (successor to Muhammad), Uthman ibn Affan, in 656. He was succeeded by Muhammad's son-in-law and scribe, Ali ibn Abi Talib, whose right to rule was challenged on the battlefield by A'ishah, Muhammad's widow, and by Mu'awiyah ibn Abi Sufyan, the governor of Damascus and a kinsman of Uthman's. The partisan conflict continued until 661, when Ali was himself assassinated and Mu'awiyah became caliph. In Islamic history, this episode is known as the first *fitnah*, or test.

4926. Islamic fundamentalists were the Kharijites, a sect founded by Ibn Wahb that broke away from the larger body of Muslims in Arabia in 657, during the first Islamic civil war (its name means "seceders"). Its members insisted on the absolute authority of the Qur'an and its literal interpretation. They forbade luxuries of all kinds, including games and music. They also held the view that the presence of sinners in the community put all believers at risk of damnation, and hence held it necessary to exclude and punish grave sinners. The Kharijites considered theirs to be the only true form of Islam and felt justified in attacking Muslims outside their group.

4927. Sectarian controversy in Islam arose during the civil war that erupted after the assassination in 656 of Islam's third caliph, Uthman ibn Affan. After the inconclusive Battle of Siffin in 657, the fourth caliph, Ali ibn Abi Talib, and his challenger, Mu'awiyah ibn Abi Sufyan, submitted the conflict to a panel of arbitrators. A group of Muslims led by Ibn Wahb, believing that arbitration was contrary to Muhammad's teaching in the Qur'an, formed a separate group to campaign against both sides. Known as the Kharijites (from the Arabic word *kharaju*, meaning 'secession,"), they assassinated Ali in 661 and continued to harass Mu'awiyah when he became caliph. They held the Qur'an, literally interpreted, to be the ultimate authority for all action, demanded the death penalty for any Muslim who committed a grave sin, and rejected as illegitimate all other Muslim sects.

4928. Permanent schism in Islam resulted from the quarrel over the future of Islam that broke out in 632 after the death of its founder, Muhammad. The essential question was whether issues should be decided by community consensus or by a charismatic leader in a line of authority originating with Muhammad. Adherents of the latter view, called Shi'ites, found themselves undercut when Ali ibn Abi Talib, Muhammad's son-in-law, was prevented from

RELIGION—ISLAM—*continued*

becoming his successor by the Muslims of Medina (now in Saudi Arabia). The result was several years of turbulence and civil war, culminating in the killing in 680 of Ali's son Husayn by the Umayyad caliphs against whom he intended to lead a rebellion. The Shi'ites maintained and elaborated their doctrinal differences with the Sunni (orthodox) majority and now constitute approximately a tenth of the world's Muslim population, concentrated in Iran.

4929. Check to Muslim expansion in western Europe was the Battle of Poitiers (also called the Battle of Tours) in 732, when a cavalry force under the Frankish ruler Charles Martel turned back a Muslim raid led by Abd ar-Rahman, the governor of Córdoba, Spain. Other factors in the failure of the Muslims to extend their conquest into the territory that is modern France included a revolt by the Berbers of North Africa and internecine strife.

4930. Biography of Muhammad was the *Sirah,* written by Muhammad ibn Ishaq ibn Yasar ibn Khiyar in Baghdad (in modern Iraq) circa 750. It was compiled from stories collected by Ibn Ishaq's father and grandfather, and from traditions related to Ibn Ishaq on his travels in the Muslim world. It was best known in the revised edition produced half a century later by Ibn Hisham, which influenced the intense doctrinal controversy then growing in Islam over the question of whether the Qur'an was eternal or created.

4931. Sufi mystics were preceded by pious Muslims who reacted to the wealth and power of the Islamic world under the Umayyad caliphs (661–749) by adopting ascetic practices, including meditation on the Qur'an's description of Judgment Day. In the late ninth century, the woman poet Rabi'ah al-Adawiyah, known as Rabi'ah of Basra (in modern Iraq), gave the movement an impetus toward mysticism by introducing the idea of loving and constant devotion to God.

4932. Establishment of Islamic jurisprudence was effected by Abu Abd Allah Muhammad ibn Idris ash-Shafi'i, an Arabian-born law scholar whose major work, the *Rifalah,* was written between 815 and 820 in Cairo, Egypt. To distinguish among the various practices that had taken root since the time of the prophet Muhammad in the seventh century, ash-Shafi'i introduced methods of establishing the authen-

ticity of laws and traditions, using the four "roots of law": Qur'an, *Hadith* (legends about Muhammad), consensus, and analogy. His work formed the basis for the *Shari'a,* the revealed Islamic law.

4933. Islamic inquisition was imposed by al-Ma'mun (Abu al-Abbas Abd Allah al-Ma'mun ibn ar-Rashid), the seventh caliph of the Abbasid dynasty, born in Baghdad (in modern Iraq), who came to power in 813 amid a succession dispute that resulted in a civil war. His wish to unify Islam both politically and doctrinally led al-Ma'mun to require all his subjects to adopt the position of the Mu'tazilites, philosophers who declared that reason and science should be given at least equal weight with Qur'anic revelation. Their position was adamantly opposed by traditionalists. In 833, al-Ma'mun put his prefect of police in charge of a campaign to force the traditionalists to accept the more liberal doctrine. Although al-Ma'mun died that same year, the campaign continued until 849.

4934. Statement of Sufi doctrine was contained in *Fusus al-hikam (The Bezels of Wisdom),* penned in 1229 by the Spanish-born Islamic philosopher Ibn al-Arabi. In 27 chapters, the *Fusus al-hikam* concisely presents the philosophy of Sufism, in which the mystic believer progresses by stages toward the state of human perfection as embodied in the prophet Muhammad, and visionary union with God.

4935. West African emperor of note to make a religious pilgrimage to Mecca was Mansa Musa, the ruler of the West African empire of Mali and founder of the university at Timbuktu. A devout Muslim, he traveled to the Islamic shrine in Mecca (in present-day Saudi Arabia) in 1324, stopping in Cairo, Egypt, on the way. Mali was then the center of a flourishing gold trade. The emperor was escorted by a procession of 60,000 men, including 12,000 slaves, and a caravan of 80 camels carrying 24,000 pounds of gold.

4936. Use of the crescent as a symbol of Islam originated with the Turks in the 14th century, when Sultan Orhan (died 1360), the second ruler of the Ottoman Empire, displayed a curved shape on the flags carried by his infantry. The shape was standardized as a crescent after 1483, when the Ottoman Turks conquered Constantinople (now Istanbul, Turkey), the capital of the Byzantine Empire, whose symbol was a crescent. The crescent moon was previously used as a symbol in a variety of pagan religions. The Arabic word for the crescent is *hilal.*

4937. Islamic revivalist reform movement was launched in 1736 by Muhammad ibn Abd al-Wahhab, an Arabian theologian living in Persia. He advocated a return to the tenets of early Islam as expressed in the Qur'an and the *Hadith* (anecdotes about Muhammad), condemning all innovations as polytheistic, including the veneration of saints, the decoration of mosques, and smoking tobacco. His followers called themselves the *al-Muwahhidun*, or unitarians, from their insistence on pure monotheism. Although the movement was denounced as puritanical, it gained political support from the Sa'ud family and their kingdom, Saudi Arabia.

RELIGION—ISLAM—SCRIPTURES

4938. Authoritative text of the Qur'an was compiled at the order of the third caliph, Uthman ibn Affan, circa 651. It was a collection and arrangement of the various messages received during trance states by the founder of Islam, Muhammad, beginning around the year 610, when he was a tradesman in Mecca (in modern Saudi Arabia). These messages were memorized by his followers and recited during prayer (the word *qur'an* means "recitation" or "reading" in Arabic). The scribe Zayd ibn Thabit collected them after Muhammad's death in 632. Variant compilations were also made by other scribes. To guarantee uniformity of teaching, Uthman had Zayd ibn Thabit produce a standard edition and ordered the destruction of all others. A version of the Qur'an in which the messages, or *suras,* were arranged chronologically was made by Ali ibn Abi Talib, the fourth caliph and Muhammad's son-in-law.

4939. Printed edition of the Qur'an was made in 1530 by Pagninus Brixiensis in Rome, Italy.

4940. English translation of the Qur'an was made by G. Sale and published in England in 1734, by which time the Qur'an had already been translated into Latin (in 1143), Italian, German, Dutch, and French.

RELIGION—JAINISM

4941. Jaina saint is held by tradition to have been Rishabhanatha, born many thousands of years ago in Ayodhya, India. He was the first *Tirthankara,* or "ford-provider," meaning an enlightened being, one who has forded the ocean of suffering and achieved liberation from rebirth. He is also considered to have been the first teacher of the precepts of Jainism, the founder of marriage and funeral rites, and the originator of the 72 accomplishments (among them arithmetic and writing) and the 64 crafts

(such as weaving and pottery). The first *Tirthankara* of whom there is some historical record—the 23rd—is Parshvanatha, who may have lived in the ninth century BCE. He established a religious order whose members vowed to renounce killing, stealing, lying, and owning property. A vow of celibacy was added by Mahavira, the 24th *Tirthankara* and the one who is credited by historians with founding Jainism as a religion in the sixth century BCE.

4942. Disciples of Mahavira were eleven Brahmin Hindus who converted to Jainism, the religion of the Jina ("conqueror," referring to one who has been liberated from reincarnation through enlightenment). *Jina,* like *Mahavira* ("great hero"), was a title conferred on Vardhamana (circa 599–527 BCE), an Indian tribal prince who renounced the world and for 13 years wandered the world as a naked ascetic until, in 557 BCE, he attained enlightenment.

4943. Jaina monastic order was established in India by the founder of Jainism, Vardhamana Mahavira, circa 550 BCE. Separate monastic lineages were founded by Mahavira's eleven disciples. The order consists of monks and nuns, who live under conditions of strict asceticism in the hope of perfecting themselves and moving further on the path toward enlightenment, and groups of lay men and women, who undertake six daily duties, including worship, veneration of saints, scriptural study, observance of rules of self-control, austerities, and acts of charity.

4944. Jaina sacred texts were the *Purvas (Foundations),* which contained the teachings of the 24 Jaina world saviors, particularly Mahavira, the last, who died in India in 527 BCE. All 14 of the *Purvas* were lost. The teachings were eventually reconstructed in twelve books of mixed verse, prose, and dialogue called the *Angas (Limbs),* of which eleven survive. The earliest of these are considered by scholars to be the *Acaranga* and the *Sutrakrtanga.* They were written in the Ardhamagadhi language, a form of Prakrit.

4945. Religion to require a vegetarian diet was Jainism, a strongly ascetic religion founded in India in the early sixth century BCE by Vardhamana Mahavira. One of its central tenets is *ahimsa,* the refusal to cause injury to any living creature, which precluded both the animal sacrifices then common in Hinduism and the eating of meat. It also precludes working in any occupation that involves taking life, including fishing and butchering, so that many modern lay Jainas hold jobs in banking and commerce.

RELIGION—JAINISM—*continued*

4946. Canonization of Jaina sacred texts took place at Patna, India, towards the end of the fourth century BCE. Three additional councils were held, the last one in the mid-fourth century CE, to alter the canon. Different sects within Jainism accept variant canons.

4947. Images of the Jaina saints showing the 24 *Tirthankaras,* or world saviors, were made in the third century BCE, during the Maurya dynasty in India. The earliest known image appears to be a polished torso found at Lohanipur.

4948. Schism in Jainism took place during the lifetime of its founder, Vardhamana Mahavira, in India in the sixth century BCE, and was led by his son-in-law Jamali, but it was evidently minor. The first of consequence occurred three centuries later, during the third century BCE, when the monastic community split permanently into two factions, the Svetambaras and the Digambaras. The points of contention included the permissibility of wearing clothes and the capacity of women to attain enlightenment. To these were added, in the fourth century, questions of differing canons of sacred literature and different versions of Jain history.

4949. King to convert to Jainism was Candragupta Maurya, the first emperor of India, who reigned from 321 BCE to circa 297 BCE. After his years of conquest, during which India was united as an empire for the first time, he became a pious adherent of Jainism and adopted a strenuously ascetic life. When famine struck India, Candragupta is said to have abdicated his throne and to have chosen suicide by starvation, an honored Jaina custom.

4950. Biographies of the Jaina saints appeared in the *Kalpa-Sutra (Eon Discourse),* a text written in India in the fourth century. It includes legends and stories about the first of the 24 *Tirthankaras,* Rishabhanata, and the last three, Aristanemi, Parshvanatha, and Mahavira, as well as brief information about the others (the 19th was a princess, Mallinatha) and rules for the recitation of the book during the annual festival of Paryusana.

4951. Reform movement in Jainism of importance was started in mid-15th-century India by Lonka Saha, a lay member of the Shvetambara sect who objected to temple worship as idolatrous and unauthorized by the Jaina canon. By the 18th century, his followers had developed a separate group, the Sthanakavasi. Among other reforms, its monks and nuns adopted the custom of covering their mouths with a cloth, to prevent themselves from causing harm to insects by unintentionally inhaling them.

4952. Formal symbol of Jainism was adopted in 1975 to commemorate the 2,500th anniversary of the attainment of *nirvana* by the founder, Vardhamana Mahavira. It consists of a polygonal figure, resembling a hexagon balanced atop a triangle. Within the hexagon are a semicircle and a swastika inside a dotted rectangle; within the triangle is a raised human hand displaying the word *ahimsa.* The polygonal figure represents the *loka-akasha,* the Jaina conception of the universe, with the celestial world and the underworld intersecting at the terrestrial world, and above all (in the semicircle) the abode of liberated souls. The swastika, an ancient Indian symbol meaning *good being,* refers to four levels of rebirth (divine, human, netherworld, and animal). The dotted rectangle is a diagram drawn with rice grains during temple worship, and the upraised hand is a gesture made during temple worship. *Ahimsa* is the central Jaina tenet of doing no harm to any living thing.

RELIGION—JUDAISM

4953. Depiction of Israelites known to archeologists appears on a wall relief of the Temple of Karnak in Luxor, Egypt. The relief depicts the victorious campaign of the Pharaoh Merneptah against ancient Canaan. In 1990, Frank Yurco, an American Egyptologist with the Field Museum of Natural History in Chicago, IL, USA, identified figures in the relief as Israelites, using evidence found on an ancient monolith known as the Merneptah Stele (circa 1207 BCE). The inscription on the stele appears to read "Israel is laid waste."

4954. Jewish conquest of Jerusalem took place circa 1002 BCE, when the Israelite army under King David captured the walled enclave from the Jebusites. It was captured a second time by the Maccabees in 164 BCE, partially retaken in 1948 during the Israeli War of Independence, and taken again on June 7, 1967, during the Six-Day War, when the Israeli Army drove Jordanian forces in the Old City from the area of the Temple Mount and the Western Wall.

4955. Temple in Jerusalem was built by King Solomon on Mount Moriah, the site of the Binding of Isaac recounted in the Torah. The original Hebrew term is *Beit ha-Mikdash,* or "holy house." According to the chronology given in the Torah, construction was begun in the

Jewish year 2933 and completed on the seventh day of the month of Tishrei in 2935, corresponding to approximately 957 BCE in the Gregorian calendar. On that day, the Ark of the Covenant, containing both sets of the Ten Commandments, was placed in the building's inner chamber. Worship services involving music, prayer, and animal offerings were conducted in the Beit ha-Mikdash until 586 BCE, when it was destroyed by Babylonian forces under Nabu-kudurri-usur (Nebuchadrezzar). It was rebuilt between 538 and 515 BCE by Jews who had returned from exile in Babylonia and continued to be used until its final destruction by the Romans in 70 CE.

4956. Reference to Solomon's Temple in Jerusalem aside from the descriptions and mentions in the Jewish Scriptures is a receipt for a three-shekel donation, written in ink on an ostrakon, or fragment of pottery, from the late ninth century BCE. The receipt reads: "As Ashyahu the king commanded you to give into the hand of Zechariah silver of Tarshish for the House of YHWH: shekels ///." Ashyahu is probably Yehoash, king of Yehudah, the southern Jewish kingdom, from 835 to 801 BCE. Zechariah was a kohen (priest) of that era.

4957. Lost tribes of Israel were the tribes of Gad, Reuben, and part of the tribe of Manasseh. They were banished in the Jewish year 3187 (circa 734 BCE) by the Assyrian king Tiglath-pileser III, who had conquered their lands in the northern part of Israel. The remaining tribes in the Kingdom of Israel—Asher, Dan, Ephraim, Issachar, Naftali, Shimon, Zevulun, and the rest of Manasseh—were conquered and dispersed by 721 BCE. The twelve tribes of Israel were descended from the sons of the Hebrew patriarch Jacob. Two of them—Yehudah and Benjamin—remained unconquered in a separate kingdom and became the ancestors of today's Jews.

4958. Object from Solomon's Temple in Jerusalem to be recovered by archeologists was a tiny ivory pomegranate that appears to have been the head of a ceremonial scepter. The inscription, carved in the Old Hebrew script that was used in ancient Israel circa 700 BCE, reads: "Holy to the kohanim [priests] belonging to the House of YHWH" (although some scholars prefer an alternate reading, "House of Asherah," which would make the pomegranate a ritual object from a Canaanite pagan temple). It was first identified in 1979 by the French paleographer André Lemaire, who saw it in the shop of an antiquities dealer in Jerusalem. The piece was smuggled out of the country in the early

1980s and was exhibited in Paris. In 1988 it was recovered by officials of the Israel Museum, who purchased it for US$550,000. The Temple (in Hebrew, the Beit ha-Mikdash) was built by King Solomon (Shlomo ha-Melekh) in the tenth century BCE.

4959. Physical evidence of a person mentioned in the Jewish scriptures was the fingerprint of Berekhyahu (Baruch), the scribe of the prophet Yirmeyahu (Jeremiah), found on a bulla, or clay seal, dating to circa 600 BCE. The inscription on the bulla reads: "Belonging to Berekhyahu, son of Neriyahu, the scribe." Berekhyahu is mentioned by name in the Book of Jeremiah (36:4–8): "So Jeremiah called Baruch son of Neriah, and Baruch wrote down in the scroll, at Jeremiah's dictation, all the words which the Lord had spoken to him." The provenance of the bulla is unknown.

4960. Anti-Semitic libel of record was contained in the chronicle written by the Egyptian priest-historian Manetho circa 300 BCE, or perhaps as late as 250 BCE. The work has not survived in the original, but it is cited, and refuted, in the treatise *Contra Apionem (Against Apion)*, written by the Jewish historian and general Flavius Josephus (Joseph ben Matthias) in the first century CE. According to Josephus, Manetho claimed that the Hebrew leader Moshe (Moses) was a renegade Egyptian priest and that the people he led out of Egypt were lepers, plague-carriers, and other diseased and reviled outcasts. The slur was repeated as truth thereafter by many later anti-Jewish authors, including Karl Marx and Adolf Hitler.

4961. Rebellion for religious freedom of record was the Makabiah (or Maccabee) rebellion that began in 168 BCE at Modin, in present-day Israel. At that time, the kingdom was controlled by the Hellenized Syrians under the Seleucid ruler Antiochus IV Epiphanes, who outlawed the practice of Judaism and desecrated the Beit ha-Mikdash, the Jerusalem Temple, by erecting within it a statue of Zeus. Although many Jews were Hellenized themselves, a revolt of religious Jews led by Mattityahu ben Yochanan and then by his third son, Yehudah (known as Yehudah ha-Maccabi, or Judah the Hammer), succeeded in 164 BCE in liberating and rededicating the Temple. This is the event commemorated in the Jewish holiday of Chanukah.

4962. Synagogues as places of prayer and study, separate from the central place of Jewish worship in Jerusalem, originated among the Jewish captives taken from Yehudah (modern Israel and Palestinian Authority) to Babylon (modern Iraq) beginning in 597 BCE. According

RELIGION—JUDAISM—*continued*

to tradition, the first synagogue to be founded there was Shef ve-Yativ in Nehardea. The earliest reference to a synagogue comes from the third century BCE and appears on a marble dedication slab from Shedia, a site near Alexandria, Egypt. The earliest known synagogue building, uncovered in 1997 near the town of Jericho, was part of a winter palace constructed circa 50 CE by the Hasmonean (Maccabean) dynasty. Synagogues are properly called by the Hebrew titles *Beit Tefillah, Beit Midrash,* and *Beit Knesset,* meaning, respectively, "house of prayer," "house of study," and "house of assembly."

4963. Royal converts to Judaism were King Izates II and Queen Helena, the monarchs of Adiabene, a state in northern Mesopotamia (in modern-day Iraq). They, their sons, and many of their nobles became Jews in 35 CE. They sent their sons to Jerusalem to be educated, and the family gave material support to the Judean revolt against Rome that began in 65.

4964. Center of Jewish learning outside Jerusalem was the yeshivah (academy) at Yavneh, a town near the coast of Judea (present-day Israel) that served as the religious, political and judicial center for Jews worldwide until 425. Sometime between 68 and 70 CE, the rabbi and scholar Yochanan ben Zakkai was smuggled in a coffin out of Jerusalem, which was then under siege by three Roman legions under the general and future emperor Titus. Ben Zakkai received permission from the Roman authorities to establish a center of learning in the outlying town of Yavneh. The Mishnah, the earliest codification of Jewish law, was compiled there circa 200. Yavneh also became the seat of the Sanhedrin (the assembly of Jewish jurists), which was disbanded by the Roman government in 425. Authority in matters of Jewish law was then transferred to the academies of Sura and Pumbedita in Babylonia and eventually to cities in Europe.

4965. Depiction of a menorah was carved into the Arch of Titus in the Forum in Rome, Italy, erected circa 81 CE by the Emperor Domitian to commemorate the destruction of Jerusalem and the enslavement of the Jews by his brother, the Roman general (and subsequently emperor) Titus. A relief panel shows a victory procession carrying the seven-branched golden candelabrum, the Menorah, that Titus had looted from the Beit ha-Mikdash (Temple of Solomon) in Jerusalem.

4966. Anti-Semitic blood libel was invented by the Greek writer Apion, as related in Book II of *Contra Apionem (Against Apion),* a refutation of Apion written circa 85 by the Jewish historian Flavius Josephus (Joseph ben Matthias). According to Josephus, Apion claimed that Jews practiced human sacrifice and cannibalism in their religious rituals. Although the charge was false, the blood libel was picked up and developed by Christian writers and repeatedly used as an excuse for the slaughter of Jews for the next 2,000 years.

4967. Jewish kingdom to be established since biblical times was Khazaria, the kingdom of the Khazars, located in what is now Kazakhstan, eastern Ukraine, and southern Russia. Sometime around 740, Bulan, the Khazar khagan, or king, adopted Judaism. Later khagans, notably Ovadia, encouraged the establishment of synagogues and centers of learning and included Jews in the supreme council. By circa 950, Judaism was the dominant faith in the Khazari kingdom. The Khazars were conquered circa 1016 by an alliance of Byzantine and Russian armies, but are thought to have become one of the founding populations of Ashkenazi Jewry, the Jews of eastern and northern Europe.

4968. Law requiring Jews to wear an identifying mark was imposed in 850 by the Muslim Abbasid caliph al-Mutawakkil on the Jews of Babylonia (modern Iraq) and on other minority groups living there. The decree required them to wear a yellow patch on their clothing or a yellow headcovering.

4969. Bar mitzvah ceremony was observed in Europe as a rite of passage for Jewish boys from approximately the 13th century. A Jewish boy automatically becomes a *bar mitzvah* ("son of the commandments") at the age of 13, at which time he is fully responsible as an adult for the observance of Jewish laws and customs. The ceremony involved calling the boy to read from the Torah during the morning service, after which a festive celebration usually was held.

4970. Burning of the Talmud by Christian authorities took place at Paris, France, in 1242. Every copy of the Talmud in France, amounting to 24 wagon-loads of handwritten volumes, had been confiscated two years earlier by order of Pope Gregory IX. All were destroyed, along with other religious books taken from Jews.

4971. Expulsion of Jews from a European country took place in England in 1290. On July 18, King Edward I of England, under pressure from his barons and the Church, announced the expulsion of all the Jews and the confiscation of their homes and property. The English Jews, numbering about 4,000, left the country by November, most with little more than the shirts on their backs. Jews did not return to England in any numbers until 1659.

4972. Chassidic master was Israel ben Eliezer, the Ba'al Shem Tov (Master of the Good Name), who founded Chassidism circa 1750 in southeastern Poland. A poor laborer in his early days, he gained a reputation as a healer and a man of insight, preaching an emotional and mystical brand of Judaism that had wide appeal. His teachings, as interpreted by his many disciples, formed the basis for numerous Chassidic sects, each with its own leader, called a tzaddik. The word "chassidism" comes from the Hebrew for "piety."

4973. Reform Jewish services were held by Israel Jacobson, a layman, in Seesen, Brunswick, Germany, in 1809. Reform Judaism denied divine authorship of the Torah, rejected *halakhah* (Jewish law) as outmoded, and emphasized prophetic teachings on social justice. Its services were modeled after those of Protestant Christians, and the traditional Hebrew liturgy was rewritten in the local language. The movement spread to many German cities and to other countries.

4974. Conservative rabbi was Zechariah Frankel, who in 1854 became head of the Jewish Theological Seminary in Breslau, Germany (now Wroclaw, Poland). Frankel developed what he called a "Positive-Historical" approach to Judaism, one that accepted the authority of Jewish tradition but called for the evolution of Jewish law to meet changing historical conditions.

4975. Use of the term "anti-Semitism" was popularized by the German journalist and political agitator Wilhelm Marr. Marr was the author of a widely read tract, "The Victory of Jewry over Germandom" (1873), in which he sought to blame the Jews for the economic and political unrest in Europe in the 1870s. In 1879 he founded the first anti-Semitic political party, the League for Anti-Semitism.

4976. Mass aliyah (emigration) to Israel in modern times, in which a wave of Jewish immigrants from the Diaspora returned to settle in their ancestral homeland, took place between 1882 and 1903. The Hebrew term *aliyah* means "ascent." Jewish communities had continued to exist in the Holy Land, an area now divided between Israel and the Palestinian Authority, since the destruction of Judea by the Romans in the second century CE.

4977. Bat mitzvah ceremony was celebrated in 1922 by Judith Kaplan Eisenstein, the daughter of the Lithuanian-born American rabbi Mordechai Menachem Kaplan, founder of the Reconstructionist branch of Judaism. A Jewish girl automatically becomes a *bat mitzvah* ("daughter of the commandments") at the age of twelve. In traditional Jewish communities there is no formal celebration associated with it. Judith Kaplan Eisenstein's ceremony was modeled after the bar mitzvah ceremony.

4978. Dead Sea Scrolls to be discovered were accidently found in 1947 in a cave at Khirbat Qumran in the Judean desert (in what is now Israel) by a young Bedouin shepherd named Muhammad Dib. Dubbed Cave I by scholars, this first cache of documents, written in ancient Hebrew and Aramaic, included a scroll of the Book of Isaiah, a commentary on the Book of Habakkuk, and a scroll containing a text known as *The War of the Sons of Light Against the Sons of Darkness*. Mar Athanasius Yeshue Samuel, the former bishop of Jerusalem, obtained the first of the scrolls in 1947 and brought them to world attention.

4979. Airlift of endangered Jews to Israel was Operation Magic Carpet, which began on November 8, 1949. It brought some 40,000 Jews to Israel from Yemen.

4980. Branch of Judaism to accept patrilineal descent in determining whether an individual is Jewish was introduced in the United States in 1983 by the Reform movement. According to Jewish law, Jewish descent passes through the mother. Patrilineal descent is not accepted as valid by other branches of Judaism.

4981. Synagogue firebombing in Germany since World War II was carried out by neo-Nazis in Lübeck on March 25, 1994. It was the first such incident since Kristallnacht on November 9–10, 1938, when Nazi rioters destroyed 177 synagogues in Germany.

RELIGION—JUDAISM—SCRIPTURES

4982. Commandment in the Torah is *p'ru ur'vu*, "be fruitful and multiply," given to Adam and Eve in the Garden of Eden. The verse occurs in the biblical book called *Bereshit* in Hebrew and Genesis in Latin. According to Jewish tradition, the text of the Torah was dictated by God to Moses at Mount Sinai, in present-day Egypt, circa 1250 BCE.

4983. Public reading of a book of the Bible since the traditional time of its revelation took place in 621 BCE, when Josiah, king of the southern Israelite kingdom of Yehudah (Judah), gathered his subjects in the Beit ha-Mikdash (the Temple in Jerusalem) and read aloud to them a book that had been recently found there, identified by many scholars as *Devarim,*, or Deuteronomy, the fifth book of the Torah. The result was the abolition of idolatry and the reintroduction of authentic Jewish religious practices.

4984. Canonization of biblical books was begun circa 444 BCE (or, according to some scholars, as late as 397 BCE), when Ezra the Scribe, leader of a group of Jews returning to Jerusalem from exile in Babylon, read "the book of the Law of Moses" to the assembled people during Sukkot (the Feast of Tabernacles), with the aim of reinforcing their return to strict religious practice. The text he read was probably the book of *Devarim* (Deuteronomy), the fifth book of the Torah.

4985. Translation of the Jewish Bible was made orally, phrase by phrase, in the synagogues of Judah (now Israel and the Palestinian Authority) and the communities of the Diaspora, notably that of Babylonia. As more Jews began speaking Aramaic—the common language of the Persian Empire from about the fifth century BCE—the synagogues provided interpreters during public readings of the Torah and prophetic texts, which were read in the original Hebrew. This practice eventually gave rise to written versions, called Targums (from *meturgeman*, "translator"). A translation into Greek for the use of the Jews living in Alexandria, Egypt, known as the Septuagint, was made in the mid-third century BCE.

4986. Compilation of Jewish oral laws was the Mishnah, edited by Yehudah ha-Nasi (Judah the Prince) at Yavneh, in Roman-occupied Judea (modern Israel), and completed circa 189 CE. In 63 tractates divided into six orders, it presents laws transmitted orally by scholars for hundreds of years. The word *mishnah* means "repetition," referring to the acts of memorization and transmission.

4987. Kabbalistic text was the *Sefer ha-Yetzirah (Book of Creation)*. Jewish religious tradition ascribes its authorship to Avraham, the first Jew (thus the book is sometimes referred to as *Otiyyot de Avraham Avinu*, or "Alphabet of Our Father Abraham"). Modern scholars believe that the text, written in Hebrew with some elements of Aramaic, probably appeared circa 300 CE in the Holy Land (present-day Israel). The *Sefer ha-Yetzirah* is the earliest known Jewish mystical work and contains cosmogonical concepts essential to the later development of Kabbalah. It regards creation as a process in which God's wisdom and power are released into the world through the channels represented by the 22 letters of the Hebrew alphabet and the ten interconnected divine qualities known as the *sefirot*.

4988. Talmud to be compiled was the Talmud Yerushalmi (Jerusalem Talmud), redacted in Jerusalem, Judea (modern Israel), circa 400. The Talmud is the authoritative explication of Jewish law, which had previously been transmitted orally from scholar to scholar. It comprises two parts: the Mishnah, the earliest compilation of oral teachings, written in Hebrew and redacted circa 189 by Yehudah ha-Nasi in Yavneh, and the Gemara, a collection of debates and commentaries on the text of the Mishnah, written in Aramaic and added over the next three centuries. The version of the Talmud that is most used today is the more extensive and complete Talmud Bavli (Babylonian Talmud), redacted in Babylonia (now Iraq) circa 500.

4989. Code of Jewish law was the *Halakhot pesuqot (The Laws as Decided)*, written in Aramaic in 760 CE by Yehudai bar Nakhman, the Gaon (head) of the yeshivah at Sura, Babylonia (in modern Iraq). The first to be accepted as the standard codification by Jews of all communities was the *Shulkhan 'Arukh (The Set Table)*, compiled circa 1564 in Safed (Tzefat, in present-day Israel) by the Sephardic rabbi and mystic Yosef ben Ephraim Karo from his own more comprehensive work *Beit Yosef (House of Joseph)*. Karo synthesized the *halakhic* (legal) decisions of the earlier scholars Moshe ben Maimon (Maimonides), Isaac Alfasi, and Asher ben Yehiel into an authoritative digest of Jewish law. The *Shulkhan 'Arukh* was adapted for use by Ashkenazic (northern and eastern European) Jewry in 1571 by Rabbi Moshe Isserles of Kraków, Poland. Religious Jews continue to regard it as authoritative.

4990. Jewish prayer book was the *Siddur Rav Amram (Order of Prayers of Rabbi Amram),* compiled circa 850 by Amram bar Sheshna, the Gaon (head) of the Talmudic academy in Sura, Babylonia (now Iraq). His collection, made at the request of the Jews of Spain, formed the basis for the modern prayerbooks used by the two main branches of Jews, the Sephardim and the Ashkenazim. Prior to his time, Jews recited the traditional prayers by heart.

4991. Printed edition of the Psalms in Hebrew was made in 1477, probably at Bologna, Italy. Excerpts from the commentary on the Psalms by the twelfth-century French rabbi David Kimchi (the Radak) were provided, verse by verse. The original Hebrew name for the Psalms is *Tehillim,* meaning "praises."

4992. Printed edition of the Talmud was an edition of the Talmud Bavli (Babylonian Talmud) printed in Spain circa 1482. The modern standard version was produced in Vilna (now Vilnius, Lithuania) circa 1886, with the pages laid out in a kind of textual antiphony: each displays a central column of texts from the Mishnah and the accompanying Gemara, surrounded by other columns containing scholarly commentaries from rabbis of widely varying times and places. The older version of the Talmud, the Talmud Yerushalmi (Jerusalem Talmud), was first printed in Venice, Italy, in 1524.

4993. Printed edition of the Torah was made in Bologna, Italy, in 1482, by Avraham ben Hayyim di Tintori and Yosef ben Avraham Caravita. The complete Jewish Bible, known as the Tanakh (an acronym for *Torah, Neviim, Ketuvim,* or "Law, Prophets, and Writings"), was printed at Soncino, Italy, in 1488 by Yehoshua Shlomo Soncino and his nephews, Moshe and Gershom, and is known as the Soncino Bible.

4994. Yiddish translation of the Jewish Bible from the original Hebrew began in 1490 with a translation in manuscript of *Tehillim* (the Psalms). Printed editions of the Torah in Yiddish were published in 1544 in the German cities of Augsburg and Konstanz.

RELIGION—SHINTO

4995. Shinto rituals are thought to have originated in the nature worship and shamanism practiced by Japan's prehistoric Yayoi culture circa 250 BCE. The word "Shinto"—derived from the Chinese characters *shen dao,* meaning "way of the gods"—was not adopted until the advent of Buddhism in the seventh century CE, when a defining term became necessary. Shinto revolves around the worship of the *kami,* the life-forces manifested in natural phenomena, as well as in important human beings (such as ancestors) and certain man-made objects.

4996. Account of the Shinto religion appeared in the *Kojiki (Chronicle of Ancient Things),* Japan's first book of history, compiled in 712. The book, written in Japanese using Chinese characters, contained a collection of myths, legends, customs, and rituals from early Shinto religion, which gave it the character of a sacred text for later practitioners of Shinto. Additional information about Shinto was contained in a second chronicle from the same era, the *Nihon shoki* or *Nihon gi (Chronicles of Japan),* compiled in 720 in Chinese. The first text was commissioned by the empress Gemmei, the second by her daughter, the empress Gensho. The cosmological myths, chiefly about the sun goddess Amaterasu and her trickster brother Susanoo, helped to establish a genealogy and chain of authority for Japan's ruling families.

4997. Shinto temple to Hachiman was built in 725 in northern Kyushu, Japan, where the city of Usa grew up around it. Hachiman, the most popular of the Shinto deities, is both the god of war and the protector of human life. When Mahayana Buddhism came to Japan and began to merge with Shinto, Hachiman was the first of the Shinto *kami,* or numinous beings, to be adopted into the Buddhist pantheon, receiving the title Daibosatsu ("future Buddha").

4998. Shinto reform movement was Ise Shinto, founded at the Ise Shrine in the 13th century to remove the Mahayana Buddhist influences that had overtaken Japan's indigenous religion. Its theology was explained in a five-volume treatise, the *Shinto gobusho.*

4999. Shinto sect was Kurozumi-Kyo, founded by the Shinto priest Munetada Kurozumi in the early 19th century. The sect was devoted to the sun goddess Amaterasu, in Japanese tradition the ancestor of the imperial family. In 1846 it received official recognition from the Japanese government, which had adopted Shinto as a state cult. The movement called Sect Shinto gave rise to 13 groups during the Meiji period, from 1868 to 1912.

5000. Establishment of State Shinto as the official religion of Japan took place during the Meiji Restoration, which began in 1868. Worship at Shinto shrines was made compulsory. The shrines themselves were administered by the national government, the teaching of Shinto was required in all schools, and great emphasis

RELIGION—SHINTO—*continued*

was placed on the divinity of the emperor and the necessity for strict obedience to his will—a factor in the militarization of Japanese society. State Shinto was abolished by the occupying Allied powers after Japan's defeat in 1945.

RELIGION—SIKHISM

5001. Sikh guru was Nanak, a mystic and wandering hymn singer from Sultanpur in the Punjab region (now divided between India and Pakistan), where Hinduism and Islam were in contention. In 1499 he had a religious experience during which he received a call to teach a new religious pathway that was neither Hindu nor Muslim, though it incorporated elements of both religions. The word *sikh* used by his followers means "disciple." He was the first of ten Sikh gurus.

5002. Sikh community and place of worship was founded circa 1520 by Nanak, the first Sikh guru, at Kartarpur, in the Punjab (in present-day India).

5003. Sectarian dissenters in Sikhism were the Udasis, followers of Shri Chand, the son of the founder of Sikhism, Guru Nanak. Circa 1525, they founded a monastic order, the first among the Sikhs, that closely resembled Hindu ascetic orders, including a celibacy requirement and the use of Sanskrit in worship. They did not adopt the uniform, including uncut hair, that since 1699 has given mainstream Sikhs a distinctive appearance. The name Udasi comes from a Sanskrit word meaning "renounce".

5004. Sikh sacred book was the *Adi Granth (First Book)*, also known as *Granth Sahib,* compiled in 1604 by Arjun, the fifth Sikh guru, at the city of Amritsar in the Punjab (now part of India). The book contains nearly 6,000 hymns in the Punjabi and Hindi languages, composed by Nanak, the founder of the religion, and his first four successors, as well as by poets and saints from both Hinduism and Islam. In 1704 the Granth was accorded the status of guru, or religious leader, in place of a human leader.

5005. Sikh temple at Amritsar was built in 1604 by Guru Arjun, fifth of the Sikh gurus, in Amritsar, the city founded by his predecessor, Ram Das, in the Punjab region of India. The temple, or *gurdwara,* was built on an island in a tank of sacred water called the *amrita-saras,* or pool of nectar. It was destroyed during the Afghan invasions and reconstructed several times. Its official name is the Harimandir, but the gold foil covering its dome has given it the name Golden Temple.

5006. Sikh martyr was Arjun, the fifth guru, the compiler of the *Adi Granth,* Sikhism's sacred text, and the builder of the Golden Temple at Amritsar, India. When Jahangir succeeded Akbar as head of the Mughal empire of India in 1606, he abandoned Akbar's policy of toleration toward the Sikhs. Arjun was accused of aiding a rebel prince, of teaching falsehoods, and and of including in the *Adi Granth* things that gave offense to Islam. He was tortured to death in Lahore (in present-day Pakistan) on May 30, 1606.

5007. Sikh guru who was a temporal leader as well as a spiritual leader was Hargobind, the sixth guru of the Sikhs. He ruled from the Akal Takht ("Immortal Throne"), which he built in 1609 at the Sikh city of Amritsar, in the Punjab region of India.

5008. Sikh military victories took place after 1627, when Shah Jahan took the throne of India's Mughal Empire. Considering the Sikhs a threat, he sent four armies against them, all of which were turned back by the Sikhs under the generalship of their sixth guru, Hargobind. Imprisoned for twelve years under Shah Jahan's predecessor, Jahangir, Hargobind was a master swordsman and rider who instituted military training among the Sikhs. They became a still more formidable force under the tenth guru, Gobind Singh, who reconstituted them as a military brotherhood in 1699. Their first offensive war against the Mughals began in 1709 under Banda Singh Bahadur, who was defeated.

5009. Sikhs to take the name "Singh" were the five volunteers who joined together as the Khalsa brotherhood on April 13, 1699, at Anandpur, Punjab, India. The Khalsa, founded by Gobind Rai (thereafter called Gobind Singh), the tenth Sikh guru, was a brotherhood of warriors. Its democratic nature was symbolized by the adoption of the surname Singh, meaning "lion," by all the men, and of Kaur, or "princess," by the women.

5010. Sikh kingdom was founded in 1801 when a chieftain named Ranjit Singh proclaimed himself maharajah of the Punjab, whose capital city, Lahore, he had captured in 1799. In 20 years of fighting, he succeeded in bringing all of the Punjab under his control and in gaining recognition from the British, whose invasion of Afghanistan he assisted. The state collapsed a few years after his death. The Punjab was later divided between India and Pakistan.

5011. Sikh revival movement was the Singh Sabha ("Singh Society"), formed in Amritsar, India, in 1873 as a response to the efforts of Christian missionaries and Hindu revivalists who were actively proselytizing Sikhs. The society founded a number of schools and colleges, including Khalsa College at Amritsar, and mounted a political campaign for legal recognition of Sikh marriages and temples.

5012. Sikh international convention was held on April 3, 1999, in the Meadowlands Convention Center in Secaucus, NJ, USA. Some 6,000 Sikhs gathered to celebrate the 300th anniversary of the Khalsa, the military fraternity of Sikh religious adherents, which was established on April 13, 1699, by the tenth Sikh guru, Gobind Singh, in the Punjab region of India.

RELIGION—TAOISM

5013. Philosopher of Taoism was Laozi (in Wade-Giles transliteration, Lao-tzu), meaning "Master Lao," the title given to Li Erh. According to the *Shih-chi (Historial Records),* China's earliest comprehensive historical account, Li Erh was a sage who lived in the sixth century BCE and served as the imperial archivist. His name was attached to the foremost work of Taoist thought, the *Tao-tê Ching (Classic of the Way of Power),* now considered to have been the work of numerous authors. His legendary wisdom gradually earned for Laozi the status of a worshipped deity.

5014. Taoist book of teachings was probably the *Zhuangzi,* a book named after its author, who lived in China from 369 to 286 BCE and whose name in Wade-Giles transliteration is Chuang-tzu. The book, also called the *Nan-hua chenching (The Pure Classic of Nan-hua),* explains the doctrine of the Tao, the eternal and unlimited One that encompasses all things. It contains the famous passage in which Zhuangzi relates how he awakened from sleep unable to say whether he was a philosopher dreaming that he was a butterfly or a butterfly dreaming that he was a philosopher. Formerly it was thought that the earliest Taoist book was the *Tao-tê Ching (Classic of the Way of Power),* attributed to the sage Laozi in the sixth century BCE, but scholars are now inclined to think that the *Tao-tê Ching* was long in compilation and reached its final form in the third century BCE.

5015. Taoist religious community was the T'ien-shih Tao (the Way of the Celestial Master), founded in 142 CE in the Szechwan province of China by Chang Ling, the first Taoist patriarch, on the basis of a revelation from the deified philosopher Laozi, from whom he received authority to teach the principles and perform the rituals of Taoism, especially as set forth in the *Tao-tê Ching (Classic of the Way of Power).* The group's members, divided into 24 or more parishes, practiced a form of healing involving confession of sins and ceremonial purification.

5016. Popular religious rebellion in China was the Yellow Turban Rebellion, an uprising against the degenerating Han dynasty that began in eastern China in 184 under a Taoist faith healer, Chang Chüeh, and continued for some 20 years. It was closely followed by the Five Pecks of Rice movement, led by Chang Lu, the third patriarch of Taoism, who broke away from the Han and set up an independent state in what is now Szechwan and Shensi provinces, using his army to spread rebellion throughout Szechwan. The movement, which became the model for future religion-based campaigns, took its name from the Taoist practice of tithing five pecks of rice. The rebellion ended in 215.

5017. Taoist state was set up circa 200 CE by Chang Lu, the third Taoist patriarch, in Hanchung (now part of the Chinese provinces of Szechwan and Shensi), from which its army fomented the rebellion against the Han dynasty known as the Five Pecks of Rice.

RELIGION—ZOROASTRIANISM

5018. Prophet of Zoroastrianism was the Iranian religious reformer and visionary Zarathushtra (in Greek, Zoroaster). Although Zoroastrian tradition holds that he lived in the sixth century BCE, many scholars place him much earlier, between 1500 and 1200 BCE. In that era, the Iranians were pastoral nomads who lived on the steppes of what is now southern Russia. Zarathushtra was a hereditary priest of their ancient religion who experienced a series of amplifying revelations. His chief teaching concerned the struggle between the Creator, Ahura Mazda (Orimazd), an eternal God of wisdom and justice, and his evil adversary, Angra Mainyu (Ahriman), with this world as their battlefield, peopled by human beings who have free choice to ally themselves with one or the other. Zarathushtra also preached an apocalypse in which a World Savior, born of a virgin mother, presides over the final victory of goodness, the resurrection of the dead, the last judgment, the salvation of the virtuous, and the perfection of Ahura Mazda's kingdom on earth.

RELIGION—ZOROASTRIANISM—*continued*

5019. Establishment of Zoroastrianism as state religion was effected in the Persian Empire, founded by Cyrus the Great in 550 BCE. It was accepted as the state religion in the area that is now Iran twice more, by the Parthians (circa 141 BCE to 224 CE) and by the Sasanians (224–651).

5020. Zoroastrian religious texts are collected in the *Avesta,* the sacred scripture of the Zoroastrian religion. Its oldest section, the *Gathas,* a group of hymns written by the prophet Zarathushtra, is generally taken to date from the sixth century BCE, although some scholars prefer to date them six to nine centuries earlier than that. By the time the 21 books of the *Avesta* were canonized and put into writing in Persia circa the fifth century CE, Avestan had long ceased to be a spoken language. A special alphabet based on Aramaic, via Pahlavi, had to be invented for it, and no other literature in it exists. Most of the *Avesta* disappeared during the foreign conquests of Persia, but its contents were summarized in the ninth-century book *Denkart.*

5021. Heresy in Zoroastrianism was Zurvanism, which maintained that the good Creator God of Zoroastrianism, Ahura Mazda, and his adversary, the evil spirit Angra Mainyu, were sons of a single father, Zurvan, meaning "time." Scholars differ as to when and where Zurvanism appeared, some saying as early as the fifth century BCE in Persian Babylonia, others in Persia itself (now Iran) during the Sasanian period (third to seventh centuries CE).

5022. Mass migration by Zoroastrians took place in the late ninth century, after their homeland, Persia (now Iran), was conquered by the Arabs, who uprooted Zoroastrianism as the state religion and established Islam in its stead. A large group of Zoroastrians crossed the Arabian Sea and settled in 936 at Sanjan, Gujarat (now part of India). They eventually built communities along the coast and flourished particularly in Bombay. The name by which they are known in India, "Parsi," means "Persian." The oldest of their sacred fires has been burning continuously at the coastal village of Udwada since the tenth century.

5023. Scholarly treatise on Zoroastrianism was written in Latin and published in 1700 by the English clergyman and early Assyriologist Thomas Hyde, who had made a special study of Persian inscriptions (it was Hyde who coined the word "cuneiform").

5024. Zoroastrian reform movement was the Zoroastrian Reform Society, founded in 1851 in Bombay, India, by followers who hoped to modernize the religion.

ROBOTS AND AUTOMATONS

5025. Automaton known from historical references was a wooden model of a pigeon built by Archytas of Tarentum (now Taranto, Italy), who lived circa 400–350 BCE. The pigeon apparently spun around while hanging from a bar. Power was supplied by steam or a stream of air. Neither the object nor a depiction survives.

5026. Book on robotics was the *Shui shih t'u Ching (Book of Hydraulic Elegancies),* published during the Sui dynasty in China circa 600 CE. The book discusses methods for making mechanical birds, beasts, and human figures powered by water.

5027. King knighted by an automaton was Alfonso XI, king of Castile (now part of Spain) from 1325 to 1350. To stimulate the growth of Castilian chivalry, in 1332 Alfonso decided to become a knight, but this presented a seemingly insuperable problem: He could not knight himself, nor could any man of lesser status administer the knighthood to him. Alfonso's ingenious solution was to have an automaton of St. James bestow the honor on him.

5028. Android-maker of record was by Hans Bullmann of Nuremberg (now in Germany) circa 1525. His male and female figures were driven by clockwork; some of them played musical instruments. An android is an automaton in human form.

5029. Mechanical duck was built in 1737 by the French mechanical engineer and robotics pioneer Jacques de Vaucanson. This ingenious automaton, containing hundreds of parts, was in the form of a life-size duck, and could not only imitate in a lifelike manner the flying and swimming motions of a duck, but also contained a simulated digestive system which digested and excreted pellets of artificial food. Openings in the body allowed viewers to see the digestive system in action; the intestines were made of india rubber tubing, probably the first rubber tubing ever made.

5030. Androids capable of a variety of tasks were designed and built by inventors Henri Louis Jacquet-Droz and son between 1772 and 1775. Their androids, motivated by cam linkages, air pressure hoses, and other sophisticated mechanisms, included the Writer, which could write messages of up to 40 letters; the Artist, which could sketch four drawings, and the Harmonium Player, a female android that played five musical pieces. All three figures have been preserved in the Neuchâtel History Museum in Neuchâtel, Switzerland.

5031. Robot as a term for an automaton was used in 1917, coined by Czech playwright Karel Capek in his play *Opilek.* Capek derived the word from the Czech word for slave, "robotnik." The word came into popular use in 1921, after Capek used it in the title of his play *R.U.R. (Rossum's Universal Robots).*

5032. Industrial robot that was practical was the Unimate, developed by two Americans, physicist Joseph F. Engelberger and engineer George C. Devol. The first unit to be produced was installed in 1961 at a General Motors plant in the United States to work with heated die-casting machines. That year, Engelberger and Devol founded Unimation, the first commercial company to make robots, and Devol filed the first American robot patent.

5033. Industrial robot organization was the Japanese Industrial Robot Association, founded in 1971 to promote the use of robots in factories.

5034. Robotics journal was *The Industrial Robot,* the first international journal of robotics, which began publication in Great Britain in 1973.

5035. Human killed by a robot was an American, Robert Williams, a worker at the Ford Motor plant in Flat Rock, MI, USA. On January 25, 1979, he was killed instantly when a robot activated unexpectedly and hit him in the head with its arm. The robot was manufacturered by Unit Handling Systems, which paid an indemnity to Williams's estate of US$10 million.

5036. Autonomous security robot was ROBART I, developed in 1980–82 at the U.S. Naval Postgraduate School in Monterey, CA, USA. This early system mounted a video camera and other sensors and navigated along preprogrammed patrol routes. It was able to detect suspected intruders but it lacked the ability to assess and filter out nuisance alarms.

5037. Robot nurse was Melkong (Medical Electric King Kong), invented in 1983 by Japanese robotics researcher Funakubo Hiroyasu. Melkong could pick up and carry patients from bed to bed or support them for bathing or a change of clothes.

5038. Battlefield robot was the Robotic Ranger, fabricated in 1984 by the Grumman Aerospace Corporation of Long Island, NY, USA, under contract to the U.S. Army's Missile Command. The remotely directed robot was designed to fire anti-tank weapons; it was first tested in the field in 1985. Another battlefield robot, the Prowler ("Programmable Robot Observer with Local Enemy Response"), designed by the American robotocs firm Robot Defense Systems, was also fire-tested that year.

5039. Speech-activated robot capable of understanding a wide range of sentences was the Speech-Actuated Manipulator, developed in 1989 by M. Brown, B. Buntschuh, and J. Wilpon at the Bell Telephone Laboratories in Holmdel, NJ, USA. Operators issued instructions to SAM over the phone; it could understand 300 billion sentences using speech-recognition routines processed by eight computers, and would ask for a restatement if it did not understand the instruction. The robot performed actions with a manipulator arm and "saw" with the help of two video cameras and eight computers.

5040. Robot to perform surgery was Robodoc, the world's first robotic device that actively performed surgical procedures. It was developed by two Americans, Howard "Hap" Paul, a veterinarian-surgeon at the Sacramento Animal Medical Group in Carmichael, CA, USA, and William Bargar, an orthopedic surgeon at Sutter General Hospital, Sacramento, CA, USA, and was manufactured by Integrated Surgical Systems. Robodoc was capable of cutting bone 40 times more precisely than human doctors. In 1995, the US$500,000 robot was authorized by the U.S. Food and Drug Administration to perform 300 hip replacement procedures on humans.

5041. Cyborg was Kevin Warwick, the first man to receive a computer implant, an event long predicted by science fiction. On August 24, 1998, Warwick, a professor of cybernetics at the University of Reading, England, had a glass capsule containing a transponder, a silicon microprocessor, and a battery surgically implanted into his arm. The chip was able to activate radio-controlled computer equipment in Warwick's office. The word "cyborg," short for "cybernetic organism," was coined by Manfred Clynes in 1960.

S

SCIENCE

5042. Scientists attached to armed forces were the botanists, zoologists, geologists, geographers, and physicians who accompanied the armies of Alexander the Great on his campaigns of military conquest beginning in 335 BCE. In his youth in Macedonia, Alexander had been a student of the Greek philosopher and scientist Aristotle.

5043. Arabic translations of scientific manuscripts were made in the eighth century, after the Muslim conquests in Europe, Africa, and Asia had brought the Muslims into contact with a wide variety of learned civilizations. Indian and Persian astronomical treatises were among the first texts to be translated. In the early ninth century, the seventh Abbasid caliph, al-Ma'mun, founded a library and research center in Baghdad (in present-day Iraq), the *Bayt al-Hikmah* (House of Wisdom), whose translation department was staffed mainly by Christian experts in Greek and Syriac.

5044. Collector of Greek scientific manuscripts was Hunayn ibn Ishaq al-Ibadi (sometimes Latinized to Johannitius), a Nestorian Christian who served as chief physician to the court of Caliph al-Mutawakkil in Baghdad (in present-day Iraq) and who traveled widely to collect classical Greek manuscripts of medicine, science, and philosophy. At his translation school in Baghdad, Greek manuscripts were rendered into Syriac and Arabic by a staff of 90 scholars, including Muslims, Jews, Christians, and Zoroastrians. A number of important Greek works, particularly by the physician Galen, exist only in these translations. Hunayn ibn Ishaq's *Questions and Answers,* a summary of Galen's teachings, was published circa 850.

5045. Muslim polymath was Abu Ali al-Husayn ibn abd Allah ibn Sina (called Avicenna in the West), scholar, scientist, philosopher, and court physician to the prince of Hamadan, Persia (now Iran), circa 1000. He was the author of more than 200 treatises on all subjects, the product of his custom of writing 50 pages each night. His reputation rests on two encyclopedic works, the *Kitab ash-shifà (Book of Healing),* which covers logic, mathematics, astronomy, music, metaphysics, and the natural sciences, and *Al-Qanun fi at-tibb (The Canon of Medicine),* a comprehensive textbook that continued to be used in the medical schools of western Europe until 1650.

5046. Renaissance man was the Humanist scholar Leon Battista Alberti, secretary at the papal court in Rome, Italy, from 1432 to 1464, whose fields of accomplishment included mathematics, Latin, moral philosophy, architecture, painting, poetry, musical composition, performance on the organ, cartography, cryptography, and the development of the Italian language.

5047. Scientific academy was the Academia Secretorum Naturae ("Secret Academy of Nature"), also called the Accademia dei Segreti, founded in Naples, Italy, circa 1575 by Giambattista della Porta. Its members were naturalists whose interests combined science and magic. Their experiments were recounted in various editions of Porta's *Magia naturalis.* Porta himself made contributions to optics, cryptology, meteorology, agronomy, astronomy, and engineering.

5048. Scientific association sanctioned by a national government was the Royal Society of London for the Promotion of Natural Knowledge, usually referred to as the Royal Society of London, founded in 1660 and chartered by King Charles II in 1662 and 1663. The first women to be admitted as members were X-ray crystallographer Kathleen Yardley Lonsdale and microbiologist Marjory Stephenson, both elected in 1945.

5049. Scientific research voyage was organized and led by Edmond Halley, the English astronomer, naval captain, and secretary of the Royal Society. With the backing of the British Admiralty, Halley departed from England on October 20, 1698, commanding the sloop H.M.S *Paramore.* The only goal of the two-year mission was to measure the variations of the compass in the South Atlantic and to chart the Earth's magnetic field. In 1701 Halley published the results of his expedition in the first magnetic charts of the Atlantic and Pacific oceans.

5050. Scientists attached to armed forces in modern times were the naturalists, engineers, medical men, scholars, and artists, members of the French Army's Commission of Science and Arts, who were attached to the forces under Napoléon Bonaparte that conquered Egypt in 1798. They made a thorough and detailed catalog of Egypt's topography, geography, climate, flora, fauna, minerals, archeological treasures (most famously, the Rosetta Stone), history, and people. Their discoveries were recorded in the *Description de l'Égypte,* published between 1808 and 1825.

5051. Scientific hoax of international notoriety was the Piltdown Man hoax of 1912. On December 18, 1912, Charles Dawson, a member of the Sussex Archaeological Society, and Arthur Smith Woodward, a geologist at the British Museum, claimed to have discovered a fossilized human skull, the first found in England, at Piltdown Common near Lewes, Sussex. Their claim was universally accepted, and Piltdown Man (*Eoanthropus dawsoni*) was prominently featured in subsequent anthropological literature. The hoax was not revealed until 1954, when two Oxford University professors, Joseph S. Weiner and Wilfrid Edward Le Gros Clark, with Kenneth P. Oakley of the British Museum, proved that the fossils were actually a modern human cranium and the jawbone of an orangutan that had been altered, stained, and planted in the ground by Dawson and probably one or more confederates. Among the figures who have been tentatively implicated in the hoax are Pierre Teilhard de Chardin, the French Jesuit priest and paleontologist, who was one of the first to view the fossils *in situ*, and Arthur Conan Doyle, author of the Sherlock Holmes and Professor Challenger stories.

SCIENCE—ARCHEOLOGY

5052. Archeologist was Nabu-na'id (Nabonidus), king of Babylonia from 556 to 539 BCE. An antiquarian and devotee of the Old Babylonian god Sin, he excavated buried shrines and temples, restored the great ziggurat of the Babylonian city of Ur (now Tel-el-Muqayyar, Iraq), and amassed a notable collection of antiquities. These formed the basis of the world's first museum, which was operated by his daughter Ennigaldi-Nanna.

5053. Archeological digs in Egypt were made by a group of French scholars, historians, engineers, and surveyors who arrived in 1798, attached to the army of invasion led by Napoléon. Their discoveries were recorded in the *Description de l'Égypte,* published between 1808 and 1825. One of these discoveries—the Rosetta Stone, a monument displaying a decree of Ptolemy V Epiphanes in three languages—led to the decipherment of hieroglyphics by Jean-François Champollion in 1822.

5054. Hieroglyphic writing from Egypt to be deciphered was an inscription carved on the Rosetta Stone, a piece of black basalt that was found near the town of Rosetta (now Rashid), Egypt, in 1799 by a member of Napoléon's military expedition. The inscription concerned a decree promulgated in 196 BCE by Ptolemy V Epiphanes, the Macedonian king of Egypt, in which he granted a variety of benefactions, pardons, and remittances of debts and taxes. It was given in Greek, Egyptian hieroglyphics, and demotic (a simplified cursive form of hieroglyphic script). The English physician and physicist Thomas Young identified some of the hieroglyphs as royal names in 1813–14. The remainder of the decipherment was accomplished in 1821–22 by Jean-François Champollion, professor at the University of Grenoble, France, who realized that hieroglyphs were neither alphabetic, syllabic, nor determinative (standing for a single idea), but a combination of all three.

5055. Cuneiform writing from Mesopotamia to be deciphered was an inscription carved on a high cliff face near the village of Bisitun, Iran (formerly Behistun, Persia), at the order of King Darius I, the Achaemenid king who ruled the Persian empire from 522 to 486 BCE. The inscription, which recounts the killings, battles, and political conflicts that accompanied Darius's rise to power, was carved on the rock in three cuneiform languages: Old Persian, Babylonian, and Elamite. Over a period of years, beginning in 1835, it was copied by Sir Henry Creswicke Rawlinson, an English army officer working for the East India Company. Rawlinson deciphered the first two paragraphs of the Old Persian text by 1837 and completed the work in 1851, laying the groundwork for the decipherment, by himself and others, of Babylonian and Elamite.

5056. Archeological digs in Mesopotamia were made by Paul-Émile Botta, the French consul in Ottoman Mesopotamia (modern Iraq), and Austen Henry Layard, a British government agent in the same area, who separately undertook to find the ancient city of Nineveh. In 1843, Botta made the first major archeological find in Mesopotamia when he uncovered the palace of Sargon II, king of Assyria in the eighth century BCE, at Dur Sharrukin (now Khorsabad). Layard, after discovering several Assyrian palaces at Nimrud beginning in 1845, excavated a mound in 1849 that proved to be the ruins of Nineveh, including the palace of Sennacherib (Sin-akhkhe-eriba), the son of Sargon II. Botta and Layard were preceded by Claudius James Rich, a British East India Company administrator stationed in Baghdad, who surveyed the site of ancient Babylon in 1811, made sketches and a map, and collected objects, but did not carry out deep excavations.

SCIENCE—ARCHEOLOGY—continued

5057. Popular book about archeology was *Nineveh and Its Remains,* published by the English archeologist Sir Austen Henry Layard in 1849. It described his discovery and excavation of the capital city of ancient Assyria and of Shanina-la-ishu, the palace of Sennacherib (Sin-akhkhe-eriba).

5058. Excavator of Troy was Frank Calvert, a British expatriate and diplomat who purchased about half of the great mound at Hisarlik, Turkey, which he suspected was the location of the ancient city of Troy. Calvert began excavations there circa 1858, 15 years before the German archeologist Heinrich Schliemann began digging there at Calvert's invitation, and announced his findings to the scholarly community in London in 1865. In 1996, Calvert's heirs filed a claim to a portion of Schliemann's Trojan treasures. They maintained that Schliemann had made valuable discoveries—a set of ceremonial axes—on Calvert's land in 1890 but had smuggled them to Berlin, Germany, without sharing the proceeds. The axes were believed by Western archeologists to have been lost at the end of World War II. In 1994, it was revealed that they were in the collection of the Pushkin Museum in Moscow, Russia.

5059. Underwater excavation of a shipwreck took place in 1900 in waters off the island of Antikythera, Greece, near Crete. Sponge divers had located a wreck at a depth of approximately 170 feet (50 to 60 meters). A salvage operation was undertaken by the divers, directed by their captain, Dimitrios Kondos, with the help of the Greek navy. The primitive diving equipment of the time made the operation extremely hazardous. All of the divers suffered from nitrogen narcosis (the bends). Sections of planking and other items were recovered. Later investigations by Jacques-Yves Cousteau in 1953 and 1976 uncovered the hull under a layer of mud. Also found were a trove of gold ingots, a monumental bronze statue of a youth sculpted circa 400 BCE, and the Antikythera Mechanism, the first known astronomical calculator. The ship is believed to have been a merchant vessel, possibly based in Pergamon (now Bergama, Turkey), from circa 85 BCE.

5060. Archeological study of a New World site that was comprehensive was conducted between 1915 and 1929 at Pecos, NM, USA, by Alfred Vincent Kidder, an American archeologist who also developed many of the methods of modern stratigraphy. He published his research in *Introduction to the Study of Southwestern Archaeology* (1924).

5061. Woman archeologist of distinction was Kathleen (Mary) Kenyon, born in Wrexham, Clwyd, Wales, in 1906. She led excavations of Jericho (then in Jordan, now under the Palestinian Authority) between 1952 and 1956, uncovering proof of the city's great antiquity (circa 7000 BCE). She also served as director of the British School of Archaeology in Jerusalem, Israel, from 1951 to 1966.

5062. Remains documented by holography were those of "Lindow Man," a 2300-year-old Iron Age mummy unearthed in 1983 from Lindow Moss, a peat bog in Cheshire, England. A pulsed laser hologram was used to record his form and then to reconstruct it by the Forensic Science Department of Scotland Yard.

SCIENCE—ASTRONOMY

5063. Astronomical monument known to archeologists may be a stone circle at Nabta in southern Egypt believed to date to circa 5000 BCE, perhaps 2,000 years earlier than Stonehenge. The site was excavated by Fred Wendorf, an American archeologist at Southern Methodist University in Dallas, TX, USA, and astrophysicist J. McKim Malville of the University of Colorado, and an account was published in the journal *Nature* in April 1998. The sprawling stone complex contains ten standing stones, each about 9 feet (2.7 meters) high, 30 rock-lined ovals, and a calendar circle with smaller standing stones that marked the position of the summer solstice.

5064. Observations of Venus were recorded by the Old Babylonians circa 3000 BCE.

5065. Astrological system was developed as early as 2500 BCE by the Sumerians and other Mesopotamian peoples.

5066. Zodiacal horoscope derived from the division of the heavens into twelve equal zodiacal "houses" or "signs" ranged along the ecliptic (the plane of the earth's orbit) was developed by Babylonian astronomers before 450 BCE. The earliest evidence of the zodiac is on a cuneiform horoscope dated to 419 BCE that is probably an adaptation of a much older work. Ancient Greek historians also credited the Greek astronomer Oenopides with inventing the zodiacal system in circa 485 BCE.

5067. Accurate method of determining the sizes of and distances to celestial bodies based on geometry was developed by the Greek philosopher and mathematician Aristarchus of Samos in his only surviving work, *On the Sizes and Distances of the Sun and Moon,* dated to circa 250 BCE.

5068. Heliocentric world system was proposed in the third century BCE by the Greek philosopher and mathematician Aristarchus of Samos, who posited that the earth and the planets make circular orbits around the sun. Two earlier Greek philosophers, Philolaus and Hicetas, both of the fifth century BCE, held the view that the earth revolves around a fiery center, but this was not identified as the sun. The heliocentric theory of the universe was revived in 1444 by Nicholas of Cusa, worked out in detail in the 16th century by Nicolaus Copernicus (Mikolaj Kopernik), and supported in the 17th century by the observations of Galileo Galilei.

5069. Sunspot observations were made in China in 165 BCE, according to the Chinese book *The Ocean of Jade*. Official Chinese sunspot observations began in 28 BCE; the data were used in astrological forecasts.

5070. Depictions of a comet by a Western civilization were stamped onto coins minted during the reign of the first Roman emperor, Augustus Caesar. These commemorated the appearance of a comet in 17 BCE that, according to Augustus and his supporters, was the spirit of Julius Caesar returning to mark his approval of Rome's new leader. As such, the coins were also an early example of political propaganda.

5071. Galaxy to be described in print was M31, the Andromeda Galaxy in the constellation Andromeda, the nearest spiral galaxy to our own and the only one visible with the naked eye. An astronomical poem by the fourth century Roman nobleman Rufus Festus Avienus, in which he describes Andromeda's bonds as "thin clouds," may possibly contain the earliest written reference to it. The first astronomical work to describe the galaxy was the star catalog *The Book of the Fixed Stars*, published in 964 by the Muslim astronomer as-Sufi. He, like later observers, believed it to be a celestial nebula (cloud). In 1611, the German astronomer Simon Marius was the first to observe the Andromeda galaxy by telescope. In his journal, he described it as looking like "a candle seen at night through a horn." The German philosopher Immanuel Kant was the first to suggest that the Andromeda nebula was in fact a distant body of stars that was not part of the Milky Way. This theory was not confirmed until the 20th century by a team of observers at the Mount Wilson Observatory in California, USA, under the American astronomer Edwin Powell Hubble.

5072. Reference to sunspots in Western literature is contained in Einhard's *Vita Karoli Magni (Life of Charles the Great)*, a biography of Charlemagne written circa 830.

5073. Observation of a supernova was made by Chinese astronomers on July 4, 1054, in the constellation of Taurus. The supernova, an exploding star about 5,000 light years from earth, was so bright that it was visible in the daytime for 23 days. The site of the explosion is now marked by an expanding, glowing cloud of gas called the Crab Nebula (catalog numbers NGC 1952 and M1). It was discovered by the English astronomer John Bevis in 1731. Pulsar NP 0532, all that remains of the exploding star's core, was found at the center of the nebula in 1969. It was the first pulsar known to have been formed from a supernova.

5074. Observation of the occultation of a star by the moon was recorded in 1497 by Nicolaus Copernicus (Mikolaj Kopernik), the Polish astronomer and developer of the heliocentric world system.

5075. Discovery of a variable star was made in 1596 by the German astronomer David Fabricius. He observed, without a telescope, periodic variations in the magnitude of the star known as Mira Ceti, in the constellation Cetus. Variable stars are stars that periodically change brightness, color, or magnetic field strength. Variable stars may vary owing to internal processes (intrinsic variables) or because they are periodically occluded by an orbiting partner. Mira Ceti was the first intrinsic variable star to be discovered.

5076. Celestial objects discovered by telescope were the largest satellites of Jupiter, called the Galilean satellites after their discoverer, the Italian astronomer Galileo Galilei, and first described in his 1610 book *Siderius nuncius (The Starry Messenger)*. Galileo originally suggested that they be named the Medicean stars after his patron, Cosimo II de' Medici. Their present names, Io, Europa, Ganymede, and Callisto, were chosen by the German astronomer Simon Marius, who discovered them independently in the same year.

5077. Planetary transit to be observed was the transit of Mercury across the disk of the sun, observed and recorded in 1631 by the French scientist and philosopher Pierre Gassendi (also spelled Gassend).

5078. Estimate of the velocity of light was made in 1676 by the Danish astronomer Ole Christensen Römer. Working at the Royal Observatory in Paris, France, Römer noted that the predicted intervals between eclipses of the moons of Jupiter became shorter as Jupiter moved closer to the earth, and longer as Jupiter moved away. Reasoning that the difference was

SCIENCE—ASTRONOMY—*continued*

related to the time needed for light to travel from Jupiter to the earth, and knowing the approximate distance between Jupiter and the earth for the precise times of each predicted eclipse, he calculated that the speed of light was 140,000 miles (225,000 kilometers) per second, a remarkably accurate figure for the era. Modern observations place the speed of light in a vacuum at 186,282 miles (299,793 kilometers) per second.

5079. Calculation of the orbit of a comet was made by the English astronomer Edmond Halley in his treatise *A Synopsis of the Astronomy of Comets,* published in 1705. He showed that three comets sighted in 1531, 1607, and 1682 were in fact the same celestial body (now called Halley's Comet) passing near the earth in three successive visitations, and correctly predicted the comet's return in 1758. Halley also described the parabolic orbits of 23 other comets using observational data in historical accounts dating from 1337 to 1698.

5080. Planet to be mapped was Venus. A Roman astronomer, Francesco Bianchini, drew what he imagined to be the surface features of Venus in 1726 and 1727, and used his observations to make estimates of the length of its day and the angle of its axis of rotation. In fact, Venus is permanently shrouded in clouds and its surface is not visible from the earth with optical instruments.

5081. Person to propose the existence of galaxies was the German philosopher Immanuel Kant. In his book *Allgemeine Naturgeschichte und Theorie des Himmels (General Natural History and Theory of the Heavens),* published in 1755, he speculated that stars revolve around a gravitational center just as planets revolve around the sun, and that clouds of stars exist outside the Milky Way. He was the first to suggest that one such star cloud was the nebula in Andromeda (now known as M31, the Andromeda galaxy), the only galaxy easily visible to the naked eye in the Northern Hemisphere.

5082. Planet discovered since ancient times was Uranus, the seventh planet from the sun, discovered by the German-born English astronomer and musician William Herschel, the founder of stellar astronomy, on March 13, 1781. Scanning the skies with a large telescope of his own design, Herschel noted a large, unfamiliar green star in the constellation Gemini that he thought at first might be a comet. Other observations proved that it was a new planet

orbiting beyond Saturn. Herschel wanted to name his discovery "Georgium Sidus" (George[s Star) after King George III, but astronomers eventually assigned it a name from Greek mythology: Uranus, the father of Saturn.

5083. Woman astronomer who was paid for her work was the German-born English observationalist Caroline Lucretia Herschel, who performed much of the calculations for her brother William's astronomical work as well as making significant discoveries of her own. In 1787, King George III granted her an annual stipend of £50.

5084. Observation of Neptune of record was made by the French astronomer Joseph-Jérome Le Français de Lalande in 1795. Lalande carefully noted the body's change of position in the sky over two successive nights but failed to draw the obvious conclusion that he was observing a planet. Neptune was officially discovered on September 23, 1846, by Johann Gottfried Galle, the German astronomer.

5085. Asteroid to be discovered was Ceres, the largest known minor planet, discovered on January 1, 1801, by Giuseppe Piazzi, a monk, astronomer, and professor of mathematics, at the observatory at Palermo, Italy. Piazzi's observations, which he had to break off prematurely because of illness, were insufficient to establish Ceres's orbit, and it took a year of systematic searching for other astronomers to find it again.

5086. Measurement of the distance to a star was made in 1838 by the German astronomer and mathematician Friedrich Wilhelm Bessel. Bessel was directing a program of astrometrics at the Königsberg Obervatory in Königsberg, Prussia (now Kaliningrad, Russia), when he noted that the star 61 Cygni appeared to move in an ellipse every year. He correctly concluded that the ellipse was actually due to the change in viewpoint (or parallax) as the earth moved around the sun, and knowing the size of the earth's orbit, was able to calculate that 61 Cygni was 10.3 light-years away.

5087. Sunspot cycle to be observed was described in 1843 by Samuel Heinrich Schwabe, a German apothecary and astronomical hobbyist. Searching for a planet inside the orbit of Mercury, Schwabe made careful drawings of the solar disk from 1826 to 1843, forming the first continuous record of sunspot activity. He posited a ten-year cycle of waxing in the number of sunspots. (The cycle is now known to be eleven years long, or 22 years for the full cycle of waxing and waning sunspot activity.)

5088. Photograph of the sun was taken in 1845 by Jean-Bernard-Léon Foucault, the French physicist and inventor.

5089. Systematic observations of galaxies were carried out beginning in 1845 by the William Parsons Rosse, third Earl of Rosse, the leading Irish astronomer of the 19th century, using the 58-foot (17.7-meter) Leviathan, a 72-inch (1.8-meter) reflector telescope in Birr Castle, Ireland. At that time, the Leviathan was the largest telescope in the world. With this instrument, Rosse discovered that many nebulae possessed a spiral shape; these are now known to be galaxies.

5090. Recognition of Neptune as a planet is attributed to the German astronomer Johann Gottfried Galle. His observation was made on September 23, 1846, at the Berlin Observatory. Previously, the existence of an undiscovered planet that perturbed the orbit of Uranus had been predicted by the British mathematician and astronomer John Couch Adams and the French astronomer Urbain Jean-Joseph Leverrier.

5091. Comet named after a woman was named in 1848 in honor of Maria Mitchell, who had discovered it the year before. Mitchell, from Nantucket, MA, USA, was the first woman in the United States to become a professional astronomer, specializing in the study of sunspots, and the first woman to be elected to the American Academy of Arts and Sciences.

5092. Observations of stellar spectra were made by the English astrophysicist William Huggins from his private observatory at Tulse Hill, London. Using a spectroscope attached to a telescope, he determined in 1863 that stars are made of the same elements as the sun and the earth. Huggins also discovered in 1864 that many nebulae are made of luminous gas.

5093. Astronomer to use electronic instruments was Joel Stebbins, the director of the University of Illinois Observatory in the United States. Working with the American physicist F.C. Brown, between 1905 and 1907 he invented a light-sensitive selenium photometer that could be attached to the eyepiece of a telescope and could measure the brightness of stars down to the third magnitude.

5094. Cosmic ray to be discovered was detected in 1925 by American physicist Robert Andrews Millikan at the California Institute of Technology, Pasadena, CA, USA. The formal announcement of the discovery was made on November 11, 1925, before the National Academy of Sciences assembled in convention at Madison, WI, USA.

5095. Movie showing another planet was made in October 1926 by the American astronomer William Hammond Wright at the Lick Observatory, Mount Hamilton, CA, USA, with the aid of the Crossley telescope, and showed the planet Mars. Another was made in September 1927 of Jupiter. Exposures were made every three minutes, so that at the rate of 32 frames a minute, the movement of the planet took as many seconds on the screen as it did hours in the sky. The photographs were taken in several colors, ranging from ultraviolet to infrared, and illustrated alterations in the appearance of the planets.

5096. Astronomical photograph taken from an airplane was made on June 29, 1927, during a total solar eclipse over Britain. The London fog was too thick to allow observation, so a photograph of the solar eclipse was snapped by a photographer flying above the fog in a British Imperial Airways twin-engine airplane.

5097. Planet found beyond Neptune was Pluto, discovered at the Lowell Observatory, Flagstaff, AZ, USA, on February 18, 1930, by Clyde William Tombaugh, on photographic plates made as part of a long-term systematic search begun under the direction of the late Dr. Percival Lowell. Lowell had mathematically predicted the location of the planet many years before, almost exactly in the position where it was ultimately found. Even after the planet had been observed many times, the announcement of its discovery was withheld until March 13, 1930, the anniversary of Lowell's birth (and of William Herschel's discovery of Uranus in 1781).

5098. Radio waves from space to be observed were discovered in 1931 by Karl Guthe Jansky, an American physicist and engineer at the Bell Telephone Laboratories in Holmdel, NJ, USA. Asked to identify and classify sources of radio interference, Jansky found one source of static that moved across the sky each day. He eventually found that this source emanated from the center of the galaxy in the constellation of Sagittarius. Jansky moved on to other work when Bell Telephone rejected his proposal for a dish-shaped radio telescope 100 feet (30 meters) wide.

SCIENCE—ASTRONOMY—*continued*

5099. Radio astronomer was American radio engineer Grote Reber, who in 1937 built the world's first radio telescope in his backyard in Wheaton, IL, USA. With the scope, a bowl-shaped antenna 31 feet (9 meters) in diameter, he discovered the first point radio sources in the sky. He worked virtually alone in the field until after World War II, when radiotelescopy became a valuable and widespread tool for astronomers.

5100. Radar signal bounced off the sun was transmitted on April 7, 1959, at Stanford University, Stanford, CA, USA, by Professor Von Russel Eshleman, Lieutenant Colonel Robert Charles Barthle, and Dr. Philip Benjamin Gallagher, who used a 40,000-watt transmitter. The signals reached the sun's corona about a half million miles (800,000 kilometers) above the visible part of the sun. They required 1,000 seconds for transmission in both directions.

5101. Scientific program to search for extra-terrestrial life was Project Ozma, conducted over a four-month period in 1960 at the National Radio Astronomy Observatory in Green Bank, WV, USA. American astrophysicist Frank D. Drake was the lead researcher. Two nearby stars, Tau Ceti and Epsilon Eridani, both about eleven light years from the earth, were scanned on radio bands for signals indicating intelligent life, but none was discovered.

5102. Quasar to be observed was discovered by Allan Rex Sandage, an American astronomer with the Mount Wilson and Palomar Observatories, Palomar, CA, USA. In 1961, Sandage and radio astronomer Thomas A. Matthews recorded signals from an extremely distant star-like object that was a strong emitter of radio waves, and located it with a large optical telescope. To describe the new object, Sandage coined the term quasar, short for "quasi-stellar radio source."

5103. Observational confirmation of the Big Bang theory was made in 1965 by the German-American astrophysicist Arno Allan Penzias and the American radio astronomer Robert Woodrow Wilson. Performing radio observations of the outer Milky Way, they noted an omnipresent low-level thermal temperature of about 3 degrees Kelvin. This, it is now agreed, was the fossil radiation from the primeval explosion of the universe known popularly as the Big Bang. Penzias and Wilson shared the 1978 Nobel Prize in Physics for this work. The Big Bang theory of the creation of the universe was proposed in 1948 by the Russian-born

American physicist and cosmologist George Anthony Gamow. Gamow conceived of the cosmos as beginning in a perfectly dense singularity containing everything in the universe. All of space, time, matter, and energy was created when this singularity exploded, leaving a residual energy trace that, Gamow predicted, would still be detectable today.

5104. Discovery of pulsars was made in 1967 by the radio astronomers Jocelyn Bell Burnell and Antony Hewish at the University of Cambridge, England. A pulsar (from "pulsating radio star") is a neutron star that rotates up to thousands of times per second while emitting an intense beam of radio waves from its magnetic poles. As the beam sweeps past the earth, the star appears to pulse rapidly.

5105. Black hole to be detected was Cygnus X-1, a strong X-ray source that is 11,000 light years away from earth. It was discovered in 1971 in the constellation Cygnus by the *Uhuru* X-ray research satellite, a USA-built instrument that was launched from a site in Kenya. Cygnus X-1 is detectable primarily by the X-ray emissions of the matter accelerating into it. It orbits a blue supergiant called HDE 226868 about 5.6 times per day, and is slowly consuming its companion at the rate of one hundred billion tons of gas daily.

5106. Discovery of the rings of Jupiter was made indirectly by the U.S.-built *Pioneer 11* spacecraft in 1974. At a distance of about 1.6 Jovian radii, the probe detected a fall-off in the density of charged particles, evidence of a possible ring. The existence of the rings was confirmed in 1979 by the *Voyager I* spacecraft, which also obtained the first close-up pictures.

5107. Discovery of the rings of Uranus was made by terrestrial instruments when the planet passed between a star and the earth on March 10, 1977. Further observations showed that the planet possesses ten narrow rings shepherded by several small satellites.

5108. Pulsar found outside the Milky Way was discovered in the Large Magellanic Cloud, a satellite galaxy of the Milky Way, in 1984.

5109. Discovery of a planet orbiting another star was made by Michel Mayor, of Geneva Observatory in Switzerland, and his graduate assistant Didier Queloz. Using the facilities at Haute-Provence Observatory in southern France, the researchers measured the patterns of the Doppler shift of 142 sun-like stars. One star, 51 Pegasi, in the constellation Pegasus, possessed a Doppler shift that indicated the presence of a giant planet orbiting closer to the star than Mercury orbits the sun. The discovery was announced on October 6, 1995.

5110. Discovery of antimatter in space of substantial mass was made by the Compton Gamma Ray Observatory launched from the U.S. space shuttle *Atlantis* on April 7, 1991. In 1997, scientists announced that a large cloud of antimatter measuring roughly 4,000 light-years by 3,500 light years had been found some 30,000 light years away, near the core of the Milky Way.

5111. Discovery of water on the moon was made by the Lunar Prospector orbiting robot probe, launched by the American space agency NASA in January 1998 to map gravity anomalies and geological deposits on the moon. On March 5, 1998, principal investigator Alan Binder announced in Mountain View, CA, USA, that a neutron spectrometer aboard the probe had located major deposits of hydrogen in shaded craters at the moon's north and south poles, indicating the presence of water ice crystals. The ice was thought to comprise about 1 percent of each cubic yard (cubic meter) of soil in the craters, totaling perhaps several hundred million tons of water altogether.

5112. Discovery of solar tornadoes as wide as the earth was made by the European Space Agency's *SOHO* (Solar Observer High Orbit) spacecraft in April 1998. Winds of hot gas inside the tornadoes were swirling at thousands of miles per hour. *SOHO* was launched into space on December 2, 1995.

5113. Computer model of the growth of the universe was developed by the Virgo Consortium, an international team of astronomers, and computed on the Cray supercomputer at the Max Planck Society Computing Center in Garching, Germany. The model, publicly introduced in June 1998 by August Evrard of the University of Michigan, MI, USA, at a meeting of the American Astronomical Society in San Diego, CA, USA, depicted how the structures of the universe, including stars and galaxies, evolved from ripples in space-time following the creation of the universe in a giant explosion some 12 to 15 billion years ago. The simulation presented a view of the entire visible universe, believed at that time to be 10 billion light years across.

5114. Gamma-ray burster visible live was detected by astronomical satellites on January 23, 1999, and photographed by an observatory in New Mexico, USA, as it occurred. The burster, located about 9 billion light years away, lasted for 100 seconds and was the biggest explosion ever seen, briefly outshining the rest of the universe. Astronomers believed that the earth happened to be in the way of the main output beam from the event, which was why the radiation burst appeared so intense.

5115. Professorship dedicated to the search for extraterrestrial life was the Watson and Marilyn Alberts Chair for the Search for Extraterrestrial Life, an academic post established at the University of California at Berkeley, CA, USA, in February 1999 with a $500,000 endowment. The first professor named to the post was astronomer and electrical engineer William Welch, who oversaw the construction of a large array of radiotelescopes for making observations 24 hours a day.

5116. Solar system with multiple planets to be discovered other than our own is a system of three planets in orbit around the star Upsilon Andromedae, about 44 light-years from the earth in the constellation Andromeda. Its discovery was announced in April 1999. The innermost planet, which was discovered in 1996, has about three-quarters the mass of Jupiter and is so close to the star that it completes an orbit in the equivalent of 4.6 earth days. The middle planet has at least twice the mass of Jupiter and completes an orbit every 242 earth days. The outermost planet has at least four times the mass of Jupiter and completes an orbit about once every four earth years. The planets, too small to be seen with a telescope, were detected by studying the effects of their gravitational pulls on Upsilon Andromedae. Their existence was discovered independently by two teams of astronomers, one at San Francisco State University, San Francisco, CA, USA, and the other at Harvard-Smithsonian Center for Astrophysics, Cambridge, MA, and the National Center for Atmospheric Research, Boulder, CO.

SCIENCE—ASTRONOMY—BOOKS AND TREATISES

5117. Astrological treatise known was the cuneiform text *Enuma Anu Enlil,* which was devoted to the intrepretation of celestial omens. It was begun in Babylon (in present-day Iraq) circa 1700 BCE, but was not completed until circa 1000 BCE. Tablets of the work were unearthed in the ruins of Nineveh in the library of the Assyrian king Ashurbanipal (Asur-bani-apli), who reigned in the seventh century BCE.

SCIENCE—ASTRONOMY—BOOKS AND TREATISES—*continued*

5118. Star catalog was compiled by Babylonian stargazers in what is now Iraq circa 1700 BCE.

5119. Star catalog that was comprehensive and accurate was compiled in 129 BCE by Hipparchus, a Greek of Bithynia on the Isle of Rhodes. According to Ptolemy, in 134 BCE Hipparchus had observed a moving star (possibly a comet) and, struck by the surprising impermanence of the heavens, was inspired to document all the known stars. His catalog included the celestial longitudes and latitudes of about 850 stars, with each star rated on a six-point scale of apparent brightness.

5120. Treatise on astronomy that was widely influential was the *Almagest* of Ptolemy (in Latin, Claudius Ptolemaeus), the Alexandrian astronomer and mathematician. It was completed circa 140 CE and served as the standard reference for North African, Arab, and European astronomers until the birth of modern astronomy in the 16th century. The *Almagest* was the first book to set out in detail the Ptolemaic or geocentric view of the structure of the solar system, in which all celestial bodies orbit the earth via an elaborate system of cycles and epicycles.

5121. Treatise on meteorites of serious scientific merit was *On the Origin of Iron-masses,* published in 1794 by the German astronomer Ernst F.F. Chladni. Chladni's assertion that iron rocks falling from the sky caused visible fireballs was dismissed as superstition by the French Academy, the reigning scientific body in Europe, until a spectacular meteor shower later that year over Siena, Italy, proved him to be correct.

5122. Astronomical journal was the *Geographical Ephemeris,* founded in 1798 by the Hungarian astronomer Franz Xaver von Zach.

5123. Photographic star catalog was the *Cape Photographic Durchmusterung,* compiled between 1885 and 1890 by David Gill, royal astronomer at the Royal Observatory, Cape Town, South Africa. It lists more than 450,000 stars in the southern sky.

SCIENCE—ASTRONOMY—ECLIPSES

5124. Total solar eclipse to be recorded is widely believed to have been noted on October 22, 2136 BCE, by Chinese astronomers. However, the earliest surviving records known with certainty to refer to a solar eclipse are a set of oracle bones, found near An-yang in northeastern China, that date from the Shang dynasty, circa 1760–1100 BCE. In one typical oracle, the bones report: "On day *kuei-yu,* it was inquired: 'The Sun was eaten in the evening; is it good?'"

5125. Recorded sequence of eclipse observations is contained in the *Ch'un-ch'iu (Spring and Autumn Annals),* which chronicles Chinese history from the Chou dynasty in 722 to 481 BCE. The *Ch'un-ch'iu* records 36 solar eclipses, including the year of the ruler, lunar month, and day of the 60-day cycle. Nearly all the eclipses can be dated by modern astronomers, providing an accurate independent dating method for historians.

5126. Total solar eclipse observed in Europe of record occurred on April 6, 648 BCE, and was noted in a poem by the Greek writer Archilochus, who wrote: "Nothing there is beyond hope, nothing that can be sworn impossible, nothing wonderful, since Zeus, father of the Olympians, made night from mid-day, hiding the light of the shining Sun, and sore fear came upon men."

5127. Prediction of a solar eclipse was long thought to have been made by Thales of Miletus (in present-day Turkey), the mathematician, geometer, and natural scientist who is considered the first Greek philosopher. According to his younger contemporary, the philosopher Xenophanes, a battle between the Lydians and Medians came to a sudden halt because of a solar eclipse that Thales had predicted. If this account is correct, and some modern scholars doubt its trustworthiness, it refers to an eclipse that took place on May 28, 585 BCE.

SCIENCE—ASTRONOMY—PLANETARIUMS

5128. Planetarium was the Gottorp Globe, built in 1664 by Andreas Busch in Gottorp, Schleswig (now in Germany). It was a 3.5-ton hollow celestial sphere, 10 feet (3 meters) in diameter, with a gilded star map on its interior. Water-driven gears powered the large device, which rotated once a day and contained within it an observing platform for twelve persons.

5129. Planetarium of the modern type with a motorized planetarium device that projected luminous moving sky images onto the interior of a large dome was invented by Walter Bauersfeld, chief designer at the Carl Zeiss Works, Jena, Germany. Five years of development led to the opening of the Carl Zeiss Planetarium, on the roof of the Zeiss plant, in August 1923.

5130. Planetarium in the Western Hemisphere was the Adler Planetarium and Astronomical Museum, presented to the city of Chicago, IL, USA, by Max Adler, an American businessman. The dome was 68 feet (20.7 meters) in diameter and seated 450 people. It was under the direction of Professor Philip Fox and was opened to the public on May 10, 1930. The projector was manufactured by Carl Zeiss Works.

SCIENCE—ASTRONOMY—TELESCOPES AND OBSERVATORIES

5131. National observatory in Europe was Uraniborg, founded by the Danish astronomer Tycho Brahe, astronomer to King Frederick II of Denmark, on the Baltic island of Ilven in 1576. Uraniborg was outiftted with the best astronomical instruments of the time, including crystal globes with the celestial bodies marked on them and giant rulers and circles to measure the angles between the planets and stars. All observations were made by the naked eye, as no one had yet thought of using lenses to study the heavens. Among the discoveries made at Uraniborg was proof that a comet seen in 1577 was farther away than the moon. Tycho also made a catalogue of the exact positions of 1000 stars, and recorded careful observations of the 1572 supernova in Cassiopeia.

5132. Telescope was probably invented by the German-Dutch spectacle-maker Hans Lippershey circa 1608. Recognizing the telescope's usefulness in war, he offered his *kijker* ("looker") to the Estates of Holland on October 2, 1608.

5133. Examination of the night sky with a telescope was made by Galileo Galilei, the great Italian astronomer. Galileo did not invent the telescope, but in 1609 he built the first one with sufficient resolving power to be useful for astronomical observation. Late that year, from his home in Padua, Italy, he looked at the moon and was astonished to find that it was not smooth, but had sharp mountains and rugged craters. He also saw, as he wrote, "stars in myriads which have never been seen before," as well as individual stars in the Milky Way, the rings of Saturn, and four moons—now called the Galilean satellites—orbiting Jupiter. In 1610, Galileo published his findings in *Siderius nuncius (The Starry Messenger)*.

5134. Reflecting telescope was invented by the English physicist Sir Isaac Newton and donated to the Royal Society of London in 1671. Newton's design employed a concave mirror at the rear of the telescope to gather and reflect light to the eyepiece. All earlier telescopes, including Galileo's, were refractors—they used a refracting lens at the front of the instrument to gather light.

5135. Permanent observatory in the Southern Hemisphere was founded near Sydney, Australia, between 1821 and 1825 by General Thomas Makdougall Brisbane, a British army officer and the governor of New South Wales. Brisbane also set himself the task of determining the positions of all stars down to eighth magnitude between declination −33 degrees and the south celestial pole. Much of the work was actually done by Brisbane's assistant, James Dunlop. The resulting data, published in 1835 and known as the *Brisbane Catalogue*, was the first thorough survey of the southern sky.

5136. Large reflecting mirror was the 72-inch (1.8-meter) objective mirror in the Leviathan, a telescope completed in 1845 at Birr Castle, Ireland, under the supervision of William Parsons Rosse, the leading Irish astronomer of the 19th century. The all-metal mirror, cast in a special alloy of tin and copper, weighed 4 tons and was by far the largest telescope mirror that had ever been built. A larger mirror was not cast until 1917.

5137. Vatican observatory was constructed outside Rome, Italy, in 1935 at the direction of Pope Pius XI. A small group of Catholic astronomers performed regular observations there until 1980, when seeing conditions became too poor because of smog and light pollution. A new papal instrument, the Vatican Advanced Technology Telescope, was inaugurated in September 1993 at Turkey Flat, AZ, USA.

5138. Major radio telescope was built at the Jodrell Bank Experimental Station at Jodrell Bank, near Manchester, England, and began operation on October 4, 1957, to track the launch of *Sputnik I*. It was designed by the English astronomer Alfred Charles Bernard Lovell, who had begun early radio telescope research there just after World War II. The steerable dish antenna was 250 feet (76 meters) in diameter and could detect longwave radio emissions in excess of 50 meters.

5139. X-ray astronomy satellite was *Uhuru*, launched on December 12, 1970, from a site in Kenya.

SCIENCE—ASTRONOMY—TELESCOPES AND OBSERVATORIES—continued

5140. Director of the Royal Greenwich Observatory in Greenwich, England, was the British astronomer Margaret Burbage. She was appointed to the post in 1972.

5141. Radio telescope in space was lofted by the Soviet Union on *Salyut 6* in July 1977. Designated KRT 10, it had a 33-foot (10-meter) dish and was designed to record radio waves in the centimeter and decimeter lengths.

5142. Large radio interferometer was the Very Large Array, located near Socorro, NM, USA. It consists of 27 parabolic radio receiver dishes that are mounted on rails in a Y-pattern with arms about 13 miles (21 kilometers) long. Each dish is 82 feet (25 meters) in diameter and can be aimed and moved along its rail from a central control room. Using interferometric principles, a computer integrates the individual signals recorded by each dish into one signal that appears to have been recorded by a single dish with a diameter of 17 miles (27 kilometers). The VLA is operated by the U.S. National Radio Astronomy Observatory and began operation in 1980.

5143. Infrared astronomy satellite was the IRAS, built by a Dutch-American consortium and launched on January 25, 1983. Its main instrument was a 24-inch (60-centimeter) Ritchey-Chretien Cassegrain telescope, which focused onto infrared detectors operating at wavelengths of 100, 60, 24, and 12 microns. The telescope was contained in a cryogenic tank of liquid helium at a temperature of 2 degrees Kelvin. Slow venting from the tank ended the satellite's operational life on November 21, 1983. It produced images of hundreds of infrared objects, including the center of the galaxy.

5144. Orbiting observatory of importance was the Hubble Space Telescope, named after American astronomer Edwin Powell Hubble. The US$1.5 billion orbiting optical observatory was launched from the space shuttle *Discovery* on April 15, 1990, in an orbit 381 miles (613 kilometers) above the earth. Fourteen feet (4 meters) wide and 43 feet (13 meters) long, the Hubble contained a 94.5-inch (240-centimeter) primary mirror and five main instrument packages, plus additional cameras sensitive to various parts of the electromagnetic spectrum. Early technical problems, including a flaw in the primary mirror, were repaired in December 1993 by a team of astronauts on the space shuttle *Endeavor.*

SCIENCE—BIOLOGY

5145. Treatise on insects was *De Animalibus insectis (Of Insect Animals),* published in 1602 by the Italian naturalist Ulisse Aldrovandi, professor of natural history at the University of Bologna from 1561.

5146. Microscopic observation of protozoa, bacteria, and human cells was performed in September 1674 by Antoni van Leeuwenhoek, a draper and amateur lensmaker of Delft, the Netherlands. Leeuwenhoek used a powerful single-lens microscope of his own design to examine a drop of pond water, where he saw to his surprise a host of creatures he called "small animalcules." In another drop of water he observed bacteria. "I saw very plainly that these were little eels, or worms," he wrote in a letter to the Royal Society of London, "lying all huddled up together and wriggling . . . and the whole water seemed to be alive with these multifarious animalcules. This was, for me, among all the marvels that I have discovered in nature, the most marvelous of all." In later investigations, Leeuwenhoek was the first to record the existence of red blood cells, the fibers of muscles, the lens of the eye, and human sperm.

5147. Entomological collection in Europe of importance was assembled by the Dutch naturalist Jan Swammerdam, who is considered to be the founder of modern entomology. Swammerdam was the first to systematically examine his specimens under the microscope. He published his findings in 1682 in *Algemeene Verhandeling van bloedeloose diertjens (The Natural History of Insects).*

5148. Taxonomic system based on scientific principles was described in *Synopsis Methodica Animalium Quadrupedum et Serpentini Generis (A Synopsis of Types of Four-legged Animals and Snakes),* published in 1693 by the English naturalist John Ray (or Wray). Ray established the species as the basic unit of taxonomy, and insisted on the need to consider all relevant anatomical and life-cycle traits in determining the classification of a species.

5149. Organism classification system still in use was devised by the Swedish botanist and explorer Carolus Linnaeus (Carl von Linné) and described by him in his treatise *Systema Naturae,* published in 1735. In 1753 he published *Species Plantarum,* a comprehensive classification of known plants, which he followed in 1758 with a classification system for animals. Linnaeus was also the inventor of the modern standard system of species nomenclature, which gives every organism two Latin names, one for the genus and one for the species.

5150. Proof of regeneration in an organism was made by the Swiss naturalist Abraham Trembley in the 18th century, while making observations of the freshwater hydra, *Chlorohydra viridissima,* a tiny polyp whose body consists of a mouth surrounded by tentacles. When he cut up a hydra, each piece grew into a complete individual. Trembley also found that a new individual could be made from two pieces grafted together. His monograph on the subject was published in 1744.

5151. Systematic and comprehensive work of natural history was *Histoire naturelle, générale et particulière (Natural History, General and Particular),* by the naturalist Georges-Louis Leclerc, Count of Buffon, of Montbard, France. In this work, which was published in 36 volumes (out of a projected 50 volumes) between 1749 and 1804, Buffon attempted to catalog and describe all of nature, so far as it was then understood. He was the first scientist to suspect that species could become extinct, the first to describe earth's development as a succession of stages, the first to suggest that the solar system was produced by the collision of a comet with the sun, and one of the first to make ethnological studies of a variety of peoples in Africa, the Pacific Islands, and the Americas.

5152. Theory of evolution was developed by Swiss naturalist Charles Bonnet. In his 1769 treatise *La Palingénésie philosophique (The Philosophical Revival),* he tried to account for the fossil record by proposing that the earth suffers periodic catastrophes that kill most living things, while the survivors advance a notch toward more advanced forms. Bonnet was the first to apply the term "evolution" to biology.

5153. Head transplant was the transference of the head of a snail onto the body of another snail, both of the same species, achieved by the Italian biologist Lazzaro Spallanzani circa 1770.

5154. Physical anthropologist was Johann Friedrich Blumenbach, professor of medicine at the University of Göttingen in Germany from 1776 to 1835. Blumenbach, the author of treatises on comparative anatomy and physiology, inaugurated the study of human beings as a species of animal, with attention to the effects on humans of biped posture, forward binocular vision, opposable thumbs, and an enlarged cranium. He produced an early classification system in which humanity was grouped by cranial size into five families, which he called American, Caucasian, Mongolian, Malayan, and Ethiopian.

5155. Artificial insemination was developed beginning in 1780 by the Italian biologist Lazzaro Spallanzani, a professor at the University of Pavia. He first worked with newts and frogs, and in 1783 achieved the first artificial insemination when he successfully transferred semen from a spaniel to a female hunting dog.

5156. Biological expedition to Amazonia by a native South American was led by Alexandre Rodrigues Ferreira, a Brazilian-born naturalist who between 1783 and 1792 was the first person to systematically collect biological specimens and record extensive observations of Amazonian flora and fauna. Rodrigues Ferreira departed from Rio de Janeiro, made his way up the Madeira and Negro rivers, and eventually arrived close to the Apaporis river. He recounted his discoveries in *Viagem Filosófica à Amazonas (Philosophical Journey to Amazonia).*

5157. Comparative anatomist to make important contributions to the discipline in its modern form was Georges-Léopold-Chrêtien-Frédéric-Dagobert, Baron Cuvier (1769–1832), the French naturalist. Cuvier's *Leçons d'anatomie comparée (Lessons on Comparative Anatomy),* published in 1800–05, presented his theory of the "correlation of parts," in which he claimed that the organs in an animal are all interrelated, and that an animal's internal and external structures are functionally determined by its way of life. Cuvier was also the first to classify fossils, making him the first comparative paleontologist.

5158. Amino acid to be discovered was asparagine, isolated from the asparagus plant by the French chemist Nicolas-Louis Vauquelin in 1806.

5159. Observation of the egg cell of a mammal was made by the pioneering German-Russian embryologist Karl Ernst Ritter von Baer. In 1827, he published *De Ovi Mammalium et Hominis Genesi (On the Mammalian Egg and the Origin of Man),* in which he established that all mammals develop from ova (eggs). His *Über Entwickelungsgeschichte der Thiere (On the Development of Animals),* published in Germany between 1828 and 1837, was the first important work of comparative embryology.

SCIENCE—BIOLOGY—*continued*

5160. Observation of a cell nucleus was made by the Scottish botanist Robert Brown in 1831, when he noted a central body in the cells of orchids of genuses *Orchidaceae* and *Asclepiadaceae*. He called this structure the "nucleus" of the cell.

5161. Theory of physiological reflexes was propounded by the London physician Marshall Hall. His study of the nervous system of newts, published in 1837, led Hall to envision the spinal cord as an interlinked system of reflex arcs (units of stimulus and response) coordinated by the brain. His ideas were denounced by the Royal Society, but later proven valid.

5162. Treatise on biophysics was *Die medizinische Physik (Medical Physics)*, published in 1856 by the German physicist Adolf Fick. It contained a detailed discussion of the fundamental laws governing diffusion and osmosis in living tissue.

5163. Study of insect behavior was *Souvenirs entomologiques (Entomological Recollections)*, published between 1879 and 1907 by the French entomologist Jean-Henri Fabre. Based on many years of observation during his retirement in the village of Serignan, France, Fabre's ten-volume work was the first study of living insects in their natural habitats. English versions appeared as *The Life of the Fly* (1913); *The Life of the Spider* (1914); and *The Life of the Weevil* (1922).

5164. Virus to be isolated for study was the tobacco mosaic virus, investigated by the Russian scientist Dmitry I. Ivanovsky in 1892 and the Dutch botanist Martinus Willem Beijerinck in 1898. Both noticed that it was possible to infect tobacco plants with the tobacco mosaic disease by preparing from a diseased plant a fluid that contained no bacteria or other known infectious agents. Beijerinck was the first to realize that the agent was biological; he called it a *contagium vivum fluidum.*

5165. Hormone to be discovered was secretin, a substance released by cells in the duodenum that stimulates the production of digestive juices in the pancreas. Its existence was demonstrated in 1902 by Ernest Henry Starling and William Bayliss, physiologists at University College, London, England, in an experiment on anesthetized dogs. The word "hormone" was coined by Starling in 1905 from a Greek word meaning "to set in motion."

5166. Primate research station was the Anthropoid Station on Tenerife in Spain's Canary Islands, established in October 1912 with funding from the Albert Samson Foundation of Berlin, Germany. The station was designed for the study of the physiology and psychology of anthropoid apes. Eugen L. Teuber, the first director, was replaced in 1913 by Wolfgang Kohler, a Docent and founder of gestalt psychology from the University of Frankfurt. Under Kohler, the station performed experiments, such as a series testing the ability of chimpanzees to use tools to obtain bananas, that were fundamental to the development of primatology.

5167. Vitamin to be identified was vitamin B1 (thiamine), discovered in 1912 by the Polish chemist Casimir Funk. Doctors had known for some time that eating a diet mainly of polished rice caused a disease called beriberi, and that switching to a diet of unpolished rice (rice with the outer layer intact) prevented and cured the disease. Seeking the substance in unpolished rice that prevented beriberi, Funk isolated an amine (a nitrogen-containing compound) that he called *vitamine* ("life amine"). This term, without the final "e" came to be the general name for all vitamins, whether they contained amines or not.

5168. Neurotransmitter to be identified was acetylcholine. In 1914, Henry Hallett Dale, an English pharmacologist and physiologist working in London, found evidence suggesting that acetylcholine, a substance he had isolated in ergot, also occurred naturally in the body and was responsible for conveying impulses across the synapses between nerve endings. His suggestion was confirmed in 1921 by the physiologist Otto Loewi of Frankfurt am Main, Germany, in experiments with frog hearts, and in 1929 by Dale using acetylcholine from horses. The two shared the 1936 Nobel Prize in Physiology or Medicine.

5169. Protein characterized by amino acid sequence was bovine insulin, the structure of which was elucidated in 1955 after a ten-year effort by British biochemist Frederick Sanger. Insulin is a hormone that controls the absorption of glucose by cells. In the course of his research, Sanger developed methods for determining the structure of proteins and other complex molecules. He was awarded the Nobel Prize in Chemistry in 1958 for his work on insulin and shared a second chemistry prize in 1980 for his contributions to the technique of nucleotide sequencing.

5170. Scientific observations of primate behavior in the wild were conducted beginning in 1960 by Jane van Lawick Goodall at the Gombe Stream National Park in Tanzania. Her detailed observations of the resident chimpanzees uncovered many previously unknown aspects of their behavior, such as that chimps are omnivores, use tools in the wild, and possess a highly developed social structure.

5171. Nation to authorize patents on animals was the United States. Patents on nonhuman animals created by reproductive technologies were authorized by the U.S. government on April 16, 1987.

5172. Patent on an animal was awarded to Harvard University, Cambridge, MA, USA, in April 1988. Developed by American geneticists Philip Leder and Timothy A. Stewart, the animal was a genetically engineered "oncomouse" that was highly susceptible to breast cancer. The use of oncomice in testing anticancer therapies was intended to reduce the number of animals used in medical experimentation and to improve the accuracy of experimental results. E.I. du Pont de Nemours and Company, Wilmington, DE, USA, had commercial rights to the animals and initially sold them for US$50 each.

5173. Mammals born from an egg grown in vitro were mice engineered by developmental biologists John Eppig and Marilyn O'Brien of the Jackson Laboratory in Bar Harbor, ME, USA. Eppig and O'Brien first grew the whole ovaries of newborn mice in culture, then isolated the egg-cell precursors called primordial oocytes. The oocytes were matured in culture dishes, fertilized with mouse sperm from adult males, and transplanted into surrogate mother mice, who gave birth to two males. The results were published in the January 1996 issue of the journal *Biology of Reproduction.*

5174. Isolation of human embryonic stem cells was made by John D. Gearhart and colleagues of Johns Hopkins Medical Institutions in Baltimore, MD, USA. The accomplishment was announced in July 1997. Stem cells have the capacity to develop into any body tissue, including blood, bone, nerve, and skin cells.

5175. High-security pathogen laboratory in Europe was opened in 1998 at the site of the former Pasteur Institute in Lyon, France. It was designed to facilitate research into some of the world's most deadly viruses, notably Lassa fever. The first director was Susan Fisher-Hoch, a virologist formerly of the Centers for Disease Control and Prevention in Atlanta, GA, USA.

SCIENCE—BIOLOGY—BOTANY

5176. Flower fossil was made in 1998 in limestone and ash deposits in an ancient lakebed near Beipaio, China. The fossil, an impression of a thin, branchlike flower bearing pod-shaped fruit with seeds, was dated to 142 million years ago by Chinese researchers.

5177. Plant-collecting expedition was ordered by Queen Hatshepsut of Egypt circa 1495 BCE. A team of laborers went to Punt (present-day Somalia), where they dug up 32 incense trees, packed their roots (still enclosed in soil balls) into wicker baskets suspended from carrying poles, and conveyed them by ship to Egypt. Most of them were planted in the terraced garden at Hatshepsut's temple at Deir el-Bahri, near Thebes, in holes that were cut into the rock, lined with clay, and filled with mud from the Nile. Drawings on the temple walls depict the expedition, which is also the first known instance of the transportation of trees.

5178. Botanist is considered to be Theophrastus of Eresus, the Greek scientist who succeeded Aristotle as head of the Peripatetic school of philosophy circa 322 BCE. Theophrastus was the author of some 200 treatises on botany in which he discussed more than 500 plants and grouped them according to genera. He was the first to make an accurate report of sexual reproduction in flowering plants.

5179. Botanical illustrations were drawn in a work of pharmacology by the Greek herbalist Crateuas, physician to Mithridates VI, king of the Anatolian province of Pontus (now part of Turkey), who reigned 120–63 BCE. Crateuas made accurate drawings of plants to illustrate his medical text. The drawings are known only from copies made circa 500 CE.

5180. Monograph on a fruit tree was the work of Ts'ai Hsiang, a Chinese horticulturalist. In 1059, he wrote *Li-chih-p'u,* a seven-chapter study of the litchi, including its cultivation, trade, and natural history.

5181. Heated conservatory for plants was constructed in 1550 by Daniele Barbaro. It was built on the grounds of the Botanical Gardens in Padua, Italy, the oldest botanical garden extant, and was used to keep plants from freezing during the winter. In all likelihood, it had glass windows.

5182. Treatise on forestry in English of importance was *Sylva, or a Discourse of Forest-trees, and the Propagation of Timber* (1664) by the English diarist John Evelyn. Evelyn was a member of the Royal Society and produced the study for the commissioners of the British

SCIENCE—BIOLOGY—BOTANY—*continued*

Navy. The book contains detailed descriptions of England's native trees and discourses on their cultivation and use. The author argues that wise forest management is a matter of overriding strategic importance to any nation dependent on wooden ships for commerce and protection. *Sylva* went through many editions well into the 19th century.

5183. Scientifically accurate treatise on sex in plants was *The Anatomy of Plants* (1682), by the English botanist and physician Nehemiah Grew. In this book, Grew gave the first printed identification of the stamen as the male sex organ of the flower and the pistil as the female sex organ. Woodcuts of the cell structure of plant tissue illustrated his discoveries.

5184. International Botanical Congress took place in 1867 in Paris, France. It was organized by the eminent Swiss botanist Alphonse-Louis-Pierre-Pyrame de Candolle, who held the chair of botany and was director of the botanical gardens at the University of Geneva from 1842 to 1893. The main work of the congress was to develop a standardized botanical nomenclature. International Botanical Congresses are now held every four or six years.

SCIENCE—BIOLOGY—CLONING

5185. Nuclear transplantation in a vertebrate was achieved in 1952 by Robert Briggs and Thomas J. King of the Institute for Cancer Research and Lankenau Hospital Research Institute in Philadelphia, PA, USA. They transplanted a nucleus from one cell of *Xenopus laevis,* a species of African clawed frog, into another cell. The technique of nuclear transplantation was later used to produce the first cloned adults.

5186. Cloned animal was a frog, created by British molecular biologist John B. Gurdon in 1970. He transplanted the nucleus of a intestinal cell from a tadpole into a frog's egg that had had its nucleus removed. The egg developed into an adult frog that had the tadpole's genome in all of its cells, and was therefore a clone of the tadpole.

5187. Mammal cloned from adult cells was Dolly, a ewe born in July 1996 at the Roslin Institute, a research facility in Roslin, Scotland, with research assistance from biotechnology company PPL Therapeutics. The work was performed by a team of biologists led by Ian Wilmut. A nucleus from a mammary cell of an adult ewe was transplanted into an enucleated egg extracted from a second ewe. The nucleus was fused with its new host by administering electrical pulses. When the egg began to divide and develop into an embryo, it was implanted into a surrogate mother ewe, where it gestated normally. Dolly was the genetic twin of the ewe that donated the mammary cell nucleus.

5188. Human cloning company was Valiant Venture Ltd., founded in 1997 by a well-funded Swiss-based religious sect known as the Raelian Movement. Valiant Venture, which was located in the Bahamas, offered a service called Clonaid to assist parents who wished to have a child cloned from one of them. The minimum fee for human cloning was US$200,000. A US$50,000 service, "Insuraclone," provided safe storage of cells from a family member to allow the future creation of a clone in case of death. Valiant Venture's first scientific director was French chemist Brigitte Boisselier. The Raelian Movement's stated goal was to "enable mankind to reach eternal life." The reported cloning of a human cell did not take place until 1998.

5189. Cloning of a primate from an embryo was announced on March 2, 1997, by M. Susan Smith and Donald Wolf of the Oregon Regional Primate Research Center, Beaverton, OR, USA. Two rhesus monkeys were cloned by the process known as nuclear transfer, which produced two genetically identical monkeys from chromosomes extracted from a single monkey embryo.

5190. Mammal born to a cloned mother was a female lamb named Bonnie, offspring of Dolly, the world's first cloned mammal, and David, a naturally born Welsh Mountain ram. Bonnie was born on April 13, 1998, at the Roslin Institute in Scotland.

5191. Cow clones were announced on December 8, 1998, by a team of researchers led by Yukio Tsunoda of Kinki University in Nara, Japan. Combining 99 cow's eggs with cow intestinal cells collected from a slaughterhouse, the researchers created 38 genetically identical viable embryos. Ten of these were transferred to surrogate mother cows, and eight calves were born. Four of the calves survived birth.

5192. Human cloning to be publicized was announced on December 16, 1998, by Kim Seung-bo, Lee Bo-yon, and colleagues at the infertility clinic of Kyunghee University Hospital in Seoul, South Korea. The researchers cultivated a human embryo using an unfertilized egg and a somatic cell donated by a woman. The embryo was allowed to divide into four cells before the experiment was stopped. Earlier researchers had combined material from human and animal cells, but the South Korean team was the first to publicize a successful procedure using all human cell material.

SCIENCE—BIOLOGY—GENETICS

5193. Treatise on laws of heredity was "Versuche über Pflanzenhybriden (Experiments with Plant Hybrids)," published in 1866 in the journal of the society of naturalists of Brünn, Austria (now Brno, Czech Republic) by the Augustinian monk Gregor Mendel, born Johann Mendel in Heinzendorf, Austrian Silesia (now Hyncice, Czech Republic). The paper summarized Mendel's hybridization experiments with garden peas, begun in 1856, that led him to formulate the basic laws of heredity.

5194. Observation of chromosomes in the nucleus of a cell was made in 1888 by the German anatomist Wilhelm von Waldeyer-Hartz, who also named them.

5195. Researcher to describe the role of the human sex chromosomes was the American-born researcher Nettie Stevens. In 1905, while still a graduate student, she published a monograph titled "Studies in Spermatogenesis, with Especial Reference to the Accessory Chromosome," in which she accurately identified the X- and Y-chromosomes and described their role in determining the sex of an embryo.

5196. Radiation mutations to be artificially created were made by Hermann Joseph Muller, a geneticist at the University of Texas, Austin, TX, USA. In 1927, he irradiated fruit flies (*Drosophila*) with X-rays and charted the mutations of their subsequent generations, thereby demonstrating that mutations are the result of changes in individual genes. For his work, he was awarded the Nobel Prize in Physiology or Medicine in 1946.

5197. Human breeding program was the Lebensborn (Fountain of Life) Society, an effort by Nazi Germany to breed a "superior race" of pure-blooded Aryans. Under the direction of the head of the SS, Heinrich Himmler, SS men and women with Nordic features were bred together. The mothers were accommodated in special Nazi nursing homes—the first was founded at Steinhoring, near Munich, on December 12, 1935—and the babies were either kept by the mothers or adopted by approved Nazi families. Several thousand children (the exact number is unknown) were born in this program.

5198. Evidence that DNA is the genetic material was discovered by Oswald Theodore Avery, a Canadian-born American bacteriologist, in 1944 at the Rockefeller Institute, New York, NY, USA. In a series of experiments, Avery, with his colleagues C.M. MacLeod and M. McCarty, determined that the "transforming principle" that conveyed heritable characteristics from one generation of bacteria to the next was a nucleic acid called deoxyribonucleic acid, or DNA.

5199. Elucidation of the structure of DNA was achieved in early 1953 by the American molecular biologist James Dewey Watson, the British physicist-turned-biologist Francis Harry Compton Crick, and the X-ray crystallographers Maurice Wilkins and Rosalind Franklin. Using X-ray diffraction data prepared by Franklin and Wilkins, Watson and Crick determined that a molecule of deoxyribonucleic acid (DNA), a substance already known to be the carrier of heritable genetic information, had to be constructed as flat pairs of nucleotides twisted into a double helix, a structure that would allow the molecule to easily self-replicate. The discovery was published in a letter to the British journal *Nature* on April 25, 1953. The three men shared the 1962 Nobel Prize in Physiology or Medicine (Franklin had died in 1958).

5200. Artificial gene was produced in 1973 by Har Gobind Khorana at the Massachusetts Institute of Technology, Cambridge, MA, USA. The gene, created in a series of replications using transfer-ribonucleic acid, was a 207-base-pair chain identical to a virus gene.

5201. Gene splicing was performed in 1973 by the American molecular biologist Paul Berg of the medical school at Stanford University, Stanford, CA, USA. He developed techniques for splicing DNA from a virus or plasmid into selected areas of bacterial or animal DNA. The recombinant DNA was then introduced into a host cell, where it produced proteins that the unmodified cell could not. For this work, Berg shared the 1980 Nobel Prize in Chemistry with Walter Gilbert and Frederick Sanger.

5202. DNA chain polymerization was invented in 1983 by American researcher Kary B. Mullis, a staff chemist for the Cetus Corporation in Emeryville, CA, USA. The DNA polymerase chain reaction enabled Mullis to replicate an entire chain of deoxyribonucleic acid (DNA) as many times as needed from a single original DNA strand. The technique had

SCIENCE—BIOLOGY—GENETICS—continued

many practical applications in genetic engineering, human genome mapping, DNA fingerprinting, evolutionary science, and genetic diagnosis. Mullis won the 1993 Nobel Prize in Chemistry for his work.

5203. Human chromosome gene-linkage maps were published in October 1992 in the journals *Nature* and *Science*. A Y-chromosome map was prepared by David Page of the Whitehead Institute for Biomedical Research, Cambridge, MA, USA. A map of chromosome 21 prepared by Daniel Cohen, director of the Center for the Study of Human Polymorphism in Paris, France, was also published.

5204. Map of the human genome was prepared in rudimentary detail by researchers under Daniel Cohen in 1993 at the Center for the Study of Human Polymorphism in Paris, France. A fully detailed map was expected to be completed circa 2001.

5205. Complete DNA sequencing of a free-living organism was achieved by a team led by J. Craig Venter of the Institute for Genomic Research in Gaithersburg, MD, USA, and Hamilton O. Smith of the Johns Hopkins University School of Medicine, Baltimore, MD, USA. In May 1997, the researchers announced that they had determined the complete genetic blueprint of *Hemophilus influenzae,* a bacterium that can cause human infections, including a form of meningitis. The organism's DNA was comprised of 1,830,137 base pairs, containing coded instructions for 1,743 genes.

5206. Gene linked with high intelligence was the I.G.F. 2, or insulin growth factor 2, receptor gene, whose presence in highly intelligent individuals was elucidated in 1998 by American behavioral geneticist Robert Plomin and colleagues at the Institute of Psychiatry in London, England. Plomin made the discovery by comparing the DNA of students with high IQ to the DNA of children with average IQ.

5207. Lamb with human genes was Polly, a genetically engineered Poll Dorset sheep born in July 1998 at a research facility in Roslin, Scotland. A medical research team led by Keith Campbell of PPL Theraputics and Ian Wilmut of the Roslin Institute mixed human genetic material with that of fetal sheep cells and inserted the engineered DNA mixture into the nucleus of a sheep egg. That cell developed into a new sheep with the human genetic material in every cell.

5208. DNA sequencing of a multicellular organism was achieved by researchers under John E. Sulston of the Sanger Center, Cambridge, England, and Robert H. Waterston of Washington University, St. Louis, MO, USA. On December 11, 1998, the team announced that it had completed the genome sequencing of *Caenorhabditis elegans,* a species of roundworm. The worm's genome contained 19,099 genes in 402 gene clusters.

SCIENCE—BIOLOGY—PALEONTOLOGY

5209. Dinosaur eggs to be discovered were found in the Gobi Desert of Mongolia during a 1921–22 expedition sponsored by the American Museum of Natural History in New York, NY, USA, and led by the American explorer and naturalist Roy Chapman Andrews. In the summer of 1922, a member of the expedition named Gary Olsen unearthed a circular clutch of 13 intact dinosaur eggs near the Flaming Cliffs in the central Gobi. The rock in which the eggs were embedded was removed and sent to the museum, where the eggs were fully uncovered and examined. Originally they were thought to have been laid by early horned dinosaurs of the genus *Protoceratops,* but recent research suggests that the eggs were those of *Oviraptor philoceratops,* a small bipedal predator.

5210. Fossil illustrations were contained in the *Historiae animalium,* published in 1551 by Swiss physician and naturalist Conrad von Gesner.

5211. Marinosaur fossil unearthed in its entirety and carefully examined by naturalists was that of an ichthyosaur discovered and excavated at Lyme Regis, England, in 1810 by the English fossil hunter Mary Anning.

5212. Woman paleontologist was the young Englishwoman Mary Anning, who collected and sold fossils to support herself and her widowed mother. In 1810, at the age of twelve, she found the first authenticated ichthyosaur skeleton in the seaside cliffs at Lyme Regis, England, and sold the skull to a university professor for £23. In 1824, the Duke of Buckingham paid her £150 for the skeleton of a plesiosaur. She also unearthed the first known pterodactyl skeleton in 1828.

5213. Published record of dinosaur fossil remains was a note by Nathan Smith in the *American Journal of Science and Arts,* dated 1820. It described fossils unearthed in 1818 by a Connecticut farmer, Solomon Ellsworth, Jr., while he was digging a well. The bones were later identified as belonging to the primitive prosauropod Anchisaurus, who lived in the late Triassic-early Jurassic period.

5214. Scientific paper using the term "dinosaur" was written in 1841 for the *Proceedings* of the British Association for the Advancement of Science by the English naturalist and anatomist Richard Owen. In this report he described his examination of teeth and bones of two extinct saurians and coined the term *dinosauria* (Latin for "terror lizards") for the class of unknown reptiles to which he believed they belonged. He described his findings more thoroughly in *A History of British Fossil Reptiles,* published 1849–84. Owen is also noted for his notorious upside-down reconstruction of the first archeopteryx fossil, an error that was not recognized until 1954.

5215. Scientific description of *Tyrannosaurus rex* was published in 1902 by paleontologist Barnum Brown of the American Museum of Natural History, New York, NY, USA. Brown, a highly successful fossil hunter, unearthed the fossils of a huge carnivorous dinosaur in the Hell Creek Formation of east-central Montana, USA and gave the new species its name, which means "tyrant lizard king." *T. rex* thrived during the Cretaceous Period and became extinct 65 million years ago.

5216. Fossilized embryo of a carnivorous dinosaur to be discovered was that of an oviraptor, a small saurischian who lived approximately 70 to 80 million years ago, during the Cretaceous period. The embryo was discovered in the Gobi Desert of Mongolia and identified by Mark A. Norell, associate curator of vertebrate paleontology at the American Museum of Natural History in New York, NY, USA. The first oviraptor bones were unearthed in 1922 lying on top of a nest of what were originally thought to be dinosaur eggs laid by the small horned dinosaur *Protoceratops*. Assuming that the animal had died in the act of stealing the eggs from the nest, the American paleontologist and museum administrator Henry Fairfield Osborn gave it the scientific name *Oviraptor philoceratops* ("egg-stealer likes ceratops"). However, the embryo found by Norell was inside an egg identical to the ones found in 1922, indicating that the oviraptor was not stealing the eggs but had laid them. Norell's findings were published in the November 4, 1994, issue of the journal *Science.*

SCIENCE—CHEMISTRY

5217. Alchemist was an Egyptian, Bolos of Mende, who lived circa 200 BCE and wrote under the name Democritus. He was the author of *Physica et mystica (Natural and Mystical Things),* a treatise on the use of colors and dyes that includes formulas for making gold and silver. Alchemy was practiced in China and India as well as in the Hellenistic world.

5218. Distillation apparatus for alchemists was a type of double boiler invented by the first-century alchemist Maria the Jewess, also known as Miriam the Prophetess. Though she probably lived in the Egyptian city of Alexandria, Maria may have come from Harran, Syria, a center of alchemical speculation.

5219. Alchemical theory to be set forth in detail appears in the work of the Egyptian writer Zosimos of Panopolis, who lived in the third century CE. His ideas centered around the existence of spirits within material bodies that can be manipulated and transformed through the use of activating substances and distillation processes.

5220. Discovery of an element was made by the German chemist and alchemist Hennig Brand. Reportedly, Hennig was in search of the philosopher's stone, a magical substance able to change ordinary metals into gold, when in 1669 he extracted from urine a waxy white substance that glowed in the dark. He named it phosphorus ("light bearer"), but did not publish his discovery. Phosphorus was rediscovered in 1680 by the English chemist Robert Boyle.

5221. Temperature scale that was widely adopted was invented circa 1700 by Gabriel Daniel Fahrenheit, a Polish-born instrumentmaker living in Amsterdam, the Netherlands. The Fahrenheit scale is based on 32 degrees for the freezing point of water and 212 degrees for the boiling point of water, with the average temperature of the human body at 98.6 degrees.

5222. Centigrade temperature scale that contained 100 degrees between the freezing and boiling points of water was developed in 1742 by the astronomer Anders Celsius of Uppsala, Sweden.

SCIENCE—CHEMISTRY—*continued*

5223. Chemist to identify a substance using a microscope was probably Andreas Sigismund Marggraf, director of the chemical laboratory of the German Academy of Sciences, Berlin, Germany, from 1754 to 1760. In 1747, Marggraf used a microscope to examine the crystallized juice he had extracted from sugar beets and thus proved that it is chemically identical to juice extracted from sugar cane. His discovery paved the way for the founding of the sugar industry.

5224. Discovery of oxygen was made in 1772 by the chemist Carl Wilhelm Scheele of Uppsala, Sweden. He gave it the name "fire-air" and described it in his book *Abhandlung von der Luft und dem Feuer (Chemical Observations and Experiments on Air and Fire)*. Because the book was not published until 1777, credit for the discovery was given to the English physical scientist and political theorist Joseph Priestley, who isolated oxygen in 1774 by heating red mercuric oxide. Recognition of oxygen's status as an element, its presence in the atmosphere, and its function in breathing and combustion was made soon after by Antoine-Laurent Lavoisier, the great French chemist.

5225. Modern chemist was the French scientist Antoine-Laurent Lavoisier, considered the "father of modern chemistry." Lavoisier's meticulous quantitative investigations into the nature of the four traditional elements—earth, water, air, and fire—led him to the discovery, announced in a paper of November 1, 1772, and in subsequent works, of the process of oxidation. It was Lavoisier who banished the phlogistical theory of chemical action, who solidified the modern concepts of elements and compounds, who proposed that matter was always conserved in a reaction, and who suggested that reactions could be expressed as equations. Active in the French Revolution, he came under suspicion during the Reign of Terror and was guillotined in Paris in 1793. His most influential work was the classic text *Traité élémentaire de chimie (Elementary Treatise on Chemistry)*, published in 1789.

5226. Analysis of air was conducted by the British chemist Henry Cavendish in 1783. He determined that air is made of 20.8 percent oxygen and 78.2 percent nitrogen, with 1 percent of other gases.

5227. Determination of the chemical composition of water was made by the eccentric English chemist and physicist Henry Cavendish in 1784–85. Building on earlier experiments by Joseph Priestley, Cavendish noted that a small amount of moisture is produced when a mixture of hydrogen gas (which he called "inflammable air") and ordinary air is ignited by a spark. Cavendish analyzed the moisture and found it to be water, created when hydrogen and oxygen in the air form a compound. The Scottish engineer James Watt came to the same conclusion at about the same time, and a controversy erupted in the Royal Society over who had priority in the discovery. It was ultimately resolved in favor of Cavendish.

5228. General reference work of modern chemistry was the *Dictionary of Chemistry,* completed in 1795 by the English chemist and inventor William Nicholson and published by Richard Phillips. The first work of chemical reference to attain the status of a standard work in the field was the *Handbuch der theoretischen Chemie (Handbook of Theoretical Chemistry,)* published in 1817–19 by the German chemist Leopold Gmelin. It was still in print at the end of the 20th century.

5229. Periodic table of the elements was constructed by the English chemist and physicist John Dalton in 1803. Dalton, the originator of modern atomic theory, had determined the atomic weights of a number of elements and displayed them in tabular form, using symbols to represent them. A more elaborate arrangement of the periodic table was devised in 1869 by the Russian chemist Dmitry Ivanovich Mendeleyev to indicate the chemical relationships of the various kinds of elements based on their atomic number and weight.

5230. Liquified gas that had been believed to be incapable of liquefaction was hydrogen sulfide, prepared by the English chemist, physicist, and master experimentalist Michael Faraday in 1818 by cooling the gas under pressure.

5231. Teaching laboratory for chemists was founded in 1827 at the University of Giessen, Germany, by Justus, Freiherr von Liebig, a pioneering German organic chemist who spent his own fortune on equipment and materials. It was the first laboratory in which modern techniques of chemical research were taught systematically.

5232. Organic compound synthesized from an inorganic substance was urea, produced from ammonium cyanate, an inorganic compound, in 1828 by Friedrich Wöhler, chemistry instructor at the municipal technical school in Berlin, Germany.

5233. Nitroglycerin was developed in 1847 by the Italian chemist Ascanio Sobrero, who first called it pyroglycerin ("fire-oil"). Little further work was done with the highly volatile and explosive substance until the Swedish chemists Immanuel Nobel and his son Alfred developed a means of manufacturing it. In 1867 Alfred Nobel produced his first recipe for dynamite, which contained 75 percent nitroglycerin and 25 percent *kieselguhr* (a porous siliceous earth). This was the first stable nitroglycerin-based explosive.

5234. International Chemical Congress was held in 1860 at Karlsruhe, Germany. The main importance of the meeting was the eventual adoption, at the suggestion of the Italian scientist Stanislao Cannizzaro, of a standard method for determining atomic weights based on the work of Amedeo Avogadro.

5235. Element discovered in space was helium, discovered in 1868 by the French astronomer Pierre Janssen. During a solar eclipse, Janssen conducted spectroscopic examination of the solar chromosphere and observed a bright yellow line in the chromospheric spectrum. Later that year, the line was first identified as belonging to a previously unknown element by the English astronomer Joseph Norman Lockyer. Lockyer and chemist Edward Frankland named the new element helium, after *helios,* the Greek word for sun.

5236. Liquid oxygen was prepared on December 2, 1877, by Louis-Paul Cailletet, an ironmaster and chemist in Burgundy, France. Having designed and built a pump capable of producing hundreds of atmospheres of pressure, he abruptly dropped the pressure in a sealed capillary tube containing a quantity of gaseous oxygen from 300 atmospheres to 1 atmosphere, which also reduced the temperature in the tube to below −297 degrees F (−183 degrees C), the liquid point of the gas. Within a day or so of Cailletet's experiment, a Swiss scientist, Raoul-Pierre Pictet, independently obtained samples of the pale blue liquid using a similar approach.

5237. Process for liquefying mixed gases was developed in 1895 by Karl von Linde, a German industrialist and inventor. His efficient system for gaseous liquefication used alternate compression and expansion with intermediate cooling, enabling him to prepare pure liquefied oxygen and nitrogen from ordinary air.

5238. Frozen hydrogen was obtained by the Scottish chemist James Dewar in 1899. He used an improved version of Karl von Linde's gas-liquefying apparatus to bring a sample of hydrogen gas below its melting point of −434.6 degrees F (−259.2 degrees C), and kept the hydrogen frozen in a vacuum flask of his own design.

5239. Liquid helium was prepared by the Dutch physicist Heike Kamerlingh Onnes in 1908 at the Cryogenic Laboratory at the University of Leiden.

5240. Researcher to discover an entire grouping of elements in the periodic table was William Ramsay, a Scottish physical chemist. From 1887 he was the chair of inorganic chemistry at the University of London. In 1894 Ramsay and his coworker Lord Rayleigh announced the discovery of argon, one of the inert or noble gases, so called because they do not combine chemically with other elements. Over the next decade he discovered all the other members of the inert group—helium, neon, krypton, xenon, and niton (now called radon), the last detected in 1910.

5241. Element to be analyzed by mass spectrometer was neon, a sample of which was examined in 1919 by English physicist Francis William Aston of Cambridge University, Cambridge, England. He found that in nature, neon is composed of two isotopes, neon 20 and neon 22. For his work in inventing the mass spectrograph, which separates and measures atoms of different masses, Aston received the Nobel Prize in Chemistry in 1922.

5242. Macromolecules were long-chain polymers discovered in isoprene, a kind of synthetic rubber, by the German chemist Hermann Staudinger with J. Fritschi in 1922. For his discovery, Staudinger, who went on to found an Institute for Macromolecular Chemistry at the Albert Ludwig University of Freiburg im Breisgau, won the 1953 Nobel Prize in Chemistry. His work laid the foundation for the subsequent development of the plastics industry and molecular biology.

5243. Element produced artificially was technetium, a radioactive metal produced in 1937 by the Italian mineralogist Carlo Perrier and the Italian-American physicist Emilio Segrè. A small sample of a long-lived isotope of technetium was created by bombarding a sample of molybdenum with deuterons in the cyclotron at the University of Berkeley, CA, USA. Perrier and Segrè named the element technetium (Greek for "artificial").

SCIENCE—CHEMISTRY—*continued*

5244. Superfluid was the liquid isotope of helium called helium 4. In 1938, Soviet physicist Pyotr Kapitsa was the first to describe the bizarre behavior of helium 4 when it is cooled to below 2.18 degrees Kelvin (−270.97 degrees C), which he called the "lambda transition." As a superfluid, its viscosity disappears, enabling it to flow through capillaries too small for any other liquid. It maintains no friction with its container, so that thin films of helium 4 can spontaneously flow up and over the sides of an open beaker. Its thermal conductivity also increases to more than 1,000 times that of copper.

5245. Element heavier than uranium was created at the University of California at Berkeley, CA, USA, by Edwin Mattison McMillan and Philip Hauge Abelson. Their announcement was made on June 8, 1940. Called neptunium (element 93, symbol Np, atomic weight 237), it was the first element created in the laboratory that was heavier than the heaviest naturally occurring element.

5246. Three-dimensional molecular structure to be elucidated was that of cholesteryl iodide, a complex organic molecule, described in 1945 from work done in 1941–42 by the British biochemist and X-ray crystallographer Dorothy Crowfoot Hodgkin. Such work with large molecules was believed by some to be impossible because of the extremely formidable calculations required to determine their structures. In later work, Hodgkin was the first to use computers for molecular analysis.

5247. Artificial diamond was produced in 1955 at the General Electric Company facility in Schenectady, NY, USA, based on high-pressure techniques developed by the American high-pressure physicist Percy Williams Bridgman at Harvard University, Cambridge, MA, USA. Graphite (pure carbon) and a metallic catalyst were subjected to pressures exceeding 100,000 atmospheres and temperatures above 3,100 degrees F (1,700 degrees C), producing small samples of pure black diamond. A claim by the French inventor Henri Moisson that he synthesized diamonds in an electric furnace in 1894 is generally not accepted by historians.

5248. Molecule analyzed with the use of a computer was vitamin B-12 in the form of cyanocobalamin, a substance that aids in the development of red blood cells. The geometry of the molecule was elucidated by the British biochemist and X-ray crystallographer Dorothy Crowfoot Hodgkin in a research effort lasting from 1948 to 1956. An early British-built digital computer was used to perform the calculations needed to translate the X-ray crystallographic data into a three-dimensional picture.

5249. Discovery of quasicrystals was made in 1982 by the Israeli researcher Daniel S. Schechtman at the National Bureau of Standards (now the National Institute of Standards and Technology) in Gaithersburg, MD, USA. Schechtman was working with an unusual alloy of aluminum, nickel, and cobalt. He found that the alloy exhibited five-fold symmetry when analyzed with X-ray crystallography. This had previously been considered impossible because pentagons, decagons, icosahedrons, and other shapes with sides or facets in multiples of five cannot be made to completely fill a surface or solid, as squares, cubes, and other regular shapes do in ordinary crystals. Electron micrographs indicated that the alloy's quasicrystalline structure is composed of stacked, overlapping decagons of atoms, giving the compound some of the characteristics of a crystalline solid and some of the characteristics of an amorphous glass.

SCIENCE—EARTH SCIENCES

5250. Continental land was discovered in 1995 at Pilbara craton in northwestern Australia by geologist Roger Buick of the University of Sydney. The piece of continental crust, the oldest ever found, was radioactively dated to 3.5 billion years ago, almost a billion years older than previous estimates of continental formation.

5251. Fossil oil was discovered in 1998 in the fossil remains of oil-forming bacteria in rocks 3 billion years old. The rocks came from Australia, South Africa, and Canada. Electron microscope examination of the rock samples under ultraviolet light revealed microscopic droplets of oil trapped within mineral grains. The oil was some 1.5 billion years older than the oldest previously known fossil oil. Adriana Dutkiewicz of CSIRO Petroleum, Birger Rasmussen of the University of Western Australia, and Roger Buick of the University of Sydney published the finding on October 28, 1998, in the scientific journal *Nature*.

5252. Geographical book was the *Ges periodos,* also called the *Periegesis (Tour Round the World,* a two-volume work written circa 550 BCE by the Greek geographer and historian Hecataeus of Miletus, Turkey. It described the geography and ethnography of the Mediterranean world, including parts of Europe and North Africa.

5253. Theory that the earth is a sphere was put forward by the Greek philosopher and mathematician Pythagoras, originally of Samos, Greece, and later (circa 530 BCE) of Croton (modern Crotone, Italy), or by the philosophers who were his students.

5254. Estimate of the circumference of the earth was made in the fourth century BCE by the Macedonian Greek philosopher Aristotle, who accepted the theory of a spherical earth put forward by his predecessor, Pythagoras. He put the figure at approximately 400,000 stadia, the equivalent of 38,285 miles (61,600 kilometers) to 53,449 miles (86,000 kilometers).

5255. Treatise on rocks and minerals was *De lapidibus (On Stones),* written early in the third century BCE by Theophrastus of Eresus, the Greek scientist and philosopher who is better known as the founder of botany.

5256. Scientific calculation of the Earth's circumference was made circa 240 BCE by Eratosthenes of Cyrene (present-day Shahhat, Libya), the Greek astronomer and mathematician. Eratosthenes used common spherical geometry to calculate the circumference. By measuring the difference in the angle of shadows cast at noon in the Egyptian cities of Syene (modern Aswan) and Alexandria, and also knowing the distance in stadia from the two cities, he calculated a circumference for the earth of 250,000 stadia, or about 28,745 miles (46,250 kilometers), a figure respectably close to the modern value of 24,900 miles (40,064 kilometers).

5257. Weathervane known to archeologists was a bronze vane in the shape of a Triton that was affixed to the top of the Tower of the Winds, a marble octagon 42 feet (12.8 meters) high that was built in Athens, Greece, by the astronomer Andronicus of Cyrrhus circa 100 BCE. The chief function of the tower, which was also called the Horologium, was to keep time, using a sundial on the exterior and a water clock within.

5258. Description of an earthquake was set down circa 25 CE by the Greek geographer Strabo. In his *Geography,* he wrote of an earthquake and tsunami in circa 373 BCE that caused the town of Eliki (probably the lost city of Helike, Greece) to subside into the Gulf of Corinth. "For the sea was raised by an earthquake and it submerged Eliki, and also the temple of Elikonian Poseidon, whom the Ionians worship even to this day. . . .And Eratosthenes says that he himself saw the place, and that the ferrymen say that there was a bronze Poseidon in the strait, standing erect, holding a sea horse in his hand, which was perilous for those who fished with nets. And Herakleides says that the submersion took place by night in his time, and, although the city was twelve stadia [about 1.5 kilometers] distant from the sea, this whole district together with the city was hidden from sight; and two thousand men who had been sent by the Achaians were unable to recover the dead bodies."

5259. Seismograph for recording earthquake tremors was invented by the Chinese astronomer, poet, and mathematician Chang Heng in 132 CE. His device consisted of an urn in which was suspended a very heavy pendulum. Eight arms were attached to the pendulum, one for each point of the compass. Around the outside of the urn were eight carvings representing dragons, each of which was connected to one of the arms. A ball was fixed in the jaws of each dragon. Arranged in a circle around the urn were eight carvings of frogs with their mouths wide open. When the vibration from an earth tremor disturbed the pendulum, it would swing towards one of the arms, causing the ball to drop into the mouth of the frog below.

5260. Use of the word "fossil" appeared in *De natura fossilium (On Natural Fossils)* published in 1546 by Georgius Agricola (born Georg Bauer), a German scholar and scientist. By fossils, Agricola meant anything that could be dug up from the ground.

5261. Anemometer for measuring air speed was invented by English physicist Robert Hooke in 1644. His device counted the turns of a horizontal bladed rotor exposed to the wind.

5262. Scientist lowered into a volcano was Athanasius Kircher, the German Jesuit priest and scholar. In 1665, he descended by rope into the crater of Vesuvius, near Naples, Italy, to examine it shortly after an eruption. He later proposed in a geology textbook that the earth had a fiery furnace at its center.

5263. Treatise on geology was *De solido intra solidum naturaliter contento dissertationis prodromus (The Prodromus of Nicolaus Steno's Dissertation Concerning a Solid Body Enclosed by Process of Nature Within a Solid),* published in 1669 by Nicolaus Steno (Niels Steensen), a Danish physician and theologian. Steno was the

SCIENCE—EARTH SCIENCES—*continued*

first to propose that fossils are the remains of ancient life; that certain rocks are produced by sedimentation; that lower layers in rock strata are older than those above them; and that each type of mineral crystal has a characteristic angle between its corresponding faces.

5264. Evidence that the earth is an oblate spheroid was observed during a 1672 French expedition to Cayenne (now in French Guiana), when it was noticed that a pendulum clock that kept accurate time in Paris was 2.5 minutes a day slower in locations near to the equator. This was explained in 1687 by Isaac Newton in the *Philosophiae Naturalis Principia Mathematica (Mathematical Principles of Natural Philosophy)*. Newton theorized that the earth was actually a flattened (oblate) spheroid, owing to the effect of centrifugal force on the earth's spinning mass, with a circumference that was wider along the equatorial axis than along the polar axis. Gravity at the poles, which are closer to the center of the mass, would therefore be stronger than gravity at the more distant equator, causing a pendulum in the equatorial regions to rock slightly more slowly.

5265. Seismologist to develop a modern theory of the cause and actions of earthquakes was the English scientist John Michell. His "Conjectures Concerning the Cause, and Observations upon the Phenomena of Earthquakes," the first modern seismological treatise, was presented to the Royal Society of London in 1760. In it he located the underwater epicenter of the Lisbon earthquake of 1755 and suggested that such earthquakes were produced by the release of high-pressure subterranean steam.

5266. Lightning rod on a public building in Europe was affixed to the steeple of the Church of St. Jacob in Hamburg (now in Germany) in 1769. The lightning rod, which prevents damage to structures by channeling lightning into the ground, was invented in 1752 by the American scientist and statesman Benjamin Franklin.

5267. Measurement of the mass and density of the earth was made by the British Astronomer Royal, Nevil Maskelyne, in 1774. He used a method called the Attraction of Mountains, which involved measuring the gravitational deflection of a long plumb line toward the large mass of a nearby mountain, and inferring from that the mass of the entire earth. The experiment was performed in Scotland on Schiehallion Mountain in North Perthshire. He

obtained a mass of about 5 million million million tons (reasonably close to the accepted figure of 5.98 times 10^{24} kilograms), as well as a mean density for the earth of approximately 4.5 times that of water.

5268. Measurement of altitude by instrument took place in 1783, when the French physicist and mathematician Jacques-Alexandre-César Charles sent a barometer up in a balloon, intending the use air pressure readings as an index of altitude.

5269. Wind intensity scale was the Beaufort Wind Force Scale, devised in 1805 by Rear-Admiral Sir Francis Beaufort based on his observations of the effects of the wind on the rigging of a man-of-war. A Beaufort number of 0 refers to windless conditions, in which the sea is like glass. A Beaufort number of 12 is given to hurricane conditions with a white, foamy sea. The scale was adopted by the British Navy in 1838 and in 1874 by the International Meteorological Committee for use when telegraphing weather conditions.

5270. National geologic survey was the Geological Survey of Great Britain, undertaken beginning in 1835 under the direction of economic geologist Henry Thomas De la Beche.

5271. National weather service was founded by Joseph Henry, the first director of the Smithsonian Institution in Washington, DC, USA, in 1848. Henry assembled a network of volunteer weather observers who kept in touch by telegraph and used their data to create a daily weather map of the United States that showed for the first time the structure and movement of weather patterns.

5272. Scale of earthquake intensity was developed by the English geologist Robert Mallet in 1857. His system was not widely adopted.

5273. Oceanographic expedition was conducted by the British corvette H.M.S. *Challenger* from December 7, 1872, to May 26, 1876. The *Challenger* expedition, which visited every ocean during a voyage of 68,890 nautical miles (127,600 kilometers), was commissioned by the British Admiralty and the Royal Society and commanded by Captain George Strong Nares. C. Wyville Thomson was the chief scientist. The expedition's findings, including many thousands of readings of oceanic temperature, ocean currents, and basin depth, as well as detailed marine biological studies, were published between 1880 and 1895 in a 50-volume document, *Report on the Scientific Results of the Voyage of H.M.S Challenger.*

5274. Climatological classification system was prepared by the Russian-born Austrian geographer Vladimir Peter Köppen in 1884, using temperature differences to define the distinct climate regions of the world. Later versions of Köppen's system, the last of which was published in 1930, also took account of seasonal changes in temperature and precipitation.

5275. Tornado expert was the American meteorologist John Park Finley, a sergeant in the U.S. Army. In the 1880s, he assembled the world's first extensive scientific observations of tornadoes and attempted to make the first tornado forecasts based on meteorological conditions. Finley also provided one of the most vivid early descriptions of tornadoes: "A single experience of this awful convulsion of the elements suffices to fasten the memory of its occurrence upon the mind with such a dreadful force that no effort can efface the remembrance of it. The destructive violence of this storm exceeds in its power, fierceness, and grandeur all other phenomena of the atmosphere."

5276. Meteorologist to name tropical storms was the English-born Australian meteorologist and astronomer Clement Lindley Wragge, who was Queensland Government Meteorologist from 1887 to 1902. Wragge favored obscure biblical names such as Talmon and Uphaz.

5277. Weather balloons were lofted in 1898 by the French meteorologist Léon-Philippe Teisserenc de Bort, formerly chief of the Administrative Center of National Meteorology in Paris, from his private observatory near Versailles, France. His unmanned balloons found evidence of a previously unknown layer of the atmosphere, which he named the stratosphere.

5278. Meteor crater identified as such was Barringer Meteor Crater in northern Arizona, USA. American engineer Daniel M. Barringer recognized the crater's extraterrestrial origin in 1905. It was formed more than 25,000 years ago by a meteorite approximately 100 feet (30 meters) in diameter that hit the earth with an impact equivalent to the detonation of 3.5 million tons of TNT.

5279. Photographic record of the state of the earth was the work of French financier Albert Kahn. In 1910, he proposed an "Archives of the Planet" that would be a "photographic inventory of the surface of the globe, as inhabited and worked by man, as it was at the beginning of the century." Kahn employed scores of photographers and filmmakers to send him autochrome images from all over the world. Approximately 72,000 plates were made, and 462,000 feet (140,000 meters) of film were shot. The ambitious project was never completed.

5280. Evidence for continental drift was presented in 1912 by the originator of the theory of continental drift, German meteorologist, geophysicist, and Arctic explorer Alfred Lothar Wegener, before the German geological Association in Frankfurt. Wegener's book *Die Entstehung der Kontinente und Ozeane (The Origin of Continents and Oceans)*, published in 1915, detailed his theory of how the continents have shifted position over hundreds of millions of years. Wegener cited fossil evidence as well as the obvious jigsaw-puzzle-like fit of most of the large land-masses. Wegener's hypothesis was not widely accepted until long after his death in 1930; it is now commonly subsumed under as the theory of plate tectonics.

5281. Calculation of the accurate age of the earth was made in 1913 by the Irish scientist John Joly at Trinity College, Dublin, with the aid of English physicist Ernest Rutherford at Cambridge University in England. Joly first estimated that the Devonian period began approximately 400 million years ago, based on the half-life of radioactive zircon and alanite, and thus was able to estimate a total age for the earth of 4.5 billion (thousand million) years. This figure is still generally accepted.

5282. Treatise on geochemistry was the *Geochemische Verteilungsgesetze der Elemente (The Geochemical Laws of the Distribution of the Elements)*, published in eight volumes between 1923 and 1938 by the Swiss-born Norwegian mineralogist Victor Moritz Goldschmidt. Goldschmidt's careful studies of thermal and injection metamorphism were the foundation of modern geochemistry and inorganic crystal chemistry. He was also the first to attempt a realistic estimate of the relative cosmic abundances of the elements.

5283. Deep-sea exploration vessel was the bathysphere, developed by the Americans William Beebe and Otis Barton in the early 1930s. A reinforced steel sphere with windows, an air supply, and a telephone, it was suspended by cable from a ship. The first descent by Beebe and Barton was made off the coast of Bermuda on June 11, 1930, when the bathysphere reached a depth of 1,300 feet (400 meters).

SCIENCE—EARTH SCIENCES—*continued*

5284. Aerial photograph showing the lateral curvature of the horizon and the beginning of the stratosphere was taken by U.S. Army captain Albert William Stevens from the gondola of the stratosphere balloon *Explorer 11*, which was sent up on November 11, 1935, by the National Geographic Society and the United States Army Air Corps. The photograph was made from an altitude of 13.71 miles (22 kilometers) above sea level. It was the first photograph of the horizon taken from such a great altitude; the first photograph for which the line of sight was entirely in the stratosphere; and the first photograph showing the extreme top of the "dust sphere" that marks the dividing line between the lower atmosphere with its clouds and dust and the stratosphere, which is clear. The balloon took off from Rapid City, SD, USA, and landed 8 hours 13 minutes later at White Lake, SD.

5285. Self-contained underwater breathing apparatus was the Aqualung, developed in 1943 by the French naval engineers and divers Jacques Yves Cousteau and Émil Gagnan. The first fully automatic compressed-air breathing system, it enabled divers for the first time to swim freely underwater without being tethered to an air supply at the surface.

5286. Hurricane reconnaissance flights were undertaken in 1947 by the U.S. Weather Bureau and U.S. Air Force, which sent two Air Force flights into the severe hurricane that developed in the Atlantic Ocean during September 12–20, 1947. Robert H. Simpson was the chief researcher from the Weather Bureau.

5287. International Geophysical Year was held in 1957–58. Scientists from 67 nations cooperated in a wide variety of data-gathering initiatives. These included building global seismograph networks, launching weather satellites and space probes (including the first artificial satellites, *Sputnik* and *Explorer*), and mounting scientific expeditions to the Arctic and Antarctic.

5288. Worldwide satellite-based weather observation system was the Television and Infra-Red Observation Satellite system, whose first satellite was launched on April 1, 1960, from Cape Canaveral, FL, USA, by NASA, the U.S. space agency. The TIROS satellites employed television cameras and infrared detectors to track storm systems and transmit pictures to receiving stations on earth, enabling meteorologists to forecast weather conditions round-the-clock.

5289. Tornado intensity scale was the Fujita-Pearson Tornado Scale (often called the F-scale), developed by the American metorologists T. Theodore Fujita and Alan Pearson and first applied in 1971. The F-scale is used to rate the intensity of a tornado by examining the damage after it has passed over a man-made structure. The scale runs from F0, the least intense tornado, to F5, a violent tornado of extreme destructiveness.

5290. Weather service to name tropical storms with male and female names was the Commonwealth of Australia Bureau of Meteorology, which began the practice of naming cyclones equally with male and female names in 1975.

5291. Ocean-mapping satellite was *Seasat 1*, launched by the United States on June 26, 1978. Its mission was to radar-map the surface of the ocean, providing precise information on tides, currents, storms, undersea seismic activity, and other phenomena that affect sea level. It sampled the sea height every 3 kilometers along its orbital track, which covered the majority of the ocean surface every three days. A global ocean-surface map was later prepared from the data.

5292. Three-dimensional maps of subterranean rifts were views of the African Rift, the longest rift below dry land, created by researchers of the Kenya Rift International Seismic Project. Seismic waves created by an array of underground explosions and by distant earthquakes were used to compile tomographic images of the rift's deep geologic structure, of which several were released in 1993.

5293. Impending volcanic eruption detected from space was the eruption on May 20, 1998, of the Pacaya volcano in Guatemala, which rained ash on Guatemala City and surrounding areas. In a program funded by Hawaii's state government and the Earth Observing System operated by the U.S. National Aeronautics and Space Administration, a computer at the University of Hawaii was used to monitor and analyze satellite data from two Geostationary Environmental Satellites for areas on the earth's surface that were rising in temperature. A hot spot centered on Pacaya was detected on May 13.

SCIENCE—INSTRUMENTS

5294. Compound microscope containing both an objective and an eyepiece was developed in Holland between 1590 and 1608. Historians of science disagree as to who should receive credit for the invention: Hans Jansen, his son Zacharias Jansen, or Hans Lippershey, all of whom were spectacle-makers. Early versions of the compound microscope were inferior in clarity and resolving power to the single-lens instruments used by the pioneering Dutch microscopist Antoni van Leeuwenhoek some 70 years later.

5295. Thermometer was invented circa 1592 by the Italian physicist and astronomer Galileo Galilei. It was an inverted glass container with a long neck that held a liquid. Changes in the temperature of the container produced changes in the volume of the air inside it, altering the level of the liquid in the neck.

5296. Clinical thermometer was an adaptation of a design by Galileo Galilei, made in 1612 by Santorio Santorio (also known as Sanctorius), professor of medical theory at the University of Padua, Italy. Santorio also adapted timekeeping mechanisms invented by Galileo to make the first pulse clock in 1602. Another student of Galileo's, the physician and rabbi Yosef Shlomo (Joseph Solomon) Delmedigo of Prague (in the present-day Czech Republic), described two thermometer designs in his 1629 Hebrew book *Ma'yan Ganim*. One was an air thermometer, an open-ended tube partly filled with liquid, and the other a sealed liquid thermometer filled with brandy.

5297. Barometer for measuring atmospheric pressure and predicting the weather was invented in 1643 in Florence, Italy, by Evangelista Torricelli, the secretary of Galileo, who had originally suggested the idea to him. Torricelli fashioned a long glass tube that was open at one end and sealed at the other. He filled the tube with mercury and turned it upside down into a bowl. The mercury partly flowed into the bowl, leaving a vacuum at the sealed top of the tube—the first time a sustained vacuum had been created. Daily observation led Torricelli to the realization that the level of mercury in the tube rose and fell with the weather.

5298. Air pump was invented in 1650 by the German physicist and engineer Otto von Guericke. Guericke used his invention to investigate the nature and properties of a vacuum. His most famous experiment was held in 1654 for Emperor Ferdinand III at Regensburg, Germany. Guericke put two copper bowls together to make a sphere, pumped out the air they enclosed, then showed that two horses pulling in opposite directions could not separate the bowls—even though all that held them together was the pressure of the surrounding air.

5299. Treatise on barometry was a pamphlet on the construction and use of simple barometers, published in 1688 by John Smith, a London clockmaker.

5300. Mercury thermometer was invented in 1714 by Gabriel Daniel Fahrenheit, a Polish-born instrument-maker living in Amsterdam, the Netherlands. Its basic design was identical to that of the modern household thermometer: a sealed glass tube with a graduated capillary bore and a reservoir bulb at one end for the mercury. Fahrenheit invented the alcohol-based thermometer in 1709.

5301. Achromatic microscope that eliminated chromatic and spherical aberration, thus improving the observer's ability to judge the colors and shapes of cells and other specimens, was invented by the English optician Joseph Jackson Lister in 1830. Using sets of compound objective lenses that he ground himself, Lister made the first accurate observations of the true "lozenge" shape of the red blood cell. Lister was the father of the pioneer in aseptic surgery, Joseph Lister.

5302. Standard laboratory burner was the Bunsen burner, invented by two German chemists, Robert Bunsen and Peter Desdega, in 1855, and still widely used. The burner's simple design consists of an upright metal tube on a base, with an inlet for flammable gas at the bottom and vents partway up that can be adjusted to regulate the amount of air that mixes with the gas as it rises to the top of the tube, where it is ignited with a sparker or match. Careful mixing of gas and air in the right proportions results in a flame of about 2,700 degrees F (1,500 degrees C).

5303. Vacuum flask was the invention of the Scottish physicist and chemist Sir James Dewar, professor at the Royal Institution of Great Britain, London, and the University of Cambridge. He developed his double-walled Dewar flask in 1892 to store liquid gases at low temperatures. The evacuated space between the walls prevents conduction of heat. The flask was later adapted for household use as the Thermos bottle.

5304. Transmission electron microscope employing electron beams and electromagnetic lenses in lieu of light beams and glass lenses was developed in 1931–33 in Berlin, Germany, by the physicist and electrical engineer Ernst August Friedrich Ruska. Another German, Rheinhold Rudenberg, filed the first patent for an electron microscope, but he did not construct a working device. The first commercial electron microscope was introduced in Germany by Siemens-Reiniger-Werke AG in 1939. A somewhat similar design was invented by the Russian-American inventor Vladimir Kosma Zworykin of the RCA Laboratory, Camden, NJ,

SCIENCE—INSTRUMENTS—*continued*

USA, and was first publicly demonstrated by Ladislaus Morton on April 20, 1940, at the American Philosophical Society convention in Philadelphia, PA, USA. The instrument was 10 feet (3 meters) high, weighed about 1,000 pounds (454 kilograms), and magnified up to 100,000 diameters.

5305. Scanning tunneling electron microscope was developed in 1947 by the German physicist Gerd Binnig and the Swiss physicist Heinrich Rohrer, both of the International Business Machines research division in Zürich, Switzerland. The scanning tunneling microscope can provide highly detailed, three-dimensional images of living creatures as well as of objects as small as atoms.

5306. Electronic nose able to differentiate among certain smells was developed in 1994 by Neotronics, a research firm based in Bishop's Stortford, Hertfordshire, England. The device was able to detect the difference between fresh and stale crackers. It could also differentiate between Champagne and white wine. The nose's twelve olfactory sensors consisted of electrically conductive polymers called polypyroles.

SCIENCE—MEASUREMENT

5307. Measure of weight of record was the beqa, used during the Amratian period of predynastic Egypt circa 3800 BCE. According to discoveries made at Naqadah, Egypt, by the British archeologist Flinders Petrie, the beqa was measured with cylindrical weights of roughly 7 ounces (198 grams).

5308. Unit of length of record was an unnamed standard unit of approximately 2.7 feet (0.8 meters) used by the megalithic tomb-builders of Europe circa 3500 BCE, according to research by British archeologist Alexander Thom.

5309. Unit of linear measure was the cubit, usually taken to be the distance between the elbow and the tip of the middle finger, about 18 inches (45.7 centimeters). It may date from 3000 BCE; it is mentioned in the Bible and was used by the Hebrews, Egyptians, Sumerians, and Babylonians. The oversized Egyptian royal cubit, 20.6 inches (52.4 centimeters) in length, was divided into seven smaller units called palms, with each palm divided into four digits.

5310. Mile was the *mille passus,* which came into general use in the Roman world by circa 150 BCE. It measured 1,000 paces. As each pace was considered to be 5 feet long (the length of two steps), the Roman mile was 5,000 feet long.

5311. Definition of an inch was given circa 1150 by Scotland's King David I, who ruled that one "ynche" was equal in width to the base of a man's thumbnail, figured by taking the average of the thumbnail breadths of a small, a middle-sized, and a large man. The word "inch" comes from the Latin *uncia,* a twelfth, referring to the twelfth part of one Roman foot.

5312. Statute mile did not attain its present length of 5,280 feet until 1593, when the English Parliament under Elizabeth I passed a statue declaring the mile to be equal to eight furlongs (an English furlong was 660 feet long).

5313. International measurement standards were formulated by the International Organization for Standardization, founded in Geneva, Switzerland, in 1946 with the goal of setting international technical standards in such areas as units of measurement, industrial processes, and information technology. These standards are accepted by the appropriate body of the approximately 80 member nations.

5314. International system of measurement was the Système Internationale (SI), developed by an international convention held in Paris, France, in 1960. It adopted six fundamental units of measure, all based on the metric system: the meter, the kilogram, the second, the degree Kelvin, the ampere (the basic unit of electricity), and the candela (a measure of luminosity).

SCIENCE—OPTICS

5315. Modern theory of the visual process was developed circa 1010 by the mathematician and physicist Alhazen, born Abu Ali al-Hasan ibn al-Haytham in Basra (now in Iraq). In his treatise on optics, known in Latin as *Opticae thesaurus Alhazeni libri vii,* he deduced that light coming from an illuminated object forms an image in the eye. The work also dealt with refraction, reflection, binocular vision, the rainbow, and atmospheric refraction. It strongly influenced the work of early European scientists, including Roger Bacon, Robert Grosseteste, and John Pecham.

5316. Parabolic mirror was invented by the Croatian physicist Marin Getaldic (1568–1626), born in Dubrovnik on the Dalmatian coast in what is now Croatia. The most outstanding Croatian scientist of his time, he was a pioneer in the algebraization of geometry, and was in regular contact with Galileo. Getaldic constructed circa 1600 a large convex mirror, roughly 2 feet (0.6 meters) in diameter, with a parabolic curve. The mirror is preserved in the National Maritime Museum in London, England. It is possible that Getaldic used this mirror to fashion a reflecting telescope, well before Isaac Newton independently invented one (incorporating a spherical concave mirror as the objective) in 1671.

5317. Achromatic lens was invented by English jurist, mathematician, and astronomer Chester Moor Hall in 1729. He combined a concave flint-glass lens with a convex crown-glass lens into a lens doublet that did not exhibit the chromatic aberration (color fringing) that plagued single lenses. In 1733 he built a series of small refracting telescopes using his lens; they were the first that were free of color distortion.

5318. Hologram was produced in 1962 by the American radar researchers Emmett Leith and Juris Upatnieks of the University of Michigan, USA, building on theoretical work done in 1948 by British/Hungarian physicist Dennis Gabor. Gabor had been unable to produce an actual hologram, a kind of three-dimensional photograph, because a suitable source of coherent light had not yet been invented. Leith and Upatnieks decided to combine Gabor's ideas on light interferometry with their research into side-looking radar. Using a laser (invented two years earlier) and off-axis split-beam techniques from the radar research, the Americans created the first true three-dimensional flat image, a transmission hologram of a toy train and bird. The image could only be viewed when illuminated by a laser beam. Also in 1962, the first hologram viewable with the light from an ordinary light bulb was invented by Soviet physicist Uri N. Denisyuk in Leningrad (now St. Petersburg, Russia). His white-light reflection hologram was the first that did not need illumination by a laser for viewing. Gabor coined the term "hologram" from the Greek words *holos* ("whole") and *gramma* ("message").

5319. Single-picture stereogram or Autostereogram, in which a hidden three-dimensional image was viewable without the need for a stereoscope was created in 1979 by the American researcher Christopher W. Tyler. Tyler, who later became associate director of the Smith-Kettlewell Eye Research Institute in San Francisco, CA, USA, had been the student of the psychologist and engineer Bela Julesz, the inventor of the random-dot stereogram, who did early theoretical work into the psychology of three-dimensional perception at the Bell Telephone Research Laboratory in Holmdel, NJ, USA. An autostereogram is a single two-dimensional image that typically appears to be made of random colored dots. When viewed correctly by focusing the eyes "behind" the image, the visual system is fooled into thinking that it is seeing a three-dimensional image.

SCIENCE—PHYSICS

5320. Atomic theory was advanced by the fifth-century BCE Greek philosopher Leucippus of Miletus (in present-day Turkey). He proposed the existence of an eternal empty space in which small indivisible particles, called atoms (from the Greek *atoma*, meaning "indivisible"), whirl about in constant motion. The whirling of atoms is, according to Leucippus, all that can be perceived by the senses. His student, Democritus of Abdera, concluded that the universe is made of only two things: the Void (space) and Being (matter), which is made up entirely of infinitesimal, fundamental particles called *atomon*. All physical phenomena could be explained by different characteristics of the atomon, such as their color, shape, or arrangement. The ideas of Democritus, though very modern in some details, did not constitute a scientific theory, as they were not based on observation and experiment. When the English physicist John Dalton proposed the first scientific atomic theory in 1803, based on his many years of chemical experimentation, he retained the word "atom" for the small particles of which all elements and compounds are composed.

5321. Treatise on magnetism was *Epistola Petri Peregrini de Maricourt ad Sygerum de Foucaucourt, militem, de magnete (Letter of Peter Peregrinus of Maricourt to Sygerus of Foucaucourt, Soldier, on the Magnet)*, written in the mid-13th century by the French scholar Pierre Pèlerin de Maricourt. It described the properties of the lodestone (magnetite), including the existence of magnetic poles, and offered a new design for a floating compass.

5322. Gravity experiment establishing that objects of differing masses fall at the same speed was published in 1586 by the Dutch engineer, inventor, and mathematician Simon Stevin. Stevin dropped two lead balls, one ten times as heavy as the other, a distance of 30 feet; both

SCIENCE—PHYSICS—*continued*

hit the ground at the same time. Stevin's report, which refuted the Aristotelian assertion that objects of different weights fall at different speeds, preceded by three years the beginning of Galileo Galilei's famous studies of gravity.

5323. Demonstration of static electricity was made by William Gilbert, physician to Elizabeth I of England. He demonstrated that magnetism can be induced in many materials by rubbing (static electrical charge), that "rays of magnetic force" extend in a field around a magnet, that iron can be magnetized by another magnet (magnetization by induction), and that magnetism is transmitted through a bar of iron from one end to the other (the flow of electric current through a conductor). He is also credited with first applying the name "electrica" or "electrics" to materials charged by rubbing. His *De Magnete* was published in 1600.

5324. Measurement of the speed of sound was made circa 1630 by the French scientist and philosopher Pierre Gassendi (also spelled Gassend). On a still day, he stood far away from a firing gun and timed the difference between seeing the muzzle flash and hearing the sound of the shot. Gassendi obtained a value for the speed of sound of 1,569.6 feet (478.4 meters) per second—about 50 percent higher than the actual value of 1,086.9 feet (331.29 meters) per second on a cold day. Gassendi inferred correctly that light travels at an essentially infinite speed compared to sound, and that the frequency of a sound does not affect its speed.

5325. Statement of a physical law as an equation with two dependent variables was Boyle's law (known in France as Mariotte's law, after the physicist Edme Mariotte), formulated in England in 1662 by the Irish-born chemist Robert Boyle. Boyle's law states that pressure and volume in a quantity of gas are inversely related. It is written $PV = P'V'$, where P and V are the pressure and volume in a vessel under one set of conditions and P' and V' are the pressure and volume under another set of conditions.

5326. Accurate measurement of the speed of sound was undertaken in 1738 by the Academy of Sciences in Paris, France. Using 18th-century measuring tools, researchers were able to obtain a value for the speed of sound of 1,089 feet (332 meters) per second, virtually identical to the accepted value of 1,086.9 feet (331.29 meters) per second on a cold day obtained in the 1960s.

5327. Physicist who was a woman was Laura Bassi of Bologna, Italy. Beginning in 1732, she did research in electricity while serving as lecturer in universal philosophy at the University of Bologna and rearing twelve children. The university appointed her professor of experimental physics in 1776.

5328. Proposal of the existence of gravitational singularities was made in a 1784 letter to the Royal Society of London by the English geologist and astronomer John Michell, considered the father of modern seismology. Michell imagined a sphere 500 times as big as the sun, with such a strong gravitational field that nothing could escape it, not even light. "Supposing light to be attracted by the same force in proportion to its inertiae," he wrote, "all light emitted from such a body would be made to return towards it, by its own proper gravity." Gravitational singularities, better known as black holes, were predicted in 1916 by Albert Einstein's general theory of relativity. Their nature was further investigated by the German astrophysicist Karl Schwarzschild, the American physicist J. Robert Oppenheimer, and others. The term "black hole" was coined in 1969 by the American astronomer John Archibald Wheeler.

5329. Absolute scale of temperature is the Kelvin scale, named for the Scottish physicist William Thomson, Baron Kelvin of Largs, who first proposed an absolute temperature scale in 1848. The Kelvin scale, measured in kelvins, places its zero point at absolute zero, the coldest possible temperature (459.67 degrees F, -273.15 degrees C). The kelvin is the base unit of temperature measurement in the International System (SI) of measurement.

5330. Discovery of X-rays was made inadvertently on November 8, 1895, by Wilhelm Conrad Röntgen (or Roentgen), professor of physics and rector of the Julius Maximilian University of Würzburg, Germany. Röntgen had covered an electrified cathode ray tube with black paper as part of an experiment when he noticed a faint fluorescence from a barium platinocyanide-coated screen across the room. He inferred correctly that the glow was caused by an unknown form of high-energy radiation emitted from the tube, which he called "X-radiation."

5331. Discovery of electrons was made by the English physicist Joseph John Thomson and announced on April 30, 1897, at the Royal Institution in London, England. Experimenting with an evacuated cathode tube, Thomson observed that the cathode rays (an electron beam) that caused the tube to glow bore a negative charge, that they could be measured by their heating effects, and that they were deflected by an electric field as well as by a magnetic field. Thomson concluded that the cathode rays were composed of "corpuscles" that were essentially the same particles no matter what gas or cathode metal was used to produce them.

5332. Theory that light consists of particles was proposed by the German physicist Max Karl Ernst Ludwig Planck on December 14, 1900. Light, claimed Planck, radiates not as waves, as Isaac Newton had claimed, but in particles or packets called quanta, with the energy of each quantum determined by its frequency times the value of a constant, h, now called Planck's constant. The value of h in meter-kilogram-second units is 6.6260755 x 10^{34} joule-second. Planck's work is the basis for quantum theory, and in 1918 won him the Nobel Prize in Physics.

5333. Modern theory of atomic structure was proposed in 1904 by the Japanese physicist Hantaro Nagaoka. In his model, electrons rotated in rings about a small central nucleus, much like the rings of Saturn. His theory was dismissed by most contemporary physicists because it appeared to suggest that atoms were inherently unstable. Evidence in favor of Hantaro's model was discovered in 1911 by the English physicist Ernest Rutherford, who in a series of elegant experiments proved that the nucleus of the atom is extremely small and dense and is surrounded by a much larger and less dense cloud of electrons. In 1913 the Danish physicist Niels Bohr suggested that electrons orbit the nucleus in concentric quantum shells that correspond to the electrons' energy levels.

5334. Superconductor known to physicists was mercury. In 1911, the Dutch physicist Heike Kamerlingh Onnes, director of the Cryogenic Laboratory at the University of Leiden, discovered that mercury cooled to just above 4 degrees Kelvin (-269 degrees C), a few degrees short of absolute zero, exhibited almost no electrical resistance.

5335. Mass spectrometer was invented by the English physicist Joseph John Thomson in 1913 in Cambridge, England. His version of this instrument, called the parabola spectrograph, identified samples of chemical substances by ionizing them and sorting their ions in a magnetic field. In 1919, the English physicist Francis William Aston invented a similar device, now called the mass spectrograph, with which he demonstrated the existence of isotopes.

5336. Scientific proof of the general theory of relativity was obtained during the total eclipse of the sun in 1919. An expedition to the Gulf of Guinea led by the British astronomer Arthur Stanley Eddington measured the direction of a star close to the sun and found that its apparent position was deflected by the sun's gravitational field in the amount predict by Albert Einstein's theory.

5337. Discovery of protons was made independently by the German physicist Wilhelm Wien in 1898 and the English physicist Joseph John Thomson in 1910. Both were investigating the properties of ionized particle beams. Thomson identified a single positively charged particle identical in mass to the hydrogen atom (which contains a single proton in its nucleus). In 1920 Ernest Rutherford, the founder of modern atomic theory, named this particle the proton.

5338. Discovery of antimatter was made in 1932 in a magnetic cloud chamber at the California Institute of Technology, Pasadena, CA, USA. The observer, physicist Carl David Anderson, noticed that one of the cosmic rays in the chamber left a trail that curved in the wrong direction. It was a particle with the mass and energy of a electron, but with a positive charge rather than a negative charge. Anderson gave the particle the name "positron." When a positron comes into contact with a normal electron, both are annihilated, releasing a flash of energy.

5339. Discovery of neutrons was made in 1932 by the English experimentalist James Chadwick at the Cavendish Laboratory of Cambridge University, where he was investigating the transmutation of elements. Chadwick was bombarding beryllium with alpha particles when he observed the emission of unknown radiation capable of dislodging protons from other atoms. From this he deduced the existence of a particle, which he called the neutron, with approximately the mass of a proton but with no electrical charge. Chadwick received the Nobel Prize in Physics in 1935 for his discovery.

5340. Artificial transmutation of an element was achieved in April 1932 at the Cavendish Laboratory of Cambridge University, Cambridge, England, when John Douglas Cockcroft and Ernest Thomas Sinton Walton used a particle accelerator of their own invention (now known as a Cockcroft-Walton generator) to train a beam of protons on lithium atoms,

SCIENCE—PHYSICS—*continued*

smashing each lithium atom into two helium atoms. Cockcroft and Walton shared the 1951 Nobel Prize in Physics for "the transmutation of atomic nuclei by artificially accelerated atomic particles."

5341. Antimatter particles to be artificially created were positrons (positively charged particles with the same mass as electrons). They were created in 1933 at the California Institute of Technology, Pasadena, CA, USA, by Carl David Anderson, using a process of gamma irradiation. He had discovered the existence of antimatter the year before. Anderson, who received a Nobel Prize in Physics in 1936, was also the co-discoverer in 1936 of the meson, a particle intermediate in mass between the proton and electron.

5342. Artificial radioisotope was produced in France in 1934 by physicists Jean-Frédéric and Irène Joliot-Curie. They bombarded the stable isotope aluminum-27 with alpha particles and converted it into a new radioactive isotope, phosphorus-30.

5343. Cyclotron spiral atom smasher was developed by Ernest Orlando Lawrence at the University of California, Berkeley, CA, USA, in 1934 to study the nuclear structure of the atom. A magnetic whirling machine using a 73-metric-ton magnet produced 10-million- to 15-million-volt rays and sent a stream of high-energy bullets from the nuclei of helium gas atoms or alpha particles in the form of a beam of light a foot from the machine.

5344. Nuclear chain reaction patent was based on work by the Hungarian expatriate physicist Leo Szilard. In October 1933, Szilard was crossing a London street when it came to him that "a chain reaction might be set up if an element could be found that would emit two neutrons when it swallowed one neutron." The idea became a classified British patent in 1935, seven years before a chain reaction was actually demonstrated by Enrico Fermi at the University of Chicago, Chicago, IL, USA, on December 2, 1942.

5345. Prediction of the existence of mesons was made in 1935 by the Japanese physicist Yukawa Hideki, a lecturer at Osaka Imperial University in Osaka, Japan, who postulated a particle that mediated the strong interaction between nucleons (the particles of the atomic nucleus). This particle, the pi meson or pion, was

discovered in 1947. Several other types of mesons of varying mass have been found; the first was observed in cosmic ray interactions in 1937 by American scientists. Yukawa was awarded the Nobel Prize in Physics in 1949.

5346. Self-sustaining nuclear chain reaction demonstration was made on December 2, 1942, by the Italian-American physicist Enrico Fermi and his staff at the Metallurgical Laboratory of the University of Chicago, Chicago, IL, USA, before approximately 40 persons. Neutrons, spontaneously released by atoms of metallic uranium or uranium oxide that were embedded in a suitable pattern throughout a block of graphite, were permitted to collide with neighboring atoms of uranium or uranium oxide, causing these neighboring atoms to split. The split atoms released additional neutrons, which caused further reactions with still other uranium atoms, and so on at a rapidly increasing rate.

5347. Synchrotron was constructed by the General Electric Research Laboratory, Schenectady, NY, USA, by Dr. Herbert Chermside Pollock and Willem Fredrik Westendorp, and installed at the Radiation Laboratory, University of California, Berkeley, CA, USA, where it released its full energy on January 17, 1949. It was invented by Edwin Mattison McMillan of the university. It weighed about 7 metric tons and had a betatron-type magnet and accelerated electrons that had negative charges.

5348. Discovery of nonsymmetric particle interaction was made in 1957 at Columbia University, New York City, NY, USA, by the Chinese-born American physicist Chien-shiung Wu. Observing the decay of the radioactive isotope cobalt-60, Wu discovered a preferred spatial direction for the emission of electrons. She therefore proved that for some weak nuclear interactions, spatial parity (and perhaps temporal parity) is not preserved. Previously, all particle interactions were thought to be completely symmetrical.

5349. Observation of neutrinos was made by American physicists Frederick Reines and Clyde L. Cowan, Jr., in 1956. A neutrino is a subatomic particle of the lepton class, with little or no mass and a neutral charge. Reines and Cowan, then with the Los Alamos National Laboratory, constructed a neutrino detector at the Savannah River laboratories in South Carolina, USA. A nuclear reactor emitted neutrinos into a 105-gallon (400-liter) tank of water and cadmium chloride. Scintillation detectors were able to record the collisions of secondary particles produced when a neutrino collided with a proton. The neutrino's discovery had been predicted by Wolfgang Pauli in 1930. Reines and Cowan shared the 1995 Nobel Prize in Physics.

5350. International conference of atomic scientists was the Pugwash Conference on Science and World Affairs, held in July 1957 at the estate of the American philanthropist Cyrus Eaton in the village of Pugwash, Nova Scotia, Canada. At the urging of Bertrand Russell, Albert Einstein, and other prominent scientists, the physicists gathered to consider ways to reduce the global danger from nuclear weapons. Later Pugwash Conferences were held in the Soviet Union, Great Britain, Yugoslavia, India, Czechoslovakia, Romania, Sweden, and the United States, among other countries.

5351. Discovery of quarks was made by American astronomers Jerome Friedman and Henry Kendall of the Massachusetts Institute of Technology, Cambridge, MA, USA, and Richard Taylor of the Stanford Linear Accelerator Center, Stanford, CA, USA, during experiments performed at the SLAC between 1967 and 1973. They found unexpectedly large numbers of electrons being scattered at large angles—clear evidence for hard subparticles, called quarks, within protons. The existence of quarks, the building blocks of subatomic particles, was first proposed in the early 1960s by Murray Gell-Mann of the California Institute of Technology, Pasadena, CA, USA, who took the name from James Joyce's linguistically playful novel *Finnegans Wake*. Friedman, Kendall, and Taylor received the 1990 Nobel Prize in Physics for their work.

5352. Superconducting materials of ceramic oxide were discovered by Swiss physicist Karl Alex Müller and German physicist Johannes Georg Bednorz, both of the International Business Machines (IBM) Zürich Research Laboratory in Zürich, Switzerland. In 1986, they induced superconductivity in a barium-lanthanum-copper oxide at a temperature of 35 Kelvins (−396 degrees F, −242 degrees C), well above absolute zero (−459.67 degrees F, −273.15 degrees C). Within a few months, they produced ceramic oxides capable of superconductivity at 100 Kelvins (−280 degrees F, −173 degrees C). The two researchers were awarded the 1987 Nobel Prize in Physics for their discovery.

5353. Superconducting material that operated at temperatures above the boiling point of nitrogen was developed in February 1987 by research teams under Paul Chu of the University of Houston, Houston, TX, USA, and Maw-Kuen Wu at the University of Alabama, Huntsville, AL, USA. Previously, the operation of superconductors required frigid temperatures near absolute zero that were hard to reach and maintain. Searching for superconductors that could perform at higher temperatures, the researchers mixed yttrium, barium, copper, and oxygen to form a compound that lost its electrical resistance at 90 degrees Kelvin (−297 degrees F), an unprecedentedly high temperature and well above the key boiling point of nitrogen (−384 degrees F, −195.8 degrees C). The discovery was officially reported in the March 2, 1988, issue of *Physical Review Letters*.

5354. Physical manipulation of individual atoms was achieved by Donald M. Eigler and Erhard K. Schweizer of the IBM Almaden Research Center, San Jose, CA, USA. In January 1990, it was announced that the two had used a scanning tunneling microscope to position 35 individual atoms of xenon on a nickel surface to spell the initials "IBM." An electron micrograph of the initials clearly showed "bumps" indicating the presence of individual atoms.

5355. Feynman Prize in Nanotechnology was awarded on October 14, 1993, at the Third Foresight Conference on Molecular Nanotechnology to Charles Musgrave, a Ph.D. candidate in chemistry at the California Institute of Technology in Pasadena, CA, USA. Musgrave had created a nanotechnology tool for "the abstraction of hydrogen from diamond surfaces by a radical species attached to a mechanical positioning device for synthesis of atomically precise diamond-like structures." The US$10,000 Feynman Prize in Nanotechnology is awarded to the "researcher whose recent work has most advanced the development of molecular nanotechnology." It is named after the Nobel Prize-winning American physicist Richard P. Feynman, who was the first to seriously propose research in nanotechnology, in 1959.

5356. Teleportation experiment in which a range of physical properties was instantaneously transferred from one physical entity to another was demonstrated successfully by researchers on October 23, 1998, at the California Institute of Technology in Pasadena, CA, USA. A team led by physics professor Jeff Kimble replicated the quantum properties of a beam of light in another light beam across a laboratory bench,

SCIENCE—PHYSICS—*continued*

taking advantage of the quantum property known as entanglement, in which photons or other particles somehow share characteristics and fates even though they may exist at opposite ends of the universe. Earlier experiments in Austria and Italy performed a similar feat with single photons.

SCIENCE—SOCIAL SCIENCES

5357. Sociologist may have been Abu Zayd Abd ar-Rahman ibn Khaldun (known as Ibn Khaldun), the foremost Islamic historian and philosopher of history. In his masterwork, the *Muqaddimah (Introduction to History),* written in the castle of Qal'at ibn Salamah, near the present-day town of Frenda, Algeria, and completed circa 1379, he developed what he called *ilm al-umran,* or "the science of culture," a clear forerunner of modern sociology. Ibn Khaldun defined *ilm al-umran* as concerning "the social transformations that succeed each other in the nature of society."

5358. Treatise to describe an entire economy was the *Tableau économique,* written in 1758 by the French physician and economist François Quesnay, leader of the physiocrats, the first known school of political economy. The *Tableau* displayed in diagrammatic fashion the relationships between classes in French society and the flow of capital among them. Quesnay's analysis, which strongly emphasized the benefits of laissez-faire government and free market competition, anticipated that of 20th-century British economist John Maynard Keynes.

5359. Treatise on economics was *An Inquiry into the Nature and Causes of the Wealth of Nations,* published in London, England, in 1776. The author was the Scottish philosopher Adam Smith, already famous for his earlier work *The Theory of Moral Sentiments. The Wealth of Nations* was a comprehensive analysis of the ways in which societies and their political institutions respond to changes in material conditions. It included an important discussion of competition as the mechanism that promotes and regulates economic activities—the first detailed description of laissez-faire capitalism. The modern science of economics is considered to have begun with its publication.

5360. Graphs displaying economic data were 44 illustrations that appeared in *The Commercial and Political Atlas,* published in London in 1786 by the English political economist William Playfair. One of the illustrations was a bar graph, the first ever published, which displayed comparative data on Scotland's trade with 17 countries in 1781. The remaining 43 graphics were time-series plots, the first application of this form in economics. (One chart, for example, compared the value of imports versus exports in England over a period of years.) About his new method of depicting financial information, Playfair wrote: "The amount of mercantile transactions in money, and of profit or loss, are capable of being as easily represented in drawing, as any part of space, or as the face of a country; though, till now, it has not been attempted."

5361. Theory of culture was proposed by the German anthropologist Gustav Friedrich Klemm, director of the royal library at Dresden, Saxony. In his ten-volume work *Allgemeine Kulturgeschichte der Menschheit (General Cultural History of Mankind),* published between 1843 and 1852, and his *Allgemeine Kulturwissenschaft (General Science of Culture),* published in 1854–55, Klemm explicated a process by which peoples evolve from a savage state to a condition of freedom.

5362. Treatise positing the existence of prehistoric matriarchies was *Das Mutterrecht (The Mother Right),* published in 1861. The author was the Swiss scholar Johann Jakob Bachofen, an anthropologist and jurist who perceived remnants of a matrilinear social order in Roman law.

5363. Kinship study was *Systems of Consanguinity and Affinity of the Human Family* (1871), a comparative study of kinship organization in a wide variety of cultures. The author was Lewis Henry Morgan, a lawyer and state legislator from Rochester, NY, USA. The book was prompted by Morgan's pioneering ethnographic research among the Seneca tribe of Native Americans, published in 1851 as *The League of the Ho-déno-sau-nee, or Iroquois.*

SEX AND GENDER

5364. Symbols of the feminine are rock engravings from the Aurignacian period, circa 30,000 BCE, that show abstract representations of the human vulva. They have been found in three caves—Abri Blanchard, Abri Castanet, and La Ferrassie—near Les Eyzies in the Dordogne region of southern France. Some archeologists believe that they are intended to express the creative power of a fertility goddess.

5365. Feminist author in medieval Europe was Christine de Pisan (or Pizan), who as a young widow in Paris became the first woman to earn her livelihood as a professional writer. In 1399, with her long poem *Épistre du dieu d'amours (Letter from the God of Loves),* she became the first woman to participate in the *querelle des dames,* the literary debate over the question of whether women are inferior to men. She elaborated on this theme in *Le Livre de la cité des dames (The Book of the City of Ladies),* published in 1405, in which three ladies, Reason, Rectitude, and Justice, offer rebuttals to the idea of women's inferiority by bringing examples from history of women who acted virtuously, nobly, or heroically.

5366. Statute establishing that men and women are equal under the law was the Statute of Lithuania, promulgated in 1529. The first law in Europe that defined the rights of women as human beings and not simply as bearers of children, it established the value of a woman's life and limb at twice that of a man of the same rank. The statute guaranteed individual legal responsibility and equality before the law for men and women. The Second Statute of Lithuania (1566) doubled the terms of imprisonment for offenses against the wife, widow, or daughter of a nobleman. A Third Statute, promulgated in 1588, acknowledged the right of Lithuanian women to choose their partners freely.

5367. Religious group advocating complete equality between men and women was the Shakers, founded circa 1770 by the English mystic and visionary Ann Lee (called Mother Ann Lee by her followers). Lee believed herself to be the embodied female aspect of God, as well as the second incarnation of Christ. With a handful of followers, she established in 1776 a "Shaking Quaker" community in America at Niskeyuna (now Watervliet, NY, USA). Among the cardinal principles of the Shakers were absolute celibacy, equal status for the sexes in worship, work, and property ownership, and equal opportunity for men and women to lead the community.

5368. Influential feminist tract was *A Vindication of the Rights of Women,* written in 1792 by the English writer Mary Wollstonecraft. Wollstonecraft was strongly influenced by the libertarian ideals of the French Revolution. In her closely reasoned book, she argued that women deserved the same personal and political rights as men, including freedom from oppression and the right to a full education.

5369. Woman to become a public speaker in Japan was Toshiko Kishida, who went on a nationwide lecture tour in 1882 on behalf of the Liberal Party, calling for a program of social reforms that included expanded rights for women. Political activities by women were made illegal five years later. Before her brief career as a speaker, Toshiko Kishida was the first commoner to be appointed lady-in-waiting to an empress of Japan.

5370. Sex-change operation using modern medical methods was performed in 1930 by Werner Kreuz, a professor at the Women's Hospital in Dresden, Germany. The patient was Einar Wegener of Denmark, who had been cross-dressing for years and had taken on the identity of a woman under the name Lili Elbe. In a series of operations, Wegener had his vocal chords altered, received a transplant of ovaries from a 26-year-old woman (possibly the first case of hormone therapy), and had his male sex organs removed. An attempt to transplant a uterus in 1931 was unsuccessful and Wegener died soon after, probably from tissue rejection shock.

5371. Center for the study of human sexuality was the Institut für Sexual Wissenschaft, founded by the pioneering homosexual rights advocate Magnus Hirschfeld in Berlin, Germany, circa 1935. It was burned by the Nazis in 1939.

5372. Sex-change operation that was successful was performed by Christian Hamburger at Gentofte Hospital, Copenhagen, Denmark, on September 24, 1951, after a course of hormone treatments. The patient was George Jorgensen of New York, NY, USA, 25 years old, who later adopted the name Christine Jorgensen. Two additional operations were needed to complete the change.

5373. Scientific study of the physiology of human sexuality was *Human Sexual Response* (1966) by the American sex researchers William Howell Masters and Virginia Eshelman Johnson. It contained the first extensive research conducted under laboratory conditions into the sexual reactions of the human body.

5374. Surrogate partner therapy was invented by the American sex researchers William Howell Masters and Virginia Eshelman Johnson, of St. Louis, MO, USA. As a part of their therapeutic practice aimed at relieving sexual dysfunction, they employed trained women to substitute for the sexual partner of male clients.

SEX AND GENDER—*continued*

The term "surrogate partner" was first used in their study *Human Sexual Inadequacy* (1970). Some much earlier precursors of the technique have been suggested, such as the practice of temple prostitution in many pagan religions.

5375. World Conference on Women was held in 1975 in Mexico City, Mexico. Attendees at the conference, which examined the condition of and prospects for women throughout the world, proclaimed 1976–1985 as the "United Nations Decade for Women." The Second World Conference on Women was held in 1980 in Copenhagen, Denmark. It called for women's participation in politics and decision making, and for the elimination of discrimination in law and policy. The Third World Conference on Women was held in 1985 in Nairobi, Kenya, and the Fourth World Conference on Women was held in 1995 in Huairou, China.

5376. International agreement barring discrimination against women was the Convention on the Elimination of All Forms of Discrimination Against Women, adopted by the United Nations General Assembly on December 18, 1979. As of 1999, 161 nations had ratified the convention.

5377. Sexual harassment case at the United Nations was brought by Catherine Claxton, an American woman employed at the United Nations headquarters in New York, NY, USA, against Luís María Gómez, a high-ranking Argentine official. On March 6, 1994, an international judge appointed by UN secretary-general Boutros Boutros-Ghali found in favor of Claxton.

5378. Women's shelter in Central Africa was founded in Harare, Zimbabwe, in 1996 by the Musasa Project, an African women's organization fighting gender violence. The shelter provided a safe place for women fleeing partner violence as well as offering trained counselors and legal advice.

SEX AND GENDER—HOMOSEXUALITY

5379. Lesbian known by name is traditionally considered to be Sappho, the Greek lyric poet and educator who lived circa 610–580 BCE on the Aegean island of Lesbos. In her poetry, she often expresses passionate feelings toward women.

5380. Homosexual rights organization was the Wissenschaftlich-humanitäres Komitee (Scientific-Humanitarian Committee), founded in 1897 by Magnus Hirschfeld in Berlin, Germany. The committee lobbied for reform of anti-homosexual laws, published homosexual rights literature, and opened local chapters in Germany, the Netherlands, and Austria.

5381. Movie with a homosexual theme was *Anders als die Anderen,* directed in Berlin, Germany, in 1919 by Richard Oswald during a brief period after World War I when films were not being censored by the German government. It starred Conrad Veidt and Reinhold Schunzel.

5382. International congress on homosexual rights was held by the World League of Sexual Reform in Berlin, Germany, in 1921. The league was founded by Magnus Hirschfeld, considered the founder of the modern homosexual rights movement.

5383. Homosexual civil rights law was passed on December 16, 1977, by the Canadian province of Quebec. The province's Charter of Human Rights, which bars discrimination against a variety of groups, was amended to include homosexuals.

5384. Country to legalize homosexual marriage was Denmark, which did so in May 1989. Eleven gay marriages, the first legal homosexual marriages in the world, were performed on October 1, 1989, in Copenhagen. The first couple to be wed was Ivan Larsen, a priest, and Ove Carlsen, a child psychologist.

5385. National constitution to specifically protect the rights of homosexuals was the revised South African constitution, passed by the Constitutional Assembly in 1996.

SEX AND GENDER—PROSTITUTION

5386. Brothel of record was opened in 594 BCE in Athens, Greece, by the archon and reformer Solon. The customers were free male citizens; the prostitutes were slaves. Cult prostitution associated with pagan temples had been practiced for centuries. This was the first house of prostitution with no religious purpose.

5387. Prostitute known by name appears to have been Rhodopis, who was born circa the sixth century BCE in Thracia (an area now divided among the modern nations of Bulgaria, Turkey, and Greece). A slave, she was ordered to work as a prostitute in Egypt. After her freedom was bought by Charaxus of Mytilene, the brother of the famous poet Sappho, Rhodopis continued to work as a prostitute and eventually became rich.

5388. Home for repentant prostitutes where they could receive training in a different trade was the Filles-Dieu, founded circa 1200 by William of Auvergne, the bishop of Paris.

5389. Public brothel sponsored by a university was the Abbaye, established in Toulouse, France, circa 1400. The brothel was a profit-making venture to produce income for the University of Toulouse and the municipal government. The prostitutes wore white scarves as an identifying mark when they went out in public. After a dispute with the townspeople, they were put under the personal protection of King Charles VI, who ordered his symbol, the royal *fleur-de-lis,* placed over the brothel door.

5390. Striptease of record took place on February 9, 1893, when an artist's model disrobed for a group of students at the Bal des Quatre Arts, an art school in Paris, France. She was arrested and fined 100 francs, causing a student riot in the Latin Quarter.

5391. Striptease before a paying audience in a public theater of record took place on March 13, 1894, at the Divan Fayouau in Paris, France. A young woman acted out various events that required undressing, such as having a bath, being examined by a doctor, and finding a flea in her undergarments.

SHIPS AND BOATS

5392. Depictions of ships were made in Egypt in the fourth millennium BCE. One, drawn on the wall of a tomb in the city of Memphis, shows a papyrus ship being steered down a river. The other, painted on a vase, shows a masted sailboat with what appears to be a roofed shelter for passengers.

5393. Reference to a ship with a name appears in an inscription of 2613 BCE that recounts the shipbuilding achievements of the fourth-dynasty Egyptian pharaoh Sneferu. He was recorded as the builder of a cedarwood vessel called *Praise of the Two Lands.*

5394. Anchor was a large stone, basket of stones, or a bag of gravel tied to a rope. Such primitive anchors were in use by sailors in Asia and Europe circa 2500 BCE.

5395. Ship of record is the Cheops Ship, built for the Egyptian pharaoh Khufu (Cheops) circa 2500 BCE. It was discovered in 1954 by a team of Egyptologists led by Kamal el-Mallakh, an Egyptian architect and archeologist employed by the Egyptian Antiquities Service. Excavating two long pits south of the Great Pyramid at Giza, Egypt, el-Mallakh smelled the odor of cedar wood. Uncovering the first pit, he found an ancient but complete and perfectly preserved galley, the first known, built almost entirely of cedar. The ship had been disassembled into approximately 1,200 pieces. These were reassembled over a 13-year period by Haj Ahmed Youssef Moustafa, the Antiquities Service's director of restoration. The largest, as well as the oldest and best-preserved vessel known from antiquity, the Cheops Ship measured 143 feet (43.6 meters) long, 18.7 feet (5.7 meters) wide, and 4.9 feet (1.5 meters) deep, and may have been Khufu's funerary barge. In 1982, the ship was mounted in its own museum next to the pyramid.

5396. Underwater shipwreck known to archeologists is the Dokos wreck, located in waters 60 to 85 feet (18 to 26 meters) deep in the Aegean Sea off the island of Dokos, Greece. Although the ship has disappeared, the site is known from 500 clay vases and hundreds of other ceramic items found on the sea floor. These are believed to have been the cargo of a merchant vessel that plied a well-established sea route between Africa and the Gulf of Argos circa 2200 BCE. The site was discovered by Peter Throckmorton in 1975.

5397. Sunken treasure ship of record is the Ulu Burun wreck, found in 1983 off Ulu Burun, Turkey, by a Turkish sponge diver who noticed what looked like "metal biscuits with ears" on the sea floor. The wreck, in dangerous waters 140 to 200 feet (43 to 61 meters) deep, was excavated by Don Frey and a team of marine archeologists from the Bodrum Museum, Turkey, and the Institute of Nautical Archeology at Texas A&M University. The cargo included 350 copper ingots with round handles, each weighing about 60 pounds (27 kilograms); 170 ingots of cobalt-blue glass from Syria; lengths of hippopotamus and elephant ivory; and many items of gold jewelry, including a scarab pendant depicting Queen Nefertiti of Egypt. The wreck has been dated to circa 1350 BCE.

5398. Work boats known are the Ferriby boats. The first was discovered in 1937 by E.V. and C.W. Wright in the Humber estuary near North Ferriby, England. Two more were found, one in 1941 and a second in 1963. Dated by radiocarbon testing to circa 1300 BCE, the boats were made of adze-hewn oak planks caulked with moss and were probably used as fishing or ferry boats. The North Ferriby site contained other boat pieces and parts of a winch, indicating that it may have been used as a boatyard, the first known.

SHIPS AND BOATS—*continued*

5399. Bireme galley with two tiers of sweeps on each side was introduced to the eastern Mediterranean by the Phoenicians circa 700 BCE. The tiers of oars were staggered so that the oars of the upper tier did not interfere with the oars of the lower tier. It was used primarily as a trading vessel.

5400. Collapsible boats were river boats used by traders in ancient Sumeria, in southern Mesopotamia (now Iraq). These were boats of hides stretched over wooden frames that were used for travel downstream, then knocked down and packed upstream by donkey. Hide boats carrying stone down the Tigris River are depicted on a wall relief found at Nineveh dating to circa 700 BCE.

5401. Metal anchor was probably the single-palm grapnel of cast bronze, used by the Greeks and other seafaring peoples of the Mediterranean circa 600 BCE.

5402. Trireme galley with three tiers of sweeps on each side was based on the Phoenician bireme and was introduced by the Greeks circa 500 BCE. An outrigger was added that enabled the rowers of the third tier of oars to sit above and outside the other two tiers of rowers.

5403. Clinker-built boats using lapstrake, or overlapping hull planks, appeared in Europe before 400 BCE. The Hjörtspring boat (dated to circa 350 BCE, a wooden warship that was part of a votive deposit found in a small bog in southeast Denmark, is the earliest-known example of a clinker-built vessel. Previously, boats were constructed using edge-to-edge planking.

5404. Rudder hinged vertically and attached to the sternpost of a ship was introduced in northern European vessels in the late twelfth century. The first depictions of ships with rudders were made on the island of Gotland, near Sweden, and in the cathedral at Winchester, England, circa 1180.

5405. Drydock for cleaning and repairing ships below the waterline was built at Portsmouth, England, in 1540 by order of King Henry VIII.

5406. Ship evaluation association was Lloyd's Register of Shipping, founded in 1760 to serve marine insurance underwriters associated with the English insurance company Lloyd's of London by investigating and describing the available ships. In 1764 it began publishing the *Register Book,* an annual list of large merchant ships. The organization sets standards for construction and maintenance of merchant ships and collects data on their use.

5407. Iceboat known from the written record is a Dutch drawing of 1768, depicting a sloop fixed with runners.

5408. Personal flotation device of record was a canvas waistcoat filled with cork, invented by the Abbé de Lachapelle in France circa 1769.

5409. Steamboat to move successfully under its own power was the *Pyroscaphe,* built by Claude-François-Dorothée, Marquis de Jouffroy d'Abbans, and tested in 1783 on the Saône River near Lyon, France. It was 138 feet (46 meters) long and was equipped with twin paddle wheels driven by a large and heavy steam engine, which allowed it to make headway upstream for 15 minutes, until the engine's vibrations broke it apart. An earlier model by Jouffroy had paddles shaped like ducks' feet, which proved to be inefficient. The French Revolution prevented Jouffroy from patenting his idea, and it was eclipsed by the work of the American steamboat inventors Robert Fulton and John Fitch. Fitch's steamboat, which had wooden paddles arranged six on a side like oars, became the first steamboat to carry a human being when it traveled along the Delaware River at a speed of 3 miles per hour on August 27, 1787.

5410. Unsinkable boat was patented in 1785 by Lionel Lukin, a coachbuilder in London, England. His model had cork linings and watertight air flotation compartments.

5411. Lifeboat designed and built for lifesaving purposes was Henry Greathead's *Original,* a double-ended boat, 30 feet (91.4 meters) long and propelled by ten oarsmen. In 1789 Greathead's boat won a competition offered by the city of Newcastle, England, for a highly buoyant rescue craft that could right itself when capsized.

5412. Seagoing iron-hulled vessel was the steamship *Aaron Manby,* built for service on the Seine River in France by the English industrialist Aaron Manby, his son Charles Manby, and sea captain Charles Napier. The flat-bottomed craft, 120 feet (36.6 meters) long and 17.2 feet (5.2 meters) wide, was made of iron plate attached to iron ribs, and was powered by dual paddlewheels. On June 10, 1822, the *Aaron Manby* succeeded in crossing the English Channel from England to Le Havre, France. It saw service as a riverboat until 1855.

5413. International Code signals for communicating between ships at sea by flags were published in England in 1857.

5414. Ship outfitted with interior electric lights was the Inman Steamship Company's *City of Berlin,* built in 1875 by Caird & Company, Greenock, Scotland. In December 1879, the passenger ship was outfitted with four electric lights in the main saloon and two in steerage, yielding "a brilliancy hitherto unknown in the steerage part of any vessel," according to the *Liverpool Journal of Commerce.*

5415. Motorboat was invented by the Belgian-born French engineer Jean-Joseph-Étienne Lenoir, one of the inventors of the internal-combustion engine. He built a boat using his liquid-fueled, two-cycle engine in 1886.

5416. Steam turbine-powered ship was the yacht *Turbinia,* built in 1894 at the C.A. Parsons Works at Newcastle upon Tyne, England. It was powered by a multistage steam turbine invented by Charles Algernon Parsons; the power plant had no reciprocating parts. The *Turbinia* measured 103 feet (31 meters) long and in 1897 attained a top speed of 34.5 knots.

5417. Hydrofoil boat was designed and built in 1905 by Italian helicopter and airship pioneer Enrico Forlanini. The experimental vessel was designed to rise up out of the water on ladderlike winged surfaces called hydrofoils, reducing drag as it was propelled along the surface at high speed by powerful engines. It achieved a top speed of 38 knots. Forlanini licensed his invention to an American, Alexander Graham Bell. With a Canadian, Frederick W. "Casey" Baldwin, Bell tested his first successful hydrofoil design, the *HD-4,* in August 1918 on Lake Baddeck, Nova Scotia, Canada. On September 9, 1919, the *HD-4* set a world-record speed of 70.86 miles (114 kilometers) per hour.

5418. Radio distress call from a ship at sea was transmitted from the British liner *Republic,* built for the Dominion Line in 1903. On January 23, 1909, en route to provide relief to victims of an earthquake in Italy, the *Republic* collided in the mid-Atlantic with the Italian liner *Florida,* which was carrying 838 earthquake survivors. Three passengers on the *Republic* and three crew members on the *Florida* were killed, and the *Republic* was severely damaged. At the order of Captain William Inman Sealby, the *Republic*'s radioman, John R. Binns, broadcast the CQD distress call. Seven ships responded to the call.

5419. Hovercraft was the *SR.N1,* developed in England and first tested May 30, 1959. It was based on ground-effect research by English engineer Christopher Cockerell, who developed a system in which air jetted at a downward angle from a slot around the circumference of a hull created a high-pressure cushion underneath, lifting the craft a few inches above the ground. The *SR.N1* carried three passengers over level ground or still waters; forward propulsion was supplied by directable fans.

5420. Nuclear-powered surface ship was the Soviet icebreaker *Lenin,* built at the Baltic Shipbuilding and Engineering Works, Leningrad, USSR (now St. Petersburg, Russia) and commissioned in 1959. The heavily built ship was 439.7 feet (134 meters) long, 90.7 feet (27.6 meters) wide, and displaced 13,366 gross tons. Its nuclear-powered steam turbines fed 30,200 horsepower to three screws and were capable of pushing the *Lenin* through ice roughly 5 feet (1.4 meters) thick at a speed of 2 knots.

5421. Hovercraft passenger service offered on a regular basis began operating on July 20, 1962. The hovercraft, a Vickers-Armstrong VA-3 with room for 24, took travelers along the Dee Estuary in Wales and England. The service was operated by British United Airways.

5422. Ship with sailing wings was the *Skin-Aitoku-Maru,* launched in 1980 by Nippon Kokan of Japan. This diesel-powered cargo vessel featured large upright folding metal wings. When the wind was right, these provided thrust that reduced fuel costs by up to 50 percent.

5423. Commercial vessel powered by magnetohydrodynamics was the *Yamata I,* designed by physicist Yoshiro Saji and launched on January 27, 1992. The craft was powered by superconducting magnets arranged on the hull that created a powerful magnetic field in seawater, propelling the vessel forward. Development assistance was provided by the Japanese Foundation for Shipbuilding Advancement in Tsukuba, Japan.

5424. Canoe museum was founded by John Jennings in Peterborough, Ontario, Canada, and opened in 1998. The collection of 600 canoes was arranged to document the history of Northwest water travel.

SHIPS AND BOATS—COMMERCIAL

5425. Transatlantic steamboat service was started by the *Great Western* and the *Sirius,* both of which arrived in New York, NY, USA on April 23, 1838. The *Sirius* made the trip from London in 19 days and the *Great Western* from Bristol in 15 days. They were built by Isambard Kingdom Brunel, the celebrated English engineer.

SHIPS AND BOATS—COMMERCIAL—
continued

5426. Tramp steamer was the collier S.S. *John Bowes,* launched on July 30, 1852, at Jarrow, England.

5427. Oil tanker was the *Charles* out of Antwerp, Belgium, which plied between Europe and the United States from 1869 to 1872. It contained 59 iron tanks, arranged in rows at the bottom of its hold in the 'tween decks. Its bulk capacity was 7,000 barrels (717 metric tons).

5428. Refrigerator ship was a French freighter, the *Frigorifique,* which was outfitted in 1877 with a cooling unit designed by Charles Teller.

5429. Round-the-world steamboat passenger service was inaugurated by the S.S. *President Harrison* of the Dollar Steamship Line, which sailed from San Francisco, CA, USA, in February 1924. Previous trips were made irregularly by cruise steamers.

SHIPS AND BOATS—NAVIGATION

5430. Navigation at night using the stars as reference points was developed by the Phoenicians, skilled mariners who dominated the Mediterranean by 1000 BCE.

5431. Compass was invented before 1100, probably independently by mariners in China and Europe. Records indicate that the Chinese mariners were using a magnetic compass circa 1100, western Europeans by 1187, and Arabs by 1220. The earliest compasses incorporated a sliver of lodestone (magnetite) floating on a stick in water. The natural magnetic field of the lodestone would align itself with magnetic north. Later it was found that a magnetized steel needle would perform the same function.

5432. Cross staff for finding the latitude at sea was invented in France by the Jewish navigator Jacob ben Makir circa 1300. The device consisted of a staff about 3 feet (1 meter) in length, marked with a scale of degrees. The mariner held up the staff to his eye and moved a shorter sliding crosspiece so that its top was level with the pole star and its bottom was aligned with the horizon. The latitude could be read on the degree scale at the intersection of the staff and the crosspiece.

5433. Astronomical observatory for navigation was the Royal Greenwich Observatory in Greenwich, England (a suburb of southeast London), founded in 1675 by King Charles II. It was expressly established to provide sailors with precise astronomical data for navigation, timekeeping, and the location of celestial bodies.

5434. Almanac of navigation published by a national government was the *Connaissance des temps (Information About the Times),* founded in Paris, France, in 1679. It contained navigation tables for finding longitude by observing the eclipses of Jupiter's satellites.

5435. Lightship used as a beacon for ships was put in place in England, in the Thames estuary near the mouth of the Medway River, in 1732. It was a converted Dutch merchant ship, the *Nore.* The first lightships built for the purpose were made in 1820.

5436. Tables of the moon's motions for navigation were compiled by the astronomer Johann Tobias Mayer, director of the observatory at the Georg-August Academy in Göttingen (now in Germany), and first published in 1755. His tables of predictive lunar motions were so accurate that navigators could use them to determine longitude at sea, and formed the basis for the lunar tables in the first edition of the British Navy's *Nautical Almanac,* published in 1767.

5437. Sextant was developed in England in 1757 by John Campbell as an improvement on the earlier octant. The sextant measures the angle between the horizon and the altitude of the sun, moon, a star, or another celestial body for which the precise celestial location is already known from a published table. It became the standard instrument in marine navigation for determining the latitude of the user. In conjunction with a chronometer, it can be used to find the longitude as well.

5438. Gyrocompass that was practical was invented by German engineer Hermann Anschütz-Kaempfe in 1907–08. The English scientist William Thomson, Lord Kelvin, made an earlier but unsuccessful attempt to design a working gyrocompass in 1883. A properly aligned gyrocompass always points to true, rather than magnetic, north.

5439. Remote detection system using sound was an early form of sonar (SOund NAvigation and Ranging) demonstrated in 1915 in France by Paul Langevin. He developed his system, which found the range of distant underwater objects by bouncing sound waves off of them, to detect icebergs.

SHIPS AND BOATS—NAVIGATION—
   LIGHTHOUSES

5440. Lighthouse of importance was the Pharos of Alexandria, Egypt, one of the Seven Wonders of the World. It was built circa 280 BCE, during the reign of Ptolemy II Philadelphus, by the engineer Sostratus of Cnidus. Located on the island of Pharos in Alexandria's harbor, the lighthouse was a marble tower about 350 feet (107 meters) high, with a spiral ramp leading to the top, where a fire fueled by wood and vegetable oil was kept burning at night. The fire could be seen from a distance of 30 miles across the Mediterranean. Late in the 14th century, the tower collapsed into the sea during an earthquake. Its submerged ruins were identified and explored by archeologists in 1995. Another manmade lighthouse may have preceded it at Sigeum (modern Yenisehir, Turkey), in 660 BCE.

5441. Lighthouse surrounded by water was the huge lighthouse built from 1584 to 1611 by the French architect and engineer Louis de Foix. It was anchored on the small island of Cordouan in the Gironde estuary near Bordeaux. The magnificently appointed stone structure was 135 feet (41 meters) in diameter at the base and 100 feet (30 meters) high and took 27 years to complete. By that time, the weight of the tower had pushed the island below sea level, leaving the lighthouse totally surrounded by water.

5442. Lighthouse in the open sea was the Eddystone Light, a wooden tower 120 feet high that was constructed in 1696–99 on the Eddystone Rocks, located in the English Channel about 14 miles from Plymouth, England. It was fastened to the rock by twelve iron stanchions. In 1703 the tower was destroyed in a storm, together with its builder, Henry Winstanley

5443. Lighthouse with a revolving light was built at Carlsten, Sweden, in 1781. The light was operated by a clockwork mechanism.

5444. Laser lighthouse went into operation at Point Danger, New South Wales, Australia, in 1970. A laser was used for its ability to provide a highly directional and very bright beam.

SHIPS AND BOATS—SUBMARINES

5445. Diving bell was known from antiquity. The first report, possibly apocryphal, of a diver submerging in a bell-shaped enclosure that contained a supply of air was that of Alexander the Great's descent in a diving bell built by Colimpha circa 330 BCE. A more detailed account dating from the same period was contained in *Problemata (Problems)* (attributed to the Greek philosopher Aristotle but probably by one of his followers), in which an early diving bell is described: "They contrive a means of respiration for divers, by means of a container sent down to them; naturally the container is not filled with water, but air, which constantly assists the submerged man."

5446. Diving apparatus for practical underwater work was invented in 1535 by the Italian engineer Guglielmo de Lorena. His device, consisting of an air chamber that fitted onto the shoulders and was supported by slings from a boat or structure on the surface, allowed a diver to work underwater for an hour in a lake near Rome, Italy.

5447. Submarine was demonstrated by the Dutch inventor Cornelis Jacobszoon Drebbel (or van Drebbel) to King James I of England. The vessel's hull was a wooden frame skinned with greased leather. Oars that protruded through the hull were sealed with tight leather flaps. Breathing air was pumped in through tubes. In a series of trials on the Thames River between 1620 and 1624, Drebbel successfully navigated underwater from Westminster to Greenwich at a depth of up to 16 feet (5 meters). James I may have been a passenger on one trip, which would make him the first head of state to travel in a submarine.

5448. Diving bell with supplementary air supply was patented in 1691 by the British astronomer Edmond Halley, then secretary of the Royal Society of London. The bell, which contained a volume of air of approximately 60 cubic feet (1.7 cubic meters), was made of wood coated with lead. A valve allowed air to be vented out while a barrel could be tapped to provide an additional supply of fresh air. A glass window at the top provided illumination.

5449. Diving suit was invented by an Englishman, John Lethbridge, in 1715. Made of leather, it covered the body entirely and contained enough air to allow a diver 30 minutes of breathing in water 30 feet (9.14 meters) deep.

5450. Submersible supplied with air pumped from the surface was suggested by the French physicist Denis Papin in 1689, but a working version was not built until 1799, when English civil engineer John Smeaton introduced his "diving chest." It used a forcing pump to replenish the air supply under pressure.

5451. Breathing apparatus for submarine escape was the Davis underwater escape apparatus, a small cylinder of compressed oxygen with a watertight mouthpiece. It was first used for emergency rescue on June 9, 1931, when the British submarine *Poseidon* sank off the coast of China. Six sailors used the Davis device to ascend safely to the surface.

SHIPS AND BOATS—SUBMARINES—continued

5452. Free-moving deep-sea submersible was the bathyscaphe, an untethered craft designed to precisely rise or descend in water like a balloon in air. Maneuverability was supplied by ballast chambers containing gasoline (which was less compressible than the air used in earlier submarines) and two props driven by electric motors. The crew was protected by a pressurized gondola. It was developed by Swiss aeronaut and engineer Auguste Piccard, who applied his experience as a high-altitude balloonist, and was financed by an industry consortium. The first successful manned bathyscaphe trials took place in 1953–54, including a descent off the coast of Dakar, Senegal, to 13,000 feet (4,000 meters) in the bathyscaphe *FNRS 3* on February 15, 1954.

5453. Dive to the bottom of the ocean took place on January 23, 1960, when the French inventor and submariner Jacques Piccard and U.S. Navy lieutenant Don Walsh descended 35,800 feet (10,912 meters) in a bathyscaphe to the bottom of the Mariana Trench in the Pacific, the deepest place in the ocean.

SHIPS AND BOATS—VOYAGES

5454. Steamboat to make an ocean voyage was the *Phoenix,* 100 feet long, built at Hoboken, NJ, USA, by Robert Livingston Stevens with his father, John Stevens. On June 10, 1809, it went from New York City to Philadelphia, PA, USA, by sea, navigating the Atlantic from Sandy Hook to Cape May, NJ, USA, under the command of Moses Rogers.

5455. Steamboat to cross an ocean was the *Savannah,* a 350-ton wooden craft designed by an American, Daniel Dod of Elizabeth, NJ, USA, and built in New York. The powerplant was a single inclined direct-acting low-pressure steam engine of a mere 90 horsepower that drove a small paddlewheel; the ship was also fully rigged with sails. The *Savannah,* captained by Moses Rogers, sailed on May 22, 1819, from Savannah, GA, USA, and arrived at Liverpool, England, on June 20. Steam power was used for only 80 hours of the 27 days 11 hours it took to make the crossing.

5456. Steamship to cross an ocean from east to west was the paddle steamer *Sirius,* built for the St. George Steam Packet Company by Robert Menzies and Son, Leith, Scotland, in 1837. In 1838, it was chartered by the British and American Navigation Company in a race with the *Great Western* to become the first steamship to cross the Atlantic to New York City.

Under the command of Lieutenant Richard Roberts, RN, the *Sirius* left Cork, Ireland, on April 4, 1838, and arrived in New York on April 22. The passage took 18 days, 10 hours, at an average speed of 6.7 knots. The *Great Western* arrived the next day.

5457. World tour by a woman traveling alone was made by the American reporter Elizabeth Cochrane, better known as Nellie Bly, who made the tour in 1889–90 as a stunt for the *New York World,* trying to beat the record set by the hero of Jules Verne's novel *Around the World in Eighty Days.* She left New York, NY, USA, on November 14, 1889, sailing from Hoboken, NJ, USA, on the *Augusta Victoria* for Southampton, England, and continued traveling eastward on a variety of conveyances, including boats, rickshaws, and mules. The *World* published daily reports on her progress. Bly returned to New York City with much fanfare on January 25, 1890, on a chartered express train. The tour took 72 days 6 hours 11 minutes 14 seconds, of which 56 days 12 hours 41 minutes were spent in actual travel.

5458. Round-the-world solo sailing journey was accomplished by the Canadian mariner Captain Joshua Slocum, who sailed from Boston, MA, USA, on April 24, 1895, in a restored fishing sloop called *The Spray.* It was 36 feet 9 inches (11.1 meters) long, 14 feet 2 inches (4.3 meters) wide, and 4 feet 2 inches (1.2 meters) deep. Its cost was US$554. The round trip of 46,000 miles (74,000 kilometers), along a route that took the craft to Nova Scotia, the Azores, Gibraltar, South America, Samoa, Australia, South Africa, and the West Indies, was completed on July 3, 1898, when Slocum sailed into the harbor at Fairhaven, MA, USA, where the ship had been built circa 1800. In 1909 Slocum and *The Spray* were lost at sea en route from New England to Grand Cayman, the Bahamas.

5459. Steamboat to pass through the Panama Canal was the American-built craneboat *Alex. La Valley,* a self-propelled steamer, which made the trip on January 7, 1914. Commercial traffic was inaugurated on August 15, 1914. The first passage of commercial cargo took place on May 18–19, 1914. The first vessel to make a direct continuous voyage from ocean to ocean through the canal was the American tug *Mariner,* on May 19, 1914.

5460. Raft trip across the Pacific of record was the Kon-Tiki Expedition, led by Norwegian explorer and anthropologist Thor Heyerdahl. In 1947, to test his theory that seafaring peoples from South America had colonized Polynesia, Heyerdahl and a crew of five sailed a balsa-wood craft, the *Kon-Tiki,* from the coast of Peru to Raroia Reef in the Tuamotu archipelago of French Polynesia—a voyage of 4,300 miles (6,900 kilometers) across open ocean.

5461. Transatlantic solo boat journey by a woman was made by Ann Davidson in a 23-foot sailboat, the *Felicity Ann,* which left Plymouth, England, on May 18, 1952, and arrived at Miami, FL, USA, on August 12, 1953. Davidson made stops en route at Douarnenez, France; Vigo, Spain; Gilbraltar; and Dominica, Antigua, Nevis, St. Thomas, and Nassau, British West Indies.

5462. Circumnavigation of the world by a submarine was made by the U.S.S. *Gudgeon,* which sailed from Pearl Harbor, HI, on July 8, 1957, visited Asian, African, and European ports, and returned to Hawaii on February 21, 1958. It traveled approximately 25,000 miles (40,225 kilometers) in 228 days. The *Gudgeon* was 269 feet (82 meters) long, had a complement of 83 and a 2,050-ton (1,859 metric-ton) displacement, and was launched on June 11, 1952, at the Portsmouth Naval Shipyard, Portsmouth, NH, USA. It was commissioned on November 21, 1952.

5463. Crossing of the North Pole underwater by a submerged submarine was accomplished on August 3, 1958, by the nuclear-powered submarine U.S.S. *Nautilus* under the command of Commander William Robert Anderson. The submarine carried 116 persons, including 14 officers, 98 crewmen, and 4 civilian scientists. It left Pearl Harbor, HI, on July 23, 1958, crossed the Pacific Ocean through the Bering Strait, surfaced, and went under the ice cap at Point Barrow, Alaska, on August 1, 1958, at 11:15 P.M. EDT. Traveling 1,830 miles (2,944 kilometers) under the ice in 96 hours, it arrived under the North Pole on August 3. The *Nautilus* then continued its voyage, reaching Iceland on August 7.

5464. Circumnavigation of the earth by a submerged submarine was accomplished by the U.S.S. *Triton,* which left New London, CT, USA, on February 16, 1960, crossed the equator on February 24, and completed the submerged circumnavigation on April 25, having traveled 41,500 miles (66,774 kilometers) in 84 days. It returned to New London on May 11. The hull of the submarine was submerged during the entire trip, but the upper portion broached the surface twice. The nuclear-powered *Triton* was 447 feet (136 meters) long and had a 37-foot (11-meter) beam. Its submerged displacement was 7,750 tons (7,029 metric tons). It carried a crew of 13 officers and 135 men and was commanded by Captain Edward Latimer Beach. The *Triton* was laid down on May 21, 1956, launched on August 19, 1958, and commissioned on November 10, 1959.

5465. Solo voyage around the world was completed by the English yachtsman Francis Charles Chichester in 1966–67. Chichester's boat was the ketch *Gipsy Moth IV,* which was 53 feet (16.2 meters) long. Chichester left Plymouth, England, on August 27, 1966, and arrived in Sydney, Australia, 107 days and 14,100 miles (22,687 kilometers) later. He embarked from Sydney on January 29, 1967. On the second leg of his trip, which lasted 119 days and covered 15,517 miles (24,972 kilometers), Chichester returned to Plymouth around Cape Horn; it was the longest nonstop voyage ever made in a small sailboat.

5466. Transatlantic solo trip by rowboat was made by the British sailor John Fairfax, who left Las Palmas in Spain's Canary Islands, off the coast of Morocco, in the *Britannia,* a 22-foot rowboat, on January 20, 1969. He was swept down to the Cape Verde Islands, crossed the Atlantic, and landed in the surf at Hollywood, FL, USA, at 1:48 P.M. on July 19, after a 180-day voyage.

5467. Solo nonstop voyage around the world was completed by the British yachtsman Robin Knox-Johnston on April 22, 1969. He made the voyage from Falmouth, England, back to Falmouth in just 312 days.

5468. Transpacific sailboat crossing by a woman was made by an American, Sharon Sites Adams, who sailed from Yokohama, Japan, on May 12, 1969, in a 31-foot fiberglass ketch, the *Sea Sharp.* She arrived at San Diego, CA, USA, on July 25, having covered a distance of approximately 5,620 miles (9,043 kilometers) in 74 days 17 hours 15 minutes.

5469. Re-enactment of a Viking voyage to the New World was Vinland Revisited, a recreation of the voyage of Leif Eriksson circa 1000 from Greenland to L'Anse aux Meadows, Newfoundland, Canada. A newly built Viking ship called *Gaia* embarked on May 17, 1991, from Bergen, Norway, stopped at Orkney, Shetland, the Faeroe Islands, Iceland, and Greenland, and reached L'Anse aux Meadows on August 2, 1991. The project cost US$4 million and was financed by the governments of Norway and Iceland and by Norwegian shipping magnate Knut Kloster.

SHIPS AND BOATS—VOYAGES—continued

5470. Solo crossing of the Gulf of Mexico in a paddled boat was made by an American, Arthur Hebert, in a 17-foot (5-meter) kayak. He left Mexico's Yucatán Peninsula on May 16, 1998, and reached Louisiana, USA, on June 4. The kayak drifted into the Mississippi River, where Hebert was picked up by a Coast Guard cutter.

SLAVERY

5471. Slavery appears to have been practiced in all areas of the world from the beginning of recorded history. The earliest mention of slavery as an institution, and of the various social rights of slaves, is in the Babylonian law code of Hammurabi from circa 1792–50 BCE. Slavery in China began at about the same time, during the Shang dynasty (circa 1760-1100 BCE).

5472. Slave revolt of record took place in 464 BCE in Sparta, Greece. After an earthquake nearly demolished the city, the helots (state-owned serfs) of Messenia, a neighboring city-state under harsh Spartan rule, rose up and attacked their masters. Driven back by Spartan forces under King Archidamus, the helots mounted a stubborn defense on the slopes of Mount Ithome in Messenia. The Spartans called in help from their allies the Athenians and crushed the rebellion.

5473. Slave society in which slaves were essential was that of classical Athens, Greece. Once slavery of citizens was outlawed circa 594 BCE, Athenians acquired increasing numbers of foreign slaves through war with Persia and trade with other Aegean peoples. Slaves made up about a third of the population of the city by circa 450. The prosperous Athenian way of life, with its strong emphasis on the political and creative freedom of citizens, was wholly dependent on the leisure that widespread slave labor made possible. Philip II of Macedonia, the father of Alexander the Great, released most of the Athenian slaves after defeating Athens at the battle of Chaeronea (338 BCE).

5474. Serfs in Europe were the *coloni,* tenant farmers of the late Roman empire who, though not technically enslaved, were bound by law to donate their labor to a nobleman or landowner. A law promulgated by the emperor Constantine the Great in 332 CE required serfs to remain on the land and to submit to the demands of the lord and his agents. A system of serfdom existed in China from ancient times.

5475. African slave trade began among African peoples before the beginning of recorded history. African slaves began to be transported to Islamic trans-Saharan and Indian Ocean slave markets, and then overseas to other parts of the Islamic world, beginning circa 650 CE.

5476. Revolt of African slaves of record was the Zanj revolt that began in 869 CE. It began in Basra (in present-day Iraq), where several thousand enslaved black Africans had been put to work draining marshes. Joined by black soldiers who had defected from the Muslim army, they repulsed a series of military attacks and took control of what is now southern Iraq and part of Iran. They were defeated in 883.

5477. European country to enter the African slave trade was Portugal, which began in the mid-15th century to purchase slaves on the west coast of Africa. The first slaves to be sold in Lisbon were ten men and women whom the Portuguese had received as a ransom for several Moors they had kidnapped on the coast of North Africa in 1441. They were followed in 1443 by two hundred black Africans who were kidnapped by the explorer Gil Eanes on his pioneering voyages to Africa's west coast. Although Prince Henry the Navigator ordered his captains in 1455 to stop capturing Africans, the practice continued.

5478. African slave kingdom in India was founded in Bengal in 1486. A group of African slaves organized a rebellion, killed the sultan of Bengal, and replaced him with their leader, who took the name Barbak Shah. The kingdom lasted, amid a series of assassinations, until 1494, when the Africans were conquered and exiled from Bengal.

5479. Slaves in the New World (other than indigenous people enslaved by other indigenous people) were African slaves brought over by Christopher Columbus on his second voyage, in 1493. They were followed by European slaves imported by Spanish settlers of the colony in Santo Domingo on the island of Hispaniola (now the capital of the Dominican Republic). In 1502, Nicolás de Ovando, the first royal governor of the West Indies, received official authorization from the queen of Spain to import African slaves "born in the power of Christians." Ovando had already instituted a system of peonage for the natives of the island, but Africans were brought in because they were believed to make more productive laborers than the Indians.

5480. Laws authorizing African slaves in the New World were the Laws of Burgos, promulgated by Spain on December 27, 1512. Ironically, black slavery was authorized by the crown to correct what was seen in Spain as a social injustice: the enforced serfdom, under the *encomienda* system, of Native Americans in Cuba and Spain's other New World territories.

5481. African slaves in South America arrived in northeast Brazil in 1538. Slaves were imported by the Portuguese colonizers following a papal bull of 1537 that forbade the enslavement of the natives. The Atlantic slave trade to Brazil was not made illegal until 1850, and it continued illegally for some decades after.

5482. Communities of escaped African slaves on a large scale were formed on the West Indian island of Hispaniola (modern Haiti and Dominican Republic) in the early 1500s. By 1542, these settlements were home to some 3,000 escaped slaves, out of a total African population on Hispaniola of about 30,000. Slaves who escaped to live in the wilderness, or with indigenous people, were known as "maroons," from the Spanish *cimarrón,* meaning "wild."

5483. African slave to earn a degree from a European university was Juan Latino, born on Africa's Barbary Coast in 1516 and sold into slavery in Seville, Spain, at the age of twelve. He was allowed to study alongside the young Duke de Sesa, whose attendant he was, and went with him to Granada, where he learned Latin and Greek. The University of Granada awarded him one degree in 1546 and the master of arts degree in 1556.

5484. Book about human rights and slavery in the New World was the *Brevísima relación de la destrucción de las Indias (A Brief Report on the Destruction of the Indies),* published in Spain in 1552. The author was the Spanish priest Bartolomé de Las Casas, the first priest ordained in the New World, who had spent years as a missionary in lands that are now Venezuela, the Dominican Republic, and Mexico, attempting to protect the enslaved Indians. In the *Brevísima relación,* he warned that God's wrath would destroy the Spanish for the sins they were committing in the Americas.

5485. Political philosopher to reject slavery was the French jurist Jean Bodin, the author of *Six livres de la République* (1576; published in English in 1606 as *The Six Bookes of a Commonweale),* in which he explored the proper foundations of sovereign government and legal authority. He was the first to express the opinion that slavery is immoral.

5486. Code for the treatment of slaves in European colonies was the *Code Noir,* or the Black Code, established in March 1685 by King Louis XIV of France. The code included some 60 articles regulating the lives of black slaves in the French colonies of the West Indies and the Indian Ocean. It was later extended to cover Louisiana. The articles specified the prohibitions and punishments applicable to slaves and required slaveowners to Christianize their slaves.

5487. Pope to condemn the African slave trade was Pope Innocent XI, who issued a condemnation on March 20, 1686. He was influenced by a 1684 petition describing the cruelties of the trade that was written by Lourenço da Silva e Mendonça, an Afro-Brazilian who claimed to be descended from Kongo royalty.

5488. Protest against slavery made by a religious group in the New World was made in 1688 by the Mennonites, a pacifist German Protestant sect that had emigrated to the Quaker colony of Pennsylvania, in what is now the United States, some years before. They issued a public statement denouncing slavery as a form of theft and through their leader, Franz Daniel Pastorius, presented it to the Quakers, who eventually took it to heart, becoming active abolitionists.

5489. Autobiography by an African slave to have a major impact on the abolition movement was *The Interesting Narrative of the Life and Adventures of Olaudah Equiano or Gustavus Vassa, the African,* published in England in 1789. Equiano was born in Benin, West Africa, circa 1750. At the age of twelve he was kidnapped and taken as a slave to English settlements in the West Indies, where he was freed some years later. He joined England's antislavery movement and wrote his autobiography to popularize the cause. It was highly popular, going through eight editions in five years. His description of his childhood was the first account in English of West African life.

5490. African refuge for former slaves was Freetown, Sierra Leone, founded in 1787 by the English social activist Granville Sharp, who had helped to bring about the abolition of slavery in Britain in 1772. The site was purchased from the ruler of Sierra Leone's Temne tribe. Freetown took in members of the Black Poor, destitute former slaves who had been emancipated in Britain. Other people who were resettled in Freetown included Africans rescued from slave ships, "maroons" (escaped slaves) from Britain's colony in Jamaica, blacks who

SLAVERY—*continued*

had fought on the British side during the rebellion of its American colonists, and former slaves of American loyalists from South Carolina who had fled to Nova Scotia, Canada, during the Revolutionary War.

5491. Freed African slaves repatriated to Africa sailed in 1787 from Portsmouth, England, to a site in Sierra Leone that had been purchased from the Temne tribe by a group of British abolitionists and philanthropists headed by Granville Sharp. The settlement, later called Freetown, was founded as a refuge for former slaves who had gained their freedom in England (where slavery had been abolished in 1772), but who had no way to support themselves there.

5492. Large-scale uprising of African slaves in the New World was the slave insurrection against the French that began in Haiti in 1791 and made its greatest strides under the generalship of the freed slave known as Toussaint-Louverture (born François-Dominique Toussaint), who specialized in guerrilla tactics. By 1801, his army had invaded the neighboring Spanish colony of Santo Domingo, freed its slaves, and brought the entire island of Hispaniola under his control. Although the French deported and imprisoned Toussaint-Louverture in 1802, Haiti declared its independence in 1804, the first Latin American country to do so.

5493. European country to outlaw slavery was Denmark, in 1792.

5494. International agreement to eliminate slave trading was reached by several European states, notably Belgium, Great Britain, France, and Germany, at the Conference of Berlin, which took place between November 15, 1844, and February 26, 1885, in Berlin, Germany. The main work of the conference was to divide up the Congo region of West Africa among the colonizing nations of Europe. Among the other matters decided was to end the African slave trade by putting pressure on those Muslim leaders who profited from it.

5495. Advocate of black pride was the Brazilian writer Luis Gonzaga de Pinto Gama (1830–82), whose poems and other writings celebrated the beauty of African women and the accomplishments of African culture. The son of a free black woman and a white Portuguese aristocrat, Gama was sold into slavery as a child and afterwards became a lawyer who specialized in defending escaped slaves.

SOCIAL WELFARE

5496. National public welfare law in Europe of record was the Act for the Relief of the Poor, the first of the so-called Poor Laws, codified in 1597–98 and enacted by the English Parliament in 1601. It was administered through parish overseers and offered workhouse jobs for laborers and relief for the poor and ill who were unable to work.

5497. Housing project in an inner-city neighborhood was founded in 1864 in St. Marylebone, a borough of London, England, by Octavia Hill, using funds loaned by the art critic and social theorist John Ruskin. Hill created low-cost housing for impoverished slum dwellers by buying decrepit tenements, renovating them, and managing them. She also provided social services and training to the residents of her own and other projects.

5498. Domestic violence law was Britain's Matrimonial Causes Act of 1878. Under English common law, husbands had the right to use a moderate degree of physical force to "correct" their wives. This law allowed women to obtain a separation order against violent and abusive husbands.

5499. Settlement house was Toynbee Hall, founded in 1884 in London, England, by Canon Samuel Augustus Barnett of St. Jude's Church. The refurbished building, which was next to the church, was to be used as a residence hall for students and others engaged in social service to the poor, working-class neighborhoods of Whitechapel.

5500. Juvenile court was established in Adelaide, Australia, in 1890. Cases were heard by the Police Magistrate or two justices of the peace. The first such court to hear a large number of cases was the Juvenile Court of Cook County, known as the Chicago Juvenile Court, authorized in Chicago, IL, USA, on April 21, 1899, and opened on July 1, 1899, with Richard Stanley Tuthill as judge. During the first year, about 2,300 cases were heard. Cases involving girls were tried by a female judge, Mary Margaret Bartelme, beginning on March 3, 1913.

5501. Family court was the the domestic relations division of the City Court of Buffalo, NY, USA, which opened for business on January 1, 1910, to handle such matters as juvenile delinquency, guardianship issues, establishment of paternity, and child support.

5502. Walk to raise funds for charity took place on December 26, 1959, when 21 walkers set out from Letchworth, Hertfordshire, England, to raise funds for the World Refugee Fund. Each walker was sponsored by donors who pledged to give money for each mile completed. The organizer was Kenneth Johnson, who stayed on the course for 50 miles. The World Refugee Fund received about £20 from the event.

SPACE

5503. Space travel by rocket was proposed in 1656 in *Histoire comique des états et empires de la lune (Comic History of the States and Empires of the Moon)* by the French fabulist Cyrano de Bergerac. Cyrano put forward the rocket as one means to get to the moon; he also suggested traveling there by balloon.

5504. Rocket engine was patented in 1895 by the Peruvian inventor Pedro Poulet. His 4-inch (10-centimeter) engine was fueled by kerosene, with nitrogen peroxide as the oxidizer.

5505. Rocket flight using liquid fuel was made on March 16, 1926, at Auburn, MA, USA, under the direction of American rocketry pioneer Robert Hutchins Goddard. Pressure was produced internally by an outside pressure tank, and after launching by an alcohol heater on the rocket. The rocket traversed 184 feet (56 meters) in 2.5 seconds, moving along the trajectory at about 60 miles (97 kilometers) per hour. The flight was reported to the Smithsonian Institution in Washington, DC, on May 5, 1926. As early as 1920, Goddard, working under a grant from Clark University, Worcester, MA, had demonstrated the lifting force of rockets using liquid oxygen and ether.

5506. Vehicle to break the sound barrier was a rocket built by the American Rocket Society and flown on September 9, 1934, at Marine Park, Staten Island, New York, NY, USA.

5507. Rocket to reach outer space was a two-stage rocket consisting of a Wac Corporal set in the nose of a German V-2 captured by American forces during World War II. It was fired on February 24, 1949, from the White Sands Proving Ground, NM, USA, by a team of German and American scientists under Dr. Wernher von Braun. It reached an altitude of 250 miles.

5508. Object to escape the earth's gravity was the Soviet unmanned space probe *Luna 1,* launched on January 2, 1959, from the Baikonur space center in south-central Kazakhstan. It flew past the moon and entered an orbit around the sun.

5509. Telecast from space showing the earth was transmitted on August 14, 1959, when the cameras in the paddlewheel satellite *Explorer 6* sent back pictures showing a 20,000-square-mile (5,180,000-hectare) area of the earth. The satellite was launched on August 7 and had a total weight of 142 pounds (64 kilograms).

5510. Multinational space agency was the European Space Agency, formed on July 31, 1973, at Brussels, Belgium, out of the European Launcher Development Organisation and the European Space Research Organisation. The original members were Austria, Belgium, Denmark, France, Germany, Ireland, Italy, the Netherlands, Norway, Spain, Sweden, Switzerland, and the United Kingdom. The first director-general was Roy Gibson, who served from 1975 to 1981.

5511. Commercial space program was developed in the 1980s by the European Space Agency, though Arianespace, a private marketing company with headquarters in Every, France. The ESA program, funded by 36 European aerospace firms and eleven European banks, was based on the Ariane booster rocket. The first successful Ariane launch was *Ariane 5,* which lifted off on June 16, 1983, from a facility at the French Space Center, Kourou, French Guiana. The payload was two satellites.

5512. International space station was *Freedom,* a joint project of the U.S. space agency, NASA, and its partners, including the European Space Agency (a consortium of 13 countries), Canada, and Japan. The station was originally proposed in a 1984 speech by U.S. president Ronald Wilson Reagan. An agreement of cooperation with the international partners was signed in 1985. It was named "Freedom" in 1988 by President Reagan. Russia joined the project in 1993 when it agreed to merge its *Mir* space station program with the Western effort. Construction began in space on November 20, 1998, and was expected to continue until circa 2012.

5513. Meteorite captured on video was videotaped on October 9, 1992, by scores of parents in New York, USA, who were attending their children's outdoor high school sports events. They saw a streak across the sky and used their home video cameras to record it. The football-sized meteorite came down in Peekskill, NY, and crushed part of a car.

5514. Space probe with ion-drive engine as its primary propulsion system was *Deep Space 1,* launched in October 1998 from Cape Canaveral, FL, USA, by the American space agency, NASA. The ion drive, which produced thrust by bombarding a block of xenon with electrici-

SPACE—*continued*

ty to generate a stream of ionized particles, was far less powerful than conventional chemical rocket propellants, but it could sustain thrust for many months. The probe was slated to fly by asteroid 1992 KD in July 1999. *Deep Space 1* was also the first robot space probe with an intelligent guidance system able to make some mission decisions on its own.

5515. Module of the International Space Station to be placed in space was the Zarya navigation and propulsion module, built in Russia and financed by the United States. It was lofted into space atop a Proton rocket on November 20, 1998, from the Baikonur, Kazakhstan, and assumed an orbit 219 miles (353 kilometers) above the earth.

5516. Ocean platform for rocket launching was the Odyssey, built by an international aerospace consortium led by Boeing Company of Seattle, WA, USA. The platform, a modified oil rig, was assembled in the United States and towed out to the mid-Pacific about 1,500 miles southeast of the Hawaiian islands. On March 27, 1999, a three-stage rocket called *Sea Launch,* built by the Russian and Ukrainian members of the consortium, lifted off from the platform carrying a 5-ton dummy payload for deployment in geosynchronous orbit. The launch was broadcast live over the Internet.

5517. Space mission headed by women was a planetary exploration project sponsored by the U.S. National Aeronautics and Space Administration in the late 1990s. The team, working at the Jet Propulsion Laboratory in Pasadena, CA, USA, built two electronic microprobes with the intention of launching them in December 1999 on the Mars Polar Lander. The microprobes, each surrounded by an aeroshell, were designed to crash into Mars at a speed of 400 miles per hour, burrow into the surface, and relay information about the planet's soil composition. The mission was run by project manager Sarah A. Gavit, chief mission engineer Kari A. Lewis, and lead scientist Suzanne E. Smrekar.

SPACE—LUNAR EXPLORATION

5518. Radar signal to the moon was beamed by the U.S. Army Signal Corps on January 10, 1946, from the Evans Signal Laboratories, Belmar, NJ, USA. The experiment was supervised by U.S. Army lieutenant colonel John H. De Witt. An echo was received 2.4 seconds later that consisted of a 180-cycle note of a quarter-second duration.

5519. Spacecraft to reach the moon was the Soviet probe *Luna 2,* which was launched from the Baikonur cosmodrome in Kazakhstan on September 12, 1959. It impacted on the lunar surface on September 13.

5520. Photographs of the dark side of the moon were transmitted to earth by the Soviet space probe *Luna 3,* launched on October 4, 1959. On October 5, it entered orbit around the moon and began sending pictures of the dark side, which is not visible from the earth.

5521. Spacecraft to make a soft landing on the moon was the Soviet craft *Luna 9,* which landed on the lunar surface on February 3, 1966.

5522. Photographs from the surface of the moon were transmitted via radio to earth by the Soviet *Luna 9* space probe on February 6, 1966. They were received by the large radiotelescope at the Jodrell Bank Experimental Station at Jodrell Bank, near Manchester, England.

5523. Spacecraft to return from lunar orbit was *Zond 5,* a Soviet moon probe, which returned from the moon in September 1968 and made a soft landing in the Soviet Union.

5524. Astronauts to orbit the moon were three Americans, Frank Borman, James Arthur Lovell, Jr., and William Alison Anders, who made ten lunar orbits in *Apollo 7,* launched by a three-stage Saturn 5 rocket from Cape Canaveral, FL, USA, at 7:51 A.M. on December 21, 1968. The spacecraft reentered the atmosphere and splashed down in the Pacific Ocean 147 hours 11 seconds later.

5525. Astronauts to land on the moon were two Americans, Neil Alden Armstrong and Edwin Eugene Aldrin, Jr., the first human beings to set foot on land beyond the earth. Together with Michael Collins, they were lifted off in *Apollo 11* at 9:32 A.M. by a Saturn 5 rocket on July 16, 1969, from Kennedy Space Center, Cape Canaveral, FL, USA, with Armstrong as flight commander. The flight reached the moon on Sunday, July 20. Collins remained in orbit as pilot of the command module *Columbia* while the other two, with Aldrin as pilot, descended to the surface of the moon in the lunar module *Eagle.* At 4:17:42 P.M. EDT the *Eagle* touched down on the moon's Mare Tranquillitatis (Sea of Tranquility). At 10:56 P.M. Armstrong came down the ladder, placed his foot on the moon, and said: "That's one small step for [a] man, one giant leap for mankind." He was joined on the lunar surface by Aldrin at 11:14 P.M. They placed a plaque on the moon and erected an 8-foot (2.4-meter) aluminum staff with a nylon United States flag. They also set up scientific instruments, collected rocks, and took photographs. At 1:34 P.M. on July 21 the *Eagle* lifted off the lunar surface to rejoin the mother ship. The *Columbia* splashed down at 12:50 P.M. EDT on July 24 in the Pacific Ocean, about 920 miles southwest of Hawaii. The astronauts were taken on board the U.S.S. *Hornet* at 2:12 P.M. and entered a mobile quarantine facility, where they remained until August 11.

5526. Lunar rover was the Soviet wheeled robot *Lunakhod I,* which landed on the moon in 1970.

5527. Soil samples from the moon were returned to earth by the Soviet lunar probe *Luna 16,* launched on September 12, 1970.

5528. Astronauts to ride a vehicle on the moon were two American astronauts, U.S. Air Force colonel David Randolph Scott and U.S. Air Force lieutenant colonel James Benson Irwin. On July 31, 1971, they rode the four-wheeled electric cart Rover, an LRV (Lunar Roving Vehicle), alongside Hadley Hills, a moon canyon 1,200 feet (366 meters) deep. With Major Alfred Merrill Worden, they were launched on July 26, 1971, at 9:34 A.M. from Cape Canaveral, FL, USA, in *Apollo 15* and returned to earth on August 7.

SPACE—MANNED FLIGHTS

5529. Human in space was probably the Soviet cosmonaut Aleksei Ledovski, although his flight was never acknowledged by the Soviet Union or by its successor, the Commonwealth of Independent States. According to intelligence obtained by the U.S. government, Ledovski was launched into space in 1957 from a site in southern Russia. His craft was probably destroyed by the heat of reentry into the earth's atmosphere. The Soviet Union is thought to have launched a number of secret manned flights in the later 1950s, none of which ended with the safe return of the pilot.

5530. Living creature launched into orbit was a female sled dog, Laika, who was shot into space inside the Soviet satellite *Sputnik II* on November 3, 1957, at Baikonur, Kazakhstan. Laika was sealed in a small capsule containing medical equipment for monitoring her heartbeat and other vital signs. She died in orbit.

5531. Animals to survive a space flight were Able and Baker, two small female monkeys, one a rhesus, the other a spider monkey, who survived a 15-minute flight in separate containers in the nose cone of an American-built Jupiter rocket launched on May 28, 1959, from Cape Canaveral, FL, USA. The cone was shot 300 miles (483 kilometers) into space and was recovered about 90 minutes later off the island of Antigua by U.S. Navy frogmen from the tug U.S.S. *Kiowa.*

5532. Living creatures launched into orbit who returned safely to earth were two dogs, Strelka and Belka, contained in the Soviet satellite *Sputnik V,* which was launched on August 19, 1960, from the USSR's Baikonur space center in south-central Kazakhstan. The satellite orbited for 24 hours and then reentered the atmosphere. The dogs were ejected in an escape pod and lowered by parachute to a ground landing.

5533. Human to return safely from space was the cosmonaut Yury Alekseyevich Gagarin, a lieutenant in the Soviet air force. Gagarin's *Vostok 1* spacecraft was launched from the USSR's Baikonur space center in Kazakhstan on April 12, 1961. It reached an apogee of 187 miles (301 kilometres) and made one earth orbit in 89 minutes. The spaceship spun dangerously out of control near the end of its single orbit but made a successful reentry and was recovered later that day in the Soviet Union. Gagarin was awarded the Order of Lenin and proclaimed a Hero of the Soviet Union and Pilot Cosmonaut of the Soviet Union. He died in the crash of a jet aircraft in 1968.

5534. Two manned craft in space simultaneously were the Soviet-built *Vostok 3* spacecraft, launched August 11, 1962, from the Baikonur space center in Kazakhstan, and the *Vostok 4,* launched a day later. *Vostok 3* was piloted by Andriyan Grigoryevich Nikolayev. *Vostok 4* was piloted by Pavel R. Popovich. The two vessels maneuvered within visual range and made radio contact, but did not dock in space.

5535. Woman to fly in space was Soviet cosmonaut Valentina Vladimirovna Nikolayeva Tereshkova. She was recruited for the cosmonaut program in 1961. After receiving a commission in the Soviet Air Force, she was selected as the prime pilot for the flight of *Vostok 6.* The solo mission was launched on June 16, 1963, and completed 48 orbits in 71 hours.

SPACE—MANNED FLIGHTS—*continued*

5536. Spacecraft to carry more than one crew member was the Soviet-built *Voskhod 1,* which lifted off on October 12, 1964, from the Baikonur space center in Kazakhstan. Aboard for the 24-hour flight were three cosmonauts: Soviet spacecraft designer Konstantin Petrovich Feoktistov, physician Boris Borisovich Yegorov (the first doctor in space), and the pilot, Vladimir Mikhaylovich Komarov.

5537. Space walk was performed by Soviet cosmonaut Aleksei A. Leonov, copilot of *Voskhod 2,* launched on March 18, 1965, from the Baikonur space center in Kazakhstan. Later that day, the spacesuited Leonov entered an inflatable airlock and left the ship through the outer hatch for a ten-minute space walk. The 17-orbit flight lasted 26 hours 2 minutes 17 seconds and ended with an off-course landing in a remote pine forest in the Ural Mountains.

5538. Rendezvous in space took place on December 15, 1965, between two American Gemini spacecraft. *Gemini 6* carried Captain Walter Marty Schirra, Jr., and Major Thomas Patten Stafford, and *Gemini 7* carried Major Frank Borman and Lieutenant Commander James Arthur Lovell, Jr. The two *Gemini* craft flew in formation within 20 to 100 feet of each other for 5 hours 16 minutes, during which the astronauts photographed one another's crafts, sighted a fire in Madagascar, and conversed.

5539. Civilian space traveler to orbit the earth was an American test pilot, Neil Alden Armstrong, who orbited for 10 hours 42 minutes in *Gemini 8,* accompanied by U.S. Air Force major David Randolph Scott. The spacecraft was launched at 9 A.M. on March 16, 1966, from Cape Canaveral, FL, USA. It achieved the world's first docking in space, with an unmanned Agena spacecraft, and splashed down on March 17.

5540. Docking of two spacecraft was effected on March 16, 1966, by the U.S.-built *Gemini 8,* which made a rendezvous and docking on its fourth orbit, 6.5 hours after launching, with an unmanned Agena target vehicle launched at 9 A.M. the same day. *Gemini 8* was launched from Cape Canaveral, FL, at 10:41 A.M. by a two-stage Titan II. It made seven orbits in 10 hours 42 minutes, landing in the Pacific Ocean at 10:23 P.M. EST near Okinawa, where it was picked up 3.5 hours after splashdown and hauled onto the deck of U.S.S. *Leonard F. Mason* at 1:38 A.M. on March 17. Neil Alden Armstrong was the command pilot and Major David Randolph Scott the pilot.

5541. Human to die during a space flight whose death was acknowledged by his government was the Soviet cosmonaut Vladimir Mikhaylovich Komarov. Komarov was the sole crew member of the *Soyuz 1* mission that lifted off on April 23, 1967, from the Soviet space center in Baikonur, Kazakhstan. On April 24, he attempted a reentry after the 18th orbit, but the spacecraft became tangled in its main parachute and plummeted to earth at a velocity of several hundred kilometers per hour. Komarov's ashes were placed in the wall of the Kremlin. The first unconfirmed death in space was probably that of Soviet cosmonaut Aleksei Ledovski, who, according to American intelligence reports, died in the Soviet Union's first secret attempt at manned spaceflight in 1957.

5542. Live telecast from space was made on October 14, 1968, during the flight of *Apollo 7,* which had been launched on October 11 from the Kennedy Space Center at Cape Canaveral, FL, USA. The astronauts, Captain Walter Marty Schirra, Jr., Major Donn Fulton Eisele, and Major Ronnie Walter Cunningham, showed views of the inside of the capsule and views through the windows.

5543. International astronaut rescue agreement was the Agreement on the Rescue of Astronauts, the Return of Astronauts and the Return of Objects Launched into Outer Space. It was fully ratified in December 1968 by the signatories, the United States, the United Kingdom, and the Union of Soviet Socialist Republics.

5544. Docking of two manned spacecraft took place in earth orbit on January 16, 1969, between *Soyuz 4* and *Soyuz 5,* launched by the Soviet Union on successive days from the Baikonur space center in Kazakhstan. Two cosmonauts left *Soyuz 5,* transferred to *Soyuz 4,* and landed in that craft. It was the first transfer of personnel from one spacecraft to another.

5545. Welding and smelting in space was performed by the Soviet cosmonauts Georgy Stepanovich Shonin and Valery Kubasov of *Soyuz 6,* launched from the Soviet Union on October 11, 1969. During the five-day mission, they conducted various space-welding and smelting tests.

5546. Space station was *Salyut 1,* built by the Soviet Union and launched on April 19, 1971. The cylindrical craft weighed 19,000 pounds (8,619 kilograms), measured 25 feet (7.6 meters) long, and contained crew quarters, areas for scientific experiments, and storage compartments for air and food. *Salyut 1*'s first occupants were cosmonauts Vladislav Nikolayevich Volkov, Georgi Dobrovolsky, and Viktor Patsayev, who spent three weeks aboard the station in June 1971. All three were killed when a faulty valve let the air out of their capsule during reentry. *Salyut 1* burned up in the earth's atmosphere in October 1971.

5547. Launch failure of a manned spacecraft took place on April 5, 1975, when a Soviet-built booster rocket carrying the *Soyuz 18A* spacecraft malfunctioned before reaching orbit. The *Soyuz,* crewed by cosmonauts Vasily Grigoryevich Lazarev and Oleg Makarov, landed far off-course in the Altai Mountains of Siberia and toppled into a ravine. The parachute lines snagged on the way down, catching the craft and saving both men, who were later rescued.

5548. International space mission was the *Apollo-Soyuz* Test Project, conducted in July 1975 by the Soviet Union and the United States to demonstrate international cooperation in space docking and rescue. Two spacecraft took part in the mission: a three-man *Apollo* crewed by Thomas P. Stafford, Vance D. Brand, and Deke Slayton, and a two-man *Soyuz* craft crewed by Aleksei Arkhipovich Leonov and Valery Nikolayevich Kubasov. Both were launched on July 15, 1975. Docking by means of a custom U.S.-built module took place over the Atlantic Ocean on July 17 at 12:09 P.M. EDT. Over a two-day period, the crews went back and forth between the two ships and completed geodetic, astronomical, medical, and technical experiments. The craft detached on July 19 and landed separately, the *Soyuz* in Kazakhstan on July 21 and the *Apollo* in the Pacific Ocean on July 24.

5549. Space traveler who was not of USSR or U.S. citizenship was the Czech cosmonaut Vladimir Remek. Remek was launched into space from the Baikonur cosmodrome in Kazakhstan on March 2, 1978, aboard *Soyuz 28.* His crewmate was a Russian, Aleksei Gubarev. The spaceship docked for seven days with the *Salyut 6* space station and landed safely on March 10.

5550. Space traveler of African descent was Cuban cosmonaut Arnaldo Tamayo-Mendez. In September 1980, he was a crew member aboard the Soviet spacecraft *Soyuz 38* on a mission to the space station *Salyut 6.*

5551. Reusable manned spacecraft was the U.S. space shuttle *Columbia,* piloted by astronauts Robert L. Crippen and John W. Young, which was launched at 7 A.M. on April 12, 1981, from Cape Canaveral, FL, USA. The weight of the shuttle was 80 tons (73 metric tons). After a flight of 54 hours 22 minutes, including 36 orbits, the shuttle touched down on the dry lake bed at Edwards Air Force Base, Muroc, CA, on April 14, 1981, at 10:21 A.M. Development of the hybrid spacecraft-airplane cost almost US$10 billion and took nine years. The first free atmospheric flight by the space shuttle took place on August 12, 1977, when the shuttle *Enterprise* was lifted to a height of 25,000 feet (7,620 meters) by a Boeing 747 airplane and glided back to Edwards Air Force Base, Muroc, CA, piloted by astronauts C. Gordon Fullerton and Fred W. Haise, Jr.

5552. European Space Agency astronaut in space was a German, Ulf Merbold, a member of the six-person Spacelab mission of November–December 1983. He flew aboard the U.S. space shuttle *Columbia,* launched on November 28 from Cape Canaveral, FL, USA.

5553. Space travelers to fly free in space were two American astronauts, U.S. Navy captain Bruce McCandless and U.S. Army lieutenant colonel Robert Stewart. On February 7, 1984, while in orbit over the earth, McCandless exited the space shuttle *Challenger* and maneuvered freely, without a tether, using a rocket pack of his own design. Stewart also used the rocket pack to fly untethered later that day.

5554. Woman to walk in space was the Soviet cosmonaut Svetlana Savitskaya. On July 17, 1984, during the orbital flight of the *Soyuz T-12,* she spent 3.5 hours outside the craft. The first space walk by an American woman astronaut took place on October 11, 1984, when Kathryn D. Sullivan exited the space shuttle *Challenger* on a tether and flew in space for 3.5 hours.

5555. Canadian astronaut was Marc Garneau of Quebec City. He joined the Canadian Space Agency in 1983 and was selected to be Canada's first astronaut in space in March 1984. Garneau was a payload specialist on mission 41-G aboard the American space shuttle *Challenger* for a seven-day flight on October 6–13, 1984.

5556. Astronaut who was a mother was an American, Dr. Anna L. Fisher, a member of the crew of the U.S. space shuttle *Discovery* mission that lifted off on November 16, 1984, from Cape Canaveral, FL, USA. She participated in the world's first satellite retrieval and repair operation.

SPACE—MANNED FLIGHTS—*continued*

5557. Medical emergency in space took place during the Soviet-built *Soyuz T-14* mission in November 1985. The crew returned to earth ahead of schedule on November 12, after the mission commander, Vladimir Vasyutin, developed an acute inflammatory infection that was probably prostatitis.

5558. Simultaneous space walk by three astronauts took place in May 1992, when astronauts aboard the American space shuttle *Endeavor* rescued the Intelsat 6/F3 communications satellite from a useless low orbit. Three astronauts—U.S. Navy commander Pierre Thuot, U.S. Air Force lieutenant colonel Thomas Aker, and civilian Richard J. Hieb—were forced to improvise an alternate method of stabilizing the spinning satellite before they could attach it to a new motor that boosted it into a higher orbit. The space walk lasted 8 hours and 29 minutes, a new record.

5559. Husband and wife to fly in space together were two Americans, mission specialist N. Jan Davis, an engineer, and Air Force lieutenant colonel Mark C. Lee, who served as crew members aboard the mission of the U.S. space shuttle *Endeavor* that began on September 12, 1992. Although NASA, the U.S. space agency, has a rule forbidding married couples to take part in the same mission, the rule was waived for Davis and Lee because they had no children and both had trained as astronauts for several years before they were married.

5560. American to be launched into space aboard a Russian spacecraft was astronaut Norman Earl Thagard, who along with two cosmonauts lifted off from the Baikonur cosmodrome in Kazakhstan on March 14, 1995, aboard a *Soyuz* spacecraft. Thagard spent several months abord the Russian space station *Mir* before returning to earth on July 7, 1995, aboard the U.S. space shuttle *Atlantis.*

5561. Spacecraft launched by the United States to dock with a Russian space station was U.S. space shuttle *Atlantis,* commanded by U.S. Navy captain Robert L. Gibson. At 8 A.M. on June 29, 1995, the shuttle docked with the Russian space station *Mir* 245 miles (394 kilometers) above the earth, forming the largest structure ever assembled in space up to that time. The *Atlantis* was 122 feet (37 meters) long, the *Mir* 112 feet (34 meters) long. The station's two Russian cosmonauts and one American astronaut, combined with the shuttle's five Americans and two Russians, also constituted the largest human population that had ever been in orbit.

5562. Woman astronaut to live in a space station was American biochemist Dr. Shannon W. Lucid of Bethany, OK, USA. On March 24, 1996, Lucid transferred from the U.S. space shuttle *Atlantis* to the Russian space station *Mir* for a planned five-month stay. It was the first time that the shuttle returned to earth with one less person aboard than had been present at the launch. Lucid remained on the station for 188 days, the longest space sojourn by any woman until that time. Her return was delayed more than six weeks by emergency repairs to the booster rockets of the *Atlantis* and by a hurricane. She came home in the *Atlantis,* which touched down at Edwards Air Force Base, Muroc, CA, USA, on September 26, 1996.

5563. Joint space walk by American and Russian astronauts took place in earth orbit on April 29, 1997, when astronaut Jerry L. Linenger and cosmonaut Vasily Tsibliyev collected cosmic dust samples and installed a radiation meter outside the Russian space station *Mir.*

5564. Bureaucrat in space was the Russian lawyer Yuri Baturin, a former defense adviser to Russian Federation president Boris Yeltsin. On August 13, 1998, Baturin and cosmonauts Gennady Padalka and Sergei Avdeyev lifted off from the Baikonur cosmodrome in Kazakhstan aboard a *Soyuz* spacecraft on a mission to the Russian space station *Mir.* Baturin's role in the mission was not specified by Russian authorities.

5565. Humans to enter the International Space Station were American astronaut Colonel Robert D. Cabana and Russian cosmonaut Sergei K. Krikalev, who departed the U.S. space shuttle *Endeavor* and entered the Unity and Zarya modules of the space station *Freedom* on December 10, 1998. The two modules, the first to be lofted into orbit 250 miles (400 kilometers) above the earth, had been joined together by *Endeavor* earlier in the week. *Freedom* was a joint project of the United States, Russia, the European Space Agency, Canada, and Japan.

5566. Woman to command a space mission was U.S. Air Force colonel Eileen Marie Collins, who joined NASA in July 1991. On July 23, 1999, she commanded four crew members aboard the space shuttle *Columbia* as it lifted off from Cape Canaveral, FL, USA, to loft the Chandra X-Ray Observatory into a high elliptical earth orbit. Previously, she served as pilot on the shuttle mission STS-63, which docked with the Russian space station *Mir* in the first flight of the joint Russian-American space program, and piloted another space shuttle flight to *Mir* in May 1997.

SPACE—PLANETARY EXPLORATION

5567. Mars probe was *Mars 1*, successfully launched from the USSR's Baikonur space center in Kazakhstan on November 1, 1962, after a series of failures. *Mars 1* was lost before it reached Mars. Two companion probes failed on the launch pad.

5568. Spacecraft placed in solar orbit to investigate interplanetary space between the orbits of the earth and Venus was the American-built probe *Pioneer 5*, launched on March 11, 1960, from Cape Canaveral, FL, USA, by a three-stage Thor-Able IV rocket. The payload was a 26-inch (66 centimeter) sphere plus four vanes covered by 4,800 solar cells with a total weight of 94.8 pounds (43 kilograms), including approximately 40 pounds (18 kilograms) of instruments. The spacecraft orbited the sun in 311.6 days. Its velocity at the third-stage burnout was 24,689 miles (39,725 kilometers) per hour. It was 74.9 million miles (121 million kilometers) from the sun in perigee and 92.3 million miles (149 million kilometers) in apogee. Its last message was received on June 26, 1960, when it had transmitted data for 138.9 hours.

5569. Spacecraft to transmit close up photographs of Mars was the American space probe *Mariner 4*, launched at 9:22 A.M. on November 28, 1964, from Cape Canaveral, FL, by a two-stage Atlas-Agena D rocket. On July 14, 1965, when the 574-pound (261-kilogram) spacecraft was 134 million miles (216 million kilometers) away from earth and 10,500 miles (16,895 kilometers) from Mars, it sent a transmission of photographs consisting of 8.3 dots per second of varying degrees of darkness. The transmission lasted for 8.5 hours and depicted the regions on Mars known as Cebrenia, Arcadia, and Amazonis.

5570. Spacecraft to reach another planet was the Soviet planetary probe *Venera 3*, which crash-landed on Venus on March 1, 1966.

5571. Spacecraft to make a soft landing on another planet was *Venera 4*, a Soviet space probe, which landed on the surface of Venus on October 18, 1967. The planet's hot, corrosive atmosphere rendered the probe inoperative within an hour, but not before it had transmitted back to earth the first detailed data on the chemical composition of the Venusian upper atmosphere.

5572. Spacecraft to carry an extraterrestrial message intended to be read by living beings elsewhere in the universe was *Pioneer 10*, the American planetary probe that was launched from Cape Canaveral, FL, USA, on March 2, 1972, by NASA, the U.S. space agency. Bolted to the probe's exterior wall was a gold-anodized plaque that carried a number of illustrations: drawings of a human man and woman, a star map marked with the location of the sun, and a second map showing the flight path of *Pioneer 10*. The message was designed by the American astronomer Carl Sagan. *Pioneer 10* left the solar system on June 14, 1983.

5573. Close-up photographs of Jupiter were taken on December 3, 1973, by the U.S.-built planetary probe *Pioneer 10*. The satellite had been launched on March 2, 1972, from Cape Canaveral, FL, USA.

5574. Photographs from the surface of another planet were transmitted back to earth by the Soviet planetary probe *Venera 9*, which dropped an instrument capsule by parachute onto the surface of Venus on October 22, 1975.

5575. Photograph taken on Mars was a 340-degree panorama taken by the two cameras aboard the 1,300-pound (590-kilogram), 10-foot (3-meter) *Viking 1* lander, which was launched on August 20, 1975, and landed on Chryse Planitia (the "Plain of Gold") on Mars on July 20, 1976. The pictures, taken on July 20, were transmitted to the *Viking* mother ship in orbit around Mars, which sent them to the Jet Propulsion Laboratory in Pasadena, CA, USA, via a radio telescope in Spain.

5576. Spacecraft to land on Mars was the American planetary probe *Viking 1*, launched on August 20, 1975, from Cape Canaveral, FL, USA. Its sister craft *Viking 2* was launched on September 9, 1975. *Viking 1* touched down on Mars on July 20, 1976, and began sending photographs back to earth. The probe operated for 6.5 years. *Viking 2* landed on September 3, 1976, and functioned for 3.5 years.

5577. Spacecraft to leave the solar system was the U.S.-built planetary probe *Pioneer 10*, launched on March 2, 1972, from Cape Canaveral, FL, USA. It left the solar system on June 14, 1983, and sent back the first data from interstellar space. On March 2, 1997, the 25th anniversary of the launch, *Pioneer 10* became the world's oldest functioning spacecraft. It was also the man-made object farthest from earth, having traveled a distance of 6 billion miles

SPACE—PLANETARY EXPLORATION—
continued

(9.7 thousand million kilometers). NASA officially ended the mission on March 31, 1997, but *Pioneer 10* continued to travel. In the year 34,600, the probe will pass within three light-years of the star Ross 246.

5578. Space probe in a polar trajectory around the sun was *Ulysses,* a joint project of the European Space Agency and the United States National Aeronautics and Space Administration. It was launched from Cape Canaveral, FL, USA, in 1990. The *Ulysses* mission was designed to explore the solar wind, the sun's magnetic field, and cosmic rays.

5579. Images taken from outside the solar system were received on February 14, 1990, from the *Voyager I* spacecraft, an unmanned U.S. interplanetary probe launched on September 5, 1977, from Cape Canaveral, FL, USA. It visited Jupiter in 1979 and Saturn in 1980 before assuming a trajectory upward from the ecliptic plane and out of the solar system. The image showed a part of the solar system as viewed from "above."

5580. Photograph taken close-up of an asteroid in space was taken on October 29, 1991, by the American space probe *Galileo,* and showed the asteroid Gaspara. The *Galileo* was launched from the U.S. space shuttle *Atlantis* on October 18, 1989, on a multi-year mission to Jupiter.

5581. Photograph of the surface of Pluto was taken from earth orbit by the U.S.-built Hubble Space Telescope and made public in March 1996. It showed major features of the planet's icy surface. Previously, the planet could only be seen from earth-based instruments as a fuzzy dot with no distinguishing details.

5582. Robot to conduct a roving exploration of the surface of another planet was Sojourner, a 25-pound (11-kilogram), six-wheeled robot designed to explore and analyze the surface of Mars. The *Pathfinder* mission, the American spacecraft that carried Sojourner into space, was launched from Cape Canaveral, FL, USA, on December 4, 1996. On July 4, 1997, *Pathfinder* landed on the Ares Vallis, an ancient Martian floodplain. Upon landing, the craft was renamed the Sagan Memorial Station, in honor of the late American astronomer Carl Sagan. On July 6, Sojourner rolled away from *Pathfinder* and began conducting an analysis of soil and rocks in the immediate area. The US$23 million robot was named for Sojourner Truth, the African-American abolitionist.

5583. Traffic accident on Mars took place on July 9, 1997, when the American robot rover Sojourner bumped into "Yogi," a large rock, while trying to park. Sojourner succeeded in examining Yogi with an alpha proton X-ray spectrometer. It was brought to Mars by *Pathfinder,* a spacecraft launched by NASA from Cape Canaveral, FL, USA, on December 4, 1996. The spacecraft landed on Mars on July 4.

SPACE—SATELLITES

5584. Artificial satellite was *Sputnik 1,* launched by the Soviet Union on October 4, 1957, from the space station at Baikonur, Kazakhstan. The spherical satellite weighed 184 pounds (84 kilograms) and orbited the earth once every 96 minutes. Its apogee (highest orbital point from earth) was 584 miles (942 kilometers) and its perigee (lowest orbital point) was 143 miles (230 kilometers). *Sputnik I* burned up in the earth's atmosphere in early 1958.

5585. Satellite powered by photovoltaic cells was *Vanguard I,* launched on March 17, 1958, by the U.S. Signal Corps. The satellite power system (0.1 watts output, powering a 5-milliwatt backup transmitter) operated for eight years.

5586. International satellite was the United States–United Kingdom satellite *Ariel 1,* launched at 1 P.M. on April 26, 1962, from the Atlantic Missile Range, Cape Canaveral, FL, USA, by a Thor-Delta booster. The 132-pound (60 kilogram) cylinder payload was 23 inches (58 centimeters) in diameter and less than 11 inches (28 centimeters) long. It carried six British experiments: three to measure electron density, temperatures, and the composition of positive ions in the ionosphere; two to monitor intensity of radiation from the sun; and one to measure cosmic rays.

5587. Commercial satellite was *Telstar 1,* an active relay-communications satellite that was designed and built by the Bell Telephone Laboratories for the American Telephone and Telegraph Company. An application permit was filed with the U.S. government on October 21, 1960, and an experimental license was granted on January 19, 1961. The satellite was launched by NASA on July 10, 1962, at 4:35 A.M. from Cape Canaveral, FL, USA, using a three-stage Thor-Delta rocket. The satellite payload was a sphere 34.5 inches (88 centimeters) in diameter that weighed 170 pounds (77 kilograms). Orbit time was 157.8 minutes.

5588. Geosynchronous satellite was *Syncom 2,* launched by NASA at 10:33 A.M. on July 26, 1963, from the Atlantic Missile Range, Cape Canaveral, FL, USA. It was conceived and designed by the Hughes Aircraft Company. The cylinder was 28 inches (71 centimeters) in diameter and 15.5 inches (39 centimeters) high and weighed 147 pounds (67 kilograms). Its orbital period was 23.9 hours, putting it approximately in synchrony with the rotation of the earth. Its apogee was 22,239 miles (35,783 kilometers) and its perigee 22,230 miles (35,768 kilometers).

5589. International satellite consortium was the International Telecommunications Satellite Organization (INTELSAT), also called the International Telecommunications Satellite Consortium, founded on August 20, 1964, by a group of 18 nations led by the United States. INTELSAT provides commercial satellite communications services to more than 180 member and nonmember countries, territories, and dependencies and administers a worldwide network of geosynchronous communications satellites and ground stations.

5590. Satellite launched by the Chinese space program was *DFH-1,* a 381-pound (173-kilogram) test satellite. It was lofted atop a Long March booster on April 24, 1970, from the Jiuquan launch site near the Gobi Desert. The satellite was capable of radio-broadcasting a single propaganda song, "Dong Fang Hong" ("The East Is Red").

5591. Satellite launched from the earth to orbit another planet was *Mariner 9,* an unmanned American spacecraft that was sent to Mars to photograph the surface and to study the planet's thin atmosphere, clouds and hazes, surface chemistry, and seasonal changes. The satellite entered Martian orbit on November 13, 1971. It mapped 70 percent of the planet's surface.

5592. Earth-observing satellite that could see through clouds and darkness was *Radarsat 1,* built by the Canadian Space Agency. It was launched on November 4, 1995, from NASA's Western Range facility in California, USA, and was controlled from the Mission Control Center at St.-Hubert, Quebec, Canada. *Radarsat 1* was the first radar-based earth-observing satellite; it employed synthetic aperture radar capable of penetrating the atmosphere and returning highly detailed images of the earth from polar orbit.

5593. Civilian spy satellite was *EarlyBird 1,* built by EarthWatch Inc. of Longmont, CO, USA, and launched into earth orbit in December 1997 from the Svobodny Cosmodrome, a military base in eastern Russia. Sensors abord the satellite were capable of resolving objects on the ground as small as 10 feet (3 meters) long.

SPORTS AND RECREATION

5594. Depiction of a ball game appears on a fresco painted on the walls of Beni Hasan, Egypt, a rock tomb from the Twelfth dynasty (circa 1900 BCE). It shows players riding on the backs of other people as they toss a ball back and forth.

5595. Ball game of record was *tlachtli* (or *tlachco*), also called *pitz* or *ulama,* a game combining elements of handball, volleyball, American football, and basketball. It was played from Honduras to what is now the southern United States from before circa 1500 BCE. Many variations were developed through the game's roughly 3,500-year history, but certain aspects tended to remain constant. The playing field was a narrow rectangular court with slanting walls. Two teams faced each other across a center line and scored points by keeping a hard rubber ball in play by hitting it with their hips, buttocks, and knees and by caroming it off the walls. As the game evolved, players began wearing protective gear on their bodies and legs and special belts fitted with pieces that helped them travel with the ball without using their hands or feet. Another addition was a stone or wooden ring hung at midcourt. If the ball passed through the ring, the game ended, often with the ritual sacrifice of one of the teams, which were sometimes composed of war captives. The game also had religious and political dimensions that are not well understood. A late version was *ollamalitzli,* played by the Aztecs of central Mexico in the 15th and 16th centuries. A description of the game appeared in *De Orbe Novo (On the New World,* written in 1530 by Pietro Martire d'Anghiera, an Italian-born Spanish royal chaplain and historian. Another eyewitness account of the Aztec game was offered by Fray Diego Durán in his *Historia de las Indias de la Nueva España e Islas de Tierra Firma (History of the Indies of New Spain)* of circa 1580. Modern athletes of Aztec and Maya descent have attempted to revive the game in the late 20th century, without human sacrifice.

SPORTS AND RECREATION—*continued*

5596. Ball court known to archeologists was a court for *tlachtli,* a ball game indigenous to Mesoamerica. The court was discovered in 1995 by a team of archeologists excavating Paso de la Amada, a village in Chiapas, Mexico, and has been dated to circa 1400 BCE, some 500 years older than the oldest previously known *tlachtli* court, also found in Mexico. The design of the Chiapas court was very similar to those of courts dating from as late as the 16th century CE: two long earthen platforms with slanted walls enclosing a narrow playing field. In the basic game, two teams vied to pass a rubber ball past a centerline without using their hands or feet.

5597. Lacrosse was played by Native Americans of the northeastern part of North America from as early as 1000 CE. Called *baggataway* or *tewaraathon,* it was played with a wooden stick with a curve or loop that held a net made of animal skin. The ball was made of animal hide stuffed with hair. Team sizes and rules of play differed from tribe to tribe, with some groups providing extensive training and coaching for their athletes. The rules of modern lacrosse were codified in 1867 by a Canadian, George W. Beers.

5598. Field hockey was played in various forms in ancient Egypt, Persia, Greece, and Rome, and a somewhat similar stick-and-ball game was invented by the Aztecs of Mexico. The first modern men's field hockey club was Blackheath, founded circa 1861 in London, England.

5599. Thomas Cup in badminton was awarded in 1949 to Malaya (now Malaysia). The Thomas Cup, the world trophy in badminton, was donated in 1939 by George Thomas, president of the International Badminton Federation.

5600. Sky-diving championships were held in 1951 in Yugoslavia under the auspices of the Fédération Aéronautique Internationale.

5601. Angler to hold world records for every billfish species was an American, Deborah Maddux Dunaway. She held International Game Fish Association world records for every species of billfish found in the Atlantic and Pacific oceans. Dunaway earned this distinction in 1993 when, after a 3.5-hour struggle, she caught a 26.5‡pound (12-kilogram) short-billed spearfish off Kona, HI, USA.

SPORTS AND RECREATION—AIR RACING

5602. International balloon race was the James Gordon Bennett race, inaugurated in Paris, France, in 1906. Bennett, the founding publisher of the *New York Herald,* offered an international trophy for annual long-distance flights. The race has been held in the United States since 1983.

5603. International airplane race was the Bennett Trophy race, held at Reims, France, from August 22 to 28, 1909. The sponsor was American newspaper publisher James Gordon Bennett.

5604. Air race from England to Australia was the Great London-to-Australia Air Derby, sponsored by Australian prime minister W.M. "Billy" Hughes and held in 1919. A prize of £10,000 was offered to the first Australians to complete the 11,000-mile (17,699-kilometer) journey in 30 days or less. Six planes competed. The race was won by Australian pilots Ross and Keith Smith and mechanics Jim Bennett and Wally Shiers, flying a twin-engine Vickers Vimy biplane.

SPORTS AND RECREATION—ARENAS

5605. Olympic stadium was built in Olympia, Greece, for the original Olympic Games, held from at least 776 BCE (the date of the first Olympic competition to be documented) through 394 CE. The stadium was a flat track, 660 feet (200 meters) long and 100 feet (30 meters) wide, where the footrace was held. (The Greek word *stade,* from which the word "stadium" is derived, refers to the length of the course.) Raised areas on either side—one a natural hill, the other a manmade mound—afforded seating for spectators. Nearby was the hippodrome, for horse racing, and the Altris, a sacred grove of trees.

5606. Giant sports arena was the Circus Maximus in Rome, an open-air structure with seats on three sides, originally used for chariot races and later for contests pitting humans against wild animals. In the first century BCE, during the time of Julius Caesar, it could hold 150,000 people. It was repeatedly enlarged until the time of the Emperor Constantine (306–337), when it seated an estimated 250,000 spectators and measured about 2,000 by 600 feet (610 by 190 meters).

5607. Full-size stadium with retractable roof was the SkyDome stadium in downtown Toronto, Ontario, Canada, which was opened to the public on June 3, 1989. The steel retractable roof consists of three movable panels, of which one rotates 180 degrees while the others telescoped straight forward. The panels run on a system of steel tracks and 76 bogies, each powered by 10-horsepower motors. The panels move at a rate of 71 feet (22 meters) per minute and require about ten minutes to open or close. The roof spans 8 acres (3 hectares), rises 282 feet (86 meters) at its highest point from the level of the field, and encloses a volume of 56.5 million cubic feet (1.6 million cubic meters). Along with the sports arena, which has seating for 58,000 spectators, the SkyDome houses an in-house hotel, restaurants, and a retail mall. It was funded by the province of Ontario and Metro Toronto and by a consortium of 28 companies.

5608. Portable velodrome of Olympic size was the 110-ton cycle velodrome used at the 1996 Olympic Games in Atlanta, Georgia, USA. The modular track, which met all the official requirements of a permanent bicycle track, could be disassembled in sections and moved to another venue.

SPORTS AND RECREATION—BASEBALL

5609. Baseball probably developed from the English game of rounders, which received its first mention in 1744 in the children's book *A Little Pretty Pocket-Book*. Rounders developed in the USA into a game called town ball (also known as cat ball). It was given its modern form in the 1840s by Alexander Joy Cartwright of New York, NY, USA, the man who laid out the diamond-shaped baseball field and came up with the rule allowing a baseman to tag a runner out. The story of the invention of baseball in Cooperstown, NY, USA, by Abner Doubleday is a myth.

5610. Baseball team was the Knickerbocker Club of New York, organized on September 23, 1845, in New York, NY, USA, by Alexander Joy Cartwright. Duncan F. Curry was the club's first president. The club played its first game in June 1846, losing 23–1. A previous team that played an earlier form of baseball was the Olympic Club of Philadelphia, PA, which played town ball from July 4, 1833, to the year 1860, when they changed to standard baseball.

5611. Rules for baseball standardizing the game were adopted in May 1858 in New York City, NY, USA, by the National Baseball Association. The rules provided that the bat was not to exceed 2.5 inches in diameter and the ball 10.5 inches in circumference, the latter to weigh 6.5 ounces. The game was to last nine innings or until one team won 21 runs. Previously each team had played under its own set of rules. Three delegates from each of the following clubs attended the meeting: Atlantic, Baltic, Bedford, Continental, Eagle, Empire, Excelsior, Eckford, Gotham, Harmony, Knickerbocker, Nassau, Olympic, Putnam, and Union.

5612. Racial integration of professional baseball was achieved in Canada a year before it was in the United States, and by the same player, Jackie Robinson. In 1946, Robinson became the first African-American player to join the Montreal Royals farm club, leading the team to the crown of the Little World Series. The following year he moved to New York, NY, USA, to join the Brooklyn Dodgers, who named him the season's rookie of the year. He won the Most Valuable Player award in 1949.

5613. Little League World Series was played in 1947 in Williamsport, PA, USA, where Little League was invented. The first Little League World Series title to be forfeited was played in Williamsport in August 1992. The winning team, from Zamboanga, the Philippines, was stripped of the championship after league officials learned that it had violated the rules by fielding many over-age players, a number of whom were not from Zamboanga. The title was awarded to their opponents, a team from Long Beach, CA, USA.

5614. Little League baseball teams outside the United States were chartered in Canada in 1951. The first leagues were located in Cape Breton, Nova Scotia, and Vancouver, British Columbia. By 2000, Little League Baseball involved 3 million children ages 6 through 18 in more than 80 countries.

5615. Major-league American baseball teams to play in Communist Cuba were the Cincinnati Reds and the Los Angeles Dodgers, who played each other in Havana, Cuba, in March 1959, shortly after the Cuban Communist revolution in which Fidel Castro seized power. Castro himself was a great fan of the game and was known as a talented pitcher. Relations quickly soured between the two countries, and a major-league American team did not play again in Cuba until March 28, 1999, when the Baltimore Orioles defeated an all-star Cuban team 3–2 in Havana's Latinoamericano Stadium.

SPORTS AND RECREATION—BASE-BALL—*continued*

5616. Team from outside the United States to win the World Series was the Toronto Blue Jays, a Canadian team, who beat the Atlanta Braves in six games to win the 89th World Series in October 1992. Games 1, 2, and 6 were played at Atlanta–Fulton County Stadium in Atlanta, GA, USA; Games 3, 4, and 5 were played at the SkyDome in Toronto, Canada. Each of the first two games was won on a home run by a backup catcher: Damon Berryhill of Atlanta in Game 1, and Ed Sprague of Toronto in Game 2. Four of the six games in the series were decided by a single run, and three of them were won in the winner's final at-bat.

SPORTS AND RECREATION—BASKET-BALL

5617. Basketball was invented in 1891 by James Naismith, a physical education instructor at the International Young Men's Christian Association Training School (now called Springfield College) in Springfield, MA, USA, who had been asked by his department head to devise an indoor team game that would be exciting but not brutal. Naismith's game was originally played with peach baskets mounted on poles. It was necessary for the players to use a ladder to remove the ball from the basket. The first game was played at the YMCA gymnasium in December 1891. The first public game was played on March 11, 1892. Similar games were played by the Olmec in Mexico many centuries earlier.

5618. Rules for basketball were published on January 15, 1892, in *The Triangle,* the school newspaper of the International Young Men's Christian Association Training School, Springfield, MA, USA. The author was James Naismith, the teacher who invented the game. The rules were standardized in 1894.

5619. Basketball in the Philippines was played in 1905 when the sport was introduced to girls by American physical education teachers at the Young Men's Christian Association center in Manila.

SPORTS AND RECREATION—BICY-CLING

5620. Bicycle was a wooden vehicle known as the *draisienne,* after its inventor, Baron Karl de Drais de Sauerbrun. Though it had wheels, it had no pedals. Riders had to push their feet against the ground to make the vehicle move forward. It was shown to the public in Paris, France, in April 1818.

5621. Bicycle capable of speed was made in Dumfriesshire, Scotland, in 1839 by a blacksmith, Kirkpatrick Macmillan. It was operated by a pair of cranks, swung back and forth by the rider's feet, which worked a set of levers that rotated the iron-rimmed wheels. The bicycle won a race against a post carriage in 1842.

5622. Bicycle with rotating pedals was the *vélocipède,* built in 1861 in Paris, France, by Pierre and Ernest Michaux, father and son. The machine had a wood and iron frame and foot-powered cranks that were modeled on the design of a vertical grindstone.

5623. Bicycle with spoked wheels was made in 1861 by James Starley, foreman at the Coventry Sewing Machine Company, Coventry, England, which had undertaken to produce 400 "velocipedes." In addition to introducing a new design, with a high front wheel and a small back wheel, Starley made his bicycles lighter by equipping their iron wheels with tautened wire spokes. His lightest machines weighed about 21 pounds. Earlier machines weighed as much as 160 pounds.

5624. International bicycle race was staged on May 31, 1868. The course of 3,936 feet (1,200 meters) was laid out in St.-Cloud Park, near Paris, France, and attracted competitors from around Europe. The winner was an English cyclist, James Moore. The first bicycling world championships were held in 1893 for amateurs and in 1895 for professional cyclists.

5625. Bicycle road race took place in France in November 1869, when some 200 riders set out on a course from Rouen to Paris, a distance of 83 miles (133.57 kilometers). James Moore, an English cyclist who had already won the first international bicycle race on record, reached the goal after 10 hours 25 minutes.

5626. Pneumatic tires for bicycles were patented in 1888 by the Scottish inventor John Boyd Dunlop, who was then a veterinary surgeon in Belfast, Ireland.

5627. International bicycling association was the International Cyclist Association, founded in 1892 by cyclists from England, France, Belgium, Denmark, the Netherlands, Germany, Canada, and the United States.

5628. Tour de France was established in 1903 by the French reporter and cycling enthusiast Henri Desgrange. Considered the most prestigious road race in cycling, it runs about 2,500 miles (4000 kilometers) through France, Belgium, Spain, Italy, Germany, and Switzerland. The first winner was a Frenchman, Maurice Garin.

5629. Recumbent bicycle of importance was the two-wheel Velocar, designed and built by French inventor Charles Mochet. Mochet had sold a four-wheeled pedalcar with some success in the 1920s, but found that the fastest and most stable design was a two-wheeled version, developed circa 1930, that was similar to the long-wheelbase recumbent bicycle designs of the late 20th century. Riding a Velocar, Paul Morand won the Paris–Limoges race in 1933, the first race won with such a vehicle, and on July 7, 1933, Francis Faure set a new world record by riding a Velocar 27.9 miles (45.055 kilometers) in an hour. Recumbents were permanently banned from world bicycle racing on April 1, 1934, in a controversial decision by the 58th Congress of the Union Cycliste International.

5630. Bicyclist to go faster than 50 miles per hour in a certified speed trial was bicyclist Fred Markham. On May 6, 1979, in a men's 200-meter flying start speed trial for solo riders held by the International Human Powered Vehicle Association in Ontario, Canada, Markham pedaled a Gardner Martin-designed recumbent bicycle, the "Easy Racer," to a speed of 50.84 miles (81.82 kilometers) per hour.

SPORTS AND RECREATION—BOBSLED

5631. Bobsled competition took place in 1898 on the Cresta Run at St. Moritz, Switzerland. The first modern bobsled design had been developed in St. Moritz in 1888.

5632. Bobsled world championship was the four-man bobsled competition in the first Olympic Winter Games, held in 1924 at Chamonix, France. Two-man bobsled championships began in 1931.

SPORTS AND RECREATION—BOWLING

5633. Bowling game is known from an Egyptian child's tomb of circa 2500 BCE. The grave contained nine pins and a stone ball. The ball was rolled under three arches before striking the pins.

5634. Bowling game in modern times evolved from a religious ritual performed in local churches in what is now Germany, possibly as early as the fourth century. To encourage a feeling of victory over sin, monks would set up a wooden club in a passageway of the cloister and try to knock it over by rolling a stone at it. The club was called a *kegil* in Old High German, giving rise to the modern English term "kegler" for "bowler."

5635. Indoor bowling lane for recreational bowling was constructed circa 1455 in London, England.

5636. International bowling competition was held in Hannover, Germany, circa 1891.

SPORTS AND RECREATION—BOXING

5637. Boxing dates from the ancient Greek world circa 1500 BCE, before the time of the Trojan War; it is mentioned as a sport in Homer's *Iliad,* believed to date to circa 800 BCE. Boxing was made part of the ancient Olympic Games circa 688 BCE.

5638. Boxing gloves are visible on the earliest Greek depictions of boxers, from circa 1500 BCE. They were wrappings of soft leather and were meant to protect the hand. The Romans later introduced knobbed leather mitts that were designed for bludgeoning.

5639. Boxing bout since ancient times was held in England in 1681. Regular bareknuckle matches were held in Lodnon beginning in 1698.

5640. Heavyweight boxing champion was the English bareknuckle fighter James Figg, whose career lasted from circa 1719 to 1730. The 6-foot (1.8-meter) boxer weighed in at 185 pounds (84 kilograms) and is believed to have only lost one match.

5641. School of pugilism was Figg's Amphitheatre, opened in London, England, circa 1730 by James Figg, the world's first heavyweight boxing champion. Figg taught boxing as well as wrestling, swordfighting, and cudgeling.

5642. Boxing rules were developed by the English prizefighter Jack Broughton, a pupil of the first heavyweight champion, Jack Figg In 1743, he devised a set of rules that barred holds and blows below the waist and hitting a man after he was down. Broughton's rules were superseded in 1838 by the London Prize Ring rules. Broughton was also the first to introduced padded gloves to the sport. In his last fight, he was blinded in both eyes by a backhand punch.

5643. Boxer to emphasize skill over brute strength was the Jewish fighter Daniel Mendoza, of London, England, who became the English heavyweight champion in 1791. His boxing style combined good timing, rapid punching, and decisive use of opportunities, rather than old-fashioned brawling.

5644. World heavyweight boxing championship was held on April 17, 1860, at Farnborough, Hampshire, England, between American boxer John C. Heenan and British champion Tom Sayers. The 42-round fight ended when both fighters were too bloodied to continue and the crowd broke into the ring.

SPORTS AND RECREATION—BOXING— *continued*

5645. Amateur boxing championships were held in 1867 in England under the Marquis of Queensberry rules. The first championships under an amateur governing body were staged in 1881 by the British Amateur Boxing Association.

5646. Asian boxer to win a world championship was the Philippine fighter Pancho Villa, who won the flyweight title in 1923.

5647. World heavyweight champion to regain his title after losing it was the African-American boxer Floyd Patterson, who first won the title after knocking out Archie Moore in five rounds in Chicago, IL, USA, on November 30, 1956. Ingemar Johansson of Sweden took the championship by downing Patterson in three rounds in New York City on June 26, 1959. On June 20, 1960, Patterson knocked out Johansson in a rematch in New York, becoming the first person ever to win the world heavyweight boxing championship twice.

SPORTS AND RECREATION—BULL-FIGHTING

5648. Bullfighting dates from the Minoan period (circa 3000–1100 BCE) on Crete (part of present-day Greece), according to colorful frescoes that show Cretan boys and girls leaping over the sharp horns of bulls.

5649. Running of the bulls in Pamplona, Spain, took place in July 1521. The practice is an integral part of the city's Fiesta de San Fermín, which begins on July 6 and honors Pamplona's patron saint, its first bishop. In the *encierro* ("enclosing") of the bulls, crowds of boys and men (rarely women) run before a herd of bulls being driven down the city's narrow streets. Anyone who is insufficiently agile runs the risk of being trampled and gored. Most of the bulls later die in the bullfights held daily during the festival.

5650. Matador of renown was the 18th-century bullfighter Francisco Romero of Málaga, Spain. Romero is said to have first used the bullfighter's red cape, the *muleta,* as early as 1726, and was the first to kill a bull face to face.

5651. Permanent bullring in modern times was built in Madrid, Spain, in 1743.

5652. Bullfighting school was founded in 1830 by Pedro Romero in Seville, Spain. Pedro, the grandson of renowned matador Francisco Romero, claimed to have killed 5,600 bulls in the ring.

5653. Woman bullfighter of renown in Europe was Cristina Sánchez of Spain. On May 25, 1996, at the 23,000-seat bullring, Las Ventas, in Madrid, she became a *matador de toros* after killing a huge bull, Pocabarbos. She was the first woman in the history of European bullfighting to take the *alternativa* (the occasion on which a matador kills his or her first bull), the rite of passage after which a bullfighter is considered established.

SPORTS AND RECREATION—CRICKET

5654. Cricket match was probably played in 1679 in Sussex, England. The records show that two eleven-man teams (the standard team size in modern cricket) met there; the winning team took home a prize of 50 guineas. Rules for cricket may have been codified as early as 1709, the date of the first intercounty match. Cricket is played primarily in the former British colonies, including India, South Africa, the West Indies, Australia, New Zealand, Pakistan, Sri Lanka, and Zimbabwe (formerly the British colony of Rhodesia).

5655. Cricket club was the Hambledon Club, founded circa 1750. Matches were held in Hampshire, England, on Broadhalfpenny Down. The Marylebone Cricket Club, formed in London in 1787, soon eclipsed the Hambledon Club in importance and is today the international governing body of the sport.

5656. Sahara Cup cricket contest was a five-match cricket series played in September 1996 by teams from India and Pakistan. It was hosted in Toronto, Canada, by the Toronto Cricket, Skating and Curling Club. The first officially approved international cricket matches to be held in Canada, the Sahara Cup was broadcast to 2 billion people on three continents. Pakistan won the series despite being 1–2 down.

SPORTS AND RECREATION—CROQUET

5657. Croquet developed from the French mallet-and-hoop game of paille-maille (or pall-mall), played from at least the 13th century. The modern English form of the game, also called association croquet, was invented in England in 1857.

5658. World croquet championships were held in 1989 at the Hurlingham Club, London, England.

SPORTS AND RECREATION—FOOTBALL (AMERICAN)

5659. International football game was played on December 6, 1873, in New Haven, CT, USA. The team from Yale University defeated a team from Eton College, England, with a score of two goals to one.

5660. Professional football game was played on September 3, 1895, in Latrobe, PA, USA, between the Latrobe Young Men's Christian Association and the Jeannette Athletic Club, Jeannette, PA, USA, which Latrobe won 12–0. Latrobe's captain was Harry Ryan and Jeannette's was "Posie" Flowers. Since the regular quarterback was unable to play, John K. Brallier of Indiana, PA, USA, was paid US$10 and expenses to fill in. The following year four men were paid, and in 1897 the entire team was paid.

5661. World championship professional football game was played on December 17, 1933, at Wrigley Field, Chicago, IL, USA, between two American teams. The Chicago Bears of the Western Division defeated the New York Giants of the Eastern Division of the National Football League 23–21.

5662. Super Bowl football game between the National Football League and the American Football League for the world championship was played on January 15, 1967, at the Memorial Coliseum, Los Angeles, CA, USA, before 63,036 spectators. The Green Bay Packers (NFL) defeated the Kansas City Chiefs (AFL) 35–10. The winning Packers received US$15,000 each, the Chiefs US$7,500 each.

SPORTS AND RECREATION—GOLF

5663. Golf course appears to have been the Old Course at St. Andrews, Fife, Scotland. Although the Royal and Ancient Golf Club (originally called the Society of St. Andrews Golfers) was not founded there until 1754, most historians of the sport believe that people were playing golf at St. Andrews as early as the 15th century. A 1457 parliamentary decree required that "Fute-ball and Golfe be utterly cryed downe," apparently because the Scots preferred those sports to archery practice. The Royal and Ancient Golf Club, known as the R. and A., is now the foremost golfing authority in the world.

5664. Golfer known by name was King James IV of Scotland, who ruled from 1488 to 1513. Although in 1491 he enacted a decree suppressing both golf and football (rugby), the account books of the Lord High Treasurer from the first decade of the 1500s contain an entry for purchase of "golf clubbis and ballis" for the king.

5665. Woman to play golf of record was Mary, Queen of Scots. In 1567, she caused an uproar by playing the game a few days after her husband's murder.

5666. Golfing association was the Company of Gentlemen Golfers, now called the Honourable Company of Edinburgh Golfers, headquartered at Muirfield in East Lothian, Scotland. It was founded in Edinburgh in 1744 by "several Gentlemen of Honour skillful in the ancient and healthfull exercise of Golf." John Rattray, a local surgeon, was the first winner of the Company's annual competition. The first set of rules for golf were set down in the minutes of the organization in 1751.

5667. Golf course outside Scotland was the Royal North Devon Club, founded in England in 1864.

5668. Women's golf tournament was held on June 13, 1893, at Royal Lytham, England.

5669. Winner of the Grand Slam was the American amateur Bobby Jones, born Robert Tyre Jones, Jr., in Atlanta, GA, USA. In 1930 Jones won the British Open and British Amateur and the U.S. Open and U.S. Amateur championships, having already won nine championships in those tournaments beginning in 1923.

SPORTS AND RECREATION—GYMNASTICS

5670. Gymnastics club was founded in Berlin, Germany, in 1811 by Friedrich Ludwig Jahn, a high school teacher. Jahn was convinced that his country's military security depended on producing young people who were both physically fit and intensely patriotic. His club, called the *turnverein* ("gymnastics society"), served both purposes. Similar clubs were opened in other German cities until 1819, when gymnastics was banned by the government. Gymnastics equipment invented by Jahn included the parallel bars, the side horse, the vaulting horse, the horizontal bar, the rings, and the balance beam.

5671. Gymnastics treatise was *Deutsche Turnkunst zur Einrichtung der Turnplätze (A Treatise on Gymnastics)*, written by Friedrich Ludwig Jahn, the founder of modern gymnastics, and Ernst Eiselen. It was published in Germany in 1816.

5672. Trampoline of modern design was developed in 1936 by the American gymnast George Nissen.

SPORTS AND RECREATION—GYMNASTICS—*continued*

5673. Uneven parallel bars used in international competition were demonstrated in the gymnastic program of the 1936 Summer Olympic Games in Berlin, Germany. The apparatus is 7 feet 11 inches (2.4 meters) high at the top bar. The lower bar is 5 feet 3 inches (1.6 meters) high. The first gold medalist in the uneven bars was Margit Korondi of Hungary, who scored 19.400 in the event at the 1952 Summer Olympic Games in Helsinki, Finland.

5674. Trampoline international competition was held as part of the Pan-American Games of 1955. West Germany (now part of unified Germany) hosted the first open international trampolining competition in 1962, and the first world championships took place in England in 1964.

5675. International trampoline governing body was the International Trampoline Association, founded in 1964 in England following the first world trampoline championships.

SPORTS AND RECREATION—HANDBALL

5676. Handball-style game was thermae, a form of the game played against the walls of the public baths (also called *thermae*) of ancient Rome circa 100 CE.

5677. International handball match was held in 1887 between Philip Casey, the Irish-born American national champion, and John Lawlor, the Irish national champion. The first game was in Ireland on August 4, and the last in the United States on November 29. Casey won eleven games to six.

SPORTS AND RECREATION—HORSE RACING

5678. Horse races held regularly were part of the ancient Olympic Games, held at Olympia, in the ancient Greek city-state of Elis. Four-hitch chariot and bareback races were held from circa 700 BCE. By that date, horse racing was also a popular sport in North Africa, Persia, central Asia, and China, although there are no reliable records of races regularly held.

5679. Irish racing probably developed from horse races run as early as 50 CE at the Curragh (from the Gaelic *cuireach,* or racecourse), a plain of 5,000 pastoral acres in what is now County Kildare, Ireland. There is written evidence of chariot races held there in the third century. A Curragh breeding society was established in 1760. In the late 20th century, the Curragh Racecourse and Training Grounds was the center of Irish racing and breeding. Its modern flat track hosted the annual running of the Irish Derby (now the Budweiser Irish Derby).

5680. Racing purse of record was £40, offered to English knights competing in a 3-mile (4.8-kilometer) race held circa 1190, during the reign of Richard I the Lion-Heart.

5681. Thoroughbreds known as such were three Arabian stallions, the Byerly Turk, the Darley Arabian, and the Godolphin Barb, all named after their owners. The horses were brought to England between 1689 and 1730 and sired numerous racers. Nearly all modern thoroughbreds are descended from them. These, however, were not the first Arabians brought to Britain. Roman horse breeders brought Arab and Barb horses to the islands before 250 CE, and in the first half of the 17th century, 43 mares—the so-called Royal Mares—formed a breeding stock whose descendants were the first to be entered in the General Stud Book.

5682. English Derby was run on May 4, 1780, at Epsom Downs, Surrey, England, over a course of 1.5 miles (2.4 kilometers). The race was named for Edward Stanley, the twelfth earl of Derby. The modern race is limited to three-year-old colts and fillies, and is run the first Wednesday in June.

5683. Stakes horse race in North America was the King's Plate, first run at Trois-Rivières, Quebec, Canada, in June 1836. It carried a purse of 50 guineas put up by King William IV, and was open to horses bred in the Lower-Canada province who had never won a stakes race before.

5684. Traveling van for horses was designed by an Englishman, Lord George Bentinck, to convey his racehorses from one racetrack to another, thus sparing them the fatigue of walking. The van, which was pulled by a team of post horses, was a padded box with room inside for two animals. It was first used in September 1836, when a thoroughbred named Elis was trundled more than 200 miles from Goodwood, Sussex, to Doncaster, Yorkshire, to run in the St. Leger race, which he won.

5685. Grand National Handicap Steeplechase was held in 1839 at Aintree, near Liverpool, England. Inaugurated by an innkeeper, William Lynn, it was called the Grand National from 1847. The race runs 4 miles 855 yards (7,180 meters), twice around a triangular course, and has 31 jumps (fences), some of which are extremely hazardous. Horses are handicapped at up to 12 stone 7 pounds (175 pounds, or 79 kilograms).

5686. Kentucky Derby was run at the Churchill Downs Course at Louisville, KY, USA, on May 17, 1875. The winner was Aristides, with Oliver Lewis as the jockey, who took the purse of US$2,850. Aristides covered the 1.5-mile (2.4-kilometer) course in 2 minutes 37.75 seconds.

5687. Flat horse race in North America was the Washington, DC, International, first held at Laurel Racetrack in Maryland, USA, in November 1952. The annual race is 1.5 miles (2.4 kilometers) long and is open to horses at least three years of age.

5688. Woman jockey in the Grand National steeplechase held in Great Britain was Charlotte Brew, who in 1977 rode her own horse, Barony Fort. The Grand National is held annually at Aintree, England.

5689. Winner of the Prix d'Amérique who was a woman was Swedish driver Helen Johansson, who won harness racing's most prestigious event in January 1996 at the Hippodrome de Vincennes, Paris, France. She was the first woman to compete in the event. Johansson was guiding Ina Scot, who had previously won 31 consecutive races in Sweden.

SPORTS AND RECREATION—ICE HOCKEY

5690. Ice hockey game played under rules similar to those of the present-day game was held in 1855 in Kingston, Ontario, Canada, by two teams from the Royal Canadian Rifle regiment.

5691. Ice hockey game played indoors was held in 1875 at the Victoria Skating Rink in Montreal, Canada. McGill University fielded both teams. According to an account in *The Daily British Whig,* the teams took time out from play to batter each other about the head and legs and smash the wooden benches, becoming so violent that "the lady spectators fled in confusion."

5692. Ice hockey rules were written down by W.F. Robertson, a student at McGill University in Montreal, Canada. He was a founder of the McGill University Hockey Club, the first ice hockey club, which was formed in 1877. Robertson's rules, derived from field hockey, called for nine players on a team and mandated the use of a square puck.

5693. Woman to become a professional hockey player was Manon Rheaume, a 20-year-old French Canadian goalie from Quebec, Canada. In September 1992, she became the first woman to play in a National Hockey League (NHL) game when she minded the net for an American team, the Tampa Bay Lightning, in the first period of an exhibition contest. She gave up two goals and made seven saves. She was later signed by Tampa Bay to a three-year contract with the club's minor-league affiliate, the Atlanta Knights.

SPORTS AND RECREATION—INTERNATIONAL GAMES

5694. Commonwealth Games were held in 1930 in Hamilton, Ontario, Canada, for competitors from the member nations of the British Commonwealth. These included the United Kingdom, Canada, Australia, New Zealand, and Jamaica. The Commonwealth Games were originally called the British Empire Games.

5695. Maccabiah Games for Jewish athletes of all nationalities were held in British Palestine (later Israel) in 1932. The Olympic-style games, which included track and field, water sports, boxing, polo, soccer, tennis, and other events, were sponsored by the World Maccabi Union, an international Jewish sports organization.

5696. Pan-American Games were held in Buenos Aires, Argentina, in 1951 under the auspices of the Organización Deportiva Panamericana, or Pan American Sports Organization, based in Mexico City, Mexico. The games were patterned after the Olympic Games and had the sanction of the International Olympic Committee but were limited to athletes from the countries of the Americas. At Buenos Aires, approximately 2,000 athletes from 20 nations participated in 19 sports. Forty-two nations participated in the 1999 games in Winnipeg, Canada.

5697. Special Olympics for athletes with mental disabilities was held on July 20, 1968, at Soldier Field in Chicago, IL, USA. Approximately 1,000 athletes took part in the games. By 1998, there were Special Olympics programs in 143 countries holding 16,000 sports events annually.

SPORTS AND RECREATION—INTERNATIONAL GAMES—*continued*

5698. Gay Games were held in San Francisco, CA, USA, beginning August 28, 1982, in the midst of a lawsuit by the United States Olympic Committee to ban the Games from using the name "Gay Olympics." They were organized by Tom Waddell, a decathlon competitor at the 1968 Olympic Games in Mexico City, to focus world attention on sports achievements by homosexual athletes. Ten countries—Australia, Belgium, Canada, England, France, Ireland, Israel, New Zealand, West Germany (now Germany), and the United States—fielded competitors in 17 athletic events. The Gay Games are held every four years, each time in a different city. The first to be held outside North America took place August 1–8, 1998, in Amsterdam, the Netherlands, with 15,000 participants competing in 29 events, including ice hockey, volleyball, body-building, swimming, and dancing.

5699. Nemean Games in modern times were held in Nemea, Greece, on June 1, 1996, in a newly restored stadium dating to the fourth-century BCE. Athletic festivals were held at Nemea by the ancient Greeks until shortly before the beginning of the Common Era.

SPORTS AND RECREATION—MARTIAL ARTS

5700. Depiction of swordsmen fencing is found at the funerary temple built circa 1190 BCE by Pharaoh Ramses III of Egypt at Medinat Habu. Among the reliefs that decorate the walls is one showing swordsmen engaged in a fencing match. They are shown wearing face, ear, and chest protectors and using swords with blunted points, indicating that the scene depicts sport or practice, rather than combat.

5701. Kung fu master is traditionally considered to be the Indian Buddhist priest Bodhidharma, known to the Chinese as Ta Mo and in Japan as Daruma Daishi, who arrived in the Honan Province of China circa 525 CE. There he established a school of self-defense at the Shaolin Ssu Monastery. Ta Mo's fighting style, dubbed kung fu (*gongfu* in Pinyin), the Chinese term for "skill," combined ancient forms of Chinese boxing with exercises from Indian yoga that were based on the movements of the 18 main animals in the Indo-Chinese iconography (the tiger, leopard, snake, dragon, crane, and others). Shaolin kung fu is considered by most historians of martial arts to be ancestral to the forms of karate later developed in China, Okinawa, Korea, and Japan.

5702. Fencing guild was the Association of St. Marcus, better known as the Marxbrüder, which was formed in Löwenburg, Germany, in the 15th century. It received official recognition from the Emperor Frederick III in 1480 and may have existed for a century before that.

5703. Capoeira practitioners were Angolan slaves brought to work Brazilian plantations by the Portuguese circa 1700. The gymnastic movements of capoeira fighting combined handstands, somersaults, and flips with much high-kicking. Adversaries often attacked each other with blades strapped to the feet. Modern forms of capoeira, practiced mainly in Brazil, are more dancelike, with close passing movements and high kicks timed to the music of the berimbau, or musical bow.

5704. Modern savaté was developed in Paris, France, by Charles Lecour in 1845. Lecour distilled this kick-boxing fighting art, which he called *la boxe française,* from two older forms of street fighting: *chausson marseillais,* which depended almost exclusively on high kicks, and savaté (Middle French for "old shoe,"), which used a combination of open-handed blows and low kicks. The first rulebook for the modern sport of savaté was published in 1899.

5705. Judo was developed from the ancient Japanese martial art jujutsu by Jigoro Kano, founder of the modern sport. Kano's first dojo, which he called the kodokan, was opened in Tokyo, Japan, in 1882. Judo was described by Kano as the way of "gentleness or giving way in order to ultimately gain the victory." The style involves throws, pins, holds, choke-holds and armlocks, and aims to turn the momentum and force of an opponent against him. It was first introduced to the Olympic Games in 1964.

5706. Aikido was developed in 1942 by the Japanese martial arts master Morihei Ueshiba, who combined techniques from jujutsu, Daito-ryu aikijutsu, and traditional Japanese sword and spear fighting. Noted for its flowing circular movements and emphasis on locking and throwing moves, aikido was intended as a purely spiritual and defensive art (*aikido* is Japanese for "way of spiritual harmony"). A later form of aikido, Tomiki aikido, was developed by Ueshiba's student Tomiki Kenji as a competition style; this is the form taught most widely today.

5707. Modern tae kwon do was developed in the 1940s and 1950s, chiefly by the South Korean general Choi Hong Hi, from the ancient Korean fighting style of tae kyon (developed circa 50 BCE), and from shotokan karate, imported from Japan during the Japanese occupation of Korea from 1910 to 1945. Choi Hong Hi named the style *tae kwon do* ("art of kicking and punching") in 1957. It is characterized by the use of high standing, spinning, and jumping kicks as well as hand blows. The first students of tae kwon do were the Korean military, but in 1965 the Korean Tae kwon do Association (later the World Tae kwon do Federation) was founded with Choi as president.

5708. World judo champion who was not Japanese was Anton Geesink of Utrecht, the Netherlands. He won the 1961 world championship in Tokyo, Japan, which was considered a stunning upset, and took the gold medal in judo in the 1964 Summer Olympics in Tokyo. Geesink won a third and final world title in 1965, as well as 13 European titles.

SPORTS AND RECREATION—MOTOR RACING

5709. Automobile race that was not merely a reliability test was held in France on June 11–14, 1895. The race course was a circuit of 732 miles (1,178 kilometers) from Paris to Bordeaux and back. The first to cross the finish line was Émile Levassor, driving a two-seater Panhard et Levassor at an average speed of 15 miles (24 kilometers) per hour. However, his car did not meet the race requirements, and he was disqualified.

5710. Closed-circuit road race was the Course de Périgueux, held in 1898 under the auspices of the Automobile Club de France. The race was a single lap of 90 miles (145 kilometers).

5711. Motorcycle race was held on September 20, 1898, under the auspices of the Automobile Club de France. Eight riders competed in the race, which followed a 94-mile (152-kilometer) course from Paris to Nantes and back. The winning time of 4 hours 10 minutes 37 seconds was clocked by a rider named Chevalier on a Michelin-Dion tricycle.

5712. Land speed record was set by the French driving enthusiast Count Gaston de Chasseloup-Laubat. On December 18, 1898, he set a world record of 39.24 miles (62.78 kilometers) per hour on the 2-kilometer course at Achères, France, with an electric vehicle.

5713. Driver to exceed 100 kilometers per hour was the Belgian auto racer Camille Jenatzy. On April 29, 1899, Jenatzy achieved a speed of 105.87 kilometers per hour (65.79 miles per hour) on the 2-kilometer course at Achères, France. The car was an electrically powered, torpedo-like vehicle named *La Jamais Contente* ("The Never-Satisfied").

5714. International road race was the Bennett Trophy race of 1901, organized by the Automobile Club de France. Three national automobile clubs competed for a prize offered by James Gordon Bennett, owner of the *New York Herald,* an American newspaper.

5715. Car to exceed 100 miles per hour was a Gobron Brillié driven by the French racer Louis Rigolly. In 1904, Rigolly reached a speed of 103.55 miles (166.6 kilometers) per hour at the track in Ostend, Belgium.

5716. Grand Prix race was run on June 27, 1906, at Le Mans, France. The winner was Ferenc Szisz of Hungary, who drove a Renault. Unlike the Bennett Trophy race, established in France in 1901, the Le Mans Grand Prix was open to manufacturers' teams rather than national teams.

5717. Motorcycle race of importance was the Tourist Trophy race, first run in 1907 on the Isle of Man. A short triangular course was set up, and stock touring cycles were used. In 1911, the course was lengthened to 37.75 miles (61 kilometers) and extended into the mountainous interior of the island. In 1911, the first trophies on the Mountain Circuit were awarded to P.J. Evans, who won the Junior 350cc riding a Humber at 41.45 miles (66.7 kilometers) per hour, and to O.C. Godfrey, who won the Senior 500cc on an Indian at 47.63 miles (76.6 kilometers) per hour.

5718. Rally race was sponsored in 1907 by the French daily newspaper *Le Matin.* The race started in Beijing, China, on June 10, 1907, and was won on August 11, when an Italian entry, the *Italia,* crossed the finish line in Paris, France, after traveling a distance of about 7,500 miles (12,000 kilometers). The cars were required to pass through a set of checkpoints along the route.

5719. Twenty-four-hour automobile endurance race was the Grand Prix d'Endurance, run on May 26–27, 1923, at Le Mans, France, site of the first Grand Prix race. It was won by the French team of A. Lagache and R. Leonard, who drove a Chenard-Walcker car. The race was organized by Georges Durand, Emile Coquille, and Charles Faroux.

5720. Rocket car was developed in 1928 by German industrialist and inventor Fritz von Opel, scion of the Opel car manufacturing company, with associates Max Valier and Friedrich Wilhelm Sander. The first test of the Opel-Rak 1, as the vehicle was called, took place on March 15, 1928.

SPORTS AND RECREATION—MOTOR RACING—*continued*

5721. Monocoque chassis for Formula 1 racing cars was introduced in 1963 for the Lotus 25, designed by Colin Chapman, for Lotus Cars Ltd., the British sports car manufacturer. The one-piece chassis, made of aluminum, added superior strength and stiffness while weighing less than a tubular chassis. Driven by Jim Clark, the Lotus 25 won seven Grand Prix and Lotus's first world championship.

5722. Racing car designed to take advantage of ground effects aerodynamics was the Formula 1 Lotus 78, built in 1976 by Lotus Cars Ltd. of England. The body included skirts that created a low-pressure zone underneath that kept the car "vacuumed" to the road. Side pods acted like inverted wings that further pressed the car onto the road. The result was much improved traction and tighter cornering. In 1978, the world championship was won by Lotus with Mario Andretti driving the 78's successor, the Lotus 79.

5723. Dakar Rallye was held in 1979. The race of 6626 miles (10,568 kilometers) was run from Paris, France, via Granada, Spain, to the Atlantic coast city of Dakar in Senegal. Motorcycle and car teams participated. The first winners were French biker Cyril Neveu on a Yamaha and the French team of Genestier/Terbiaut/LeMordant in a four-wheel-drive Range Rover. The prize money consisted of 1.7 million francs, plus bonuses offered by motor sport companies. Seven women on motorcycles also competed: Martine de Cortanze, Pascale Geurie, Martine Renier, Christine Martin-Lefort, Marie Ertaud, and Corrine Koppenhague.

5724. Race for solar-powered vehicles was the Pentax World Solar Challenge, first held in November 1987 along a 2,000-mile (3,100-kilometer) course from Darwin to Adelaide, Australia. It was the first transcontinental solar-powered vehicle race. The winner was the *Sunraycer,* built by General Motors of Detroit, MI, USA, at a cost of US$15 million. The *Sunraycer* completed the course 590 miles (950 kilometers) ahead of the other participants, at an average speed of 44 miles (71 kilometers) per hour.

5725. Car to break the sound barrier was a British-built rocket car, the *Thrust SSC,* powered by two Rolls-Royce engines generating 100,000 horsepower of thrust. On October 13, 1997, at a 13-mile (21-kilometer) course at the Black Rock Desert near Gerlach, NV, USA,

Royal Air Force pilot Andy Green drove the Thrust SSC to 764.138 miles (1,229.498 kilometers) per hour, slightly over Mach I, the speed of sound. Other teams had claimed to exceed the speed of sound in a land vehicle, but this was the first time the sound barrier had been broken with accredited independent third-party verification. The *Thrust SSC* was owned by Richard Noble.

SPORTS AND RECREATION—MOUNTAINEERING

5726. Account of mountain climbing of importance was written by the Italian poet Francesco Petrarca (Petrarch), who lived mainly in Italy from 1304 to 1374. In April 1336, "to see what so great an elevation had to offer," he climbed the peak of Mount Ventoux in Provence, France, which is 6,263 feet (1,909 meters) high. In a letter to the Augustinian monk Dionigi di San Sepolcro, he later wrote: "I stood like one dazed, I beheld the clouds under our feet, and what I had read of Athos and Olympus seemed less incredible as I myself witnessed the same things from a mountain less famous."

5727. Alpine mountaineer was Horace-Bénédict de Saussure, professor of physics and philosophy at the Academy of Geneva in Switzerland. Beginning in 1760, he made a series of pioneering ascents in the Swiss Alps. His *Voyages dans les Alpes (Travels in the Alps),* published in several volumes between 1779 and 1796, introduced the word "geology" into scientific nomenclature.

5728. Ascent of Mont Blanc was achieved on August 8, 1786, by two Frenchmen, the physician Michel-Gabriel Baccard and his porter, Jacques Balmat. At 15,782 feet (4,807 meters), Mont Blanc, which spans territory between France and Switzerland, is the highest mountain in western Europe. The climbers collected a reward for the feat from French naturalist Horace Bénédict de Saussure, who climbed the mountain himself the following year.

5729. Alpine mountaineer who was a woman was Maria Paradis of Chamonix, Switzerland, who reached the summit of Mont Blanc, the highest peak in western Europe, on July 14, 1808. The idea was suggested to her by Jacques Balmat, who had participated in the first successful ascent of the mountain some 22 years earlier.

5730. Ascent of the Matterhorn was achieved on July 14, 1865, by a seven-man British team led by English mountaineer Edward Whymper, who had made seven previous attempts. The climb turned deadly on the descent when one climber slipped and pulled down three more to their deaths. Whymper and two guides were saved only because the rope broke. The Matterhorn, which at 14,692 feet (4,478 meters) high is the third highest mountain in western Europe, is located in the Pennine Alps on the border between Switzerland and Italy.

5731. Ascent of Mount Elbrus in the Caucasus Range in Russia, the highest point on the continent of Europe, took place in 1868, when a British team reached the lower of the twin peaks. The higher one was climbed in 1874. Elbrus is an extinct volcano 18,510 feet (5,642 meters) high.

5732. Ascent of Mount Kilimanjaro was made in 1889 by a team led by the German geographer Hans Meyer. They conquered the 19,340-foot (5,895-meter) summit of Kibo, the taller of the snowcapped volcano's two peaks. Kilimanjaro is the highest mountain in Africa and is located in northeastern Tanzania.

5733. Ascent of Aconcagua in the Andes range was made by the Swiss mountaineer Matthias Zürbriggen in 1897, 14 years after it was first attempted. Mount Aconcagua, in Argentina, is the highest mountain in South America and the highest in the Western Hemisphere, rising 22,834 feet (6,960 meters) above sea level.

5734. Ascent of Mount Kenya by Europeans was achieved by a party under the leadership of the British geographer Sir Halford John Mackinder, who reached the summit in 1899. Mount Kenya (Kirinyaga in Swahili), Africa's second-highest mountain, is located in central Kenya. It is an extinct volcano 17,058 feet (5,199 meters) high.

5735. Ascent of Mount McKinley (Denali) in the Alaska Range was made in 1913 by a six-member American team led by Hudson Stuck. Mount McKinley, in the state of Alaska, USA, is 20,320 feet (6,194 meters) high, the highest peak in North America.

5736. Ascent of Annapurna in the Himalaya was accomplished on the first attempt, in the spring of 1950, by a French expedition led by Maurice Herzog. On June 3, Herzog and Louis Lachenal reached the summit, 26,504 feet (8,078 meters) above sea level. The climb cost Herzog all his fingers and toes, which were frostbitten. The world's tenth highest mountain, Annapurna is located in Nepal. It was the first peak higher than 8,000 meters to be climbed.

5737. Ascent of Mount Everest was achieved by Edmund Percival Hillary of New Zealand and the Nepalese Sherpa mountaineer Tenzing Norgay, two members of an expedition sponsored by the Royal Geographical Society and the Joint Himalayan Committee of the Alpine Club. The expedition, outfitted with special cold-weather gear and breathing equipment for the thin atmosphere, headed up the Khumbu Icefall and Glacier, the West Cwm, and the Lhotse Face to the South Col, where the highest of their eight camps was established. On May 29, 1953, Hillary and Norgay climbed the Southeast Ridge to the summit. Mount Everest is called Chomolungma in Tibetan and Sagarmatha in Nepali; both names mean "Goddess Mother of the World.". It is the highest point on earth, rising 29,028 feet (8,848 meters) from the Great Himalaya Range between Nepal, Tibet, and China. The first attempt to climb the mountain was made in 1921.

5738. Ascent of Nanga Parbat (Diamir) in the Himalaya was completed by Herman Buhl, part of a two-man German team, on July 3, 1953, when he crawled to the summit after a 17-hour final push. The first attempt on Nanga Parbat, the world's ninth highest mountain, was made in 1895. It rises to 26,660 feet (8,126 meters) in Kashmir, in territory claimed by both India and Pakistan.

5739. Ascent of K2 (Mount Godwin Austen) was led by the Italian geologist Ardito Desio in 1954. His team of Italian climbers consisted of five scientists, a doctor, a photographer, and twelve others. Two of the climbers, Achille Compagnoni and Lino Lacedelli, followed the Abruzzi Ridge route and reached the summit on July 31, 1954. K2, at 28,250 feet (8,611 meters) tall, is the world's second highest mountain. In 1856, T.G. Montgomerie of the British Survey of India became the first European to see it. He gave the peak the designation K2 because it was the second mountain to be surveyed in the Karakoram Range. Its local names are Dapsang and Chogori. It is located in Kashmir, in territory disputed by India and Pakistan. The first attempt to climb the peak was made in 1902 by a Swiss-British-Austrian team.

5740. Ascent of Cho Oyu in the Himalaya was made by two Austrian mountaineers, Herbert Tichy and Joseph Joechler, and a Sherpa climber, Pasang Dawa, who reached the summit on October 14, 1954, without using bottled oxygen. Cho Oyu stands in northeast Nepal, 26,750 feet (8,153 meters) high, the world's eighth highest mountain.

SPORTS AND RECREATION—MOUNTAINEERING—*continued*

5741. Ascent of Makalu in the Himalaya was accomplished in May 1955 by a French group under Jean Franco. Two team members, Jean Couzy and Lionel Terray, reached the summit on May 15, followed by the rest of the team on May 16. Makalu is located in northeast Nepal. It is the world's fifth highest peak, at 27,824 feet (8,481 meters) above sea level. The first attempt to climb it was made in 1954.

5742. Ascent of Kanchenjunga in the Himalaya was made in 1955 by a British team led by Charles Evans. On May 25, two climbers, Joe Brown and George Band, climbed almost to the summit, stopping seven feet short at the request of the government of Sikkim, where the mountain is held sacred. The third highest mountain in the world, Kanchenjunga stands 28,208 feet (8,598 meters) above sea level, on the border between Sikkim (now a state in India) and Nepal. The first attempt on Kanchenjunga was made in 1905 by a Swiss-French-British team, which lost four members in an avalanche.

5743. Ascent of Manaslu (Kutang) in the Himalaya was accomplished on May 9, 1956, by a twelve-member Japanese group led by Yuko Maki. Manaslu is the seventh highest peak in the world, rising to 26,760 feet (8,156 meters) in western Nepal.

5744. Ascent of Lhotse in the Himalaya was completed on May 18, 1956, by Ernst Reiss and Fritz Luchsinger, members of a Swiss team led by Albert Eggler. Lhotse is the fourth highest mountain in the world, reaching 27,923 feet (8,511 meters) above sea level on the border between Tibet and Nepal.

5745. Ascent of Dhaulagiri was completed on May 13, 1960, by sportswriter Max Eiselin and an eleven-member team. Dhaulagiri, in Nepal, is 26,810 feet (8,172 meters) above sea level, the sixth highest peak in the world. In 1802 it became the first of the Himalayan mountains to be identified as more than 25,000 feet high.

5746. Ascent of the Vinson Massif in Antarctica, 16,067 feet (4,897 meters) high and the highest point on the continent, was made on December 20, 1966, by a ten-member American expedition led by Nicholas Clinch.

5747. Woman to reach the summit of Mount Everest was the Japanese climber Tabei Junko, deputy leader of an all-female expedition. After surviving an avalanche that buried her under a huge block of ice, she reached the summit via the Southeast Ridge on May 16, 1975. She was accompanied by Ang Tsering of Nepal.

5748. Ascent of Mount Everest without bottled oxygen was achieved on the afternoon of May 8, 1978, by the Italian mountaineer Reinhold Messner and the Austrian mountaineer Peter Habeler. It was a feat long considered impossible, even by experienced mountaineers, who normally use containers of oxygen for breathing on the climb of 29,028 feet (8,848 meters). The two men suffered severe chest pains and extreme lethargy as the atmosphere thinned at the higher elevations. "I am nothing more than a single narrow gasping lung, floating over the mists and summits," wrote Messner in 1979, describing his sensations on reaching the summit.

5749. Solo ascent of Mount Everest was achieved by Reinhold Messner of Italy in 1980. He reached the summit, 29,028 feet (8,848 meters) above sea level, via the North Col to the North Face. Unlike most Everest climbers, Messner did not use contained oxygen for breathing, even at the highest elevations where the air is very thin. It was his second ascent of Everest without breathing apparatus.

5750. Mountaineer to ascend the world's three tallest peaks was the Italian climber Reinhold Messner. He reached the summit of Mount Everest, 29,028 feet (8,848 meters) in height, in 1978; of K2, 28,250 feet (8,611 meters) high, in 1979; and of Kanchenjunga, 28,208 feet (8,598 meters) high, in 1982. All of Messner's ascents were completed without breathing equipment. The three peaks are located in the Himalaya Range on the border between China and Nepal.

5751. Mountaineer to climb the highest peak on every continent was Dick Bass of Texas, USA, a wealthy amateur climber who paid more experienced climbers to guide him. In 1985, he reached the summit of Mount Everest, the highest point in Asia and in the world, with the help of David Breashears, an American mountaineer. Everest is 29,028 feet (8,848 meters) high. Bass had previously reached the tops of Mount Aconcagua in Argentina, South America (22,834 feet, 6,960 meters); Mount McKinley, also known as Denali, in Alaska, USA, North America (20,320 feet, 6,194 meters); Mount Kilimanjaro in Tanzania, Africa (19,340 feet, 5,895 meters); Mount Elbrus in Russia, Europe (18,510 feet, 5,642 meters); the Vinson Massif in Antarctica (16,067 feet, 4,897 meters); and Mount Kosciusko in Australia, considered to be part of Oceania (7,310 feet, 2,228 meters). Bass's claim was challenged by Patrick Morrow, a Canadian mountaineer who accomplished the same feat, substituting the Carstensz Pyramid, also called Puncak Jaya, in Indonesia (16,535 feet, 5,040 meters) for Mount Kosciusko, which is less than half its height.

5752. Man to climb all 14 of the world's tallest mountains was the Italian mountaineer Reinhold Messner. By 1986, he had reached the summits of every mountain in the world higher than 26,250 feet (8,000 meters), including Mount Everest. All the climbs were made without breathing apparatus, and usually without support climbers.

5753. Woman to climb Mount Everest solo without bottled oxygen was New Zealander Lydia Bradey, who reached the summit in 1988.

5754. Sherpa expedition to Everest was the 1991 Sherpa Everest Expedition, all of whose members belonged to the Sherpa ethnic enclave in Nepal. Sherpas have accompanied most Everest attempts as guides and porters.

5755. Woman to climb the highest peak on every continent was a French climber, Christine Janin. She climbed Mount Everest in Asia, Mount McKinley in North America, Mount Kilimanjaro in Africa, the Vinson Massif in Antarctica, Mount Elbrus in Europe, and the Carstensz Pyramid in Oceania. On December 25, 1992, she completed the feat by reaching the summit of Mount Aconcagua in South America.

SPORTS AND RECREATION—OLYMPIC GAMES

5756. Olympic Games were held at Olympia, in the ancient Greek city-state of Elis, traditionally dated to circa 1300 BCE. They were staged as part of a religious festival to honor Zeus, and according to legend were founded by Herakles, the son of Zeus and the mortal woman Alcmene. The first Olympic Games of which there are extensive records were the games of 776 BCE, which are said to have been founded by Herakles of Ida under the sponsorship of three kings: Iphitus of Elis, Lycurgus of Sparta, and Cleosthenes of Pisa.

5757. Olympic champion of record was Coroebus of Elis, a cook by profession. He was the winner of the 200-yard sprint race in the first documented Olympic Games, held in 776 BCE at Mount Olympus, near his hometown.

5758. Pentathlon was incorporated into the ancient Greek Olympic games in 708 BCE. It consisted of five events: the long jump, the javelin throw, the discus throw, a running race, and wrestling.

5759. Olympic games for women were the Heraea, athletic events for women in ancient Greece. They were administered by married women for maiden competitors and held every four years at the stadium at Olympia, in Elis, to honor Hera, the wife of Zeus. According to the Greek travel writer Pausanias, the games consisted of footraces, with "the course of the stadium shortened for [the maidens] by about one-sixth of its length." Pausanias added that "To the winning maidens they give crowns of olive and a portion of the cow sacrificed to Hera." The inauguration date of the Heraea Games is unknown, but Pausanias wrote of them circa 160 CE.

5760. Olympic Games in the modern era were proposed by the French educator and sportsman Baron Pierre de Coubertin in 1892, with the intention of building peaceful relations among nations. With financial support from George Averoff, an Egyptian businessman, the first modern Olympiad met in Athens, Greece, in April 1896. Teams were sent by eight European countries—Denmark, England, France, Germany, Greece, Hungary, and Switzerland. An unofficial team from the United States also participated, winning nine of the twelve track-and-field events. In addition, competitions were held in cycling, fencing, gymnastics, shooting, swimming, and tennis.

5761. Olympic marathon in modern times was run as part of the first modern Olympic games, held in Athens, Greece, in April 1896. The route, from the town of Marathon to the stadium in Athens, was planned as a tribute to Pheidippides, the legendary messenger of 490 BCE who brought the news of the Greek victory at Marathon over the Persians. The winner of the modern marathon was the Greek athlete Spiridon Loues.

5762. Olympic champion in the modern era was James B. Connolly, who received the first gold medal of the first modern Olympic Games on April 6, 1896, in Athens, Greece. He won the hop, step, and jump (now called the triple jump) with a jump of 45 feet. Connolly, a student at Harvard University in Cambridge, MA, USA, was one of ten American men who traveled to Athens to compete in the Olympic Games unofficially, since the United States had not yet organized a national Olympic Committee.

SPORTS AND RECREATION—OLYMPIC GAMES—*continued*

5763. Child to win a gold medal in the Olympic Games was a Dutch boy whose name was never recorded. He served as coxswain in the pair-oared shell rowed by R. Klein and F.A. Brandt in Paris, France, in 1900. The team set a record of 7 minutes 34.2 seconds that remained unbroken until 1960. The child, who was no older than ten, was substituted for an adult because he weighed less.

5764. Woman athlete to win an Olympic medal was the English tennis champion Charlotte Cooper. She won the women's singles lawn tennis competition at the 1900 Olympic Games in Paris, France, the first games in which women participated. Cooper was also a five-time singles winner at Wimbledon (1895, 1896, 1898, 1901, and 1908).

5765. Olympic Games in the Western Hemisphere were held in St. Louis, MO, USA, in 1904.

5766. Olympic Games to be canceled for political reasons were the Games of 1916. They could not be held because many of the nations of Europe were competing with each other on the battlefields of World War I.

5767. Athlete of African descent to win a gold medal in an individual event was the African-American track and field star William DeHart Hubbard, who won the long jump competition at the 1924 Summer Olympic Games in Paris, France, with a leap of 24 feet 5.125 inches (approximately 7.5 meters). At the 1908 Games in London, England, another African American, John Baxter Taylor, Jr., won a medal as a member of the American relay team running the 1,600-meter medley.

5768. Winter Olympic Games were held in 1924 in Chamonix, France. Fewer than 300 athletes from 16 countries competed in 16 events.

5769. Winter Olympic Games in the Western Hemisphere were the third Games, held in Lake Placid, NY, USA, in 1932. Participating were 274 men and 32 women athletes from 17 countries.

5770. Sportsman to win individual gold medals in four successive Olympic Games was Paul B. Elvstrom of Denmark, who captured the yachting event in the Firefly class in the 1948 summer Games and the Finn class in the Games of 1952, 1956, and 1960.

5771. Woman athlete of African descent to win a medal in the Olympic Games was Audrey Patterson, who earned a bronze medal in the 200-meter sprint at the 1948 Olympics in London, England.

5772. Woman athlete of African descent to win an Olympic gold medal was the American athlete Alice Coachman of Albany, GA, USA. At the 1948 Summer Olympics in London, England, she jumped 5 feet 6.125 inches (1.68 meters) in the women's high-jump competition on her first attempt, winning her the gold.

5773. Woman athlete to win four gold medals in one Olympic Games was the Dutch track and field athlete Francina Blankers-Koen of Amsterdam, the Netherlands. At the 1948 Summer Olympic Games in London, England, she won the 100-meter and 200-meter sprints and the 80-meter hurdles. She also shared a gold medal as the anchor of the Dutch team in the 100-meter relay. She was also the first mother to win Olympic gold.

5774. Gymnast to achieve a perfect score was the Swiss gymnast Hans Eugster, who scored a perfect 10.00 in the compulsory parallel bars event at the 1950 World Championships in Basel.

5775. Olympic marathon winner who had never run a marathon was the Czech runner Emil Zátopek, who won the event in the 1952 Olympic Games, held in Helsinki, Finland. Although he had never run the race before, he set an Olympic record of 2 hours 23 minutes 3.2 seconds over the 26 miles 385 yards (42,195 meters) of the course.

5776. Woman athlete to take the Olympic oath at the opening ceremony was Italian downhill skier Giuliana Chenal-Minuzzo, at the 1956 Winter Olympics in Cortina d'Ampezzo, Italy.

5777. Olympic Games in the Southern Hemisphere were held in November and December 1956 in Melbourne, Australia. Because of an Australian quarantine against the importation of horses, the equestrian events were held in Stockholm, Sweden.

5778. Olympic Games in Asia were held in 1964 in Tokyo, Japan. More than 5,000 athletes from 94 countries competed in 162 events.

5779. Person to win the same Olympic event three times was the Australian sprint-swimmer Dawn Fraser. She won the 100-meter freestyle event in the 1956, 1960, and 1964 Olympics and held the 100-meter world record of 58.9 seconds for 16 years, from February 29, 1964, to January 8, 1972.

5780. Runner to win the Olympic marathon twice was the Ethiopian athlete Abebe Bikila. In 1960, at the Summer Olympic Games in Rome, Italy, Bikila gave his native land its first Olympic medal by winning the marathon in a time of 2:15:17, a world record. At the 1964 Olympics in Tokyo, Japan, he won again with a time of 2:12:12, setting another world record

5781. Summer Olympic Games in Latin America were the 19th Games, held in Mexico City, Mexico, in 1968. Participating were 4,750 male and 781 female competitors from 112 countries.

5782. Woman athlete to light the Olympic flame was Mexican hurdler Norma Enriqueta Basilio de Sotela, who lit the flame in the stadium at the 1968 Summer Olympic Games in Mexico City, Mexico.

5783. Winter Olympic Games in Asia were the eleventh Games, held in 1972 in Sapporo, Japan. The 35 participating countries sent a total of 1,015 men and 217 women athletes.

5784. Boycotts of the Olympic Games for political reasons were conducted in July 1976, when the Games were held in Montreal, Canada. A group of 32 nations from Africa and Asia, led by Tanzania, withheld their teams to protest the fact that New Zealand had sent its national rugby team to play in South Africa, a country with an official domestic policy of racial discrimination. On July 16, the day after the Games opened, Taiwan withdrew its team to protest the decision of Olympic authorities to apply the name "Republic of China" to mainland China (the Communist nation officially known as the People's Republic of China), rather than to itself.

5785. Gymnast to achieve a perfect score in the Olympic Games was the Romanian Nadia Comaneci. In July 1976, she was awarded seven perfect 10.00 scores in all, plus the gold medals for the balance beam and the uneven bars, at the Summer Olympic Games in Montreal, Canada.

5786. Mother-daughter Olympic medalists were Elizabeta Bagrinaseva and her daughter Irina Nazarova, both of the Soviet Union. At the 1952 Summer Olympic Games, Bagrinaseva won the medal in the women's discus event. At the 1980 Summer Games, Nazarova shared the gold medal in the women's 400-meter relay event.

5787. Black African woman athlete to win an Olympic gold medal was the hurdler Nawal El Moutawakil of Morocco. She won the gold medal in the 400-meter hurdles at the 1984 Summer Olympic Games in Los Angeles, CA, USA.

5788. Heptathlon event was held at the Summer Olympic Games in Los Angeles, CA, USA, in 1984. The heptathlon is a two-day women's athletic competition that consists of seven events: the 100-meter hurdles, the high jump, the shot put, the 200-meter run, the broad jump, the javelin throw, and the 800-meter run. The first gold medalist was Glynis Nunn of Australia, with a score of 6,390.

5789. Olympic marathon for women was staged at the 1984 Summer Olympic Games in Los Angeles, CA, USA. Joan Benoit Samuelson of Portland, ME, USA, was the winner.

5790. Woman to compete in both the Summer and Winter Olympic Games was an American, Connie Carpenter Phinney, who won the women's individual bicycling road race event in the 1984 Summer Games, held in Los Angeles, CA, USA. She had also competed as a speed skater in the 1972 Winter Games in Sapporo, Japan.

5791. Women's cycling event was the 79K road race, which took place on on July 29, 1984, at the Summer Olympic Games in Los Angeles, CA, USA. The gold medal was won by an American, Connie Carpenter Phinney.

5792. Heptathlon two-time gold medalist was the American athlete Jackie Joyner-Kersee. She won the event at the Summer Olympic Games in Seoul, Korea, in 1988 with a score of 7,215, and again in 1992 in Barcelona, Spain, with a score of 7,044.

5793. African woman athlete to win the Olympic women's marathon was the Ethiopian runner Fatuma Roba, who won the event at the 1996 Summer Olympic Games in Atlanta, GA, USA, with a time of 2 hours 26 minutes 5 seconds and the biggest margin in the marathon's four-race history.

5794. Hong Kong athlete to win a gold medal at the Olympic Games was the windsurfer Lee Lai-Shan, who won a gold medal in the women's boardsailing competition at the Summer Olympic Games held in Atlanta, GA, USA, in 1996. Athletes had been sent by the British crown colony of Hong Kong to the Olympics since 1952. The team sent to Atlanta was the last before China resumed sovereignty over the city on July 1, 1997.

SPORTS AND RECREATION—OLYMPIC GAMES—*continued*

5795. Olympics to have an official World Wide Web site was the 26th Olympiad, held in Atlanta, GA, USA, in 1996. The Internet site carried results of competition for every Olympic sport, as well as a wide variety of information for participants and spectators.

5796. Women's Olympic volleyball event was held at the Summer Olympic Games in Atlanta, GA, USA. The gold medalists were Jackie Silva and Sandra Pires of Brazil, who secured a 12–11, 12–6 victory in the final. These were the first gold medals ever awarded to Brazilian women.

5797. Runner to win both the 200-meter and the 400-meter races at the same Olympic games was the American Michael Johnson, who achieved that feat on August 2, 1996, at the Summer Olympic Games in Atlanta, GA, USA. Johnson also set a new world record in the 200-meter race, with a time of 19.32 seconds.

SPORTS AND RECREATION—POLO

5798. Equestrian sport was polo, first played in ancient Persia (now Iran) as training for elite cavalry units. In its early development polo was often played with as many as 100 riders on each team. The first written account describes a game between Persian and Turkoman tribesmen circa 600 BCE.

5799. European polo club was the Cachar Polo Club, founded in 1859 by British tea planters in Silchar, Assam, in northeastern India.

5800. International polo competition was the Westchester Cup, first held in 1886 between the championship teams of the United States and England. England won the cup that year; the United States first won in 1909.

5801. World polo championships were staged in 1989 in Berlin, Germany. The U.S. team defeated Great Britain 7–6.

SPORTS AND RECREATION—RUGBY

5802. Rugby match was played in 1823 at Rugby School in England. During a game of football (a forerunner of what would later be called association football, or soccer), the ball was picked up and run in by William Webb Ellis. It was a violation of the rules but one that proved popular with players and fans. Other versions of the game's origin put the date at circa 1839. The first rulebook for the new game was published at the school in 1846.

5803. International rugby game was played between McGill University of Montreal, Canada, and Harvard University, Cambridge, MA, USA. The match was held at Jarvis Field, Cambridge, MA, USA, on May 14, 1874. The teams played rugby football under Harvard's rules, which stated that every goal constituted a game. McGill arrived with 11 men and Harvard with 15, four of whom were dropped to equalize the teams. Harvard won three games, the first two lasting about five minutes and the third about twelve minutes. This game marked the first instance in which an admission fee was charged at a collegiate sporting event. The proceeds were used for lavishly entertaining the McGill team. A second match was played the following day, and a third match was played in the fall in Montreal.

SPORTS AND RECREATION—SKATING

5804. Ice skates were developed circa 1000 BCE in Scandinavia. Archeological sites reveal that early skates were made from the shank or rib bones of elk, reindeer, or other large animals.

5805. Roller skates are believed to have been invented in 1759 by Joseph Merlin, a Belgian maker of musical instruments, although they may have been in use in the Netherlands some decades earlier. Merlin's design had one row of two wheels, making his skates the first in-line roller skates as well. He is reported to have made a grand rolling entrance into a London costume party and crashed headlong into a mirror.

5806. Skating rink was opened on January 7, 1876, by its developer, John Gamgee of London, England. It was a small rink measuring only about 400 square feet (37 square meters).

SPORTS AND RECREATION—SKIING

5807. Nordic skier of importance was probably Sondre Nordheim, from Telemark in Norway. In 1866 he perfected the Christiania turn and parallel stop, and, later, the Telemark turn. He also improved the maneuverability of nordic skis by shortening them, carving a waist into them, and improving their bindings.

5808. Alpine skier of international renown was the Norwegian explorer, oceanographer, and statesman Fridtjof Nansen. On August 15, 1888, he led a team of six Norwegians across the Greenland ice cap from east to west, arriving at Ameralik fjord on the west coast on September 26. His account fired the imagination of skiers across Europe, though Nansen himself dismissed the exploit that made him famous as a mere "ski tour."

5809. Ski course was planned out in 1906 by skier Viktor Sohm at Zürs, Austria.

5810. Downhill ski race of record was held at Arlberg, Austria, on January 6, 1911.

5811. Ski school was opened circa 1920 at St. Anton in the Arlberg region of the Austrian alps by Hannes Schneider, known for his development of the modern techniques of downhill skiing. He pursued a two-tiered educational program, with a beginners' level for tourists and an advanced level to train future instructors in his method.

5812. Slalom race was held at Mussen, Switzerland, in 1922. It was organized by the British skier Arnold Lunn.

SPORTS AND RECREATION—SOCCER (ASSOCIATION FOOTBALL)

5813. Soccer-type football games have been played since antiquity in many parts of the world. In most such games, two teams attempt to kick, push, or pass a ball or other round object toward the opponent's goal. Perhaps the earliest known game that bears a strong resemblance to modern soccer (association football) was episkuros, or harpaston, played in ancient Greece as early as circa 500 BCE. In Rome, it was called harpastum and was played from circa 150 BCE. Roman legions brought the game to other cultures of Europe, including Britain circa 44 CE. A similar game is known from China (206 BCE).

5814. Rules for soccer (association football) were developed at the University of Cambridge, England, in 1843, drawing upon various sets of rules devised by university students who had played the game as schoolboys. The Cambridge Rules formed the basis for the first uniform rule book for association football published by the London Football Association in 1863.

5815. Soccer club was founded in 1857 in Sheffield, England, as the Sheffield Football Club.

5816. World Cup soccer championship was held in Uruguay in 1930 under the auspices of the Fédération Internationale de Football Association. Thirteen countries fielded teams out of the 41 FIFA members. In the final, which was held on July 30 at the new Centenario Stadium in Montevideo, Uruguay defeated Argentina 4–2. Guillermo Stábile of Argentina was the top scorer, with eight goals. The 68,000 spectators (some accounts put the number at closer to 93,000) were frisked for weapons before being allowed into the stadium—the first time this was considered necessary in an international championship event.

SPORTS AND RECREATION—SWIMMING

5817. Heated swimming pool is believed to have been built circa 40 BCE by the famously wealthy Roman diplomat Gaius Cilnius Maecenas at his palace and gardens on the Esquiline Hill in Rome.

5818. Schools to require swimming instruction were those of 17th-century Japan.

5819. International swimming championship was a 440-yard (402-meter) race, held annually beginning in 1846 in Australia.

5820. Man to swim the English Channel was an Englishman, Captain Matthew Webb. On August 24–25, 1875, he made the crossing from Dover, England, to Calais, France, a distance of 20.5 miles (33 kilometers), in 21 hours 45 minutes, using the breaststroke. Three months earlier, in May 1875, an American swimmer, Paul Boynton, had crossed the Channel in 23 hours 30 minutes, but because he was wearing a flotation suit, the credit for the first crossing is usually given to Webb.

5821. Man to swim 100 meters in under a minute was the swimming champion and movie actor Johnny Weissmuller (born Jonas Weissmuller in Freidorf, Romania). On July 9, 1922, at the Neptune Beach Tank, Alameda, CA, USA, he clocked a time of 58.3 seconds in the 100-meter freestyle sprint. In the 1924 Olympics, he won a gold medal with a time of 59 seconds, and repeated the performance in 1928 for another gold medal with a time of 58.6 seconds.

5822. Woman to swim the English Channel was Gertrude Caroline Ederle of New York, NY, USA. On August 6, 1926, she swam from Cap Gris-Nez, France, to Dover, England, a distance of 35 miles (56 kilometers), in 14 hours 31 minutes. She broke the men's record by almost two hours.

5823. Swimmer to cross the Irish Sea was Thomas Blower of Nottingham, England. In 1947 it took him 15 hours 25 minutes to swim a 25-mile route from Donaghadee, Northern Ireland, to Portpatrick, Scotland.

5824. Swimmer to cross the Strait of Gibraltar was Daniel Carpio, a Peruvian swimmer who crossed the Strait from Spain to Spanish Morocco (now part of independent Morocco) on July 22, 1948. The eight-mile swim took 9 hours 20 minutes.

SPORTS AND RECREATION—SWIMMING—*continued*

5825. Swimmer to cross the English Channel in both directions was Antonio Abertondo of Argentina. On September 20, 1961, he set out from England, reaching the shore of France after a swim of 18 hours 50 minutes. He took a four-minute rest and then set out on the return trip, which took 24 hours 16 minutes.

5826. Underwater swim across the English Channel from France to England was made by American ship designer and boat captain Fred Baldasare on July 10–11, 1962, the day after he made the first underwater swim from Sicily to Italy across the Messina Strait. Over the next six months, Baldasare, an expert scuba-diver, became the first to swim underwater across the Oresund Strait from Denmark to Sweden, nonstop both ways across the Bosphorus between Asia and Europe, the full length of the Bosphorus from the Black Sea to the Sea of Marmara, across the Hellespont from Asia to Europe, across Algeciras Bay from Gibraltar to Spain, across the Strait of Gibraltar from Europe to Africa, and the full length of the Strait of Gibraltar from the Atlantic to the Mediterranean (the first such swim either underwater or surface). Baldasare specialized in long-distance swims made entirely underwater, including eating and drinking, without a shark cage.

5827. Swim from Mexico to Cuba was completed on June 1, 1998, by Australian marathon swimmer Susan Maroney. Spending most of her time in a shark-proof cage, Maroney took more than 30 hours to swim the 123 miles (200 kilometers) from Isla Mujeres, Mexico, to Las Tumbas Beach in western Cuba, a world distance record for unassisted, open-water swimming.

SPORTS AND RECREATION—TABLE TENNIS

5828. Table tennis was developed in London, England, circa 1895. English gamesman James Gibbs introduced the use of lightweight celluloid balls circa 1891, and the game was commercialized shortly thereafter. The game's other name, Ping-Pong, is a trademark of game manufacturer Parker Brothers of Salem, MA, USA.

5829. Table tennis international association was the Fédération Internationale de Tennis de Table (International Table Tennis Federation), founded in 1926 by the national associations of Austria, Czechoslovakia, England, Denmark, Germany, Hungary, India, Sweden, and Wales.

5830. Table tennis world championship was held in London, England, in 1927. It was won by Hungary.

SPORTS AND RECREATION—TENNIS

5831. Court tennis was a form of handball known as *jeu de paume* ("palm game"), played in the twelfth century by members of the French royal court. Court tennis, also known as real or royal tennis, is a racket sport that requires an indoor court with inward-sloping roofs.

5832. Lawn tennis has been played in England at least since the late 18th century. A reference to such a game appeared in the pages of England's *Sporting Magazine* in 1793.

5833. Tennis club was founded in Leamington, England, in 1872 by Harry Gem.

5834. Tennis rule book was *Sphairistikè, or Lawn Tennis,* by the English sportsman Walter Clopton Wingfield, published in 1873.

5835. World tennis championship was the All-England Championship (or Wimbledon Championship), first held in the summer of 1877 on one of the croquet lawns of the All-England Croquet and Lawn Tennis Club in Wimbledon, England. The first women's championship was held there in 1884.

5836. Grand Slam winner in tennis was an American, Don Budge, who captured the 1938 titles in the four major singles competitions in tennis: the Australian Open, the French Open, Wimbledon, and the U.S. Open.

5837. Grand Slam doubles winners in tennis were two Australians, Frank Sedgeman and Ken McGregor. They earned the honor in 1951 after winning the men's doubles titles in the Australian Open, the French Open, Wimbledon, and the U.S. Open.

5838. Woman tennis player to win the Grand Slam was the American tennis champion Maureen Catherine Connolly, popularly known as "Little Mo," who won the honor in 1953 after winning all four major women's singles competitions at Wimbledon, the U.S. Open, the Australian Open, and the French Open.

5839. Federation Cup in tennis was awarded in an elimination tournament that was held in London, England, in 1963, under the auspices of the International Lawn Tennis Federation. Teams from 16 nations participated. The Federation Cup is the top trophy of women's amateur team tennis.

5840. Latin American tennis player to become the top ranked player in the world was Marcelo Ríos, a native of Santiago, Chile. He turned professional in 1994 and was ranked the number one men's singles player in the world in 1998.

SPORTS AND RECREATION—TRACK AND FIELD

5841. Marathon took place circa 490 BCE, after the Athenians decisively routed the Persians in the Battle of Marathon, fought on the Marathon plain of northeastern Attica. According to legend, a Greek soldier ran nonstop 22.5 miles (36.2 kilometers) from the site of the battle to the city of Athens, where he died of exhaustion after gasping out the message "Rejoice—we conquer!" The name of the messenger is often given as Pheidippides. According to the Greek historian Herodotus, that was the name of a trained runner who was dispatched from Athens before the battle to request the assistance of Sparta. Herodotus claims that Pheidippides was able to make the 150-mile (241-kilometer) trip in two days.

5842. Modern pentathlete was the Dutch track-and-field star Francina Blankers-Koen of Amsterdam, the Netherlands. In 1951, she set a modern pentathlon record of 4,692 points. The modern pentathlon consists of five events: the shot put, the high jump, the 200-meter sprint, the 80-meter hurdles, and the long jump.

5843. Person to run a mile in less than four minutes was an Englishman, Roger Gilbert Bannister, a medical student at Oxford University. On May 6, 1954, at a dual meet in Oxford, he broke what was thought to be an insuperable psychological and physical barrier when he achieved a time of 3:59.4. Bannister was knighted in 1975.

5844. Asian athlete to win a World Cup gold medal in track and field was Chinese women's shotput champion Huang Zhihong. She won the 1989 World Cup track and field event at Barcelona, Spain, with a throw of 68 feet 0.25 inches (20.73 meters).

5845. Muslim woman athlete to win a track and field world championship was the Algerian runner Hassiba Boulmerka, who won the women's 1,500-meter final at the 1991 world championships in Tokyo, Japan. She was also the first African woman to win a world championship. Some traditional Muslims denounced her for running with bare legs, which is forbidden for women by Islamic custom. In 1992, at the Summer Olympic Games in Barcelona, Spain, she became the first Algerian to win an Olympic gold medal, taking the women's 1,500-meter with a time of 3:55:30.

5846. Runner over the age of 40 to break the four-minute mile was Ireland's Eamonn Coghlan. On February 20, 1994, at the age of 41, Coghlan ran a mile in 3:58.15 at Harvard University's indoor track in Allston, MA, USA. This was more than a second faster than Roger Bannister's historic breaking of the four-minute-mile barrier in 1954.

5847. Boston Marathon in which both champions were African athletes was the race of 1997. Lameck Aguta was the seventh consecutive men's champion from Kenya, with a finishing time of 2 hours 10 minutes 34 seconds. Fatuma Roba of Ethiopia became the first African women's champion with a time of 2 hours 26 minutes 23 seconds.

SPORTS AND RECREATION— TRIATHLON

5848. Triathlon was the 1974 Mission Bay Triathlon, held in California, USA. It consisted of a foot race of 2.8 miles (4.5 kilometers), a bike race of 5 miles (8 kilometers), a swim of 0.25 miles (0.4 kilometers), a run of 2 miles (3.2 kilometers), and another quarter-mile swim.

5849. Ironman triathlon was the Hawaii Ironman competition of February 18, 1978, held on the Big Island, Hawaii, USA. It consisted of a swim of 2.4 miles (3.9 kilometers), a bike ride of 112 miles (180 kilometers), and a full 26.2-mile (42-kilometer) marathon run. There were 14 contestants, all men; the winner was Gordon Haller, a former U.S. Navy pentathlete.

5850. Triathlon in Europe was held in Nice, France, in 1982. The first official triathlon races, under the auspices of L'Union Internationale de Triathlon, were held at Avignon, France, in August 1989.

SPORTS AND RECREATION—WALKING AND WHEELING

5851. Man to walk 100,000 kilometers whose achievement is on record was the Romanian athlete Dimitru Dan. He was participating in a competition sponsored by the Touring Club de France that began on April 10, 1910. At the start, there was a field of 200 entrants. Dan was the only one to complete the race, which he did in 1916, having walked an average of 27 miles (43 kilometers) per day.

SPORTS AND RECREATION—WALKING
AND WHEELING—*continued*

5852. Round-the-world journey on foot of
record was made by an American, David
Kunst, who walked 14,450 miles (23,250 kilometers) across four continents between June 20,
1970, and October 5, 1974. Another American,
George Matthew Schilling, claimed to have
made a round-the-world walk beginning on August 3, 1897, but his achievement has not been
verified.

**5853. Walk from the southernmost to the
northernmost points of the Americas** was
achieved on September 18, 1983, when British
walker George Meegan arrived in northern
Alaska after a 2,426-day traverse of the Americas. He departed on January 26, 1977, from
Ushuaia on the Beagle Channel in Tierra del
Fuego, Argentina, and traveled 19,019 miles on
foot to Prudhoe Bay in northern Alaska, the
northernmost inhabited point of the North
American land mass.

5854. Circumnavigation by wheelchair was
achieved by a Canadian, Rick Hansen, who was
paralyzed from the waist down. Beginning on
March 21, 1985, he wheeled 24,902 miles
(39,944 kilometers) from Vancouver, British
Columbia, Canada, through 34 countries, and
back to Vancouver on May 22, 1987.

SPORTS AND RECREATION—WATER
RACING

5855. International yacht race took place in
England on August 22, 1851, under the auspices of the Royal Yacht Squadron. The course
circled the Isle of Wight, a distance of 53 miles
(85 kilometers). The winner was *America,*
owned by an American syndicate headed by
Commodore John Cox Stevens of the New
York Yacht Club, designed by George Steers,
and built by William Henry Brown of New
York. It was 101 feet 9 inches (31 meters)
overall, with a beam of 23 feet 11 inches (7
meters). The mainmast measured 81 feet (25
meters). *America* covered the course in 10
hours 37 minutes, defeating 14 other contestants. It received a trophy valued at £100 sterling and known as the Queen's Cup, in honor
of Queen Victoria.

5856. Across-the-ocean race was held in 1866
from Sandy Hook, CT, USA, to Cowes, Isle of
Wight, England, with the sponsorship of the
New York Yacht Club. Three schooners participated: the *Fleetwing,* the *Vesta,* and the *Henrietta,* all approximately 105 feet (32 meters) in
length The race was won in 13 days of sailing
by the *Henrietta,* owned by James Gordon Bennett, an American newspaper publisher.

**5857. International motorboat racing compe-
tition** was the Harmsworth Cup, founded by
the British publishing magnate Alfred Harmsworth in 1903. The first annual motorboating
competition, it was open to national entries under 40 feet (12 meters) in length. The first
Harmsworth Cup (actually a bronze plaque)
was won by *Napier I,* a British boat captained
by S.F. Edge, which attained a speed of 19.53
miles (31.4 kilometers) per hour over the two
heats of the race.

5858. Solo transatlantic sailboat race was run
from Plymouth, England, to New York, NY,
USA, in 1960. The winner was the English
yachtsman Francis Charles Chichester, sailing
the *Gipsy Moth III,* who made the passage in
40 days.

**5859. International challenger to win the
America's Cup in yacht racing** was the Australian yacht *Australia II,* which defeated the
American entry *Liberty* in 1983. The *Australia
II*'s innovative wing-keel, designed by Ben
Lexcen, was given credit for the win. It was
the first time the United States lost the cup after defending it successfully 24 times in the
race's 132-year history.

**5860. Watercraft to win the Dupont Water
Prize** for a human-powered boat capable of
traveling 20 knots for 100 meters, or to the
team with the fastest speed on record as of December 31, 1992, was the *Cavitator,* an air-
propeller-driven hydrofoil built and piloted by
Mark Drela of the Massachusetts Institute of
Technology in Cambridge, MA, USA. In a
speed trial on October 27, 1991, on the Charles
River in Boston, MA, USA, the *Cavitator*
achieved a speed of 18.50 knots (21.3 miles per
hour or 34.3 kilometers per hour). The record
still stood on the deadline date and the
US$25,000 Dupont Water Prize was awarded to
Drela's team in the spring of 1993.

**5861. All-woman America's Cup yacht-
racing crew** in the 144-year history of the race
were the members of the crew of *America III,*
which entered the 1995 competition. The yacht
was owned by American businessman Bill
Koch and cost US$20 million to own and oper-
ate. The crew of 26 was chosen on January 12,
1995, from 687 applicants, including both sea-
soned sailors and female athletes from other
sports. Leslie Egnot served as captain. *America
III* won the first race of the Citizen Cup defender trials, but ultimately lost that race to the
PACT 95 crew, skippered by Kevin Mahaney.
The 1995 America's Cup was won by the Royal New Zealand Yacht Squadron.

SPORTS AND RECREATION—WATER SPORTS

5862. Surfers were the Polynesian settlers of the Hawaiian Islands, who began to ride carved wooden boards off Hawaiian beaches circa 750 CE.

5863. Water polo was originally played by participants who rode on barrels painted to look like ponies while they hit a ball with sticks. The first rules for modern water polo were published in Scotland in 1877 and organized the game along the lines of soccer (association football).

5864. International water polo match was played in 1890 in London, England, between Scotland and England. The match was won by Scotland.

5865. Modern surfer was George Freeth of Waikiki, Hawaii. In 1907, he gave a series of highly publicized surfing exhibitions at Redondo Beach, CA, USA.

5866. Windsurfing equipment was patented in 1968 by two Americans, surfing enthusiast Hoyle Schweitzer and sailor Jim Drake, who invented the first practical free-sail system with no rigging. Their design was called the Windsurfer, from which the sport took its name. The early Windsurfer boards measured 12 feet (3.5 meters) long and weighed 60 pounds (27 kilograms).

SPORTS AND RECREATION—WRESTLING

5867. Wrestling matches were held in Egypt and Babylonia, as attested by seals and other pictorial evidence dating from about 3000 BCE. The athletes pictured are engaged in belt wrestling, a style of wrestling still practiced widely in the 20th century.

5868. Reference to wrestling in literature takes place in the *Epic of Gilgamesh,* the world's first known epic poem, composed in Sumer (in modern Iraq) circa 2000 BCE. The wrestlers are Gilgamesh, the Sumerian king who is the poem's protagonist, and his friend Enkidu.

5869. Wrestler of note was a Greek athlete, Milon (or Milo) of Croton (now Crotone, Italy), a military leader of the late sixth century BCE, famous for his strength. Milon won 32 wrestling contests, including six victories in the Pythian Games and six in the Olympic Games.

5870. Sumo grand champion or *yokozuna* was Akashi Shiganosuke, victor in the national Japanese competition of 1632, during the Tokugawa shogunate. Sumo wrestling is often called Japan's national sport.

5871. Greco-Roman wrestling in modern times in the modern style was developed in Paris, France, circa 1860. Greco-Roman wrestling emphasizes holds with the arms and disallows holds below the waist or tripping or wrapping with the legs. A competition in the sport was held at the first modern Olympic Games, the 1896 Olympics in Athens, Greece.

5872. Sumo champion not born in Japan was Konishiki, who was born in Samoa and began his competitive career in Hawaii. In 1982, he began competing in Japan, and in 1984 had achieved promotion to the top-ranked *Makunouchi* division. In 1987, the Sumo Kyokai (the governing body of sumo) promoted him to *ozeki* or champion, the sport's second highest rank. Konishiki hoped to be considered for elevation to the highest rank, *yokozuna* (grand champion), achieved by only 62 men in the history of sumo, but this did not occur. He retired in 1998.

T

TELECOMMUNICATIONS—FAXES

5873. Fax process was invented by the Scottish psychologist Alexander Bain in 1843. That year, he received a British patent for "improvements in producing and regulating electric currents and improvements in timepieces and in electric printing and signal telegraphs." Bain's invention used two synchronous pendulums, one for transmission and one for reception, each of which oscillated over a rotating drum. A text message or image created in an electrically conductive material was wrapped around the sending drum. A needle on the sending pendulum picked up impulses only where there was conductive material. The receiving needle made marks on photosensitive paper corresponding to the signals from the sending needle. Frederick Blakewell, an English physicist, demonstrated a working model at the London Great Exhibition of 1851. With this patent, Bain was also the first to propose the idea of scanning an image—breaking it up into small parts for transmission—that is the basis for all graphical telecommunications, including television.

5874. Fax system for commercial use was the Pantelegraph, introduced by Giovanni Caselli, an Italian inventor, in 1863. Like the fax process invented by Alexander Bain in 1843, Caselli's Pantelegraph employed a system of rotating drums scanned by synchronized, elec-

TELECOMMUNICATIONS—FAXES—continued

trically charged pendulums. The original document was wrapped onto the transmitting drum and scanned by the transmitting pendulum. The receiving drum was wrapped in paper soaked in potassium cyanide, which changed color when electrically charged by the tip of the pendulum. This resulted in images with high fidelity to the original. The first commercial transmission using his system was made on May 16, 1865, over the telegraph line connecting Lyon and Paris, France.

5875. Fax transmission of photographs was developed by Arthur Korn, a German physicist, and first demonstrated in 1902. Unlike earlier electromechanical systems, the Korn system used a selenium photocell to scan the original photograph, which was wrapped on a glass drum. At the receiver, a light controlled by the transmitted signal recorded the transmitted image onto photographic film. Newspapers were the first to adopt his system; in 1906, the first news photograph transmissions over telegraph lines took place between Munich and Berlin.

5876. Transatlantic radio fax transmission of a photograph took place on June 11, 1922, when a photograph of Pope Pius XI was transmitted from Rome, Italy, by Arthur Korn, a German physicist and the inventor of the first system for faxing photographs. The picture, a halftone 7 by 9.5 inches (18 by 24.3 centimeters), was received 40 minutes after transmission at Bar Harbor, ME, USA, by Chief Radioman Edmund H. Hansen of the U.S. Navy. Light falling on a selenium cell produced a group of shaded dots that formed a halftone. It was published in the *New York World* the same day.

5877. Transcontinental radio fax transmission was made on May 6, 1925 across the United States. It was also the first transpacific radio fax transmission. Photographs of war games and of a general, an admiral, and a governor were transmitted by Alfred J. Koenig from Honolulu, Hawaii (then a territory of the United States), using a transmitter designed by Captain Richard Howland Ranger. The photographs went to Kahuku, Hawaii, by wire; to Marshall, CA, USA, by radio; to Bolinas, CA, by radio; to Riverhead, NY, by radio; and finally to New York City by wire. The total distance was 5,136 miles (8,264 kilometers).

5878. Desktop fax machine was the Magnafax Telecopier, introduced in April 1966 by the Xerox Corporation of Stamford, CT, USA. The 46-pound (21-kilogram) device, the first that was priced within range of a majority of businesses, was also the first that could operate over standard phone lines.

5879. International fax standard was set in 1974 by the International Telegraph and Telephone Consultative Committee (CCITT), a committee of the United Nations. The standard, called Group 1 fax, set the parameters by which fax machines in different countries or from different manufacturers could connect to one another, which previously had not been possible. The Group 1 fax standard used a modulated analog signal to carry information. It was possible to send a one-page document in about six minutes at a resolution of 100 lines per inch, a marked improvement over earlier transmission speeds.

5880. International digital fax standard was Group 3 fax, adopted in 1980 by the International Telegraph and Telephone Consultative Committee (CCITT). Fax machines compliant with the Group 3 standard used a modem and a standard bit-compression scheme for the digital transmission of images, rather than the older analog-modulation method of Group 1 and Group 2 fax equipment. Using Group 3, a page of text or graphics could be transmitted in less than a minute at a speed of 2,400 to 14,400 bits per second (bps) to any compatible device. An improved Group 4 standard requiring high-speed data lines was proposed by CCITT in 1984.

5881. Color fax machine was introduced by the Sharp Corporation of Tokyo, Japan, in 1990.

TELECOMMUNICATIONS—NETWORKS

5882. National broadcasting monopoly was granted to the British Broadcasting Corporation, a public corporation established in 1927 under royal charter. The BBC was granted a complete monopoly of all aspects of broadcasting in the British Isles, including radio and television; in exchange, it was not allowed to broadcast commercials, self-promotional material, or its own political or social commentary. The first director general of the BBC was John Reith (later Lord Reith), who served from 1927 to 1938. The BBC's monopoly on television ended in 1954, and on radio in 1972.

5883. Proposal for global satellite telecommunications was contained in the article "Extra-Terrestrial Relays," written in 1945 for the magazine *Wireless World* by Arthur Charles Clarke, an English radar instructor and technician with the Royal Air Force. Clarke's description of a global telecommunications network based on radio transceiver satellites in geosynchronous earth orbit was met with skepticism at first, but it was less than 20 years later that the first geosynchronous satellite, *Syncom 2,* was launched by NASA, the U.S. space agency. Clarke went on to become one of the best-known science fiction writers.

5884. Communications satellite was *Echo 1,* a 26.5-inch magnesium sphere launched by an American Thor-Delta rocket at 5:39 A.M. on August 12, 1960, from Cape Canaveral, FL, USA. The satellite went into orbit at 7:45 A.M. after the three stages of the rocket had been fired successfully. A taped message was transmitted from Goldstone, CA, bounced off the satellite, and received by the Bell Telephone laboratory at Holmdel, NJ.

5885. Geosynchronous commercial communications satellite was *Early Bird,* later called *INTELSAT 1,* the first satellite operated by the International Telecommunications Satellite Organization. It was launched on April 6, 1965, from Cape Kennedy, FL, USA, and placed in a stationary equatorial orbit over the Atlantic Ocean.

5886. Lightwave-based telecommunications system to provide a full range of service, including voice, data, and video, was an experimental underground line installed in 1977 in Chicago, IL, USA. The system used laser beams transmitted via glass fibers that each carried the equivalent of 672 voice channels. It was developed by researchers at the Bell Telephone Laboratories in Holmdel, NJ, USA.

5887. Privately owned global satellite network was PanAmSat, founded in 1984 by the Spanish-American entrepreneur René Anselmo as a commercial alternative to the United States government-owned international satellite monopoly. In 1988, PanAmSat launched the PAS-1 Atlantic Ocean Region satellite, becoming the world's first private-sector international satellite service provider. In 1995, PanAmSat began offering global satellite service.

5888. Fiber-optic transoceanic cable was the transatlantic TAT-8, a joint venture of DGT in France, British Telecom, and the American Telephone & Telegraph Company (AT&T). Completed in 1988, it linked the United States with Great Britain and France, and was capable of carrying thousands of simultaneous television, telephone, and data transmissions.

5889. Wireless city was the rural town of Quitaque, TX, USA. In December 1992, the installation of a completely wireless phone system employing digital radio transmission was completed by an American telecommunications firm, Inter-Digital Communications Corporation. All of the town's 400 telephones beamed conversations via dish antennas to a radio transmission tower 10 miles away in the town of Turkey, TX. From there, the calls were routed to their destinations.

5890. Commercial cable system capable of carrying simultaneous TV, telephony, and high-speed data was launched in June 1996 by the Australian firm of Optus Vision, a partly owned cable television subsidiary of Optus Communications.

5891. Open international telecommunications agreement was the Basic Telecommunications Services Accord, concluded on February 15, 1997, by 69 nations meeting under the auspices of the World Trade Organization. The agreement, which took effect on January 1, 1998, for most signatories, opened telecommunication markets to all competitors and committed governments to end telecommunications tariffs and state telephone monopolies.

5892. Commercial communications satellite to circle the moon was *AsiaSat 3,* launched by the Chinese telecommunications company AsiaSat from Kazakhstan on December 25, 1997. Originally, the satellite was believed to have been lost after its fourth booster failed, but it was redirected in late April and early May 1998 by the American aerospace firm Hughes Global Services into a slingshot orbit around the moon that sent it back into a useful high earth orbit. It was the first time such a procedure had been attempted for a commercial satellite.

5893. China–USA undersea telecommunications cable went into operation at the end of 1999. The fiber-optic cable was a joint venture of several global telecommunications companies, including the Nippon Telegraph and Telephone Corporation of Japan.

TELECOMMUNICATIONS— NETWORKS—*continued*

5894. Japan–USA undersea cable network was slated to begin operation in mid-2000. A joint venture of American and Japanese telecommunications companies, the fiber-optic cable submarine network connected Japan with the U.S. mainland via Hawaii.

TELECOMMUNICATIONS—RADIO

5895. Radio waves were generated by the German physicist, engineer, and mathematician Heinrich Rudolph Hertz, professor of physics at the Karlsruhe Polytechnic in Berlin. In 1887, Hertz used oscillating circuits to transmit and receive radio waves, and calculated the velocity of the waves, confirming the prediction of physicist James Clerk Maxwell that electromagnetic waves travel at the speed of light. Hertz also confirmed that light and heat are forms of electromagnetic radiation. The first discovery that electromagnetic waves move through air had been made several years earlier by the London-born experimenter David Edward Hughes, the inventor of the carbon microphone. A loose connection in a telephone receiver alerted Hughes to the fact that electrical signals could travel between sending and receiving circuits even if they were unconnected. However, Hughes did not publish his work, and Hertz is given credit for the discovery.

5896. Radio inventor has long been claimed by historians from the former Soviet Union to be Aleksandr Stepanovich Popov, a Russian inventor. At a meeting of the Russian Physical and Chemical Society that took place on May 7, 1895, Popov demonstrated a receiver that could detect radio waves produced by lightning charges many miles away. On March 24, 1896, Popov demonstrated the transmission and reception of information by wireless telegraphy—more than three months before a similar demonstration by the Italian-Irish inventor Guglielmo Marconi in England. However, it was Marconi who obtained the world's first radio patent (on June 2, 1896), and who was the indispensable figure in the worldwide commercialization of radio technology.

5897. Radio patent was British patent No.12039, granted on June 2, 1896, to radio pioneer Guglielmo Marconi.

5898. Wireless radio manufacturing company was the Wireless Telegraph and Signal Company, Ltd., incorporated in England in July 1897. The principal owner was Guglielmo Marconi, the developer of radio. (The firm's name was changed in 1900 to the Marconi Wireless Telegraph Company, Ltd.).

5899. Permanent wireless installation was constructed by the Marconi Wireless Telegraph Co., Ltd., in November 1897 at The Needles on the Isle of Wight, Great Britain, under the direction of Guglielmo Marconi.

5900. Wireless station for international communications was established in 1899 at South Foreland, England, by the Wireless Telegraph and Signal Company, Ltd., owned by Guglielmo Marconi. The station was built to maintain regular communications with a similar installation 31 miles (50 kilometers) away in Wimereux, France.

5901. Transoceanic radio message was sent on December 12, 1901, from Poldhu, Cornwall, England, and received at St. John's, Newfoundland, Canada, by Guglielmo Marconi, the developer of radio. The message, which traveled some 2,000 miles (3,200 kilometers), was simply the Morse-code signal for the letter "s." Marconi thereby proved that wireless communication was not limited by the curvature of the earth to a distance of less than 200 miles (322 kilometers).

5902. Transoceanic radio broadcast was sent in code on January 19, 1903, between Cape Cod, MA, USA, and Poldhu, Cornwall, England. Greetings were exchanged between British king Edward VII and American president Theodore Roosevelt. Experimental broadcasts had been made earlier.

5903. Transatlantic radio message of the regular westward service was sent in code by British Privy Councillor Lord Avebury, formerly Sir John Lubbock, to the *New York Times* newspaper from Clifden, Ireland, via Glace Bay, Nova Scotia, on October 17, 1907, on the regular Marconi transatlantic service. The message included the statement: "Trust introduction wireless more closely unite people States Great Britain who seem form one Nation though under two Governments and whose interests are really identical."

5904. SOS signal sent in an emergency was transmitted on June 11, 1909, from the Cunard liner S.S. *Slavonia,* which was grounded off the Azores. The first famous SOS message was transmitted from the luxury liner *Titanic* on April 14–15, 1912, after the ship struck an iceberg while en route to New York City from Southampton, England. A nearby ship, the Leyland liner *Californian,* failed to notice the distress call because its radioman was not on duty. The Cunard liner *Carpathia* did acknowledge the SOS but was unable to reach the scene until 1 hour and 20 minutes after the *Titanic* sank.

5905. Transpacific radio conversation was transmitted on October 6, 1911, from the steamer *Chive Maru* to the wireless station on Hokkaido Island in the northern part of Japan and thence to the Hillcrest station, San Francisco, CA, USA, approximately 6,000 miles (9,654 kilometers) away. The operators exchanged messages.

5906. Radio station call letters were assigned by the International Radiotelegraphic Conference, held in London, England, in 1912. Originally, station call letters were assigned according to the initial letter of the country name, so that French stations started with F, German stations with A or D (for Aleman or Deutschland), and British stations with B. This system generally lapsed in the 1930s, except in the United States, Canada, and Mexico.

5907. Radiotelegraph message from Great Britain to Australia was sent in 1918 from a long-wave station in Caernarvon, Wales, operated by the Marconi Wireless Telegraph Company, to a second station in Australia. The transmission distance was 11,000 miles (17,700 kilometers).

5908. Radio broadcast of live music took place on June 15, 1920, when a concert featuring the singer Dame Nellie Melba was broadcast by Guglielmo Marconi from Writtle, Chelmsford, England. It was picked up by radio receivers throughout Europe as well as by ships in the Atlantic.

5909. French-language commercial AM radio station was CKAC of Montreal, Canada, which began broadcasting in 1922.

5910. Transoceanic radio voice broadcast took place on December 31, 1923, when station KDKA of Pittsburgh, PA, USA, broadcast the voice of Dr. Harry Phillips Davis, vice president of the Westinghouse Electric and Manufacturing Company, via short wave. It was received by 2AZ, a station operated by the Metropolitan Vickers Company, Manchester, England, and rebroadcast to London. The first experiments with transoceanic voice broadcast date to 1915, when the American Telephone & Telegraph Company sent a radio signal modulated by speech captured by a microphone from Arlington, VA, USA, to Paris, France. However, the signal was not successfully reconstituted in audible spoken form.

5911. Round-the-world radio broadcast was accomplished in 0.125 seconds on June 30, 1930, by a series of radio relays. An American, Clyde Decker Wagoner, spoke into a short-wave microphone from station W2XAD, Schenectady, NY, USA. His voice was relayed to Holland, to Java, to Australia, across the Pacific Ocean to North America, and back to Schenectady.

5912. Radio broadcast heard in both the Arctic and the Antarctic regions was made on September 23, 1934, by W2XAF, the short-wave station of the General Electric Company, Schenectady, NY, USA. The program, broadcast by the New York Coffee House, was sent to the American illustrator Rockwell Kent, who was near Labrador. It was also heard by American explorer Richard Evelyn Byrd, who was with his second Antarctic expedition at Little America.

5913. Transistor radio receiver to be mass-produced was the Regency Radio, manufactured by the Regency Division of Industrial Development Engineering Associates, Indianapolis, IN, USA. The first shipments to dealers were made in October 1954. The receiver was about the size of an index card and weighed 12 ounces (372 grams). It had no tubes but instead contained four transistors. It was powered entirely by a 22.5-volt B battery.

5914. Pocket transistor radio was introduced in 1957 by Tokyo Tsushin Kogyo (Tokyo Telecommunications Engineering Corporation, now Sony KK), a consumer electronics firm founded in Tokyo, Japan, in 1946 by Ibuka Masaru and Morita Akio.

5915. Radio broadcast using an orbiting satellite was made on December 19, 1958, when a tape recording of the voice of U.S. president Dwight David Eisenhower delivering Christmas greetings was broadcast on frequencies of 107.97 and 107.94 megacycles from a rocket revolving around the earth.

5916. Transatlantic undersea radio conversation took place on October 2, 1965, between American aquanauts in *Sealab 2,* at a depth of 205 feet (62 meters) in the Pacific Ocean off La Jolla, CA, USA, and French divers in *Conshelf 3,* at a depth of 330 feet (101 meters) in the Mediterranean Sea off Cap Ferrat, France.

TELECOMMUNICATIONS—RADIO—continued

5917. Packet radio network to use the same transmission protocols as the Internet was ALOHAnet, developed by the American researcher Norman Abramson of the University of Hawaii, USA. It was put into operation in July 1970 and was connected to the ARPANET, the first national Internet, in 1972.

TELECOMMUNICATIONS—TELEGRAPH

5918. Long-distance communication system using an alphabet was described by the Greek historian Polybius circa 140 BCE. The 24 letters of the Greek alphabet were arranged on a grid so that each letter could be identified by a pair of numerals derived from its location on the x and y axes. The messages were transmitted by operators holding varying numbers of torches in each hand.

5919. Visual telegraph that was widely used was the mechanical semaphore invented in 1791 by two French brothers, Claude and Ignace Chappe. The Chappes constructed chains of hilltop towers, spaced 3 to 6 miles (5 to 10 kilometers) apart, each just within the line of sight of two others. The towers were outfitted with pairs of movable arms mounted on a crossbeam. Moving the arms and tilting the crossbeam clockwise or counterclockwise—essentially a magnified, mechanical version of flag waving—provided a sufficient number of positions to represent the numerals and letters of the alphabet. Skilled signalers were able to transmit 50 characters in one hour from Toulon to Paris. Sending the same message by horseback would have taken three to four days.

5920. Message transmitted by visual telegraph line was sent in 1793 across a 30-mile stretch of France, using the 22 stations of the Paris–Lille line. It notified the Convention, France's revolutionary government, that its armies had conquered the town of Condé. The reply read: "We congratulate the brave republican soldiers and give order that Condé, bearing up to now the name of the hated nobility, should be called for ever Nord-Libre," meaning "Free North." The line to Lille was the first to be put up by the inventor of the visual telegraph, Claude Chappe.

5921. Primitive telegraph system was constructed in 1827 by an American, Harrison Gray Dyar, who operated a 2-mile (3-kilometer) telegraph system at the racecourse at Long Island City, NY (now part of Queens, New York City), USA. Iron wire attached to glass insulators on wooden posts enabled the current to produce a red mark on litmus paper at the receiving station. The lapse of time between the sparks indicated the different letters.

5922. Telegraph message was an announcement of the presidential and vice presidential candidates chosen by the Whig political party at their national convention, which met at Baltimore, MD, USA, at the end of April, 1844. On May 1, a train left Baltimore for Washington, DC, carrying news of the results. A telegraph operator at Annapolis Junction, on the railway route, asked for the information and transmitted it to Samuel Finley Breese Morse, the inventor of Morse code, who was waiting for it at the Washington railroad station. The message was: "The ticket is Clay and Frelinghuysen." The message arrived an hour before the train. This message predated by more than three weeks Morse's famous message of May 24, 1844, "What hath God wrought," sent from the Supreme Court room in the Capitol in Washington, DC, to Alfred Vail at the Mount Clare station of the Baltimore and Ohio Railroad Company in Baltimore.

5923. Commercial telegraph service was inaugurated on May 24, 1844, by the American artist and inventor Samuel Finley Breese Morse, who sent a message from the Supreme Court room in the Capitol, Washington, DC, USA, to Alfred Vail at the Mount Clare station of the Baltimore and Ohio Railroad Company, Baltimore, MD, USA. Vail retransmitted it to Morse. The message, "What hath God wrought," was selected from the 23rd verse of the 23rd chapter of the biblical Book of Numbers by Annie Ellsworth, daughter of the commissioner of patents.

5924. Underwater telegraph cable that was practical was laid by Ezra Cornell, an associate of Samuel Finley Breese Morse, the developer of telegraphy. In 1845 he laid 12 miles of cable enclosed in lead pipes across the Hudson River, connecting Fort Lee, NJ, USA, with New York City. This cable was carried away by ice in 1846. Before the cable was installed, messages for Philadelphia, PA, USA, and Washington, DC, USA, were carried across the Hudson by messengers in boats.

5925. Undersea telegraph cable ran from Portpatrick, Scotland, to Donaghadee, Ireland, and was completed by the Magnetic Telegraph Company in 1853. The project was overseen by English engineer Charles Tilston Bright, who later helped lay the first transoceanic cable.

5926. Transatlantic telegraph cable was completed on August 5, 1858, through the efforts of the Atlantic Telegraph Company, founded by the English engineer Charles Tilston Bright and two Americans, Cyrus West Field and J.W. Brett. On July 28, 1858, a splice was made in mid-ocean, and on the following day four ships belonging to Britain and the United States paid out the cable as they sailed for home—the British ships *Agamemnon* and *Valorous,* bound for Valentia, Ireland, and the American vessels *Niagara* and *Gorgon,* bound for Trinity Bay, Newfoundland, Canada. These destinations were to be the terminals of the cable. The cable was 1,950 statute miles (3,138 kilometers) long and more than two-thirds of it was laid more than 2 miles (3 kilometers) deep. The cable was weak and the current insufficient, and service was suspended on September 1, 1858.

5927. Transatlantic telegraph messages were introductory and complimentary greetings exchanged by U.S. president James Buchanan and Great Britain's Queen Victoria on August 16, 1858, along the first transatlantic telegraph cable, which was completed on August 5, 1858. The 90-word message took 67 minutes to transmit in full.

5928. Multiplexing signal switching system was developed in 1871 by French inventor Jean-Maurice-Émile Baudot. In his system, a single line could be switched (multiplexed) among several simultaneous users by an electromechanical distributor that was divided into sectors. Each sector encoded the signal in binary form, using a 32-symbol telegraph code, later called Baudot's Code, and sent it to the proper destination. Baudot's invention formed the basis for modern telecommunications switching systems.

5929. Telegraph message sent around the world by commercial telegraph was "This message sent around the world," sent at 7 P.M. on August 20, 1911, from the 17th floor of the New York Times building, New York, NY, USA, by the *New York Times* newspaper and received by the *Times* at 7:16:30 P.M. The message traveled over 28,613 miles (46,038 kilometers) and 16 relays by way of the Azores, Gibraltar, Bombay, Philippine Islands, Midway, Guam, Honolulu, and San Francisco.

5930. International telecommunications conglomerate was created in 1928 with the merger of two American companies, Commercial Cable-Postal Telegraph, owned by businessman Clarence Mackay, and International Telephone and Telegraph. Under the ITT name, the combined firm operated cables between New York, Miami, and Cuba and across the Atlantic and Pacific oceans.

TELECOMMUNICATIONS—TELEPHONE

5931. Voice synthesizer was demonstrated to the public on December 22, 1845, at the Musical Fund Hall in Philadelphia, PA, USA, by Joseph Faber, an inventor recently arrived from Germany. His device took 17 years to develop. It consisted of a keyboard that by mechanical means operated a series of reeds, bellows, and chambers, designed to work like the human mouth, tongue, teeth, glottis, larynx, and lungs. Passing air through the device produced 16 basic phonemes, enough to pronounce accurately any word in any European language. The machine's slow, sepulchral voice seemed to emerge from a mechanical head that was fixed to the frame. In 1846, Phineas T. Barnum exhibited Faber's invention, dubbed the Euphonium, in London, where it was viewed by Melville Bell, the father of Alexander Graham Bell, inventor of the telephone.

5932. Treatise on telephony was published by the Belgian-born French inventor Charles Bourseul in 1854 in the magazine *L'Illustration de Paris.* Bourseul tinkered with various telegraph systems before beginning experiments with the electrical transmission of the human voice. He invented an early microphone, but was unable to build a satisfactory speaker, and did not patent his work.

5933. Words heard on a telephone were "Mr. Watson, come here, I want you," spoken into a telephone on March 10, 1876, by Alexander Graham Bell and received at another telephone set by his associate Thomas Augustus Watson on a different floor of Bell's home in Boston, MA, USA.

5934. Telephone for domestic use was installed in April 1877 at the home of Charles Williams, Jr., of Somerville, MA, USA, at the corner of Arlington and Lincoln streets. Williams also had a telephone installed at the same time in his office at 109 Court Street, Boston, MA, USA.

TELECOMMUNICATIONS— TELE-PHONE—*continued*

5935. International commercial telephone service was begun on July 1, 1881, when service was inaugurated by the National Bell Telephone Company of the State of Maine between Calais, ME, USA, and St. Stephen, New Brunswick, Canada, two points separated by the St. Croix River, the international boundary line between the United States and Canada.

5936. Transatlantic message over radio telephone was transmitted on October 21, 1915, from Arlington, VA, to Paris. The voice of B.B. Webb was heard by Herbert E. Shreeve and Austen M. Custis of the American Telephone and Telegraph Company and by Lieutenant Colonel Ferrie of the French government at a receiving station installed in the Eiffel Tower.

5937. Transatlantic commercial telephone service was established between New York, NY, USA, and London, England. It was inaugurated on January 7, 1927, when Walter Sherman Gifford, president of the American Telephone and Telegraph Company, who was in New York, talked to Sir George Evelyn Pemberton Murray, secretary of the British Post Office, who was in London. Thirty-one commercial calls were made the first day. The charge was US$75 for a three-minute conversation. The first private conversation was made by Adolph Simon Ochs, publisher of the *New York Times,* to Geoffrey Dawson, editor of the *Times* of London. The messages were transmitted from Rocky Point, NY, USA.

5938. Telephone conversation to travel around the world was held on April 25, 1935, between Walter Sherman Gifford, president of the American Telephone Company, in his office in New York, NY, USA, and T.G. Miller, a company vice president, who was in an office about 50 feet away. The call was routed over 23,000 miles (37,007 kilometers) of telephone wire as well as by radio through San Francisco, Java, Amsterdam, and London and back to New York.

5939. Touch-tone phone system that used tones in the voice frequency range rather than pulses generated by rotary dials was installed in Baltimore, MD, USA, in 1941. Under the experimental system, developed by the Bell Telephone Laboratories in Holmdel, NJ, USA, individuals made calls using ordinary rotary dialing phones; operators in a central switching office pushed the buttons to send calls along trunk lines. The first commercial touch-tone phones were shown at the 1962 World's Fair in Seattle, WA, USA.

5940. Telephone answering machine was the Ipsophone, manufactured in 1949 by Buhrle and Company, Oerlikon, Switzerland. The washing-machine-sized device, which weighed more than 300 pounds, allowed callers to access their messages from a remote telephone using a security code. Despite the Ipsophone's size and cost, many were purchased by observant Jews who used the device to receive phone messages on the Sabbath, when touching phones and other electrical devices is forbidden.

5941. Direct-dial telephone network that eliminated the need for human switchboard operators on standard telephone calls was invented by researchers at the Bell Telephone Laboratories in Holmdel, NJ, USA. The world's first such commercial system was installed in Englewood, NJ, USA, in 1951.

5942. Fiber optic cable for the efficient transmission of light was developed by an Indian physicist, Narinder S. Kapany, in 1955. The fibers consisted of an inner transmitting core, made of highly transparent glass, and an outer reflective cladding. Long lengths of fiber optic cable for telecommunications use were not available until the 1970s.

5943. Transatlantic telephone call using the transoceanic cable took place on September 25, 1956, when Cleo Frank Craig, chairman of the board of the American Telegraph and Telephone Company, who was in New York, NY, USA, spoke to Dr. Charles Hill, the British postmaster general, who was at Lancaster House, London. The cable, designed to carry 36 conversations at the same time, was the joint undertaking of the Bell System, the British Post Office (operator of the telephone service in Great Britain), and the Canadian Overseas Telecommunications Corporation.

5944. Transpacific telephone service using the transoceanic cable began on June 18, 1964, when U.S. president Lyndon Baines Johnson in Washington, DC, USA, spoke to Japanese premier Hayato Ikeda in Tokyo, Japan. The cable, with a capacity of 138 voice channels, stretched 5,300 nautical miles (9,816 kilometers) from Oahu, HI, USA, to Japan via Midway, Wake, and Guam, and joined existing cables to the United States mainland, Canada, and Australia. Partners in the US$80-million cable project were the American Telephone and Telegraph Company, Kokusai Denshin Denwa Company of Japan, the Hawaiian Telephone Company, and RCA Communications.

5945. International direct-dial service was available from New York City to London beginning March 1, 1970. The service was a joint venture of the American Telephone & Telegraph Company and the British General Post Office.

5946. Cellular telephone system was put into service in Tokyo, Japan, in 1979.

5947. Commercial satellite telephone installation on an airplane was approved by the International Maritime Satellite Organization (Inmarsat) and installed in 1990 on a Gulfstream 4 business jet. The system was made by Racal and worked by relaying signals between the aircraft and a ground telecommunications network through the Inmarsat geostationary satellite system.

5948. Personal portable phone capable of making a call from anywhere in the world was introduced in 1996 by Comsat Mobile Communications of Bethesda, MD, USA. Called the Planet 1, it was the size of a laptop computer with a phone attached. The phone sent signals into space that were captured by an orbiting satellite and transmitted to the destination. The phone retailed for US$2,995.

TELECOMMUNICATIONS—TELEVISION

5949. Complete television system was the mechanical system devised by the German inventor Paul Nipkow, who obtained a German patent in 1884. Nipkow's system used the photoconductive properties of the element selenium to convert brightly illuminated scenes to a low-voltage signal that could be transmitted by wire and then reconverted to an image on a receiver. A mechanical scanning device consisting of a rotating disk with 18 holes was used at both sending and receiving ends to break down and reconstitute the image into 18 horizontal lines of resolution.

5950. All-electronic television system was proposed in 1908 by Scottish electrical engineer Alan Campbell Swinton and presented in 1911 to the Röntgen Society of London. Swinton's television system was to employ cathode ray tubes with magnetic line scanning systems in camera and receiver, essentially as in modern television, but much of the actual technology had not yet been invented.

5951. Televised images to be publicly displayed were the heads of two ventriloquist's dummies, which appeared on a screen before an audience at the Royal Institution, London, England, on January 27, 1926. The dummies were operated by the Scottish inventor John Logie Baird, who was demonstrating a mechanical scanning system that he had developed from designs made in 1884 by Paul Gottlieb Nipkow. The scanner broke up an image of a moving person into a series of electronic impulses that could be transmitted by cable to a distant viewing screen as a low-resolution pattern of light and dark. The event was the first public demonstration of moving television images.

5952. International television transmission was sent over phone lines from London, England, to Hartsdale, NY, USA, by Scottish television pioneer John Logie Baird on January 13, 1928.

5953. Transoceanic radio signal conveying a television image was received on February 8, 1928, at Hartsdale, NY, USA, by Robert M. Hart, owner of shortwave station W2CVJ. The sound vision, a picture of Mrs. Mia Howe, was sent across the ocean from 2 KZ, Purley, England, a station with two kilowatts of power, by John Logie Baird of the Baird Television Development Company of London, using short radio waves.

5954. Color television system was pioneered by John Logie Baird, a Scottish electrical engineer, in 1928, but the first color system that was practical was invented in 1929 by a team under Herbert Ives at the Bell Telephone Laboratories in Holmdel, NJ, USA. It broke down the image into three colors, red, blue, and green, using three scanning passes, and transmitted each color signal on a separate channel.

5955. Person to be interviewed on television was the Irish actress Peggy O'Neil, who spoke on camera from the Ideal Home Exhibition held in Southampton, England, on April 29, 1930. Asked her opinion of television, she replied: "Television is certainly very fascinating. . . . to say the least, it's very wonderful."

5956. Demonstration of home reception of television was given in New York, NY, USA, on August 20, 1930, when a half-hour program broadcast from two stations was received on screens placed in a store in the Hotel Ansonia at Broadway and 73rd Street, in the Hearst Building at Eighth Avenue and 57th Street, and in a residence at 98 Riverside Drive. On these screens appeared the images of performers talking and singing in the studios of the Jenkins W2XCR television station at Jersey City, NJ, and the De Forest W2XCD station at Passaic, NJ. The distance, approximately 6 miles (10 kilometers), was the greatest over which pictures had yet been transmitted by television. The caricaturist Al Hirschfeld was master of ceremonies.

TELECOMMUNICATIONS— TELEVISION—continued

5957. Closed-circuit sporting event was a college baseball game played at Waseda University in Tokyo, Japan, on February 17, 1931. The game was transmitted by wire to the university's electrical laboratory, where it was viewed by Professor Tadaoki Yamamoto and his students. The first public telecast of a team game was broadcast from Waseda University on September 27, 1931.

5958. Television announcer who was a woman was Elizabeth Cowell, who announced for the British Broadcasting Corporation beginning on August 31, 1935.

5959. Regular broadcast high-definition television service was inaugurated from London, England, on November 2, 1936, by the British Broadcasting Corporation under the direction of John Reith.

5960. Electronic television system that was practical was invented by the Russian-American electrical engineer Vladimir Kosma Zworykin, a researcher at the Radio Corporation of America (RCA), who received the two essential television patents in the United States on December 20, 1938. One patent was for the iconoscope, a cathode-ray transmitting tube that formed the heart of all television cameras until the late 1980s. The second patent was for the kinescope, or cathode-ray receiving tube, the device that displays the image on all televisions and most computer monitors. Such devices had been predicted as early as 1908, but Zworykin was the first to develop practical implementations of them.

5961. Olfactory television set was Smellovision, developed by the Swiss inventor Hans Laube in 1945. A "smell pack" incorporated into the set was designed to give off odors that enhanced the programming on the screen.

5962. International television broadcast of importance was that of the coronation of Queen Elizabeth II of the United Kingdom and Northern Ireland, held at Westminster Abbey on June 2, 1953. It was broadcast live to the United Kingdom, France, the Netherlands, and West Germany.

5963. Europe-wide television programming was offered by Eurovision, a live network created by linking television stations in Belgium, Denmark, France, Germany, Great Britain, Italy, the Netherlands, and Switzerland. The first broadcast was live from the Festival of Flowers in Montreux, Switzerland, on June 6, 1954.

5964. Video tape recorder for sounds and pictures was manufactured by the Ampex Corporation, Redwood City, CA, USA, and demonstrated simultaneously in Redwood City and Chicago, IL, USA, on April 14, 1956. The tape, 2 inches (5 centimeters) wide, moved at a speed of 15 inches (38 centimeters) per second. A single 14-inch (36-centimeter) reel accommodated a 65-minute recording. The developers were Charles P. Ginsberg, Charles E. Anderson, and Ray Dolby. The Columbia Broadcasting System purchased three of the video tape recorders at US$75,000 each in 1956.

5965. Helical-scan video tape recorder was demonstrated in September 1959 by the Japanese electronics firm Tokyo Shibaura Denki KK, the Toshiba Corporation, headquartered in Tokyo. The Toshiba prototype had one head. Sony KK and the Japan Victor Corporation (JVC), a subsidiary of Matsushita, further developed the product, with the first helical scan color VTR with two heads being shown by JVC in 1961. This was the basic design later used in the first VHS video cassette recorders.

5966. Transoceanic telecast by satellite was transmitted on July 10, 1962, from Andover, ME, USA. It was bounced off the American-built orbiting relay communications satellite *Telstar 1* and was received at various stations in Europe and the United States. The following day, a telecast from Pleumeur-Bodou, France, was received at Andover by means of the horn-shaped receiving antenna. The satellite was launched on July 10 from Cape Canaveral, FL, USA.

5967. Worldwide live television program was "Our World," shown in 26 countries on June 25, 1967, via four satellites. The two-hour production involved 10,000 technicians and 300 cameras in 14 countries on five continents. It opened with glimpses of births in Mexico, Canada, Denmark, and Japan. The rest of the program featured clips of conductor Leonard Bernstein and pianist Van Cliburn rehearsing a Rachmaninoff concerto at New York City's Lincoln Center, the Beatles recording a song in London, a rehearsal of *Lohengrin* in Bayreuth, Germany, the making of a movie in Italy, and other presentations. The program cost about US$5 million.

5968. Professional video cassette format was U-Matic, a three-quarter-inch cassette system developed jointly by three Japanese electronics firms, Sony KK, the Japan Victor Company, and Matsushita Denki Sangyo KK (Matsushita Electric Industrial Company). It was introduced for sale to broadcasters and industrial customers in 1970.

5969. High-definition digital videocassette recorder for use by the television industry was introduced by the Toshiba Corporation of Japan in late 1993. The VCR was developed in cooperation with BTS Broadcast Television Systems of Germany. It could record up to 64 minutes of high-definition digital video and audio data on a metal-particle tape 0.75 inches (19 millimeters) wide.

5970. Digital wireless cable television system was launched in October 1996 in Manitoba, Canada, by SkyCable Inc., a wholly owned subsidiary of the Craig Broadcast Systems. The system employed no ground cable, but depended entirely on satellite service.

5971. Simultaneous television and radio broadcast of music from five continents took place on February 7, 1998 (U.S. time), when five choral groups sang the "Ode to Joy" from Ludwig von Beethoven's *Ninth Symphony* for the opening ceremony of the 1998 Winter Olympic Games, held in Nagano, Japan. The participating choruses were the Tanglewood Festival Chorus, directed by John Oliver and broadcasting from the General Assembly Hall of the United Nations headquarters in New York City; a Chinese choir in Beijing's Forbidden City; the Ernst Senff Choir at the Brandenburg Gate in Berlin, Germany; three combined choirs in Cape Town, South Africa; and the Sydney Philharmonia Choir at the Sydney Opera House, Sydney, Australia. Instrumental accompaniment was broadcast from Nagano Prefecture Cultural Hall by five orchestras under the direction of Japanese-born conductor Seiji Ozawa. The chief technical engineer was an American, Mark Schubin.

TELECOMMUNICATIONS—VIDEOPHONE

5972. Videophone was developed very early in the development of television. In 1936, the German Post Office established a public television-telephone service between Berlin, Leipzig, Nuremberg, and Hamburg. Coaxial cables carried low-resolution video images of the callers along with the their voices, carried by a standard telephone signal. The service was discontinued in 1940.

5973. Color videophone for home use was introduced by the American Telephone & Telegraph Company in 1992. The AT&T Videophone 2500 was capable of sending and receiving video calls over existing phone lines without any other special equipment. It was a standard-size telephone, with a fold-up panel holding a small liquid crystal display screen and camera lens. A hood could be lowered over the camera for privacy. The unit initially sold for US$1,499.

5974. Internet video conference between an aircraft and a ground location was Project LINK, which took place on September 20, 1995, between NASA's Kuiper Airborne Observatory and the Exploratorium museum in San Francisco, CA, USA. The video conference, developed by Eureka Scientific, Inc., was designed to allow students to explore the differences between the ground and the air environment.

THEATER

5975. Actor to perform a role was the sixth-century Athenian dramatist Thespis, who is traditionally considered to be the inventor of acting as we know it. According to Aristotle's *Poetics,* Greek drama was entirely choral until Thespis, winner of the prize for tragedy at the Great Dionysia of circa 534 BCE, began to read dramatic speeches on stage, making him the first protagonist, or leading actor. He also invented dialogue when he began to exchange words with the leader of the chorus. Aeschylus is credited with introducing the practice of dialogue between two actors.

5976. Play to flop was *The Capture of Miletus,* a tragedy by a Greek writer, Phrynichus, that was produced in Athens in 492 BCE as part of the city's annual springtime arts festival, the City Dionysia. The plot concerned the destruction of the city of Miletus (in present-day Turkey) by the Persians two years earlier. Audiences disliked the play intensely and Phrynichus was forced to pay a fine.

5977. Dialogues in drama or fiction, as a literary device to contrast two worldviews, are the Sicilian mimes, which date to circa 425 BCE. According to Plato, whose works contain the only mention of them, the Sicilian mimes were written by Sophron of Syracuse. The original texts have not survived.

5978. Stage clowns appeared in Greek comedy productions circa the fifth century BCE. Their role was to get laughs by mimicking the lead characters and acting as buffoons.

THEATER—*continued*

5979. Latin comedy and tragedy were adapted in 240 BCE by Lucius Livius Andronicus from Greek plays for the Ludi Romani (Roman games), the yearly games held in honor of Jupiter. These were the first dramatic performances known to have been given in ancient Rome. The names of the plays are not known. Andronicus, a Greek war captive from Tarentum in southern Italy, is often called the "father of Roman literature."

5980. Suppression of a theatrical performance of record occurred in the Roman Republic in 204 BCE, when the satirist and poet Gnaeus Naevius, the first native Italian playwright, presented a play critical of certain public officials. He was convicted of slander, imprisoned, and possibly exiled.

5981. European playwright since classical times, and the first known playwright who was a woman, was the Saxon canoness Hrosvitha of Gandersheim (now in Germany), who died circa 1000. She was the author of six comedies in Latin—*Abraham, Callimachus, Dulcitius, Gallicanus, Pafnutius,* and *Sapientia*—all concerning the lives of Christian virgin martyrs. Her manuscripts were lost until 1500, when they were found by the German scholar Konradus Celtis.

5982. Morality play extant is *The Castell of Perseverance,* written in England circa 1425. Morality plays, popular in medieval Europe, were allegorical representations in Christian terms of the human choice between good and evil.

5983. Elizabethan acting troupe was the Earl of Leicester's Men, founded by the Earl in 1559. The company made its first appearance before the court of Queen Elizabeth in 1560 and began performing in its own London playhouse, James Burbage's The Theatre, in 1576.

5984. Kabuki performance was given in 1603 in Kyoto, Japan, where a group of actresses led by a woman named Okuni introduced a new kind of dance drama involving elaborate spectacle, sensuous dances, and much audience-actor interaction. It immediately became popular among ordinary Japanese and gave rise to troupes of imitators. Women were banned from performing kabuki in 1629 because so many of the actresses were prostitutes; since 1652, all actors have been adult males.

5985. Play staged in the New World was probably *La Théâtre de Neptune en la Nouvelle France,* performed on November 14, 1606, at Port Royale (now Annapolis Royal, Nova Scotia, Canada), by French players.

5986. Celebrity actress with an international following was Sarah Bernhardt, born Henriette-Rosine Bernard, who first won a devoted following in her native Paris. In 1879 she began traveling the world, performing leading roles in plays by Racine, Shakespeare, Dumas, and Eugène Scribe and cultivating a reputation as an extravagant libertine. A quarter of a million mourners attended her funeral in 1923.

5987. Absurdist play was *Ubu Roi (King Ubu),* by the French dramatist and poet Alfred Jarry. It was first produced on December 10, 1896, at the Théâtre de l'Oeuvre in Paris by the director Aurélian-Marie Lugné-Poe. Jarry conceived the work at the age of 15 to poke fun at a hated schoolmaster. It relates the grotesque adventures of the character Père Ubu, King of Poland, in anarchic and scatalogical imagery that so scandalized the audience and critics that the play was forced to close after two performances.

THEATER—STAGING

5988. Stage makeup is thought to have been invented by Thespis, the Greek poet and dramatist who became the first actor to take an individual role circa 534 BCE. Although Greek performers, like most performers in the ancient world, covered their features with masks, Thespis is said to have decorated his face with red cinnabar and white lead.

5989. Indoor theater was the Théâtre de l'Hôtel de Bourgogne, in Paris, France. A hall in the Hôtel de Bourgogne was converted for theatrical use in 1548 by the Confrérie de la Passion, a society of merchants and craftsmen with a 150-year monopoly on the production of mystery plays.

5990. Set designer of note was the late-16th-century Mannerist artist Giuseppe Arcimboldo (or Arcimboldi) of Milan, Italy. A resident of Prague (now the capital of the Czech Republic), he designed sets for the court theater of the Habsburg rulers Maximilian II and his son Rudolf II, Holy Roman Emperors and kings of Bohemia and Hungary, whom he also served as court painter. He is better known for his paintings, precursors of Surrealism, in which he made human faces out of compositions of objects.

5991. Elizabethan theater and the first public playhouse in England was The Theatre, in Shoreditch, London, built by James Burbage and John Brayne for the acting company known as the Earl of Leicester's Men. The building, which featured theatrical productions and athletic competitions from 1576 to 1598, was a roofless yard surrounded by three levels of seating galleries. Some of its timbers were used in the construction of the Globe Theatre, home of many of Shakespeare's plays.

5992. Indoor theater built for stage productions was the Teatro Olimpico in Vicenza, Italy, constructed by the Accademia Olimpica. Andrea Palladio, the architect, modeled it on the theaters of ancient Rome, adding a flat ceiling on which was painted a view of the sky. The first play to be performed there, on March 3, 1585, was *Oedipus Rex,* by Sophocles.

5993. Theater with a permanent proscenium arch was the Teatro Farnese in Parma, Italy, built by Giovanni Battista Aleotti in 1618–19 in the palace of the Farnese noble family. The stage area was framed by a proscenium arch decorated with statues and paintings. It also contained a curtain which was used only for theatrical effect, rather than for hiding scene changes, since the scenery was rearranged in full view of the spectators. The Teatro Farnese became the prototype for most modern playhouses.

5994. Description of stage lighting in a book appears in Joseph Furtenbach's *Sciena d'Comoedia,* published in Augsburg, Germany, in 1628. The theaters of his day used tallow candles and oil lamps to illuminate the stage. Furtenbach described how to achieve even theatrical lighting through the use of footlights and massed lights at the sides of the stage.

5995. Theater illuminated by gaslight was the Lyceum Theatre in London, England, which was converted to gas by Frederick Winsor in 1803.

5996. Theater with its own gas generator was the Chestnut Street Theatre in Philadelphia, PA, USA, which switched to gaslight in 1816.

5997. Theatrical spotlight was limelight, invented in 1816 by Scottish-born engineer Thomas Drummond, although it was not used in theaters as a spotlight until 1837. The device produced a bright light by heating calcium, in the form of a block of lime, in an oxyhydrogen flame. The addition of lenses allowed the operator to train a beam of light on a moving actor. Limelight could also be used to simulate moonlight, water, and other natural effects.

5998. Theater entirely lit by electric lights was the Savoy, built in London, England, in 1881 by the theatrical impresario Richard D'Oyly Carte to house his productions of works by Gilbert and Sullivan. Earlier experiments with electric lighting for stage illumination had been conducted at the Paris Opéra in 1846, but the Savoy was the first theater to make full and permanent use of the new technology.

5999. Modern theater in the round was the Penthouse Theatre at the University of Washington, Seattle, WA, USA, designed by Glenn Hughes and completed in 1940. The audience was seated in tiers completely surrounding a central performing space.

TIME—CALENDARS

6000. Calendar extant may have been inscribed on a 30,000-year-old bone known as the Blanchard Plaque, found in Abri Blanchard, Dordogne, France. According to the British paleoastronomer Alexander Marshack, marks on the bone represent a record of two lunations (periods of the moon) with indications of the moon's phase and possibly even its location in the sky.

6001. Twenty-four-hour days were invented by the ancient Egyptians circa 3500 BCE. However, the Egyptian hours varied in length according to the season, so that daylight hours were longer in summer and shorter in winter. A day with 24 equal hours was instituted by the Babylonians circa 300 BCE.

6002. Calendar with a year of 365 days was the Egyptian civil calendar, established circa 3000 BCE. Based approximately on the solar year, it also featured years and months of fixed duration, with twelve months of 30 days each plus five additional days at the end of the year. The Julian calendar developed in Roman times was closely based on the Egyptian model.

6003. Chinese calendar was in use from at least 1400 BCE, according to evidence on oracle bones found near An-yang in northeastern China that date from the Shang dynasty, circa 1760–1100 BCE. The ancient Chinese calendar was based on a year of 365.25 days and a lunation of 29.5 days, with ten- and twelve-day "weeks" grouped in 60-cycle periods. The naming of Chinese years by a totem animal, as in the Year of the Dragon, began in the Zhou dynasty circa 1000 BCE.

TIME—CALENDARS—*continued*

6004. Calendar developed in the Americas is thought to have been in use as early as circa 1000 BCE by the early chiefdom cultures that spread from the Valley of Mexico through the present Mexican states of Morelos, Veracruz, Oaxaca, and Chiapas and down along the west coast of Guatemala and El Salvador. This calendar was based on a year of 260 days, and differed extensively from the later and better-known Mayan calendar. Monument 3, unearthed at the San José Mogote in the Oaxaca Valley of Mexico and dated to between 604 and 504 BCE, is the earliest known stone carving containing references to this calendar. Monument 3 also contains the first known use of a Mesoamerican day-name, for an individual called Earthquake 1. (A day-name was a name based on the person's date of birth).

6005. Year in the Muslim calendar was the year in which Muhammad, the founder of Islam, traveled from Mecca to Yathrib (now Medina, Saudi Arabia), the journey that is called the *hijrah* in Arabic and is known in the West as the Hegira. That year was 622 on the Gregorian calendar. The Muslim calendar was probably instituted by Umar ibn al-Khattab, the second caliph, circa 639, after the need for a dating system became apparent. The lunar months observed in pre-Muslim Arabia were retained under different names.

6006. Jewish calendar extant is the Gezer Calendar, made in the city of Gezer, Israel, in the late tenth century BCE, most likely during the reign of King Solomon. It describes eight agricultural seasons within a cycle of twelve lunar months. The Jewish calendar in its modern form was publicized circa 356 CE by Rabbi Hillel II, leader of the Sanhedrin (the Great Assembly) at Tiberias in present-day Israel. The Sanhedrin was responsible for calculating the holidays of the Jewish calendar, a lunisolar system with complex intercalations that was derived in part from the Babylonian calendar of the sixth century BCE. Hillel published the method of calculation so that distant Jewish communities in the Diaspora could calculate the correct days for the festivals on their own, without waiting to hear the declarations of the Sanhedrin.

6007. Calendar adopted worldwide was the Gregorian calendar, a reform of the older Julian solar calendar promulgated by Pope Gregory XIII in 1582. To restore the proper date of the vernal equinox, which had fallen back to the beginning of March owing to inaccuracies in the Julian calendar, Gregory advanced the calendar ten days after October 4, 1582. The Gregorian calendar also adjusted the addition of leap years so that the calendar was astronomically accurate for 20,000 years. It was adopted in 1583 by Italy, Portugal, Spain, and the Catholic German principalities, and by all other states in Europe and the Americas by 1923. Japan adopted the Gregorian calendar in 1873, and China in 1912. Nearly all former European colonies have also adopted it. Many Muslim nations and Israel officially reckon dates by their own religious calendars, but typically conduct business using the Gregorian system.

6008. Islamic country to adopt a solar year was Turkey under the Ottomans. In 1677, it switched from the lunar months of the Muslim calendar to the solar months of the Julian calendar, though retaining the Muslim numbering of years. In 1929, during the modernizing campaign of Mustafa Kemal Atatürk, the country adopted the Gregorian calendar completely.

6009. National revolutionary calendar was the French Republican calendar, based on the Alexandrian adaptation of the ancient Egyptian calendar by Pierre-Sylvain Maréchal. A version of Maréchal's calendar was presented by Charles Gilbert Romme to the National Convention in Paris, which approved it on October 5, 1793, and made it public on November 24. The new era was deemed to have begun on September 22, 1792, the date of the foundation of the Republic, with each new year to begin on the autumnal equinox as observed from the Paris Observatory. The year contained twelve months of 30 days, with five additional days (*sanculotides*) each year, and a leap year with six sanculotides every four years. More radically, each month had three "weeks" of ten days; each day had ten hours; each hour had 100 minutes; and each minute had 100 seconds. All units of time were given new names, such as Thermidor for the month falling roughly in July–August; these were supplied by the playwright Philippe-François-Nazaire Fabre d'Églantine. The new calendar, which dispensed with all religious holidays, was never popular and was abandoned on January 1, 1806, although it was revived briefly by the Paris Commune in 1871.

6010. Eight-day week of record in modern times was decreed by the U.S. government for Alaska following its purchase of the territory from Russia in 1867. Previously, Alaska had been considered to be the easternmost territory of Russia, and therefore local Alaska clock time was in advance of clock time in eastern

Siberia. When ownership of the land passed to the United States, Alaskan clocks were set back a day so that local time would be behind the westernmost clock time in the United States, thereby creating a single eight-day week.

6011. Identification of years in the Chinese calendar by the names of totem animals such as the Dragon or Rat began in the Zhou dynasty circa 1000 BCE.

TIME—ERAS AND DATES

6012. Event in Greek history to be dated was the Olympic Games, held in Olympia, Greece, in 776 BCE. The date was identified through calculations made by the philosopher and mathematician Hippias, who grew up in Elis, not far from Olympia. Hippias is also known as the inventor of the quadratrix curve.

6013. Definite date in the history of the Indian subcontinent is 327 BCE, the year in which India was invaded by the Greek armies of Alexander the Great. Alexander reached as far as the Beas River in northern India before his overworked troops mutinied and forced a withdrawal.

6014. Calculation of the date of creation in the Bible is contained in the *Seder olam rabbah (Order of the World)* by Rabbi Yosi ben Chalafta, a Jewish scholar of Roman Palestine (now Israel) in the second century CE. He calculated a date of Monday, October 7, 3761 BCE (in the Julian calendar), using internal evidence provided by the genealogies and histories in the Jewish scriptures, as well as known dates in post-biblical Jewish history. This date refers to an abstract "first molad" or instant in which the first lunation of creation began (i.e., the beginning of the very first lunar month, with which the lunisolar Jewish calendar had to begin). By this reckoning, the instant of first creation was actually about 1.5 days earlier, at 6 P.M. on Saturday, October 5, 3761 BCE, the beginning of the first day.

6015. Work of history to use BC and AD was *De ratione temporum (On the Reckoning of Time)* of the Venerable Bede, written circa 725 in Northumbria, England. The Bede based his "Christian Era" dating system on the one invented by the Roman abbot Dionysius Exiguus (also known as Denis the Little) circa 525. The abbreviations stand for "before Christ" and *anno Domini* ("in the year of our Lord").

6016. Dynamical time scale for determining the orbital motions of celestial bodies was Ephemeris Time, defined in 1952 by the International Astronomical Union. Ephemeris Time was based on the earth's orbital motion as determined by accurate (but nonrelativistic) solar tables published in 1898 by the American astronomer Simon Newcomb. It was superseded in 1984 by a more accurate standard, Barycentric Time, that took into account the relativistic motions of bodies in the solar system.

6017. Relativistic time scale was Barycentric Dynamical Time, a celestial time measurement system defined in 1984 by the International Astronomical Union as a replacement for the less-accurate Ephemeris Time. The motion equations of Barycentric Dynamical Time are based on the center of mass of the solar system and take into account refinements required by the general theory of relativity, which earlier dynamical time systems did not.

TIME—TIMEPIECES

6018. Reference to a sundial is found in the Jewish scriptures in the book of 2 Kings. The text makes reference to a sundial set up by Achaz, king of Yehudah (Judah; modern-day Israel and the Palestinian Authority) in the eighth century BCE. When his son and successor Chizkiyahu (Hezekiah) asks the prophet Yeshayahu (Isaiah) for a sign from heaven, the shadow on the sundial moves backwards 10 degrees.

6019. Hourglass is first mentioned in a play by the comic Athenian playwright and poet Baton circa 250 BCE, but was certainly known many centuries earlier.

6020. Large mechanical clock of record was invented by the Chinese Tantric Buddhist monk and mathematician Yixing circa 700. Water flowing through the clock turned a wheel once each day. Torches inside the mechanism kept the works from freezing in winter.

6021. Astronomical clock of large size was the "Cosmic Engine" built in China in 1092 by Su Song. Intended to tell time by simulating the movements of the sun and moon, the intricate device was more than 30 feet (10 meters) high.

6022. Mechanical clock in Europe was installed by the Austin (Augustinian) canons at Dunstable Priory, Bedfordshire, England, in 1283.

6023. Public clock to strike the hours was built in Milan, Italy, in 1335.

6024. Alarm clock still extant is a wall clock from Würzburg, Germany, dating to circa 1350. It was probably originally made for a monastery. The clock is preserved in Würzburg's Mainfränkisches Museum.

TIME—TIMEPIECES—*continued*

6025. Mechanical clock still extant is the clock at Salisbury Cathedral in England, built circa 1386. In 1929, it was found by T.R. Robinson in the tower and later restored to working condition.

6026. Pocket watch is thought by some historians to have been created in 1510 in Nuremberg (Nürnberg), Germany, by locksmith Peter Henlein, who had invented an essential part of the mechanism, the mainspring, about ten years earlier. The mainspring replaced the system of weights used in clocks and thus made possible a lightweight, portable timepiece. Henlein's first model was spherical. Later models were disks, some 4 to 6 inches (100 to 150 millimeters) in diameter and 3 inches (75 millimeters) high.

6027. Pendulum clock was invented in 1641 by Vincenzio Galilei, the son of Galileo. He was the first to realize that the pendulum, with its regular period of oscillation (first noted by his father), would make an efficent and accurate regulator of clock movement. Vincenzio's design for a clock that used a pendulum escapement was much improved in 1656 by the Dutch mathematician and astronomer Christiaan Huygens. The weight-driven, pendulum-regulated escapement led to smaller and less expensive wall clocks that could be priced within reach of a wider public.

6028. Minute hand appeared on watches in Europe circa 1670.

6029. Clock capable of keeping accurate time at sea was the chronometer invented by 18th-century Yorkshire-born carpenter turned clockmaker John Harrison, who devoted his life to the effort. Vying for a prize of £20,000 offered by the British Board of Longitude for the construction of a clock that would keep time at sea, enabling navigators for the first time to accurately calculate longitude, Harrison began work in 1728 and submitted three instruments before his fourth was accepted by the Board in 1762. Accurate to within .01 second per day, Harrison's chronometer no. 4 was the first timepiece designed to compensate for the expansion and contraction effects of varying temperatures. It was also the first clock to keep time accurately while it was being wound. Harrison did not receive full payment from the Board until 1773, three years before his death.

6030. Quartz clock based on the regular oscillation of a quartz crystal in an electrical circuit was the invention of the Canadian-born telecommunications engineer Warren Marrison. His first quartz clock design was developed in 1927 at Bell Laboratories in Holmdel, NJ, USA. It proved to be more accurate than the best existing mechanical clocks.

6031. Clock to operate by nuclear power was the Atomicron, made by the National Company, Malden, MA, USA, and exhibited on October 2, 1956, at the Overseas Press Club, New York City. It was 84 inches (2 meters) high, 22 inches (56 centimeters) wide, and 18 inches (48 centimeters) deep, and was priced at US$50,000. Its "pendulum" was the cesium atom, which oscillates at a constant frequency of 9,192,631,830 megacycles a second.

6032. Battery-powered wristwatch was the Hamilton Electric 500, introduced by the Hamilton Watch Company of Lancaster, PA, USA, in January 1957. Instead of a mainspring, the watch was powered by a tiny battery. It was designed by Hamilton's director of research, John Van Horn, after whom the first production models were named, together with chief physicist Philip Biemiller and master technician James Reese.

6033. Electronic wristwatch was the Accutron "Spaceview D", introduced on October 25, 1960, by the Bulova Watch Company of Switzerland and New York, NY, USA. It used a tuning fork as an oscillator instead of the hairspring and balance-wheel oscillator found in conventional watches. The tuning fork vibrated 360 times per second. Gears converted the vibrating motion of the tuning fork to rotary motion to turn the hands on the analog dial. The Accutron was accurate to within one minute per month. It was designed by Max Hetzel, William Bennett, Egbert Van Haaften and William Mutter.

6034. Quartz wristwatch was the Quartz 35 SQ Astron, produced by the Japanese watchmaking firm of Seiko. It was introduced in Tokyo on December 25, 1969. The Astron had an analog dial and sold for 450,000 yen (US$1,250). The oscillator was a quartz crystal vibrating at 8,192 times per second, and the movement was accurate to within about five seconds per month, or a minute per year. Analog quartz watch technology was developed in 1967 by the central research organization of the Swiss watch industry, Centre Électronique Horloger in Neuchâtel, Switzerland, but Swiss quartz watches were not available commercially until 1970.

6035. Digital quartz wristwatch was the Pulsar, sold beginning in late 1972 by HMW (previously the Hamilton Watch Company) of Lancaster, PA, USA. The Pulsar had no standard dial; it indicated the time of day in flashing red light-emitting diode numerals displayed when the owner pushed a button. It was initially sold in jewelry stores for US$2,100. The Pulsar was developed by HMW and Electro/Data, Inc., under the direction of John Bergey.

6036. Calculator watch was introduced by Pulsar, at that time the Time Computer division of HMW of Lancaster, PA, USA, in 1975. The Pulsar calculator watch counted hours, minutes, and seconds, kept track of the month and date, and featured a tiny calculator panel with add, subtract, multiply, divide, percent, and memory functions. A small plastic tool was provided to push the recessed keys. The watch sold for US$600, or in gold cases for US$3,950.

6037. Television wristwatch was introduced by Seiko of Tokyo, Japan, in the fall of 1983. It featured a liquid crystal video display that showed blue pictures on a light gray background, and was able to receive UHF and VHF TV channels and FM radio.

6038. Radio-controlled wristwatch that could synchronize automatically to broadcast radio signals based on atomic time standards was introduced in 1991 by Junghans Uhren GmbH of Germany. The Mega 1 automatically updated its time according to signals broadcast from a transmitter near Frankfurt, Germany. The updating function was only available within the range of the transmitter and only for the Central Europe time zone.

6039. Watch that told time in Catalan was developed by Michael McCready and Xavier Casanovas and marketed in Europe in 1996. The watch displayed time markings in quarter hours, as is the custom in the Spanish region of Catalonia.

TOOLS AND HARDWARE

6040. Adhesives were used in the Middle East tens of thousands of years ago. Stone tools found at Umm el Tlel in the Syrian desert in 1995–96 exhibit traces of a glue-like material, bitumen, apparently used to attach them to a handle. The implements have been dated to circa 34000 BCE by their discoverers, Eric Boeda and colleagues of the University of Paris, France.

6041. Axe was one of the earliest tools, with pressure-flaked flints used as handleless axes beginning in the early Paleolithic period. Axes acquired wooden or bone hafts by circa 30,000 BCE. The shaft-hole axe (with a hole in the cutting head for the haft) was developed in Mesopotamia (now Iraq) by circa 5000 BCE, and the first metal axes, made of copper, were in use in Egypt by circa 4000 BCE. The *Odyssey* of Homer, believed to date to circa 800 BCE, contains the first literary mention of the iron-bladed axe.

6042. Hammer was, along with the axe, one of the earliest tools to be invented. The oldest forms of hammers were simply handheld stones chosen because they possessed a flattened end. Wooden or bone clubs fashioned with a heavy, flattened head were in use by the Paleolithic period in many parts of the Old World. The hafted hammer, with a grooved stone head that helped hold in place a lashed-on wooden branch, paralleled the development of the stone axe, and dates from the Neolithic period, perhaps 10,000 BCE. The clawed hammer for driving and extracting nails was a Roman invention.

6043. Nails made of bronze were used in Sumeria (now Iraq) circa 3300 BCE.

6044. Drill was the bow drill. It had been independently invented in most parts of the Old World by the beginning of the Bronze Age, and was certainly in use in Egypt by circa 3000 BCE. A string or gut was looped around the bit, usually of sharpened hardwood or bone with a flint or metal tip. The string was drawn back and forth by a wooden bow, turning the bit. The auger, a metal bit with a twisted or spooned end and a crosswise handle (like the modern gimlet), was probably invented by the Romans. Larger versions were braced against the chest. The carpenter's brace appeared in Europe by circa 1400. The common hand drill, with a geared crank and a screw chuck to hold standardized steel drill bits, is a 19th-century invention.

6045. Plastering tools had a long period of development beginning at least circa 2500 BCE. The ancient Egyptians, Greeks, Etruscans, Hindus, and Maya all employed plastering techniques for their temples and other structures to provide a suitably smooth surface for wall paintings. Plasterer's tools essentially identical to those used today were pictured in wall murals found in the ruins of the Roman town of Pompeii, buried on August 24, 79 CE, in a volcanic eruption. Many of Pompeii's houses exhibit extravagant wall murals on plaster.

TOOLS AND HARDWARE—*continued*

6046. Lock was unearthed on the remains of a door in the ruins of the palace of Khorsabad near ancient Nineveh (now in Iraq). Of the pin tumbler type, it consists of a large wooden door bolt pierced with holes. A lock assembly contains wooden pins that drop down into the holes to secure the lock; a wooden key with pegs that matched the holes was used to lift the pins and open the door. The lock has been dated to circa 2000 BCE.

6047. Saw capable of cutting wood efficiently was developed by the ancient Egyptians circa 2000 BCE. Older saws, consisting simply of a wooden shaft into which were bound pieces of flint, bone, or teeth, had been in use from circa 12,000 BCE, but these were highly inefficient.

6048. Pulley and tackle block was probably invented by the Pythagorean philosopher and scientist Archytas of Tarentum (now Taranto, Italy), who lived circa 400–350 BCE.

6049. Scissors were developed during the Bronze Age. The first extant example of a two-bladed, one-piece bronze scissor with a c-type spring joining the handles (often called spring shears) was found in Egypt and dates to circa 300 BCE.

6050. Steel saws were introduced by Roman craftsmen during the period of the Republic. Pliny the Elder, in his *Historia naturalis (Natural History),* completed in Rome circa 77 CE, noted that Roman metal saws possessed teeth that were alternately bent left and right, a practice followed to widen the kerf (cut) and make it easier to pull the saw while cutting. Romans also made use of large tensioned frame saws for cutting planks. This type of saw, essentially unchanged in design, is still in use today.

6051. Plane in its simplest form—a sharp stone for scraping and smoothing wood—has been used by all woodworking peoples since the Paleolithic period. The familiar woodworking plane with an angled metal blade held in a block was possibly invented by the Romans; the first known examples are from Pompeii, Italy, and date to before 79 CE. In form remarkably like the modern hand plane, the Roman versions had an iron sole (bottom) and iron blade and wooden handgrips and were up to 17 inches (44 centimeters) long.

6052. Folding knife with multiple tools extant is a multibladed tool of Roman design dating from circa 250 CE, in the collection of the Fitzwilliam Museum in Cambridge, England. A precursor of the modern Swiss Army knife, the tool contains a folding knife, a three-pronged fork, a spoon, an awl or prong, a small spoon for spices, and a toothpick. All fold into a single lyre-shaped handle.

6053. Spirit level was invented in France by Melchisédech Thévenot circa 1660, according to correspondence between Thévenot and the Dutch mathematician Christiaan Huygens. Thévenot published a description of his device in 1681.

6054. Steel scissors were developed in 1761 in Sheffield, England, by English metalsmith Robert Hinchliffe. His cast steel scissors were the first that could be mass produced.

6055. Pruning shears were invented in France in 1815 by the Marquis Bertrand de Moleville, an exiled minister of King Louis XVI.

6056. Powered wood shapers were developed to prepare the hundreds of thousands of premade wooden parts needed to assemble the Crystal Palace, the huge pavilion of glass, iron, and wood that housed the Great Exhibition, which opened May 1, 1851, in Hyde Park, London, England. Steam-powered shapers, with rotating steel cutters in a wide variety of shapes, were used to make such elements as the sash bars for the roof, of which some 200 miles (320 kilometers) were needed. Within 20 years, shapers were in general use in woodshops all over Britain.

6057. Electric drill for industrial use was patented in 1889 by Arthur James Arnot of Melbourne, Australia.

6058. Flashlight was manufactured by the American Electric and Novelty Manufacturing Company of New York, NY, USA, which started in business in 1896. The first flashlight was produced about 1898. The model consisted of a paper tube with metal fittings, a rough brass stamping used for a reflector, without any lens, and a spring contact switch. The lamp was handmade, as was the battery. The company later changed its name to the American Eveready Company and subsequently became a part of the National Carbon Company.

6059. Swiss Army knife was patented in Switzerland on June 12, 1897, by the Swiss cutlery maker Karl Elsener, who since 1891 had been making multibladed knives for the Swiss Army at his factory in Ibach near Schwyz in Switzerland. It was a light pocketknife for officers and featured a blade, awl, can opener, screwdriver, a second small blade, and a corkscrew. Elsener's essential innovation was to use only two springs for the six blades, thus creating a compact but versatile tool that could be easily carried in a pocket.

6060. Electric hand drill was invented in 1914 by S. Duncan Black and Alonzo G. Decker, founders of the Black and Decker Corporation of Towson, MD, USA. The bulky but portable drill weighed 24 pounds and had a pistol grip and trigger switch. Black and Decker introduced the world's first portable half-inch electric drill in 1916 and the world's first cordless electric drill, powered by self-contained nickel-cadmium cells, in 1961. In 1968 it developed the Apollo Lunar Surface Drill, the first cordless drill used on the moon. The power head for the drill was designed to remove core samples from the lunar surface.

6061. Aerosol spray can was invented by Julian Seth Kahn of New York, NY, USA, who received a U.S. patent on August 22, 1939, for an "apparatus for mixing a liquid with gas." It was equipped with an inexpensive disposable valve mechanism. Under controlled pressure, it dispensed such items as whipped cream, paints, pharmaceuticals, and insecticides.

TOOLS AND HARDWARE—LAWN MOWERS

6062. Lawn mower was the idea of Edwin Budding, an English textile engineer, who based it on a device used for trimming the nap on cloth. His patented design was manufactured by John Ferrabee of the Phoenix Iron Works, near Stroud, Gloucestershire, beginning in 1830. Before this invention, lawns were trimmed with scythes and flattened with rollers.

6063. Lawn mower that was practical was invented by Elwood McGuire of Richmond, IN, USA, in the 1890s. He attached a set of sharp blades to a rotating reel with a cutting bed at the center. The grass was clipped off as it came between the bed and the blades.

6064. Power mowers for cutting grass were designed and built in 1897 by the Benz Company, Stuttgart, Germany, and the Coldwell Lawn Mower Company, Newbury, NY, USA. Both models used gasoline motors and neither was commercially produced.

6065. Hovercraft lawn mower was the Flymo, introduced in 1963 by the Flymo Company of England. The whirling horizontal cutting blade also acted as a fan, creating a cushion of air that lifted the body of the mower a few inches above the ground.

W

WEAPONS

6066. Weapon known to archeologists is a broken wooden spear. It was unearthed in 1911 by S. Hazzledine Warren at Clacton-on-Sea, England. It is believed to date to circa 200,000 BCE.

6067. Metal helmets were manufactured in Mesopotamia of copper-and-arsenic bronze, beginning approximately in 3000 BCE. More often, Mesopotamian and Egyptian soldiers wore helmets of leather.

6068. Battering rams were employed by the Assyrians circa 900 BCE. They attached a spear or some other projectile to a shield-covered wagon, wheeled it up to the city walls, and pushed it back and forth to make a breach.

6069. Siege engines for attacking city walls were developed by the Assyrians circa 800 BCE. Relief sculptures from that era show a wheeled wooden tower with an upper deck and a long pointed arm projecting forward and upward. While soldiers prised the mortar from the walls, archers stationed on the platform picked off the city's defenders.

6070. Crossbows were invented in China, where they have been found in graves dating from the fifth century BCE. The earliest form was a single wooden bow fixed to a grooved stock. The bolt was held in the groove and fired by a trigger mechanism.

6071. Catapult was, according to tradition, a kind of giant crossbow invented circa 399 BCE by Greek engineers in the employ of Dionysius the Elder, tyrant of Syracuse, Sicily, in anticipation of a war with Carthage. It was called the *gastrophetes*, Greek for "belly shooter," because soldiers drawing the weapon had to brace it against their stomachs.

6072. Chain mail is shown on Greek reliefs of the third century BCE. Mail was made by sewing iron rings on leather or fabric garments.

6073. Solar energy weapons may have been devised by the Greek mathematician, scientist, and engineer Archimedes, who played a key role in the defense of Syracuse, Sicily, during its siege by Roman forces in 213–212 BCE. According to contemporary accounts, Archimedes burned the besieging Roman ships by focusing sunlight on them with an array of concave bronze mirrors. Historians had long viewed this feat as apocryphal, but in 1973 the Greek engi-

WEAPONS—*continued*

neer Ioannis Sakkas proved that it was technically possible. Sakkas arranged for 50 sailors to focus the light from 31 bronze-coated concave mirrors onto a wooden ship floating 160 feet away, setting it ablaze.

6074. Plate armor that was practical was the *lorica segmentata,* or segmented iron shirt, worn by Roman legionnaires in the first century CE. It replaced the *lorica hamata,* or mail shirt.

6075. Greek fire is thought to have been invented by a Syrian Jewish architect, Callinicus of Heliopolis (now Baalbek, Lebanon), who brought the secret formula to the Byzantine Greeks in 673, during the reign of Constantine IV Pogonatus, after leaving Syria as a refugee from the Muslims. Although the exact composition of Greek fire is no longer known, it most probably contained naphthene palmitate, the chief ingredient of napalm. It clung as it burned and could not be extinguished by water. Byzantine mariners kept containers of Greek fire handy to spray and catapult onto their opponents.

6076. Flame throwers were deployed by the Chinese in 919. They used a highly flammable gunpowder paste to ignite petroleum.

6077. Trebuchet was in use by circa 1004 in China, about 200 years before similar machines appeared in Europe. These huge siege machines, which were capable of flinging heavy rocks or other missiles great distances, were manned by up to 100 soldiers. Propulsive energy was provided by a heavy counterweight fixed to the end of a long pivoting arm. At the other end of the arm was a basket or sling to hold the missile. When the counterweight was dropped, the arm moved rapidly in a vertical arc and hurled the missile.

6078. Bayonet is said to have been invented by French peasants who ran out of ammunition for their arquebuses while they were chasing bandits and in a fit of ingenuity stuck the handles of their knives into the muzzles, creating makeshift spears. Knives equipped with plugs for this purpose, instead of handles, were made in Bayonne, France, beginning in 1649.

6079. Poison gas to be employed with significant effect was chlorine gas. It was released by the Germans on April 22, 1915, along a four-mile (6-kilometer) front at the second battle of Ypres, Belgium, during World War I. Although thousands of canisters of gas were used, causing some 15,000 French and Algerian casualties, the Germans hesitated to put their own forces into the gassed zone and failed to follow up on the attack. The Germans had previously tried the gas against the Russians in Poland, without success.

6080. Mustard gas use in war occurred on July 12, 1917, at Ypres in Belgium, when German forces lobbed shells containing the yellow, choking gas into Allied trenches. Mustard gas is a vesicant (blistering agent) made from carbon, hydrogen, sulfur, and chlorine.

6081. Nerve gas was Tabun, an organophosphorus agent related to insecticides, developed by the German chemical conglomerate Interessengemeinschaft Farbenindustrie Aktiengesellschaft (I.G. Farben) in 1936. It was never used in battle.

6082. Computer virus as a weapon of war was reportedly used in January 1991 in the initial stages of the Gulf War by American intelligence agents to cripple Iraqi air-defense command computers.

6083. Register of international arms sales and transfers was the United Nations Register on Conventional Arms, established in December 1991 by the United Nations General Assembly. The register tracked international arms transfers and national production and stockpiles of conventional arms as well as relevant military policies. In its initial form, it did not track weapons of mass destruction, including nuclear arms.

WEAPONS—EXPLOSIVES

6084. Gunpowder was black powder, discovered in the ninth century by Chinese alchemists seeking the elixir of immortality. It was known as *huo pao,* "the fire drug." The ingredients, in their approximate proportions, were 10 percent sulfur, 15 percent charcoal, and 15 percent saltpeter (potassium nitrate). Saltpeter is found in the soil of many parts of China and later became known in Europe as "Chinese snow."

6085. Grenade was apparently used by the Chinese in the year 1231 against Mongol attackers who were digging a tunnel to the base of a city wall. The tunnel was roofed with ox skins. The defenders lowered a chain on which was suspended a weapon they called *chen tien lei,* "heaven-shaking thunder," an iron can filled with black powder. The explosion destroyed the tunnel and everyone in it.

6086. Mine barrage was the invention of an American, David Bushnell, who conceived the idea of floating kegs containing explosives and equipped with a gunlock and hammer that would ignite upon contact with ships. In August 1777, during the American Revolutionary War, he attached a series of mines together in Black Point Bay, near New London, CT, USA. Members of the crew of the British frigate *Cerberus,* commanded by Captain J. Symons, noticed a rope alongside their ship. They hauled it in, not realizing that a mine was attached to the other end. They hoisted the mine on board and it exploded, killing three of the crew and blowing a fourth into the water.

6087. Exploding shell was the invention of Henry Shrapnel, an English artillery officer. In 1784, he hit upon the idea of placing a fused charge inside an artillery shell, and filling the shell casing with small lead pellets or bullets. The fuse was timed to explode when the shell neared the enemy, spraying lethal shot (shrapnel) over a large area. Shrapnel shells first saw wide use in the Napoleonic Wars.

6088. Remote-controlled explosive mine activated by electricity was the invention of Pavel Lvovich Silling, a Russian engineer, who demonstrated it to generals of the Russian army at the Neva River near St. Petersburg in 1812. By sending electric current along a wire, he produced a spark that detonated the mine. Silling's device was used soon thereafter in the defense of St. Petersburg against Napoléon's invasion.

6089. Smokeless gunpowder was guncotton, an explosive formed by the nitration of cotton fiber in nitric and sulfuric acid, accidently discovered in 1845 by the German chemist Christian Friedrich Schönbein while mopping up an acid spill with his wife's cotton apron. The formula was improved and made more stable in 1884 by a French inventor, Paul Vieille.

6090. Torpedo that was self-propelled was developed for the Austrian Navy between 1864 and 1867 by English engineer Robert Whitehead, based upon earlier work done by an Austrian naval officer named Luppis. Whitehead's early designs, propelled by a compressed-air engine driving a single screw, could travel at 6 knots (7 miles per hour), and had a range of up to 700 yards (640 meters). The torpedo was 14 feet (4 meters) long and carried a charge of explosive in its nose.

6091. Military use of TNT was during the Russo-Japanese War of 1904–1905. Powerful, stable, and inexpensive, TNT made the ideal high-explosive for mines and artillery shells, and became the most widely used military explosive of the 20th century.

6092. Aerial bombs were cans of nitroglycerin dropped by Italian aviators during air raids on the Libyan town of Ain Zara in 1911.

6093. Shaped charge used in war was employed with great success by the Germans during the glider attack on May 10, 1940, against Eben-Emael, a massive Belgian fortification anchoring the Albert Canal defensive line. German paratroopers equipped with portable shaped charges, which directionally focused the blast effect on a small area, were able to penetrate Belgian bunkers that would have been proof against larger conventional explosives.

WEAPONS—GUNS AND ARTILLERY

6094. Depiction of a gun was a wall carving in a Buddhist cave in the Chinese province of Szechuan. It was discovered in 1985 by the British Sinologist Joseph Needham. Dating to 1128 CE, the carving depicts a demonic warrior holding a bombard that is belching flames. A nearby figure holds a grenade. The carving predates by some two centuries similar weapons depicted in European documents.

6095. European to publish a recipe for gunpowder was the English experimental scientist and Franciscan friar Roger Bacon. In 1242, he gave precise directions for making black powder and noted its likely usefulness in war.

6096. Cannon with bamboo barrels appear on the inventory of the Imperial Arsenal of Yangchow, China, in 1259. They shot stones. Cannon barrels fabricated of thick layers of paper and glue were also made in China during that era.

6097. Depiction of a gun in Europe appears in the Holkham Codex, also known as *De officiis regum (On the Duties of Kings),* a manuscript made for King Edward III of England by Walter de Millemete in 1326. It shows a knight in chain mail firing a bottle-shaped gun mounted on a trestle table. The gun is perhaps 3 feet long (1 meter) and has a large arrow stuffed into its bore. The knight is seen in the act of applying a glowing piece of metal to the gun's touchhole, using something resembling a tongs.

6098. Metal cannon was a cast-bronze barrel 14 inches (340 millimeters) long and weighing 15.5 pounds (7 kilograms), made in China in March 1332.

6099. Gun carriage was invented by two French brothers, Jean and Gaspard Bureau, circa 1440. It was a wheeled wooden platform, drawn by a team of horses or mules, on which a cannon was mounted.

WEAPONS—GUNS AND ARTILLERY—
continued

6100. Muskets were used by Spanish infantry circa 1450. These were matchlock weapons, weighing 25 pounds (10 kilograms), that fired a lead ball weighing about 1.5 ounces (42 grams) and needed to rest on a support for accurate fire. Awkward as they were, the first muskets were far superior to the older arquebuses and fired a ball heavy enough to penetrate any suit of armor.

6101. Accidental shooting of record took place in 1515 in Constance (now in Germany). According to a contemporary account, a man named Laux Pfister was handling a wheel-lock pistol when it went off accidently, wounding a prostitute he had just hired. A court required him to pay her medical expenses and provide her with a lifetime pension.

6102. Treatise on ballistics was *Nova Scientia (A New Science)*, written in 1535 by the Venetian mathematician Niccolò Fontana Tartaglia (or Tartalea). The book's descriptions of the mathematics of falling bodies included the first firing tables for artillery.

6103. Cartridges were made of paper and contained only gunpowder; the bullet was loaded separately. They were in use by the Swedish Army before 1630.

6104. Nation to ban firearms was Japan under the Tokugawa shogunate. After guns were introduced to Japan in 1543 by Portuguese sailors, feudal Japan quickly developed a large gun industry, producing some of the best-made firearms in the world. However, widespread use of guns was seen by the shogunate as a threat to the traditional social position of the samurai class, and their use was increasingly restricted. By 1633, trade in firearms was forbidden (as was trade with foreigners in general), and the few guns that were made were reserved to the shoguns themselves. The ban lasted until the early 19th century.

6105. Revolver pistol with a revolving cylinder was invented circa 1680 by an Englishman, J. Dafte, who produced a bronze horse pistol with a revolving barrel.

6106. Machine gun may have been the gun patented by the English gunsmith James Puckle in 1718. A cross between a flintlock musket and a revolver, it featured a revolving cylinder that fed bullets into the gun's firing chamber. It could fire 63 rounds in 7 minutes, compared to the 7 or so rounds a musketman was capable of firing in the same time.

6107. Breechlock rifle used in war was the Ferguson flintlock, produced by the Scottish gunmaker Patrick Ferguson, a major in the British Army, and first demonstrated in public on June 1, 1776. The British Army ordered 200 of the rifles, which could be fired at a rate of up to six times a minute, and used them in the American War of Independence.

6108. Breech-loading gun was invented in 1786 by the English gunsmith Henry Nock at his shop in London. His design was a variation of the smoothbore musket, constructed with a chamber at the rear of the barrel that could be opened to quickly load powder and shot.

6109. Breech-loading military rifle that proved pivotal in battle was the bolt-action Dreyse rifle or "needle gun" invented by Prussian gunmaker Johann Nikolas Dreyse in 1841. Employing a long, needle-like firing pin to detonate the charge, the accurate and easy-to-load rifle, which could be fired from a prone position, was adopted by the Prussian Army in 1848.

6110. Breech-loading, rifle-bored cannon was invented in 1855 by an Englishman, William George Armstrong. The barrels of Armstrong's cannon were rifled with long, helical strips of wrought iron welded into the bore, which imparted spin to the shell and thus improved its stability in flight, and were reinforced on the outside with heat-shrunken steel rings at the areas of greatest stress. He also invented a breech-loading mechanism that could accommodate an elongated projectile. His design was adopted by the British Army in 1859. Armstrong's factory later became the munitions firm Vickers Armstrong Ltd., one of the largest in Britain.

6111. Machine gun that was practical was invented by Charles E. Barnes of Lowell, MA, USA, who obtained a U.S. patent on July 8, 1856, on an "improved automatic cannon." It was operated by a crank, the speed of firing depending upon the speed with which the crank was turned.

6112. Breech-loading artillery used in combat were 18-pound cannon built by British munitions manufacturer William Armstrong. During the Opium Wars, Armstrong's artillery were used on August 12, 1860, by the British Army to bombard Sinho, China, in an effort to force Beijing to admit foreign diplomats.

6113. Rapid-fire machine gun was the Gatling gun, invented by American inventor Richard Jordan Gatling of Indianapolis, IN, USA, who obtained a U.S. patent on November 4, 1862, on "an improvement in revolving battery guns." The first gun, which fired 250 shots a minute, was made in Indianapolis.

6114. Automatic pistol was a 7.63-millimeter weapon designed by the American gunsmith Hugo Borchardt in 1893 for the German firm of Ludwig Loewe & Co. (later the Deutsche Waffen- und Munitionsfabriken). A sliding mechanism powered by the recoil of the previous shot ejected the spent cartridge, cocked the hammer, and loaded a fresh cartridge from a magazine in the handgrip.

6115. Dum-dum bullets were developed at Dum-Dum, a suburb of Calcutta, India, by the British Army circa 1897 for the .303 military cartridges. The bullets were hollow-tipped and mushroomed on impact, causing large wounds.

6116. Submachine gun widely used in battle was the Maschinen Pistole 1918 Bergmann, designed by Hugo Schmeisser and issued to German troops toward the end of World War I. The short-barreled MP18 used 9-millimeter rounds and could fire about 400 rounds per minute. The energy of gases expelled during the firing of a round was used to blow the spent cartridge back and out of the gun while automatically loading another cartridge into the chamber, thus enabling a constant rate of fire. The first submachine gun to be manufactured was the .45-caliber Thompson submachine gun, known as the "Tommy gun," invented in the United States by John Taliaferro Thompson in 1915. It was not issued to Allied troops during the war.

6117. Assault rifle was the German Sturmgewehr MP44, designed by Hugo Schmeisser in 1944 for the German Army. It fired a lighter weight 7.92-millimeter cartridge at a rapid rate; 30 rounds were held in a curved magazine. About 430,000 were manufactured. It was the basis for the Russian AK-47, designed by Mikhail Timofeyevich Kalashnikov in 1947, of which an estimated 70 million had been produced by 1995.

6118. Gun that could fire one million rounds a minute was "Metal Storm," invented by Michael O'Dwyer of Brisbane, Australia, and publicly demonstrated in 1997. The Metal Storm design employed no moving parts, no gunpowder, and no shell casings. It consisted of one or more barrels packed with small-caliber bullets separated by wads of propellant. An electrical charge applied along the barrel successively ignited the propellant wads, projecting the bullets at an extremely high rate of fire. A prototype fired 180 nine-millimeter bullets in 0.01 second, equivalent to about 1 million rounds per minute. The inventor envisioned the new gun design as being especially useful for clearing land mines by densely spraying entire open areas with bullets.

WEAPONS—MECHANIZED

6119. Assault vehicle was a ladder on wheels that could be pushed against city walls, allowing attackers to climb up and over. Such a scaling ladder is shown on an Egyptian tomb painting dated circa 2500 BCE.

6120. Armored car was developed in 1902 by the French firm of Charron, Girardot, and Voight. It featured an internal combustion engine, armor plated sides, and a small gun in a turret.

6121. Self-propelled tank effectively used in war was the British Mark I tank, known as "Big Willie," designed by Lieutenant Colonel E.D. Swinton and built by William Foster & Co., Ltd. It first saw combat on August 15, 1916, at the first Battle of the Somme during World War I. A long, narrow tracked vehicle primarily designed to cross trenches, it was lightly armed with small-caliber cannon and machine guns and lacked a top turret.

6122. Amphibious assault vehicle that was effectively and widely used was the LVT (Landing Vehicle Tracked), developed for the U.S. Marines in 1943–44 in the Pacific theater of World War II. The armored LVT(A)-4 model, which was equipped with a 75mm howitzer and several machine guns, could ferry assault troops thousands of yards to shore and then provide light armored support.

WEAPONS—NUCLEAR

6123. Atomic bomb explosion occurred on July 16, 1945, in a desert area at Alamogordo Air Base, 120 miles southeast of Albuquerque, NM, USA, and was observed by U.S. Army officials and members of the Manhattan Project research team. The shot, designated "Trinity," part of Operation Trinity, was detonated on a 100-foot (30-meter) steel tower. The yield was approximately 18 kilotons, equivalent to the explosive force of 18,000 tons of TNT.

WEAPONS—NUCLEAR—*continued*

6124. Atomic bomb explosion underwater took place on July 24, 1946, in the Pacific Ocean, three miles off Bikini Atoll in the Marshall Islands. The bomb was dropped from an American airplane at a height of 7,000 feet (2,134 meters) and exploded 90 feet (27 meters) underwater. The shot, designated "Baker," was part of Operation Crossroads. It resulted in the sinking of ten vessels (including the battleship *Arkansas*) that were set up as a target.

6125. Ban-the-bomb demonstrations took place in Times Square, New York, NY, USA, in July 1946, a few days after the United States conducted its first underground nuclear weapons test at Bikini, an atoll of the Marshall Islands in the central Pacific.

6126. Atomic bomb detonated by a country other than the United States was the RDS-1, code-named "First Lightning," a plutonium-based fission device developed by the Soviet Union and exploded on August 29, 1949, at the Polygon test site, near the city of Semipalatinsk (now Semey, Kazakhstan). Soviet technicians under the direction of physicist Igor Vasilyevich Kurchatov designed the RDS-1 as an exact copy of the Gadget/Fat Man bomb developed by the United States in 1945. The RDS-1 was suspended 110 feet (33 meters) above the ground on a gallows-shaped rig built at the detonation site. Many tons of earth and debris were thrown up by the 15-kiloton explosion, producing a huge cloud of radioactive fallout that landed on the collective farms of Russia's Altai region, northeast of the bomb site. Tens of thousands of field workers received doses of radiation orders of magnitude higher than those received by people near the nuclear reactor accident at Chernobyl, the Ukraine, in 1986.

6127. Remote detection of a nuclear weapons test was conducted by the U.S. Office of Naval Research in 1949. At the request of the U.S. Atomic Energy Commission, the ONR developed a system that detected radioactive fallout in rainwater. This system detected the explosion of the RDS-1 (known as Joe-1 in the United States), exploded by the Soviet Union on August 29, 1949, at the Polygon test site, near the city of Semipalatinsk (now Semey, Kazakhstan).

6128. Atomic bomb explosion underground was detonated on November 29, 1951, at Frenchman Flat, NV, USA, and witnessed by a group consisting of some members of Congress and some military officers headed by Chief of Staff General Joseph Lawton Collins. The explosion, which produced a hole about 800 feet (244 meters) in diameter and 100 feet (30 meters) deep, was designated as "Uncle," a part of Operation Buster-Jangle.

6129. Hydrogen bomb was constructed by the United States under the direction of Hungarian-American physicist Edward Teller and detonated on October 31, 1952, at the Elugelab Atoll at the Eniwetok Proving Ground, Marshall Islands. It was designated as "Mike," part of Operation Ivy.

6130. Hydrogen bomb detonated by a country other than the United States was the RDS-6s, developed by the Soviet Union about eight and a half months after the first American thermonuclear bomb was detonated at Enewetak. It was tested on August 12, 1953, at the Polygon test site, near Semipalatinsk (now Semey, Kazakhstan). It had a yield of 400 kilotons. About 80 percent of the yield was derived from fission, and only 20 percent from the fusion reaction. Soviet physicist Andrei Sakharov was the lead theoretical designer of the device.

WEAPONS—ROCKETS AND MISSILES

6131. Rockets powered by gunpowder were invented by Chinese military engineers, possibly as early as the eleventh century, during the Sung dynasty. They were hollow bamboo tubes packed with powder and fixed to incendiary arrows.

6132. Mass-produced rockets for warfare were developed by William Congreve, a British Army artillery officer. Congreve got the idea from observing the rockets used by the Indian prince Hyder Ali against the British in 1792 and 1799. In 1805 he produced a standardized rocket that was 40.5 inches (103 centimeters) long and was capable of hitting a target 6,000 feet (1,830 meters) away. These were used in the Napoleonic Wars and in the 1814 attack on Fort McHenry that inspired Francis Scott Key to write the "Star Spangled Banner," the national anthem of the United States. Later versions of the Congreve rocket were able to deliver a 20-pound warhead of black powder about 3 miles (5 kilometers).

6133. Handheld rocket launcher was developed by Captain L.A. Skinner and C.N. Hickman and produced on June 14, 1942, by the General Electric Company, Bridgeport, CT, USA, for use as an anti-tank weapon by American forces during World War II. Dubbed the "bazooka," after a crude wind instrument made of pipes invented by American comedian Bob Burns, it weighed 12 pounds (5 kilograms) and was operated by a two-man team. It consisted of a smooth-bore steel tube about 50 inches (1.3 meters) long and 2.5 inches (6.3 centimeters) in diameter, open at both ends. Attached to the tube were a shoulder stock and front and rear grips for the gunner, together with sights and an electric battery that set off the rocket-propelled charge when the launcher trigger was squeezed. The rocket was nearly 2 feet (0.6 meters) long. It fired about 300 yards (330 meters). The first 5,000 bazookas were completed within 30 days.

6134. Ballistic missile test flight was completed successfully on October 3, 1942, by Nazi Germany when its V-2 rocket ascended to 53 miles (85 kilometers) in altitude from a research base near the village of Peenemünde in northeastern Germany. General Walter Robert Dornberger, military head of the program, reportedly said to research director Wernher von Braun, "Do you realize what we accomplished today? Today the space ship was born!"

6135. Cruise missile used in war was the German-built V-1, a pilotless jet plane loaded with explosives that was launched in great numbers against London and other English cities from 1944 to 1945. More than 8,000 V-1s were aimed at British civilian targets from German launch sites in the Pas de Calais on the northern coast of Nazi-occupied France. From the first assault on June 13, 1944, to the final launch on March 29, 1945, the V-1 caused massive damage to buildings and more than 6,000 deaths. As the first strategic missile—Nazi leader Adolf Hitler described the V-1 as a "revenge weapon" meant to break British morale—it was, however, a failure.

6136. Intercontinental ballistic missile was the SS-6 Sapwood (NATO designation), a multistage ICBM test-launched by the Soviet Union in 1957. The maximum range of the SS-6 was under 3,500 miles (5,600 kilometers), and it could only reach targets in the United States from Soviet bases above the Arctic Circle. In 1960, an SS-6 engine explosion killed hundreds of observers, including the chief of the Soviet strategic missile program, Mitrofan Ivanovich Nedelin.

6137. Submarine-launched ballistic missile was the Polaris missiles, developed by the United States Navy and first launched from the nuclear-powered submarine U.S.S. *George Washington* on November 15, 1960 while it was on patrol off the coast of Charleston, SC, USA. The two-stage, solid-fueled Polaris was 31 feet (9.4 meters) long and 4.5 feet (1.4 meters) in diameter. It carried a single nuclear warhead and was launched from below the surface. A later model was capable of delivering three warheads to three separate targets.

6138. Satellite-based ICBM-launch warning system was the Missile Defense Alarm System, a network of reconnaissance satellites developed by the United States and deployed beginning in 1960. MIDAS became operational on July 12, 1961. The MIDAS satellites used infra-red detectors to spot the hot launch plumes of Soviet intercontinental ballistic missiles.

Subject Index

The subject Index is an alphabetical listing of all the subjects mentioned in the entries (excluding most proper names of people and places, which are covered in the Names and Geographical indexes). To find an entry in the main body of the text, please search for the italicized indexing number.

A

abbey
in Western Europe, *4850*
Abbey of St.-Denis (Paris), *1184*
abolition movement
autobiography by African slave to have major impact on, *5489*
Aboriginal Australians
elected to Australian Parliament, *2656*
performer to achieve international success, *4451*
real estate owned by, in modern times, *4667*
religion, *4728*
aboriginal peoples
Arctic, ambassador to, *3150*
abortion
by vacuum aspiration, *2362*
modern nation to make abortion freely available, *2366*
pill, *2373*
absurdist play, *5987*
Academic American Encyclopedia, *1732, 3388*
Académie Française
Black African member of, *3338*
Academy Awards
film made by a studio outside the United States to win an Academy Award, *4304*
performer in foreign film to win
Best Actor, *4323*
Best Actress, *4322*
acanthus ornamentation
buildings with, *1173*
Acapulco Black Film Festival, *4345*
accidental shooting, *6101*
accidents
See
airplane accidents
automobile accidents
nuclear accidents
accordion, *4416*
harmonicas, *4402*
acetylcholine, *5168*

achromatic lens, *5317*
achromatic microscope, *5301*
Aconcagua
ascent, *5733*
actors and actresses
actor, *5975*
celebrity with international following, *5986*
makeup for, *2724*
movie character with worldwide appeal, *4320*
movie star, *4319*
performer in foreign film to win Academy Award for
Best Actor, *4323*
Best Actress, *4322*
voice double, *4321*
actuarial tables
actuarial table, *2419*
scientific effort to relate age and mortality in large population, *1868*
acupuncture
for dental problems, *3794*
adding machine, *1662*
adhesives, *6040*
Adoration of the Magi (holiday), *3017*
Adventists, *4838*
Adventures of Tom Sawyer, The (Twain), *3362*
advertisements
advertisement, *1449*
cigarette, showing woman smoking, *1455*
circular, *1451*
personal ad placed by individual in search of marriage, *2397*
printed poster, *1450*
prints made for marketing and advertising purposes, *1452*
advertising agencies
advertising agency, *1453*
international, *1454*
advice column, *4454*
Aeneid (Virgil)
blank verse in English, *3416*
aerial bombardment and warfare
air battle that was strategically important, *4222*

airplane flights—*Continued*

launch of heavier-than-air machine entirely under own power, *1356*
London to Delhi scheduled flight, *1363*
manned rocket-plane flight, *1367*
over North Pole, *2321*
over ocean, *1357*
Paris to New York nonstop, *1368*
scheduled commercial jet, *1346*
seaplane, *1358*
to land at North Pole, *2324*
to land at South Pole, *2327*
transpacific nonstop, *1369*
United States to Australia, *1366*
woman to fly over North Pole, *2326*
women
    to fly faster than speed of sound, *1382*
    to fly solo from England to Australia, *1373*
Wright Brothers, *1354*
    See also
    round-the-world flights
    transatlantic airplane flights
    transpacific flights

airplane hijacking, *1798*
international terrorist organization to use skyjacking, *1800*

airplane races
from England to Australia, *5604*
international, *5603*

airplanes and aircraft
aerobats, *1314*
all-metal, *1316*
amphibious, *1312*
astronomical photograph taken from, *5096*
black box flight recorder, *1327*
bombing experiment, *4204*
bombing raid from, *4206*
complete aerial turn in airplane, *1355*
ejection seat, *1323*
    that was propelled by explosives, *1324*
fighter plane, *4212*
flying model, *1307*
heavy night bomber, *4213*
long-distance passenger plane, *1317*
military, *4203*
ornithopter, *1334*
person to travel more than 500 miles per hour, *1322*
powered by human motion, *1330*
    to cross English Channel, *1331*
powered solely by propfan engines, *1335*
practical design for fixed-wing aircraft, *1308*
radial engine, *1309*
rocket-propelled, *1318*
solar-powered, to cross English Channel, *1332*
sport airplane, *1319*
terrorist bomb attack on, *1801*
use of, in war, *4205*

See also
aerial bombardment and warfare
commercial air services
and types of aircraft e.g. dirigibles, jet planes, etc.

airships
See
balloons and airships
dirigibles
hot-air balloons

Akkadian Empire, *2675*
Sargon of Akkad, *2763*

alchemy
alchemists, *5217*
    distillation apparatus for, *5218*
theory, *5219*

alcoholic beverages
alcohol, *4020*
champagne, *2483*
cocktail, *2485*
distilled liquor, *2478*
grog, *2484*
in military rations, *4113*
koumiss, *2509*
legal regulation of trade in, *2476*
martini, *2490*
rum, *2482*
whisky, *2479*
    distillery, *2488*
wine, *2475*
    pasteurized, *2536*
wine cooler, *2480*
    See also
    beer

Alcoholics Anonymous (AA)
self-help program for substance abusers, *4027*

Aldine Press, *3358, 4707*

Alexandria, Library at
classification system of all knowledge, *1810*
critical edition of works of Homer, *3328*

Alexandria, School of, *4776*

algebra
common symbols, *3740*
mathematician to use, *3737*
systematic notation, *3743*

Algonkian language
grammar and primer in, *3536*

alimony payments, *2399*

All Saints Day
Halloween, *3025*

alliances
See
international alliances

Almagest (Ptolemy), *5120*
treatise on, *3735*

almanacs
farmer's, *1002*

altarpiece
from Western Europe showing the Annunciation, *1272*

aluminum, *3669*
in commercial quantities, *3671*

aluminum automobile
mass-produced, *3256*

aluminum can
pull-top, *2523*

Alzheimer's disease
case of, *3844*

Amazon River
scientific exploration, *2295*

Amazonian flora and fauna
biological expedition by native South American, *5156*

ambassadors
British, to United States, *3145*
to Arctic aboriginal peoples, *3150*
woman accredited as, *3148*

ambulances
ambulance, *4010*
motorized, *4015*

America
letter containing description of, *2282*
newspaper published in British colonies in, *4496*

American automobile manufacturers
joint venture between Japanese auto manufacturers and, *3253*

American Civil War
See
Civil War, American

American Wilderness Experience (California)
wilderness park in a mall, *2262*

America's Cup
all-women yacht racing crew, *5861*
international challenger to win, in yacht racing, *5859*

Amharic writing, *3521*

amino acids
protein characterized by amino acid sequence, *5169*
to be discovered, *5158*

ammonia factory, *1494*

amphetamine, *3935*

amphibious aircraft, *1312*

amphibious assault vehicle, *6122*

amplifier tube
electronic, *2012*

Anabaptist church, *4819*
adult baptisms in modern times, *4818*

Analects (Confucius), *4895*

anaphylaxis
description of, *3843*

anarchist, *2662*

anastigmatic lens
that was commercially successful, *4582*

anatomically-correct humans
depictions, *1263*

anatomists
since antiquity to dissect human bodies, *3957*
to break with Galen, *3958*
to dissect human cadavers, *3946*

anatomy
comparative anatomist, *5157*
treatise
based on dissection, *3774*
with accurate illustrations, *3776*
x-ray photograph of, *3902*

anchors
anchor, *5394*
metal, *5401*

anchovies
canned fish, *2533*

Andean empire, *2686*
account of, from insider's perspective, *3010*

androids, *5028*
capable of variety of tasks, *5030*

Andromeda Galaxy, *5071*

anemometer, *5261*

anesthesia
anesthetic, *3758*
local, *3764*
ether, use in childbirth, *2343*
in surgery
hospital to use, *3763*
modern use, *3761*
medieval doctor to advocate use of, *3759*
modern use, in dentistry, *3762*
nitrous oxide, discovery of anesthetic properties of, *3760*
Queen to deliver child under, *2344*

angled fortifications, *1187*

Anglican church
college in Africa, *4800*
Communion church, *4821*
meeting of heads of Catholic church and, *4805*
priest who was not of European descent, *4834*
saint, *4831*
Sunday school, *4799*
women priests, *4843*
to be officially ordained, *4846*

Anglo-Saxons
king to call himself "King of the English", *2928*
to arrive in England, *4636*

animal experimentation
law regulating, *1140*

animal nutrition
agricultural research station, *1004*

apes and monkeys—*Continued*
  primate research station, *5166*
  to survive space flight, *5531*
Aphrodite of Cnidus, *1297*
Apostles' Creed, *4778*
appendectomy, *4046*
Appian Way, *1585*
Apple Computer
  personal computer with graphical user interface, *1731*
apples, *1027*
appliances
  See
    cookware and appliances
aquaculture, *1005*
  cultured pearls, *1009*
  fish breeding, *1008*
  oyster farm, *1006*
Aqualung, *5285*
aquariums
  for public display, *1163*
  oceanarium, *1164*
aqueducts
  aqueduct, *2129*
  raised, of great length, *2133*
  Roman, *2132*
Arab League, *3134*
Arab poet
  to write in colloquial style, *3547*
Arab states
  political association, *3134*
Arabic books, *3545*
  dictionary, *3546*
Arabic history
  of the world, *3007*
Arabic language
  Christian writer in, *4793*
  scientific manuscripts translated into, *5043*
Arawakan Indians
  New World inhabitants forcibly taken to Old World, *2283*
Arbor Day, *3036*
arc lamp, *2091*
arch dam, *2159*
Archbishop of Canterbury, *4791*
archeology
  archeologist, *5052*
  cuneiform writing from Mesopotamia to be deciphered, *5055*
  digs in Egypt, *5053*
  digs in Mesopotamia, *5056*
  excavator of Troy, *5058*
  hieroglyphic writing from Egypt to be deciphered, *5054*
  popular book about, *5057*
  remains documented by holography, *5062*
  study of New World site, *5060*

underwater excavation of shipwreck, *5059*
  woman archeologist of distinction, *5061*
architectural model
  of Jerusalem, *1192*
architectural theory
  treatise, *1188*
architecture
  See
    buildings and structures
    cooling systems
    heating systems
    and names of types of buildings and architectural elements e.g. basilica, domes, etc.
archives
  International Congress of Archivists, *1822*
  national system, *1817*
Arctic region
  airplane flight to land at North Pole, *2324*
  ambassador to aboriginal peoples, *3150*
  discovery of North Pole, *2325*
  European explorer in North America to reach, by land, *2314*
  explorer to set foot on both North and South Poles, *2328*
  flight over North Pole, *2321*
  radio broadcast heard in, *5912*
  surface ship to reach North Pole, *2329*
  woman to fly over North Pole, *2326*
Argand burner
  modern, *3088*
argon, *5240*
armed forces
  African army with standardized training and tactics, *4128*
  air forces
    independent, *4131*
    military, *4127*
    modern, *4130*
  armored soldiers on sub-Saharan Africa, *4123*
  defeat of European colonial power by African, *4177*
  drill book, *4126*
  joint peacetime military exercises between Brazil and Argentina, *4133*
  medical officers in armed forces, *4121*
  modern, to use military drill, *4125*
  national standing, in Europe, *4124*
  NATO joint military exercises in former Warsaw Pact nation, *4132*
  newspaper, *4504*
  scientists attached to, *5042*
    in modern times, *5050*
  slave, *4122*
  troop transport, *4157*
  with trained nursing staff to treat wounded, *4129*
    See also
      navies

astrology—*Continued*
  treatise, *5117*
  zodiacal horoscope, *5066*

astronauts
  Canadian, *5555*
  child whose parents had both flown in space, *2393*
  European Space Agency astronaut in space, *5552*
  international rescue agreement, *5543*
  joint space walk by American and Russian, *5563*
  simultaneous walk by three, *5558*
  to land on moon, *5525*
  to orbit moon, *5524*
  to ride vehicle on moon, *5528*
  who was a mother, *5556*
  woman, to live in space station, *5562*

astronomical charts
  printed, *3629*

astronomy
  Antikythera Mechanism, *5059*
  astronomer to use electronic equipment, *5093*
  back hole to be detected, *5105*
  comets
    calculation of orbit of, *5079*
  computer model of growth of universe, *5113*
  cosmic ray to be discovered, *5094*
  discovery of antimatter in space, *5110*
  estimate of velocity of light, *5078*
  extraterrestrial life
    professorship dedicated to search for, *5115*
    scientific program to search for, *5101*
  gamma-ray burster visible live, *5114*
  heliocentric world system, *5068*
  journal, *5122*
  large radio interferometer, *5142*
  meteorites
    captured on video, *5513*
    treatise, *5121*
  monument, *5063*
  observational confirmation of Big Bang theory, *5103*
  observatories
    for navigation, *5433*
    national, in Europe, *5131*
    orbiting, *5144*
    permanent, in Southern Hemisphere, *5135*
    Royal Greenwich Observatory, *5140*
    Vatican, *5137*
  photograph taken from an airplane, *5096*
  planetariums, *5128*
    in Western Hemisphere, *5130*
    of modern type, *5129*
  radar signal bounced off sun, *5100*
  radio astronomer, *5099*
  radio waves from space to be observed, *5098*
  satellites
    infrared, *5143*
    x-ray, *5139*
  star catalog, *5118*
    photographic, *5123*
    that was comprehensive and accurate, *5119*
  time scales
    dynamical, *6016*
    relativistic, *6017*
  treatise that was widely influential, *5120*
  woman astronomer who was paid for her work, *5083*
    See also
  moon
  planets and stars
  space
  sun
  telescopes

asylums
  for mentally ill, *3987*
  in Europe, *3988*

atheism
  religious movements, *4737*

Atlantic and St. Lawrence Railroad, *3272*

Atlantis (space shuttle)
  launched by U.S. to dock with Russian space station, *5561*

atlases
  comprehensive digital, of human body, *3908*
  maps and charts, *3618*
  star, to include coordinates, *3631*

atomic bomb explosions, *6123*
  in country other than U.S., *6126*
  over enemy territory, *4232*
  underground, *6128*
  underwater, *6124*

atomic theory, *5320*
  modern theory of atomic structure, *5333*

atoms
  physical manipulation of individual, *5354*

auctions
  Old Master painting sold for more than US$10 million, *1288*

Augsburg Confession
  Lutheran churches, *4820*

Australia Day, *3031*

Australian newspaper
  weekly, *4502*

Australian Parliament
  Aboriginal Australian elected to, *2656*
  woman to become member, *2655*

Australopithicus afarensis
  hominid species known to be ancestor of modern humans, *4613*

authors
  known by name, *3326*

autopsy
of well-known individual, *1866*
Autostereogram, *5319*
avalanches
20th century, to kill 10,000 people, *1925*
to kill more than 1,000 people, *1917*
Avesta, *5020*
Avestan language
text in, *3496*
avocados
cultivation, *1054*
axe, *6041*
axe heads, ceremonial
Southeast Asian decorative artwork, *1243*
aye-aye
born in captivity, *1124*
Ayurvedic medicine
texts of, *3770*
Aztecs
conquistador, *4653*
hot cocoa, *2547*
priest-king, *2950*

B

B1 vitamin, *5167*
baby bottles, *2379*
baby carriages
baby carriage, *2383*
collapsible stroller, *2394*
perambulator, *2385*
backgammon, *2567*
bacteria
microscopic observation, *5146*
bacterial infections
patient to be given penicillin, *3936*
synthetic drug to treat, *3931*
badminton
Thomas Cup in, *5599*
Baedeker guidebooks, *3394*
Baha'i leader, *4741*
bakeries
commercial, *2526*
balance of trade and payments
England, *1543*
ball court, *5596*
ball games
ball game, *5595*
depiction, *5594*
handball-style, *5676*
ballerinas
professional, *1856*
to dance on toes, *1860*
to wear tutu, *1861*

virtuoso, *1858*
ballet
Ballet Russes, *1862*
codification of five basic positions, *1855*
entirely danced, *1857*
International Ballet Competition, *1864*
modern choreographer, *1863*
to combine dancing, music, and acting, *1854*
woman to choreograph her own, *1859*
ballistic missiles
intercontinental, *6136*
submarine equipped with, *4275*
test flight, *6134*
ballistics
treatise, *6102*
balloon race
international, *5602*
balloons and airships
airship, *1396*
animals sent aloft, *1393*
casualties, *1890*
circumnavigation of world by balloon
nonstop, *1413*
flight instrument extant, *1397*
flight over water, *1399*
human ascent into stratosphere, *1408*
hydrogen, *1392*
ascent in, *1395*
letter sent by, *4679*
rigid, *1403*
steam-powered, *1401*
transatlantic balloon flights, *1410*
solo, *1411*
transpacific balloon flight, *1412*
used for wartime reconnaissance, *1400*
weather, *5277*
woman to ascend in untethered, *1398*
See also
dirigibles
hot-air balloons
ballpoint pen, *3593*
widely used, *3596*
ban-the-bomb demonstrations, *6125*
bananas
cultivation, *1029*
in New World, *1040*
band (music), *4365*
Band-Aid, *3878*
bandages
small, with built-in adhesive, *3878*
surgical adhesive, *3876*
Bandung Conference (1955), *3163*
banjos, *4403*
bank holidays, *3035*
bank notes, *2447*
Bank of England, *2406*
bank robbery
Internet bank robber, *1807*

cells
    isolation of human embryonic stem, 5174
    microscopic observation of protozoa, bacteria, and, 5146
    observation of egg cell of mammal, 5159
    observation of nucleus of, 5160
comparative anatomist, 5157
expedition to Amazonia by native South American, 5156
head transplant, 5153
high-security pathogen laboratory in Europe, 5175
hormone to be discovered, 5165
insects
    entomological collection in Europe, 5147
    study of behavior, 5163
    treatise on, 5145
mammals born from egg grown in vitro, 5173
neurotransmitter to be identified, 5168
organism classification system, 5149
physical anthropologist, 5154
primates
    research station, 5166
    scientific observations of behavior in wild, 5170
proof of regeneration in an organism, 5150
protein characterized by amino acid sequence, 5169
systematic and comprehensive work of natural history, 5151
taxonomic system based on scientific principles, 5148
theory of evolution, 5152
theory of physiological reflexes, 5161
virus to be isolated, 5164
vitamin to be identified, 5167
    See also
    botany
    cloning
biophysics
    treatise, 5162
bipolar disorder
    description of, 3829
    See also
    pigeons
birds
    transatlantic crossing by, 1114
Birdseye frozen food
    for mass market, 2542
bireme galley, 5399
birth
    See
    pregnancy and childbirth
birth control
    comprehensive treatise on contraception and birth, 2357

condoms, 2358
    designed to be worn by a woman, 2374
    recommendation that condoms be used for birth control, 2359
    thermoformed plastic, 2375
contraceptives, 2356
country to limit births as national policy, 2372
family planning clinics, 2363
    state-supported, 2369
intrauterine device (IUD), 2367
    copper, 2371
manual, 2360
pamphlet on, from feminist perspective, 2365
pill, 2370
rhythm method, 2368
vaginal cap, 2361
vasectomy, 2364
    See also
    abortion
birth defects
    epidemic, caused by a drug, 1908
birth registry
    national, 4601
Bissell carpet sweeper, 3062
Black and Decker
    electric hand drill, 6060
black box flight recorder, 1327
Black Death, 1903
black hole
    to be detected, 5105
black nationalist movement, 2660
black pride
    advocate of, 5495
Black September organization
    massacre at Olympic Games, 1799
black tulip, 1057
Blanc, Mont
    ascent, 5728
Blanchard Plaque, 6000
blanket
    electric, 3069
blasting cap, 3683
blimps
    See
    dirigibles
blind persons
    guide dogs, 1157
    reading system for, 2008
    school for blind children, 2007
blood
    artificial, 4102
blood bank, 4100
blood circulation
    See
    circulatory system

types of buildings and architectural elements e.g. basilica, domes, etc.

Bulgarian writing, *3505*

bull
transgenic, *1123*

bullet train line, *3282*

bulletin board
personal computer, *1704*

bullfighting, *5648*
matador of renown, *5650*
permanent bullring, *5651*
running of bulls, *5649*
school, *5652*
woman bullfighter of renown in Europe, *5653*

bumpers, car, *3235*

Bunsen burner, *5302*

burials
burial, *1869*
canopic jars, *1875*
cemetery, *1874*
ceremony, *1870*
coffins, *1872*
cast-iron, *1880*
embalming by injecting arteries with preservative, *1879*
mausoleum, *1877*
mummies, *1871*
Native American to be buried in Europe, *1878*
necropolis in North America, *1876*
sarcophagi, *1873*
space, *1885*

Burma
See
Myanmar

buses and bus service
bus service, *3209*
motorized, *3213*
with internal-combustion engine, *3218*

bustles, *1631*

butter, *2507*
clarified, *2507*

buttons and fasteners
buttons, *1640*
cut-steel, *1641*
hook and loop, *1644*
metal snap, *1642*
zipper that was practical, *1643*

Byzantine Empire
woman to rule, *2772*

C

cabaret, *4441*

cabbage, *1023*
Chinese cabbage, *1033*

Cable News Network (CNN), *4465*

cable systems
commercial, capable of carrying simultaneous TV, telephony, and high-speed data, *5890*
digital wireless television system, *5970*
Japan–USA undersea cable network, *5894*

cacao cultivation, *1024*

caissons, for bridges
closed or pneumatic, *2143*
open, *2140*

cake, *2544*
wedding, recipe for, *2548*

calculator watch, *6036*

calculators
automatic, to factor whole numbers, *1664*
electronic digital, *1665*
electronic pocket, *2030*
mechanical calculator, *1660*
for astronomical use invented in modern times, *1661*
See also
computers

calculus
Newton (Sir Isaac) and, *3748*
treatise, *3748*

calendars
adopted worldwide, *6007*
calendar, *6000*
Chinese, *6003*
developed in Americas, *6004*
Jewish, *6006*
national revolutionary, *6009*
printed, *3353*
with year of 365 days, *6002*
year in Muslim, *6005*
See also
eras and dates

caliph, *2927*

calligraphy, *3310*

Calvinist (Reformed) church, *4822*

Cambodian Empire, *2774*

camcorder, *2036*

camels
cross-breeding of llama with, *1127*
domesticated, *1147*
saddle, *1150*

cameras and camera equipment
anastigmatic lens that was commercially successful, *4582*
digital still, *4588*
flash powder, *4580*
instant, *4587*
magic lantern, *4576*
obscura, *4575*
portrait, *4578*
stroboscopic lamp, *4585*
thirty-five millimeter

cells—*Continued*
  observation of egg cell of mammal, *5159*
  observation of nucleus, *5160*
  observations of chromosomes in, *5194*
cellular telephone system, *5946*
celluloid
  synthetic plastic that was widely used in industry, *1490*
Celts
  bards, *3329*
cement, *2150*
  Portland, *2152*
cemetery, *1874*
Centigrade temperature scale, *5222*
central bank, *2406*
central heating system
  for buildings, *1208*
Central Intelligence Agency (U.S.)
  overthrow of democratic foreign government arranged by, *4143*
centrifuge, *3877*
ceramic oxide
  superconducting materials of, *5352*
ceramics
  thermoplastic, *3653*
cereal crop, *1010*
cereal food
  mass-produced, for infants, *2391*
Ceres (asteroid), *5085*
Cesarean operation, *2335*
  fully documented, *2339*
chain mail, *6072*
chairs
  inflatable, *3095*
  tubular steel, *3091*
champagne, *2483*
Chanel No. 5
  designer perfume, *2748*
Chanukah, *3015*
chartered airplane flight, *1337*
Chassidism
  master, *4972*
check(money), *2448*
checkers, *2568*
  book, *2572*
  military game, *2570*
cheese, *2508*
  factory, *2510*
Chelmno extermination camp (Poland), *1772*
Chemical Bank (N.Y.)
  automatic teller machine (ATM), *2416*
chemical disaster
  to cause large loss of life, *1958*
chemical gases
  mustard, *6080*
  nerve, *6081*

  poison, *6079*
chemistry
  analysis of air, *5226*
  artificial diamond, *5247*
  chemist to identify substance using microscope, *5223*
  determination of composition of water, *5227*
  discovery of quasicrystals, *5249*
  elements
    artificial transmutation of an, *5340*
    discovered in space, *5235*
    discovery of an, *5220*
    discovery of oxygen, *5224*
    frozen hydrogen, *5238*
    heavier than uranium, *5245*
    inert group, *5240*
    liquid helium, *5239*
    liquid oxygen, *5236*
    periodic table of, *5229*
    produced artificially, *5243*
    to be analyzed by mass spectrometer, *5241*
    treatise on geochemistry, *5282*
  general reference work of modern, *5228*
  International Chemical Congress, *5234*
  liquefied gas, *5230*
  macromolecules, *5242*
  modern chemist, *5225*
  molecule analyzed with use of computer, *5248*
  nitroglycerin, *5233*
  Nobel Prize, *4523*
    Asia, *4527*
    Latin America, *4525*
    North America, *4524*
    Oceania, *4526*
  organic compound synthesized from inorganic substance, *5232*
  process for liquefying mixed gases, *5237*
  superfluid, *5244*
  teaching laboratory for chemists, *5231*
  temperature scales
    Centigrade, *5222*
    Fahrenheit, *5221*
  three-dimensional molecular structure, *5246*
    See also
  alchemy
chemotherapeutic drug, *3929*
Cherokee language
  Native North American language to be given its own written form, *3540*
chess
  black player to become grandmaster, *2602*
  chess-like game, *2597*
  international tournament, *2598*
  world champion, *2599*
    defeated by computer, *2601*
    who was a woman, *2600*
cheval glass, *2742*

Christianity—*Continued*
  book of mysticism by a woman, *4797*
  celibacy rule for priests, *4782*
  Christians, *4770*
  church order, *4775*
  college in Africa, *4800*
  convent, *4790*
  creeds, *4778*
    ecumenical, *4787*
  Crusading order of knights, *4795*
  ecumenical conference, *4802*
  establishment as state religion, *4781*
  formal attempt to define nature of Jesus, *4788*
  Gnostic, *4773*
  Gospel, *4774*
  heretical sectarian movement, *4777*
  historian of Christian church, *4785*
  institution of higher learning, *4776*
  legal recognition of Christians in Roman Empire, *4783*
  martyr, *4771*
  missionaries
    center of activity, *4772*
    in China, *4792*
    international ecumenical organization, *4803*
    society, *4798*
  monastery, *4784*
  monk, *4780*
  Mormon church, *4801*
  radical reformer, *4796*
  rule book for monastic life, *4786*
  scholastic, *4794*
  Stylite, *4789*
  Sunday school, *4799*
  Unification Church teachings, *4804*
  writer in Arabic, *4793*
    See also
    Orthodox Christianity
    Protestantism
    Roman Catholicism
Christmas, *3023*
  cards, *4673*
  Nativity, Feast of, *3024*
  Santa Claus, *3019*
  trees, *3029*
chromium
  discovery of, *3667*
chromosomes
  human sex, researcher to describe role of, *5195*
  observations, *5194*
chronometer, *6029*
Chrysler Building (N.Y.)
  skyscraper more than 1,000 feet high, *1227*
Chunnel, *2198*

Church of England, *4821*
churches
  See
  cathedrals and churches
cigarette advertisement
  showing woman smoking, *1455*
cigarette-rolling machine, *1068*
cigarette smoking
  anti-smoking crusader, *4023*
  connection between tobacco and cancer, *4024*
  Europeans to smoke tobacco, *4022*
  nicotine chewing gum, *4030*
  self-help program for substance abusers, *4027*
cigarettes, *1065*
  factory, *1067*
Cincinnati Reds, *5615*
cinematographers
  of lasting influence, *4290*
  woman, *4303*
circle
  mathematical definition of, *3732*
circuits
  integrated, *2018*
  printed, *2015*
circulatory system
  description of, *3943*
  description of pulmonary blood circulation, *3953*
circumnavigations
  Africa, *2303*
  Antarctica, *2310*
  Australia, *2309*
  Britain, *2304*
  by wheelchair, *5854*
  polar, of earth, *2311*
  world, *2305*
    by a sea captain, *2306*
    by a woman, *2307*
    by submarine, *5462*
    by submerged submarine, *5464*
    commercial airmail letter, *4686*
    west to east, *2308*
    See also
  round-the-world flights
Circus Maximus, *5606*
circuses
  clown, *2206*
  elephants, *2207*
  Europe, *2204*
  fire with large loss of life, *1952*
  flying trapeze act, *2209*
  human cannonball, *2210*
    family act, *2214*
  known by that name, *2205*
  modern, *2203*
  monkey, *2202*
  three-ring, *2211*

clowns—*Continued*
   stage, *5978*
clubs
   for gentlemen, *1834*
   service, *1839*
coach (transportation), *3208*
coal mine, *3680*
cocaine
   use as local anesthetic, *3764*
cocktails
   cocktail, *2485*
   Manhattan, *2490*
   martini, *2490*
cocoa
   cacao cultivation, *1024*
   hot, *2547*
coconut processing equipment, *1092*
codeine, *3924*
coelacanth
   caught alive, *1115*
coffee
   drinking, *2495*
   espresso machine, *3071*
   instant, *2499*
      freeze-dried, *2500*
   percolator, *3059*
   sweet and light, *2497*
   used as stimulant, *2494*
   "Viennese style", *2497*
coffee house, *1462*
"coffee presidents"
   Brazil, *2790*
coffins, *1872*
   cast-iron, *1880*
coinage
      See
   money and coinage
coke-smelted iron, *3664*
cold cream, *2717*
"cold war"
   use of term, *4191*
collapsible boats, *5400*
collars
   ruffed, *1615*
colleges and universities
   Africa, *1987*
   China, *1982*
   Christian, in Africa, *4800*
   Europe, *1986*
   European, to admit women as students, *1996*
   foreigner to be appointed professor in German university, *1997*
   Internet university to receive accreditation, *2003*
   long-distance, without classrooms, *2000*
   modern, *1991*
      in Caribbean, *1999*

   museum, *1825*
   nation to put all its universities on Internet, *2002*
   New World, *1989*
   on-line course of study, *2001*
   permanent institution of higher education in liberal arts, *1981*
   professor who was a woman, *1988*
   scholar of African descent to earn a doctorate from a European university, *1992*
   scholarly societies, *1985*
   still in existence, *1984*
   technical, *1993*
   to enroll women and men on equal terms, *1994*
   Western world, *1983*
   woman appointed to faculty of French university, *1998*
   woman to earn degree of Doctor of Philosophy, *1990*
   women's, *1995*
colophon
   in printed book, *3351*
color blindness
   treatise, *3839*
color photography
   process, *4579*
      that was practical, *4583*
Colorado beetle
   species import ban, *2242*
Columbia (space shuttle)
   reusable manned spacecraft, *5551*
Columbus Day, *3033*
combs, *2727*
comedies
   Latin, *5979*
comedy (movie), *4346*
   slapstick, *4347*
comets
   calculation of orbit of, *5079*
   depiction, *5070*
   named after a woman, *5091*
comfort women
   reparations for forced prostitution, *1779*
comic opera, *4429*
comics
   books featuring color cartoons previously published in newspapers, *4469*
   strips
      in a magazine, *4467*
      in daily newspaper, *4470*
      published as booklet, *4466*
      with ongoing character, *4468*
   superhero, *4472*
   with adventure hero, *4471*
commercial air services
   air transport company, *1336*
   airline meals, *1338*
   airliner widely used, *1320*

D

E

F

Fabergé Easter egg, *1248*
fables
with morals, *3438*
facial tissues, *2721*
factories
ammonia, *1494*
beet sugar, *2549*
cheese, *2510*
cigarette, *1067*
glass, in Americas, *3646*
in which workers paid for services of a reader, *1506*
Japanese-owned automobile, in U.S., *3252*
lace, *3708*
margarine, *2538*
model, run on humanitarian principles, *1501*
olive oil, *2525*
pencil, *3584*
to obtain uranium from gold, *3675*
factory ship
for whaling, *3124*
Fahrenheit temperature scale, *5221*
false eyes, *3978*
family court, *5501*
family hotel, *1465*
family names, *3483*
family planning clinics, *2363*
state-supported, *2369*
famines
caused by government ideology, *1950*
famine, *1912*
to kill more than 1 million people, *1922*
fans
mechanical ventilating, *3052*
farmers' almanac, *1002, 4735*
farms
oyster, *1006*
farthingale
hoop skirt, *1613*
See also
clothing and fashion
and types of clothing and accessories e.g.
hats, jewelry, etc.
fashion magazine, *1610*
fashion models
society model, *1622*
fast-food outlets, *1460*
Faust legend, *3479*
fax
international standard, *5879*
faxes
color machine, *5881*
desktop machine, *5878*
international digital standard, *5880*

process, *5873*
system for commercial use, *5874*
transcontinental radio transmission, *5877*
transmission of photographs, *5875*
by transatlantic radio, *5876*
Federation Cup
in tennis, *5839*
felt-tip pen, *3598*
female figurine of the "Venus" type, *1293*
feminine, the
symbols of, *5364*
feminism
author in medieval Europe, *5365*
influential tract, *5368*
pamphlet on birth control, *2365*
fencing
depiction of swordsmen, *5700*
guild, *5702*
Fermat's last theorem
mathematical proof, *3756*
ferries
to sink with large loss of life, *1941*
ferris wheel, *2213*
fertilizers
agricultural research station, *1004*
guano, *1096*
synthetic, *1095*
Feynman Prize in Nanotechnology, *5355*
fiber
synthetic, *3721*
produced entirely from chemicals, *3724*
produced in a factory, *3722*
suitable for making cloth, *3723*
fiber optic cable, *5942*
fiber-optic transoceanic cable, *5888*
fiberglass
production automobile with fiberglass body, *3243*
field hockey, *5598*
Fields Medal (mathematics), *3753*
fighter plane, *4212*
Filene's (Boston)
automatic price reductions on merchandise, *1518*
Filipino immigrants
continuous settlements of Asians in North America, *4662*
film projector
magic lantern, *4576*
film rolls
camera to use, *4581*
films
See
actors and actresses
animated films and cartoons
movies and films

food
> frozen, for mass market, *2542*
> international standards for quality of, *4018*
> irradiation, *2522*
> product to be pasteurized, *2536*
>> *See also*
>> cookbooks
>> cookware and appliances
>> dairy foods
>> snacks and sweets
>> spices and savories
>> and types of food e.g. margarine, pasta
>> etc.

food processor, *3072*

food purity law, *2472*
> still observed, *2473*

foot care
> chiropodist, *3966*

football
> international game, *5659*
> professional games, *5660*
>> world championship, *5661*
> soccer-type games, *5813*
> Super Bowl game, *5662*
>> *See also*
>> soccer

footprints
> human, *4619*

Ford Motor Company
> plastic car, *3242*

foreign debt
> Third World country to default on, *2417*

foreign films
> performer in, to win Academy Award for
>> Best Actor, *4323*
>> Best Actress, *4322*

forensic investigation and detection, *1760*
> conviction for murder based on photographic evidence of marks on bullet, *1756*
> genetic fingerprinting method, *1758*
> retinal print identification system, *1757*
>> *See also*
>> DNA evidence
>> fingerprints

forensic pathologist, *3955*

forestry
> treatise on, in English, *5182*

fork, *3100*

formula (for infants)
> mass-produced, *2387*

fortifications
> angled, *1187*

fortress
> artillery, *1189*

fortune-telling
> dice, *2603*
> Tarot cards, *2582*

fossil fuels
> commercial petrochemical plant for fluid catalytic-cracking, *2110*
> fluid catalytic- cracking process, *2109*
> horizontal oil drilling, *2112*
> international oil pipeline, *2108*
> kerosene, *2104*
> multistep crude oil refining, *2106*
> natural gas wells, *2100*
> oil-from-coal plant, *2111*
> oil seeps, *2099*
> oil well, *2105*
> subsea gas pipeline in Asia, *2114*
> synthetic gasoline plant, *2107*
> underwater natural gas production station, *2113*

fossils
> embryo of carnivorous dinosaur to be discovered, *5216*
> flower, *5176*
> hominids
>> Asia, *4621*
>> Europe, *4622*
> *Homo erectus*, *4616*
> human remains in Americas, *4627*
> illustrations, *5210*
> marinosaur fossil unearthed in its entirety, *5211*
> oil, *5251*
> published record of dinosaur remains, *5213*
> use of the word, *5260*

Foundling Hospital of London, *3891*

fountain pen, *3592*

four-color map problem, *3754*

Franciscans, *4857*

Franco-Prussian War, *4140*

Frankenstein; or the Modern Prometheus (Shelley), *3448*

Franks
> King of France, *2925*

free-trade region, *1549*
> encompassing North America, *1552*

Freedom (international space station), *5512*
> humans to enter, *5565*
> module to be placed in space, *5515*

freedom of speech
> constitutional guarantee, *2648*
> law guaranteeing, *2646*

freemasons
> grand lodge, *1836*
> woman to become, *1837*

Freetown (Sierra Leone)
> African refuge for former slaves, *5490*
> freed African slaves repatriated to Africa, *5491*

freeze-dried coffee, *2500*

freight elevator, *1203*

hats
  bowler, *1649*
  elaborate medieval headdresses, *1646*
  poke bonnet, *1648*
  top hat, *1647*
Hausa writing, *3539*
Havana Bienal, *1256*
haymaker, *1084*
head cabbage, *1023*
head transplant, *5153*
headdresses
  elaborate medieval, *1646*
heads of state
  Argentina, *2993*
  Chancellor of Germany, *2996*
  Chile, *2991*
  Cyprus, *2999*
  Doge of Venice, *2984*
  Dominican Republic, *2994*
  Fascist dictator, *2998*
  free Ecuador, *2992*
  General secretary of Communist Party of
    former Soviet Union, *2997*
  Guatemala, *2995*
  Hong Kong, *3001*
  Imam of Oman, *2985*
  Mozambique, *3000*
  Paraguay, *2990*
  shogun, *2986*
  to meet in on-line chat session, *3165*
  to order an automobile, *3226*
  united Afghanistan, *2989*
    names of types of heads of state e.g. em-
      perors and empresses, presidents, etc.
health
      See
    public health and sanitation
health-care facility
  with labyrinth, *4095*
health diet
  popular, *4084*
health resorts, *4081*
heart
  human
    anatomically correct image of, *3900*
    electrocardiogram, *3903*
  prehistoric painting of, of mammal, *3899*
    the cardiac headings
heart, artificial
  in an animal, *4066*
  transplant of
    into human being, *4072*
    that was intended to be permanent, *4074*
heart-lung machine, *4068*
heart operations
      See
    cardiac surgery
heart transplant, *4071*

heat pump, *2064*
heated swimming pool, *5817*
heating stoves, *3050*
heating systems
  central, for buildings, *1208*
  hot-water, *1210*
heavier-than-air machines
  flight, *1353*
  launch of, entirely under own power, *1356*
Hebrew language
  ancient language revived for modern use,
    3302
  dictionary, *3563*
  printed book, *3564*
  printed edition of Psalms, *4991*
Hebrew writing, *3562*
helicopters
  autogiro, *1423*
  flight, *1422*
  free flight indoors, *1425*
  powered by human motion, *1429*
  solo round-the-world flight, *1428*
  that was successful, *1426*
  transatlantic flight, *1427*
  woman pilot, *1424*
heliocentric world system, *5068*
helium, *5235*
  liquid, *5239*
  superfluid, *5244*
helmets
  metal, *6067*
Helsinki Human Rights Day, *3044*
hematocrit, *3877*
hemostatic technique
  to stop surgical bleeding, *4038*
Henry VI, Part I (Shakespeare), *3421*
Heptathlon
  event, *5788*
  two-time gold medallist, *5792*
Heraea (athletic events), *5759*
heraldry, *2706*
  device worn by an English King, *2707*
heredity
  treatise on laws of, *5193*
heresy
  auto-da-fé, *4863*
  Christian sectarian movement, *4777*
  Hindu heresies, *4905*
  in Zoroastrianism, *5021*
  pope tried for, after his death, *4852*
  Protestant heretic, *4824*
heroin, *3927*
  methadone maintenance program for addicts,
    4029
herring
  salted, *2527*
Hertz Drive-Ur-Self System, *3238*

horse collar, *1075*

horse-drawn seed drill, *1078*

horse races
    English Derby, *5682*
    flat, in North America, *5687*
    Grand National Handicap Steeplechase, *5685*
        woman jockey in, *5688*
    held regularly, *5678*
    Irish racing, *5679*
    Kentucky Derby, *5686*
    purse, *5680*
    stakes, in North America, *5683*
    thoroughbreds, *5681*
    traveling van for horses, *5684*
    winner of Prix d'Amérique who was a woman, *5689*

horse riding, *1144*

horses
    for transport, *1146*
    New World, *1107*
    North American mainland, *1108*
    saddle, *1151*

horseshoes
    reference to, *1153*

horticulture
    See
    gardens and gardening
    plants and flowers

Horyu Temple complex
    wooden buildings, *1180*

hospice
    teaching and research, for dying, *3896*

Hospitallers of St. John of Jerusalem, *4795*

hospitals
    Asia, *3880*
    Christian, *3882*
    clinical rounds, *3892*
    for unwanted newborns, *3891*
    free dispensary for poor, *3890*
    Islamic, *3885*
    isolation, for plague victims, *3888*
    medieval, in Europe, *3884*
    military, *3881*
        in Europe since antiquity, *3889*
    national railway, *3898*
    Protestant, *3893*
    public, in Europe, *3883*
    solar-powered, *3897*
    teaching, *3887*
    teaching and research hospice for dying, *3896*
    to keep charts for patients, *3886*
    women's
        founded by women, *3894*
        staffed by women physicians, *3895*

hostels
    for pilgrims, *1457*

hot-air balloons
    ascent in, *1394*
    hot-air balloon, *1390*
    statement of principle, *1389*
    that was successful, *1391*

hot cocoa, *2547*

hot-water heating system, *1210*

hotels
    bridal suite in, *2398*
    family, *1465*
    floating resort, *1471*
    hospice for Christian pilgrims, *1458*
    hostels for pilgrims, *1457*
    inns, *1456*
    major chain, *1468*
    railway, *1467*
    taller than 1,000 feet, *1472*
    with staff psychologist, *4006*

hourglass, *6019*

house and home
    household detergent, *3111*
    household management book, *3049*
    housekeeping magazine, *3048*
        See also
    furniture
    stoves
    and names of household implements e.g. carpet sweeper, pots, etc.

houses
    apartment, *1221*
    brick, *1215*
    fully computerized, *1223*
    known to archeologists, *1214*
    post-and-lintel construction, *1220*
    powered by solar cells, *1222*
    rectangular, *1216*
    town house, *1219*
    tract, *1218*
    with interior courtyard, *1217*

housing project
    in inner-city neighborhood, *5497*

hovercraft, *5419*
    lawn mower, *6065*
    passenger service, *5421*

Hoyle's rules for card games, *2589*

Hubble Space Telescope, *5144*

human anatomy
    See
    anatomy

human antibodies
    See
    antibodies

human body
    comprehensive digital atlas of, *3908*
    magnetic resonance image of, *3907*

human breeding program, *5197*

human cannonball, *2210*
    family act, *2214*

I

J

Kabbalah
  text, *4987*
Kanchenjunga
  ascent, *5742*
Kannada writing, *3497*
karma
  statement of Hindu doctrine of reincarnation, *4903*
Kashmiri writing, *3522*
Kellogg-Briand Pact, *3171*
Kelvin scale, *5329*
Kentucky Derby, *5686*
Kenwood Chef food processor, *3072*
Kenya, Mount
  ascent, *5734*
kerosene
  for illumination purposes, *2104*
Kharijites, *4926*
Khazaria, *4967*
Khmer Empire, *2774*
kibbutz, *1570*
kidney dialysis, *4090*
kidney stones
  ultrasonic disintegrator, *4093*
Kilimanjaro, Mount
  ascent, *5732*
  European explorers to sight, *2298*
kindergarten, *1973*
kinetic sculpture, *1300*
  in which motion was main esthetic factor, *1301*
  mobiles, *1302*
King Arthur legend
  Holy Grail
    version of, *3472*
  prose works in French language, *3555*
  reference
    in historical work, *3470*
    in literature, *3469*
King James version, of Bible
  edition, *4891*
kingdoms
    See
  emperors and empresses
  empires and dynasties
kings and monarchs
  Albania, *2973*
  Armenia, united, *2923*
  Aztec, *2950*
  Belgium, *2963*
  Bhutan, *2959*
  biography of European king, *2930*
  British
    to live in Buckingham Palace, *2965*
    to visit United States, *2976*
  Bulgaria, modern, *2969*
  constitutional

  modern Greece, *2964*
  coronation
    conducted in English, *2957*
    televised, *2979*
  crowned by automaton, *5027*
  Egypt, *2971*
  Emir of Kuwait, *2961*
  England and Scotland, *2958*
  France, *2925*
  Germany, *2929*
  Hawaii, *2962*
  Hungary, *2938*
  Inca, *2943*
  Iraq, *2975*
  Italy, *2924*
  Jordan, *2977*
  Kaiser of united German Reich, *2967*
  King David, reference outside the Bible, *2922*
  Korea, *2920*
  Lao people, *2949*
  Libya, *2978*
  Luxembourg, *2935*
    Grand Duchy, *2966*
  Montenegro, *2970*
  Morocco, *2980*
  Muslim caliph, *2927*
  Myanmar, *2940*
  Norway, *2932*
  pharaoh, *2919*
  Poland, *2939*
  Portugal, *2941*
  Prince of Wales, *2947*
  Romania, *2968*
  Saudi Arabia, *2974*
  Scotland, *2931*
  sheikh of Bahrain, *2982*
  Spain, *2954*
  sultans, *2936*
    Brunei, *2983*
    Oman, *2960*
    Ottoman Empire, *2948*
  Swaziland, *2981*
  Sweden, *2937*
  Thailand, *2972*
  Tibet, *2926*
  to call himself "King of the English", *2928*
  to convert to Jainism, *4949*
  tsar of all Russia, *2953*
  Vietnam, *2933*
  women
    England, *2956*
    France, *2944*
    Georgia, *2942*
    Luxembourg, *2945*
    Muslim leader, *2946*
    pharaoh, *2921*
    Poland, *2952*
    Russia, *2934*
    Scandinavian countries, *2951*

L

laughing gas (nitrous oxide)
  discovery of anesthetic properties of, *3760*
  use in dentistry, *3762*
laundromat, *1520*
lawn-care manual, *2620*
lawn mowers, *6062*
  hovercraft, *6065*
  power, *6064*
  that was practical, *6063*
lawn tennis, *5832*
laws and legislation
  African slaves in New World, *5480*
  against enhanced bosoms, *1611*
  animal experimentation, *1140*
  Bank Holidays Act of 1875, *3035*
  child labor, *1502*
  codes
      code, *2644*
      Jewish law, *4989*
      national, of laws of war, *4120*
      uniform national, *2649*
  copyright, *3334*
  cruelty to animals, *1138*
  domestic violence, *5498*
  Electoral Act (New Zealand), *2639*
  environmental lawsuit, *2240*
  European legislator of African descent, *2652*
  food purity, *2472*
  food purity law
      still observed, *2473*
  forbidding freezing of corpse for future resuscitation, *1884*
  general patent, *1541*
  guaranteeing freedom of speech, *2646*
  Hindu law code, *4906*
  homosexual civil rights, *5383*
  international environmental, *2248*
  international maritime, *1527*
  Internet, *1721*
  Islamic jurisprudence, *4932*
  marriage and divorce, *2395*
  marriage and divorce laws
      marital property reform, *2400*
  national public health legislation, *2241*
  national public welfare law in Europe, *5496*
  permitting assisted suicide, *1889*
  protection for trade secrets, *1439*
  regulation of trade in alcoholic beverages, *2476*
  requiring doctors to report cases of occupational disease, *1508*
  requiring Jews to wear identifying mark, *4968*
  species import ban, *2242*
  statute establishing that men and women are equal under the law, *5366*
  sumptuary laws, *1603*
      medieval, *1609*
  waste disposal, *2238*
  water pollution, *2266*

See also
  international laws and rights
lead pencil
  depiction of, *3583*
lead poisoning
  description of, *3830*
  occupational disease, *3828*
League of Nations, *3186*
  international civil service, *3147*
Lebensborn (Fountain of Youth) Society, *5197*
leeches
  anticoagulant, *3920*
legal drama, *3443*
legislation
      See
  laws and legislation
Leica 1 camera, *4584*
lemurs
  captive-bred, returned to Madagascar, *1128*
length, unit of, *5308*
lenses
  achromatic, *5317*
  anastigmatic, that was commercially successful, *4582*
      See also
  contact lenses
Lepanto, Battle of
  major naval battle decided by firepower, *4246*
leprosy
  contagious disease to be brought under control in Europe, *3832*
Leviathan telescope
  large reflecting mirror in, *5136*
Leyden (Leiden) jar
  storage device for electricity, *2080*
Lhotse
  ascent, *5744*
libel
  anti-Semitic, *4960*
  blood, anti-Semitic, *4966*
liberal arts
  permanent institution of higher education in, *1981*
libraries, *1809*
  Asia, *1812*
  Carnegie library, *1820*
  catalog, *1811*
  children's, *1819*
  classification system of all knowledge, *1810*
  International Congress of Archivists, *1822*
  international library organization, *1821*
  national archive system, *1817*
  public, in Europe, *1815*
  to possess 100 million items, *1823*
  with books shelved upright, *1814*
Library of Congress, *1823*
library school, *1818*

London Stock Exchange, *2428*
    women to trade on floor of, *2433*
London zoo, *1162*
L'Oréal Company
    commercial hair dye, *2735*
Los Angeles Dodgers, *5615*
lost-slipper motif
    in folktale, *3465*
lottery
    colony financed by, *4661*
    modern, run by national government, *2610*
    national, *2607*
    public, with cash prizes, *2605*
"Love Me Do" (song), *4446*
LSD
    synthetic hallucinogen, *4028*
Luna (Soviet space probe), *5508*
Lunar Prospecting orbiting robot probe, *5111*
lunar rover, *5526*
Lusitania, R.M.S., *1932*
lutes, *4400*
Lutheran churches, *4820*
    Protestant religious order, *4836*
lyres, *4399*

M

macadamia nut orchards, *1055*
Maccabees
    rebellion of, *4961*
Maccabiah Games, *5695*
machine guns, *6106*
    rapid-fire, *6113*
    that was practical, *6111*
machines
    device to transmit power through gearing, *2186*
    for printing wallpaper, *4711*
    homeostatic, *2184*
    simple, still in use, *2183*
        types of machines e.g. automobiles, engines and motors etc.
macromolecules, *5242*
mad cow disease
    epidemic, *1910*
Mag-Lev train, *3283*
magazines and periodicals
    astronomical journal, *5122*
    children's, *4479*
    comic strip in, *4467*
    for popular entertainment, *4475*
    illustrated, *4476*
    in Native American language, *4480*

known by that name, *4478*
    magazine, *4473*
    online, peer-reviewed journal, *4483*
    periodical, *4474*
    picture, *4481*
    robotics, *5034*
    stamp, *4695*
    to put a hologram on its cover, *4482*
    women's, edited by a woman, *4477*
magic lantern, *4576*
magic square, *3727*
magic tricks
    books explaining, *2218*
magicians
    to use electricity in act, *2217*
    whose act included mind-reading tricks, *2216*
magnetic resonance image (MRI)
    of human body, *3907*
    scanner, *3907*
magnetic surgery system, *4065*
magnetic wire recording device, *2045*
magnetism
    treatise, *5321*
magnetohydrodynamics
    commercial vessel powered by, *5423*
magnets
    electromagnet, *2083*
mah-jongg, *2575*
    rummy card games, *2593*
Mahabharata (Hindu poem)
    reference to dice in, *2604*
Mahavira
    disciples of, *4942*
mail
        See
    airmail
    postage stamps
    postal service
mail-order catalog, *1512*
mailing list
    computer network, *1701*
Mainz Psalter
    book printed in color, *3350*
    colophon printed in a book, *3351*
Maithili writing, *3523*
maize
    cultivation, *1019*
Makalu
    ascent, *5741*
malaria
    recognition of vector of, *3842*
Malay writing, *3510*
Malayalam writing, *3504*
malpractice
    regulation for physicians, *3942*
mambo, *1853*

mesmerism
hypnosis, *3990*
Meso-American culture, *4634*
mesons
prediction of existence of, *5345*
Mesropian Bible, *3494*
Messiah (oratorio), *4388*
metal airplane, *1316*
metal anchor, *5401*
metal cannon, *6098*
metal cans, *2518*
galvanized metal trash can, *4036*
metal helmets, *6067*
metal lamps, *3076*
metal pen, *3581*
metal plate engraving, *1291*
metal sculpture
welded, *1303*
metal snap fasteners, *1642*
metal statue, *1295*
metal stirrups, *1154*
"Metal Storm" (gun), *6118*
metallurgy
textbook, *3663*
meteor crater, *5278*
meteorites
captured on video, *5513*
treatise, *5121*
methadone maintenance program
for heroin addicts, *4029*
methane plant, *2061*
methanol
automobile fueled by, *3255*
Methodists
religious group, *4833*
World Methodist Council, *4841*
metronome, *4414*
metropolis, *1556*
Mexican–American trail, *4658*
Mexican Revolution
use of aircraft carriers in war, *4259*
Mexican War
army newspaper, *4504*
micrometer, *2188*
microprocessor, *1678*
microscopes
achromatic, *5301*
chemist to identify substance using, *5223*
compound, *5294*
electron
scanning tunneling, *5305*
transmission, *5304*
observation of protozoa, bacteria, and human cells, *5146*

Microsoft
commercial software for personal computers, *1730*
microwave oven, *3073*
Middle Ages
doctor to advocate use of anesthesia, *3759*
educational center to transmit Greek scientific heritage, *1962*
elaborate headdresses, *1646*
feminist author in Europe, *5365*
hospital in Europe, *3884*
sumptuary laws, *1609*
treatise on medicine written in Europe, *3771*
midwifery
book in English language written by a woman, *3427*
comprehensive treatise on contraception and birth, *2357*
manual for midwives, *2336*
physician to teach obstetrics and, *2341*
See also
wet-nursing
mile, *5310*
statute, *5312*
military academy
Europe, *4118*
military aircraft, *4203*
military airmail
international route, *4682*
military game, *2570*
military hospitals, *3881*
in Europe since antiquity, *3889*
military-industrial complex, *4119*
military intelligence
agency, *4139*
cryptanalyst, *4135*
woman, *4137*
espionage, treatise, *4138*
intelligence-gathering operation, *4134*
modern war won through superior, *4140*
overthrow of democratic foreign government arranged by CIA, *4143*
reconnaissance satellite system, *4144*
signal intelligence satellite, *4145*
sound recordings used to transmit coded messages in wartime, *4141*
spy ring, *4136*
military law
national code of laws of war, *4120*
military medals
for valor, *4115*
military radar, *2013*
military surgery
treatise on, *4045*
military technology
illustrated manual, *4117*
military uniforms
designed by an artist, *4148*

Monel, *3673*
money and coinage, *2442*
    bank notes, *2447*
    bill of exchange, *2438*
    cash register, *2454*
    cashless community in which electronic cash
      cards replaced bills and coins, *2463*
    check, *2448*
    copper coins in England, *2450*
    copper-nickel coins, *2453*
    currency board in Africa, *2429*
    digitally drawn currency note, *2462*
    dollar coin, *2451*
    electronic cash cards, *2461*
    government coinage, *2437*
    guinea, *2449*
    hyperinflation, *4277*
    IOU promissory note, *2436*
    mill-driven coin press, *2443*
    mint fully mechanized, *2446*
    minted in Canada, *2456*
    minted with steam-powered machinery, *2452*
    national in Oceania to have its own modern,
      2458
    numismatics treatise, *2441*
    paper money, *2440*
    penny, *2439*
    plastic money, *2460*
    shilling, *2444*
    thaler, *2445*
    traveler's checks, *2455*
    unified currency in Europe, *2464*
      See also
      credit cards
money market
    West African, *2431*
Mongols
    invasion of Japan, *4163*
Monitor (ship)
    naval battle between ironclad vessels, *4255*
monkeys
    See
      apes and monkeys
monks and hermits
    Buddhist, *4745*
    Christian, *4780*
    Stylite, *4789*
monoclonal antibodies, *4091*
Monosodium glutamate (MSG), *2563*
monotheism
    religious reformer, *4736*
Monte Carlo, casino, *2233*
Montecassino (abbey), *4850*
Montessori school, *1977*
moon
    astronauts to land on, *5525*
    astronauts to orbit, *5524*
    astronauts to ride a vehicle on, *5528*

    commercial communications satellite to cir-
      cle, *5892*
    discovery of water on, *5111*
    lunar rover, *5526*
    map of, *3622*
    observation of occultation of a star by the,
      5074
    photographs
      of dark side, *5520*
      surface of moon, *5522*
    radar signal to, *5518*
    soil samples from, *5527*
    spacecraft to make soft landing on, *5521*
    spacecraft to reach, *5519*
    spacecraft to return from orbit of, *5523*
    table of motions of, for navigation, *5436*
moon concrete, *2155*
moon rock
    smuggled, *1808*
Moonstone, The (Collins), *3454*
morality play, *5982*
Moravia, kingdom of, *2683*
Moravian Church community, *4832*
Mormon church, *4801*
morphine
    heroin, *3927*
    isolation of, *3923*
morris dancing, *1844*
mortality tables
    actuarial table, *2419*
mortar, hydraulic, *2151*
mosaic
    depicting flower arrangement, *1268*
mosque, *4921*
mosquito-eradication project, *4016*
mother goddess, *4729*
Mother Goose nursery rhymes, *3431*
motion pictures
    See
      movies and films
motor home, *3220*
motor vehicles
    See
      automobile accidents
      automobiles and motor vehicles
      See also
      engines and motors
motorboats, *5415*
    international racing competition, *5857*
motorcycle accident
    person killed in, *1895*
motorcycle races, *5711*
    Dakar Rallye, *5723*
    of importance, *5717*
motorcycles
    designed to be a motor vehicle, *3219*
    mass-produced, *3217*

N

nationwide poisoning epidemic, *1909*
Native Americans
  barbecue, *2529*
  Bible translated into indigenous American
    language, *4892*
  European to join, *4651*
  grammar and primer in indigenous North
    American language, *3536*
  language to be given its own written form,
    3540
  magazine in language of, *4480*
  music by indigenous American peoples to
    be recorded, *4373*
  New World inhabitants forcibly taken to Old
    World, *2283*
  premier of Nunavat, *2918*
  publication in, printed in American colonies,
    3425
  to be buried in Europe, *1878*
  to cross Atlantic, *2274*
Nativity, Feast of
  mention of, *3024*
natural history
  systematic and comprehensive work, *5151*
***Nautilus*, U.S.S.,** *4273, 5463*
naval admiral
  woman who was, *4239*
naval ships and battles
  aircraft carriers
    adapted from conventional warship,
      4261
    attack, *4264*
    built as such, *4265*
    landing of plane on ship under way,
      4262
    nuclear-powered, *4276*
    to be sunk by surface ships, *4270*
    use of, in war, *4259*
    with a through-deck runway, *4263*
  battleship powered by steam turbines, *4258*
  British ship to bear initials H.M.S., *4252*
  civilian ship sunk in World War II, *4267*
  fought with cannon broadsides, *4245*
  in which Greek fire was used, *4243*
  iron-hulled warship, *4254*
  ironclad ships, *4247*
    battle between, *4255*
    in modern times, *4253*
    naval battles in which they participated,
      4248
  Japanese casualty in World War II, *4271*
  major battle decided by firepower, *4246*
  major battle fought by Dutch navy, *4250*
  mock, *2219*
  modern conflict in which Asian power de-
    feated European power, *4257*
  naval battle, *4238*
  naval shot of World War II, *4266*
  nuclear-powered warship, *4274*
  periscope, *4256*

rams, *4241*
sea battle fought solely by air power, *4272*
smokescreen in, *4249*
submarines
  blockade, *4260*
  built for use in war, *4251*
  equipped with ballistic missiles, *4275*
  nuclear-powered, *4273*
U-boat captured in World War II, *4268*
Viking raid, *4244*
warship, *4240*
naval uniform, *4149*
navies
  Muslim, *4242*
navigation
  almanac of, published by national govern-
    ment, *5434*
  astronomical observatory for, *5433*
  at night, *5430*
  compass, *5431*
    gyrocompass, *5438*
  cross staff, *5432*
  lightship, *5435*
  remote detection system using sound, *5439*
  sextant, *5437*
  tables of moon's motions for, *5436*
    See also
    circumnavigations
    lighthouses
Nazi Germany
  American flag to fly over defeated Nazi
    Empire, *4190*
  book burning, *3364*
  death camps, *1772*
    revolt by prisoners, *1773*
    to be liberated in World War II, *1774*
  human breeding program, *5197*
  national euthanasia program, *1771*
  war criminals convicted of crimes against
    humanity, *1776*
necropolis
  in North America, *1876*
Nemean Games
  in modern times, *5699*
neo-Confucianism
  philosopher, *4899*
neoclassic architecture, *1194*
neon, *5241*
neon lamps
  building illuminated by, *2095*
Neptune
  recognition as a planet, *5090*
Neptune (planet)
  observation, *5084*
  planet found beyond, *5097*
neptunium, *5245*
nerve gas, *6081*
Nescafé freeze-dried coffee, *2500*

fast, *2121*
destruction of, as act of war, *4193*
Europe, *2115*

nuclear submarines
nuclear submarine lost at sea, *1942*
warship to sink with nuclear weapons aboard, *1943*

Nuclear Test Ban Treaty, *3176*

nuclear transplantation
in vertebrate, *5185*

nuclear waste
deep underground storage site, *2257*
disaster to cause large loss of life, *1955*
nation heavily polluted by, *2270*

nuclear weapons
atomic bomb explosions, *6123*
   in country other than U.S., *6126*
   underground, *6128*
   underwater, *6124*
ban-the-bomb demonstrations, *6125*
hydrogen bombs, *6129*
   detonated by country other than U.S., *6130*
nonproliferation treaty for weapons of mass destruction, *3179*
remote detection of a test, *6127*
Strategic Arms Limitation Treaty (SALT I), *3180*
test moratorium, *3174*

numbers and number systems
decimal system, treatise advocating use of, *3742*
factoring of 100-digit number, *3755*
irrational, *3730*
method of finding prime numbers, *3733*
sexagesimal, *3726*
use of the terms "billion" and "trillion", *3739*
use of zero, *3738*

numismatics
treatise, *2441*

nuns
Buddhist, *4748*
   Chinese woman to become, *4758*
Doctor of the Church who was a woman, *4876*

Nuremberg Tribunal
definition of rape as crime against humanity, *1775*

nursery rhymes
Mother Goose, *3431*
printed collection, *3430*

nurses
army with trained nursing staff to treat wounded, *4129*
religious order of, *3964*
robot, *5037*
woman to be awarded British Order of Merit, *3974*

nursing schools, *3858*
for professional nurses, *3861*

nuts
macadamia nut orchards, *1055*
peanuts, *1037*

nylon
synthetic fiber produced entirely from chemicals, *3724*

O

oats, *1028*

obelisks, *1259*

Oberammergau passion play
performance, *4861*

Oberlin Collegiate Institute (Ohio)
college to enroll women and men on equal terms, *1994*

oboe, *4409*

obstetrical forceps, *2340*

obstetrics
   See
   pregnancy and childbirth

occupational disease, *3828*

occupational medicine
physician to specialize in, *3965*
treatise, *3783*

ocean and sea voyages
by steamboat, *5454*
   crossing the ocean, *5455*
Christopher Columbus, *2281*
detailed account of, *2273*
direct sea voyage from Western Europe to Asia, *2285*
discovery of Greenland, *2275*
European expedition to round the southern tip of Africa, *2280*
European traveler to reach Chinese frontier, *2276*
European traveler to set foot on North American continent after Vikings, *2284*
European travelers in Japan, *2291*
eyewitness account by European traveler of life in African interior, *2288*
for scientific research, *5049*
major Chinese voyage of exploration and diplomacy, *2277*
Native Americans to cross Atlantic, *2274*
New World inhabitants forcibly taken to Old World, *2283*
raft trip across, *5460*
re-enactment of Viking voyage to New World, *5469*
round-the-world solo sailing journey, *5458*
solo, around the world, *5465*
solo crossing of Gulf of Mexico in paddled boat, *5470*

P

tried for heresy after his death, *4852*
> *See also*
> papal indulgences and bulls

poppy
use as narcotic drug, *3918*

Popular Front for the Liberation of Palestine (PFLP)
international terrorist organization to use skyjacking, *1800*

popular music
cabaret, *4441*
collection of folk ballads, *4439*
Communist song of international popularity, *4440*
wartime song popular with both sides of the conflict, *4442*
> *See also*
> rock music

population growth
country with more than 1 billion people, *4608*
treatise, *4602*
> that had wide influence, *4603*
> *See also*
> world population

porcelain, *3643*
dentures, *3808*
made for Chinese imperial council, *3645*
manufactured in Europe, *3648*

portable personal computer, *1684*

portable televisions
all-transistor, *2026*
flat-screen pocket, *2033*

portable wooden building, *1170*

portraits
camera, *4578*
caricatures, *1280*
full-length double, *1275*
Old Master painting sold at auction for more than US$10 million, *1288*
satirical, *1279*

Portuguese writing, *3516*

post-and-lintel construction
house, *1220*

postage meter, *4676*

postage stamps, *4689*
airmail, *4698*
album, *4694*
catalogs, *4693*
collectors, *4690*
> handbook for, *4696*
commemorative, *4697*
dealer, *4692*
depicting basketball, *4699*
magazine for, *4695*
with serrated edges, *4691*

postal giro system, *2411*

postal service
centralized system, *4669*

Christmas cards, *4673*
complaint by postal deliverer, *4668*
international dogsled mail, *4678*
international postal congress, *4675*
junk mail, *4677*
prepaid envelopes, *4671*
prepaid postcards, *4674*
system to carry prepaid mail, *4672*
to carry private mail, *4670*
> *See also*
> airmail
> postage stamps

postcards
prepaid, *4674*

poster kiosks, *4459*

potato cultivation, *1032*

pots, *3097*

potter's wheel, *3633, 3636*

pottery, *3632*
kiln, *3634*

potty
depiction, *2380*

poultry litter
as fuel, *2074*

pound lock
on a canal, *2135*

power loom, *3716*

powered wood shapers, *6056*

prayer
of thanksgiving for crops, *4735*

prayer book
Jewish, *4990*

Praying Through the Window campaign, *4845*

prefabricated building, *1191*

pregnancy and childbirth
artificial insemination of human being, *2342*
Cesarean operation, *2335*
> fully documented, *2339*
comprehensive treatise on contraception and birth, *2357*
ether as anesthetic in, *2343*
frozen embryo to come successfully to birth, *2351*
incubator for premature babies, *2337*
international program to promote safe birth, *2352*
manual for midwives, *2336*
nonuplets, *2347*
obstetrical forceps, *2340*
octuplets, *2355*
physician to teach obstetrics and midwifery, *2341*
pregnancy test, *2334*
pregnant woman, depiction, *2332*
Queen to deliver child under anesthesia, *2344*
quintuplets, *2345*

printers and printing—*Continued*
machine for printing wallpaper, *4711*
movable type, *4703*
music printed from movable type, *4706*
photoengraving, *4716*
rotary, roll-fed, *4718*
rub process, *4701*
screen, *4717*
typeface made in Europe in non-Roman alphabet, *4705*
woman, *4710*
xerography, *4724*
color copier, *4726*
copy machine, *4725*

printing presses
flatbed, *4714*
licenses for, *4708*
Linotype machine, *4722*
machine capable of casting individual letters of type, *4723*
New World, *4709*
newspaper folding device, *4720*
printing press, *4704*
rotary, steam-driven, *4715*
steam-powered, *4713*

prison reformer, *1738*

prisoners of war
accidental sinking of ships carrying, *1938*

privatization campaign, *1447*

Prix d'Amérique
winner of, who was a woman, *5689*

probation system
for criminals of all ages, *1739*

product designer, modern, *3090*

production line
mechanized, *1483*

programmable logic controller (PLC), *2189*

Project Ozma, *5101*

promissory note, *2436*

Prontosil
sulfa drug, *3934*

property laws
marital property reform law, *2400*

Prophet's Mosque, *4921*

prosthetic devices
artificial eardrum, *3983*
artificial hip, *3985*
below-knee leg prosthesis, *3984*
false eyes, *3978*
glass eyes, *3982*
iron hand, *3980*
mechanical arm, *3981*
written record of prosthesis, *3979*

prostitutes and prostitution
brothel, *5386*
forced, reparations for, *1779*
home for repentant prostitutes, *5388*
known by name, *3465*

prostitute, *5387*

proteins
characterized by amino acid sequence, *5169*

Protestant Reformation
Catholic monastic order founded after, *4868*
date in, *4814*

Protestantism
Bible society, *4835*
heretic, *4824*
hospital, *3893*
hymnbook
containing hymns in English, *4823*
hymnbooks, *4813*
liturgies, *4816*
major statement of theological doctrine, *4815*
reformer to abolish the Mass, *4817*
religious order, *4836*
service in New World, *4828*
Universal Week of Prayer, *4837*
names of specific sects e.g. Anglican church, Baptists, etc.

Proto-Indo-European languages, *3298*

protons
discovery of, *5337*

protozoa
microscopic observation, *5146*

pruning shears, *6055*

psalms
in metrical form, *4385*
printed edition of, in Hebrew, *4991*

psychiatry and psychology
asylums for mentally ill, *3987*
in Europe, *3988*
behaviorist, *4002*
clinical depression and bipolar disorder description, *3829*
course in scientific psychology, *3995*
drug treatment for mental illness, *3986*
experimental psychology
laboratory, *3998*
work of, *3994*
hotel with staff psychologist, *4006*
humane treatment for mentally ill, *3991*
hypnosis, *3990*
phrenologist, *3993*
postgraduate center for psychiatric education, *3862*
psychologist to relate known physiological facts to psychological phenomena, *3996*
psychology journal, *3997*
refuge for mentally ill patients, *3992*
standardized intelligence test, *4001*
use of term "psychology", *3989*

psychoanalysis
psychoanalyst, *3999*
woman, *4003*
treatise, *4000*

Russian Orthodox church
Patriarch of Moscow, *4810*
who was not Russian by birth, *4811*
Russian Revolution of 1917, *2673*
Russian writing, *3511*
Russo-Japanese War
military use of TNT, *6091*
modern conflict in which Asian power defeated European power, *4257*
rye, *1013*

S

Sabbath
celebrated on Sunday, *3022*
saddle
camels, *1150*
horses, *1151*
stirrup, *1152*
Safe Motherhood Initiative (Kenya), *2352*
safety elevator, *1205*
safety fuse, *3682*
safety matches, *3106*
safety pin, *3105*
safety razors, *2753*
to be commercially manufactured, *2754*
sagas, *3441*
legal drama, *3443*
sailboat races
solo transatlantic, *5858*
saints
Anglican, *4831*
gypsy to be beatified by Catholic Church, *4881*
Hindu poet-saints of *bhakti* devotional movement, *4909*
Jaina, *4941*
biographies, *4950*
images of, *4947*
Orthodox, from Russia, *4809*
Roman Catholic
canonized by a pope, *4853*
from New World, *4872*
sales tax, *2465*
salmon
canned, *2533*
salted herring, *2527*
Salvation Army
activities, *4839*
San Francisco Conference
United Nations conference, *3188*
sandals, *1651*
Sandinistas
woman to become president of Nicaragua, *2848*

sandwich, *2530*
sanitation
See
public health and sanitation
Sanskrit
grammar, *3571*
major source of international folktales, *3468*
text, *3570*
Santa Claus, *3019*
Santa Maria del Fiore (Florence)
Renaissance architect of importance, *1186*
sarcophagi, *1873*
sardines
canned, *2533*
sarin nerve gas
terrorist attack using, *1802*
saser, *2024*
sash windows, *1193*
satellite systems
ICBM-launch warning system, *6138*
reconnaissance, *4144*
signal intelligence satellite, *4145*
satellites
artificial, *5584*
civilian spy, *5593*
commercial, *5587*
earth-observing, that could see through clouds and darkness, *5592*
geosynchronous, *5588*
infrared astronomy, *5143*
international, *5586*
consortium, *5589*
launched by Chinese space program, *5590*
launched from earth to orbit another planet, *5591*
ocean-mapping, *5291*
powered by photovoltaic cells, *5585*
worldwide satellite-based weather observation system, *5288*
x-ray astronomy, *5139*
See also
communications satellites
satire
in English, *3420*
satirical portrait, *1279*
satyagraha
nonviolent act of civil disobedience of international significance, *3155*
sauce
Worcestershire, *2561*
savaté
modern, *5704*
savings bank, *2407*
sawmills
steam-powered, *1479*
water-powered, *1476*
saws
saw, *6047*

seat belts, *3227*
  compulsory, *4019*
  production automobiles with, *3247*
seaweed
  cultivation, *1007*
secret service
  to specialize in codebreaking, *3401*
secret society
  Communist, *2671*
secretin, *5165*
sedan, *3237*
seed drill
  horse-drawn, *1078*
seed planting
  grain drill, *1071*
seeing-eye dogs
    See
    guide dogs
seige engines
  trebuchet, *6077*
seigecraft
  treatise, *4116*
seismograph, *5259*
self-contained underwater breathing apparatus (SCUBA), *5285*
self-guided car, *3259*
self-help programs
  for substance abusers, *4027*
self-immolation
  by Buddhist monk, *1886*
self-rising flour, *2534*
self-sharpening plow, *1083*
semiconductors
  epitaxy fabrication, *2019*
seminaries
  New World, *4867*
Septuagint, *4882*
  translation of Jewish Bible, *4985*
septuplets
  to survive birth, *2353*
serfs, *5474*
serial killer, *1785*
sericulture
  silk, *3701*
serrated walls
  angled fortifications, *1187*
service club, *1839*
settlement house, *5499*
Seven Samurai, The (film), *4305*
Seven Wonders of the World
  lighthouse of importance, *5440*
  list, *1176*
sewage system, *4032*
sewer
  still in use, *4033*

sewing machine
  that was practical, *1486*
sex and gender
  center for study of human sexuality, *5371*
  in plants, scientifically accurate treatise on, *5183*
  religious group advocating complete equality between men and women, *5367*
  scientific study of physiology of human sexuality, *5373*
  sex-change operation, *5370*
    that was successful, *5372*
  statute establishing that men and women are equal under the law, *5366*
  surrogate partner therapy, *5374*
  symbols of the feminine, *5364*
    See also
    feminism
    homosexuality
    prostitution
sex-change operation, *5370*
  that was successful, *5372*
sex chromosomes
  gene-linkage maps, *5203*
  human
    researcher to describe role of, *5195*
sex scandals
  political, *2627*
sexagesimal number system, *3726*
sextant, *5437*
sexual harassment
  case at United Nations, *5377*
shaduf
  water-lifting device, *1094*
Shakers
  group advocating equality between men and women, *5367*
Shakespeare's plays
  censored edition, *3433*
  Henry VI, Part I, *3421*
shaman
  portrait, *4727*
shampoo, *2729*
Shang dynasty, *2677*
shaper, *1485*
shaving instruments
    See
    razors and shaving instruments
shawls, *1604*
sheep-shearing machine, *1137*
sheepdog trials, *1156*
sheikh
  of Bahrain, *2982*
sherbet
  frozen desserts, *2546*
Sherpa expedition
  to Everest, *5754*

travel and tourism—*Continued*
transatlantic voyages and crossings

travel books
dictionary for tourists, *3368*
guidebooks, *3394*
illustrated with original photographs, *3393*
vocabulary list, *3392*

travel writers
Russian, *3391*
travel writer, *3390*

traveler's checks, *2455*

Treasury of the Cnidians, *1172*

treaties
global, to regulate fishing on high seas, *3126*
international trade in rare animals, *1142*
South Pacific Nuclear Free Zone Treaty, *3140*
See also
international treaties
North Atlantic Treaty Organization (NATO)

Treblinka (Poland)
revolt by prisoners in Nazi death camp, *1773*

trebuchet, *6077*

trees
See
plants and flowers
Arbor Day, *3036*
Christmas, *3029*
fruit, monograph on, *5180*
of which there is historical record, *2615*

trial by jury, *1736*
British jury to consider evidence overseas, *1740*
televised trial, *4463*

triathlon, *5848*
Europe, *5850*
Ironman, *5849*

trigonometry
treatise on, *3735*

"trillion"
use of term, *3739*

trireme galley, *5402*

Tristram Shandy (Sterne), *3446*

Triton, U.S.S., *5464*

triumphal arch, *1260*

trivia board game
of international popularity, *2579*

Trojan War
confederation of Greek city states, *2678*

troop transport, *4157*

troubadour, *4363*

trousers
See
pants

Troy
excavator, *5058*

trumpet, *4401*
museum, *4425*

tsars
to travel outside Russia, *2777*

tuba, *4418*

tubular steel chair, *3091*

tulips
black, *1057*
cultivated by florists, *1045*

tumors
hyperthermia for treating, *4078*
See also
cancer

tunneling machine
that could turn 90 degrees, *2197*

tunnels
automobile, *2193*
canal, *2190*
mountain, *2192*
rail, longer than 50 kilometers, *2196*
road, longer than 10 miles, *2195*
undersea, *2194*
underwater, *2191*
link between Great Britain and Europe, *2198*

turbine, *2161*
gas, patent, *2167*

turbocharged engine
for mass-produced automobile, *3251*

turbojet aircraft, *1321*

Turkish horticultural treatise, *2619*

Turkish writing, *3501*

turquoise
hard-rock mining operation, *3679*

twenty-four hour days, *6001*

typefaces and fonts
italics, *4707*
made in Europe in non-Roman alphabet, *4705*
printed book decorated with ornaments, *3356*

typewriters
book manuscript written on, *3362*
correction fluid for, *3597*
patent, *3585*
that was practical, *3590*
to be marketed, *3591*

typewritten letter, *3324*

tyrannosaurus
scientific description of, *5215*

U

U-boat
  captured on World War II, *4268*
ultralight airplane
  transatlantic flight by, *1386*
ultrasonic disintegrator
  used in medicine, *4093*
ultraviolet (UV) radiation
  increase over populated area, *2253*
ultraviolet solid-state laser, *2023*
Umayyad dynasty, *2685*
  Islamic hospital, *3885*
umbrellas
  waterproof, *1619*
underground photographs, *4596*
undersea tunnel, *2194*
underwater personal computers, *1689*
underwater photograph, *4594*
underwater shipwreck, *5396*
underwater tunnels, *2191*
  Chunnel, *2198*
uneven parallel bars, *5673*
Unification Church
  teachings, *4804*
unions
  general, not confined to one trade, *1504*
  nation to legalize trade, *1507*
  strike by workers, *1500*
    See also
    guilds
unit of length, *5308*
unit of linear measure, *5309*
Unitarian church, *4827*
United Nations
  Armed Forces awarded Nobel Prize for
    Peace, *4544*
  Atomic Energy Commission
    chairman, *3190*
  Codex Alimentarius Commission, *4018*
  Commission on Crime Prevention and Crim-
    inal Justice, session, *1796*
  condemnation of anti-Semitism by, *3201*
  Conference on International Organization,
    3188
  Conference on Straddling Fish Stocks and
    Highly Migratory Fish Stocks, *3126*
  Convention on the Law of the Sea, *2248*
  Decade for Women, *5375*
  deputy Secretary-general, *3204*
  Development Programme
    ranking of countries by human develop-
      ment, *3199*
  Earth Summit, *2251*
  embargo, *3194*
  environmental conference, *2246*

  General Assembly
    meeting, *3192*
    president of, who was a woman, *3195*
    representative of nongovernmental orga-
      nization to address plenary session of,
      3197
  international maritime organization, *3193*
  International Year of the World's Indige-
    nous People, *3200*
  manhunt, *1795*
  meeting to establish, *3187*
  member nations, *3189*
  military action, *4192*
  Register on Conventional Arms, *6083*
  sanctioned force sent uninvited to a sover-
    eign country, *4197*
  Secretary-general, *3191*
    from an Asian nation, *3196*
    from black African nation, *3203*
  sexual harassment case at, *5377*
  UNESCO General conferences, *3162*
  world bank, *2413*
  World Heritage List sites, *3198*
  World Trade Organization, director-general,
    3202
United Nations Day, *3040*
"United States of Europe"
  call for, *3135*
UNIVAC I, *1671*
universal literacy
  call for, in modern times, *1965*
Universal Week of Prayer, *4837*
universe
  computer model of growth of, *5113*
universities
    See
    colleges and universities
Unix
  multi-user operating system, *1727*
unsinkable boat, *5410*
Up-Helly-Aa fire festival, *3020*
Upanishads
  Brahman, *4904*
  didactic verses, *3437*
  karmic reincarnation, *4903*
Ur-Nammu
  law code, *2644*
uranium
  element heavier than, *5245*
  factory to obtain, from gold, *3675*
Uranus (planet), *5082*
  discovery of rings, *5107*
urban areas
  housing project in, *5497*
Urdu writing, *3532*
urea, *5232*
used-car dealership, *1517*

Utopia
reference to, *3478*
Utopian town planner, *1561*

V

V-block engine, *2175*
vaccines and inoculation
poliomyelitis, *3912*
rabies, *3911*
smallpox, *3909*
to be chemically synthesized, *3913*
tooth decay, *3822*
vaccine, *3910*
vacuum
investigation of properties, *5298*
vacuum aspiration
abortion by, *2362*
vacuum flask, *5303*
vaginal cap, *2361*
vampirism
World Dracula Congress, *3481*
vanilla
artificial flavoring, *2539*
vascular sutures, *4054*
vasectomy, *2364*
Vatican Council, *4875*
Vatican observatory, *5137*
vedalia beetle, *1100*
Vegemite, *2564*
vegetarian, *2469*
principles, *2471*
vehicular death
ballooning casualties, *1890*
hang-glider fatality, *1893*
person killed in motorcycle accident, *1895*
person run over by train, *1891*
See also
airplane accidents
automobile accidents
ship wrecks and sinkings
Velcro, *1644*
vélocipède, *5622*
velodrome
portable, of Olympic size, *5608*
vending machines
commercial, *1510*
in modern times, *1516*
vending machine, *1509*
Venice Biennale
international art exhibition, *1251*
ventriloquist, *2215*
Venus (planet)
observations, *5064*

planet to be mapped, *5080*
spacecraft to make soft landing on another planet, *5571*
spacecraft to reach another planet, *5570*
"Venus" type female figurine, *1293*
Veronal
barbiturate, *3925*
Very Large Array, *5142*
Vesuvius, Mount
eruption, *1914*
scientist lowered into volcano, *5262*
veterinary schools, *3857*
chiropractic, *3864*
VHS videocassette recorder, *2031*
Via Appia (Appian Way), *1585*
Victoria, Lake
European explorer to find source of White Nile, *2300*
video
music, *4450*
satellite-delivered digital system for education, *1979*
video cassette format
professional, *5968*
video entertainment system
family car with, *3260*
video games, *2577*
designer of renown, *2578*
hand-held, *2039*
video tape recorders
for sound and pictures, *5964*
helical-scan, *5965*
home, *2027*
Video Walkman, *2038*
videocassette recorders
for home use, *2028*
high-definition digital, *5969*
pocket, and television, *2038*
VHS, *2031*
videoconferencing
on Internet, between aircraft and ground location, *5974*
videodisc, *2029*
system that was commercially successful, *2034*
videophone, *5972*
color, for home use, *5973*
Vietnamese writing, *3524*
Vikings
discovery of Greenland, *2275*
raid by, *4244*
Up-Helly-Aa fire festival, *3020*
voyage to New World
re-enactment, *5469*
Vindication of the Rights of Women, A (Wollstonecraft), *5368*
Vinland
European settlement in North America, *4643*

war—*Continued*

kites used in warfare, *4201*

lasting more than three centuries, *4194*

major land battle decided by volley fire, *4168*

major land battles decided by firepower, *4166*

military aircraft, *4203*

military clash between China and a western power, *4172*

military victory of Islam, *4159*

modern, won through military intelligence, *4140*

national code of laws of, *4120*

offensive operation by NATO, *4200*

peacekeeper to die in Somalia, *4199*

pilot captured during, *4208*

scalping, *4156*

statement of principle of medical neutrality during, *3127*

telegraph used in, *4174*

to receive extensive newspaper coverage, *4175*

to receive news coverage, *4167*

treatise on, *4155*

treaty banning use of weather as weapon of, *3181*

troop transport, *4157*

United Nations military action, *4192*

United Nations–sanctioned force sent uninvited to a sovereign country, *4197*

use of airplanes in, *4205*

use of term "cold war", *4191*

woman to lead rebellion against Roman Empire, *4158*

woman to wear armor while leading men in battle, *4154*

world war, *4170*

> *See also*
> aerial bombardment and warfare
> armed forces
> civil wars
> genocide and war crimes
> guns and artillery
> naval ships and battles
> navies
> rockets and missiles
> weapons and explosives
> and names of wars e.g. Trojan War, World War II, etc.
> the military headings

war correspondent, **4456**

to file dispatches by telegraph, *4458*

war crimes

> *See*
> genocide and war crimes

war photographers, **4460**

who was a woman, *4462*

Warsaw Pact

country to attempt to withdraw, *3173*

former members to join NATO, *3143*

signatories, *3172*

warships

aircraft carrier adapted from conventional warship, *4261*

battleship powered by steam turbines, *4258*

iron-hulled, *4254*

ironclad, *4247*

> battle between, *4255*
> in modern times, *4253*
> naval battles in which they participated, *4248*

nuclear-powered, *4274*

rams, *4241*

sunk by air attack in wartime, *4269*

warship, *4240*

washing machine, **3054**

waste disposal

deep underground nuclear waste storage site, *2257*

law, *2238*

watches

> *See*
> clocks and watches

water

carbonated, *2531*

determination of chemical composition of, *5227*

water desalinization

city in North America to use seawater as its sole water supply, *2245*

country to depend mainly on, *2244*

plant, *1489*

process, *1475*

water-lifting device, **1094**

water mills

undershot, *2186*

water mill, *2185*

water pollution

law, *2266*

oil spills

> from commercial tanker, *2269*
> on ocean, *2268*

water polo, **5863**

international match, *5864*

water-powered sawmill, **1476**

water purification plant, **4011**

water supply

chlorinated, city with, *4014*

waterbed, **3094**

Waterman Company

fountain pen, *3592*

watermark, **3692**

waterproof umbrellas, **1619**

waterwheel turbine, **2059**

Watson Brake complex

human construction in New World, *4632*

Watt steam engine, **2165**

X

Y

Z

Zen Buddhism, *4759*
  popularizer of, in the West, *4764*
Zeppelin flights, *1405*
  Graf Zeppelin, *1407*
zero
  use of, *3738*
zipper
  that was practical, *1643*
zodiacal horoscope, *5066*
zoo(s), *1158*
  Europe, *1161*
  large, *1159*
  public, *1162*

  Western Hemisphere, *1160*
Zoroastrianism
  establishment as state religion, *5019*
  heresy in, *5021*
  holidays, *3013*
  mass migrations, *5022*
  prophet, *5018*
  reform movement, *5024*
  religious texts, *5020*
  scholarly treatise, *5023*
Zulus
  army with standardized training and tactics, *4128*
  newspaper, *4512*
  writing, *3543*
  written history, *3011*

Index by Years

Following is a chronlogical listing of entries, arranged by year. To find an entry in the main body of the text, please search for the italicized indexing number.

569

26,000 BCE

Agriculture, *1001*

25,000 BCE

Depiction of a pregnant woman, *2332*
Evidence of weaving, *3696*
Whistles, *4397*

23,000 BCE

Female figurine of the "Venus" type, *1293*

20,000 BCE

Representations of death, *1865*

18,000 BCE

Shaving instruments, *2749*

17,300 BCE

Cord, *3697*

15,000 BCE

Portrait of a shaman, *4727*

13,000 BCE

Depiction of a woman in labor, *2333*

11,000 BCE

Human remains in the Americas, *4627*

10,500 BCE

Human habitation in the Americas, *4628*

10,000 BCE

Animal domesticated for food, *1129*
Bread, *2524*
Cereal crop, *1010*
Hammer, *6042*
Pottery, *3632*

9700 BCE

Site of organized human activity in North America, *4629*

9600 BCE

Skeleton of a domesticated dog, *1104*

9500 BCE

Rice, *1011*

9150 BCE

Person with dwarfism, *3824*

9000 BCE

Einkorn domestication, *1012*

Houses, *1214*
Permanent settlement, *4630*

8000 BCE

Copper tools, *3654*
Depiction of organized warfare, *4151*
Depictions of anatomically correct human, *1263*
Houses made of brick, *1215*
Walled town, *1555*

7300 BCE

Brain surgery, *4037*

7000 BCE

Cattle herders, *1130*
Cloth fragment, *3698*
Metropolis, *1556*
Rectangular houses, *1216*

6500 BCE

Cloth made of animal fiber, *3699*
Plaster statues, *1294*
Rye, *1013*

6000 BCE

Beans, *1014*
Crops cultivated in the New World, *1015*
Large-scale irrigation project, *1093*
Religion, *4728*
Sugar cane cultivation, *1059*

5500 BCE

Sickle, *1069*

5000 BCE

Astronomical monument, *5063*
Intoxicating drug, *4020*
Skeleton of a black African, *4620*

4500 BCE

Gold artifacts, *3655*
Olive oil factory, *2525*
Potter's wheel, *3633*
Seals for fastening and recording, *3576*

4000 BCE

African rock art, *1233*
Barley, *1016*
Beer, *2474*
Combs, *2727*
Floor coverings, *3075*
Garment to undergo changes of fashion, *1594*
Grape cultivation, *1017*
Hoe, *1070*
Horse riding, *1144*
Long-distance sea trading along regular routes, *1523*

2800 BCE—*continued*
Paper, *3687*

2780 BCE

Beekeeping, *1134*

2737 BCE

Tea, *2491*

2700 BCE

Acupuncture for dental problems, *3794*
Famine, *1912*
Ink, *3578*
Maize cultivation, *1019*
Millet, *1020*
Recommendation to treat physical disorders
    with exercise and massage, *4079*
Regional superpower, *2674*
Smelted iron artifact, *3661*

2650 BCE

Large stone structure, *1167*
Physician known by name, *3941*

2613 BCE

Reference to a ship with a name, *5393*

2600 BCE

Dentist, *3795*
Sphinx, *1258*

2500 BCE

Anchor, *5394*
Aquaculture, *1005*
Assault vehicle, *6119*
Bowling game, *5633*
Calligraphy, *3310*
Cemetery, *1874*
City in continuous existence, *1557*
City planned on a grid, *1558*
Domesticated camels, *1147*
Evidence of Hinduism, *4900*
Incinerators, *2236*
Lutes, *4400*
Oil presses, *1473*
Plastering tools, *6045*
Sewage system, *4032*
Sexagesimal number system, *3726*
Shampoo, *2729*
Ship, *5395*
Silk, *3701*
Structure more than 100 meters tall, *1224*
Tract houses, *1218*

2449 BCE

Obelisks, *1259*

2400 BCE

Glass objects, *3637*
Religion to offer divine judgment and salvation,
    4730

2334 BCE

Emperor, *2763*
Empire, *2675*

2333 BCE

King of Korea, *2920*

2325 BCE

Religious text, *4731*

2300 BCE

Author known by name, *3326*
Complaint by a postal deliverer, *4668*
Go, *2566*
Landscape in art, *1264*
Legend of a resurrected deity, *4732*
Maps, *3600*
Metal statue, *1295*
Verses in honor of a deity, *4733*

2285 BCE

Library, *1809*

2200 BCE

Cake, *2544*
Magic square, *3727*
Orange cultivation, *1021*
Underwater shipwreck, *5396*
Water-lifting device, *1094*

2160 BCE

Use of canopic jars, *1875*

2136 BCE

Total solar eclipse to be recorded, *5124*

2100 BCE

Corset, *1599*
High heels, *1650*
Law code, *2644*
Literature for children, *3434*
Multi-story building, *1168*
Pear orchards, *1022*
Pharmacopoeia of medicinal herbs, *3787*
Written record of wet-nursing, *2377*

2097 BCE

Zoo, *1158*

2025 BCE

Town house, *1219*

Zoroastrian holidays, *3013*
Zoroastrian religious texts, *5020*

495 BCE

Buddhist nun, *4748*

492 BCE

Play to flop, *5976*

490 BCE

Marathon, *5841*

484 BCE

Choreographers, *1841*

483 BCE

Buddhist Council, *4749*
Buddhist monastic rule, *4750*
Buddhist monument, *4751*

480 BCE

International maritime law, *1527*
Woman cryptanalyst, *4137*

479 BCE

Admiral who was a woman, *4239*
Philosopher to advocate teaching and social activism as a way of life, *4557*

475 BCE

Transposition cipher, *3396*

464 BCE

Slave revolt, *5472*

460 BCE

Treatise on geometry, *3731*

450 BCE

Atomic theory, *5320*
Book of poetry in a Chinese language, *3550*
Confucian text, *4895*
Slave society, *5473*
Trade guilds, *1528*
Treatise on war, *4155*
Zodiacal horoscope, *5066*

444 BCE

Canonization of biblical books, *4984*

432 BCE

Buildings with acanthus ornamentation, *1173*

431 BCE

Hospitals in Asia, *3880*

430 BCE

Epidemic, *1899*
Utopian town planner, *1561*

425 BCE

Dialogues, *5977*
Narrative secular history book of importance, *3002*
Planned genocide, *1765*
Scalping, *4156*

400 BCE

Camera obscura, *4575*
Canal in China of importance, *2131*
Carpeting, *3080*
Chinese historical archive, *3003*
Cynic, *4558*
Grammarian, *3296*
Hair lightening, *2732*
Heresy in Zoroastrianism, *5021*
Knotting as a technique of making carpets, *3704*
Sanskrit grammar, *3571*
Stage clowns, *5978*
Treatise on espionage, *4138*

399 BCE

Catapult, *6071*

393 BCE

Permanent institution of higher education in the liberal arts, *1981*

390 BCE

Bill of exchange, *2438*

377 BCE

Description of disease as a matter of science, *3827*
Treatise on human ecology, *2237*

375 BCE

Literary critic, *3327*
Schism in Buddhism, *4752*
Treatise on hunting, *3123*

370 BCE

Pulley and tackle block, *6048*

360 BCE

Treatise on cryptography, *3397*
Treatise on siegecraft, *4116*

354 BCE

Mausoleum, *1877*

350 BCE

Alphabet to include vowels, *3316*
Automaton, *5025*
Central heating system for buildings, *1208*
Clinker-built boats, *5403*
Cookbook, *2501*
Desalination process, *1475*
Estimate of the circumference of the earth, *5254*
Explicator of orthodox Confucianism, *4896*
Fables with morals, *3438*
Gynecologist who was a woman, *3945*
Occupational disease, *3828*
Philosophical encyclopedia, *3376*
Punctuation, *3317*
Reference to tea, *2492*
Sculpture of the goddess Aphrodite in the nude, *1297*

335 BCE

Scientists attached to armed forces, *5042*

330 BCE

Diving bell, *5445*

328 BCE

School for mirror artisans, *2738*

327 BCE

Definite date in the history of the Indian subcontinent, *6013*

326 BCE

Banana cultivation, *1029*

325 BCE

Canonization of Jaina sacred texts, *4946*
Taoist book of teachings, *5014*

324 BCE

Circumnavigation of Britain, *2304*
Detailed account of a long sea voyage, *2273*

322 BCE

Botanist, *5178*

321 BCE

Emperor of India, *2766*

320 BCE

Sighting of a mermaid, *3466*
Waste-disposal law, *2238*

312 BCE

Paved long-distance road, *1585*

Roman aqueduct, *2132*

310 BCE

Skeptic, *4559*

306 BCE

Epicurean, *4560*

303 BCE

Professional barbers, *2752*

300 BCE

Anatomist to dissect human cadavers, *3946*
Anti-Semitic libel, *4960*
Bestiary, *3467*
Flying model airplane, *1307*
Food purity law, *2472*
Homeostatic machine, *2184*
Images of the Jaina saints, *4947*
Iron for smoothing clothes, *3051*
Mathematical definition of a circle, *3732*
Molded glass, *3640*
Reed pen, *3580*
Schism in Jainism, *4948*
Scissors, *6049*
Stoic, *4561*
Tamil writing, *3487*
Text of Chinese medicine, *3767*
Treatise on rocks and minerals, *5255*

297 BCE

King to convert to Jainism, *4949*

284 BCE

Critical edition of the works of Homer, *3328*

280 BCE

Lighthouse of importance, *5440*
Troop transport, *4157*
Western physician to take a pulse, *3947*

278 BCE

Dragon Boat races in China, *3014*
Poet in a Chinese language, *3551*

275 BCE

Surgery to repair a cleft lip, *4039*

261 BCE

Buddhist inscriptions, *4753*
Establishment of Buddhism as a state religion, *4754*

260 BCE

Buddhist national leader, *2767*

Yin-Yang philosophical school, *4562*

251 BCE

Country outside India to accept Buddhism, *4755*

250 BCE

Accurate method of determining the sizes of and distances to celestial bodies, *5067*
Chain mail, *6072*
Christian Bible, *4882*
Classification system of all knowledge, *1810*
Hairless dog breeds, *1117*
Heliocentric world system, *5068*
Hourglass, *6019*
Library catalog, *1811*
Organ, *4405*
Shawls, *1604*
Shinto rituals, *4995*
Translation of the Jewish Bible, *4985*

245 BCE

Tree of which there is historical record, *2615*

241 BCE

Warship, *4240*

240 BCE

Latin comedy and tragedy, *5979*
Method of finding prime numbers, *3733*
Scientific calculation of the Earth's circumference, *5256*

235 BCE

Epic translated into Latin, *3568*

230 BCE

Calculation of pi (π), *3734*

221 BCE

Emperor of China, *2768*
Libraries in Asia, *1812*

218 BCE

Iron hand, *3980*

212 BCE

Solar energy weapons, *6073*

204 BCE

Suppression of a theatrical performance, *5980*

200 BCE

Alchemist, *5217*
Commercial bakeries, *2526*

Organist, *4361*
Parchment, *3688*
Planned city in South America, *1562*
Punctuation system, *3318*
Saddle for horses, *1151*
Sinhalese writing, *3488*
Statement of the principle of hot-air ballooning, *1389*
Surveyors, *2126*
Yoga textbook, *3768*

199 BCE

Concrete, *2149*

196 BCE

Triumphal arch, *1260*

184 BCE

Basilica, *1174*
Epic composed in Latin, *3569*

183 BCE

Encyclopedia for young adults, *3377*

179 BCE

Stone bridge, *2137*

175 BCE

Attempt to reconcile Judaism and philosophy, *4563*
Rams, *4241*

165 BCE

Sunspot observations, *5069*

164 BCE

Chanukah, *3015*
Rebellion for religious freedom, *4961*

153 BCE

New Year to begin on January 1, *3016*

150 BCE

Basilica still extant, *1175*
Biography of the Buddha, *4756*
Cement, *2150*
Kites, *1414*
List of Seven Wonders of the World, *1176*
Mile, *5310*

140 BCE

Long-distance communication system using an alphabet, *5918*
Raised aqueduct of great length, *2133*

130 BCE

Anticoagulant, *3920*

130 BCE—*continued*

Establishment of Confucianism as the state religion, *4897*

129 BCE

Star catalog that was comprehensive and accurate, *5119*

125 BCE

Stirrup, *1152*

124 BCE

Civil service examinations, *2628*
University in China, *1982*

110 BCE

Oyster farm, *1006*

105 BCE

Chinese historian of importance, *3004*

100 BCE

Art presenting a continuous narrative, *1234*
Authoritative Hindu law code, *4906*
Botanical illustrations, *5179*
Craft guilds, *1529*
Firefighting devices, *1573*
Insecticide, *1097*
Kites used in warfare, *4201*
Major intercontinental road, *1586*
Major source of international folktales, *3468*
Military hospitals, *3881*
Pairs of fitted shoes, *1652*
Reference to horseshoes, *1153*
Roller bearings, *3291*
Statement of the Hindu doctrine of *dharma*, *4907*
Trade between the Mediterranean world and East Africa, *1530*
Vending machine, *1509*
Water mill, *2185*
Weathervane, *5257*

95 BCE

King of united Armenia, *2923*

80 BCE

Mechanical calculator, *1660*

63 BCE

Shorthand, *3319*

60 BCE

Druid, *4738*

59 BCE

News posters, *4484*

50 BCE

Bards, *3329*
Buddhist religious texts, *4765*
Giant sports arena, *5606*
Pali text, *3489*
Synagogues, *4962*

49 BCE

Surgery to repair perforated or obstructed intestines, *4040*

48 BCE

Medical officers in the armed forces, *4121*

46 BCE

Mock naval battle, *2219*

44 BCE

Autopsy of a well-known individual, *1866*

40 BCE

Heated swimming pool, *5817*
Winnowing machine, *1072*

27 BCE

Emperor of Rome, *2769*

25 BCE

Description of an earthquake, *5258*

17 BCE

Depictions of a comet, *5070*

10 BCE

Blown glass, *3641*

2 BCE

Book on cosmetics, *2715*

1 BCE

Plum cultivation, *1031*

1

Apartment houses, *1221*
Domesticated ducks, *1135*
Lanterns, *3081*
Pineapple cultivation, *1030*

6

Organized police force, *1788*
Sales tax, *2465*

25

Freight elevators, *1203*

Plate armor, *6074*

27

Device to transmit power through gearing, *2186*
Public bathing, *2716*

33

Christians, *4770*

35

Royal converts to Judaism, *4963*

36

Christian martyr, *4771*

40

Center of Christian missionary activity, *4772*

50

Brassiere, *1605*
Distillation apparatus for alchemists, *5218*
Gnostic, *4773*
Images of the Buddha, *4757*
Irish racing, *5679*
Medical text written by a woman, *3769*
Plow with a moldboard, *1073*
Texts of Ayurvedic medicine, *3770*

58

Deification of K'ung Fu-tzu (Confucius), *4898*

60

Hostels for pilgrims, *1457*
Woman to lead a rebellion against the Roman Empire, *4158*

62

Native Americans to cross the Atlantic, *2274*

64

Concrete dome, *1177*
Fireproofing, *1574*
Gospel, *4774*
Papal throne, *3082*
Pope, *4847*

70

Center of Jewish learning outside Jerusalem, *4964*
Lock for river navigation, *2134*
Topiary gardening, *2616*

75

Turbine, *2161*

77

Encyclopedia of importance, *3378*

Pharmacopoeia widely used, *3788*
Steel saws, *6050*

79

Metal pen, *3581*
Plane, *6051*
Thimbles, *3099*
Volcanic eruption, *1914*
Window glass, *3642*

80

Sports spectacular, *2220*

82

Depiction of a menorah, *4965*

85

Anti-Semitic blood libel, *4966*

98

Account of Germanic religion, *4739*

100

Book, *3339*
Buddhist manuscripts, *4766*
Full-length mirrors, *2739*
Greenhouses, *1074*
Handball-style game, *5676*
Important text of Mahayana Buddhism, *4767*
Iron tooth, *3798*
Jewish physician, *3948*
Trade between China and southeast Asia, *1531*

105

Rag paper, *3689*

106

Chinese woman historian, *3005*

125

Depiction of a flower arrangement, *1268*

128

Monumental concrete structure, *1178*

132

Seismograph, *5259*

140

Treatise on astronomy that was widely influential, *5120*
Treatise on trigonometry, *3735*

142

Taoist religious community, *5015*

150

Calculation of the date of creation in the Bible, *6014*
Christian church order, *4775*
Christian institution of higher learning, *4776*
Comprehensive treatise on contraception and birth, *2357*
Description of clinical depression and bipolar disorder, *3829*
Heretical Christian sectarian movement, *4777*
Sports arena disaster, *1946*

159

Writing system invented in the New World, *3320*

160

Olympic games for women, *5759*

165

Smallpox epidemic in Europe, *1900*

166

Trade between Rome and China, *1532*

180

Cold cream, *2717*
Epiphany (Adoration of the Magi), *3017*
Mechanical ventilating fan, *3052*

189

Compilation of Jewish oral laws, *4986*

200

Christian creed, *4778*
Cultivation of potato, *1032*
Endocrinologists, *3949*
Popular religious rebellion in China, *5016*
Rub printing process, *4701*
Scandinavian writing, *3490*
Taoist state, *5017*
Woman poet in a Chinese language, *3552*

217

Antipope, *4848*

218

Elephants taken on a sea voyage, *1106*

220

Actuarial table, *2419*
Encyclopedia compiled in Asia, *3379*

248

Commentary on the *I Ching*, *4564*

250

Alchemical theory, *5219*
Folding knife with multiple tools, *6052*
Metal stirrups, *1154*
Writing in runes, *3321*

269

St. Valentine's Day, *3018*

280

Christian church built for the purpose, *4779*

286

Christian monk, *4780*

300

Bikini, *1606*
Galaxy to be described in print, *5071*
Handkerchief, *2718*
Kabbalistic text, *4987*
Santa Claus, *3019*
Surgical procedure in North America, *4041*

303

Establishment of Christianity as the state religion, *4781*

306

Celibacy rule for Christian priests, *4782*

311

Legal recognition of Christians in the Roman Empire, *4783*

315

Christian monastery, *4784*
Historian of the Christian church, *4785*
Rule book for Christian monastic life, *4786*

320

Hindu temple, *4908*
Up-Helly-Aa fire festival, *3020*

325

Coptic writing, *3491*
Easter, *3021*
Ecumenical Christian creed, *4787*
Formal attempt to define the nature of Jesus, *4788*
Sunday sabbath, *3022*

331

Christian hospitals, *3882*

332

Serfs, *5474*

600

Book on robotics, *5026*
Chess-like game, *2597*
Dental implant operations, *3799*
Hindu poet-saints of the *bhakti* devotional movement, *4909*
King of Tibet, *2926*
Major city of the New World, *1563*
Mon and Khmer writing, *3499*
Pagoda, *1179*
Prose work in English, *3404*
Quill pen, *3582*
Reference to the King Arthur legend in literature, *3469*
Slavic state, *2683*

610

Biography written by a woman, *3330*

611

Jihad, *4919*

618

Government bulletins regularly issued, *2629*
Porcelain, *3643*
Silk tapestry, *3083*

622

Convert to Islam, *4920*
Islamic state, *2684*
Mosque, *4921*
Year in the Muslim calendar, *6005*

624

Military victory of Islam, *4159*
Muslim expulsion of Jews, *4922*

629

Diplomatic contact between Africa and China, *3144*
Introduction of Buddhism to Tibet, *4760*

630

Suspension bridge with iron chains, *2139*
Tolerated minorities under Islam, *4923*

632

Muslim caliph, *2927*

633

Expansion of Islam outside Arabia, *4924*
Telugu writing, *3500*

635

Christian missionaries in China, *4792*

644

Windmills, *2056*

649

Muslim navy, *4242*

650

African slave trade, *5475*
Sighting of Antarctica, *2312*

651

Arabic book, *3545*
Authoritative text of the Qur'an, *4938*

656

Civil war in Islam, *4925*

657

Islamic fundamentalists, *4926*
Sectarian controversy in Islam, *4927*

658

Poet in English, *3405*

659

Use of silver amalgam to fill dental cavities, *3800*

661

Muslim dynasty, *2685*

673

Greek fire, *6075*
Naval battle in which Greek fire was used, *4243*

680

Description of lead poisoning, *3830*
Permanent schism in Islam, *4928*
Tonsillectomy, *4043*

690

Empress of China to rule in her own right, *2771*

700

Epic poem in English, *3406*
Large mechanical clock, *6020*
Major settlement built of stone in sub-Saharan Africa, *1564*
Settlers in Madagascar, *4637*

704

Printed book, *3340*

1024—*continued*

Pocket, *1608*

1040

State-run company, *1536*

1042

King to practice curing of the "king's evil", *3952*

1044

King of Myanmar, *2940*

1048

Movable type, *4703*

1050

Flagellation sects, *4855*
Yiddish writing, *3573*

1054

Observation of a supernova, *5073*

1057

Russian writing, *3511*

1059

Monograph on a fruit tree, *5180*

1064

Printed astronomical charts, *3629*

1066

Tournament between armed knights, *2221*

1070

Turkish horticultural treatise, *2619*

1073

Neo-Confucian philosopher, *4899*

1075

Scholarly societies, *1985*
University in Europe, *1986*

1077

Christian scholastic, *4794*

1090

Fork, *3100*

1092

Assassins, *1784*

Astronomical clock of large size, *6021*

1095

Crusade, *4160*

1096

Autograph handwritten by a known individual in Europe, *3322*
Jewish martyrs massacred by the Crusaders, *4161*

1099

Flood to cause massive loss of life, *1915*

1100

Book written in the Americas, *3342*
Compass, *5431*
Popular health diet, *4084*
Rockets powered by gunpowder, *6131*
Tidal-powered mill, *2057*

1101

Troubadour, *4363*

1106

Russian travel writer, *3391*

1110

Jewish scientific encyclopedia, *3380*

1113

Crusading order of knights, *4795*

1125

Gujarati texts, *3512*
History of Iceland in Icelandic, *3008*

1128

Depiction of a gun, *6094*

1130

European heraldry, *2706*

1131

Flying buttresses, *1183*

1136

Polish writing, *3513*
Teaching hospital, *3887*

1137

Stained glass, *3644*

1139

Christian radical reformer, *4796*

King of Portugal, *2941*

1140

Treatise on crafts by a practicing artisan, *1246*

1144

Building in the Gothic style, *1184*

1145

Legend of Prester John, *3471*

1149

Numismatics treatise, *2441*

1150

Cookbook in English, *2502*
Court tennis, *5831*
Definition of an inch, *5311*
Dominoes, *2571*
Guild of perfume makers, *2745*
Hindi writing, *3514*
Juggernaut, *4911*
Oriya writing, *3515*
Pigeon post system, *1155*
Sagas, *3441*

1152

Book of Christian mysticism by a woman, *4797*

1153

Restaurant still extant, *1459*

1154

Pope born in England, *4856*

1159

European traveler to reach the Chinese frontier, *2276*

1160

Encyclopedia compiled by a woman, *3381*
Minstrel tale, *3442*

1163

Barber surgeons, *4044*
Cathedral in the Gothic style, *1185*

1166

Hyperinflation, *4277*

1170

Woman poet to write in French, *3554*

1176

Eisteddfod, *3027*

1180

Rudder, *5404*
Version of the Holy Grail legend, *3472*

1184

Woman to rule Georgia, *2942*

1187

Statement of the principle of medical neutrality in wartime, *3127*

1189

Heraldic device worn by an English king, *2707*

1190

Racing purse, *5680*

1192

Portuguese writing, *3516*
Shogun, *2986*

1198

Municipal bank, *2403*

1200

Andean empire, *2686*
Bar mitzvah ceremony, *4969*
Brussels sprouts commercially grown, *1035*
Dijon mustard, *2559*
Fortress in the New World, *4162*
Home for repentant prostitutes, *5388*
Hungarian writing, *3517*
Inca, *2943*
Keeper of the Holy Grail, *3473*
Legal drama, *3443*
Major road system in the Americas, *1587*
Powdered milk, *2509*
Prose works in the French language, *3555*
Shinto reform movement, *4998*
Stock market, *2425*
Tomato cultivation, *1036*

1208

Hymn for which an exact date is known, *4382*

1210

Christian mendicant orders, *4857*

1212

Rule for Christian monastic life written by a woman, *4858*

1219

Flag of a people, *2708*

1220

Thai capital, *2687*

1224

Buddhist priest to be married, *4762*

1226

Woman to rule France, *2944*
Woman to rule Luxembourg, *2945*

1229

International trade fairs, *1537*
Statement of Sufi doctrine, *4934*

1231

Grenade, *6085*
Official Christian inquisition, *4859*

1235

Emperor of Mali, *2775*

1236

Muslim leader who was a woman, *2946*

1242

Burning of the Talmud by Christian authorities, *4970*
European to publish a recipe for gunpowder, *6095*

1247

Inquisition directed against Jews, *4860*
Treatise on forensic autopsy, *1749*

1250

Assamese writing, *3518*
Description of pulmonary blood circulation, *3953*
Japanese dentists, *3802*
Licensing requirement for physicians, *3853*
Medieval doctor to advocate the use of anesthesia, *3759*
Treatise on magnetism, *5321*

1252

Florin, *2442*

1254

Card games in Europe, *2581*

1258

Prince of Wales, *2947*
Sultan of the Ottoman Empire, *2948*

1259

Cannon, *6096*

1260

Canon, *4383*

Salted herring, *2527*

1264

Oil paintings, *1271*

1270

Appearance in literature of legendary Germanic heroes, *3474*
Black African state to be well documented, *2688*
Medieval sumptuary laws, *1609*
Paper mill in Europe, *3691*
Watermark, *3692*

1273

Urban air pollution, *2263*

1274

Invasion of Japan, *4163*

1275

Czech writing, *3519*
Joint-stock bank, *2404*

1277

Company in England, *1538*

1283

Comic opera, *4429*
Drawing and quartering, *1741*
Mechanical clock in Europe, *6022*

1287

Eyeglasses, *4103*

1290

Expulsion of Jews from a European country, *4971*
Marathi writing, *3520*

1295

Frozen desserts, *2546*
Pasta, *2528*

1300

Blood transfusion, *4096*
Cross staff, *5432*
Fashion magazine, *1610*
Fast-food outlets, *1460*
Glass mirrors, *2740*
Picture books, *3343*
Porcelain made for the Chinese imperial council, *3645*
Professional caterers, *1461*

1302

Forensic postmortem, *1750*

1303

Shipping tax based on tonnage, *1539*

1305

Standard shoe sizes, *1654*

1306

Lawn-care manual, *2620*

1307

Building more than 500 feet high, *1225*

1309

Bonsai, *2621*

1313

Contagious disease to be brought under control in Europe, *3832*

1316

King of the Lao people, *2949*
Treatise on human anatomy based on dissection, *3774*

1320

University in Africa, *1987*

1324

West African emperor of note to make a religious pilgrimage to Mecca, *4935*

1326

Depiction of a gun in Europe, *6097*

1331

Cannon used in warfare, *4164*

1332

King knighted by an automaton, *5027*
Metal cannon, *6098*

1333

Church altarpiece from western Europe showing the Annunciation, *1272*

1335

Public clock to strike the hours, *6023*
Wind-driven vehicle, *3205*

1336

Account of mountain climbing, *5726*

1340

Outbreak of the Black Death, *1903*

Wheelbarrow, *1076*

1343

Humanist, *4567*

1344

Amharic writing, *3521*

1348

Municipal board of health, *4007*
Thread-the-needle dance, *1842*

1350

Alarm clock still extant, *6024*
European city with a municipal health officer, *4008*
Kashmiri writing, *3522*
Maithili writing, *3523*
Mechanical wire-drawing equipment, *1477*
Tarot cards, *2582*

1352

Depiction of eyeglasses, *4104*

1360

Stringed instrument played by a keyboard, *4407*
Use of the crescent as a symbol of Islam, *4936*

1364

Oberammergau passion play performance, *4861*

1370

Law against enhanced bosoms, *1611*
Perfume containing alcohol, *2746*

1373

Pound lock on a canal, *2135*

1376

Aztec priest-king, *2950*
Woman to rule the Scandinavian countries, *2951*

1377

Isolation hospital for plague victims, *3888*
Polyphonic mass, *4384*
Reference to the Robin Hood legend, *3475*

1378

Antipope during the Great Schism, *4862*

1379

Nomenclator, *3399*
Sociologist, *5357*

1382

Bank exchange, *2405*
English translation of the Bible, *4884*

1384

Woman to rule Poland, *2952*

1385

Elaborate medieval headdresses, *1646*

1386

Mechanical clock still extant, *6025*

1389

Woman to write professionally, *3331*

1390

University professor who was a woman, *1988*

1391

Dalai Lama, *4763*

1395

Novellas in English, *3407*

1399

Feminist author in medieval Europe, *5365*

1400

Bookkeeping manual, *1441*
German prose work, *3559*
Public brothel sponsored by a university, *5389*
Silk carpet, *3085*

1402

Illustrated manual of military technology, *4117*
Printed playing cards, *2583*

1403

Insane asylum in Europe, *3988*
Quarantine, *4009*

1404

Peoples of the Canary Islands, *4645*

1405

Major Chinese voyage of exploration and diplomacy, *2277*

1410

Armored soldiers in sub-Saharan Africa, *4123*

1413

Club for gentlemen, *1834*

King of England after the Norman Conquest who could read and write English, *3408*

1416

Dancing master, *1843*

1420

Commander to coordinate mobile armored artillery, infantry, and cavalry as one tactical unit, *4165*
International and multicultural academy for explorers, *2278*

1421

Patent, *1540*

1422

English-only rule, *3409*
Oil painters, *1273*
Woman physician to receive university training, *3954*

1423

Printed European illustration, *1290*

1425

Clothes designer, *1612*
Morality play, *5982*
Painting composed with one-point perspective, *1274*

1427

Income tax, *2466*

1430

Wheeled carts on rails, *3263*

1432

Renaissance man, *5046*

1433

Sea chart of southern Asian and Indian waters, *3607*

1434

Explorers to pass Cape Bojador since antiquity, *2279*
Full-length double portrait, *1275*

1435

Parliament on the European continent, *2651*
Renaissance concept of the artist, *1235*
Scientific explanation of perspective in art, *1276*

1436

Autobiography in English, *3410*

1474—continued

General patent law, *1541*
Use of compressed air for materials transport, *1478*

1475

Book printed in the English language, *3354*
Coffee house, *1462*
Drypoint engraving, *1292*
Printed cookbook, *2503*

1476

Music printed from movable type, *4706*
Publisher in English, *3412*

1477

Book printed in England that bears a date, *3355*
Diamond engagement ring, *2396*
Printed advertising poster, *1450*
Printed edition of the Psalms in Hebrew, *4991*

1478

Printed book decorated with type ornaments, *3356*

1480

Dictionary for tourists, *3368*
Fencing guild, *5702*
Vocabulary list for travelers to a foreign country, *3392*

1481

Auto-da-fé, *4863*
City to require a privy in each house, *4034*
Illustrated book in English, *3357*

1482

Printed edition of the Talmud, *4992*
Printed edition of the Torah, *4993*

1485

Military unit to wear a complete uniform, *4146*
Parachute, *1430*
Treatise on the theory of architecture, *1188*
Use of the terms "billion" and "trillion", *3739*

1486

African slave kingdom in India, *5478*
Witchcraft encyclopedia, *3476*

1488

European expedition to round the southern tip of Africa, *2280*
Witch image, *3477*

1490

Cast-iron stoves, *3053*

Forensic pathologist, *3955*
Printed editions of Greek classics, *3358*
Secular play in English, *3413*
Yiddish translation of the Jewish Bible, *4994*

1492

Epidemic in the New World, *1904*
Europeans to smoke tobacco, *4022*
Expedition of Christopher Columbus, *2281*
Jews in the New World, *4646*
King and Queen of Spain, *2954*
Letter containing a description of America, *2282*
Peanuts, *1037*
Terrestrial globe, *3612*

1493

Eyewitness report to become a best-seller, *4453*
Horses in the New World, *1107*
Limes in the New World, *1038*
New World inhabitants forcibly taken to the Old World, *2283*
Pineapples in the Old World, *1039*
Slaves in the New World, *5479*
Sugar cane brought to the New World, *1062*

1494

Town founded by a European in the New World, *4647*
Treatise on double-entry bookkeeping, *1442*
Treaty in which the entire world was partitioned, *3167*
War to receive news coverage, *4167*
Whisky, *2479*

1495

Cases of syphilis, *3833*

1496

Permanent European settlement in the New World, *4648*

1497

European traveler to set foot on the North American continent after the Vikings, *2284*
Observation of the occultation of a star by the moon, *5074*
Treatise on military surgery, *4045*

1498

Common algebraic symbols, *3740*
Direct sea voyage from Western Europe to Asia, *2285*
European explorer to land on the South American continent, *2286*
Toothbrushes with bristles, *2759*

1499

Sikh guru, *5001*

1500

Cesarean operation, *2335*
Cooling system for buildings, *1209*
Dentures retained by adhesion, *3803*
Golfer, *5664*
Lamp with a chimney, *3086*
Map showing the Spanish discoveries in the New World, *3613*
Mill-driven coin press, *2443*
Poker-type card game, *2585*
Shirts, *1614*
Year the world population exceeded 500 million, *4600*

1501

Italics, *4707*
Protestant hymnbook, *4813*

1502

Licenses for printing presses, *4708*

1503

King to practice dentistry, *3804*

1504

Explorer saved by an eclipse, *2287*
Shilling, *2444*

1506

Secret service to specialize in codebreaking, *3401*

1507

Eyewitness account by a European traveler of life in the African interior, *2288*
Map to use the name "America" for the New World, *3614*

1508

Contact lenses, *4105*
Hornbooks, *1963*
Mechanical prosthetic arm, *3981*

1509

Wallpaper, *3087*
Wife of Henry VIII of England, *2955*

1510

Colonial palace in the New World, *4649*
European settlements in South America, *4650*
European to join a Native American people, *4651*
Pocket watch, *6026*

1512

Catholic priest ordained in the New World, *4864*

Laws authorizing African slaves in the New World, *5480*
Naval battle fought with cannon broadsides, *4245*

1513

European explorers to see the Pacific Ocean, *2289*
Manual for midwives, *2336*

1514

Cathedral in the New World, *4865*

1515

Accidental shooting, *6101*
Artillery fortress, *1189*
Ventriloquist, *2215*

1516

Bananas in the New World, *1040*
Food purity law still observed, *2473*
Ghetto, *1565*
Reference to Utopia, *3478*

1517

Date in the Protestant Reformation, *4814*
Reading glasses, *4106*

1518

Cigarettes, *1065*
Printed cryptology book, *3402*

1519

Easter Mass in Central America, *4866*
European settlement on the west coast of the New World, *4652*
History of West Africa, *3009*
Horses on the North American mainland, *1108*
Hot cocoa, *2547*
Orange cultivation in the New World, *1041*
Thaler, *2445*
Zoo in the Western Hemisphere, *1160*

1520

Estonian writing, *3525*
Euchre, *2586*
Renaissance sculptor of note who was a woman, *1298*
Sikh community, *5002*

1521

Conquistador, *4653*
Major statement of Protestant theological doctrine, *4815*
Rumanian writing, *3526*
Running of the bulls, *5649*

1522

Circumnavigation of the world, *2305*
Polyglot Bible, *4886*

1523

Protestant liturgies, *4816*
Protestant reformer to abolish the Mass, *4817*

1525

Adult baptisms in modern times, *4818*
Anabaptist church, *4819*
Android-maker, *5028*
Grade levels in schools, *1964*
New Testament printed in English, *4887*
Sectarian dissenters in Sikhism, *5003*

1526

Scottish Gaelic collection of writings, *3527*

1527

Lace pattern books, *3707*
National standing army in Europe, *4124*

1529

Empire to unite the Indian subcontinent, *2690*
Statute establishing that men and women are
　equal under the law, *5366*

1530

Call for universal literacy in modern times,
　1965
Description of syphilis, *3834*
Glossary of English words explained in En-
　glish, *3414*
Lutheran churches, *4820*
Printed edition of the Qur'an, *4939*
Public lottery with cash prizes, *2605*
Royal palace in Europe to integrate public and
　private functions in one unified structure,
　1190
Textbook of dentistry, *3775*
Tomatoes in the Old World, *1042*
Toxicologist, *3956*

1532

Cryptogram written in the New World, *3403*
Germ warfare for purposes of genocide, *1766*

1533

Autopsy by Europeans in the New World, *1867*

1534

Anglican Communion church, *4821*
Military regulation concerning uniforms, *4147*
Translation of the complete Christian Bible into
　a modern European language, *4888*

1535

Diving apparatus for practical underwater work,
　5446
European industry in the Americas, *4654*
Printed edition of the complete Christian Bible
　in English, *4889*
Treatise on ballistics, *6102*

1536

Calvinist (Reformed) church, *4822*
Journey across North America, *2290*
News agency, *4513*
Seminary in the New World, *4867*

1537

Anatomist since antiquity to dissect human
　bodies, *3957*
Anatomist to break with Galen, *3958*
Map to name North and South America, *3615*
Military surgeon to treat gunshot wounds with-
　out cautery, *3959*

1538

African slaves in South America, *5481*
University in the New World, *1989*

1539

Book printed in the Western Hemisphere, *3359*
Hymnbook containing hymns in English, *4823*
Printing press in the New World, *4709*
Psalms in metrical form, *4385*
Punjabi writing, *3528*

1540

Book of printed star charts, *3630*
Catholic monastic order founded after the be-
　ginning of the Protestant Reformation, *4868*
Drydock, *5405*
Ruffed collars, *1615*

1541

News sheet printed in the New World, *4486*
Satirical portrait, *1279*

1542

Communities of escaped African slaves, *5482*
Maps showing Australia, *3616*

1543

European travelers in Japan, *2291*
Finnish writing, *3529*
Public schools in the modern era, *1966*
Treatise on human anatomy with accurate illus-
　trations, *3776*

1544

Women admitted to a guild of dentists, *3805*

1571

Major naval battle decided by firepower, *4246*

1572

Military hospital in Europe since antiquity, *3889*

1573

Artist of note to be investigated by the Inquisition, *1239*

1575

African state to be ruled as a colony of a European state, *2691*
Dance notation, *1845*
Scientific academy, *5047*
Set designer, *5990*

1576

Autobiography in English by a man, *3419*
Elizabethan theater, *5991*
European city in southern Africa, *4656*
National observatory in Europe, *5131*
Political philosopher to reject slavery, *5485*
Satire in English, *3420*

1577

Governor-general of the Dutch Republic, *2988*

1578

Map of the Alps, *3619*
Prefabricated building, *1191*

1579

Protestant service in the New World, *4828*

1580

Dentistry instruction, *3854*
Modern epidemiologist, *3961*
Sea captain to circumnavigate the world, *2306*
Western European women to wear pants, *1616*

1581

Ballet to combine dancing, music, and acting, *1854*

1582

Calendar adopted worldwide, *6007*
Catholic edition of the Bible in a vernacular language, *4890*

1583

English-speaking colony in the New World, *4657*

1585

Indoor theater built for stage productions, *5992*

Latvian writing, *3534*
Treatise advocating the use of the decimal system, *3742*

1586

Bottled beer, *2481*
Gravity experiment, *5322*

1587

Concerti, *4386*
Faust legend, *3479*

1588

Book about shorthand in English, *3323*
Incubator for premature babies, *2337*
Marine disaster costing more than 10,000 lives, *1930*
Naval uniform, *4149*
Star atlas to include coordinates, *3631*

1589

Clothing patterns, *1617*
Knitting machine, *3714*
Patriarch of Moscow, *4810*
Play by William Shakespeare, *3421*
Politician to offer a chicken in every pot, *2630*

1590

Architectural model of Jerusalem, *1192*
Compound microscope, *5294*

1591

Domestic tragedy in English, *3422*
Systematic algebraic notation, *3743*

1592

Glass factory in the Americas, *3646*
Ironclad ships, *4247*
Naval battles in which ironclad vessels participated, *4248*
Smokescreen in a battle, *4249*
Thermometer, *5295*

1593

Library with books shelved upright, *1814*
Statute mile, *5312*

1594

Flush toilet, *4035*
Modern army to use military drill, *4125*

1595

Lace factory, *3708*

1596

Catholic martyrs who were Japanese, *4869*

1616—*continued*

Poet laureate of England, *3424*
Treatise on sign language, *3781*
Voyage around Cape Horn, *2292*

1617

Attempted murder by poisoned book, *1786*
Catholic saint from the New World, *4872*
Native American to be buried in Europe, *1878*
Pharmacists, *3963*

1618

Avalanche to kill more than 1,000 people, *1917*
Landslide to kill more than 1,000 people, *1918*
National pharmacopoeia in English, *3790*
Theater with a permanent proscenium arch, *5993*

1619

Orangery, *2622*
Orphan export program, *2382*
Whaling town, *3125*

1620

Deaf person educated in lip-reading and speaking, *2005*
Newspaper in the English language, *4490*
Submarine, *5447*

1621

Newspaper published in England, *4491*

1622

Newspaper in England that was successful, *4492*

1623

Dictionary called by that name, *3371*
Literary salon, *3332*
Nation to enact a national patent system, *1544*

1624

Mechnical calculator for astronomical use invented in modern times, *1661*

1625

Comprehensive text on international law, *3151*
Glass eyes, *3982*
Restaurant to offer forks, *1463*

1627

Sikh military victories, *5008*
Treatise on library science, *1816*

1628

Blood transfusions in Europe, *4097*

Description of stage lighting, *5994*
Embalming by injecting the arteries with preservative, *1879*

1629

Cultivation of New World crops in Africa, *1047*

1630

Cartridges, *6103*
Measurement of the speed of sound, *5324*
Obstetrical forceps, *2340*
Sash windows, *1193*

1631

Free election in North America, *2635*
Major land battle decided by volley fire, *4168*
Official newspaper of a government, *4493*
Planetary transit to be observed, *5077*

1632

Sumo grand champion, *5870*

1633

Brazilian general of African descent, *4169*
Dutch painter of note who was a woman, *1282*
Nation to ban firearms, *6104*
Religious order of nurses, *3964*

1635

Free dispensary for the poor, *3890*

1636

Sugar cane commercial production, *1063*

1637

Exponent symbols, *3745*
Facial tissues, *2721*
Opera house, *4433*
Waterproof umbrellas, *1619*

1638

Practical theory of pedagogy, *1967*

1639

Constitution in the New World, *2645*

1640

Artificial eardrum, *3983*
Pears in the New World, *1048*

1641

Law against cruelty to animals, *1138*
Pendulum clock, *6027*

1642

Adding machine, *1662*

Cribbage, *2587*
Disastrous flood caused by war, *1947*
European explorer to see New Zealand, *2293*

1643

Barometer, *5297*

1644

Anemometer, *5261*

1645

Mint fully mechanized, *2446*
Newspaper in continuous publication, *4494*
Publication in English printed in the American colonies, *3425*
World war, *4170*

1647

Hydraulic press, *2187*

1648

Expedition to sail around the northernmost point of Asia, *2313*

1649

Bayonet, *6078*
Missionary society, *4798*
Quaker meetings, *4830*

1650

Air pump, *5298*
Bridge card game, *2588*
King of Bhutan, *2959*
Male hairdresser to style women's hair, *2733*
Schools to require swimming instruction, *5818*
Space travel by rocket, *5503*
Strawberry cultivation, *1049*

1652

Swahili writing, *3535*

1653

Minuet, *1846*
Prepaid envelopes, *4671*

1654

Magic lantern, *4576*
Slide rule, *3746*

1655

Recommendation that condoms be used for birth control, *2359*

1656

Commercial newspaper in continuous publication, *4495*

Opera in English, *4434*

1657

Oboe, *4409*

1658

Bank notes, *2447*
Illustrated school textbook, *1968*

1659

Check, *2448*
Debating society, *1835*
Opera in French, *4435*

1660

Band, *4365*
Pencil factory, *3584*
Spirit level, *6053*
Tartan plaids, *3709*

1661

Anglican saint, *4831*
Bible translated into an indigenous American language, *4892*
Christian missionaries in Tibet, *4873*
Codification of the five basic ballet positions, *1855*
Treatise on air pollution, *2264*

1662

Bus service, *3209*
Scientific association sanctioned by a national government, *5048*
Statement of a physical law as an equation with two dependent variables, *5325*

1663

Electric generator, *2078*
Guinea, *2449*
Magazine, *4473*
Steam-powered sawmill, *1479*

1664

Planetarium, *5128*
Treatise on forestry in English, *5182*

1665

Periodical continuously published, *4474*
Scientist lowered into a volcano, *5262*
Stradivarius violin, *4410*

1666

Grammar and primer in an indigenous North American language, *3536*

1667

Art exhibition in Europe, *1249*

1667—*continued*

Blood transfusion in Europe in which the patient survived, *4098*

Chief of police, *1789*

Peace treaty among European powers to arbitrate world trade, *3168*

1668

Thesaurus in English, *3372*

1669

Discovery of an element, *5220*

Treatise on geology, *5263*

1670

Cookbook known to have been written by a woman, *2504*

Minute hand, *6028*

Woman to write professionally in English, *3426*

1671

Book in the English language written by a woman, *3427*

Reflecting telescope, *5134*

Theft of the British Crown Jewels, *1804*

1672

Copper coins in England, *2450*

Evidence that the earth is an oblate spheroid, *5264*

Magazine for popular entertainment, *4475*

1673

Piston engine, *2162*

1674

Microscopic observation of protozoa, bacteria, and human cells, *5146*

1675

Astronomical observatory for navigation, *5433*

Champagne, *2483*

Prints made for marketing and advertising purposes, *1452*

1676

Estimate of the velocity of light, *5078*

Fire insurance company, *2420*

1677

Islamic country to adopt a solar year, *6008*

Washing machine, *3054*

1678

Woman to earn the degree of Doctor of Philosophy, *1990*

1679

Almanac of navigation published by a national government, *5434*

Cricket match, *5654*

Pressure cooker, *3055*

Treatise on binary mathematics, *3747*

1680

Pashto writing, *3537*

Revolver pistol, *6105*

1681

Animal exterminated by human action in historical times, *1109*

Ballerina to dance professionally, *1856*

Ballet entirely danced, *1857*

Boxing bout, *5639*

Canal tunnel, *2190*

1682

Entomological collection in Europe, *5147*

History of dance, *1847*

Scientifically accurate treatise on sex in plants, *5183*

1683

Coffee sweet and light, *2497*

University museum, *1825*

1684

Treatise on calculus, *3748*

1685

Code for the treatment of slaves in European colonies, *5486*

Dentistry textbook in English, *3782*

Licensing requirement for dentists, *3855*

Normal school for training teachers, *1969*

Open caisson, *2140*

Primer for teaching reading in English, *1970*

1686

Meteorological map of the world, *3620*

National birth registry, *4601*

Pope to condemn the African slave trade, *5487*

Wire-screen sifter for grain, *1077*

1687

Glass mirrors free of distortion, *2741*

1688

Marine insurance underwriters, *2421*

Protest against slavery made by a religious group in the New World, *5488*

Treatise on barometry, *5299*

1689

Woman intellectual in the New World, *3333*

1715—*continued*

New Testament printed in Asia, *4893*

1716

Government complaint box, *2631*

1717

Freemason grand lodge, *1836*

1718

Machine gun, *6106*

1719

Heavyweight boxing champion, *5640*
Novel in English, *3428*

1720

Patent for a moldboard sheathed in iron, *1079*
Pirate alleged to have made prisoners walk the plank, *1787*
Stock market brought down by speculation mania, *2427*

1721

Prime minister, *2870*

1722

European explorer to land on Easter Island (Rapa Nui), *2294*
Moravian Church community, *4832*

1723

Opera diva, *4436*

1726

Ballerina virtuoso, *1858*
Matador of renown, *5650*
Planet to be mapped, *5080*

1727

Eyeglass frames, *4107*

1728

Autobiography of a European artist, *1240*
Dental drill for cavities, *3807*
Thoroughbreds, *5681*

1729

Achromatic lens, *5317*
Conduction of electricity along a wire, *2079*

1730

School of pugilism, *5641*

1731

Magazine known by that name, *4478*

1732

Encyclopedia of music, *4367*
Lightship, *5435*
Threshing machine, *1080*

1733

Baby carriage, *2383*
Fish breeding, *1008*

1734

English translation of the Qur'an, *4940*
Scholar of African descent to earn a doctorate from a European university, *1992*
Woman to choreograph her own ballets, *1859*

1735

Account of rubber production, *1050*
Organism classification system, *5149*

1736

Appendectomy, *4046*
Islamic revivalist reform movement, *4937*

1737

Mechanical duck, *5029*
Storm to kill more than 100,000 people, *1921*

1738

Accurate measurement of the speed of sound, *5326*
Methodist religious group, *4833*

1739

Physician to teach obstetrics and midwifery, *2341*

1740

Grog, *2484*

1741

Hospital for unwanted newborns, *3891*

1742

Centigrade temperature scale, *5222*
Compendium of rules for a game, *2589*
Performance of the oratorio *Messiah*, *4388*

1743

Boxing rules, *5642*
Orchestra of the modern type, *4368*
Orchestra still in existence, *4369*
Passenger elevator, *1204*
Permanent bullring, *5651*
Scientific exploration of the Amazon River, *2295*

1764—*continued*

Treatise on criminal justice and its reform, *1737*

1765

Anglican priest who was not of European descent, *4834*
Collection of folk ballads, *4439*
Mail-order catalog, *1512*
Restaurant known by that term, *1464*
Savings bank, *2407*
Watt steam engine, *2165*

1766

Law guaranteeing freedom of speech, *2646*

1767

Masonry stove, *3056*
Woman to circumnavigate the world, *2307*

1768

Circus monkey, *2202*
General encyclopedia in the English language, *3384*
Iceboat, *5407*

1769

Explosion to cause great loss of life, *1948*
Famine to kill more than 1 million people, *1922*
Lightning rod on a public building in Europe, *5266*
Modern circus, *2203*
Motor vehicle, *3211*
Motor vehicle accident, *3212*
Personal flotation device, *5408*
Recipe for a wedding cake, *2548*
Theory of evolution, *5152*

1770

Head transplant, *5153*
Modern wheelchair designed for hospital use, *3868*
Religious group advocating complete equality between men and women, *5367*

1772

Androids capable of a variety of tasks, *5030*
Carbonated water, *2531*
Discovery of oxygen, *5224*
Dressmaker with a flourishing export business, *1621*
European explorer in North America to reach the Arctic by land, *2314*
Modern chemist, *5225*
Patent on colored ink, *3587*

1773

Bank clearinghouse, *2408*

Prison reformer, *1738*
Stock exchange known by that name, *2428*

1774

Family hotel, *1465*
Hypnosis, *3990*
Measurement of the mass and density of the earth, *5267*

1775

Circumnavigation of the world from west to east, *2308*
Occupational carcinogen to be identified, *3837*
Reaming machine, *1480*
Society model, *1622*

1776

Breechlock rifle, *6107*
Cocktail, *2485*
Greyhound racing, *1110*
Independent nation in the New World, *2692*
Physical anthropologist, *5154*
Physicist who was a woman, *5327*
Submarine built for use in war, *4251*
Treatise on economics, *5359*

1777

Hot-water heating system, *1210*
Mine barrage, *6086*
National flag, *2709*
Society for the protection of dramatists' rights, *3335*

1779

International drug trade, *4025*
Steam engine still in working order, *2166*

1780

Artificial insemination, *5155*
Circus in Europe, *2204*
English Derby, *5682*
Freestanding full-length mirror, *2742*
Sunday school, *4799*

1781

Book of Mother Goose nursery rhymes, *3431*
Bridge constructed entirely of cast iron, *2142*
Lighthouse with a revolving light, *5443*
Magician whose act included mind-reading tricks, *2216*
Planet discovered since ancient times, *5082*

1782

Circus known by that name, *2205*
Luxury restaurant, *1466*

1783

Analysis of air, *5226*

1794—*continued*
Military air force, *4127*
Soft drink business, *2532*
Technical college, *1993*
Treatise on color blindness, *3839*
Treatise on meteorites, *5121*

1795

Cannery, *2517*
General reference work of modern chemistry, *5228*
Observation of Neptune, *5084*

1796

Hydraulic press, *1481*
Lithograph, *4712*
National archive system, *1817*
Refuge for mentally ill patients, *3992*
Vaccine, *3910*

1797

Coins minted with steam-powered machinery, *2452*
Communist, *2670*
Discovery of chromium, *3667*
Parachutist to jump from a flying craft, *1432*
Screw-threading metal lathe, *1482*
Top hat, *1647*

1798

Archeological digs in Egypt, *5053*
Extraction of beryllium, *3668*
Industrial trade show, *1545*
Scientists attached to armed forces in modern times, *5050*
Treatise on human population growth that had a wide influence, *4603*

1799

Clothes dryer, *3058*
Discovery of the anesthetic properties of nitrous oxide (laughing gas), *3760*
Graduated income tax, *2467*
Large terrestrial mammal exterminated by human action in historical times, *1111*
Library school, *1818*
Mechanical reaper, *1082*
Model factory run on humanitarian principles, *1501*
Practical design for a fixed-wing aircraft, *1308*
Submersible supplied with air pumped from the surface, *5450*
Weather maps, *3623*

1800

Astronomical journal, *5122*
Battery, *2081*

Bone china, *3649*
Coffee percolator, *3059*
Comparative anatomist, *5157*
Mechanized production line, *1483*
Metronome, *4414*
Micrometer, *2188*
Modern bow for playing musical instruments, *4415*
Parisian couturier, *1623*
Pinochle, *2590*
Scientific treatise on histology, *3785*
Screws and bolts mass-produced in standard sizes, *1484*
Uniform national law code, *2649*

1801

Asteroid to be discovered, *5085*
Beet sugar factory, *2549*
Education for children with mental retardation, *2009*
Sikh kingdom, *5010*

1802

Child labor law, *1502*
Fuel cell, *2058*
Identification of fluoride as a tooth-decay preventive, *3811*
Melodrama in English, *3432*
Phrenologist, *3993*

1803

Children's library, *1819*
Circumnavigation of Australia, *2309*
Large building illuminated by gas, *2102*
Periodic table of the elements, *5229*
Self-sharpening plow, *1083*
Steam locomotive, *3264*
Steam-powered printing press, *4713*
Theater illuminated by gaslight, *5995*

1804

Automated loom, *3717*
Bible society, *4835*
Emperor of France, *2779*
Hausa writing, *3539*
Independent nation in Latin America, *2694*
Year the world population exceeded 1 billion, *4604*

1805

Educational reformer to stress individual development, *1971*
Isolation of morphine, *3923*
Mass-produced rockets for warfare, *6132*
Matches, *3102*
Modern use of anesthesia in surgery, *3761*
Wind intensity scale, *5269*

1806

Amino acid to be discovered, *5158*

Carbon paper, *3693*
Circus clown, *2206*
Cotton thread, *3710*
Presidential bank in India, *2409*

1807

Arc lamp, *2091*
Censored edition of Shakespeare, *3433*

1808

Alpine mountaineer who was a woman, *5729*
Cast-iron coffin, *1880*
Emergency parachute jump, *1433*
Guerrilla war, *4171*

1809

Composer able to make a living entirely by writing music of his own choice, *4370*
Grapefruit plantation, *1052*
Gynecological surgery, *4047*
National teacher-training program, *1972*
Ombudsman, *2632*
Reform Jewish services, *4973*
Steamboat to make an ocean voyage, *5454*
Treatise on aerodynamics, *1305*

1810

King of Hawaii, *2962*
Marinosaur fossil unearthed in its entirety, *5211*
Metal cans, *2518*
Woman paleontologist, *5212*

1811

Anti-technology riots, *1503*
City with more than 1 million inhabitants, *1566*
Flatbed press, *4714*
Gymnastics club, *5670*

1812

Collection of folktales from oral tradition, *3480*
Public power utility, *2103*
Remote-controlled explosive mine, *6088*

1813

Craps game, *2609*
Playing deck with double-headed face cards, *2591*

1814

Nocturne, *4389*
Steam-driven rotary press, *4715*
Steam locomotive in regular use, *3265*

1815

Black nationalist movement, *2660*
Cheese factory, *2510*

Modern massage technique, *4087*
Pruning shears, *6055*

1816

African army with standardized training and tactics, *4128*
Circus elephants, *2207*
Fire extinguisher, *1575*
Gymnastics treatise, *5671*
Latin American novel, *3457*
Leader of independent Paraguay, *2990*
Stethoscope, *3869*
Theater with its own gas generator, *5996*

1817

Cholera pandemic, *1906*
Detective bureau, *1791*
Modern encyclopedia of philosophy, *4568*
Synthetic fertilizer, *1095*

1818

Bicycle, *5620*
Leader of independent Chile, *2991*
Liquified gas, *5230*
Pigeon racing, *1112*
Poke bonnet, *1648*
Science-fiction novel, *3448*

1819

Canned fish, *2533*
Chocolate for eating, *2550*
Short story in the modern era, *3449*
Steamboat to cross an ocean, *5455*

1820

Electromagnet, *2082*
Haymaker, *1084*
Published record of dinosaur fossil remains, *5213*

1821

Accordion, *4416*
Circumnavigation of Antarctica, *2310*
Native North American language to be given its own written form, *3540*
Permanent observatory in the Southern Hemisphere, *5135*

1822

Conductor to use a baton, *4371*
Hieroglyphic writing from Egypt to be deciphered, *5054*
Photoengraving, *4716*
Seagoing iron-hulled vessel, *5412*
Traps for human trespassers in gardens, *2623*

1823

Electromagnet that could support more than its own weight, *2083*

1823—*continued*
Rugby match, *5802*
Waterproof raincoat, *1624*
Whisky distillery, *2488*

1824

Constitutional president of Mexico, *2782*
Portland cement, *2152*
Public opinion poll, *2633*

1825

Aluminum, *3669*
Steam locomotive passenger service, *3266*
Talking doll, *2384*
Theorists of socialism, *2661*
Treaty between a South American country and a North American country, *3169*

1826

Friction matches, *3103*
Gas stove that was practical, *3060*
Hemispheric diplomatic conference, *3158*
Internal-combustion engine, *2168*
Manual on birth control, *2360*
Photograph, *4589*
President of the Argentine republic, *2783*
Public zoo, *1162*
Shaper, *1485*
Yiddish play to be performed, *3574*

1827

Asian newspaper in English, *4500*
Christian college in Africa, *4800*
Description of global warming, *2239*
Endoscope, *3870*
Observation of the egg cell of a mammal, *5159*
Primitive telegraph system, *5921*
Printed photograph, *4590*
Teaching laboratory for chemists, *5231*
Waterwheel turbine, *2059*

1828

Chocolate cocoa and candy, *2551*
Egyptian newspaper, *4501*
European explorer to visit Timbuktu, *2297*
Leader of free Ecuador, *2992*
Modern Hindu reform movement, *4913*
Organic compound synthesized from an inorganic substance, *5232*
Steel pen point, *3588*

1829

Bathing suit for women, *1625*
Comic strip published as a booklet, *4466*
Concertina, *4417*
Corrugated iron, *3670*
Leader of united, independent Argentina, *2993*

Modern police force, *1792*
Steam-powered fire engine, *1576*
Typewritten letter, *3324*
Water purification plant, *4011*

1830

Achromatic microscope, *5301*
All-steam railway service, *3269*
Bullfighting school, *5652*
Circus trailer, *2208*
International rail line, *3267*
Lawn mower, *6062*
Mormon church, *4801*
Person run over by a train, *1891*
President of Ecuador, *2784*
Sewing machine that was practical, *1486*
Thermostat, *1211*
Train station, *3268*
Woven elastic webbing, *3711*

1831

Building with a patented cooling system, *1212*
King of Belgium, *2963*
Motorized bus service, *3213*
Observation of a cell nucleus, *5160*
Safety fuse, *3682*
Weekly Australian newspaper, *4502*

1832

Ballerina to dance on her toes, *1860*
Ballerina to wear a tutu, *1861*
Codeine, *3924*
Environmental lawsuit, *2240*
Private detective agency, *1793*

1833

Afro-Brazilian newspaper, *4503*
College to enroll women and men on equal terms, *1994*
Comprehensive study of Proto-Indo-European, *3298*
Constitutional monarch of modern Greece, *2964*
General union, *1504*
President of Colombia, *2785*
Train wreck, *1931*

1834

Direct-current electric motor, *2169*
Universal computing machine, *1666*

1835

Hypodermic syringe, *3871*
Iron railroad track, *3270*
Magazine in a Native American language, *4480*
Modern news service, *4514*
National geologic survey, *5270*
Silvered hand mirror, *2743*
Tuba, *4418*

Worcestershire sauce, *2561*

1836

Glass fiber, *3650*
Investigative reporter, *4457*
Novel to be serialized, *3450*
Nursing school, *3858*
Protestant hospital, *3893*
Protestant religious order, *4836*
Stakes horse race in North America, *5683*
Traveling van for horses, *5684*

1837

British monarch to live in Buckingham Palace, *2965*
College for women, *1995*
Cuneiform writing from Mesopotamia to be deciphered, *5055*
Electric vehicle, *3214*
Kindergarten, *1973*
Theatrical spotlight, *5997*
Theory of physiological reflexes, *5161*

1838

Measurement of the distance to a star, *5086*
Steamship to cross an ocean from east to west, *5456*
Transatlantic steamboat service, *5425*
Vaginal cap, *2361*

1839

Bicycle capable of speed, *5621*
Dentistry journal, *3812*
Fuel cell that was practical, *2060*
Grand National Handicap Steeplechase, *5685*
Military clash between China and a western power, *4172*
Modern stethoscope, *3872*
National effort to prevent drug addiction, *4026*
Nitrogen-rich bulk fertilizer, *1096*
Photographic process that was practical, *4577*
Railway hotels, *1467*

1840

Anarchist, *2662*
Correspondence course, *1974*
Dental college, *3859*
Large-scale use of a pesticide, *1098*
Postage stamps, *4689*
Postal system to carry prepaid mail, *4672*
Wood pulp paper, *3694*

1841

Breech-loading military rifle, *6109*
Constitutional president of Honduras, *2786*
Incandescent lamp, *2092*
Modern detective story, *3451*
Photography studio in Europe open to the public, *4591*

Portrait camera, *4578*
Professional organization of pharmacists, *3968*
Scientific paper using the term "dinosaur", *5214*
Stamp collector, *4690*

1842

Can-can dance, *1848*
Modern lager beer, *2489*
Photographs of a historic event, *4592*
Picture magazine, *4481*
Scientific treatise on public health, *3786*
Steam forge hammer, *1487*
Underwater tunnel, *2191*

1843

Agricultural research station, *1004*
Air transport company, *1336*
Archeological digs in Mesopotamia, *5056*
Christmas cards, *4673*
Computer programmer, *1725*
Existentialist work, *4569*
Fax process, *5873*
Grain stripper, *1085*
Millionaire, *1443*
Rules for soccer (association football), *5814*
Sunspot cycle to be observed, *5087*
Theory of culture, *5361*

1844

Book illustrated with photographs, *3361*
Brazilian novel, *3458*
Bridal suite in a hotel, *2398*
Commercial telegraph service, *5923*
International agreement to eliminate slave trading, *5494*
Leader of the independent Dominican Republic, *2994*
Modern use of anesthesia in dentistry, *3762*
Paper patterns for clothing printed full size, *1626*
Polka, *1849*
Telegraph message, *5922*
Vulcanized rubber, *1488*

1845

Art photographs, *4593*
Criminal caught by telegraph, *1751*
Image of human tissue made from life, *3901*
Large reflecting mirror, *5136*
Magician to use electricity in his act, *2217*
Modern savaté, *5704*
Municipal recreation park, *1567*
Photograph of the sun, *5088*
Pneumatic tires, *3292*
Rubber bands, *3104*
Self-rising flour, *2534*
Silver amalgam tooth filling in modern times, *3813*

1845—*continued*

Smokeless gunpowder, *6089*
Systematic observations of galaxies, *5089*
Underwater telegraph cable that was practical, *5924*
Voice synthesizer, *5931*
Wire news service, *4515*

1846

Army newspaper, *4504*
Baseball team, *5610*
Hospital to use anesthesia in surgery, *3763*
International swimming championship, *5819*
Newspaper cooperative, *4516*
Recognition of Neptune as a planet, *5090*
Saxophone, *4419*
Shinto sect, *4999*
Uniforms in military khaki, *4150*
Universal Week of Prayer, *4837*

1847

Communist secret society, *2671*
Concourse in a train station, *3271*
Ether as an anesthetic in childbirth, *2343*
Leader of independent Guatemala, *2995*
Modern transverse flute, *4420*
Nitroglycerin, *5233*
President of Liberia, *2787*

1848

Absolute scale of temperature, *5329*
Chewing gum, *2552*
Comet named after a woman, *5091*
Communist political platform, *2672*
European explorers to sight Mount Kilimanjaro, *2298*
European legislator of African descent, *2652*
Medical school for women, *3860*
National public health legislation, *2241*
National weather service, *5271*
Perambulator, *2385*
Prime minister of Denmark's first parliamentary government, *2871*
Prime minister of Hungary, *2873*
Prime minister of Sardinia-Piedmont, *2872*
Republic in Africa, *2695*
Use of antisepsis, *4048*

1849

Aerial bombardment of a city, *4202*
Bowler hat, *1649*
Dry cleaning, *1627*
Popular book about archeology, *5057*
Safety pin, *3105*
Woman physician in modern times to earn a degree from a medical school, *3969*

1850

Advocate of black pride, *5495*

African national newspapers, *4505*
Civil war to cause 20 million deaths, *4173*
Closed or pneumatic caisson, *2143*
Color photography process, *4579*
Crinolines, *1628*
Iron-frame building in Europe, *1195*
Xhosa writing, *3541*

1851

Condensed milk, *2511*
Glass building, *1196*
International chess tournament, *2598*
International yacht race, *5855*
Ophthalmoscope, *3873*
Powered wood shapers, *6056*
World's Fair, *2223*
Zoroastrian reform movement, *5024*

1852

Aeronautical society, *1306*
Beehive with removable frames, *1086*
Department store, *1514*
Housekeeping magazine, *3048*
Safety elevator, *1205*
Screen printing, *4717*
Steam-powered airship, *1401*
Tramp steamer, *5426*
Travel book illustrated with original photographs, *3393*
Woman in Europe to receive official permission to wear pants, *1629*

1853

Aquarium for public display, *1163*
Blue jeans, *1630*
Cigarette factory, *1067*
International railroad in North America, *3272*
Manned glider flight that was successful, *1416*
Queen to deliver a child under anesthesia, *2344*
Telegraph used in warfare, *4174*
Undersea telegraph cable, *5925*
War correspondent to file dispatches by telegraph, *4458*
War to receive extensive newspaper coverage, *4175*

1854

Aluminum in commercial quantities, *3671*
Army with a trained nursing staff to treat its wounded, *4129*
Conservative rabbi, *4974*
Epidemic map, *3624*
Postage stamps with serrated edges, *4691*
Poster kiosks, *4459*
Travel guidebooks, *3394*
Treatise on telephony, *5932*
War photographers, *4460*

1855

Breech-loading, rifle-bored cannon, *6110*

1864—*continued*

European-born emperor of a North American country, *2780*
Golf course outside Scotland, *5667*
Head of state to order an automobile, *3226*
Housing project in an inner-city neighborhood, *5497*
International agreements on the humane treatment of soldiers and civilians in wartime, *3170*
International Communist labor organization, *1505*
International medical relief organization, *4012*
Observations of stellar spectra, *5092*
Periscope, *4256*
Salvation Army activities, *4839*

1865

Abortion by vacuum aspiration, *2362*
Antiseptic surgery, *4049*
Ascent of the Matterhorn, *5730*
Blasting cap, *3683*
European university to admit women as students, *1996*
Fax system for commercial use, *5874*
Railway speed limit, *3273*
Roll-fed rotary press, *4718*
Woman physician in England, *3970*

1866

Across-the-ocean race, *5856*
Battle decided by the use of breech-loading infantry rifles, *4176*
Clinical thermometer in current use, *3874*
Factory in which the workers paid for the services of a reader, *1506*
National school system to require manual training, *1976*
Nordic skier, *5807*
Treatise on laws of heredity, *5193*
Woman dentist with a degree from a dental school, *3814*

1867

Amateur boxing championships, *5645*
Animated picture machine, *4324*
Baha'i leader, *4741*
Dental spittoon with running water, *3815*
Dining-car service, *3274*
Dynamite mining demonstration, *3684*
Eight-day week, *6010*
International advertising agency, *1454*
International Botanical Congress, *5184*
King of Luxembourg, *2966*
Mass-produced infant formula, *2387*
Patents for reinforced concrete, *2153*
Police procedural, *3453*
Prime minister of the Dominion of Canada, *2876*

Torpedo, *6090*
Treatise on antiseptic surgery, *4050*
Typewriter that was practical, *3590*
Woman to vote in an election, *2636*

1868

Ascent of Mount Elbrus, *5731*
Canada Day (Dominion Day), *3034*
Detective novel, *3454*
Element discovered in space, *5235*
Establishment of State Shinto, *5000*
Hook and ladder truck, *1577*
International bicycle race, *5624*
Motorcycle, *3215*
Sheep-shearing machine, *1137*

1869

Bicycle road race, *5625*
Bustles, *1631*
Hydroelectric generator, *2084*
Letterpress halftone reproduction of a photograph, *4719*
Margarine, *2537*
Oil tanker, *5427*
Prepaid postcards, *4674*
Synthetic plastic that was widely used in industry, *1490*
Vatican Council, *4875*

1870

Daily newspaper in Japan, *4506*
Modern war won through superior military intelligence, *4140*
Mountain tunnel, *2192*
Newspaper folding device, *4720*
Petroleum jelly, *3926*
Pneumatic subway, *3286*
Sneakers, *1656*
Typewriter to be marketed, *3591*

1871

Bank holidays, *3035*
Chancellor of Germany, *2996*
Communist song of international popularity, *4440*
Corrugated paper, *3695*
Electric generator that was commercially successful, *2085*
Kaiser of a united German Reich, *2967*
Kinship study, *5363*
Margarine factory, *2538*
Multiplexing signal switching system, *5928*
Nation to legalize trade unions, *1507*
Treatise on animism, *4742*

1872

Arbor Day, *3036*
Jehovah's Witnesses, *4840*

Museum of traditional life, *1827*
Oceanographic expedition, *5273*
Tennis club, *5833*

1873

International football game, *5659*
Multistep crude oil refining, *2106*
Psychologist to relate known physiological facts to psychological phenomena, *3996*
Sheepdog trials, *1156*
Sikh revival movement, *5011*
Smog disaster, *1949*
Tennis rule book, *5834*

1874

Antivivisection prosecution, *1139*
Artificial flavoring, *2539*
Barbed wire, *1089*
Exhibition of impressionist paintings, *1250*
International postal congress, *4675*
International rugby game, *5803*
Organic pesticide, *1099*
Steam sterilization of cans, *2519*
Steel bridge, *2144*
Tempered glass manufacturing process, *3651*
Treatise on cremation, *1881*
Woman to earn a doctorate in mathematics, *3751*

1875

Book manuscript written on a typewriter, *3362*
Book on poker, *2592*
Dental drill powered by electricity, *3816*
European explorer to cross Africa from coast to coast, *2301*
French Impressionist artist who was a woman, *1284*
Ice hockey game played indoors, *5691*
Kentucky Derby, *5686*
Life-support system, *3875*
Literary agent, *3336*
Man to swim the English Channel, *5820*
Modern Hindu reform movement that rejected Western influence, *4915*
Rummy card games, *2593*
Westerners to promote Hindu ideas, *4916*
Yoruba writing, *3542*

1876

Caribbean Spanish-language poet who was a woman, *3459*
Carpet sweeper, *3062*
Crematorium, *1882*
Disease known to be caused by a specific microbe, *3840*
Electric rail and street lamps, *2093*
Four-stroke internal-combustion engine, *2171*
Law regulating animal experimentation, *1140*
Milk chocolate, *2553*

Psychology journal, *3997*
Skating rink, *5806*
Words heard on a telephone, *5933*

1877

Centrifugal cream separator, *2512*
Human cannonball, *2210*
Ice hockey rules, *5692*
Liquid oxygen, *5236*
Photographs showing action, *4597*
Refrigerator ship, *5428*
Sound recording device, *2040*
Species import ban, *2242*
Telephone for domestic use, *5934*
Water polo, *5863*
World tennis championship, *5835*

1878

Domestic violence law, *5498*
Electric company, *2086*
Family planning clinic, *2363*
Mechanical cream separator, *1090*
Modern dancer, *1850*
Phonograph, *2041*
Probation system for criminals of all ages, *1739*
Sugar cubes, *2554*

1879

Boycott, *1444*
Cash register, *2454*
Cave paintings to be discovered, *1285*
Celebrity actress with an international following, *5986*
Disease proven to be transmitted by insects, *3841*
Electric locomotive, *3275*
Experimental psychology laboratory, *3998*
Funicular railway, *3276*
Musical encyclopedia in English, *4372*
National park, *2258*
Private home fully illuminated with electric lights, *2094*
Ship outfitted with interior electric lights, *5414*
Study of insect behavior, *5163*
Two-stroke internal-combustion engine, *2172*
Use of the term "anti-Semitism", *4975*

1880

Artificial language, *3299*
Cigarette-rolling machine, *1068*
Electric elevator, *1207*
Navigation of the Northeast Passage, *2315*
Safety razor to be commercially manufactured, *2754*
Synthetic indigo, *3720*
Tango, *1851*

1881

Cabaret, *4441*

1881—*continued*

Carnegie library, *1820*
Centrifugal cream separator with a continuous flow, *2513*
Efficiency expert, *1445*
English translations of early Buddhist texts, *4769*
Halftone printing plate, *4721*
International commercial telephone service, *5935*
King of Romania, *2968*
Rubber tires, *3293*
Theater entirely lit by electric lights, *5998*
Woman executed in Russia for political terrorism, *1797*
World Methodist Council, *4841*

1882

Flip book, *4325*
International Polar Year, *2316*
Judo, *5705*
Labor Day, *3037*
Mass aliyah (emigration) to Israel, *4976*
Postgraduate center for psychiatric education, *3862*
Store lit by electricity, *1515*
Surgical adhesive bandage, *3876*
Three-ring circus, *2211*
Woman to become a Freemason, *1837*
Woman to become a public speaker in Japan, *5369*

1883

Alternating-current electric motor, *2173*
Galvanized metal trash can, *4036*
Motorcycle with an internal-combustion engine, *3216*
Orient Express service, *3277*
Postal giro system, *2411*
Solar cell, *2062*
State-sponsored social security system, *2423*
Synthetic fiber, *3721*
Transmission of electricity through high-voltage cable, *2087*

1884

Climatological classification system, *5274*
Complete television system, *5949*
Dirigible, *1402*
Edition of the *Oxford English Dictionary*, *3375*
Fabergé Easter egg, *1248*
Foreigner to be appointed professor in a German university, *1997*
Fountain pen, *3592*
Linotype machine, *4722*
Local anesthetic, *3764*
Martini, *2490*
Roller coaster, *2212*
Settlement house, *5499*

Synthetic fiber produced in a factory, *3722*

1885

Carriage propelled by dogs, *3210*
Japanese woman to become a physician, *3971*
Modern city with a downtown commercial area, *1568*
Motion picture, *4278*
Pasteurized milk, *2514*
Photographic star catalog, *5123*
Prime minister of Japan, *2877*
Rabies vaccine, *3911*
Seat belt, *3227*
Skyscraper, *1226*
Spark plug, *2174*
Tornado expert, *5275*
Vending machine in modern times, *1516*

1886

Biological pest control, *1100*
Dishwasher, *3063*
Hindu woman to earn a medical degree, *3972*
International copyright agreement, *3152*
International polo competition, *5800*
Metal snap fastener, *1642*
Motorboat, *5415*
Photo interview, *4571*
Rule book of bridge, *2594*
Women's organization in Japan, *1838*
World chess champion, *2599*

1887

City with a woman mayor, *1569*
Contact lenses for correcting defective vision, *4109*
Dictation device, *2042*
Flash powder, *4580*
Flood to cause more than 1 million deaths, *1923*
Impressionist musical composition, *4390*
International handball match, *5677*
Machine capable of casting individual letters of type, *4723*
Meteorologist to name tropical storms, *5276*
Radio waves, *5895*

1888

Alpine skier, *5808*
Ballpoint pen, *3593*
Beauty contest, *2199*
Camera to use film rolls, *4581*
Chop suey, *2540*
Commemorative postage stamp, *4697*
Observation of chromosomes, *5194*
Phonograph record, *2043*
Pneumatic tires for bicycles, *5626*
Railway in China, *3278*
Staff cartoonist on a newspaper, *4461*
Yiddish literary annual, *3575*

1895—*continued*

Table tennis, *5828*
Universal system for phonetic transcription, *3300*
X-ray photograph of human anatomy, *3902*

1896

Absurdist play, *5987*
Car theft, *1805*
Car with an electric starter, *3234*
City with a chlorinated water supply, *4014*
Comic strip with an ongoing character, *4468*
Cookbook with standardized measurements, *2506*
Defeat of a European colonial power by African military forces, *4177*
Dental X-rays, *3818*
Film director who was a woman, *4284*
Flashlight, *6058*
Flight of a heavier-than-air machine, *1353*
Hang-glider fatality, *1893*
Heart operation, *4052*
Movie exhibition in a theater to a paying audience, *4353*
Movie theater, *4354*
Narrative film, *4285*
Olympic champion in the modern era, *5762*
Olympic Games in the modern era, *5760*
Olympic marathon in modern times, *5761*
Radio inventor, *5896*
Radio patent, *5897*
Subway on the European continent, *3288*

1897

Ascent of Aconcagua, *5733*
Bumpers, *3235*
Cigarette advertisement showing a woman smoking, *1455*
Condensed soup, *2541*
Discovery of electrons, *5331*
Dum-dum bullets, *6115*
European politician to adopt a platform of anti-Semitism, *2664*
Homosexual rights organization, *5380*
Permanent wireless installation, *5899*
Power mowers, *6064*
Radiator, *2178*
Rigid airship, *1403*
Swiss Army knife, *6059*
Taxicabs, *3236*
Used-car dealership, *1517*
Wireless radio manufacturing company, *5898*
World Zionist Congress, *2665*

1898

Bobsled competition, *5631*
Closed-circuit road race, *5710*
Diesel engine built for commercial service, *2179*

Driver fatally injured in an automobile accident, *1894*
Explorers to winter in Antarctica, *2317*
Film festival, *4339*
Heroin, *3927*
Land speed record, *5712*
Magnetic wire recording device, *2045*
Motorcycle race, *5711*
Sedan, *3237*
Underground hydroelectric plant, *2089*
Weather balloons, *5277*

1899

Ascent of Mount Kenya, *5734*
Aspirin, *3928*
Bouillon cubes, *2562*
Children's museum, *1829*
Driver to exceed 100 kilometers per hour, *5713*
Frozen hydrogen, *5238*
Fruit exporting company, *1546*
International court, *3153*
Juvenile court, *5500*
Passenger fatally injured in an automobile accident, *1896*
Person killed in a motorcycle accident, *1895*
Police dog unit, *1794*
Reinforced concrete bridge, *2145*
Shipboard newspaper, *4508*
Treatise on psychoanalysis, *4000*
Vasectomy, *2364*
Wireless station for international communications, *5900*
Woman to die in the electric chair, *1746*

1900

Avocado cultivation, *1054*
Child to win a gold medal in the Olympic Games, *5763*
Credit union in the Western Hemisphere, *2412*
Dirigible that was commercially and militarily successful, *1404*
Electric arc furnace, *1493*
Films synchronized with speech, *4286*
Fire truck with an internal-combustion engine, *1578*
International Congress of Comparative Law, *3154*
International dentistry assocation, *3819*
Motorized ambulances, *4015*
Paper clip, *3110*
Prime minister of Australia, *2878*
Theory that light consists of particles, *5332*
Underwater excavation of a shipwreck, *5059*
Woman athlete to win an Olympic medal, *5764*
Zeppelin flight, *1405*
Zulu writing, *3543*

1901

Artificial insemination center, *1119*

Blood types to be discovered, *4099*
Corporation worth US$1 billion, *1547*
Fingerprint bureau, *1754*
Free dental clinic for poor children, *3820*
International road race, *5714*
Laparoscopic surgery, *4053*
Mosquito-eradication project to control disease, *4016*
Motorcycle designed to be a motor vehicle, *3219*
Nobel Prize for Literature, *4530*
Nobel Prize for Peace, *4538*
Nobel Prize in Chemistry, *4523*
Nobel Prize in Physics, *4545*
Nobel Prize in Physiology or Medicine, *4549*
Pentecostal churches, *4842*
Road designed for motor vehicles, *1589*
Transoceanic radio message, *5901*

1902

Armored car, *6120*
Country to electrify its main-line tracks, *3279*
Daily shipboard newspaper, *4509*
Description of anaphylaxis, *3843*
Fax transmission of photographs, *5875*
Hormone to be discovered, *5165*
Motor home, *3220*
President of Cuba, *2791*
Science fiction film, *4348*
Scientific description of *Tyrannosaurus rex*, *5215*
Stuffed toy bear, *2388*
Vascular sutures, *4054*
Volcanic eruption of the 20th century, *1924*

1903

Airplane flight, *1354*
Constitutional president of Panama, *2792*
Democratic president of Uruguay, *2793*
Electrocardiogram, *3903*
International motorboat racing competition, *5857*
Mineral separation by flotation, *3677*
Movie star, *4319*
Movie theater in Asia, *4355*
Movie western, *4349*
National speed limit, *3221*
Newspaper illustrated exclusively with photographs, *4510*
Postage meter, *4676*
Radial aviation engine, *1309*
Tabloid newspaper, *4511*
Tour de France, *5628*
Transoceanic radio broadcast, *5902*
Woman to win a Nobel Prize, *4518*
Zulu newspaper, *4512*

1904

Car to exceed 100 miles per hour, *5715*

Comic books featuring color cartoons previously published in newspapers, *4469*
Comic strip in a daily newspaper, *4470*
Complete aerial turn in an airplane, *1355*
Electron tube diode, *2010*
Geothermal power station, *2063*
Ice cream cone, *2515*
Iced tea, *2498*
Mass-produced double-sided recording discs, *2046*
Modern theory of atomic structure, *5333*
Olympic Games in the Western Hemisphere, *5765*
Radar, *2011*

1905

African Pygmies to visit Europe, *4665*
Astronomer to use electronic instruments, *5093*
Basketball in the Philippines, *5619*
Chemotherapeutic drug, *3929*
Dental hygienist, *3821*
Expedition to sail through the Northwest Passage, *2318*
Fire extinguisher for chemical fires, *1579*
Genocide in the 20th century, *1768*
Hydrofoil boat, *5417*
Junk mail, *4677*
Meteor crater, *5278*
Military use of TNT, *6091*
Modern conflict in which an Asian power defeated a European power, *4257*
Monel, *3673*
Researcher to describe the role of the human sex chromosomes, *5195*
Service club, *1839*
Standardized intelligence test, *4001*
Star of Africa, *3678*
Synthetic fiber suitable for making cloth, *3723*
Woman to win the Nobel Prize for Peace, *4539*

1906

Animated cartoon, *4326*
Battleship powered by steam turbines, *4258*
Bubble gum, *2555*
Case of Alzheimer's disease, *3844*
Feature-length motion picture, *4288*
Film composer, *4287*
Grand Prix race, *5716*
Instant coffee, *2499*
International balloon race, *5602*
Launch of a heavier-than-air machine entirely under its own power, *1356*
Music synthesizer powered by electricity, *4422*
Newsreel, *4350*
Nobel Prize for Peace winner from North America, *4540*
Permanent wave hairstyle, *2734*
Ski course, *5809*
Stenography machine, *3594*

1906—*continued*

Woman appointed to the faculty of a French university, *1998*

1907

Catalytic converter for automobile engines, *2267*
Craps bookie, *2611*
Electronic amplifier tube, *2012*
Gyrocompass, *5438*
Helicopter flight, *1422*
Household detergent, *3111*
Modern air force, *4130*
Modern surfer, *5865*
Montessori school, *1977*
Motorcycle race of importance, *5717*
Nobel Prize in Physics winner from North America, *4546*
Nonviolent act of civil disobedience of international significance, *3155*
Novel in an African vernacular language, *3460*
Popularizer of Zen Buddhism in the West, *4764*
Public sculpture honoring a car race, *1299*
Rally race, *5718*
Silkscreen printing for fabrics, *3718*
Symphony incorporating continuous choral and orchestral elements, *4391*
Transatlantic radio message of the regular westward service, *5903*
Woman to be awarded the British Order of Merit, *3974*
Women elected as members of a Parliament, *2653*

1908

Airplane accident that was fatal, *1897*
All-electronic television system, *5950*
Boy scout troop, *2389*
Coins minted in Canada, *2456*
Detonating cord, *3685*
King of modern Bulgaria, *2969*
Liquid helium, *5239*
Major hotel chain, *1468*
Monosodium glutamate (MSG), *2563*
Vegemite, *2564*

1909

Airplane flight over the ocean, *1357*
Animated character to appear in a series of cartoons, *4327*
Automatic price reductions on merchandise, *1518*
Ballets Russes, *1862*
Commercial hair dye, *2735*
Drugstore chain, *1519*
Glider club, *1419*
Glider pilot who was a woman, *1420*
International airplane race, *5603*
Jewish city founded in Israel in modern times, *4666*

Kibbutz, *1570*
Military aircraft, *4203*
One-piece bathing suit, *1634*
Pilot's licenses, *1310*
Radio distress call from a ship at sea, *5418*
SOS signal sent in an emergency, *5904*
Treatment for syphilis, *3930*
Woman to win the Nobel Prize for Literature, *4531*

1910

Airplane bombing experiment, *4204*
Bathroom scale, *2723*
Building illuminated by neon lamps, *2095*
Criminal caught by radio, *1755*
Electric discharge lamp, *2096*
Family court, *5501*
International ecumenical missionary organization, *4803*
King of independent Montenegro, *2970*
Laparoscopic surgery on a human being, *4055*
Makeup specifically for movie actors, *2724*
Modern encyclopedia for children, *3385*
Movie palace, *4356*
Nonrepresentational modern paintings, *1286*
Photographic record of the state of the earth, *5279*
Prime minister of the Union of South Africa, *2879*
Researcher to discover an entire grouping of elements, *5240*
Seaplane flight, *1358*
Synthetic drug to treat bacterial infections, *3931*
Woman to receive a pilot's license, *1311*

1911

Aerial bombs, *6092*
Airmail flight by airplane, *4680*
Billionaire businessman, *1446*
Bombing raid from an aircraft, *4206*
Cellophane, *3112*
Chartered airplane flight, *1337*
Double feature, *4289*
Downhill ski race, *5810*
Explorer to reach the South Pole, *2319*
National parks service, *2259*
Nobel Prize winner to win the award twice, *4519*
President of China, *2795*
President of the Republic of Portugal, *2794*
Superconductor, *5334*
Telegraph message sent around the world by commercial telegraph, *5929*
Transpacific radio conversation, *5905*
Use of airplanes in war, *4205*

1912

Airplane accident involving a woman that was fatal, *1898*

Amphibious aircraft, *1312*
Aviator wounded in combat by ground fire, *4207*
Composer of jazz music, *4376*
Currency board in Africa, *2429*
Diesel locomotive, *3280*
Evidence for continental drift, *5280*
Modern political party for Africans, *2666*
Nobel Prize in Physiology or Medicine winner from North America, *4550*
Parachute jump from an airplane, *1434*
Pilot captured during war, *4208*
Primate research station, *5166*
Radio station call letters, *5906*
Rotary cultivator, *1091*
Scientific hoax of international notoriety, *5051*
Vitamin to be identified, *5167*
Woman to pilot an airplane over the English Channel, *1313*

1913

Aerobats, *1314*
Animation made by the cel process, *4328*
Ascent of Mount McKinley (Denali), *5735*
Calculation of the accurate age of the earth, *5281*
Caribbean novel in English, *3461*
Cinematographer of lasting influence, *4290*
Crossword puzzle, *2574*
Dramatic films shot in Africa, *4291*
Film archive, *4293*
Kinetic sculpture, *1300*
Mass spectrometer, *5335*
Nobel Prize for Literature winner from Asia, *4532*
Parachute jump from an airplane by a woman, *1435*
Refrigerators, *3066*
Thirty-five-millimeter camera that was commercially successful, *4584*
Tracking shot, *4292*
Transatlantic crossing by a bird, *1114*
Zipper that was practical, *1643*

1914

Aerial bombardment of a city by airplane, *4209*
Airliner, *1315*
Airplane pilots killed in combat, *4210*
Alkaline dry cell battery, *2090*
Ammonia factory, *1494*
Behaviorist, *4002*
Bombing raids, *4211*
Building of glass bricks, *1198*
Casualty of World War I, *4178*
Chemical anticoagulant, *3932*
Color feature film, *4294*
Electric hand drill, *6060*
Modern ballet choreographer, *1863*
Movie character with worldwide appeal, *4320*

Nation with a substantial number of women physicians, *3975*
Neurotransmitter to be identified, *5168*
Nobel Prize in Chemistry winner from North America, *4524*
Pamphlet on birth control from a feminist perspective, *2365*
Recording of a complete symphony, *4392*
Regular airmail service, *4681*
Stainless steel, *3674*
Steamboat to pass through the Panama Canal, *5459*
Traffic lights, *1590*
Use of aircraft carriers in war, *4259*

1915

All-metal airplane, *1316*
Description of syphilis, *3834*
Fighter plane, *4212*
Genocide squads, *1769*
Induced cancer, *3845*
International ice show star, *2224*
Mechanical pencil, *3595*
Nobel Prize in Physics winner from Oceania, *4547*
Passenger liner sunk by a submarine, *1932*
Poison gas, *6079*
Raggedy Ann doll, *2390*
Remote detection system using sound, *5439*
Sound recordings used to transmit coded messages in wartime, *4141*
Submarine blockade, *4260*
Transatlantic message over radio telephone, *5936*
Woman psychoanalyst, *4003*

1916

Animation in color, *4329*
Anti-art movement, *1252*
Avalanche of the 20th century to kill 10,000 people, *1925*
Battle with more than 1 million casualties, *4180*
Germ warfare in modern times, *4179*
Guide dogs, *1157*
Heavy night bomber, *4213*
Man to walk 100,000 kilometers, *5851*
Olympic Games to be canceled for political reasons, *5766*
Self-propelled tank, *6121*

1917

Aircraft carrier adapted from a conventional warship, *4261*
Airmail stamps, *4698*
Billion-pound loan, *2457*
Communist revolution, *2673*
Cosmetics entrepreneur of note, *2725*
Feature-length animated film, *4330*

1917—*continued*

International military airmail route, *4682*

Jazz record, *4377*

Landing of a plane on a ship under way, *4262*

Long-distance passenger plane, *1317*

Massed tank attack, *4181*

Mustard gas, *6080*

Rail accident in which more than 500 people were killed, *1933*

Robot, *5031*

Supreme War Council of the World War I Allies, *4182*

1918

Aircraft carrier attack, *4264*

Aircraft carrier with a through-deck runway, *4263*

Flight from Cairo to Calcutta, *1359*

Independent air force, *4131*

Musical instrument to create sound with electromagnetic fields, *4423*

President of Czechoslovakia, *2796*

President of independent Poland, *2797*

Prime minister of independent Latvia, *2798*

Prime minister of Yugoslavia, *2880*

Radiotelegraph message from Great Britain to Australia, *5907*

Regular civil airmail service, *4683*

Rent-a-car business, *3238*

Submachine gun widely used in battle, *6116*

Train disaster caused by the use of narcotics, *1934*

Woman accredited as a minister to a foreign power, *3146*

Worldwide pandemic, *1907*

1919

Air race from England to Australia, *5604*

Airline in continuous operation, *1341*

Airline meals, *1338*

Automatic calculator to factor whole numbers, *1664*

Commercial book club, *3363*

Element to be analyzed by mass spectrometer, *5241*

Flight from England to Australia, *1362*

General association of nations, *3186*

Intercontinental passenger service, *1340*

International airmail service, *4684*

International civil service, *3147*

London to Paris scheduled passenger airplane service, *1339*

Motorized trailer, *3222*

Movie with a homosexual theme, *5381*

Nonstop transatlantic airplane flight, *1361*

Pop-up toaster, *3067*

President of independent Estonia, *2800*

President of independent Finland, *2799*

Roadside telephone, *1591*

Scientific proof of the general theory of relativity, *5336*

Skydiver, *1436*

Transatlantic airplane flight, *1360*

Transatlantic dirigible flight, *1406*

Woman to become a member of the British Parliament, *2654*

1920

Blow dryer for hair, *2736*

Crash of a passenger airliner, *1935*

Discovery of protons, *5337*

Kinetic sculpture in which motion was the main esthetic factor, *1301*

Landslide to kill more than 100,000 people, *1926*

Mah-jongg, *2575*

Marital property reform law, *2400*

Mobiles, *1302*

Modern nation to make abortions freely available, *2366*

Modern pyramid scheme, *1806*

President of the federal republic of Austria, *2802*

President of Turkey, *2801*

Radio broadcast of live music, *5908*

Reference to the Iron Curtain, *3128*

Ski school, *5811*

Standardized sizes for bras, *1635*

Surrealist text, *3455*

Swimsuit beauty contest, *2200*

1921

Airline ticket and reservation office, *1342*

Airplane bombing experiment to sink a battleship, *4215*

Arms limitation conference, *3160*

Conviction for murder based on photographic evidence of marks on a bullet, *1756*

Designer perfume, *2748*

Diesel locomotive in regular service, *3281*

Expressway for automobiles, *1592*

International congress on homosexual rights, *5382*

Isolation of insulin, *3933*

Labor concentration camp, *1770*

Macadamia nut orchards, *1055*

Movie studio to produce 100 feature films, *4295*

Prime minister of Northern Ireland, *2881*

Small bandage with built-in adhesive, *3878*

Theorist of air warfare, *4214*

Woman to become a member of the Australian Parliament, *2655*

1922

Aircraft carrier built as such, *4265*

Airliner collision, *1936*

Bat mitzvah ceremony, *4977*

Commercial talking motion picture, *4296*
Film studio in China, *4297*
Freeze frame, *4298*
French-language commercial AM radio station, *5909*
General secretary of the Communist Party of the former Soviet Union, *2997*
Geodesic dome, *1199*
Human cannonball family act, *2214*
King of independent Egypt, *2971*
Macromolecules, *5242*
Man to swim 100 meters in under a minute, *5821*
Military radar experiment, *2013*
Modern art festival in South America, *1253*
Slalom race, *5812*
Snowmobile, *3223*
Topology book, *3752*
Transatlantic radio fax transmission of a photograph, *5876*
Written history in Zulu, *3011*

1923

Asian boxer to win a world championship, *5646*
Autogiro, *1423*
Muslim country to adopt a secular government, *2696*
Planetarium of the modern type, *5129*
Transoceanic radio voice broadcast, *5910*
Treatise on geochemistry, *5282*
Troop movement by airplane, *4216*
Twenty-four-hour automobile endurance race, *5719*
Woman accredited as an ambassador, *3148*

1924

Archeological study of a New World site, *5060*
Athlete of African descent to win a gold medal in an individual event, *5767*
Bobsled world championship, *5632*
Dogsled crossing of the Northwest Passage, *2320*
Frozen food for the mass market, *2542*
Gas chamber, *1747*
Musical composition to incorporate a phonograph recording in a live performance, *4393*
Oil pastels, *1287*
Photography booth, *4572*
Round-the-world steamboat passenger service, *5429*
Surrealist manifesto, *1241*
Winter Olympic Games, *5768*

1925

Communist wire service, *4517*
Constitutional monarch of Thailand, *2972*
Cosmic ray to be discovered, *5094*
Fascist dictator, *2998*

Movie shown on an airplane, *4299*
National park in Africa, *2260*
Photoelectric cell, *2014*
Stock exchange member who was a woman, *2430*
Surrealist exhibition, *1254*
Tornado to cause more than 500 deaths, *1927*
Transcontinental radio fax transmission, *5877*
Tubular steel chair, *3091*

1926

Aerosol can, *3113*
Containers of yogurt with fruit mixed in, *2516*
Dance notation to precisely indicate movement and rhythm, *1852*
Flight over the North Pole, *2321*
Movie accompanied by prerecorded sound to be released as a feature film, *4300*
Movie showing another planet, *5095*
Rocket flight using liquid fuel, *5505*
Table tennis international association, *5829*
Televised images to be publicly displayed, *5951*
Woman to swim the English Channel, *5822*

1927

Air conditioner for home use, *3068*
Apparatus used to treat respiratory failure, *4088*
Arteriogram, *3904*
Astronomical photograph taken from an airplane, *5096*
Automobile tunnel, *2193*
Electric blanket, *3069*
Heat pump, *2064*
London to Delhi scheduled aircraft flight, *1363*
National broadcasting monopoly, *5882*
Quartz clock, *6030*
Radiation mutations to be artificially created, *5196*
Stroboscopic lamp for high-speed photography, *4585*
Synthetic gasoline plant, *2107*
Table tennis world championship, *5830*
Transatlantic commercial telephone service, *5937*
Transatlantic solo airplane flight, *1364*
Vitamin to be commercially synthesized and manufactured, *2543*
Voice double, *4321*
Welded metal sculpture, *1303*
World chess champion who was a woman, *2600*
Year the world population exceeded 2 billion, *4605*

1928

Animation with sound, *4331*
Antiwar treaty, *3171*
Flight from the United States to Australia, *1366*

1928—*continued*

Flying bush doctor, *3976*
International dogsled mail, *4678*
International telecommunications conglomerate, *5930*
International television transmission, *5952*
Intrauterine device (IUD), *2367*
King of Albania, *2973*
Mass-produced cereal food for infants, *2391*
Recording tape, *2047*
Rocket car, *5720*
Rocket-propelled airplane, *1318*
Sulfa drug, *3934*
Transatlantic east-west nonstop airplane flight, *1365*
Transoceanic radio signal conveying a television image, *5953*
Underground film, *4351*
Visual encyclopedia for children, *3386*

1929

Cardiac catheterization, *4089*
Circumnavigation by air, *1407*
Color television system, *5954*
Comic strip with an adventure hero, *4471*
Electroencephalogram, *3905*
Manned rocket-plane flight, *1367*
Movie musical, *4352*
Movie with both sound and color, *4301*
Newsreel theater, *4357*
Rhythm method, *2368*
Tape recorder, *2048*

1930

Cellophane transparent tape, *3114*
Commonwealth Games, *5694*
Computing device with electronic components, *1667*
Deep-sea exploration vessel, *5283*
Demonstration of home reception of television, *5956*
Dinosaur eggs to be discovered, *5209*
European jazz musician to win international recognition, *4378*
International bridge match, *2595*
Motorized clothes dryer, *3070*
Multiplex theater, *4358*
Nobel Prize for Literature winner from North America, *4533*
Non-Western nation to become fully industrialized, *2697*
Organic gardening, *2625*
Paris to New York nonstop airplane flight, *1368*
Person to be interviewed on television, *5955*
Planet found beyond Neptune, *5097*
Planetarium in the Western Hemisphere, *5130*
Recumbent bicycle, *5629*
Round-the-world radio broadcast, *5911*
Sex-change operation, *5370*

Skyscraper more than 1,000 feet high, *1227*
State-supported family planning clinics, *2369*
Winner of the Grand Slam, *5669*
World Cup soccer championship, *5816*

1931

Blood bank, *4100*
Breathing apparatus for submarine escape, *5451*
Closed-circuit sporting event, *5957*
Constitutional president of Spain, *2803*
Electric shaver, *2755*
Human ascent into the stratosphere, *1408*
Infrared photograph, *4598*
One-armed pianist of international stature, *4374*
Radio waves from space to be observed, *5098*
Skyscraper with more than 100 stories, *1228*
Starter motor, *2180*
Transpacific nonstop airplane flight, *1369*

1932

Amphetamine, *3935*
Annual film festival, *4340*
Artificial language based entirely on English, *3301*
Artificial transmutation of an element, *5340*
Commercial pilot who was a woman, *1343*
Discovery of antimatter, *5338*
Discovery of neutrons, *5339*
Foam-rubber padded seating, *3092*
Germ warfare against civilians in modern times, *4183*
Industrial scientist to win a Nobel Prize, *4520*
International disarmament conferences, *3161*
King of independent Iraq, *2975*
King of Saudi Arabia, *2974*
Maccabiah Games, *5695*
National gasoline tax, *2468*
Severe famine caused by government ideology, *1950*
Transatlantic solo airplane flight by a woman, *1370*
Transatlantic westbound solo nonstop flight, *1371*
Use of the term "International Style", *1200*
Winter Olympic Games in the Western Hemisphere, *5769*

1933

Antimatter particles to be artificially created, *5341*
Bridge with piers sunk in the open sea, *2146*
Drive-in movie theater, *4359*
Nationwide highway system, *1593*
Nazi book burning, *3364*
Poliomyelitis vaccine, *3912*
Round-the-world solo airplane flight, *1372*
Sport airplane, *1319*
Transmission electron microscope, *5304*
World championship professional football game, *5661*

1934

Anti-apartheid novel, *3462*
Artificial radioisotope, *5342*
Cyclotron, *5343*
Fluorescent lamp, *2097*
Front-wheel-drive car, *3240*
International oil pipeline, *2108*
Laundromat, *1520*
Nation in Oceania to have its own modern coinage, *2458*
President of the Soviet Writers' Union, *3337*
Quintuplets, *2345*
Radio broadcast heard in both the Arctic and the Antarctic regions, *5912*
Regularly scheduled transoceanic flights, *1344*
Shock therapy for treating mental illness, *4004*
Stamp depicting basketball, *4699*
Subcompact car designed to be fuel-efficient, *3239*
Vehicle to break the sound barrier, *5506*
Woman to fly solo from England to Australia, *1373*

1935

Aerial photograph showing the lateral curvature of the horizon and the beginning of the stratosphere, *5284*
Center for the study of human sexuality, *5371*
Electric guitar, *4424*
Human breeding program, *5197*
National film archive, *4302*
Nuclear chain reaction patent, *5344*
Paparazzo, *4573*
Prediction of the existence of mesons, *5345*
Self-help program for substance abusers, *4027*
Tape recorder to use plastic tape, *2049*
Telephone conversation to travel around the world, *5938*
Television announcer who was a woman, *5958*
Transpacific airmail flight, *4685*
Transpacific solo airplane flight by a woman, *1374*
Vatican observatory, *5137*

1936

Commercial airliner widely used, *1320*
Diesel passenger car, *3241*
English-speaking country to abolish the death penalty, *1748*
Fields Medal, *3753*
Nerve gas, *6081*
Nobel Prize for Peace winner from Latin America, *4541*
Plastic contact lenses, *4110*
Prefrontal lobotomy, *4056*
Printed circuit, *2015*
Regular broadcast high-definition television service, *5959*
Single-lens reflex (SLR) 35-millimeter camera, *4586*

Tape recording of a live concert, *2050*
Trampoline, *5672*
Transatlantic commercial airship, *1409*
Uneven parallel bars, *5673*
Videophone, *5972*

1937

Artificial heart in an animal, *4066*
Electroshock therapy, *4005*
Element produced artificially, *5243*
Feature-length animated film directed by a woman, *4332*
Feature-length animated film made by the cel process, *4333*
Fluid catalytic cracking process, *2109*
Freeze-dried instant coffee, *2500*
Letter to circumnavigate the world by commercial airmail, *4686*
Radio astronomer, *5099*
Synthetic fiber produced entirely from chemicals, *3724*
Treatise on computing theory, *1659*
Woman helicopter pilot, *1424*
Woman to serve as a combat pilot, *4217*

1938

Coelacanth caught alive, *1115*
Comic book superhero, *4472*
Electronic television system that was practical, *5960*
Grand Slam winner in tennis, *5836*
Helicopter free flight indoors, *1425*
Occanarium, *1164*
Premier of Thailand, *2882*
President of the Republic of Ireland (Éire), *2804*
Rail bridge higher than 500 feet, *2147*
Superfluid, *5244*
Toothbrush with synthetic bristles, *2761*
Vinyl shower curtains, *3093*
Wartime song popular with both sides of the conflict, *4442*
Xerography, *4724*

1939

Aerosol spray can, *6061*
Attack of World War II, *4184*
Bomb to land on German soil in World War II, *4218*
British monarchs to visit the United States, *2976*
Civilian ship sunk in World War II, *4267*
Declaration of war in World War II, *4186*
Electronic digital calculator, *1665*
Live electronic music, *4394*
National euthanasia program, *1771*
Naval shot of World War II, *4266*
Shot of World War II, *4185*
Transatlantic airmail service, *4687*

1939—*continued*

Turbojet aircraft, *1321*
U-boat captured in World War II, *4268*

1940

Air battle that was strategically important, *4222*
Aircraft carrier to be sunk by surface ships, *4270*
Electronic warfare in the air, *4219*
Element heavier than uranium, *5245*
Glider assault, *4220*
Helicopter that was successful, *1426*
Modern theater in the round, *5999*
Paratrooper assault on a fortified area, *4221*
Photographic collection in a museum, *1830*
Recording of piano on tape, *2051*
Shaped charge used in war, *6093*
Warship sunk by air attack in wartime, *4269*

1941

Aerosol product, *3115*
Aircraft units staffed entirely by women, *4223*
Death camp, *1772*
International oil embargo, *3129*
Japanese naval casualty in World War II, *4271*
Major airborne assault, *4224*
Person to travel more than 500 miles per hour, *1322*
Photographic pictorial biography, *4574*
Plastic car, *3242*
Programmable electronic binary computer, *1668*
Round-the-world flight by a commercial airplane, *1375*
Self-heating cans, *2520*
Silicon solar cell, *2065*
Touch-tone phone system, *5939*
War photographer who was a woman, *4462*

1942

Aikido, *5706*
Ballistic missile test flight, *6134*
Battle with more than 2 million deaths, *4187*
British civilian medal conferred on a country, *2698*
Commercial petrochemical plant for fluid catalytic cracking, *2110*
Ejection seat, *1323*
Handheld rocket launcher, *6133*
Oil spills on the ocean, *2268*
Patient to be given penicillin, *3936*
Sea battle fought solely by air power, *4272*
Self-sustaining nuclear chain reaction demonstration, *5346*
Vessel to cross the Northwest Passage west to east, *2322*
Woman to be awarded the Iron Cross, *4225*
Women pilots to down enemy aircraft in combat, *4226*

1943

Amphibious assault vehicle, *6122*
Ballpoint pen widely used, *3596*
Blimp lost in combat, *4228*
Chaff to jam radar, *4227*
Ejection seat that was propelled by explosives, *1324*
Electromechanical cryptographic decoder, *4142*
Environmental restoration plan for an industrial site, *2243*
Firestorm, *1951*
Kidney dialysis, *4090*
President of Syria, *2805*
Refugee ship disaster, *1937*
Revolt by prisoners at a Nazi death camp, *1773*
Self-contained underwater breathing apparatus, *5285*
Synthetic hallucinogen, *4028*

1944

Accidental sinking of ships carrying prisoners of war, *1938*
Allied soldier killed in combat on D-Day, *4188*
Anglican woman priest, *4843*
Assault rifle, *6117*
Circus fire with large loss of life, *1952*
Cruise missile used in war, *6135*
Evidence that DNA is the genetic material, *5198*
Jet fighter, *4229*
Meeting to establish the United Nations, *3187*
Operation to cure congenital heart disease, *4057*
Platypus born in captivity, *1120*
President of the modern Republic of Iceland, *2806*
Systemic pesticide, *1101*
Undersea tunnel, *2194*

1945

Afterburner, *2181*
American flag to fly over the defeated Nazi empire, *4190*
Atomic bomb explosion, *6123*
Atomic bomb explosion over enemy territory, *4232*
Definition of rape as a crime against humanity, *1775*
Jet bomber, *4230*
Jet-propelled landing on an aircraft carrier, *1376*
Marine disaster costing the lives of more than 10,000 noncombatants, *1939*
Meeting of American and Soviet troops in World War II, *4189*
Member nations of the United Nations, *3189*
Nazi death camp to be liberated in World War II, *1774*
Nobel Prize for Literature winner from Latin America, *4534*

Nobel Prize in Physiology or Medicine winner from Oceania, *4551*
Olfactory television set, *5961*
Plastic container for kitchen use, *3116*
Political association of Arab states, *3134*
Proposal for global satellite telecommunications, *5883*
Rocket-propelled warplane, *4231*
Three-dimensional molecular structure, *5246*
United Nations conference, *3188*
World bank, *2413*

1946

Atomic bomb explosion underwater, *6124*
Ban-the-bomb demonstrations, *6125*
Call for a united democratic Europe, *3135*
Chairman of the United Nations Atomic Energy Commission, *3190*
Espresso machine, *3071*
General-purpose computer that was fully electronic, *1669*
Grand Prix of the Cannes International Film Festival, *4341*
International measurement standards, *5313*
King of Jordan, *2977*
Meeting of the United Nations General Assembly, *3192*
Modern bikini, *1636*
Nuclear reactor in Europe, *2115*
President of the Philippines, *2807*
Racial integration of professional baseball, *5612*
Radar signal to the moon, *5518*
Radiation-induced cataracts, *3846*
Secretary general of the United Nations, *3191*
Solar furnace of commercial size, *2066*
Unification Church teachings, *4804*
War criminals convicted of crimes against humanity, *1776*
Woman cinematographer, *4303*

1947

Airplane to fly faster than the speed of sound, *1377*
Canasta, *2596*
Commercial round-the-world airplane flight, *1345*
Dead Sea Scrolls to be discovered, *4978*
Food processor, *3072*
General conference of the United Nations Educational, Scientific and Cultural Organization, *3162*
Hurricane reconnaissance flights, *5286*
Instant camera, *4587*
Little League World Series, *5613*
Microwave oven, *3073*
Nobel Prize in Physiology or Medicine winner from Latin America, *4552*
Prime minister of India, *2884*
Prime minister of Pakistan, *2885*
Prime minister of Sri Lanka, *2883*

Raft trip across the Pacific, *5460*
Regional cooperative in Oceania, *3136*
Scanning tunneling electron microscope, *5305*
Swimmer to cross the Irish Sea, *5823*
United Nations Day, *3040*
Woman to win the Nobel Prize in Physiology or Medicine, *4553*
Women to winter in Antarctica, *2323*

1948

Airplane hijacking, *1798*
Ancient language revived for modern use, *3302*
Country to depend mainly on water from desalination, *2244*
International maritime organization, *3193*
International organization for promoting health, *4017*
Long-playing (LP) phonograph records, *2052*
Musique concrète, *4395*
Premier of North Korea, *2886*
President of South Korea, *2808*
Prime minister of independent Myanmar, *2887*
Prime minister of Israel, *2888*
Refugee ship fire to cause large loss of life, *1940*
Sportsman to win individual gold medals in four successive Olympic Games, *5770*
Steel-belted radial-ply automobile tire, *3295*
Swimmer to cross the Strait of Gibraltar, *5824*
Transatlantic eastward flight by jet airplane, *1378*
Transistor, *2016*
Use of the term "cold war", *4191*
Woman athlete of African descent to win a medal in the Olympic Games, *5771*
Woman athlete of African descent to win an Olympic gold medal, *5772*
Woman athlete to win four gold medals in one Olympic Games, *5773*

1949

Airlift of endangered Jews to Israel, *4979*
Atomic bomb detonated by a country other than the United States, *6126*
Corneal graft, *4058*
Film made by a studio outside the United States to win an Academy Award, *4304*
Modern university in the Caribbean, *1999*
Nobel Prize in Physics winner from Asia, *4548*
Peacetime alliance of European and North American nations, *3137*
President of Indonesia, *2810*
President of Israel, *2809*
Ramjet aircraft, *1325*
Remote detection of a nuclear weapons test, *6127*
Rocket to reach outer space, *5507*
Round-the-world nonstop flight by an airplane, *1379*
Running shoes, *1657*

1949—*continued*

Synchrotron, *5347*
Telephone answering machine, *5940*
Thomas Cup in badminton, *5599*

1950

Airmail service by jet aircraft, *4688*
Ascent of Annapurna, *5736*
Copy machine, *4725*
Disposable diapers, *2392*
Floppy disk, *1670*
Gymnast to achieve a perfect score, *5774*
HIV infections, *3847*
International Congress of Archivists, *1822*
Organ transplant from one human to another that was successful, *4067*
Rolodex, *1521*
Transatlantic nonstop jet airplane flight, *1380*
United Nations military action, *4192*

1951

Atomic bomb explosion underground, *6128*
Correction fluid for typists, *3597*
Direct-dial telephone network, *5941*
Electronic computer for commercial use, *1671*
Grand Slam doubles winners in tennis, *5837*
International pharmacopoeia, *3791*
King of independent Libya, *2978*
Legal definition of genocide, *1777*
Little League baseball teams outside the United States, *5614*
Mambo, *1853*
Milk carton, *2521*
Miss World contest, *2201*
Modern pentathlete, *5842*
Nobel Prize in Physiology or Medicine winner from Africa, *4554*
Pan-American Games, *5696*
Rock and roll song, *4443*
Sex-change operation that was successful, *5372*
Sky-diving championships, *5600*
United Nations embargo, *3194*

1952

Airplane flight to land at the North Pole, *2324*
Artificial lens for surgical insertion into the eye, *4111*
Bank to issue a credit card, *2414*
Birth to be televised for the public, *2346*
Discovery of the North Pole, *2325*
Dynamical time scale, *6016*
Factory to obtain uranium from gold, *3675*
Flat horse race in North America, *5687*
Hydrogen bomb, *6129*
Jet airliner, *1326*
Nuclear power plant disaster, *1953*
Nuclear transplantation in a vertebrate, *5185*
Olympic marathon winner who had never run a marathon, *5775*

Performance of a *Son et lumière* show, *2225*
Rock concert, *4444*
Scheduled commercial jet flight, *1346*
Tranquilizer, *3937*
Transatlantic helicopter flight, *1427*
Transatlantic solo boat journey by a woman, *5461*
Transpacific nonstop jet airplane flight, *1381*
Woman archeologist of distinction, *5061*

1953

Ascent of Mount Everest, *5737*
Ascent of Nanga Parbat (Diamir), *5738*
Commercial jet airplane pilot who was a woman, *1347*
Elucidation of the structure of DNA, *5199*
Ferry to sink with large loss of life, *1941*
Geodesic dome with a commercial use, *1201*
Heart-lung machine, *4068*
Hydrogen bomb detonated by a country other than the United States, *6130*
International animal protection society, *1141*
International television broadcast, *5962*
President of the United Nations General Assembly who was a woman, *3195*
Professional soldier to be awarded a Nobel Prize for Peace, *4542*
Televised coronation, *2979*
Woman tennis player to win the Grand Slam, *5838*
Woman to fly faster than the speed of sound, *1382*

1954

Ascent of Cho Oyu, *5740*
Ascent of K2 (Mount Godwin Austen), *5739*
Birth-control pill, *2370*
Civilian nuclear power plant, *2116*
Electron-beam welding, *1495*
Europe-wide television programming, *5963*
Free-moving deep-sea submersible, *5452*
Jazz festival, *4379*
Nonstick cookware, *3117*
Oil-from-coal plant, *2111*
Overthrow of a democratic foreign government arranged by the U.S. Central Intelligence Agency, *4143*
Person to run a mile in less than four minutes, *5843*
Prime minister of Sudan, *2889*
Rotary internal-combustion engine, *2182*
Round-the-world flights over the North Pole on a regularly scheduled air route, *1383*
Slow motion action sequence, *4305*
Solar cells that were practical, *2067*
Transistor radio receiver to be mass-produced, *5913*
West African money market, *2431*
Worldwide rock-and-roll hit, *4445*

1955

Artificial diamond, *5247*
Ascent of Kanchenjunga, *5742*
Ascent of Makalu, *5741*
Edition of the *Guinness Book of World Records*, *2226*
Fiber optic cable, *5942*
Film to win the Palme d'Or at the Cannes International Film Festival, *4342*
Meeting of the nonaligned movement, *3163*
Nuclear-powered submarine, *4273*
Pilot to bail out of an airplane flying at supersonic speed, *1437*
Protein characterized by amino acid sequence, *5169*
Signatories of the Warsaw Pact, *3172*
Trampoline international competition, *5674*
Woman to fly over the North Pole, *2326*

1956

Airplane flight to land at the South Pole, *2327*
Ascent of Lhotse, *5744*
Ascent of Manaslu (Kutang), *5743*
Clock to operate by nuclear power, *6031*
Constitutional president of the Republic of Egypt, *2811*
Containerized shipping, *1548*
Country to attempt to withdraw from the Warsaw Pact, *3173*
Discovery of nonsymmetric particle interaction, *5348*
King of independent Morocco, *2980*
Molecule analyzed with the use of a computer, *5248*
Nobel Prize winner to win twice in the same field, *4521*
Nuclear power plant, *2117*
Nuclear reactor in Asia, *2118*
Observation of neutrinos, *5349*
Olympic Games in the Southern Hemisphere, *5777*
Supersonic bomber, *4233*
Transatlantic telephone call using the transoceanic cable, *5943*
Video tape recorder for sounds and pictures, *5964*
Woman athlete to take the Olympic oath at the opening ceremony, *5776*

1957

Artificial satellite, *5584*
Battery-powered wristwatch, *6032*
Circumnavigation of the world by a submarine, *5462*
Film festival in the Western Hemisphere, *4343*
Free-trade region, *1549*
Hook and loop fastener, *1644*
Human in space, *5529*
Intercontinental ballistic missile, *6136*

International conference of atomic scientists, *5350*
International Geophysical Year, *5287*
Laser, *2017*
Living creature launched into orbit, *5530*
Major nuclear power plant accident, *1954*
Major radio telescope, *5138*
Modern tae kwon do, *5707*
Nuclear waste disaster to cause large loss of life, *1955*
Performance of a *Son et lumière* show in Britain, *2227*
Pocket transistor radio, *5914*
President of independent Tunisia, *2812*
Prime minister of Ghana, *2890*
Prime minister of Malaysia, *2891*
Production automobile with a fiberglass body, *3243*
Round-the-world nonstop flight by a jet airplane, *1384*
Sub-Saharan African colony to gain its independence, *2699*
Trousers with permanent pleats, *1637*

1958

Black box flight recorder, *1327*
Crossing of the North Pole underwater by a submerged submarine, *5463*
Food irradiation, *2522*
Integrated circuit, *2018*
Japanese auto manufacturer to export cars to the U.S. market, *3244*
Nuclear weapons test moratorium, *3174*
Pacemaker successfully implanted in a patient, *4059*
President of Guinea, *2813*
President of the European Parliament, *2814*
Prime minister of Nigeria, *2892*
Radio broadcast using an orbiting satellite, *5915*
Round-the-world airline service, *1348*
Satellite powered by photovoltaic cells, *5585*
Snorkel fire truck, *1580*
Transoceanic jetliner service, *1349*

1959

All-plastic building, *1202*
Animals to survive a space flight, *5531*
Bank credit card to gain national acceptance, *2415*
Breeder reactor, *2119*
Computer-aided manufacturing system, *1496*
Epidemic of birth defects caused by a drug, *1908*
Float glass, *3652*
Helical-scan video tape recorder, *5965*
Hovercraft, *5419*
Major-league American baseball teams to play in Communist Cuba, *5615*

1959—*continued*

Movie premiered simultaneously in major cities throughout the world, *4306*
Nuclear-powered surface ship, *5420*
Nuclear-powered warship, *4274*
Object to escape the earth's gravity, *5508*
Photographs of the dark side of the moon, *5520*
Prime minister of Singapore, *2893*
Radar signal bounced off the sun, *5100*
Reconnaissance satellite system, *4144*
Spacecraft to reach the moon, *5519*
Steamroller, *1497*
Submarine equipped with ballistic missiles, *4275*
Telecast from space showing the earth, *5509*
Transoceanic cryogenic shipping, *1550*
Walk to raise funds for charity, *5502*

1960

All-transistor portable television, *2026*
Ascent of Dhaulagiri, *5745*
Botanical garden display under a geodesic dome, *2626*
Circumnavigation of the earth by a submerged submarine, *5464*
Communications satellite, *5884*
Dive to the bottom of the ocean, *5453*
Electronic wristwatch, *6033*
Epitaxy fabrication, *2019*
Felt-tip pen, *3598*
International system of measurement, *5314*
Leader of independent Cyprus, *2999*
Living creatures launched into orbit who returned safely to earth, *5532*
Mars probe, *5567*
Nobel Prize for Peace winner from Africa, *4543*
Plastic bags, *3118*
President of independent Madagascar, *2819*
President of independent Niger, *2820*
President of Senegal, *2815*
President of the Central African Republic, *2822*
President of the Democratic Republic of the Congo, *2818*
President of the Ivory Coast (Côte d'Ivoire), *2816*
President of the Republic of Chad, *2821*
President of the Republic of Mali, *2823*
President of the United Republic of Cameroon, *2817*
Prime minister of the Democratic Republic of the Congo, *2894*
Prime minister who was a woman, *2895*
Programmable logic controller, *2189*
Scientific observations of primate behavior in the wild, *5170*
Scientific program to search for extraterrestrial life, *5101*
Signal intelligence satellite, *4145*
Solar thermal power plant, *2068*

Solo transatlantic sailboat race, *5858*
Somali writing, *3544*
Spacecraft placed in solar orbit, *5568*
Submarine-launched ballistic missile, *6137*
Working laser, *2020*
World heavyweight champion to regain his title after losing it, *5647*
Worldwide satellite-based weather observation system, *5288*
Year the world population exceeded 3 billion, *4606*

1961

All-news radio station, *4464*
Computer-generated short film, *4334*
Electric toothbrush, *2762*
Explorer to set foot on both the North and South Poles, *2328*
Hatchback automobile, *3245*
Human to return safely from space, *5533*
Industrial robot that was practical, *5032*
Nuclear-powered aircraft carrier, *4276*
Performance of a *Son et lumière* show in Africa, *2228*
Performer in a foreign language film to win the Academy Award for Best Actress, *4322*
President of independent Gabon, *2824*
President of independent Mauritania, *2825*
President of Togo, *2826*
Prime minister of Sierra Leone, *2896*
Quasar to be observed, *5102*
Satellite-based ICBM-launch warning system, *6138*
Soft contact lens, *4112*
Swimmer to cross the English Channel in both directions, *5825*
Tape cassette, *2053*
Televised trial, *4463*
Treaty to govern the use of a continent, *3175*
World judo champion who was not Japanese, *5708*

1962

Beatles recording to become a hit, *4446*
Car with hidden headlights, *3246*
Commercial satellite, *5587*
Computer game, *2576*
Containership facility, *1551*
Hologram, *5318*
Hovercraft passenger service, *5421*
International satellite, *5586*
Performance of a *Son et lumière* show in the United States, *2229*
President and prime minister of the Yemen Arab Republic (North Yemen), *2829*
President of Rwanda, *2828*
President of Tanzania, *2827*
Prime minister of Algeria, *2897*
Prime minister of independent Jamaica, *2898*
Prime minister of independent Uganda, *2899*

Prime minister of the Republic of Trinidad and Tobago, *2900*
Pull-top aluminum can, *2523*
Secretary general of the United Nations from an Asian nation, *3196*
Transoceanic telecast by satellite, *5966*
Two manned craft in space simultaneously, *5534*
Underwater swim across the English Channel, *5826*

1963

Democratically elected president of the Dominican Republic, *2830*
Digital computer animation, *4335*
Federation Cup in tennis, *5839*
Film directed by an African to be distributed outside Africa, *4307*
Geosynchronous satellite, *5588*
Hovercraft lawn mower, *6065*
International standards for food quality, *4018*
Japanese company to sell stock on United States stock exchanges, *2432*
Liver transplant, *4069*
Monocoque chassis for Formula 1 racing cars, *5721*
Nobel laureate who was the sole winner of awards in two different categories, *4522*
Nuclear arms–control treaty, *3176*
Nuclear engineer, *2128*
Nuclear submarine lost at sea, *1942*
Prenatal blood transfusion, *4101*
President of Nigeria, *2831*
Prime minister of Kenya, *2901*
Production automobiles with seat belts, *3247*
Self-immolation by a Buddhist monk, *1886*
Supercomputer, *1672*
Telephone hot line between nations, *3149*
Tokamak, *2120*
Woman to fly in space, *5535*

1964

Bullet train line, *3282*
Child whose parents had both flown in space, *2393*
Dot-matrix printer, *1673*
Human cancer-causing virus to be discovered, *3848*
International Ballet Competition, *1864*
International satellite consortium, *5589*
International trampoline governing body, *5675*
Meeting of the Palestine Liberation Organization, *2667*
Modern rice hybrid that was successful, *1056*
Olympic Games in Asia, *5778*
Operating system, *1726*
Person to win the same Olympic event three times, *5779*
Premier of Belize, *2902*
President of Zambia, *2832*

Runner to win the Olympic marathon twice, *5780*
Soccer (association football) disaster, *1956*
Spacecraft to carry more than one crew member, *5536*
Transpacific telephone service using the transoceanic cable, *5944*
Transplant of an animal organ into a human being, *4070*

1965

Computer art exhibition, *1255*
Geosynchronous commercial communications satellite, *5885*
Home video tape recorder, *2027*
International treaty prohibiting racial discrimination, *3156*
Methadone maintenance program for heroin addicts, *4029*
Minicomputer, *1674*
Miniskirt, *1638*
Observational confirmation of the Big Bang theory, *5103*
Performance of a *Son et lumière* show in Asia, *2230*
Prime minister of independent Lesotho, *2903*
Rendezvous in space, *5538*
Space walk, *5537*
Spacecraft to transmit close-up photographs of Mars, *5569*
Stealth aircraft, *4234*
Transatlantic undersea radio conversation, *5916*
Waterbed, *3094*

1966

Ascent of the Vinson Massif, *5746*
Civilian space traveler to orbit the earth, *5539*
Computer modem that was practical, *1675*
Country to withdraw from the North Atlantic Treaty Organization (NATO), *3177*
Desktop fax machine, *5878*
Docking of two spacecraft, *5540*
Inflatable chair, *3095*
Kwanzaa, *3041*
Meeting of the heads of the Anglican and Catholic churches, *4805*
Nobel Prize for Literature winner from the Middle East, *4535*
Photographs from the surface of the moon, *5522*
President of Botswana, *2833*
Prime minister and president of Guyana, *2904*
Prime minister of Malawi, *2905*
Reversed sounds, *4447*
Scientific study of the physiology of human sexuality, *5373*
Spacecraft to make a soft landing on the moon, *5521*
Spacecraft to reach another planet, *5570*

1967

Car with a rotary engine, *3248*
Caribana Festival, *3042*
City in North America to use seawater as its sole water supply, *2245*
Discovery of pulsars, *5104*
Discovery of quarks, *5351*
Freezing of a corpse for future resuscitation, *1883*
Heart transplant, *4071*
Human to die during a space flight, *5541*
King of independent Swaziland, *2981*
Massacre at the Olympic Games, *1799*
McDonald's restaurant outside the United States, *1469*
Oil spill from a commercial tanker, *2269*
Rock music festival, *4448*
Solo voyage around the world, *5465*
Spacecraft to make a soft landing on another planet, *5571*
Super Bowl football game, *5662*
Teaching and research hospice for the dying, *3896*
Telecommunications tower higher than 500 meters, *1229*
Tidal electric generator plant, *2069*
Treaty on the use of space, *3178*
Worldwide live television program, *5967*

1968

Astronauts to orbit the moon, *5524*
Book set into type completely by electronic composition, *3365*
Car with a computer chip, *3249*
Computer mouse, *1676*
International astronaut rescue agreement, *5543*
International terrorist organization to use skyjacking, *1800*
Liquid crystal display, *2021*
Live telecast from space, *5542*
Nonproliferation treaty for weapons of mass destruction, *3179*
Spacecraft to return from lunar orbit, *5523*
Special Olympics, *5697*
Summer Olympic Games in Latin America, *5781*
Warship to sink with nuclear weapons aboard, *1943*
Windsurfing, *5866*
Woman athlete to light the Olympic flame, *5782*

1969

African film festival, *4344*
Art holograms, *1242*
Astronauts to land on the moon, *5525*
Bank to install an automatic teller, *2416*
Booker Prize, *3456*
Computer network, *1694*

Country to make seat belts compulsory, *4019*
Docking of two manned spacecraft, *5544*
Holographic movie, *4308*
Interactive museum, *1831*
Multiuser operating system, *1727*
Nobel Prize in Economics, *4528*
Pesticide disaster in Europe, *1957*
Plan for European economic and monetary union, *3138*
Prime minister of Libya, *2906*
Quartz wristwatch, *6034*
Solo nonstop voyage around the world, *5467*
Supersonic jet airliner, *1328*
Synthetic fabric that was waterproof and breathable, *3725*
Transatlantic solo trip by rowboat, *5466*
Transpacific sailboat crossing by a woman, *5468*
Transplant of an artificial heart into a human being, *4072*
Videocassette recorder for home use, *2028*
Videodisc, *2029*
Welding and smelting in space, *5545*

1970

Bar code system for marking industrial products, *1498*
Cloned animal, *5186*
Collapsible baby stroller, *2394*
Copper IUD, *2371*
Doctor of the Church who was a woman, *4876*
Headlight washer/wiper, *3250*
IMAX film, *4309*
International direct-dial service, *5945*
Jumbo jet, *1329*
Laser lighthouse, *5444*
Lunar rover, *5526*
Nobel Prize in Chemistry winner from Latin America, *4525*
Nobel Prize in Economics winner from North America, *4529*
Packet radio network, *5917*
President of Gambia, *2834*
Professional video cassette format, *5968*
Satellite launched by the Chinese space program, *5590*
Soil samples from the moon, *5527*
Spreadsheet program, *1728*
Storm to kill 1 million people, *1928*
Surrogate partner therapy, *5374*
Twisted nematic liquid crystal display (LCD), *2022*
X-ray astronomy satellite, *5139*

1971

Astronauts to ride a vehicle on the moon, *5528*
Black hole to be detected, *5105*
Electronic mail message, *1695*
Electronic mail message to use the @ ("at") sign, *1696*

Electronic pocket calculator, *2030*
Floppy disk widely used, *1677*
Industrial robot organization, *5033*
Long-distance university without classrooms, *2000*
Microprocessor, *1678*
Nonuplets, *2347*
President of Equatorial Guinea, *2835*
Radiation surgery, *4060*
Satellite launched from the earth to orbit another planet, *5591*
Sheikh of independent Bahrain, *2982*
Space station, *5546*
Tornado intensity scale, *5289*

1972

Aboriginal Australian elected to the Australian Parliament, *2656*
African song that was an international pop hit, *4449*
Artificial hip, *3985*
CAT scan, *3906*
City with more than 10 million inhabitants, *1571*
Computer-to-computer conversation in English, *1697*
Digital quartz wristwatch, *6035*
Director of the Royal Greenwich Observatory, *5140*
International encyclopedia in Japanese, *3387*
International environmental conference, *2246*
International networking conference, *1698*
Multiplex hologram, *4310*
Prime minister of Bangladesh, *2907*
Spacecraft to carry an extraterrestrial message, *5572*
Strategic Arms Limitation Treaty, *3180*
Video game, *2577*
Winter Olympic Games in Asia, *5783*

1973

Animated film to win an award at the Cannes International Film Festival, *4336*
Artificial gene, *5200*
Australian real estate owned by aborigines in modern times, *4667*
Close-up photographs of Jupiter, *5573*
Color xerographic copier, *4726*
Gene splicing, *5201*
Home powered by solar cells, *1222*
International Internet connections, *1699*
Multinational space agency, *5510*
National computer network, *1700*
Nobel Prize for Literature winner from Oceania, *4536*
Oil embargo in peacetime, *3130*
Personal computer, *1679*
Personal computer kit, *1680*
Radial keratotomy, *4061*
Robotics journal, *5034*

Town buried by a volcano in modern times, *1929*
Treaty on the international trade in rare animals, *1142*
Women to trade on the floor of the London Stock Exchange, *2433*

1974

Discovery of the rings of Jupiter, *5106*
International fax standard, *5879*
Personal computer operating system, *1729*
Privatization campaign, *1447*
Representative of a nongovernmental organization to address a plenary session of the United Nations General Assembly, *3197*
Retail item priced by a bar code scanner, *1522*
Round-the-world journey on foot, *5852*
Triathlon, *5848*
Woman to become president of a nation, *2836*
Year the world population exceeded 4 billion, *4607*

1975

Calculator watch, *6036*
Commercial software for personal computers, *1730*
Disposable razor, *2756*
Formal symbol of Jainism, *4952*
International space mission, *5548*
Launch failure of a manned spacecraft, *5547*
Live broadcast from the British Parliament, *2657*
Mailing list, *1701*
Monoclonal antibodies, *4091*
Music video, *4450*
Nationwide poisoning epidemic, *1909*
Nobel Prize in Chemistry winner from Oceania, *4526*
Organization to promote human-powered transportation, *3206*
Photographs from the surface of another planet, *5574*
President of Benin, *2837*
President of independent Cape Verde, *2840*
President of the People's Republic of Angola, *2838*
President of the Seychelles, *2839*
Prime minister of independent Suriname, *2908*
Ruler of independent Mozambique, *3000*
Smart card, *2459*
Surface ship to reach the North Pole, *2329*
Weather service to name tropical storms with male and female names, *5290*
Woman to reach the summit of Mount Everest, *5747*
World Conference on Women, *5375*

1976

Boycotts of the Olympic Games, *5784*

1976—*continued*

Computer network linking two continents, *1702*

Feature film incorporating digital computer graphics, *4337*

Gymnast to achieve a perfect score in the Olympic Games, *5785*

Head of state to send an e-mail message, *1703*

Holographic film system, *4311*

Photograph taken on Mars, *5575*

Racing car designed to take advantage of ground effects aerodynamics, *5722*

Significant mathematical problem solved by computer, *3754*

Spacecraft to land on Mars, *5576*

Supersonic airliner to enter regular service, *1350*

Supersonic jet service across the Atlantic Ocean, *1351*

Turbocharged engine for a mass-produced automobile, *3251*

VHS videocassette recorder, *2031*

Voice reader, *3303*

1977

Aircraft powered by human motion, *1330*

Aviation disaster in which more than 500 people were killed, *1944*

Discovery of the rings of Uranus, *5107*

Homosexual civil rights law, *5383*

Latin American country with an environmental ministry, *2247*

Lightwave-based telecommunications system, *5886*

Magnetic resonance image of a human body, *3907*

Personal computer that was commercially successful, *1681*

Personal computer trade show, *1682*

Radio telescope in space, *5141*

Treaty banning the use of the weather as a weapon of war, *3181*

Video game designer of renown, *2578*

Woman jockey in the Grand National steeplechase, *5688*

1978

Ascent of Mount Everest without bottled oxygen, *5748*

Ironman triathlon, *5849*

Mass cult suicide in modern times, *1887*

Medicine produced using recombinant DNA, *3938*

Ocean-mapping satellite, *5291*

Peace treaty between an Arab nation and Israel, *3182*

Personal computer bulletin board, *1704*

Pope born in Poland, *4877*

Prime minister of Dominica, *2909*

Space traveler who was not of USSR or U.S. citizenship, *5549*

Test-tube baby, *2348*

Transatlantic balloon flight, *1410*

World Heritage List sites, *3198*

1979

Aircraft powered by human motion to cross the English Channel, *1331*

Artificial blood, *4102*

Bicyclist to go faster than 50 miles per hour, *5630*

Black tulip, *1057*

Cellular telephone system, *5946*

Compact disc players, *2032*

Country to limit births as national policy, *2372*

Dakar Rallye, *5723*

Direct election of the European Parliament, *2658*

Flat-screen pocket television, *2033*

Fundamentalist Islamic republic, *2700*

Human killed by a robot, *5035*

International agreement barring discrimination against women, *5376*

MUD (multi-user dominion), *1705*

Personal stereo cassette player, *2035*

Pope to visit a Communist country, *4878*

President of the European Parliament who was directly elected, *2841*

Prime minister of St. Vincent and the Grenadines, *2912*

Prime minister of the Islamic Republic of Iran, *2910*

Single-picture stereogram, *5319*

Trivia board game of international popularity, *2579*

Videodisc system that was commercially successful, *2034*

Woman to serve as prime minister of Great Britain, *2911*

1980

All-news television network, *4465*

Autonomous security robot, *5036*

Freshwater national park, *2261*

Horizontal oil drilling, *2112*

Human antibodies produced artificially, *3939*

International digital fax standard, *5880*

Large radio interferometer, *5142*

Mother-daughter Olympic medalists, *5786*

Museum of brass instruments, *4425*

Power plant using solar cells, *2070*

Prime minister of Zimbabwe, *2913*

Reduced Instruction Set Computer (RISC), *1683*

Road tunnel longer than 10 miles, *2195*

Ship with sailing wings, *5422*

Solar-powered airplane to cross the English Channel, *1332*

Solo ascent of Mount Everest, *5749*

Space traveler of African descent, *5550*

Total Internet crash, *1706*

1985—*continued*

Genetic fingerprinting method, *1758*
International space station, *5512*
Medical emergency in space, *5557*
Mountaineer to climb the highest peak on every continent, *5751*
Nation to put all its universities on the Internet, *2002*
Recording on audio CD to sell 1 million copies worldwide, *2054*
Registered Internet domain, *1711*

1986

Encyclopedia on CD-ROM, *1732*
Epidemic of mad cow disease, *1910*
Genetically engineered plants, *1058*
Hypertext computer application, *1733*
Man to climb all 14 of the world's tallest mountains, *5752*
Modern integrated pest management program in Asia, *1102*
Moon concrete, *2155*
Nicotine chewing gum, *4030*
Nobel Prize for Literature winner from Africa, *4537*
One Sky, One World international kite flying event, *1421*
Regional nuclear-free zone, *3140*
Round-the-world nonstop airplane flight without refueling, *1385*
Superconducting materials of ceramic oxide, *5352*
War lasting more than three centuries, *4194*

1987

Amorphous silicon solar cell, *2071*
Country with more than 1 billion people, *4608*
Digital Audio Tape (DAT), *2055*
International program to promote safe birth, *2352*
Murderer apprehended on DNA evidence alone, *1759*
Museum of art by women, *1832*
Nation to authorize patents on animals, *5171*
Nobel Prize in Physiology or Medicine winner from Asia, *4555*
Palm identification system, *1760*
Race for solar-powered vehicles, *5724*
Sumo champion not born in Japan, *5872*
Superconducting material that operated at temperatures above the boiling point of nitrogen, *5353*
Suspect cleared of a crime by DNA evidence, *1761*
Year in which the number of Internet hosts exceeded 10,000, *1712*
Year the world population exceeded 5 billion, *4609*

1988

Abortion pill, *2373*
Computer hacker to be convicted, *1713*
Cyber café, *1470*
Factoring of a 100-digit number, *3755*
Fiber-optic transoceanic cable, *5888*
Floating resort hotel, *1471*
Leader of a modern Muslim nation who was a woman, *2914*
Mag-Lev train, *3283*
Nobel Prize for Peace awarded to the United Nations Armed Forces, *4544*
Patent on an animal, *5172*
Plastic money, *2460*
Pocket videocassette recorder and television, *2038*
Rail tunnel longer than 50 kilometers, *2196*
Temperature of 100 million degrees Kelvin, *2122*
Underwater natural gas production station, *2113*
Widespread worm attack on the Internet, *1714*
Woman to climb Mount Everest solo without bottled oxygen, *5753*
World AIDS Day, *1911*

1989

Asian athlete to win a World Cup gold medal in track and field, *5844*
Commercial-scale thermal solar energy installations, *2072*
Country to legalize homosexual marriage, *5384*
Full-size stadium with retractable roof, *5607*
Fully computerized house, *1223*
Handheld video game, *2039*
Helicopter powered by human motion, *1429*
High school for space scientists, *1978*
Internet index, *1715*
Interspecies birth of a cat, *1121*
Jungle canopy walkway for tourists, *2249*
Old Master painting sold at auction for more than US$10 million, *1288*
Pipeline fire, *1959*
Speech-activated robot, *5039*
Woman to motorcycle from the United States to Tierra del Fuego, *3224*
World croquet championships, *5658*
World polo championships, *5801*
Year in which the number of Internet hosts exceeded 100,000, *1716*

1990

Big cats born by in vitro fertilization, *1122*
Coconut processing equipment, *1092*
Color fax machine, *5881*
Commercial provider of Internet dial-up access, *1717*
Commercial satellite telephone installation on an airplane, *5947*
Country to have more suburbanites than city and rural dwellers combined, *4610*

Death by suicide machine, *1888*

Deployment of the NATO rapid reaction force in a member country, *4195*

Expedition to cross Antarctica by dogsled and foot, *2330*

Free election in which Muslim fundamentalists obtained a majority, *2640*

Gene therapy, *4094*

Global hypermedia information system, *1718*

Global language, *3304*

Goldman Environmental Prizes, *2250*

Human stampede to cause massive loss of life, *1960*

Images taken from outside the solar system, *5579*

International Earth Day, *3043*

Law forbidding the freezing of humans for future resuscitation, *1884*

Orbiting observatory, *5144*

Patriarch of Moscow who was not Russian by birth, *4811*

Physical manipulation of individual atoms, *5354*

President of Communist Poland who was chosen in a free representative election, *2846*

President of independent Kazakhstan, *2847*

President of independent Lithuania, *2849*

President of Namibia, *2850*

Pyroelectric ear thermometer, *3879*

Ranking of countries by human development, *3199*

Shoe made from recycled materials, *1658*

Space probe in a polar trajectory around the sun, *5578*

Thermoplastic ceramics, *3653*

Transatlantic flight by an ultralight airplane, *1386*

Traverse of Antarctica on foot, *2331*

Veterinary chiropractic school, *3864*

Woman to become president of Nicaragua, *2848*

Woman to become president of the Republic of Ireland (Éire), *2851*

Year in which the total number of computers in the world exceeded 100,000,000, *1688*

1991

African–African American Summit, *3164*

Computer virus as a weapon of war, *6082*

Deliberate use of environmental warfare, *4196*

Democratically elected leader of Russia, *2854*

Destruction of an attacking missile by a defensive missile in combat, *4235*

Home-built supersonic jet, *1333*

Incumbent African president defeated in a democratic election, *2641*

Leader of independent Turkmenistan, *2860*

Muslim woman athlete to win a track and field world championship, *5845*

National railway hospital, *3898*

Ornithopter, *1334*

Photograph taken close-up of an asteroid in space, *5580*

Premier of France who was a woman, *2915*

President of Azerbaijan, *2856*

President of independent Georgia, *2853*

President of independent Slovenia, *2855*

President of independent Ukraine, *2861*

President of Kyrgyzstan, *2858*

President of Moldova, *2857*

President of Tajikistan, *2859*

President of Uzbekistan, *2852*

Radio-controlled wristwatch, *6038*

Re-enactment of a Viking voyage to the New World, *5469*

Register of international arms sales and transfers, *6083*

Sherpa expedition to Everest, *5754*

United Nations–sanctioned force sent uninvited to a sovereign country, *4197*

Watercraft to win the Dupont Water Prize, *5860*

1992

Aboriginal Australian performer to achieve international success, *4451*

Aye-aye born in captivity, *1124*

Catechism of the Catholic Church since the Renaissance, *4879*

Color videophone for home use, *5973*

Commercial vessel powered by magnetohydrodynamics, *5423*

Director of the World Evangelical Fellowship who was not from the West, *4844*

Earth Summit, *2251*

Ethnic violence in the former Soviet Empire, *4198*

Helsinki Human Rights Day, *3044*

Heptathlon two-time gold medalist, *5792*

Human chromosome gene-linkage maps, *5203*

Husband and wife to fly in space together, *5559*

International map of the world, *3625*

Library to possess 100 million items, *1823*

Meteorite captured on video, *5513*

Nation heavily polluted by nuclear waste, *2270*

Online, peer-reviewed journal, *4483*

Open Skies treaty, *3183*

Person to adopt a symbol as a name, *3484*

Philosophy café, *4570*

Pope to become a recording star, *4375*

Portable fuel cell, *2073*

Production automobile fueled by methanol, *3255*

Robotic brain surgeon, *4062*

Satellite-delivered digital video system for education, *1979*

Simultaneous space walk by three astronauts, *5558*

1992—*continued*

Team from outside the United States to win the World Series, *5616*

Transgenic bull, *1123*

Transplant of a baboon liver into a human being, *4076*

Wireless city, *5889*

Woman to become a professional hockey player, *5693*

Woman to become prime minister of Poland, *2916*

Woman to climb the highest peak on every continent, *5755*

Year in which the number of Internet hosts exceeded 1,000,000, *1719*

1993

Angler to hold world records for every billfish species, *5601*

Canadian prime minister who was a woman, *2917*

Commercial electric plant using poultry litter as fuel, *2074*

Condom designed to be worn by women, *2374*

Electronic light bulb, *2098*

Electronic memory using a single electron, *1690*

Feature film broadcast on the Internet, *4313*

Feature film released on CD-ROM, *4312*

Feynman Prize in Nanotechnology, *5355*

Free multiparty elections in the Arabian peninsula, *2642*

Global evangelical rally, *4845*

Green Cross organization, *2252*

Humor museum, *2231*

International Year of the World's Indigenous People, *3200*

Large mammal discovered since World War II, *1116*

Map of the human genome, *5204*

Mathematical proof of Fermat's last theorem, *3756*

National government to have a World Wide Web presence, *2634*

Peacekeeper to die in Somalia, *4199*

President of Eritrea, *2864*

President of independent Slovakia, *2863*

President of the Czech Republic, *2862*

Session of the United Nations Commission on Crime Prevention and Criminal Justice, *1796*

Supersonic airline co-pilot who was a woman, *1352*

Three-dimensional maps of subterranean rifts, *5292*

Tunneling machine that could turn 90 degrees, *2197*

Ultraviolet solid-state laser, *2023*

Ultraviolet (UV) radiation increase over a populated area, *2253*

Underwater personal computer, *1689*

United Nations manhunt, *1795*

1994

Aircraft powered solely by propfan engines, *1335*

Ambassador to Arctic aboriginal peoples, *3150*

Anglican women priests to be officially ordained, *4846*

Black African president of South Africa, *2865*

Catholic member of the British royal family since the 17th century, *4880*

Condemnation of anti-Semitism by the United Nations, *3201*

Electronic nose, *5306*

Elephant hospital, *1143*

Fossilized embryo of a carnivorous dinosaur to be discovered, *5216*

Free-trade region encompassing North America, *1552*

Fusion reactor to generate 10 megawatts of power, *2123*

High-definition digital videocassette recorder, *5969*

International conference of multimedia publishers, *1734*

Internet bank robber, *1807*

Law specifically permitting assisted suicide, *1889*

Multinational coordinated air strikes by NATO, *4236*

Murderer executed on DNA evidence, *1762*

NATO joint military exercises in a former Warsaw Pact nation, *4132*

Nonracial democratic elections in South Africa, *2643*

Offensive operation by NATO, *4200*

President of the Republic of Belarus, *2866*

Runner over the age of 40 to break the four-minute mile, *5846*

Saser, *2024*

Sexual harassment case at the United Nations, *5377*

Synagogue firebombing in Germany since World War II, *4981*

Underwater link between Great Britain and Europe, *2198*

Virtual financial services company, *2418*

Visit by an American president to a country on the U.S. list of terrorist states, *3131*

White lion born in the Western Hemisphere, *1125*

White witch doctor, *3977*

1995

All-woman America's Cup yacht-racing crew, *5861*

American to be launched into space aboard a Russian spacecraft, *5560*

City with more than 20 million inhabitants, *1572*

Comprehensive study of worldwide biodiversity, *2254*

Director-general of the World Trade Organization, *3202*

Discovery of a planet orbiting another star, *5109*

Earth-observing satellite that could see through clouds and darkness, *5592*

Electronic cash cards, *2461*

Encyclopedia of integer sequences, *3757*

Estonian Biennial, *1257*

Feature film that was entirely computer-animated, *4338*

Global treaty to regulate fishing on the high seas, *3126*

Gorilla born by in vitro fertilization, *1126*

Internet video conference between an aircraft and a ground location, *5974*

Mass-produced aluminum automobile, *3256*

Real-time car navigation system, *3257*

Robot to perform surgery, *5040*

Spacecraft launched by the United States to dock with a Russian space station, *5561*

Subsea gas pipeline in Asia, *2114*

Terrorist attack using military poison gas, *1802*

Thermoformed plastic condom, *2375*

Transpacific solo balloon flight, *1412*

Vaccine to be chemically synthesized, *3913*

Wave-powered electricity generator for commercial use, *2075*

Web ring, *1720*

World Dracula Congress, *3481*

Year more encyclopedias were distributed on CD-ROM than in print, *3389*

1996

African woman athlete to win the Olympic women's marathon, *5793*

Chief executive of Hong Kong, *3001*

Commercial cable system capable of carrying simultaneous TV, telephony, and high-speed data, *5890*

Continental nuclear-free zone, *3141*

Copyright law covering the Internet, *1721*

Court-ordered wiretap on a computer network, *1763*

Digital wireless cable television system, *5970*

Digitally drawn currency note, *2462*

Disk drive to store 1 billion bits of data per square inch, *1691*

Electric car to be mass-produced, *3258*

Heads of state to meet in an on-line chat session, *3165*

Hong Kong athlete to win a gold medal at the Olympic Games, *5794*

Human action to affect the earth's planetary motion, *2255*

International Festival of the Sea, *3045*

International pipe organ festival, *4426*

Joint peacetime military exercises between Brazil and Argentina, *4133*

List of the world's most endangered historical sites, *2256*

Mammal cloned from adult cells, *5187*

Mammals born from an egg grown in vitro, *5173*

National constitution to specifically protect the rights of homosexuals, *5385*

Nemean Games in modern times, *5699*

Olympics to have an official World Wide Web site, *5795*

Personal portable phone capable of making a call from anywhere in the world, *5948*

Photograph of the surface of Pluto, *5581*

Portable velodrome of Olympic size, *5608*

President of the Palestinian Authority, *2867*

Reparations for forced prostitution, *1779*

Runner to win both the 200-meter and the 400-meter races at the same Olympic games, *5797*

Sahara Cup cricket contest, *5656*

Three-dimensional display screen, *2025*

War criminals indicted for rape, *1778*

Watch that told time in Catalan, *6039*

Winner of the Prix d'Amérique who was a woman, *5689*

Woman astronaut to live in a space station, *5562*

Woman bullfighter of renown in Europe, *5653*

Woman to become president of the Parliamentary Assembly of the Council of Europe, *2659*

Women's Olympic volleyball event, *5796*

Women's shelter in Central Africa, *5378*

World chess champion defeated by a computer, *2601*

1997

Acapulco Black Film Festival, *4345*

Accurate recreation of the last flight of Amelia Earhart, *1387*

Boston Marathon in which both champions were African athletes, *5847*

Captive-bred lemurs returned to Madagascar, *1128*

Car to break the sound barrier, *5725*

Cashless community in which electronic cash cards replaced bills and coins, *2463*

Civilian spy satellite, *5593*

Cloning of a primate from an embryo, *5189*

Commercial ship to sail from China to Taiwan, *1553*

Complete DNA sequencing of a free-living organism, *5205*

Comprehensive digital atlas of the human body, *3908*

Cross-breeding of a llama with a camel, *1127*

Discovery of antimatter in space, *5110*

Transatlantic crossing by an robot airplane, *1388*

Tribal state in Canada with self-government, *2701*

Virtual autopsies, *3865*

Virtual-reality reconstruction of a crime scene, *1764*

Visit made by South Korean tourists to North Korea, *3132*

Woman fighter pilot to fire a missile in combat, *4237*

Woman to become president of Switzerland, *2868*

World's fair with a marine theme, *2232*

1999

Airplane equipped with its own parachute, *1438*

Black chess player to become a grandmaster, *2602*

British jury to consider evidence overseas, *1740*

Businessman worth US$100 billion, *1448*

China–USA undersea telecommunications cable, *5893*

Computerized robot to grade essays on a standardized test, *1980*

Day on which the Dow Jones industrial average broke 10,000 points, *2434*

Day on which the Dow Jones industrial average broke 11,000 points, *2435*

Digital projection of a major motion picture, *4317*

Eastern European country to elect a woman as president, *2869*

Family car with its own video entertainment system, *3260*

Feature film to premiere simultaneously in a theater and on the Internet, *4315*

Former Warsaw Pact nations to join NATO, *3143*

Fuel cell car, *3262*

Gamma-ray burster visible live, *5114*

Illuminated Bible manuscript from the modern era, *4894*

International meetings of ministers in Antarctica, *3166*

Internet university to receive accreditation, *2003*

Language to have its entire literature available on computer, *3306*

Major motion picture to be produced and exhibited entirely with digital technology, *4318*

Movie to make more than US$100 million in 5 days, *4316*

Nonstop circumnavigation of the world by balloon, *1413*

Ocean platform for rocket launching, *5516*

Performer in a foreign language film to win the Academy Award for Best Actor, *4323*

Pope to visit a mainly Christian Orthodox country, *4812*

Premier of Nunavat, *2918*

Production car with a night-vision system, *3261*

Professorship dedicated to the search for extra-terrestrial life, *5115*

Scented suits, *1639*

Serving leader of a sovereign nation indicted for war crimes by an international tribunal, *1783*

Sikh international convention, *5012*

Solar service stations for electric vehicles, *2076*

Solar system with multiple planets to be discovered, *5116*

Space mission headed by women, *5517*

Three-dimensional computer model of an Old Master sculpture, *1304*

Three-dimensional map of Mars, *3627*

Unified currency in Europe, *2464*

Woman to command a space mission, *5566*

Writing by brain wave, *3325*

Year the world population exceeded 6 billion, *4611*

2000

Country to officially celebrate the year 2000, *3047*

Country whose rail system was completely electrified, *3284*

Dam higher than 1,000 feet, *2160*

Japan–USA undersea cable network, *5894*

2001

Building more than 1,500 feet in height, *1230*

Index by Days

Following is a chronological listing of entries, arranged by month and day. (Many entries are identified only by year.) To find an entry in the main body of the text, please search for the italicized number.

January 7

1714 Typewriter patent, *3585*
1785 Balloon flight over open water, *1399*
Letter sent by airmail, *4679*
1876 Skating rink, *5806*
1914 Steamboat to pass through the Panama Canal, *5459*
1927 Transatlantic commercial telephone service, *5937*
1929 Comic strip with an adventure hero, *4471*

January 8

1656 Commercial newspaper in continuous publication, *4495*
1889 Electric tabulating machine, *1663*
1912 Modern political party for Africans, *2666*
1927 London to Delhi scheduled aircraft flight, *1363*

January 9

1839 Photographic process that was practical, *4577*
1894 Movie to be copyrighted, *4280*
1953 Ferry to sink with large loss of life, *1941*

January 10

1863 Subway, *3285*
1946 Radar signal to the moon, *5518*

January 11

1569 National lottery, *2607*
1935 Transpacific solo airplane flight by a woman, *1374*

January 13

1501 Protestant hymnbook, *4813*
1924 Photography booth, *4572*
1928 International television transmission, *5952*
1942 Ejection seat, *1323*
1976 Voice reader, *3303*

January 14

1639 Constitution in the New World, *2645*
1958 Round-the-world airline service, *1348*
1994 Catholic member of the British royal family since the 17th century, *4880*

January 15

1892 Rules for basketball, *5618*
1967 Super Bowl football game, *5662*

January 16

1957 Round-the-world nonstop flight by a jet airplane, *1384*

1969 Docking of two manned spacecraft, *5544*

January 17

1949 Synchrotron, *5347*
1996 Heads of state to meet in an on-line chat session, *3165*

January 18

64 Papal throne, *3082*
1871 Kaiser of a united German Reich, *2967*
1991 Destruction of an attacking missile by a defensive missile in combat, *4235*

January 19

1903 Transoceanic radio broadcast, *5902*

January 20

1969 Transatlantic solo trip by rowboat, *5466*
1996 President of the Palestinian Authority, *2867*
Woman to become president of the Parliamentary Assembly of the Council of Europe, *2659*

January 21

1525 Anabaptist church, *4819*
1970 Jumbo jet, *1329*
1976 Supersonic airliner to enter regular service, *1350*

January 22

1876 Crematorium, *1882*

January 23

1849 Woman physician in modern times to earn a degree from a medical school, *3969*
1909 Radio distress call from a ship at sea, *5418*
1960 Dive to the bottom of the ocean, *5453*
1964 Transplant of an animal organ into a human being, *4070*
1999 Gamma-ray burster visible live, *5114*

January 24

1556 Earthquake to cause massive loss of life, *1916*

January 25

1905 Star of Africa, *3678*

February 11

1899 Person killed in a motorcycle accident, *1895*

February 12

1818 Leader of independent Chile, *2991*
1898 Driver fatally injured in an automobile accident, *1894*
1961 Explorer to set foot on both the North and South Poles, *2328*
1990 Traverse of Antarctica on foot, *2331*

February 14

269 St. Valentine's Day, *3018*
1946 General-purpose computer that was fully electronic, *1669*
1990 Images taken from outside the solar system, *5579*

February 15

1113 Crusading order of knights, *4795*
1954 Free-moving deep-sea submersible, *5452*
1997 Open international telecommunications agreement, *5891*

February 16

1937 Synthetic fiber produced entirely from chemicals, *3724*
1960 Circumnavigation of the earth by a submerged submarine, *5464*
1982 Woman to become president of Malta, *2844*

February 17

1600 Scientist executed by the Catholic Church, *4870*
1931 Closed-circuit sporting event, *5957*

February 18

1911 Airmail flight by airplane, *4680*
1920 Swimsuit beauty contest, *2200*
1930 Planet found beyond Neptune, *5097*
1978 Ironman triathlon, *5849*

February 19

1878 Phonograph, *2041*

February 20

1994 Runner over the age of 40 to break the four-minute mile, *5846*

February 21

1866 Woman dentist with a degree from a dental school, *3814*

1947 Instant camera, *4587*
1995 Transpacific solo balloon flight, *1412*

February 23

1905 Service club, *1839*

February 24

1835 Magazine in a Native American language, *4480*
1943 Refugee ship disaster, *1937*
1949 Rocket to reach outer space, *5507*

February 25

1899 Passenger fatally injured in an automobile accident, *1896*
1990 Woman to become president of Nicaragua, *2848*

February 26

1870 Pneumatic subway, *3286*
1949 Round-the-world nonstop flight by an airplane, *1379*
1955 Pilot to bail out of an airplane flying at supersonic speed, *1437*

February 27

425 University in the Western world, *1983*

February 28

1994 Offensive operation by NATO, *4200*

February 29

1504 Explorer saved by an eclipse, *2287*

March

1332 Metal cannon, *6098*
1493 Eyewitness report to become a bestseller, *4453*
1536 Journey across North America, *2290*
1679 Treatise on binary mathematics, *3747*
1685 Code for the treatment of slaves in European colonies, *5486*
1847 Leader of independent Guatemala, *2995*
1918 Regular civil airmail service, *4683*
1942 Patient to be given penicillin, *3936*
1957 Prime minister of Ghana, *2890*
1959 Major-league American baseball teams to play in Communist Cuba, *5615*
1983 Identification of the AIDS virus, *3849*
1984 Magazine to put a hologram on its cover, *4482*

March 16—*continued*

Docking of two spacecraft, *5540*

1999 Day on which the Dow Jones industrial average broke 10,000 points, *2434*

March 17

1958 Satellite powered by photovoltaic cells, *5585*

1999 Fuel cell car, *3262*

March 18

1895 Bus with an internal-combustion engine, *3218*

1906 Launch of a heavier-than-air machine entirely under its own power, *1356*

1925 Tornado to cause more than 500 deaths, *1927*

1931 Electric shaver, *2755*

1965 Space walk, *5537*

1967 Oil spill from a commercial tanker, *2269*

March 20

1686 Pope to condemn the African slave trade, *5487*

1899 Woman to die in the electric chair, *1746*

1998 National Internet holiday, *3046*

March 21

1617 Native American to be buried in Europe, *1878*

1952 Rock concert, *4444*

1985 Circumnavigation by wheelchair, *5854*

1990 President of Namibia, *2850*

1999 Nonstop circumnavigation of the world by balloon, *1413*

Performer in a foreign language film to win the Academy Award for Best Actor, *4323*

March 22

1907 Nonviolent act of civil disobedience of international significance, *3155*

1945 Political association of Arab states, *3134*

March 23

1841 Photography studio in Europe open to the public, *4591*

1966 Meeting of the heads of the Anglican and Catholic churches, *4805*

March 24

1843 Air transport company, *1336*

1896 Radio inventor, *5896*

1934 Front-wheel-drive car, *3240*

1992 Open Skies treaty, *3183*

1994 White lion born in the Western Hemisphere, *1125*

1996 Woman astronaut to live in a space station, *5562*

March 25

1436 Renaissance architect of importance, *1186*

1993 Supersonic airline co-pilot who was a woman, *1352*

1994 Synagogue firebombing in Germany since World War II, *4981*

March 27

1855 Kerosene, *2104*

1914 Chemical anticoagulant, *3932*

1977 Aviation disaster in which more than 500 people were killed, *1944*

1999 Ocean platform for rocket launching, *5516*

March 30

1858 Pencil with an attached eraser, *3589*

March 31

1912 Aviator wounded in combat by ground fire, *4207*

1998 Stellarator, *2124*

April

1336 Account of mountain climbing, *5726*

1818 Bicycle, *5620*

1828 European explorer to visit Timbuktu, *2297*

1836 Investigative reporter, *4457*

1841 Modern detective story, *3451*

1877 Telephone for domestic use, *5934*

1896 Olympic Games in the modern era, *5760*

Olympic marathon in modern times, *5761*

1914 Use of aircraft carriers in war, *4259*

1919 President of independent Estonia, *2800*

1923 Troop movement by airplane, *4216*

1925 Movie shown on an airplane, *4299*

1927 Apparatus used to treat respiratory failure, *4088*

1932 Artificial transmutation of an element, *5340*

1936 Single-lens reflex (SLR) 35-millimeter camera, *4586*

1966 Desktop fax machine, *5878*

1968 Book set into type completely by electronic composition, *3365*

May 10

1930 Planetarium in the Western Hemisphere, *5130*
1933 Nazi book burning, *3364*
1940 Glider assault, *4220*
Paratrooper assault on a fortified area, *4221*
Shaped charge used in war, *6093*
1994 Black African president of South Africa, *2865*

May 11

1610 European buried in the Imperial City, *4871*
1867 King of Luxembourg, *2966*

May 12

1857 Women's hospital staffed by women physicians, *3895*
1926 Flight over the North Pole, *2321*
1969 Transpacific sailboat crossing by a woman, *5468*

May 13

1607 Permanent English settlement in America, *4659*
Tobacco cultivation by a European, *1066*
1830 President of Ecuador, *2784*
1887 Dictation device, *2042*
1906 Woman appointed to the faculty of a French university, *1998*
1960 Ascent of Dhaulagiri, *5745*
1998 Deep underground nuclear waste storage site, *2257*

May 14

1874 International rugby game, *5803*
1948 Prime minister of Israel, *2888*
1955 Signatories of the Warsaw Pact, *3172*

May 15

1911 Double feature, *4289*
1955 Ascent of Makalu, *5741*
1991 Premier of France who was a woman, *2915*

May 16

1865 Fax system for commercial use, *5874*
1882 Flip book, *4325*
1888 Phonograph record, *2043*
1975 Woman to reach the summit of Mount Everest, *5747*

May 17

1861 Economy package tour, *2235*

1875 Kentucky Derby, *5686*
1985 Recording on audio CD to sell 1 million copies worldwide, *2054*

May 18

1631 Free election in North America, *2635*
1914 Regular airmail service, *4681*
1952 Transatlantic solo boat journey by a woman, *5461*
1953 Woman to fly faster than the speed of sound, *1382*
1956 Ascent of Lhotse, *5744*
1977 Treaty banning the use of the weather as a weapon of war, *3181*

May 19

1909 Ballets Russes, *1862*
1998 Rock concert on Mount Everest, *4452*

May 20

1498 Direct sea voyage from Western Europe to Asia, *2285*
1927 Transatlantic solo airplane flight, *1364*
1932 Transatlantic solo airplane flight by a woman, *1370*
1939 Transatlantic airmail service, *4687*
1941 Major airborne assault, *4224*
1998 Impending volcanic eruption detected from space, *5293*

May 21

1993 President of Eritrea, *2864*

May 22

1968 Warship to sink with nuclear weapons aboard, *1943*
1993 Feature film broadcast on the Internet, *4313*

May 23

1785 Bifocal eyeglasses, *4108*
1924 Dogsled crossing of the Northwest Passage, *2320*
1999 Movie to make more than US$100 million in 5 days, *4316*

May 24

1844 Commercial telegraph service, *5923*
1964 Soccer (association football) disaster, *1956*
1976 Supersonic jet service across the Atlantic Ocean, *1351*

May 25

1829 Typewritten letter, *3324*

June 3—*continued*

1998 AIDS vaccine tested internationally, *3914*

June 4

1783 Hot-air balloon that was successful, *1391*

1784 Woman to ascend in an untethered balloon, *1398*

1990 Death by suicide machine, *1888*

1998 Solo crossing of the Gulf of Mexico in a paddled boat, *5470*

June 5

1959 Prime minister of Singapore, *2893*

1981 Test-tube twins, *2349*

June 6

1846 Army newspaper, *4504*

1933 Drive-in movie theater, *4359*

1944 Allied soldier killed in combat on D-Day, *4188*

1954 Europe-wide television programming, *5963*

June 7

1494 Treaty in which the entire world was partitioned, *3167*

1887 Machine capable of casting individual letters of type, *4723*

1890 Comic strip in a magazine, *4467*

1939 British monarchs to visit the United States, *2976*

1965 Home video tape recorder, *2027*

1979 Direct election of the European Parliament, *2658*

1980 Power plant using solar cells, *2070*

1981 Destruction of a nuclear reactor as an act of war, *4193*

1990 Patriarch of Moscow who was not Russian by birth, *4811*

June 8

1900 Films synchronized with speech, *4286*

1928 Flight from the United States to Australia, *1366*

1940 Aircraft carrier to be sunk by surface ships, *4270*

Element heavier than uranium, *5245*

1964 Child whose parents had both flown in space, *2393*

1983 Test-tube triplets, *2350*

June 9

1803 Circumnavigation of Australia, *2309*

1923 Autogiro, *1423*

1931 Breathing apparatus for submarine escape, *5451*

1975 Live broadcast from the British Parliament, *2657*

June 10

1809 Steamboat to make an ocean voyage, *5454*

1822 Seagoing iron-hulled vessel, *5412*

1935 Self-help program for substance abusers, *4027*

1943 Ballpoint pen widely used, *3596*

1966 Reversed sounds, *4447*

June 11

1509 Wife of Henry VIII of England, *2955*

1895 Automobile race, *5709*

1909 SOS signal sent in an emergency, *5904*

1922 Transatlantic radio fax transmission of a photograph, *5876*

1928 Rocket-propelled airplane, *1318*

1930 Deep-sea exploration vessel, *5283*

1963 Self-immolation by a Buddhist monk, *1886*

June 12

1897 Swiss Army knife, *6059*

1913 Animation made by the cel process, *4328*

1979 Aircraft powered by human motion to cross the English Channel, *1331*

June 13

1874 Tempered glass manufacturing process, *3651*

1893 Women's golf tournament, *5668*

1944 Cruise missile used in war, *6135*

1971 Nonuplets, *2347*

June 14

1777 National flag, *2709*

1919 Nonstop transatlantic airplane flight, *1361*

1942 Handheld rocket launcher, *6133*

1951 Electronic computer for commercial use, *1671*

1983 Spacecraft to leave the solar system, *5577*

June 15

1219 Flag of a people, *2708*

1844 Vulcanized rubber, *1488*

1869 Synthetic plastic that was widely used in industry, *1490*

June 30—*continued*
1948 Transistor, *2016*
1980 Woman to become president of a nation in a democratic election, *2842*

July

1518 Printed cryptology book, *3402*
1521 Running of the bulls, *5649*
1525 New Testament printed in English, *4887*
1709 Women's magazine edited by a woman, *4477*
1775 Circumnavigation of the world from west to east, *2308*
1834 Direct-current electric motor, *2169*
1870 Modern war won through superior military intelligence, *4140*
1881 Carnegie library, *1820*
1892 Crime solved using fingerprints, *1753*
1897 Wireless radio manufacturing company, *5898*
1905 Synthetic fiber suitable for making cloth, *3723*
1934 International oil pipeline, *2108*
1943 Chaff to jam radar, *4227*
1957 International conference of atomic scientists, *5350*
1960 Prime minister who was a woman, *2895*
1962 President of Rwanda, *2828*
1964 International Ballet Competition, *1864*
1967 Caribana Festival, *3042*
1970 Packet radio network, *5917*
1976 Boycotts of the Olympic Games, *5784*
     Gymnast to achieve a perfect score in the Olympic Games, *5785*
1977 Radio telescope in space, *5141*
1979 President of the European Parliament who was directly elected, *2841*
1981 IBM-compatible personal computer, *1685*
1992 Transplant of a baboon liver into a human being, *4076*
1995 Electronic cash cards, *2461*
1996 Mammal cloned from adult cells, *5187*
1997 Isolation of human embryonic stem cells, *5174*
     Teraflop computer, *1692*
1998 Lamb with human genes, *5207*

July 1

1868 Canada Day (Dominion Day), *3034*
1881 International commercial telephone service, *5935*
1907 Modern air force, *4130*
1916 Battle with more than 1 million casualties, *4180*

1968 Nonproliferation treaty for weapons of mass destruction, *3179*
1974 Woman to become president of a nation, *2836*
1979 Personal stereo cassette player, *2035*

July 2

1900 Dirigible that was commercially and militarily successful, *1404*
     Zeppelin flight, *1405*
1943 Revolt by prisoners at a Nazi death camp, *1773*
1990 Human stampede to cause massive loss of life, *1960*

July 3

1667 Peace treaty among European powers to arbitrate world trade, *3168*
1866 Battle decided by the use of breech-loading infantry rifles, *4176*
1913 Transatlantic crossing by a bird, *1114*
1953 Ascent of Nanga Parbat (Diamir), *5738*
1971 Radiation surgery, *4060*
1977 Magnetic resonance image of a human body, *3907*

July 4

1054 Observation of a supernova, *5073*
1776 Independent nation in the New World, *2692*
1874 Steel bridge, *2144*
1937 Woman helicopter pilot, *1424*
1946 President of the Philippines, *2807*

July 5

1791 British ambassador to the United States, *3145*
1865 Railway speed limit, *3273*
1975 President of independent Cape Verde, *2840*

July 6

1885 Rabies vaccine, *3911*
1915 Sound recordings used to transmit coded messages in wartime, *4141*
1919 Transatlantic dirigible flight, *1406*
1944 Circus fire with large loss of life, *1952*
1966 Prime minister of Malawi, *2905*
1997 Robot to conduct a roving exploration of the surface of another planet, *5582*

July 7

1960 Working laser, *2020*

July 24

1824 Public opinion poll, *2633*
1946 Atomic bomb explosion underwater, *6124*

July 25

1909 Airplane flight over the ocean, *1357*
1978 Test-tube baby, *2348*

July 26

1941 International oil embargo, *3129*
1963 Geosynchronous satellite, *5588*

July 27

1909 Military aircraft, *4203*
1944 Jet fighter, *4229*

July 28

1862 European explorer to find the source of the White Nile, *2300*
1885 Vending machine in modern times, *1516*
1946 Ban-the-bomb demonstrations, *6125*

July 29

1952 Transpacific nonstop jet airplane flight, *1381*
1980 Human antibodies produced artificially, *3939*
1984 Women's cycling event, *5791*

July 30

1852 Tramp steamer, *5426*
1930 World Cup soccer championship, *5816*
1943 Ejection seat that was propelled by explosives, *1324*

July 31

1910 Criminal caught by radio, *1755*
1954 Ascent of K2 (Mount Godwin Austen), *5739*
1971 Astronauts to ride a vehicle on the moon, *5528*
1973 Multinational space agency, *5510*

August

1777 Mine barrage, *6086*
1864 International agreements on the humane treatment of soldiers and civilians in wartime, *3170*
1897 World Zionist Congress, *2665*
1923 Planetarium of the modern type, *5129*
1941 Plastic car, *3242*

1957 Prime minister of Malaysia, *2891*
1960 Plastic bags, *3118*
President of independent Niger, *2820*
1963 Supercomputer, *1672*
1971 Sheikh of independent Bahrain, *2982*
1990 Transatlantic flight by an ultralight airplane, *1386*
1991 President of Azerbaijan, *2856*
1995 Wave-powered electricity generator for commercial use, *2075*
1998 Virtual-reality reconstruction of a crime scene, *1764*

August 1

1861 Iron-hulled warship, *4254*
1992 Helsinki Human Rights Day, *3044*

August 2

1622 Newspaper in England that was successful, *4492*
1917 Landing of a plane on a ship under way, *4262*
1991 Re-enactment of a Viking voyage to the New World, *5469*
1996 Runner to win both the 200-meter and the 400-meter races at the same Olympic games, *5797*

August 3

1492 Expedition of Christopher Columbus, *2281*
Letter containing a description of America, *2282*
1943 Firestorm, *1951*
1958 Crossing of the North Pole underwater by a submerged submarine, *5463*

August 4

1496 Permanent European settlement in the New World, *4648*
1956 Nuclear reactor in Asia, *2118*
1983 President of Burkina Faso, *2845*
1995 Global treaty to regulate fishing on the high seas, *3126*

August 5

1498 European explorer to land on the South American continent, *2286*
1858 Transatlantic telegraph cable, *5926*
1914 Traffic lights, *1590*
1926 Movie accompanied by prerecorded sound to be released as a feature film, *4300*
1963 Nuclear arms–control treaty, *3176*
1982 Solo helicopter voyage around the world, *1428*

August 6

1890	Electric chair, *1745*
1926	Woman to swim the English Channel, *5822*
1932	Annual film festival, *4340*
1945	Atomic bomb explosion over enemy territory, *4232*

August 7

1588	Marine disaster costing more than 10,000 lives, *1930*

August 8

1709	Hot-air balloon, *1390*
1786	Ascent of Mont Blanc, *5728*
1945	Definition of rape as a crime against humanity, *1775*

August 9

1859	Escalator, *1206*
1884	Dirigible, *1402*

August 10

1512	Naval battle fought with cannon broadsides, *4245*
1896	Hang-glider fatality, *1893*

August 11

1645	Publication in English printed in the American colonies, *3425*
1907	Rally race, *5718*
1960	President of the Republic of Chad, *2821*

August 12

1860	Breech-loading artillery, *6112*
1865	Antiseptic surgery, *4049*
1953	Hydrogen bomb detonated by a country other than the United States, *6130*
1960	Communications satellite, *5884*
1962	Two manned craft in space simultaneously, *5534*
1982	Terrorist bomb attack on an airplane, *1801*

August 13

1521	Conquistador, *4653*
1960	President of the Central African Republic, *2822*
1998	Bureaucrat in space, *5564*

August 14

1457	Book printed in color, *3350*

1959	Colophon in a printed book, *3351*
	Telecast from space showing the earth, *5509*

August 15

1456	Printed edition of the Bible, *4885*
1888	Alpine skier, *5808*
1916	Self-propelled tank, *6121*
1947	Prime minister of India, *2884*
	Prime minister of Pakistan, *2885*
1948	President of South Korea, *2808*
1962	Containership facility, *1551*

August 16

1858	Transatlantic telegraph messages, *5927*
1960	Leader of independent Cyprus, *2999*

August 17

1895	Pedestrian killed by an automobile, *1892*
1975	Surface ship to reach the North Pole, *2329*
1978	Transatlantic balloon flight, *1410*

August 18

1932	Transatlantic westbound solo nonstop flight, *1371*
1998	Heart surgery broadcast on the Internet, *4063*

August 19

1942	Battle with more than 2 million deaths, *4187*
1960	Living creatures launched into orbit who returned safely to earth, *5532*
1998	Open-heart surgery streamed live on the World Wide Web, *4064*

August 20

1911	Telegraph message sent around the world by commercial telegraph, *5929*
1930	Demonstration of home reception of television, *5956*
1964	International satellite consortium, *5589*
1971	Electronic pocket calculator, *2030*
1982	Third World country to default on its foreign debt, *2417*

August 21

1944	Meeting to establish the United Nations, *3187*
1998	Transatlantic crossing by an robot airplane, *1388*

August 22

1848   European legislator of African descent, *2652*
1849   Aerial bombardment of a city, *4202*
1851   International yacht race, *5855*
1939   Aerosol spray can, *6061*

August 23

476   King of Italy, *2924*
1977   Aircraft powered by human motion, *1330*

August 24

79   Volcanic eruption, *1914*
     Window glass, *3642*
1875   Man to swim the English Channel, *5820*
1911   President of the Republic of Portugal, *2794*
1949   Peacetime alliance of European and North American nations, *3137*
1981   Digital still camera, *4588*
1998   Cyborg, *5041*

August 25

1919   London to Paris scheduled passenger airplane service, *1339*

August 26

1884   Linotype machine, *4722*

August 27

1783   Hydrogen balloon, *1392*
1859   Oil well, *2105*
1928   Antiwar treaty, *3171*
1939   Turbojet aircraft, *1321*
1991   President of Moldova, *2857*

August 28

1910   King of independent Montenegro, *2970*
1982   Gay Games, *5698*

August 29

1949   Remote detection of a nuclear weapons test, *6127*

August 30

1617   Catholic saint from the New World, *4872*
1914   Aerial bombardment of a city by airplane, *4209*

August 31

1935   Television announcer who was a woman, *5958*

1939   Attack of World War II, *4184*
1991   President of Kyrgyzstan, *2858*

September

1674   Microscopic observation of protozoa, bacteria, and human cells, *5146*
1836   Traveling van for horses, *5684*
1839   Railway hotels, *1467*
1854   Epidemic map, *3624*
1894   Antitoxin laboratory operated by a public health department, *4013*
1897   Used-car dealership, *1517*
1898   Diesel engine built for commercial service, *2179*
1938   Toothbrush with synthetic bristles, *2761*
1957   Laser, *2017*
1959   Helical-scan video tape recorder, *5965*
1961   Hatchback automobile, *3245*
1968   Spacecraft to return from lunar orbit, *5523*
1969   Prime minister of Libya, *2906*
1980   Space traveler of African descent, *5550*
1988   Computer hacker to be convicted, *1713*
     Underwater natural gas production station, *2113*
1992   Robotic brain surgeon, *4062*
     Woman to become a professional hockey player, *5693*
1994   NATO joint military exercises in a former Warsaw Pact nation, *4132*
1996   Sahara Cup cricket contest, *5656*
1997   Cashless community in which electronic cash cards replaced bills and coins, *2463*
     International Conservative Congress, *2669*
1998   Rock opera, *4438*

September 1

1913   Aerobats, *1314*
1919   Intercontinental passenger service, *1340*
1928   King of Albania, *2973*
1939   Naval shot of World War II, *4266*
     Shot of World War II, *4185*

September 3

1895   Professional football game, *5660*
1930   Paris to New York nonstop airplane flight, *1368*
1939   Civilian ship sunk in World War II, *4267*
     Declaration of war in World War II, *4186*
1998   Genocide conviction by an international court, *1782*

September 25

1513 European explorers to see the Pacific Ocean, *2289*
1690 Newspaper published in the British colonies in America, *4496*
1877 Centrifugal cream separator, *2512*
1956 Transatlantic telephone call using the transoceanic cable, *5943*

September 26

1580 Sea captain to circumnavigate the world, *2306*

September 27

1825 Steam locomotive passenger service, *3266*
1892 Matchbooks, *3109*
1912 Composer of jazz music, *4376*
1962 President and prime minister of the Yemen Arab Republic (North Yemen), *2829*

September 28

1864 International Communist labor organization, *1505*
1869 Hydroelectric generator, *2084*

September 29

1957 Nuclear waste disaster to cause large loss of life, *1955*

September 30

1929 Manned rocket-plane flight, *1367*

October

1187 Statement of the principle of medical neutrality in wartime, *3127*
1283 Drawing and quartering, *1741*
1863 Prime minister of independent Romania, *2875*
1870 Typewriter to be marketed, *3591*
1892 Gym suit for girls, *1632*
1902 Daily shipboard newspaper, *4509*
1926 Movie showing another planet, *5095*
1939 Electronic digital calculator, *1665*
     National euthanasia program, *1771*
1954 Transistor radio receiver to be mass-produced, *5913*
1962 Beatles recording to become a hit, *4446*
1972 Computer-to-computer conversation in English, *1697*
     International networking conference, *1698*
1982 Camcorder, *2036*
1988 Temperature of 100 million degrees Kelvin, *2122*

1992 Ethnic violence in the former Soviet Empire, *4198*
     Human chromosome gene-linkage maps, *5203*
     Team from outside the United States to win the World Series, *5616*
1993 Global evangelical rally, *4845*
1996 International pipe organ festival, *4426*
     Joint peacetime military exercises between Brazil and Argentina, *4133*
1997 Non-NATO ally of the United States in the Western Hemisphere, *3142*
1998 Space probe with ion-drive engine, *5514*
     Thought control of a computer, *1735*
     Virtual autopsies, *3865*

October 1

1869 Prepaid postcards, *4674*
1946 War criminals convicted of crimes against humanity, *1776*
1964 Bullet train line, *3282*

October 2

1608 Telescope, *5132*
1956 Clock to operate by nuclear power, *6031*
1965 Transatlantic undersea radio conversation, *5916*

October 3

1932 King of independent Iraq, *2975*
1942 Ballistic missile test flight, *6134*

October 4

1582 Calendar adopted worldwide, *6007*
1881 Centrifugal cream separator with a continuous flow, *2513*
1957 Artificial satellite, *5584*
     Major radio telescope, *5138*
1958 Transoceanic jetliner service, *1349*

October 5

1793 National revolutionary calendar, *6009*
1852 Beehive with removable frames, *1086*
1883 Orient Express service, *3277*
1908 King of modern Bulgaria, *2969*
1914 Airplane pilots killed in combat, *4210*
1931 Transpacific nonstop airplane flight, *1369*
1948 Musique concrète, *4395*
1959 Photographs of the dark side of the moon, *5520*
1974 Round-the-world journey on foot, *5852*

October 27

1980 Total Internet crash, *1706*
1991 Leader of independent Turkmenistan, *2860*
Watercraft to win the Dupont Water Prize, *5860*
1994 Visit by an American president to a country on the U.S. list of terrorist states, *3131*

October 29

1465 Typeface made in Europe in a non-Roman alphabet, *4705*
1991 Photograph taken close-up of an asteroid in space, *5580*

October 30

1869 Letterpress halftone reproduction of a photograph, *4719*
1888 Ballpoint pen, *3593*

October 31

1952 Hydrogen bomb, *6129*
1956 Airplane flight to land at the South Pole, *2327*
Country to attempt to withdraw from the Warsaw Pact, *3173*

October 3l

1994 Ambassador to Arctic aboriginal peoples, *3150*

November

1492 Europeans to smoke tobacco, *4022*
1869 Bicycle road race, *5625*
1888 Railway in China, *3278*
1897 Permanent wireless installation, *5899*
1905 Genocide in the 20th century, *1768*
1952 Flat horse race in North America, *5687*
1956 Olympic Games in the Southern Hemisphere, *5777*
1958 Nuclear weapons test moratorium, *3174*
1974 Representative of a nongovernmental organization to address a plenary session of the United Nations General Assembly, *3197*
1987 Race for solar-powered vehicles, *5724*
1990 Global hypermedia information system, *1718*
Woman to become president of the Republic of Ireland (Éire), *2851*
1995 Comprehensive study of worldwide biodiversity, *2254*
1997 Captive-bred lemurs returned to Madagascar, *1128*

1998 Visit made by South Korean tourists to North Korea, *3132*

November 1

837 Halloween, *3025*
1772 Modern chemist, *5225*
1848 Medical school for women, *3860*
1894 Music by indigenous American peoples to be recorded, *4373*
1911 Bombing raid from an aircraft, *4206*

November 2

1929 Newsreel theater, *4357*
1936 Regular broadcast high-definition television service, *5959*
1988 Widespread worm attack on the Internet, *1714*

November 3

1840 Dental college, *3859*
1957 Living creature launched into orbit, *5530*
1978 Prime minister of Dominica, *2909*
1982 Traffic accident in which more than 2,000 people were killed, *1945*

November 4

1862 Rapid-fire machine gun, *6113*
1994 Fossilized embryo of a carnivorous dinosaur to be discovered, *5216*
1995 Earth-observing satellite that could see through clouds and darkness, *5592*

November 5

1605 Guy Fawkes Day, *3030*

November 6

1917 Communist revolution, *2673*
1945 Jet-propelled landing on an aircraft carrier, *1376*

November 7

1875 European explorer to cross Africa from coast to coast, *2301*

November 8

1602 Public library in Europe, *1815*
1827 Asian newspaper in English, *4500*
1833 Train wreck, *1931*
1837 College for women, *1995*
1895 Discovery of X-rays, *5330*
1949 Airlift of endangered Jews to Israel, *4979*

November 11

1925 Cosmic ray to be discovered, *5094*

December—*continued*

1922	Aircraft carrier built as such, *4265*
1938	Coelacanth caught alive, *1115*
	Premier of Thailand, *2882*
1943	Electromechanical cryptographic decoder, *4142*
1951	King of independent Libya, *2978*
1968	International astronaut rescue agreement, *5543*
1969	Plan for European economic and monetary union, *3138*
1973	Oil embargo in peacetime, *3130*
1979	Fundamentalist Islamic republic, *2700*
	Prime minister of St. Vincent and the Grenadines, *2912*
1984	Chemical disaster to cause large loss of life, *1958*
1989	Fully computerized house, *1223*
1991	President of independent Ukraine, *2861*
	Register of international arms sales and transfers, *6083*
1992	Wireless city, *5889*
1993	Electronic memory using a single electron, *1690*
1996	Chief executive of Hong Kong, *3001*
	Copyright law covering the Internet, *1721*
1997	Civilian spy satellite, *5593*
	Disk drive to store 10 billion bits of data per square inch, *1693*
	Mining claim on the ocean floor, *3686*
	Septuplets to survive birth, *2353*
1999	Space mission headed by women, *5517*

December 1

1783	Ascent in a hydrogen balloon, *1395*
1917	Supreme War Council of the World War I Allies, *4182*
1919	Woman to become a member of the British Parliament, *2654*
1988	Leader of a modern Muslim nation who was a woman, *2914*
	World AIDS Day, *1911*

December 2

1620	Newspaper in the English language, *4490*
1804	Emperor of France, *2779*
1877	Liquid oxygen, *5236*
1941	Round-the-world flight by a commercial airplane, *1375*
1942	Self-sustaining nuclear chain reaction demonstration, *5346*
1952	Birth to be televised for the public, *2346*

1982	Transplant of an artificial heart that was intended to be permanent, *4074*

December 3

1833	College to enroll women and men on equal terms, *1994*
1939	Bomb to land on German soil in World War II, *4218*
1948	Refugee ship fire to cause large loss of life, *1940*
1967	Heart transplant, *4071*
1973	Close-up photographs of Jupiter, *5573*
1997	Land mine treaty, *3185*

December 4

1154	Pope born in England, *4856*
1996	Electric car to be mass-produced, *3258*

December 5

1829	Leader of united, independent Argentina, *2993*
1909	Glider pilot who was a woman, *1420*

December 6

1873	International football game, *5659*
1983	Book to sell at auction for more than US$10 million, *3366*

December 7

1872	Oceanographic expedition, *5273*
1998	Smuggled moon rock, *1808*

December 8

1941	Death camp, *1772*
	Japanese naval casualty in World War II, *4271*
1998	Cow clones, *5191*

December 10

1896	Absurdist play, *5987*
1919	Flight from England to Australia, *1362*
1956	Nobel Prize winner to win twice in the same field, *4521*
1963	Nobel laureate who was the sole winner of awards in two different categories, *4522*
1988	Nobel Prize for Peace awarded to the United Nations Armed Forces, *4544*
1989	Helicopter powered by human motion, *1429*
1997	International regulation of greenhouse gas emissions, *2271*

December 26—*continued*

1959   Walk to raise funds for charity, *5502*
1966   Kwanzaa, *3041*

December 27

1512   Laws authorizing African slaves in the New World, *5480*
1945   World bank, *2413*
1949   President of Indonesia, *2810*

December 28

1895   Movies shown commercially, *4283*

December 30

1959   Submarine equipped with ballistic missiles, *4275*

December 31

1600   Multinational corporation, *1542*
1923   Transoceanic radio voice broadcast, *5910*

Index to Personal Names

Following is a listing of personal names in the main body of the text, arranged alphabetically by last name. To find an entry in the main body of the text, please search for the italicized indexing number.

A

A-lo-pen: Christian missionaries in China, *4792*

Abbot, Gilbert: Hospital to use anesthesia in surgery, *3763*

Abbott, Scott: Trivia board game of international popularity, *2579*

Abd Allah ibn Sa'd ibn Abi Sarh: Muslim navy, *4242*

Abd ar-Rahman *See* ar-Rahman, Abd

Abelson, Philip Hauge: Element heavier than uranium, *5245*

Abertondo, Antonio: Swimmer to cross the English Channel in both directions, *5825*

Abraham ben Garton ben Yitzhak *See* Garton ben Yitzhak, Abraham ben

Abramovitz, Sholem: Yiddish literary annual, *3575*

Abramson, Norman: Packet radio network, *5917*

Abruzzo, Ben: Transatlantic balloon flight, *1410*

Abu al-Atahiyah: Arab poet to write in a colloquial style, *3547*

Abu al-Qasim: Oral surgeon, *3801*

Abu Ali al-Hasan: Modern theory of the visual process, *5315*

Abu Bakr: Convert to Islam, *4920*

Abu Bakr, Caliph: Expansion of Islam outside Arabia, *4924*
Muslim caliph, *2927*

Abu Daoud: Massacre at the Olympic Games, *1799*

Abu Lu'lu'a: Windmills, *2056*

Abul Kasim: Illustrated surgical treatise, *3773*

Acamapichtli: Aztec priest-king, *2950*

Achard, Franz Karl: Beet sugar factory, *2549*

Achaz: Reference to a sundial, *6018*

Achong, B.G.: Human cancer-causing virus to be discovered, *3848*

Adam de la Halle: Comic opera, *4429*

Adams, Ansel: Photographic collection in a museum, *1830*

Adams, John Couch: Recognition of Neptune as a planet, *5090*

Adams, John Quincy: Public opinion poll, *2633*

Adams, Sharon Sites: Transpacific sailboat crossing by a woman, *5468*

Adgar, Charles: Sound recordings used to transmit coded messages in wartime, *4141*

Adkins, Janet: Death by suicide machine, *1888*

Adler, Max: Planetarium in the Western Hemisphere, *5130*

Adovasio, Jim: Evidence of weaving, *3696*

Adrian IV, Pope: Pope born in England, *4856*

Aeneas Tacticus: Treatise on cryptography, *3397*

Aesop: Fables with morals, *3438*

Aethelberht I: Prose work in English, *3404*

Aethelred, King of England: Customs paid by importers, *1534*

Aethelstan, King of Wessex and Mercia: King to call himself "King of the English", *2928*

Afonso I, King of Portugal: King of Portugal, *2941*

Africanus, Leo: European explorer to visit Timbuktu, *2297*

Afwerki, Isaias: President of Eritrea, *2864*

Agnesi, Maria Gaetana: Woman mathematician of renown since antiquity, *3749*

Agnodice: Gynecologist who was a woman, *3945*

Agnon, Shmuel Yosef: Nobel Prize for Literature winner from the Middle East, *4535*

Agricola, Georgius: Metallurgy textbook, *3663*
Mineralogy textbook, *3676*
Use of the word "fossil", *5260*

Agricola, Mikael: Finnish writing, *3529*

Aguta, Lameck: Boston Marathon in which both champions were African athletes, *5847*

Ahidjo, Ahmadou: President of the United Republic of Cameroon, *2817*

Ahiram: Alphabetic inscription in a writing system ancestral to modern Western alphabets, *3314*

Ahlfors, Lars Valerian: Fields Medal, *3753*

Ahmes: Treatise on mathematics, *3728*

Aidarusi, Sayyid: Swahili writing, *3535*

Airlangga: Malay writing, *3510*

A'ishah: Civil war in Islam, *4925*

Akayesu, Jean-Paul: Genocide conviction by an international court, *1782*

Akayev, Askar: President of Kyrgyzstan, *2858*

Akbar: Sikh martyr, *5006*

Aker, Thomas: Simultaneous space walk by three astronauts, *5558*

Akhenaton: Monotheistic religious reformer, *4736*

al-Farabi: Islamic philosopher with a following in the West, *4566*

Al Khalifah, Isa ibn Sulman, Sheikh of Bahrain: Sheikh of independent Bahrain, *2982*

al-Rashid, Harun, Caliph *See* Harun al-Rashid, Caliph

Albert, Prince: Top hat, *1647*

Alberti, Leon Battista: Angled fortifications, *1187*
Cipher wheel, *3400*
Modern treatise on geography, *3609*
Peep shows, *2222*
Renaissance concept of the artist, *1235*
Renaissance man, *5046*
Scientific explanation of perspective in art, *1276*
Treatise on the theory of architecture, *1188*

Alberts, Watson and Marilyn: Professorship dedicated to the search for extraterrestrial life, *5115*

Albucasis: Illustrated surgical treatise, *3773*
Oral surgeon, *3801*

Alcmaeon: Researcher to conduct human dissections for scientific purposes, *3944*

Alcock, John Williams: Nonstop transatlantic airplane flight, *1361*

Aldrin, Edwin Eugene "Buzz", Jr.: Astronauts to land on the moon, *5525*

Aldrovandi, Ulisse: Treatise on insects, *5145*

Alega, Joan de: Clothing patterns, *1617*

Aleichem, Sholem: Yiddish literary annual, *3575*

Aleotti, Giovanni Battista: Theater with a permanent proscenium arch, *5993*

Alexander II, Tsar: Head of state to order an automobile, *3226*

Alexander III, Tsar: Fabergé Easter egg, *1248*

Alexander the Great: Banana cultivation, *1029*
Definite date in the history of the Indian subcontinent, *6013*
Diving bell, *5445*
Empire to span multiple continents, *2679*
Long-distance road, *1582*
Scientists attached to armed forces, *5042*

Alexander VI, Pope: Treaty in which the entire world was partitioned, *3167*

Alexis II, Patriarch: Patriarch of Moscow who was not Russian by birth, *4811*

Alexius Comnenus, Emperor of Byzantium: Crusade, *4160*

Alfonso XI, King of Castile: King knighted by an automaton, *5027*

Alfred the Great: English translation of a biblical text, *4883*

Algaze, Guillermo: Tract houses, *1218*

Alhaj, Abdul Rahman Putra: Prime minister of Malaysia, *2891*

Alhazen: Modern theory of the visual process, *5315*

Ali ibn Abi Talib: Civil war in Islam, *4925*
Permanent schism in Islam, *4928*

Ali ibn Abi Talib, Caliph: Sectarian controversy in Islam, *4927*

Ali Mohammad, Mirza: Baha'i leader, *4741*

Ali Pasha: Major naval battle decided by firepower, *4246*

Allbutt, Thomas Clifford: Clinical thermometer in current use, *3874*

Allen, Bryan: Aircraft powered by human motion, *1330*
Aircraft powered by human motion to cross the English Channel, *1331*

Allen, Charles: Dentistry textbook in English, *3782*

Allen, Paul Gardner: Commercial software for personal computers, *1730*

Allen, Thomas: Life insurance company, *2422*

Allen, William Cardinal: Catholic edition of the Bible in a vernacular language, *4890*

Alpharabius; Avennasar *See* al-Farabi

Alvarez d'Avila, Don Juan: Major naval battle fought by the Dutch navy, *4250*

Alvise, G. and A.: Printed book decorated with type ornaments, *3356*

Alzheimer, Alois: Case of Alzheimer's disease, *3844*

Amaral, Tarsila do: Modern art festival in South America, *1253*

Amati, Andrea: Violin, *4408*

Amda Siyon: Black African state to be well documented, *2688*

Amda Tseyon: Amharic writing, *3521*

Ames, Nathan: Escalator, *1206*

Amherst, Jeffery: Germ warfare for purposes of genocide, *1766*

Amin, Idi: Prime minister of independent Uganda, *2899*

Amo, Anton Wilhelm von: Scholar of African descent to earn a doctorate from a European university, *1992*

Amram bar Sheshna, Rabbi: Jewish prayer book, *4990*

Amundsen, Roald: Explorers to winter in Antarctica, *2317*
Flight over the North Pole, *2321*

Amundsen, Roald Engelbregt Gravning: Expedition to sail through the Northwest Passage, *2318*
Explorer to reach the South Pole, *2319*

Anathapindika: Buddhist monastery, *4747*

Aristarchus of Samos:—*continued*
Heliocentric world system, *5068*
Aristobulus of Paneas: Attempt to reconcile Judaism and philosophy, *4563*
Aristophanes of Byzantium: Punctuation system, *3318*
Aristotle: Desalination process, *1475*
Diving bell, *5445*
Estimate of the circumference of the earth, *5254*
Scientists attached to armed forces, *5042*
Western philosopher, *4556*
Arjun, Guru: Sikh martyr, *5006*
Sikh sacred book, *5004*
Sikh temple at Amritsar, *5005*
Arkhangelsky, Aleksandr A.: Scheduled commercial jet flight, *1346*
Arkwright, Richard: Anti-technology riots, *1503*
Armas, Carlos Castillo: Overthrow of a democratic foreign government arranged by the U.S. Central Intelligence Agency, *4143*
Armati, Armato Degli: Eyeglasses, *4103*
Armstrong, Neil Alden: Astronauts to land on the moon, *5525*
Civilian space traveler to orbit the earth, *5539*
Docking of two spacecraft, *5540*
Armstrong, William: Breech-loading artillery, *6112*
Arnot, Arthur James: Electric drill, *6057*
Aronson, Max: Movie star, *4319*
Arp, Jean: Anti-art movement, *1252*
Arrhenius, ante August: Description of global warming, *2239*
Arriaga, Manoel José de: President of the Republic of Portugal, *2794*
Arron, Henck Alphonsus Eugène: Prime minister of independent Suriname, *2908*
Artemisia: Mausoleum, *1877*
Artemisia I of Halicarnassus: Admiral who was a woman, *4239*
Arthur, King: Reference to the King Arthur legend in literature, *3469*
Aryabhata I: Mathematician to use algebra, *3737*
Arzimovich, Lev Andreyevich: Tokamak, *2120*
Asahara, Shoko: Terrorist attack using military poison gas, *1802*
Ashley, Maurice: Black chess player to become a grandmaster, *2602*
Ashmole, Elias: University museum, *1825*
Ashurbanipal: Astrological treatise, *5117*
Epic, *3435*
Asklepios: Health resorts, *4081*
Asóka: Buddhist inscriptions, *4753*
Buddhist national leader, *2767*
Establishment of Buddhism as a state religion, *4754*

Aspdin, Joseph: Portland cement, *2152*
Assad, Hafez al-: Visit by an American president to a country on the U.S. list of terrorist states, *3131*
Astley, Philip: Modern circus, *2203*
Aston, Francis William: Element to be analyzed by mass spectrometer, *5241*
Mass spectrometer, *5335*
Astor, Lady: Woman to become a member of the British Parliament, *2654*
Astor, Mary: Movie accompanied by prerecorded sound to be released as a feature film, *4300*
Atalos III: Art presenting a continuous narrative, *1234*
Atanasoff, John Vincent: Electronic digital calculator, *1665*
Atanassova, Maria: Commercial jet airplane pilot who was a woman, *1347*
Atatürk, Mustafa Kemal: Islamic country to adopt a solar year, *6008*
Muslim country to adopt a secular government, *2696*
President of Turkey, *2801*
Woman to serve as a combat pilot, *4217*
Athanasius the Athonite, St.: Orthodox monastery, *4808*
Atkinson, John: Wrapped soap for sale, *2722*
Attlee, Clement: Labor party, *2663*
Aubrey, John: Debating society, *1835*
Augustine of Canterbury, St.: Archbishop of Canterbury, *4791*
Prose work in English, *3404*
Augustus Caesar: Depictions of a comet, *5070*
Emperor of Rome, *2769*
Organized police force, *1788*
Ausonius, Decimus Magnus: Water-powered sawmill, *1476*
Austin: Archbishop of Canterbury, *4791*
Averoff, George: Olympic Games in the modern era, *5760*
Avery, Oswald Theodore: Evidence that DNA is the genetic material, *5198*
Avicenna: Muslim polymath, *5045*
Avienus, Rufus Festus: Galaxy to be described in print, *5071*
Avogadro, Amedeo: International Chemical Congress, *5234*
Avraham bar Hiyya: Jewish scientific encyclopedia, *3380*
Aydid, Muhammad Farah: United Nations manhunt, *1795*
Aymand, Claudius: Appendectomy, *4046*
Azhari, Isma'il al-: Prime minister of Sudan, *2889*
Azikiwe, Nnamdi: President of Nigeria, *2831*

B

Ba'al Shem Tov: Chassidic master, *4972*

Babbage, Charles: Universal computing machine, *1666*

Babcock, Joseph P.: Mah-jongg, *2575*

Babeuf, François-Noël: Communist, *2670*

Babur: Empire to unite the Indian subcontinent, *2690*

Baby Fae: Transplant of a baboon heart into a human being, *4075*

Baccard, Michel-Gabriel: Ascent of Mont Blanc, *5728*

Bachioni, Romolo: Film composer, *4287*

Bachofen, Johann Jakob: Treatise positing the existence of prehistoric matriarchies, *5362*

Bacon, Roger: European to publish a recipe for gunpowder, *6095*

Badler, Virginia R.: Alcoholic beverages in military rations, *4113*
Wine, *2475*

Baedeker, Karl: Travel guidebooks, *3394*

Baer, Karl Ernst Ritter von: Observation of the egg cell of a mammal, *5159*

Baeyer, Adolf von: Barbiturate, *3925*
Synthetic indigo, *3720*

Bagrinaseva, Elizabeta: Mother-daughter Olympic medalists, *5786*

Baha' Allah: Baha'i leader, *4741*

Bahadur, Banda Singh: Sikh military victories, *5008*

Bailey, Leonard L.: Transplant of a baboon heart into a human being, *4075*

Bailey, William: Washing machine, *3054*

Baillou, Guillaume de: Modern epidemiologist, *3961*

Bain, Alexander: Fax process, *5873*
Psychologist to relate known physiological facts to psychological phenomena, *3996*
Psychology journal, *3997*

Baird, John Logie: Color television system, *5954*
International television transmission, *5952*
Televised images to be publicly displayed, *5951*
Transoceanic radio signal conveying a television image, *5953*

Bakay, Roy: Thought control of a computer, *1735*

Bakewell, Robert: Livestock breeder, *1118*

Bakunin, Mikhail: International Communist labor organization, *1505*

Bala: Punjabi writing, *3528*

Balagtas, Francisco: Tagalog writing, *3533*

Balbo, Count Cesare: Prime minister of Sardinia-Piedmont, *2872*

Balboa, Vasco Núñez de: European explorers to see the Pacific Ocean, *2289*
European settlements in South America, *4650*

Baldaia, Alfonso Gonçalvo: Explorers to pass Cape Bojador since antiquity, *2279*

Baldasare, Fred: Underwater swim across the English Channel, *5826*

Baldwin, Frederick W. "Casey": Hydrofoil boat, *5417*

Balewa, Abubakar Tafawa: Prime minister of Nigeria, *2892*

Balmat, Jacques: Alpine mountaineer who was a woman, *5729*
Ascent of Mont Blanc, *5728*

Balzer, Stephen Marius: Radial aviation engine, *1309*

Ban Ku: Chinese woman historian, *3005*

Ban Zhao: Chinese woman historian, *3005*

Band, George: Ascent of Kanchenjunga, *5742*

Banda, Hastings Kamuzu: Prime minister of Malawi, *2905*

Bandaranaike, Sirimavo Ratwatte Dias: Prime minister who was a woman, *2895*

Bannister, Roger Gilbert: Person to run a mile in less than four minutes, *5843*

Banting, Frederick Grant: Isolation of insulin, *3933*

Banzer, Marcus: Artificial eardrum, *3983*

Barbak Shah: African slave kingdom in India, *5478*

Barbara, Agatha: Woman to become president of Malta, *2844*

Barbaro, Daniel: Heated conservatory for plants, *5181*

Barber, John: Gas turbine patent, *2167*

Bardeen, John: Nobel Prize winner to win twice in the same field, *4521*
Transistor, *2016*

Bardi, Giovanni: Opera known by that name, *4430*

Baré: Woman to circumnavigate the world, *2307*

Bargar, William: Robot to perform surgery, *5040*

Barker, Will G.: Newsreel, *4350*

Barnack, Oskar: Thirty-five-millimeter camera that was commercially successful, *4584*

Barnard, Christiaan Neethling: Heart transplant, *4071*

Barnes, Charles E.: Machine gun that was practical, *6111*

Barnett, Samuel Augustus: Settlement house, *5499*

Barnum, P.T.: Three-ring circus, *2211*
Voice synthesizer, *5931*

Barol, A.: Gas station, *3233*

Barr, Y.M.: Human cancer-causing virus to be discovered, *3848*

Barraquer, José: Corneal graft, *4058*

Barringer, Daniel M.: Meteor crater, *5278*

Barrymore, John: Movie accompanied by prerecorded sound to be released as a feature film, *4300*

Barsimson, Jacob: Jews in the New World, *4646*

Bartelme, Mary Margaret: Juvenile court, *5500*

Barthle, Robert Charles: Radar signal bounced off the sun, *5100*

Bartle, Richard: MUD (multi-user dominion), *1705*

Barton, Edmund: Prime minister of Australia, *2878*

Barton, Otis: Deep-sea exploration vessel, *5283*

Baruch: Physical evidence of a person mentioned in the Jewish scriptures, *4959*

Baruch, Bernard: Chairman of the United Nations Atomic Energy Commission, *3190*
Use of the term "cold war", *4191*

Basil of Caesarea, St.: Christian hospitals, *3882*

Basil the Great, St.: Bestiary, *3467*

Basilio de Sotela, Norma Enriqueta: Woman athlete to light the Olympic flame, *5782*

Bass, Dick: Mountaineer to climb the highest peak on every continent, *5751*

Bassi, Laura: Physicist who was a woman, *5327*

Bastian, Gert: Green Party seats in a national government, *2668*

Bateman, Hester Needham: Woman silversmith to register her own hallmark, *1247*

Baton: Hourglass, *6019*

Batten, Jane Gardner: Woman to fly solo from England to Australia, *1373*

Batthya'ny, Count Lajos: Prime minister of Hungary, *2873*

Baturin, Yuri: Bureaucrat in space, *5564*

Baudelaire, Charles: Modernist poetry, *3452*

Baudonivia: Biography written by a woman, *3330*

Baudot, Jean-Maurice-Émile: Multiplexing signal switching system, *5928*

Bauer, Andreas: Steam-driven rotary press, *4715*

Bauer, Georg: Metallurgy textbook, *3663*
Mineralogy textbook, *3676*

Bauer, Yevgeny: Tracking shot, *4292*

Bauersfeld, Walter: Planetarium of the modern type, *5129*

Baulieu, Étienne-Émile: Abortion pill, *2373*

Baybars: Slave army, *4122*

Bayliss, William: Hormone to be discovered, *5165*

Bazargan, Mehdi: Prime minister of the Islamic Republic of Iran, *2910*

Beach, Alfred Ely: Pneumatic subway, *3286*

Beard, Richard: Photography studio in Europe open to the public, *4591*

Beatles, The: Feature film released on CD-ROM, *4312*

Beau de Rochas, Alphonse-Eugène: Four-stroke internal-combustion engine, *2171*

Beauchamp, George: Electric guitar, *4424*
Electric guitar, *4424*

Beauchamp, Pierre: Codification of the five basic ballet positions, *1855*

Beaufort, Francis: Wind intensity scale, *5269*

Beaujoyeux, Balthasar de: Ballet to combine dancing, music, and acting, *1854*

Beaumarchais, Pierre-Augustin Caron: Society for the protection of dramatists' rights, *3335*

Beauvilliers, Antoine: Luxury restaurant, *1466*

Beaux, Ernst: Designer perfume, *2748*

Beccaria, Cesare: Call for abolition of the death penalty, *1742*
Treatise on criminal justice and its reform, *1737*

Becquerel, Henri: Nobel Prize winner to win the award twice, *4519*
Woman to win a Nobel Prize, *4518*

Becquet, Henri: Airmail flight by airplane, *4680*

Bede, Jim: Home-built supersonic jet, *1333*

Bede, St.: Anglo-Saxons to arrive in England, *4636*
Easter, *3021*
Reference to the King Arthur legend in a historical work, *3470*
Work of history to use BC and AD, *6015*

Bedford, James H.: Freezing of a corpse for future resuscitation, *1883*

Bednorz, Johannes Georg: Superconducting materials of ceramic oxide, *5352*

Beebe, William: Deep-sea exploration vessel, *5283*

Beecham, Thomas: Tape recording of a live concert, *2050*

Beers, George W.: Lacrosse, *5597*

Beethoven, Ludwig von: Composer able to make a living entirely by writing music of his own choice, *4370*

Beeton, Isabella: Household management book, *3049*
Housekeeping magazine, *3048*
Recipes to be tested, *2505*

Beeton, Samuel: Housekeeping magazine, *3048*

Begin, Menachem: Peace treaty between an Arab nation and Israel, *3182*

Behaim, Martin: Terrestrial globe, *3612*

Behn, Aphra: Woman to write professionally in English, *3426*

Behring, Emil Adolf von: Nobel Prize in Physiology or Medicine, *4549*

Beiersdorf, Paul: Surgical adhesive bandage, *3876*

Beijerinck, Martinus Willem: Virus to be isolated, *5164*

Bell, Alexander Graham: Hydrofoil boat, *5417*

Voice synthesizer, *5931*

Words heard on a telephone, *5933*

Bell, Andrew: General encyclopedia in the English language, *3384*

Bell, Chichester: Dictation device, *2042*

Bell, John: War correspondent, *4456*

Bell, Melville: Voice synthesizer, *5931*

Bellingshausen, Fabian Gottlieb von: Circumnavigation of Antarctica, *2310*

Bellonte, Maurice: Paris to New York nonstop airplane flight, *1368*

Belloy, Jean-Baptiste de: Coffee percolator, *3059*

Belshazzar: Cryptanalyst, *4135*

Spy ring, *4136*

Ben Bella, Ahmed: Prime minister of Algeria, *2897*

Ben-Gurion, David: Prime minister of Israel, *2888*

Ben-Yehudah, Eliezer: Ancient language revived for modern use, *3302*

Ben Zakkai, Yochanan: Center of Jewish learning outside Jerusalem, *4964*

Bendersky, Gordon: Anatomically correct image of the human heart, *3900*

Benedict of Nursia, St.: Abbey in Western Europe, *4850*

Benedict, William Pershing: Airplane flight to land at the North Pole, *2324*

Benesch, Alfred A.: Traffic lights, *1590*

Benigni, Roberto: Performer in a foreign language film to win the Academy Award for Best Actor, *4323*

Benivieni, Antonio: Forensic pathologist, *3955*

Benjamin of Rome: Printed book in Hebrew, *3564*

Benjamin of Tudela: European traveler to reach the Chinese frontier, *2276*

Bennett, J.M.: Flight from England to Australia, *1362*

Bennett, James Gordon: Across-the-ocean race, *5856*

International airplane race, *5603*

International balloon race, *5602*

International road race, *5714*

Investigative reporter, *4457*

Bennett, Jim: Air race from England to Australia, *5604*

Bennett, William: Electronic wristwatch, *6033*

Bennigsen, Leonty Leontyevich: Playing deck with double-headed face cards, *2591*

Benoist, Thomas: Airliner, *1315*

Bentinck, Lord George: Traveling van for horses, *5684*

Beowulf: Epic poem in English, *3406*

Berekhyahu: Physical evidence of a person mentioned in the Jewish scriptures, *4959*

Berg, Paul: Gene splicing, *5201*

Berger, Hans: Electroencephalogram, *3905*

Berger, Lee: Human footprints, *4619*

Berger-Levrault, Oscar: Stamp catalogs, *4693*

Bergès, Aristide: Hydroelectric generator, *2084*

Bergey, John: Digital quartz wristwatch, *6035*

Berlanga, Tomás de: Bananas in the New World, *1040*

Berlichingen, Götz von: Mechanical prosthetic arm, *3981*

Berlin, Heinrich: Writing system invented in the New World, *3320*

Berlin, Samuel H.: Transatlantic telephone call using the transoceanic cable, *5943*

Berliner, Emile: Phonograph record, *2043*

Bernacchi, Antonio: Castrato of note, *4432*

Bernadotte, Jean: Playing deck with double-headed face cards, *2591*

Bernardi, Micheline: Modern bikini, *1636*

Berners-Lee, Tim: Global hypermedia information system, *1718*

Bernhardt, Sarah: Celebrity actress with an international following, *5986*

Films synchronized with speech, *4286*

Bernolák, Anton: Slovak writing, *3538*

Berry, Albert: Parachute jump from an airplane, *1434*

Berry, Marcellus Fleming: Traveler's checks, *2455*

Bert, Paul: Life-support system, *3875*

Bertin, Rose: Dressmaker with a flourishing export business, *1621*

Besant, Annie: Westerners to promote Hindu ideas, *4916*

Besant, Walter: Literary agent, *3336*

Besnard, M.V.: Skeleton of a black African, *4620*

Bessel, Friedrich Wilhelm: Measurement of the distance to a star, *5086*

Bessemer, Henry: Mass production of steel, *3672*

Best, Charles H.: Isolation of insulin, *3933*

Béthencourt, Jean de: Peoples of the Canary Islands, *4645*

Beukelszoon, William: Salted herring, *2527*

Bevis, John: Observation of a supernova, *5073*

Bhabha, Homi Jehangir: Nuclear reactor in Asia, *2118*

Bhutto, Benazir: Leader of a modern Muslim nation who was a woman, *2914*

Bi Zheng: Movable type, *4703*

Bianchini, Francesco: Planet to be mapped, *5080*

Bichat, Marie-François-Xavier: Scientific treatise on histology, *3785*

Bickford, William: Safety fuse, *3682*

Biemiller, Philip: Battery-powered wristwatch, *6032*

Bikila, Abebe: Runner to win the Olympic marathon twice, *5780*

Bilge: Turkish writing, *3501*

Billings, John and Evelyn: Rhythm method, *2368*

Binder, Alan: Discovery of water on the moon, *5111*

Binet, Alfred: Standardized intelligence test, *4001*

Bingen, Hildegard of: Book of Christian mysticism by a woman, *4797*

Bingham, Caleb: Children's library, *1819*

Bini, Lucio: Electroshock therapy, *4005*

Binnig, Gerd: Scanning tunneling electron microscope, *5305*

Binns, John R.: Radio distress call from a ship at sea, *5418*

Biow, Hermann: Photographs of a historic event, *4592*

Biran, Avraham: Reference to King David, *2922*

Birdseye, Clarence: Frozen food for the mass market, *2542*

Biro, Lazlo: Ballpoint pen widely used, *3596*

Bismarck, Otto von: Chancellor of Germany, *2996*

State-sponsored social security system, *2423*

Bissaker, Robert: Slide rule, *3746*

Bissell, Melville Reuben: Carpet sweeper, *3062*

Bitzer, George William "Billy": Cinematographer of lasting influence, *4290*

Bjarni Herjölffson: European traveler to sight North America, *4641*

Björnsson, Sveinn: President of the modern Republic of Iceland, *2806*

Blache, Alice Guy: Film director who was a woman, *4284*

Narrative film, *4285*

Black, S. Duncan: Electric hand drill, *6060*

Blackburn, John: Transatlantic telephone call using the transoceanic cable, *5943*

Blackton, James Stuart: Animated cartoon, *4326*

Blackwell, Elizabeth: Woman physician in modern times to earn a degree from a medical school, *3969*

Blaese, Michael: Gene therapy, *4094*

Blair, David: Feature film broadcast on the Internet, *4313*

Blair, Tony: British prime minister to address the Parliament of the Irish Republic, *3133*

Blakewell, Frederick: Fax process, *5873*

Blalock, Alfred: Operation to cure congenital heart disease, *4057*

Blanchard, Jean-Pierre Francois: Balloon flight over open water, *1399*

Letter sent by airmail, *4679*

Blanche of Castile: Woman to rule France, *2944*

Blankers-Koen, Francina: Modern pentathlete, *5842*

Woman athlete to win four gold medals in one Olympic Games, *5773*

Blanquart-Evrard, Louis-Désiré: Travel book illustrated with original photographs, *3393*

Blattner, Louis: Tape recorder, *2048*

Blavatsky, Helena: Westerners to promote Hindu ideas, *4916*

Blechynden, Richard: Iced tea, *2498*

Blekinsop, John: Steam locomotive in regular use, *3265*

Blériot, Louis: Airplane flight over the ocean, *1357*

Blix, Magnus Gustav: Centrifuge, *3877*

Blood, Thomas: Theft of the British Crown Jewels, *1804*

Blower, Thomas: Swimmer to cross the Irish Sea, *5823*

Blücher, Gebhard Leberecht: Playing deck with double-headed face cards, *2591*

Blumenbach, Johann Friedrich: Physical anthropologist, *5154*

Bly, Nellie: World tour by a woman traveling alone, *5457*

Bocchi, Dorotea: University professor who was a woman, *1988*

Bodhidharma: Kung fu master, *5701*

Zen Buddhism, *4759*

Bodin, Jean: Political philosopher to reject slavery, *5485*

Bodley, Thomas: Public library in Europe, *1815*

Boeda, Eric: Adhesives, *6040*

Boeing, William Edward: International airmail service, *4684*

Boerhaave, Hermann: Clinical teacher, *3856*

Böhm, Theobald: Modern transverse flute, *4420*

Bohr, Niels: Modern theory of atomic structure, *5333*

Boileau, Louis-Auguste: Department store, *1514*

Boisselier, Brigitte: Human cloning company, *5188*

Bolesław I, King of Poland: King of Poland, *2939*

Bolívar, Simón: Hemispheric diplomatic conference, *3158*

Leader of free Ecuador, *2992*

President of Colombia, *2785*

Bolkiah, Pengiran Muda Hassanal, Sultan of Brunei: Sultan of independent Brunei, *2983*

Bolos of Mende: Alchemist, *5217*

Bombardier, Joseph-Armand: Snowmobile, *3223*

Bonet, Juan Pablo: Deaf person educated in lip-reading and speaking, *2005*

Bonheur, Rosa: Woman in Europe to receive official permission to wear pants, *1629*

Bonifacio, G.: Treatise on sign language, *3781*

Bonner, Neville: Aboriginal Australian elected to the Australian Parliament, *2656*

Bonnet, Charles: Theory of evolution, *5152*

Bonnet, Stede: Pirate alleged to have made prisoners walk the plank, *1787*

Bonsack, James A.: Cigarette-rolling machine, *1068*

Booth, Catherine: Poke bonnet, *1648*
Salvation Army activities, *4839*

Booth, William: Salvation Army activities, *4839*

Booty, Frederick: Stamp catalogs, *4693*

Bopp, Franz: Comprehensive study of Proto-Indo-European, *3298*

Borchardt, Hugo: Automatic pistol, *6114*

Borden, Gail: Condensed milk, *2511*

Bordini, Faustina: Opera diva, *4436*

Borgononi, Theodoric: Medieval doctor to advocate the use of anesthesia, *3759*

Borman, Frank: Astronauts to orbit the moon, *5524*
Rendezvous in space, *5538*

Borron, Robert de: Keeper of the Holy Grail, *3473*
Prose works in the French language, *3555*

Bosch, Juan: Democratically elected president of the Dominican Republic, *2830*

Botha, Louis: Prime minister of the Union of South Africa, *2879*

Botta, Paul-Émile: Archeological digs in Mesopotamia, *5056*

Böttger, Johann Friedrich: Porcelain manufactured in Europe, *3648*

Boucicaut, Aristide: Department store, *1514*

Boudicca: Woman to lead a rebellion against the Roman Empire, *4158*

Boulanger, A.: Restaurant known by that term, *1464*

Boulmerka, Hassiba: Muslim woman athlete to win a track and field world championship, *5845*

Boulton, Matthew: Coins minted with steam-powered machinery, *2452*
Cut-steel button, *1641*

Boumedienne, Houari: Prime minister of Algeria, *2897*

Bouquet, Henry: Germ warfare for purposes of genocide, *1766*

Bourguiba, Habib ibn Ali: President of independent Tunisia, *2812*

Bourke-White, Margaret: War photographer who was a woman, *4462*

Bourne, Nicholas: Newspaper in England that was successful, *4492*

Bourseul, Charles: Treatise on telephony, *5932*

Boursier du Courdray, Angélique le: Woman to write a book on childbirth, *2338*

Boursier, Louise: Woman to write a book on childbirth, *2338*

Bowditch, E.B.: Oil well, *2105*

Bowdler, Harriet: Censored edition of Shakespeare, *3433*

Bowdler, Thomas: Censored edition of Shakespeare, *3433*

Bowerman, Bill: Shoe made from recycled materials, *1658*

Bowler, Thomas: Bowler hat, *1649*

Boyce, Joseph: Mechanical reaper, *1082*

Boycott, Charles Cunningham: Boycott, *1444*

Boyd, Louise Arner: Woman to fly over the North Pole, *2326*

Boyle, Robert: Discovery of an element, *5220*
Statement of a physical law as an equation with two dependent variables, *5325*

Boynton, Paul: Man to swim the English Channel, *5820*

Brabant, Louis: Ventriloquist, *2215*

Bradey, Lydia: Woman to climb Mount Everest solo without bottled oxygen, *5753*

Bragg, William Henry: Nobel Prize in Physics winner from Oceania, *4547*

Bragg, William Lawrence: Nobel Prize in Physics winner from Oceania, *4547*

Bragi the Old: Scandinavian writing, *3490*

Brahe, Tycho: National observatory in Europe, *5131*

Brain, C.K.: Human use of fire, *4617*

Brakespear, Nicholas: Pope born in England, *4856*

Brallier, John K.: Professional football game, *5660*

Bramah, Joseph: Beer-pump handle, *2486*
Hydraulic press, *1481*

Brand, Hennig: Discovery of an element, *5220*

Brand, Vance D.: International space mission, *5548*

Brandenberger, J.E.: Cellophane, *3112*

Brandt, F.A.: Child to win a gold medal in the Olympic Games, *5763*

Brattain, Walter Houser: Transistor, *2016*

Braun, Werner von: Ballistic missile test flight, *6134*

Braun, Wernher von: Rocket to reach outer space, *5507*

Bray, John Randolph: Animation made by the cel process, *4328*

Brayne, John: Elizabethan theater, *5991*

Brazauskas, Algirdas: President of independent Lithuania, *2849*

Brearley, Harry: Stainless steel, *3674*

Breashears, David: Mountaineer to climb the highest peak on every continent, *5751*

Brendel, Walter: Ultrasonic disintegrator used in medicine, *4093*

Brenston, Jackie: Rock and roll song, *4443*

Breslaw, Philip: Magician whose act included mind-reading tricks, *2216*

Breton, Andre: Surrealist manifesto, *1241*
Surrealist text, *3455*

Brett, J.W.: Transatlantic telegraph cable, *5926*

Breuer, Josef: Psychoanalyst, *3999*

Breuer, Marcel: Tubular steel chair, *3091*

Brew, Charlotte: Woman jockey in the Grand National steeplechase, *5688*

Brezhnev, Leonid: Strategic Arms Limitation Treaty, *3180*

Briand, Aristide: Antiwar treaty, *3171*

Bridgman, Percy Williams: Artificial diamond, *5247*

Briggs, Claire: Comic strip in a daily newspaper, *4470*

Briggs, Robert: Nuclear transplantation in a vertebrate, *5185*

Bright, Charles Tilston: Transatlantic telegraph cable, *5926*
Undersea telegraph cable, *5925*

Bright, Timothy: Book about shorthand in English, *3323*

Brisbane, Thomas Makdougall: Permanent observatory in the Southern Hemisphere, *5135*

Britten, Benjamin: One-armed pianist of international stature, *4374*

Brixiensis, Pagninus: Printed edition of the Qur'an, *4939*

Broadwick, Georgia: Parachute jump from an airplane by a woman, *1435*

Brodie, Maurice: Poliomyelitis vaccine, *3912*

Brodrick, Geraldine: Nonuplets, *2347*

Brotheridge, Daniel: Allied soldier killed in combat on D-Day, *4188*

Broughton, Jack: Boxing rules, *5642*

Brown, Alan: Mass-produced cereal food for infants, *2391*

Brown, Arthur Whitton: Nonstop transatlantic airplane flight, *1361*

Brown, Barnum: Scientific description of *Tyrannosaurus rex*, *5215*

Brown, Dorcas: Horse riding, *1144*
Wheel, *3289*

Brown, F.C.: Astronomer to use electronic instruments, *5093*

Brown, Harold P.: Electric chair, *1745*

Brown, Joe: Ascent of Kanchenjunga, *5742*

Brown, Joe E.: Movie with both sound and color, *4301*

Brown, Louise: Test-tube baby, *2348*

Brown, M.: Speech-activated robot, *5039*

Brown, Mount: Stamp catalogs, *4693*

Brown, Robert: Observation of a cell nucleus, *5160*

Brown, William Henry: International yacht race, *5855*

Bruchsal, Alexander: Shilling, *2444*

Brunel-Deschamps, Eliette: Paintings, *1262*

Brunel, Isambard Kingdom: Steam forge hammer, *1487*
Transatlantic steamboat service, *5425*

Brunel, Marc Isambard: Mechanized production line, *1483*
Underwater tunnel, *2191*

Brunelleschi, Filippo: Patent, *1540*

Renaissance architect of importance, *1186*
Scientific explanation of perspective in art, *1276*

Bruno, Giordano: Scientist executed by the Catholic Church, *4870*

Brunschwig, Hieronymus: Treatise on military surgery, *4045*

Brutus, Lucius Junius: Republic, *2680*

Buchanan, Franklin: Naval battle between ironclad vessels, *4255*

Buchanan, James: Transatlantic telegraph messages, *5927*

Buckland, Rodney: Suspect cleared of a crime by DNA evidence, *1761*

Buddha, Gautama: Buddhist missionaries, *4744*
Buddhist monastery, *4747*
Buddhist monks, *4745*
Buddhist monument, *4751*
Buddhist nun, *4748*
Pali text, *3489*
Statement of Buddhist doctrine, *4746*

Budding, Edwin: Lawn mower, *6062*

Budge, Don: Grand Slam winner in tennis, *5836*

Buffon, George-Louis Leclerc, count of: Systematic and comprehensive work of natural history, *5151*

Buhl, Herman: Ascent of Nanga Parbat (Diamir), *5738*

Buick, Roger: Fossil oil, *5251*

Bulan: Jewish kingdom to be established since biblical times, *4967*

Bull, John: Grain stripper, *1085*

Buller, Walter: International bridge match, *2595*

Bullmann, Hans: Android-maker, *5028*

Bullock, William: Newspaper folding device, *4720*
Roll-fed rotary press, *4718*

Bunsen, Robert: Standard laboratory burner, *5302*

Buntschuh, B.: Speech-activated robot, *5039*

Buñuel, Luis: Underground film, *4351*

Burbage, James: Elizabethan acting troupe, *5983*
Elizabethan theater, *5991*

Burbage, Margaret: Director of the Royal Greenwich Observatory, *5140*

Bureau, Gaspard: Gun carriage, *6099*

Bureau, Jean: Gun carriage, *6099*

Burgmuller, Friedrich: Polka, *1849*

Burgos, Gaspard: Method for teaching the deaf to speak, read, and write, *2004*

Burke, Robert: European explorer to cross the Australian continent, *2299*

Burke, Thomas: Olympic Games in the modern era, *5760*

Burkitt, Denis Parsons: Human cancer-causing virus to be discovered, *3848*

Burleson, Donald: Computer hacker to be convicted, *1713*

Burnell, Jocelyn Bell: Discovery of pulsars, *5104*

Burnham, Linden Forbes Sampson: Prime minister and president of Guyana, *2904*

Burpee, Washington Atlee: Chartered airplane flight, *1337*

Burroughs, Edgar Rice: Comic strip with an adventure hero, *4471*

Major motion picture to be produced and exhibited entirely with digital technology, *4318*

Burstein, Jill: Computerized robot to grade essays on a standardized test, *1980*

Burt, William Austin: Typewritten letter, *3324*

Burton, Charles: Perambulator, *2385*

Busbecq, Ghislain de: Flower cultivated by florists, *1045*

Busch, Adolphus: Diesel engine built for commercial service, *2179*

Busch, Andreas: Planetarium, *5128*

Buschmann, Friedrich: Accordion, *4416*

Bush, George Herbert Walker: Free-trade region encompassing North America, *1552*

Bush, Vannevar: Computing device with electronic components, *1667*

Bushnell, David: Mine barrage, *6086*

Submarine built for use in war, *4251*

Bushnell, Nolan K.: Video game, *2577*

Bussy, Antoine: Extraction of beryllium, *3668*

Bustamante, Alexander: Prime minister of independent Jamaica, *2898*

Butler, James: Wire-screen sifter for grain, *1077*

Butler, Robert: Geriatrics department, *3863*

Butter, Nathaniel: Newspaper in England that was successful, *4492*

Byng, Julian: Massed tank attack, *4181*

Byrd, Richard: Flight over the North Pole, *2321*

Byrd, Richard Evelyn: Radio broadcast heard in both the Arctic and the Antarctic regions, *5912*

Byron, O.H.: Martini, *2490*

C

Ca' da Mosto, Alvise: Eyewitness account by a European traveler of life in the African interior, *2288*

Cabana, Robert D.: Humans to enter the International Space Station, *5565*

Cabeza de Vaca, Alvar Núñez: Journey across North America, *2290*

Cabot, John: European traveler to set foot on the North American continent after the Vikings, *2284*

International Festival of the Sea, *3045*

Map showing the Spanish discoveries in the New World, *3613*

Cadolle, Madame: Brassiere, *1605*

Caedmon: Poet in English, *3405*

Caesar, Augustus: Depictions of a comet, *5070*

Organized police force, *1788*

Sales tax, *2465*

Caesar, Julius: Autopsy of a well-known individual, *1866*

Giant sports arena, *5606*

Medical officers in the armed forces, *4121*

Mock naval battle, *2219*

News posters, *4484*

Caesaria, St.: Convent, *4790*

Caesarius, St.: Convent, *4790*

Cage, John Milton: Live electronic music, *4394*

Cahill, Thaddeus: Music synthesizer powered by electricity, *4422*

Cahill, Thomas: Map of any part of the Americas, *3608*

Cailler, François-Louis: Chocolate for eating, *2550*

Cailletet, Louis-Paul: Liquid oxygen, *5236*

Caillie, René: European explorer to visit Timbuktu, *2297*

Caius Martius: Topiary gardening, *2616*

Calcar, Jan Stephan van: Treatise on human anatomy based on dissection, *3774*

Treatise on human anatomy with accurate illustrations, *3776*

Calenda, Costanza: Woman physician to receive university training, *3954*

Calixtus, St.: Antipope, *4848*

Callimachus of Athens: Buildings with acanthus ornamentation, *1173*

Callimachus of Cyrene: Classification system of all knowledge, *1810*

Library catalog, *1811*

Callinicus of Heliopolis: Greek fire, *6075*

Calvert, Frank: Excavator of Troy, *5058*

Calvin, John: Calvinist (Reformed) church, *4822*

Presbyterian church, *4825*

Protestant heretic, *4824*

Psalms in metrical form, *4385*

Camargo, Marie: Ballerina virtuoso, *1858*

Cambacérès, Jean-Jacques Régis de: Uniform national law code, *2649*

Cambert, Robert: Opera in French, *4435*

Cameron, James: Film to earn US$1 billion worldwide, *4314*

Cameron, Verney Lovett: European explorer to cross Africa from coast to coast, *2301*

Cammann, George P.: Stethoscope, *3869*

Camoës, Luís Vaz de: Modern epic poems, *3445*

Campbell, John: Sextant, *5437*

Campbell, Keith: Lamb with human genes, 5207

Campbell, Kim: Canadian prime minister who was a woman, 2917

Canaday, Rudd: Multiuser operating system, 1727

Candolle, Alphonse-Louis-Pierre-Pyrame de: International Botanical Congress, 5184

Candragupta Maurya: Emperor of India, 2766
King to convert to Jainism, 4949

Cannizzaro, Stanislao: International Chemical Congress, 5234

Cano, Juan Sebastian del: Circumnavigation of the world, 2305

Cantrell, J.F.: Laundromat, 1520

Capek, Karel: Robot, 5031

Caraka: Texts of Ayurvedic medicine, 3770

Carasso, Isaac: Containers of yogurt with fruit mixed in, 2516

Caravita, Yosef ben Avraham: Printed edition of the Torah, 4993

Carbonell, Eudald: Evidence of cannibalism, 4618

Cardano, Gerolamo: Book on gambling techniques, 2606

Carissan, Eugène Olivier: Automatic calculator to factor whole numbers, 1664

Carlile, Richard: Manual on birth control, 2360

Carlin, Steve: Childbirth streamed live on the Internet, 2354

Carlsen, Ove: Country to legalize homosexual marriage, 5384

Carlson, Chester Floyd: Xerography, 4724

Carnegie, Andrew: Carnegie library, 1820

Carnot, Lazare: Technical college, 1993

Carol I, King of Romania: King of Romania, 2968

Carolus, Johann: Printed newspapers published regularly, 4488

Carothers, Wallace Hume: Synthetic fiber produced entirely from chemicals, 3724

Carpio, Daniel: Swimmer to cross the Strait of Gibraltar, 5824

Carracci, Annibale: Caricatures, 1280

Carrel, Alexis: Nobel Prize in Physiology or Medicine winner from North America, 4550
Vascular sutures, 4054

Carrera, Rafael: Leader of independent Guatemala, 2995

Carrier, Willis Haviland: Air conditioner for home use, 3068

Carriera, Rosalba: Pastellist, 1283

Carrington, Louis H.: Transpacific nonstop jet airplane flight, 1381

Carswell, John: Scottish Gaelic collection of writings, 3527

Carter, Jimmy: Nuclear power plant disaster, 1953

Cartwright, Alexander Joy: Baseball, 5609
Baseball team, 5610

Cartwright, Edmund: Power loom, 3716

Casanovas, Xavier: Watch that told time in Catalan, 6039

Caselli, Giovanni: Fax system for commercial use, 5874

Casey, Philip: International handball match, 5677

Cassini, Cesar-François: Mapping survey of a country, 3621

Castle, Irene: Permanent wave hairstyle, 2734

Castro, Fidel: Major-league American baseball teams to play in Communist Cuba, 5615

Catherine of Aragon: Wife of Henry VIII of England, 2955

Cato, Marcus Portius: Encyclopedia for young adults, 3377

Cato, Milton: Prime minister of St. Vincent and the Grenadines, 2912

Cato the Elder: Basilica, 1174
Encyclopedia for young adults, 3377

Catullus: Reference to horseshoes, 1153

Caus, Salomon de: Orangery, 2622

Cave, Edward: Magazine known by that name, 4478

Cavendish, Henry: Analysis of air, 5226
Determination of the chemical composition of water, 5227

Cawdrey, Robert and Thomas: Dictionary of the English language, 3370

Cawl, Faarax M.I.: Somali writing, 3544

Caxton, William: Book printed in England that bears a date, 3355
Book printed in the English language, 3354
Dictionary for tourists, 3368
Illustrated book in English, 3357
Printed advertising poster, 1450
Publisher in English, 3412
Vocabulary list for travelers to a foreign country, 3392

Cayley, George: Manned glider flight that was successful, 1416
Practical design for a fixed-wing aircraft, 1308
Treatise on aerodynamics, 1305

Celer: Concrete dome, 1177

Cellini, Benvenuto: Autobiography of a European artist, 1240

Cellon, George: Avocado cultivation, 1054

Celsius, Anders: Centigrade temperature scale, 5222

Celtis, Konradus: European playwright, 5981

Cerf, Vinton: International networking conference, 1698
National computer network, 1700

Cerletti, Ugo: Electroshock therapy, 4005

Cézanne, Paul: Exhibition of impressionist paintings, 1250

Chrétien de Troyes: Version of the Holy Grail legend, *3472*

Christ, Carol P.: Celebration of the Mysteries at Eleusis in modern times, *4743*

Christianson, Ward: Personal computer bulletin board, *1704*

Christine de Pisan: Feminist author in medieval Europe, *5365*
Woman to write professionally, *3331*

Christophe, Henri: Independent nation in Latin America, *2694*

Chrysler, Walter P.: Skyscraper more than 1,000 feet high, *1227*

Chu, Paul: Superconducting material that operated at temperatures above the boiling point of nitrogen, *5353*

Chukwu, Nkem: Octuplets, *2355*

Chuquet, Nicholas: Use of the terms "billion" and "trillion", *3739*

Churchill, Winston: Call for a united democratic Europe, *3135*
Reference to the Iron Curtain, *3128*

Cicero, Marcus Tullius: Druid, *4738*

Cid, El: Autograph handwritten by a known individual in Europe, *3322*

Cierva, Juan de la: Autogiro, *1423*

Claghorn, E.J.: Seat belt, *3227*

Clare of Assisi, St.: Rule for Christian monastic life written by a woman, *4858*

Clark, Barney B.: Transplant of an artificial heart that was intended to be permanent, *4074*

Clark, James and Patrick: Cotton thread, *3710*

Clark, Jim: Monocoque chassis for Formula 1 racing cars, *5721*

Clark, Joseph: Physician to understand the necessity for hygiene, *3967*

Clark, Julia: Airplane accident involving a woman that was fatal, *1898*

Clark, Wilfrid Edward Le Gros: Scientific hoax of international notoriety, *5051*

Clarke, Arthur Charles: Proposal for global satellite telecommunications, *5883*

Claude, Georges: Building illuminated by neon lamps, *2095*
Electric discharge lamp, *2096*

Claudius Caecus, Appius: Paved long-distance road, *1585*
Roman aqueduct, *2132*

Claxton, Catherine: Sexual harassment case at the United Nations, *5377*

Cleisthenes: Democracy, *2681*

Clement: Christian institution of higher learning, *4776*

Clement of Alexandria: Epiphany (Adoration of the Magi), *3017*

Clement VII, Pope: Antipope during the Great Schism, *4862*

Clerk, Dugald: Two-stroke internal-combustion engine, *2172*

Clinch, Nicholas: Ascent of the Vinson Massif, *5746*

Clinton, William Jefferson: Visit by an American president to a country on the U.S. list of terrorist states, *3131*

Clovis I, King of the Franks: King of France, *2925*

Clusius, Carolus: Flower cultivated by florists, *1045*

Clynes, Manfred: Cyborg, *5041*

Coachman, Alice: Woman athlete of African descent to win an Olympic gold medal, *5772*

Cochrane, A.A.: Iron-hulled warship, *4254*

Cochrane, Elizabeth: World tour by a woman traveling alone, *5457*

Cochrane, Josephine: Dishwasher, *3063*

Cockcroft, John Douglas: Artificial transmutation of an element, *5340*

Cocke, John: Reduced Instruction Set Computer (RISC), *1683*

Cockeram, Henry: Dictionary called by that name, *3371*

Cockerell, Christopher: Hovercraft, *5419*

Cogan, David G.: Radiation-induced cataracts, *3846*

Coghlan, Eamonn: Runner over the age of 40 to break the four-minute mile, *5846*

Cohen, Daniel: Human chromosome gene-linkage maps, *5203*
Map of the human genome, *5204*

Cohl, Emile: Animated character to appear in a series of cartoons, *4327*

Coignet, François: Reinforced concrete structure, *1197*

Coke, William: Bowler hat, *1649*

Cole, Henry: Christmas cards, *4673*
World's Fair, *2223*

Colebrook, Leonard: Sulfa drug, *3934*

Colle, Giovanni: Blood transfusions in Europe, *4097*

Collins, Eileen Marie: Woman to command a space mission, *5566*

Collins, Joseph Lawton: Atomic bomb explosion underground, *6128*

Collins, Michael: Astronauts to land on the moon, *5525*

Collins, Robert: Physician to understand the necessity for hygiene, *3967*

Collins, William Wilkie: Detective novel, *3454*

Collison, John: Rule book of bridge, *2594*

Colmar, Charles Xavier Thomas de: Adding machine, *1662*

Columbus, Bartholomeo: Permanent European settlement in the New World, *4648*

Columbus, Christopher: Cases of syphilis, *3833*

Coverdale, Miles: Hymnbook containing hymns in English, *4823*
Printed edition of the complete Christian Bible in English, *4889*
Cowan, Clyde L., Jr.: Observation of neutrinos, *5349*
Cowan, Edith Dircksey: Woman to become a member of the Australian Parliament, *2655*
Cowell, Elizabeth: Television announcer who was a woman, *5958*
Craig, Cleo Frank: Transatlantic telephone call using the transoceanic cable, *5943*
Craig, James: Prime minister of Northern Ireland, *2881*
Cranfield, Lionell: Balance of trade and payments for a nation, *1543*
Crary, Albert Paddock: Explorer to set foot on both the North and South Poles, *2328*
Crasser, Jeremias: News agency, *4513*
Crateuas: Botanical illustrations, *5179*
Crawford, Jane Todd: Gynecological surgery, *4047*
Cray, Seymour R.: Supercomputer, *1672*
Crémieux, Hector: Operetta, *4437*
Crescentius, Petrus de: Lawn-care manual, *2620*
Cresson, Edith: Premier of France who was a woman, *2915*
Crichton, Michael: Feature film incorporating digital computer graphics, *4337*
Crick, Francis Harry Compton: Elucidation of the structure of DNA, *5199*
Crippen, Harvey: Criminal caught by radio, *1755*
Crippen, Robert L.: Reusable manned spacecraft, *5551*
Cristofori, Bartolomeo di Francesco: Pianoforte, *4412*
Croesus: Government coinage, *2437*
Crompton, Rookes Evelyn Bell: Electric radiator, *1213*
Private home fully illuminated with electric lights, *2094*
Cronkite, Walter: Inflatable chair, *3095*
Cronstedt, Axel Fredrik: Nickel obtained in a pure sample, *3666*
Cronstedt, Carl Johan: Masonry stove, *3056*
Cros, Émile-Hortensius-Charles: Sound recording device, *2040*
Crosland, Alan: Movie accompanied by prerecorded sound to be released as a feature film, *4300*
Movie with both sound and color, *4301*
Cross, C.S.: Synthetic fiber suitable for making cloth, *3723*
Cross, Lloyd: Multiplex hologram, *4310*
Cruz, Juana Inés de la: Woman intellectual in the New World, *3333*
Csetibius: Organist, *4361*
Ctesibius: Organ, *4405*

Cuellar, Javier Pérez de: President of Namibia, *2850*
Cuffe, Paul: Black nationalist movement, *2660*
Cugnot, Nicolas-Joseph: Motor vehicle, *3211*
Motor vehicle accident, *3212*
Culbertson, Ely: International bridge match, *2595*
Cullinan, Thomas M.: Star of Africa, *3678*
Culver, Kenneth: Gene therapy, *4094*
Cunningham, Ronnie Walter: Live telecast from space, *5542*
Curie, Marie: Nobel Prize winner to win the award twice, *4519*
Woman appointed to the faculty of a French university, *1998*
Woman to win a Nobel Prize, *4518*
Curie, Pierre: Nobel Prize winner to win the award twice, *4519*
Woman to win a Nobel Prize, *4518*
Curtis, John: Chewing gum, *2552*
Curtiss, Glenn Hammond: Airplane bombing experiment, *4204*
Cusi, Meshullam: Printed book in Hebrew, *3564*
Custis, Austen M.: Transatlantic message over radio telephone, *5936*
Cuvier, Georges-Léopold-Chrêtien-Frédéric-Dagober Baron: Comparative anatomist, *5157*
Cuzzoni, Francesca: Opera diva, *4436*
Cygnäus, Uno: National school system to require manual training, *1976*
Cyrano de Bergerac: Space travel by rocket, *5503*
Cyril, St.: Russian writing, *3511*
Cyrus the Great: Empire to span multiple continents, *2679*
Establishment of Zoroastrianism as state religion, *5019*
Spy ring, *4136*

D

da Saló, Gaspare: Violin, *4408*
Dacey, Ralph: Magnetic surgery system, *4065*
Dacko, David: President of the Central African Republic, *2822*
Daddah, Moktar Ould: President of independent Mauritania, *2825*
Dafte, J.: Revolver pistol, *6105*
Dagmar, Tsaritsa: Fabergé Easter egg, *1248*
Daguerre, Louis-Jacques-Mandé: Photographic process that was practical, *4577*
Daimler, Gottlieb Wilhelm: Carburetor, *2177*
Motorcycle with an internal-combustion engine, *3216*
Production automobile with a gas-powered internal-combustion engine, *3229*

V-block engine, *2175*

Dale, Henry Hallett: Neurotransmitter to be identified, *5168*

Dali, Salvador: Underground film, *4351*

Dalton, John: Atomic theory, *5320*
Periodic table of the elements, *5229*
Treatise on color blindness, *3839*

Damadian, Raymond: Magnetic resonance image of a human body, *3907*

Damian, Peter: Flagellation sects, *4855*

Dan, Dimitru: Man to walk 100,000 kilometers, *5851*

Dandolo, Duchess Giovanna: Lace, *3706*

D'Andrea, Novella: University professor who was a woman, *1988*

Daniel: Cryptanalyst, *4135*

Daniel of Kiev: Russian travel writer, *3391*

Darazi, Muhammad ibn Isma'il ad-: Druze imam, *4740*

Darby, Abraham: Coke-smelted iron, *3664*

Darby III, Abraham: Bridge constructed entirely of cast iron, *2142*

Darius I: Cuneiform writing from Mesopotamia to be deciphered, *5055*
Empire to span multiple continents, *2679*
Suez canal, *2130*
Westerner to visit India, *2272*

Darlington, Jennie: Women to winter in Antarctica, *2323*

Dassler, Adolf: Running shoes, *1657*

Dauksa, Mikalojus: Lithuanian writing, *3530*

Daumier, Honoré: Aerial photographs, *4595*

Davenant, William: Opera in English, *4434*

Davenport, Thomas: Direct-current electric motor, *2169*

Dávid, Ferenc: Unitarian church, *4827*

David I, King of Scotland: Definition of an inch, *5311*

David III of Wales: Drawing and quartering, *1741*

David, King of Israel: Reference to King David, *2922*

Davids, Thomas William Rhys: English translations of early Buddhist texts, *4769*

Davidson, Ann: Transatlantic solo boat journey by a woman, *5461*

Davidson, Robert: Electric vehicle, *3214*

Davis, Harry Phillips: Transoceanic radio voice broadcast, *5910*

Davis, N. Jan: Husband and wife to fly in space together, *5559*

Davy, Humphrey: Discovery of the anesthetic properties of nitrous oxide (laughing gas), *3760*

Davy, Humphry: Arc lamp, *2091*
Fuel cell, *2058*

Dawa, Pasang: Ascent of Cho Oyu, *5740*

Dawks, Ichabod: Evening newspaper, *4497*

Dawson, Charles: Scientific hoax of international notoriety, *5051*

Dawson, Geoffrey: Transatlantic commercial telephone service, *5937*

Dayananda Sarasvati: Modern Hindu reform movement that rejected Western influence, *4915*

De Forest, Lee: Electronic amplifier tube, *2012*

De Havilland, Geoffrey: Jet airliner, *1326*

de Klerk, F.W.: Black African president of South Africa, *2865*

De la Beche, Henry Thomas: National geologic survey, *5270*

de la Reynie, Gabriel-Nicholas: Chief of police, *1789*

de Lumley, Henri: Site of human habitation in Europe, *4623*

de Luna Victoria, Francisco Xavier: Catholic bishop of African descent in the New World, *4874*

de Moleyns, Frederick: Incandescent lamp, *2092*

De Witt, John H.: Radar signal to the moon, *5518*

Deagan, Kathleen: Spanish settlement in North America, *4655*

Debussy, Claude: Impressionist musical composition, *4390*

Decker, Alonzo G.: Electric hand drill, *6060*

Defoe, Daniel: Novel in English, *3428*

Degas, Edgar: Exhibition of impressionist paintings, *1250*

Degeyter, Pierre: Communist song of international popularity, *4440*

Delaborde, J.B.: Electrified musical instrument, *4413*

DeLaurier, James: Ornithopter, *1334*

della Porta, Giambattista: Incubator for premature babies, *2337*
Steam engine, *2163*

Delmedigo, Yosef Shlomo (Joseph Solomon): Clinical thermometer, *5296*

Delprat, Guillaume: Mineral separation by flotation, *3677*

Democritus of Abdera: Atomic theory, *5320*

Denis, Jean-Baptiste: Blood transfusion in Europe in which the patient survived, *4098*

Denisyuk, Uri N.: Art holograms, *1242*
Hologram, *5318*

Denner, Johann Christoph: Clarinet, *4411*

Deprez, Marcel: Transmission of electricity through high-voltage cable, *2087*

Deraismes, Maria: Woman to become a Freemason, *1837*

Deroche, Elise: Woman to receive a pilot's license, *1311*

Desbarats, George Edouard: Letterpress halftone reproduction of a photograph, *4719*

Descartes, René: Contact lenses, *4105*
Exponent symbols, *3745*

Desdega, Peter: Standard laboratory burner, *5302*

Desgrange, Henri: Tour de France, *5628*

Desio, Ardito: Ascent of K2 (Mount Godwin Austen), *5739*

Desjardins, Alphonse: Credit union in the Western Hemisphere, *2412*

Dessalines, Jean-Jacques: Independent nation in Latin America, *2694*

Deutsch, Peter: Internet index, *1715*

Deville, Henri Sainte-Claire: Aluminum in commercial quantities, *3671*

Devol, George C.: Industrial robot that was practical, *5032*

Devonshire, Duke of: Baby carriage, *2383*

DeVries, William C.: Transplant of an artificial heart that was intended to be permanent, *4074*

Dew, Walter: Criminal caught by radio, *1755*

Dewar, James: Frozen hydrogen, *5238*
Vacuum flask, *5303*

Dezhnev, Semyon Ivanov: Expedition to sail around the northernmost point of Asia, *2313*

Dge-'dun-grub-pa: Dalai Lama, *4763*

Diaghilev, Serge: Ballets Russes, *1862*

Dias, Bartolomeu: European expedition to round the southern tip of Africa, *2280*

Dias de Novais, Paulo: African state to be ruled as a colony of a European state, *2691*
European city in southern Africa, *4656*

Dias, Henrique: Brazilian general of African descent, *4169*

Díaz de Vivar, Rodrigo: Autograph handwritten by a known individual in Europe, *3322*

Dib, Muhammad: Dead Sea Scrolls to be discovered, *4978*

Dibango, Manu: African song that was an international pop hit, *4449*

Dickens, Charles: Novel to be serialized, *3450*

Dickson, Earle: Small bandage with built-in adhesive, *3878*

Dickson, William Kennedy Laurie: Movie comedy, *4346*
Movie to be copyrighted, *4280*

Diemer, Walter: Bubble gum, *2555*

Diesel, Rudolf: Diesel engine built for commercial service, *2179*

Diesel, Rudolf Christian Karl: Diesel engine, *2176*

Dionne Quintuplets: Quintuplets, *2345*

Dionysius Exiguus: Work of history to use BC and AD, *6015*

Dionysius the Elder: Catapult, *6071*

Diori, Hamani: President of independent Niger, *2820*

Dioscorides, Pedanius: Pharmacopoeia widely used, *3788*

Dirks, Rudolph: Comic books featuring color cartoons previously published in newspapers, *4469*

Dischinger, Franz: Geodesic dome, *1199*

Diskay, Joseph: Voice double, *4321*

Disney, Walt: Animation with sound, *4331*
Feature-length animated film made by the cel process, *4333*

Divitiacus: Druid, *4738*

Dobrovolsky, Georgi: Space station, *5546*

Dod, Daniel: Steamboat to cross an ocean, *5455*

Dolby, Ray: Video tape recorder for sounds and pictures, *5964*

Dole, Vincent: Methadone maintenance program for heroin addicts, *4029*

Domagk, Gerhard: Sulfa drug, *3934*

Dominic de Guzmán, St.: Christian mendicant orders, *4857*

Domitian: Depiction of a menorah, *4965*

Dong Yuan: Monumental landscape painting, *1270*

Donne, Alfred: Image of human tissue made from life, *3901*

Donneau de Vizé, Jean: Magazine for popular entertainment, *4475*

Donnolo, Shabbetai: Treatise on medicine written in medieval Europe, *3771*

Donovan, Marion: Disposable diapers, *2392*

Dorantes de Carranca, Andres: Journey across North America, *2290*

Dornberger, Walter Robert: Ballistic missile test flight, *6134*

Dorrance, John T.: Condensed soup, *2541*

d'Orville, Albert: Christian missionaries in Tibet, *4873*

Dos Santos, Renaldo: Arteriogram, *3904*

Doughty, Thomas: Periscope, *4256*

Douglas, Jesse: Fields Medal, *3753*

Douhet, Giulio: Theorist of air warfare, *4214*

Dove, Arthur: Nonrepresentational modern paintings, *1286*

Dowsing, H.J.: Electric radiator, *1213*

Doyle, Arthur Conan: Movie shown on an airplane, *4299*
Scientific hoax of international notoriety, *5051*

D'Oyly Carte, Richard: Theater entirely lit by electric lights, *5998*

Drais de Sauerbrun, Baron Karl de: Bicycle, *5620*

Drake, Edwin Laurentine: Oil well, *2105*

Drake, Francis: Protestant service in the New World, *4828*
Sea captain to circumnavigate the world, *2306*

Drake, Frank D.: Scientific program to search for extraterrestrial life, *5101*

Drake, Jim: Windsurfing, *5866*

Drake, Karen: Septuplets to survive birth, *2353*

Drebbel, Cornelis Jacobszoon: Submarine, *5447*

Dreifuss, Ruth: Woman to become president of Switzerland, *2868*

Drela, Mark: Watercraft to win the Dupont Water Prize, *5860*

Dresser, Betsy L.: Gorilla born by in vitro fertilization, *1126*
Interspecies birth of a cat, *1121*

Dresser, Christopher: Modern product designer, *3090*

Drew, Richard Gurley: Cellophane transparent tape, *3114*

Dreyse, Johann Nikolas: Breech-loading military rifle, *6109*

Drinker, Philip: Apparatus used to treat respiratory failure, *4088*

Driscoll, Bridget: Pedestrian killed by an automobile, *1892*

Drummond, Thomas: Theatrical spotlight, *5997*

Dryden, John: Poet laureate of England, *3424*

Du Camp, Maxime: Travel book illustrated with original photographs, *3393*

Duarte, Juan Pablo: Leader of the independent Dominican Republic, *2994*

Dube, John Langalibalele: Zulu newspaper, *4512*
Zulu writing, *3543*

Dubernard, Jean-Michel: Hand transplant, *4077*

Dubois de Chémant, Nicolas: Porcelain dentures, *3808*

Dubois, Eugene: Fossils of *Homo erectus*, *4616*

Dubus-Bonnel, Ignace: Glass fiber, *3650*

Duchamp, Marcel: Anti-art movement, *1252*
Kinetic sculpture, *1300*

Duchâteau, Alexis: Porcelain dentures, *3808*

Duchesne-Guillemin, Jacques: Musical notation, *4360*

Dufek, John: Airplane flight to land at the South Pole, *2327*

Duke of Zhou: Homeostatic machine, *2184*

Dunant, Jean-Henri: International agreements on the humane treatment of soldiers and civilians in wartime, *3170*
International medical relief organization, *4012*
Nobel Prize for Peace, *4538*

Dunaway, Deborah Maddux: Angler to hold world records for every billfish species, *5601*

Duncan, Isadora: Modern dancer, *1850*

Dunlop, James: Permanent observatory in the Southern Hemisphere, *5135*

Dunlop, John Boyd: Pneumatic tires for bicycles, *5626*

Dunning, E.H.: Landing of a plane on a ship under way, *4262*

Dunton, John: Advice column, *4454*

Dupuy de Lôme, Stanislas-Charles-Henri-Laurent: Ironclad warship in modern times, *4253*

Durán, Diego: Ball game, *5595*

Durand, Georges: Twenty-four-hour automobile endurance race, *5719*

Durand, Peter: Metal cans, *2518*

Durrani, Ahmad Shah: Leader of united Afghanistan, *2989*

Dutkiewicz, Adriana: Fossil oil, *5251*

Dyar, Harrison Gray: Primitive telegraph system, *5921*

E

Eads, James Buchanan: Steel bridge, *2144*

Eanes, Gil: European country to enter the African slave trade, *5477*
Explorers to pass Cape Bojador since antiquity, *2279*

Earhart, Amelia: Transatlantic solo airplane flight by a woman, *1370*
Transpacific solo airplane flight by a woman, *1374*

Eastman, George: Camera to use film rolls, *4581*
Free dental clinic for poor children, *3820*

Eaton, Cyrus: International conference of atomic scientists, *5350*

Ebers, Georg Moritz: Medical texts, *3766*

Eckener, Hugo: Circumnavigation by air, *1407*

Eckert, J. Presper, Jr.: Electronic computer for commercial use, *1671*
General-purpose computer that was fully electronic, *1669*

Ecuyer, Captain: Germ warfare for purposes of genocide, *1766*

Eddington, Arthur Stanley: Scientific proof of the general theory of relativity, *5336*

Ederle, Gertrude Caroline: Woman to swim the English Channel, *5822*

Edge, S.F.: International motorboat racing competition, *5857*

Edgerton, Harold Eugene "Doc": Stroboscopic lamp for high-speed photography, *4585*

Edison, Thomas Alva: Alkaline dry cell battery, *2090*
Electric company, *2086*
Electron tube diode, *2010*
Incandescent lamp, *2092*
Movie exhibition in a theater to a paying audience, *4353*
Movie studio, *4279*
Movie to be copyrighted, *4280*
Phonograph, *2041*

Edison, Thomas Alva:—*continued*
Sound recording device, *2040*

Edward I, King of England: Expulsion of Jews from a European country, *4971*
Shipping tax based on tonnage, *1539*
Standard shoe sizes, *1654*
Urban air pollution, *2263*

Edward III, King of England: Depiction of a gun in Europe, *6097*

Edward the Confessor, King of England: King to practice curing of the "king's evil", *3952*

Edward VII, King of England: Star of Africa, *3678*
Transoceanic radio broadcast, *5902*

Edwards, Robert: Test-tube baby, *2348*

Egas Moniz, António Caetano de Abreu Freire: Prefrontal lobotomy, *4056*

Eggler, Albert: Ascent of Lhotse, *5744*

Egnot, Leslie: All-woman America's Cup yacht-racing crew, *5861*

Ehrlich, Paul: Synthetic drug to treat bacterial infections, *3931*
Treatment for syphilis, *3930*

Eichengreen, Arthur: Aspirin, *3928*

Eichmann, Adolf: Televised trial, *4463*

Eiffel, Alexandre-Gustave: Department store, *1514*

Eigler, Donald M.: Physical manipulation of individual atoms, *5354*

Eilmer: Manned glider flight, *1415*

Einhard: Biography of a European king, *2930*
Reference to sunspots in Western literature, *5072*

Einstein, Albert: International conference of atomic scientists, *5350*
Proposal of the existence of gravitational singularities, *5328*
Scientific proof of the general theory of relativity, *5336*

Einthoven, Willem: Electrocardiogram, *3903*

Eisele, Donn Fulton: Live telecast from space, *5542*

Eiselen, Ernst: Gymnastics treatise, *5671*

Eiselin, Max: Ascent of Dhaulagiri, *5745*

Eisenhower, Dwight David: Nazi death camp to be liberated in World War II, *1774*
Open Skies treaty, *3183*
Overthrow of a democratic foreign government arranged by the U.S. Central Intelligence Agency, *4143*
Peacetime alliance of European and North American nations, *3137*
Radio broadcast using an orbiting satellite, *5915*

Eisenstein, Judith Kaplan: Bat mitzvah ceremony, *4977*

Eisler, Paul: Printed circuit, *2015*

El Moutawakil, Nawal: Black African woman athlete to win an Olympic gold medal, *5787*

Eliezer, Israel ben *See* Israel ben Eliezer

Eliot, John: Bible translated into an indigenous American language, *4892*
Missionary society, *4798*

Elisha: Case of mouth-to-mouth resuscitation, *4080*

Elizabeth I, Queen of England: Anglican Communion church, *4821*
Elizabethan acting troupe, *5983*
European ruler to bathe regularly, *2720*
Flush toilet, *4035*
Multinational corporation, *1542*
National lottery, *2607*
Puritans, *4826*
Sea captain to circumnavigate the world, *2306*
Statute mile, *5312*

Elizabeth II, Queen of England: Head of state to send an e-mail message, *1703*
International television broadcast, *5962*
Televised coronation, *2979*
Underwater link between Great Britain and Europe, *2198*

Elizabeth, Queen of Hungary: Perfume containing alcohol, *2746*

Elizabeth, the Queen Mother: British monarchs to visit the United States, *2976*

Ellis, William Webb: Rugby match, *5802*

Ellsworth, Annie: Commercial telegraph service, *5923*

Ellsworth, Lincoln: Flight over the North Pole, *2321*

Ellsworth, Solomon, Jr.: Published record of dinosaur fossil remains, *5213*

Elmqvist, Rune: Pacemaker successfully implanted in a patient, *4059*

Elsener, Karl: Swiss Army knife, *6059*

Elvstrom, Paul B.: Sportsman to win individual gold medals in four successive Olympic Games, *5770*

Empiricus, Sextus: Skeptic, *4559*

Emre, Yunus: Turkish writing, *3501*

Emtage, Alan: Internet index, *1715*

En-lil-ti: Personal name, *3482*

Ende: Woman miniaturist, *1269*

Engelbart, Douglas C.: Computer mouse, *1676*

Engelberger, Joseph F.: Industrial robot that was practical, *5032*

Engels, Friedrich: Communist political platform, *2672*
Communist secret society, *2671*

Enheduanna: Author known by name, *3326*
Verses in honor of a deity, *4733*

Ennigaldi-Nanna: Museum, *1824*

Ennius, Quintus: Epic composed in Latin, *3569*

Épée, Charles-Michel de l': School for deaf education, *2006*

Epicurus of Samos: Epicurean, *4560*

Epiphanius of Constantia: Bestiary, *3467*

Eppig, John: Mammals born from an egg grown in vitro, *5173*

Epstein, M.A.: Human cancer-causing virus to be discovered, *3848*

Equiano, Olaudah: Autobiography by an African slave to have a major impact on the abolition movement, *5489*

Eratosthenes: Method of finding prime numbers, *3733*

Eratosthenes of Cyrene: Scientific calculation of the Earth's circumference, *5256*

Ercilla y Zúñiga, Alonso de: Modern epic poems, *3445*

Erik the Red: Discovery of Greenland, *2275*
Settlers in Greenland, *4642*

Eriksdottir, Freydis: European settlement in North America, *4643*

Eriksson, Leif: European settlement in North America, *4643*
Map of any part of the Americas, *3608*
Re-enactment of a Viking voyage to the New World, *5469*

Eriksson, Thorvald: European settlement in North America, *4643*

Ermengem, Émile van: Outbreak of botulism, *3838*

Ermesinde, Countess: Woman to rule Luxembourg, *2945*

Ernst, Max: Surrealist exhibition, *1254*

Eshinni: Buddhist priest to be married, *4762*

Eshleman, Von Russel: Radar signal bounced off the sun, *5100*

Estevánico: Journey across North America, *2290*

Esther, Queen: Planned genocide, *1765*

Étienne, Jean-Louis: Expedition to cross Antarctica by dogsled and foot, *2330*

Etinger, Shloyme: Yiddish play to be performed, *3574*

Euclid: Mathematical definition of a circle, *3732*

Eugénie, Empress of France: Crinolines, *1628*

Eugster, Hans: Gymnast to achieve a perfect score, *5774*

Eupalinus of Megara: Hydraulic engineer, *2125*

Euripides: Choreographers, *1841*

Eustachio, Bartolomeo: Treatise on dental anatomy, *3778*

Evans, Charles: Ascent of Kanchenjunga, *5742*

Evans, P.J.: Motorcycle race of importance, *5717*

Evans, Thomas W.: Silver amalgam tooth filling in modern times, *3813*

Evatt, H. V.: Chairman of the United Nations Atomic Energy Commission, *3190*

Evelyn, John: Greenhouses, *1074*
Treatise on air pollution, *2264*
Treatise on forestry in English, *5182*

Everitt, Percival: Vending machine in modern times, *1516*

Evrard, August: Computer model of the growth of the universe, *5113*

Ezra the Scribe: Canonization of biblical books, *4984*

F

Fa-hsien: Suspension bridge, *2138*

Fa Ngum: King of the Lao people, *2949*

Faber, Joseph: Voice synthesizer, *5931*

Fabergé, Peter Karl: Fabergé Easter egg, *1248*

Fabiola, St.: Hospice for Christian pilgrims, *1458*
Public hospital in Europe, *3883*

Fabre d'Églantine, Philippe-François-Nazaire: National revolutionary calendar, *6009*

Fabre, Henri: Seaplane flight, *1358*

Fabre, Jean-Henri: Study of insect behavior, *5163*

Fabricius ab Aquapendente, Hieronymus: Works on comparative embryology, *3779*

Fabricius, David: Discovery of a variable star, *5075*

Factor, Max: Makeup specifically for movie actors, *2724*

Fae, Baby: Transplant of a baboon heart into a human being, *4075*

Faggin, Federico: Microprocessor, *1678*

Fagunwa, Daniel Olorunfemi: Yoruba writing, *3542*

Fahrenheit, Gabriel Daniel: Mercury thermometer, *5300*
Temperature scale, *5221*

Fairfax, John: Transatlantic solo trip by rowboat, *5466*
Weekly Australian newspaper, *4502*

Fallopio, Gabriele: Condoms, *2358*

Fansler, Percival: Airliner, *1315*

Faraday, Michael: Liquified gas, *5230*

Farina, Jean-Baptiste: Eau de cologne, *2747*

Farman, Maurice and Henri: Long-distance passenger plane, *1317*

Farmer, Fannie Merritt: Cookbook with standardized measurements, *2506*

Farnworth, Arthur: Trousers with permanent pleats, *1637*

Faroux, Charles: Twenty-four-hour automobile endurance race, *5719*

Fauchard, Pierre: Dental drill for cavities, *3807*

Gell-Mann, Murray: Discovery of quarks, *5351*

Gem, Harry: Tennis club, *5833*

Gendutrup: Dalai Lama, *4763*

Geoffrey, Count of Anjou: European heraldry, *2706*

Geoffroi de Preully, Baron: Tournament between armed knights, *2221*

George II, King of England: Museum operated as a public institution, *1826*

George VI, King of England: British civilian medal conferred on a country, *2698*
British monarchs to visit the United States, *2976*

Gerbert of Aurillac: French-born pope, *4854*

Geremek, Bronislav: Former Warsaw Pact nations to join NATO, *3143*

Gerlache de Gomery, Adrien Victor Joseph de: Explorers to winter in Antarctica, *2317*

Gerone II, King of Syracuse: Troop transport, *4157*

Gersdorff, Hans von: Illustrated surgical treatise, *3773*

Gesner, Abraham: Kerosene, *2104*

Gesner, Conrad: Depiction of a lead pencil, *3583*
Modern bibliography, *1813*

Gesner, Conrad von: Fossil illustrations, *5210*

Getaldic, Marin: Parabolic mirror, *5316*

Gheyn, Jacob de: Army drill book, *4126*

Ghiberti, Lorenzo: Autobiography of an artist, *1236*

Gibbon, John H., Jr.: Heart-lung machine, *4068*

Gibbs, James: Table tennis, *5828*

Gibson, Robert L.: Spacecraft launched by the United States to dock with a Russian space station, *5561*

Gibson, Roy: Multinational space agency, *5510*

Gibson, William: Cyberspace description, *1708*

Gierek, Edward: Pope to visit a Communist country, *4878*

Giffard, Henri: Steam-powered airship, *1401*

Gifford, Walter Sherman: Telephone conversation to travel around the world, *5938*
Transatlantic commercial telephone service, *5937*

Gilbert, Humphrey: English-speaking colony in the New World, *4657*

Gilbert, Joseph Henry: Agricultural research station, *1004*

Gilbert, William: Demonstration of static electricity, *5323*

Gildas: Reference to the King Arthur legend in a historical work, *3470*

Gilgamesh: Epic, *3435*
Reference to wrestling in literature, *5868*

Gill, David: Photographic star catalog, *5123*

Ginsberg, Charles P.: Video tape recorder for sounds and pictures, *5964*

Girard, Louis: Iron tooth, *3798*

Glas, Louis: Jukebox, *2044*

Glidden, Joseph Farwell: Barbed wire, *1089*

Gnam-ri srong-brtsan: King of Tibet, *2926*

Gobind Singh: Sikhs to take the name "Singh", *5009*

Goddard, John Frederick: Photography studio in Europe open to the public, *4591*

Goddard, Robert Hutchins: Rocket flight using liquid fuel, *5505*

Godfrey, O.C.: Motorcycle race of importance, *5717*

Godoy y Alcayaga, Lucila: Nobel Prize for Literature winner from Latin America, *4534*

Godunov, Boris: Patriarch of Moscow, *4810*

Goebbels, Josef: Nazi book burning, *3364*

Goes, Hugo: Wallpaper, *3087*

Gokchen, Sabiha: Woman to serve as a combat pilot, *4217*

Goldman, Arnold J.: Commercial-scale thermal solar energy installations, *2072*

Goldman, Richard and Rhoda: Goldman Environmental Prizes, *2250*

Goldmark, Peter: Long-playing (LP) phonograph records, *2052*

Goldschmidt, Victor Moritz: Treatise on geochemistry, *5282*

Golze, Hermann: Bus with an internal-combustion engine, *3218*

Gómez, Luís María: Sexual harassment case at the United Nations, *5377*

Gondard, Maurice: Starter motor, *2180*

González, Julio: Welded metal sculpture, *1303*

Goodall, Jane van Lawick: Scientific observations of primate behavior in the wild, *5170*

Goodhue, Lyle D.: Aerosol product, *3115*

Goodyear, Charles: Sneakers, *1656*
Vulcanized rubber, *1488*

Goosen, Hendrick: Coelacanth caught alive, *1115*

Gorbachev, Mikhail: Green Cross organization, *2252*

Gordon, Hugh: Commercial round-the-world airplane flight, *1345*

Gore, Robert: Synthetic fabric that was waterproof and breathable, *3725*

Gore, Wilbert L.: Synthetic fabric that was waterproof and breathable, *3725*

Gorgas, William Crawford: Mosquito-eradication project to control disease, *4016*

Gorgo: Woman cryptanalyst, *4137*

Göring, Hermann: Air battle that was strategically important, *4222*

Gorky, Maksim: President of the Soviet Writers' Union, *3337*

Gorlitz, Dr.: Guide dogs, *1157*

Gould, Francis Carruthers: Staff cartoonist on a newspaper, *4461*

Gould, Gordon: Laser, *2017*

Gowers, Bruce: Music video, *4450*

Grafenberg, Ernst: Intrauterine device (IUD), *2367*

Gramme, Zénobe-Théophile: Electric generator that was commercially successful, *2085*

Grassi, Giovanni: Recognition of the vector of malaria, *3842*

Gray, Charles: European explorer to cross the Australian continent, *2299*

Gray, J.E.: Stamp catalogs, *4693*

Gray, Stephen: Conduction of electricity along a wire, *2079*

Greathead, Henry: Lifeboat, *5411*

Grebel, Konrad: Adult baptisms in modern times, *4818*
  Anabaptist church, *4819*

Green, Andy: Car to break the sound barrier, *5725*

Green, George: Prenatal blood transfusion, *4101*

Green, George F.: Dental drill powered by electricity, *3816*

Green, Norvin: Electric company, *2086*

Greenberg, Bernie: Guide to E-mail etiquette, *1710*

Greenwood, John: Powered dental drill, *3810*

Grégoire, Marc: Nonstick cookware, *3117*

Gregory I the Great, Pope: Gregorian chant, *4381*

Gregory III, Pope: Halloween, *3025*

Gregory IV, Pope: Halloween, *3025*

Gregory IX, Pope: Burning of the Talmud by Christian authorities, *4970*
  Official Christian inquisition, *4859*

Gregory, Samuel: Medical school for women, *3860*

Gregory the Illuminator, St.: Establishment of Christianity as the state religion, *4781*

Gregory XIII, Pope: Calendar adopted worldwide, *6007*

Greiner, Friedrich: Taxicabs, *3236*

Grew, Nathaniel: Epsom salt (magnesium sulfate), *3922*

Grew, Nehemiah: Scientifically accurate treatise on sex in plants, *5183*

Grey, Earl: Coins minted in Canada, *2456*

Grey, Lady Jane: Woman to rule England, *2956*

Greymantle, Geoffrey: Stone castles, *1182*

Griffo, Francesco: Italics, *4707*

Grimaldi, Joseph: Circus clown, *2206*

Grimm, Jacob and Wilhelm: Collection of folktales from oral tradition, *3480*

Grisegonelle, Geoffroi *See* Fulk Nerra

Gromyko, Andrei: Chairman of the United Nations Atomic Energy Commission, *3190*

Gropius, Walter: Tubular steel chair, *3091*

Grose, Francis: Dictionary of English slang, *3374*

Grotius, Hugo: Comprehensive text on international law, *3151*

Grove, George: Musical encyclopedia in English, *4372*

Grove, William R.: Fuel cell that was practical, *2060*

Grubert, Marie: Woman dentist with a degree from a dental school, *3814*

Grueber, Johannes: Christian missionaries in Tibet, *4873*

Gruelle, John: Raggedy Ann doll, *2390*

Grufudd, David ap: Drawing and quartering, *1741*

Gruhl, Herbert: Green Party seats in a national government, *2668*

Gruyon, Felix: Vasectomy, *2364*

Gubarev, Aleksei: Space traveler who was not of USSR or U.S. citizenship, *5549*

Guericke, Otto von: Air pump, *5298*
  Electric generator, *2078*

Guerrero, Gonzalo: European to join a Native American people, *4651*

Guerrero, Manuel Amador: Constitutional president of Panama, *2792*

Guglielmo de Lorena: Diving apparatus for practical underwater work, *5446*

Guido de Vigevano: Wind-driven vehicle, *3205*

Guillard, Charlotte: Woman printer, *4710*

Guillaume de Machaut: Polyphonic mass, *4384*

Guillotin, Joseph-Ignace: Execution by guillotine, *1744*

Gurdon, John B.: Cloned animal, *5186*

Gusmão, Bartholomeu de: Hot-air balloon, *1390*

Gustav I Vasa, King of Sweden: National standing army in Europe, *4124*

Gustavus Adolphus, King of Sweden: Major land battle decided by volley fire, *4168*

Gutenberg, Johannes: Best-seller, *3348*
  Book printed in color, *3350*
  Book printed in Europe, *3344*
  Book printed in Europe that survives in its complete form, *3349*
  Printed edition of the Bible, *4885*
  Printed New Year's greeting, *3028*
  Printing press, *4704*
  Text printed in Europe bearing a date, *3347*

Gutermuth, Hans: Glider club, *1419*

Guthrie, Francis: Significant mathematical problem solved by computer, *3754*

Guyton de Morveau, Louis Bernard: Military air force, *4127*

H

Haakonson, Kiki: Miss World contest, *2201*

Haarman, Wilhelm: Artificial flavoring, *2539*

Habash, Georges: International terrorist organization to use skyjacking, *1800*

Habeler, Peter: Ascent of Mount Everest without bottled oxygen, *5748*

Hadrian: Depiction of a flower arrangement, *1268*

Monumental concrete structure, *1178*

Hageman, Geert: Black tulip, *1057*

Hahn, Ulrich: Music printed from movable type, *4706*

Hainisch, Michael Arthur Josef Jakob: President of the federal republic of Austria, *2802*

Haise, Fred W., Jr.: Reusable manned spacecraft, *5551*

Haken, Wolfgang: Significant mathematical problem solved by computer, *3754*

Haki: Up-Helly-Aa fire festival, *3020*

Haldane, T.G.N.: Heat pump, *2064*

Halévy, Ludovic: Operetta, *4437*

Haley, Bill: Worldwide rock-and-roll hit, *4445*

Hall, Charles: Waterbed, *3094*

Hall, Chester Moor: Achromatic lens, *5317*

Hall, G.J.: Labor party, *2663*

Hall, Marshall: Theory of physiological reflexes, *5161*

Hallam, Clint: Hand transplant, *4077*

Haller, Gordon: Ironman triathlon, *5849*

Halley, Edmond: Calculation of the orbit of a comet, *5079*

Diving bell with supplementary air supply, *5448*

Meteorological map of the world, *3620*

Scientific effort to relate age and mortality in a large population, *1868*

Scientific research voyage, *5049*

Hamburger, Christian: Sex-change operation that was successful, *5372*

Hamilton, William: Plastic bags, *3118*

Hammon, Briton: Autobiography by an African slave to have a major impact on the abolition movement, *5489*

Hammond, George: British ambassador to the United States, *3145*

Hammurabi: Banking regulations, *2401*

Contract terms for wet-nursing, *2378*

Drug treatment for mental illness, *3986*

Legal protection for trade secrets, *1439*

Legal regulation of the trade in alcoholic beverages, *2476*

Malpractice regulation for physicians, *3942*

Marriage and divorce laws, *2395*

Slavery, *5471*

Hamzah ibn Ali, Caliph: Druze imam, *4740*

Han Si: Kites, *1414*

Hancock, Thomas: Waterproof raincoat, *1624*

Hancock, Walter: Motorized bus service, *3213*

Handel, George Frideric: Performance of the oratorio *Messiah*, *4388*

Handy, William Christopher "W.C.": Composer of jazz music, *4376*

Haney, Chris: Trivia board game of international popularity, *2579*

Hannibal: Elephants taken on a sea voyage, *1106*

Hanno: Voyage of colonization, *4635*

Hansen, Edmund H.: Transatlantic radio fax transmission of a photograph, *5876*

Hansen, Rick: Circumnavigation by wheelchair, *5854*

Hantaro Nagaoka: Modern theory of atomic structure, *5333*

Harald I Fairhair, King of Norway: King of Norway, *2932*

Hardy, James D.: Transplant of an animal organ into a human being, *4070*

Hargobind, Guru: Sikh guru who was a temporal leader, *5007*

Sikh military victories, *5008*

Hargrave, Lawrence: Box kite, *1417*

Manned flight by kite, *1418*

Hargreaves, James: Anti-technology riots, *1503*

Machine to spin yarn on more than one spindle, *3715*

Harington, John: Flush toilet, *4035*

Harley, Edward and Robert: Museum operated as a public institution, *1826*

Harmer, Barbara: Supersonic airline co-pilot who was a woman, *1352*

Harmsworth, Alfred: International motorboat racing competition, *5857*

Newspaper illustrated exclusively with photographs, *4510*

Tabloid newspaper, *4511*

Harris, Benjamin: Newspaper published in the British colonies in America, *4496*

Harris, Chapin A.: Dental college, *3859*

Dentistry journal, *3812*

Harris, Jeremy: Ornithopter, *1334*

Harris, John: Encyclopedic dictionary, *3373*

Harris, Paul Percy: Service club, *1839*

Harrison, James: Frozen meat for commercial sale, *2535*

Harrison, James Jonathan: African Pygmies to visit Europe, *4665*

Harrison, John: Clock capable of keeping accurate time at sea, *6029*

Hart, Robert M.: Transoceanic radio signal conveying a television image, *5953*

Hartley, David: Use of the term "psychology", *3989*

Harun al-Rashid, Caliph: Elephants taken on a sea voyage, *1106*

Harvey, John W.: Nuclear submarine lost at sea, *1942*

Harvey, William: Description of pulmonary blood circulation, *3953*

Harvey, William:—*continued*
Embalming by injecting the arteries with preservative, *1879*
Hatshepsut: Pharaoh who was a woman, *2921*
Plant-collecting expedition, *5177*
Haultin, Pierre: Music printed from movable type, *4706*
Haüy, Valentin: Reading system for blind people, *2008*
School for blind children, *2007*
Havas, Charles-Louis: Modern news service, *4514*
Havel, Václav: President of the Czech Republic, *2862*
Hayakawa Tokuji: Mechanical pencil, *3595*
Hayden, Horace H.: Dentistry journal, *3812*
Hayes, Daniel: Hook and ladder truck, *1577*
Hayes, Denis: International Earth Day, *3043*
Hazilius, Artur: Museum of traditional life, *1827*
Open-air museum, *1828*
Hearne, Samuel: European explorer in North America to reach the Arctic by land, *2314*
Hebert, Arthur: Solo crossing of the Gulf of Mexico in a paddled boat, *5470*
Hecataeus of Miletus: Geographical book, *5252*
Narrative secular history book of importance, *3002*
Heckel, Paul: Hypertext computer application, *1733*
Hedin, Sven: Centrifuge, *3877*
Heelan, Bill: Internet index, *1715*
Heemskerk, Jacob van: Major naval battle fought by the Dutch navy, *4250*
Heenan, John C.: World heavyweight boxing championship, *5644*
Hegel, Georg Wilhelm Friedrich: Modern encyclopedia of philosophy, *4568*
Heilmeier, George: Liquid crystal display, *2021*
Heinkel, Ernst: Turbojet aircraft, *1321*
Helena of Adiabene: Royal converts to Judaism, *4963*
Helmholtz, Hermann von: Ophthalmoscope, *3873*
Helwys, Thomas: Baptist church, *4829*
Hemacandra: Gujarati texts, *3512*
Hemming, Edmund: Mechanical street sweeper, *1588*
Hempleman-Adams, David: Person to complete the "Explorer's Grand Slam", *2302*
Hendee, George M.: Motorcycle designed to be a motor vehicle, *3219*
Hengest: Anglo-Saxons to arrive in England, *4636*
Henlein, Peter: Pocket watch, *6026*
Hennebique, François: Reinforced concrete bridge, *2145*
Reinforced concrete building system, *2154*

Hennings, Emmy: Anti-art movement, *1252*
Henry, Edward: Fingerprint bureau, *1754*
Henry II, Emperor of Germany: Great Seal, *2705*
Henry II, Holy Roman Emperor: Pocket, *1608*
Henry II, King of France: Ballet to combine dancing, music, and acting, *1854*
Henry III, King of England: Prince of Wales, *2947*
Henry IV, King of France: Politician to offer a chicken in every pot, *2630*
Henry, Joseph: National weather service, *5271*
Henry the Navigator of Portugal, Prince: Post for trade between Europe and Africa, *1554*
Henry the Navigator, Prince: European country to enter the African slave trade, *5477*
International and multicultural academy for explorers, *2278*
Henry V, King of England: English-only rule, *3409*
King of England after the Norman Conquest who could read and write English, *3408*
Henry VII, King of England: Military unit to wear a complete uniform, *4146*
Shilling, *2444*
Henry VIII, King of England: Anglican Communion church, *4821*
Drydock, *5405*
Military regulation concerning uniforms, *4147*
Royal palace in Europe to integrate public and private functions in one unified structure, *1190*
Women admitted to a guild of dentists, *3805*
Henson, Maria Rosa: Reparations for forced prostitution, *1779*
Henson, Matthew Alexander: Discovery of the North Pole, *2325*
Henson, William S.: Air transport company, *1336*
Herakles of Ida: Olympic Games, *5756*
Herjölffson, Bjarni *See* Bjarni Herjölffson
Hermann, Emmanuel: Prepaid postcards, *4674*
Herndon, Hugh, Jr.: Transpacific nonstop airplane flight, *1369*
Hero of Alexandria: Turbine, *2161*
Vending machine, *1509*
Herodotus: Narrative secular history book of importance, *3002*
Scalping, *4156*
Herophilus: Anatomist to dissect human cadavers, *3946*
Western physician to take a pulse, *3947*
Héroult, Paul-Louis-Toussaint: Electric arc furnace, *1493*
Herrad of Landsberg: Encyclopedia compiled by a woman, *3381*

Herschel, Caroline Lucretia: Woman astronomer who was paid for her work, 5083

Herschel, William: Planet discovered since ancient times, 5082
Register of fingerprints, 1752

Hertz, Heinrich Rudolph: Radio waves, 5895

Hertz, John D.: Rent-a-car business, 3238

Herzl, Theodor: Jewish city founded in Israel in modern times, 4666
World Zionist Congress, 2665

Herzog, Jesus Silva: Third World country to default on its foreign debt, 2417

Herzog, Maurice: Ascent of Annapurna, 5736

Hesi-Re: Dentist, 3795

Hesiod: Written versions of the Greek myths, 3464

Hetherington, John: Top hat, 1647

Hetzel, Max: Electronic wristwatch, 6033

Heun, Manfred: Einkorn domestication, 1012

Hevelius, Johannes: Map of the moon, 3622

Hewish, Antony: Discovery of pulsars, 5104

Heydrich, Reinhard: Attack of World War II, 4184

Heyerdahl, Thor: Raft trip across the Pacific, 5460

Hezelo: Flying buttresses, 1183

Hicetas: Heliocentric world system, 5068

Hickman, C.N.: Handheld rocket launcher, 6133

Hieb, Richard J.: Simultaneous space walk by three astronauts, 5558

Higgs, Thomas: Machine to spin yarn on more than one spindle, 3715

Highen, James: Sheep-shearing machine, 1137

Higinbotham, William: Video game, 2577

Hilda, St.: Poet in English, 3405

Hildebrand, Heinrich and Wilhelm: Motorcycle to be mass-produced, 3217

Hill, Charles: Transatlantic telephone call using the transoceanic cable, 5943

Hill, John: Connection between tobacco and cancer, 4024
Gossip columnist, 4455

Hill, Levi: Color photography process, 4579

Hill, Octavia: Housing project in an inner-city neighborhood, 5497

Hill, Rowland: Postage stamps, 4689
Postal system to carry prepaid mail, 4672

Hillaire, Christian: Paintings, 1262

Hillary, Edmund Percival: Ascent of Mount Everest, 5737

Hillel II, Rabbi: Jewish calendar, 6006

Himmler, Heinrich: Human breeding program, 5197

Hinchliffe, Robert: Steel scissors, 6054

Hinton, Christopher: Nuclear power plant, 2117

Hipparchus: Star catalog that was comprehensive and accurate, 5119

Hippias: Event in Greek history to be dated, 6012

Hippocrates: Description of disease as a matter of science, 3827
Occupational disease, 3828
Treatise on human ecology, 2237

Hippocrates of Chios: Treatise on geometry, 3731

Hippodamus: Utopian town planner, 1561

Hippolytus, St.: Antipope, 4848

Hirschfeld, Al: Demonstration of home reception of television, 5956

Hirschfeld, Magnus: Center for the study of human sexuality, 5371
Homosexual rights organization, 5380

Hitchcock, Henry-Russell: Use of the term "International Style", 1200

Hitler, Adolf: Cruise missile used in war, 6135
National euthanasia program, 1771
Subcompact car designed to be fuel-efficient, 3239
Woman to be awarded the Iron Cross, 4225

Hiyya, Avraham bar See Avraham bar Hiyya

Hobbs, Lucy Beaman: Woman dentist with a degree from a dental school, 3814

Hoby, Lady Margaret: Diary in English, 3423

Hodgkin, Dorothy Crowfoot: Molecule analyzed with the use of a computer, 5248
Three-dimensional molecular structure, 5246

Hoe, Richard: Newspaper folding device, 4720

Hoff, Jacobus Henricus van't: Nobel Prize in Chemistry, 4523

Hoff, Ted: Microprocessor, 1678

Hofmann, Albert: Synthetic hallucinogen, 4028

Holcroft, Thomas: Melodrama in English, 3432

Holladay, Wilhelmina Cole: Museum of art by women, 1832

Holland, Clifford Milburn: Automobile tunnel, 2193

Holland, Greg: Transatlantic crossing by an robot airplane, 1388

Hollingshead, Richard Milton, Jr.: Drive in movie theater, 4359

Homer: Boxing, 5637
Epic translated into Latin, 3568

Homfray, Samuel: Steam locomotive, 3264

Honda Soichiro: Japanese-owned automobile factory in the United States, 3252

Hooke, Robert: Anemometer, 5261

Horney, Karen Danielsen: Woman psychoanalyst, 4003

Horsa: Anglo-Saxons to arrive in England, 4636

Horszowski, Mieczyslaw: Recording of piano on tape, 2051

Horthy, Miklós: Woman accredited as a minister to a foreign power, 3146

Hosford, Mary: College to enroll women and men on equal terms, *1994*

Hoskins, John: Washing machine, *3054*

Hotteterre, Jean: Oboe, *4409*

Houdry, Eugène: Fluid catalytic cracking process, *2109*

Hounsfield, Godfrey: CAT scan, *3906*

Houphouët-Boigny, Félix: President of the Ivory Coast (Côte d'Ivoire), *2816*

Houssay, Bernardo Alberto: Nobel Prize in Physiology or Medicine winner from Latin America, *4552*

Howard, A.C.: Rotary cultivator, *1091*

Howard, Albert: Organic gardening, *2625*

Howard, Edward: Naval battle fought with cannon broadsides, *4245*

Howard, Henry, Earl of Surrey: Blank verse in English, *3416*

Howard, John: Prison reformer, *1738*
Sheep-shearing machine, *1137*

Howe, Mia: Transoceanic radio signal conveying a television image, *5953*

Hoyle, Edmond: Compendium of rules for a game, *2589*

Hrosvitha: European playwright, *5981*
Hungarian writing, *3517*
Woman poet to write in German, *3558*

Hu, Jan: Protestant hymnbook, *4813*

Huang Zhihong: Asian athlete to win a World Cup gold medal in track and field, *5844*

Hubbard, Edward: International airmail service, *4684*

Hubbard, William DeHart: Athlete of African descent to win a gold medal in an individual event, *5767*

Hubble, Edwin Powell: Galaxy to be described in print, *5071*
Orbiting observatory, *5144*

Hublin, Jean-Jacques: Physical handicap in an adult, *3823*

Huggins, William: Observations of stellar spectra, *5092*

Hugh, Bishop of Gebal: Legend of Prester John, *3471*

Hugh of Provence: Depiction of eyeglasses, *4104*

Hugh of Semur, Abbot: Flying buttresses, *1183*

Hughes, Charles: Circus known by that name, *2205*

Hughes, David Edward: Radio waves, *5895*

Hughes, Glenn: Modern theater in the round, *5999*

Hughes, W.M. "Billy": Air race from England to Australia, *5604*

Hülsenbeck, Richard: Anti-art movement, *1252*

Hülsmeyer, Christian: Radar, *2011*

Humann, Karl: Art presenting a continuous narrative, *1234*

Humboldt, Alexander von: Weather maps, *3623*

Humerelli: Political sex scandal, *2627*

Hunayn ibn Ishaq: Collector of Greek scientific manuscripts, *5044*

Hünefeld, Günther von: Transatlantic east-west nonstop airplane flight, *1365*

Hung Hsiu-ch'üan: Civil war to cause 20 million deaths, *4173*

Hung Tsun: Numismatics treatise, *2441*

Hunt, David: Serving leader of a sovereign nation indicted for war crimes by an international tribunal, *1783*

Hunt, Walter: Safety pin, *3105*

Hunzinger, George: Folding metal-framed furniture, *3089*

Huret, Monsieur: Carriage propelled by dogs, *3210*

Hurtado de Mendoza, Diego: Picaresque novel, *3444*

Hus, Jan: Moravian Church community, *4832*

Husayn, Abdullah ibn, King of Jordan: King of Jordan, *2977*

Huskisson, William: Person run over by a train, *1891*

Hussein, Saddam: Deliberate use of environmental warfare, *4196*

Huth, Edward J.: Online, peer-reviewed journal, *4483*

Hutten, Ulrich von: Description of syphilis, *3834*

Huydecoper, Jonkheer: War lasting more than three centuries, *4194*

Huygens, Christiaan: Pendulum clock, *6027*
Piston engine, *2162*
Spirit level, *6053*

Hyatt, Isaiah Smith: Synthetic plastic that was widely used in industry, *1490*

Hyatt, John Wesley: Synthetic plastic that was widely used in industry, *1490*

Hyde, Douglas: President of the Republic of Ireland (Éire), *2804*

Hyde, Thomas: Scholarly treatise on Zoroastrianism, *5023*

Hyder Ali: Mass-produced rockets for warfare, *6132*

Hypatia: Woman mathematician to win renown, *3736*

I

I Yin: Doctrine of the Five Flavors, *2470*

Ibn an-Nafis: Description of pulmonary blood circulation, *3953*

Ibn Firnas: Manned glider flight, *1415*

ibn Ishaq ibn Yasar ibn Khiyar, Muhammad: Biography of Muhammad, *4930*

J

Jannus, Antony: Airliner, *1315*
Parachute jump from an airplane, *1434*
Jansen, Hans: Compound microscope, *5294*
Jansen, Zacharias: Compound microscope, *5294*
Jansky, Karl Guthe: Radio waves from space to be observed, *5098*
Janssen, Pierre: Element discovered in space, *5235*
Jarry, Alfred: Absurdist play, *5987*
Jarvik, Robert K.: Transplant of an artificial heart that was intended to be permanent, *4074*
Jawara, Dawda Kairaba: President of Gambia, *2834*
Jayavarman II: Khmer emperor, *2774*
Jeffers, Harry Celestine: Transatlantic helicopter flight, *1427*
Jeffreys, Alec J.: Genetic fingerprinting method, *1758*
Jeffries, John: Balloon flight over open water, *1399*
Flight instrument, *1397*
Letter sent by airmail, *4679*
Jellicoe, G.A.: Environmental restoration plan for an industrial site, *2243*
Jenatzy, Camille: Driver to exceed 100 kilometers per hour, *5713*
Jenner, Edward: Vaccine, *3910*
Jenney, William Le Baron: Skyscraper, *1226*
Jennings, John: Canoe museum, *5424*
Jeremiah: Physical evidence of a person mentioned in the Jewish scriptures, *4959*
Jerez, Rodrigo de: Europeans to smoke tobacco, *4022*
Jernigan, Joseph Paul: Comprehensive digital atlas of the human body, *3908*
Jespersen, Otto: Universal system for phonetic transcription, *3300*
Jessen, Ernst: Free dental clinic for poor children, *3820*
Jesus: Christmas, *3023*
Mention of the Feast of the Nativity, *3024*
Jesus of Nazareth: Center of Christian missionary activity, *4772*
Christians, *4770*
Jiménez de Cisneros, Cardinal Francisco: Polyglot Bible, *4886*
Jiménez Malla, Ceferino: Gypsy (Rom) to be beatified by the Catholic Church, *4881*
Jimmu Tenno: Emperor of Japan, *2765*
Jinnah, Muhammad Ali: Prime minister of Pakistan, *2885*
Jñanadeva: Marathi writing, *3520*
Job, St.: Patriarch of Moscow, *4810*
Jobs, Steven: Personal computer that was commercially successful, *1681*
Joechler, Joseph: Ascent of Cho Oyu, *5740*
Johanson, Donald: Hominid species, *4613*

Johansson, Helen: Winner of the Prix d'Amérique who was a woman, *5689*
Johansson, Ingemar: World heavyweight champion to regain his title after losing it, *5647*
John, Count of Nassau-Siegen: Army drill book, *4126*
John I Tzimisces: Orthodox monastery, *4808*
John II, Emperor of Byzantium: Teaching hospital, *3887*
John II the Good, King of France: Stringed instrument played by a keyboard, *4407*
John of Nassau-Siegen: Military academy in Europe, *4118*
John, Patrick Roland: Prime minister of Dominica, *2909*
John Paul II, Pope: Catechism of the Catholic Church since the Renaissance, *4879*
Pope born in Poland, *4877*
Pope to become a recording star, *4375*
Pope to visit a Communist country, *4878*
Pope to visit a mainly Christian Orthodox country, *4812*
John VIII, Pope: Pope to be assassinated, *4851*
John XV, Pope: Catholic saint canonized by a pope, *4853*
Johnson, Clarence Leonard "Kelly": Stealth aircraft, *4234*
Johnson, Henry: Martini, *2490*
Johnson, Kenneth: Walk to raise funds for charity, *5502*
Johnson, Lyndon Baines: Transpacific telephone service using the transoceanic cable, *5944*
Johnson, Michael: Runner to win both the 200-meter and the 400-meter races at the same Olympic games, *5797*
Johnson, Philip Cortelyou: Use of the term "International Style", *1200*
Johnson, Virginia Eshelman: Scientific study of the physiology of human sexuality, *5373*
Surrogate partner therapy, *5374*
Johnston, Leslie: Big cats born by in vitro fertilization, *1122*
Joliot-Curie, Jean-Frédéric and Irène: Artificial radioisotope, *5342*
Jolly, Jean-Baptiste: Dry cleaning, *1627*
Joly, John: Calculation of the accurate age of the earth, *5281*
Color photographic process that was practical, *4583*
Jonathan, Leabua: Prime minister of independent Lesotho, *2903*
Jones, Albert L.: Corrugated paper, *3695*
Jones, Bobby: Winner of the Grand Slam, *5669*
Jones, Brian: Nonstop circumnavigation of the world by balloon, *1413*

Kelling, Georg: Laparoscopic surgery, 4053

Kellogg, Frank B.: Antiwar treaty, 3171

Kellogg, Mary Fletcher: College to enroll women and men on equal terms, 1994

Kells, C. Edmund: Dental X-rays, 3818

Kelly, Ned: Feature-length motion picture, 4288

Kelly, Petra: Green Party seats in a national government, 2668

Kemmler, William: Electric chair, 1745

Kempe, Margery: Autobiography in English, 3410

Ken, William: Baby carriage, 2383

Kendall, Henry: Discovery of quarks, 5351

Kennedy, Phillip: Thought control of a computer, 1735

Kennelly, A.E.: Electric chair, 1745

Kenneth I MacAlpin, King of Scotland: King of Scotland, 2931

Kent, Rockwell: Radio broadcast heard in both the Arctic and the Antarctic regions, 5912

Kenyatta, Jomo: Prime minister of Kenya, 2901

Kenyon, Kathleen (Mary): Woman archeologist of distinction, 5061

Kenyon, W. Johnson: Small bandage with built-in adhesive, 3878

Keogh, Oonagh: Stock exchange member who was a woman, 2430

Kérékou, Mathieu: Incumbent African president defeated in a democratic election, 2641

President of Benin, 2837

Kerr, Gordon Campbell: Birth to be televised for the public, 2346

Kerr, Robert: IMAX film, 4309

Key, Francis Scott: Mass-produced rockets for warfare, 6132

Keynes, John Maynard: Treatise to describe an entire economy, 5358

Khafre: Sphinx, 1258

Khaldun, Ibn See Ibn Khaldun

Khalil ibn Ahmad, al-: Dictionary of Arabic, 3546

Treatise on cryptanalysis, 3398

Khama, Seretse: President of Botswana, 2833

Khan, Genghis: Powdered milk, 2509

Khnumhotep II: Specimen of cryptology, 3395

Khomeini, Ayatollah Ruhollah: Fundamentalist Islamic republic, 2700

Khomyakov, Valeria: Women pilots to down enemy aircraft in combat, 4226

Khorana, Har Gobind: Artificial gene, 5200

Khosrow I Anushirvan: Medieval educational center to transmit the Greek scientific heritage, 1962

Khri-srong-lde-btsan: Buddhist monastery in Tibet, 4761

Khrisong Detsen: Buddhist monastery in Tibet, 4761

Khufu: Ship, 5395

Structure more than 100 meters tall, 1224

Khushhal Khan Khatak: Pashto writing, 3537

Khwarizmi, Muhammad ibn Musa al-: Use of zero, 3738

Kidder, Alfred Vincent: Archeological study of a New World site, 5060

Kierkegaard, Soren Abbye: Existentialist work, 4569

Kikisch, Arthur: Recording of a complete symphony, 4392

Kilby, Jack: Integrated circuit, 2018

Kildall, Gary: Personal computer operating system, 1729

Kim Il-sung: Premier of North Korea, 2886

Kim Seung-bo: Human cloning, 5192

Kimble, Jeff: Teleportation experiment, 5356

Kimbu: Physicians in Japan, 3950

Kindi, Ya'qub ibn Ishaq as-Sabah al-: Islamic philosopher, 4565

King, Augusta Ada Byron, countess of Lovelace: Computer programmer, 1725

King, Charles: Movie musical, 4352

King, Charles Brady: Pneumatic hammer, 1492

King, John: European explorer to cross the Australian continent, 2299

King, Thomas J.: Nuclear transplantation in a vertebrate, 5185

Kingsford-Smith, Charles: Flight from the United States to Australia, 1366

Kipfer, Paul: Human ascent into the stratosphere, 1408

Kircher, Athanasius: Magic lantern, 4576

Scientist lowered into a volcano, 5262

Kirkeby, Anker: Film archive, 4293

Kishida, Toshiko: Woman to become a public speaker in Japan, 5369

Kittinger, Joe: Transatlantic solo balloon flight, 1411

Klee, Paul: Surrealist exhibition, 1254

Kleimack, J.J.: Epitaxy fabrication, 2019

Klein, R.: Child to win a gold medal in the Olympic Games, 5763

Kleinas, Danielius: Lithuanian writing, 3530

Kleist, Ewald Georg von: Storage device for electricity, 2080

Klemm, Gustav Friedrich: Theory of culture, 5361

Kloster, Knut: Re-enactment of a Viking voyage to the New World, 5469

Knaus, Hermann: Rhythm method, 2368

Knopfler, Mark: Recording on audio CD to sell 1 million copies worldwide, 2054

Knopp, Gustav: Hydroponic garden, 2624

Knorozov, Yury Valentinovich: Writing system invented in the New World, 3320

Knox, John: Scottish Gaelic collection of writings, 3527

Knox-Johnston, Robin: Solo nonstop voyage around the world, *5467*

Koch, Bill: All-woman America's Cup yacht-racing crew, *5861*

Koch, Carl: Feature-length animated film directed by a woman, *4332*

Koch, Robert: Disease known to be caused by a specific microbe, *3840*

Koenig, Alfred J.: Transcontinental radio fax transmission, *5877*

Koenig, Friedrich: Flatbed press, *4714*
Steam-driven rotary press, *4715*
Steam-powered printing press, *4713*

Kogalniceanu, Mihail: Prime minister of independent Romania, *2875*

Köhl, Hermann: Transatlantic east-west nonstop airplane flight, *1365*

Köhler, Georges: Monoclonal antibodies, *4091*

Kohler, Wolfgang: Primate research station, *5166*

Kolff, Willem Johan: Kidney dialysis, *4090*

Kollantai, Aleksandra: Woman accredited as an ambassador, *3148*

Kollár, Jan: Slovak writing, *3538*

Koller, Carl: Local anesthetic, *3764*

Kolshitsky, Franz Georg: Coffee sweet and light, *2497*

Komar, Victor: Holographic film system, *4311*

Komarov, Vladimir Mikhaylovich: Human to die during a space flight, *5541*
Spacecraft to carry more than one crew member, *5536*

Komenský, Jan Ámos: Practical theory of pedagogy, *1961*

Kondos, Dimitrios: Underwater excavation of a shipwreck, *5059*

Kongfuzi: Book of poetry in a Chinese language, *3550*
Confucian text, *4895*
Establishment of Confucianism as the state religion, *4897*
Philosopher to advocate teaching and social activism as a way of life, *4557*

Konishiki: Sumo champion not born in Japan, *5872*

Köppen, Vladimir Peter: Climatological classification system, *5274*

Korn, Arthur: Fax transmission of photographs, *5875*
Transatlantic radio fax transmission of a photograph, *5876*

Korolkov, Jevgenij: Internet bank robber, *1807*

Korondi, Margit: Uneven parallel bars, *5673*

Kotruljic, Benko: Bookkeeping manual, *1441*

Kovác, Michal: President of independent Slovakia, *2863*

Kovalevskaya, Sofya Vasilyevna: Woman to earn a doctorate in mathematics, *3751*

Kozlovsky, Nikolay: Tracking shot, *4292*

Kramer, Heinrich: Witchcraft encyclopedia, *3476*

Kramer, Stanley: Movie premiered simultaneously in major cities throughout the world, *4306*

Krapf, Ludwig: European explorers to sight Mount Kilimanjaro, *2298*

Kravchuk, Leonid: President of independent Ukraine, *2861*

Krebs, Artur: Dirigible, *1402*

Krens, Thomas: Multinational art museum, *1833*

Kreusi, John: Phonograph, *2041*
Sound recording device, *2040*

Kreuz, Werner: Sex-change operation, *5370*

Krikalev, Sergei K.: Humans to enter the International Space Station, *5565*

Kroitor, Roman: IMAX film, *4309*

Krosgk, Schwerin von: Reference to the Iron Curtain, *3128*

Kubasov, Valery: Welding and smelting in space, *5545*

Kubasov, Valery Nikolayevich: International space mission, *5548*

Kublai Khan: Invasion of Japan, *4163*

Kucan, Milan: President of independent Slovenia, *2855*

Kuchma, Leonid: President of independent Ukraine, *2861*

Kül: Turkish writing, *3501*

Kunst, David: Round-the-world journey on foot, *5852*

Kunz, Michael: Site of organized human activity in North America, *4629*

Kupka, František: Nonrepresentational modern paintings, *1286*

Kurapento, Jordaki: Emergency parachute jump, *1433*

Kurchatov, Igor Vasilyevich: Atomic bomb detonated by a country other than the United States, *6126*
Nuclear reactor in Europe, *2115*

Kurosawa, Akira: Slow motion action sequence, *4305*

Kurozumi, Munetada: Shinto sect, *4999*

Kurzweil, Raymond: Voice reader, *3303*

Kushshihar: Political sex scandal, *2627*

Kuwatli, Shukri al-: President of Syria, *2805*

Kyeser, Conrad: Illustrated manual of military technology, *4117*

L

La Condamine, Charles-Marie de: Account of rubber production, *1050*
Scientific exploration of the Amazon River, *2295*

La Sale, Antoine de: Novel in the French language, *3556*

La Salle, St. Jean-Baptiste de: Normal school for training teachers, *1969*

Laban, Rudolf: Dance notation to precisely indicate movement and rhythm, *1852*

Labrouste, Henri: Iron-frame building in Europe, *1195*

Lacedelli, Lino: Ascent of K2 (Mount Godwin Austen), *5739*

Lachapelle, Abbé de: Personal flotation device, *5408*

Lachenal, Louis: Ascent of Annapurna, *5736*

Lacy, Alexander: Children's book in English, *3418*

Laënnec, René-Théophile-Hyacinthe: Stethoscope, *3869*

Lafontaine, Henri-Marie: International library organization, *1821*

Lafontaine, Mlle.: Ballerina to dance professionally, *1856*

Lagache, A.: Twenty-four-hour automobile endurance race, *5719*

Lagerlöf, Selma Ottiliana Lovisa: Woman to win the Nobel Prize for Literature, *4531*

Laire, Abbé: Library school, *1818*

Lalande, Joseph-Jérome Le Français de: Observation of Neptune, *5084*

Lalla: Kashmiri writing, *3522*

Lallier, Justin: Stamp albums, *4694*

Laloux, René: Animated film to win an award at the Cannes International Film Festival, *4336*

Lamas, Carlos Saavedra: Nobel Prize for Peace winner from Latin America, *4541*

Land, Edwin Herbert: Instant camera, *4587*

Landau, Remy: Spreadsheet program, *1728*

Landsbergis, Vytautas: President of independent Lithuania, *2849*

Landsteiner, Karl: Blood types to be discovered, *4099*

Langenscheidt, Gustav: Correspondence school, *1975*

Langevin, Paul: Remote detection system using sound, *5439*

Langhorne, Nancy Witcher: Woman to become a member of the British Parliament, *2654*

Langland, William: Reference to the Robin Hood legend, *3475*

Langley, Samuel Pierpont: Flight of a heavier-than-air machine, *1353*
Radial aviation engine, *1309*

Langmuir, Irving: Industrial scientist to win a Nobel Prize, *4520*

Langstroth, Lorenzo Lorraine: Beehive with removable frames, *1086*

Lanier, Richard: Site of organized human activity in North America, *4629*

Lansky, Aaron: Language to have its entire literature available on computer, *3306*

Lanston, Tolbert: Machine capable of casting individual letters of type, *4723*

Lao-tzu: Philosopher of Taoism, *5013*

Laozi: Philosopher of Taoism, *5013*
Taoist religious community, *5015*

Larrey, Baron Dominique-Jean: Ambulance, *4010*

Larsen, Ivan: Country to legalize homosexual marriage, *5384*

Larsson, Arne: Pacemaker successfully implanted in a patient, *4059*

Las Casas, Bartolomé de: Book about human rights and slavery in the New World, *5484*
Catholic priest ordained in the New World, *4864*

Lasseter, John: Feature film that was entirely computer-animated, *4338*

Latham, Woodville: Movie recorded on film to be shown on a screen, *4282*

Latino, Juan: African slave to earn a degree from a European university, *5483*

Laube, Hans: Olfactory television set, *5961*

Laurent, Alexander: Fire extinguisher for chemical fires, *1579*

Laurent, François, Marquis d' Arlandes: Ascent in a hot-air balloon, *1394*

Lauterbur, Paul C.: Magnetic resonance image of a human body, *3907*

Laval, Carl Gustaf Patrik de: Centrifugal cream separator with a continuous flow, *2513*
Mechanical cream separator, *1090*

Laveran, Charles-Louis-Alphonse: Recognition of the vector of malaria, *3842*

Lavinde, Gabrieli di: Nomenclator, *3399*

Lavoisier, Antoine-Laurent: Discovery of oxygen, *5224*
Modern chemist, *5225*

Lawes, John Bennet: Agricultural research station, *1004*

Lawler, Richard Harold: Organ transplant from one human to another that was successful, *4067*

Lawlor, John: International handball match, *5677*

Lawrence, Ernest Orlando: Cyclotron, *5343*

Lawrence, Florence: Movie star, *4319*

Layard, Austen Henry: Archeological digs in Mesopotamia, *5056*
Popular book about archeology, *5057*

Layard, Henry: Epic, *3435*

Lazarev, Vasily Grigoryevich: Launch failure of a manned spacecraft, *5547*

Lazzara, Robert: Heart surgery broadcast on the Internet, *4063*

Le Maire, Jakob: Voyage around Cape Horn, *2292*

le Neve, Ethel: Criminal caught by radio, *1755*

Le Prince, Louis: Motion picture, *4278*
Le Thanh Tong, Emperor of Vietnam: Vietnamese writing, *3524*
Lea, John Wheeley: Worcestershire sauce, *2561*
Leakey, Meave: Hominid species, *4613*
Leary, Timothy: Space burial, *1885*
Leblanc, Alfred: Pilot's licenses, *1310*
Lecour, Charles: Modern savaté, *5704*
Leder, Philip: Patent on an animal, *5172*
Ledovski, Aleksei: Human in space, *5529*
  Human to die during a space flight, *5541*
Leduc, René: Ramjet aircraft, *1325*
Lee, Ann: Religious group advocating complete equality between men and women, *5367*
Lee Bo-yon: Human cloning, *5192*
Lee Kuan Yew: Prime minister of Singapore, *2893*
Lee Lai-Shan: Hong Kong athlete to win a gold medal at the Olympic Games, *5794*
Lee, Mark C.: Husband and wife to fly in space together, *5559*
Lee, William: Knitting machine, *3714*
Leeuwenhoek, Antoni van: Microscopic observation of protozoa, bacteria, and human cells, *5146*
Lefebvre, André: Front-wheel-drive car, *3240*
Lefebvre, Camille: Public sculpture honoring a car race, *1299*
Lefeldt, Wilhelm C.L.: Centrifugal cream separator, *2512*
Leggo, William Augustus: Letterpress halftone reproduction of a photograph, *4719*
Lehmann, Caspar: Cut glass, *3647*
Lehner, Tom: Tooth decay vaccine, *3822*
Lehwess, E.E.: Motor home, *3220*
Leibniz, Gottfried Wilhelm von: Treatise on binary mathematics, *3747*
  Treatise on calculus, *3748*
Leip, Hans: Wartime song popular with both sides of the conflict, *4442*
Leith, Emmett: Hologram, *5318*
Leloir, Luis F.: Nobel Prize in Chemistry winner from Latin America, *4525*
Lemaire, André: Object from Solomon's Temple in Jerusalem, *4958*
Lemoine, Louis: Steamroller, *1497*
Lemp, Julius: Civilian ship sunk in World War II, *4267*
Lenin, Vladimir Ilyich: Communist revolution, *2673*
  Socialist women's newspaper, *4507*
Lennon, John: Reversed sounds, *4447*
Lenoir, Jean-Joseph-Étienne: Automobile, *3225*
  Head of state to order an automobile, *3226*
  Internal-combustion engine that was commercially successful, *2170*
  Motorboat, *5415*

Spark plug, *2174*
Lenormand, Louis-Sébastien: Parachutist, *1431*
Lenstra, Arjen: Factoring of a 100-digit number, *3755*
Lentsch, Carl G.O.: Centrifugal cream separator, *2512*
Leo Africanus: University in Africa, *1987*
Leo III, Emperor of Byzantium: Ban on the use of icons in Christian worship, *4807*
Leo III, Pope: Holy Roman Emperor, *2773*
Leo X, Pope: Reading glasses, *4106*
León, Pedro Ponce de: Method for teaching the deaf to speak, read, and write, *2004*
Leonard, R.: Twenty-four-hour automobile endurance race, *5719*
Leonardo da Vinci: Contact lenses, *4105*
  Cooling system for buildings, *1209*
  Helicopter powered by human motion, *1429*
  Lamp with a chimney, *3086*
  Mechanical ventilating fan, *3052*
  Mill-driven coin press, *2443*
  Parachute, *1430*
Leonidas: Woman cryptanalyst, *4137*
Leonov, Aleksei A.: Space walk, *5537*
Leonov, Aleksei Arkhipovich: International space mission, *5548*
Leopold I, King of Belgium: King of Belgium, *2963*
Léotard, Jules: Flying trapeze act, *2209*
Leroy, Louis: Exhibition of impressionist paintings, *1250*
Leroy, Monsieur: Parisian couturier, *1623*
Lester, Richard: Feature film released on CD-ROM, *4312*
Lethbridge, John: Diving suit, *5449*
Leucippus of Miletus: Atomic theory, *5320*
Levassor, Émile: Automobile race, *5709*
Levens, Peter: Rhyming dictionary, *3369*
Leverrier, Urbain Jean-Joseph: Recognition of Neptune as a planet, *5090*
Levin, Vladimir: Internet bank robber, *1807*
Lewis, Julie: Shoe made from recycled materials, *1658*
Lewis, Kari A.: Space mission headed by women, *5517*
Lewis, Oliver: Kentucky Derby, *5686*
Lewis, Sinclair: Nobel Prize for Literature winner from North America, *4533*
Lexcen, Ben: International challenger to win the America's Cup in yacht racing, *5859*
Leyster, Judith: Dutch painter of note who was a woman, *1282*
Lhermite, Jehan: Wheelchair, *3867*
Li Tzu-cheng: Disastrous flood caused by war, *1947*
Liaquat Ali Khan: Prime minister of Pakistan, *2885*
Licklider, J.C.R.: Computer network, *1694*

Lie, Trygve Halvdan: Secretary general of the United Nations, *3191*

Lieber, Francis: National code of the laws of war, *4120*

Liebig, Justus von: Teaching laboratory for chemists, *5231*

Liebig, Justus von, Baron: Mass-produced infant formula, *2387*
Silvered hand mirror, *2743*

Lihung Chang: Chop suey, *2540*

Lilienthal, Otto: Hang-glider fatality, *1893*

Lillie, Malcolm C.: Brain surgery, *4037*

Lima, Almeida: Prefrontal lobotomy, *4056*

Lin, T.D.: Moon concrete, *2155*

Lin Tse-hsü: Military clash between China and a western power, *4172*

Lincoln, Abraham: Photographic pictorial biography, *4574*

Lincoln, William E.: Animated picture machine, *4324*

Lind, James: Clinical trial, *4085*
Vitamin-deficiency disease to be cured, *3836*

Lindbergh, Charles Augustus: Transatlantic solo airplane flight, *1364*

Linde, Karl von: Process for liquefying mixed gases, *5237*

Lindfield, Henry: Driver fatally injured in an automobile accident, *1894*

Linenger, Jerry L.: Joint space walk by American and Russian astronauts, *5563*

Linetski, Yoyel: Yiddish literary annual, *3575*

Ling, Per Henrik: Modern massage technique, *4087*

Lingyi, Zhong: Buddhist site of importance in China, *4758*

Linnaeus, Carolus: Organism classification system, *5149*

Lipman, Hyman L.: Pencil with an attached eraser, *3589*

Lippershey, Hans: Compound microscope, *5294*
Telescope, *5132*

Lippisch, Alexander Martin: Rocket-propelled airplane, *1318*
Rocket-propelled warplane, *4231*

Lisser, E.G. de: Caribbean novel in English, *3461*

Lister, Joseph: Antiseptic surgery, *4049*
Treatise on antiseptic surgery, *4050*

Lister, Joseph Jackson: Achromatic microscope, *5301*

Livingstone, David: European explorer to cross Africa from coast to coast, *2301*

Livy: Clean-shaven society, *2751*

Lloyd, Edward: Marine insurance underwriters, *2421*

Llywelyn ap Gruffudd, Prince of Wales: Prince of Wales, *2947*

Loar, H.H.: Epitaxy fabrication, *2019*

Loar, Lloyd: Electric guitar, *4424*

Lockyer, Joseph Norman: Element discovered in space, *5235*

Loening, Grover Cleveland: Amphibious aircraft, *1312*

Loewi, Otto: Neurotransmitter to be identified, *5168*

Long, Crawford Williamson: Modern use of anesthesia in surgery, *3761*

Lonka Saha: Reform movement in Jainism, *4951*

Lonsdale, Kathleen Yardley: Scientific association sanctioned by a national government, *5048*

Lorant, Stefan: Photographic pictorial biography, *4574*

Loren, Sophia: Performer in a foreign language film to win the Academy Award for Best Actress, *4322*

Lorena, Guglielmo de *See* Guglielmo de Lorena

Lorenzetti, Ambrogio: Thread-the-needle dance, *1842*

Lorillard, Pierre: Millionaire, *1443*

Lorraine, Marguerite de: Ballet to combine dancing, music, and acting, *1854*

Lothair: French writing, *3553*

Loud, John J.: Ballpoint pen, *3593*

Loudon, John Claudius: Traps for human trespassers in gardens, *2623*

Loues, Spiridon: Olympic marathon in modern times, *5761*

Louis the German: French writing, *3553*

Louis the German, King of Germany: King of Germany, *2929*

Louis XIII, King of France: Waterproof umbrellas, *1619*

Louis XIV, King of France: Casino game, *2608*
Code for the treatment of slaves in European colonies, *5486*
Dentists with professional credentials, *3806*
Minuet, *1846*

Louis XV, King of France: Passenger elevator, *1204*

Louise de Marillac, St.: Religious order of nurses, *3964*

Louisi, Mathieu: European legislator of African descent, *2652*

Love, Bessie: Movie musical, *4352*

Lovelace, Ada: Computer programmer, *1725*

Lovell, Alfred Charles Bernard: Major radio telescope, *5138*

Lovell, James Arthur, Jr.: Astronauts to orbit the moon, *5524*
Rendezvous in space, *5538*

Low, David: Chiropodist, *3966*
Family hotel, *1465*

Lowell, Percival: Planet found beyond Neptune, *5097*

M

Mahavira, Vardhamana:—*continued*
Religion to require a vegetarian diet, *4945*
Schism in Jainism, *4948*

Mahendra: Country outside India to accept Buddhism, *4755*

Mahler, Gustav: Symphony incorporating continuous choral and orchestral elements, *4391*

Mahmud of Ghazna, Sultan: Sultan, *2936*

Mahone, Paula: Septuplets to survive birth, *2353*

Mahoney, John Friend: Treatment for syphilis, *3930*

Maiman, Theodore Harold: Working laser, *2020*

Maimon, Moshe ben *See* Maimonides

Maimonides: Attempt to reconcile Judaism and philosophy, *4563*

Makarios III, Archbishop: Leader of independent Cyprus, *2999*

Makarov, Oleg: Launch failure of a manned spacecraft, *5547*

Maki, Yuko: Ascent of Manaslu (Kutang), *5743*

Makir, Jacob ben *See* Jacob ben Makir

Malfatti, Anita: Modern art festival in South America, *1253*

Mallakh, Kamal el-: Ship, *5395*

Mallet, Robert: Scale of earthquake intensity, *5272*

Malory, Thomas: Keeper of the Holy Grail, *3473*

Malske, Johann George: Electric locomotive, *3275*

Malthus, Thomas: Treatise on human population growth that had a wide influence, *4603*

Ma'mun, Caliph al-: Arabic translations of scientific manuscripts, *5043*
Islamic inquisition, *4933*

Manasse, Mark: Factoring of a 100-digit number, *3755*

Manby, Aaron: Seagoing iron-hulled vessel, *5412*

Manby, Charles: Seagoing iron-hulled vessel, *5412*

Manby, George: Fire extinguisher, *1575*

Mancelius, Georgius: Latvian writing, *3534*

Mancham, James R.: President of the Seychelles, *2839*

Manco Capac, Inca: Inca, *2943*

Mandela, Nelson Rolihlahla: Black African president of South Africa, *2865*
Nonracial democratic elections in South Africa, *2643*

Mandeville, Bernard Xavier Philippe de Marigny de: Craps game, *2609*

Manet, Édouard: French Impressionist artist who was a woman, *1284*

Manetho: Anti-Semitic libel, *4960*

Manley, Mary de la Rivière: Women's magazine edited by a woman, *4477*

Manly, Charles Matthews: Radial aviation engine, *1309*

Mannerheim, Lars August: Ombudsman, *2632*

Mannheim, Amédée: Modern slide rule, *3750*

Mansa Musa: University in Africa, *1987*
West African emperor of note to make a religious pilgrimage to Mecca, *4935*

Mansart, Jules Hardouin: Open caisson, *2140*

Manson, Patrick: Disease proven to be transmitted by insects, *3841*

Mansur, Caliph Abu Ja'far al-: Islamic hospital, *3885*

Manutius, Aldus: Italics, *4707*
Printed editions of Greek classics, *3358*

Marcius Rex: Raised aqueduct of great length, *2133*

Marconi, Guglielmo: Permanent wireless installation, *5899*
Radio broadcast of live music, *5908*
Radio inventor, *5896*
Radio patent, *5897*
Radiotelegraph message from Great Britain to Australia, *5907*
Shipboard newspaper, *4508*
Transoceanic radio message, *5901*
Wireless radio manufacturing company, *5898*
Wireless station for international communications, *5900*

Maréchal, Pierre-Sylvain: National revolutionary calendar, *6009*

Margai, Milton Augustus Striery: Prime minister of Sierra Leone, *2896*

Marggraf, Andreas Sigismund: Chemist to identify a substance using a microscope, *5223*
Sugar from beets, *1064*

Margrete, Queen of Denmark: Woman to rule the Scandinavian countries, *2951*

Mari Diata: Emperor of Mali, *2775*

Maria the Jewess: Distillation apparatus for alchemists, *5218*

Maria Theresa, Empress of Austria: Zoo in Europe, *1161*

Marie de France: Woman poet to write in French, *3554*

Mariotte, Edme: Statement of a physical law as an equation with two dependent variables, *5325*

Marius, Simon: Celestial objects discovered by telescope, *5076*
Galaxy to be described in print, *5071*

Markham, Fred: Bicyclist to go faster than 50 miles per hour, *5630*

Marlowe, Christopher: Faust legend, *3479*

Maroney, Susan: Swim from Mexico to Cuba, *5827*

Marot, Clément: Psalms in metrical form, *4385*

Marr, Wilhelm: Use of the term "anti-Semitism", *4975*

Marrison, Warren: Quartz clock, *6030*

Marshack, Alexander: Calendar, *6000*

Marshall, George Catlett: Professional soldier to be awarded a Nobel Prize for Peace, *4542*

Marston, Thomas: Map of any part of the Americas, *3608*

Martel, Charles: Check to Muslim expansion in western Europe, *4929*

Martial: Greenhouses, *1074*

Martin, Gardner: Bicyclist to go faster than 50 miles per hour, *5630*

Martin, Glenn: Parachute jump from an airplane by a woman, *1435*

Martin, Gregory: Catholic edition of the Bible in a vernacular language, *4890*

Martínez, Saturnino: Factory in which the workers paid for the services of a reader, *1506*

Martini, Simone: Church altarpiece from western Europe showing the Annunciation, *1272*

Martonyi, Janos: Former Warsaw Pact nations to join NATO, *3143*

Marvell, Andrew: Debating society, *1835*

Marwil, A.R. von: Regular civil airmail service, *4683*

Marx, Karl: Communist political platform, *2672*

Communist secret society, *2671*

International Communist labor organization, *1505*

Mary I, Queen of England: Woman to rule England, *2956*

Mary of Burgundy: Diamond engagement ring, *2396*

Mary, Queen of Scots: Woman to play golf, *5665*

Masaccio: Painting composed with one-point perspective, *1274*

Masaryk, Tomás: President of Czechoslovakia, *2796*

Mashtots, St. Mesrop: Armenian writing, *3494*

Maskelyne, Nevil: Measurement of the mass and density of the earth, *5267*

Mason, Rex: Comic strip with an adventure hero, *4471*

Master of the Housebook: Drypoint engraving, *1292*

Masters, William Howell: Scientific study of the physiology of human sexuality, *5373*
Surrogate partner therapy, *5374*

Mas'udi, Abu al-Hasan Ali al-: Muslim settlement in East Africa, *4638*

Matignon, Madame de: Society model, *1622*

Matney, Timothy: Tract houses, *1218*

Matsushita, Konosuke: Flat-screen pocket television, *2033*

Matthews, Thomas A.: Quasar to be observed, *5102*

Matthias, Archduke of Habsburg: Governor-general of the Dutch Republic, *2988*

Mattityahu ben Yochanan: Rebellion for religious freedom, *4961*

Mattityahu, Yochanan ben *See* Yochanan ben Mattityahu

Mauchly, John W.: Electronic computer for commercial use, *1671*
General-purpose computer that was fully electronic, *1669*

Maudslay, Henry: Mechanized production line, *1483*
Micrometer, *2188*
Screw-threading metal lathe, *1482*
Screws and bolts mass-produced in standard sizes, *1484*

Maurice de Sully: Cathedral in the Gothic style, *1185*

Maurice of Nassau: Modern army to use military drill, *4125*

Maurice of Saxony: Public schools in the modern era, *1966*

Mausolus of Caria: Mausoleum, *1877*

Maximianus, Gaius Galerius Valerius: Legal recognition of Christians in the Roman Empire, *4783*

Maximilian, Archduke: Diamond engagement ring, *2396*

Maximilian Joseph, Ferdinand, Emperor of Mexico: European-born emperor of a North American country, *2780*

Maximinus: Antipope, *4848*

Maxwell, Lily: Woman to vote in an election, *2636*

May, Phil: Rock opera, *4438*

Mayall, J.E.: Art photographs, *4593*

Maybach, Wilhelm: Carburetor, *2177*
Motorcycle with an internal-combustion engine, *3216*
Radiator, *2178*
V-block engine, *2175*

Mayer, Johann Tobias: Tables of the moon's motions for navigation, *5436*

Mayor, Michel: Discovery of a planet orbiting another star, *5109*

Mays, Stephen and Amanda: Test-tube twins, *2349*

Mazor, Stan: Microprocessor, *1678*

Mazvydas, Martynas: Lithuanian writing, *3530*

M'ba, Léon: President of independent Gabon, *2824*

Mbotela, James: Swahili writing, *3535*

McCandless, Bruce: Space travelers to fly free in space, *5553*

McCarty, M.: Evidence that DNA is the genetic material, *5198*

McCaughey, Bobbi and Kenny: Septuplets to survive birth, *2353*

McCormick, Katherine Dexter: Birth-control pill, *2370*

McCready, Michael: Watch that told time in Catalan, *6039*

McDowell, Ephraim: Gynecological surgery, *4047*

McGovern, Vincent Howard: Transatlantic helicopter flight, *1427*

McGregor, Ken: Grand Slam doubles winners in tennis, *5837*

McGuire, Elwood: Lawn mower that was practical, *6063*

McKean, Thomas: President of a nation, *2781*

McKinney, Curtis R.: Human remains in the Americas, *4627*

McLean, Malcolm: Containerized shipping, *1548*

McLendon, Gordon: All-news radio station, *4464*

McMillan, Edwin Mattison: Element heavier than uranium, *5245*
Synchrotron, *5347*

Medici, Cosimo I de': Academy of fine arts, *1238*

Medicis, Catherine de: Ballet to combine dancing, music, and acting, *1854*

Medwall, Henry: Secular play in English, *3413*

Mee, Arthur: Modern encyclopedia for children, *3385*
Visual encyclopedia for children, *3386*

Meegan, George: Walk from the southernmost to the northernmost points of the Americas, *5853*

Meeker, Jotham: Magazine in a Native American language, *4480*

Megasthenes: Sighting of a mermaid, *3466*

Mège-Mouriès, Hippolyte: Margarine, *2537*

Mehmed II: Major land battles decided by firepower, *4166*

Melanchthon, Philipp: Grade levels in schools, *1964*
Lutheran churches, *4820*
Major statement of Protestant theological doctrine, *4815*
Public schools in the modern era, *1966*

Melba, Nellie: Radio broadcast of live music, *5908*

Méliès, Georges: Narrative film, *4285*
Science fiction film, *4348*

Mellaart, James: Metropolis, *1556*

Mellon, Paul: Map of any part of the Americas, *3608*

Menakhem ben Saruq: Dictionary in the Hebrew language, *3563*

Menches, Charles E.: Ice cream cone, *2515*

Mencius: Explicator of orthodox Confucianism, *4896*

Mendel, Gregor: Treatise on laws of heredity, *5193*

Mendeleyev, Dmitry Ivanovich: Periodic table of the elements, *5229*

Mendonça, Lourenço da Silva e: Pope to condemn the African slave trade, *5487*

Mendoza, Daniel: Boxer to emphasize skill over brute strength, *5643*

Menéndez de Avilés, Pedro: Spanish settlement in North America, *4655*

Menes: Crowns, *2703*
Inscription identifying a historical personage by name, *3308*
Pharaoh, *2919*

Menestrier, Claude-François: History of dance, *1847*

Mengzi: Explicator of orthodox Confucianism, *4896*

Menilek II, King of Ethiopia: Defeat of a European colonial power by African military forces, *4177*

Menzies, Michael: Threshing machine, *1080*

Menzies, Robert: Steamship to cross an ocean from east to west, *5456*

Merbold, Ulf: European Space Agency astronaut in space, *5552*

Mercator, Gerardus: Map to name North and South America, *3615*
Mercator projection, *3617*

Mercury, Freddie: Music video, *4450*

Mergenthaler, Ottmar: Linotype machine, *4722*

Merlin, John Joseph: Modern wheelchair designed for hospital use, *3868*

Merlin, Joseph: Roller skates, *5805*

Mesmer, Franz Anton: Hypnosis, *3990*

Messiha, Khalil: Flying model airplane, *1307*

Messner, Reinhold: Ascent of Mount Everest without bottled oxygen, *5748*
Man to climb all 14 of the world's tallest mountains, *5752*
Mountaineer to ascend the world's three tallest peaks, *5750*
Solo ascent of Mount Everest, *5749*
Traverse of Antarctica on foot, *2331*

Mestral, Georges de: Hook and loop fastener, *1644*

Metellus Celer, Quintus: Native Americans to cross the Atlantic, *2274*

Methodius, St.: Russian writing, *3511*

Metrodora: Medical text written by a woman, *3769*

Meusnier, Jean-Baptiste-Marie: Airship, *1396*

Meyer, Hans: Ascent of Mount Kilimanjaro, *5732*

Mhlophe, Ntombhe: White witch doctor, *3977*

Michaux, Ernest: Bicycle with rotating pedals, *5622*

Michaux, Pierre: Bicycle with rotating pedals, *5622*

Michelangelo: Academy of fine arts, *1238*
Military uniform designed by an artist, *4148*
Satirical portrait, *1279*
Three-dimensional computer model of an Old Master sculpture, *1304*

Michelin, André and Édouard: Pneumatic automobile tire, *3294*

Michell, John: Proposal of the existence of gravitational singularities, *5328*
Seismologist to develop a modern theory of the cause and actions of earthquakes, *5265*

Michelson, Albert Abraham: Nobel Prize in Physics winner from North America, *4546*

Michtom, Morris: Stuffed toy bear, *2388*

Midland Woman: Human remains in the Americas, *4627*

Mietke, Adolf: Flash powder, *4580*

Mignet, Henri: Sport airplane, *1319*

Mikimoto, Kokichi: Cultured pearls, *1009*

Mikoyan, Anastas Ivanovich: Country to attempt to withdraw from the Warsaw Pact, *3173*

Miletus, Thales of: Description of static electricity, *2077*

Mill, Henry: Typewriter patent, *3585*

Millemete, Walter de: Depiction of a gun in Europe, *6097*

Miller, Ann: Big cats born by in vitro fertilization, *1122*

Miller, Anne Sheafe: Patient to be given penicillin, *3936*

Miller, Robert: Thermoformed plastic condom, *2375*

Miller, T.G.: Telephone conversation to travel around the world, *5938*

Miller, William: Adventists, *4838*

Miller, Willoughby D.: Foreigner to be appointed professor in a German university, *1997*
Recognition of the true cause of tooth decay, *3817*

Millikan, Robert Andrews: Cosmic ray to be discovered, *5094*

Milon of Croton: Wrestler of note, *5869*

Milosevic, Slobodan: Serving leader of a sovereign nation indicted for war crimes by an international tribunal, *1783*

Milstein, César: Monoclonal antibodies, *4091*

Milton, John: Debating society, *1835*

Milutinovic, Milan: Serving leader of a sovereign nation indicted for war crimes by an international tribunal, *1783*

Minamoto, Yoritomo, Shogun of Japan: Shogun, *2986*

Minkoff, Lawrence: Magnetic resonance image of a human body, *3907*

Miriam the Prophetess: Distillation apparatus for alchemists, *5218*

Miró, Joan: Surrealist exhibition, *1254*

Misselden, Edward: Balance of trade and payments for a nation, *1543*

Mistral, Gabriela: Nobel Prize for Literature winner from Latin America, *4534*

Misurata, Volpi de: Annual film festival, *4340*

Mitchell, John: Steel pen point, *3588*

Mitchell, Maria: Comet named after a woman, *5091*

Mitchell, William "Billy": Airplane bombing experiment to sink a battleship, *4215*

Mitterrand, François: Underwater link between Great Britain and Europe, *2198*

Miyamoto, Shigeru: Video game designer of renown, *2578*

Mochanov, Yuri A.: Humans in Siberia, *4624*

Mochet, Charles: Recumbent bicycle, *5629*

Moctezuma II: Easter Mass in Central America, *4866*
Zoo in the Western Hemisphere, *1160*

Modena, Tommaso da: Depiction of eyeglasses, *4104*

Moëns, Jean-Baptiste Constant: Handbook for stamp collectors, *4696*
Stamp catalogs, *4693*
Stamp dealer, *4692*

Mofolo, Thomas Mokopu: Novel in an African vernacular language, *3460*

Mohamad, Mahathir: Heads of state to meet in an on-line chat session, *3165*

Mohammad, Mirza Ali *See* Baha' Allah

Mohr, Linda: Frozen embryo to come successfully to birth, *2351*

Moir, John: Canned fish, *2533*

Moizo, Lieutenant: Pilot captured during war, *4208*

Mojmir I: Slavic state, *2683*

Moleville, Bertrand de: Pruning shears, *6055*

Moll, Joseph: Communist secret society, *2671*

Mollison, James A.: Transatlantic westbound solo nonstop flight, *1371*

Molotov, Vyacheslav Mikhailovich: Signatories of the Warsaw Pact, *3172*

Molson, John: Brewery in the Western Hemisphere, *2487*

Moltke, Adam Wilhelm, Count: Prime minister of Denmark's first parliamentary government, *2871*

Mondino de' Luzzi: Treatise on human anatomy based on dissection, *3774*

Mondino dei Liucci: Anatomist since antiquity to dissect human bodies, *3957*

Monet, Claude: Exhibition of impressionist paintings, *1250*

Monge, Gaspard: Technical college, *1993*

Monier, Joseph: Patents for reinforced concrete, *2153*
Reinforced concrete building system, *2154*

Moniz, António Caetano de Abreu Freire Egas: Arteriogram, *3904*

Monod, Théodore: Skeleton of a black African, *4620*

Montagnier, Luc: Diagnostic test for AIDS, *3850*

Identification of the AIDS virus, *3849*

Montagu, John, the 4th Earl of Sandwich: Sandwich, *2530*

Montanus: Heretical Christian sectarian movement, *4777*

Montessori, Maria: Montessori school, *1977*

Monteverdi, Claudio: Opera house, *4433*

Orchestra, *4364*

Orchestration, *4387*

Montgolfier, Jacques-Étienne: Animals sent aloft in a balloon, *1393*

Ascent in a hot-air balloon, *1394*

Emergency parachute jump, *1433*

Hot-air balloon that was successful, *1391*

Woman to ascend in an untethered balloon, *1398*

Montgolfier, Joseph-Michel: Animals sent aloft in a balloon, *1393*

Ascent in a hot-air balloon, *1394*

Emergency parachute jump, *1433*

Hot-air balloon that was successful, *1391*

Woman to ascend in an untethered balloon, *1398*

Montgomerie, T.G.: Ascent of K2 (Mount Godwin Austen), *5739*

Montu, Captain: Aviator wounded in combat by ground fire, *4207*

Moon, Sun Myung: Unification Church teachings, *4804*

Moore, Archie: World heavyweight champion to regain his title after losing it, *5647*

Moore, J. Ross: Motorized clothes dryer, *3070*

Moore, James: Bicycle road race, *5625*

International bicycle race, *5624*

Morain, François: Automatic calculator to factor whole numbers, *1664*

Morand, Paul: Recumbent bicycle, *5629*

More, Thomas: Reference to Utopia, *3478*

Moreno, Roland: Smart card, *2459*

Morey, Samuel: Internal-combustion engine, *2168*

Morgagni, Giovanni: Treatise on autopsies, *3784*

Morgan, Garrett A.: Traffic lights, *1590*

Morgan, George: Person killed in a motorcycle accident, *1895*

Morgan, John Pierpont: Corporation worth US$1 billion, *1547*

Morgan, Lewis Henry: Kinship study, *5363*

Morgan, Piers: Naval battle fought with cannon broadsides, *4245*

Morisot, Berthe: Exhibition of impressionist paintings, *1250*

French Impressionist artist who was a woman, *1284*

Morita, Akio: All-transistor portable television, *2026*

Japanese company to sell stock on United States stock exchanges, *2432*

Personal stereo cassette player, *2035*

Pocket transistor radio, *5914*

Moritz, Johann Gottfried: Tuba, *4418*

Morosini, Duchess Morosina: Lace factory, *3708*

Morris, Robert T., Jr.: Widespread worm attack on the Internet, *1714*

Morrison, James Beall: Dental drill powered by electricity, *3816*

Morrow, Patrick: Mountaineer to climb the highest peak on every continent, *5751*

Morse, Samuel Finley Breese: Commercial telegraph service, *5923*

Underwater telegraph cable that was practical, *5924*

Morton, Cardinal John: Secular play in English, *3413*

Morton, Julius Sterling: Arbor Day, *3036*

Morton, Ladislaus: Transmission electron microscope, *5304*

Morton, William Thomas Green: Hospital to use anesthesia in surgery, *3763*

Modern use of anesthesia in dentistry, *3762*

Moses: Intelligence-gathering operation, *4134*

Moshe ben Maimon: Attempt to reconcile Judaism and philosophy, *4563*

Motley, Eric: Miss World contest, *2201*

Mott, John Raleigh: Ecumenical conference, *4802*

Moustafa, Haj Ahmed Youssef: Ship, *5395*

Mqhayi, Samuel Edward Krune: Xhosa writing, *3541*

Mu Tsung: Card games, *2580*

Mu'awiyah I, Caliph: Civil war in Islam, *4925*

Muslim dynasty, *2685*

Muslim navy, *4242*

Sectarian controversy in Islam, *4927*

Mugabe, Robert Gabriel: Prime minister of Zimbabwe, *2913*

Muhammad: Convert to Islam, *4920*

Islamic state, *2684*

Military victory of Islam, *4159*

Mosque, *4921*

Muslim caliph, *2927*

Muslim ritual, *4918*

Tolerated minorities under Islam, *4923*

Muhammad V, King of Morocco: King of independent Morocco, *2980*

Mujib, Sheikh: Prime minister of Bangladesh, *2907*

Müller, F.E.: Contact lenses for correcting defective vision, *4109*

Muller, Hermann Joseph: Radiation mutations to be artificially created, *5196*

Müller, Karl Alex: Superconducting materials of ceramic oxide, 5352

Müller, Paul Hermann: Organic pesticide, 1099

Mullis, Kary B.: DNA chain polymerization, 5202

Mulroney, Brian: Free-trade region encompassing North America, 1552

Murasaki, Shikibu: Novel, 3440

Murdock, William: Illumination by gas, 2101
Large building illuminated by gas, 2102

Murray, George Evelyn Pemberton: Transatlantic commercial telephone service, 5937

Murray, James: Edition of the Oxford English Dictionary, 3375
Synthetic fertilizer, 1095

Musgrave, Charles: Feynman Prize in Nanotechnology, 5355

Musick, Edwin Charles: Transpacific airmail flight, 4685

Musschenbroek, Pieter van: Storage device for electricity, 2080

Mussolini, Benito Amilcare Andrea: Fascist dictator, 2998

Musurus, Marcus: Printed editions of Greek classics, 3358

Mutalibov, Ayaz: President of Azerbaijan, 2856

Mu'tasim, Caliph al-: Slave army, 4122

Mutawakkil, Caliph al-: Law requiring Jews to wear an identifying mark, 4968

Mutter, William: Electronic wristwatch, 6033

Muul, Illar: Jungle canopy walkway for tourists, 2249

Muybridge, Eadweard: Photographs showing action, 4597

Myers, Jacob H.: Voting machines, 2638

N

Nabiyev, Rahman: President of Tajikistan, 2859

Nabonidus: Archeologist, 5052

Nachman, Rabbi Moshe ben: Printed book in Hebrew, 3564

Nadar: Aerial photographs, 4595
Exhibition of impressionist paintings, 1250
Photo interview, 4571
Underground photographs, 4596

Nadel, Daniel: Cord, 3697

Naevius, Gnaeus: Suppression of a theatrical performance, 5980

Nagelmackers, Georges: Orient Express service, 3277

Nagy, Imre: Country to attempt to withdraw from the Warsaw Pact, 3173

Naismith, James: Basketball, 5617
Rules for basketball, 5618

Naito, Ryochi: Artificial blood, 4102

Nakamatsu, Yoshiro: Floppy disk, 1670

Nakaoka Tei: Dentures retained by adhesion, 3803

Nanak: Sikh sacred book, 5004

Nanak, Guru: Punjabi writing, 3528
Sikh community, 5002
Sikh guru, 5001

Nannaya: Telugu writing, 3500

Nansen, Fridtjof: Alpine skier, 5808

Napier, Charles: Seagoing iron-hulled vessel, 5412

Napier, John: Logarithm tables, 3744

Napoléon Bonaparte: Archeological digs in Egypt, 5053
Emperor of France, 2779
Guerrilla war, 4171
Playing deck with double-headed face cards, 2591
Scientists attached to armed forces in modern times, 5050
Uniform national law code, 2649

Napoléon III: European-born emperor of a North American country, 2780

Nares, George Strong: Oceanographic expedition, 5273

Narmer: Inscription identifying a historical personage by name, 3308

Nasmyth, James: Shaper, 1485
Steam forge hammer, 1487

Nasser, Gamal Abdel: Constitutional president of the Republic of Egypt, 2811
Meeting of the nonaligned movement, 3163

Naudé, Gabriel: Treatise on library science, 1816

Naveh, Joseph: Reference to King David, 2922

Nazarbayev, Nursultan Abishevich: President of independent Kazakhstan, 2847

Nazarova, Irina: Mother-daughter Olympic medalists, 5786

N'Djocké, Emmanuel Dibango: African song that was an international pop hit, 4449

Nearchus: Sugar in Europe, 1060

Nebuchadrezzar: Cryptanalyst, 4135
Temple in Jerusalem, 4955

Necho II: Circumnavigation of Africa, 2303

Nedelin, Mitrofan Ivanovich: Intercontinental ballistic missile, 6136

Needham, Joseph: Depiction of a gun, 6094

Neferites: Dentist, 3795

Nehru, Jawaharlal: Meeting of the nonaligned movement, 3163
National railway hospital, 3898
Prime minister of India, 2884

Nehru, Pandit Jawaharlal: Nuclear reactor in Asia, 2118

Nelmes, Sarah: Vaccine, 3910

Nelson, Prince Rogers: Person to adopt a symbol as a name, 3484

Nelson, Robert F.: Freezing of a corpse for future resuscitation, *1883*

Nennius: Reference to the King Arthur legend in a historical work, *3470*

Nero: Concrete dome, *1177*

Nesmith, Betsy: Correction fluid for typists, *3597*

Nessler, Karl Ludwig: Permanent wave hairstyle, *2734*

Nesterov, Petr Nikolaevich: Aerobats, *1314*

Neto, António Agostinho: President of the People's Republic of Angola, *2838*

Neuserre: Obelisks, *1259*

Neustadter, Arnold: Rolodex, *1521*

Neveu, Cyril: Dakar Rallye, *5723*

Newbery, John: Book of Mother Goose nursery rhymes, *3431*
  Children's fiction book in English, *3429*
  Children's magazine, *4479*
  Marketing strategy aimed at children, *1511*

Newby, P.H.: Booker Prize, *3456*

Newcomb, John: Wire-screen sifter for grain, *1077*

Newcomb, Simon: Dynamical time scale, *6016*

Newcomen, Thomas: Commercially successful steam engine, *2164*

Newman, Larry: Transatlantic balloon flight, *1410*

Newman, Maxwell H.A.: Electromechanical cryptographic decoder, *4142*

Newton, Isaac: Encyclopedic dictionary, *3373*
  Evidence that the earth is an oblate spheroid, *5264*
  Parabolic mirror, *5316*
  Reflecting telescope, *5134*
  Treatise on calculus, *3748*

Ngo Quyen: King of Vietnam, *2933*

Nguema, Francisco Macías: President of Equatorial Guinea, *2835*

Nguyen Binh Khiem: Vietnamese writing, *3524*

Nguyen Trai: Vietnamese writing, *3524*

Nhat Chi Mai: Self-immolation by a Buddhist monk, *1886*

Nicander of Colophon: Anticoagulant, *3920*

Nicephorus II Phocas: Orthodox monastery, *4808*

Nicholas I, King of Montenegro: King of independent Montenegro, *2970*

Nicholas of Cusa: Heliocentric world system, *5068*

Nicholas of Hereford: English translation of the Bible, *4884*

Nicholas, St.: Santa Claus, *3019*

Nichols, Ruth Rowland: Commercial pilot who was a woman, *1343*

Nicholson, William: General reference work of modern chemistry, *5228*

Nicuesa, Diego de: European settlements in South America, *4650*

Niepce, Joseph-Nicéphore: Photoengraving, *4716*
  Photograph, *4589*
  Printed photograph, *4590*
  Printed photograph, *4590*

Nightingal, Florence: Army with a trained nursing staff to treat its wounded, *4129*

Nightingale, Florence: Nursing school, *3858*
  School for professional nurses, *3861*
  Woman to be awarded the British Order of Merit, *3974*

Nijinsky, Vaslav: Ballets Russes, *1862*

Nikola, Andriyan Grigoryevich: Two manned craft in space simultaneously, *5534*

Nikolayev, Andrian: Child whose parents had both flown in space, *2393*

Nikolayeva, Yelena Andrianovna: Child whose parents had both flown in space, *2393*

Nipkow, Paul: Complete television system, *5949*

Nishikawa, Tokichi: Cultured pearls, *1009*

Nissen, George: Trampoline, *5672*

Nixon, Richard M.: Strategic Arms Limitation Treaty, *3180*

Nixon, Richard Milhous: Smuggled moon rock, *1808*

Niyazov, Saparmurad: Leader of independent Turkmenistan, *2860*

Nizam al-Mulik: Assassins, *1784*

Nkrumah, Kwame: Prime minister of Ghana, *2890*
  Sub-Saharan African colony to gain its independence, *2699*

Nobel, Alfred: Blasting cap, *3683*
  Dynamite mining demonstration, *3684*
  Mountain tunnel, *2192*
  Nitroglycerin, *5233*

Nobile, Umberto: Flight over the North Pole, *2321*

Noble, Richard: Car to break the sound barrier, *5725*

Noble, Rollie: American flag to fly over the defeated Nazi empire, *4190*

Nock, Henry: Breech-loading gun, *6108*

Noir, Foulques le *See* Fulk Nerra

Nordenskjóld, Nils Adolf Erik: Navigation of the Northeast Passage, *2315*

Nordheim, Sondre: Nordic skier, *5807*

Norell, Mark A.: Fossilized embryo of a carnivorous dinosaur to be discovered, *5216*

Norgay, Tenzing: Ascent of Mount Everest, *5737*

Northcliffe, Lord: Tabloid newspaper, *4511*

Norton, Thomas: Dramatic tragedy in English, *3417*

Nowell, Alexander: Bottled beer, *2481*

Nowell, April: Artwork, *1231*

Noyce, Robert: Integrated circuit, *2018*

Nu, U Thakin: Prime minister of independent Myanmar, *2887*

Nuchterlein, Karl: Single-lens reflex (SLR) 35-millimeter camera, *4586*

Nufer, Jacob: Cesarean operation, *2335*

Nujoma, Samuel: President of Namibia, *2850*

Numan, Eppo: Transatlantic flight by an ultralight airplane, *1386*

Nunn, Glynis: Heptathlon event, *5788*

Nyerere, Julius Kambarage: President of Tanzania, *2827*

Nyswander, Marie: Methadone maintenance program for heroin addicts, *4029*

O

Oakley, Kenneth P.: Scientific hoax of international notoriety, *5051*

Obadiah, Manasseh: Printed book in Hebrew, *3564*

Oberkampf, Christophe-Philippe: Machine for printing wallpaper, *4711*

Obote, Apollo Milton: Prime minister of independent Uganda, *2899*

O'Brien, Marilyn: Mammals born from an egg grown in vitro, *5173*

Obrig, Theodore: Plastic contact lenses, *4110*

Ochs, Adolph Simon: Transatlantic commercial telephone service, *5937*

O'Connor, Tommy: Wartime song popular with both sides of the conflict, *4442*

Octavian: Emperor of Rome, *2769*

Odlum, Jacqueline Cochran: Woman to fly faster than the speed of sound, *1382*

Odo, St.: Musical notation using letters of the alphabet, *4362*

Odoacer, King of Italy: King of Italy, *2924*

Odoric de Pordenone, St.: Fast-food outlets, *1460*

Professional caterers, *1461*

O'Dwyer, Michael: Gun that could fire one million rounds a minute, *6118*

Oeben, Jean-François: Modern wheelchair designed for hospital use, *3868*

Oelschlägel, Charlotte: International ice show star, *2224*

Oenopides: Zodiacal horoscope, *5066*

Oersted, Hans Christian: Aluminum, *3669*

Offa, King of Mercia: King to call himself "King of the English", *2928*

Penny, *2439*

Offenbach, Jacques: Operetta, *4437*

Ogden, C.K.: Artificial language based entirely on English, *3301*

Ogino, Ginko: Japanese woman to become a physician, *3971*

Ogino, Kyusaka: Rhythm method, *2368*

Ogle, Henry: Mechanical reaper, *1082*

Ohain, Hans von: Turbojet aircraft, *1321*

O'Higgins, Bernardo: Leader of independent Chile, *2991*

Ohl, Russell: Silicon solar cell, *2065*

Ojdanic, Dragoljub: Serving leader of a sovereign nation indicted for war crimes by an international tribunal, *1783*

Ojeda, Alonso de: European settlements in South America, *4650*

Okalik, Paul: Premier of Nunavut, *2918*

Okuni: Kabuki performance, *5984*

Oland, Warner: Movie accompanied by prerecorded sound to be released as a feature film, *4300*

Voice double, *4321*

Old, Archie J., Jr.: Round-the-world nonstop flight by a jet airplane, *1384*

Oldenburg, Baroness: Poke bonnet, *1648*

Olga, St.: Orthodox saint from Russia, *4809*

Woman to rule a part of Russia, *2934*

Oliver, Elizabeth: Childbirth streamed live on the Internet, *2354*

Oliver, Sean: Childbirth streamed live on the Internet, *2354*

Olivier, Laurence Kerr: Film made by a studio outside the United States to win an Academy Award, *4304*

Olmo, Andres de: Nahuatl grammar, *3531*

Olof Skötkonung, King of Sweden: King of all Sweden, *2937*

Olsen, George: Dinosaur eggs to be discovered, *5209*

Olsen, Ole: Film archive, *4293*

Olson, Lennart: Human antibodies produced artificially, *3939*

Olympio, Sylvanus: President of Togo, *2826*

O'Malley, Troy: Virtual-reality reconstruction of a crime scene, *1764*

Oñate, Juan de: Mexican–American trail, *4658*

O'Neil, Peggy: Person to be interviewed on television, *5955*

Ong, H.S.: Talking bathroom scale, *2726*

Onnes, Heike Kamerlingh: Liquid helium, *5239*

Superconductor, *5334*

Opel, Fritz von: Manned rocket-plane flight, *1367*

Rocket car, *5720*

Oppenheimer, Frank: Interactive museum, *1831*

Oppenheimer, J. Robert: Chairman of the United Nations Atomic Energy Commission, *3190*

Proposal of the existence of gravitational singularities, *5328*

Opper, Frederick Burr: Comic books featuring color cartoons previously published in newspapers, *4469*

Orata, Sergius: Oyster farm, *1006*

Ordóñez, José Batlle y: Democratic president of Uruguay, *2793*

Orestes: King of Italy, *2924*

Orhan, Sultan: Use of the crescent as a symbol of Islam, *4936*

Origen: Christian institution of higher learning, *4776*

Orso, Doge of Venice: Doge of Venice, *2984*

Ortelius, Abraham: Atlas, *3618*

Osborn, Henry Fairfield: Fossilized embryo of a carnivorous dinosaur to be discovered, *5216*

Osborn, James Butler: Submarine equipped with ballistic missiles, *4275*

Osborne, Adam: Portable personal computer, *1684*

Osei Tutu: Emperor of the Ashanti, *2778*

O'Shaughnessy, William: Telegraph used in warfare, *4174*

Osman I, Sultan: Sultan of the Ottoman Empire, *2948*

Oswald, Richard: Movie with a homosexual theme, *5381*

Otis, Elisha Graves: Safety elevator, *1205*

Otlet, Paul: International library organization, *1821*

Ott, Fred: Movie comedy, *4346*
Movie to be copyrighted, *4280*

Otto, Bishop of Friesling: Legend of Prester John, *3471*

Otto, King of Greece: Constitutional monarch of modern Greece, *2964*

Otto, Nikolaus August: Four-stroke internal-combustion engine, *2171*

Ötzi: Tattoos, *1596*
Vegetarian, *2469*

Ousmane Sembène *See* Sembène, Ousmane

Outcault, Richard: Comic strip with an ongoing character, *4468*

Ovadia: Jewish kingdom to be established since biblical times, *4967*

Ovando, Nicolás de: Slaves in the New World, *5479*

Ovid: Book on cosmetics, *2715*

Owen, Earl: Hand transplant, *4077*

Owen, Richard: Scientific paper using the term "dinosaur", *5214*

Owen, Robert: General union, *1504*
Model factory run on humanitarian principles, *1501*
Theorists of socialism, *2661*

Ozawa, Toru: Terrorist bomb attack on an airplane, *1801*

P

Pachomius, St.: Christian monastery, *4784*
Rule book for Christian monastic life, *4786*

Pacioli, Luca: Treatise on double-entry bookkeeping, *1442*

Padmasambhava: Buddhist monastery in Tibet, *4761*

Pagano, Matio: Lace pattern books, *3707*

Page, David: Human chromosome gene-linkage maps, *5203*

Page, Frederick Handley: Heavy night bomber, *4213*

Painter, George R.: Map of any part of the Americas, *3608*

Pakington, John: Iron-hulled warship, *4254*

Palladio, Andrea: Academy of fine arts, *1238*
Indoor theater built for stage productions, *5992*

Palma, Tomás Estrada: President of Cuba, *2791*

Palmer, Donald D., Jr.: One Sky, One World international kite flying event, *1421*

Palmer, Henry Robinson: Corrugated iron, *3670*

Pammachius, St.: Hospice for Christian pilgrims, *1458*

Pandit, Vijaya Lakshmi: President of the United Nations General Assembly who was a woman, *3195*

Pangborn, Clyde: Transpacific nonstop airplane flight, *1369*

Panini: Grammarian, *3296*
Sanskrit grammar, *3571*

Pannartz, Arnold: Typeface made in Europe in a non-Roman alphabet, *4705*

Pantaenus: Christian institution of higher learning, *4776*

Papin, Denis: Pressure cooker, *3055*
Submersible supplied with air pumped from the surface, *5450*

Paracelsus: Toxicologist, *3956*

Paradis, Maria: Alpine mountaineer who was a woman, *5729*

Paravisinus, Dionysius: Typeface made in Europe in a non-Roman alphabet, *4705*

Pardo, René: Spreadsheet program, *1728*

Paré, Ambroise: Military surgeon to treat gunshot wounds without cautery, *3959*

Parham, Charles: Pentecostal churches, *4842*

Pariser, Alan: Rock music festival, *4448*

Park, William Hallock: Antitoxin laboratory operated by a public health department, *4013*

Parkes, Alexander: Synthetic plastic, *3107*

Parnell, Charles: Boycott, *1444*

Parshvanatha: Jaina saint, *4941*

Parsons, Charles Algernon: Steam turbine-powered ship, *5416*

Pascal, Blaise: Adding machine, *1662*
Bus service, *3209*
Hydraulic press, *2187*

Paschal II, Pope: Crusading order of knights, *4795*

Pasha, Ali *See* Ali Pasha

Pashnin, O.G.: Surface ship to reach the North Pole, *2329*

Passy, Frédéric: Nobel Prize for Peace, *4538*

Passy, Paul: Universal system for phonetic transcription, *3300*

Pasteur, Louis: Food product to be pasteurized, *2536*
Pasteurized milk, *2514*
Rabies vaccine, *3911*

Pastorius, Franz Daniel: Protest against slavery made by a religious group in the New World, *5488*

Patañjali: Yoga textbook, *3768*

Patarroyo, Manual: Vaccine to be chemically synthesized, *3913*

Paterson, Andrew Barton ("Banjo"): Plastic money, *2460*

Patsayev, Viktor: Space station, *5546*

Patterson, Audrey: Woman athlete of African descent to win a medal in the Olympic Games, *5771*

Patterson, Floyd: World heavyweight champion to regain his title after losing it, *5647*

Patton, George Smith: American flag to fly over the defeated Nazi empire, *4190*
Nazi death camp to be liberated in World War II, *1774*

Paul, Howard "Hap": Robot to perform surgery, *5040*

Paul, Jacques and Nicholas: Soft drink business, *2532*

Paul, Les: Electric guitar, *4424*

Paul of Aegina: Description of lead poisoning, *3830*
Tonsillectomy, *4043*

Paul, St.: Center of Christian missionary activity, *4772*

Paul VI, Pope: Meeting of the heads of the Anglican and Catholic churches, *4805*

Pauli, Wolfgang: Observation of neutrinos, *5349*

Pauling, Linus Carl: Nobel laureate who was the sole winner of awards in two different categories, *4522*

Paulus, Friedrich: Battle with more than 2 million deaths, *4187*

Pausanias: Olympic games for women, *5759*

Pausanius: Transposition cipher, *3396*

Pavlova, Anna: Ballets Russes, *1862*

Paxton, Joseph: Glass building, *1196*

Pearson, Alan: Tornado intensity scale, *5289*

Pearson, Charles: Subway, *3285*

Pearson, Gerald L.: Solar cells that were practical, *2067*

Peary, Robert Edwin: Discovery of the North Pole, *2325*

Pease, Edward: Steam locomotive passenger service, *3266*

Pease, Pamela S.: Internet university to receive accreditation, *2003*

Pecock, Reginald: Proposal to purify the English language, *3411*

Peel, Robert: Modern police force, *1792*

Pégoud, Celestin Adolphe: Aerobats, *1314*

Pèlerin de Maricourt, Pierre: Treatise on magnetism, *5321*

Pelletier, Joseph: Execution by guillotine, *1744*

Penzias, Arno Allan: Observational confirmation of the Big Bang theory, *5103*

Pepionkh: Cake, *2544*

Pepy I: Metal statue, *1295*

Percy, Thomas: Collection of folk ballads, *4439*

Pereira, Aristides: President of independent Cape Verde, *2840*

Perelman, Eliezer Yitzhak: Ancient language revived for modern use, *3302*

Pérez de Cuellar, Javier: Nobel Prize for Peace awarded to the United Nations Armed Forces, *4544*

Pérez Prado, Dámaso: Mambo, *1853*

Peri, Jacopo: Opera known by that name, *4430*
Opera whose music is still extant, *4431*

Pérignon, Dom Pierre: Champagne, *2483*

Perkin, William Henry: Synthetic dye, *3719*

Perkins, Jacob: Building with a patented cooling system, *1212*
Frozen meat for commercial sale, *2535*

Perkins, Larry: Transcontinental trip by a solar-powered vehicle, *3207*

Perón, Isabel Martínez De: Woman to become president of a nation, *2836*

Perovskaya, Sofia L.: Woman executed in Russia for political terrorism, *1797*

Perret, Jean-Jacques: Safety razor, *2753*

Perrier, Carlo: Element produced artificially, *5243*

Perrin, Pierre: Opera in French, *4435*

Perrins, William: Worcestershire sauce, *2561*

Perronet, Jean-Rodolphe: Engineering school, *2127*

Perrot, Bernard: Glass mirrors free of distortion, *2741*

Perry, James: Steel pen point, *3588*

Perry, Stephen: Rubber bands, *3104*

Pestalozzi, Johann Heinrich: Educational reformer to stress individual development, *1971*
National teacher-training program, *1972*

Peter, Daniel: Milk chocolate, *2553*

Peter, St.: Papal throne, *3082*
Pope, *4847*

Peter the Great: Tsar to travel outside Russia, *2777*

Petrarch: Account of mountain climbing, *5726*
Humanist, *4567*

Petrie, Flinders: Measure of weight, *5307*

Petrucci, Ottaviano del: Music printed from movable type, *4706*

Petzval, Josef Max: Portrait camera, *4578*

Pfister, Albrecht: Illustrated books printed in Europe, *3352*

Pfister, Laux: Accidental shooting, *6101*

Pfleumer, Fritz: Recording tape, *2047*

Phalareus, Demetrius: Fables with morals, *3438*

Pheidippides: Marathon, *5841*

Pherecydes of Soros: Greek prose work, *3561*

Phibunsongkhram, Luang: Premier of Thailand, *2882*

Philip II, King of Spain: Marine disaster costing more than 10,000 lives, *1930*
Wheelchair, *3867*

Philip III, King of France: Medieval sumptuary laws, *1609*

Philip IV, King of France: Contagious disease to be brought under control in Europe, *3832*

Philip IV the Fair, King of France: Stock market, *2425*

Philip of Macedon: Permanent institution of higher education in the liberal arts, *1981*

Philippe, Odette: Grapefruit plantation, *1052*

Phillip, Arthur: Convicts deported to Australia, *4663*

Philolaus: Heliocentric world system, *5068*

Phinney, Connie Carpenter: Woman to compete in both the Summer and Winter Olympic Games, *5790*
Women's cycling event, *5791*

Phipps, James: Vaccine, *3910*

Phrynichus: Play to flop, *5976*

Piacenza, Domenico da: Dancing master, *1843*

Piazzi, Giuseppe: Asteroid to be discovered, *5085*

Picasso, Pablo: Surrealist exhibition, *1254*

Piccard, Auguste: Dive to the bottom of the ocean, *5453*
Free-moving deep-sea submersible, *5452*
Human ascent into the stratosphere, *1408*

Piccard, Bertrand: Nonstop circumnavigation of the world by balloon, *1413*

Piccard, Jacques: Dive to the bottom of the ocean, *5453*

Piccolomini, Alessandro: Book of printed star charts, *3630*

Pickup, Edith: Swimsuit beauty contest, *2200*

Pictet, Raoul-Pierre: Liquid oxygen, *5236*

Pilâtre de Rozier, Jean-François: Ascent in a hot-air balloon, *1394*
Ballooning casualties, *1890*

Pilkington, Alastair: Float glass, *3652*

Piłsudski, Józef Klemens: President of independent Poland, *2797*

Pincus, Gregory: Birth-control pill, *2370*

Pinel, Philippe: Humane treatment of the mentally ill, *3991*

Pino, Mario: Human habitation in the Americas, *4628*

Pinochet, Augusto: Privatization campaign, *1447*

Pires, Sandra: Women's Olympic volleyball event, *5796*

Pirhum: IOU promissory note, *2436*

Pisanello, Il: Clothes designer, *1612*

Pitchfork, Colin: Murderer apprehended on DNA evidence alone, *1759*

Pitman, Isaac: Correspondence course, *1974*

Pitt, William: Graduated income tax, *2467*

Pius IX, Pope: Vatican Council, *4875*

Pius VII, Pope: Emperor of France, *2779*

Pius XI, Pope: Vatican observatory, *5137*

Pixérécourt, Guilbert de: Melodrama in English, *3432*

Pizarro, Francisco: Germ warfare for purposes of genocide, *1766*

Place, Martha M.: Woman to die in the electric chair, *1746*

Planck, Max Karl Ernst Ludwig: Theory that light consists of particles, *5332*

Plato: Dialogues, *5977*
Literary critic, *3327*
Philosophical encyclopedia, *3376*
Theorists of socialism, *2661*

Playfair, William: Graphs displaying economic data, *5360*

Plesman, Albert: Airline in continuous operation, *1341*

Pliny the Elder: Encyclopedia of importance, *3378*
Tallow soap, *2714*
Topiary gardening, *2616*

Pliny the Younger: Volcanic eruption, *1914*

Plomin, Robert: Gene linked with high intelligence, *5206*

Plouffe, Simon: Encyclopedia of integer sequences, *3757*

Pocahontas: Native American to be buried in Europe, *1878*

Poe, Edgar Allan: Modern detective story, *3451*

Pollaiuolo, Antonio: Engraving on metal plate, *1291*

Pollock, Herbert Chermside: Synchrotron, *5347*

Polo, Marco: Frozen desserts, *2546*
Major intercontinental road, *1586*
Pasta, *2528*

Polybius: Long-distance communication system using an alphabet, *5918*

Poma de Ayala, Felipe Guamán: Account of the Andean world from an insider's perspective, *3010*

Pomerance, Carl: Factoring of a 100-digit number, *3755*

Pompey: King of united Armenia, *2923*

Poniatowski, Stanislaw II August, King of Poland: Written national constitution outside of the United States, 2647
Pontian, St.: Antipope, 4848
Pontormo, Jacopo da: Old Master painting sold at auction for more than US$10 million, 1288
Ponzi, Charles: Modern pyramid scheme, 1806
Popov, Aleksandr Stepanovich: Radio inventor, 5896
Popovich, Pavel R.: Two manned craft in space simultaneously, 5534
Porsche, Ferdinand: Subcompact car designed to be fuel-efficient, 3239
Porsenna, Lars: Republic, 2680
Porta, Giambattista della: Scientific academy, 5047
Porte, Juan: Circus in Europe, 2204
Porter, Edwin S.: Movie western, 4349
Posidonios of Apamea: Bards, 3329
  Druid, 4738
Post, Wiley Hardeman: Round-the-world solo airplane flight, 1372
Potiquet, Alfred: Stamp catalogs, 4693
Pott, Percivall: Occupational carcinogen to be identified, 3837
Potter, Charles: Mineral separation by flotation, 3677
Pottier, Eugéne: Communist song of international popularity, 4440
Poubelle, Eugene: Galvanized metal trash can, 4036
Poulet, Pedro: Rocket engine, 5504
Poulsen, Valdemar: Magnetic wire recording device, 2045
Prajadhipok: Constitutional monarch of Thailand, 2972
Prall, Elizabeth Smith: College to enroll women and men on equal terms, 1994
Pravaz, Charles Gabriel: Hypodermic syringe, 3871
Praxiteles: Sculpture of the goddess Aphrodite in the nude, 1297
Price, George: Premier of Belize, 2902
Priestley, Joseph: Carbonated water, 2531
  Discovery of oxygen, 5224
  Discovery of the anesthetic properties of nitrous oxide (laughing gas), 3760
  Rubber eraser, 3586
Prieur, Jean-Yves: Saser, 2024
Prince: Person to adopt a symbol as a name, 3484
Princip, Gavrilo: Casualty of World War I, 4178
Priscus, Lucius Tarquinius: Clean-shaven society, 2751
Pritchard, Thomas: Bridge constructed entirely of cast iron, 2142
Proctor, Bernard E.: Food irradiation, 2522

Prokofiev, Sergey Sergeyevich: One-armed pianist of international stature, 4374
Properzia de Rossi: Renaissance sculptor of note who was a woman, 1298
Protic, Stojan: Prime minister of Yugoslavia, 2880
Proudhon, Pierre-Joseph: Anarchist, 2662
Prouskouriakoff, Tatiana: Writing system invented in the New World, 3320
Prudhomme, René-François-Armand Sully: Nobel Prize for Literature, 4530
Ptacek, Stephen R.: Solar-powered airplane to cross the English Channel, 1332
Ptolemy (Claudius Ptolemaeus): Treatise on astronomy that was widely influential, 5120
  Treatise on trigonometry, 3735
Ptolemy I Soter: Library catalog, 1811
Ptolemy V Epiphanes: Archeological digs in Egypt, 5053
  Hieroglyphic writing from Egypt to be deciphered, 5054
Pu-abi: Jewelry, 1595
Puckle, James: Machine gun, 6106
Pulsifer, Alden William: International dogsled mail, 4678
Puma, Waman: Account of the Andean world from an insider's perspective, 3010
Purcell, Henry: Composer to write more than 100 hours of music, 4366
Pusey, Joshua: Matchbooks, 3109
Pushkova, Galina: Woman cinematographer, 4303
Pyrrho of Elis: Skeptic, 4559
Pythagoras: Irrational number, 3730
  Law against cruelty to animals, 1138
  Theory that the earth is a sphere, 5253
  Woman mathematician, 3729
Pytheas: Detailed account of a long sea voyage, 2273
Pytheas of Massalia: Circumnavigation of Britain, 2304
Pythius: Banker, 2402

Q

Qaddafi, Muammar al-: King of independent Libya, 2978
  Massacre at the Olympic Games, 1799
  Prime minister of Libya, 2906
Qin Shi Huangdi: Emperor of China, 2768
Qu Yuan: Dragon Boat races in China, 3014
  Poet in a Chinese language, 3551
Quang Duc: Self-immolation by a Buddhist monk, 1886
Quant, Mary: Miniskirt, 1638
Quaque, Philip: Anglican priest who was not of European descent, 4834

Queloz, Didier: Discovery of a planet orbiting another star, *5109*

Quesnay, François: Treatise to describe an entire economy, *5358*

Quibell, J.E.: Inscription identifying a historical personage by name, *3308*

Quimby, Harriet: Woman to pilot an airplane over the English Channel, *1313*

Quinquet, Monsieur: Lamp with a chimney, *3086*

Quinty, Pierre de: Lace pattern books, *3707*

Qurrah, Theodorus Abu: Christian writer in Arabic, *4793*

R

Rabi'ah al-Adawiyah: Sufi mystics, *4931*

Rabin, Yitzhak: Peace treaty between an Arab nation and Israel, *3182*

Rabinowitz, Sherrie: Cyber café, *1470*

Radegund, St.: Biography written by a woman, *3330*

Radon, J.: CAT scan, *3906*

Rahman, Mujibur: Prime minister of Bangladesh, *2907*

Raikes, Robert: Sunday school, *4799*

Rais, Gilles de: Serial killer, *1785*

Ramakrishna Paramahansa: Hindu missionary in the West, *4917*
Prophet to declare that all religions are true, *4914*

Ramazzini, Bernardino: Physician to specialize in occupational medicine, *3965*
Treatise on occupational medicine, *3783*

Rambeau, Catharine: Woman to motorcycle from the United States to Tierra del Fuego, *3224*

Rambouillet, Madame de: Literary salon, *3332*

Ramon, Yehoshua: Rams, *4241*

Ramos, Fidel: Heads of state to meet in an online chat session, *3165*

Ramsay, William: Researcher to discover an entire grouping of elements, *5240*

Ramses II: Apples, *1027*

Ramses III: Public park, *1560*

Ramsey, Arthur Michael, Archbishop of Canterbury: Meeting of the heads of the Anglican and Catholic churches, *4805*

Ramusio, Gian Battista: European author to write about tea, *2496*

Ranger, Richard Howland: Transcontinental radio fax transmission, *5877*

Ranjit Singh: Sikh kingdom, *5010*

Ransome, Robert: Cast iron plow, *1081*
Self-sharpening plow, *1083*

Raphael: Reading glasses, *4106*

Rashi: Printed book in Hebrew, *3564*

Rashid, Mohammed: Terrorist bomb attack on an airplane, *1801*

Rasmussen, Birger: Fossil oil, *5251*

Rasmussen, Knud Johan Victor: Dogsled crossing of the Northwest Passage, *2320*

Ratdolt, Erhard: Printed book with a separate title page, *3353*

Rausing, Ruben: Milk carton, *2521*

Ravel, Maurice: One-armed pianist of international stature, *4374*

Rawlinson, Henry Creswicke: Cuneiform writing from Mesopotamia to be deciphered, *5055*

Ray, John: Encyclopedic dictionary, *3373*
Taxonomic system based on scientific principles, *5148*

Raymond, Pierre-Albert: Metal snap fastener, *1642*

Razi, Abu Bakr Muhammad ibn Zakariyà ar-: Muslim physician, *3951*
Treatise on smallpox, *3831*

Raziya, Queen of Delhi: Muslim leader who was a woman, *2946*

Read, Albert Cushing: Transatlantic airplane flight, *1360*

Reagan, Ronald Wilson: International space station, *5512*

Reard, Louis: Modern bikini, *1636*

Reber, Grote: Radio astronomer, *5099*

Rebmann, Johannes: European explorers to sight Mount Kilimanjaro, *2298*

Recorde, Robert: Equal sign, *3741*

Reed, Walter: Mosquito-eradication project to control disease, *4016*

Reese, James: Battery-powered wristwatch, *6032*

Regiomontanus: Ephemeris, *3611*
Printed book with a separate title page, *3353*

Rehehausen, Johann Georg: Latvian writing, *3534*

Rehn, Louis: Heart operation, *4052*

Rei, August: President of independent Estonia, *2800*

Reid, Chris: White witch doctor, *3977*

Reines, Frederick: Observation of neutrinos, *5349*

Reinhardt, Jean-Baptiste "Django": European jazz musician to win international recognition, *4378*

Reiniger, Lotte: Feature-length animated film directed by a woman, *4332*

Reiss, Ernst: Ascent of Lhotse, *5744*

Reith, John: National broadcasting monopoly, *5882*
Regular broadcast high-definition television service, *5959*

Reitsch, Hanna: Helicopter free flight indoors, *1425*
Person to travel more than 500 miles per hour, *1322*

Woman helicopter pilot, *1424*

Woman to be awarded the Iron Cross, *4225*

Remek, Vladimir: Space traveler who was not of USSR or U.S. citizenship, *5549*

Renard, Charles: Dirigible, *1402*

Renaudot, Théophraste: Free dispensary for the poor, *3890*

Official newspaper of a government, *4493*

Renault, Louis: Sedan, *3237*

Renoir, Pierre-Auguste: Exhibition of impressionist paintings, *1250*

Respighi, Ottorino: Musical composition to incorporate a phonograph recording in a live performance, *4393*

Revenaugh, Daniell: Two-lid piano, *4428*

Reynaud, Leyonce: Concourse in a train station, *3271*

Rhazes: Muslim physician, *3951*

Plaster of Paris for medical use, *4083*

Treatise on smallpox, *3831*

Rheaume, Manon: Woman to become a professional hockey player, *5693*

Rhee, Syngman: President of South Korea, *2808*

Rhind, Alexander Henry: Treatise on mathematics, *3728*

Rhodopis: Lost-slipper motif in a folktale, *3465*

Prostitute, *5387*

Rhys, Siôn David: Welsh writing, *3498*

Ricci, Matteo: European buried in the Imperial City, *4871*

Riccioli, Giovanni Battista: Map of the moon, *3622*

Rich, Claudius James: Archeological digs in Mesopotamia, *5056*

Richard I, King of England: Heraldic device worn by an English king, *2707*

Racing purse, *5680*

Richards, Dickinson W.: Cardiac catheterization, *4089*

Richards, Theodore William: Nobel Prize in Chemistry winner from North America, *4524*

Richardson, Lunsford: Junk mail, *4677*

Richelieu, Cardinal: Official newspaper of a government, *4493*

Richelieu, Duc de: Mayonnaise, *2560*

Richer, James: Passenger fatally injured in an automobile accident, *1896*

Richet, Charles Robert: Description of anaphylaxis, *3843*

Rickenbacker, Adolph: Electric guitar, *4424*

Rickover, Hyman George: Nuclear-powered submarine, *4273*

Ridley, Harold: Artificial lens for surgical insertion into the eye, *4111*

Ridley, John: Grain stripper, *1085*

Rigolly, Louis: Car to exceed 100 miles per hour, *5715*

Rinuccini, Ottavio: Opera known by that name, *4430*

Opera whose music is still extant, *4431*

Ríos, Marcelo: Latin American tennis player to become the top ranked player in the world, *5840*

Riquet, Pierre: Canal connecting the Atlantic to the Mediterranean, *2136*

Canal tunnel, *2190*

Rishabhanatha: Jaina saint, *4941*

Rist, Johann: Magazine, *4473*

Ritchie, Dennis: Multiuser operating system, *1727*

Ritty, James J.: Cash register, *2454*

Rivadavia, Bernardino: President of the Argentine republic, *2783*

Roach, Archie: Aboriginal Australian performer to achieve international success, *4451*

Roba, Fatuma: African woman athlete to win the Olympic women's marathon, *5793*

Boston Marathon in which both champions were African athletes, *5847*

Robert, Anne-Jean: Hydrogen balloon, *1392*

Robert-Houdin, Jean-Eugène: Books that explained magic tricks, *2218*

Magician to use electricity in his act, *2217*

Robert-Houdin, Paul: Performance of a *Son et lumière* show, *2225*

Robert, Nicholas-Louis: Ascent in a hydrogen balloon, *1395*

Hydrogen balloon, *1392*

Roberts, David: Human footprints, *4619*

Roberts, Edward: Personal computer kit, *1680*

Roberts, Joseph Jenkins: President of Liberia, *2787*

Republic in Africa, *2695*

Roberts, Richard: Steamship to cross an ocean from east to west, *5456*

Robertson, W. F.: Ice hockey rules, *5692*

Robin Hood: Reference to the Robin Hood legend, *3475*

Robinson, Jackie: Racial integration of professional baseball, *5612*

Robinson, Mary: Woman to become president of the Republic of Ireland (Éire), *2851*

Robinson, Robert: Tranquilizer, *3937*

Robinson, T.R.: Mechanical clock still extant, *6025*

Robiquet, Pierre-Jean: Codeine, *3924*

Rocca, Nick La: Jazz record, *4377*

Rock, John: Birth-control pill, *2370*

Rock, William T.: Movie theater, *4354*

Rockefeller, John David: Billionaire businessman, *1446*

Rodchenko, Aleksandr Mikhailovich: Mobiles, *1302*

Roddenberry, Gene: Space burial, *1885*

Rodiana, Honorata: Woman to paint frescoes, *1278*

Rodrigues Ferreira, Alexandre: Biological expedition to Amazonia by a native South American, *5156*

Rodríguez de Tío, Lola: Caribbean Spanish-language poet who was a woman, *3459*

Rodríguez, José Joaquín: Free, democratic elections in Central America, *2637*

Roger of Helmarshausen: Treatise on crafts by a practicing artisan, *1246*

Rogers, Moses: Steamboat to cross an ocean, *5455*

Steamboat to make an ocean voyage, *5454*

Roggeveen, Jakob: European explorer to land on Easter Island (Rapa Nui), *2294*

Rohrer, Heinrich: Scanning tunneling electron microscope, *5305*

Rojas, Francisca: Crime solved using fingerprints, *1753*

Romaine, Robert: Self-propelled rotary cultivator, *1087*

Römer, Ole Christensen: Estimate of the velocity of light, *5078*

Romero, Francisco: Matador of renown, *5650*

Romero, Pedro: Bullfighting school, *5652*

Romme, Charles Gilbert: National revolutionary calendar, *6009*

Ronne, Edith "Jackie": Women to winter in Antarctica, *2323*

Röntgen, Wilhelm Conrad: Dental X-rays, *3818*

Discovery of X-rays, *5330*

Nobel Prize in Physics, *4545*

X-ray photograph of human anatomy, *3902*

Roosevelt, Theodore: Modern conflict in which an Asian power defeated a European power, *4257*

Nobel Prize for Peace winner from North America, *4540*

Stuffed toy bear, *2388*

Transoceanic radio broadcast, *5902*

Roper, Sylvester Hayward: Motorcycle, *3215*

Rosa de Lima, St.: Catholic saint from the New World, *4872*

Rosas, Juan Manuel de: Leader of united, independent Argentina, *2993*

Rosenthal, Ida Kaganovich: Standardized sizes for bras, *1635*

Roslin, Eucharius: Manual for midwives, *2336*

Ross, I.M.: Epitaxy fabrication, *2019*

Ross, Ronald: Recognition of the vector of malaria, *3842*

Rosse, William Parsons: Large reflecting mirror, *5136*

Systematic observations of galaxies, *5089*

Rotheim, Erik: Aerosol can, *3113*

Rothschild, Mayer Amschel: Mail-order catalog, *1512*

Rotz, Jean: Maps showing Australia, *3616*

Rousseau, Jean-Jacques: Educational reformer to stress individual development, *1971*

Rouvroy, Claude-Henri de: Theorists of socialism, *2661*

Roxas y Acuña, Manuel: President of the Philippines, *2807*

Roy, Ram Mohun: Modern Hindu reform movement, *4913*

Royer de la Bastie, François: Tempered glass manufacturing process, *3651*

Rubinstein, Helena: Cosmetics entrepreneur of note, *2725*

Rudd, Caroline Mary: College to enroll women and men on equal terms, *1994*

Rudenberg, Rheinhold: Transmission electron microscope, *5304*

Rudolf of Nuremberg: Mechanical wire-drawing equipment, *1477*

Rudolph, Paul: Anastigmatic lens that was commercially successful, *4582*

Rufus of Samaria: Jewish physician, *3948*

Ruggiero, Renato: Director-general of the World Trade Organization, *3202*

Rugiati, Pastrengo: Oil spill from a commercial tanker, *2269*

Rumford, Benjamin Thomson, Count von: Cooking stove that was practical, *3057*

Ruska, Ernst August Friedrich: Transmission electron microscope, *5304*

Ruskin, John: Housing project in an inner-city neighborhood, *5497*

Russell, Bertrand: International conference of atomic scientists, *5350*

Russell, Charles Taze: Jehovah's Witnesses, *4840*

Russell, Steve: Computer game, *2576*

Russell, William Howard: War correspondent to file dispatches by telegraph, *4458*

War to receive extensive newspaper coverage, *4175*

Rustaveli, Shota: Georgian writing, *3495*

Rutan, Richard: Round-the-world nonstop airplane flight without refueling, *1385*

Rutherford, Ernest: Calculation of the accurate age of the earth, *5281*

Discovery of protons, *5337*

Modern theory of atomic structure, *5333*

Rutherford, John: Clinical rounds in hospitals, *3892*

Ryan, Harry: Professional football game, *5660*

Ryan, T.J.: Labor party, *2663*

S

Sabah bin Jabir bin Adhbi, Emir of Kuwait: Emir of Kuwait, *2961*

Sacchi, Bartolomeo: Printed cookbook, *2503*

Sachs, Ferdinand: Hydroponic garden, *2624*

Sackville, Thomas: Dramatic tragedy in English, *3417*

Sadat, Anwar: Constitutional president of the Republic of Egypt, *2811*
Peace treaty between an Arab nation and Israel, *3182*

Sagan, Carl: Robot to conduct a roving exploration of the surface of another planet, *5582*
Spacecraft to carry an extraterrestrial message, *5572*

Sahagún, Bernardino de: Encylopedia of ancient Mexico, *3382*

Sa'id, Oman Ahmad ibn, Sultan of Oman: Sultan of Oman, *2960*

Sainovic, Nikola: Serving leader of a sovereign nation indicted for war crimes by an international tribunal, *1783*

Saji, Yoshiro: Commercial vessel powered by magnetohydrodynamics, *5423*

Sakamura, Ken: Fully computerized house, *1223*

Sakel, Manfred: Shock therapy for treating mental illness, *4004*

Sakharov, Andrei: Hydrogen bomb detonated by a country other than the United States, *6130*

Sakharov, Andrey D.: Tokamak, *2120*

Sakkas, Ioannis: Solar energy weapons, *6073*

Saladin: Statement of the principle of medical neutrality in wartime, *3127*

Salah ad-Din Yusuf ibn Ayyub *See* Saladin

Salameh, Ali Hassan: Massacre at the Olympic Games, *1799*

Salamini, Francesco: Einkorn domestication, *1012*

Sale, G.: English translation of the Qur'an, *4940*

Salinas de Gortari, Carlos: Free-trade region encompassing North America, *1552*

Sallal, Abd Allah as-: President and prime minister of the Yemen Arab Republic (North Yemen), *2829*

Sallé, Marie: Woman to choreograph her own ballets, *1859*

Salmon, Robert: Haymaker, *1084*

Salter, Susanna Medora: City with a woman mayor, *1569*

Salwala, Soraida: Elephant hospital, *1143*

Samas-Musezib: IOU promissory note, *2436*

Samuel, Mar Athanasius Yeshue: Dead Sea Scrolls to be discovered, *4978*

Samuelson, Joan Benoit: Olympic marathon for women, *5789*

Samuelson, Paul Anthony: Nobel Prize in Economics winner from North America, *4529*

Sánchez, Cristina: Woman bullfighter of renown in Europe, *5653*

Sanchez, Raphael: Letter containing a description of America, *2282*

Sandage, Allan Rex: Quasar to be observed, *5102*

Sandeman, John Glas: Vending machine in modern times, *1516*

Sandtner, Jacob: Architectural model of Jerusalem, *1192*

Sanger, Frederick: Protein characterized by amino acid sequence, *5169*

Sanger, Margaret: Birth-control pill, *2370*
Pamphlet on birth control from a feminist perspective, *2365*

Sanghamittha: Country outside India to accept Buddhism, *4755*

Sánkara: Hindu monastic order, *4910*

Sankara, Thomas: President of Burkina Faso, *2845*

Santana, Pedro: Leader of the independent Dominican Republic, *2994*

Santander, Francisco de Paula: President of Colombia, *2785*

Santangel, Luis de: Letter containing a description of America, *2282*

Santorio, Santorio: Clinical thermometer, *5296*
Physician to use precise measuring instruments, *3962*
Treatise on basal metabolism, *3780*

Santos-Dumont, Alberto: Launch of a heavier-than-air machine entirely under its own power, *1356*

Sappho: Lesbian, *5379*

Sarasvati, Dayananda *See* Dayananda Sarasvati

Sarasvati, Mena: Assamese writing, *3518*

Sargent, Alonzo: Train disaster caused by the use of narcotics, *1934*

Sargent, Elise: Can-can dance, *1848*

Sargon: Emperor, *2763*

Sargon of Akkad: Empire, *2675*

Saruq, Menakhem ben *See* Menakhem ben Saruq

Saulak, Muhammad: Major naval battle decided by firepower, *4246*

Saunders, Cicely: Teaching and research hospice for the dying, *3896*

Saunders, Joe W.: Human construction in the New World, *4632*

Saussure, Horace Benedict de: Alpine mountaineer, *5727*
Ascent of Mont Blanc, *5728*

Sautet, Marc: Philosophy café, *4570*

Sautuola, Marcelino de: Cave paintings to be discovered, *1285*

Sautuola, Maria: Cave paintings to be discovered, *1285*

Savery, Thomas: Steam engine, *2163*

Savitskaya, Svetlana: Woman to walk in space, *5554*

Sawoniuk, Anthony: British jury to consider evidence overseas, *1740*

Sax, Antoine-Joseph: Saxophone, *4419*

Sax, Antoine-Joseph:—continued
Tuba, 4418
Sayers, Tom: World heavyweight boxing championship, 5644
Scappi, Bartolema: Printed cookbook, 2503
Schaeffer, Claude-Frédéric-Armandat: Alphabet, 3313
Schaeffer, Pierre: Musique concrète, 4395
Schawlow, Arthur Leonard: Laser, 2017
Schechtman, Daniel S.: Discovery of quasicrystals, 5249
Scheele, Carl Wilhelm: Discovery of oxygen, 5224
Schenck, Robert C.: Book on poker, 2592
Scheurl, Christoph: News agency, 4513
Schiaparelli, Elsa: Zipper that was practical, 1643
Schickard, Wilhelm: Mechnical calculator for astronomical use invented in modern times, 1661
Schilling, David Carl: Transatlantic eastward flight by jet airplane, 1378
Transatlantic nonstop jet airplane flight, 1380
Schilling, George Matthew: Round-the-world journey on foot, 5852
Schirra, Walter Marty, Jr.: Live telecast from space, 5542
Rendezvous in space, 5538
Schittler, Emil: Tranquilizer, 3937
Schleyer, Johann Martin: Artificial language, 3299
Schlick, Count of: Thaler, 2445
Schmeisser, Hugo: Assault rifle, 6117
Submachine gun widely used in battle, 6116
Schmied, Egbert: Ultrasonic disintegrator used in medicine, 4093
Schneider, Hannes: Ski school, 5811
Schöffer, Peter: Book printed in color, 3350
Book printed in Europe that survives in its complete form, 3349
Colophon in a printed book, 3351
Printed edition of the Bible, 4885
Text printed in Europe bearing a date, 3347
Schomburgk, Hans Hermann: Dramatic films shot in Africa, 4291
Schönbein, Christian Friedrich: Smokeless gunpowder, 6089
Schouten, Willem Corneliszoon: Voyage around Cape Horn, 2292
Schubin, Mark: Simultaneous television and radio broadcast of music from five continents, 5971
Schueller, Eugène: Commercial hair dye, 2735
Schultz, Norbert: Wartime song popular with both sides of the conflict, 4442
Schuman, Robert: President of the European Parliament, 2814
Schunzel, Reinhold: Movie with a homosexual theme, 5381

Schwabe, Samuel Heinrich: Sunspot cycle to be observed, 5087
Schwartz, David: Rigid airship, 1403
Schwarzenberg, Karl Philipp: Playing deck with double-headed face cards, 2591
Schwarzschild, Karl: Proposal of the existence of gravitational singularities, 5328
Schweiger, Walter: Passenger liner sunk by a submarine, 1932
Schweitzer, Hoyle: Windsurfing, 5866
Schweizer, Erhard K.: Physical manipulation of individual atoms, 5354
Schweppe, Jacob: Soft drink business, 2532
Schwimmer, Rosike: Woman accredited as a minister to a foreign power, 3146
Sclienting, Wilhelm: Airplane pilots killed in combat, 4210
Scott, David Randolph: Astronauts to ride a vehicle on the moon, 5528
Civilian space traveler to orbit the earth, 5539
Docking of two spacecraft, 5540
Scott, George H.: Transatlantic dirigible flight, 1406
Scultetus, Joannis: Glass eyes, 3982
Scylax of Caryanda: Periplus, 3604
Westerner to visit India, 2272
Sealby, William Inman: Radio distress call from a ship at sea, 5418
Sedgeman, Frank: Grand Slam doubles winners in tennis, 5837
Segalas, Pierre: Endoscope, 3870
Segré, Emilio: Element produced artificially, 5243
Seishu, Hanaoka: Modern use of anesthesia in surgery, 3761
Seleucus Nicator: Sighting of a mermaid, 3466
Selfridge, Thomas Etholen: Airplane accident that was fatal, 1897
Semaw, Sileshi: Tools, 4614
Sembène, Ousmane: Film directed by an African to be distributed outside Africa, 4307
Semen, Waldo: Vinyl shower curtains, 3093
Semmelweis, Ignaz Philipp: Use of antisepsis, 4048
Senanayake, Don Stephen: Prime minister of Sri Lanka, 2883
Senefelder, Aloys: Lithograph, 4712
Senghor, Léopold Sédar: Black African member of the Académie Française, 3338
President of Senegal, 2815
Senn, Nicholas: Surgeon to use gloves, 4051
Sennacherib: Aqueduct, 2129
Parking penalty, 1584
Senning, Ake: Pacemaker successfully implanted in a patient, 4059
Sequoyah: Native North American language to be given its own written form, 3540
Sergius, Marcus: Iron hand, 3980

Serpollet, Leon: License plate, *3228*

Serturner, Friedrich Wilhelm Adam Ferdinand: Isolation of morphine, *3923*

Servetus, Michael: Description of pulmonary blood circulation, *3953*
Protestant heretic, *4824*

Severus: Concrete dome, *1177*

Sewell, E.R.: Passenger fatally injured in an automobile accident, *1896*

Sewell, Henry: Prime minister of New Zealand, *2874*

Seymour, William J.: Pentecostal churches, *4842*

Shafi'i, Abu Abd Allah Muhammad ibn Idris ash-: Establishment of Islamic jurisprudence, *4932*

Shah Jahan: Sikh military victories, *5008*

Shaka Zulu: African army with standardized training and tactics, *4128*

Shakespeare, William: Play by William Shakespeare, *3421*

Shallit, Jeffrey: Automatic calculator to factor whole numbers, *1664*

Shapiro, Ben: Rock music festival, *4448*

Sharp, Cecil: Morris dancing, *1844*

Sharp, Granville: African refuge for former slaves, *5490*
Freed African slaves repatriated to Africa, *5491*

Sharp, Harry: Vasectomy, *2364*

Sharp, James: Gas stove that was practical, *3060*

Sharp, Jane: Book in the English language written by a woman, *3427*

Sharvit, Jacob: Olive oil factory, *2525*

Shaw, Louis Agassiz: Apparatus used to treat respiratory failure, *4088*

Shefer, Reva: Holocaust reparations from a neutral nation, *1780*

Sheffield, Washington Wentworth: Toothpaste tube, *2760*

Sheldon, John P.: Typewritten letter, *3324*

Shelley, Mary Wollstonecraft: Science-fiction novel, *3448*

Shen Nung: Tea, *2491*

Sheptoon La-Pha: King of Bhutan, *2959*

Sheridan, Charles: Heart surgery broadcast on the Internet, *4063*

Sheshna, Amram bar, Rabbi *See* Amram bar Sheshna, Rabbi

Shiers, W.H.: Flight from England to Australia, *1362*

Shiers, Wally: Air race from England to Australia, *5604*

Shiganosuke, Akashi: Sumo grand champion, *5870*

Shima, Masatoshi: Microprocessor, *1678*

Shimura, Takashi: Slow motion action sequence, *4305*

Shinran: Buddhist priest to be married, *4762*

Shipton, Mother: Witch image, *3477*

Shockley, William: Transistor, *2016*

Sholes, Christopher Latham: Typewriter that was practical, *3590*

Shonin, Georgy Stepanovich: Welding and smelting in space, *5545*

Shotoku, Prince: Wooden buildings, *1180*

Shrapnel, Henry: Exploding shell, *6087*

Shreeve, Herbert E.: Transatlantic message over radio telephone, *5936*

Shrewbury, Earl of: Military regulation concerning uniforms, *4147*

Shri Chand: Sectarian dissenters in Sikhism, *5003*

Shriver, A.K.: Steam sterilization of cans, *2519*

Shugart, Alan: Floppy disk widely used, *1677*

Shulgi: Zoo, *1158*

Shuqeiri, Ahmad: Meeting of the Palestine Liberation Organization, *2667*

Shushanik, St.: Georgian writing, *3495*

Shuster, Joe: Comic book superhero, *4472*

Shute, Nevil: Movie premiered simultaneously in major cities throughout the world, *4306*

Siddhartha Gautama: Atheistic religious movements, *4737*
Biography of the Buddha, *4756*
Buddhist missionaries, *4744*
Buddhist monastery, *4747*
Buddhist monks, *4745*
Buddhist nun, *4748*
Statement of Buddhist doctrine, *4746*

Siegel, Jerry: Comic book superhero, *4472*

Siegfried, Count of Ardennes: Ruler of Luxembourg, *2935*

Siemens, Werner von: Electric locomotive, *3275*

Sikorsky, Igor Ivan: Helicopter that was successful, *1426*

Sikwayi: Native North American language to be given its own written form, *3540*

Sillen, Andrew: Human use of fire, *4617*

Silling, Pavel Lvovich: Remote-controlled explosive mine, *6088*

Silva, Jackie: Women's Olympic volleyball event, *5796*

Sima Qian: Chinese historian of importance, *3004*

Simeon the Elder: Stylite, *4789*

Simon, Helmut: Tattoos, *1596*
Vegetarian, *2469*

Simon Magus: Gnostic, *4773*

Simon, Mary May: Ambassador to Arctic aboriginal peoples, *3150*

Simon, Samuel: Silkscreen printing for fabrics, *3718*

Simon, Théodore: Standardized intelligence test, *4001*

Simons, Elwyn: Animal believed to be the ancestor of apes, monkeys, and humans, *4612*

Aye-aye born in captivity, *1124*

Simplicius: Treatise on geometry, *3731*

Simpson, George B.: Electric cooktop, *3061*

Simpson, James Young: Abortion by vacuum aspiration, *2362*

Simpson, Robert H.: Hurricane reconnaissance flights, *5286*

Sims, James Marion: Women's hospital founded by women, *3894*

Sjostrand, Sten: Floating resort hotel, *1471*

Skelton, R.A.: Map of any part of the Americas, *3608*

Skinner, L.A.: Handheld rocket launcher, *6133*

Škoda, Josef: Modern stethoscope, *3872*

Slattery, Francis A.: Warship to sink with nuclear weapons aboard, *1943*

Slayton, Deke: International space mission, *5548*

Sloane, Hans: Museum operated as a public institution, *1826*

Sloane, Neil J.A.: Encyclopedia of integer sequences, *3757*

Smeaton, John: Hydraulic mortar, *2151*

Submersible supplied with air pumped from the surface, *5450*

Smellie, William: General encyclopedia in the English language, *3384*

Physician to teach obstetrics and midwifery, *2341*

Smith, Adam: Treatise on economics, *5359*

Smith, Bruce: Crops cultivated in the New World, *1015*

Smith, Captain John: Permanent English settlement in America, *4659*

Smith, Dick: Solo helicopter voyage around the world, *1428*

Smith, Edwin: Medical texts, *3766*

Smith, George Franklin: Pilot to bail out of an airplane flying at supersonic speed, *1437*

Smith, Hamilton O.: Complete DNA sequencing of a free-living organism, *5205*

Smith, J.L.B.: Coelacanth caught alive, *1115*

Smith, John: Treatise on barometry, *5299*

Whisky distillery, *2488*

Smith, Joseph: Mormon church, *4801*

Smith, Keith: Air race from England to Australia, *5604*

Smith, Keith Macpherson: Flight from England to Australia, *1362*

Smith, M. Susan: Cloning of a primate from an embryo, *5189*

Smith, Nathan: Published record of dinosaur fossil remains, *5213*

Smith, Oberlin: Recording tape, *2047*

Smith, Robert Holbrook: Self-help program for substance abusers, *4027*

Smith, Ross: Air race from England to Australia, *5604*

Smith, Ross Macpherson: Flight from Cairo to Calcutta, *1359*

Flight from England to Australia, *1362*

Smith, Willis Warren: Drive-in movie theater, *4359*

Smrekar, Suzanne E.: Space mission headed by women, *5517*

Smyth, John: Baptist church, *4829*

Sneferu: Reference to a ship with a name, *5393*

Snegur, Mircea: President of Moldova, *2857*

Snoddy, Gloria: Heart surgery broadcast on the Internet, *4063*

Snow, John: Epidemic map, *3624*

Snowden, Mrs. Philip: Reference to the Iron Curtain, *3128*

Sobhuza II, King of Swaziland: King of independent Swaziland, *2981*

Sobrero, Ascanio: Nitroglycerin, *5233*

Soglo, Nicéphore: Incumbent African president defeated in a democratic election, *2641*

Sohm, Viktor: Ski course, *5809*

Solomon, King of Israel: Hebrew writing, *3562*

Jewish calendar, *6006*

Object from Solomon's Temple in Jerusalem, *4958*

Temple in Jerusalem, *4955*

Solomon, Lauren: Personal computer kit, *1680*

Solomon, Les: Personal computer kit, *1680*

Solon: Brothel, *5386*

Democracy, *2681*

Sommeiller, Germain: Mountain tunnel, *2192*

Soncino, Yehoshua Shlomo: Printed edition of the Torah, *4993*

Sonni Ali: Emperor of Songhai, *2776*

Sophocles: Choreographers, *1841*

Sophron of Syracuse: Dialogues, *5977*

Sopwith, Tom: Chartered airplane flight, *1337*

Soranus of Ephesus: Comprehensive treatise on contraception and birth, *2357*

Soro, Giovanni: Secret service to specialize in codebreaking, *3401*

Sostratus of Cnidus: Lighthouse of importance, *5440*

Soucaret, Bertha: Beauty contest, *2199*

Soufflot, Jacques-Germain: Neoclassic architecture, *1194*

Soupault, Philippe: Surrealist text, *3455*

Sousa, Tomé de: Governor-general of Brazil, *2987*

Sowande, J. Sobowole: Yoruba writing, *3542*

Soyinka, Akinwande Oluwole "Wole": Nobel Prize for Literature winner from Africa, *4537*

Spallanzani, Lazzaro: Artificial insemination, *5155*

Head transplant, *5153*

Sparling, Marcus: War photographers, *4460*

Speciale, Pietro: Sugar mill in Europe, *1061*

Speke, John Hanning: European explorer to find the source of the White Nile, *2300*

Spencer, Percy: Microwave oven, *3073*

Spencer, Timothy Wilson: Murderer executed on DNA evidence, *1762*

Speusippus: Philosophical encyclopedia, *3376*

Spilsbury, John: Jigsaw puzzle, *2573*

Spina, Alessandro di: Eyeglasses, *4103*

Spinelli, Parri: Artist to draw freely with pen on paper, *1277*

Spitzer, Victor: Comprehensive digital atlas of the human body, *3908*

Spode, Josiah: Bone china, *3649*

Spohr, Louis: Conductor to use a baton, *4371*

Sprenger, Jakob: Witchcraft encyclopedia, *3476*

Srong-brtsan-sgam-po: Introduction of Buddhism to Tibet, *4760*

Ssu-ma Ch'ien: Chinese historian of importance, *3004*

Stáble, Guillermo: World Cup soccer championship, *5816*

Städtler, Friedrich: Pencil factory, *3584*

Stafford, Thomas P.: International space mission, *5548*

Stafford, Thomas Patten: Rendezvous in space, *5538*

Stahlberg, Kaarlo Juho: President of independent Finland, *2799*

Stalin, Josef: General secretary of the Communist Party of the former Soviet Union, *2997*

Modern nation to make abortions freely available, *2366*

Severe famine caused by government ideology, *1950*

Stampar, Andrija: International organization for promoting health, *4017*

Stanford, Leland: Photographs showing action, *4597*

Stanislaw II August Poniatowski, King of Poland: Written national constitution outside of the United States, *2647*

Stanley, Edward, Earl of Derby: English Derby, *5682*

Starkweather, Gary: Laser printer for business, *1687*

Starley, James: Bicycle with spoked wheels, *5623*

Starling, Ernest Henry: Hormone to be discovered, *5165*

Starzl, Thomas Earl: Liver transplant, *4069*

Statler, Ellsworth Milton: Major hotel chain, *1468*

Staudinger, Hermann: Macromolecules, *5242*

Stearn, C.H.: Synthetic fiber suitable for making cloth, *3723*

Stebbins, Joel: Astronomer to use electronic instruments, *5093*

Steers, George: International yacht race, *5855*

Steger, Will: Expedition to cross Antarctica by dogsled and foot, *2330*

Stein, Aurel: Rag paper, *3689*

Stein, Robert: International conference of multimedia publishers, *1734*

Steinitz, Wilhelm: World chess champion, *2599*

Steinweg, Henry Engelhard: Steinway piano, *4421*

Stelzner, Carl Ferdinand: Photographs of a historic event, *4592*

Steno, Nicolaus: Treatise on geology, *5263*

Stephen, St.: Christian martyr, *4771*

Stephen, St., of Hungary: King of Hungary, *2938*

Stephen VII, Pope: Pope tried for heresy after his death, *4852*

Stephenson, George: International rail line, *3267*

Steam locomotive in regular use, *3265*

Steam locomotive passenger service, *3266*

Stephenson, George and Robert: Person run over by a train, *1891*

Stephenson, Marjory: Scientific association sanctioned by a national government, *5048*

Steptoe, Patrick: Test-tube baby, *2348*

Sterne, Laurence: Stream of consciousness as a literary technique, *3446*

Stevens, Albert William: Aerial photograph showing the lateral curvature of the horizon and the beginning of the stratosphere, *5284*

Stevens, John: Steamboat to make an ocean voyage, *5454*

Stevens, John Cox: International yacht race, *5855*

Stevens, Nettie: Researcher to describe the role of the human sex chromosomes, *5195*

Stevens, Robert Livingston: Steamboat to make an ocean voyage, *5454*

Stevenson-Menchik, Vera Francevna: World chess champion who was a woman, *2600*

Stevin, Simon: Gravity experiment, *5322*

Treatise advocating the use of the decimal system, *3742*

Stewart, Robert: Space travelers to fly free in space, *5553*

Stewart, Timothy A.: Patent on an animal, *5172*

Stieber, Wilhelm: Modern war won through superior military intelligence, *4140*

Stieff, Margaret: Stuffed toy bear, *2388*

Stohr, M.: Electron-beam welding, *1495*

Stojiljkovic, Vlajko: Serving leader of a sovereign nation indicted for war crimes by an international tribunal, *1783*

Stoker, Bram: World Dracula Congress, *3481*

Stolyar, A.D.: Brain surgery, *4037*

Stone, Constance: Woman physician in Australia, *3973*

Stone, Victoria: Health-care facility with a labyrinth, *4095*

Strabo: Description of an earthquake, *5258*

Strabo, Walahfrid: Gardening book, *2618*

Stradivari, Antonio: Stradivarius violin, *4410*

Strauss, Joseph Baermann: Bridge with piers sunk in the open sea, *2146*

Strauss, Levi: Blue jeans, *1630*

Strauss, Richard: One-armed pianist of international stature, *4374*

Streitwieser, Franz: Museum of brass instruments, *4425*

Stringfellow, John: Air transport company, *1336*

Strite, Charles: Pop-up toaster, *3067*

Struger, Odo J.: Programmable logic controller, *2189*

Stuck, Hudson: Ascent of Mount McKinley (Denali), *5735*

Student, Kurt: Major airborne assault, *4224*

Stumpf, Johannes: Map of the Alps, *3619*

Sturgeon, William: Electromagnet that could support more than its own weight, *2083*

Sturluson, Snorri: King of Norway, *2932*

Stylites, Simeon, St.: Stylite, *4789*

Su Kung: Use of silver amalgam to fill dental cavities, *3800*

Su Song: Astronomical clock of large size, *6021*

Su Sung: Printed astronomical charts, *3629*

Suchocka, Hanna: Woman to become prime minister of Poland, *2916*

Sucklin, John: Cribbage, *2587*

Sucre, Antonio José de: Leader of free Ecuador, *2992*

Suess, Randy: Personal computer bulletin board, *1704*

Sufi, as-: Galaxy to be described in print, *5071*

Suger, Abbot: Building in the Gothic style, *1184*
Stained glass, *3644*

Suiko Tenno: Empress of Japan, *2770*

Sukarno: President of Indonesia, *2810*

Sullivan, Kathryn D.: Woman to walk in space, *5554*

Sullivan, W.N.: Aerosol product, *3115*

Sulston, John E.: DNA sequencing of a multicellular organism, *5208*

Sun Tzu: Treatise on espionage, *4138*
Treatise on war, *4155*

Sun Yixian (Sun Yat-Sen): President of China, *2795*

Sundback, Gideon: Zipper that was practical, *1643*

Sundiata: Emperor of Mali, *2775*

Superbus, Lucius Tarquinius: Republic, *2680*

Surrey, Henry Howard, Earl of: Blank verse in English, *3416*

Susini, Luis: Cigarette factory, *1067*

Susruta: Surgery to repair perforated or obstructed intestines, *4040*
Texts of Ayurvedic medicine, *3770*

Suttner, Bertha Félicie Sophie von: Woman to win the Nobel Prize for Peace, *4539*

Suzuki, Daisetsu Teitaro: Popularizer of Zen Buddhism in the West, *4764*

Swammerdam, Jan: Entomological collection in Europe, *5147*

Swan, Joseph: Incandescent lamp, *2092*
Synthetic fiber, *3721*

Sweynheym, Conrad: Typeface made in Europe in a non-Roman alphabet, *4705*

Swinnerton, James: Comic books featuring color cartoons previously published in newspapers, *4469*

Swinton, Alan Campbell: All-electronic television system, *5950*

Swinton, E.D.: Self-propelled tank, *6121*

Sylvester II, Pope: French-born pope, *4854*

Szent-Györgyi, Albert von: Vitamin-deficiency disease to be cured, *3836*

Szilard, Leo: Nuclear chain reaction patent, *5344*

Szisz, Ferenc: Grand Prix race, *5716*

T

Tabari, Abu Jafar Muhammad ibn Jarir at-: Arabic history of the world, *3007*

Tabora, Diogenes: Feature-length animated film, *4330*

Tacayhamo: Andean empire, *2686*

Tacitus, Cornelius: Account of Germanic religion, *4739*
Woman to lead a rebellion against the Roman Empire, *4158*

Tacon, Paul: Depiction of organized warfare, *4151*

Taglioni, Maria: Ballerina to dance on her toes, *1860*
Ballerina to wear a tutu, *1861*

Tagore, Rabindranath: Nobel Prize for Literature winner from Asia, *4532*

T'ai Tsung: Christian missionaries in China, *4792*

Tainter, Charles: Dictation device, *2042*

Tait, Margaret: Gym suit for girls, *1632*

Taizong: Printed edition of the Buddhist canon, *4768*

Takagi, Takeo: Sea battle fought solely by air power, *4272*

Takashina Takakane: Bonsai, *2621*

Talbot, William Henry Fox: Book illustrated with photographs, *3361*

Screen printing, *4717*

Taliesin: Welsh writing, *3498*

Tamara, Queen of Georgia: Woman to rule Georgia, *2942*

Tamayo-Mendez, Arnaldo: Space traveler of African descent, *5550*

Tamba Yasuyori: Japanese medical book, *3772*

Tambano Furiyori: Japanese dentists, *3802*

Tambano Kaneyasu: Japanese dentists, *3802*

Tamm, Igor Y.: Tokamak, *2120*

Tangun: King of Korea, *2920*

Tartaglia, Niccolò Fontana: Treatise on ballistics, *6102*

Tasman, Abel Janszoon: European explorer to see New Zealand, *2293*

Tate, Henry: Sugar cubes, *2554*

Taussig, Helen Brooke: Operation to cure congenital heart disease, *4057*

Taut, Bruno: Building of glass bricks, *1198*

Tavrisov, A.A.: Multistep crude oil refining, *2106*

Tawell, John: Criminal caught by telegraph, *1751*

Tayler, William: Advertising agency, *1453*

Taylor, Estelle: Movie accompanied by prerecorded sound to be released as a feature film, *4300*

Taylor, Florence: Glider pilot who was a woman, *1420*

Taylor, Frederick Winslow: Efficiency expert, *1445*

Taylor, John Baxter, Jr.: Athlete of African descent to win a gold medal in an individual event, *5767*

Taylor, Richard: Discovery of quarks, *5351*

Taylor, Robert: Computer network, *1694*

Tcherepnin, Nikolay Nikolayevich: Ballets Russes, *1862*

Teilhard de Chardin, Pierre: Scientific hoax of international notoriety, *5051*

Teisserenc de Bort, Léon-Philippe: Weather balloons, *5277*

Teller, Charles: Refrigerator ship, *5428*

Teller, Edward: Hydrogen bomb, *6129*

Teoctist, Patriarch of Romania: Pope to visit a mainly Christian Orthodox country, *4812*

Tepl, Johannes von: German prose work, *3559*

Teresa of Ávila: Doctor of the Church who was a woman, *4876*

Tereshkova, Valentina Vladimirovna Nikolayeva: Child whose parents had both flown in space, *2393*
Woman to fly in space, *5535*

Terray, Lionel: Ascent of Makalu, *5741*

Tesla, Nikola: Alternating-current electric motor, *2173*

Thackeray, William Makepeace: World's Fair, *2223*

Thagard, Norman Earl: American to be launched into space aboard a Russian spacecraft, *5560*

Thäis: Organist, *4361*

Thales: Western philosopher, *4556*

Thales of Miletus: Prediction of a solar eclipse, *5127*

Thant, U: Secretary general of the United Nations from an Asian nation, *3196*

Thatcher, Margaret Hilda: Prime minister, *2870*
Woman to serve as prime minister of Great Britain, *2911*

Theano: Woman mathematician, *3729*

Theiler, Max: Nobel Prize in Physiology or Medicine winner from Africa, *4554*

Theodora, Empress of Byzantium: Feast of Orthodoxy, *3026*

Theodosius II, Emperor of Rome: University in the Western world, *1983*

Theophilus Presbyter: Treatise on crafts by a practicing artisan, *1246*

Theophrastus of Eresus: Botanist, *5178*
Treatise on rocks and minerals, *5255*

Theremin, Leon Sergeyevich: Musical instrument to create sound with electromagnetic fields, *4423*

Thespis: Actor, *5975*
Stage makeup, *5988*

Theuerer, H.C.: Epitaxy fabrication, *2019*

Thévenot, Melchisédech: Spirit level, *6053*

Thimonnier, Barthélemy: Sewing machine that was practical, *1486*

Tholstrup, Hans: Transcontinental trip by a solar-powered vehicle, *3207*

Thom, Alexander: Unit of length, *5308*

Thomas, George: Thomas Cup in badminton, *5599*

Thomas, Harold: Chemotherapeutic drug, *3929*

Thompson, Henry: Treatise on cremation, *1881*

Thompson, John Taliaferro: Submachine gun widely used in battle, *6116*

Thompson, Ken: Multiuser operating system, *1727*

Thompson, Lemarcus Adna: Roller coaster, *2212*

Thompson, Leonard: Isolation of insulin, *3933*

Thompson, William: Underwater photograph, *4594*

Thomson, C. Wyville: Oceanographic expedition, *5273*

Thomson, Joseph John: Discovery of electrons, *5331*
Discovery of protons, *5337*
Mass spectrometer, *5335*

Thomson, Robert William: Pneumatic tires, *3292*

Thomson, William, Baron Kelvin of Largs: Absolute scale of temperature, *5329*

Thomson, William, Baron Kelvin of Largs:— *continued*

Gyrocompass, *5438*

Thorfinnson, Snorri: Child born of European parents in North America, *4644*

Thorgilsson, Ari: History of Iceland in Icelandic, *3008*

Thornton, F. Martin: Color feature film, *4294*

Thorvaldson, Erik *See* Erik the Red Erik the Red

Thou, Jacques-Auguste de: Library with books shelved upright, *1814*

Thouret, M.: Artificial insemination of a human being, *2342*

Throckmorton, Peter: Underwater shipwreck, *5396*

Thucydides: Epidemic, *1899*

Thuot, Pierre: Simultaneous space walk by three astronauts, *5558*

Thutmose III: Glass bottle, *3639*
Palace, *1169*

Thutmose IV: Tapestry, *3078*

Tibbets, Paul Warfield, Jr.: Atomic bomb explosion over enemy territory, *4232*

Tiberius, Mauricius Flavius: Metal stirrups, *1154*

Tible, Elizabeth: Woman to ascend in an untethered balloon, *1398*

Tichy, Herbert: Ascent of Cho Oyu, *5740*

Tiemann, Ferdinand: Artificial flavoring, *2539*

Tiglath-pileser III: Lost tribes of Israel, *4957*

Tigranes II the Great: King of united Armenia, *2923*

Tikkana: Telugu writing, *3500*

Tim-Oi Lee, Florence: Anglican woman priest, *4843*

Timagenes of Alexandria: Bards, *3329*

Tinbergen, Jan: Nobel Prize in Economics, *4528*

Tintoretto: Academy of fine arts, *1238*

Tintori, Avraham ben Hayyim di: Printed edition of the Torah, *4993*

Tiridates III, King of Armenia: Establishment of Christianity as the state religion, *4781*

Tiro, Marcus Tullius: Shorthand, *3319*

Titian: Academy of fine arts, *1238*

Tito, Josip Broz: Meeting of the nonaligned movement, *3163*

Tito, Teburoro: Country to officially celebrate the year 2000, *3047*

Titus: Depiction of a menorah, *4965*
Sports spectacular, *2220*

Togo Heihachiro: Modern conflict in which an Asian power defeated a European power, *4257*

Tokugawa, Yoshimune: Government complaint box, *2631*

Tokurai: Physicians in Japan, *3950*

Tombalbaye, N'Garta François: President of the Republic of Chad, *2821*

Tombaugh, Clyde William: Planet found beyond Neptune, *5097*

Tomiki Kenji: Aikido, *5706*

Tomlinson, Ray: Electronic mail message, *1695*
Electronic mail message to use the @ ("at") sign, *1696*

Tomyris: Woman to wear armor while leading men in battle, *4154*

Tonegawa, Susumu: Nobel Prize in Physiology or Medicine winner from Asia, *4555*

Töpffer, Rodolphe: Comic strip published as a booklet, *4466*

Topor, Roland: Animated film to win an award at the Cannes International Film Festival, *4336*

Torquemada, Antonio: Checkers book, *2572*

Torres, Luis de: Europeans to smoke tobacco, *4022*

Torricelli, Evangelista: Barometer, *5297*

Touré, Ahmed Sékou: President of Guinea, *2813*

Tournachon, Gaspard-Félix: Aerial photographs, *4595*
Exhibition of impressionist paintings, *1250*
Photo interview, *4571*
Underground photographs, *4596*

Tourte, François: Modern bow for playing musical instruments, *4415*

Toussaint, Charles: Correspondence school, *1975*

Toussaint-Louverture: Large-scale uprising of African slaves in the New World, *5492*

Townes, Charles Hard: Laser, *2017*

Townley, Houghton: Comic strip in a magazine, *4467*

Toyama, Syuichi: Rice, *1011*

Toyotomi, Hideyoshi: Catholic martyrs who were Japanese, *4869*
Naval battles in which ironclad vessels participated, *4248*

Trautmann, Jeremiah: Cesarean birth fully documented, *2339*

Trembley, Abraham: Proof of regeneration in an organism, *5150*

Trevithick, Robert: Steam locomotive, *3264*

Trithemius, Johannes: Printed cryptology book, *3402*

Trotha, Lothar von: Genocide in the 20th century, *1768*

Troung Trong Tri: Personal computer, *1679*

Trubshaw, Roy: MUD (multi-user dominion), *1705*

Truman, Harry S: Overthrow of a democratic foreign government arranged by the U.S. Central Intelligence Agency, *4143*
United Nations military action, *4192*

Truth, Sojourner: Robot to conduct a roving exploration of the surface of another planet, *5582*

Ts'ai Hsiang: Monograph on a fruit tree, *5180*

Ts'ai Lun: Rag paper, *3689*

Ts'ai Yen: Woman poet in a Chinese language, *3552*

Tschirnhaus, Ehrenfried Walter von: Porcelain manufactured in Europe, *3648*

Tsering, Ang: Woman to reach the summit of Mount Everest, *5747*

Tsibliyev, Vasily: Joint space walk by American and Russian astronauts, *5563*

Tsiranana, Philibert: President of independent Madagascar, *2819*

Tsunoda, Yukio: Cow clones, *5191*

Tuke, William: Refuge for mentally ill patients, *3992*

Tull, Jethro: Horse-drawn seed drill, *1078*

Tumason, Kolbein: Hymn for which an exact date is known, *4382*

Tung Chee-hwa: Chief executive of Hong Kong, *3001*

Tupolev, Alexey Alexeyevich: Supersonic jet airliner, *1328*

Tupolev, Andrey Nikolayevich: Scheduled commercial jet flight, *1346*

Turing, Alan Matheson: Electromechanical cryptographic decoder, *4142*
Treatise on computing theory, *1659*

Turner, Benjamin Bracknell: Book illustrated with photographs, *3361*

Turner, D.A.: Gas chamber, *1747*

Turner, Ted: All-news television network, *4465*

Turner, William Thomas: Passenger liner sunk by a submarine, *1932*

Tutankhamen: Clothes made of tapestry weaving, *1600*
Gloves, *1601*
Military game, *2570*
Trumpet, *4401*

Tuthill, Richard Stanley: Juvenile court, *5500*

Twain, Mark: Book manuscript written on a typewriter, *3362*

Twinning, Alexander C.: Frozen meat for commercial sale, *2535*

Tykot, Robert: Long-distance sea trading along regular routes, *1523*

Tyler, Christopher W.: Single-picture stereogram, *5319*

Tylor, Edward Burnett: Treatise on animism, *4742*

Tyndale, William: Glossary of English words explained in English, *3414*
New Testament printed in English, *4887*

Tzara, Tristan: Anti-art movement, *1252*

U

Uchermann, Karl: Postage meter, *4676*

Udall, Nicholas: Comedy written in English, *3415*

Udobi, Iyke Louis: Octuplets, *2355*

Ueshiba, Morihei: Aikido, *5706*

Ugyen Wangchuk: King of Bhutan, *2959*

Ui-te-Rangiora: Sighting of Antarctica, *2312*

Ulfilas: German writing, *3557*

Ulloa, Antonio de: Isolation of platinum, *3665*

Ulm, Charles T.P.: Flight from the United States to Australia, *1366*

Ulmanis, Guntis: Prime minister of independent Latvia, *2798*

Ulmanis, Karlis: Prime minister of independent Latvia, *2798*

Ulrich, St.: Catholic saint canonized by a pope, *4853*

Uluj Ali: Major naval battle decided by firepower, *4246*

Umar ibn al-Khattab, Caliph: Expansion of Islam outside Arabia, *4924*
Year in the Muslim calendar, *6005*

Unas: Religious text, *4731*

Upatnieks, Juris: Hologram, *5318*

Ur-Nammu: Law code, *2644*
Multi-story building, *1168*

Urban, Charles: Color feature film, *4294*

Urban II, Pope: Crusade, *4160*

Urban VI, Pope: Antipope during the Great Schism, *4862*

Ure, Andrew: Thermostat, *1211*

Usman dan Fodio: Hausa writing, *3539*

Uthman ibn Affan: Sectarian controversy in Islam, *4927*

Uthman ibn Affan, Caliph: Authoritative text of the Qur'an, *4938*
Civil war in Islam, *4925*
Expansion of Islam outside Arabia, *4924*

Uthman ibn Fudi: Hausa writing, *3539*

Uthmar ibn Affan, Caliph: Arabic book, *3545*

Utnapishtim: Flood story, *3463*

V

Vaaler, Johann: Paper clip, *3110*

Vail, Alfred: Commercial telegraph service, *5923*

Valentine, St.: St. Valentine's Day, *3018*

Valfyer, M. de: Prepaid envelopes, *4671*

Valle, Federico: Feature-length animated film, *4330*

Van Alen, William: Skyscraper more than 1,000 feet high, *1227*

Van Buren, Martin: Typewritten letter, *3324*

van den Heuvel, Martinus: Prints made for marketing and advertising purposes, *1452*

van den Keere, Pieter: Newspaper in the English language, *4490*

van der Post, Laurens: Anti-apartheid novel, *3462*

Van Eyck, Hubert: Oil painters, *1273*

Van Eyck, Jan: Full-length double portrait, *1275*

Oil painters, *1273*

van Geen, John: Computer modem that was practical, *1675*

Van Haaften, Egbert: Electronic wristwatch, *6033*

Van Hoevenbergh, Henry: Flip book, *4325*

Van Horn, John: Battery-powered wristwatch, *6032*

van Houten, Konraad Johannes: Chocolate cocoa and candy, *2551*

Vasari, Giorgio: Academy of fine arts, *1238*

Book about the High Renaissance, *1237*

Vassa, Gustavus: Autobiography by an African slave to have a major impact on the abolition movement, *5489*

Vasyutin, Vladimir: Medical emergency in space, *5557*

Vaucanson, Jacques de: Automated loom, *3717*

Mechanical duck, *5029*

Vauquelin, Nicolas-Louis: Amino acid to be discovered, *5158*

Discovery of chromium, *3667*

Extraction of beryllium, *3668*

Vaux, Roland de: Dead Sea Scrolls to be discovered, *4978*

Veblen, Oswald: Topology book, *3752*

Veidt, Conrad: Movie with a homosexual theme, *5381*

Veil, Simone: President of the European Parliament who was directly elected, *2841*

Velasco, Luís de: Deaf person educated in lipreading and speaking, *2005*

Veldeke, Heinrich von: Dutch writing, *3507*

Venable, James M.: Modern use of anesthesia in surgery, *3761*

Vencer, Agustin, Jr.: Director of the World Evangelical Fellowship who was not from the West, *4844*

Venter, J. Craig: Complete DNA sequencing of a free-living organism, *5205*

Ventris, Michael: Greek writing, *3560*

Verduyn, Pieter Andriannszoon: Below-knee leg prosthesis, *3984*

Vernon, Edward: Grog, *2484*

Veronese, Paolo: Artist of note to be investigated by the Inquisition, *1239*

Vesalius, Andreas: Anatomist to break with Galen, *3958*

Skeleton prepared by a medical researcher, *3960*

Treatise on human anatomy with accurate illustrations, *3776*

Vespucci, Amerigo (Americus): Map to use the name "America" for the New World, *3614*

Victor, St.: Pope, *4847*

Victoria, Guadalupe: Constitutional president of Mexico, *2782*

Victoria, Queen of England: British monarch to live in Buckingham Palace, *2965*

Bustles, *1631*

Queen to deliver a child under anesthesia, *2344*

Transatlantic telegraph messages, *5927*

Vidocq, François-Eugène: Detective bureau, *1791*

Private detective agency, *1793*

Vieille, Paul: Smokeless gunpowder, *6089*

Viète, François: Systematic algebraic notation, *3743*

Vigevano, Guido de *See* Guido de Vigevano

Vignoles, Charles: Iron railroad track, *3270*

Vike-Freiberga, Vaira: Eastern European country to elect a woman as president, *2869*

Vilga, Edward: Feature film to premiere simultaneously in a theater and on the Internet, *4315*

Villa, Pancho: Asian boxer to win a world championship, *5646*

Villafranca, Blasius: Wine cooler, *2480*

Vincent de Paul, St.: Religious order of nurses, *3964*

Vishpla: Written record of a prosthesis, *3979*

Vitruvius: Device to transmit power through gearing, *2186*

Freight elevators, *1203*

Vivekananda: Hindu missionary in the West, *4917*

Vivian, John Henry: Environmental lawsuit, *2240*

Voigtländer, Friedrich: Portrait camera, *4578*

Volkov, Vladislav Nikolayevich: Space station, *5546*

Volta, Alessandro Giuseppe Antonio Anastasio: Battery, *2081*

Von Ehr II, James R.: Nanotechnology company, *1499*

Vuia, Trajan: Launch of a heavier-than-air machine entirely under its own power, *1356*

W

Waddell, Tom: Gay Games, *5698*

Wagenseil, Johann Christoph: Encyclopedia for children, *3383*

Wagoner, Clyde Decker: Round-the-world radio broadcast, *5911*

White, Patrick Victor Martindale: Nobel Prize for Literature winner from Oceania, *4536*

White, Timothy: Hominid species, *4613*

Whitehead, Robert: Torpedo, *6090*

Whitlock, David: Comprehensive digital atlas of the human body, *3908*

Whitney, John, Sr.: Computer-generated short film, *4334*

Whittle, Frank: Jet fighter, *4229*

Whittle, Thomas, Jr.: European child born in Australia, *4664*

Whitworth, Joseph: Screws and bolts mass-produced in standard sizes, *1484*

Whymper, Edward: Ascent of the Matterhorn, *5730*

Whythorne, Thomas: Autobiography in English by a man, *3419*

Wichterle, Otto: Soft contact lens, *4112*

Widman, Johannes: Common algebraic symbols, *3740*

Wien, Wilhelm: Discovery of protons, *5337*

Wieprecht, Wilhelm: Tuba, *4418*

Wigner, Eugene Paul: Nuclear engineer, *2128*

Wilde, Friedrich: Vaginal cap, *2361*

Wiles, Andrew: Mathematical proof of Fermat's last theorem, *3756*

Wilhelm I, Kaiser: Kaiser of a united German Reich, *2967*

Wilhelm IV, Duke of Bavaria: Food purity law still observed, *2473*

Wilkins, Charles: Hindu text translated into English, *4912*

Wilkins, John: Thesaurus in English, *3372*

Wilkins, Maurice: Elucidation of the structure of DNA, *5199*

Wilkinson, Eugene Parks: Nuclear-powered submarine, *4273*

Wilkinson, John: Bridge constructed entirely of cast iron, *2142*
Cast-iron coffin, *1880*
Reaming machine, *1480*

William, Count of Poitiers: Troubadour, *4363*

William III, King of England: Central bank, *2406*

William III, King of Luxembourg: King of Luxembourg, *2966*

William IV, King of England: Stakes horse race in North America, *5683*

William Louis of Nassau: Modern army to use military drill, *4125*

William of Auvergne: Home for repentant prostitutes, *5388*

William of Malmesbury: Manned glider flight, *1415*

Williams, Charles, Jr.: Telephone for domestic use, *5934*

Williams, Eric Eustace: Prime minister of the Republic of Trinidad and Tobago, *2900*

Williams, Hugh C.: Automatic calculator to factor whole numbers, *1664*

Williams, Kendra: Woman fighter pilot to fire a missile in combat, *4237*

Williams, Paul "Hucklebuck": Rock concert, *4444*

Williams, Robert: Human killed by a robot, *5035*

Willoughby, Sharon: Veterinary chiropractic school, *3864*

Wills, William: European explorer to cross the Australian continent, *2299*

Wilmut, Ian: Lamb with human genes, *5207*
Mammal cloned from adult cells, *5187*

Wilpon, J.: Speech-activated robot, *5039*

Wilson, Harold: Long-distance university without classrooms, *2000*

Wilson, Robert Woodrow: Observational confirmation of the Big Bang theory, *5103*

Wilson, William Griffith: Self-help program for substance abusers, *4027*

Wilson, Woodrow: General association of nations, *3186*

Wingfield, Walter Clopton: Tennis rule book, *5834*

Winkel, Dietrich Nikolaus: Metronome, *4414*

Winn, John H.: Craps bookie, *2611*

Winsor, Frederick: Theater illuminated by gaslight, *5995*

Winstanley, Henry: Lighthouse in the open sea, *5442*

Winthrop, John: Free election in North America, *2635*

Wirth, Christian: National euthanasia program, *1771*

Withering, William: Cardiac stimulant, *4086*

Wittgenstein, Paul: One-armed pianist of international stature, *4374*

Wöhler, Friedrich: Extraction of beryllium, *3668*
Organic compound synthesized from an inorganic substance, *5232*

Wojtyla, Karol: Pope born in Poland, *4877*
Pope to visit a Communist country, *4878*
Pope to visit a mainly Christian Orthodox country, *4812*

Wolf, Donald: Cloning of a primate from an embryo, *5189*

Wolfmüller, Alois: Motorcycle to be mass-produced, *3217*

Wollstonecraft, Mary: Influential feminist tract, *5368*

Wolseley, Frank: Sheep-shearing machine, *1137*

Wolstenholme, Mr.: Balance of trade and payments for a nation, *1543*

Wood, Kenneth: Food processor, *3072*

Wood, Thomas: University museum, *1825*

Woodward, Arthur Smith: Scientific hoax of international notoriety, *5051*

Wooley, Hannah: Cookbook known to have been written by a woman, *2504*

Woolley, Leonard: Board game, *2565*
Museum, *1824*

Worden, Alfred Merrill: Astronauts to ride a vehicle on the moon, *5528*

Worden, John Lorimer: Naval battle between ironclad vessels, *4255*

Wozniak, Stephen: Personal computer that was commercially successful, *1681*

Wragge, Clement Lindley: Meteorologist to name tropical storms, *5276*

Wright, E.V. and C.W.: Work boats, *5398*

Wright, John Michael: Tartan plaids, *3709*

Wright, Orville: Airplane accident that was fatal, *1897*
Airplane flight, *1354*
Military aircraft, *4203*

Wright, Wilbur: Airplane flight, *1354*
Complete aerial turn in an airplane, *1355*
Military aircraft, *4203*

Wright, William Hammond: Movie showing another planet, *5095*

Wu, Chien-shiung: Discovery of nonsymmetric particle interaction, *5348*

Wu, Maw-Kuen: Superconducting material that operated at temperatures above the boiling point of nitrogen, *5353*

Wu Wang: Chinese ruler to invoke the Mandate of Heaven, *2764*

Wu Ze-tian: Empress of China to rule in her own right, *2771*

Wu Zhou: Empress of China to rule in her own right, *2771*

Wudi: Establishment of Confucianism as the state religion, *4897*
University in China, *1982*

Wundt, Wilhelm: Course in scientific psychology, *3995*
Experimental psychology laboratory, *3998*
Work of experimental psychology, *3994*

Wycliffe, John: English translation of the Bible, *4884*

Wynne, Arthur: Crossword puzzle, *2574*

X

Xenophanes: Prediction of a solar eclipse, *5127*

Xenophon: Treatise on hunting, *3123*

Xirsi, Cali Xuseen: Somali writing, *3544*

Xuanzang: Suspension bridge with iron chains, *2139*

Y

Yablochkov, Pavel Nikolayevich: Electric rail and street lamps, *2093*

Yajima, Kajiko: Women's organization in Japan, *1838*

Yajñavalkya: Statement of the Hindu doctrine of karmic reincarnation, *4903*

Yamagiwa, Katsusaburo: Induced cancer, *3845*

Yamamoto, Tadaoki: Closed-circuit sporting event, *5957*

Yamshchikova, Olga: Women pilots to down enemy aircraft in combat, *4226*

Yannas, Ioannis V.: Transplant of artificial skin, *4073*

Yeager, Charles Elwood "Chuck": Airplane to fly faster than the speed of sound, *1377*

Yeager, Jeana: Round-the-world nonstop airplane flight without refueling, *1385*

Yegorov, Boris Borisovich: Spacecraft to carry more than one crew member, *5536*

Yehoash: Reference to Solomon's Temple in Jerusalem, *4956*

Yehudah ben Mattityahu, ha-Maccabi: Chanukah, *3015*
Rebellion for religious freedom, *4961*

Yehudah ha-Nasi: Compilation of Jewish oral laws, *4986*

Yeltsin, Boris Nikolayevich: Democratically elected leader of Russia, *2854*
Treaty between the North Atlantic Treaty Organization (NATO) and Russia, *3184*

Yi Sun-Shin: Ironclad ships, *4247*
Naval battles in which ironclad vessels participated, *4248*
Smokescreen in a battle, *4249*

Yikunno Amlak: Black African state to be well documented, *2688*

Yirmeyahu: Physical evidence of a person mentioned in the Jewish scriptures, *4959*

Yixing: Large mechanical clock, *6020*

Yochanan ben Mattityahu: Chanukah, *3015*

Yochanan, Mattityahu ben *See* Yehudah ben Mattityahu, ha-Maccabi

Young, John W.: Reusable manned spacecraft, *5551*

Young, Robert: Boy scout troop, *2389*

Young, Thomas: Hieroglyphic writing from Egypt to be deciphered, *5054*

Yü, Emperor: Magic square, *3727*

Yuan Shikai: President of China, *2795*

Yudin, Sergey: Blood bank, *4100*

Yukawa, Hideki: Nobel Prize in Physics winner from Asia, *4548*
Prediction of the existence of mesons, *5345*

Yurco, Frank: Depiction of Israelites, *4953*

Z

Zaburu, François Sopite: Factory ship for whaling, *3124*

Zacchini, Ildebrando: Human cannonball family act, *2214*

Zach, Franz Xaver von: Astronomical journal, *5122*

Zacuto, Abraham: Explorer saved by an eclipse, *2287*

Zajac, Edward: Digital computer animation, *4335*

Zakrzewska, Marie Elizabeth: Women's hospital staffed by women physicians, *3895*

Zamenhof, Ludwik Lejzer: Artificial language, *3299*

Zamora, Nicetor Alcála: Constitutional president of Spain, *2803*

Zangen, Fritz von: Airplane pilots killed in combat, *4210*

Zarathushtra: Prophet of Zoroastrianism, *5018*
Text in the Avestan language, *3496*
Zoroastrian holidays, *3013*
Zoroastrian religious texts, *5020*

Zátopek, Emil: Olympic marathon winner who had never run a marathon, *5775*

Zayd ibn Thabit: Arabic book, *3545*

Zayn-ul-Abidin: Cashmere, *3705*

Zazel: Human cannonball, *2210*

Zeidler, Othmar: Organic pesticide, *1099*

Zeller, Carl August: National teacher-training program, *1972*

Zeno of Citium: Stoic, *4561*

Zenodotus of Ephesus: Critical edition of the works of Homer, *3328*

Zeppelin, Ferdinand, Graf von: Dirigible that was commercially and militarily successful, *1404*
Zeppelin flight, *1405*

Zetkin, Clara: Socialist women's newspaper, *4507*

Zheng He: Major Chinese voyage of exploration and diplomacy, *2277*
Sea chart of southern Asian and Indian waters, *3607*

Zhu, Toufo: HIV infections, *3847*

Zhuangzi: Taoist book of teachings, *5014*

Ziegenbalg, Bartholomäus: New Testament printed in Asia, *4893*

Zinzendorf, Nicholas Ludwig von: Moravian Church community, *4832*

Zipper, Jaime: Copper IUD, *2371*

Ziusudra: Flood story, *3463*

Zizka, Jan: Commander to coordinate mobile armored artillery, infantry, and cavalry as one tactical unit, *4165*

Zog I, King of Albania: King of Albania, *2973*

Zoser: Large stone structure, *1167*

Zosimos of Panopolis: Alchemical theory, *5219*

Zou Yan: Yin-Yang philosophical school, *4562*

Zukertort, Johannes: World chess champion, *2599*

Zumárraga, Juan de: Book printed in the Western Hemisphere, *3359*
Printing press in the New World, *4709*
Seminary in the New World, *4867*

Zürbriggen, Matthias: Ascent of Aconcagua, *5733*

Zuse, Konrad: Programmable electronic binary computer, *1668*

Zwingli, Huldreich: Protestant reformer to abolish the Mass, *4817*

Zwingli, Huldrych: Protestant liturgies, *4816*

Zworykin, Vladimir Kosma: Electronic television system that was practical, *5960*
Transmission electron microscope, *5304*

Geographical Index

The following is a listing of key locations in the main body of the text, arranged alphabetically by nation, state or province, and city. To find an entry in the main body of the text, please search for the italicized indexing number. Locations are identified by their current name; for example, events that took place in Mesopotamia are indexed under Iraq.

AFGHANISTAN

Buddhist manuscripts, *4766*
Images of the Buddha, *4757*
Leader of united Afghanistan, *2989*
Pashto writing, *3537*
Sultan, *2936*
Traffic accident in which more than 2,000 people were killed, *1945*
Windmills, *2056*

ALBANIA

King of Albania, *2973*
Signatories of the Warsaw Pact, *3172*

Valona

International military airmail route, *4682*

ALGERIA

Free election in which Muslim fundamentalists obtained a majority, *2640*
Muslim woman athlete to win a track and field world championship, *5845*
Prime minister of Algeria, *2897*
Recognition of the vector of malaria, *3842*

Frenda

Sociologist, *5357*

ANGOLA

African state to be ruled as a colony of a European state, *2691*
Banjos, *4403*
Capoeira practitioners, *5703*
President of the People's Republic of Angola, *2838*
World war, *4170*

Benguela

European explorer to cross Africa from coast to coast, *2301*

Luanda

Cultivation of New World crops in Africa, *1047*
European city in southern Africa, *4656*

ANTARCTICA

Ascent of the Vinson Massif, *5746*
Circumnavigation of Antarctica, *2310*
Expedition to cross Antarctica by dogsled and foot, *2330*
Explorer to reach the South Pole, *2319*
Explorer to set foot on both the North and South Poles, *2328*
Explorers to winter in Antarctica, *2317*
Highly detailed map of Antarctica, *3626*
International meetings of ministers in Antarctica, *3166*
International Polar Year, *2316*
Person to complete the "Explorer's Grand Slam", *2302*
Traverse of Antarctica on foot, *2331*
Treaty to govern the use of a continent, *3175*

Little America

Radio broadcast heard in both the Arctic and the Antarctic regions, *5912*

Stonington Island

Women to winter in Antarctica, *2323*

ANTIGUA

Animals to survive a space flight, *5531*

ARABIA

Sea chart of southern Asian and Indian waters, *3607*

ARCTIC

Airplane flight to land at the North Pole, *2324*

737

Rhythm method, *2368*
Rotary cultivator, *1091*
Solo helicopter voyage around the world, *1428*
Swim from Mexico to Cuba, *5827*
Trousers with permanent pleats, *1637*
Underwater personal computer, *1689*
Vegemite, *2564*
Weather service to name tropical storms with male and female names, *5290*
Woman to become a member of the Australian Parliament, *2655*
Woman to fly solo from England to Australia, *1373*

Narrabeen Beach

Glider pilot who was a woman, *1420*

New South Wales

Box kite, *1417*
Commemorative postage stamp, *4697*
Manned flight by kite, *1418*

Point Danger

Laser lighthouse, *5444*

Sydney

Australia Day, *3031*
Australian real estate owned by aborigines in modern times, *4667*
Circumnavigation of Australia, *2309*
European child born in Australia, *4664*
Frozen meat for commercial sale, *2535*
Nobel Prize in Chemistry winner from Oceania, *4526*
Nonuplets, *2347*
Permanent observatory in the Southern Hemisphere, *5135*
Round-the-world airline service, *1348*
Solo voyage around the world, *5465*
Swimsuit beauty contest, *2200*
Transcontinental trip by a solar-powered vehicle, *3207*
Weekly Australian newspaper, *4502*

Northern Territory

Arnhem Land

Religion, *4728*

Darwin

Flight from England to Australia, *1362*

Queensland

Flying bush doctor, *3976*

Virtual-reality reconstruction of a crime scene, *1764*

Brisbane

Flight from the United States to Australia, *1366*
Gun that could fire one million rounds a minute, *6118*

South Australia

Adelaide

Nobel Prize in Physics winner from Oceania, *4547*
Nobel Prize in Physiology or Medicine winner from Oceania, *4551*
Race for solar-powered vehicles, *5724*
Test-tube triplets, *2350*

Victoria

Melbourne

Black box flight recorder, *1327*
Cosmetics entrepreneur of note, *2725*
Double feature, *4289*
Electric drill, *6057*
European explorer to cross the Australian continent, *2299*
Feature-length motion picture, *4288*
Frozen embyro to come successfully to birth, *2351*
International advertising agency, *1454*
Olympic Games in the Southern Hemisphere, *5777*
Platypus born in captivity, *1120*
Sheep-shearing machine, *1137*
Test-tube twins, *2349*
Woman physician in Australia, *3973*

Western Australia

Jinmium

Art depiction, *1232*

Pilbara

Continental land, *5250*

AUSTRIA

Aerial bombardment of a city, *4202*
Ascent of Cho Oyu, *5740*
Ascent of Mount Everest without bottled oxygen, *5748*
Balloon used for wartime reconnaissance, *1400*
Battle decided by the use of breech-loading infantry rifles, *4176*
CAT scan, *3906*

AUSTRIA—*continued*

Climatological classification system, *5274*
Daily newspaper, *4498*
Homosexual rights organization, *5380*
Local anesthetic, *3764*
Medicine kit, *3916*
Nation to abolish capital punishment, *1743*
Postal giro system, *2411*
Prepaid postcards, *4674*
President of the federal republic of Austria, *2802*
Printed circuit, *2015*
Programmable logic controller, *2189*
Symphony incorporating continuous choral and orchestral elements, *4391*
Tattoos, *1596*
Teleportation experiment, *5356*
Torpedo, *6090*
Tsar to travel outside Russia, *2777*
Vegetarian, *2469*
Witchcraft encyclopedia, *3476*
Woman to win the Nobel Prize for Peace, *4539*
World chess champion, *2599*
Written national constitution outside of the United States, *2647*

Arlberg

Downhill ski race, *5810*

Linz

American flag to fly over the defeated Nazi empire, *4190*
National euthanasia program, *1771*

St. Anton

Ski school, *5811*

Vienna

Blood types to be discovered, *4099*
Circus in Europe, *2204*
Coffee sweet and light, *2497*
Composer able to make a living entirely by writing music of his own choice, *4370*
European politician to adopt a platform of anti-Semitism, *2664*
Flower cultivated by florists, *1045*
One-armed pianist of international stature, *4374*
Phrenologist, *3993*
Portrait camera, *4578*
Psychoanalyst, *3999*
Regular civil airmail service, *4683*
Session of the United Nations Commission on Crime Prevention and Criminal Justice, *1796*
Shock therapy for treating mental illness, *4004*
Treatise on psychoanalysis, *4000*
Use of antisepsis, *4048*
Zoo in Europe, *1161*

Zürs

Ski course, *5809*

AZERBAIJAN

Grape cultivation, *1017*
President of Azerbaijan, *2856*
Woman to rule Georgia, *2942*

BAHAMAS

Human cloning company, *5188*

BAHRAIN

Sheikh of independent Bahrain, *2982*
Supersonic airliner to enter regular service, *1350*

BANGLADESH

Bengali writing, *3508*
Nationwide poisoning epidemic, *1909*
Prime minister of Bangladesh, *2907*
Storm to kill 1 million people, *1928*

BARBADOS

Modern university in the Caribbean, *1999*
Pirate alleged to have made prisoners walk the plank, *1787*
Rum, *2482*
Sugar cane commercial production, *1063*

BELARUS

President of Israel, *2809*
President of the Republic of Belarus, *2866*

Domachevo

British jury to consider evidence overseas, *1740*

BELGIUM

Anatomist to break with Galen, *3958*
Automobile, *3225*
Bombing raids, *4211*
Copper-nickel coins, *2453*
Deployment of the NATO rapid reaction force in a member country, *4195*
Diamond engagement ring, *2396*
Driver to exceed 100 kilometers per hour, *5713*
Drypoint engraving, *1292*
European jazz musician to win international recognition, *4378*
Full-length double portrait, *1275*
Glider assault, *4220*

Handbook for stamp collectors, *4696*
Head of state to order an automobile, *3226*
International rail line, *3267*
King of Belgium, *2963*
Lace, *3706*
Modern wheelchair designed for hospital use, *3868*
Motorboat, *5415*
Oil painters, *1273*
Outbreak of botulism, *3838*
Philosophy café, *4570*
Pigeon racing, *1112*
Roller skates, *5805*
Shaped charge used in war, *6093*
Skeleton prepared by a medical researcher, *3960*
Spark plug, *2174*
Stamp catalogs, *4693*
Treatise on telephony, *5932*
Wheelchair, *3867*

Antwerp

Atlas, *3618*
Oil tanker, *5427*
Printed edition of the complete Christian Bible in English, *4889*

Bruges

Book printed in the English language, *3354*
Stock exchange, *2426*

Brussels

Brussels sprouts commercially grown, *1035*
Chemical anticoagulant, *3932*
International library organization, *1821*
Multinational space agency, *5510*
Peacetime alliance of European and North American nations, *3137*
Stamp dealer, *4692*

Fleurus

Balloon used for wartime reconnaissance, *1400*

Ghent

Police dog unit, *1794*

Liège

Luxury spa, *2719*

Malines

Military hospital in Europe since antiquity, *3889*

Ostend

Car to exceed 100 miles per hour, *5715*

Spa

Beauty contest, *2199*

Ypres

Mustard gas, *6080*
Poison gas, *6079*

BELIZE

Goldman Environmental Prizes, *2250*
Premier of Belize, *2902*

BENIN

Autobiography by an African slave to have a major impact on the abolition movement, *5489*
Incumbent African president defeated in a democratic election, *2641*
President of Benin, *2837*

BERMUDA

Deep-sea exploration vessel, *5283*

BHUTAN

King of Bhutan, *2959*

BOLIVIA

Cultivation of potato, *1032*
Green Cross organization, *2252*
Hemispheric diplomatic conference, *3158*
Planned city in South America, *1562*

BORNEO

Long-distance sea trading along regular routes, *1523*

BOSNIA-HERZEGOVINA

Offensive operation by NATO, *4200*
War criminals indicted for rape, *1778*

Sarajevo

Casualty of World War I, *4178*

BOTSWANA

President of Botswana, *2833*

BRAZIL

Advocate of black pride, *5495*

BRAZIL—*continued*

African slaves in South America, *5481*
Afro-Brazilian newspaper, *4503*
Biological expedition to Amazonia by a native South American, *5156*
Brazilian general of African descent, *4169*
Brazilian novel, *3458*
Capoeira practitioners, *5703*
Governor-general of Brazil, *2987*
Joint peacetime military exercises between Brazil and Argentina, *4133*
Launch of a heavier-than-air machine entirely under its own power, *1356*
Portuguese writing, *3516*
President of Brazil, *2790*
Scientific exploration of the Amazon River, *2295*
Women's Olympic volleyball event, *5796*
World war, *4170*

Minas Gerais

Gold rush in the New World, *3681*

Rio de Janeiro

Earth Summit, *2251*

Sao Paolo

Modern art festival in South America, *1253*

BRITAIN

Air battle that was strategically important, *4222*
Aircraft carrier adapted from a conventional warship, *4261*
Aircraft carrier to be sunk by surface ships, *4270*
Aircraft carrier with a through-deck runway, *4263*
Alimony payments, *2399*
Antivivisection prosecution, *1139*
Appendectomy, *4046*
Army with a trained nursing staff to treat its wounded, *4129*
Artificial language based entirely on English, *3301*
Ascent of Kanchenjunga, *5742*
Ascent of Mount Elbrus, *5731*
Bards, *3329*
Battleship powered by steam turbines, *4258*
Billion-pound loan, *2457*
Bombing raids, *4211*
Booker Prize, *3456*
Breathing apparatus for submarine escape, *5451*
Breech-loading artillery, *6112*
Breechlock rifle, *6107*
British ambassador to the United States, *3145*
British civilian medal conferred on a country, *2698*

British jury to consider evidence overseas, *1740*
British monarchs to visit the United States, *2976*
British prime minister to address the Parliament of the Irish Republic, *3133*
British ship to bear the initials H.M.S., *4252*
Bustles, *1631*
Car to break the sound barrier, *5725*
Car with an electric starter, *3234*
Chaff to jam radar, *4227*
Chemotherapeutic drug, *3929*
Circumnavigation of Britain, *2304*
Civilian ship sunk in World War II, *4267*
Clinical trial, *4085*
Cloned animal, *5186*
Convicts deported to Australia, *4663*
Declaration of war in World War II, *4186*
Detailed account of a long sea voyage, *2273*
Domestic violence law, *5498*
Dum-dum bullets, *6115*
Elucidation of the structure of DNA, *5199*
Epidemic of birth defects caused by a drug, *1908*
Epidemic of mad cow disease, *1910*
Fiber-optic transoceanic cable, *5888*
Fighter plane, *4212*
Film made by a studio outside the United States to win an Academy Award, *4304*
Fire extinguisher, *1575*
Food processor, *3072*
Graduated income tax, *2467*
Halloween, *3025*
Heavy night bomber, *4213*
Hologram, *5318*
Human cancer-causing virus to be discovered, *3848*
Independent air force, *4131*
Independent nation in the New World, *2692*
International astronaut rescue agreement, *5543*
International drug trade, *4025*
International satellite, *5586*
Jet airliner, *1326*
Labor party, *2663*
Landing of a plane on a ship under way, *4262*
Law regulating animal experimentation, *1140*
Law requiring doctors to report cases of occupational disease, *1508*
Mass-produced rockets for warfare, *6132*
Massed tank attack, *4181*
Military clash between China and a western power, *4172*
Modern encyclopedia for children, *3385*
Music video, *4450*
Nation to legalize trade unions, *1507*
National broadcasting monopoly, *5882*
National geologic survey, *5270*
National public health legislation, *2241*
Nuclear weapons test moratorium, *3174*
Oceanographic expedition, *5273*
Passenger liner sunk by a submarine, *1932*

CANADA—*continued*

Free-trade region encompassing North America, *1552*

Highly detailed map of Antarctica, *3626*

IMAX film, *4309*

International map of the world, *3625*

Labor Day, *3037*

Lacrosse, *5597*

Letterpress halftone reproduction of a photograph, *4719*

Little League baseball teams outside the United States, *5614*

Map showing the Spanish discoveries in the New World, *3613*

Monel, *3673*

Movie to make more than US$100 million in 5 days, *4316*

Nation to put all its universities on the Internet, *2002*

National fiber-optic Internet, *1724*

National parks service, *2259*

Native Americans to cross the Atlantic, *2274*

Pan American Day, *3039*

Premier of Nunavat, *2918*

Prime minister of the Dominion of Canada, *2876*

Quartz clock, *6030*

Racial integration of professional baseball, *5612*

Round-the-world solo sailing journey, *5458*

Spreadsheet program, *1728*

Thermoformed plastic condom, *2375*

Transatlantic telephone call using the transoceanic cable, *5943*

Trivia board game of international popularity, *2579*

Vessel to cross the Northwest Passage west to east, *2322*

Labrador

Radio broadcast heard in both the Arctic and the Antarctic regions, *5912*

Transatlantic east-west nonstop airplane flight, *1365*

Alberta

Brewery in the Western Hemisphere, *2487*

British Columbia

European explorer to cross North America north of Mexico, *2296*

Law forbidding the freezing of humans for future resuscitation, *1884*

Tribal state in Canada with self-government, *2701*

Richmond

McDonald's restaurant outside the United States, *1469*

Vancouver

Circumnavigation by wheelchair, *5854*

Fuel cell car, *3262*

Victoria

International airmail service, *4684*

Manitoba

Digital wireless cable television system, *5970*

New Brunswick

Pennefield

Transatlantic westbound solo nonstop flight, *1371*

St. Stephen

International commercial telephone service, *5935*

Newfoundland

English-speaking colony in the New World, *4657*

European traveler to set foot on the North American continent after the Vikings, *2284*

Map of any part of the Americas, *3608*

Transatlantic crossing by an robot airplane, *1388*

Transatlantic telegraph cable, *5926*

Transoceanic radio message, *5901*

Harbor Grace

Transatlantic solo airplane flight by a woman, *1370*

L'Anse aux Meadows

Child born of European parents in North America, *4644*

European settlement in North America, *4643*

Re-enactment of a Viking voyage to the New World, *5469*

St. John's

Nonstop transatlantic airplane flight, *1361*

Northwest Territories

European explorer in North America to reach the Arctic by land, *2314*

Nova Scotia

Annapolis Royal

Play staged in the New World, *5985*

CHILE—*continued*

Santiago

Latin American tennis player to become the top ranked player in the world, *5840*

CHINA

Acupuncture for dental problems, *3794*
Anglican woman priest, *4843*
Animal believed to be the ancestor of apes, monkeys, and humans, *4612*
Asthma medication, *3917*
Astronomical clock of large size, *6021*
Attempted murder by poisoned book, *1786*
Beans, *1014*
Bonsai, *2621*
Book of poetry in a Chinese language, *3550*
Book on robotics, *5026*
Breathing apparatus for submarine escape, *5451*
Brush and ink for writing, *3579*
Camera obscura, *4575*
Canal in China of importance, *2131*
Cannon, *6096*
Card games, *2580*
Chief executive of Hong Kong, *3001*
China–USA undersea telecommunications cable, *5893*
Chinese cabbage, *1033*
Chinese historian of importance, *3004*
Chinese historical archive, *3003*
Chinese prose work, *3549*
Chinese ruler to invoke the Mandate of Heaven, *2764*
Chinese woman historian, *3005*
Chinese writing, *3548*
Chop suey, *2540*
Civil service examinations, *2628*
Civil war to cause 20 million deaths, *4173*
Coal mine, *3680*
Commentary on the *I Ching*, *4564*
Commercial communications satellite to circle the moon, *5892*
Commercial ship to sail from China to Taiwan, *1553*
Compass, *5431*
Confucian text, *4895*
Country to limit births as national policy, *2372*
Country with more than 1 billion people, *4608*
Crossbows, *6070*
Deification of K'ung Fu-tzu (Confucius), *4898*
Disease proven to be transmitted by insects, *3841*
Distilled liquor, *2478*
Doctrine of the Five Flavors, *2470*
Domesticated ducks, *1135*
Dominoes, *2571*
Dragon Boat races in China, *3014*
Earthquake to cause massive loss of life, *1916*

Emperor of China, *2768*
Empress of China to rule in her own right, *2771*
Encyclopedia compiled in Asia, *3379*
Endocrinologists, *3949*
Establishment of Confucianism as the state religion, *4897*
European traveler to reach the Chinese frontier, *2276*
Evidence of Chinese religion, *4734*
Explicator of orthodox Confucianism, *4896*
Eyeglasses, *4103*
Family names, *3483*
Film studio in China, *4297*
Flame throwers, *6076*
Flood to cause more than 1 million deaths, *1923*
Go, *2566*
Grenade, *6085*
Gunpowder, *6084*
Harmonicas, *4402*
Heating stoves, *3050*
Homeostatic machine, *2184*
Horse races held regularly, *5678*
Hyperinflation, *4277*
Identification of years in the Chinese calendar by the names of totem animals, *6011*
Important text of Mahayana Buddhism, *4767*
Inoculation against smallpox, *3909*
Insecticide, *1097*
International drug trade, *4025*
Invasion of Japan, *4163*
Kites, *1414*
Kites used in warfare, *4201*
Lacquer, *1244*
Language spoken by more than 1 billion people, *3305*
Large mechanical clock, *6020*
Large political state in Asia, *2677*
Large zoo, *1159*
Libraries in Asia, *1812*
Lock for river navigation, *2134*
Magic lantern, *4576*
Magic square, *3727*
Mah-jongg, *2575*
Major Chinese voyage of exploration and diplomacy, *2277*
Mechanical ventilating fan, *3052*
Meeting to establish the United Nations, *3187*
Metal cannon, *6098*
Metal stirrups, *1154*
Military clash between China and a western power, *4172*
Millet, *1020*
Monograph on a fruit tree, *5180*
Monumental landscape painting, *1270*
Mountaineer to ascend the world's three tallest peaks, *5750*
Movable type, *4703*
Multivolume printed book series, *3341*

CHINA—*continued*

Hong Kong

Subsea gas pipeline in Asia, *2114*

Kaifeng

Disastrous flood caused by war, *1947*
Restaurant still extant, *1459*

Kansu

Landslide to kill more than 100,000 people, *1926*

Lu-shun

Modern conflict in which an Asian power defeated a European power, *4257*

Macao

Airplane hijacking, *1798*

Nanjing

Germ warfare against civilians in modern times, *4183*

Nanking

Sea chart of southern Asian and Indian waters, *3607*

Shanghai

Building more than 1,500 feet in height, *1230*
Refugee ship fire to cause large loss of life, *1940*

Shantung

Yin-Yang philosophical school, *4562*

Sinho

Breech-loading artillery, *6112*

Szechuan

Depiction of a gun, *6094*

Szechwan

Popular religious rebellion in China, *5016*
Taoist religious community, *5015*

Wushan

Hominids in Asia, *4621*

Xian

Christian missionaries in China, *4792*
Diplomatic contact between Africa and China, *3144*
Major intercontinental road, *1586*

Yungang

Buddhist site of importance in China, *4758*

Zhengzhou

Fast-food outlets, *1460*
Professional caterers, *1461*

Zhoukoudian

Burial, *1869*

COLOMBIA

European settlements in South America, *4650*
Fruit exporting company, *1546*
President of Colombia, *2785*
Treaty between a South American country and a North American country, *3169*
Vaccine to be chemically synthesized, *3913*

Bogotá

Corneal graft, *4058*

Río Pinto

Isolation of platinum, *3665*

CONGO

African Pygmies to visit Europe, *4665*
International agreement to eliminate slave trading, *5494*
National park in Africa, *2260*
Pope to condemn the African slave trade, *5487*
President of the Democratic Republic of the Congo, *2818*
Prime minister of the Democratic Republic of the Congo, *2894*

Kinshasa

HIV infections, *3847*

COOK ISLANDS

Rarotonga

Regional nuclear-free zone, *3140*

COSTA RICA

Free, democratic elections in Central America, *2637*

DENMARK—*continued*

Magnetic wire recording device, *2045*
Modern theory of atomic structure, *5333*
National observatory in Europe, *5131*
Prime minister of Denmark's first parliamentary government, *2871*
Scandinavian writing, *3490*
Sex-change operation, *5370*
Sportsman to win individual gold medals in four successive Olympic Games, *5770*
Suspension bridge spanning more than 5,000 feet, *2148*
Treatise on geology, *5263*
Universal system for phonetic transcription, *3300*
Woman to rule the Scandinavian countries, *2951*
Writing in runes, *3321*

Copenhagen

Film archive, *4293*
Round-the-world flights over the North Pole on a regularly scheduled air route, *1383*
Sex-change operation that was successful, *5372*
Typewriter to be marketed, *3591*

Hjörtspring

Clinker-built boats, *5403*

Greenland

Alpine skier, *5808*
Settlers in Greenland, *4642*

Julianehb

Discovery of Greenland, *2275*

Upernavik

Dogsled crossing of the Northwest Passage, *2320*

DJIBOUTI

President of Djibouti, *2843*

DOMINICA

Prime minister of Dominica, *2909*

DOMINICAN REPUBLIC

Asian spice to be cultivated successfully in the New World, *1043*
Autopsy by Europeans in the New World, *1867*
Bananas in the New World, *1040*
Barbecue, *2529*

Book about human rights and slavery in the New World, *5484*
Communities of escaped African slaves, *5482*
Democratically elected president of the Dominican Republic, *2830*
Explorer saved by an eclipse, *2287*
Leader of the independent Dominican Republic, *2994*
New World inhabitants forcibly taken to the Old World, *2283*
Orange cultivation in the New World, *1041*
Sugar cane brought to the New World, *1062*
Town founded by a European in the New World, *4647*

Santo Domingo

Cathedral in the New World, *4865*
Catholic priest ordained in the New World, *4864*
Colonial palace in the New World, *4649*
Horses in the New World, *1107*
Internet access point in Latin America, *1722*
Permanent European settlement in the New World, *4648*
Slaves in the New World, *5479*
University in the New World, *1989*

DUBAI

Cross-breeding of a llama with a camel, *1127*

ECUADOR

Leader of free Ecuador, *2992*
Major road system in the Americas, *1587*
President of Ecuador, *2784*
Scientific exploration of the Amazon River, *2295*

Maldonado

Solar-powered hospital, *3897*

EGYPT

Advanced beer-brewing methods, *2477*
African state outside Egypt, *2676*
Alchemical theory, *5219*
Alchemist, *5217*
Anesthetic, *3758*
Anti-Semitic libel, *4960*
Apples, *1027*
Archeological digs in Egypt, *5053*
Assault vehicle, *6119*
Axe, *6041*
Barley, *1016*
Beekeeping, *1134*
Bowling game, *5633*
Bronze artifact, *3657*

ENGLAND—*continued*

Environmental restoration plan for an industrial site, *2243*

Epic poem in a vernacular European language, *3439*

Epic poem in English, *3406*

Equal sign, *3741*

European heraldry, *2706*

European ruler to bathe regularly, *2720*

European to publish a recipe for gunpowder, *6095*

Exploding shell, *6087*

Expulsion of Jews from a European country, *4971*

Faust legend, *3479*

Fax process, *5873*

Flatbed press, *4714*

Flight from England to Australia, *1362*

Flood to cause massive loss of life, *1915*

Flush toilet, *4035*

Folding knife with multiple tools, *6052*

Fuel cell, *2058*

Fuel cell that was practical, *2060*

Gas turbine patent, *2167*

General reference work of modern chemistry, *5228*

Global hypermedia information system, *1718*

Glossary of English words explained in English, *3414*

Golf course outside Scotland, *5667*

Gothic novel, *3447*

Grog, *2484*

Guinea, *2449*

Haymaker, *1084*

Heavyweight boxing champion, *5640*

Heraldic device worn by an English king, *2707*

Hieroglyphic writing from Egypt to be deciphered, *5054*

Hindu missionary in the West, *4917*

Hindu text translated into English, *4912*

Hoop skirts with panniers, *1620*

Hovercraft, *5419*

Hovercraft lawn mower, *6065*

Hovercraft passenger service, *5421*

Hydraulic mortar, *2151*

Hydraulic press, *1481*

Iced tea, *2498*

Image of human tissue made from life, *3901*

Incandescent lamp, *2092*

Influential feminist tract, *5368*

International Code signals, *5413*

International motorboat racing competition, *5857*

International polo competition, *5800*

International trampoline governing body, *5675*

Iron railroad track, *3270*

Jet fighter, *4229*

Jigsaw puzzle, *2573*

Keeper of the Holy Grail, *3473*

King of England after the Norman Conquest who could read and write English, *3408*

King of England and Scotland, *2958*

King to call himself "King of the English", *2928*

King to practice curing of the "king's evil", *3952*

Lawn tennis, *5832*

Lightship, *5435*

Liquified gas, *5230*

Machine gun, *6106*

Machine to spin yarn on more than one spindle, *3715*

Major nuclear power plant accident, *1954*

Manned glider flight, *1415*

Marine disaster costing more than 10,000 lives, *1930*

Mass production of steel, *3672*

Mechanical clock still extant, *6025*

Mechanical reaper, *1082*

Mechanical street sweeper, *1588*

Mechanical ventilating fan, *3052*

Metal cans, *2518*

Meteorological map of the world, *3620*

Military regulation concerning uniforms, *4147*

Missionary society, *4798*

Modern oil lamp, *3088*

Modern product designer, *3090*

Modern theory of atomic structure, *5333*

Molecule analyzed with the use of a computer, *5248*

Monocoque chassis for Formula 1 racing cars, *5721*

Morality play, *5982*

Morris dancing, *1844*

Motorized bus service, *3213*

Movie character with worldwide appeal, *4320*

Musical encyclopedia in English, *4372*

Nation to enact a national patent system, *1544*

National lottery, *2607*

National public welfare law in Europe, *5496*

National speed limit, *3221*

Naval uniform, *4149*

Novel in English, *3428*

Novellas in English, *3407*

Nuclear power plant, *2117*

Obstetrical forceps, *2340*

Opera in English, *4434*

Organic gardening, *2625*

Orphan export program, *2382*

Package tour of Europe, *2234*

Patent for a moldboard sheathed in iron, *1079*

Patent on colored ink, *3587*

Peace treaty among European powers to arbitrate world trade, *3168*

Periodic table of the elements, *5229*

Personal ad placed by an individual in search of marriage, *2397*

Planet discovered since ancient times, *5082*

Play by William Shakespeare, *3421*

ENGLAND—*continued*

Woman to choreograph her own ballets, *1859*
Woman to fly solo from England to Australia, *1373*
Woman to rule England, *2956*
Woman to write professionally in English, *3426*
Women admitted to a guild of dentists, *3805*
World chess champion, *2599*
World heavyweight boxing championship, *5644*

Abbot's Langley

Pope born in England, *4856*

Addiscombe

Electromagnet that could support more than its own weight, *2083*

Aintree

Grand National Handicap Steeplechase, *5685*
Woman jockey in the Grand National steeplechase, *5688*

Bath

Correspondence course, *1974*

Berkeley

Vaccine, *3910*

Birmingham

Coins minted with steam-powered machinery, *2452*
Large building illuminated by gas, *2102*
Motorized trailer, *3222*
Steel pen point, *3588*
Synthetic plastic, *3107*

Bishop's Stortford

Electronic nose, *5306*

Blackwall

Iron-hulled warship, *4254*

Bletchley Park

Electromechanical cryptographic decoder, *4142*

Bradley

Cast-iron coffin, *1880*

Bristol

Anglican women priests to be officially ordained, *4846*

European traveler to set foot on the North American continent after the Vikings, *2284*
International Festival of the Sea, *3045*
Transatlantic steamboat service, *5425*
Woman physician in modern times to earn a degree from a medical school, *3969*

Calverton

Knitting machine, *3714*

Cambridge

Artificial transmutation of an element, *5340*
Computer programmer, *1725*
Discovery of neutrons, *5339*
Discovery of pulsars, *5104*
DNA sequencing of a multicellular organism, *5208*
Element to be analyzed by mass spectrometer, *5241*
Mass spectrometer, *5335*
Mathematical proof of Fermat's last theorem, *3756*
Rules for soccer (association football), *5814*
Universal computing machine, *1666*
Wallpaper, *3087*

Canterbury

Archbishop of Canterbury, *4791*
Christian scholastic, *4794*
Penny, *2439*
Secular play in English, *3413*

Chatsworth

Baby carriage, *2383*

Chelmsford

Electric toaster, *3065*
Radio broadcast of live music, *5908*

Cheshire

Remains documented by holography, *5062*

Chicester

Proposal to purify the English language, *3411*

Clacton-on-Sea

Weapon, *6066*

Coalbrookdale

Coke-smelted iron, *3664*

Colchester

MUD (multi-user dominion), *1705*

Cornwall

Oil spill from a commercial tanker, *2269*
Transoceanic radio message, *5901*

Coventry

Bicycle with spoked wheels, *5623*
Synthetic fiber suitable for making cloth, *3723*

Culham

Temperature of 100 million degrees Kelvin, *2122*

Derby

Afterburner, *2181*

Dishley

Livestock breeder, *1118*

Doncaster

Float glass, *3652*
Traveling van for horses, *5684*

Dover

Airplane flight over the ocean, *1357*
Balloon flight over open water, *1399*
Letter sent by airmail, *4679*
Man to swim the English Channel, *5820*
Woman to pilot an airplane over the English Channel, *1313*
Woman to swim the English Channel, *5822*

Dunstable

Mechanical clock in Europe, *6022*

Eccles

Person run over by a train, *1891*

Epsom Springs

Epsom salt (magnesium sulfate), *3922*

Eton

International football game, *5659*

Exeter

Person killed in a motorcycle accident, *1895*

Falmouth

Solo nonstop voyage around the world, *5467*

Folkestone

Aircraft powered by human motion to cross the English Channel, *1331*

Gloucester

Underwater link between Great Britain and Europe, *2198*

Sunday school, *4799*

Gravesend

Native American to be buried in Europe, *1878*

Greenwich

Astronomical observatory for navigation, *5433*
Director of the Royal Greenwich Observatory, *5140*

Hampshire

Cricket club, *5655*

Harrow

Passenger fatally injured in an automobile accident, *1896*

Isle of Man

Parliament, *2650*

Isle of Wight

Across-the-ocean race, *5856*

Jarrow

Tramp steamer, *5426*

Kent

Prose work in English, *3404*

Killingworth

Steam locomotive in regular use, *3265*

Knaresborough

Witch image, *3477*

Leamington

Tennis club, *5833*

Leeds

Clinical thermometer in current use, *3874*
Portland cement, *2152*

Leicester

Genetic fingerprinting method, *1758*

ENGLAND—Leicester—*continued*
Virtual autopsies, *3865*

Leicestershire

Murderer apprehended on DNA evidence alone, *1759*
Suspect cleared of a crime by DNA evidence, *1761*

Letchworth

Walk to raise funds for charity, *5502*

Lincoln

Building more than 500 feet high, *1225*

Lindisfarne

Viking raid, *4244*

Liverpool

All-steam railway service, *3269*
Steamboat to cross an ocean, *5455*
Train station, *3268*

London

Advertising agency, *1453*
Advice column, *4454*
Air race from England to Australia, *5604*
Air transport company, *1336*
Airline meals, *1338*
All-electronic television system, *5950*
Aquarium for public display, *1163*
Astronomical photograph taken from an airplane, *5096*
Athlete of African descent to win a gold medal in an individual event, *5767*
Bank clearinghouse, *2408*
Bible society, *4835*
Blank verse in English, *3416*
Book of Mother Goose nursery rhymes, *3431*
Book on poker, *2592*
Book printed in England that bears a date, *3355*
Book to sell at auction for more than US$10 million, *3366*
Bottled beer, *2481*
Bowler hat, *1649*
Boxer to emphasize skill over brute strength, *5643*
Breech-loading gun, *6108*
British monarch to live in Buckingham Palace, *2965*
Buddhist manuscripts, *4766*
Building with a patented cooling system, *1212*
Carbon paper, *3693*
Carbonated water, *2531*
Central bank, *2406*

Check, *2448*
Children's book in English, *3418*
Children's fiction book in English, *3429*
Children's magazine, *4479*
Christmas cards, *4673*
Circus clown, *2206*
Circus known by that name, *2205*
Circus monkey, *2202*
City with more than 1 million inhabitants, *1566*
Club for gentlemen, *1834*
Colony financed by a lottery, *4661*
Color feature film, *4294*
Comedy written in English, *3415*
Comic strip in a magazine, *4467*
Communist secret society, *2671*
Compendium of rules for a game, *2589*
Concertina, *4417*
Connection between tobacco and cancer, *4024*
Coronation of a monarch conducted in English, *2957*
Corrugated iron, *3670*
Crash of a passenger airliner, *1935*
Criminal caught by radio, *1755*
Cummerbund, *1633*
Debating society, *1835*
Dictionary of the English language, *3370*
Discovery of electrons, *5331*
Diving bell with supplementary air supply, *5448*
Economy package tour, *2235*
Edition of the *Guinness Book of World Records*, *2226*
Electric blanket, *3069*
Electric subway, *3287*
Electron tube diode, *2010*
Elizabethan acting troupe, *5983*
Elizabethan theater, *5991*
English-only rule, *3409*
Epidemic map, *3624*
Evening newspaper, *4497*
Eyeglass frames, *4107*
Family hotel, *1465*
Federation Cup in tennis, *5839*
Field hockey, *5598*
Fingerprint bureau, *1754*
Flight instrument, *1397*
Freemason grand lodge, *1836*
Gene linked with high intelligence, *5206*
General union, *1504*
Glass building, *1196*
Gossip columnist, *4455*
Graphs displaying economic data, *5360*
Guy Fawkes Day, *3030*
Gym suit for girls, *1632*
Heat pump, *2064*
High school for space scientists, *1978*
Highway robber of note who was a woman, *1803*
Hormone to be discovered, *5165*
Hospital for unwanted newborns, *3891*

Household management book, *3049*
Housekeeping magazine, *3048*
Housing project in an inner-city neighborhood, *5497*
Human cannonball, *2210*
Hymnbook containing hymns in English, *4823*
Illustrated book in English, *3357*
Illustrated magazine, *4476*
Indoor bowling lane, *5635*
Insane asylum in Europe, *3988*
International bridge match, *2595*
International chess tournament, *2598*
International Communist labor organization, *1505*
International direct-dial service, *5945*
International Internet connections, *1699*
International television broadcast, *5962*
International television transmission, *5952*
International water polo match, *5864*
Life insurance company, *2422*
Literary agent, *3336*
Live broadcast from the British Parliament, *2657*
London to Paris scheduled passenger airplane service, *1339*
Magazine known by that name, *4478*
Magician whose act included mind-reading tricks, *2216*
Manual on birth control, *2360*
Marine insurance underwriters, *2421*
Marketing strategy aimed at children, *1511*
Melodrama in English, *3432*
Micrometer, *2188*
Military unit to wear a complete uniform, *4146*
Miniskirt, *1638*
Miss World contest, *2201*
Modern circus, *2203*
Modern police force, *1792*
Movie shown on an airplane, *4299*
Movie theater, *4354*
Multinational corporation, *1542*
Municipal recreation park, *1567*
Museum operated as a public institution, *1826*
Nation in Oceania to have its own modern coinage, *2458*
National pharmacopoeia in English, *3790*
Neurotransmitter to be identified, *5168*
New Testament printed in English, *4887*
Newspaper illustrated exclusively with photographs, *4510*
Newspaper in England that was successful, *4492*
Newspaper published in England, *4491*
Newsreel, *4350*
Novel to be serialized, *3450*
Nuclear chain reaction patent, *5344*
Observations of stellar spectra, *5092*
Occupational carcinogen to be identified, *3837*
Oil paintings, *1271*
Pedestrian killed by an automobile, *1892*

Perambulator, *2385*
Performance of a *Son et lumière* show in Britain, *2227*
Periodical continuously published, *4474*
Permanent wave hairstyle, *2734*
Pharmacists, *3963*
Photography studio in Europe open to the public, *4591*
Physician to teach obstetrics and midwifery, *2341*
Picture magazine, *4481*
Postage stamps, *4689*
Powered wood shapers, *6056*
Prefabricated building, *1191*
Primer for teaching reading in English, *1970*
Printed advertising poster, *1450*
Printed collection of nursery rhymes, *3430*
Professional organization of pharmacists, *3968*
Proposal of the existence of gravitational singularities, *5328*
Public power utility, *2103*
Public zoo, *1162*
Publisher in English, *3412*
Radio station call letters, *5906*
Railway hotels, *1467*
Recipes to be tested, *2505*
Reflecting telescope, *5134*
Regular broadcast high-definition television service, *5959*
Researcher to discover an entire grouping of elements, *5240*
Rock opera, *4438*
Round-the-world airline service, *1348*
Royal palace in Europe to integrate public and private functions in one unified structure, *1190*
Rubber bands, *3104*
Rubber tires, *3293*
Rule book of bridge, *2594*
Salvation Army activities, *4839*
Scheduled commercial jet flight, *1346*
School for professional nurses, *3861*
School of pugilism, *5641*
Scientific association sanctioned by a national government, *5048*
Scientific treatise on public health, *3786*
Screw-threading metal lathe, *1482*
Screws and bolts mass-produced in standard sizes, *1484*
Seismologist to develop a modern theory of the cause and actions of earthquakes, *5265*
Settlement house, *5499*
Ship evaluation association, *5406*
Skating rink, *5806*
Smog disaster, *1949*
Staff cartoonist on a newspaper, *4461*
Stamp collector, *4690*
Steam-driven rotary press, *4715*
Steam-powered fire engine, *1576*
Steam-powered sawmill, *1479*

Woman to lead a rebellion against the Roman Empire, *4158*

North Ferriby

Work boats, *5398*

Northampton

Gas stove that was practical, *3060*

Northumbria

Work of history to use BC and AD, *6015*

Nottingham

Anti-technology riots, *1503*
Swimmer to cross the Irish Sea, *5823*

Odiham

Transatlantic eastward flight by jet airplane, *1378*

Oxford

Edition of the *Oxford English Dictionary*, *3375*
Methodist religious group, *4833*
Person to run a mile in less than four minutes, *5843*
Public library in Europe, *1815*
Treatise on animism, *4742*
University museum, *1825*
University to teach rural agriculture, *1003*

Oxfordshire

Horse-drawn seed drill, *1078*

Piltdown Common

Scientific hoax of international notoriety, *5051*

Plymouth

Circumnavigation of the world from west to east, *2308*
Lighthouse in the open sea, *5442*
Sea captain to circumnavigate the world, *2306*
Solo transatlantic sailboat race, *5858*
Solo voyage around the world, *5465*
Transatlantic airplane flight, *1360*
Transatlantic solo boat journey by a woman, *5461*
Woman to become a member of the British Parliament, *2654*

Portsmouth

Drydock, *5405*

Freed African slaves repatriated to Africa, *5491*
Mechanized production line, *1483*

Purley

Transoceanic radio signal conveying a television image, *5953*

Reading

Book illustrated with photographs, *3361*
Cyborg, *5041*

Redhill

Dynamite mining demonstration, *3684*

Rochester

Closed or pneumatic caisson, *2143*

Rothamsted

Agricultural research station, *1004*

Roundhay

Motion picture, *4278*

Royal Lytham

Women's golf tournament, *5668*

Sheffield

Soccer club, *5815*
Stainless steel, *3674*
Steel scissors, *6054*

Shrewsbury

Drawing and quartering, *1741*

Shropshire

Reference to the Robin Hood legend, *3475*

South Foreland

Wireless station for international communications, *5900*

Southampton

Person to be interviewed on television, *5955*

Stockton-on-Tees

Friction matches, *3103*

Stoke-upon-Trent

Bone china, *3649*

ENGLAND—*continued*

Stratford-upon-Avon

Foam-rubber padded seating, *3092*

Stroud

Lawn mower, *6062*

Suffolk

Commercial electric plant using poultry litter as fuel, *2074*

Surrey

Computerized pen, *3599*

Sussex

Cricket match, *5654*

Swaffham

Greyhound racing, *1110*

Swindon

Electronic cash cards, *2461*

Westminster

Dictionary for tourists, *3368*

Weymouth Bay

Underwater photograph, *4594*

Whitby

Poet in English, *3405*

Wimbledon

CAT scan, *3906*
World tennis championship, *5835*

Winchester

Rudder, *5404*

York

Refuge for mentally ill patients, *3992*

Yorkshire

Manned glider flight that was successful, *1416*

Cornwall

Poldhu

Transoceanic radio broadcast, *5902*

Redruth

Illumination by gas, *2101*

Shropshire

Coalbrookedale

Bridge constructed entirely of cast iron, *2142*

Surrey

Epsom Downs

English Derby, *5682*

EQUATORIAL GUINEA

President of Equatorial Guinea, *2835*

ERITREA

President of Eritrea, *2864*

ESTONIA

Circumnavigation of Antarctica, *2310*
Estonian writing, *3525*
President of independent Estonia, *2800*

Saaremaa

Estonian Biennial, *1257*

Tallinn

Patriarch of Moscow who was not Russian by birth, *4811*

ETHIOPIA

African woman athlete to win the Olympic women's marathon, *5793*
African written language, *3492*
Amharic writing, *3521*
Black African state to be well documented, *2688*
Boston Marathon in which both champions were African athletes, *5847*
Coffee used as a stimulant, *2494*
Legend of Prester John, *3471*
Runner to win the Olympic marathon twice, *5780*

Adowa

Defeat of a European colonial power by African military forces, *4177*

Gona

Tools, *4614*

FRANCE—*continued*

Electron-beam welding, *1495*
Element discovered in space, *5235*
Endoscope, *3870*
European heraldry, *2706*
European legislator of African descent, *2652*
Expedition to cross Antarctica by dogsled and foot, *2330*
Exponent symbols, *3745*
Extraction of beryllium, *3668*
Fast breeder reactor, *2121*
Fiber-optic transoceanic cable, *5888*
Fighter plane, *4212*
Film director who was a woman, *4284*
Fire extinguisher for chemical fires, *1579*
Fluid catalytic cracking process, *2109*
Four-stroke internal-combustion engine, *2171*
Freestanding full-length mirror, *2742*
Freeze frame, *4298*
Front-wheel-drive car, *3240*
Glass fiber, *3650*
Glass mirrors free of distortion, *2741*
Gregorian chant, *4381*
Guerrilla war, *4171*
Guild of perfume makers, *2745*
Gun carriage, *6099*
Head of state to order an automobile, *3226*
Hieroglyphic writing from Egypt to be deciphered, *5054*
High heels, *1650*
History of dance, *1847*
Holy Roman Emperor, *2773*
Hoop skirts with panniers, *1620*
Hydraulic press, *2187*
Hydroelectric generator, *2084*
Hypodermic syringe, *3871*
International rail line, *3267*
International road race, *5714*
Jewish martyrs massacred by the Crusaders, *4161*
Jigsaw puzzle, *2573*
Keeper of the Holy Grail, *3473*
King of France, *2925*
Library school, *1818*
Life-support system, *3875*
Machine for printing wallpaper, *4711*
Major land battles decided by firepower, *4166*
Man to walk 100,000 kilometers, *5851*
Mapping survey of a country, *3621*
Margarine, *2537*
Mayonnaise, *2560*
Measurement of altitude by instrument, *5268*
Measurement of the speed of sound, *5324*
Mechanical duck, *5029*
Medieval sumptuary laws, *1609*
Military air force, *4127*
Military-industrial complex, *4119*
Military surgeon to treat gunshot wounds without cautery, *3959*
Millionaire, *1443*

Modern bow for playing musical instruments, *4415*
Modern chemist, *5225*
Modern slide rule, *3750*
Modern wheelchair designed for hospital use, *3868*
Modernist poetry, *3452*
Motion picture, *4278*
Motor vehicle, *3211*
Motte-and-bailey castles, *1181*
Mountain tunnel, *2192*
Multiplexing signal switching system, *5928*
Musical notation, *4360*
National archive system, *1817*
National Internet holiday, *3046*
Nobel Prize for Literature, *4530*
Nobel Prize for Peace, *4538*
Nobel Prize winner to win the award twice, *4519*
Nonstick cookware, *3117*
Novel in the French language, *3556*
Oboe, *4409*
Observation of Neptune, *5084*
Official Christian inquisition, *4859*
Official newspaper of a government, *4493*
Opera in French, *4435*
Oral surgeon, *3801*
Pants, *1607*
Parachutist, *1431*
Parisian couturier, *1623*
Patents for reinforced concrete, *2153*
Peace treaty among European powers to arbitrate world trade, *3168*
Periplus, *3604*
Personal computer, *1679*
Personal flotation device, *5408*
Photo interview, *4571*
Photograph, *4589*
Photograph of the sun, *5088*
Photographic process that was practical, *4577*
Photographic record of the state of the earth, *5279*
Pilot's licenses, *1310*
Plan for European economic and monetary union, *3138*
Planetary transit to be observed, *5077*
Pneumatic automobile tire, *3294*
Police procedural, *3453*
Political philosopher to reject slavery, *5485*
Politician to offer a chicken in every pot, *2630*
Premier of France who was a woman, *2915*
Prepaid envelopes, *4671*
Presbyterian church, *4825*
President of the European Parliament, *2814*
Pressure cooker, *3055*
Printed photograph, *4590*
Prose works in the French language, *3555*
Pruning shears, *6055*
Psalms in metrical form, *4385*
Ramjet aircraft, *1325*

Recumbent bicycle, *5629*
Reference to a reading group, *3346*
Reference to sunspots in Western literature, *5072*
Refrigerator ship, *5428*
Reinforced concrete building system, *2154*
Remote detection system using sound, *5439*
Representations of death, *1865*
Roller bearings, *3291*
Rubber eraser, *3586*
Ruffed collars, *1615*
Safety razor, *2753*
Science fiction film, *4348*
Scientific exploration of the Amazon River, *2295*
Scientists attached to armed forces in modern times, *5050*
Seagoing iron-hulled vessel, *5412*
Self-contained underwater breathing apparatus, *5285*
Self-propelled tank, *6121*
Shawls, *1604*
Silver amalgam tooth filling in modern times, *3813*
Slapstick movie comedy, *4347*
Smart card, *2459*
Sound recording device, *2040*
Space travel by rocket, *5503*
Spark plug, *2174*
Spirit level, *6053*
Sport airplane, *1319*
Stamp catalogs, *4693*
Starter motor, *2180*
Steamroller, *1497*
Stethoscope, *3869*
Stock market, *2425*
Strawberry cultivation, *1049*
Stringed instrument played by a keyboard, *4407*
Supersonic airliner to enter regular service, *1350*
Surrealist manifesto, *1241*
Swimmer to cross the English Channel in both directions, *5825*
Systematic algebraic notation, *3743*
Tarot cards, *2582*
Technical college, *1993*
Tempered glass manufacturing process, *3651*
Theorists of socialism, *2661*
Tidal electric generator plant, *2069*
Tour de France, *5628*
Tournament between armed knights, *2221*
Treatise on magnetism, *5321*
Treatise to describe an entire economy, *5358*
Underwater swim across the English Channel, *5826*
Unified currency in Europe, *2464*
Uniform national law code, *2649*
Use of the terms "billion" and "trillion", *3739*
Vascular sutures, *4054*
Ventriloquist, *2215*

Veterinary school, *3857*
Visual telegraph, *5919*
War to receive news coverage, *4167*
Water-powered sawmill, *1476*
Waterproof umbrellas, *1619*
Waterwheel turbine, *2059*
Woman poet to write in French, *3554*
Woman to become a Freemason, *1837*
Woman to circumnavigate the world, *2307*
Woman to climb the highest peak on every continent, *5755*
Woman to receive a pilot's license, *1311*
Woman to rule France, *2944*
Woman to win a Nobel Prize, *4518*
Woman to write a book on childbirth, *2338*
World bank, *2413*

Abri Blanchard

Calendar, *6000*

Achères

Driver to exceed 100 kilometers per hour, *5713*
Land speed record, *5712*

Alençon

Motorized ambulances, *4015*

Alsace

Cast-iron stoves, *3053*

Amplepuis

Sewing machine that was practical, *1486*

Anjou

Stone castles, *1182*

Annonay

Hot-air balloon that was successful, *1391*

Arles

Archbishop of Canterbury, *4791*
Convent, *4790*

Auvergne

French-born pope, *4854*

Avignon

Nomenclator, *3399*

Bayonne

Bayonet, *6078*

FRANCE—*continued*

Bec

Christian scholastic, *4794*

Benouville

Allied soldier killed in combat on D-Day, *4188*

Besançon

Synthetic fiber produced in a factory, *3722*

Blois

Magician to use electricity in his act, *2217*
Performance of a *Son et lumière* show, *2225*

Bordeaux

Gas station, *3233*
Lighthouse surrounded by water, *5441*

Boulogne

Ballooning casualties, *1890*

Boulogne-Billancourt

Hatchback automobile, *3245*
Sedan, *3237*

Brest

Naval battle fought with cannon broadsides, *4245*

Burgundy

Liquid oxygen, *5236*

Calais

Airplane flight over the ocean, *1357*
Company in England, *1538*
Man to swim the English Channel, *5820*
Underwater link between Great Britain and Europe, *2198*

Cambrai

Massed tank attack, *4181*

Cannes

Film to win the Palme d'Or at the Cannes International Film Festival, *4342*
Grand Prix of the Cannes International Film Festival, *4341*
International conference of multimedia publishers, *1734*

Cap Gris-Nez

Aircraft powered by human motion to cross the English Channel, *1331*
Woman to swim the English Channel, *5822*

Cape Ferrat

Transatlantic undersea radio conversation, *5916*

Chalais-Meudon

Dirigible, *1402*

Chalon-sur-Saône

Photoengraving, *4716*

Chamonix

Bobsled world championship, *5632*
Winter Olympic Games, *5768*

Chantambre

Iron tooth, *3798*

Châtellerault

Reinforced concrete bridge, *2145*

Clermont

Crusade, *4160*

Clermont-Ferrand

Steel-belted radial-ply automobile tire, *3295*

Cluny

Flying buttresses, *1183*
Musical notation using letters of the alphabet, *4362*

Cologne

Lace pattern books, *3707*

Coquainvilliers

Helicopter flight, *1422*

Cormeilles-en-Vexin

Solar-powered airplane to cross the English Channel, *1332*

Dijon

Dijon mustard, *2559*

Douai

Catholic edition of the Bible in a vernacular language, *4890*

FRANCE—Paris—*continued*

Aluminum in commercial quantities, *3671*
Anti-art movement, *1252*
Antiwar treaty, *3171*
Art exhibition in Europe, *1249*
Artificial insemination of a human being, *2342*
Ascent in a hot-air balloon, *1394*
Athlete of African descent to win a gold medal in an individual event, *5767*
Automobile, *3225*
Automobile club, *3232*
Automobile race, *5709*
Ballerina to dance on her toes, *1860*
Ballerina to dance professionally, *1856*
Ballerina to wear a tutu, *1861*
Ballerina virtuoso, *1858*
Ballet entirely danced, *1857*
Ballets Russes, *1862*
Bicycle, *5620*
Bicycle road race, *5625*
Bicycle with rotating pedals, *5622*
Building illuminated by neon lamps, *2095*
Building in the Gothic style, *1184*
Burning of the Talmud by Christian authorities, *4970*
Bus service, *3209*
Cabaret, *4441*
Can-can dance, *1848*
Cannery, *2517*
Car theft, *1805*
Cathedral in the Gothic style, *1185*
Celebrity actress with an international following, *5986*
Chief of police, *1789*
Child to win a gold medal in the Olympic Games, *5763*
Circus elephants, *2207*
Circus trailer, *2208*
Codification of the five basic ballet positions, *1855*
Coffee percolator, *3059*
Communist, *2670*
Communist political platform, *2672*
Communist song of international popularity, *4440*
Comprehensive text on international law, *3151*
Comprehensive treatise on pathology and physiology, *3777*
Concourse in a train station, *3271*
Contact lenses for correcting defective vision, *4109*
Containers of yogurt with fruit mixed in, *2516*
Dakar Rallye, *5723*
Dental drill for cavities, *3807*
Dentistry instruction, *3854*
Dentists with professional credentials, *3806*
Department store, *1514*
Designer perfume, *2748*
Detective bureau, *1791*
Diagnostic test for AIDS, *3850*

Dry cleaning, *1627*
Economy package tour, *2235*
Electrified musical instrument, *4413*
Emperor of France, *2779*
Engineering school, *2127*
Estimate of the velocity of light, *5078*
Execution by guillotine, *1744*
Exhibition of impressionist paintings, *1250*
Fax system for commercial use, *5874*
Feminist author in medieval Europe, *5365*
Films synchronized with speech, *4286*
Flying trapeze act, *2209*
Food product to be pasteurized, *2536*
Free dispensary for the poor, *3890*
French Impressionist artist who was a woman, *1284*
Galvanized metal trash can, *4036*
General association of nations, *3186*
General conference of the United Nations Educational, Scientific and Cultural Organization, *3162*
Greco-Roman wrestling in modern times, *5871*
Home for repentant prostitutes, *5388*
Human chromosome gene-linkage maps, *5203*
Humane treatment of the mentally ill, *3991*
Hydrogen balloon, *1392*
Identification of the AIDS virus, *3849*
Impressionist musical composition, *4390*
Indoor theater, *5989*
Industrial trade show, *1545*
Internal-combustion engine that was commercially successful, *2170*
International balloon race, *5602*
International bicycle race, *5624*
International Botanical Congress, *5184*
International Congress of Archivists, *1822*
International Congress of Comparative Law, *3154*
International dentistry assocation, *3819*
International socialist workers' holiday, *3038*
International system of measurement, *5314*
Iron-frame building in Europe, *1195*
Kinetic sculpture, *1300*
Library with books shelved upright, *1814*
License plate, *3228*
Literary salon, *3332*
Long-distance passenger plane, *1317*
Luxury restaurant, *1466*
Magazine for popular entertainment, *4475*
Magician to use electricity in his act, *2217*
Male hairdresser to style women's hair, *2733*
Map of the human genome, *5204*
Matches, *3102*
Mint fully mechanized, *2446*
Modern bikini, *1636*
Modern epidemiologist, *3961*
Modern news service, *4514*
Modern savaté, *5704*
Motion picture of importance, *4281*
Motor home, *3220*

Motor vehicle accident, *3212*
Motorboat, *5415*
Motorcycle race, *5711*
Movie palace, *4356*
Movies shown commercially, *4283*
Musique concrète, *4395*
Narrative film, *4285*
National revolutionary calendar, *6009*
Neoclassic architecture, *1194*
Nonrepresentational modern paintings, *1286*
Open caisson, *2140*
Operetta, *4437*
Orient Express service, *3277*
Parachutist to jump from a flying craft, *1432*
Paris to New York nonstop airplane flight, *1368*
Pasteurized milk, *2514*
Philosophy café, *4570*
Physical handicap in an adult, *3823*
Police station, *1790*
Polka, *1849*
Porcelain dentures, *3808*
Postgraduate center for psychiatric education, *3862*
Private detective agency, *1793*
Public sculpture honoring a car race, *1299*
Rabies vaccine, *3911*
Rally race, *5718*
Reading system for blind people, *2008*
Recommendation that condoms be used for birth control, *2359*
Reinforced concrete structure, *1197*
Religious order of nurses, *3964*
Restaurant known by that term, *1464*
Restaurant to offer forks, *1463*
Saser, *2024*
Saxophone, *4419*
School for blind children, *2007*
School for deaf education, *2006*
Scientific treatise on histology, *3785*
Shopping mall, *1513*
Society for the protection of dramatists' rights, *3335*
Society model, *1622*
Stained glass, *3644*
Stamp albums, *4694*
Standardized intelligence test, *4001*
Steam-powered airship, *1401*
Striptease, *5390*
Striptease before a paying audience in a public theater, *5391*
Supersonic jet service across the Atlantic Ocean, *1351*
Surrealist exhibition, *1254*
Surrealist text, *3455*
Transatlantic balloon flight, *1410*
Transatlantic message over radio telephone, *5936*
Transatlantic solo airplane flight, *1364*

Transmission of electricity through high-voltage cable, *2087*
Treatise on library science, *1816*
Treatise on telephony, *5932*
Underground film, *4351*
Underground photographs, *4596*
Welded metal sculpture, *1303*
Winner of the Prix d'Amérique who was a woman, *5689*
Wire news service, *4515*
Woman appointed to the faculty of a French university, *1998*
Woman athlete to win an Olympic medal, *5764*
Woman in Europe to receive official permission to wear pants, *1629*
Woman printer, *4710*
Woman to choreograph her own ballets, *1859*
Woman to write professionally, *3331*
Woven elastic webbing, *3711*

Pecq

Hot-water heating system, *1210*

Pleumeur-Bodou

Transoceanic telecast by satellite, *5966*

Poitiers

Biography written by a woman, *3330*
Check to Muslim expansion in western Europe, *4929*
Troubadour, *4363*

Poix

Airliner collision, *1936*

Provence

Playing cards using the four modern suits, *2584*

Reims

International airplane race, *5603*
Normal school for training teachers, *1969*
Polyphonic mass, *4384*

Rouen

Bicycle road race, *5625*
Knitting machine, *3714*

St. Dié

Map to use the name "America" for the New World, *3614*

Serignan

Study of insect behavior, *5163*

FRANCE—*continued*

Strasbourg

Book printed in Europe, *3344*
Call for a united democratic Europe, *3135*
Christmas trees, *3029*
Direct election of the European Parliament, *2658*
Free dental clinic for poor children, *3820*
French writing, *3553*
Law against enhanced bosoms, *1611*
President of the European Parliament who was directly elected, *2841*
Printed newspapers published regularly, *4488*
Printing press, *4704*
Treatise on military surgery, *4045*

Toulon

Ironclad warship in modern times, *4253*

Toulouse

Intercontinental passenger service, *1340*
International pipe organ festival, *4426*
Public brothel sponsored by a university, *5389*

Tours

Check to Muslim expansion in western Europe, *4929*

Troyes

Version of the Holy Grail legend, *3472*

Vallon-Pont-d'Arc

Paintings, *1262*

Versailles

Animals sent aloft in a balloon, *1393*
Minuet, *1846*
Passenger elevator, *1204*
Supreme War Council of the World War I Allies, *4182*
Weather balloons, *5277*

Vienne

Inquisition directed against Jews, *4860*

Wimereux

Wireless station for international communications, *5900*

FRENCH GUIANA

Cayenne

Evidence that the earth is an oblate spheroid, *5264*

Kourou

Commercial space program, *5511*

FRENCH POLYNESIA

Raft trip across the Pacific, *5460*

Gambier Islands

Human societies destroyed by overpopulation, *4599*

GABON

President of independent Gabon, *2824*

GAMBIA

Currency board in Africa, *2429*
President of Gambia, *2834*

GEORGIA

General secretary of the Communist Party of the former Soviet Union, *2997*
Georgian writing, *3495*
President of independent Georgia, *2853*
Woman to rule Georgia, *2942*

Dmanisi

Hominid remains in Europe, *4622*

GERMANY

Accidental shooting, *6101*
Accordion, *4416*
Account of Germanic religion, *4739*
Aerial bombardment of a city by airplane, *4209*
Air battle that was strategically important, *4222*
Air pump, *5298*
Aircraft carrier to be sunk by surface ships, *4270*
Airplane pilots killed in combat, *4210*
Anglo-Saxons to arrive in England, *4636*
Artificial eardrum, *3983*
Artificial flavoring, *2539*
Artificial language, *3299*
Ascent of Nanga Parbat (Diamir), *5738*
Aspirin, *3928*
Assault rifle, *6117*
Automatic pistol, *6114*
Barbiturate, *3925*
Bathroom scale, *2723*
Battle decided by the use of breech-loading infantry rifles, *4176*
Beet sugar factory, *2549*
Blimp lost in combat, *4228*
Bookplate, *3345*

GERMANY—*continued*

Photography booth, 4572

Picture books, 3343

Plan for European economic and monetary union, 3138

Plastic contact lenses, 4110

Playing deck with double-headed face cards, 2591

Pocket, 1608

Poison gas, 6079

Porcelain manufactured in Europe, 3648

Postal service to carry private mail, 4670

Printed cryptology book, 3402

Printed map in Europe, 3610

Printed playing cards, 2583

Process for liquefying mixed gases, 5237

Production automobile with a gas-powered internal-combustion engine, 3229

Protestant liturgies, 4816

Public schools in the modern era, 1966

Radar, 2011

Radiator, 2178

Radio-controlled wristwatch, 6038

Recording tape, 2047

Reference to the Iron Curtain, 3128

Regularly scheduled transoceanic flights, 1344

Rocket car, 5720

Rocket-propelled airplane, 1318

Rocket-propelled warplane, 4231

Roller bearings, 3291

Running shoes, 1657

Shaped charge used in war, 6093

Shot of World War II, 4185

Smokeless gunpowder, 6089

Solar service stations for electric vehicles, 2076

Standard laboratory burner, 5302

State-sponsored social security system, 2423

Steam-driven rotary press, 4715

Steam-powered printing press, 4713

Storage device for electricity, 2080

Submachine gun widely used in battle, 6116

Submarine blockade, 4260

Sunspot cycle to be observed, 5087

Surgical adhesive bandage, 3876

Synthetic gasoline plant, 2107

Systemic pesticide, 1101

Talking doll, 2384

Tape recorder, 2048

Tape recording of a live concert, 2050

Televised trial, 4463

Textbook of dentistry, 3775

Theory that light consists of particles, 5332

Toxicologist, 3956

Trampoline international competition, 5674

Transatlantic radio fax transmission of a photograph, 5876

Translation of the complete Christian Bible into a modern European language, 4888

Treatise on binary mathematics, 3747

Treatise on biophysics, 5162

Treatise on calculus, 3748

Treatise on crafts by a practicing artisan, 1246

Treatise on meteorites, 5121

Treatment for syphilis, 3930

U-boat captured in World War II, 4268

Use of the term "anti-Semitism", 4975

Use of the word "fossil", 5260

V-block engine, 2175

Vaginal cap, 2361

Videophone, 5972

Voice synthesizer, 5931

Warship sunk by air attack in wartime, 4269

Wartime song popular with both sides of the conflict, 4442

Weather maps, 3623

Wheeled carts on rails, 3263

Witchcraft encyclopedia, 3476

Woman psychoanalyst, 4003

Woman to be awarded the Iron Cross, 4225

Woman to become president of the Parliamentary Assembly of the Council of Europe, 2659

Wood pulp paper, 3694

Augsburg

Catholic saint canonized by a pope, 4853

Human ascent into the stratosphere, 1408

News agency, 4513

Yiddish translation of the Jewish Bible, 4994

Bad Cannstatt

Motorcycle with an internal-combustion engine, 3216

Bamberg

Illustrated books printed in Europe, 3352

Berlin

Anti-art movement, 1252

Art presenting a continuous narrative, 1234

Center for the study of human sexuality, 5371

Chemist to identify a substance using a microscope, 5223

Correspondence school, 1975

Electric locomotive, 3275

Expressway for automobiles, 1592

Feature-length animated film directed by a woman, 4332

Foreigner to be appointed professor in a German university, 1997

Gymnastics club, 5670

Hang-glider fatality, 1893

Helicopter free flight indoors, 1425

Homosexual rights organization, 5380

International agreement to eliminate slave trading, 5494

International congress on homosexual rights, 5382

Licensing requirement for dentists, *3855*
Movie with a homosexual theme, *5381*
Multinational art museum, *1833*
Nazi book burning, *3364*
Organic compound synthesized from an inorganic substance, *5232*
Poster kiosks, *4459*
Programmable electronic binary computer, *1668*
Radio waves, *5895*
Recognition of Neptune as a planet, *5090*
Recognition of the true cause of tooth decay, *3817*
Recording of a complete symphony, *4392*
Rhythm method, *2368*
Rigid airship, *1403*
Sugar from beets, *1064*
Tape recorder to use plastic tape, *2049*
Transmission electron microscope, *5304*
Tuba, *4418*
Uneven parallel bars, *5673*
World polo championships, *5801*

Bingen

Book of Christian mysticism by a woman, *4797*
Pesticide disaster in Europe, *1957*

Blankenburg

Kindergarten, *1973*

Bremen

Mag-Lev train, *3283*
Woman helicopter pilot, *1424*

Breslau

Scientific effort to relate age and mortality in a large population, *1868*

Brunswick

Reform Jewish services, *4973*
Savings bank, *2407*

Buxheim

Printed European illustration, *1290*

Coblenz

Travel guidebooks, *3394*

Cologne

Building of glass bricks, *1198*
Eau de cologne, *2747*
Einkorn domestication, *1012*
European tapestry, *3084*
International rail line, *3267*

International trade fairs, *1537*
New Testament printed in English, *4887*

Danzig

Map of the moon, *3622*

Darmstadt

Glider club, *1419*

Dessau

All-metal airplane, *1316*

Dresden

Book written in the Americas, *3342*
Laparoscopic surgery, *4053*
Sex-change operation, *5370*
Single-lens reflex (SLR) 35-millimeter camera, *4586*
Theory of culture, *5361*

Dusseldorf

Household detergent, *3111*
Nursing school, *3858*
Protestant hospital, *3893*
Protestant religious order, *4836*

Eichstätt

Illustrated manual of military technology, *4117*

Eisleben

Grade levels in schools, *1964*

Frankfurt

Fashion magazine, *1610*
Heart operation, *4052*

Frankfurt am Main

City to require a privy in each house, *4034*
International trade fairs, *1537*
Mail-order catalog, *1512*
Neurotransmitter to be identified, *5168*
Synthetic drug to treat bacterial infections, *3931*
Transatlantic commercial airship, *1409*

Freising

Municipal bank, *2403*

Friedrichshafen

Bombing raids, *4211*

GERMANY—Friedrichshafen—*continued*
Dirigible that was commercially and militarily successful, *1404*
Transatlantic commercial airship, *1409*
Zeppelin flight, *1405*

Gandersheim

European playwright, *5981*
Woman poet to write in German, *3558*

Garching

Computer model of the growth of the universe, *5113*

Giessen

Silvered hand mirror, *2743*
Teaching laboratory for chemists, *5231*

Gleiwitz

Attack of World War II, *4184*

Gotha

Nazi death camp to be liberated in World War II, *1774*

Göttingen

Physical anthropologist, *5154*
Tables of the moon's motions for navigation, *5436*
Woman to earn a doctorate in mathematics, *3751*

Gottorp

Planetarium, *5128*

Halle

Modern university, *1991*

Hamburg

Fire insurance company, *2420*
Firestorm, *1951*
International Polar Year, *2316*
Lightning rod on a public building in Europe, *5266*
Magazine, *4473*
Photographs of a historic event, *4592*

Hannover

International bowling competition, *5636*

Heidelberg

Course in scientific psychology, *3995*

Orangery, *2622*
Work of experimental psychology, *3994*

Helgoland

Bomb to land on German soil in World War II, *4218*
Desalination plant, *1489*

Herrnhut

Moravian Church community, *4832*

Hohenburg

Encyclopedia compiled by a woman, *3381*

Jena

Anastigmatic lens that was commercially successful, *4582*
Geodesic dome, *1199*
Planetarium of the modern type, *5129*

Karlsruhe

International Chemical Congress, *5234*

Königsberg

Ophthalmoscope, *3873*

Konstanz

Yiddish translation of the Jewish Bible, *4994*

Leckwitz

Meeting of American and Soviet troops in World War II, *4189*

Leipzig

Common algebraic symbols, *3740*
Experimental psychology laboratory, *3998*
International trade fairs, *1537*
Major land battle decided by volley fire, *4168*
Orchestra still in existence, *4369*

Löwenburg

Fencing guild, *5702*

Lübeck

European city with a municipal health officer, *4008*
Marine disaster costing the lives of more than 10,000 noncombatants, *1939*
Synagogue firebombing in Germany since World War II, *4981*

GERMANY—Wittenberg—*continued*

Major statement of Protestant theological doctrine, *4815*

Scholar of African descent to earn a doctorate from a European university, *1992*

Wolfenbüttel

Printed newspapers published regularly, *4488*

Wolfsburg

Subcompact car designed to be fuel-efficient, *3239*

Worms

Manual for midwives, *2336*
Yiddish writing, *3573*

Wuppertal-Elberfeld

Sulfa drug, *3934*

Württemberg

Map to use the name "America" for the New World, *3614*

Würzburg

Alarm clock still extant, *6024*
Contact lenses for correcting defective vision, *4109*
Discovery of X-rays, *5330*
X-ray photograph of human anatomy, *3902*

GHANA

Anglican priest who was not of European descent, *4834*
Currency board in Africa, *2429*
Dramatic films shot in Africa, *4291*
Emperor of the Ashanti, *2778*
Prime minister of Ghana, *2890*
Secretary-general of the United Nations from a black African nation, *3203*
Sub-Saharan African colony to gain its independence, *2699*
West African money market, *2431*

GREECE

Actor, *5975*
Alphabet to include vowels, *3316*
Automaton, *5025*
Botanist, *5178*
Boxing, *5637*
Boxing gloves, *5638*
Buttons, *1640*

Central heating system for buildings, *1208*
Chain mail, *6072*
Christian creed, *4778*
Circumnavigation of Britain, *2304*
Classification system of all knowledge, *1810*
Constitutional monarch of modern Greece, *2964*
Cookbook, *2501*
Critical edition of the works of Homer, *3328*
Definite date in the history of the Indian subcontinent, *6013*
Desalination process, *1475*
Description of an earthquake, *5258*
Description of clinical depression and bipolar disorder, *3829*
Description of disease as a matter of science, *3827*
Description of lead poisoning, *3830*
Description of static electricity, *2077*
Detailed account of a long sea voyage, *2273*
Dialogues, *5977*
Diving bell, *5445*
Electrotherapy, *4082*
Epidemic, *1899*
Fables with morals, *3438*
Geographical book, *5252*
Greek prose work, *3561*
Hair lightening, *2732*
Health resorts, *4081*
Iron for smoothing clothes, *3051*
Irrational number, *3730*
Library catalog, *1811*
Literary critic, *3327*
Long-distance communication system using an alphabet, *5918*
Marathon, *5841*
Medical text written by a woman, *3769*
Metal anchor, *5401*
Naval battle, *4238*
Occupational disease, *3828*
Pharmacopoeia widely used, *3788*
Prediction of a solar eclipse, *5127*
Punctuation, *3317*
School for mirror artisans, *2738*
Scientific calculation of the Earth's circumference, *5256*
Scientists attached to armed forces, *5042*
Sighting of a mermaid, *3466*
Soccer-type football games, *5813*
Stage clowns, *5978*
Stage makeup, *5988*
Tonsillectomy, *4043*
Total solar eclipse observed in Europe, *5126*
Treatise on geometry, *3731*
Treatise on human ecology, *2237*
Treatise on hunting, *3123*
Treatise on rocks and minerals, *5255*
Trireme galley, *5402*
Turbine, *2161*
Utopian town planner, *1561*
Water mill, *2185*

ICELAND

Account of Germanic religion, *4739*
Appearance in literature of legendary Germanic heroes, *3474*
Crossing of the North Pole underwater by a submerged submarine, *5463*
History of Iceland in Icelandic, *3008*
Hymn for which an exact date is known, *4382*
Legal drama, *3443*
President of the modern Republic of Iceland, *2806*
Re-enactment of a Viking voyage to the New World, *5469*
Sagas, *3441*
Woman to become president of a nation in a democratic election, *2842*

Heimaey

Town buried by a volcano in modern times, *1929*

Reykjavik

Settlement in Iceland, *4640*

Thingvellir

Parliament, *2650*

INDIA

Airmail flight by airplane, *4680*
Anticoagulant, *3920*
Ascent of K2 (Mount Godwin Austen), *5739*
Ascent of Kanchenjunga, *5742*
Ascent of Nanga Parbat (Diamir), *5738*
Assamese writing, *3518*
Atheistic religious movements, *4737*
Authoritative Hindu law code, *4906*
Banana cultivation, *1029*
Bengali writing, *3508*
Biographies of the Jaina saints, *4950*
Biography of the Buddha, *4756*
Buddhist inscriptions, *4753*
Buddhist missionaries, *4744*
Buddhist monastic rule, *4750*
Buddhist national leader, *2767*
Buddhist religious texts, *4765*
Butter, *2507*
Buttons, *1640*
Caste system in Hinduism, *4901*
Chess-like game, *2597*
Cummerbund, *1633*
Definite date in the history of the Indian subcontinent, *6013*
Didactic verses, *3437*
Disciples of Mahavira, *4942*
Domesticated chickens, *1131*
Emperor of India, *2766*

Empire to unite the Indian subcontinent, *2690*
English settlement in India, *4660*
Establishment of Buddhism as a state religion, *4754*
Evidence of Hinduism, *4900*
Fiber optic cable, *5942*
Food purity law, *2472*
Formal symbol of Jainism, *4952*
Grammarian, *3296*
Gujarati texts, *3512*
Hindi writing, *3514*
Hindu heresies, *4905*
Hindu missionary in the West, *4917*
Hindu monastic order, *4910*
Hindu poet-saints of the *bhakti* devotional movement, *4909*
Hindu religious text, *4902*
Hindu temple, *4908*
Hindu text translated into English, *4912*
Hindu woman to earn a medical degree, *3972*
Hymns, *4380*
Images of the Buddha, *4757*
Images of the Jaina saints, *4947*
Important text of Mahayana Buddhism, *4767*
Interspecies birth of a cat, *1121*
Jaina monastic order, *4943*
Jaina sacred texts, *4944*
Jaina saint, *4941*
Juggernaut, *4911*
Kannada writing, *3497*
Kashmiri writing, *3522*
King to convert to Jainism, *4949*
Kung fu master, *5701*
Maithili writing, *3523*
Major source of international folktales, *3468*
Malayalam writing, *3504*
Marathi writing, *3520*
Marijuana smoking, *4021*
Mass-produced rockets for warfare, *6132*
Modern Hindu reform movement that rejected Western influence, *4915*
Mustard used as a spice, *2557*
National railway hospital, *3898*
Nationwide poisoning epidemic, *1909*
Nobel Prize for Literature winner from Asia, *4532*
Oriya writing, *3515*
Pashto writing, *3537*
Plastic surgery, *4042*
President of the United Nations General Assembly who was a woman, *3195*
Presidential bank in India, *2409*
Prime minister of India, *2884*
Printed cloth, *3702*
Punjabi writing, *3528*
Reference to dice games in literature, *2604*
Reform movement in Jainism, *4951*
Religion to require a vegetarian diet, *4945*
Rice, *1011*
Sahara Cup cricket contest, *5656*

INDIA—*continued*
Sanskrit grammar, *3571*
Sanskrit text, *3570*
Schism in Buddhism, *4752*
Schism in Jainism, *4948*
Sea trade between India and Mesopotamia, *1524*
Shawls, *1604*
Sikh international convention, *5012*
Sikh kingdom, *5010*
Sikh martyr, *5006*
Sikh military victories, *5008*
Spinning wheel, *3713*
State-supported family planning clinics, *2369*
Statement of the Hindu doctrine of *Brahman*, *4904*
Statement of the Hindu doctrine of *dharma*, *4907*
Statement of the Hindu doctrine of karmic reincarnation, *4903*
Stirrup, *1152*
Surgery to repair perforated or obstructed intestines, *4040*
Suspension bridge, *2138*
Suspension bridge with iron chains, *2139*
Tamil writing, *3487*
Telugu writing, *3500*
Texts of Ayurvedic medicine, *3770*
Uniforms in military khaki, *4150*
Vegetarian principles, *2471*
Westerner to visit India, *2272*
Westerners to promote Hindu ideas, *4916*
World war, *4170*
Written record of a prosthesis, *3979*
Yoga textbook, *3768*
Zen Buddhism, *4759*

Ajanta

Frescoes, *1266*

Amritsar

Sikh guru who was a temporal leader, *5007*
Sikh revival movement, *5011*
Sikh sacred book, *5004*
Sikh temple at Amritsar, *5005*

Anandpur

Sikhs to take the name "Singh", *5009*

Arrah

Register of fingerprints, *1752*

Begumpett

Recognition of the vector of malaria, *3842*

Bengal

African slave kingdom in India, *5478*

Cholera pandemic, *1906*
Famine to kill more than 1 million people, *1922*
Storm to kill more than 100,000 people, *1921*

Bhopal

Chemical disaster to cause large loss of life, *1958*

Bombay

Mass migration by Zoroastrians, *5022*
Methane plant, *2061*
Zoroastrian reform movement, *5024*

Calcutta

Comparative linguist, *3297*
Dum-dum bullets, *6115*
Flight from Cairo to Calcutta, *1359*
Modern Hindu reform movement, *4913*
Prophet to declare that all religions are true, *4914*

Delhi

London to Delhi scheduled aircraft flight, *1363*
Muslim leader who was a woman, *2946*
Performance of a *Son et lumière* show in Asia, *2230*

Kapilavastu

Buddhist nun, *4748*

Kartarpur

Sikh community, *5002*

Kashmir

Cashmere, *3705*

Kasia

Buddhist monument, *4751*

Kozhikode

Direct sea voyage from Western Europe to Asia, *2285*

Kusumapura

Mathematician to use algebra, *3737*

Patna

Canonization of Jaina sacred texts, *4946*

Punjab

Sectarian dissenters in Sikhism, *5003*

IRAN

Bisitun

Gondeshapur

Hamadan

Rayy

IRAN—*continued*

Shush

Long-distance road, *1582*

Susa

Planned genocide, *1765*

Teheran

Fundamentalist Islamic republic, *2700*

Vresk

Rail bridge higher than 500 feet, *2147*

IRAQ

Aquaculture, *1005*
Aqueduct, *2129*
Arab poet to write in a colloquial style, *3547*
Archeological digs in Mesopotamia, *5056*
Astrological system, *5065*
Astrological treatise, *5117*
Axe, *6041*
Banking regulations, *2401*
Battering rams, *6068*
Battle for which a precise date is known, *4152*
Beasts of burden, *1145*
Beer, *2474*
Border wall, *4114*
Cereal crop, *1010*
Code of Jewish law, *4989*
Collapsible boats, *5400*
Computer virus as a weapon of war, *6082*
Contract terms for wet-nursing, *2378*
Copper tools, *3654*
Cryptanalyst, *4135*
Curling iron, *2730*
Deliberate use of environmental warfare, *4196*
Deployment of the NATO rapid reaction force in a member country, *4195*
Description of epilepsy, *3826*
Description of tooth decay, *3793*
Destruction of a nuclear reactor as an act of war, *4193*
Destruction of an attacking missile by a defensive missile in combat, *4235*
Drug treatment for mental illness, *3986*
Emperor, *2763*
Empire, *2675*
Epic, *3435*
Farmers' almanac, *1002*
Flood story, *3463*
Floor coverings, *3075*
Germ warfare, *4153*
Glass objects, *3637*
Glassmaking formula, *3638*
Gold artifacts, *3655*

Grain drill, *1071*
Hair styling, *2731*
Hand mirrors, *2737*
Harness, *1149*
Hoe, *1070*
Horses for transport, *1146*
House with an interior courtyard, *1217*
House with post-and-lintel construction, *1220*
International trade in ice, *1525*
IOU promissory note, *2436*
Islamic philosopher, *4565*
Jewish prayer book, *4990*
King of independent Iraq, *2975*
Landscape in art, *1264*
Large-scale irrigation project, *1093*
Law requiring Jews to wear an identifying mark, *4968*
Legal protection for trade secrets, *1439*
Legal regulation of the trade in alcoholic beverages, *2476*
Legend of a resurrected deity, *4732*
Lock, *6046*
Lutes, *4400*
Lyres, *4399*
Malpractice regulation for physicians, *3942*
Marriage and divorce laws, *2395*
Metal helmets, *6067*
Modern theory of the visual process, *5315*
Mother goddess, *4729*
Nails, *6043*
New Year's festival, *3012*
Observations of Venus, *5064*
Oriental carpet design, *3079*
Parasol, *1602*
Parking penalty, *1584*
Personal name, *3482*
Pickles, *2558*
Picture writing, *3307*
Pigeon post system, *1155*
Popular book about archeology, *5057*
Potter's wheel, *3636*
Pottery kiln, *3634*
Prayer of thanksgiving for crops, *4735*
Reference to a windbreak, *2612*
Reference to wrestling in literature, *5868*
Royal converts to Judaism, *4963*
Sea trade between India and Mesopotamia, *1524*
Seals for fastening and recording, *3576*
Sexagesimal number system, *3726*
Siege engines, *6069*
Simple machine still in use, *2183*
Slavery, *5471*
Spy ring, *4136*
Star catalog, *5118*
Stylus, *3577*
Synagogues, *4962*
Synthetic material of any kind, *3635*
Talmud to be compiled, *4988*
Tampons, *2713*

Unit of linear measure, *5309*
Use of bicarbonate of soda as an antacid, *3915*
Vocabulary list, *3367*
Water-lifting device, *1094*
Woman fighter pilot to fire a missile in combat, *4237*
World map still extant, *3605*
Written language that used symbols, *3309*
Zodiacal horoscope, *5066*

Baghdad

Arabic history of the world, *3007*
Arabic translations of scientific manuscripts, *5043*
Biography of Muhammad, *4930*
Collector of Greek scientific manuscripts, *5044*
Hospital to keep charts for patients, *3886*
Islamic inquisition, *4933*
Muslim physician, *3951*
Public pharmacy, *3921*
Slave army, *4122*
Use of zero, *3738*

Basra

Dictionary of Arabic, *3546*
Revolt of African slaves, *5476*
Sufi mystics, *4931*
Treatise on cryptanalysis, *3398*

Erech

Depiction of a wheel, *3290*

Eshnunna

Smelted iron artifact, *3661*

Hit

Oil seeps, *2099*

Kirkuk

International oil pipeline, *2108*
Troop movement by airplane, *4216*

Mosul

Manicure set, *2712*

Niffer

City map, *3601*
Literature, *3436*
Pharmacopoeia of medicinal herbs, *3787*

Nuzi

Maps, *3600*

Shanidar

Burial ceremony, *1870*

Tel-el-Muqayyar

Archeologist, *5052*
Author known by name, *3326*
Board game, *2565*
Depiction of milking, *1133*
Harps, *4398*
Jewelry, *1595*
Lamps, *3074*
Law code, *2644*
Literature for children, *3434*
Manicure set, *2712*
Metal lamps, *3076*
Multi-story building, *1168*
Museum, *1824*
Musical notation, *4360*
Paved streets, *1581*
Town house, *1219*
Verses in honor of a deity, *4733*
Written record of wet-nursing, *2377*
Zoo, *1158*

Yorghan Tepe

Political sex scandal, *2627*

IRELAND

Bank holidays, *3035*
Boycott, *1444*
Edition of the *Guinness Book of World Records*, *2226*
International handball match, *5677*
Irish Gaelic writing, *3493*
Irish racing, *5679*
Large reflecting mirror, *5136*
Nocturne, *4389*
Passenger liner sunk by a submarine, *1932*
President of the Republic of Ireland (Éire), *2804*
Prime minister of Northern Ireland, *2881*
Runner over the age of 40 to break the four-minute mile, *5846*
Settlement in Iceland, *4640*
Statement of a physical law as an equation with two dependent variables, *5325*
Synthetic fertilizer, *1095*
Systematic observations of galaxies, *5089*
Woman to become president of the Republic of Ireland (Éire), *2851*

Belfast

Aircraft carrier adapted from a conventional warship, *4261*
Pneumatic tires for bicycles, *5626*

IRELAND—*continued*
Clifden

Nonstop transatlantic airplane flight, *1361*
Transatlantic radio message of the regular westward service, *5903*

Cork

Steamship to cross an ocean from east to west, *5456*

Donaghadee

Swimmer to cross the Irish Sea, *5823*
Undersea telegraph cable, *5925*

Dublin

British prime minister to address the Parliament of the Irish Republic, *3133*
Calculation of the accurate age of the earth, *5281*
Color photographic process that was practical, *4583*
Performance of the oratorio *Messiah*, *4388*
Physician to understand the necessity for hygiene, *3967*
Stock exchange member who was a woman, *2430*
Transatlantic east-west nonstop airplane flight, *1365*

Londonderry

Transatlantic solo airplane flight by a woman, *1370*

Portmarnock

Transatlantic westbound solo nonstop flight, *1371*

Valentia

Transatlantic telegraph cable, *5926*

ISRAEL

Airlift of endangered Jews to Israel, *4979*
Ancient language revived for modern use, *3302*
Anti-Semitic blood libel, *4966*
Anti-Semitic libel, *4960*
Artwork, *1231*
Bestiary, *3467*
Calculation of the date of creation in the Bible, *6014*
Case of mouth-to-mouth resuscitation, *4080*
Center of Jewish learning outside Jerusalem, *4964*
Commandment in the Torah, *4982*

Cord, *3697*
Cryptanalyst, *4135*
Dead Sea Scrolls to be discovered, *4978*
Destruction of a nuclear reactor as an act of war, *4193*
Discovery of quasicrystals, *5249*
Gnostic, *4773*
Intelligence-gathering operation, *4134*
International terrorist organization to use skyjacking, *1800*
Jewish physician, *3948*
Kabbalistic text, *4987*
Keeper of the Holy Grail, *3473*
Kibbutz, *1570*
Lost tribes of Israel, *4957*
Maccabiah Games, *5695*
Mass aliyah (emigration) to Israel, *4976*
Massacre at the Olympic Games, *1799*
Nobel Prize for Literature winner from the Middle East, *4535*
Oil embargo in peacetime, *3130*
Olive oil factory, *2525*
Peace treaty between an Arab nation and Israel, *3182*
Physical evidence of a person mentioned in the Jewish scriptures, *4959*
Pope, *4847*
Portable wooden building, *1170*
President of Israel, *2809*
Prime minister of Israel, *2888*
Reference to a sundial, *6018*
Reference to King David, *2922*
Sickle, *1069*
Synagogues, *4962*
Tallow soap, *2714*
Translation of the Jewish Bible, *4985*
Unit of linear measure, *5309*

Ain Mallaha

Skeleton of a domesticated dog, *1104*

Athlit

Rams, *4241*

Caesarea

Historian of the Christian church, *4785*

Gezer

Hebrew writing, *3562*
Jewish calendar, *6006*

Jericho

Walled town, *1555*

Jerusalem

Canonization of biblical books, *4984*

ITALY—*continued*

Old Master painting sold at auction for more than US$10 million, *1288*
Orchestration, *4387*
Pasta, *2528*
Peep shows, *2222*
Pendulum clock, *6027*
Performer in a foreign language film to win the Academy Award for Best Actor, *4323*
Performer in a foreign language film to win the Academy Award for Best Actress, *4322*
Reading glasses, *4106*
Solo ascent of Mount Everest, *5749*
Star atlas to include coordinates, *3631*
Steam engine, *2163*
Sugar in Europe, *1060*
Tarot cards, *2582*
Tattoos, *1596*
Teleportation experiment, *5356*
Theorist of air warfare, *4214*
Thermometer, *5295*
Thimbles, *3099*
Treatise on autopsies, *3784*
Treatise on basal metabolism, *3780*
Treatise on dental anatomy, *3778*
Treatise on double-entry bookkeeping, *1442*
Treatise on medicine written in medieval Europe, *3771*
Treatise on occupational medicine, *3783*
Treatise on sign language, *3781*
Treatise on the theory of architecture, *1188*
Use of airplanes in war, *4205*
Vegetarian, *2469*
War to receive news coverage, *4167*
Wind-driven vehicle, *3205*
Woman mathematician of renown since antiquity, *3749*
Women Renaissance artists to attain renown, *1281*

Assisi

Rule for Christian monastic life written by a woman, *4858*

Bologna

Anatomist since antiquity to dissect human bodies, *3957*
Bank exchange, *2405*
Caricatures, *1280*
Castrato of note, *4432*
Forensic postmortem, *1750*
Physicist who was a woman, *5327*
Printed edition of the Psalms in Hebrew, *4991*
Printed edition of the Torah, *4993*
Renaissance sculptor of note who was a woman, *1298*
Scholarly societies, *1985*
Treatise on human anatomy based on dissection, *3774*

Treatise on insects, *5145*
University in Europe, *1986*
University professor who was a woman, *1988*

Brescia

Christian radical reformer, *4796*
Explosion to cause great loss of life, *1948*
Typeface made in Europe in a non-Roman alphabet, *4705*
Violin, *4408*

Brindisi

International military airmail route, *4682*
Paved long-distance road, *1585*

Cassino

Abbey in Western Europe, *4850*

Chiavenna

Landslide to kill more than 1,000 people, *1918*

Cividale del Friuli

Cannon used in warfare, *4164*

Civitavecchia

Artillery fortress, *1189*

Como

Battery, *2081*

Cortina d'Ampezzo

Woman athlete to take the Olympic oath at the opening ceremony, *5776*

Cosenza

Person with dwarfism, *3824*

Cremona

Stradivarius violin, *4410*
Woman to paint frescoes, *1278*

Crotone

Researcher to conduct human dissections for scientific purposes, *3944*
Theory that the earth is a sphere, *5253*
Woman mathematician, *3729*
Wrestler of note, *5869*

Fabriano

Paper mill in Europe, *3691*

Watermark, *3692*

Ferrera

Dancing master, *1843*

Florence

Academy of fine arts, *1238*
Autobiography of an artist, *1236*
Barometer, *5297*
Book about the High Renaissance, *1237*
Florin, *2442*
Forensic pathologist, *3955*
Humane treatment of the mentally ill, *3991*
Income tax, *2466*
Opera known by that name, *4430*
Opera whose music is still extant, *4431*
Painting composed with one-point perspective, *1274*
Parachute, *1430*
Patent, *1540*
Pianoforte, *4412*
Public lottery with cash prizes, *2605*
Renaissance architect of importance, *1186*
Renaissance concept of the artist, *1235*
Scientific explanation of perspective in art, *1276*
Three-dimensional computer model of an Old Master sculpture, *1304*

Genoa

European traveler to set foot on the North American continent after the Vikings, *2284*
Frozen desserts, *2546*
Joint-stock bank, *2404*

Herculaneum

Volcanic eruption, *1914*

Larderello

Geothermal power station, *2063*

Lucca

Medieval doctor to advocate the use of anesthesia, *3759*

Mantua

Cooling system for buildings, *1209*
Orchestra, *4364*

Milan

Call for abolition of the death penalty, *1742*
Crematorium, *1882*
Inflatable chair, *3095*

Municipal board of health, *4007*
Public clock to strike the hours, *6023*
Set designer, *5990*
Treatise on criminal justice and its reform, *1737*
Typeface made in Europe in a non-Roman alphabet, *4705*

Modena

Physician to specialize in occupational medicine, *3965*

Montenotte

Transatlantic solo balloon flight, *1411*

Naples

Cases of syphilis, *3833*
Comic opera, *4429*
Funicular railway, *3276*
Identification of fluoride as a tooth-decay preventive, *3811*
Oyster farm, *1006*
Scientific academy, *5047*
Scientist lowered into a volcano, *5262*
Woman physician to receive university training, *3954*

Padua

Anatomist to break with Galen, *3958*
Clinical thermometer, *5296*
Examination of the night sky with a telescope, *5133*
Heated conservatory for plants, *5181*
Physician to specialize in occupational medicine, *3965*
Physician to use precise measuring instruments, *3962*
Woman to earn the degree of Doctor of Philosophy, *1990*
Works on comparative embryology, *3779*

Palermo

Asteroid to be discovered, *5085*

Parma

Opera diva, *4436*
Self-guided car, *3259*
Theater with a permanent proscenium arch, *5993*

Pavia

Artificial insemination, *5155*
Head transplant, *5153*

Piovi di Sacco

Printed book in Hebrew, *3564*

ITALY—*continued*

Pola

City with a chlorinated water supply, *4014*

Pompeii

Basilica still extant, *1175*
Metal pen, *3581*
Plane, *6051*
Plastering tools, *6045*
Volcanic eruption, *1914*
Window glass, *3642*

Porto

Hospice for Christian pilgrims, *1458*

Pozzuoli

Cement, *2150*
Concrete, *2149*

Reggio di Calabria

Printed book in Hebrew, *3564*

Rome

Account of Germanic religion, *4739*
Actuarial table, *2419*
Antipope, *4848*
Apartment houses, *1221*
Autopsy of a well-known individual, *1866*
Backgammon, *2567*
Barber surgeons, *4044*
Basilica, *1174*
Book, *3339*
Book on cosmetics, *2715*
Brassiere, *1605*
Catechism of the Catholic Church since the Renaissance, *4879*
Catholic index of forbidden books, *4849*
Catholic monastic order founded after the beginning of the Protestant Reformation, *4868*
Catholic saint canonized by a pope, *4853*
Christian radical reformer, *4796*
Christmas, *3023*
Clean-shaven society, *2751*
Commercial bakeries, *2526*
Concrete dome, *1177*
Craft guilds, *1529*
Depiction of a menorah, *4965*
Depictions of a comet, *5070*
Diving apparatus for practical underwater work, *5446*
Drill, *6044*
Druid, *4738*
Emperor of Rome, *2769*
Encyclopedia for young adults, *3377*

Encyclopedia of importance, *3378*
Epic composed in Latin, *3569*
Epic translated into Latin, *3568*
Eyewitness report to become a best-seller, *4453*
Fireproofing, *1574*
Folding knife with multiple tools, *6052*
Freight elevators, *1203*
Frozen desserts, *2546*
Full-length mirrors, *2739*
Galaxy to be described in print, *5071*
Giant sports arena, *5606*
Gospel, *4774*
Greenhouses, *1074*
Hammer, *6042*
Handball-style game, *5676*
Handkerchief, *2718*
Heated swimming pool, *5817*
Holy Roman Emperor, *2773*
Iron hand, *3980*
King of Italy, *2924*
Latin comedy and tragedy, *5979*
Latin writing, *3567*
Legal recognition of Christians in the Roman Empire, *4783*
Major intercontinental road, *1586*
Medical officers in the armed forces, *4121*
Meeting of the heads of the Anglican and Catholic churches, *4805*
Mention of the Feast of the Nativity, *3024*
Mile, *5310*
Military hospitals, *3881*
Military uniform designed by an artist, *4148*
Mock naval battle, *2219*
Modern treatise on geography, *3609*
Montessori school, *1977*
Monumental concrete structure, *1178*
Music printed from movable type, *4706*
New Year to begin on January 1, *3016*
News posters, *4484*
Organized police force, *1788*
Pairs of fitted shoes, *1652*
Papal throne, *3082*
Paved long-distance road, *1585*
Permanent international war crimes court, *1781*
Pharmacopoeia widely used, *3788*
Planet to be mapped, *5080*
Plate armor, *6074*
Pope, *4847*
Pope to be assassinated, *4851*
Pope to become a recording star, *4375*
Pope to condemn the African slave trade, *5487*
Pope tried for heresy after his death, *4852*
Printed book in Hebrew, *3564*
Printed cookbook, *2503*
Printed edition of the Qur'an, *4939*
Professional barbers, *2752*
Public bathing, *2716*
Public hospital in Europe, *3883*
Raised aqueduct of great length, *2133*
Recording of piano on tape, *2051*

JAPAN—*continued*

Usa

Shinto temple to Hachiman, *4997*

Wakayama

Dentures retained by adhesion, *3803*

Yokohama

Transpacific sailboat crossing by a woman, *5468*

Yokota Air Base

Transpacific nonstop jet airplane flight, *1381*

JORDAN

Dam, *2156*
King of Jordan, *2977*
Meeting of the Palestine Liberation Organization, *2667*
Non-NATO ally of the United States in the Western Hemisphere, *3142*
Tolerated minorities under Islam, *4923*

Ain Ghazal

Plaster statues, *1294*

Aqaba

Christian church built for the purpose, *4779*

KAZAKHSTAN

Commercial communications satellite to circle the moon, *5892*
Horse riding, *1144*
Jewish kingdom to be established since biblical times, *4967*
Nation heavily polluted by nuclear waste, *2270*
President of independent Kazakhstan, *2847*
Wheel, *3289*

Almaty

Apples, *1027*

Baikonur

Artificial satellite, *5584*
Bureaucrat in space, *5564*
Docking of two manned spacecraft, *5544*
Human to die during a space flight, *5541*
Human to return safely from space, *5533*
Living creature launched into orbit, *5530*

Living creatures launched into orbit who returned safely to earth, *5532*
Mars probe, *5567*
Module of the International Space Station to be placed in space, *5515*
Object to escape the earth's gravity, *5508*
Space walk, *5537*
Spacecraft to carry more than one crew member, *5536*
Spacecraft to reach the moon, *5519*
Two manned craft in space simultaneously, *5534*

Pazyryk

Carpeting, *3080*
Knotting as a technique of making carpets, *3704*

Semey

Atomic bomb detonated by a country other than the United States, *6126*
Hydrogen bomb detonated by a country other than the United States, *6130*
Remote detection of a nuclear weapons test, *6127*

KENYA

African violets, *1053*
Ascent of Mount Kenya, *5734*
Black hole to be detected, *5105*
Boston Marathon in which both champions were African athletes, *5847*
Goldman Environmental Prizes, *2250*
Muslim settlement in East Africa, *4638*
Prime minister of Kenya, *2901*
Swahili writing, *3535*
Three-dimensional maps of subterranean rifts, *5292*
Trade between the Mediterranean world and East Africa, *1530*
X-ray astronomy satellite, *5139*

Kibwezi

Solar-powered hospital, *3897*

Nairobi

International program to promote safe birth, *2352*

KIRIBATI

Country to officially celebrate the year 2000, *3047*

KOREA

Chinese cabbage, *1033*

Epidemic in Japan, *1902*
Ironclad ships, *4247*
King of Korea, *2920*
Korean writing, *3509*
Naval battles in which ironclad vessels participated, *4248*
Physicians in Japan, *3950*
Smokescreen in a battle, *4249*

Seoul

Heptathlon two-time gold medalist, *5792*

KUWAIT

Country to depend mainly on water from desalination, *2244*
Deliberate use of environmental warfare, *4196*
Emir of Kuwait, *2961*

KYRGYZSTAN

President of Kyrgyzstan, *2858*

LAOS

King of the Lao people, *2949*
Large mammal discovered since World War II, *1116*

LATVIA

Holocaust reparations from a neutral nation, *1780*
Latvian writing, *3534*
Prime minister of independent Latvia, *2798*

Riga

Eastern European country to elect a woman as president, *2869*

LEBANON

Blown glass, *3641*
Political association of Arab states, *3134*
Tallow soap, *2714*

Baalbek

Greek fire, *6075*

Jubayl

Alphabetic inscription in a writing system ancestral to modern Western alphabets, *3314*
Legend of Prester John, *3471*
Travel writer, *3390*

Sidon

Dental bridges, *3792*

List of Seven Wonders of the World, *1176*

LESOTHO

Novel in an African vernacular language, *3460*
Prime minister of independent Lesotho, *2903*

LIBERIA

President of Liberia, *2787*
Republic in Africa, *2695*

LIBYA

Bombing raid from an aircraft, *4206*
Caravans across the Sahara, *1526*
King of independent Libya, *2978*
Method of finding prime numbers, *3733*
Prime minister of Libya, *2906*
Simple machine still in use, *2183*

Ain Zara

Aerial bombs, *6092*

El Azizia

Pilot captured during war, *4208*
Use of airplanes in war, *4205*

Shahhat

Scientific calculation of the Earth's circumference, *5256*

Tobruk

Aviator wounded in combat by ground fire, *4207*

LITHUANIA

President of independent Lithuania, *2849*
Statute establishing that men and women are equal under the law, *5366*
Woman to rule Poland, *2952*

Vilnius

Printed edition of the Talmud, *4992*

LUXEMBOURG

King of Luxembourg, *2966*
Ruler of Luxembourg, *2935*
Woman to rule Luxembourg, *2945*

MACAO

Anglican woman priest, *4843*

MACEDONIA

Definite date in the history of the Indian subcontinent, *6013*
Scientists attached to armed forces, *5042*

MADAGASCAR

Aye-aye born in captivity, *1124*
Captive-bred lemurs returned to Madagascar,
1128
President of independent Madagascar, *2819*
Road designed for motor vehicles, *1589*
Settlers in Madagascar, *4637*

MALAWI

Freshwater national park, *2261*
Prime minister of Malawi, *2905*

MALAYSIA

Goldman Environmental Prizes, *2250*
Heads of state to meet in an on-line chat ses-
sion, *3165*
Japanese naval casualty in World War II, *4271*
Long-distance sea trading along regular routes,
1523
New Testament printed in Asia, *4893*
Prime minister of Malaysia, *2891*
Southeast Asian decorative artwork, *1243*
Talking bathroom scale, *2726*
Telephone conversation to travel around the
world, *5938*
Thomas Cup in badminton, *5599*

Borneo

Jungle canopy walkway for tourists, *2249*

MALI

Caravans across the Sahara, *1526*
Emperor of Mali, *2775*
Emperor of Songhai, *2776*
Empire in sub-Saharan Africa, *2682*
President of the Republic of Mali, *2823*
Trading empire in central Africa, *1533*
West African emperor of note to make a reli-
gious pilgrimage to Mecca, *4935*

Asselar

Skeleton of a black African, *4620*

Timbuktu

European explorer to visit Timbuktu, *2297*
History of West Africa, *3009*
University in Africa, *1987*

MALTA

British civilian medal conferred on a country,
2698
Crusading order of knights, *4795*
Human cannonball family act, *2214*
Representation of a plant growing in a pot,
2613
Structures, *1166*
Woman to become president of Malta, *2844*

MARSHALL ISLANDS

Bikini

Atomic bomb explosion underwater, *6124*
Ban-the-bomb demonstrations, *6125*

Eniwetok

Hydrogen bomb, *6129*

MAURITANIA

Empire in sub-Saharan Africa, *2682*
Nonstop circumnavigation of the world by bal-
loon, *1413*
President of independent Mauritania, *2825*
Trading empire in central Africa, *1533*

MAURITIUS

Animal exterminated by human action in historical times, *1109*
Code for the treatment of slaves in European
colonies, *5486*

MEXICO

Anatomically correct image of the human heart,
3900
Avocado cultivation, *1054*
Aztec priest-king, *2950*
Ball court, *5596*
Ball game, *5595*
Book written in the Americas, *3342*
Conquistador, *4653*
Constitutional president of Mexico, *2782*
Continuous settlements of Asians in North
America, *4662*
Cotton clothing, *1597*
Crops cultivated in the New World, *1015*
Cryptogram written in the New World, *3403*
Encylopedia of ancient Mexico, *3382*
European-born emperor of a North American
country, *2780*
European to join a Native American people,
4651
Free-trade region encompassing North America,
1552

Hairless dog breeds, *1117*
Hot cocoa, *2547*
Journey across North America, *2290*
Latin American novel, *3457*
Maize cultivation, *1019*
Major city of the New World, *1563*
Meso-American culture, *4634*
Nahuatl grammar, *3531*
Necropolis in North America, *1876*
Peaches in the New World, *1046*
Peanuts, *1037*
Rummy card games, *2593*
Satellite-delivered digital video system for education, *1979*
Third World country to default on its foreign debt, *2417*
Tomato cultivation, *1036*
University in the New World, *1989*

Acapulco

Acapulco Black Film Festival, *4345*

Chiapas

Catholic priest ordained in the New World, *4864*

Isla Mujeres

Swim from Mexico to Cuba, *5827*

Matamoros

Army newspaper, *4504*

Mexico City

Book printed in the Western Hemisphere, *3359*
Easter Mass in Central America, *4866*
Mexican–American trail, *4658*
News sheet printed in the New World, *4486*
Pan-American Games, *5696*
Printing press in the New World, *4709*
Seminary in the New World, *4867*
Summer Olympic Games in Latin America, *5781*
Woman athlete to light the Olympic flame, *5782*
Woman intellectual in the New World, *3333*
World Conference on Women, *5375*
Zoo in the Western Hemisphere, *1160*

Oaxaca

Calendar developed in the Americas, *6004*
Civilian president of Mexico, *2789*

Puebla

European industry in the Americas, *4654*

Tijuana

All-news radio station, *4464*

Veracruz

Use of aircraft carriers in war, *4259*
Writing system invented in the New World, *3320*

Yucatán

Horses on the North American mainland, *1108*
Solo crossing of the Gulf of Mexico in a paddled boat, *5470*

MOLDOVA

President of Moldova, *2857*

MONACO

Film festival, *4339*

Monte-Carlo

European luxury casino and seaside resort, *2233*

MONGOLIA

Powdered milk, *2509*
Turkish writing, *3501*

Gobi Desert

Dinosaur eggs to be discovered, *5209*
Fossilized embryo of a carnivorous dinosaur to be discovered, *5216*

MONTENEGRO

King of independent Montenegro, *2970*

MORAVIA

Slavic state, *2683*

Pekarna

Lamps, *3074*

MOROCCO

Black African woman athlete to win an Olympic gold medal, *5787*
Ghetto, *1565*
King of independent Morocco, *2980*
Physical handicap in an adult, *3823*
Swimmer to cross the Strait of Gibraltar, *5824*

Amsterdam

Airline ticket and reservation office, *1342*
Army drill book, *4126*
Baptist church, *4829*
Family planning clinic, *2363*
Gay Games, *5698*
Illustrated school textbook, *1968*
Mercury thermometer, *5300*
Modern pentathlete, *5842*
Newspaper in the English language, *4490*
Star of Africa, *3678*
Telephone conversation to travel around the world, *5938*
Temperature scale, *5221*
Woman athlete to win four gold medals in one Olympic Games, *5773*

Breda

Peace treaty among European powers to arbitrate world trade, *3168*

Delft

Enameled cookware, *3101*
Microscopic observation of protozoa, bacteria, and human cells, *5146*

Haarlem

Dutch painter of note who was a woman, *1282*

The Hague

International court, *3153*

Kampen

Kidney dialysis, *4090*

Leiden

Flower cultivated by florists, *1045*
Liquid helium, *5239*
Superconductor, *5334*

Moerdijk

Paratrooper assault on a fortified area, *4221*

Rotterdam

Nobel Prize in Economics, *4528*

Tiel

Merchant guild, *1535*

Utrecht

World judo champion who was not Japanese, *5708*

Vreeswijk

Pound lock on a canal, *2135*

NEW ZEALAND

Ascent of Mount Everest, *5737*
English-speaking country to abolish the death penalty, *1748*
European explorer to see New Zealand, *2293*
Humans in New Zealand, *4639*
International meetings of ministers in Antarctica, *3166*
Major airborne assault, *4224*
National nuclear-free zone, *3139*
National voting rights for women, *2639*
Prime minister of New Zealand, *2874*
Sighting of Antarctica, *2312*
Woman to climb Mount Everest solo without bottled oxygen, *5753*
Woman to fly solo from England to Australia, *1373*

Auckland

Prenatal blood transfusion, *4101*

NICARAGUA

President of a Central American country born in the United States, *2788*
Woman to become president of Nicaragua, *2848*

NIGER

Emperor of Songhai, *2776*
President of independent Niger, *2820*

NIGERIA

Armored soldiers in sub-Saharan Africa, *4123*
Bronze artifacts in sub-Saharan Africa, *1245*
Currency board in Africa, *2429*
Hausa writing, *3539*
Nobel Prize for Literature winner from Africa, *4537*
Octuplets, *2355*
President of Nigeria, *2831*
Prime minister of Nigeria, *2892*
Sculptures in sub-Saharan Africa, *1296*
Transatlantic crossing by a bird, *1114*

Lagos

Yoruba writing, *3542*

NORTH KOREA

Premier of North Korea, *2886*

POLAND—*continued*

Pope born in Poland, *4877*
Pope to visit a Communist country, *4878*
President of Communist Poland who was chosen in a free representative election, *2846*
President of independent Poland, *2797*
Unitarian church, *4827*
Vitamin to be identified, *5167*
Woman appointed to the faculty of a French university, *1998*
Woman to become prime minister of Poland, *2916*
Woman to rule Poland, *2952*
Written national constitution outside of the United States, *2647*

Gdansk

Naval shot of World War II, *4266*
Shot of World War II, *4185*

Gniezno

Polish writing, *3513*

Kraków

Code of Jewish law, *4989*
Regular civil airmail service, *4683*

Szczecin

Guide dogs, *1157*

Treblinka

Revolt by prisoners at a Nazi death camp, *1773*

Warsaw

Artificial language, *3299*
Emergency parachute jump, *1433*
Woman to win a Nobel Prize, *4518*

Wroclaw

Conservative rabbi, *4974*
Disease known to be caused by a specific microbe, *3840*

Zloczew

Paparazzo, *4573*

PORTUGAL

Arteriogram, *3904*
Brazilian general of African descent, *4169*
Clothing patterns, *1617*
Cultivation of New World crops in Africa, *1047*

European travelers in Japan, *2291*
Explorers to pass Cape Bojador since antiquity, *2279*
Global empire, *2689*
King of Portugal, *2941*
Peanuts, *1037*
Post for trade between Europe and Africa, *1554*
Prefrontal lobotomy, *4056*
President of the Republic of Portugal, *2794*

Azores

SOS signal sent in an emergency, *5904*

Lisbon

Direct sea voyage from Western Europe to Asia, *2285*
European country to enter the African slave trade, *5477*
European expedition to round the southern tip of Africa, *2280*
Gold rush in the New World, *3681*
Letter containing a description of America, *2282*
Modern epic poems, *3445*
Portuguese writing, *3516*
Seismologist to develop a modern theory of the cause and actions of earthquakes, *5265*
Transatlantic airmail service, *4687*
Transatlantic airplane flight, *1360*
World's fair with a marine theme, *2232*

Sagres

Eyewitness account by a European traveler of life in the African interior, *2288*
International and multicultural academy for explorers, *2278*

Terreiro do Paco

Hot-air balloon, *1390*

PUERTO RICO

Caribbean Spanish-language poet who was a woman, *3459*
Labor Day, *3037*

ROMANIA

Germ warfare in modern times, *4179*
Gymnast to achieve a perfect score in the Olympic Games, *5785*
King of Romania, *2968*
Launch of a heavier-than-air machine entirely under its own power, *1356*
Man to walk 100,000 kilometers, *5851*
Pope to visit a mainly Christian Orthodox country, *4812*

Prime minister of independent Romania, *2875*
Refugee ship disaster, *1937*
World Dracula Congress, *3481*

Freidorf

Man to swim 100 meters in under a minute, *5821*

RUMANIA

Rumanian writing, *3526*

RUSSIA

Aerobats, *1314*
American to be launched into space aboard a Russian spacecraft, *5560*
Artificial heart in an animal, *4066*
Artificial insemination center, *1119*
Ascent of Mount Elbrus, *5731*
Atomic bomb detonated by a country other than the United States, *6126*
Bureaucrat in space, *5564*
Child whose parents had both flown in space, *2393*
Circumnavigation of Antarctica, *2310*
Civilian nuclear power plant, *2116*
Civilian spy satellite, *5593*
Climatological classification system, *5274*
Communist revolution, *2673*
Democratically elected leader of Russia, *2854*
Discovery of chromium, *3667*
Eight-day week, *6010*
Electric arc welding, *1491*
Ethnic violence in the former Soviet Empire, *4198*
Expedition to sail around the northernmost point of Asia, *2313*
Fabergé Easter egg, *1248*
Head of state to order an automobile, *3226*
Holographic film system, *4311*
Humans to enter the International Space Station, *5565*
Hydrogen bomb detonated by a country other than the United States, *6130*
Jewish kingdom to be established since biblical times, *4967*
Joint space walk by American and Russian astronauts, *5563*
Military use of TNT, *6091*
Modern ballet choreographer, *1863*
Modern conflict in which an Asian power defeated a European power, *4257*
Module of the International Space Station to be placed in space, *5515*
Mother-daughter Olympic medalists, *5786*
Musical instrument to create sound with electromagnetic fields, *4423*
Nation with a substantial number of women physicians, *3975*

Observation of the egg cell of a mammal, *5159*
Orthodox saint from Russia, *4809*
Periodic table of the elements, *5229*
Plum cultivation, *1031*
President of the Soviet Writers' Union, *3337*
Prophet of Zoroastrianism, *5018*
Radio inventor, *5896*
Russian writing, *3511*
Scalping, *4156*
Scheduled commercial jet flight, *1346*
Spacecraft launched by the United States to dock with a Russian space station, *5561*
Standardized sizes for bras, *1635*
Tokamak, *2120*
Tracking shot, *4292*
Treaty between the North Atlantic Treaty Organization (NATO) and Russia, *3184*
Tsar to travel outside Russia, *2777*
Virus to be isolated, *5164*
War to receive extensive newspaper coverage, *4175*
Wheel, *3289*
Woman accredited as an ambassador, *3148*
Woman executed in Russia for political terrorism, *1797*
Woman to earn a doctorate in mathematics, *3751*
Woman to fly in space, *5535*
Woman to rule a part of Russia, *2934*
World chess champion defeated by a computer, *2601*
World chess champion who was a woman, *2600*
Written national constitution outside of the United States, *2647*

Archangelsk

Labor concentration camp, *1770*

Baku

Multistep crude oil refining, *2106*

Chelyabinsk

Nuclear waste disaster to cause large loss of life, *1955*

Gorky

Motor home, *3220*

Kaliningrad

Lithuanian writing, *3530*
Measurement of the distance to a star, *5086*

Kiev

Russian travel writer, *3391*

RUSSIA—*continued*

Moscow

All-plastic building, *1202*
Electric rail and street lamps, *2093*
Kinetic sculpture in which motion was the main esthetic factor, *1301*
Mobiles, *1302*
Nuclear reactor in Europe, *2115*
Patriarch of Moscow, *4810*
Patriarch of Moscow who was not Russian by birth, *4811*
Radial keratotomy, *4061*
Telecommunications tower higher than 500 meters, *1229*
Tsar, *2953*

St. Petersburg

Internet bank robber, *1807*
Nuclear-powered surface ship, *5420*
Remote-controlled explosive mine, *6088*

Uta

Pipeline fire, *1959*

Volgograd

Battle with more than 2 million deaths, *4187*
Women pilots to down enemy aircraft in combat, *4226*

Yakutsk

Humans in Siberia, *4624*

RWANDA

Genocide conviction by an international court, *1782*
President of Rwanda, *2828*

SAMOA

Sumo champion not born in Japan, *5872*

SARDINIA-PIEDMONT

Prime minister of Sardinia-Piedmont, *2872*

SAUDI ARABIA

Arabic book, *3545*
Authoritative text of the Qur'an, *4938*
Camel saddle, *1150*
Civil war in Islam, *4925*
Deliberate use of environmental warfare, *4196*
Destruction of an attacking missile by a defensive missile in combat, *4235*

Domesticated camels, *1147*
Islamic fundamentalists, *4926*
Islamic revivalist reform movement, *4937*
King of Saudi Arabia, *2974*
Muslim caliph, *2927*
Permanent schism in Islam, *4928*
Sectarian controversy in Islam, *4927*
Thoroughbreds, *5681*

Badr

Military victory of Islam, *4159*

Mecca

Convert to Islam, *4920*
Human stampede to cause massive loss of life, *1960*
Jihad, *4919*
Muslim ritual, *4918*
West African emperor of note to make a religious pilgrimage to Mecca, *4935*

Medina

Islamic state, *2684*
Mosque, *4921*
Muslim expulsion of Jews, *4922*
Year in the Muslim calendar, *6005*

SCOTLAND

Absolute scale of temperature, *5329*
All-electronic television system, *5950*
Breechlock rifle, *6107*
Civilian ship sunk in World War II, *4267*
Clinical trial, *4085*
Definition of an inch, *5311*
Disease proven to be transmitted by insects, *3841*
European explorer to find the source of the White Nile, *2300*
Fax process, *5873*
Frozen hydrogen, *5238*
Golfer, *5664*
Heat pump, *2064*
International water polo match, *5864*
King of England and Scotland, *2958*
King of Scotland, *2931*
King to practice dentistry, *3804*
Logarithm tables, *3744*
Observation of a cell nucleus, *5160*
Pneumatic tires, *3292*
Pneumatic tires for bicycles, *5626*
Psychologist to relate known physiological facts to psychological phenomena, *3996*
Psychology journal, *3997*
Researcher to discover an entire grouping of elements, *5240*
Tartan plaids, *3709*
Theatrical spotlight, *5997*

Traps for human trespassers in gardens, *2623*
Treatise on economics, *5359*
Treatise on human population growth, *4602*
Treatise on mathematics, *3728*
Vacuum flask, *5303*
Vitamin-deficiency disease to be cured, *3836*
Water polo, *5863*
Waterproof raincoat, *1624*
Wave-powered electricity generator for commercial use, *2075*
Whisky, *2479*
Woman to play golf, *5665*

Aberdeen

Canned fish, *2533*
Literary agent, *3336*

Dounreay

Breeder reactor, *2119*

Dumfriesshire

Bicycle capable of speed, *5621*

Dunfermline

Carnegie library, *1820*

Edinburgh

Abortion by vacuum aspiration, *2362*
Clinical rounds in hospitals, *3892*
Electric vehicle, *3214*
General encyclopedia in the English language, *3384*
Golfing association, *5666*
International ecumenical missionary organization, *4803*

Firth of Forth

Transatlantic dirigible flight, *1406*

Glasgow

Antiseptic surgery, *4049*
Boy scout troop, *2389*
Thermostat, *1211*
Treatise on antiseptic surgery, *4050*

Glenlivet

Whisky distillery, *2488*

Greenock

Ship outfitted with interior electric lights, *5414*

Lanark

Physician to teach obstetrics and midwifery, *2341*

Leith

Steamship to cross an ocean from east to west, *5456*

Lismore

Scottish Gaelic collection of writings, *3527*

North Perthshire

Measurement of the mass and density of the earth, *5267*

Orkney Islands

Latrines, *4031*

Outer Hebrides

Transatlantic crossing by an robot airplane, *1388*

Paisley

Cotton thread, *3710*

Portpatrick

Swimmer to cross the Irish Sea, *5823*
Undersea telegraph cable, *5925*

Roslin

Lamb with human genes, *5207*
Mammal born to a cloned mother, *5190*
Mammal cloned from adult cells, *5187*

St. Andrews

Golf course, *5663*

SEA

Accidental sinking of ships carrying prisoners of war, *1938*
Aircraft carrier attack, *4264*
Amphibious assault vehicle, *6122*
Angler to hold world records for every billfish species, *5601*
Atomic bomb explosion underwater, *6124*
Bireme galley, *5399*
Blimp lost in combat, *4228*
Chartered airplane flight, *1337*
Coelacanth caught alive, *1115*
Country to officially celebrate the year 2000, *3047*
Daily shipboard newspaper, *4509*
Dive to the bottom of the ocean, *5453*
European explorers to see the Pacific Ocean, *2289*

Black African president of South Africa, *2865*
Booker Prize, *3456*
European expedition to round the southern tip of Africa, *2280*
Fossil oil, *5251*
Large terrestrial mammal exterminated by human action in historical times, *1111*
Meat-eating hominids, *4615*
Modern political party for Africans, *2666*
National constitution to specifically protect the rights of homosexuals, *5385*
Nobel Prize for Peace winner from Africa, *4543*
Nobel Prize in Physiology or Medicine winner from Africa, *4554*
Nonracial democratic elections in South Africa, *2643*
Prime minister of the Union of South Africa, *2879*
Regular airmail service, *4681*
Voyage around Cape Horn, *2292*
White witch doctor, *3977*
Written history in Zulu, *3011*
Zulu writing, *3543*

Alice

Xhosa writing, *3541*

Cape Town

Coelacanth caught alive, *1115*
Heart transplant, *4071*
Human footprints, *4619*
Meat-eating hominids, *4615*
Photographic star catalog, *5123*

Durban

Zulu newspaper, *4512*

Johannesburg

Nonviolent act of civil disobedience of international significance, *3155*
Scheduled commercial jet flight, *1346*

Krugersdorp

Factory to obtain uranium from gold, *3675*

Sasolburg

Oil-from-coal plant, *2111*

Swartkrans

Human use of fire, *4617*

Transvaal

Star of Africa, *3678*

SOUTH KOREA

Arbor Day, *3036*
Modern tae kwon do, *5707*
President of South Korea, *2808*
United Nations military action, *4192*

Donghae

Visit made by South Korean tourists to North Korea, *3132*

Pusan

Ferry to sink with large loss of life, *1941*

Seoul

Human cloning, *5192*
Scented suits, *1639*
Transpacific solo balloon flight, *1412*

SOVIET UNION (FORMER)

Aircraft units staffed entirely by women, *4223*
Art holograms, *1242*
Artificial satellite, *5584*
Atomic bomb detonated by a country other than the United States, *6126*
Civilian nuclear power plant, *2116*
Commercial jet airplane pilot who was a woman, *1347*
Communist song of international popularity, *4440*
Communist wire service, *4517*
Docking of two manned spacecraft, *5544*
Food irradiation, *2522*
General secretary of the Communist Party of the former Soviet Union, *2997*
Holographic film system, *4311*
Human in space, *5529*
Human to die during a space flight, *5541*
Human to return safely from space, *5533*
Hydrogen bomb detonated by a country other than the United States, *6130*
Intercontinental ballistic missile, *6136*
International astronaut rescue agreement, *5543*
International space mission, *5548*
Launch failure of a manned spacecraft, *5547*
Living creature launched into orbit, *5530*
Living creatures launched into orbit who returned safely to earth, *5532*
Lunar rover, *5526*
Mars probe, *5567*
Medical emergency in space, *5557*
Meeting to establish the United Nations, *3187*
Modern nation to make abortions freely available, *2366*
Nuclear weapons test moratorium, *3174*
Object to escape the earth's gravity, *5508*
Photographs from the surface of another planet, *5574*

Asturias

Prehistoric painting to show the heart of a mammal, *3899*

Ávila

Doctor of the Church who was a woman, *4876*
Printed map in Europe, *3610*

Barbastro

Gypsy (Rom) to be beatified by the Catholic Church, *4881*

Barcelona

Asian athlete to win a World Cup gold medal in track and field, *5844*
Containers of yogurt with fruit mixed in, *2516*
Eyewitness report to become a best-seller, *4453*
Heptathlon two-time gold medalist, *5792*
Intercontinental passenger service, *1340*
Jewish scientific encyclopedia, *3380*
Welded metal sculpture, *1303*

Bilbao

Multinational art museum, *1833*

Burgos

Picaresque novel, *3444*

Canary Islands

Peoples of the Canary Islands, *4645*

Castile

Deaf person educated in lip-reading and speaking, *2005*
Hoop skirt, *1613*

Catalonia

Watch that told time in Catalan, *6039*

Cervera

Dance notation, *1845*

Córdoba

Check to Muslim expansion in western Europe, *4929*
Dictionary in the Hebrew language, *3563*
Illustrated surgical treatise, *3773*
Manned glider flight, *1415*
Oral surgeon, *3801*

Elvira

Celibacy rule for Christian priests, *4782*

Getafe

Autogiro, *1423*

Granada

African slave to earn a degree from a European university, *5483*
Narcotic drugs, *3918*

Las Palmas

Transatlantic solo trip by rowboat, *5466*

Madrid

Permanent bullring, *5651*
Woman bullfighter of renown in Europe, *5653*

Málaga

Matador of renown, *5650*

Minorca

Mayonnaise, *2560*

Palos

Expedition of Christopher Columbus, *2281*

Pamplona

Running of the bulls, *5649*

Seville

Auto-da-fé, *4863*
Bullfighting school, *5652*
Cigarettes, *1065*
Circumnavigation of the world, *2305*
Quill pen, *3582*

Tenerife

Aviation disaster in which more than 500 people were killed, *1944*
Primate research station, *5166*

Tordesillas

Treaty in which the entire world was partitioned, *3167*

Tudela

European traveler to reach the Chinese frontier, *2276*

Valencia

Checkers book, *2572*

SRI LANKA

Buddhist religious texts, *4765*
Country outside India to accept Buddhism, *4755*
Cricket match, *5654*
English translations of early Buddhist texts, *4769*
Hospitals in Asia, *3880*
Pali text, *3489*
Prime minister of Sri Lanka, *2883*
Prime minister who was a woman, *2895*
Sighting of a mermaid, *3466*
Sinhalese writing, *3488*

Anuradhapura

Tree of which there is historical record, *2615*

ST. VINCENT AND THE GRENADINES

Prime minister of St. Vincent and the Grenadines, *2912*
Volcanic eruption of the 20th century, *1924*

SUDAN

African state outside Egypt, *2676*
Cattle herders, *1130*
Prime minister of Sudan, *2889*
Sculptures in sub-Saharan Africa, *1296*

SURINAME

Jews in the New World, *4646*
Prime minister of independent Suriname, *2908*

SWAZILAND

King of independent Swaziland, *2981*

SWEDEN

Blasting cap, *3683*
Cartridges, *6103*
Centrifuge, *3877*
Description of global warming, *2239*
Diesel locomotive in regular service, *3281*
Ejection seat that was propelled by explosives, *1324*
Headlight washer/wiper, *3250*
King of all Sweden, *2937*
Law guaranteeing freedom of speech, *2646*
Marital property reform law, *2400*
Masonry stove, *3056*
Mechanical cream separator, *1090*
Milk carton, *2521*
Miss World contest, *2201*
National birth registry, *4601*
National standing army in Europe, *4124*

Navigation of the Northeast Passage, *2315*
Newspaper in continuous publication, *4494*
Nickel obtained in a pure sample, *3666*
Nicotine chewing gum, *4030*
Nitroglycerin, *5233*
Nobel Prize for Literature, *4530*
Nobel Prize for Literature winner from North America, *4533*
Nobel Prize for Peace winner from North America, *4540*
Nobel Prize in Chemistry, *4523*
Nobel Prize in Chemistry winner from North America, *4524*
Nobel Prize in Economics winner from North America, *4529*
Nobel Prize in Physics, *4545*
Nobel Prize in Physics winner from North America, *4546*
Nobel Prize in Physiology or Medicine, *4549*
Nobel Prize in Physiology or Medicine winner from North America, *4550*
Nobel Prize winner to win the award twice, *4519*
Nobel Prize winner to win twice in the same field, *4521*
Ombudsman, *2632*
Organism classification system, *5149*
Parliament on the European continent, *2651*
Pinochle, *2590*
Plastic bags, *3118*
Radiation surgery, *4060*
Scandinavian writing, *3490*
Turbocharged engine for a mass-produced automobile, *3251*
Voice double, *4321*
Winner of the Prix d'Amérique who was a woman, *5689*
Woman to rule the Scandinavian countries, *2951*
Woman to win a Nobel Prize, *4518*
Woman to win the Nobel Prize for Literature, *4531*
World heavyweight champion to regain his title after losing it, *5647*

Carlsten

Lighthouse with a revolving light, *5443*

Göteborg

Anti-skid system, *3254*
Production automobiles with seat belts, *3247*

Gotland

Rudder, *5404*

Jönköping

Safety matches, *3106*

SWITZERLAND—*continued*

Mussen

Slalom race, *5812*

Neuchâtel

Androids capable of a variety of tasks, *5030*

Oerlikon

Telephone answering machine, *5940*

Plurs

Avalanche to kill more than 1,000 people, *1917*

St. Gall

Garden plan, *2617*
Gregorian chant, *4381*

St. Gotthard

Road tunnel longer than 10 miles, *2195*

St. Moritz

Bobsled competition, *5631*

Samaden

Electric oven, *3064*

Schwyz

Swiss Army knife, *6059*

Sigershauffen

Cesarean operation, *2335*

Vevey

Chocolate for eating, *2550*
Freeze-dried instant coffee, *2500*
Milk chocolate, *2553*

Winterthur

Diesel locomotive, *3280*

Yverdon

Educational reformer to stress individual development, *1971*
National teacher-training program, *1972*

Zürich

Adult baptisms in modern times, *4818*

Anabaptist church, *4819*
Anti-art movement, *1252*
Call for a united democratic Europe, *3135*
European university to admit women as students, *1996*
Fields Medal, *3753*
Paper patterns for clothing printed full size, *1626*
Printed edition of the complete Christian Bible in English, *4889*
Protestant reformer to abolish the Mass, *4817*
Scanning tunneling electron microscope, *5305*
Superconducting materials of ceramic oxide, *5352*

SYRIA

Arch dam, *2159*
Battering rams, *6068*
Christian church order, *4775*
Curling iron, *2730*
Dam still extant, *2158*
Description of pulmonary blood circulation, *3953*
Expansion of Islam outside Arabia, *4924*
Germ warfare, *4153*
Hair styling, *2731*
Plum cultivation, *1031*
Political association of Arab states, *3134*
President of Syria, *2805*
Siege engines, *6069*

Aleppo

Stylite, *4789*

Damascus

City in continuous existence, *1557*
Civil war in Islam, *4925*
Islamic hospital, *3885*
Islamic philosopher with a following in the West, *4566*
Muslim dynasty, *2685*
Muslim navy, *4242*
Visit by an American president to a country on the U.S. list of terrorist states, *3131*

Harran

Distillation apparatus for alchemists, *5218*

Heliopolis

Greek fire, *6075*

Ras Shamra

Hymns, *4380*

Ras Sharma

Alphabet, *3313*

TUNISIA—*continued*

Tunis

Elephants taken on a sea voyage, *1106*

TURKEY

Anticoagulant, *3920*
Arch dam, *2159*
Banker, *2402*
Bear cub sanctuary, *1165*
Botanical illustrations, *5179*
Boxing, *5637*
Christian hospitals, *3882*
City planned on a grid, *1558*
City with uniform plot sizes, *1559*
Deployment of the NATO rapid reaction force
in a member country, *4195*
Einkorn domestication, *1012*
Flower cultivated by florists, *1045*
Fork, *3100*
Garment to undergo changes of fashion, *1594*
Genocide squads, *1769*
Government coinage, *2437*
Grape cultivation, *1017*
Heretical Christian sectarian movement, *4777*
Islamic country to adopt a solar year, *6008*
Major naval battle decided by firepower, *4246*
Mausoleum, *1877*
Muslim country to adopt a secular government,
2696
Muslim navy, *4242*
President of Turkey, *2801*
Sultan of the Ottoman Empire, *2948*
Turkish horticultural treatise, *2619*
Turkish writing, *3501*
Use of airplanes in war, *4205*
Woman to serve as a combat pilot, *4217*
Wrought iron, *3662*

Ankara

Brocading technique, *3703*

Antioch

Center of Christian missionary activity, *4772*
Christians, *4770*

Bergama

Cold cream, *2717*
Parchment, *3688*

Bodrum

Admiral who was a woman, *4239*
Narrative secular history book of importance,
3002

Cappadocia

Description of clinical depression and bipolar
disorder, *3829*

Çatalhüyük

Cloth made of animal fiber, *3699*
Metropolis, *1556*

Cayonu

Cloth fragment, *3698*

Demre

Santa Claus, *3019*

Hallan Cemi

Animal domesticated for food, *1129*

Hisarlik

Excavator of Troy, *5058*

Hissarlik

Confederation of Greek city-states, *2678*

Istanbul

Baha'i leader, *4741*
Ban on the use of icons in Christian worship,
4807
Coffee house, *1462*
Crusade, *4160*
Feast of Orthodoxy, *3026*
Greek fire, *6075*
Major land battles decided by firepower, *4166*
Naval battle in which Greek fire was used,
4243
Orient Express service, *3277*
Outbreak of plague, *1901*
Patriarchates of the Orthodox Church, *4806*
Refugee ship disaster, *1937*
Rule book of bridge, *2594*
Teaching hospital, *3887*
Trade guilds, *1528*
University in the Western world, *1983*
Use of the crescent as a symbol of Islam, *4936*
Woman to rule the Byzantine Empire, *2772*

Izmir

Long-distance road, *1582*

Iznik

Easter, *3021*
Ecumenical Christian creed, *4787*

Formal attempt to define the nature of Jesus, *4788*

Sunday sabbath, *3022*

Kadeköÿ

Patriarchates of the Orthodox Church, *4806*

Miletus

Atomic theory, *5320*
Description of static electricity, *2077*
Geographical book, *5252*
Prediction of a solar eclipse, *5127*
Utopian town planner, *1561*
Western philosopher, *4556*
World map, *3603*

Pergamon

Art presenting a continuous narrative, *1234*

Scutari

Army with a trained nursing staff to treat its wounded, *4129*

Selçuk

Comprehensive treatise on contraception and birth, *2357*

Titris Hoyuk

Tract houses, *1218*

Ulu Burun

Sunken treasure ship, *5397*

Yenisehir

Lighthouse of importance, *5440*

Zawi Chenui

Houses, *1214*
Permanent settlement, *4630*

TURKMENISTAN

Leader of independent Turkmenistan, *2860*
Woman to wear armor while leading men in battle, *4154*

Ashgabat

Solar thermal power plant, *2068*

UGANDA

European explorer to find the source of the White Nile, *2300*

Human cancer-causing virus to be discovered, *3848*
Prime minister of independent Uganda, *2899*

UKRAINE

Aircraft powered solely by propfan engines, *1335*
Brain surgery, *4037*
Horse riding, *1144*
Jewish kingdom to be established since biblical times, *4967*
Nobel Prize for Literature winner from the Middle East, *4535*
Ocean platform for rocket launching, *5516*
Orthodox saint from Russia, *4809*
Outbreak of the Black Death, *1903*
President of independent Ukraine, *2861*
Telegraph used in warfare, *4174*
War correspondent to file dispatches by telegraph, *4458*
War photographers, *4460*
War to receive extensive newspaper coverage, *4175*
Woman to rule a part of Russia, *2934*

Feodosiya

Germ warfare, *4153*

Kiev

Russian writing, *3511*
Yiddish literary annual, *3575*

Odessa

Regular civil airmail service, *4683*

Zhitomir

Yiddish play to be performed, *3574*

UNITED STATES

Accidental sinking of ships carrying prisoners of war, *1938*
Aerosol product, *3115*
African–African American Summit, *3164*
AIDS vaccine tested internationally, *3914*
Airplane flight to land at the North Pole, *2324*
Airplane flight to land at the South Pole, *2327*
All-woman America's Cup yacht-racing crew, *5861*
American flag to fly over the defeated Nazi empire, *4190*
American to be launched into space aboard a Russian spacecraft, *5560*
Amphetamine, *3935*
Amphibious aircraft, *1312*
Amphibious assault vehicle, *6122*

UNITED STATES—*continued*

Stenography machine, *3594*
Strategic Arms Limitation Treaty, *3180*
Strawberry cultivation, *1049*
Submachine gun widely used in battle, *6116*
Submarine-launched ballistic missile, *6137*
Sunflowers, *1044*
Supersonic bomber, *4233*
Telephone hot line between nations, *3149*
Three-ring circus, *2211*
Tornado expert, *5275*
Tornado intensity scale, *5289*
Tornado to cause more than 500 deaths, *1927*
Trampoline, *5672*
Transatlantic telegraph messages, *5927*
Transdermal patch, *4092*
Traveler's checks, *2455*
Treaty banning the use of the weather as a weapon of war, *3181*
Treaty between a South American country and a North American country, *3169*
Triathlon, *5848*
Trivia board game of international popularity, *2579*
Use of aircraft carriers in war, *4259*
VHS videocassette recorder, *2031*
Visit by an American president to a country on the U.S. list of terrorist states, *3131*
Voice double, *4321*
Walk from the southernmost to the northernmost points of the Americas, *5853*
War criminals convicted of crimes against humanity, *1776*
War photographer who was a woman, *4462*
Warship to sink with nuclear weapons aboard, *1943*
Washing machine, *3054*
Wilderness park in a mall, *2262*
Windsurfing, *5866*
Woman fighter pilot to fire a missile in combat, *4237*
Woman psychoanalyst, *4003*
Woman tennis player to win the Grand Slam, *5838*
Woman to become a professional hockey player, *5693*
Woman to fly over the North Pole, *2326*
Woman to pilot an airplane over the English Channel, *1313*
Woman to walk in space, *5554*
Woman to win the Nobel Prize in Physiology or Medicine, *4553*
World Methodist Council, *4841*
Worldwide rock-and-roll hit, *4445*
Writing system invented in the New World, *3320*

Alabama

Florence

Composer of jazz music, *4376*

Huntsville

Superconducting material that operated at temperatures above the boiling point of nitrogen, *5353*

Alaska

Ascent of Mount McKinley (Denali), *5735*
Eight-day week, *6010*
Site of organized human activity in North America, *4629*

Anchorage

Transpacific nonstop jet airplane flight, *1381*

Point Barrow

Crossing of the North Pole underwater by a submerged submarine, *5463*
Dogsled crossing of the Northwest Passage, *2320*

Arizona

Meteor crater, *5278*

Flagstaff

Planet found beyond Neptune, *5097*

California

Commercial airliner widely used, *1320*

Alameda County

Surgical procedure in North America, *4041*

Berkeley

Cyclotron, *5343*
Element heavier than uranium, *5245*
Element produced artificially, *5243*
Professorship dedicated to the search for extraterrestrial life, *5115*
Synchrotron, *5347*
Two-lid piano, *4428*
Waterbed, *3094*

Burbank

Feature film that was entirely computer-animated, *4338*

Major motion picture to be produced and exhibited entirely with digital technology, *4318*

Carmichael

Robot to perform surgery, *5040*

Cupertino

Personal computer that was commercially successful, *1681*

Personal computer with a graphical user interface, *1731*

Davis

Map of any part of the Americas, *3608*

Duarte

Medicine produced using recombinant DNA, *3938*

Emeryville

DNA chain polymerization, *5202*

Hollywood

Cinematographer of lasting influence, *4290*

Commercial talking motion picture, *4296*

Makeup specifically for movie actors, *2724*

Movie musical, *4352*

Movie studio to produce 100 feature films, *4295*

La Jolla

Transatlantic undersea radio conversation, *5916*

Loma Linda

Transplant of a baboon heart into a human being, *4075*

Long Beach

Kwanzaa, *3041*

Los Angeles

All-news radio station, *4464*

Black African woman athlete to win an Olympic gold medal, *5787*

Computer network, *1694*

Electric guitar, *4424*

Feature-length animated film made by the cel process, *4333*

Film made by a studio outside the United States to win an Academy Award, *4304*

Heptathlon event, *5788*

Olympic marathon for women, *5789*

Parachute jump from an airplane by a woman, *1435*

Pentecostal churches, *4842*

Performer in a foreign language film to win the Academy Award for Best Actor, *4323*

Performer in a foreign language film to win the Academy Award for Best Actress, *4322*

Pilot to bail out of an airplane flying at supersonic speed, *1437*

Round-the-world flights over the North Pole on a regularly scheduled air route, *1383*

Super Bowl football game, *5662*

Woman to compete in both the Summer and Winter Olympic Games, *5790*

Women's cycling event, *5791*

Malibu

Working laser, *2020*

Merced

Round-the-world nonstop flight by a jet airplane, *1384*

Monterey

Autonomous security robot, *5036*

Personal computer operating system, *1729*

Rock music festival, *4448*

Mount Hamilton

Movie showing another planet, *5095*

Mountain View

Discovery of water on the moon, *5111*

Integrated circuit, *2018*

Transgenic bull, *1123*

Muroc

Airplane to fly faster than the speed of sound, *1377*

Reusable manned spacecraft, *5551*

Round-the-world nonstop airplane flight without refueling, *1385*

Woman astronaut to live in a space station, *5562*

Woman to fly faster than the speed of sound, *1382*

Oakland

Accurate recreation of the last flight of Amelia Earhart, *1387*

Flight from the United States to Australia, *1366*

Transpacific solo airplane flight by a woman, *1374*

Video game, *2577*

Colorado

Colorado Springs

Global evangelical rally, *4845*

Denver

Birth to be televised for the public, *2346*
Comprehensive digital atlas of the human body, *3908*
Liver transplant, *4069*

Englewood

Internet university to receive accreditation, *2003*

Longmont

Civilian spy satellite, *5593*

Telluride

Power transmission installation using alternating current, *2088*

Connecticut

Bridgeport

Dental hygienist, *3821*
Handheld rocket launcher, *6133*

Danbury

Encyclopedia distributed via data network, *3388*
Encyclopedia on CD-ROM, *1732*

Groton

Nuclear-powered submarine, *4273*
Submarine equipped with ballistic missiles, *4275*

Hartford

Book manuscript written on a typewriter, *3362*
Circus fire with large loss of life, *1952*
Constitution in the New World, *2645*
Modern use of anesthesia in dentistry, *3762*

New Haven

International football game, *5659*
Map of any part of the Americas, *3608*
Patient to be given penicillin, *3936*

New London

Circumnavigation of the earth by a submerged submarine, *5464*

Mine barrage, *6086*
Toothpaste tube, *2760*

Salisbury

Children's library, *1819*

Sandy Hook

Across-the-ocean race, *5856*

Saybrook

Submarine built for use in war, *4251*

Stamford

Desktop fax machine, *5878*
Electric shaver, *2755*

Stratford

Helicopter that was successful, *1426*

Waterbury

Can opener, *3108*

Delaware

Wilmington

Synthetic fabric that was waterproof and breathable, *3725*
Synthetic fiber produced entirely from chemicals, *3724*
Toothbrush with synthetic bristles, *2761*

District of Columbia

Washington

Arms limitation conference, *3160*
Commercial telegraph service, *5923*
Computer-to-computer conversation in English, *1697*
Electric cooktop, *3061*
Flat horse race in North America, *5687*
Flight of a heavier-than-air machine, *1353*
Fuel cell car, *3262*
Genetically engineered plants, *1058*
International Conservative Congress, *2669*
International networking conference, *1698*
Library to possess 100 million items, *1823*
Machine capable of casting individual letters of type, *4723*
Magazine to put a hologram on its cover, *4482*
Meeting to establish the United Nations, *3187*
Military radar experiment, *2013*
Modern congress of nations in the Americas, *3159*

UNITED STATES—District of Columbia—
Washington—*continued*

Museum of art by women, *1832*
Music by indigenous American peoples to be recorded, *4373*
National code of the laws of war, *4120*
National weather service, *5271*
Online, peer-reviewed journal, *4483*
Pan American Day, *3039*
Peacetime alliance of European and North American nations, *3137*
Plaster statues, *1294*
Supersonic jet service across the Atlantic Ocean, *1351*
Telegraph message, *5922*
Transpacific telephone service using the trans-oceanic cable, *5944*
Treaty to govern the use of a continent, *3175*
Use of the term "cold war", *4191*

Florida

Cape Canaveral

Animals to survive a space flight, *5531*
Astronaut who was a mother, *5556*
Astronauts to land on the moon, *5525*
Astronauts to orbit the moon, *5524*
Astronauts to ride a vehicle on the moon, *5528*
Civilian space traveler to orbit the earth, *5539*
Close-up photographs of Jupiter, *5573*
Commercial satellite, *5587*
Communications satellite, *5884*
Docking of two spacecraft, *5540*
European Space Agency astronaut in space, *5552*
Geosynchronous satellite, *5588*
Husband and wife to fly in space together, *5559*
Images taken from outside the solar system, *5579*
International satellite, *5586*
Live telecast from space, *5542*
Orbiting observatory, *5144*
Rendezvous in space, *5538*
Reusable manned spacecraft, *5551*
Robot to conduct a roving exploration of the surface of another planet, *5582*
Satellite launched from the earth to orbit another planet, *5591*
Space probe in a polar trajectory around the sun, *5578*
Space probe with ion-drive engine, *5514*
Space travelers to fly free in space, *5553*
Spacecraft launched by the United States to dock with a Russian space station, *5561*
Spacecraft placed in solar orbit, *5568*
Spacecraft to carry an extraterrestrial message, *5572*
Spacecraft to land on Mars, *5576*
Spacecraft to leave the solar system, *5577*

Spacecraft to transmit close-up photographs of Mars, *5569*
Telecast from space showing the earth, *5509*
Woman to command a space mission, *5566*
Worldwide satellite-based weather observation system, *5288*

Cape Kennedy

Geosynchronous commercial communications satellite, *5885*

Hollywood

Transatlantic solo trip by rowboat, *5466*

Key West

City in North America to use seawater as its sole water supply, *2245*

Lantana

Woman to motorcycle from the United States to Tierra del Fuego, *3224*

Miami

Smuggled moon rock, *1808*
Transatlantic solo boat journey by a woman, *5461*

North Fort Myers

Round-the-world journey on foot, *5852*

Orlando

Childbirth streamed live on the Internet, *2354*
Major motion picture to be produced and exhibited entirely with digital technology, *4318*
Open-heart surgery streamed live on the World Wide Web, *4064*

St. Augustine

Oceanarium, *1164*
Spanish settlement in North America, *4655*

St. Petersburg

Airliner, *1315*

Tampa

Airliner, *1315*

Georgia

Albany

Woman athlete of African descent to win an Olympic gold medal, *5772*

Athens

Factoring of a 100-digit number, *3755*

Atlanta

African woman athlete to win the Olympic women's marathon, *5793*
All-news television network, *4465*
Olympics to have an official World Wide Web site, *5795*
Portable velodrome of Olympic size, *5608*
Runner to win both the 200-meter and the 400-meter races at the same Olympic games, *5797*
Team from outside the United States to win the World Series, *5616*
Winner of the Grand Slam, *5669*
Women's Olympic volleyball event, *5796*

Decatur

Thought control of a computer, *1735*

Jefferson

Modern use of anesthesia in surgery, *3761*

Savannah

Steamboat to cross an ocean, *5455*

Hawaii

Ironman triathlon, *5849*
Surfers, *5862*

Honolulu

Terrorist bomb attack on an airplane, *1801*
Transcontinental radio fax transmission, *5877*
Transpacific solo airplane flight by a woman, *1374*

Kona

Angler to hold world records for every billfish species, *5601*

Pearl Harbor

Circumnavigation of the world by a submarine, *5462*

Waikiki

Modern surfer, *5865*

Illinois

Significant mathematical problem solved by computer, *3754*

Champaign

Nobel Prize winner to win twice in the same field, *4521*

Chicago

Cloth fragment, *3698*
Comic strip in a daily newspaper, *4470*
Condom designed to be worn by women, *2374*
Drugstore chain, *1519*
Factoring of a 100-digit number, *3755*
Ferris wheel, *2213*
Juvenile court, *5500*
Lightwave-based telecommunications system, *5886*
Modern city with a downtown commercial area, *1568*
Nobel Prize in Physics winner from North America, *4546*
Organ transplant from one human to another that was successful, *4067*
Personal computer bulletin board, *1704*
Planetarium in the Western Hemisphere, *5130*
Refrigerators, *3066*
Rent-a-car business, *3238*
Rock and roll song, *4443*
Self-sustaining nuclear chain reaction demonstration, *5346*
Service club, *1839*
Skyscraper, *1226*
Snorkel fire truck, *1580*
Special Olympics, *5697*
Video tape recorder for sounds and pictures, *5964*
World championship professional football game, *5661*

De Kalb

Barbed wire, *1089*

Hillsdale

Veterinary chiropractic school, *3864*

Shelbyville

Dishwasher, *3063*

Springfield

Airplane accident involving a woman that was fatal, *1898*

Wheaton

Radio astronomer, *5099*

UNITED STATES—*continued*
Indiana

Evansville

Vitamin to be commercially synthesized and manufactured, *2543*

Indianapolis

Raggedy Ann doll, *2390*
Rapid-fire machine gun, *6113*
Transistor radio receiver to be mass-produced, *5913*
Vasectomy, *2364*

Ivanhoe

Train disaster caused by the use of narcotics, *1934*

New Harmony

Theorists of socialism, *2661*

Richmond

Lawn mower that was practical, *6063*

Iowa

Ames

Electronic digital calculator, *1665*

Des Moines

Septuplets to survive birth, *2353*

Kansas

Argonia

City with a woman mayor, *1569*

Topeka

Pentecostal churches, *4842*

Kentucky

Danville

Gynecological surgery, *4047*

Louisville

Kentucky Derby, *5686*

Monticello

Oil seeps, *2099*

Louisiana

Solo crossing of the Gulf of Mexico in a paddled boat, *5470*

Baton Rouge

Commercial petrochemical plant for fluid catalytic cracking, *2110*

Lake Charles

Transoceanic cryogenic shipping, *1550*

New Orleans

Craps game, *2609*
Dental X-rays, *3818*

Maine

Andover

Transoceanic telecast by satellite, *5966*

Bangor

Chewing gum, *2552*

Bar Harbor

Mammals born from an egg grown in vitro, *5173*
Transatlantic radio fax transmission of a photograph, *5876*

Calais

International commercial telephone service, *5935*

Caribou

Transatlantic solo balloon flight, *1411*

Eastern Egg Rock

Transatlantic crossing by a bird, *1114*

Lewiston

International dogsled mail, *4678*

Limestone

Transatlantic nonstop jet airplane flight, *1380*

Portland

International railroad in North America, *3272*

Presque Isle

Transatlantic balloon flight, *1410*

Maryland

Annapolis Junction

Telegraph message, *5922*

Baltimore

Behaviorist, *4002*
Commercial telegraph service, *5923*
Complete DNA sequencing of a free-living organism, *5205*
Dental college, *3859*
Dentistry journal, *3812*
Isolation of human embryonic stem cells, *5174*
Linotype machine, *4722*
Mass-produced rockets for warfare, *6132*
Operation to cure congenital heart disease, *4057*
Touch-tone phone system, *5939*

Bethesda

Gene therapy, *4094*
Identification of the AIDS virus, *3849*
Personal portable phone capable of making a call from anywhere in the world, *5948*

Gaithersburg

Complete DNA sequencing of a free-living organism, *5205*
Discovery of quasicrystals, *5249*

Greenbelt

Human action to affect the earth's planetary motion, *2255*

Towson

Electric hand drill, *6060*

Massachusetts

Allston

Runner over the age of 40 to break the four-minute mile, *5846*

Amherst

Language to have its entire literature available on computer, *3306*

Auburn

Rocket flight using liquid fuel, *5505*

Boston

Autobiography by an African slave to have a major impact on the abolition movement, *5489*
Automatic price reductions on merchandise, *1518*
Boston Marathon in which both champions were African athletes, *5847*
Cookbook with standardized measurements, *2506*
Dentist's chair, *3809*
Ether as an anesthetic in childbirth, *2343*
Hospital to use anesthesia in surgery, *3763*
Law against cruelty to animals, *1138*
Medical school for women, *3860*
Missionary society, *4798*
Modern pyramid scheme, *1806*
Modern use of anesthesia in dentistry, *3762*
Newspaper published in the British colonies in America, *4496*
Nuclear submarine lost at sea, *1942*
Olympic Games in the modern era, *5760*
Probation system for criminals of all ages, *1739*
Publication in English printed in the American colonies, *3425*
Round-the-world solo sailing journey, *5458*
Transplant of artificial skin, *4073*
Words heard on a telephone, *5933*

Cambridge

Artificial diamond, *5247*
Artificial gene, *5200*
Bible translated into an indigenous American language, *4892*
Computer-aided manufacturing system, *1496*
Computer game, *2576*
Computing device with electronic components, *1667*
Court-ordered wiretap on a computer network, *1763*
Discovery of quarks, *5351*
Fields Medal, *3753*
Food irradiation, *2522*
Grammar and primer in an indigenous North American language, *3536*
Human chromosome gene-linkage maps, *5203*
International rugby game, *5803*
Nobel Prize in Chemistry winner from North America, *4524*
Patent on an animal, *5172*
Political sex scandal, *2627*
Stroboscopic lamp for high-speed photography, *4585*
Voice reader, *3303*
Watercraft to win the Dupont Water Prize, *5860*

Cape Cod

Transoceanic radio broadcast, *5902*

Chicopee

Transatlantic helicopter flight, *1427*

UNITED STATES—Massachusetts—*continued*

Eastham

Pears in the New World, *1048*

Fairhaven

Round-the-world solo sailing journey, *5458*

Gloucester

Frozen food for the mass market, *2542*

Lexington

Microwave oven, *3073*

Lowell

Machine gun that was practical, *6111*

Malden

Clock to operate by nuclear power, *6031*

Maynard

Minicomputer, *1674*

Nantucket

Comet named after a woman, *5091*

Northampton

IOU promissory note, *2436*

Pittsfield

Adventists, *4838*

Plymouth

Puritans, *4826*

Roxbury

Motorcycle, *3215*

Salem

Table tennis, *5828*

Saugus

Escalator, *1206*

Shrewsbury

Birth-control pill, *2370*

Somerville

Telephone for domestic use, *5934*

South Hadley

College for women, *1995*

Springfield

Basketball, *5617*
Motorcycle designed to be a motor vehicle, *3219*
Rules for basketball, *5618*

Weymouth

Ballpoint pen, *3593*

Woburn

Guide to E-mail etiquette, *1710*
Registered Internet domain, *1711*

Michigan

Hologram, *5318*

Dearborn

Plastic car, *3242*
Production automobile fueled by methanol, *3255*

Detroit

Death by suicide machine, *1888*
Electric car, *3230*
Electric car to be mass-produced, *3258*
Family car with its own video entertainment system, *3260*
Joint venture between Japanese and American automobile manufacturers, *3253*
Pneumatic hammer, *1492*
Production car with a night-vision system, *3261*
Race for solar-powered vehicles, *5724*
Typewritten letter, *3324*

Flat Rock

Human killed by a robot, *5035*

Grand Rapids

Carpet sweeper, *3062*

Kalamazoo

Dental drill powered by electricity, *3816*

Mount Clemens

Transatlantic eastward flight by jet airplane, *1378*

UNITED STATES—Oregon—*continued*

Ashland

Web ring, *1720*

Beaverton

Cloning of a primate from an embryo, *5189*

Portland

Shoe made from recycled materials, *1658*

Pennsylvania

Protest against slavery made by a religious group in the New World, *5488*

Elkins Park

Anatomically correct image of the human heart, *3900*

Erie

Evidence of weaving, *3696*

Harrisburg

Public opinion poll, *2633*

Heightstown

Train wreck, *1931*

Lancaster

Battery-powered wristwatch, *6032*
Calculator watch, *6036*
Digital quartz wristwatch, *6035*

Latrobe

Professional football game, *5660*

Philadelphia

Artwork, *1231*
Bifocal eyeglasses, *4108*
Bubble gum, *2555*
Dental drill powered by electricity, *3816*
Dental spittoon with running water, *3815*
Electric car, *3230*
Electronic computer for commercial use, *1671*
General-purpose computer that was fully electronic, *1669*
Heart-lung machine, *4068*
Nuclear transplantation in a vertebrate, *5185*
Pencil with an attached eraser, *3589*
Performance of a *Son et lumière* show in the United States, *2229*

Phonograph record, *2043*
Steamboat to make an ocean voyage, *5454*
Theater with its own gas generator, *5996*
Three-dimensional computer model of an Old Master sculpture, *1304*
Voice synthesizer, *5931*
White lion born in the Western Hemisphere, *1125*
World chess champion defeated by a computer, *2601*

Pittsburgh

Jehovah's Witnesses, *4840*
Self-heating cans, *2520*
Transoceanic radio voice broadcast, *5910*
Transplant of a baboon liver into a human being, *4076*

Pottstown

Museum of brass instruments, *4425*

Titusville

Oil well, *2105*

Williamsport

Little League World Series, *5613*

Rhode Island

Newport

Jazz festival, *4379*

Providence

Animated picture machine, *4324*

South Dakota

Rapid City

Aerial photograph showing the lateral curvature of the horizon and the beginning of the stratosphere, *5284*

White Lake

Aerial photograph showing the lateral curvature of the horizon and the beginning of the stratosphere, *5284*

Tennessee

Vonore

Native North American language to be given its own written form, *3540*

Texas

Mountaineer to climb the highest peak on every continent, *5751*

Austin

Radiation mutations to be artificially created, *5196*

Dallas

Electronic pocket calculator, *2030*
Integrated circuit, *2018*

Fort Worth

Computer hacker to be convicted, *1713*
Laundromat, *1520*
Round-the-world nonstop flight by an airplane, *1379*
Solo helicopter voyage around the world, *1428*

Houston

Octuplets, *2355*
Open-heart surgery streamed live on the World Wide Web, *4064*
Superconducting material that operated at temperatures above the boiling point of nitrogen, *5353*
Traffic accident on Mars, *5583*
Transplant of an artificial heart into a human being, *4072*

Quitaque

Wireless city, *5889*

Richardson

Nanotechnology company, *1499*

Utah

Natural Bridges National Monument

Power plant using solar cells, *2070*

Salt Lake City

Transplant of an artificial heart that was intended to be permanent, *4074*

Vermont

Brandon

Direct-current electric motor, *2169*

Virginia

Arlington

Transatlantic message over radio telephone, *5936*

Arlington Heights

Airplane accident that was fatal, *1897*

Danville

Woman to become a member of the British Parliament, *2654*

Fort Myer

Military aircraft, *4203*

Hampton Roads

Airplane bombing experiment to sink a battleship, *4215*
Naval battle between ironclad vessels, *4255*

Jamestown

Anti-smoking crusader, *4023*
Colony financed by a lottery, *4661*
Permanent English settlement in America, *4659*
Tobacco cultivation by a European, *1066*

Newport News

Nuclear-powered aircraft carrier, *4276*

Richmond

Cigarette advertisement showing a woman smoking, *1455*

Washington

Redmond

Businessman worth US$100 billion, *1448*

Seattle

Commercial software for personal computers, *1730*
Heart surgery broadcast on the Internet, *4063*
International airmail service, *4684*
Jumbo jet, *1329*
Language spoken by more than 1 billion people, *3305*
Live electronic music, *4394*
Modern theater in the round, *5999*
Ocean platform for rocket launching, *5516*
Touch-tone phone system, *5939*
Underground hydroelectric plant, *2089*

Walla Walla

Tract houses, *1218*

Wenatchee

Transpacific nonstop airplane flight, *1369*

UNITED STATES—*continued*

West Virginia

Green Bank

Scientific program to search for extraterrestrial life, *5101*

Wisconsin

Chippewa Falls

Computer with a parallel architecture, *1686*
Supercomputer, *1672*

Green Bay

One Sky, One World international kite flying event, *1421*

Madison

Cosmic ray to be discovered, *5094*

Milwaukee

Programmable logic controller, *2189*
Surgeon to use gloves, *4051*
Typewriter that was practical, *3590*

Oshkosh

Home-built supersonic jet, *1333*

Racine

Blow dryer for hair, *2736*

URUGUAY

Canasta, *2596*
Democratic president of Uruguay, *2793*

Montevideo

World Cup soccer championship, *5816*

UZBEKISTAN

President of Uzbekistan, *2852*

Samarkand

Paper mill in the Muslim world, *3690*

VATICAN

Doctor of the Church who was a woman, *4876*
Meeting of the heads of the Anglican and Catholic churches, *4805*

Pope born in Poland, *4877*
Pope to become a recording star, *4375*
Pope to visit a Communist country, *4878*

VENEZUELA

Book about human rights and slavery in the New World, *5484*
European explorer to land on the South American continent, *2286*
Latin American country with an environmental ministry, *2247*
Weather maps, *3623*

VIETNAM

King of Vietnam, *2933*
Large mammal discovered since World War II, *1116*
Major Chinese voyage of exploration and diplomacy, *2277*
Southeast Asian decorative artwork, *1243*
Trade between China and southeast Asia, *1531*
Vietnamese writing, *3524*

Ho Chi Minh City

Self-immolation by a Buddhist monk, *1886*

WALES

Bank holidays, *3035*
Bible society, *4835*
Coal mine, *3680*
Comparative linguist, *3297*
General union, *1504*
Hovercraft passenger service, *5421*
Prince of Wales, *2947*
Reference to the King Arthur legend in a historical work, *3470*
Reference to the King Arthur legend in literature, *3469*
Sheepdog trials, *1156*
Steam locomotive, *3264*
Woman archeologist of distinction, *5061*

Caernarvon

Radiotelegraph message from Great Britain to Australia, *5907*

Cardiff

Welsh writing, *3498*

Cardigan

Eisteddfod, *3027*

Swansea

Environmental lawsuit, *2240*

GEOGRAPHICAL INDEX

YEMEN

Airlift of endangered Jews to Israel, *4979*
Coffee drinking, *2495*
Free multiparty elections in the Arabian peninsula, *2642*
President and prime minister of the Yemen Arab Republic (North Yemen), *2829*

YUGOSLAVIA

Prime minister of Yugoslavia, *2880*
Serving leader of a sovereign nation indicted for war crimes by an international tribunal, *1783*
Sky-diving championships, *5600*

ZAMBIA

President of Zambia, *2832*

ZIMBABWE

Prime minister of Zimbabwe, *2913*

Harare

Women's shelter in Central Africa, *5378*

Masvingo

Major settlement built of stone in sub-Saharan Africa, *1564*